ATTENTION and PERFORMANCE VII

Proceedings of the Seventh International Symposium on Attention and Performance
Sénanque, France, August 1-6, 1976

ATTENTION and PERFORMANCE VII

Edited by

Jean Requin

*Département de Psychobiologie Expérimentale
Institut de Neurophysiologie et Psychophysiologie
du Centre National de la Recherche Scientifique
Marseille, France*

 LAWRENCE ERLBAUM ASSOCIATES, PUBLISHERS

1978   Hillsdale, New Jersey

DISTRIBUTED BY THE HALSTED PRESS DIVISION OF
JOHN WILEY & SONS
New York   Toronto   London   Sydney

Lawrence Erlbaum Associates, Inc., Publishers
62 Maria Drive
Hillsdale, New Jersey 07642

Distributed solely by Halsted Press Division
John Wiley & Sons, Inc., New York

Library of Congress Cataloging in Publication Data

International Symposium on Attention and Performance,
    7th, Abbey of Sénanque, 1977.
    Attention and performance VII.

    Includes bibliographical references and indexes.
    1. Attention—Congresses. 2. Performance—
Congresses. I. Requin, Jean. II. Title.
BF321.I57 1977   153.7   78-13662
ISBN 0-470-26521-3

Printed in the United States of America

Contents

List of Contributors and Participants   xvii

Group Photo   xxii

Preface   xxv

PART I: TIME IN PERCEPTION

1. Temporal Factors in Visual Information Processing:
    A Tutorial Review
        Charles W. Eriksen and Derek W. Schultz **3**

        I.   Introduction   3
        II.   Temporal Integration   4
        III. Retinal Locus, Acuity and Processing Time   6
        IV.   Visual Persistence   8
        V.   Visual Masking   11
        VI.   Cognitive Masking   16
        VII. Conclusions   20
              References   20

2. Time Factors in the Processing of Visual
    Movement Information
        Claude Bonnet **25**

        I.   Introduction   25
        II.   Temporal Processing in Visual Motion
              Perception   27

229040

    III. Neuro-Sensory Adaptation (NSA)   32
    IV. Temporal Summation in Movement
          After-Effects   36
     V. Conclusion   38
          References   39

3.   Interdependence Between the Processing of Temporal and Non-Temporal Information
        Ewart A. C. Thomas and Nancy E. Cantor **43**

      I. Introduction   43
     II. Method   47
    III. Results   48
    IV. Some Assumptions About Information
          Processing   51
     V. Applications of Assumptions to Data   55
    VI. Concluding Remarks   58
          References   61

4.   The Formation of Auditory Streams
        Albert S. Bregman **63**

      I. Introduction   63
     II. Similarity   66
    III. Simplicity (Good Form)   67
    IV. Good Continuation   68
     V. Competition of Organizations   69
    VI. Closure and Belongingness   70
   VII. Common Fate and Spectral
          Decomposition   71
  VIII. Subject-Controlled Factors   73
          References   74

5.   On the Time It Takes to Tell Things Apart
        Raymond S. Nickerson **77**

      I. Introduction   77
     II. Same Versus Different Response Times   78
    III. Some Hypotheses Regarding the Relative
          Shortness of Same RT   79
    IV. Further Evidence that Same and Different
          Judgments are Different   83
     V. Some Related Findings   84
    VI. Conclusions   85
          References   86

6. The Making of the Present: A Tutorial Review
   John A. Michon **89**

      I.   Introduction   90
      II. The Conscious Present   90
      III. Processing Sequential Information   93
      IV. Why We Perceive Pattern: Tuning   99
      V. Summary and Conclusions   105
      References   107

PART II: WORD PERCEPTION AND READING

7. Visual Search and Reading: Eye Movements and Functional Visual Field: A Tutorial Review
   Herman Bouma **115**

      I.   Introduction   116
      II. Functional Visual Field   119
      III. Control of Eye Saccades   131
      IV. Integration of Successive Information   138
      References   143

8. Foveal and Parafoveal Cues in Reading
   Keith Rayner **149**

      I.   Introduction   149
      II. Experiment 1   151
      III. Experiment 2   156
      IV. General Discussion   159
      References   161

9. Non-Analytic Correspondences and Pattern in Word Pronunciation
   Lee R. Brooks **163**

      I.   Introduction   163
      II. A Demonstration of Implicit Learning   167
      III. The Manipulation of Visual Patterning   172
      IV. Sound-Correlated Patterning and Visual Similarity   174
      References   176

10. **Implicit Speech in the Reading of Numbers and Meaningless Syllables**
    Joël Pynte **179**

      I. Introduction   179
      II. Experiment 1   180
      III. Experiment 2   186
      IV. Conclusion   191
      References   191

11. **The Origins of Mixed Errors**
    Tim Shallice and Janina McGill **193**

      I. Introduction   193
      II. Segmentation Errors   196
      III. Preliminary Experiment   197
      IV. Main Experiment   200
      V. General Discussion   204
      Appendix 1   206
      Appendix 2   207
      References   207

12. **Word Recognition and Production: Reciprocity in Clinical and Normal Studies**
    Anthony J. Marcel and Karalyn E.Patterson **209**

      I. Introduction   210
      II. From Grapheme to Phoneme   211
      III. Knowing the Meaning but not the Word   212
      IV. The Locus of Word Class Effects   218
      V. Concluding Discussion and Comments   223
      References   225

PART III: SPEECH PERCEPTION AND CODING

13. **There May Be Nothing Peculiar to Perceiving in a Speech Mode**
    James E. Cutting **229**

      I. Introduction   229
      II. Categorical Perception   230
      III. Boundary Shifts Due to Selective Adaptation   235
      IV. Left-Hemisphere Effects Due to Cerebral Specialization   236

V. Asymmetric Interference with Redundancy
Gain   236
VI. The Speech Mode and the Auditory-Phonetic
Distinction   237
References   240

14. Spatial Constraints on Attention to Speech
José Morais **245**

I. Does Speech Perception Depend on Speaker
Direction?   245
II. Spatial Position Versus Ear of Entry   247
III. Enlarging the Picture of Auditory Spatial
Effects   250
IV. Listening with the Ears or with the Whole
Body   252
V. Auditory Spatial Effects Depend on Correct
Allocation of Voluntary Attention   255
VI. Implications of the Preceding Findings for a
Theory of the Auditory Spatial Effects   257
References   259

**15. Laterality and Localization: A "Right Ear Advantage"
for Speech Heard on the Left**
*Christopher J. Darwin, Peter Howell, and
Susan A. Brady* **261**

I. Introduction   261
II. Method   264
III. Results   267
IV. Discussion   271
References   277

16. Speech Timing and Intelligibility
A. W. F. Huggins **279**

I. Introduction   279
II. The Main Factors Affecting Speech
Timing   280
III. A Model for Speech Timing   288
IV. Speech Timing and the Deaf   291
V. The Contribution of Speech Timing to
Intelligibility   292
References   296

17. An Experimental Study of Writing, Dictating, and Speaking
John D. Gould **299**

    I. Introduction   299
    II. Training   301
    III. Experiment 1   302
    IV. Experiment 2   306
    V. Experiment 3   308
    VI. Experiment 4   312
    VII. General Discussion   316
    References   318

18. Audition and Speech Coding in Short-Term Memory: A Tutorial Review
Robert G. Crowder **321**

    I. Introduction   322
    II. Phonological Coding   322
    III. Echoic Memory   329
    IV. Phonological Coding and Echoic Memory Distinguished   334
    References   340

PART IV: HEMISPHERE DIFFERENCES

19. Functional Cerebral Space: A Model for Overflow, Transfer and Interference Effects in Human Performance: A Tutorial Review
Marcel Kinsbourne and Robert E. Hicks **345**

    I. Introduction   345
    II. The Neurological Basis of Differences in Functional Distance   347
    III. Simultaneous Imitative Effects   349
    IV. Sequential Transfer Effects   350
    V. Simultaneous Interference Effects   351
    VI. Perceptual Interference   354
    VII. Facilitation Effects and the Biasing of Divided Attention   355
    VIII. Is Functional Distance Necessarily Transitive?   356
    IX. Implication of the Functional Space Model for the Possible Adaptive Value of Hemispheric Specialization of Function   357
    X. Overview   359
    References   359

20. Factors Affecting Face Recognition in the Cerebral Hemispheres: Familiarity and Naming
Carlo Umiltà, Daniela Brizzolara, Patrizia Tabossi, and Hugh Fairweather **363**

    I.   Introduction   363
    II.   Method   366
    III.   Results   367
    IV.   Discussion   370
        References   373

21. Verbal and Pictorial Processing by Hemisphere as a Function of the Subject's Verbal Scholastic Aptitude Test Score
Neal E. A. Kroll and David J. Madden **375**

    I.   Introduction: Visual Field Differences and Information Processing   375
    II.   Experiment 1: Verbal Test Stimuli Projected to Left or Right VF   378
    III.   Experiment 2: Pictorial TS Projected to LVF or RVF   382
    IV.   Discussion   388
        References   389

22. Between-Hand vs Within-Hand Choice-RT: A Single Channel of Reduced Capacity in the Split-Brain Monkey
Yves Guiard and Jean Requin **391**

    I.   Introduction   392
    II.   Procedure   394
    III.   Experiment 1   397
    IV.   Experiment 2   401
    V.   Experiment 3   404
    VI.   General Discussion   406
        References   409

23. Individual Differences in Reading Strategies in Relation to Handedness and Cerebral Asymmetry
Gillian Cohen and Roger Freeman **411**

    I.   Introduction   412
    II.   Experiment 1   413
    III.   Experiment 2   418
    IV.   Experiment 3   420
        References   425

PART V: RESPONSE AND PHYSIOLOGICAL PROCESSES

24. **The Neurophysiology of Human Attention:**
     A Tutorial Review
     Terence W. Picton, Kenneth B. Campbell,
     Jacinthe Baribeau-Braun, and Guy B. Proulx **429**

           I. Introduction   430
          II. Evoked Potentials During Auditory
               Vigilance   431
         III. Problems of General Arousal   434
          IV. Cortical Negative Shifts   435
           V. Levels of Selection   441
          VI. The Early Processing of Sensory
               Information   444
         VII. The Nature of the N100 Component of the
               Evoked Potential   447
        VIII. The Late Components of the Evoked
               Potential   450
          IX. The Nature of the Parietocentral Late
               Positive Wave   452
           X. Tentative Conclusions   459
               References   460

25. **The Psychophysiology of Anticipation**
     Peter J. Lang, Arne Öhman, and Robert F. Simons **469**

           I. Introduction   469
          II. Two-Stimulus Anticipation Paradigm   471
         III. The Heart Rate Response   471
          IV. Experimental Studies on Heart Rate
               Response   473
           V. The Cortical Slow Wave   477
          VI. Experimental Studies on Cortical Slow
               Wave   478
         VII. Conclusions   481
               References   483

26. **Sequential Effects of Distracting Stimuli in a Selective**
     Attention Reaction Time Task
     Anthony G. Greenwald and Karl E. Rosenberg **487**

           I. Introduction   487
          II. Logic of Using SART Data to Infer Memory
               for the Content of the Unattended
               Channel   488

III. Effect of Proportion of Conflict Trials in an
Extended Sequence   489
IV. Effects of Sequences of Agreement and
Conflicts   490
V. Further Study of Agreement-Conflict
Sequences   493
VI. Memory for Unattended Information   497
VII. Relation Between SART and Information
Reduction Tasks   497
VIII. Taxonomy of 2-Trial Sequential Effects in
SART   498
References   503

27. Selective Attention as a Motor Program
Jean-Marie Coquery **505**

I. Introduction   506
II. Modifications of Sensory Transmission
During Movement   506
III. Attention and Orienting Reactions   510
IV. Effects of Selective Attention on Spinal
Reflexes   512
References   513

28. Storage Codes for Movement Information
George E. Stelmach and Hugh D. McCracken **515**

I. Introduction   515
II. Experiment 1   517
III. Experiment 2   521
IV. Experiment 3   525
V. Experiment 4   527
VI. General Discussion   530
References   533

29. On the Temporal Control of Rhythmic Performance
Dirk Vorberg and Rolf Hambuch **535**

I. Introduction   535
II. Wing's Model   537
III. Experiment   538
IV. Results   540
V. Extensions of the Basic Model   542
VI. Tests of the Models   549
VII. Discussion   552
References   554

30. **Issues in the Theory of Action: Degrees of Freedom, Coordinative Structures and Coalitions**
Michael T. Turvey, Robert E. Shaw, and William Mace **557**

    I. The Problems of Context-Conditioned Variability and Degrees of Freedom   558
    II. The Concept of Coordinative Structure   563
    III. Toward a Definition of Coalitions   573
    References   593

PART VI: THEORIES AND MODELS

31. **An Adaptive Module for Simple Judgment**
Douglas Vickers **599**

    I. A General Decision Module for Response Frequency and Time in Simple Judgments   600
    II. Confidence in Simple Judgments   611
    III. The Problem of Adaptation   612
    References   616

32. **The Relative Judgment Theory of the Psychometric Function**
Stephen W. Link **619**

    I. Introduction   619
    II. The Theory of Relative Judgment   620
    III. Kellogg's Experiment   624
    IV. The Shallice and Vickers Experiments   626
    V. The Link (1971) Experiment   628
    References   630

33. **A Model for the Visual Recognition of Words of Three Letters**
Don Bouwhuis **631**

    I. Introduction   631
    II. Reading Versus Recognition   632
    III. Eye Position and Visual Interference   634
    IV. The Recognition Model   636
    V. An Experimental Test   638
    VI. Results   639
    VII. Discussion   641
    References   644

34. The Word Frequency Effect: A New Theory
Michel Treisman and Peter A. Parker **645**

    I.   Introduction   645
    II. A Theory of the Perceptual Identification of
        Complex Stimuli   649
    III. A Computer Simulation of the Model   654
    IV. An Experimental Test of Perceptual Identification
        Theory   657
        Glossary of Symbols   672
        References   674

**35. Visual Search, Visual Attention, and the Attention
Operating Characteristic**
George Sperling and Melvin J. Melchner **675**

    I.   Visual Search under a Single Attentional
        State   676
    II. Visual Search under Multiple Attentional
        States   678
    III. The Attention Operating Characteristic
        (AOC)   682
        References   686

**36. Model Acceptability and the Use of Bayes-Fiducial
Methods for Validating Models**
*Henry Rouanet, Dominique Lépine, and
Daniel Holender* **687**

    I.   Inadequacy of Significance Tests for
        . Validating Models   687
    II. Fiducial Inference and the Notion of
        Acceptability   690
    III. Fiducial (or Bayes-Fiducial) Inference;
        Fiducial and Confidence Methods   694
    IV. Fiducial Analysis of Holender and
        Bertelson's Data; Inferences on Population
        Parameters   695
    V. Comments and Conclusions   699
        Appendix   699
        References   701

Author Index   **703**

Subject Index   **719**

Contributors and Participants

The name of a conference participant who did not contribute to this volume is preceded by an asterisk. The name of a contributor who did not participate in the conference is indicated with a dagger.

*Dr. Jesus Alegria, Université Libre de Bruxelles, Laboratoire de Psychologie Expérimentale, Bruxelles, Belgium

*Dr. Vera Bakalska, Institute of Physiology, Bulgarian Academy of Sciences, Academy G. Bouthcer Str. Bl. 1, Sofia 1113, Bulgaria

†Dr. Jacinthe Baribeau-Braun, Ottawa General Hospital, Department of Medicine, 43 Bruyere Street, Ottawa, Ontario K1N 5C8, Canada

*Dr. Paul Bertelson, Université Libre de Bruxelles, Laboratoire de Psychologie Expérimentale, Bruxelles, Belgium

Dr. Claude Bonnet, Université René Descartes, Laboratoire de Psychologie Expérimentale et Comparée, 28, rue Serpente, 75600, Paris, France

Dr. Herman Bouma, Institute for Perception Research, Postbus 513, Den Dolech 2, Eindhoven, The Netherlands

Dr. Dominic Bouwhuis, Institute for Perception Research, Insulindelaan 2, Eindhoven 4502, The Netherlands

†Dr. Susan A. Brady, University of Sussex, Laboratory of Experimental Psychology, Brighton, BN 1 9 Q G, England

Dr. Albert S. Bregman, McGill University, Department of Psychology, P. O. Box 60 70, Station A, Montreal, Québec, Canada

†Dr. Daniela Brizzolara, Universita di Padova, Istituto di Psicologia, Piazza Capitaniato 5, Padova 35100, Italy

Dr. Lee Brooks, McMaster University, Department of Psychology, Hamilton, Ontario, Canada

†Dr. Kenneth B. Campbell, Ottawa General Hospital, Department of Medicine, 43 Bruyere Street, Ottawa, Ontario K1N 5C8, Canada

†Dr. Nancy E. Cantor, Stanford University, Department of Psychology, Stanford, California 94305, USA

Dr. Gillian Cohen, University of Oxford, Department of Experimental Psychology, South Parks Road, Oxford OX1 3UD, England

Dr. Jean-Marie Coquery, Université de Lille I, Laboratoire de Psychophysiologie, SN 4, B. P. 36, 59650 Villeneuve d'Ascq, France

Dr. Robert G. Crowder, Yale University, Department of Psychology, New Haven, Connecticut 06520, USA

Dr. James E. Cutting, Wesleyan University, Psychological Laboratory, Middleton, Connecticut 06457, USA

Dr. Christofer J. Darwin, University of Sussex, Laboratory of Experimental Psychology, Brighton BN 1 9 QG, England

*Dr. Stanislav Dornic, University of Stockholm, Department of Psychology, Post Box 6706, S 113 85, Stockholm, Sweden

*Dr. Henri Durup, Institut de Neurophysiologie et Psychophysiologie du C.N.R.S., Département de Psychologie Animale, 31, chemin Joseph-Aiguier, 13274 Marseille Cedex 2, France

†Dr. Charles W. Eriksen, University of Illinois, Department of Psychology, Champaign, Illinois 61820, USA

†Dr. Hugh Fairweather, Universita di Bologna, Istituto di Psicologia, Viale Berti-Pichat 5, bologna 40127, Italy

†Dr. Roger H. Freeman, University of Oxford, Department of Experimental Psychology, South Parks Road, Oxford OX1 3UD, England

Dr. John D. Gould, IBM, Thomas J. Watson Research Center, P. O. Box 218, Yorktown Heights, New York 10598, USA

Dr. Anthony G. Greenwald, The Ohio State University, Department of Psychology, 404 C West 17th Avenue, Columbus, Ohio 43210, USA

Dr. Yves Guiard, Institut de Neurophysiologie et Psychophysiologie du C.N.R.S., Département de Psychobiologie Expérimentale, 31, chemin Joseph-Aiguier, 13274 Marseille Cedex 2, France

†Dr. Rolf Hambuch, Universitat Konstanz, Fachbereich Psychologie und Soziologie, D 7750 Konstanz, Postfach 7733, Germany

Dr. Robert Hicks, The Hospital for Sick Children, 555 University Avenue, Toronto, Ontario MRG 1X8, Canada

Dr. Daniel Holender, Université Libre de Bruxelles, Laboratoire de Psychologie Expérimentale, 117, av. Adolphe Buyl, 1050 Bruxelles, Belgium

†Dr. Peter Howell, University of Sussex, Laboratory of Experimental Psychology, Brighton, BN1 9QG, England

Dr. A. W. F. Huggins, Bolt, Beranek and Newman Inc., 50 Moulton Street, Cambridge, Massachusetts 02138, USA

*Dr. Daniel Kahneman, The Hebrew University of Jerusalem, Department of Psychology, Jerusalem, Israel

†Dr. Marcel Kinsbourne, The Hospital for Sick Children, 555 University Avenue, Toronto, Ontario MRG 1X8, Canada

*Dr. Sylvan Kornblum, University of Michigan, Mental Health Research Institute, 205 N. Forest Avenue, Ann Arbor, Michigan 48104, USA

Dr. Neal E. Kroll, University of California, Department of Psychology, Davis, California 95616, USA

*Dr. David LaBerge, University of Minnesota, Department of Psychology, Elliot Hall, Minneapolis, Minnesota 55455, USA

Dr. Peter J. Lang, University of Wisconsin, Department of Psychology, Madison, Wisconsin 53706, USA

Dr. Dominique Lépine, Université René Descartes, Laboratoire de Psychologie Expérimentale et Comparée, 28, rue Serpente, 75600 Paris, France

Dr. Stephen W. Link, McMaster University, Department of Psychology, Hamilton, Ontario, Canada

†Dr. Hugh McCracken, University of Wisconsin, Motor Behavior Laboratory, 2000 Observatory Drive, Madison, Wisconsin 53706, USA

†Dr. William Mace, Trinity College, Hartford, Connecticut 06106, USA

†Dr. Janina McGill, The National Hospital for Nervous Diseases, Psychology Department, Queen Square, London WC 1N 3BG, England

Dr. David Madden, University of California, Department of Psychology, Davis, California 95616, USA

Dr. Anthony J. Marcel, Applied Psychology Unit, 15 Chaucer Road, Cambridge CB2 2EF, England

†Dr. Melvin J. Melchner, Bell Laboratories, 600 Mountain Avenue, Murray Hill, New Jersey 07974, USA

Dr. John A. Michon, University of Groningen, Institute of Experimental Psychology, P. O. Box 14, Haren GN 8100, The Netherlands

*Dr. Stephen Monsell, University of Oxford, Department of Experimental Psychology, South Parks Road, Oxford OX1 3PS, England

Dr. José Morais, Université Libre de Bruxelles, Laboratoire de Psychologie Expérimentale, 117, av. Adolphe Buyl, 1050 Bruxelles, Belgique

Dr. Raymond S. Nickerson, Bolt, Beranek and Newman Inc., 50 Moulton Street, Cambridge, Massachusetts 02138, USA

†Dr. Arne Öhman, Institute of Psychology, University of Bergen, Post Box 25, N-5014, Bergen, Norway

*Dr. Jacques Paillard, Institut de Neurophysiologie et Psychophysiologie du C.N.R.S., Département de Psychophysiologie Générale, 31, Chemin Joseph Aiguier, 13274 Marseille Cedex 2, France

†Dr. Peter A. Parker, University of Oxford, Department of Experimental Psychology, South Parks Road, Oxford OX1 3UD, England

†Dr. Karalyn Patterson, Applied Psychology Unit, 15 Chaucer Road, Cambridge CB2 2EF, England

Dr. Terence W. Picton, Ottawa General Hospital, Department of Medicine, 43 Bruyere Street, Ottawa, Ontario K1N 5C8, Canada

†Dr. Guy B. Proulx, Ottawa General Hospital, Department of Medicine, 43 Bruyere Street, Ottawa, Ontario K1N 5C8, Canada

Dr. Joël Pynte, Université de Provence, Département de Psychologie, 29, rue Schuman, 13621 Aix en Provence Cedex, France

Dr. Keith Rayner, University of Rochester, Department of Psychology, River Station, Rochester, New York 14627, USA

Dr. Jean Requin, Institut de Neurophysiologie et Psychophysiologie du C.N.R.S., Département de Psychobiologie Expérimentale, 31, chemin Joseph-Aiguier, 13274 Marseille Cedex 2, France

†Dr. Karl E. Rosenberg, The Ohio State University, Department of Psychology, 404 C West 17th Avenue, Columbus, Ohio 43210, USA

†Dr. Henry Rouanet, Université René Descartes, UER de Mathématiques, 12 rue Cujas, 75005, Paris, France

*Dr. Andries F. Sanders, Institute for Perception TNO, Kampurg 5, Soesterberg, The Netherlands

†Dr. Dereck W. Schultz, University of Illinois, Department of Psychology, Champaign, Illinois 61820, USA

*Dr. Andras Semjen, Académie des Sciences de Hongrie, Institut de Psychologie, Szondy-u 83–85, Budapest VI, Hungary

Dr. Timothy Shallice, The National Hospital for Nervous Diseases, Psychology Department, Queen Square, London WC 1N 3BG, England

†Dr. Robert Shaw, University of Connecticut, Department of Psychology, Storrs, Connecticut 06268, USA

†Dr. Robert F. Simons, University of Wisconsin, Department of Psychology, Madison, Wisconsin 53706, USA

Dr. George Sperling, Bell Laboratories, 600 Mountain Avenue, Murray Hill, New Jersey 07974, USA

Dr. George E. Stelmach, University of Wisconsin, Motor Behavior Laboratory, 2000 Observatory Drive, Madison, Wisconsin 53706, USA

*Dr. Saul Sternberg, Bell Laboratories, 600 Mountain Avenue Murray Hill, New Jersey 07974, USA

†Dr. Patrizia Tabossi, Universita di Padova, Istituto di Psicologia, Piazza Capitaniato 5, Padova 35100, Italy

Dr. Ewart A. C. Thomas, Stanford University, Department of Psychology, Stanford, California 94305, USA

*Dr. Anne Treisman, University of Oxford, Department of Experimental Psychology, South Parks Road, Oxford OX1 3UD, England

Dr. Michel Treisman, University of Oxford, Department of Experimental Psychology, South Parks Road, Oxford OX1 3UD, England

Dr. Michael T. Turvey, University of Connecticut, Department of Psychology, Storrs, Connecticut 06268, USA

Dr. Carlo A. Umiltà Universita di Padova, Istituto di Psicologia, Piazza Capitaniato 5, Padova 35100, Italy

Dr. Douglas Vickers, University of Adelaide, Department of Psychology, Adelaide, South Australia 5001, Australia

Dr. Dirk Vorberg, Universitat Konstanz, Fachbereich Psychologie und Soziologie, D 775 Konstanz, Postfach 7733, Germany

*Dr. Alan T. Welford, University of Adelaide, Department of Psychology, Adelaide, South Australia 5001, Australia

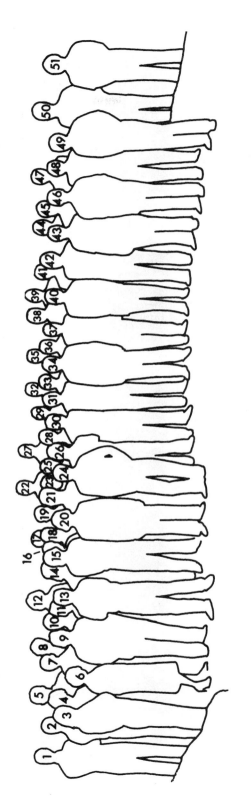

1. A. W. F. Huggins
2. K. Rayner
3. T. Shallice
4. A. Treisman
5. J. D. Gould
6. V. Bakalska
7. H. Bouma
8. R. S. Nickerson
9. J. Morais
10. D. Laberge
11. Y. Guiard
12. D. Lépine
13. A. J. Marcel
14. G. Cohen
15. P. Bertelson
16. T. W. Picton
17. J. A. Michon

18. C. Umiltà
19. S. Kornblum
20. G. Sperling
21. D. Holender
22. D. Bouwhuis
23. J. Pynte
24. A. G. Greenwald
25. S. Sternberg
26. J. Alegria
27. N. E. A. Kroll
28. C. Bonnet
29. A. T. Welford
30. J. M. Coquery
31. H. Durup
32. A. S. Bregman
33. G. E. Stelmach
34. D. J. Madden

35. S. Dornic
36. D. Vorberg
37. M. Treisman
38. S. Monsell
39. L. Brooks
40. R. G. Crowder
41. M. T. Turvey
42. D. Vickers
43. S. W. Link
44. A. F. Sanders
45. J. E. Cutting
46. C. J. Darwin
47. R. Hicks
48. D. Kahneman
49. P. J. Lang
50. J. Paillard
51. J. Requin

Preface

The organization of the Seventh International Symposium on Attention and Performance marks a double anniversary. It not only was held 10 years after Andries Sanders took the initiative of bringing together a small group of human performance specialists, it also marked the beginnings of a new, formal association. Only now can we fully appreciate how much Sanders' initiative foreshadowed the fundamental direction of interest that has dominated experimental psychology over the last 10 years. It is now clear that the satisfaction expressed by the participants of that first conference, and by those of the next five equally successful conferences, was due, at least in part, to the style chosen for holding the meetings (i.e., small, intimate, deliberately open-ended, free from academic tradition or formalism), which seemed particularly suited to creative work and scientific discussion. This satisfaction expressed, in part, fulfillment of a deeply felt need: Many research workers, faced with the rapid development of ideas resulting from an even more rapid accumulation of new data, were rather distressed to see their work still rigidly classified in terms of psychological "functions" and were willing to take part in the dynamic forces that periodically restructure disciplines, temporarily concentrating research efforts on new problems and problem areas.

Thus it was logical that those responsible for the successful organization of the six preceding meetings (and the regular and internationally valued publication of their proceedings) wished to perpetuate in the statutes of an association[1] the tone and precepts that were at the heart of this success. Hence

---

[1]The first ad hoc organizing Committee consisted of Drs. W. G. Koster, S. Kornblum, P. M. A. Rabbitt, A. F. Sanders, S. Sternberg, and A. T. Welford.

the new "International Association for the Study of Attention and Performance" was created, whose objectives are to "increase and disseminate scientific knowledge in the area of human attention, performance, and information processing, and to foster international communication in this area." Although some people warned the organizers of formalizing what had been until then a succession of spontaneous improvisations building on previous success, the idea was enthusiastically received by most of our colleagues, who saw in it a way to perpetuate the spirit of Attention and Performance.

The organization of the seventh of these meetings was, thus, the first scientific expression of the new association. In this context, the organizer's mission was both simple and perilous: simple, in that it did not require as much imagination and improvisation as it did imitation (by borrowing well-tried formulas of his predecessors), and perilous, in that confidence in the excellence of the technical material presented did not guarantee the main objective (i.e., that a certain style and atmosphere prevail). From this viewpoint, he can be criticized for having minimized the risks by choosing to organize the meeting in the Abbey of Sénanque, whose 12-century stones, drenched by the Mediterranean sun, were his precious and ever-present collaborators. Whereas it is not our role to determine whether this volume displays "continuity in the absence of directives," which was one of the charms of the preceding meetings, we can, however, affirm that the organization of *Attention and Performance VII* was determined with this idea in mind.

But spontaneity was not the only aim. Indeed, a constant concern was to prevent disciplinary and methodological divisions from dominating the thematic structure of the meeting. This sprang less from feelings of marginality in a pychophysiologist organizer than from the hope of catalyzing the somewhat static position of experimental psychology in France. Scientific psychology, an area that is particularly active internationally, has found it particularly difficult to develop in a country where the humanities and sciences have been traditionally opposed and where the academic context still condones the gulf between the social and biological sciences. Where the development and autonomy of psychology over the last 25 years required a demonstration of its scientific respectability, it has been difficult to prevent protectionist attempts at preserving methodological unity at the expense of a somewhat restrictive definition of its subject matter. Anglo-Saxon and American readers, especially, may find such considerations rather out of date. The reality that they represent remains, however, a sensitive area for many French research workers. This is particularly true for those who have chosen to work at the juncture of psychological and physiological disciplines, and who regard the future promise of this position as worth its present discomfort.

The organization of this book can be seen as a reconciliation of the three main goals that served as guidelines in setting up the conference. The first goal, which I called "spontaneity," was obviously suited to emphasize currently more dynamic areas of experimental psychology. This explains the large place given to so-called "cognitive psychology." To a large extent this may cover little more than the recent and legitimate infatuation for studying complex information processing related to language. This is well represented in the two sections where problems of word perception, reading, speech perception, and speech production are developed. The second goal was to exemplify the necessary complementary relationship of psychologists and physiologists in the convergence of problematics and levels of analysis. This appears particularly in the constitution of the two sections devoted, on the one hand, to functional differences between the cerebral hemispheres, and, on the other hand, to the role played by attentional processes in the preparation and programming of sensorimotor activity. The third goal was the wish to counter extreme empirical approaches, which often lead to underestimation of the heuristic value of theoretical developments and attempts at formalization. This clearly underlies the organization of the first and last sections. The first is devoted to the temporal patterning of perceptual processes, an area where the sophistication of experimental studies is especially suitable to fostering speculation; the last is entirely devoted to some new advances in the field of models. As initiated by the *Attention and Performance IV* volume, each of these sections except the last is opened and/or concluded by a "tutorial" paper. This is conceived more as a sifting of information in the field than as a true review paper, and it is aimed at giving each section more coherence, as well as serving as a guideline for nonspecialist readers.

The organization of the Seventh International Symposium on Attention and Performance could not have been undertaken without the financial aid of the "Délégation Générale a la Recherche Scientifique et Technique" and the "Centre National de la Recherche Scientifique"; it could not have been accomplished without the efficient technical assistance graciously allotted by the "Institut de Neurophysiologie et Psychophysiologie," or without the collaboration and advice of the members of the Executive Committee of the Association, and the support of Paul Bertelson, who was constantly available to the organizer of the congress and, later, to the editor of this volume.[2] Lastly, my thanks go to those who had the heavy and delicate task of reading, in a spirit of total cooperation, the different contributions that make up this book: D. A. Allport, R. J. Audley, A. D. Baddeley, D. Bamber, P. Bertelson, D. E. Broadbent, J. M. Coquery, J. C. Falmagne, D. M. Green, A. W. F. Huggins, D. Kahneman, S. Keele, M. Kinsbourne, S. Kornblum, D. LaBerge, D. Lépine, A. M. Liberman, S. W. Link, A. J. Marcel, D. E. Meyer,

[2]S. Dornic, S. Kornblum, J. Requin, A. F. Sanders, S. Sternberg, A. M. Treisman, and A. T. Welford form the actual Executive Committee of the "International Association for the Study of Attention and Performance."

B. C. J. Moore, J. Morton, R. Näätänen, R. S. Nickerson, J. Paillard, R. W. Pew, P. M. A. Rabbitt, T. Shallice, L. H. Shaffer, G. Sperling, E. A. C. Thomas, A. M. Treisman, M. Treisman, L. Van Noorden, and H. G. Vaughan. . . . without forgetting the person who undertook to improve, with not too much severity, those few pages of which the editor is co-author. The editor maintains the privilege, which he would share if he could, of being the only one to be fully acquainted with the interesting book, which could be published, of the correspondence between and among the editor and the authors and all those whose useful suggestions and kind criticisms were greatly responsible for the merits of this book.

JEAN REQUIN

ATTENTION and
PERFORMANCE VII

Proceedings of the Seventh International Symposium
on Attention and Performance
Sénanque, France, August 1-6, 1976

TIME IN
PERCEPTION

1 Temporal Factors in Visual Information Processing: A Tutorial Review

Charles W. Eriksen
Derek W. Schultz

Department of Psychology
University of Illinois
Champaign Illinois

ABSTRACT

This paper reinterprets several phenomena of visual information processing from the perspective of finite temporal resolution in vision. At the outset, it is argued that stimulus information both accumulates and decays gradually over time. From this contention, the visual icon is reinterpreted to be nothing more than the epiphenomenal manifestation of decaying sensory information in higher cortical centers, and not a separate precognitive information storage register. The nature of visual masking is then discussed, and it is concluded that there is no convincing evidence for the existence of erasure or interruption processes in vision. There is, however, evidence for a "cognitive" masking effect that reflects the limited-capacity nature and finite temporal resolution of the visual processing system.

I. INTRODUCTION

Models of visual information processing must be developed within the constraints set by the physiological nature of the visual system. In this paper we intend to examine several of the research topics of visual information processing in relation to salient characteristics of this system and in doing so, to outline a perspective on visual information processing models. Specifically, the visual system, like all biological systems, responds as a function of time. Since Ganz (1975) recently has provided an excellent review of the temporal integrative characteristics of human vision, we do not intend to duplicate his coverage.

Rather, we wish to emphasize a few conclusions that follow from his more detailed review of the research literature.

The primary thesis we will argue is that the visual system has a limited capacity for temporal resolution. Responses in the eye and the visual tracts of the primary projection areas do not produce square wave responses, even when stimulated by a square wave stimulus. Maximum response in the visual system does not occur with the onset of the stimulus; it develops over an appreciable length of time (in the context of information processing models) — 100 msec or more. We are familiar with this summation as Bloch's Law, and the critical duration refers to the time interval over which complete reciprocity holds for time and intensity. That is, within the critical duration the same visual effect can be obtained, for example, by doubling the intensity of the stimulus as by doubling its duration. For brightness, the value of the critical duration has been found in various investigations to be on the order of approximately 100 msec (see Ganz, 1975). But for form perception, the work of Kahneman and his associates (Kahneman, 1964; Kahneman & Norman, 1964; Kahneman, Norman, & Kubovy, 1967) has suggested a critical duration on the order of 300–400 msec. So we see that the time required for a visual input to achieve maximum clarity is not trivial.

Just as important, so far as information processing research is concerned, is the fact that activity in the visual system does not terminate with the termination of the physical stimulus. There are many examples of this visual persistence, but we are perhaps most familiar with it in terms of concepts such as the icon or short-term visual store. Behavioral indices of this visual persistence can be obtained for 300 or more msec following termination of the stimulus, depending upon stimulus intensity, state of adaptation of the eye, and the postexposure luminances.

II. TEMPORAL INTEGRATION

Is Maximum stimulus clarity achieved instantaneously?

The summation of energy in the visual system over time suggests that the information available to a central processor is analogous to a developing photographic print. Just as a print develops over time when bathed, a visual sensation develops over time. As with a photographic print, gross figure–ground differentiation appears first as energy is integrated. Fine detail becomes discernable later as energy is summed sufficiently to resolve the higher acuity requirements for this detail. This is the nature of the visual input — the raw material — from which cognitive psychology must proceed.

Temporal development of the visual input was recognized by the microgenetic approach to perception (see Flavell & Draguns, 1957), but their concern was in the development of the percept itself rather than with the temporal arrival of levels of information. More directly related to the temporal development of visual information is the well-documented speed/accuracy tradeoff (Fitts, 1966; Ollman, 1966; Swensson, 1972). A speed/accuracy tradeoff implies that the conscious executive (in the sense of Newell & Simon, 1972) is capable of tapping the developing information across time. When the executive acts upon the developing visual input early in the sequence, insufficient energy summation is available to assure a high level of accuracy. Conversely, waiting until energy summation is complete results in slower response but a higher level of accuracy. These considerations are consistent with the research on cumulative models of reaction time (Pachella, 1974; Stone, 1960) and in the use of the latency operation characteristic (LOC) to measure the rate of perceptual construction (Lappin & Disch, 1972a, 1972b, 1973; Pachella & Fisher, 1969; Pew, 1969).

The temporal summation of energy in the visual register has several implications for models of information processing. First, discriminations based upon high acuity resolution will require more time; that is, aggregation of information is a direct function of processing time. Second, processing itself probably proceeds as a series of successive approximations. It seems unlikely (particularly in view of evidence like the speed/accuracy tradeoff) that processing from the sensory register awaits full development of the visual registration. How, for example, would the executive know when maximum energy summation had occurred? Instead, we might anticipate sequential stages of processing corresponding to the points in time when the information needed to satisfy increasingly demanding acuity requirements becomes available. Current speculation that "feature detectors" may have different thresholds (Estes, 1976) may turn out to reflect nothing more than the amount of energy summation required for the acuity resolution associated with that feature. At the very least, what present evidence exists as to differential thresholds for feature detectors is highly confounded with visual acuity.

Inasmuch as a percept is seen to resolve in clarity over time, questions of serial versus parallel processing need to be reconsidered. It can be argued that whether several stimuli are processed serially or simultaneously critically depends on the rate at which evidence is aggregated for each stimulus. Should the rates of information accumulation differ among the stimuli, they might be processed in parallel (i.e., information regarding them would accumulate simultaneously), but be identified serially (as the information threshold for recognition of each is surpassed). Although the constraints of this paper preclude the elaboration of implications for the serial versus parallel processing controversy, it should be noted that such a distinction seems both arbitrary and unjustifiable if the visual system lacks infinite temporal resolution.

III. RETINAL LOCUS, ACUITY AND PROCESSING TIME

Is Stimulus Availability Independent of Retinal Locus?

Research concerned with visual attentional capacity and processing rate has frequently employed linear or rectangular letter displays subtending as much as 8° of visual angle (Bjork & Estes, 1973; Egeth, Jonides, & Wall, 1972; Estes, 1974; Shaw & Weigel, 1973). Theory based on data from these studies has often assumed simultaneous availability of all letters in the display to some central cognitive processor or attentional filter. There is considerable evidence to suggest that such an assumption is seriously in error. First, acuity, even within the fovea, drops rather markedly as the locus of the stimulus is moved from the foveal center (Riggs, 1965). Second, neural bundles become increasingly interconnected outward across the retina, thereby degrading edge and contour resolution. The effect of reducing acuity is a degradation in the quality of the stimulus and Sternberg (1969), among others, has shown that reaction time to visual forms increases appreciably with stimulus degradation. Thus, retinal locus and acuity are critical variables to visual information processing research.

The effect of the retinal locus of a signal upon reaction time has a long research history (e.g., Hall & von Kries, 1879; Poffenberger, 1912). However, these studies typically used simple reaction time, usually to a light flash, and were mainly concerned with differences in reaction time to foveal versus extrafoveal stimulation. More directly relevant to information processing concerns is a recent experiment by Lefton and Haber (1974). These investigators were also concerned with the assumption made by information processing theorists that all n letters in a simultaneously presented display were simultaneously available to a central processor. Lefton and Haber measured the subject's reaction time for "same" and "different" judgments to two letters presented simultaneously. The retinal locus from foveal center to plus or minus 4° of angle was explored. Though reaction time varied nearly 100 msec from foveal center to 4° outward, there were significant nonmonotonic effects in their data. The reasons for the nonmonotonicity were not clear, but perhaps reflect the judgmental nature of the task that may have interacted with the stimulus location.

Eriksen and Schultz (1977) have recently published data that more directly reflect the effect of foveal locus upon recognition or identification time. They presented a capital letter either at the foveal center or at 3 loci to the right and left of foveal center along a horizontal meridian out to 3° of visual angle. Vocal reaction time to identify the presented letter was measured. Letters were presented in both degraded and undegraded conditions. Degradation was obtained by the superimposition of a dot matrix over the capital letter. Data from their experiment are shown in Table 1.

TABLE 1

Mean Vocal Reaction Time to Target Identification in Msec Across
Retinal Loci Under Two Levels of Stimulus Quality.

	Retinal Locus						
	$-3°$	$-2°$	$-1°$	$0°$	$1°$	$2°$	$3°$
Degraded:	560	522	491	458	493	530	563
Undegraded:	484	452	431	418	432	465	491

From the table, it is clear that retinal locus has a pronounced effect upon vocal identification time: latency increases on the order of 100 msec when the stimulus is moved from the foveal center to plus or minus 3° of angle on a horizontal meridian. Further, degrading the stimulus leads to an increase in reaction time at all foveal locations with a suggestion that degradation becomes a more potent variable as locus is moved from foveal center.

These differences in identification times as a function of foveal locus may be attributed to two different processes. First of all, neural transmission time from the retina to higher visual processing centers varies as a function of retinal locus (Doty, 1958; Kappauf, 1967; Sweet, 1953). However, the magnitude of the differences in transmission time that have been reported is appreciably less within the fovea than the approximate 100 msec obtained in our data and those of Lefton and Haber (1974).

A second and probably more important reason for the latency difference is the degradation in the information provided higher processing centers as the periphery of the fovea and nonfoveal regions are stimulated. As we have described above, due to the time-intensity reciprocity, the information in the primary visual projection area develops over time as energy is summed. As stimuli fall on retinal areas of less acuity, a longer period of energy summation would be required in order to compensate for the decreased acuity. The results obtained for the degraded stimuli are consistent with this interpretation.

Regardless of the extent to which the present effects are due to differences in neural transmission time for different retinal loci, or the need for increased energy summation time, the data clearly demonstrate that the peripheral sense organ, at least in vision, plays an important role in limiting overloads on subsequent information processing stages. Even when the visual system is stimulated simultaneously with a linear multiletter display, the characteristics of the eye ensure that the information in the display is available to a central processor or stages in a temporally distributed manner.

IV. VISUAL PERSISTENCE

Is There a Separate Visual Store?

The work of Sperling (1960) and Averbach and Coriell (1961) in the early sixties revived interest in the old phenomenon of visual persistence. The work of these investigators coincided with the resurgent interest by cognitive psychologists in perceptual processing and in the development of models thereof. Neisser (1967) popularized the term "icon" for this photographic-like internal representation of a visual stimulus and the icon soon became an integral part of many models of visual information processing, with some model builders positing that all processing of visual information proceeded from the iconic representation of the stimulus. It was not clear in many of these models how the icon differed from the sensation — the registration of the visual stimulation upon the primary projection areas in the cortex. Perhaps it didn't. But the concept of the icon carried a little more "pizzazz" than terms like "neural event" or "cortical projection of the visual stimulation." Psychologists tended to overlook the fact that, except for such occasions as lightning storms on dark nights, the average human did not need to process information from an icon, since the stimulus of interest could be fixated for relatively long periods of time.

Removal of the icon from its pedestal requires some further analysis of its characteristics. It is important whether the icon is conceived on the one hand as a separate short-term highly detailed memory system or, on the other hand, as the persistence for short durations of the neurological acitivity in higher visual centers resulting from stimulation of the retina. The distinction is acutely important for interpreting the effects of successive stimuli separated by brief interstimulus intervals. If the icon is a separate memory system, then provision exists for separate storage of each of the successive inputs. However, if the icon is not a separate system, interference or montage-like effects would be expected due to superimposition of stimuli on projection areas still responding to a prior stimulation.

We know of no compelling evidence requiring an iconic storage separate and different from the decaying stimulation trace. Furthermore, positing such a separate storage creates problems. For example, one must consider the transfer of the sensation to the iconic storage. Does the transfer occur instantaneously or sequentially, and if the latter, how many transfers are required?

In view of the previous discussion concerning the relatively slow build-up of the stimulus sensation, a concept of a separate iconic storage would necessitate postulation of exactly when in the development of this information the transfer occurs. For example, does it occur at the end of the energy summation interval, or can the transfer occur anytime throughout the build-up of information in the sensory register?

A special problem is encountered in the case of successive stimuli, where stimulus durations are short and the second stimulus follows the first within 100 or so msec. If the same retinal cells stimulated by the first stimulus are now stimulated by a succeeding stimulus, is the icon of the second stimulus stored separately from that of the first? If so, some mechanism must exist to provide feedback telling the transfer system that the previous icon is still present and, therefore, that a new storage locus for the second stimulus must be found. On the other hand, if the two stimulations share the same storage register, so that the fresh icon of the last stimulus is superimposed upon the decaying icon of the first, then the concept of a separate iconic storage is an unnecessary complication. In performance terms, such a system would gain nothing over the theoretically simpler system in which the succeeding stimulus occupies the same sensory register along with the decaying effects from the prior stimulation.

An experiment by Eriksen and Collins (1968) on icon duration and visual integration provides evidence on these hypotheses. They constructed pairs of stimuli, with each member of the pair looking like a collection of random dots. When the two members of the pair were exposed simultaneously in separate tachistoscopic fields, they superimposed in such a way as to form legible three-letter nonsense syllables. The duration of integration due to iconic persistence could then be studied by introducing variable interstimulus intervals between presentation of the two members of the pair. Recognition remained above the control level with interstimulus intervals well in excess of 100 msec. Now, if the icon of the first stimulation of "random dots" were stored separately from that of the second stimulation of "random dots," it would be difficult to understand how these two registers could be superimposed so as to reconstruct the embedded nonsense syllable. At the very least, some mechanism for superimposition of separate iconic stores on a point-for-point basis would have to be posited. Parsimony argues against this conclusion.

A separate iconic store also seems unlikely from the viewpoint of evolution. The environment from which the eye evolved poses few natural circumstances of brief duration visual signals or of rapid successive visual stimulation. Reading is perhaps the most common example where rapid sequential visual inputs are involved, but even here, rapid readers still make only three to four fixations per second. As Ganz (1975) has noted, attempts to speed up the rate of reading quickly run into interference effects when fixations are limited to 100 msec. Experimental demonstration of this limitation on perceptual rate when the same or an overlapping population of retinal receptors is stimulated by each succeeding stimulus has been presented by Eriksen and Eriksen (1971). They successively presented a letter, a digit, and a directional arrowhead at different rates in such a manner that the same or an overlapping population of retinal receptors was stimulated by each successive input. Approximately 250 msec between stimulations was required for all three stimuli to be identified with perfect accuracy.

Similar conclusions were reached by Potter and Levy (1969) using complex pictorial stimuli.

If the icon is viewed as just another manifestation of lack of fine temporal resolution by the visual system, then it represents nothing more mysterious than the persistence of decaying stimulation traces in the higher visual centers. Naturally, the existence of the icon must be acknowledged in any efforts to determine the time visual inputs are available for processing, and becomes a particular annoyance for experimental methodologies attempting to determine processing rate from inferences based upon the duration of the physical stimulus.

If the icon is the persisting decaying stimulation trace, we would expect its duration as well as its clarity to be a function of stimulus intensity as well as the adapting luminance level. As Dick (1974) has pointed out, there are few parametric data available relating duration or quality of the icon to stimulus variables. Several experiments, however, do show that the legibility and duration of the icon increase with the intensity of the visual stimulus. Eriksen and Steffy (1964) found that at low intensities, essentially no legible icon could be measured by the classical partial report technique originated by Sperling (1960).[1] Eriksen and Steffy used a dark adaptation field and a stimulus field of 3.7 fL. Though these intensities are low, they are well within the range of values used in tachistoscopic investigations. Keele and Chase (1967) also found little evidence of iconic storage at this luminance level, but when higher luminances were employed clear evidence of a legible icon was obtained.

Eriksen and Rohrbaugh (1970) used stimulus displays consisting of 12 letters arranged in a circular pattern with a probe indicator designating one of the letters. The indicator occurred either simultaneously with the display or was delayed by interstimulus intervals of 0–300 msec. Two levels of display luminance were studied: 0.7 mL and 7.0 mL. Evidence of iconic persistence was found at both intensity levels, but accuracy was uniformly higher for 7.0 mL displays and performance did not become asymptotic until a longer target-probe interval.

As the iconic representation decays following termination of the stimulus, it might be supposed that its quality at any given point during decay would be comparable to that of a stimulus presented at a lower intensity level. That such is the case is suggested by the data of Eriksen and Collins (1968). They used the previously described stimuli consisting of what appeared to be random dot patterns that formed a three-letter nonsense syllable when the two members of the pair of these patterns were tachistoscopically superimposed. They found that a simultaneous presentation of the members of the pair in which each member was at a different luminance level resulted in poorer performance than if each

---

[1]Keele and Chase (1967) suggested that the failure of Eriksen and Steffy to obtain evidence of iconic storage was due to use of too simple a task. However, if the failure to obtain positive findings were due to the simplicity of the task, then performance should have remained at a high level of accuracy as the probe stimulus was delayed by longer and longer intervals. This, however, was not the case.

member was presented at the same luminance. That is, if the two dot patterns were of unequal luminance, structuring the dot patterns to produce the embedded nonsense syllable was less readily attained. These experimenters reasoned that if the decaying trace of an iconic representation at a given moment in time were comparable to a stimulation at a lower intensity, then presentation of the second (delayed) dot pattern at a lower intensity than the first pattern should yield improved performance for the delay interval. This procedure would result in both dot patterns being closer together in luminance. Thus, if the first member of a dot pair was presented at 5 mL, then 50 msec later when the second member was presented at 2 mL (corresponding more closely to the energy of the decayed trace of the first member) better integration would occur. Their results supported the prediction at several different luminance levels.

The evidence that the iconic representation is proportional to the intensity of the stimulus and influenced by the level of the adapting luminance is commensurate with the conclusion that iconic storage does not represent a separate memory system, but is rather the stimulation trace persisting in the sensory register. If a separate storage system existed, it seems somewhat coincidental that the quality and duration of this storage could be so directly proportional to the stimulus parameters. Occam's Razor forces us to regard the visual icon as the epiphenomenon of imprecise temporal resolution in vision.

V. VISUAL MASKING

Is An Interruption or Erasure Concept Necessary?

Many recent studies of visual information processing (e.g., Averbach, 1963; Haber & Standing, 1968; Johnston & McClelland, 1973; Reicher, 1969; Sperling, 1963; Wheeler, 1970; Wing & Allport, 1972) have employed a methodology based upon the assumption that a "noise" field presented within several hundred msec following termination of a visual target either erases that target or terminates its processing. The employment of such a mask has been used in attempts to control the amount of time the target will be available for processing. Further, many authors (Averbach, 1963; Keele, 1973; Lindsey & Norman, 1972; Posner, 1973; Sperling, 1963) have constructed information processing models on the basis of data obtained by methods that depend critically on a termination assumption.

It is easy to understand why an erasure-like process has a seductive appeal. The persistence of the stimulation trace or icon after termination of the stimulus creates obstacles for attempts to determine processing times, and to delineating stages of processing. Further, the possibility that the noise elements of the mask might be competing with/or saturating feature detectors that are necessary for target recognition is intriguing. But, unfortunately, the wide acceptance of the assumption that noise masks either erase or terminate target processing is more dependent upon methodological convenience than upon impelling deduction or inexorable fact. On the contrary, there is considerable evidence to suggest that successive visual events occurring within a time span of several hundred msec either have their energy summed into a unified stimulus or result in a composite much like a montage. Thus, whether or not a noise mask would appear to terminate the processing of a preceding target would then only depend on whether the superimposition of mask features on the target would eliminate critical discriminatory detail.

Some years ago, several investigators (Eriksen, 1966; Eriksen & Collins, 1967; Eriksen & Hoffman, 1963; Kahneman, 1965; Kinsbourne & Warrington, 1962) noted the relation between many masking phenomena and the known characteristic of the visual system to sum energy over brief temporal intervals. Their research has shown that the results of masking by light flashes, noise fields, and by encircling rings can be described as integration of the target and the mask into a composite. This integration may reduce the figure—ground contrast of the target and/or obscure its distinguishing features by contour interactions or superimposition.

The role of integration has been recognized in several recent influential papers on visual masking that espouse a dual masking theory (Bongartz & Scheerer, 1976; Scheerer, 1973; Spencer & Shuntich, 1970; Turvey, 1973). These papers urge that integration occurs under certain circumstances to produce masking effects, but interruption or processing termination occurs for other masking situations. Ganz (1975), for example, attributes metacontrast masking to an erasure process.

Perhaps these authors are invoking more demons than are necessary. For a processing termination concept to remain viable, there must be specification of the particular circumstances under which it occurs. Furthermore, it must be shown that these specified circumstances are not amenable to an integration account.

Scheerer (1973), Bongartz and Scheerer (1976), and Spencer and Shuntich (1970) distinguish between integration masking and interruption masking on the basis of the interstimulus interval between target and mask. Masking by integration processes is reserved for interstimulus intervals of 150 msec or less, corresponding to the critical duration from Bloch's Law. Masking effects obtained at longer interstimulus intervals are attributed to the interruption of processing by the mask.

It is doubtful if a valid distinction between integration versus interruption masking can be made purely on interstimulus interval. Assuming that summation or integration occurs only for durations less than 150 msec overlooks the extensive research carried on by Kahneman and his associates (Kahneman, 1964; Kahneman & Norman, 1964; Kahneman et al., 1967) that demonstrates a critical duration for form perception on the order of 300—400 msec. The results from

Kahneman's laboratory and the work of van den Brink (1957) [see Ganz, 1975] have led Ganz (1975) to suggest that perceptual tasks involving higher stages of the perceptual system yield larger critical durations.

Scheerer (1973) and Spencer and Shuntich (1970) find evidence for masking at long interstimulus intervals (ISIs) only by using displays with many potential targets. They used a probe occurring either simultaneously with the display, or at intervals afterwards, to designate the specific target to the subject. As Eriksen and Rohrbaugh (1970) have pointed out, the use of multiletter displays in masking studies involves several other processes that need to be considered in interpreting the results.

In part, the integration-interruption controversy arises from inadequate explication of integration theory. As we have argued, the lack of fine temporal resolution in the visual system has two distinct manifestations. First, there is an initiation component during which the visual system is summing energy. This interval corresponds to the critical duration of Bloch's Law. Second, a decay component is apparent from iconic persistence for as long as several hundred msec, depending upon the parameters of the physical stimulus. Furthermore, we know that the subject can often continue to process information from this icon.

If a mask is presented within the summation interval for the target, we would expect energy summation to result in a unitary composite perception. This is particularly true where the mask consists of a light flash. We might distinguish this as *summation masking,* as distinct from the second phase *integrative masking,* which occurs when the target is too complex to be processed during the physical duration of the stimulus and the subject must continue processing from the iconic trace. The processing from the icon can be interfered with if the mask superimposes its neural representation upon the decaying trace of the target. The extent to which interference occurs will depend on the relative intensity of the two superimposed traces and the degree to which discriminatory detail of the target is obscured.

It is not appropriate to refer to this second type of interference as an "interruption," if the term connotes termination of target processing. Independent operations would be required to demonstrate that the effect resulted from virtual termination of processing rather than from mere *interference.* In fact, Spencer and Shuntich (1970) are aware of this possibility when they discuss the incomplete masking effects obtained by their low energy masks.

Let us apply the Eriksen and Rohrbaugh (1970) integration account to the results of the Spencer and Shuntich (1970) experiment. The experiment of these latter investigators was quite comparable to that of Eriksen and Rohrbaugh and the results were highly similar. In one condition, Spencer and Shuntich used displays consisting of 12 letters arranged in a circular pattern around a central fixation point. A visual probe, presented simultaneously with the display, designated the letter to be reported. Exposure duration was set so as to yield approximately 85% accuracy when no mask followed the display. A pattern

TABLE 2

Percentage of Correct Identifications as a Function of SOA Between Target and Mask for Each of Three Levels of Mask Energy[a]

Mask energy	Stimulus onset asynchrony in msec. between target and mask.					
	0	50	100	150	200	300
E_1	80	67	58	65	72	82
E_2	62	43	48	65	71	78
E_3	31	30	47	62	71	76

[a](From Spencer & Schuntich, 1970. Data have been interpolated from their figure).

mask was used and its intensity was varied over three levels. The mask was presented at various ISIs following termination of the display and probe. A control condition employed a single letter display in which the letters could occupy any one of the twelve positions, and again the mask at one of the three intensity levels followed the single letter display at various ISIs.[2]

Partial results from this experiment are shown in Table 2. For the single letter display, even the most intense mask did not exert an effect beyond 150 msec ISI. In the case of the 12-letter displays on the other hand, masking effects were found to extend 250 to 300 msec. Further, the ISI of maximum masking was dependent upon mask intensity: the greater the mask intensity, the shorter the ISI at which maximum masking occurred. This pattern of results is quite comparable to that obtained by Eriksen and Rohrbaugh and is consistent with their predictions.

To reinterpret the Spencer and Shuntich (1970) data, one must first consider some of the behaviors that are involved in processing a briefly exposed multi-target display using a partial report technique. Twelve unrelated letters are beyond the subject's capacity to process in a brief visual presentation. Instead, the probe enables him to select which of the potential targets is the one to be reported. But perception of the probe and the act of selection do not occur instantaneously. Averbach and Coriell (1961) estimated that as long as 200 msec are required in perceiving and selecting. Experimentation by Colegate, Hoffman, and Eriksen, (1973) and Eriksen and Hoffman (1973) has yielded comparable time estimates. It is recognized that a 200 msec interval represents not a constant perception-selection time but, given an underlying distribution of selection times, the upper tail of that selection time distribution. Further, in keeping with our discussion of iconic storage, we would expect that the stimulus representation in the icon is decaying in intensity during the period of probe perception and selection. One further consideration must be borne in mind:

[2]Spencer and Shuntich (1970) also investigated forward masking, but for the sake of brevity we will not consider this aspect to their data here. Analogous conclusions follow from their forward masking data.

masking itself is a rather fragile phenomena — it depends upon the relative energy of target and mask. In most experimental arrangements, a slight increase in target energy or a slight decrease in mask energy is sufficient to eliminate or reduce the mask effect.

We now present an integration account of the Spencer and Shuntich results. Consider first the lowest energy mask, E-1. When this mask was presented simultaneously with the target display, little or no masking occurred. The energy of the mask was insufficient to mask the greater energy of the target. Of course, in keeping with the above considerations, the subject did not immediately process the target — first he had to process the indicator to know which target to encode. For the sake of exposition, let us assume that probe perception and selection occupies on the average 100 msec. Thus, when the subject was ready to encode the target, the target trace, as well as the superimposed mask trace, had decayed in energy over this 100 msec interval. However, since both target and mask were decaying, presumably at essentially the same rate, the relative energies remained essentially the same. But, when the mask is delayed by 100 msec ISI, the subject must then encode a target that has decayed for 100 msec, upon which is superimposed a pattern mask with a much higher energy (since the mask has just arrived and has not yet decayed). Therefore, the masking effect will be greater at this ISI.

As the mask is delayed further, the probability increases that the subject will have made his selection from the probe and encoded the target before the mask arrives, so that the ascending performance at ISIs greater than 100 msec reflects the increasing probability of target encoding prior to mask arrival.

A similar explanation is applied to the results for the mid- and high-intensity mask. The prediction is that the greater the intensity of the mask, the shorter the ISI between target and mask for maximum masking. For example, with a stronger mask the target trace need not decay to as low an energy level for the mask to be maximally effective. Indeed, if the mask is intense enough, it can be made to mask the target under simultaneous target and mask presentation.

Thus, the masking effects obtained with multitarget displays and a probe are a combination of two separate effects: (1) the increasing susceptibility of the decaying target icon to masking by a constant energy mask; and (2) the increasing probability with increasing ISIs that the target will be selected and encoded before mask occurrence.

Turvey (1973) has also presented an interruption theory of masking and, like Bongartz and Scheerer (1976) and Spencer and Shuntich (1970), also recognizes masking due to integration. He conceives of interruption masking as a cognitive effect where the appearance of the second stimulus (mask) causes a central processor either to hurry the processing of the first stimulus, or to interrupt the processing of the old in order to begin processing of the new. He uses the analogy of a clerk in a store who, if only one customer is present, spends considerable time with him, but, should a second customer enter the store, cuts short or hurries the treatment of the first customer.

Turvey's evidence for two kinds of masking is based upon a number of experiments employing two kinds of masks, a random mask and a pattern mask, and both monoptic and dichoptic viewing conditions. But the literature on binocular brightness averaging and Fechner's paradox offers a much simpler interpretation of his findings on dichoptic masking. Levelt (1965) has presented considerable data and a theoretical account demonstrating that the extent to which binocular interaction occurs in the summing or averaging of brightness depends upon the contour information available in the separate eyes. The degree of summation of brightness is weighted by the amount of contour information that is received by each eye. In the absence of contour information in one eye, the luminance from that field does not interact or summate in perceived brightness. This provides a good account of why negative results have been obtained in dichoptic masking by light flashes (Battersby & Wagman, 1962; Schiller, 1965), but pattern masks have yielded dichoptic masking effects (Kinsbourne & Warrington, 1962; Schiller, 1965; Schiller & Smith, 1966).

Turvey's failure to obtain dichoptic masking with his random mask would appear to be due to its lack of contour information. The mask consisted of a random arrangement of very tiny dots. At brief exposures the energy from the field was probably insufficient to provide enough acuity resolution to detect the dots, so that the mask behaved much as a dim light flash. This would be commensurate with research in vision that has shown that fine gratings function as a gray uniform field. His pattern mask, on the other hand, consisted of a haphazard arrangement of line segments comparable in size and extent to the lines in letters. This mask provided contour information in the dichoptic situation and led to results comparable to those obtained by others using pattern masks in dichoptic arrangements.

Turvey's other evidence for an interruption process in pattern masking is not convincing. He failed to rule out the possibility of the superimposition of the pattern mask on the decaying icon of the target. The target and the mask were always arranged so that both target and mask stimulated either the same, or an overlapping, population of retinal receptors. A simple control would have been to present the target a degree or two to the left of fixation and the mask a degree or two to the right. This would have effectively ruled out any integration interpretation of obtained masking effects. To follow Turvey's analogy, it should not make a difference in the time the clerk devotes to the first customer whether the second customer comes in from the north or south door.

VI. COGNITIVE MASKING

Is There More to Masking Than Meets the Eye?

We do not intend to advance the thesis that all visual masking effects are attributable to integration. But we do submit that there is no evidence for erasure or interruption masking that cannot be accounted for more parsimoniously by integration. In fact, there is a form of *cognitive masking* that cannot be attributed to target degradation. An experiment by Eriksen and Eriksen (1974) illustrates this form of masking with reaction time as the dependent variable.

In their experiment, two sets of capital letters were used as targets: H and K, and S and C. Subjects were instructed to move a lever in one direction if the target were an H or a K and in the opposite direction if the target were an S or a C. The subjects knew that the target would always appear directly above the fixation point and were further instructed to ignore any extraneous letters that appeared flanking the targets. In the various experimental conditions target letters were presented in four ways: alone; flanked three on each side by repetitions of the same target letter; flanked by the other member of the same set as the target letter; or flanked by letters of the opposite target set. In Table 3, data from the experiment are reproduced for the condition where the flanking noise letters were 0.5° of visual angle removed from the target letter, a distance greater than has been previously shown to produce contour interference (Flom, Weymouth, & Kahneman, 1963).

As can be seen from the table, reaction time to the target was much more rapid when the target appeared without accompanying noise letters. The presence of noise letters increased reaction time even if the noise was from the same response set as the target. The most dramatic increase in reaction time occurred, however, when the noise letters were from the opposite response set.

The results cannot be attributed to interference due to adjacent contours. If contour interference were the only factor, one would expect to obtain comparable results when the noise letters were from the same response set as when they were from the opposite response set. An interpretation in terms of allocation of limited processing energy or capacity is suggested by the effect of the opposite-response set noise letters. The fact that they exert a more pronounced slowing on reaction time than noise letters from the same response set suggests that they have been processed to the point of arousing incipient interfering responses.

This latency inhibition from extraneous noise stimuli in the visual field can be obtained with a wide variety of noise. Table 4 presents data from an experiment in which the targets were the capital letters A or H and the response a lever

TABLE 3

Mean Reaction Time in Msec to Classify the Set of a Target Letter Under Four Noise Conditions[a]

Noise Conditions			
Target alone	Repetitions of target letter	Same response set as target letter	Opposite response set from target letter
406	437	445	461

[a](From Eriksen & Eriksen, 1974.)

TABLE 4

Mean Reaction Time in Msec to the Letters A and H as Dependent Upon the Kinds
of Flanking Noise Stimuli.

Noise Conditions			
Letter alone	Geometric forms	Colors	Random lines
292	330	327	319

movement in one direction or the other depending upon the target. Again, the
subjects knew the target would always appear directly above the fixation point
and they were to ignore any other stimuli that appeared in the visual field. In
this experiment, in addition to presenting the target alone, the target was flanked
in different conditions by patches of colors; by solid geometric forms such as
triangles, hexagons, and diamonds; or by random patterns of line segments the
size and width of those used in the letter strokes. Again it is seen that the presence
of extraneous stimuli in the visual field slowed reaction time to the target letter.

At this point the question arises as to whether reaction time is reflecting the
same underlying processes as accuracy. Eriksen and Eriksen (1972) have shown
that typical masking functions can be obtained with reaction time as the dependent variable in a classic ring masking paradigm. But more convincing, perhaps, is the fact that cognitive masking effects can be obtained using identification
accuracy as a dependent variable in the extraneous noise paradigms just described.
If an exposure duration is selected where the subject can identify a capital letter
with about 85% accuracy, a marked drop in accuracy is found if noise letters are
presented in the visual field simultaneously with the target letter.

A further resemblance of cognitive masking effects to typical masking functions
is found in an experiment by Eriksen and Hoffman (1972). In their experiment
the subject was required to identify as quickly as possible a target letter that
appeared on the circumference on an imaginary circle 2° in diameter centered on
the fixation point. The target could appear at any one of the 12 clock positions.
Two classes of noise signals were employed — other capital letters, or black discs
— and were presented at three levels of proximity to the target letter. At the
closest spacing, the two noise letters appeared on each side of the target in the
adjacent clock positions (0.53° angle removed). Thus, if the target appeared at
12 o'clock, noise signals appeared at 1 and 2, and 11 and 10 o'clock. At the
second spacing, noise signals were one position removed on each side of the target
(1° of angle). Thus, for the case of a 12 o'clock target, noise signals were at 2 and
3 o'clock and 10 and 9 o'clock. In the third spacing, two clock positions intervened between noise and target on each side (1.4° of angle). In another experimental manipulation, the stimulus onset asynchrony (SOA) by which the noise
followed the appearance of the target was varied from zero to 300 msec. Table
5 summarizes the data from their experiment.

TABLE 5

Mean Time to Vocalize Target Letter as a Function of SOA Between Onset of the Target and the Onset of the Noise Elements.[a]

Noise	Spacing	Stimulus onset asynchrony between target and noise in msec.					
		0	50	100	150	200	300
	0.5°	543	478	441	420	414	412
Letters	1.0°	481	462	433	418	413	411
	1.4°	481	461	431	415	413	411
	0.5°	438	435	413	411	410	410
Discs	1.0°	431	434	412	410	409	411
	1.4°	428	432	411	410	408	409

[a]For two types of noise and three angular separations between target and closest noise element. (From Eriksen & Hoffman, 1972.)

For both classes of noise, letters and discs, a typical masking function was obtained as SOA increased. Maximum slowing of reaction time occurred when the letter noise appeared simultaneously with the target. For the disc noise, reaction time had become asymptotic by an SOA of 100 msec, whereas 150 msec SOA was required for asymptote with the letter noise. At all SOAs the discs impaired reaction time less than did the letters. Further, impairment is found at all spacings of noise, although the closest spacing produces the most interference.

While we stated above that this form of "cognitive masking" was *not* explainable on the basis of integration and resultant degradation of the target, this was not to say that lack of final temporal resolution in the visual system was not manifest in the phenomenon. The Eriksen and Hoffman (1972) results, obtained when an SOA is introduced between target and noise, reveal again that visual processing is not instantaneous. Their finding that the maximum effect occurred when target and noise (mask) were simultaneous is not unique in the masking literature. In fact, masking by random or pattern noise, or by an encircling ring, typically shows maximum effect when presented simultaneously with the target.

Once the problem is placed in the context of the temporal delay in the visual system, the retroactive effects of a mask no longer need to dominate our thinking. Instead, we can turn our thoughts to the more basic question: Why is a letter more difficult to identify if encircled by a black ring or if other letters, colors, or forms are simultaneously presented in the visual field? Indeed, the ability to delay this "noise," and produce attenuation in the effect, provides us with a potent research procedure for disentangling information processing steps or stages. The finding by Eriksen and Hoffman (1972) that masking from disc noise extends over a shorter SOA than does masking from letter noise suggests that the former does not involve the more advanced stages that letter noise does. Systematically delaying the presentation of different forms of "noise" might produce differential effects on tasks involving identity matching, as opposed to name matching or category matching.

VII. CONCLUSIONS

Reexamination of various visual information processing phenomena from a perspective of temporal resolution in the visual system leads to the following conclusions:

1. The human visual processing system lacks infinite temporal resolution under both stimulus onset and offset.
2. The human processor aggregates visual stimulus information over a period of 100 msec or more, during which time energy is summed.
3. This aggregation of stimulus evidence results in gross figure-ground discrimination prior to the discernment of fine stimulus detail. Such a successive approximation to a finely detailed percept over time suggests the reinterpretation of controversies regarding serial versus parallel processing, and the existence of different thresholds for feature detectors.
4. Stimulus information arrives sequentially to a central processor. This conclusion follows from both the nature of information aggregation in vision and the gradient of acuity across the retina.
5. The visual icon is merely the epiphenomenal manifestation of a decaying stimulus trace, and must not be regarded as a precognitive storage register.
6. There is no convincing evidence for an "erasure" or "interruption" process in visual perception.
7. There is, however, evidence for a "cognitive" masking phenomenon that results from the limited-capacity nature of the visual information processing system.

ACKNOWLEDGMENTS

This research was supported by Public Health Service Research Grant MH-1206 and United States Public Health Service Research Career Program Award K6-MH-22014 to the first author.

REFERENCES

Averbach, E. The span of apprehension as a function of exposure duration. *Journal of Verbal Learning and Verbal Behavior,* 1963, *2,* 60–64.

Averbach, E., & Coriell, A. S. Short-term memory in vision. *Bell System Technical Journal,* 1961, *40,* 309–328.

Battersby, W. S., & Wagman, I. H. Neural limitations of visual excitability: IV. Spatial determinants of retrochiasmal interaction. *American Journal of Physiology*, 1962, *203*, 359–365.

Bjork, E., & Estes, W. K. Letter identification in relation to linguistic context and masking conditions. *Memory and Cognition*, 1973, *1*, 217–223.

Bongartz, W., & Scheerer, E. Two visual stores and two processing operations in tachistoscopic partial report. *Quarterly Journal of Experimental Psychology*, 1976, *28*, 203–219.

Colegate, R., Hoffman, J. E., & Eriksen, C. W. Selective encoding from multielement visual displays. *Perception and Psychophysics*, 1973, *14*, 217–224.

Dick, A. O. Iconic memory and its relation to perceptual processing and other memory mechanisms. *Perception and Psychophysics*, 1974, *16*, 575–596.

Doty, R. W. Potentials evoked in cat cerebral cortex by defuse and by punctiform photic stimuli. *Journal of Neuro-physiology*, 1958, *21*, 437–464.

Egeth, H., Jonides, J., & Wall, S. Parallel processing of multielement displays. *Cognitive Psychology*, 1972, *3*, 694–698.

Eriksen, B. A., & Eriksen, C. W. Effects of noise letters upon the identification of a target letter in a nonsearch task. *Perception & Psychophysics*, 1974, *16*, 143–149.

Eriksen, C. W. Temporal luminance summation effects in backward and forward masking. *Perception and Psychophysics*, 1966, *1*, 87–92.

Eriksen, C. W., & Collins, J. F. Some temporal characteristics of visual pattern perception. *Journal of Experimental Psychology*, 1967, *74*, 476–484.

Eriksen, C. W., & Collins, J. F. Sensory traces versus the psychological moment in the temporal organization of form. *Journal of Experimental Psychology*, 1968, *77*, 376–382.

Eriksen, C. W., & Eriksen, B. A. Visual perceptual processing rates and backward and forward masking. *Journal of Experimental Psychology*, 1971, *89*, 306–313.

Eriksen, C. W., & Eriksen, B. A. Visual backward masking as measured by voice reaction time. *Perception and Psychophysics*, 1972, *12*, 5–8.

Eriksen, C. W., & Hoffman, M. Form recognition at brief duration as a function of adapting field and interval between stimulations. *Journal of Experimental Psychology*, 1963, *66*, 485–499.

Eriksen, C. W., & Hoffman, J. E. Temporal and spatial characteristics of selective encoding from visual displays. *Perception and Psychophysics*, 1972, *12*, 201–204.

Eriksen, C. W., & Hoffman, J. E. The extent of processing of noise elements during selective encoding from visual displays. *Perception and Psychophysics*, 1973, *14*, 155–160.

Eriksen, C. W., & Rohrbaugh, J. Visual masking in multielement displays. *Journal of Experimental Psychology*, 1970, *83*, 147–154.

Eriksen, C. W., & Steffy, R. A. Short-term memory and retroactive interference in visual perception. *Journal of Experimental Psychology*, 1964, *68*, 423–434.

Eriksen, C. W., & Schultz, D. W. Retinal locus and acuity in visual information processing. *Bulletin of the Psychonomic Society*, 1977, *9*, 81–84.

Estes, W. K. Redundancy of noise elements and signals in visual detection of letters. *Perception and Psychophysics*, 1974, *16*, 53–60.

Estes, W. K. Perceptual processing in letter recognition and reading. In E. C. Carterette & M. P. Friedman (Eds.) *Handbook of perception*, Vol. IX. New York: Academic Press, 1976.

Fitts, P. M. Cognitive aspects of information processing: III. Set for speed versus accuracy. *Journal of Experimental Psychology*, 1966, *71*, 849–857.

Flavell, J. H., & Draguns, J. A microgenetic approach to perception and thought. *Psychological Bulletin*, 1957, *54*, 197–217.

Flom, M. C., Weymouth, F. W., & Kahneman, D. Visual resolution and contour interaction. *Journal of Optical Society of America*, 1963, *53*, 1026–1032.

Ganz, L. Temporal factors in visual perception. In E. C. Carterette & M. P. Friedman (Eds.) *Handbook of perception* Vol. I. New York: Academic Press, 1975.

Haber, R. N., & Standing, L. G. Clarity and recognition of masked and degraded stimuli. *Psychonomic Science,* 1968, *13,* 83–84.

Hall, G. S., & von Kries, J. Über die abhangigkeit der reactionzet vom ort des reizes. *Archives of Anatomy and Physiology: Leipzig Supplement,* 1879, 1–10.

Johnston, J. C., & McClelland, J. L. Visual factors in word perception. *Perception and Psychophysics,* 1973, *14,* 365–370.

Kahneman, D. Temporal summation in an acuity task at different energy levels – a study of the determinants of summation. *Vision Research,* 1964, *4,* 557–566.

Kahneman, D. Exposure duration and effective figure ground contrast. *Quarterly Journal of Experimental Psychology,* 1965, *17,* 308–314.

Kahneman, D., & Norman, J. The time-intensity relation in visual perception as a function of the observer's task. *Journal of Experimental Psychology,* 1964, *68,* 215–220.

Kahneman, D., Norman, J., & Kubovy, M. The critical duration for the resolution of form: Centrally or peripherally determined? *Journal of Experimental Psychology,* 1967, *73,* 323–327.

Kappauf, W. E. *On- and off-latencies in visual perception: Effects of luminance, wavelength, and retinal location.* (Grant NB-05576-01, Report #4). Champaign, Il.: University of Illinois, November, 1967.

Keele, S. W. *Attention and human performance.* Pacific Palisades, Calif: Goodyear Publishing Co., 1973.

Keele, S. W., & Chase, W. G. Short-term visual storage. *Perception and Psychophysics,* 1967, *2,* 383–386.

Kinsbourne, M., & Warrington, E. K. The effect of an aftercoming random pattern on the perception of brief visual stimuli. *Quarterly Journal of Experimental Psychology,* 1962, *14,* 223–234.

Lappin, J. S., & Disch, K. The latency operating characteristic: I Effects of stimulus probability on choice reaction time. *Journal of Experimental Psychology,* 1972, *92,* 419–427. (a)

Lappin, J. S., & Disch, K. The latency operating characteristic: II. Effects of visual stimulus intensity on choice reaction time *Journal of Experimental Psychology,* 1972, *93,* 367–372. (b)

Lappin, J. S., & Disch, K. Latency operating characteristic: III. Temporal uncertainty effects. *Journal of Experimental Psychology,* 1973, *98,* 279–285.

Lefton, L., & Haber, R. N. Information extraction from different retinal locations. *Journal of Experimental Psychology,* 1974, *102,* 975–980.

Levelt, W. J. M. Binocular brightness averaging and contour information. *British Journal of Psychology,* 1965, *56,* 1–13.

Lindsey, P. H., & Norman, D. A. *Human information processing.* New York: Academic Press, 1972.

Neisser, U. *Cognitive psychology.* New York: Appleton-Century-Crofts, 1967.

Newell, A., & Simon, H. *Human problem solving.* Englewood Cliffs, N.J.: Prentice-Hall, 1972.

Ollman, R. T. Fast guesses in choice reaction time. *Psychonomic Science,* 1966, *6,* 155–156.

Pachella, R. The interpretation of reaction time in information-processing research. In B. Kantowitz, (Ed.), *Human information processing: Tutorials in performance and cognition.* Hillsdale, N.J.: Lawrence Erlbaum Associates, 1974.

Pachella, R. G., & Fisher, D. F. Effect of stimulus degradation and similarity on the tradeoff between speed and accuracy in absolute judgments. *Journal of Experimental Psychology,* 1969, *81,* 7–9.

Pew, R. W. The speed-accuracy operating characteristic. In W. G. Koster (Ed.), *Attention and Performance II*. Amsterdam: North-Holland, 1969. (Reprinted from *Acta Psychologica, 1969, 30.*)

Poffenberger, A. T. Reaction time to retinal stimulation with special reference to time lost in conduction through nerve centers. *Archives of Psychology, 1912, 3,* 23, 1–73.

Posner, M. I. *Cognition: An introduction*. Glenview, IL: Scott, Foresman and Co., 1973.

Potter, M. C., & Levy, E. J. Recognition memory for a rapid sequence of pictures. *Journal of Experimental Psychology, 1969, 81,* 10–15.

Reicher, G. Perceptual recognition as a function of meaningfulness of stimulus material. *Journal of Experimental Psychology, 1969, 81,* 276–280.

Riggs, L. A. Visual acuity. In Graham, C. H. (Ed.), *Vision and visual perception*. New York: Wiley, 1965.

Scheerer, E. Integration, interruption and processing rate in visual backward masking: II. An experimental test. *Psychologische Forschung, 1973, 36,* 95–115.

Schiller, P. H. Monoptic and dichoptic visual masking by patterns and flashes. *Journal of Experimental Psychology, 1965, 69,* 193–199.

Schiller, P. H., & Smith, M. C. Detection in metacontrast. *Journal of Experimental Psychology, 1966, 71,* 32–39.

Shaw, P., & Weigel, G. Effects of bars and blanks on recognition of words and non-words embedded in a row of letters. *Perception and Psychophysics, 1973, 14,* 117–124.

Spencer, T., & Schuntich, R. Evidence for an interruption theory of backward masking. *Journal of Experimental Psychology, 1970, 85,* 198–203.

Sperling, G. A. The information available in brief visual presentations. *Psychological Monographs, 1960, 74,* 1–29.

Sperling, G. A. A model for visual memory tasks. *Human Facotrs, 1963, 5,* 19–31.

Sternberg, S. Memory scanning: Mental processes revealed by reaction time experiments. *American Scientist, 1969, 57,* 421–457.

Stone, M. Models for choice reaction times. *Psychometrika, 1960, 25,* 251–260.

Sweet, A. L. Temporal discrimination by the human eye. *The American Journal of Psychology, 1953, 66,* 185–198.

Swensson, R. G. The elusive tradeoff: Speed versus accuracy in visual discrimination tasks. *Perception and Psychophysics, 1972, 12,* 16–32.

Turvey, M. T. On peripheral and central processes in vision: Inferences from an information-processing analysis of masking with patterned stimuli, *Psychological Review, 1973, 80,* 1–52.

Wheeler, D. D. Processes in word recognition. *Cognitive Psychology, 1970, 1,* 59–85.

Wing, A., & Allport, D. A. Multidimensional encoding of visual form. *Perception and Psychophysics, 1972, 12,* 474–476.

2 Time Factors in the Processing of Visual Movement Information

Claude Bonnet

Laboratoire de Psychologie Expérimentale et Comparée
Université René Descartes
Paris, France

ABSTRACT

Different aspects of the role of time as a modulating variable in the processing of visual movement information are analyzed. The efficiency of such a variable in discriminating between processes is stressed.

1. In detection experiments, temporal summation processes are demonstrated that allow us to distinguish between two different Analyzing Systems that process movement information in different ways. These two processes also appear to be effective in modulating the apparent velocity of a grating.

2. The assumption of a Neuro-Sensory Adaptation (NSA) process is then questioned on the basis of the predicted temporal characteristics of the phenomena that it should produce, in particular, the movement aftereffect. From that study, it follows that two classes of visual aftereffects should be assumed. Only one of them is attributable to a NSA process.

3. Further investigation of the movement aftereffect leads to the study of temporal frequency as a factor of temporal summation. Again the results appear to be consistent with the assumption that two different Analyzing Systems are triggered depending upon the Spatial Frequency range of the stimulus.

I. INTRODUCTION

The processing of visual movement information can be considered to start with the sensory coding of the relevant features of the stimulus. According to a sensory psychophysiological approach, a *feature* is a dimension of the proximal stimulus that selectively triggers or gates (Blakemore, 1975) a specific Analyzing System. The demonstration of such a specific Analyzing System, which is assumed

25

to insure the sensory coding of a given feature, is obtained through such psychophysical paradigms as selective adaptation or subthreshold summation (see Sekuler, 1975). Neurophysiological evidence is a complementary basis for considering a stimulus dimension as a feature. In effect, the basic assumption of feature coding is that there exist cells (feature detectors) in the central nervous system that are selectively responsive to a particular dimension. In a psychophysical approach, it will not be referred to single cells (detectors) but to Analyzing Systems, i.e., to a set of neural cells sharing common properties. If among stimulus dimensions some have to be considered as trigger-features, some others are "modulating" variables, i.e., dimensions that are not coded as such, but that modulate the sensitivity of an Analyzing System to its trigger-feature. Exposure time will be shown to be such a variable in the coding and processing of the motion features.

Successive stimulations of different retinal places need to be integrated temporally in order to be perceived as a visual movement.[1] It is conceived that two different features are extracted from the same stimulation and coded separately: the velocity and the amplitude of the movement (see Bonnet, 1975; MacKay, 1973; Orban, 1975). The aim of the present paper is to examine how the study of different order of time factors would support such an assumption that two different features (velocity and amplitude) are extracted from the same stimulus.

If two separate Analyzing Systems are to be assumed, very likely each of them shares different temporal integrative properties. These properties will be examined first at threshold level, then at suprathreshold levels of the stimulus. Temporal summation appears with a single stimulation; it manifests itself as a tradeoff between some variable of the stimulus and a time dimension. That tradeoff holds over a range of durations up to a critical one, such as in the case of Bloch's law. With repeated stimulations, temporal summation produces curvilinear function so that the best sensitivity of the system corresponds to an optimal duration, as in the case of sensitivity to flicker. Both kinds of phenomena are presumably related under proper models (see Ganz, 1975).

Aside from these temporal summation effects, prolonged stimulation of the same retinal areas produces a weakening of the motion sensation in time, especially in its apparent velocity. A Neuro-Sensory Adaptation process (NSA) can explain such a phenomenon. At the cessation of the visual stimulation, a new phenomenon appears: a Movement-After-Effect (MAE) which is classically attributed to the same NSA process (Barlow & Hill, 1963). Psychophysical relationships including time factors will provide clarification of the requirements for a NSA process assumption. In effect, in the so-called "selective adaptation" paradigm, a NSA process has to be proved, since other processes can generate the same kind of results.

---

[1]In the present paper, only retinal movement on a stationary eye is considered.

Temporal summation will also appear in Movement After-Effect where two classes of phenomena will be suggested on the basis of their time constants, each of them being ascribed to a different Analyzing System.

This paper will concern itself with the suggestion that the study of time factors provides powerful paradigms for discriminating separate processes at work in the sensory coding of movement information in the visual system.

II. TEMPORAL PROCESSING IN VISUAL MOTION PERCEPTION

A. The Role of Time in the Detection of Single Sweep Targets.

Renewing previous assumptions of Brown (1955) and Leibowitz (1955a), two separate Feature Analyzing Systems have been postulated for the detection of the visual movement of a single sweep target (Bonnet, 1975). In a Displacement Analyzing System (DAS), motion detection is accomplished through the triggering of some set of amplitude detectors. The amplitude of a translation is not given at once. It is conceived as resulting from the preprocessing of the stationary components of the translation. In the simplest case, such a preprocessing would consist in generating a given level of triggering (amplitude) on the basis of the comparison between an actual stationary position (the ending point) and the sensory trace of a previous one (the starting point). Three main properties characterized such a System are: its unresponsiveness to the motion phase per se, its great dependence upon the persistency of the initial stationary (or stationary-like) position, and its dependence upon the stationary components of the stimulus. In a Movingness Analyzing System (MAS), motion detection is accomplished through the triggering of some set of velocity detectors. Temporal summation of the "energy" content of the motion phase per se is requested in order to reach the level of triggering of these velocity detectors.

A simple experimental paradigm is developed in order to test the model and to explore more thoroughly some properties of the two assumed Systems. It was more extensively described elsewhere (Bonnet, 1975; Bonnet & Renard, 1977). Basically, such a paradigm consists in comparing the motion thresholds expressed in the same units (liminal amplitude = S lim) whether the stimulus translation was *discrete* or *continuous*. In the former, the translation contains only stationary components (starting and ending points, i.e., stroboscopic motion); in the latter, it contains only a motion phase without any obvious stationary component. Each stimulus presentation consists in a single sweep of a punctiform object controlled in amplitude and duration (and hence in velocity). In the model, the MAS is triggered exclusively by the motion phase, i.e., only by a continuous translation. The DAS is triggered by the stationary components of the stimulus, i.e., in every case by a discrete translation and in some cases by a continuous one. The last event occurs when the velocity of the motion is slow enough so that the extremities of the motion track can be considered as quasi-stationary, and/or when usable stationary references are closed to the motion track.

The simplest instance of the validation of the model through that paradigm is obtained in the difference between motion thresholds for discrete and continuous translations in central and peripheral vision. The DAS is assumed to be prominent in central vision, whereas the MAS would be prominent in peripheral one. Actually, in central vision and for short exposure times, motion thresholds for discrete presentation are lower than those for a continuous one; the reverse result is observed in peripheral vision (Bonnet & Renard, 1977).

Let us compare now the effects of exposure time (for continuous translation) or of Inter-Stimulus Interval (for discrete presentation) in the two assumed Systems. When motion thresholds resulted from the prominent activity of the DAS, most of the decrease in $S\ lim$ should be attributed to the decay of the persistency of the initial stationary position. For constant station times, it has been repeatedly found (Bonnet, 1975; Kinchla & Allen, 1969; Korte, 1915; Neuhaus, 1930) that with a discrete translation, regardless of whether an apparent movement is observed, $S\ lim$ increased as a negatively accelerated function of the interstimulus interval. The function holds for all the range of ISI. In parametrically equivalent situations, continuous translation leads to different results. In the high range of exposure time (i.e., for low velocities), continuous and discrete translations give the same $S\ lim$ thresholds (Bonnet, 1975; Kinchla & Allan, 1969). However, in the low exposure time range for continuous translation, $S\ lim$ appears to be constant, whereas the exposure time is made to increase (Cohen & Bonnet, 1972; Dimmick & Karl, 1930; Johnson & Leibowitz, 1976; Leibowitz, 1955a). This is to say that at threshold a Velocity x Time tradeoff is obtained which is interpreted in terms of temporal summation by analogy with Bloch's law. As can be deduced from Leibowitz' data (1955a), the range of exposure times over which such a tradeoff holds decreases when the luminance level of the field increases. Such a result strongly reinforces the interpretation of the tradeoff in terms of a temporal summation process (see Ganz, 1975). As a matter of fact, in the range of exposure time inside which the Velocity x Time tradeoff is observed, stationary references are uneffective (Bonnet, 1975; Hanes, 1965; Leibowitz, 1955b), while beyond the exposure time at which the tradeoff is no longer observed, motion thresholds are progressively more lowered when exposure time is increased (Bonnet, 1975; Leibowitz, 1955b).

To sum up, a temporal summation does apply in the MAS processing that suggests that for such a System, detection of a visual motion is based on a "single sensory event" (Brown, 1955), i.e., a constant level of energy in the stimulus. However, temporal integration in the DAS implies comparison of a sensory trace with an actual stimulus position. The persistency of that trace depends in particular upon the station time of the stimulus: the longer the station time, the shorter the persistency. From Neuhaus's data (1930) it can be shown that at constant ISI, S lim increases when station time increases. Hence, the increase in S lim with increase in ISI (or in exposure time) can be attributed to an effect of persistency. In that respect the temporal integrative properties of the two assumed Analyzing Systems appear to be different. This assumption does not apply only in the case of single sweep targets. In effect most of the motion stimuli are repetitive and one needs to consider the temporal frequency-filter properties of the two assumed Systems.

B. Temporal Summation Processes for Moving Grating Detection.

Sinusoidal drifting gratings are the simplest stimuli for the study of the temporal frequency characteristics of the two assumed Systems. Parametrically such a stimulus is described by its Spatial Frequency (SF in cycle/degree of visual angle) and its angular Velocity (V in deg/sec). The product of the two is the Temporal Frequency (TF in cycle/sec. or Hz) with which a given retinal area is stimulated. Evidence for temporal summation in the case of such a repetitive stimulation requires the demonstration of a curvilinearity in the sensitivity function. In effect, a temporal summation process leads to assume an optimal onset-to-onset interval. For a drifting grating, such an optimal interval is the temporal period of its drift (the inverse of its TF) for which the sensitivity is maximum. Hence, some tradeoff is expected between SF and V in a given situation.

Sensitivity, measured by the liminal contrast, varies curvilinearly with the Spatial Frequency (SF) of stationary sinusoidal gratings (Campbell & Robson, 1968). Since the optimal SF, corresponding to the lower contrast threshold, decreases with the mean luminance level, no fixed value can be reported. When such a grating is made to drift, few changes in sensitivity are observed in the high SF range (i.e., beyond the optimal SF), while a high gain in sensitivity is reported in the lower SF range (Robson, 1966). Flickering stationary gratings also raised the sensitivity in the low SF range, but to a lower extent than motion (Tolhurst, Sharpe & Hart, 1973). Kulikowski and Tolhurst (1973) and Tolhurst (1973) have postulated the existence of two types of channels differentiated on the basis of their sensitivity to SF range. Some evidence was reported that such an assumption is consistent with that of the two Analyzing Systems for motion detection (Bonnet, 1977). Shortly, the Movingness Analyzing System would respond mostly in the low SF range and show a rather high degree of selectivity for TF (or Velocity), as demonstrated in selective adaptation experiments (Pantle & Sekuler, 1968; Tolhurst et al., 1973). Conversely, the Displacement Analyzing System responding mostly in the high SF range shows a rather high degree of selectivity for SF (Blakemore & Campbell, 1969).

Now, evidence for temporal integration is obtained first in the demonstration of a reciprocity of the effects between Velocity and Spatial Frequency for the optimal motion threshold. Using square wave gratings, Crook (1937) showed that the luminance threshold for detecting the direction of movement is minimal for a Temporal Frequency of about 3 Hz for different combinations of V and SF. Using sinus wave gratings, van Nes, Koenderink, Nas, and Bouman (1967) found a similar result with a somewhat longer time constant. Actually, Kelly (1971) and Breitmeyer (1973), using a different experimental procedure, showed that this optimal duration decreases with the increase in the mean luminance level. To summarize, the MAS that is most responsive to low Spatial Frequency is best activated by high velocity, whereas the DAS that is selective for Spatial Frequencies in the high range is best activated by low velocities. According to Ganz (1975), such a temporal summation would just be a form of Bloch's law. Differential optimal durations for temporal summation in the two Analyzing Systems will be examined in the next section.

C. Temporal Summation and Apparent Velocity of Drifting gratings.

If the distinction between the two Analyzing Systems is still valid at the supra-threshold level of the stimulus, one should be able to demonstrate a differential effect of the Temporal Frequency in the low and high Spatial Frequency range. In the case of ocular fixation, it has been shown that the apparent velocity of a moving pattern increases with its TF (and SF) (Brown, 1931; Cohen, 1964; Smith & Sherlock, 1957). Using square wave gratings, Diener, Wist, Dichgans, and Brandt (1976) demonstrated that the apparent velocity ($V°$) of such a movement would result from the sum of two independent effects: one due to the retinal velocity (V), the other one due to the SF or TF of the grating, so that the results could be described by the following equations:

$$V° = aV + b \text{ V SF}$$

$$V° = aV + b \text{ TF}$$

However, these authors used gratings only in the low SF range. A new experiment was done to test the validity of their conclusions over a larger SF range. Actually, with reference to the results of Robson (1966), it was assumed that the effect of TF would be more important in the low SF range than in the high one.

Subjects have to adjust the apparent velocity of a vertical sinusoidal grating drifting horizontally (SF = 0.20 c/deg) to the apparent velocity of a standard grating differing in SF and TF. The two gratings were presented cyclically for 5 sec periods, until the matching of their apparent velocities was accomplished. The drifting gratings appear successively through a 3 x 2.5° aperture in the middle of a black field. Their Michelson contrast was set at 70% and their mean luminance was 0.64 cd/m². Four SF were presented at each of four velocities covering a range of TF between 0.375 to 12 Hz. The lowest SF could not be presented at the lowest velocity. Gratings were produced on the face of oscilloscopes with standard procedures. Three Ss took part in the experiment and were presented five times with each of the 15 conditions in different sessions.[2]

For a constant standard velocity, the matched velocity increases with the Spatial Frequency and the Temporal Frequency of the standard grating. The steeper the increase, the higher the velocity (and the TF level). A single linear function does not fit the results, as seen in Fig. 1, where the results are expressed in term of the ratio of the matched/standard velocities.

Two quadratic solutions were then examined. The origin (SF = .20) was taken into account while no systematic error was observed for that matching. The fitted equations were the following:

$$V° = V\,(a + b\mathrm{SF} + c\mathrm{SF}^2) = V\,(0.89 + 1.53\mathrm{SF} - .22\,\mathrm{SF}^2) \tag{1}$$

$$V° = \mathrm{SF}\,(a + b\mathrm{SV} + c\mathrm{V}^2) = \mathrm{SF}\,(0.04 + 2.57\,\mathrm{V} - .19\,\mathrm{V}^2) \tag{2}$$

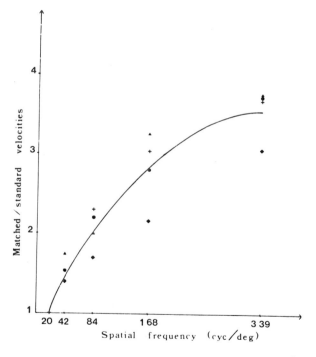

FIG. 1   Ratio of the matched/standard velocities for the different SF of standard gratings. The mean regression line is plotted together with the mean of the 3 Ss for each velocity. (3) = 44°/sec, (▲) = .89°/sec, (●) = 1.78°/sec, (♦) = 3.57°/sec.

[2]Fixation was requested and a control of the eye movements did not show any optokinetic nystagmus.

In both cases the quadratic regression is significant, however, the sum of the square differences between experimental data and the regression line is much lower for solution 1(Σ $(y - Y)^2 = 11.903$) than for solution 2 (Σ $(y - Y)^2 = 132.88$). We can then conclude that SF is responsible for most of the nonlinearity in the regression. A schematic way to summarize the results is to say that since the function is negatively accelerated, the apparent velocity is more strongly dependent upon Temporal Frequency in the lower range of SF than in the higher one. In other words, the temporal characteristics that differentiate the two Analyzing Systems presumably hold also at suprathreshold levels. Further evidence will be suggested in the next section.

III. NEURO-SENSORY ADAPTATION (NSA)

Protracted observation of the motion of a pattern produces a decline in its apparent velocity. At the cassation of the adapting motion, an apparent movement in the opposite direction is observed (Movement After-Effect, MAE). In other experimental conditions, thresholds for motion detection can also be demonstrated to be selectively raised (see in Sekuler, 1975). All these changes are classically attributed to a Neuro-Sensory Adaptation process (NSA). This assumption is rarely questioned, and in fact the expression of "selective adaptation" is used for a large range of features under experiment. Since other processes can be at work, this assumption should be questioned. In doing so, some temporal factors will be demonstrated. Bonnet, Freeman, Renard, and Shiina, (1974) have presented a first attempt to determine the psychophysical requirements for assuming a NSA process to be at work in visual aftereffects.

A. Neuro-Sensory Adaptation During the Observation of a Real Motion.

If the decline in the intensity (in the case of motion, its velocity) of a feature as a function of the duration of its observation is to be attributed to a Neuro-Sensory Adaptation process, a negatively accelerated function is to be expected (Marks, 1974). Exponential decrease in the apparent velocity of a moving pattern as a function of the duration of its observation was obtained under various experimental conditions (Goldstein, 1957; Mashhour, 1964; Matsuda, 1970; Taylor, 1963). In the experiment of Bonnet et al. (1974) further data covering a larger range of durations were obtained.

Two arithmetic spirals, 6° diameter were presented each side of the fixation point (SF = 1.8 c/deg and TF = 2Hz). A magnitude estimation technique was used, with one of the spirals as the standard and being presented only at the end of the adaptation period. Two Ss took part in the experiment and received six trials with each of the six durations of adaptation.

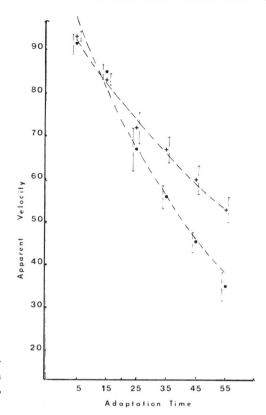

FIG. 2   Rated apparent velocity as a function of the adaptation time (in sec). Results of two Ss, six trials per duration.

Results are reported separately for each of the two *S*s in Fig. 2. While an exponential fit cannot be securely demonstrated, the results are consistent with such an assumption. A finite asymptotic value (duration) was expected, but the range of the used durations was not large enough so as to reach the critical duration of observation beyond which no more change in apparent velocity would be reported.

As in the case of brightness, in which a NSA assumption is largely accepted (Marks, 1974), the rate of decay of the exponential function should increase with the increase in the stimulus (and, therefore, apparent) velocity. That result fits the data of Mashhour (1964) and of Matsuda (1970).

B. Neuro-Sensory Adaptation and Movement Aftereffect.

In a Neuro-Sensory Adaptation model, the aftereffect should be the phenomenal counterpart of the neural recovery from adaptation (Barlow & Hill, 1963). The aftereffect, maximum at the time at which the real adapting motion stopped,

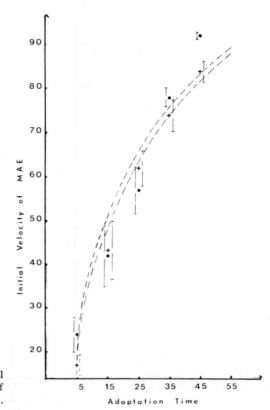

FIG. 3   Rated apparent initial
velocity of MAE as a function of
the adaptation time (in sec).

declines thereafter exponentially in time during the test period. Hence, the Movement Aftereffect can be characterized by a set of two parameters: either its
intercept and its slope (Taylor, 1963) or its intercept and its duration (Bonnet,
1973; Bonnet, Bouvier, & Petiteau, 1976; Sekuler & Pantle, 1967). The last two
parameters, most frequently used, should, under a NSA model, be related. With
some specifications (Bonnet, 1973; Bonnet et al., 1976) this result holds for
MAE (Scott & Noland, 1965; Sekuler & Pantle, 1967; Taylor, 1963).

   If the initial apparent velocity (the intercept) of the MAE is related to the
amount of NSA reached at the end of the adapting period, it should increase as
a negatively accelerated function of the duration of adaptation. The same type
of function should obviously hold for the duration of MAE. This last result was
reported in Wohlgemuth (1911), Sekuler and Pantle (1967) and Bonnet (1973).
The former was validated in Taylor (1963) and in Sekuler and Pantle (1967).
Further data were obtained in a situation complementary to the one discussed in
Section II.1.

The same *S*s, procedure and stimuli were used. The standard adaptation motion of the spiral was presented for 55 sec. The comparison adaptation motion was presented for one of the six adaptation times, so that the two motions stopped simultaneously. The *S*s rated the initial apparent velocity of the MAE corresponding to the comparison stimulus as a function of the initial velocity of the MAE corresponding to the standard stimulus.

Results are reported separately for each *S*s in Fig. 3. The exponential increase in the initial velocity of the MAE as a function of the adaptation duration is consistent with the data. Here, too, a finite asymptote (duration) is to be expected. It has not been obtained, probably because the range of durations was not large enough.

Now, the real test that a NSA process underlies both phenomena; the decline of the apparent velocity during the adaptation period and the increase in the initial apparent velocity of the MAE as a function of the adaptation duration requires the demonstration of a linear relationship (i.e., a correlation) between them. Results from the two preceding experiments when replotted show such a linear relationship for each of the two *S*s.

C. Two Classes of Visual Aftereffects.

The functions reported earlier, especially the linear relationship between initial intensity and duration of the aftereffect, are the main criteria for assuming a NSA process. In some visual aftereffects the last relationship fails to be obtained. The reason for that failure, which disproved the NSA assumption, is likely to be found in the fact that both kinds of aftereffects have different "Adaptation" time constants. Each of the functions reported above should have a finite asymptote, i.e., a duration of adaptation beyond which no more decrease in the apparent velocity of the adapting movement and no more increase in the apparent initial velocity of its MAE would be obtained. In using a threshold method, Sekuler (1975) reported that an asymptotic aftereffect is reached beyond 100 sec of adaptation duration. Related durations are reported for brightness (Marks, 1974). At variance, in the size aftereffect, Ikeda and Obonai (1953) reported that beyond 100 msec the initial aftereffect does not rise with further increases in adaptation duration. That time constant was estimated at 500 msec for Spatial Frequency aftereffect (Gorea, 1977). Nevertheless, in both cases the increase in the duration of the aftereffect as a function of the increase of the induction period of the effect still holds for durations ten times longer or more (Blakemore & Campbell, 1969; Ikeda & Obonai, 1953). Consequently, for the type of aftereffect that presumably covers all the so-called figural aftereffects, a NSA process cannot be called for.

IV. TEMPORAL SUMMATION IN
MOVEMENT AFTEREFFECTS.

It has been previously suggested that the temporal summation constants should be different for the Movingness and for the Displacement Analyzing Systems. The study of the change in MAE characteristics (intercept and/or duration) with changes in Velocity, Spatial Frequency, and/or Temporal Frequency of the adapting moving pattern will allow us to provide preliminary evidence for it.

When the adaptation duration is kept constant, MAE characteristics have been repeatedly found to vary curvilinearly as a function of the velocity (and TF) of the adapting movement (Richards, 1971; Scott & Noland, 1965; Wohlgemuth, 1911). However, contrary to Scott and Noland's assumption (1965), the velocity does not seem to be the most critical variable in the explanation of the effect. Most of the experiments have been run with a single pattern and hence with a single Spatial Frequency or a single SF spectrum. Consequently, the change in Temporal Frequency can very well account for the curvilinear function.

Pantle (1974) presented the first evidence for such an interpretation. He measured the initial velocity and the duration of MAE for two sinus drifting gratings (SF = 3 and 6 c/deg) varying over a large range of velocities and TF. For both parameters, the same optimal value of the curvilinear function is obtained for both Spatial Frequencies when plotted as a function of Temporal Frequency. The best MAE seems then to be obtained for a TF = 5 Hz, or in other words, when a Velocity x SF tradeoff of 200 msec is used as adapting stimulus. Other results found in the literature can be reanalyzed (for instance, Richards, 1971) showing that such a result applies over the high SF range, which has been assumed to activate prominently the Displacement Analyzing System.

Some data seem to indicate that a different result would be obtained when the stimulus pattern is in the low SF range, which has been assumed to activate prominently the Movingness Analyzing System. Two indicating experiments are reported.

In a first experiment, duration of MAE was measured on separate occasions for five different velocities. Under one condition, the TF was kept constant (5 Hz) and five arithmetic spirals differing in number of turns (hence in SF) were used. Under the other condition, a single spiral was used (SF = 1.6c/deg) but its TF (practically its rotation speed) was changed. Six Ss took part in the experiment and gave five replications in each of the 10 experimental conditions.

When the Temporal Frequency of the adapting motion is kept constant, the duration of the MAE declines with the increase in the adapting velocity that correlates with a decline in the pattern Spatial Frequency. This result is reported on the left panel of Fig. 4. As far as Spatial Frequency is concerned, the obtained effect is the opposite from the one obtained by Pantle (1974). However, the last author works in the high SF range, while in the present experiment we remain in the low one. When the Spatial Frequency of the pattern

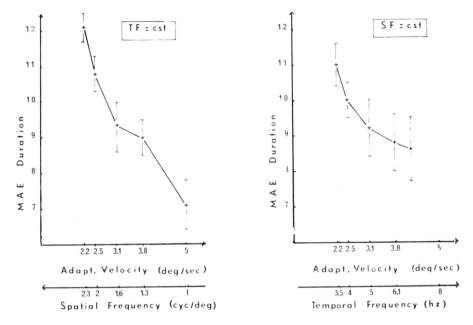

FIG. 4   Duration of MAE (in sec) of rotating spiral as a function of the adapting (radial) velocity. Left panel, TF = 5 Hz = cst; right panel, SF = 1.6c/deg = cst.

is kept constant, the same relationship between the duration of MAE and the velocity of the adapting motion is observed: the duration of MAE declines when the Temporal Frequency increases (right panel of Fig. 4). Notice that the optimal TF reported by Pantle (TF = 5 Hz) is in the middle range of the Temporal Frequencies used in the present experiment. Using drifting gratings, Sekuler (1975, p. 400) reported results analogous to those of the present experiment. The present results and their departure from Pantle's can be understood if one assumes that the Movingness Analyzing System (activated by low SF) has a longer time constant for temporal summation than the DAS. A second experiment was run to provide support to the assumption. Nine adapting conditions were used, combining 3 lower SF and 3 lower TF. Other characteristics of the experiment were identical to those of the previous one. Results appear in Fig. 5. The duration of MAE increases with the Spatial Frequency of the spiral, but now it also increases with the Temporal Frequency (and Velocity) of the adapting motion.

Confronting the data of the two experiments, it is possible to suggest that in the low SF range the best MAE is obtained when the adapting TF is around 3 Hz. Because of apparatus limitations the Velocity x SF tradeoff of the MAS at 333 msec could not have been tested directly. Preliminary data obtained by

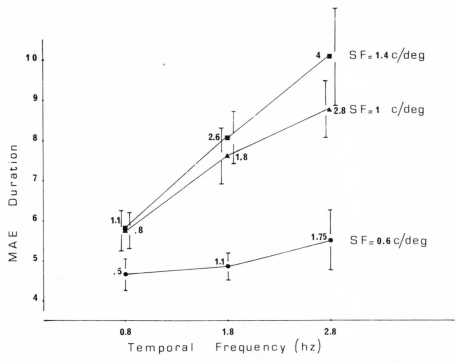

FIG. 5   Duration of MAE (in sec.) of rotating spiral as a function of the adaptating temporal frequency. SF as a parameter.

Lorscheid with sinus gratings seem to confirm both Pantle's results in the high SF range and the present conclusion in the low SF range. In other words, there exists preliminary evidence according to which the temporal summation constants for the Movingness and for the Displacement Analyzing Systems would be different.

V. CONCLUSION

Two main functions of time factors in motion perception have been reviewed. Many experimental data are obviously needed in order to complete our knowledge of the processes at work. Nevertheless, it is believed that the present conceptual framework should clarify the time constraints of the Analyzing Systems processing motion information. Many questions remain open for each function that will be raised in conclusion.

For temporal summation processes, one can wonder if there is some relationship between the Velocity x Time tradeoff (§ I.2, II.2) in the Movingness Analyzing System. Analysis of the stimulus in terms of its Fourier components in the way suggested by Ganz (1975), p. 182) may be fruitful for suggesting relationships between these processes.

The two different temporal summation constants for the two separate Analyzing Systems have to be worked out more thoroughly. In particular, it should also hold in threshold experiments. In the background of filter models, motion is considered to be a form of spatio-temporal modulation. According to Sekuler (1975), it differs from other forms, such as flicker, by the fact that it has "a directional component in either the stimulus or its percept." Using drifting gratings or rotating spiral, Watanabe et al. (1968) and Richards (1971) showed that the optimal TF for motion detection is about 3 Hz, while for flicker detection (scintillation) it is about 5 Hz. One may wonder if these results are related to the two different temporal summation constants of the two Analyzing Systems in motion integration.

The last question will concern the estimates of the Neuro-Sensory Adaptation asymptote(s). Are these estimates identical whether they are obtained from the decline of the apparent velocity during the adaptation period, or from the increase in apparent initial velocity of the MAE, or from its related duration?

REFERENCES

Barlow, H. B., & Hill, R. M. Evidence for a physiological explanation of the waterfall illusion and figural after effects. *Nature,* 1963, *200,* 1434–1435.

Blakemore, C. Central visual processing. In M. S. Gazzaniga & C. Blakemore (Eds.), *Handbook of Psychobiology,* New York: Academic Press, 1975.

Blakemore, C., & Campbell, F. W. On the existence of neurons in the human visual system selectively sensitive to the orientation and size of retinal images. *Journal of Physiology,* 1969, *203,* 237–260.

Bonnet, C. Facteurs temporels dans le mouvement consécutif visuel. *Vision Research,* 1973, *13,* 1311–1317.

Bonnet, C. A tentative model for visual motion detection. *Psychologia,* 1975, *18,* 35–50.

Bonnet, C. Visual motion detection models: Features and frequency filters. *Perception,* 1977, *6,* 491–500.

Bonnet, C., & Renard, C. La détection du mouvement visuel en vision centrale et en vision périphérique. In *Psychologie Expérimentale et Comparée: Hommage à Paul Fraisse,* Paris, P.U.F., 1977.

Bonnet, C., Freeman, R. B. Jr., Renard, C., & Shiina, K. Psychophysical requirements for an adaptation process hypothesis in visual aftereffects. *Brain Research,* 1974, special issue. (Summary of papers presented at the EBBS meeting, Paris.)

Bonnet, C., Bouvier, A., & Petiteau, H. Phases in movement after-effects and their relationship to the kinetic-figural effect: adaptation and conditioning processes. *Psychological Research,* 1976, *38,* 267–282.

Breitmeyer, B. G. A relationship between the detection of size, rate, orientation and direction in the human visual system. *Vision Research,* 1973, *13,* 41–58.

Brown, J. F. The visual perception of velocity. *Psychologische Forschung,* 1931, *14,* 199–232.

Brown, R. H. Velocity discrimination and the intensity time relation. *Journal of the Optical Society of America*, 1955, *45*, 189–192.

Campbell, F. W., & Robson, J. G. Application of Fourier analysis to the visibility of gratings. *Journal of Physiology*, 1968, *197*, 551–566.

Cohen, R. L. *Problems in motion perception*. Uppsala, Appelbergs, 1964,

Cohen, R. L., & Bonnet, C. Movement detection thresholds and stimulus durations. *Perception & Psychophysics*, 1972, *12*, 269–272.

Crook, M. N. Visual discrimination of movement. *Journal of Psychology*, 1937, *3*, 541–558.

Diener, H. C., Wist, E. R., Dichgans, J., & Brandt, T. The spatial frequency effect on perceived velocity. *Vision Research*, 1976, *16*, 169–176.

Dimmick, F. L., & Karl, J. C. The effect of exposure time upon the R. L. of visible motion. *Journal of Experimental Psychology*, 1930, *13*, 365–369.

Ganz, L. Temporal factors in visual perception. In E. C. Carterette & M. P. Friedman (Eds.) *Handbook of Perception*, Vol. V: *Seeing*. New York: Academic Press, 1975.

Goldstein, A. G. Judgments of visual acuity as a function of length of observation time. *Journal of Experimental Psychology*, 1957, *54*, 457–461.

Gorea, A. Les canaux de fréquence spatiale sont-ils susceptibles de s'adapter? *L'Année Psychologique*, 1977, *77*, 311–324.

Hanes, L. F. Discrimination of direction of movement at short exposure durations. *Dissertation Abstracts*, 1965, *25*, 7391.

Ikeda, H., & Obonai, T. The quantitative analysis of figural after-effects, I.: The process of growth and decay of figural after-effects. *Japanese Journal of Psychology*, 1953, *23*, 246–260; *24*, 29–66. (English abstracts.)

Johnson, C. A., & Leibowitz, H. W. Velocity-time reciprocity in the perception of motion: foveal and peripheral determinations. *Vision Research*, 1976, *16*, 177–180.

Kelly, D. H. Theory of flicker and transient responses. I. Uniform fields. *Journal of the Optical Society of America*, 1971, *61*, 537–546.

Kinchla, R. A., & Allan, L. G. A theory of visual movement perception. *Psychological Review*, 1969, *76*, 537–558.

Korte, A. Kinematoskopische Untersuchungen. *Zeitschrift für Psychologie*, 1915, *72*, 193–296.

Kulikowski, J. J., & Tolhurst, D. J. Psychophysical evidence for sustained and transient neurons in the human visual system. *Journal of Physiology*, 1973, *232*, 149–162.

Leibowitz, H. W. The relationship between the rate threshold for the perception of movement and luminance for various durations of exposure. *Journal of Experimental Psychology*, 1955, *49*, 209–214. (a)

Leibowitz, H. W. Effect of reference lines on the discrimination of movement. *Journal of the Opitcal Society of America*, 1955, *45*, 829–830. (b)

MacKay, D. M. Visual stability and voluntary eye movements. In R. Jung (Ed.), *Handbook of sensory physiology*, Vol. VII/3A. Berlin: Springer, 1973.

Marks, L. E. *Sensory processes: the new psychophysics*. New York: Academic Press, 1974.

Mashhour, M. *Psychophysical relations in the perception of velocity*. Stockholm: Almqvist & Wiksell, 1964.

Matsuda, F. Developmental study of time, space and velocity estimations. III. Velocity estimation. *Japanese Journal of Psychology*, 1970, *40*, 297–303.

Neuhaus, W. Experimentelle untersuchung der scheinbewegung. *Archivs für Gesamte Psychologie*, 1930, *75*, 315–458.

Orban, G. *Visual cortical mechanisms of movement perception*. Vander, Leuven, 1975.

Pantle, A. Motion after-effect magnitude as a measure of the spatiotemporal properties of direction-sensitive analyzers. *Vision Research*, 1974, *14*, 1229–1236.

Pantle, A., & Sekuler, R. Velocity sensitive mechanisms in human vision. *Vision Research,* 1968, *8,* 445–450.

Richards, W. Motion perception in man and other animals. *Brain, Behavior & Evolution,* 1971, *4,* 162–181.

Robson, J. G. Spatial and temporal contrast sensitivity of the visual system. *Journal of the Optical Society of America,* 1966, *56,* 1141–1142.

Scott, T. R., & Noland, J. H. Some stimulus dimensions of rotating spirals. *Psychological Review,* 1965, *72,* 344–357.

Sekuler, R. Visual motion perception. In E. C. Carterette & M. P. Friedman (Eds.) *Handbook of Perception,* Vol. V: *Seeing.* New York: Academic Press, 1975.

Sekuler, R., & Pantle, A. A model for after-effects of seen motion. *Vision Research,* 1967, *7,* 427–439.

Smith, O. W., & Sherlock, L. A new explanation of the velocity-transposition phenomenon. *American Journal of Psychology,* 1957, *70,* 102–105.

Taylor, M. M. Tracking the decay of the after-effect of seen rotary movement. *Perceptual and Motor Skills,* 1963, *16,* 119–129.

Tolhurst, D. J. Separate channels for the analysis of the shape and the movement of a moving visual stimulus. *Journal of Physiology,* 1973, *231,* 385–402.

Tolhurst, D. J., Sharpe, C. R., & Hart, G. The analysis of drift rate of moving sinusoidal gratings. *Vision Research,* 1973, *13,* 2545–2556.

van Nes, F. L., Koenderink, J. J., Nas, H., & Bouman, M. A. Spatio-temporal modulation transfer in the human eye. *Journal of the Optical Society of America,* 1967, *57,* 1082–1088.

Watanabe, A., Mori, T., Nagata, S., & Hiwatashi, K. Spatial sine-wave response of the human visual system. *Vision Research,* 1968, *8,* 1245–1263.

Wohlgemuth, A. On the after-effect of seen movement. *British Journal of Psychology.* Monograph Supplement, n°1, 1911.

3

Interdependence Between the Processing of Temporal and Non-Temporal Information

Ewart A. C. Thomas
Nancy E. Cantor

Department of Psychology
Stanford University
Stanford, California

ABSTRACT

An experiment is reported in which subjects were presented visually with circular arrays of letters that vary in duration, number of letters, size of array, and whether or not they contain a target letter. In Pure duration conditions, subjects judged the duration of the array, and in Pure detection conditions subjects judged whether or not the array contained the target letter. In two Mixed conditions, subjects performed both duration and detection tasks, and the conditions differed according to whether the duration task was emphasized (Map 1) or the detection task was emphasized (Map 2). Decrements in duration accuracy and changes in the effects of certain variables on perceived duration were observed in going from Pure to Mixed conditions. Detection accuracy increased with stimulus duration in the Mixed but not the Pure conditions. A model assuming that duration and detection judgments are made simultaneously in the Mixed conditions provides a good explanation of the reaction time and accuracy data from Map 1 but not Map 2. It is argued that, in the Pure duration condition, judgments are based partly on a timer that starts shortly after stimulus onset and stops shortly after stimulus offset, or as soon as a critical duration is reached, whichever occurs first. When the duration task is emphasized in a Mixed condition, duration and detection judgments are done simultaneously but with a decrement in each. When the detection task is emphasized, priority is given to this task, and the duration judgment is derived mainly from the outcome of processing in the detection task.

I. INTRODUCTION

Recent studies of the process by which a subject judges the duration of a briefly presented stimulus (≈ 100 msec duration) have attempted to clarify the role of nontemporal stimulus information in the processing of temporal information.

An empirical finding around which most of these studies have centered is known as the "filled-duration illusion," whereby a duration that is "filled" with non-temporal information is perceived as longer than an identical duration that is "empty" (see Buffardi, 1971 and Ornstein, 1969 for references to this finding). To account for this illusion, it has been suggested that the subject divides attention between time-keeping and the processing of nontemporal information, and that perceived duration is based on the output of both processes (Thomas & Brown, 1974; Thomas & Weaver, 1975). Such a division of attention can be expected to affect also the subject's perception of the presented nontemporal information. Therefore, a strong test of this assumption requires the obtaining of the subject's perceptions of temporal and nontemporal information in conditions where no division of attention is required by the task instructions (Pure conditions) and in conditions where such division is required (Mixed conditions).

This approach was used by Thomas and Cantor (1975), who presented subjects with stimuli varying in duration and size and required them to (a) judge only the duration (Pure duration condition), (b) judge only the size (Pure size condition), and (c) judge both the duration and the size of each stimulus (Mixed condition). It was found that perceived duration was the same in conditions (a) and (c), but that perceived size was less in condition (c) than (b). This led us to suggest that attention is automatically captured by nontemporal information in condition (a), so that this condition is, in effect, one of divided attention, whereas, in condition (b), attention is focused on the size estimation task. Of additional interest is the finding that varying the number of stimulus sizes from 2 to 4 did not affect perceived duration.

These results raise a number of issues that have been discussed extensively in the literature on *attention*, namely, (1) which performance measures show "attenuation" in going from Pure to Mixed conditions, and under what experimental conditions, (2) if there is a change (usually a decrement) in performance in going from Pure to Mixed conditions, is the source of this change early or late in processing, for example, is it at the perceptual or the decision-making level, (3) if attention is divided, is the division set at the start of each trial, or does it vary over the course of processing depending on the changing processing requirements of each task, and (4) what is the relative priority given to the processing of the two or more tasks whether or not attention is divided. The experimental designs used to generate relevant data vary from requiring judgments of two aspects of a single stimulus, for example, duration and size as mentioned above, and loudness and "quality" of a tone (Moore & Massaro, 1973), to requiring judgments on two channels within the same modality, for example, tracking two messages in a dichotic listening task (Broadbent, 1958; Moray, 1975), and detecting an auditory signal that can occur in one of many channels (Sorkin, Pastore, & Pohlmann, 1972), to requiring judgments in different modalities, for example, visual and auditory detection and duration tasks (Eijkman & Vendrik, 1965), visual duration judgments and auditory recognition (Massaro & Kahn, 1973), and judgments about two aspects of a visual stimulus and two aspects of an auditory stimulus (Taylor, Lindsay, & Forbes, 1967). In addition to designs involving the standard Pure and Mixed (or Focused and Divided) conditions, Shiffrin and his coworkers have used a design in which the subject simultaneously monitors several channels in one (simultaneous) condition, and monitors the channels successively in another (successive) condition (Shiffrin & Gardner, 1972; Shiffrin, Gardner, & Allmeyer, 1973; Shiffrin & Grantham, 1974). Finally, most of the studies use response accuracy as the performance measure, notable exceptions being studies by Briggs, Peters, and Fisher (1972), LaBerge (1973), and Treisman and Davies (1973), who also use reaction time measures. A selective review of the conclusions drawn from these and similar studies will serve to motivate the assumptions we will use in our subsequent discussion of the processing of temporal and nontemporal information.

The "single channel hypothesis" and a weaker version, the "Attenuation" hypothesis, which assume that all of the presented stimulus information cannot enter the recognition system at the same time, have been proposed by Broadbent (1958), Estes and Taylor (1964, 1966), and Moray (1970) to account for Pure– Mixed decrements in performance accuracy, such as that observed in the dichotic listening task (Broadbent, 1958). Massaro and Kahn (1973) found a decrement in auditory recognition accuracy when a simultaneous visual duration task was difficult enough, and argued that the decrement occurs because central processing capacity is required during the perceptual stage of processing, and when this capacity is demanded elsewhere by a difficult duration judgment, recognition accuracy is lowered. Briggs et al. (1972) found a decrement in choice reaction time and argued that dividing attention causes a decrease in the speed of sampling the stimulus at an early stage of stimulus encoding. They also suggested that the locus of the decrement might vary depending on where in the system the simultaneous task places its greatest load. On this point, Wickens (1976) has found that decrements are observed in a primary task when the secondary task places its load at the output stage (a task requiring physical force), but not when it is a perceptual (signal detection) task. Also, Allport, Antonis, and Reynolds (1972) have found that subjects can simultaneously shadow an auditory message and sight-read piano music without any decrement, and they suggest that the decrement found by Broadbent (1958) may be due to the confusability of the messages at a central processing stage rather than to a bottleneck in early stages of processing.

In contrast to these studies, other studies have found no decrements, for example, those by Eijkman and Vendrik (1965), Moore and Massaro (1973), Shiffrin and Gardner (1972), and Shiffrin et al. (1973). And Shiffrin and Grantham (1974) have interpreted these results as suggesting that, when decrements are observed, the locus of the effect occurs late rather than early in processing.

Another issue, separate from that concerning decrements, concerns the interdependence of processing in the two or more tasks of a Mixed condition. Such interdependencies can be shown by detailed analyses of performance accuracy on one task *conditional* on the values of the stimulus variables relevant to the other task, or on the level of performance on the other task. For example, Eijkman and Vendrik (1965) found that auditory (visual) detection accuracy was correlated with neither the presence versus absence of a visual (auditory) signal, nor with visual (auditory) detection accuracy. For duration judgments, though, there was a correlation between accuracy on the two tasks, leading these authors to suggest that there may be one "central duration judgment process" that receives as input peripheral neural activity initiated in different sense modalities. Also, Sorkin et al. (1972) found that detection accuracy of a signal in one auditory channel does depend on whether there is a signal in another auditory channel (note that the division of attention here is within the same modality, whereas in the Eijkman and Vendrik study it was across modalities). To account for this interaction between channels, it was suggested that processing in one channel is independent of that in the other until the signal in one channel reaches a certain level of intensity. At this point, simultaneous monitoring of the two channels is interrupted and attention is focused on the channel in which the critical intensity level was reached. During this time of focused attention, information on the other unattended channel decays.

To summarize, there is some evidence that the locus of the Pure–Mixed decrement can occur early in processing (Briggs et al., 1972; Massaro & Kahn, 1973), although most of the recent studies suggest that it occurs late in processing. For simultaneous duration judgments in two modalities and for simultaneous detection in two auditory channels, there is evidence of an interaction between the processing in the two tasks, although it is not clear which modality or channel, if any, is given priority during interdependent processing.

The study to be reported includes Pure and Mixed conditions, and varies the priority that subjects are instructed to give to the duration and detection judgments in the Mixed conditions. After presenting the data, we will examine the reasonableness of different assumptions about information processing in the Pure conditions. Then we will discuss how performance might change in going from Pure to Mixed conditions. Such changes might be seen in the *level* of accuracy or reaction time, and in the *relationship* between, say, accuracy and stimulus duration. Finally, we will examine how the interdependent processing, postulated by Sorkin et al. (1972), is affected by experimenter-given priorities of the two tasks in the Mixed conditions. To do this, we will construct a "null hypothesis" model that assumes parallel processing in the two tasks, with observed reaction time being the greater of the times required for the duration and detection judgments.

II. METHOD

Two groups of subjects participated in separate conditions of the experiment.

A. Pure Duration and Detection Conditions

1. Subjects

Thirteen Stanford University undergraduates received $2.00 for participation in individual sessions of about 1 hr.

2. Stimuli

Circular arrays of letters were presented on a Tektronix model 604 oscilloscope with P 31 fast-decay phosphor, controlled by a Nova model 820 computer. The stimulus arrays varied according to the number of letters presented on a trial (four or eight letters), the size of the circular diameter (2 cm diameter = small, 4 cm = large), the presence or absence of the target letter "F" (target/nontarget trials), and the duration of presentation (50 msec = short, 100 msec = long). Stimulus letters were 0.35 cm in height and 0.25 cm in width, and subjects sat about 2 ft 4 in from the oscilloscope. The letter positions were equally spaced on the circumference of the circle (90 $k°$ from the vertical, $k = 0, 1, 2, 3$ for small arrays, and 45 $k°$, $k = 0, 1, \ldots, 7$ for large arrays).

3. Responses

All subjects performed first in a Pure duration condition and then in a Pure detection condition. Five subjects used four-response scales: "very short," "medium short," "medium long," and "very long" in the duration condition, and "sure yes," "maybe yes," "maybe no," and "sure no" in the detection condition. Eight subjects used two-response scales, "short" and "long," and "yes" and "no" in the two conditions. The first group of subjects made the button-press responses with the index and middle fingers of the left and right hands, and the second group used the index fingers of the left and right hands. In both groups, the assignment of "short" and "long" responses to the left and right hands was counterbalanced over subjects, as was the assignment of "yes" and "no" responses. Subjects were aware of the possible changes in stimulus variables over trials and were asked to respond by pressing the appropriate button as soon as possible after stimulus offset. These buttons were spaced 1 in apart.

4. Procedure

Each session started with 32 practice trials in the duration condition. Feedback ("short" or "long" printed on the screen) was given after each response. Following the practice trials there were 96 experimental trials in this condition (2 blocks of 48 trials each). After this condition, subjects received 16 practice trials without feedback in the detection condition. These practice trials were followed by 2 blocks of 48 trials each. On each trial, the values of the four stimulus variables were chosen with probability 0.5.

B. The Mixed Conditions

1. Subjects

Eighteen Stanford University undergraduates were each paid $4.00 for participation in two individual sessions each lasting about 1 hour.

2. Stimuli

The stimuli were identical to those used in the Pure conditions.

3. Responses

Subjects in the mixed condition were asked to judge both duration (short versus long) and whether or not the stimulus was a target (yes "F" versus no "F") on each trial. Two stimulus–response maps were used, and each subject used one map during a session. In Map 1, "short" responses were made with one hand and "long" responses with the other hand, the assignment being randomized over subjects. "Yes" responses were made with the middle fingers by half of the subjects and with the index fingers by the other half of the subjects. In Map 2, "yes" responses were made with one hand and "no" responses with the other hand, randomly assigned over subjects, and "short" responses were assigned to the middle fingers for half of the subjects and to the index fingers for the other half.

4. Procedure

Both the procedure for stimulus presentation and the presentation probabilities of each stimulus type were identical to those described for the Pure conditions. The Mixed condition sessions were divided into four experimental blocks, each containing 52 trials and were preceded by a practice block of 32 trials on which feedback as to the presented duration (short or long) was given.

III. RESULTS

To save space, we present most of the data in Tables 1, 2, and 3, and summarize in this section those aspects that are of particular interest. The data from the Pure conditions were subjected to analyses of variance, with the data from the two-response group being considered separately from the four-response group data. The dependent variables were accuracy and correct reaction time (RT). For example, responses on the four response scale were collapsed into yes/no judgments and the percentage of correct responses was computed for each subject to each stimulus type. (It should be noted that the percentage of correct responses for "long" stimulus duration is a measure of perceived duration for these durations, and by subtracting the percentage on "short" durations from 100 we get

TABLE 1
Accuracy Rates and Mean Correct RT (in msec.) in the Pure Detection
Conditions for the Two- and Four-Response Scales, and for Each Value
of the Four Stimulus Variables.

Stimulus Values	Two-Response Scale		Four-Response Scale	
	Prob (Correct)	Correct RT	Prob (Correct)	Correct RT
Non-target	0.84	581	0.83	983
Target	0.88	531	0.89	668
Short	0.85	581	0.84	873
Long	0.85	531	0.88	778
Four-letter	0.94	516	0.94	728
Eight-letter	0.78	596	0.78	923
Small	0.87	549	0.89	785
Large	0.84	563	0.82	866

a measure of perceived duration for these durations.) In the Mixed conditions, the data from Maps 1 and 2 were analyzed separately. In our brief summary of these analyses the reported effects are statistically significant beyond the 0.05 level, but there are other significant effects, mainly interactions, which are not included in the summary.

1. Detection accuracy is greater for small than for large arrays and for four rather than for eight letter arrays in both the Pure and Mixed conditions (see Tables 1 and 3). In the Mixed conditions only, detection accuracy is greater on nontarget than on target trials and increases with increases in stimulus duration (see Table 3).

2. Duration judgment accuracy is greater for short than for long stimuli in both the Pure (see Table 2) and the Mixed (see Table 3) conditions. In the Pure duration condition, accuracy of judgment decreases with increases in stimulus size, and perceived duration increases with increases in the number of letters in the array (see Table 2). On the other hand, perceived duration in the Mixed condition *decreases* with increases in the number of letters and size of the stimulus array for Map 2 (see Table 3).

3. Accuracy of performance does not decrease in the detection task from the Pure to the Mixed condition, whereas a large decrement in the accuracy of duration judgments is observed in the Mixed condition. Average RT in the Mixed conditions is greater than in the Pure conditions.

4. RT in both the Pure detection and Mixed conditions is greater on non-target than on target trials and for eight rather than for four letter arrays (see Tables 1 and 3). RT increases with increases in stimulus size in both Pure conditions (see Tables 1 and 2) and in the Map 2 Mixed condition data (see Table 3). RT is greater for short than for long durations in the Pure detection condition (see Table 1) and greater for long than for short durations in the Pure duration

TABLE 2

Accuracy Rates, Perceived Duration, and Mean Correct RT (in msec)
in the Pure Duration Condition for the Two- and Four-Response Scales, and
for Each Value of the Three Stimulus Variables.

Stimulus Values	Two-Response Scale			Four-Response Scale		
	Prob (Correct)	Perceived duration	Correct RT	Prob (Correct)	Perceived duration	Correct RT
Short	0.85	0.15	509	0.84	0.15	780
Long	0.69	0.69	543	0.77	0.77	789
Four-letter	0.77	0.39	529	0.83	0.41	787
Eight-letter	0.76	0.45	523	0.79	0.50	782
Small	0.81	0.42	509	0.84	0.45	792
Large	0.73	0.42	543	0.79	0.47	777

TABLE 3

Detection and Duration Accuracy (A-Det and A-Dur), Perceived Duration
(PD), and Correct RT (in msec) in the Mixed Conditions (Maps 1 and 2)
for Each Value of the Four Stimulus Variables.

Stimulus Values	Map 1				Map 2			
	A-Det	A-Dur	PD	Correct RT	A-Det	A-Dur	PD	Correct RT
Non-target	0.88	0.71	0.45	1018	0.91	0.65	0.41	1059
Target	0.82	0.72	0.46	939	0.85	0.67	0.40	997
Short	0.83	0.76	0.24	977	0.86	0.76	0.24	1040
Long	0.87	0.67	0.67	980	0.90	0.56	0.56	1016
Four-letter	0.91	0.72	0.46	954	0.94	0.68	0.44	983
Eight-letter	0.80	0.71	0.45	1002	0.82	0.64	0.37	1073
Small	0.87	0.71	0.47	973	0.90	0.66	0.43	1009
Large	0.83	0.72	0.44	984	0.86	0.66	0.38	1047

data (see Table 2). In the Mixed condition, RT decreases with increases in stimulus duration in the Map 2 data (see Table 3). In general, the relationships between RT and the stimulus variables are similar in Map 2 and the Pure detection condition.

5. As anticipated, the pattern of results suggests that subjects did emphasize the duration task in Map 1 and the detection task in Map 2.

IV. SOME ASSUMPTIONS ABOUT INFORMATION PROCESSING

In this section we will try to make explicit our assumptions about the information processing involved in making duration and detection judgments. We will consider only a limited set of assumptions and then see which assumptions from this limited set best account for the data on reaction time and accuracy.

As stated earlier, our theoretical framework for discussing temporal judgments was constructed in an attempt to account for the effects of nontemporal stimulus information. A stimulus consisting of nontemporal information I presented for duration t is encoded as a vector, one component being the encoded duration $f_I(t)$, and the other being the encoded nontemporal information $g_t(I)$ (Thomas and Brown, 1974). Perceived duration is based on both $f(.)$ and $g(.)$. As a special case, Thomas and Weaver (1975) assume that $f(.)$ is independent of I, that the relevant aspect of $g(.)$ is the time, $g^*(I)$, to encode I, and that perceived duration is a weighted average of $f(t)$ and $g^*(I)$. The weights in the average are influenced by the amount of attention allocated to the f-processor ($\equiv$ timer) and to the g-processor. According to these assumptions, the effects of nontemporal information occur in the early stages of processing. To see if later stages, in particular the stage of response selection, also affect perceived duration, Thomas and Cantor (1975) varied the number of nontemporal stimulus categories. This variable was chosen for study because it is known to affect overall (choice) reaction time to stimuli. It was found, however, that it did not affect perceived duration. Therefore, in extending the above models to account for reaction time data, it will be necessary to specify how certain variables can selectively influence perceived duration, reaction time, and detection accuracy.

Let us consider two assumptions about how duration judgments are made.

1. Stimulus onset activates a timer and stimulus offset stops it (there are random delays between stimulus onset [offset] and timer onset [offset], such as those assumed by Sternberg and Knoll (1973) to account for temporal-order judgments). While the timer is activated, its output, which is the time since activation, is continuously available. Before each trial in a two-choice (short/long) discrimination, the subject sets a critical duration c such that a response is made as soon as the output from the timer equals c or at timer offset, whichever occurs

first. In the first case, the response "long" is given, and in the second case the response "short" is given. Errors occur because of variability in the delays between stimulus and timer onset and offset, and the error probabilities conditional on stimulus duration depend on the average value of c. If c is approximately equal to the shorter (longer) duration, the majority of errors will be made when this duration is presented.

Reaction time predictions can be derived from this assumption. In the present experiment *reaction time* (RT) *is measured from stimulus offset*. Let T_1 (T_2) be the average time (measured from stimulus onset) of timer offset when the short (long) duration is presented, and let T_1' (T_2') be the average time of timer offset when the short (long) duration is presented, *given that timer offset occurs before c*. In general, $T_1' < T_1 < c < T_2$, and, since $T_1 < T_2$, $T_1' < T_2' < c$. Also, let k be the time from timer offset or from c (whichever occurs first) to the observable response. For stimulus durations of 50 and 100 msec, the RTs, measured from stimulus offset, for the four stimulus-response combinations are

$$RT\ (S/S) \;=\; RT\ (\text{"short" response, given short duration})$$
$$=\; T_1' + k - 50, \tag{1a}$$
$$RT\ (L/S) \;=\; c + k - 50, \tag{1b}$$
$$RT\ (S/L) \;=\; T_2' + k - 100, \tag{1c}$$
$$\text{and}\quad RT\ (L/L) \;=\; c + k - 100 \tag{1d}$$

Since $T_1' < c$, RT (S/S) < RT (L/S), and since $T_2' < c$, RT (S/L) < RT (L/L). That is, correct RT is less than error RT for the short duration, and the opposite is true for the long duration. Also, RT (L/S) − RT (L/L) = 50, and RT (L/L) > RT (S/S) if $c > T_1' + 50$, a condition that is satisfied if c is close to T_2.

2. Alternatively, we could assume that the short/long decision starts at timer offset, the decision variable being the encoding $f(.)$ of the stimulus duration. Using an extension of the Theory of Signal Detectability studied by Thomas and Myers (1972), RT predictions can be derived. Suppose that the distributions of $f(.)$ are normal with the same variance, and let c denote the decision criterion. RT is assumed to be a decreasing function of the absolute difference between $f(.)$ and c. Then it can be shown that, in general, reaction time and response probability would be inversely related. In particular, if correct responses are more frequent than incorrect responses, correct RT is less than error RT for both durations; and, if the error rate is greater for the long duration than for the short duration, RT (L/L) would be greater than RT (S/S).

Concerning detection judgments (of presence ["Yes"] versus absence ["No"] of the target letter "F"), we can consider two similar assumptions.

3. Starting with stimulus onset, the subject accumulates "information" about the presence of the target and responds "Yes" as soon as the information reaches some level c_1, provided it did not previously reach a level c_2 $(< c_1)$, in which case the response would have been "no." If the information that is accumulated

is a likelihood ratio, then this is the model of choice reaction time examined extensively by Laming (1968). Otherwise, the model is the one examined by Link and Heath (1975).

The RT and accuracy predictions for the different stimulus—response pairs can be found in these references. However, for the present purposes, the following general prediction suffices. If the rate of information accumulation before level c_1 or c_2 is reached is the same before stimulus offset as after, then the RT for the long duration, RT (L) (again measured from stimulus offset) would be about 50 msec less than the RT for the short duration, RT (S).

4. Alternatively, we could assume that the Theory of Signal Detectability applies. The "information packet" from which the decision variable is extracted is obtained at a constant time after stimulus onset. RT predictions can be derived as in Assumption 2. To account for a finding that RT (L) is less than RT (S), we could assume that the information packet has better "quality" in the former case, and that, in order to achieve similar accuracy rates for the two durations, the subject spends more time processing the packet in the latter case. According to this argument, a variable that affects information quality could affect RT without affecting accuracy.

The above Assumptions refer to processing in the Pure duration and detection conditions. In the Mixed condition there are at least two additional issues, namely, whether or not processing capacity is shared between the duration and detection tasks, and which task is given priority. We now consider two possibilities that can be regarded as extremes.

5. In the Mixed condition duration information is processed in parallel with target information. However, the processing capacities allocated to the two tasks are proportions a and b of the levels in the Pure duration and Pure detection conditions, respectively. If a and b are less than 1, then we would expect a performance decrement (decrease in accuracy or increase in RT) from Pure to Mixed conditions. If a and b depend on stimulus variables, for example, number of nontargets, then the *effects* of these variables could be different in the two conditions (since, in the Pure condition, these variables would probably not affect capacity allocation). It should be noted that the assumption that a and b might depend on stimulus variables leaves open the question as to where in processing do these effects occur.

One implication of the assumption of parallel processing is that, *for a given stimulus,* the probability of correct duration and detection judgments is equal to the *product* of the probability of a correct duration judgment times that for a correct detection judgment. This is the test applied by Eijkman and Vendrik (1965) to show that auditory and visual detection judgments are made independently. Suppose that, for a given stimulus, p_a, p_b, and p_{ab} are the probabilities of correct duration, correct detection, and correct duration and detection judgments, respectively. Then the implication stated above is that $p_{ab} = p_a p_b$.

This implication *is* consistent with the possibility that p_a and p_b might covary positively across stimuli, for example, four-letter and eight-letter arrays.

6. At the other extreme, we might suppose that in the Mixed condition the subject first performs the detection task and then the duration task. Given that the subject can do only one task at a time, this ordering is reasonable because it is likely that duration information is more readily extracted from the encoding of the letters than target information is from the encoding of duration. For example, the quality of the encoding of the letters is probably directly related to duration, so it can serve as a cue for judging duration. To the extent that extracting duration information in this way, that is, from the g-processor, is less reliable than extracting it from the timer while it is activated, duration judgments would be less accurate in the Mixed than in the Pure condition. However, performance on detection should be the same in the two conditions because of the priority given to this task in the Mixed condition. This Assumption is an extreme form of the suggestion made by Sorkin et al. (1972) to account for the interaction between the processing in two auditory channels.

If the duration judgment is based on the quality of the output of the g-processor in the manner suggested above, those trials on which a correct detection judgment is made have a higher output quality than average and therefore, should have a greater *perceived duration* than average. That is, the duration judgments on correct detection trials would reflect a greater *bias* for saying "long" than the duration judgments on incorrect detection trials. There need be no difference in accuracy of duration judgments between correct and incorrect detection trials, and this mode of processing is not inconsistent with equality between p_{ab} and $p_a p_b$.

Assumptions 5 and 6 appear to be markedly different processing strategies, but both can be consistent with a given set of data on response accuracy. First, depending on the allocation of attention in Assumption 5, that is, on the values of a and b, p_a and p_b can be less than or equal to the accuracy rates in the Pure conditions. Second, both parallel and sequential processing are consistent with the equality of p_{ab} and $p_a p_b$. Because of this, we now discuss some assumptions about RT that seem to characterize Assumption 5 but not 6.

5a. In the Mixed condition let T and T' be the times required for the duration and detection judgments. Consistently with the assumption of parallel processing, we assume that T and T' are independent random variables and that observed RT is the greater of T and T'. To test the adequacy of this assumption, we first identify the means of eight RT distributions, and then derive the mean RT for various combinations of correct and incorrect duration and detection judgments.

Considering *duration* judgments, let m_{1c} and m_{1e} be the mean of T conditional on correct and incorrect judgments, respectively, for short duration, and let m_{2c} and m_{2e} be the corresponding means for the long duration. Considering *detection* judgments, let m_{3c} and m_{3e} be the mean of T' conditional on correct and incorrect judgments, respectively, for nontarget stimuli, and let m_{4c} and

m_{4e} be the corresponding means for target stimuli. For simplicity, we assume that the distributions of T and T', conditional on stimulus and response, are exponential, so that the above means m_{ic} and m_{ie} ($i = 1, \ldots, 4$) each characterize the RT distribution.

For the short and long durations ($i = 1$ and 2, respectively) we now derive the mean RT for responses that are correct duration and correct detection (T_{i1}), correct duration and incorrect detection (T_{i2}), incorrect duration and correct detection (T_{i3}), and incorrect duration and incorrect detection (T_{i4}). Then for nontarget and target stimuli ($i = 3$ and 4, respectively) we derive similarly the expressions for T_{ij}, $j = 1, \ldots, 4$. For $i = 1, \ldots, 4$, let $F_{ic}(t)$ and $F_{ie}(t)$ denote the exponential distribution functions (d.f.) with means m_{ic} and m_{ie}, respectively, and let q_i be the error rate for the ith group of stimuli.

To compute T_{11} we note that T is the correct RT for short durations and has d.f. $F = F_{1c}$, and T' is the correct detection RT and has d.f. $F' = [(1-q_3) F_{3c} + (1-q_4) F_{4c}] / (2-q_3-q_4)$, since targets and nontargets are equally likely. Since RT is the maximum of T and T', its d.f. is FF' and the mean is

$$T_{11} = \int_0^\infty (1 - FF')\, dt,$$

$$= m_{1c} + \frac{Q_3\, m_{3c}{}^2}{m_{1c} + m_{3c}} + \frac{(1 - Q_3)\, m_{4c}{}^2}{m_{1c} + m_{4c}},$$

where $Q_3 = (1-q_3) / (2-q_3-q_4)$. Similarly, to find T_{12} we note that $F = F_{1c}$ and T' is the error detection RT and has d.f. $F' = (q_3 F_{3e} + q_4 F_{4e}) / (q_3 + q_4)$. Mean RT is given by

$$T_{12} = m_{1c} + \frac{Q_4\, m_{3e}{}^2}{m_{1c} + m_{3e}} \quad \frac{(1 - Q_4)\, m_{4e}{}^2}{m_{1c} + m_{4e}},$$

where $Q_4 = q_3 / (q_3 + q_4)$. The expressions for the remaining T_{ij} have the same form and can be derived from the above expressions by changing the subscripts of m and q appropriately.

The q_i and T_{ij} can be estimated from the data, and the values of m_{ic} and m_{ie} can be found that minimize the differences between expected and observed T_{ij}. This was done using the computer subroutine STEPIT (Chandler, 1965).

V.   APPLICATIONS OF ASSUMPTIONS TO DATA

In the Pure duration condition the error rates for short and long durations were 0.15 and 0.31, respectively, when there were two response alternatives, and 0.16 and 0.23, respectively, when there were four alternatives. With two response alternatives, error and correct RT were approximately equal to 508 msec for the short duration, while error RT was less than correct RT (468 vs. 543 msec) for the long duration. With four alternatives, error and correct RT were approximately equal to 788 msec for the long duration, while error RT was greater than correct RT (849 vs. 780 msec) for the short duration. According to Assumption 1, error RT should be greater (less) than correct RT for short (long) durations, whereas, according to Assumption 2, since errors are less frequent than correct responses, error RT should be greater than correct RT for both durations. These data are more consistent with the first Assumption, although the weight of evidence is not overwhelming.

In the Pure detection condition, correct RT for short durations exceeded that for long durations by 51 msec when they were two responses, and by 96 msec when there were four responses. The differences between error RT were even greater. As pointed out earlier, this pattern of data is more consistent with Assumption 3 than Assumption 4.

We prefer to think, therefore, of duration judgments as being based on a timer that is activated by stimulus onset and that triggers a response as soon as it reaches a critical duration or is switched off by stimulus offset, whichever comes first. Also, we view the accumulation of nontemporal information as starting from stimulus onset and proceeding as a random walk until the information reaches one or other preset levels.

Turning to the data from the Mixed conditions, we noted previously that there was a decrement in accuracy of duration judgments in going from Pure to Mixed conditions, the decrement being most marked for Map 2. In terms of Assumption 5, we might say that the capacity allocated to duration judgments is less in Map 1 than that allocated in the Pure condition, and is less in Map 2 than in Map 1. It may be recalled that Thomas and Cantor (1975) found no Pure versus Mixed differences in duration judgments, and this absence of a difference may have been due to the simplicity of their size discrimination tasks, relative to the detection task used in the present study.

The overall levels of detection accuracy are comparable across Pure and Mixed conditions. However, accuracy increased with stimulus duration in both Mixed conditions but was independent of duration in the Pure condition. This change in the relation between accuracy and duration as we go from Pure to Mixed conditions suggests that processing capacity is limited and is shared between the two tasks in the the Mixed conditions. The effect of this sharing of capacity appears to be located within the first 100 msec of processing, that is, early in processing. This conclusion is in agreement with that of Briggs et al (1972).

To see if there was a correlation between the accuracy of duration judgments and that of detection judgments, 2 x 2 contingency tables (duration/detection, correct/incorrect) were computed for short durations, long durations, nontarget stimuli, and target stimuli. These tables, together with the associated mean RTs, are shown in Table 4. In all cases the hypothesis of no correlation could not be rejected.

TABLE 4

Joint Probability (P) and RT (in msec) for Maps 1 and 2, for Each of Four-Response Categories and for Selected Stimulus Values[a]

Stimulus Values	Measure	Map 1 Response Category				Map 2 Response Category			
		(1)	(2)	(3)	(4)	(1)	(2)	(3)	(4)
Nontarget	P	0.64	0.08	0.24	0.04	0.59	0.05	0.32	0.04
	RT	1018	1009	999	992	1059	1087	1071	1191
Target	P	0.60	0.13	0.22	0.05	0.57	0.09	0.29	0.05
	RT	939	1012	968	952	997	1167	1026	1089
Short	P	0.65	0.13	0.18	0.04	0.66	0.09	0.22	0.03
	RT	997	1018	1013	998	1040	1108	1082	1199
Long	P	0.59	0.08	0.28	0.05	0.52	0.05	0.38	0.05
	RT	980	1003	954	946	1016	1147	1014	1080

[a](1) correct duration, correct detection; (2) correct duration, incorrect detection; (3) incorrect duration, correct detection; and (4) incorrect duration, incorrect detection.

Finally, the parallel processing RT model of Assumption 5a was applied to the data from Maps 1 and 2, shown in Table 4. For each Map, a measure was obtained of the goodness-of-fit of the model, and this measure is distributed as X^2 with 8 degrees of freedom. For Map 1, $X^2 \cong 4.0$ (NS), indicating a good fit of the model, while for Map 2, $X^2 = 20$ ($p < .01$), indicating a poor fit of the model. For Map 1, the estimates of correct and error RT were (499, 567), (531, 481), (803, 792), and (759, 749) for short and long durations, nontarget and target stimuli, respectively.[1] It is interesting to note that the estimated error RT is greater (less) than the estimated correct RT for short (long) durations, in accordance with Assumption 1. The findings that, for the Map 2 data, Assumption 5a gives a poor fit, that detection performance is the same as in the Pure detection condition, and that duration judgments are much less accurate than in the Pure duration condition suggest that Assumption 6 gives a more accurate account than Assumption 5 of processing in this condition. That is, when the detection task is emphasized, processing in the two tasks appears to be interdependent, with priority given to the detection task.

VI. CONCLUDING REMARKS

Our original, and still primary, interest is in understanding how duration judgments are made. Because of the empirical evidence that these judgments are affected by nontemporal information, we have had to examine the dual relationships between the processing of temporal information and the processing of nontemporal information. As is the case with most discussions of information processing, our framework for discussing this duality attributes a central role to the concept of *attention*. A priori, one can imagine at least two possible effects on temporal judgments of attending to nontemporal information. The first is that attending to nontemporal information (I) enhances time-keeping (Thomas & Brown, 1974, Example 6.1.5). This might be so if time-keeping were an intermittent on—off process, such that the passage of time is encoded accurately during the "on-periods" and not encoded during the "off-periods," and that attending to I increases the length of on-periods relative to that of off-periods. It has been argued that this assumption can account for the finding that perceived duration is greater when I is presented during an interval than when the interval is empty, that is, for the filled-duration illusion.

---

[1]The relative magnitudes of the "duration" and "detection" RTs in the optimum solution depend on the initial parameter values used by STEPIT. However, the differences among m_{ic} and m_{ie} ($i = 1, 2$) and those among m_{ic} and m_{ie} ($i = 3, 4$) are independent of the initial parameter values. Our present remarks concern these differences only. The three optimum (duration RT, detection RT) solutions were approximately (200, 900), (800, 500), and (500, 800). We have chosen the last of these solutions because the data from the Pure conditions show that duration RT is less than detection RT and is much greater than 200 msec.

The second possibility is that presented information captures the attention mechanism, leading to a decrease in the reliability of time-keeping. If perceived duration is dependent on the outcomes of attending to I and of time-keeping (Thomas & Weaver, 1975), the perceived duration of a filled interval may or may not be greater than that of an empty interval depending on the "weights" given to the two outcomes. It is this assumption of divided attention that connects our thinking about time perception with the previous work on the characteristics of *attention,* which work is concerned mainly with locating the source of performance decrements due to divided attention rather than with the details of how *particular* types of information (for example, loudness, spatial location, and duration) are processed. To be sure, when duration tasks are used in attention studies (for example, Eijkman & Vendrik, 1965; Massaro & Kahn, 1973), the important feature of these tasks is the sensory modality in which the stimulus is presented, not the temporal nature of the information, although differences attributable to the latter variable have been noted. In the present experiments, judgments of temporal and nontemporal information concern a unitary visual stimulus, and one can equally well suppose that the temporal information is presented to a (visual) *channel* or to a (time-keeping) sensory *modality.* Whereas previous work on attention suggests that this is an important distinction (see, for example, Treisman, 1969), our present models ignore the distinction and focus on when the duration judgment begins, how it is affected by nontemporal variables, and how all performance measures are affected by the division of attention.

Our reaction time data from the Pure duration conditions suggest that duration judgments are based partly on a timer that starts at a short random delay after stimulus onset and stops at a short random delay after stimulus offset, or as soon as a critical duration is reached, whichever occurs first. Attending to nontemporal information might affect the "speed" of the timer or the length of the delays between stimulus and timer onset and offset. We prefer to think that the critical duration is set before each trial, but it is conceivable that it is set very soon after stimulus onset and is influenced by nontemporal factors. A different view of the basis of duration judgments has been recently proposed by Massaro and Idson (1976). Their view is that, starting at stimulus offset, duration information grows over time and tends to an asymptotic value. This growth is reflected in the increase in *accuracy* (d') of duration judgments during the interval from stimulus offset to the onset of a masking stimulus. Further work is needed to differentiate between these two models, in particular, to see which model gives a better account of both reaction time and accuracy data.

In the Mixed condition that emphasized the duration task (Map 1), our analysis of reaction time and accuracy data suggests that, for a given stimulus, duration and detection decisions are done simultaneously. However, the speed of these decisions varies across stimuli and, probably across Pure and Mixed conditions. That is, the assumption of simultaneous processing is consistent with the observed effects of nontemporal variables on perceived duration in the Map 1 condition, and with the observed differences in accuracy and in the effects of nontemporal variables between this condition and the Pure duration conditions. In the Map 2 condition, in which the detection task was emphasized, the assumption of simultaneous processing does not give a good account of the data, although the accuracy of the detection decision is independent of that of the duration decision when the data are pooled over subjects. The effects observed in this condition are very similar to those observed in the Pure detection conditions, and this has led us to suppose that, in this condition, the subject first makes the detection decision and then the duration decision. The duration decision may be based on the quality of the nontemporal information on that trial, and our assumption is that perceived duration, not accuracy, is directly related to quality. Therefore, the dependence between the two decisions need not be reflected in the correlation between the levels of accuracy.

Our finding, that detection accuracy increases with stimulus duration in the Mixed conditions, but is independent of duration in the Pure conditions, suggests that the division of attention in the former conditions causes a decrement in the rate of accumulation of the relevant information at an early stage of processing. Together with the observed decrement in duration accuracy, these data suggest that performance on both tasks is impaired by the division of attention. An interesting possibility is suggested by the estimates of hypothetical mean reaction times obtained by applying Assumption 5a to the data from Map 1. The estimated reaction times to make duration judgments are around 500 msec, the approximate value of the observed reaction time in the two-response, Pure duration condition. The estimated reaction times to make detection judgments are around 800 msec, much greater than the observed reaction times in the two-response Pure detection condition and close to those in the four-response condition. The suggestion is that, in the Mixed condition, the subject spends more time on the detection judgments in order to achieve an accuracy level comparable to that reached in the Pure conditions. Such a speed—accuracy tradeoff could explain why some attention studies do not find decrements in accuracy in divided attention conditions (for futher discussion of this point, see Wickelgren, 1974).

The observed differences between Maps 1 and 2 suggest that stimulus—response mapping affects the way stimulus information is processed, for example, whether the duration decision is made concurrently with or after the detection decision. A recent study (Cantor & Thomas, 1977) examines the role of task instructions by requiring subjects to make duration judgments while attending to the area of visually presented shapes in one condition, and to the perimeter of these shapes in another condition. It was found that perceived duration was positively correlated with area and negatively correlated with perimeter, but that these effects were the same in the two conditions. One might say that subjects in this experiment could not control their attention (in the sense of ignoring the irrelevant stimulus dimension), whereas in the present experiment some control of attention is indicated. Whether the difference between the two experiments is due to the peripheral locus of an area and perimeter decision relative to that of a detection decision or to the difference between varying the relevant stimulus dimension and varying the stimulus–response mapping remains to be seen.

ACKNOWLEDGMENTS

We are pleased to acknowledge the extensive help of Peter G. Smith in programming our experiment on the computer and in estimating the parameters of a theoretical model. This work was supported by Grant GB-43275 from the National Science Foundation.

REFERENCES

Allport, D. A., Antonis, B., & Reynolds, P. On the division of attention: A disproof of the single channel hypothesis. *Quarterly Journal of Experimental Psychology,* 1972, *24,* 225–235.

Broadbent, D. *Perception and communication.* London: Pergamon, 1958.

Briggs, G., Peters, G., & Fisher, P. On the locus of the divided attention effects. *Perception and Psychophysics,* 1972, *11,* 315–320.

Buffardi, L. Factors affecting the filled-duration illusion in the auditory, tactual, and visual modalities. *Perception and Psychophysics,* 1971, *10,* 292–294.

Cantor, N. E., & Thomas, E. A. C. The control of attention in the processing of temporal and spatial information in complex visual patterns. *Journal of Experimental Psychology: Human Perception and Performance,* 1977, *3,* 243–250.

Chandler, J. P. *Subroutine STEPIT: An algorithm that finds the values of the parameters which minimize a given continuous function.* (A copyrighted program.) J. P. Chandler, Copyright, 1965.

Eijkman, G., & Vendrik, A. J. H. Can a sensory system be specified by its internal noise? *Journal of the Acoustical Society of America,* 1965, *37,* 1102–1109.

Estes, W. K., & Taylor, H. A. A detection method and probabilistic model for assessing information processing from brief visual displays. *Proceedings of the National Academy of Sciences of the United States of America,* 1964, *52,* 446–454.

Estes, W. K., & Taylor, H. A. Visual detection in relation to display size and redundancy of critical elements. *Perception and Psychophysics,* 1966, *1,* 9–16.

LaBerge, D. Identification of two components of the time to switch attention: A test of a serial and parallel model of attention. In S. Kornblum (Ed.), *Attention and performance IV.* New York: Academic Press, 1973.

Laming, D. R. J. *Information theory of choice-reactiont imes.* New York: Academic Press, 1968.

Link, S. W., & Heath, R. A. A theory of sequential comparative judgment. *Psychometrika,* 1975, *40,* 77–106.

Massaro, D. W., & Idson, W. L. Temporal course of perceived auditory duration. *Perception and Psychophysics,* 1976, *20,* 331–352.

Massaro, D. W., & Kahn, B. J. Effects of central processing on auditory recognition. *Journal of Experimental Psychology,* 1973, *97,* 51–58.

Moore, J. J., & Massaro, D. W. Attention and processing capacity in auditory recognition. *Journal of Experimental Psychology,* 1973, *99,* 49–54.

Moray, N. Introductory experiments in auditory time sharing. Detection of intensity and frequency increments. *Journal of the Acoustical Society of America,* 1970, *47,* 1071–1073.

Moray, N. A data base for theories of selective listening. In P. M. A. Rabbit & S. Dornic (Eds.), *Attention and performance V.* London: Academic Press, 1975.

Ornstein, R. *On the experience of time.* Baltimore: Penguin, 1969.

Shiffrin, R. M., & Gardner, G. T. Visual processing capacity and attentional control. *Journal of Experimental Psychology,* 1972, *93,* 78–82.

Shiffrin, R. M., Gardner, G. T., & Allmeyer, D. H. On the degree of attention and capacity limitations in visual processing. *Perception and Psychophysics,* 1973, *14,* 231–236.

Shiffrin, R. M., & Grantham, D. W. Can attention be allocated to sensory modalities? *Perception and Psychophysics,* 1974, *15*(3), 460–474.

Sorkin, R. D., Pastore, R. G., & Pohlmann, L. D. Simultaneous two-channel signal detection. II. Correlated and uncorrelated signals. *Journal of the Acoustical Society of America,* 1972, *51,* 1960–1965.

Sternberg, S., & Knoll, R. L. The perception of temporal order: Fundamental issues and a general model. In S. Kornblum (Ed.), *Attention and performance IV.* New York: Academic Press, 1973.

Taylor, M. M., Lindsay, P. H., & Forbes, S. M. Quantification of shared capacity processing in auditory and visual discrimination. In A. Sanders (Ed.), *Attention and performance I.* Amsterdam: North-Holland, 1967.

Thomas, E. A. C., & Brown, I. Time perception and the filled-duration illusion. *Perception and Psychophysics,* 1974, *16*(3), 449–458.

Thomas, E. A. C., & Cantor, N. E. On the duality of simultaneous time and size perception. *Perception and Psychophysics,* 1975, *18,* 44–48.

Thomas, E. A. C., & Myers, J. L. Implications of latency data for threshold and nonthreshold models of signal detection. *Journal of Mathematical Psychology,* 1972, *9,* 253–285.

Thomas, E. A. C., & Weaver, W. B. Cognitive processing and time perception. *Perception and Psychophysics,* 1975, *17,* 363–367.

Treisman, A. M. Strategies and models of selective attention. *Psychological Review,* 1969, *76,* 282–299.

Treisman, A., & Davies, A. Divided attention to ear and eye. In S. Kornblum (Ed.), *Attention and performance IV.* New York: Academic Press, 1973.

Wickelgren, W. *Speed-accuracy tradeoff and information processing dynamics.* Paper presented at the meetings of the Psychonomics Society, 1974.

Wickens, C. D. The effects of divided attention on information processing in manual tracking. *Journal of Experimental Psychology: Human Perception and Performance,* 1976, *2*(1), 1–13.

4 The Formation of Auditory Streams

Albert S. Bregman

Department of Psychology
McGill University
Montreal, Canada

ABSTRACT

In a complex environment with many simultaneous sounds, auditory perception seems to be strongly affected by heuristic processes that try to "parse" the acoustic input and recover the combination of acoustic components contributed by each separate source of sound. These heuristics tend to follow principles described by Gestalt psychology. Their operation is well described by the notions of similarity, proximity, simplicity, good continuation, competition of organizations (belongingness), and common fate. The processes of judgment and pattern recognition seem to apply most easily when the elements upon which these processes operate have been grouped into the same perceptual stream by the "parsing" heuristics.

I. INTRODUCTION

Human beings have evolved in a world in which many different events can act at the same time in creating the input to their senses. Given that this is the case, the sensory systems must have evolved some ways of sorting out the input so as to recover a separate "description" of each source. Researchers in computer vision (see Winston, 1977) have recently been attacking these problems under the name of "scene analysis." Heuristic rules have been evolved to decide how regions of the optic array should be separated and combined to find the meaningful objects. The auditory system is no less in need of scene analysis heuristics. One sound can momentarily mask another; sounds from different sources mix if they occur together. If we looked at a spectrogram of any brief moment of sound, there would be a complex pattern of streaks, any pair of which could have been caused by the same source, or by different sources. Conversely, a single streak could have been the summation of two sources. Furthermore, the harmonics from one source are interlaced with the harmonics of another one. Yet it appears that the auditory system manages to pull apart the separate sources. This chapter reports some beginnings in the study of auditory scene analysis, and later discusses some relations with the study of attention.

The scene analysis processes in audition concern themselves with segregation and grouping and must successfully answer questions such as these: How many sources are shaping the input? Was some particular discontinuity a change in the sound of one source or an interruption by a second source? Should two spectral peaks be grouped to derive one sound with complex timbre, or separated to derive two sounds with simpler timbre?

The Gestalt psychologists in their study of vision, pointed out many factors that led parts of displays to group or segregate; they viewed these as the consequence of force fields in the brain. We can accept the Gestaltists' descriptions of the factors that lead to organization, but instead of viewing them as they did we can look at these processes as the heuristic use of information employed in scene analysis. To be useful, heuristics should tend to give right answers. That is, they should tend to group those parts of the input that were shaped by the same source and segregate those which were not. No one heuristic will necessarily always succeed, but if there are many of them, competing with or reinforcing one another, the right description of the input should generally emerge.

The auditory system has two types of information to work with, the monaural spectrum and the relations between the spectra in the two ears. Clearly, the localization of spectral components in space can serve as important information upon which grouping can be based. Our own research however, has focused upon information available in the monaural spectrum — the frequency and amplitude changes over time.

Two basic sets of factors interact in creating a meaningful description from the acoustic input: our general heuristics for parsing all signals and our knowledge, skills, and intentions concerning specific types of signals. The general heuristics for parsing arise from the encounter of the species with quite general regularities of the world. They concern such problems in audition as mixing and masking, and take advantage of the usefulness of similarity, proximity, good continuation, and so forth as probabilistic clues to the composition of any signal whatever. Knowledge and skills, on the other hand, are based on the learning derived from specific encounters of individuals with their environments and are concerned with the meanings of sounds. It should be emphasized here, however, that the effective use of stored knowledge and skills so as to derive meaning is highly dependent on the successful operation of the general heuristics for segregation and grouping. Presumably, when we look up the identity of an input signal in our internal "dictionaries," we look it up by means of some group of acoustic features. But which group? If we assume that two separated segments of the input are part of the same signal, we will enter our dictionary only once with

FIG. 1.   Relation of stream organization to stimulus and response factors.

properties of both segments. If we assume that they are separate signals, we will enter the dictionary twice with two separate clusters of properties. The result of the recognition process will differ in the two cases. We see that the heuristic decomposition of the signal is critical for pattern recognition. I do not want to assert that the effects go only in one direction. Stored knowledge and skills can sometimes affect the process of decomposition. Probably it is stored knowledge that enables us, for example, to decompose an utterance into a string of words. I wish only to point out that the parsing heuristics can have a strong effect upon recognition. This idea has encouraged us to temporarily ignore the listener's extraction of specific meanings, and to focus on these general heuristics for parsing the monaural spectrum.

There are two sorts of questions that arise in these studies: (1) What information in the signal is used by the parser to sort out the separate streams of sound? and (2) What perceptual and judgmental consequences can be shown to follow from this stream organization? The questions cannot be answered separately. To find out what stimulus factors lead to the segregation of acoustic components, we have to use response measures as indices of segregation. This means we have to know the perceptual or judgmental consequences of segregation. Conversely, to study these consequences we have to know how stimulus factors affect the stream organization. In practice, we assume a theoretical process called "stream organization" and try to link it to a variety of stimulus factors and response consequences as in Fig. 1. In this paper I cannot discuss in detail the many response consequences that arise from stream organization. I will simply mention them and then focus, in the rest of the chapter, on the process whereby the streams are constructed. For now I will simply make the following summary. When an acoustic input is structured into simultaneous streams, these response consequences seem to occur: (a) listeners can reliably judge the number of streams (Bregman & Dannenbring, 1973); (b) they can only recognize rapid patterns of tones that are part of the same stream (Bregman & Campbell, 1971); (c) they can only label accurately the order of tones in the same stream (Bregman & Campbell, 1971); (d) they may judge elements of one stream as overlapping in time with elements of another concurrent stream, even when this is not true (Dannenbring & Bregman, 1976); (e) rhythmic patterns will include only members of the same stream (Bregman, in press-a). All these response effects can be used as measures of stream organization. They all reflect a grouping of information into streams and segregation of the information in different streams.

The remainder of this chapter is concerned with the heuristics that structure the streams. These heuristics seem to obey Gestalt principles, and I have used these principles as guidelines in studying the processes of organization. While they are not specified well enough to serve as formal explanations, they are quite suggestive and can provide a familiar framework within which some of the major phenomena can be described.

II. SIMILARITY

The first principle states that elements will be grouped if they are similar. I have chosen to interpret similarity as similarity of spectral composition. In the very simple case of pure tones, spectral similarity can be thought of as the nearness in frequency of the tones.

The role of frequency similiarity in stream segregation can be illustrated in a simple experiment (Bregman & Campbell, 1971). Suppose we take six pure tones, each of 100 msec duration , and string them into a repetitive loop so that

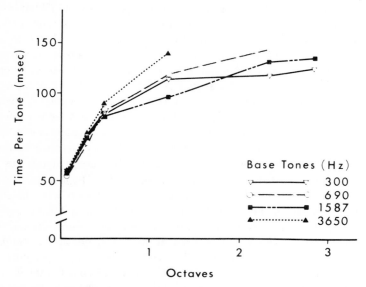

FIG. 2.   The splitting threshold, expressed as the time per tone (onset to onset) to which subjects adjusted the speed of a sequence of tones. The sequence alternated a high tone (F_2) with a low tone (F_1) in a galloping rhythm. The threshold is shown as a function of the ratio between the high and low frequencies. The parameter is the frequency of the low tone (F_1). These results are for four subjects run over a period of five days.

tones from a low range of frequencies alternate with tones from a higher range, with about an octave and a half separating the ranges. After listening to a few cycles, the stream of sound seems to split into two streams, one involving only the high tones, the other restricted to the low tones. Patterns are heard within each stream, but no pattern relating the two streams is evident. As a test of this, we can play three-tone patterns in isolation to listeners and ask them whether the three tones occur in the same order and spacing within the six-tone sequence. Subjects can answer correctly only if the three target tones are in the same stream, the high one or the low one.

The effects of frequency separation interact with those of the speed of the tonal sequence. At higher speeds of alternation, there is more splitting; streams will be restricted to narrower ranges of frequency (see Van Noorden, 1975).

This can be demonstrated by describing an unpublished experiment by G. Bernstein and myself in which subjects increased the rate of alternation of two tones until they split into two streams. The tones alternated in the pattern ABA—ABA—etc., and split at high speeds into two streams, a fast stream of A—A—A—etc., and a slower stream of B———B———, which were easily discriminated. The results are shown in Fig. 2. Two factors were varied by the experimenter, the frequency in hertz of the lower tone and the ratio between the higher and lower frequencies. Generally, as the frequencies moved closer together it required a higher rate of alternation of the tones to split the streams apart. This effect held over the entire range of frequencies that we explored; we do not see any discontinuity in our results that could be attributed to the possible crossover from a place to a periodicity-based region of pitch perception.

III. SIMPLICITY (GOOD FORM)

The preference for two-stream perception when there is a bimodal distribution of frequencies in the signal   seems like a principle of simplicity. It is as if the parsing heuristics are built to find a description that tries to minimize two things: the number of streams and the rate of change within each stream. The following experiment shows that the heuristics begin by constructing a single stream and subdivide this when the evidence for two streams becomes compelling. In short, it takes some time for a two-stream interpretation to emerge (Bregman, in press-b).

A listener is asked to speed up the rate of alternation of a continuous sequence of high and low tones until splitting occurs. In some conditions the stream of tones is continuous with no gaps. In others, a 4-sec silence is inserted after each group of four, eight, or sixteen tones. We find that the more often the silences occur, the faster the tones must be made to alternate before they split. This is shown in Fig. 3. A package (as referred to in Fig. 3) is defined as a number of tones preceded and followed by silence. As the number of tones per package

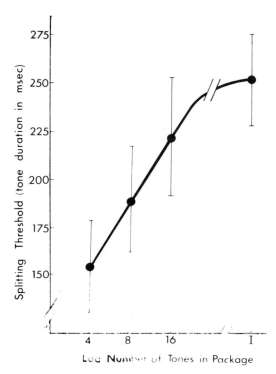

FIG. 3.   Splitting threshold in msec per tone (onset-to-onset time) as a function of number of tones per package. There were three tones, two "high" (784 and 831 Hz) and one "low" (330 Hz) presented in the sequence H_1, L, H_2, L, H_1, L, etc. As package size went up, the high and low tones segregated at slower speeds (greater tone durations).

increases, tone sequences will split at slower speeds (or longer times per tone, as in Fig. 3).

It can be assumed that the 4-sec silence resets the evidence-gathering process, so that in longer packages of tones more evidence for two streams can accumulate, and that therefore there is a greater tendency to split. Since both this factor and speed favor splitting. one of them can be traded off against the other in determining thresholds for splitting. This is the relation shown in Fig. 3.

IV. GOOD CONTINUATION

Another Gestalt factor is the effect of good continuation. If a repetitive cycle that contains an alternation between high and low tones tends to split into a high and a low stream, this splitting tendency can be reduced by connecting the sequential tones by frequency glides (Bregman & Dannenbring, 1973). Apparently one of the heuristics used by the parser involves treating any smooth and regular change as arising from a single source. Discontinuities in frequency (especially large, sudden ones) are taken to indicate a change in source.

We shall see the effects of sudden changes operating again in the illusion of continuity, but let us turn our attention now to another Gestalt principle, the idea that there are multiple organizations being structured at once and that these organizations compete for elements.

V. COMPETITION OF ORGANIZATIONS

To get at the question of whether organizations compete, we performed an experiment in which a portion of the signal consisted of four tones XABX (Bregman & Rudnicky, 1975). The complete presentation is shown in Fig. 4. Listeners judged the order of A and B. This was very difficult because the pair AB occurred quickly and was embedded in a four-tone pattern flanked by two distractor tones, labelled X. However, by moving another stream of tones, which we called the captor tones, near to the frequency of the distractor tones, we were able to capture the distractors, combine them in a separate stream, and strip them away perceptually, leaving the tones AB in a stream of their own. This made their order quite easy to judge. We have evidence here for two simultaneously structured streams, one of them, the tones AB, the subject of judgment and hence of attention, and the other one serving to strip distractors *out* of the domain of

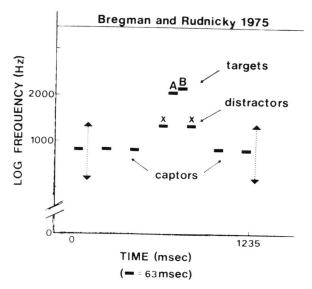

FIG. 4. Stimuli from Bregman and Rudnicky (1975). A stream of captor tones is varied in frequency (in Hz). When near the distractor (X) tones in frequency, they capture them into a stream, isolating the AB pair (targets) so that the order of AB is easy to judge.

attention. It seems that when the distractor tones were assigned a position in one organization, they were made unavailable for roles in the other organization. This can be taken to define the Gestalt notion of "belongingness."

VI. CLOSURE AND BELONGINGNESS

The principle of belongingness can be observed also in the illusion of continuity. In the simplest case, when a bit of a pure-tone signal is chopped out and a noise burst inserted to fill the gap, the pure tone is heard to continue through the gap. This case is shown in Fig. 5A. The leading edge of the noise burst, labeled X, exactly coincides with the discontinuation of the tone. We might ask this question. Since there is an acoustic discontinuity at that point in time, and since the tone no longer is present, why is the tone not heard as shutting off during the noise? The explanation may be that the discontinuity is assigned to the noise burst as defining its onset edge, perhaps because the noise is the louder signal, and that this same discontinuity cannot serve also to define the offset edge of the tone — it has to belong to one or the other, but not both. If so, this would mean that since there was no separate perceptual evidence for any boundary

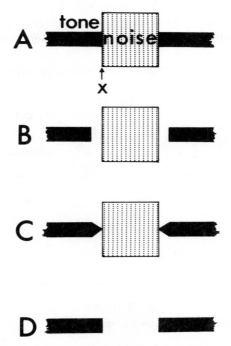

FIG. 5.   The role of the tone-noise boundary in the illusion of continuity: (A) tone ends at noise onset, (B) tone ends before noise onset, (C) tone becomes 10 db softer before noise onset, (D) no noise filling the tonal gap.

belonging to the tone itself, the perceptual description process tended to treat the tone as continuous.

This interpretation of the illusion is supported by two findings. First, if the offset of the tone precedes the onset of the noise by enough time to be perceptible, as in Fig. 5B, then no tone is heard during the noise (Elfner & Homick, 1967); second, if the tone is altered in loudness (indicated by thickness of bars in Fig. 5C) just before the noise, there is less continuation of the tone through the noise. Gary Dannenbring and I (Bregman & Dannenbring, 1977), have shown that these loudness changes can provide discontinuities independent of the leading edge of the noise, to serve as boundaries for the tone segments. The illusion of continuity is a case of what the Gestalt psychologists called perceptual closure, but looking at it from the point of view of scene analysis can be more fruitful. Viewed in these terms, we see the acoustic system making an interpretation in which the event is heard as having an occlusion or masking of one sound by another, this interpretation being based on acoustic evidence that the tone has probably been masked. If you remove the evidence for masking by, for example, taking the noise out of the gap (as in Fig. 5D), the perceptual closure does not occur despite the fact that the trajectory and hence the continuity of the tone has not been altered. We hear a tone with a gap in it, not a continuous tone (Warren, 1970).

Hence, continuity alone is not enough to produce closure. The auditory system also has to interpret the incomplete continuation as the result of some other acoustic factor, like masking, before it will generate closure. After all, we *can* hear gaps in sounds.

VII. COMMON FATE AND SPECTRAL DECOMPOSITION

I referred earlier to the problem of interpreting the interleaved spectral components in the spectrogram of a complex acoustic environment. The choice of which simultaneous components to hear as parts of some particular source will determine the perceived complexity or timbre of that source. The perception of acoustic quality, therefore, is heavily tied to the decisions of the parsing mechanisms about the grouping of components.

A Gestalt psychologist might approach the problem of the grouping of simultaneous events through the principle of common fate. This principle says that if two elements of a scene are undergoing the same kinds of changes at the same time, they are to be grouped as part of the same event. This is a good heuristic. It is likely in our world that the many frequency components arising from an acoustic source will come on and go off at more or less the same time, will glide up and down in pitch together, will be amplitude modulated together, and so on. On the other hand, this heuristic for grouping simultaneous events will not work in isolation. It will have to cooperate and compete with hueristics that create good sequential organizations.

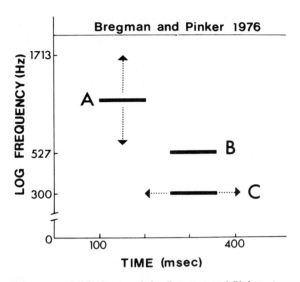

FIG. 6. Stimuli from unpublished research by Bregman and Pinker. A pure tone A alternates with a pair of tones BC. Tone A may vary in frequency (Hz), and C may vary in its asynchrony with B. Both factors affect the perceived richness of C and the stream membership of B.

Steven Pinker and I (Bregman & Pinker, in press) pitted these heuristics for simultaneous and successive grouping against one another. The stimuli are shown in Fig. 6. A single pure tone A, alternates repeatedly with a simultaneous pair, B and C. We introduced two manipulations. First, we varied the frequency of A from close to B's frequency to a much higher one. Second, we moved the lowest tone C forward and backward in time to create different degrees of asychrony with B. We reasoned that the sequential stream-forming process, working according to the heuristic of grouping by similarity, would try to unify A with B in a single stream when these tones were near in frequency, and would try to reject C into a separate stream. Opposing this process, the heuristic of grouping simultaneous frequency components by the principle of common fate would try to fuse the perception of B and C whenever their onsets and offsets were synchronous.

Our measure of the perceptual fusion of B and C was a very direct one. We told our listeners that the experiment was to investigate the perceptual "richness" or "timbre" of a sound, defined as "the quality that distinguishes, for example, the sounds of different musical instruments, producing notes of the same pitch." They were asked to concentrate on "the notes with the lowest pitch" in the recurrent cycle, and to judge them on a seven point scale with the two ends anchored by two standard tones. The pure standard was C alone, while the rich standard was B and C played together, synchronously, with slow onsets and offsets. The results are shown in Fig. 7. When B and C were synchronous, C was judged as sounding rich, with the richness dropping off as C was moved out

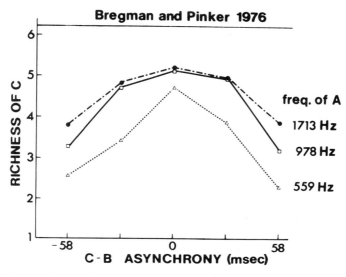

FIG. 7.   Mean ratings of richness for tone C of Figure 6 as a function of the asynchrony of B and C (a negative value indicates that C preceded B). The parameter is the frequency of A.

of synchrony with B. The closeness in frequency of A to B also had the predicted effect of reducing the perceived richness of C by stripping B off into a separate stream. Let us return to Fig. 6. We also asked listeners to judge directly whether A and B were in the same stream. As well as the usual result of a greater grouping of A and B into the same stream when they are close in frequency, we also found that the degree of synchrony of B with C made a difference; B would form a stream with A most often when B was asynchronous with C, and therefore free of C's influence. Clearly, we are observing a competition phenomenon here. The presence of A favors the insertion of B into a sequential stream according to the principle of similarity, thus acting to isolate C. The position of C, on the other hand, favors the insertion of B into a synchronous timbre structure with it according to the principle of common fate, thus acting to isolate A.

VIII. SUBJECT-CONTROLLED FACTORS

So far the discussion has centered on the information in the stimulus and how it is sorted out by general, probably innate, Gestalt-like heuristics that create organized preliminary descriptions. It is important at this point to consider the relations between these effects and the process of attention. The Gestalt psychologists accepted the idea that the observer's goals, memories, and skills could themselves make contributions to the organization of perceptual events, and employed concepts such as "einstellung" (set) to describe their effects. The effect of set on stream segregation has been demonstrated clearly by van Noorden, that is, the difference between his "temporal coherence boundary" and "fission boundary" (van Noorden, 1975). Such influences can be seen to correspond with the second sort of factor that I dealt with in the introduction to this chapter. They, too, create organization; an example I gave earlier was the dividing of an utterance into strings of recognized words.

Much of the research reported in this symposium requires the subject to make a judgment. This act of judging requires the subject to bring elements into relation with one another or with some internal standard. The fact that this is an act of organization is more easily seen in real-life cases. To judge the relative lengths of two branches on a tree, the ends of those two branches have to be segregated from the ends of all the others and brought into a perceptual relationship with one another.

In judging, in controlling action, and in planning, we select and organize aspects of our sensory input. In loose language, we pay attention to things. But we should ask the question, "What are the things that we can organize together in a single act of attention?" In audition, can we pick any arbitrary pair of spectral components out of an acoustic signal and make a judgment on them? The research I have reported has suggested that the aspects that can be brought together in a single act of attention are not at all arbitrarily selectable. We are built to pay attention to auditory sources, not to acoustic components, and it is the decomposition heuristics, organized in ways described by Gestalt psychology, that build the auditory descriptions of sources out of the complex acoustic input and, in so doing, place strong constraints on the process of attention.

ACKNOWLEDGMENTS

This research was supported by the National Research Council of Canada, The Quebec Department of Education FCAC program, and the McGill Faculty of Graduate Studies and Research. The author wishes to thank Gary Dannenbring for his collaboration over a period of five years.

REFERENCES

Bregman, A. S. Auditory streaming: Competition among alternative organizations. *Perception and Psychophysics,* in press. (a)

Bregman, A. S. Auditory streaming is cumulative. *Journal of Experimental Psychology: Human Perception and Performance,* in press. (b)

Bregman, A. S., & Campbell, J. Primary auditory stream segregation and perception of order in rapid sequences of tones. *Journal of Experimental Psychology,* 1971, *89,* 244—249.

Bregman, A. S., & Dannenbring, G. L. The effect of continuity on auditory stream segregation. *Perception and Psychophysics,* 1973, *13,* 308—312.

Bregman, A. S., & Dannenbring, G. L. Auditory continuity and amplitude edges. *Canadian Journal of Psychology,* 1977, *31,* 151—159.

Bregman, A. S., & Pinker, S. Auditory streaming and the building of timbre. *Canadian Journal of Psychology,* in press.

Bregman, A. S., & Rudnicky, A. I. Auditory segregation: Stream or streams? *Journal of Experimental Psychology: Human Perception and Performance,* 1975, *1,* 263–267.

Dannenbring, G. L., & Bregman, A. S. Stream segregation and the illusion of overlap. *Journal of Experimental Psychology: Human Perception and Performance,* 1976, *2,* 544–555.

Elfner, L. F., & Homick, J. L. Auditory continuity effects as a function of the duration and temporal location of the interpolated signal. *Journal of the Acoustical Society of America,* 1967, *42,* 576–579.

van Noorden, L. P. A. S. Temporal coherence in the perception of tone sequences. Unpublished doctoral dissertation. Eindhoven University of Technology, The Netherlands, 1975.

Warren, R. M. Perceptual restoration of missing speech sounds. *Science,* 1970, *167,* 392–393.

Winston, P. H. *Artificial intelligence.* Reading, Mass.: Addison–Wesley, 1977.

5 On the Time it Takes to Tell Things Apart

Raymond S. Nickerson

Bolt Beranek and Newman Inc.
Cambridge, Massachusetts, United States

ABSTRACT

The finding that it often takes less time to determine that two stimuli are the same than to determine that two stimuli are different is discussed. Several hypotheses that have been put forth to account for the finding are considered. It is concluded that none of these hypotheses adequately accounts for the finding, except in an ad hoc fashion, but several of them identify factors that probably play some role in determining the relationship between SAME and DIFFERENT RT. The question is raised as to how the difference between SAME and DIFFERENT RT relates to several other judgmental asymmetries that have been reported, and as to whether these assymmetries may have a common explanation.

I. INTRODUCTION

The act of comparing one thing with another and determining whether they are instances of the same thing must be a very fundamental type of perceptual activity. Without the ability to make such comparisons there could be no perception as we know it. This perhaps accounts, in part, for the considerable interest that researchers have shown in recent years in measuring the time it takes for an individual to tell whether two things are the same or different. This interest also stems to some degree, however, from the specific finding that the time required to determine that two matching stimuli are the same is often surprisingly short, compared to the time required to determine that two nonmatching stimuli differ. It is this finding that constitutes the focus for this chapter.

II. SAME VERSUS DIFFERENT RESPONSE TIMES

Attention will be limited primarily, though not exclusively, to SAME—DIF-FERENT judgment tasks that have the following properties: (a) the items to be compared are presented sequentially, (b) SAME and DIFFERENT trials occur with equal frequency, (c) SAME means physical correspondence (as opposed to same name), and (d) the difference between stimuli requiring the response DIFFERENT is large enough to be easily perceived.

Typically, when the stimuli that have been compared under these conditions have been single letters or numbers, positive responses have been faster than negative responses. This result has been obtained by many investigators (e.g., Atkinson, Holmgren, & Juola, 1969; Bamber, 1969; Johnson, 1975; Nickerson, 1965; Posner & Boies, 1971; Sloboda, 1976; Sternberg, 1969), and it has been shown to persist over several days of practice on the task (Nickerson, 1965, 1966). While the magnitude of the difference between SAME and DIFFERENT RT has varied over a range of a few tens of msec in these studies, 50 msec is representative of the differences obtained. Although this result has been most commonly found with alphanumeric stimuli, very similar results have been ob-tained with words (Fraisse, 1970; Johnson, 1975; Smith, 1967), and certain nonlinguistic visual patterns (Briggs & Blaha, 1969; Cohen, 1969; Fraisse, 1970; Tversky, 1969). What it seems to suggest is that the SAME judgment in these experiments is not the outcome of an analytic process that compares stimuli in a feature-by-feature fashion and terminates either upon finding a mismatch or after determining that there are no mismatches to be found.

Further support for the notion of a nonanalytic basis for SAME judgments comes from experiments in which subjects have been asked to compare simple nonalphanumeric stimuli that can differ with respect to a variable number of features (Egeth, 1966; Hawkins, 1969; Nickerson, 1967; Reed, 1975). Color, shape, and size are illustrative of the visual features that have been varied in these experiments; in the case of auditory stimuli, phonetic features have been used. When the two stimuli presented for comparison on a given trial are not the same, they have differed with respect to one, or a combination of two or more, of these features. Typically, DIFFERENT RT has varied inversely with the number of features with respect to which the stimuli differ, a result that *is* consistent with the assumption that the stimuli are compared by means of a self-terminating feature-by-feature analysis. Such an assumption leads one to expect SAME RT to be at least as long as the DIFFERENT RT obtained when the stimuli differ with respect to only a single feature, and, in particular, with respect to that feature associated with the longest DIFFERENT RT. This is not the result that has been obtained, however; typically, SAME RT has been considerably shorter than the longest DIFFERENT RT, and, in some cases, as short as, or shorter than, the shortest of them. In brief, the relationship that has been found between DIFFERENT RT and number of differing attributes seems to suggest a model of the comparison process that SAME RT does not fit.

An analogous finding has been obtained in experiments in which the task is to determine whether two letter strings are identical. Bamber (1969) found that the time required to judge two *n*-letter strings to be different varied inversely with the number of letters with respect to which the two strings differed. This result also suggests an analytic — this time letter-by-letter — comparison process. But, again, SAME RT was too short to be consistent with this hypothesis. Similar results have been obtained with alphanumeric stimuli by Beller (1970), with simple nonalphanumeric shapes by Donderi and Case (1970), and, in the auditory modality, with speech-like stimuli by Reed (1975).

III. SOME HYPOTHESES REGARDING THE RELATIVE SHORTNESS OF SAME RT

Several hypotheses have been put forth to account for the relative shortness of SAME RT. The following are perhaps the most prominent of these hypotheses.

A.   Stimulus-Sampling Artifact

Some investigators have pointed out that the design of SAME–DIFFERENT experiments has often involved a stimulus-sampling bias that could produce the asymmetry obtained between SAME and DIFFERENT RTs (Johnson, 1975; Krueger, 1973; Williams, 1972). If SAME and DIFFERENT stimulus pairs are presented with equal frequency, and the items comprising the pairs are sampled at random from the set of admissible possibilities in both cases, then specific SAME pairs will occur more frequently on the average than will specific DIF-FERENT pairs. This follows from the fact that given a set of *n* alternative stimuli there are only *n* ways to produce pairs of identical items, whereas there are $n(n-1)/2$ ways (ignoring order) to produce pairs whose members differ from each other. For example, one can produce only 10 two-digit numbers in which the same digit occurs twice, whereas one can produce 45 unique two-digit numbers (again ignoring order) in which the digits differ. Thus, if one thinks of a pair of items that occurs on a trial as *a* stimulus, then the well-known stimulus frequency effect provides a basis for expecting SAME RT to be shorter than DIFFERENT RT, because the individual stimuli calling for a SAME response occur more frequently than do those calling for a DIFFERENT response.

Thomas (1974) has pointed out another way in which stimulus sampling could lead to shorter SAME RTs. Given the occurrence of a particular character, say *A*, as the first stimulus of a pair, the contingent probability that the second stimulus will be that same character, *A*, is 0.5, whereas the probability that it will be any other *particular* character, say *B*, is far less than 0.5. If the subject can prepare for only one particular stimulus, his best strategy is to prepare for a repetition of the first one.

The possibility of attributing the relative shortness of SAME RT to stimulus-sampling artifacts was tested in an experiment by Nickerson (1973) in which the stimuli were selected in accordance with the following constraints: (a) SAME and DIFFERENT pairs occurred with equal frequency; (b) any given stimulus was paired only with itself (on SAME trials) or with one *particular* other stimulus (on DIFFERENT trials) so the second letter was, with equal probability, either the same as the first, or the particular other letter that was uniquely paired with it; and (c) the relative frequency of occurrence of specific SAME pairs was varied systematically, as was that of specific DIFFERENT pairs.

RT was inversely related to the relative frequency of occurrence of a stimulus pair, but at all relative frequencies SAME RT was shorter than DIFFERENT RT by about 50 msec. A shortcoming of this experiment was the fact that subjects did not receive much practice, so one might question whether the fact that different stimuli were occurring with different probabilities was subjectively meaningful. The finding that RT was sensitive to relative frequency of occurrence suggests it was.

An earlier experiment (Nickerson, 1968) was also addressed to the issue of a possible stimulus-sampling artifact. In this case only two letters (*C* and *D*) comprised the entire stimulus ensemble. On every trial one of these letters was paired either with itself or with the other letter. Again, SAME RT proved to be shorter than DIFFERENT RT by an average of about 50 msec. Thus, while stimulus-sampling statistics undoubtedly can affect performance, they do not account for the generally relative shortness of SAME RT.

B. Priming

On SAME trials, the second stimulus is a repetition of the first. Thus, its perception involves reactivation of a recently activated process. According to the priming notion, the initial activation of the process by which the stimulus is perceived primes it for the second activation. The effect of priming is to speed up the second activation relative to the first (Donderi & Zelnicker, 1969; Posner & Boies, 1971).

This hypothesis gets some support from a number of other experiments that have demonstrated stimulus-repetition effects on response time (Bertelson, 1961; Kornblum, 1969). The results of these experiments provide limited support, however, inasmuch as the difference between SAME and DIFFERENT RTs has been obtained even when the stimuli being compared are separated by several seconds (although the largest effects seem to be obtained with interstimulus intervals of a few hundred msec), whereas stimulus-repetition effects typically have been found only when the stimuli are separated by a few hundred msec at most.

C. Trace Strength

According to this hypothesis, presentation of the first of the items to be compared activates its memory representation and thereby modifies it in some way (strengthens it, tags it). The SAME—DIFFERENT decision is made by inspecting the memory representation corresponding to the second item and determining its strength. Decision time is assumed to vary inversely with the strength of the memory trace, relative to some criterion strength that divides the decision axis into SAME and DIFFERENT components (Bindra, Williams, & Wise, 1965; Krueger, 1975; Nickerson, 1972). The trace-strength hypothesis differs from that of priming in that it locates the effect in a decision process, whereas the priming hypothesis locates the effect in the encoding or perception of the second stimulus.

The trace-strength hypothesis nicely accommodates the finding that DIFFERENT RT varies inversely with the degree to which the stimuli being compared differ. Given the assumptions that the distinguishing quality of SAME and DIFFERENT stimuli is the strength of a memory trace, and that activation of a stimulus increases the strength not only of its memory trace but of those of similar stimuli as well, we would expect a DIFFERENT stimulus with a relatively strong trace (a DIFFERENT stimulus that is similar in many respects to the target) to have a high likelihood of evoking the wrong (SAME) response. Such an effect should be seen in the data, both as a relatively high incidence of errors (incorrect SAMEs), and long RTs, because of the response competition involved. Both of these results have been obtained.

By virtue of the assumption that decision time varies inversely with the difference between the strength of the stimulus trace and the criterion strength (Bindra, et al., 1965), the trace-strength hypothesis also accommodates the finding that SAME RT may vary with the degree to which the DIFFERENT stimuli differ (Nickerson, 1969). The greater the overlap between the strength index distributions for SAME and DIFFERENT pairs, the closer any given index will be to criterion, on the average, and thus the greater will be the average decision time for both SAME and DIFFERENT decisions.

The trace-strength hypothesis also has its weaknesses, however. The assumption that decision time is inversely related to the difference between the strength of a trace and a criterion strength does not provide a basis for expecting SAME RTs to be shorter than DIFFERENTs in general. RT should vary inversely with the difference between the trace strength and the criterion, independently of the side of the criterion on which the strength value lies. One might postulate a bias in the positioning of the decision criterion with respect to the SAME and DIFFERENT strength index distributions, but this requires some assumptions that are not inherent to the trace-strength notion.

D.   Response Bias

Perhaps subjects are more likely to set themselves to respond SAME than to respond DIFFERENT, and for that reason are faster on the SAME trials, but this hypothesis is not very satisfactory in the absence of an explanation of why there should be such a bias. One can point to the fact that when the words "same" and "different" are juxtaposed contrastively, they usually occur in that order, suggesting a pervasive asymmetry, at least in linguistic usage (Nickerson, 1967); however, this does not really explain the bias, if there is one. Moreover, a significant response bias in either direction should be reflected in asymmetrical error rates. For example, a bias for SAME responses should be reflected not only in short SAME RTs, but also in a higher incidence of false SAME responses than of false DIFFERENTs. Such asymmetrical error tendencies have not typically been found.

E. Confirmation Checking

Some investigators have suggested that DIFFERENT responses are relatively slow because of a double-checking procedure invoked only in their case. The assumption is that the subject makes an immediate positive response if the items being compared match; however, on some proportion of the trials on which a match is not obtained, the subject makes a second attempt to get a match, or checks to confirm the mismatch before making a negative response (Briggs & Johnsen, 1973; Burrows, 1972; Egeth, Jonides, & Wall, 1972; Howell & Stockdale, 1975; Murdock, 1971; Tversky, 1969).

While this hypothesis does accommodate the finding, one might ask why the subject should require confirmation before making a negative response, but not before making a positive one. An obvious reason for checking one decision outcome more carefully than the other would be any asymmetry in the relative ease with which the two types of errors are made. If, for example, it were much easier to make a false DIFFERENT decision than a false SAME one, the subject would do well to confirm any tentative DIFFERENT decision before making his response. But is there any reason to expect false DIFFERENTs to be generally more likely than false SAMEs? One can easily imagine instances in which the converse should be true. Consider the situation in which the DIFFERENT stimulus pairs occurring in a given session differ by differing amounts ranging from something close to a just-noticeable difference to very large differences indeed. In this case, when two very different stimuli are paired, the difference is apparent and the DIFFERENT response is relatively fast. However, when the two stimuli are the same, one should encounter difficulty in determining whether they are really the same, or differ by a very small amount.

To be sure, one can think of decision processes that are likely to require checking when they have a negative outcome, and not when the outcome is positive. This only demonstrates the plausibility of the hypothesis; it does not validate it. What is needed, if the confirmation hypothesis is to be taken seriously, is an articulation and testing of its implications for relationships other than the one it is intended to explain.

F.   Independent Processes

Several investigators have concluded that SAME and DIFFERENT decisions are mediated by independent processes. In some cases it is assumed that the process that mediates SAME decisions precedes that which mediates DIFFERENT decisions; in other cases it is assumed that the two processes occur in parallel, but that they are qualitatively different and that the SAME process is the faster. The first, and probably best known, two-process model was proposed by Bamber (1969). This model assumes that sameness is (usually) determined by a process that compares stimuli as wholes, and that difference is determined by an analytic process that compares them feature-by-feature. According to this model, the two processes occur in parallel, and the decision is made faster when the stimuli are the same because the holistic process takes less time than the analytic one.

This model accommodates the findings quite well, and it or some variant of it has been espoused by several investigators in addition to Bamber (Beller, 1970; Klatzky & Thompson, 1975; Lockhead, 1972; Pachella & Miller, 1976; Tversky, 1969). However, like all the other models that have been proposed, it is ad hoc and its validity has not yet been corroborated by findings other than the one it was intended to explain.

IV.   FURTHER EVIDENCE THAT SAME AND DIFFERENT JUDGMENTS ARE DIFFERENT

The finding that SAME response times tend to be shorter than DIFFERENT response times, or at least shorter than the dependence of DIFFERENT RT on degree of difference would lead one to expect, does not necessarily indicate that SAME and DIFFERENT judgments are mediated by different processes. What it does seem to establish is that the process by which stimuli of the type used in these experiments are determined to be identical does not involve a self-terminating, feature-by-feature, or character-by-character, analysis. If such an analysis were the basis for both SAME and DIFFERENT judgments, DIFFERENT RTs would be shorter than SAMEs because the determination of identity logically requires an exhaustive analysis, whereas the determination of a difference does not. Further evidence that SAME judgments are not mediated by an exhaustive analytic comparison of the stimuli is the fact that it takes less time to determine that two-letter strings are identical than to determine that they have at least one letter in common (Bamber, Herder, & Tidd, 1975; Nickerson & Pew, 1973). This is true even when the two strings are identical in both cases, and the difference grows with the number of letters in the string. The common-letter judgment seems to be based on an analytic self-terminating process, but the identity judgment does not.

There are several findings other than the difference between SAME and DIF-
FERENT RT that have been taken as evidence that the processes underlying
SAME and DIFFERENT judgments may differ in some fundamental sense.
Investigators have found, for example, that SAME and DIFFERENT RTs are
differentially affected by the manipulation of certain variables. In several studies,
familiarity with the stimuli has had an effect on SAME but not on DIFFERENT
RT (Ambler & Proctor, 1976, Exp. 1; Egeth & Blecker, 1971; Hock, 1973). In
one of these studies, changing from a two-response to a one-response procedure
(in which some subjects responded only on SAME trials and others only on
DIFFERENT trials) had a greater effect on SAME RT than on DIFFERENT RT
(Egeth & Blecker, 1971). In another, SAME RT, but not DIFFERENT RT, was
influenced by the symmetry of the stimuli as well as by their familiarity (Hock,
1973). Conversely, under some conditions, familiarity has been found to affect
the accuracy of DIFFERENT judgments when it did not affect that of SAMEs
(Robinson, 1969).

Krueger (1970) found that the bracketing of letters by vertical lines slowed
both SAME and DIFFERENT RTs; however, the two types of response were
differentially affected by the height of the lines and by variations in their onset—
offset times. The same investigator obtained, in one study, an effect of frequency
of occurrence of specific stimulus pairs, but only on DIFFERENT RT (Krueger,
1973). Beller (1970) found that when subjects had to decide whether all of
the letters in an n-letter string had the same name, SAME RT was independent of n; however, DIFFERENT RT increased when n was increased by adding
identical letters to the string, whereas it decreased when the added letters were
different. In a same-name letter-matching task, Pachella and Miller (1976) found
that stimulus probability had an effect on DIFFERENT RT and on SAME RT
for stimuli that matched only with respect to name, whereas it had no effect on
SAME RT for stimuli that were physically the same. Thomas (1974) has obtained
data suggesting that when stimulus probability is varied, the preparation that
occurs during the warning interval is biased toward the more probable stimulus
and that increasing the opportunity to prepare (increasing the duration of the
warning interval) facilitates SAME but not DIFFERENT RT.

All of these results may be viewed as inconsistent with the assumption that
SAME and DIFFERENT judgments are mediated by the same processes; presumably, if they were, the time to make them would be affected by the same
variables.

V.   SOME RELATED FINDINGS

Several other judgment-time asymmetries have been reported that resemble the
difference between SAME and DIFFERENT RT in some respects. It has been
found, for example, that true statements tend to be verified faster than false

statements, and affirmative statements faster than negative ones. Moreover, these two factors interact so that true affirmatives are verified faster than false affirmatives, while false negatives tend to be verified faster than true negatives (Chase & Clark, 1972; Clark & Brownell, 1975; Clark & Chase, 1972; Gough, 1965, 1966; Just & Carpenter, 1971; Slobin, 1966; Trabasso, Rollins, & Shaughnessy, 1971; Wason & Jones, 1963). Positive locative prepositions (e.g., above, before, up) are encoded and compared more rapidly than implicit negative prepositions (below, after, down) (Clark, 1973, 1974; Clark & Brownell, 1975; Clark, Carpenter, & Just, 1973; Clark & Chase, 1972). A similar asymmetry has been reported between "unmarked" adjectives (e.g., tall, high, good) and their "marked" antonyms (e.g., short, low, bad) (Clark, 1969).

The question is whether all these judgmental asymmetries have a common explanation. More to the point of this chapter is the question of whether SAME judgments are unique in any fundamental way, or does their relative speed have the same basis as that of judgments involving true affirmative assertions, positive locative prepositions, unmarked adjectives, and the like.

VI.   CONCLUSIONS

Typically, the hypotheses (such as those described in Section III) that have been put forth to account for differences between SAME and DIFFERENT RT have been generated in an ad hoc fashion. Any given hypothesis has been prompted by a particular experimental finding and proposed as an explanation of that finding. None of these hypotheses is able to account completely for all the results that have been obtained.

These hypotheses do identify, however, several factors, each of which may contribute to the SAME–DIFFERENT difference, at least in certain instances. It is clear, for example, that stimulus-sampling statistics can affect both SAME and DIFFERENT RTs and, consequently, the difference between them. Response biases, when they occur, can undoubtedly affect the relative speeds of SAME and DIFFERENT responses. And it seems likely that situations can be defined in which the subject benefits from doublechecking the basis for one or the other type of decision before making the associated response. However, the evidence seems to suggest that there is a residual difference between SAME and DIFFERENT RT to be explained even after such "peripheral" factors have been taken into account. And it may be that any model that will adequately account for the difference will have to be somewhat eclectic. Priming may be a factor, for example, at least when the interstimulus interval is relatively brief. Similarly, the strength of a fading memory trace may also play some role. And judgments of sameness and of difference may not be two sides of the same coin, but may depend on at least partially different processes. These possibilities are not mutually exclusive.

Finally, the similarity of the difference between SAME and DIFFERENT RTs to other judgmental asymmetries, such as those noted in Section V, seems unlikely to be coincidental. One question that should be considered with respect to each of these asymmetries is whether it serves some useful purpose for the individual. Is it the case, in particular, that sensitivity to the similarities between specific stimuli in one's environment is more adaptive than sensitivity to the differences between them?

REFERENCES

Ambler, B. A., & Proctor, J. D., The familiarity effect for single-letter pairs. *Journal of Experimental Psychology: Human Perception and Performance*, 1976, *2*, 222–234.

Atkinson, R. C., Holmgren, J. E., & Juola, J. F., Processing time as influenced by the number of elements in a visual display. *Perception and Psychophysics*, 1969, *6*, 321–326.

Bamber, D. Reaction times and error rates for "same"–"different" judgments of multidimensional stimuli. *Perception and Psychophysics*, 1969, *6*, 169–174.

Bamber, D., Herder, J., & Tidd, K. Reaction times in a task analogous to "same"–"different" judgment. *Perception and Psychophysics*, 1975, *18*, 321–327.

Beller, H. K. Parallel and serial stages in matching. *Journal of Experimental Psychology*, 1970, *4*, 213–219.

Bertelson, P. Sequential redundancy and speed in a serial two-choice responding task. *Quarterly Journal of Experimental Psychology*, 1961, *12*, 90–102.

Bindra, D., Williams, J. A., & Wise, J. S. Judgments of sameness and difference: Experiments on decision time. *Science*, 1965, *150*, 1625–1628. (Erratum, *Science*, 1965, *150*, 1699.)

Briggs, G. E., & Blaha, J. Memory retrieval and central comparison times in information processing. *Journal of Experimental Psychology*, 1969, *79*, 395–402.

Briggs, G. E., & Johnsen, A. M. On the nature of central processing in choice reactions. *Memory and Cognition*, 1973, *1*, 91–100.

Burrows, D. Modality effects in retrieval of information from short-term memory. *Perception and Psychophysics*, 1972, *11*, 365–372.

Chase, W. G., & Clark, H. H. Mental operations in the comparison of sentences and pictures. In L. Gregg (Ed.), *Cognition in learning and memory*. New York: Wiley, 1972.

Clark, H. H. Linguistic processes in deductive reasoning. *Psychological Review*, 1969, *76*, 387–404.

Clark, H. H. Space, time, semantics, and the child. In T. E. Moore (Ed.), *Cognitive development and the acquisition of language*. New York: Academic Press, 1973.

Clark, H. H. Semantics and comprehension. In T. A. Sebeok (Ed.), *Current trends in linguistics, Vol. 12: Linguistics and adjacent arts and sciences*. The Hague, Netherlands: Mouton, 1974.

Clark, H. H., & Brownell, H. H. Judging up and down. *Journal of Experimental Psychology: Human Perception and Performance*, 1975, *1*, 339–352.

Clark, H. H., Carpenter, P. A., and Just, M.A. On the meeting of semantics and perception. In W. G. Chase (Ed.), *Visual information processing*. New York: Academic Press, 1973.

Clark, H. H., & Chase, W. G. On the process of comparing sentences against pictures. *Cognitive Psychology*, 1972, *3*, 472–517.

Cohen, G. Pattern recognition: Differences between matching patterns to patterns and matching descriptions to patterns. *Journal of Experimental Psychology*, 1969, *82*, 427–434.

Donderi, D., & Case, B. Parallel visual processing: Constant same–different decision latency with two to fourteen shapes. *Perception and Psychophysics*, 1970, *8*, 373–375.

Donderi, D. C., & Zelnicker, D. Parallel processing in visual same–different decisions. *Perception and Psychophysics*, 1969, *5*, 197–200.

Egeth, H. E. Parallel versus serial processes in multi–dimensional stimulus discrimination. *Perception and Psychophysics*, 1966, *1*, 245–252.

Egeth, H., & Blecker, D. Differential effects of familiarity on judgments of sameness and difference. *Perception and Psychophysics*, 1971, *9*, 321–326.

Egeth, H., Jonides, J., & Wall, S. Parallel processing of multielement displays. *Cognitive Psychology*, 1972, *3*, 674–698.

Fraisse, P. Reconnaissance de l'identité physique et sémantique de dessins et de noms. *Schweizerische Zeitschrift für Psychologie und ihre Anwedungen*, 1970, *29*, 76–84.

Gough, P. B. Grammatical transformations and speed of understanding. *Journal of Verbal Learning and Verbal Behavior*, 1965, *5*, 107–111.

Gough, P. B. The verification of sentences: The effects of delay of evidence and sentence length. *Journal of Verbal Learning and Verbal Behavior*, 1966, *5*, 492–496.

Hawkins, H. L. Parallel processing in complex visual discrimination. *Perception and Psychophysics*, 1969, *5*, 56–64.

Hock, H. S. The effects of stimulus structure and familiarity on same–different comparison. *Perception and Psychophysics*, 1973, *14*, 413–420.

Howell, P., & Stockdale, J. E. Memory and display search in binary classification reaction time. *Perception and Psychophysics*, 1975, *18*, 379–388.

Johnson, N. F. On the function of letters in word identification: Some data and a preliminary model. *Journal of Verbal Learning and Verbal Behavior*, 1975, *14*, 17–29.

Just, M. A., & Carpenter, P. A. Comprehension of negation with quantification. *Journal of Verbal Learning and Verbal Behavior*, 1971, *10*, 244–253.

Klatzky, R. L., & Thompson, A. Integration of features in comparing multifeature stimuli. *Perception and Psychophysics*, 1975, *18*, 428–432.

Kornblum S. Sequential determinants of information processing in serial and discrete choice reaction time. *Psychological Review,* 1969, *76*, 113–131.

Krueger, L. E. Effect of bracketing lines on speed of "same"–"different" judgment of two adjacent letters. *Journal of Experimental Psychology*, 1970, *84*, 324–330.

Krueger, L. E. Effect of irrelevant surrounding material on speed of same–different judgment of two adjacent letters. *Journal of Experimental Psychology*, 1973, *98*, 252–259.

Krueger, L. E. The effect of an extraneous added memory set on item recognition: a test of parallel dependent vs. serial–comparison models. *Memory and Cognition*, 1975, *3*, 485–495.

Lockhead, G. R. Processing dimensional stimuli: A note. *Psychological Review*, 1972, *79*, 410–419.

Murdock, B. B. A parallel-processing model for scanning. *Perception and Psychophysics*, 1971, *10*, 289–291.

Nickerson, R. S. Response times for "same"–"different" judgments. *Perception and Motor Skills*, 1965, *20*, 15–18.

Nickerson, R. S. Response times with a memory dependent decision task. *Journal of Experimental Psychology*, 1966, *72*, 761–769.

Nickerson, R. S. "Same"–"different" response times with multi-attribute stimulus differences. *Perceptual and Motor Skills*, 1967, *24*, 543–554.

Nickerson, R. S. Note on "same"–"different" response times. *Perceptual and Motor Skills*, 1968, *27*, 565–566.

Nickerson, R. S. "Same"–"different" response times: A model and a preliminary test. In W. G. Koster (Ed.), *Attention and Performance II*. Amsterdam: North Holland, 1969.

Nickerson, R. S. Binary-classification reaction time: A review of some studies of human information-processing capabilities. *Psychonomic Monograph Supplements*, 1972, *4*, No. 17 (Whole No. 65), 275–318.

Nickerson, R. S. Frequency, recency, and repetition effects on *same* and *different* response times. *Journal of Experimental Psychology*, 1973, *101*, 330–336.

Nickerson, R. S., & Pew, R. Visual pattern matching: An investigation of some effects of decision task, auditory codability and spatial correspondence. *Journal of Experimental Psychology*, 1973, *98*, 36-43.

Pachella, R. G., & Miller, J. O. Simulus probability and same–different classification. *Perception and Psychophysics*, 1976, *19*, 29–34.

Posner, M. I., & Boies, S. J. Components of attention. *Psychological Review*, 1971, *78*, 391–408.

Reed, C. Reaction times for a same–different discrimination of vowel-consonant syllables. *Perception and Psychophysics*, 1975, *18*, 65–70.

Robinson, J. S. Familiar patterns are no easier to see than novel ones. *American Journal of Psychology*, 1969, *82*, 513–522.

Slobin, D. I. Grammatical transformations in childhood and adulthood. *Journal of Verbal Learning and Verbal Behavior*, 1966, *5*, 219–227.

Sloboda, J. A. Decision times for word and letter search: A holistic word identification model examined. *Journal of Verbal Learning and Verbal Behavior*, 1976, *15*, 93–101.

Smith, E. E. Effects of familiarity on stimulus recognition and categorization. *Journal of Experimental Psychology*, 1967, *74*, 324–332.

Sternberg, S. Memory-scanning: Mental processes revealed by reaction-time experiments. *American Scientist*, 1969, *57*, 421–457.

Thomas, E. A. C. The selectivity of preparation. *Psychological Review,* 1974, *81*, 442–464.

Trabasso, T., Rollins, H., & Shaughnessy, E. Storage and verification stages in processing concepts. *Cognitive Psychology*, 1971, *2,* 239–289.

Tversky, B. Pictorial and verbal encoding in a short-term memory task. *Perception and Psychophysics*, 1969, *6*, 225–233.

Wason, P. C., & Jones, S. Negatives: Denotation and connotation. *British Journal of Psychology*, 1963, *54*, 299–307.

Williams, J. D. The effects of practice with controlled stimulus pairs on same–different judgments. *Journal of Experimental Psychology*, 1972, *96*, 73–77.

6 The Making of the Present: A Tutorial Review

John A. Michon

Institute for Experimental Psychology
University of Groningen
The Netherlands

ABSTRACT

The core concept in this paper is the *psychological present,* commonly understood as a time interval in which sensory information, internal processing, and
concurrent behavior appear to be integrated within the same span of attention.
Understanding the relation between the temporal structure of input information and the processes that determine the dynamics of the *present* will also
make it possible to understand the way in which conscious temporal experience
(time perception) is shaped.

The *present,* in this conception, is a highly flexible tuning process that
is dynamically fitting the temporal width of the field of attention and its
phase relations to the sequential structure of the pattern of events. Thus, it
serves an important function in enabling the organism to optimize its information processing activities. It is an active, or constructive process; this
necessitates the assumption that temporal information can be extracted from
event sequences that is structurally independent of the nontemporal dimensions of information (viz., spatial and categorical attributes of stimuli).

Because the *present* is so highly adaptive, no fixed parameter values can be
expected to describe it adequately. Only under certain boundary or rest conditions may we expect the parameters of the process to adopt certain values,
related to the properties of the information processing mechanisms (scanning
rate, precategorical storage, STM, etc.). Some of the procedures that the
organism has available for extracting and parsing temporal information have
become known in recent years, and some attempts at formally describing these
procedures have been made. At the same time, there is some psychophysiological evidence to support the view that the tuning process may be controlled
by phasic changes in alertness and allocation of effort.

This conception of the role and significance of the *present* adds a new dimension to the age-old problem of the subjective flow of time. There is a considerable argument about what causes subjective time to accelerate or decel-

erate. While it is fairly common to attribute such changes to the number and complexity of events or to the processing effort involved, some contradictions remain.

I. INTRODUCTION

This chapter will consider some topics in time psychology from the standpoint of performance theory. Time psychology has been concerned with studying the human experience of time and duration for more than a century, but to a considerable extent it has done so only at a phenomenological and descriptive level. Current ways of thinking about process and structure in human performance and in cognition have only recently started to have some impact on time psychology.

It is as part of this development that I shall relate the subjective experience of what has been called the *conscious* or *specious present* to the processing of temporal information in situations in which the subject deals with sequential patterns of events at varying degrees of complication.

A sequential pattern can be defined as "a finite string of symbols that states the rules governing the indefinite continuation of a non-terminating sequence" (Simon, 1972). In other words, a sequential pattern is a (relatively compact) description of a series of events that may in principle be extended indefinitely; the description summarizes the invariant aspects of the series over time. Events in a sequential series may be regularly distributed in time, or they may occur at irregular or random instants. If, however, the description of the sequence contains rules that determine the exact temporal loci of successive events, then we may speak of a temporally specified pattern. *Temporal patterns* in the restricted sense constitute a special class of *sequential patterns,* viz., the class of patterns in which only the temporal structure of the event series is specified. We may take music as an example in which meter and rhythm are independent of, although coextensive and generally correlated with, melody, harmony, and dynamics. Thus, while meter taken by itself is a temporal pattern in the restricted sense, in music it generally appears as one aspect of a sequential pattern.

II. THE CONSCIOUS PRESENT

A. The Basic Proposition

The fundamental proposition of this paper is that the process of discovering or constructing the temporal pattern of a sequence of events is consciously experienced as the *specious present.* The specious present is understood in the sense defined by James (1890) as the time interval, a few seconds in length, in which we experience the flow of events as being simultaneously available to perceptual or cognitive analysis. In other words, the thesis proposed is the following: if, and only if, the temporal structure of a series of events is focally attended, consciousness is in a processing mode that is reflected in experience as the "specious present" (from now on I shall frequently speak of *present,* for short). As a corollary, I maintain that the actual state of the experienced present (its perceived width, persistence, etc.) will reflect the ongoing search for pattern.

B. Consciousness Regained

This invocation of conscious experience, which would have been considered unduly mentalistic 10 years ago, recently has been taken up by a number of authors (Mandler, 1975; Posner, 1975; Shallice, 1972).

Mandler defines consciousness as "a mode of processing that affects the state of a (mental) structure. Given that consciousness mode, the 'contents' of consciousness are those structures and their products that are in the conscious state" (Mandler, 1975, p. 45). Consciousness is considered as a limited-capacity attentional process, which serves such functions as evaluation, choice, grouping, and pattern recognition. Shallice (1972), who describes consciousness as the process of selecting a "dominant action system" (i.e., a dominant plan for action appropriate under the prevailing circumstances), points out that consciousness will become active only in case of conflicting lower order action systems. For instance, if a situation arises for which no appropriate action system is available, one will be constructed consciously (e.g., LaBerge, 1974). With practice such a system will gradually become inaccessible to consciousness (Mandler, 1962).

C. The Specious Present

That aspect of consciousness called the *present* has a certain width. We can still "perceive" the first two sounds of a clock striking three as "having sounded just before" when actually the third sound is *now* in progress. In other words, one main characteristic of events in the present is their availability to our attention in real time, although this is a qualified availability rather than a simultaneity. Moreover, the width of the present varies with the direction of this attention (Fraisse, 1967; James, 1890).

Sometimes the present has been described as a continuum, much like a shift-register, picking up information on one side and dropping it at the far end (James, 1890). But as Fraisse (1967) correctly noted, this is not a good description of the state of affairs: if we listen to the tic-tac of a clock we do not perceive a "tic-tac" first and then a "tac-tic" one moment later. This points to a second phenomenal characteristic of the present, which we may call segmentation. Apparently the stream of consciousness is chopped up into meaningful, or at least structurally coherent, segments. In relation to this it is observed that the content of the present is organized in ways that may be suggested by the stimuli themselves, but also as part of an integrative process, which incorporates the context (the situational present) and the implicit knowledge about the events. This was brought out, for instance, in the penetrating phenomenological analysis by the philosopher Husserl (1964) of the contents of the present.

One of the observations Husserl made was that a tone *now* sounding will continually exhibit a different phase in consciousness. That is, we first perceive it as about to begin (when we expect it), then as beginning, as having just begun, being nearly over, and so forth. In this process each earlier phase is retained in each later phase; it is integrated in the perspective of that later phase until after some time the event is "cut loose," and from then on is only experienced as being potentially retrievable. This particular form of retention should be distinguished from memory, according to Husserl. It is not open to the type of operations that we can perform on memory contents, such as rehearsing, picking out certain episodes, or "sweeping glances" with their concomitant loss of detail. Consequently, the present cannot be subject to the types of errors that our memories can show; it has the quality of the uninterpreted, and proceeds as it comes, in real time. This, in short, is a presentation very much akin to the ideas of James, and surprisingly close to what our present cognitive stance would accept as good doctrine.

D. Summary of Properties of the Present

We may summarize the phenomenal qualities of the conscious present as they emerge from more than one hundred years of empirical studies, in the following way:

1. It has a width that is highly variable and that seems to have an upper limit of 7 or 8 sec, although its average seems to be of the order of 2 or 3 sec. Its perceived width depends on the number and the sequential structure of the events in it.

2. Constituent events, in order to be perceived as independent, must be separated by at least 150—250 msec. That is, when more than five or six events per second occur, they will fuse into higher order perceived transients or dynamic events.

3. Events display a pronounced and almost irresistible tendency for temporal structure when they are between 250 and 900 msec apart, while an optimum near 600 msec is reported most often.

4. The information contained in a present is a discrete segment; its boundaries are determined by various temporal and nontemporal structural properties. When no external structure is present in the stimulus, segmentation will be imposed subjectively (grouping).

5. The contents of a present are simultaneously available and are as such continuously open for restructuring; that is, the information contained in it is open to revision under different cognitive (or at least higher order) interpretive hypotheses.

Two other qualities commonly associated with the conscious present, orientation towards past (as in shadowing), or future (anticipating), and the fine grain (time quantum) have been studied, but here opinions vary considerably, especially with regards to the time quantum.

III. PROCESSING SEQUENTIAL INFORMATION

A. Time Constants and Processes

In this section a number of facets of sequential information processing will be discussed, which will bring out the importance of temporal pattern in the organization of behavior. This discussion is limited to such phenomena as, I think, are reflected in the contents of the present, and therefore may be said to be involved in the making of the present. The following paragraphs follow the phenomenal qualities of the present as they were summarized in the previous section. Some of those processes play a considerable role in performance theory; frequently the parameters of a number of perceptual phenomena seem to converge on the same process. In other cases there is speculation to a much greater extent. Admittedly, there is a considerable oversimplification, which in part is based on the indestructable optimism of the author, who believes that the fairly narrow range displayed by some time constants under various task conditions reveal some common underlying process.

1. The time quantum

Starting at the short end, we meet the boundary between simultaneity and order perception, which may be estimated at approximately 25 msec (Hirsch & Sherrick, 1961). This must be a fairly general mechanism as it is independent of modality.

These, and similar results (as, for instance, the subjective interference patterns that can be observed in a line scan visual presentation [Allport, 1968]), have given rise to the concept of the time quantum. Thus, time is partitioned into a discrete series of episodes by an internal clock that is either triggered internally, or is driven by external events. The literature on the search for the time quantum incorporates many effects and several values (see Pöppel [1978] for a summary; also discussions by Kristofferson [1973] and Vroon [1974]). Most of the more recent studies seem to converge on the value between 20 and 30 msec. This, incidentally, compares very well with the information rates of between 30 and 50 msec hypothesized on the basis of feature scanning experiments such as Sternberg's (Cavanagh, 1972; Sternberg, 1975).

Yet the matter is still open, as no direct observations of the time quantum have been made, and also because much of the evidence is suspect, in particular that on multimodal reaction time distributions that have been taken as a primary source of evidence in the past (see Vroon [1974] for a discussion and Luce & Green [1974] for an opinion).

Although the fine grain of time plays a considerable role in the perception of sequential stimulation, as is illustrated by the delicate timing relations in speech (Huggins, 1972; Klatt, 1976; Nooteboom, 1972), these temporal relations do not concern *separate* independent events. As was stressed by Bouma (1976), Massaro (1974), and others, we are dealing in this case with dynamic changes of the signal under concern, rather than with the temporal relations between successive independent events.

2. Precategorical storage

What constitutes an independent event in time must be processed without competition of other events, which means that such an event must be allowed to occupy precategorical storage without interference. Recent work on this storage mechanism tends to converge clearly on values between 150 msec (Efron, 1970, 1973) and 550 msec (Kristofferson, 1976), with a neat 250 msec as the modal value (Averbach & Coriell, 1961; Cavanagh, 1972; Kahneman, 1973; Massaro, 1974 Posner, 1975; etc.).

For the purpose of our present discussion there are *two* event types that are of direct concern: the perceived duration of an event, and the perceived relation between two successive events, especially their *coherence* and their order.

Psychophysical studies of the perception of duration have thoroughly established that indeed the most sensitive perception is of intervals between roughly 200 and 800 msec, with an optimum around 400 msec (Eisler, 1975; Fraisse, 1967; Michon, 1964, 1967b). Whereas for synchronization behavior ranging between 200 and 800 msec precisions usually are reported on the order of 4–5% (Michon, 1967a, b), recent studies by Kristofferson (1976) and Vorberg (this volume), have shown that with (indeed very long) practice an extremely high precision can be achieved. Kristofferson found that after 2 months of daily practice a subject was capable of producing intervals in a synchronization task with variance that was constant at less than 2% between 400 and 1200 msec, increasing very slowly beyond. His conclusion is that synchronizing behavior is brought about by two independent part processes, one being the basic minimal S–R delay distribution (under certain experimental conditions this will be the approximate distribution for simple reaction times) plus a completely deterministic (zero variance!) delay process. Very fine timing is, of course, also known in complex motor skills, while – as we shall see later – the perception of temporal patterns in speech also points to a high quality processing of temporal information. A recent outburst of new experiments in this realm in psychoacoustics offers further support (cf. Plomp, 1975).

The perceptual coherence between sequentially independent events increases when the events are more than 150 msec apart. When presented at higher rates they split up in two or more independent sequences, or else they are grouped subjectively. The optimum coherence in rhythmic patterns is reached between 350 and 700 msec (Fraisse, 1956; van Noorden, 1975; Vos, 1973). Huggins (1974) studied click sequences presented alternatively to both ears and found that for low rates the subject "shadowing" the clicks will follow the switching pattern, but at five clicks or more per second, he will match his shadowing performance to one ear only, thus halving the apparent tempo. This again points to the transition of the within-span to the independent-event mode of precategorical storage.

Finally, it has been documented by several authors that the order of successive events is perceived correctly only if they do not interfere in precategorical storage. Ladefoged and Broadbent (1959), and more recently Thomas, Hill, Carroll, and Garcia (1970), Warren and his collaborators (Warren & Obusek, 1972; Warren, Obusek, Farmer & Warren, 1969), and van Noorden (1975) have shown that order perception in complex sequential patterns depends on event independence, requiring a separation of at least 200–300 msec. Warren et al. (1969) have shown the importance of the availability of cognitive labels (counting, etc.) for naming the patterns. When sequential or temporal events fall within the range of precategorical storage, grouping is inescapable. Vos (1973) pointed out that only when a verbal (or at least a symbolic) label can be assigned to such a group, it can be represented internally as a stable, independent event. The rate of producing such labels is restricted by the same mechanism, as it requires the pronunciation of at least one covert syllable (see also Perkins, 1974).

3. Primary memory or short-term memory

The next question, to be dealt with very briefly, is whether we can equate the total width of the specious present with short-term memory. Equating the upper limit of 7 ± 2 sec of the present with the 20 to 30 sec range commonly found for STM seems somewhat farfetched. Moreover, the paradigms are essentially different: the 20–30 sec estimates are obtained with a limited *static* load on memory, whereas the loads on the present are dynamic and more comparable with running memory tasks as studied by Sanders and Van Borselen (1966), or with the primary memory paradigm developed by Waugh and Norman (1965), or even with Crowder's suffix effect (Crowder 1972, Crowder & Chao-Ming Cheng, 1973).

The principal question here is: to what extent can temporal patterns be concatenated in such a way that at the end the relations can still be comprehended and the earlier parts modified in the light of the later ones? In primary memory we indeed have information available at the surface level required for such processing. What is to be understood as surface structures is a matter of some doubt, but it should be a rather primitive level. In speech it would have to be at the phonological level at most. The question "Anymore tea dear?" may escape the husband who is watching the Cup Final on TV for several seconds, but he can retrieve the message up to the intonation and syntactic patterns. An experimental test of this phenomenon is currently being carried out by Franchik (Broadbent, personal communication, 1976); this study seems to offer support for a rather long availability interval.

4. Orientation

A final distinction concerns the backward or forward orientation of attention with respect to the immediate past or the immediate future. In terms of processing, these two temporal orientations will be adopted by the subject when he is engaged in a rehearsal task and an anticipation task, respectively. I wish only to mention this aspect for the sake of completeness. There is a vast body of literature on both rehearsal and anticipation, but the role of this dual orientation on the dynamics of the specious present has not been systematically studied. (Anticipation is known to slow down the subjective flow of time though.)

B. Availability and Segmentation

One important aspect of the present is that information in it remains in a state of availability until it can be processed at a higher and more abstract level. This availability will persist until some structural boundary (a syntactic boundary or a pause, for instance) is reached. This will free the information channels for higher order analysis, upon which a new present may start. Until such a boundary is reached, the information remains available at the level of the surface structure for further (re-) interpretation, comparison, etc., but thereafter the surface information will be irretrievably lost. In Husserl's phenomenological analysis, it will be recalled, this is the point at which an experience is "cut loose" and becomes a memory.

The segmentation that occurs at structural boundaries divides the stream of consciousness into internally representable units, thus relieving the higher coding and storage processes. And because of it we always remember structurally "healthy" patterns: there is never a memory straddling two successive structural units. This observation also reduces the plausibility of explaining the present in terms of either some internal clock "ticking away" successive presents, or a new present starting whenever the preceding one is "filled." In the absence of structural boundaries in the input the subject may, however, sometimes succeed in avoiding confusion by using accidental features as boundary markers, or he may try to impose a purely subjective segmentation pattern on the input. The latter strategy will succeed only when the prosodic features of the input are minimal, as, for instance, in isochronic sequences (see Section IV.B).

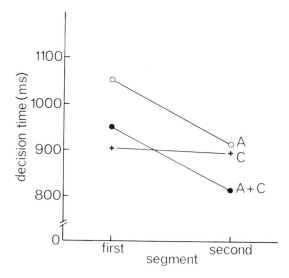

FIG. 1.   Time to decide whether a 6-frame movie fragment was *old, new,* or *paraphrase,* for fragments before or after a change in scene (A), a cut (C), or the combination of the two (A + C). (After Carroll and Bever, 1975.)

Thus, we have two organizational principles of the present: availability and segmentation. Both are open to empirical study, and both occur in the auditory and visual modalities.

Boundaries of events can be indicated by pauses and other "prosodic" features, such as intonation, or by such higher order features as syntactic and semantic aspects of the stimulus. The relative roles of pauses and prosody and of the higher order boundaries have been studied quite extensively in the past few years (Bower & Springston, 1970; Carroll & Bever, 1975; Dooling, 1974; Martin, 1972; van Katwijk, 1973; and others).

The general conclusion is that the temporal structure by itself is not a sufficient condition for segmentation. However, if a pause or a stress coincides with a higher order structural feature, then segmentation is facilitated. That is, the probability of segmentation is greater in that case than when the higher order structural boundary is presented in isolation. Thus, it seems that it is primarily the higher structural boundaries (syntactic or semantic) that determine the potential points of segmentation, but that the temporal structure will very strongly stimulate the actual process.

A good illustration of these processes is offered by a recent experiment of Carroll and Bever (1975). They used a paradigm conceived by Jarvella (1970) and further developed by Caplan (1972) to study the availability of surface information in event sequences. Using this paradigm, Carroll and Bever (1975) showed short movie sequences, each consisting of two consecutive fragments. The fragments were separated by either a "cut" or a change of action, or by a combination of the two. Subjects were then shown 6-frame sequences that were to be classified as *old, new* (not seen before), or *paraphrase* (similar but not identical to old). The *old* 6-frame sequences were either the last 6 frames before, or the first 6 after, the transition. The authors measured the response latencies for these different target sequences. Their results show clearly that both the cut (C) and the change of action (A) boundaries are effective, but C is only effective *together with A*. The differences between the A and A + C scores on the first versus the second segment indicates the greater difficulty of retrieval for the information contained in the first sequence (see Fig. 1). Apparently, we may draw the conclusion that structural boundaries serve as signals for segmentation of the ongoing present, while other, more strictly temporal, features are aiding this process. If presented exclusively by themselves they prove no sufficient cause for segmentation. Apparently, the subject must have a thorough knowledge of the structural properties of the stimulus sequences in order to make an appropriate use of the temporal information that is available in them.

C. The Role of Pauses

Given the phenomenon of segmentation as discussed in the previous section, the role of pauses deserves some separate attention. It has been argued that apart from being an organization principle inducing proximity in the events between the pauses (Bower & Winzenz, 1969; Fraisse, 1956; Garner, 1974; Vos, 1973), the pause also fulfills the role of an information bucket, in which information is collected that cannot be dealt with immediately upon presentation because it cannot be integrated into the main pattern of events. The shift phenomenon, discussed by Fodor, Bever, and Garrett (1974) is an example of this "bucket" function. Apparently, the present tends to perceptual closure achieved at the cost of shifting nonintegrated information to a pause.

Furthermore, Bower and Springston (1970), Martin (1972), and others have pointed out that extra time becomes available in a pause for extra or higher order abstraction processing. This is only the case when the pause coincides with a structural boundary, or when the segments are so long that subsegments are necessary to cope with the information. Pauses and hesitations are then introduced subjectively (but audibly) in speech *production* (Boomer, 1965; Goldman-Eisler, 1968; Martin & Strange, 1968a, b).

The particular role of the pause is illuminated by the fact that it frequently is a nonentity; that is, it goes unnoticed even though it is physically present. The phenomenon, known as the dead interval (Fraisse, 1956, 1967; McDougall, 1903) has been found to depend on the temporal structure of the task pattern, but in no case to exceed 300–400 msec (Michon, 1968, 1977). This suggests that, after processing the contents of one present, one empty "cycle" of the precategorical storage process is made before a new present is started. This result seems to be in line with the earlier discussion of the temporal parameters of the present. Also, it may point to relations with the course of preparation (Kahneman, 1973; Killeen, 1975; Posner, 1975), or with the psychological refractory period (see Kahneman's discussion, 1973). A discussion of this relation can be found in Michon (1977).

IV. WHY WE PERCEIVE PATTERN: TUNING

The perception of temporal pattern enables the organism to *tune in* on the flow of information, thus making it possible to optimize its processing activity. If the internal representation of the time course of information matches the external events, the subject may make optimal use of the peaks and pauses in the incoming information. The role of peaks and pauses in the perception of temporal structure is perhaps the most direct aspect that deals with the discovery of pattern. As in visual perception, the places at which information is at a maximum (contours) achieve a dominant perceptual quality, whereas elements that are (relatively) void of information spontaneously assume the status of "background." In this context one should consider in particular the various Gestalt grouping principles of elements that are similar in a certain way. The latter factors, studied in the well-known Gestalt laws, are discussed by Bregman (this volume).

Not only will overload of the processing channels be avoided, but temporal pattern also may help considerably in reducing the class of possible stimuli that the subject may expect, thus reducing the amount of search necessary for event recognition. Thus, we may expect the temporal structure of sequential patterns to be a powerful organizing principle.

A. Pattern Description Systems

Recent years have seen the emergence of a number of procedures or grammatical systems for describing sequential patterns in formal terms (for reference see in particular Greeno & Simon, 1974; Jones, 1974, 1976; Leeuwenberg, 1969; Martin, 1972; Restle, 1970; Simon, 1972; Vitz & Todd, 1969). In principle these are purely formal descriptive systems, although they all claim some psychological relevance. However, when psychological meaningfulness is tested by comparing the complexity of the description with the psychological complexity as measured by scaling or processing time, ambiguous results are frequently obtained. This indicates that other factors help determine perceived complexity. It is necessary for a pattern description system to take into account such factors as the load on memory and the amount of attention allocated to the various parts of the sequence. We may further expect an important influence of the speed of presentation that will constrain the possibility to apply the various rules of the pattern description. In most cases this does lead to additional assumptions, which are not a part of the descriptive system as such. Simon (1972) and Greeno and Simon (1974) have shown, however, that it is feasible to construct models which incorporate such restrictions in the system, for instance by introducing certain upper limits on the memory for part sequences.

B. Isochronic Stimulus Sequences

In the limiting case, subjects have to process sequences of strictly identical events occurring at strictly regular instants. These sequences are called isochronic. It is well known that such series, which in fact have no intrinsic patterning and consequently offer no cues for segmentation, are nevertheless perceived as being temporally structured. This phenomenon — known as subjective grouping — is also observable in the visual perception of regular tile patterns. Usually, a subject will consciously pay attention to an isochronic sequence, either because he is instructed to count events in one way or another, anticipates the arrival of the stimulus (in synchronizing task), or is continuing a particular series. This suggests that subjective grouping is employed as a strategy because it is an efficient and load reducing way of processing sequential information. Grouping enables the subject to assign a cognitive label to each group, viz., by counting or stressed tapping. Depending on the speed of the presentation, the subject will choose a labeling tempo that is close to an optimum in the perception of temporal structure, that is, at intervals close to 500 msec (Fraisse, 1956; Perkins, 1975; Vos, 1973).

C. Garner's Experiments

When we deal with event sequences that *do* have a temporal structure, such as the binary sequences studied by Garner and his associates (Garner, 1974), the question, which organization principles do account for the way in which the structure of these sequences is perceived, is raised. One thesis is that pattern perception in this case is based on some very simple rules, so simple that we may say that the organism is "preattuned" to them, and only just picking up the information contained in the sequences. Given a structuring according to figure and ground, the pattern cannot help but be noticed.

The experiments of Garner and his associates (summarized in Garner, 1974) are the single most coherent set of experiments dealing with the discovery of temporal pattern.

In these experiments subjects were presented with binary sequences of buzzes (high and low) or flashes. The sequences consisted in most cases of eight or nine events, and were repeated indefinitely until the subject was able to reproduce or describe the correct order of events in the sequence. The sequences were constructed in such a way that they contained no subgroups, and (what amounts to the same) would be different, irrespective of the starting point of the sequence chosen by the subject.

Thus, [x o o o x x o o] is such a sequence, whereas [x o o x x o o x] apparently is not. As a result, each of the cyclical orders of the elements may be perceived as an independent pattern without any a priori preference, except for the fact that certain organizations of the events will be perceptually more stable than others. For the observer it will be easier to tune in on such a stable organization.

This implies that stable patterns will be perceived more quickly, that is, with fewer repetitions and by more observers, as the preferred organization. Looking at the structural similarities of strong patterns as opposed to others whose organization remains ambiguous may help to uncover the rules underlying the organization of such binary patterns.

Garner's analysis revealed a number of very simple Gestalt-like principles that described the actual tuning behavior of the subjects to a large extent. The first principle discovered was that subjects select one of the two event types as representing a background, the other being chosen as figure. Thus, they would assign these roles to either of the following two part sequences.

sequence   . . . x o o x x x o o . . . .

part sequence a.   . . . x   x x x   . . . .

part sequence b.   . . .   o o   o o . . . .

This assignment is arbitrarily made and can be easily reversed. After having established a figure-ground relation, the perception of stable pattern is based on two structural rules: the *gap rule,* which states that the preferred end of a cycle is the longest run of ground-elements. The second rule is *runs-rule,* which states that the longest run of figure elements is preferably put at the beginning of the perceived pattern. (It will be clear that these two rules implicitly use the Gestalt laws of similarity and proximity.) These two rules may conflict, in which case the gap-rule tends to overrule the runs-rule; or there may be a conflict in a sequence, for example, if there are two gaps of length 2, as in the example just given. In these and other cases, the result will be an ambiguous pattern: some subjects choosing different organizations, or the same subjects choosing different organizations on different trials. It will also result in a large increase in the number of repetitions of the pattern needed for making a decision.

One main feature of these experiments is the high degree of spontaneity involved. The lack of preset instructions and of preliminary knowledge of the "system" insures that the patterns in this situation speak for themselves. We may indeed call this tuning; not only does the subject pick up the preferred organization of the pattern, he also discovers without difficulty the period of the cycle.

Accordingly, the rules established by Garner may be considered as fundamental principles of organization, which are supported by the results of other studies of sequential and temporal pattern (Fraisse, 1956; Restle, 1970; Vos, 1973).

D. Complex Patterns

The active imposition of a structure on the way sequences are perceived is more likely to arise when we are dealing with the more complex sequential patterns that have been studied among others by Simon and Kotovsky (1963), Vitz and Todd (1969), and Restle (1970). Restle, for instance, pointed out the importance of *runs* and trills as principles of organization in the structure of sequential patterns. In a sequence made up of events chosen from a set of ordered elements, [1, 2, . . 6] a run would be represented by a sequence like [2345], a trill by a sequence like [5454]. Restle and Brown (1970) trained subjects on a pattern learning task, either in a *runs only* condition, for example, [654354324321], or a *trills only* condition [565343323121]. They were then tested on an ambiguous series such as [2123434565], which can either be coded in terms of trills *or* of runs. It is not entirely surprising that the authors found this pattern being structured in accordance with the learned regularity.

In an analogous way, Dooling (1975) trained subjects to listen to sentences in noise that conformed to a particular prosodic pattern. After a number of sentences that had an identical rhythmic structure, he would suddenly present a sentence with an equal number of syllables but with a different rhythmic structure. Thus, after 10 sentences of the type

They are háppў péoplĕ

a sentence would follow like

They are prĕcíse ăccoúnts.

Comprehension in such cases dropped dramatically, and it was also found that the effect was strong enough to transgress word boundaries.

The most explicit attempt to relate a formal description of pattern to the perceived temporal structure of sequences of events is Martin's study (Martin 1972), which described the essence of the tuning process in terms of two principles, *relative timing* and *relative stress*. Both principles indicate that it is very unlikely (as was already argued by Lashley in 1951) that temporal patterning consists of serial concatenation.

Relative timing is the ability to compress or dilate a temporal pattern in time in such a way that the relative temporal relations between successive events are either retained or, at most, changed in a systematic way. The first occurs when we repeat a sentence at a different speed; the second will happen, for instance, in speech, when a particular vowel is followed by phoneme strings of different lengths. Subjects are found to *tune in* on changes in tempo quite easily, although it may take some "cycles" in a pattern (e.g., a few words or sentences or bars of music) before subjects "catch up" with the new rate (Huggins, 1972; Michon, 1967b).

The second aspect, discussed in Martin's paper, is relative accent, which refers to the fact that under a wide range of conditions the pattern of placements of accent (stress) is invariant. With a highly parsimonious description derived from these principles, Martin was able to describe many of the prosodic features of the English language. Thus he succeeded, among other things, in explaining the prosodic relations between stress and relative timing pattern of sentences that allow different stress patterns (viz., *I told you to gó,* vs. *I tóld you to go* or *Í told you to go*).

It has been thoroughly established by now that the perception of stress in language is based on very subtle and inconspicuous cues in the physical sound pattern. By studying the location of perceived stress in artificially inflected syllable sequences and sentences, van Katwijk (1973) has shown that it is precisely the pattern of intonation (inflection) that is a necessary (though not sufficient) condition for accent to occur. Manipulation of other speech dimensions as cues for stress require a massive effort on the part of the speaker: increments on the order of 20% in intensity or duration are required before they lead to the perception of stress.

To study the importance of tuning in speech perception, it is sufficient to disturb the temporal pattern of the message. There are several techniques to degrade either the temporal, the prosodic, the phonological, or even the syntactic structure. (For further discussion, see Huggins, this volume.)

E. The Anticipatory Role of Tuning

Thus far we have not discussed very explicitly the attentive function of the tuning process. However, tuning does not serve only to passively facilitate efficient processing. Its role is much more active, as it also helps to anticipate important events such as peaks in the flow of information. The effect of warning signals, either in a regular sequence or by repeated presentation of a single pair of signals may be considered in this light. The precision of synchronization also belongs here, but these topics fall beyond the immediate scope of the present study.

The precision of anticipation of temporally structured events has been studied extensively, and it has been established that practiced subjects are very quick to pick up a pattern: 2 or 3 cycles suffice when the rate of events is within the confines of rhythm perception, that is, if the interevent intervals are between 250 and 900 msec (Best & Bartlett, 1972; Fraisse, 1956; Michon, 1967b). With prolonged training a very high degree of precision can be obtained, as was shown by Kristofferson (1976), and as we know from musical esemble playing.

Recently Hamilton and Hockey (1974) undertook an attempt to investigate the ability to anticipate and extract critical information from certain (but not

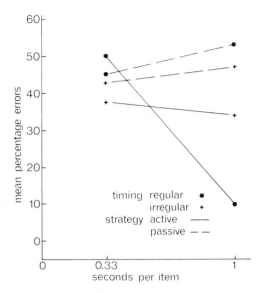

FIG. 2. The effect of timing regularity and attentional strategy on errors in recall, for slow and fast presentation rates (1 and 3 items/sec). (After Hamilton and Hockey, 1974.)

other) elements a sequence of events. In this study, the subject's task was to select for recall certain target words, letters, or numbers at the expense of others. The main question they asked was whether it is possible to induce a patterned fluctuating state of preparation to handle a sensory input. Otherwise subjects would have to use an event counting method in anticipating the next critical event (tagging), or even to accept all input words, rejecting the irrelevant ones only at the end (exhaustive storage). For this purpose they presented their subjects with sequences of 9 letters, words, or numbers in which the critical items were numbers, either in positions 2, 4, 6, and 8, or in random positions.

The results favored an interpretation in terms of the first of the three strategies. This became clear when the critical items were randomized, thus making anticipation impossible, and also when the subjects were presented with regular sequences but instructed to follow either a "passive" or an "active" strategy. However, the results differed considerably as a function of the interitem interval. In fact, when this interval was 0.375 s there was no difference between the anticipatory and the passive receptive strategy, but whereas the passive strategy gave a constant percentage of missed critical items, irrespective of the speed of presentation (0.375, 0.500 or 0.750 sec), the active strategy improved performance considerably. Similarly, the irregular timing (random order) of the critical items did not affect the results of the passive strategy but had a dramatic effect on the active strategy, albeit only if the presentation was rather slow.

As Hamilton and Hockey have argued, the results require some explanation of the tuning process that is involved here in terms of an attentive mechanism that can be triggered in a temporally patterned fashion. The same assumption has been made with respect to the perception of speech pattern, but apparently in the present case we are dealing with a comparatively slow, cognitive process that requires a considerable amount of time. This is suggested by the absence of an effect at the 375 msec interval. The process of "controlled activation," hypothesized by Hamilton and Hockey (1974), should possibly be equated to phasic arousal processes as described by Posner (1975) and Posner and Boies (1971), but in a cyclical version.

An extremely interesting and thoughtful treatment of the temporal organization of arousal and selective attention has been given by Killeen (1975). Killeen dealt with these mechanisms in a framework of temporal conditioning, a field that has undergone a rapid development in recent years. He took the amount and type of observed behavior between two successive instants at which food is delivered as indicative of the operation of two attention-related mechanisms. Briefly, after the first of these instants there is an increasing tendency to show generalized activity, indicative of the state of arousal of the organism. The rate of increase is dependent on the organism's expectancies about when the next food-delivering will occur. At the same time, however, there is also an increasing tendency for selective behavior to interfere with and inhibit general activity; this tendency is observable as a progressive reduction of generalized behavior and a display of "freezing" or other orienting behavior. This pattern of behavior shows great generality across experimental situations as well as species. Killeen demonstrated that the process is highly adaptive to the temporal structure of the feeding cycle, within a range of at least 2 min. Within this range the pattern of generalized activity is not time-locked to the feeding instant, but is posited at approximately 0.3 or 0.4 of the interfeeding interval. At the next feeding instant orienting behavior, and thus response preparation, is maximal.

Although this research refers to a somewhat specific area of behavior, it underlines the importance of tuning for the optimal organization of behavior. It is also suggestive of the sort of mechanism which is at work in the processing of sequential events.

V. SUMMARY AND CONCLUSIONS

The attentional mechanisms and the precategorical and primary memories seem to offer a parsimonious — albeit oversimplified — description of the properties of the specious present. How the present behaves depends on the organization of the event sequences and on the higher order rules available to the subject. It also seems likely that at a low level subjects adhere to principles of organization (Gestalt rules) that may be considered as referring to primary or precognitive processing.

The conscious present emerges whenever the subject is engaged in the more complex or ambiguous cases of detecting or constructing pattern. With respect to the tuning or adaptation of the organism to the temporal structure of the input, it is held that variations in the present, as it is perceived, reflect the tuning process.

This implies that we must accept the idea that there is a temporal dimension to attention. Not only is it necessary to distinguish between a spatial and a non-spatial (or categorical) component of attention (Janssen, 1976; Wertheim, 1977), a temporal component is also needed.

When the subject is paying attention to temporal relations, effort is allocated that cannot be allocated elsewhere (Hicks, Miller, & Kinsbourne, 1976; Michon, 1972; Thomas & Weaver, 1975). This runs partly counter to the position of Keele, who held that the tuning process might not require effort at all (Keele, 1975; Keele & Boies, 1973). Michon's (1966) technique of measuring mental load by a secondary interval production task seems to support this; no detrimental effect of the secondary task on the main task was found. However, Keele's conclusion may well be attributed to a difference in the degree of training of the subjects with respect to the temporal versus spatial components of the task, or to a difference in the complexity of these components — the temporal structure of many laboratory tasks does not put a heavy tax on the capacity of the system. Additionally, training in finding spatial positions (keyboard musicians, Go players) may result in an effortless processing of spatial patterns.

If we acknowledge the three-dimensional character of the attentional field, the effects of task performance on the subjective experience of the present — and of the subjective flow of time — will become accessible to more precise predictions.

A. The Time Estimation Paradigm

The foregoing analysis of the relation between the conscious present, especially its duration, and the processing of information suggests an experimental paradigm to supplement the RT paradigm commonly used in performance studies. The rationale follows directly from our principal thesis that the subjective present is a mode of information processing which reflects the processing of temporal information. Given the limited capacity of the subjects they will, when asked to estimate time, either pay attention to the *temporal* information of the situation or to their main task. When absorbed by the task, no spare capacity is available to notice the passage of time, and consequently time seems to pass quickly; when the task is simple, much attention can be spent on time passing and estimates will be long. The relation between time experience and information processing in general determines the most dramatic confrontation with time that we know: the variability of the subjective speed of time. This phenomenon has been studied in some detail (see Fraisse, 1967; Hicks, Miller, & Kinsbourne, 1976; Michon, 1972; Pöppel, 1978; Vroon, 1973a, b, for useful reviews). Only recently has a more systematic approach been adopted in which not only the effect of a particular task on experienced duration is observed, but also the specific properties of the stimuli are considered (e.g., Mo, 1975, 1976; Thomas & Cantor, 1975). Thus, Time Estimation (TE) has become a within-task instead of a between-tasks paradigm, and should be especially useful in such tasks where there is a certain temporal structure in the processing of information. For instance, if there is a pause in the input or in the processing, no "time" is added to experience, and consequently our estimate of duration would tend to decrease (Michon, 1977). One interesting application of the TE paradigm is that of Noizet and Do (1972/73), who looked at the TE for French sentences of various types and derived some distinctions between, for example, embedded versus right branching clauses, or noun phrases differing only in the use of *qui* versus *que* as a connective.

There are several candidate models that may give the TE-paradigm a good quantitative basis. Some of the more recent ones were proposed by Michon (1967b), Wing (1973), Thomas (1974; see also this volume) and most recently Vorberg and Hambuch (this volume). Of these, only Thomas (and to some extent Michon, 1967b, Ch. 5) thus far dealt explicitly with the trade-off between temporal and nontemporal information.

A consistently applicable experimental paradigm for the adoption of TE remains to be found but given such a standard procedure, it may be expected that TE will become a very useful tool, in which we will find that the large trial-to-trial variability in time estimation data, originally taken as a headache of time psychologists, does in fact reveal what we are after as performance theorists: the effects of attention and performance on the making of the present.

ACKNOWLEDGMENTS

This study was written while the author was at the Netherlands Institute for Advanced Study N.I.A.S., Wassenaar, The Netherlands.

REFERENCES

Allport, D. A. Phenomenal simultaneity and the perceptual moment hypothesis. *British Journal of Psychology,* 1968, *59,* 395–406.

Averbach, E., & Coriell, A. S. Short-term memory in vision. *Bell System Technical Journal* 1961, *40,* 309–328.

Best, P. R., & Bartlett, N. R. Effect of stimulus interval and foreperiod duration on temporal synchronization. *Journal of Experimental Psychology,* 1972, *95,* 154–158.

Boomer, D. S. Hesitation and grammatical encoding. *Language & Speech,* 1965, *8,* 148–158.

Bouma, H. Perceptieve functies. In J. A. Michon, E. G. Eijkman, & L. F. W. de Klerk (Eds.), *Handboek der psychonomie.* Deventer: Van Loghum Slaterus, 1976.

Bower, G. H., & Springston, F. Pauses as recoding points in letter series. *Journal of Experimental Psychology,* 1970, *83,* 421–430.

Bower, G. H., & Winzenz, D. Group structure, coding and memory for digit series. *Journal of Experimental Psychology Monograph* 1969, *80,* 1–17.

Caplan, D. Clause boundaries and recognition latencies for words in sentences. *Perception & Psychophysics,* 1972, *12,* 73–76.

Carroll, J. M., & Bever, T. G. Segmentation in cinema perception. *Science,* 1975, *191,* 1053–1055.

Cavanagh, J. P. Relation between the immediate memory and the memory search rate. *Psychological Review,* 1972, *79,* 525–530.

Crowder, R. G. Visual and auditory memory. In J. F. Kavanagh & I. G. Mattingly (Eds.), *Language by ear and by eye: The relationships between speech and reading.* Cambridge, Mass.: MIT Press, 1972.

Crowder, R. G., & Chao-Ming Cheng, Phonemic confusability, precategorical acoustic storage and the suffix effect. *Perception & Psychophysics,* 1973, *13,* 145–148.

Dooling, D. J. Rhythm and syntax in sentence perception. *Journal of Verbal Learning & Verbal Behavior,* 1974, *13,* 255–264.

Efron, R. The minimum duration of a perception. *Neuropsychologia,* 1970, *8,* 57–63.

Efron, R. An invariant characteristic of perceptual systems in the time domain. In S. Kornblum (Ed.), *Attention and performance IV.* New York: Academic Press, 1973.

Eisler, H. Subjective duration and psychophysics. *Psychological Review,* 1975, *82,* 429–450.

Fodor, J. A., Bever, T. G., & Garrett, M. F. *The psychology of language.* New York: McGraw-Hill, 1974.

Fraisse, P. *Les structures rythmiques.* Louvain: Studia Psychologica, 1956.

Fraisse, P. *Psychologie du temps* (2nd ed.), Paris: Presses Universitaires de France, 1967.

Garner, W. R. *The processing of information and structure.* Potomac, Md. Lawrence Erlbaum Associates, 1974.

Goldman-Eisler, F. *Psycholinguistics, experiments in spontaneous speech.* London: Academic Press, 1968.

Greeno, J. F., & Simon, H. A. Processes for sequence production. *Psychological Review,* 1974, *81,* 187–198.

Hamilton, P., & Hockey, R. Active selection of items to be remembered. *Cognitive Psychology,* 1974, *6,* 61–83.

Hicks, R. E., Miller, G. W., & Kinsbourne, M. *Prospective and retrospective judgments of temporal duration as a function of information processed.* Unpublished manuscript, 1976.

Hirsh, I. J., & Sherrick, Jr., C. E. Perceived order in different sense modalities. *Journal of Experimental Psychology,* 1961, *62,* 423–432.

Huggins, A. W. F. On the perception of temporal phenomena in speech. *Journal of the Acoustical Society of America,* 1972, *51,* 1279–1290.

Huggins, A. W. F. On perceptual integration of dichotically alternated pulse trains. *Journal of the Acoustical Society of America,* 1974, *56,* 939–934.

Husserl, E. *The phenomenology of internal time consciousness* (J. S. Churchill, trans.). The Hague: Nijhoff, 1964.

James, W. *Principles of psychology* (2 Vols.). New York: Dover, 1950 (Originally published, 1890.)

Janssen, W. H. *On the nature of the mental image.* Doctoral dissertation, University of Groningen, 1976.

Jarvella, R.J. Effects of syntax on running memory span for connected discourse. *Psychonomic Science,* 1970, *19,* 235–236.

Jones, M. R. Cognitive representations of serial pattern. In B. H. Kantowitz (Ed.), *Human information processing: Tutorials in performance and cognition.* Hillsdale, N.J.: Lawrence Erlbaum, Associates, 1974.

Jones, M. R. Levels of structure in the reconstruction of temporal and spatial serial patterns. *Journal of Experimental Psychology HLM,* 1976, *2,* 475–488.

Kahneman, D. *Attention and effort.* Englewood Cliffs, N.J.: Prentice-Hall, 1973.

Katwijk, A. van. *Accentuation in Dutch.* Doctoral dissertation, Technical University of Eindhoven, 1973.

Keele, S. W. The representation of motor programmes. In P. M. A. Rabbitt & S. Dornic (Eds.), *Attention and performance V.* London: Academic Press, 1975.

Keele, S. W., & Boies, S. J. Processing demands of sequential information. *Memory and Cognition,* 1973, *1,* 85–90.

Killeen, P. On the temporal control of behavior. *Psychological Review,* 1975, *82,* 89–115.

Klatt, D. H. Linguistic uses of segmental deviation in English: Acoustic and perceptual evidence. *Journal of the Acoustical Society of America,* 1976, *59,* 1208–1221.

Kristofferson, A. B. *Psychological timing mechanisms.* Lecture at the 4th Annual Meeting of the Lake Ontario Vision Establishment, Niagara Falls, Ontario, March, 1973.

Kristofferson, A. B. Low variance stimulus-response latencies: Deterministic internal delays? *Perception & Psychophysics,* 1976, *20,* 89–100.

Kristofferson, A. B., & Allan, L. G. Successiveness and duration discrimination. In S. Kornblum (Ed.), *Attention and performance IV.* New York: Academic Press, 1973.

LaBerge, D. Acquisition of automatic processing in perceptual and associative learning. In P. M. A. Rabbitt & S. Dornic (Eds.), *Attention and performance V.* London: Academic Press, 1974.

Ladefoged, P., & Broadbent, D. E. Auditory perception of temporal order. *Journal of the Acoustical Society of America,* 1959, *31,* 1539.

Lashley, K. S. The problem of serial order in behavior. In L. A. Jeffress (Ed.), *Cerebral mechanisms in behavior: the Hixon Symposium.* New York: Wiley, 1951.

Leeuwenberg, E. L. Quantitative specification of information in sequential patterns. *Psychological Review,* 1969, *76,* 216–220.

Luce, R. D., & Green, D. M. Detection, discrimination and recognition. In E. C. Carterette, & M. P. Friedman, (Eds.), *Handbook of perception* (Vol. II): *Psychophysical judgment and measurement.* New York: Academic Press, 1974.

Mandler, G. From association to structure. *Psychological Review,* 1962, *69,* 415–427.

Mandler, G. *Mind and emotion.* New York: Wiley, 1975.

Martin, J. G. Rhythmic (hierarchical) versus serial structure in speech and other behavior. *Psychological Review,* 1972, *79,* 487–509.

Martin, J. G., & Strange, W. Determinants of hesitations in spontaneous speech. *Journal of Experimental Psychology,* 1968, *76,* 474–479. (a)

Martin, J. G., & Strange, W. The perception of hesitation in spontaneous speech. *Perception & Psychophysics,* 1968, *3,* 427–438. (b)

Massaro, D. W. Perceptual units in speech recognition. *Journal of Experimental Psychology,* 1974, *102,* 199–208.

McDougall, R. The structure of simple rhythm forms. *Psychological Review Monograph Supplement,* 1903, *4,* 309–416.

Michon, J. A. Studies on subjective duration, I. Differential sensitivity in the perception of repeated temporal intervals. *Acta Psychologica,* 1964, *22,* 441–450.

Michon, J. A. Tapping regularity as a measure of perceptual motor load. *Ergonomics,* 1966, *9,* 401–412.

Michon, J. A. Magnitude scaling of short durations with closely spaced stimuli. *Psychonomic Science,* 1967, *9,* 359–360. (a)

Michon, J. A. *Timing in temporal tracking.* Assen: Van Gorcum, 1967. (b)

Michon, J. A. *The non-experience of short temporal intervals.* Techn. Rep. IZF 1968-12. Institute for Perception, Soesterberg, Netherlands.

Michon, J. A. Processing of temporal information and the cognitive theory of time experience. In J. T. Fraser, F. C. Haber, & G. H. Mueller (Eds.), *The study of time.* Heidelberg: Springer, 1972.

Michon, J. A. Holes in the fabric of subjective time: Figure-ground relations in event sequences. *Acta Psychologica,* 1977, *41,* 191–203.

Mo, S. S. Temporal reproduction of duration as a function of numerosity. *Bulletin of the Psychonomic Society,* 1975, *5,* 165–167.

Mo, S. S. Nonmonotonicity of temporal judgment of duration as a function of variability of size. *Bulletin of the Psychonomic Society,* 1976, *7,* 196–198.

Noizet, G., & Do, P. Estimation du temps de présentation comme indice de la complexité syntaxique des phrases. *Bulletin de Psychologie,* 1972/73, *26,* 396–404.

Noorden, L. P. A. S., van. *Temporal coherence in the perception of tone sequences.* Doctoral dissertation, Tehcnical University of Eindhoven, 1975.

Nooteboom, S. *Production and perception of vowel duration.* Doctoral dissertation. University of Utrecht, 1972.

Perkins, D. N. Coding position in a sequence by rhythmic grouping. *Memory & Cognition,* 1974, *2,* 219–223.

Plomp, R. Auditory psychophysics. *Annual Review of Psychology,* 1975, *25,* 207–232.

Pöppel, E. Time perception. In H. L. Teuber, R. Held, & H. Leibowitz (Eds.), *Handbook of sensory psychology* (Vol. 8): *Perception.* New York: Springer, 1978.

Posner, M. I. Psychobiology of attention. In M. S. Gazzaniga & C. Blakemore (Eds.), *Handbook of psychobiology.* New York: Academic Press, 1975.

Posner, M. I., & Boies, S. Components of attention. *Psychological Review,* 1971, *78,* 391–408.

Restle, F. Theory of serial pattern learning: Structural trees. *Psychological Review,* 1970, *77,* 481–495.

Restle, F., & Brown, E. R. Serial pattern learning. *Journal of Experimental Psychology,* 1970, *83,* 120–125.

Sanders, A. F., & Van Borselen, J. W. Continuing memory and information processing. *Journal of Experimental Psychology,* 1966, *71,* 844–848.

Shallice, T. Dual functions of consciousness. *Psychological Review,* 1972, *79,* 383–393.

Simon, H. A. Complexity and the representation of patterned sequences of symbols. *Psychological Review,* 1972, *79,* 369–382.

Simon, H. A., & Kotovsky, K. Human acquisition of concepts for sequential patterns. *Psychological Review,* 1963, *70,* 534–546.

Sternberg, S. Memory scanning: new findings and current controversies. *Quarterly Journal of Experimental Psychology,* 1975, *27,* 1–32.

Thomas, E. A. C., & Brown, I., Jr. Time perception and the filled duration illusion. *Perception and Psychophysics,* 1974, *16,* 449–458.

Thomas, E. A. C., & Cantor, N. E. On the duality of simultaneous time and size perception. *Perception & Psychophysics,* 1975, *18,* 44–48.

Thomas, E. A. C., & Weaver, W. B. Cognitive processing and time perception. *Perception & Psychophysics,* 1975, *17,* 363–367.

Thomas, I. B., Hill, P. B., Carroll, F. S., & Garcia, B. Temporal order in the perception of vowels. *Journal of the Acoustical Society of America,* 1970, *48,* 1010–1013.

Vitz, P. C., & Todd, I. C. A coded element model of the perceptual processing of sequential stimuli. *Psychological Review* 1969, *76,* 433–449.

Vos, P. G. M. M. *Waarneming van metrische toonreeksen.* Dissertatie, Universiteit van Nijmegen, 1973.

Vroon, P. A. Tapping rate as a measure of expectancy in terms of response and attention limitation. *Journal of Experimental Psychology,* 1973, *101,* 183–185. (a)

Vroon, P. A. *Some process variables in sequential time estimation.* Psychological Laboratory, Utrecht, Report No. 7, 1973 (b)

Vroon, P. A. Is there a time quantum in duration experience? *American Journal of Psychology,* 1974, *87,* 237–245.

Waugh, N. C., & Norman, D. A. Primary memory. *Psychological Review,* 1965, *72,* 89–104.

Warren, R. M., & Obusek, C. J. Identification of temporal order within auditory sequences. *Perception & Psychophysics,* 1972, *12,* 86–90.

Warren, R. M., Obusek, C. J., Farmer, R. M., & Warren, R. P. Auditory sequence: confusion of patterns other than speech or music. *Science,* 1969, *164,* 586–587.

Wertheim, A. H. *The influence of eye movements on the processing of visual information from moving sources.* Report Traffic Research Centre, University of Groningen, 1976.

Wertheim, A. H. Doctoral dissertation (in preparation) 1979, Institute of Experimental Psychology, University of Groningen.

Wing, A. M. *The timing of interresponse intervals by human subjects.* Unpublished doctoral dissertation, McMaster University, Hamilton, Ontario, 1973.

WORD PERCEPTION AND READING

7 Visual Search and Reading: Eye Movements and Functional Visual Field: A Tutorial Review

Herman Bouma

Institute for Perception Research IPO
Eindhoven, The Netherlands

ABSTRACT

Visual search is concerned with processes for finding specified objects of unknown position. At any given moment the retinal fovea deals with only a narrow cone of visual space outside the eye. Therefore, the fovea has to be guided to the position of interest. It is one of the functions of eccentric vision, outside the fovea, to provide such guidance. Eccentric vision, in particular the size of the functional visual field, and control of the line of sight by head and eye movements are therefore basic to an understanding of search.

If, arbitrarily, head movements and moving objects are excluded from consideration, eye movements are restricted to jumps (saccades) that are separated by eye pauses. Since the jumps are quick, useful vision occurs during eye pauses only. Vision is then based upon a series of quasi-stationary retinal images which are shifted a few times each second. These basic facts lead to the following rather straightforward division of research problems in visual tasks: (1) vision from a brief stationary image, (2) the control of eye saccades, and (3) the integration of successive images into one continuous visual impression. Of course, the relations between these three separate types of process have to be established as well.

The aim of the present contribution is to show that this view has led to fruitful research aimed at understanding both visual search and reading. The approach is advocated for further studies of visual activities.

1. Studies on vision from brief stationary images have to concentrate on eccentric rather than on foveal vision, and on presentation durations representative of eye pause durations. They should also preferably concern structured rather than homogeneous visual fields or backgrounds. The latter distinction is of importance because of the strong adverse interactions between neighboring objects, which prevent studies with homogeneous backgrounds from being representative of many conditions in daily life. These lateral interferences are

specific in the sense that certain stimulus properties interact selectively among each other over relatively long retinal distances. Although the interactions may extend not only in space but in time as well, the lateral interferences probably limit the functional visual field more than the effects of backward and forward masking.

2. Control of eye saccades is a difficult research problem in its own right. There is a wide range of processing levels where eye guidance may originate. A preliminary division might distinguish between (a) semiautonomous guidance by motor routines; (b) sensory and perceptual guidance by visual, auditory, and tactual objects and; (c) cognitive guidance by knowledge and expectation on as many different levels of complexity as one might wish to distinguish, including individually unique factors. These levels should be seen as cooperating rather than as being mutually exclusive. Indeed, eye saccades may reflect the complexities of man himself. Now that eye monitoring equipment is more generally available, the task of research might be to peel off from reality reduced situations in which relatively simple and amenable types of control appear dominant.

3. On the integration of visible information from successive images, some data exist that suggest that the visual system does not need advance information on eye saccades in order to integrate perceptually the incoming information. Some preliminary evidence suggests that eccentric recognition may sometimes be slower than foveal recognition, so that the internal recognition process may not always be all that successive.

Applications of the above research questions to processes of search and of reading are demonstrated.

I. INTRODUCTION

The main theme of this study is how ordinary vision is achieved via retinal images that shift a few times each second. These quick shifts occur when searching for new objects of unknown position, when reading, and in fact in the majority of situations in daily life where we are exploring or just looking around. It has been said that the decision most often made in one's life is where to look next (Mackworth, 1965) — an estimate would be about a hundred-thousand times a day — and this calls for a certain automaticity of control. The present study concentrates not only on "where to look next" but also on "what is seen at present," and on the remarkable notion that continuous, detailed vision is based on irregularly jumping retinal images.

To approach the subject analytically, we shall enter a few areas that until recently were largely "terra incognita". Quite a few of these remain, but a few isles of well-documented results stand out, where the dawn of insight now illuminates a somewhat entangled research situation. What I shall try to do here is to map out the known and to explore the adjoining unknown, while concentrating on questions open to adequate experimental coverage.

The problem may be briefly sketched as follows. In reading, in visual search, in visual inspection, and in visual exploration, the eyes are steady for periods of 200—800 msec, after which they rotate quickly towards a new steady position.

During the eye saccades there is no useful vision, and the continuing interest of researchers in why we do not see in the 25 msec in which the retinal image moves very fast[1] seems to skip a question more relevant to this paper, i.e., what we see from 300 msec of a steady retinal image. Over the visual field, visual information processing is not homogeneous, and we shall ask as a first question how far from fixation relevant objects can be seen. The answer will be shown to depend closely not only on the position of the target within the visual field, but also on the presence of objects other than the target. We then have to discuss processes that determine the size of the functional visual field in search and in reading (Part 1).

The processing of spatial information from areas outside the line of sight is rather limited. Although most of the visual field is covered by eccentric vision, vision is not limited proportionally because of eye saccades that bring the line of sight close to relevant objects. These eye saccades are under sophisticated control. In and around the line of sight, the visual system carries out detailed and elaborate visual processing of spatial information, and visual attention is usually directed near the line of sight.

Since the fovea covers only 3 square degrees out of the roughly 10,000 square degrees of the visual field, foveal vision is of little use unless guided toward directions of visual interest. This guidance can be provided by a great many sources and is executed by the head and eye-movement motor systems that thereby determine each successive retinal image. We shall not further discuss head movements, which come into play for rotations of the line of sight of over 30° or so (Sanders, 1963).

The second question to be asked therefore concerns the ways in which eye movements are controlled, and we shall not deal with smooth pursuit movements but shall restrict the discussion to eye saccades (Part 2).

Let us imagine that we know both what is seen from one fixation and what each next retinal image is going to be. A remaining research task would then be to understand the integration of vision from these successive images into the stable impression of the outside world that we experience. The processing of visual information continues after the retinal image has disappeared. The processings of successive retinal images therefore overlap in time and give rise to interactions of many types — the notion of continuity refers to one such interaction. Leaving interactions from sensory modalities and of a cognitive nature other than visual out of account here, our third question will inquire into timings and interactions of assumed visual information processing as evolving from successive retinal images (Part 3). Because of a lack of both experimental evidence and explicit theories, this last topic can be dealt with only briefly.

---

[1]Maximum speeds can be of the order of 400 deg/sec, depending on saccade extent. The quickly moving image is processed by the retina, which has an integration time of about 30 msec, depending on adaptation level (Roufs, 1972).

EHYP	ZVMLBQ	ODUGQR	IVMXEW
SWIQ	HSQJMF	QCDUGO	EWVMIX
UFCJ	ZTJVQR	CQOGRD	EXWMVI
WBYH	RDQTFM	QUGCDR	IXEMWV
OGTX	TQVRSX	URDGQO	VXWEMI
GWVX	MSVRQX	GRUQDO	MXVEWI
TWLN	ZHQBTL	DUZGRO	XVWMEI
XJBU	ZJTQXL	UCGROD	MWXVIE
UDXI	LHQVXM	DQRCGU	VIMEXW
HSFP	FVQHMS	QDOCGU	EXVWIM
XSCQ	MTSDQL	CGUROQ	VVWMIEX
SDJU	TZDFQB	OCDURQ	VMWIEX
PODC	QLHBMZ	UOCGQD	XVWMEI
ZVBP	QMXBJD	RGQCOU	WXVEMI
PEVZ	RVZHSQ	GRUDQO	XMEWIV
SLRA	STFMQZ	GODUCQ	MXIVEW
JCEN	RVXSQM	QCURDO	VEWMIX
ZLRD	MQBJFT	DUCOQG	EMVXWI
XBOD	MVZXLQ	CGRDQU	IVWMEX
PHMU	RTBXQH	UDRCOQ	IEVMWX
ZHFK	BLQSZX	GQCORU	WVZMXE
PNJW	QSVFDJ	GOQUCD	XEMIWV
CQXT	FLDVZT	GDQUOC	WXIMEV
GHNR	BQHMDX	URDCGO	EMWIVX
IXYD	BMFDQH	GODRQC	IVEMXW
QSVB	QHLJZT		

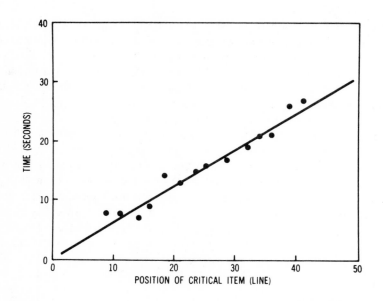

The division of problems of search and of reading into (1) recognition from a steady presentation, (2) eye saccade control, and (3) central integration including interferences of successive images, defines separate research problems but not independent visual processes. Thus, the retinal image is dependent on the momentary line of sight, which in turn depends on earlier visual information used for eye guidance. What this implies is that the relationships will ultimately have to be specified rather precisely in time.

As an intermezzo, let us consider a classical experiment by Neisser (1967) which combines aspects of search and of reading. Subjects scanned through lists of letter strings until they found a certain target letter. From string number and search time, an empirical scanning rate was calculated. This scanning rate, up to 10 lines per second, turned out not to be constant, but to depend on parameters such as length and composition of the letter strings. Search times were longer for targets in longer strings and for targets that resembled the nontargets (Fig. 1). It is useful to reconsider the experiment after some twelve years, because the empirical scanning rate leaves certain underlying search processes unspecified that can now be better understood. I refer to questions such as how many letters or strings do subjects handle in one fixation? and is there overlap in successive functional visual fields? From insight into search processes it should follow, for example, how scanning rates be expressed — such as in lines per second or in letters per second. We shall return to this experiment later.

II. FUNCTIONAL VISUAL FIELD

The functional visual field can be described as the field within which one can see an object from a single eye pause. In daylight, objects are most visible in the line of sight (foveal vision), and visibility usually decreases with increasing eccentricity. Because the fovea is very small, properties of eccentric vision determine the boundaries of the functional visual field. Figure 2 indicates current terminology of areas of various retinal eccentricities.

A first question about eccentric vision is whether it is limited by the optical quality of the retinal image. If the eye is focused at the correct distance, it turns out that the retinal image is well focused up to 30° of eccentricity (le Grand, 1966) and it has recently been established that up to an eccentricity of 60°, visual acuity is not limited by the optical quality of the retinal image (Millodot, Johnson, Lamont, & Leibowitz, 1975).

FIG. 1   Examples of search tasks as studied by Neisser. Subjects search for the presence[+] or absence[-] of a particular letter in unpronounceable strings. String length and visual similarity between target and nontargets are among the variables. From left to right the target examples are: K+, Q−, Z+, Z+. The diagram indicates a linear relation between average search time and the number of the target line (Neisser, 1967).

In eccentric vision, visual functions have received little systematic exploration, and most of the available data concern single, simple objects against a homogeneous background. The best known function concerns visual acuity, i.e. the reciprocal of the smallest detail (in minutes of arc visual angle) that can be resolved from standard optotypes, in particular the Landolt-C. The smallest detail increases with eccentricity, linearly up to about 25° and steeper thereafter (Fig. 2). Also, it is well established that color discrimination decreases rather sharply from the fovea outwards. Depending on object size, contrast sensitivity generally shows less decline. Discrimination of orientation also remains quite accurate, at least up to an eccentricity of 10° (Andriessen & Bouma, 1970) and estimation of the length as such of letter strings varies little with eccentricity (Schiepers, 1973, 1976).

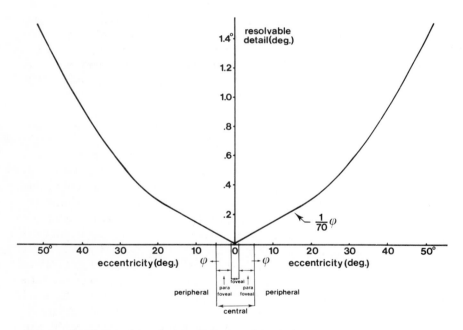

FIG. 2   Detail size of standard optotype (Landolt C) that can just be detected, as a function of retinal eccentricity. Visual acuity is defined as (detail size)$^{-1}$, where detail size is expressed in minutes of arc. Foveal acuity is normally between 1 and 2. Data combined from a number of sources among which le Grand (1966) and Sloan (1968). Terminology for angular distance from the line of sight distinugishes between foveal vision (eccentricity $\varphi <$ 1°), parafoveal vision ($1° < \varphi < 5°$), and peripheral vision ($\varphi > 5°$). Foveal and parafoveal vision combine to form central vision ($\varphi < 5°$), parafoveal and peripheral to form eccentric vision ($\varphi > 1°$). It should be kept in mind that there are no visual functions that show such sharp boundaries.

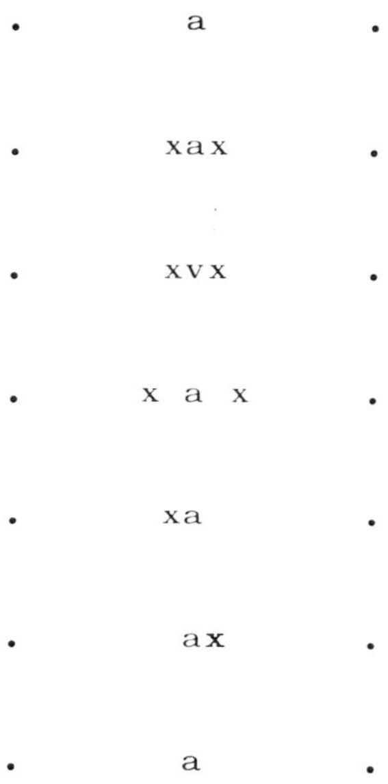

•   a   •

•   x a x   •

•   x v x   •

•   x a x   •

•   x a   •

•   a x   •

•   a   •

FIG. 3   Demonstration of lateral interference in eccentric vision. Looking successively at the dots, one sees that recognizability of the embedded letters attended to is hampered by the flanking x letters.

The above data for single objects on a homogeneous background have limited relevance for visual search, for reading, and indeed for ordinary vision in general, because they cannot be generalized to include visual objects amid other objects. Recent evidence indicates that the influence of a structured background is dramatic, and the new evidence will undoubtedly lead to changes in present views on quite a few topics, among which are the special properties of foveal vision and the design of experiments on serial position curves. We shall therefore consider in some detail recent evidence on visual detection and recognition in filled backgrounds.

A. Visual Interference and Reading

Let us start with letter recognition. Isolated single letters can be recognized in single presentations[2] about as well as visual acuity from Landolt-C standard

[2]To prevent eye saccades towards the test stimulus, the duration of presentation should be below the latency of eye reactions, the lower limit of which can be put at 150 msec. Fortunately, correct recognition scores are only slightly dependent on presentation time between values of 50 and 200 msec. A value of 100 msec therefore seems quite a good choice for tachistoscopic presentation representative of normal eye pauses.

optotypes predicts. The addition of any adjacent letters, however, makes recognition scores drop sharply. This fact has been known for some time (Mackworth, 1965; Woodworth, 1938; Woodworth & Schlosberg, 1954) but has only recently been widely documented (Bjork & Estes, 1973; Eriksen & Eriksen, 1974; Wolford & Hollingsworth, 1974), sometimes under the heading of "lateral masking."

What are the consequences for the functional visual field and what types of interference process are involved? If we just add two letters to a target letter, one at each side, recognition is seriously hampered (Fig. 3) and the functional recognition field is observed to shrink substantially to about 25% of its initial diameter (Bouma, 1970; see also Fig. 3). The effect seems to be a rather passive or automatic one, in the sense that the interference largely remains when, while maintaining proper fixation, the subject directs his visual attention towards the eccentric test letter, as one does for instance with continuous exposure (Townsend, Taylor, & Brown, 1971).

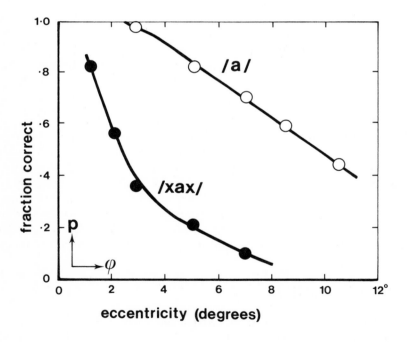

FIG. 4   Embedding randomly chosen target letters between two letters x (indicated as /xax/), makes recognition scores in eccentric vision drop sharply, as compared with the nonembedded situation (indicated as / a /). The diameter of the corresponding functional visual field shrinks to about 25% of its nonembedded value. One degree visual angle corresponds with four letter spacings (Bouma, 1970).

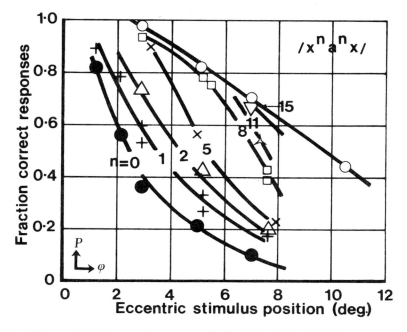

FIG. 5   When embedded target letters are gradually isolated visually by leaving n spacings open between the target and the two flanking letters, recognition improves, but only gradually. For complete visual isolation an open distance is required of about 40% of target eccentricity. One degree visual angle corresponds with four letter spacings. (Bouma, 1970).

In the case of a passive interference, one expects the interaction to lessen when distances between the target letter and adjacent letters are increased. Although this indeed proves to be true, the results are nevertheless surprising. It turns out that for embedded letters, distances toward the two adjacent letters have to be as large as 40–50% of target eccentricity before the functional field is again as wide as it is for isolated letters (Bouma, 1970; see also Fig. 5). The range over which the interference operates is therefore substantial. If we define visual isolation as the absence of interference from other stimuli, it follows that visual isolation of a target letter requires a surrounding homogeneous background with a radius of almost half the value of target eccentricity (Fig. 6). This is of consequence for the design of tachistoscopic experiments.

If interfering letters are put at one side only of the target letter, it is found that the interference is stronger when the interfering letters are at the eccentric side rather than at the foveal side. This can be interpreted in the sense that the interference is more pronounced in the direction towards the fovea than away from the fovea. When letter strings are presented (see Fig. 7), this leads to recognition scores of outward letters (farthest from the fovea) being higher than those

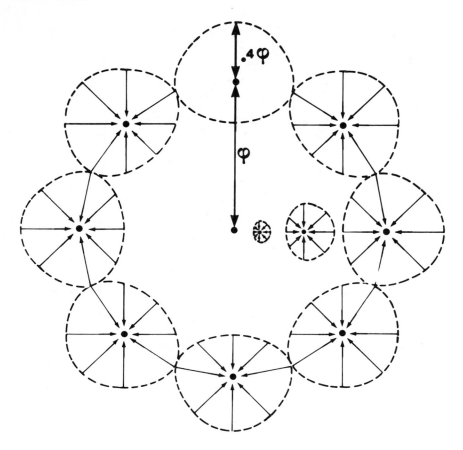

Lateral interference in eccentric vision

FIG. 6   Scheme of lateral interference extent. Recognizability of targets positioned at the centers of the indicated areas is decreased if other stimuli are present within these areas.

of inward letters (closest to the fovea). The common decrease of recognition with eccentricity is thus upset. The functional field therefore depends not only on the presence of other letters and on their distance to the target letter, but also on their relative positions on the line from fovea toward target letter (Bouma, 1973; Mackworth, 1965; Woodworth & Schlosberg, 1954).

Another property of the interference is that it may well be less in the right visual (half) field than in the left (Bouma, 1973), as shown in Fig. 7. Bouwhuis (this volume) presents evidence that the well-known right field preference for visual word recognition can quantitatively be explained from differences in letter recognition, mainly due to interference (Bouma & Bouwhuis, 1975; Bouwhuis, this volume). The higher scores for words in the right visual field (Mishkin & Forgays, 1952), which have hitherto been ascribed to better language facilities of a whole (left) hemisphere, can perhaps now be localized in a small visual portion of that hemisphere. A similar view has been put forward by Bradshaw, Gates, and Patterson (1976), who ascribe a better spatial analysis to the left cerebral hemisphere. We propose therefore, as properties of lateral visual interference: strong effects; wide range; feature specific; mainly foveally directed; little expressed in fovea; and less expressed in right than in left visual field.

There are a number of implications for the functional field in reading. First, it is limited by visual interference effects rather than by visual acuity. Second, initial and final letters of words benefit from the adjacent blank space, in particular initial letters left of fixation and final letters right of fixation. Third, the lesser degree of interference in the right visual field may be one cause of the functional field extending farther right than left of fixation. Fourth, interferences may operate over distances substantially greater than a blank spacing or the leading between lines. There is extensive benefit for initial and final portions of the printed lines. Generally, visual interference effects make functional visual fields depend on many aspects of the layout of the printed page.

The functional visual field in reading has been the subject of many earlier investigations. Estimates based on eccentric recognition of isolated words may come out at some 8 letters left and 12 letters right of fixation, depending on word length, criterion, and so on (Bouma, 1973; see also Fig. 7). As compared

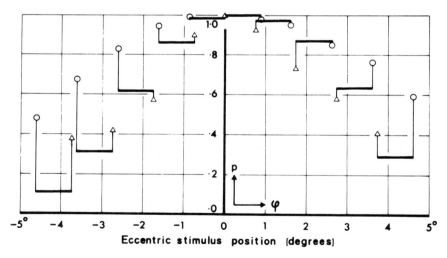

FIG. 7   In eccentric vision, recognition of outward letters of unpronounceable letter strings is higher than recognition of inward letters. This is interpreted as the interference being directed mainly towards the fovea. The bars indicate recognition scores of true words, which are higher in the right visual field. (Bouma, 1973).

with true reading, these experiments differ in having no adjacent words and consequently less visual interference on the one hand, and no syntactic and semantic benefits on the other. A discussion of the precise relation between letter perception and word perception (cf. Bouwhuis, this volume; Massaro, 1975; Smith & Spoehr, 1974) is outside the scope of the present paper. However, it may be mentioned just briefly that the so-called word superiority effect — in certain conditions a letter from a word is reported somewhat more effectively than a letter from an unpronounceable string — should be considered as additional to, and in no way in contradiction with, the present considerations.

Recent estimates obtained from actual oral and silent reading of good readers come out at a diameter of 15–20 letters (Bouma & de Voogd, 1974) and the most direct estimate with an elegant and sophisticated new method in which the line of print can be changed during an eye saccade comes out at a distance of up to 15 letters in the right visual field (McConkie & Rayner, 1975; Rayner, 1975). It is only natural that the functional field should depend upon the type of recognition: for example, one will find different values for the recognition of embedded letters, of word attributes such as word length or word-contour, and of words. It also depends on the position in the line of print or on the printed page. The interference has a direct bearing on the interpretation of serial position curves resulting from tachistoscopic experiments in which a string of many letters is presented simultaneously usually extending symmetrically into the left and right visual fields. If subjects are requested to report all letters after a single brief presentation ("full report condition") they turn out the well-known W-shaped curves: initial and final letters of the string have high scores as well as the central letters, viewed foveally; embedded letters both left and right of fixation have low scores. Generally, W turns out to be skewed, in that letters from the left visual field are reported somewhat more effectively than their counterparts in the right field, in seeming contrast with the interference, which is supposedly less in the right field.

In these experiments it would seem that two quite different processes are interwoven, that is, visual interference and limitations of memory due to overload, as has also been proposed by Estes, Allmeyer, and Reder (1976). Visual lateral interference effects are different for the various letter positions in the string and can be held responsible for the overall W shape. This adverse interference depends on such parameters as the number of letters in the string and the size and distance of the letters. A decline of memory or a limited memory capacity, on the other hand, favors letters reported first and therefore can be expected to cause a decline in scores from left to right. It would therefore seem useful to study separately (1) interference effects in situations without memory overload, and (2) memory overload in situations without visual interference, before studying their interactions in a well controlled design.

The interference effects also hold a message for the special role of foveal vision. In this view, foveal vision is not just special because visual processing provides for maximum visual acuity, but also because of the minimum of lateral interference, which gives extensive opportunities for segmentation of complex images and for recognizing their separate parts, thus providing for maximum "visual isolation." It may be that the area of minimum interference even extends slightly into the right visual field. In addition, it should be recalled that visual attention usually resides at the line of sight, providing guidance for motor control of the hands, for example.

This view on foveal function may explain my observation that foveal vision retains its special function in situations in which visual acuity does not peak, such as when the optical image is blurred or at low light levels.

B. Visual Interference and Search

In visual search, much larger retinal areas may be involved. The notion that performance in visual search tasks should be related to eccentric vision has occurred to a number of researchers, among them Johnston (1965), but the essential difference between homogeneous and filled backgrounds has not often been appreciated. The topic of tachistoscopic target detection in eccentric vision using complex backgrounds has received remarkably little research interest, although many authors use complex stimulus fields that extend outside the foveal area. However, there have been some recent papers on the subject (Engel, 1971, 1974, 1976, 1977; Grindley & Townsend, 1970; see also Fig. 8). As we have seen in

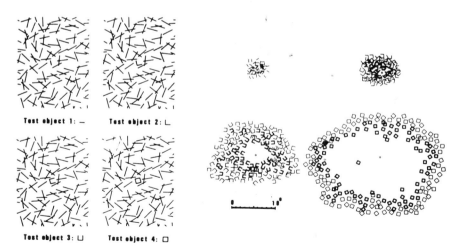

Test object 1: —   Test object 2: L

Test object 3: ⊔   Test object 4: ☐

FIG. 8   When each of four different test objects was presented against the same background of straight lines (left picture, test objects in the centers), the functional visual field within which they could be found in a single presentation come out as indicated in the right picture. Test objects drawn in bold lines were reported correctly in a single presentation, those in thin lines were not. Small central circle: fixation spot (Engel, 1971).

the case of letters, the functional visual field is generally much smaller for structured backgrounds than for homogeneous backgrounds. The results of these experiments have contributed to our understanding of the nature of lateral
interference.

The first point that has been made is that the interference is specific to certain
features of the stimulus. Thus, disk targets are particularly hampered by other
disks, and line targets by other lines. Specificities go even farther than that and
have been found for size and for luminance of disks (Engel, 1974; see also Fig. 9)

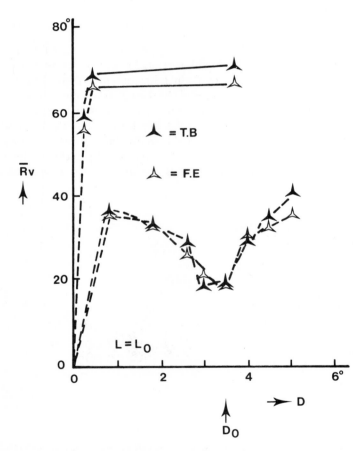

FIG. 9   Specific effects in lateral interference. The graph indicates maximum eccentricity
where the presence of a disk could be detected as a function of its diameter D. Upper curves:
homogeneous background, lower curves: background of other disks of constant diameter D_o.
Background interferes most with detection for $D = D_o$ (Engel, 1974).

and for the orientation of lines (Andriessen & Bouma, 1976). Interference is therefore not one general phenomenon, but concerns many analyzed stimulus features that interact specifically with similar features. The levels of visual analysis at which these interferences operate can therefore be specified, which opens new possibilities for investigating how this analysis proceeds.

Another important finding is that the functional visual field may be influenced by directed attention. In complex fields, but not in simple fields with homogeneous backgrounds (Shiffrin, Gardner, & Allmeyer, 1973; Shiffrin, McKay, & Shaffer, 1976) directing one's attention beforehand to a certain direction relative to fixation increases the eccentricity where the stimulus may be detected, without a noticeable decrease in other directions (Engel, 1971; Grindley & Townsend, 1968). Also, during concentration on other tasks, such as foveal recognition, the functional field has been found to shrink (Ikeda & Takeuchi, 1975). In this very special sense, the rather passive interference processes should be considered together with directed attention.

The distinction is an example of Norman and Bobrow's (1975) quite general distinction between signal-data limited processes and resource-limited processes.

What we intend to show in concluding this section is that the concepts developed so far, in particular the functional visual field as limited by lateral interferences, are of direct relevance to the understanding of visual search. A few of the many remaining problems will be pointed out.

We shall first briefly review a recent experiment by Engel (1976, 1977). As a search task, he used a complex background field consisting of identical disks and two test disks, one slightly smaller, the other slightly larger than the background disks. First, the functional visual fields of the test disks were evaluated from single tachistoscopic presentations. Next, a search experiment was run in which subjects searched for one of the test disks (target) until they found it, during which their eye movements were recorded.

The idea behind the experiment is that subjects make saccades that can be described as random (Bloomfield, 1972; Krendel & Wodinsky, 1960) until the target happens to be within the functional visual field, after which a straight saccade can bring it into foveal vision. In order to check the relevance of the functional field concept, its size in tachistoscopic recognition was compared with a size derived from actual search time distributions on the assumption of a random search strategy. This comparison demonstrates that for targets of different diameter, both values show a similar increase with increasing difference between target and background disks (Fig. 10). The value derived from the actual search is somewhat smaller than the tachistoscopic value, indicating that visual processing is somewhat more difficult in a continuous series than in a single presentation, perhaps owing to backward masking effects. An interesting side observation was that on a number of occasions the eyes were close to the target and yet moved on, only to return one saccade later. This shows that recognition had taken place too late to prevent the occurrence of the undirected eye saccade.

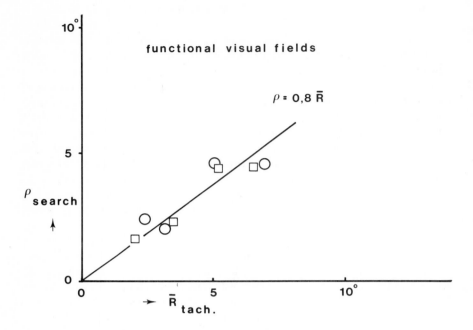

FIG. 10   Average radius ρ of the functional visual field as calculated from actual search time distributions compared with the average radius R in tachistoscopic presentation for four different sizes of target disk (Engel, 1976).

Let us finally reconsider some of Neisser's findings (1967; see also Fig. 1) and comment on them from our present point of view.

1. The increasing difficulty of finding a target letter with increasing string length is indicative of increased lateral interferences between letters, which limit the functional field of view.

2. The greater difficulty in finding target letters in the midst of other letters of similar shape may be at least partly due to increased lateral interference, which acts selectively on features shared by both targets and nontargets (cf. Estes, 1972).

3. The scanning rate of up to 10 lines per second indicates that the subjects had one eye fixation in any two or three lines, which is sufficient in the case of short lines to bring every letter once within the functional visual field.

The general conclusion is that an analysis in terms of functional visual field and of eye saccades may account for many of the findings obtained in actual visual search.

III.   CONTROL OF EYE SACCADES

Limitations of the functional field are balanced by a sophisticated control system for eye saccades, which is essential for refreshing the retinal image in visual tasks such as inspection, search, and reading. In recent years there has been remarkable progress in understanding neurophysiological control mechanisms in monkeys, which we shall not discuss. One may use Dichgans and Bizzi (1972), Robinson (1973), and Evarts (1974) as entry references. The way in which the human control system operates in complex visual tasks has so far largely resisted analysis. What stand out are the variations: variations between subjects and between repeated presentations to the same subject. This seems to call for statistical or probabilistic descriptions (Fig. 11). However, these should not make us forget

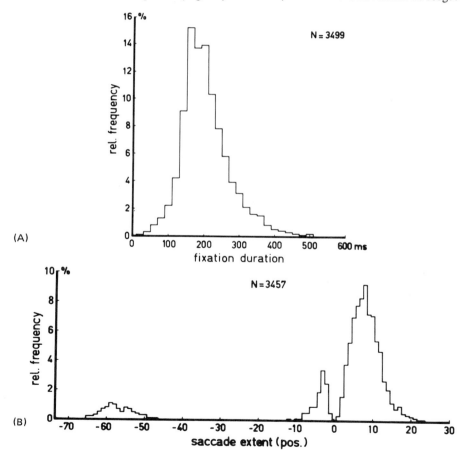

FIG. 11   Distributions of eye pause duration and of saccade extent (number of letters) in silent reading. Pooled data from 7 readers. (Andriessen & de Voogd, 1973).

that the cause of the variations has then escaped analysis, and that strictly systematic events may appear as random variations.

Eye saccades are characterized by direction and extent (vector) and by their moments of occurrence (timing). An alternative description of the same phenomena specifies fixation position and eye pause duration. The descriptions differ in that they specify position and timing in absolute or relative terms. Quite often we do not yet know which description should be preferred, i.e. which comes closest to the underlying control processes.

The evidence available in the literature is rather diverse. On the side of complex tasks there are recordings of scan paths in complex visual scenes, usually in a free inspection task (Mackworth & Morandi, 1967; Noton & Stark, 1971; Yarbus, 1967; see also Fig. 12). These are fascinating to look at, but the conclusions are restricted because of the case history aspect. Some very broad conclusions may emerge from such studies, such as that the eye has a tendency to select "informative details" (cf. Antes, 1974), or "complex parts," or"certain body parts of portraits," such as the eyes. On the other extreme there are very careful studies on latency and extent of saccades toward a simple stimulus appearing singly on a homogeneous background (Robinson, 1968, 1973; Wheeless, Boynton, & Cohen, 1966). I have only been able to find a few studies in between, with controlled complexity and well-defined problems (e.g., Gould & Peeples, 1970; Levy-Schoen, 1974; O'Regan, 1975).

Let us take a closer look at what types of control process are held to exist for initiation, timing, and vector of eye saccades. The first one to mention is spatial sensory control. From information on almost any place on the retina an eye saccade may be initiated that brings this particular place in the visual field quickly into foveal vision. Although visual stimuli in eccentric vision have been studied most extensively, auditory and tactile stimuli may elicit similar semi-automatic orienting reactions. A second category may be called cognitive control, by which is meant that the eye may be directed towards places where useful information is expected. Such eye saccades may serve perceptual processing and directed search, and may develop into skilled routine movements, such as in reading. Cognitive control may also make use of spatial-sensory control (Hochberg, 1970). A somewhat different third category involves the influence of the general state of activity of the organism, such as alertness, drowsiness, and motivational factors. Perhaps these factors modulate the general level of eye activity rather than exert control on specific eye saccades.

A. Spatial Sensory Factors

Many detailed studies have been carried out on how the eye reaches a single object presented in eccentric vision (Robinson, 1968, 1973). Response latencies are variable, but they are usually between 200 and 300 msec, and seldom below 150 msec, values which are only slightly below manual response latencies (Roufs,

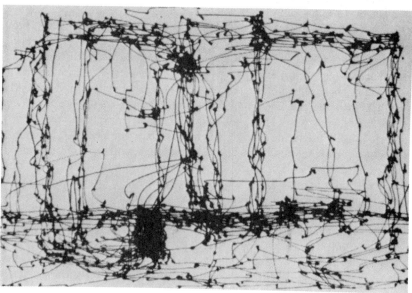

FIG. 12   Record of eye pauses and saccades during 10 min of free examination of the upper picture (Yarbus, 1967).

1974). Quite commonly, the "aimed" eye saccade itself falls somewhat short of the target and a second corrective saccade may follow very quickly, 100–200 msec after the first saccade (Becker, 1972, 1976; Prablanc & Jeannerod, 1975; Robinson, 1968, 1973). More generally, initiation and direction on the one hand and extent of the saccade on the other should perhaps be considered separately, since the extent of a normal or correction saccade can be influenced by newly appearing stimuli up to about 100 msec before its occurrence.

Thus, the timing and direction of eye saccades towards single eccentric targets can be determined by stimuli occurring 200–300 msec earlier, and saccade extent even by stimuli 100–200 msec earlier (Levy-Schoen, 1969). I draw particular attention to the fact that these latencies are about as long as eye pause durations, which, for the single stimuli considered, would mean that the saccade terminating an eye pause can just be under the influence of eccentric visual information picked up during the very same eye pause.

When two visual objects are presented simultaneously at different eccentricities, the one close to fixation tends to be fixated first, and the originally more eccentric one immediately thereafter. However, this is not a strict rule, and a closer view shows that preferences are different for different eccentric directions; for example, saccades to the left, right, or above may precede saccades to below, and saccades in the same direction as the previous one have some preference over saccades in the opposite direction (Levy-Schoen, 1974). This approach by way of multiple stimuli seems a promising one, because it explicitly considers processes of choice and of decision.

It would be useful to see if the approach could be extended towards understanding scan paths along several objects. Of course, after each saccade the retinal situation has changed and the new layout of the visual field should be considered together with the previous one, taking into account that the motor response latencies of the eyes are about as long as the eye pause durations. Scan paths along relatively simple line drawings have indeed been studied. Fixations generally stay close to the lines and concentrate on corners, and repeated scannings of a configuration may lead to fairly constant scan paths (Yarbus, 1967; Zusne & Michels, 1964; cf. Fig. 12). No detailed analyses of eye saccades and latencies in terms of visual information from consecutive retinal images have come to my knowledge, however. For relatively simple line configurations such as triangles or squares, the eye tends to fixate stationary near the center (Kaufman & Richards, 1969).

There has been some work in the literature on the stimulus attributes that provide eye guidance in eccentric vision. Generally the relatively simple "sensory" attributes, such as color or brightness seem to prevail over more complex ones such as shape (Gould & Peeples, 1970; Williams, 1967) and changes of stimuli are probably most effective. Functional visual fields for the various attributes may of course be different too, and these have not usually been considered. More generally, there is a difficulty in understanding visual eye guidance when choosing one visual object out of a few. Apart from there being more objects, a more complex visual analysis is also required, such as distinguishing a target from similar looking nontargets or recognizing digits or words. It is likely that complex visual tasks take more time and consequently have to lead to longer saccade latencies if saccades are controlled by the outcome of such complex visual analysis.

This should not make us despair about the applicability of conclusions from simple to more complex tasks. Two positive examples may be given from the field of reading. One is that the saccade towards the beginning of each next line of print falls short by a few letters and is often followed quickly by a corrective saccade quite similar to saccades to a single eccentric object. A second example is that the eyes easily skip blank areas present in a text (Abrams & Zuber, 1972), corresponding to the notion that the empty space has been detected a few eye pauses earlier. Both examples correspond closely to what would be expected from the more simple visual situations discussed earlier.

Spatial sensory and perceptual eye guidance is not restricted to vision. Auditory and tactile stimuli too may easily elicit eye saccades, and these seem to be well coordinated with the rather precise visual guidance. In particular, auditory guidance extends over the whole space around us, unlike vision, where the field is rather restricted. There seem to have been hardly any studies along these lines so far.

A different type of indirect influence on eye saccades by other senses proceeds by way of shifts of attention. For example, when attention is paid to auditory input, eye pauses tend to get longer (Gopher, 1973). Here too one would welcome more studies.

B. Cognitive Factors

If one knows where certain visual information can be found, one can direct one's eyes towards that direction. This has been rightly called cognitive guidance (Hochberg, 1970), since it is based on knowledge possessed by the subject. It is of course obvious that one has considerable freedom to move the eyes where one wishes and that instructions of many types can easily be carried out. These are very essential in daily situations, but it is difficult to assess their precise role both on their own and in connection with other types of eye guidance.

In itself, cognitive guidance is not restricted to the triggering of isolated saccades but may concern quite complex strategies. Scan paths may reflect problem solving strategies (Simon & Barenfeld, 1969) or perhaps even pattern recognition strategies (Baker & Loeb, 1973; Locher & Nodine, 1974; Noton & Stark, 1971), but there is also evidence to the contrary (Tversky, 1974). When often applied, these strategies may become rapid routine programs, as in reading and other skilled tasks.

In conclusion, since eye direction is also under voluntary control, there are as many levels of complexity in influencing them as there are in psychological functions in general. This is of course well known from daily life, where eye directions play their part in communication between humans, being taken to reflect alertness, evasiveness, interest, and deep thinking, to mention just a few. It is not surprising that the study of variations is often the most striking part of experiments on eye movements. The general availability of eye measuring equipment may well stimulate new insights not only into the control of eye saccades, but also into the many perceptual, cognitive, and attentional factors which they influence (Loftus, 1972; Tversky, 1974).

C. Eye Control in Reading

Let us now consider a few problems connected in this context with reading (Fig. 13), a subject which has recently been reviewed by Shebilske (1975). It may first be asked by what processes eye saccades are controlled and at what moment are

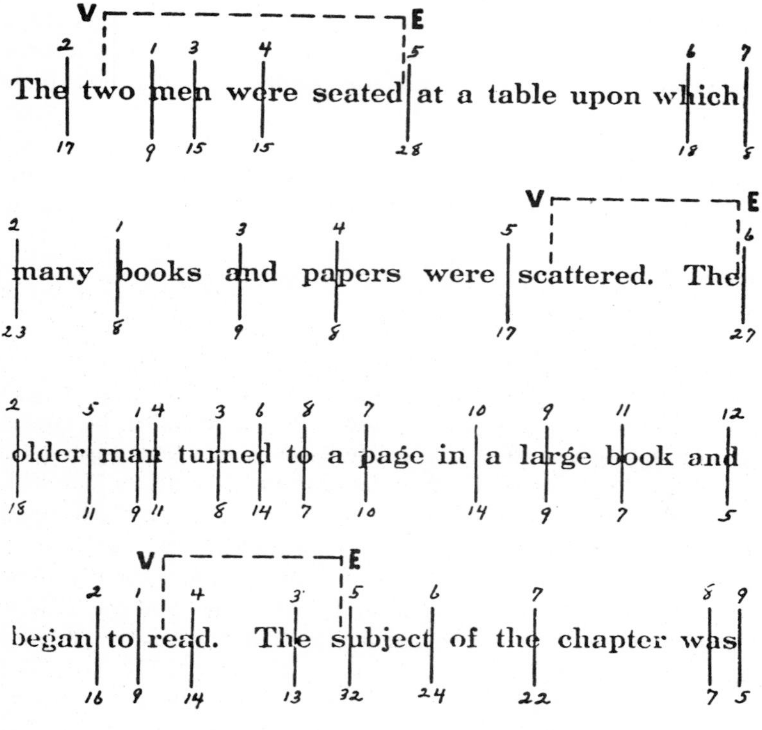

FIG. 13   Eye fixations during reading, as registered by Buswell (1920). Upper numbers indicate the order of the fixations as they occurred, lower number give fixation durations in units of 20 msec.

they triggered. One extreme view would be that timing and extent are strictly determined by a combination of foveal and eccentric vision on the one hand and text expectation on the other. For example, timing could be triggered by a successful foveal recognition, and saccade extent by a combination of eccentric vision and expectation. Each subsequent foveal input could then be optimally adapted to the needs of the reader. Indeed, the probability of fixating a certain letter depends somewhat on the length of the word to which the letter belongs (Rayner & McConkie, 1976), and short function words get relatively few fixations (O'Regan, 1975). An opposite, equally extreme view would be that each saccade is determined by a routine motor strategy and proceeds independently of current and coming text. The finding that, in reading, successive saccade extents and eye pauses are largely uncorrelated (Andriessen & de Voogd, 1973; Rayner & McConkie, 1976) can be combined with either view.

We mentioned earlier that a normal saccade latency to a single eccentric target amounts to 200–300 msec when the subject is well motivated. Fixation pauses are of the same duration, so there would just be sufficient time to take eccentric information into account. Because reading involves a more complex task requirement, this would seem too rigid a scheme for flexible reading. However, the extent of a saccade that has already been timed can still be influenced by visual information 100–200 msec before its execution. Thus, it seems just possible that in the right visual field, crude information such as word length or spacings between words can influence the extent of the next saccade. This conclusion comes close to the findings of Rayner from very sophisticated experiments in which eye saccades and retinal images were experimentally dissociated (Rayner, 1975, this volume). The timing of saccades is not critical, of course, if eccentric information can already be picked up one or more eye pauses earlier, which is for example the case with the end of each line of print.

As to control of eye pause duration, a plausible hypothesis is that the eye remains steady until recognition has satisfactorily been completed. There is a problem here because recognition latencies for words in vocal or manual reaction are of the order of at least 400 msec, a level that contrasts with the 200 msec or so for eye pauses in skilled reading. A possible solution is that only long eye pauses directly reflect processing time. Thus, in a letter search task, Gould and Carn (1973) found eye pauses of about 300 msec even after 30 days of training, and a similar finding has been reported for certain dot patterns (Gould, 1967; Gould & Dill, 1969). In pilot experiments, we found that the successive fixation of dots horizontally spaced at a few degrees visual angle produced eye pauses about 100 msec longer than in reading, probably as a result of a more precise aiming. On the other hand, in skilled routine tasks such as reading, eye pauses might be preprogrammed, and as a result, regressive saccades are necessary at the moment when recognition turns out to be insufficient, because the eye has by then already moved on. Of course, regressive saccades are a common occurrence in reading.

IV.   INTEGRATION OF SUCCESSIVE INFORMATION

Vision does not noticeably suffer from the fact that the retinal image shifts a few times per second. When exploring, searching or reading, the visual world and the text are experienced as continuous. Thus, there is a smooth integration into a stable perceptual frame of perceptual effects brought about by successive images. Because very little is known about the processes involved, this will be a short section.

Successive retinal images also affect each other's processing adversely. Such interference, usually referred to as masking, limits or hampers certain perceptual activations that otherwise would have continued after the disappearance of the retinal image. There is both forward and backward masking of complex visual stimuli, which brings about some deterioration of vision from each separate retinal image. In particular, backward masking may limit direct visual processing to a time interval of some 250 msec (Averbach & Coriell, 1961; Vanthoor & Eykman, 1973) and thus prevent certain overlaps. It seems unlikely at present that foveal recognition will be seriously hampered by backward masking from the subsequent image in eye pauses of 200 msec or more, but the data relate to relatively simple recognitions, and for eccentric vision such a statement would be premature, to say the least. The observation that the 250 msec over which backward masking is effective is about equal to the duration of normal eye pauses, makes one wonder whether the two are functionally related. It certainly seems possible that the absence of backward masking would aid recognition in cases in which the next retinal image is simply a homogeneous section of the field.

Backward masking is commonly ascribed to processes of erasure in a visual register, called iconic memory (see, for example, the recent exchange between Holding, 1975, and Coltheart, 1975). Now iconic memory cannot be as iconic as a true image or an afterimage. For all we know, no such image exists once the retina has been passed. What remain are several types of analyzed features of the stimulus, held together by ties so far unidentified. Any interactions between successive images should then be at least at the level of analyzed features. Since most of the work on backward masking concerns letters or other line configurations, the specifics of these interactions might easily have escaped attention.

However this may be, the very fact that successive retinal images are integrated into a stable frame is indicative of the fact that there can be no such thing as a complete erasure of visual information in an early stage of visual processing. The new information is combined with the earlier information, as is the case in apparent movement, where two images combine to form a single perception. The problem is what precisely is erased and what precisely survives; unfortunately, no specification can be given at present.

There are a few possible ways in which the central integration of information from successive images may be achieved, but there are few data to help us decide between them. A first hypothesis is that eye saccades are precisely reported to the visual processing system when they occur, and that, consequently, the

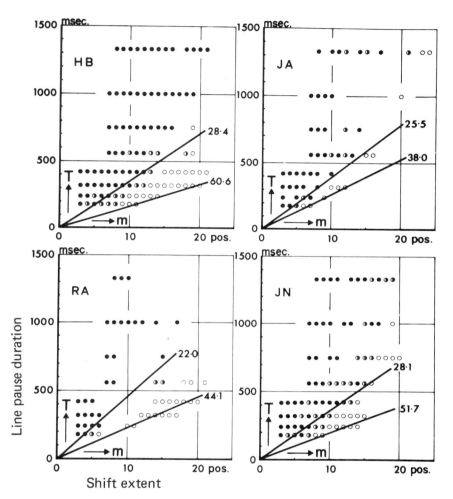

FIG. 14   Reading of normal text, where shifts of retinal images were experimentally controlled by regularly changing the display during stationary eye fixation. Dots indicate parameter values (image duration and shift extent) where reading turned out possible. The lines indicate maximum speeds attained of oral (●) and silent (o) reading, which are found to be similar to maximum speeds in ordinary viewing conditions. Four subjects (Bouma & de Voogd, 1974).

current spatial information is shifted over a similar vector, such that old and new data are combined in their proper spatial positions. Such a psychological counterpart of the physiological "corollary discharge" does exist for smooth eye movements, and its effect can be demonstrated by moving the eyes passively with one's fingers. This makes the visual world move, in contrast to the situation in which the eyes themselves follow a moving object.

A second hypothesis is that the information about the shift of the retinal image is derived from the visual information itself rather than from the eye motor system. The shifts would then be detected by comparing certain information in any two successive images and finding maximum correlations. Conspicuous objects could play special roles in such a procedure as reference points for the integration of the whole image.

A third hypothesis is that the shifts are not detected, either directly from the motor system or indirectly from a comparison of successive images. The hypothesis would be that there is an a priori stable internal representation of the visual (and auditory) world around us, which takes in information from successive images. This hypothesis comes close to the second one, except that the retinal shift does not play an explicit role and need not be the same for different objects.

There seems to be only very limited evidence to support either of the hypotheses. By providing retinal shifts in a part or in the whole of the visual field not accompanied by corresponding eye saccades, it should be possible to find out under what circumstances visual stability would depend on a match between eye saccade and retinal shift. For reading, such a situation has been attempted by training subjects to keep their eyes steady and have retinal images shift nevertheless a few times each second. Under those unnatural circumstances, both oral and silent reading proved possible with speeds quite similar to normal, natural reading (Bouma & de Voogd, 1974; see also Fig. 14). From this evidence it seems that in reading neither a precise control nor preinformation of eye saccades is necessary, although it does not exclude the possibility that saccades are precisely controlled in actual reading. The present sophisticated on-line monitoring of eye saccades, together with feedback to the presented visual information (McConkie & Rayner, 1975; Rayner, 1975), when generalized from the work on reading, should make it possible to solve problems of this type in subjectively natural viewing conditions.

When reading aloud, the voice has a certain delay relative to eye fixation, commonly referred to as eye-voice span, EVS (Buswell, 1920; Levin & Kaplan, 1970; Morton, 1964; see also Fig. 15). The notion refers to the information simultaneously present in the reader's mind. One may find it expressed in time units (0.5–1 sec), in distance units (10–20 letters), and in speech units (3–6 words), where the numbers are indicative values only. Its operational definition deserves a closer scrutiny than it has usually received — for example, parafoveal recognition and the presence or absence of backward masking have to be considered. Nevertheless, the EVS is some estimate of the information integrated. Studies that would try to analyze it in its possible components, such as word recognition, word ordering, and pronounciation, studies that monitor EVS as a function of text and pronounciation variables, and studies of EVS in special situations, such as in regressive eye saccades, would seem highly relevant to the present topic. Another estimate of how much information is dealt with simultaneously comes from an analysis of errors in speech and in oral reading, where

PLATE XXV

Continuous eye-voice relationship, Subject II₃₃

FIG. 15 Eye—voice span as measured by Buswell (1920). Upper lines indicate eye fixations as in Fig. 14, lower lines in italics represent the voice. Oblique lines connect eye fixations with the word simultaneously voiced.

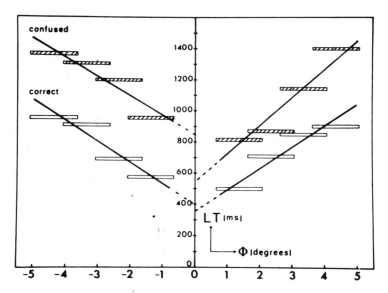

FIG. 16   Response latencies LT for visual word recognition as a function of retinal eccentricity ϕ. Upper data: incorrect responses; lower data: correct responses. Notice the steep slope of about 140 msec per degree. One degree corresponds to four letter positions (Schiepers, 1974).

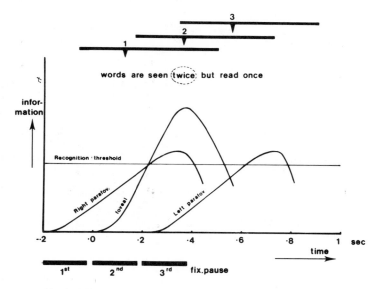

FIG. 17   Hypothetical scheme of timings in word recognition during reading, based on Fig. 16. Parafoveal recognition from the right visual half field is about simultaneous with foveal recognition of the same word from the next eye pause. The left visual half field can only contribute at a much later moment.

142

anticipations span distances up to some six syllables (Nooteboom & Cohen, 1975).

A final problem to be discussed is the timing of the stimulus information as it is picked up from successive eye pauses. Usually, it is tacitly assumed that eccentric vision needs only a marginally longer time for recognition than foveal vision. However, the evidence stems from latencies for simple tasks. It turns out that latencies for correct word recognition show a gradient of no less than 140 msec/deg (= 4 letters) (Schiepers, 1974; see also Fig. 16). If we consider a word appearing in two successive fixations, 8 letters apart, its first presentation at 2° eccentricity would take 280 msec more for recognition than its second, foveal, presentation, which would start some 250 msec later. Thus, the two successive presentations of the same word would lead to simultaneous recognition, and thus could easily be thought of as reinforcing each other (Fig. 17) on the assumption that backward masking does not interfere. It would offer an interesting confirmation of Rayner's suggestion that the information from two successive fixations is brought together in a single representation of the stimulus. It would also make it understandable why the left visual field generally contributes little in normal reading — its recognition would come no less than 400 msec after the earlier foveal recognition of the same word.

As a general conclusion, I would recommend that when considering recognition from successive retinal images, much more attention should be paid to timing than has been the case to date.

ACKNOWLEDGMENT

Thanks are due to several colleagues at IPO, who by their comments helped me to shape my thoughts as reflected in the paper. I wish to mention in particular Messrs. D. G. Bouwhuis, A. Cohen, and J. A. J. Roufs.

REFERENCES

Abrams, S. G., & Zuber, B. L. Some temporal characteristics of information processing during reading. *Reading Research Quarterly,* 1972, *8,* 40–51.

Andriessen, J. J., & Bouma, H. Just noticeable differences in slant of test lines as a function of retinal eccentricity. *IPO Annual Progress Report,* 1970, *5,* 110–113.

Andriessen, J. J., & Bouma, H. Eccentric vision: Adverse interactions between line segments. *Vision Research,* 1976, *16,* 71–78.

Andriessen, J. J., & de Voogd, A. H. Analysis of eye movement patterns in silent reading. *IPO Annual Progress Report,* 1973, *8,* 29–34.

Antes, J. R. The time course of picture viewing. *Journal of Experimental Psychology,* 1974, *103,* 62–70.

Averbach, E., & Coriell, A. S. Short-term memory in vision. *The Bell System Technical Journal,* 1961, *40,* 309–328.

Baker, M. A., & Loeb, M. Implications of measurement of eye fixations for a psychophysics of form perception. *Perception & Psychophysics,* 1973, *13,* 185–192.

Becker, W. The control of eye movements in the saccadic system. *Bibliotheca Ophtal-mologica*, 1972, *82*, 233–243.

Becker, W. Research note: Do correction saccades depend exclusively on retinal feedback? A note on the possible role of nonretinal feedback. *Vision Research*, 1976, *16*, 425–427.

Bjork, E., & Estes, W. K. Letter identification in relation to linguistic context and masking conditions. *Memory & Cognition*, 1973, *1*, 217–223.

Bloomfield, J. R. Visual search in complex fields: Size differences between target disk and surrounding discs. *Human Factors*, 1972, *14*, 139–148.

Bouma, H. Interaction effects in parafoveal letter recognition. *Nature*, 1970, *226*, 177–178.

Bouma, H. Visual interference in the parafoveal recognition of initial and final letters of words. *Vision Research*, 1973, *13*, 767–782.

Bouma, H., & Bouwhuis, D. Word recognition and letter recognition: Toward a quantitative theory for the recognition of words of three letters. *IPO Annual Progress Report*, 1975, *10*, 53–59.

Bouma, H., & de Voogd, A. H. On the control of eye saccades in reading. *Vision Research*, 1974, *14*, 273–284.

Bradshaw, J. L., Gates, A., & Patterson, K. Hemispheric differences in processing visual patterns. *Quarterly Journal of Experimental Psychology*, 1976, *28*, 667–681.

Buswell, G. T. An experimental study of the Eye–Voice Span in reading. Thesis. Chicago. *Supplementary Educational Monographs*, 1920, *17*.

Coltheart, M. Iconic Memory, a reply to Professor Holding. *Memory and Cognition*, 1975, *3*, 42–48.

Dichgans, J., & Bizzi, E. (Eds.). *Cerebral control of eye movements and motion perception*. Symposium Freiburg, Basel: Karger, 1972.

Engel, F. L. Visual conspicuity, directed attention and retinal locus. *Vision Research*, 1971, *11*, 563–576.

Engel, F. L. Visual conspicuity and selective background interference in eccentric vision. *Vision Research*, 1974, *14*, 459–471.

Engel, F. L. *Visual conspicuity as an external determinant of eye movements and selective attention*. Published thesis, Eindhoven, 1976.

Engel, F. L. Visual conspicuity, visual search and fixation tendencies of the eye. *Vision Research*, 1977, *17*, 95–108.

Eriksen, B. A., & Eriksen, C. W. Effects of noise letters upon the identification of a target letter in a nonsearch task. *Perception & Psychophysics*, 1974, *16*, 143–149.

Estes, W. K. Interactions of signal and background variables in visual processing. *Perception and Psychophysics*, 1972, *12*, 278–286.

Estes, W. K., Allmeyer, D. H., & Reder, S. M. Serial position functions for letter identification at brief and extended exposure durations. *Perception and Psychophysics*, 1976, *19*, 1–15.

Evarts, E. V. Precentral and postcentral cortical activity in association with visually triggered movement. *Journal of Neurophysiology*, 1974, *37*, 373–381.

Gopher, D. Eye movement patterns in selective listening tasks of focussed attention. *Perception and Psychophysics*, 1973, *14*, 259–264.

Gould, J. D. Pattern recognition and eye movement parameters. *Perception and Psychophysics*, 1967, *2*, 399–407.

Gould, J. D., & Carn, R. Visual search, complex backgrounds, mental counters and eye movements. *Perception and Psychophysics*, 1973, *14*, 125–132.

Gould, J. D., & Dill, A. B. Eye movement parameters and pattern discrimination. *Perception and Psychophysics*, 1969, *6*, 311–320.

Gould, J. D., & Peeples, D. R. Eye movements during visual search and discrimination of meaningless, symbol and object patterns. *Journal of Experimental Psychology*, 1970, *85*, 51–55.

le Grand, Y. *Form and space vision*. Indiana University Press, Bloomington, 1966.

Grindley, G. C., & Townsend, V. Voluntary attention in peripheral vision and its effects on acuity and differential thresholds. *Quarterly Journal of Experimental Psychology*, 1968, *20*, 11–19.

Grindley, G. C., & Townsend, V. Visual search without eye movement. *Quarterly Journal of Experimental Psychology*, 1970, *22*, 62–67.

Hochberg, J. Components of literacy: Speculations and exploratory research. In H. Levin & J. P. Williams (Eds.), *Basic studies on reading*. New York: Basic Books, 1970.

Holding, D. H. Sensory storage reconsidered + a rejoinder. *Memory and Cognition*, 1975, *3*, 31–41; 49–50.

Ikeda, M., & Takeuchi, T. Influence of foveal load on the functional visual field. *Perception & Psychophysics*, 1975, *18*, 255–260.

Johnston, D. M. Search performance as a function of peripheral acuity. *Human Factors*, 1965, *7*, 527–535.

Kaufman, L., & Richards, W. Spontaneous fixation tendencies for visual forms. *Perception and Psychophysics*, 1969, *5*, 85–88.

Krendel, E. S., & Wodinsky, J. Search in an unstructured field. *Journal of the Optical Society of America*, 1960, *50*, 562–568.

Levin, H., & Kaplan, E. L. Grammatical structure and reading. In H. Levin & J. P. Williams (Eds.), *Basic studies on reading*. New York: Basic Books, 1970.

Lévy-Schoen, A. Détermination et latence de la réponse oculomotrice a deux stimulus simultanés ou successifs selon leur excentricité relative. *l'Année Psychologique*, 1969, *69*, 373–392.

Lévy-Schoen, A. Le champ d'activité du regard: données experimentales. *l'Année Psychologique*, 1974, *74*, 43–66.

Locher, P. J., & Nodine, C. F. The role of scanpaths in the recognition of random shapes. *Perception & Psychophysics*, 1974, *15*, 308–314.

Loftus, G. R. Eye fixations and recognition memory for pictures. *Cognitive Psychology*, 1972, *3*, 525–551.

Mackworth, N. H. Visual noise causes tunnel vision. *Psychonomic Science*, 1965, *3*, 67–68.

Mackworth, N. H., & Morandi, A. J. The gaze selects informative details within pictures. *Perception and Psychophysics*, 1967, *2*, 547–552.

Massaro, D. W. Primary and secondary recognition in reading. In D. W. Massaro (Ed.), *Understanding language*. New York: Academic Press, 1975.

McConkie, G. W., & Rayner, K. The span of the effective stimulus during a fixation in reading. *Perception & Psychophysics*, 1975, *17*, 578–586.

Millodot, M., Johnson, C. A., Lamont, A., & Leibowitz, H. W. Effect of dioptrics on peripheral visual acuity. *Vision Research*, 1975, *15*, 1357–1362.

Mishkin, M., & Forgays, D. G. Word recognition as a function of retinal locus. *Journal of Experimental Psychology*, 1952, *43*, 43–48.

Morton, J. The effects of context upon speed of reading, eye movements and eye-voice span. *Quarterly Journal of Experimental Psychology*, 1964, *16*, 340–354.

Neisser, U. *Cognitive psychology*. New York: Appleton-Century-Crofts, 1967.

Nooteboom, S. G., & Cohen, A. Anticipation in speech production and its implications for perception. In A. Cohen & S. G. Nooteboom (Eds.), *Structure and process in speech perception*. Heidelberg: Springer, 1975.

Norman, D. A., & Bobrow, D. G. On data-limited and resource-limited processes. *Cognitive Psychology*, 1975, *7*, 44–64.

Noton, D., & Stark, L. Scanpaths in eye movements during pattern perception. *Science*, 1971, *171*, 308–311.

O'Regan, J. K. *Structural and contextual constraints on eye movements in reading.* Unpublished doctoral dissertation, University of Cambridge, 1975.

Prablanc, C., & Jeannerod, C. Corrective saccades: Dependence on retinal reafferent signals. *Vision Research*, 1975, *15*, 465–469.

Rayner, K. The perceptual span and peripheral cues in reading. *Cognitive Psychology*, 1975, *7*, 65–81.

Rayner, K., & McConkie, G. W. What guides a reader's eye movements? *Vision Research*, 1976, *16*, 829–837.

Robinson, D. A. The oculomotor control system: A review. *Proceedings of the IEEE*, 1968, *56*, 1032–1049.

Robinson, D. A. Models of the saccadic eye movement control system. *Kybernetik*, 1973, *14*, 71–83.

Roufs, J. A. J. Dynamic properties of vision – I. Experimental relationships between flicker and flash thresholds. *Vision Research*, 1972, *12*, 261–278.

Roufs, J. J. A. Dynamic properties of vision – V. Perception lag and reaction time in relation to flicker and flash thresholds. *Vision Research*, 1974, *14*, 853–869.

Sanders, A. F. *The selective process in the functional visual field.* Published thesis, Utrecht, 1963.

Schiepers, C. W. J. Length estimation of letter strings. *IPO Annual Progress Report*, 1973, *8*, 24–28.

Schiepers, C. W. J. Response latencies in parafoveal word recognition. *IPO Annual Progress Report*, 1974, *9*, 99–103.

Schiepers, C. W. J. Global attributes in visual word recognition. Part 1: Length perception of letter strings. *Vision Research*, 1976, *16*, 1343–1349.

Shebilske, W. Reading eye movements from an information-processing point of view. In D. W. Massaro (Ed.), *Understanding language.* New York: Academic Press, 1975.

Shiffrin, R. M., Gardner, G. T., & Allmeyer, D. H. On the degree of attention and capacity limitations in visual processing. *Perception and Psychophysics*, 1973, *14*, 231–236.

Shiffrin, R. M., McKay, D. P., & Shaffer, W. O. Attention to forty-nine spatial positions at once. *Journal of Experimental Psychology: Human Perception and Performance*, 1976, *2*, 14–22.

Simon, H. A., & Barenfeld, M. Information-processing analysis of perceptual processes in problem solving. *Psychological Review*, 1969, *76*, 473–483.

Sloan, L. L. The photopic acuity-luminance function with special reference to parafoveal vision. *Vision Research*, 1968, *8*, 901–911.

Smith, E. E., & Spoehr, K. T. The perception of printed English: A theoretical perspective. In B. H. Kantowitz (Ed.), *Human processing.* New York: Wiley, 1974.

Townsend, J. T., Taylor, S. G., & Brown, D. R. Lateral masking for letters with unlimited viewing time. *Perception & Psychophysics*, 1971, *10*, 375–378.

Tversky, B. Eye fixations in prediction of recognition and recall. *Memory and Cognition*, 1974, *2*, 275–278.

Vanthoor, F. L. J., & Eijkman, E. G. J. Time course of the iconic memory signal. *Acta Psychologica*, 1973, *37*, 79–85.

Wheeless, L. L., Boynton, R. M., & Cohen, G. H. Eye movement responses to step and pulse-step stimuli. *Journal of Optical Society of America*, 1966, *56*, 956–960.

Williams, L. G. The effects of target specification on objects fixated during visual search. *Acta Psychologica*, 1967, *27*, 355–360.

Wolford, G., & Hollingsworth, S. Lateral masking in visual information processing. *Perception and Psychophysics,* 1974, *16,* 315–320.

Woodworth, R. S. *Experimental psychology.* New York: Holt, 1938.

Woodworth, R. S., & Schlosberg, H. *Experimental psychology.* London: Methuen & Co., Ltd, 1954.

Yarbus, A. L. *Eye movements and vision.* New York: Plenum Press, 1967.

Zusne, L., & Michels, K. M. Nonrepresentational shapes and eye movements. *Perceptual and Motor Skills,* 1964, *18,* 11–20.

8

Foveal and Parafoveal Cues in Reading

Keith Rayner

Department of Psychology
University of Rochester
Rochester, New York, United States

ABSTRACT

Two experiments dealing with the use of parafoveal vision in reading and the integration of visual information over successive fixations in reading are presented. Eye position was monitored by a computer-based eye tracking system, and display changes on a cathode-ray tube were made when subjects initiated a saccade. A word was presented in parafoveal vision and subjects made an eye movement to the location of the word. As the eye was making the saccade, the computer replaced the word that was initially displayed with another word. In Experiment 1, subjects made a SAME-DIFFERENT response regarding the word that was present prior to the saccade and the word that was present after the eye movement. In Experiment 2, subjects were required to name the word that was presented after the saccade, and differences in naming times were compared as a function of the word that was present on the cathode-ray tube prior to the saccade. The results are discussed in terms of the types of visual information that readers could obtain at differing distances from the fovea, and how this information is integrated over two fixations.

I. INTRODUCTION

During reading, the horizontal line of text that falls on the retina can be divided into three areas: the foveal area, which subtends about 2° of visual angle around the reader's fixation point; the parafoveal area, which subtends about 10° of visual angle; and the peripheral area, which includes everything on the line of text beyond the parafoveal region. A recurring question in perceptual research related to reading has been to delineate the extent to which the parafoveal and the peripheral areas are useful to the skilled reader. Huey (1908) and Woodworth

(1938) devoted a considerable amount of attention to this question in their early reviews and summaries of the psychological research related to reading, and many current theories of reading (Gibson, 1969; Hochberg, 1970; McConkie & Rayner, 1976; Smith, 1971) suggest that these areas are important in reading.

There are two main ways in which information from parafoveal and peripheral vision may be useful to a reader. First, information from parafoveal and peripheral vision may be important in guiding a reader's eye movements (Rayner & McConkie, 1976). Second, information from these nonfoveal areas may facilitate reading because readers integrate visual information across separate fixations. The experiments reported here dealt with the latter issue of visual integration. Recently, Mackworth (1972) and McConkie and Rayner (1976) have presented theoretical discussions of how readers integrate information from successive fixations in reading. McConkie and Rayner suggested that during an eye fixation in reading, readers obtain visual information from parafoveal and peripheral vision and store this information in a temporary visual buffer, which they termed the Integrative Visual Buffer. The information stored in the Integrative Visual Buffer is then used as a base to which new information is added when that area (previously in parafoveal vision) is fixated. Thus, according to McConkie and Rayner, readers integrate information over successive fixations in reading so as to more rapidly process the text.

At the present time there is little data available concerning perceptual processes in reading that are specific enough to determine the extent to which readers do integrate visual information over two or more fixations. Studies by Rayner (1975) and McConkie and Rayner (1975) strongly indicated that readers obtain information such as word shape and terminal letters from parafoveal vision, and that this information facilitates reading. However, since both studies involved subjects in the task of reading connected discourse, the evidence is somewhat indirect because reading involves many subcomponent processes and semantic and syntactic constraints are involved. Also, it is important to make a distinction between information *obtained* from nonfoveal areas and information *used* from nonfoveal areas. Thus, while the Integrative Visual Buffer might hold a great deal of information about the page of text being read, the studies by Rayner (1975) and McConkie and Rayner (1975) indicated that information actually used fron nonfoveal areas is limited to words beginning less than 3° of visual angle from fixation.

The experiments to be described here were designed to determine more specifically how far into parafoveal vision readers are able to obtain certain visual characteristics of words, and how they are able to integrate this information over consecutive fixations. In order to investigate this question, the technique developed and described previously by Rayner (1975) was used. Subjects' eye movements were monitored with a computer-based eye tracking system, and display changes occurred as the subjects' eyes were in motion. Two similar tasks were used; one required a same-different judgment and the other was a voice-reaction time task. In the first task, subjects fixated on a fixation dot, and a word or letter string was flashed to parafoveal vision. Subjects were instructed to move their eyes (when they saw the word) and fixate directly on the initially presented stimulus. However, during the subject's saccade the computer often replaced the initially presented stimulus with a different word. The subject's task was to make a same-different judgment regarding the two stimuli. The theoretical assumption underlying the task was that a subject stored information in the Integrative Visual Buffer about the word displayed in parafoveal vision prior to moving his eye and would then use this information as a base to which he would add new information when his eye arrived at its destination. The more similar the initially displayed alternative was to the second word (and hence the information stored in the Integrative Visual Buffer), the greater would be the probability of responding "same." Any discrepancy between the information stored prior to the eye movement and the information present after the eye movement would lead to a higher probability of a "different" response.

The second task was very similar in some respects to the same-different task, except that the subject was instructed to name the second word as soon as he could identify it. Again, the assumption was that the subject would store visual information in the Integrative Visual Buffer prior to making his eye movement. If this stored information was consistent with the information available when his eye arrived at its destination, the naming time would be faster than if the information was inconsistent with the stored information.

II. EXPERIMENT 1

A. Materials and Apparatus

A set of 12 words with word frequency counts of 38–60 in the Kucera and Francis (1967) corpus were used as base words. The base word represented the final word that was presented to the subjects. There were four 5-letter words, four 6-letter words, and four 7-letter words. For each of the base words, five types of words or letter strings were prepared that could serve as the initially presented stimulus. The first alternative was a word (*W-Ident*) that was identical to the base word. Thus, for example, if the word *chest* was the base word, the *W-Ident* alternative would also be *chest*. The second alternative was a word (*chart*) that began and ended with the same letters and also maintained the overall word shape of the base word. This was called the *W-SL* alternative, since it was a word (*W*), and both word shape (*S*) and extreme letters (*L*) were identical to the base word. The remaining three alternatives were all nonwords (*N*) that varied in terms of graphic similarity to the base word. In the *N-SL* alternative (*chovt*), both extreme letters and word shape were maintained. All letters that differed between the *W-Ident* and *W-SL* alternatives were replaced by letters that were visually confusable with the letter in the *W-SL*. In addition, ascenders were always replaced by ascenders and descenders by descenders. The *N-L* alternative (*chfbt*) was formed by replacing every letter that differed in the *W-Ident* and *W-SL* alternatives with letters that were not visually confusable and did not share prominent distinctive features. For example, a descender was replaced by an ascender or a letter that did not extend above or below the line. Thus, the shape of the base word was altered in the *N-L* alternative, but the extreme letters remained the same. The *N-S* alternative (*ekovf*) was formed by replacing the initial and final letters that were identical in the *W* alternatives with letters that were visually confusable for those letters. Therefore, in this alternative the word shape was maintained but not the extreme letters. The confusable letters were determined from confusability matrices and groupings (Bouma, 1971; Hodge, 1962). Table 1 shows some examples of the base words and the five alternative words or letter strings. It should be noted that a relatively small set of base words was used in the experiment. This was done intentionally so that the subjects would be very familiar with the words. Thus, minimal differences between the parafoveally presented alternative and the base word should be more discernable (and lead to "different" responses) than if a large set of unfamiliar words was used.

The base words and their corresponding initially displayed alternatives appeared in lower-case type font on a VT-11 Cathode-Ray Tube (CRT) interfaced with a PDP-11 computer. The CRT had a P-31 phosphor, which had the characteristic that removing a character resulted in a drop to 1% of maximum brightness in .250 msec. The decay rate on the CRT was such that persistence from a character position that had been changed dropped below visual threshold within

TABLE 1
Examples of the Base Word and Different Alternatives
Used in Experiments 1 and 2

Base Word	W-Ident[a]	W-SL[b]	N-SL[c]	N-L[d]	N-S[e]
chest	chest	chart	chovt	chfbt	ekovf
phone	phone	plane	ptcne	psfne	qtcuc
author	author	antler	amttcr	abtsir	amttcv
palace	palace	police	pcluce	pyltce	qcluec
crossed	crossed	cruised	crmesed	crkesed	evmescb
granted	granted	guarded	gmavbed	gkabned	pmavbcb

[a]*W-Ident* = identical to the base word.

[b]*W-SL*   = a word with the same shape and end-letters as the base word.

[c]*N-SL*   = a nonword with the same shape and end-letters as the base word.

[d]*N-L*   = a nonword wtih the same end-letters as the base word.

[e]*N-S*   = a nonword with the same shape as the base word.

5 msec. The position of the eye was determined by an infrared sensing device placed in front of the subject's right eye. The signal from the eye movement monitor was sampled every msec by the computer, and so continuous on-line monitoring of eye position was possible. The characteristics of the display were such that three character spaces equaled 1° of visual angle. The subject's eye was 48.26 cm from the face of the CRT.

B. Procedure

When a subject arrived for the experiment, the purpose of the experiment was explained to him. The subject was then seated in an adjustable chair and the eye sensors were adjusted. Since the computer program in effect recalibrated each time the subject fixated on a target dot and only used the total range between a series of calibration dots when initiating a display change, it was not necessary to fix the head with a bite board. A forehead rest was used, and the subject was asked to try to keep his head still. After the eye sensors were appropriately adjusted, a series of five calibration dots appeared horizontally on the CRT. The subject was instructed to fixate each dot and push a button as he did. After the subject pushed the button the fifth time, a pattern showing where the computer had marked the subject's fixation appeared on the CRT. If the experimenter was unsatisfied with the pattern, the calibration dots appeared on the CRT again and the subject recalibrated. When the experimenter was satisfied that the pattern was reasonable, and allowed sufficient range between fixation points, he pushed a button that resulted in the pattern leaving the CRT, and a fixation dot appeared in the center of the screen. The subject then fixated the dot and pushed the button again. If he was fixated within one-half a character position of the dot, an initially displayed alternative appeared beginning either 1°, 3°, or 5° to the right of fixation. The subject was instructed to move his eyes to the location of the word and make a same-different judgment. As soon as the subject's eye moved one character space to the right of fixation, the computer immediately replaced the initially displayed word or letter string with the base word. Since the lag in the sensors was less than 4 msec and the decay rate of the CRT was less than 5 msec, the display change was made completely during the saccade. However, it is true that the eye often drifts during a fixation and if the amount of drift were greater than one character space, the computer would initiate the change. To overcome this problem, any trial in which the latency of the saccade was less than 100 msec and/or any trial in which the saccadic movement was completed in less than 15 msec was automatically repeated at the end of the series. Pilot work with the apparatus indicated that these software constraints were highly effective, and any trial in which the subject actually saw the display change occur was thus repeated later in the sequence. If the subject was not fixated within a one-half character space of the fixation dot when he pushed the button, the computer would make a loud beeping noise, after which the subject refixated and pushed the button again. The subjects found that a block of trials went most satisfactorily when they fixated generally on the dot rather than focusing all attention on the dot. Each subject went through 288 trials; on half of the trials "same" responses were correct. The subjects were specifically told that half of the trials were "different" and asked to keep that in mind when responding and to try to make about half of their responses "different."

When the subject made his same-different judgment, the experimenter pushed one button for same responses and another button for different responses. This information was stored in the computer for each trial, along with the amount of time that the intially displayed word appeared on the CRT (the reaction time of the eye) and the amount of time for the saccadic movement. The 288 trials were divided into 8 blocks of 36 trials, and each of eight subjects saw the blocks in a different order. Prior to the experimental trials, 30 warm-up trials were given. All eight subjects had normal uncorrected vision.

C. Results

For each subject, a hit rate at each of the visual angles was computed as well as the false alarm rate for each of the "different" alternatives. The respective hit rates and false alarm rates at each visual angle were then converted to a d' score. The d' score was used as the dependent measure in a 3 (visual angle) x 4 (initially displayed alternative: W-SL, N-SL, N-L, and N-S) repeated measures analysis of variance. There was a significant main effect of visual angle ($F(2, 14) = 6.99$, $p < .008$) in which the d' score was higher for words beginning 1° from fixation (1.35) than for words beginning 3° (.71) or 5° (.39) from fixation (Newman-Keuls test, $p < .05$). There was also a significant main effect of initially displayed alternatives ($F(3, 21) = 12.41, p < .0002$), and a Newman-Keuls test indicated that the means for the two SL conditions (.51 for W and .55 for N) differed from the N-L (1.01) and N-S (1.20) alternatives ($p < .01$). There was also a significant Visual Angle x Initially Displayed Alternative interaction ($F(6, 42) = 390, p < .004$) which can be observed in Fig. 1. Planned comparisons revealed that the nature of the interaction was that there were no differences between the alternatives at 5° whereas the SL conditions resulted in lower d' scores (i.e., discriminations were more difficult) closer to fixation than the N-L and N-S conditions ($F(1, 42) = 43.56, p < .001$). The overall hit rates for stimuli beginning 1°, 3°, and 5° from fixation were .86, .77, and .76, respectively. The corresponding false alarm rates were .45, .55, and .60.

In addition to the d' scores, it was also possible to analyze data on eye movements. On each trial, the computer recorded the reaction time of the eye in moving to the location of the initially presented stimulus. These data were subjected to a 3 (visual angle) x 2 (same vs. different) repeated measures analysis of variance. The latter variable refers to conditions in which the base word was replaced by itself (W-$Ident$ was initially displayed) versus conditions in which there was a change between the initially displayed alternative and the base word. There was

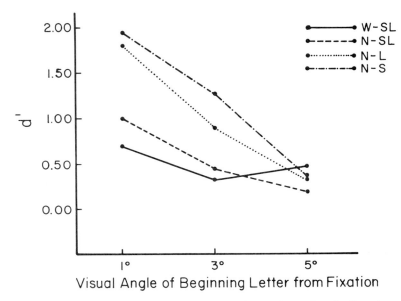

FIG. 1.   d′ scores at each visual angle for the different alternatives in Experiment 1.

no effect ($F < 1$) of this variable indicating that the nature of the initially displayed alternative did not affect latency for the eye movement. There was a
significant main effect of visual angle ($F(2, 14) = 7.67, p < .006$), and a Newman-
Keuls test ($p < .01$) indicated that the latency for a 5° movment (211 msec) was
longer than for 1° (185 msec) or 3° (186 msec) movements. The interaction was
nonsignificant ($p < .20$). The overall mean latency was 194 msec, and the means
of the 8 subjects ranged form 140 msec to 249 msec. A correlation between the
latency for the eye movement and accuracy of response was computed for each
subject. All of the correlations were low; the mean correlation was .02, suggesting
that the amount of information obtained about the initially displayed alternative
did not vary as a function of the duration of the presaccadic fixation.

The mean percentage of trials that had to be repeated due to the subject
seeing the change take place as a result of drifts was 17.6%, with a range across
subjects of 1%–35%. Finally, the mean time to execute a saccade of 1°, 3°, and
5° was 22 msec, 30 msec, and 34 msec, respectively.

D. Discussion

The results of Experiment 1 indicated that information about word shape and
terminal letters was acquired from words beginning 1° and 3° of visual angle from
fixation. Thus, there were differences in the ability to discriminate differences
among alternatives that bore varying degrees of similarity to the base word when
they began 3° or less from fixation; but discrimination performance decreased

as the stimuli began further from fixation so that by 5° of visual angle there were no differences between alternatives. Although subjects were specifically told that half of the time different responses were correct and were asked to adjust their responses accordingly, seven of the eight subjects responded "same" far more frequently than "different." The eighth subject responded "different" a high proportion of the time. All of the subjects reported that the task was extremely difficult and they were uncertain of the basis for their response. It was considerably easier for subjects to make a judgment when they actually saw a display change occur. Of course, such conditions were eliminated from the data analysis. It is worth noting that the criterion used for repeating a trial resulted in many more repeats than the number of times subjects indicated that they saw the change. Even on many of the trials that were eliminated because they were repeated, subjects responded "same."

The monitoring of eye movements resulted in data concerning the time relations in the experiment. Over all conditions in the experiment, the mean amount of time that the initially displayed alternative was physically present on the CRT was 194 msec. This value is not far different from mean fixation durations often found in reading (Rayner & McConkie, 1976). Thus, the amount of time that the initially displayed alternative could be processed on the retina approximated the lower range of reading fixation durations. The importance of the significant effect for longer saccade latency for stimuli beginning 5° from fixation than for stimuli beginning closer to fixation is unclear, because in Experiment 2 a different pattern was obtained.

Finally, at first glance, the results of Experiment 1 seem to provide support for Rayner's (1975) finding that semantic processing requires foveal or near-foveal vision. There was no difference between the W-SL and N-SL conditions when the stimuli began 1° from fixation. If semantic or lexical information were being extracted from words beginning 1° from fixation, one could reasonably expect that the additional information available from words in the W-SL condition would lead to a higher d' score than the N-SL condition. The results showed no differences. However, the nature of the same-different task may have made it possible for the subjects to make their responses purely on the basis of a visual discrimination. A strategy of responding in terms of surface visual properties alone, rather than in terms of lexical identity, would lead to an underestimation of information obtained at the lexical level. Therefore, in Experiment 2 an attempt was made to approximate more closely the reading situation by having the subjects name the base word.

III. EXPERIMENT 2

A. Materials and Apparatus

The materials and apparatus were identical to Experiment 1, except that 30 base words and their corresponding initially displayed alternatives were used. Again, the words had word frequency counts of 38—60 in the Kucera and Francis

(1967) corpus. The 30 words were equally divided between 5-, 6-, and 7-letter words.

B. Procedure

The procedure was analogous to Experiment 1, except that subjects were told to name the base word as rapidly as they could. In addition, words were presented beginning or ending 1°, 3°, or 5° to the left or right of fixation. Thus, in the experiment, the subject fixated on the fixation dot, pushed the button as he did so, and a word or letter string appeared at one of the six locations. The subject then moved his eye to the location of the initially displayed word. As soon as his eye moved one character position to the left or right of fixation, the computer replaced the initially displayed alternative with the base word. A throat-activated microphone was fastened around the subject's throat, and the computer recorded the naming time for each stimulus presentation. Altogether, there were 900 trials in the experiment which resulted from the combination of six locations in which the initially displayed alternatives and base words appeared, five conditions (W-Ident, W-SL, N-SL, N-L, and N-S), and 30 base words. The 900 trials were broken into 30 trials and within each block each word occurred once. Each condition occurred once at each visual angle (5°, 3°, and 1° left and right of fixation). Six subjects participated in the experiment. For reasons unrelated to the experiment, data were obtained on only half of the trials for two of the subjects. The data were collected in four or five 1–1½ hour sessions. Prior to each session, subjects were given a block of 30 warmup trials.

C. Results

Figure 2 shows the major results from Experiment 2. A 3 (visual angle) x 2 (left vs. right) x 5 (condition: W-Ident, W-SL, N-SL, N-L, N-S) analysis of variance on the time to name the base word after the eye movement yielded significant main effects of conditions ($F(4, 20) = 18.12, p < .0001$) and of visual angle ($F(2, 10) = 27.40, p < .001$). A Newman-Keuls test on the main effect of conditions indicated that naming time for the W-Ident condition (467.3 msec) was faster than the naming time for the N-SL condition (479.9), which was faster than the W-SL condition (490.7) and the N-L condition (493.6), which did not differ from each other ($p < .05$). The N-S condition (505.6) resulted in the slowest naming time of all conditions. A Newman-Keuls test on the main effect of visual angle indicated that all three visual angles differed significantly from each other ($p < .05$). The mean times for naming alternatives beginning 1°, 3°, and 5° from fixation was 471.5 msec, 489.6 msec, and 501.8 msec, respectively. There was also a significant interaction of Condition x Visual Angle ($F(8, 40) = 4.99, p < .001$). A planned comparison test indicated that the W-Ident and the N-SL condition differed significantly from the other three conditions at 1° and 3°, but at 5° there were no differences among conditions ($F(1, 40) = 17.00, p < .01$).

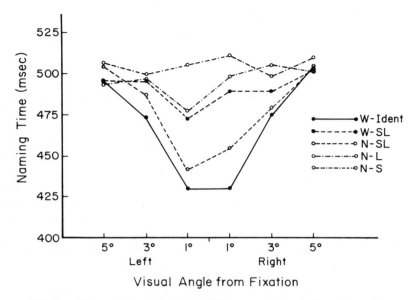

FIG. 2.   Mean naming times for the different conditions in Experiment 2.

In addition to the analysis on naming time after the eye movement, an analysis was carried out in which the dependent variable was the total time from when the initially displayed alternative appeared on the CRT until the subject named the base word. This dependent measure thus includes reaction time for the saccade, as well as time to execute the saccade. The overall results of this analysis were identical to the analysis which involved only naming time after the saccade.

Analysis of the eye movement data indicated that there were no differences in reaction time to move the eye as a function of the initially displayed alternative. There was, however, a significant main effect of visual angle ($F(2, 10) =$ 9.91, $p < .01$) and the reaction time for a 3° or 5° saccade (179 msec and 180 msec) was faster than a 1° eye movement (188 msec). This result is contradictory to the results of Experiment 1 in which it was found that saccadic latency was longer for stimuli beginning 5° from fixation than for stimuli beginning 1° or 3° from fixation. The mean time to execute a saccade of 1°, 3°, and 5° was 23 msec, 30 msec, and 35 msec, respectively. Finally, it is interesting that the only significant effect of left vs. right was for saccade time ($F(1, 5) = 24.15, p < .01$) and saccades to the right of fixation were carried out faster (28 msec) than those to the left (31 msec). Since the initial letters of words provides a great deal of information about a word, this difference is most likely due to the fact that the distance a saccade would have to cover to bring the initial part of a word onto the fovea would be greater for words presented to the left of fixation than for words presented to the right of fixation.

D. Discussion

The results of Experiment 2 are fairly consistent with the results from Experiment 1. In both experiments, performance decreased with increasing visual angle, so that there were no differences at 5° of visual angle as a function of the initially displayed alternatives. One major difference between the two experiments was the lack of a difference between the *W-SL* condition and the *N-SL* condition in Experiment 1 and differences between these conditions in Experiment 2. This difference appears to be due to the fact that in Experiment 1 responses could be made on the basis of a visual discrimination. Since the *W-SL* and *N-SL* were very similar in visual appearance there were no differences in Experiment 1, while in Experiment 2, where a naming reponse was required, there were differences between these conditions for words beginning 1° or 3° from visual angle. Thus, we can conclude that the longer naming times for the *W-SL* condition resulted from the additional information available in words since this condition involved initially presenting a word. Subjects are thus capable of lexical or semantic information from words beginning 1° and sometimes 3° from fixation.

It is worth mentioning at this point that there were individual differences in both of the experiments. For about half of the subjects in Experiment 2, when words were presented at 3° of visual angle from fixation, there were virtually no differences between the *W-Ident, W-SL,* and *N-SL* conditions. However, for the other half of the subjects the *W-SL* resulted in longer naming times at 3°. Likewise, in Experiment 1 some of the subjects showed very little difference between alternatives initially presented 3° from fixation.

Generally, the results from the experiments presented here suggest that readers are able to obtain semantic and visual information slightly further from fixation than Rayner (1975) reported in a reading task. This difference is most likely due to task differences and the fact that the stimulus is less complex in the present task and hence there is not interference from surrounding letters. It is also probable that the differences in saccadic latency found in Experiment 1 and Experiment 2 are attributable to task demands.

IV. GENERAL DISCUSSION

The results of the experiments presented here suggest that information that is useful to the reader in the Integrative Visual Buffer varies as a function of the distance from the fovea. For words beginning as far as 3° from fixation, information is available about the initial letters and word shape. On occasion, as Experiment 2 indicated, lexical information may be obtained for words beginning 3° from fixation. However, Rayner (1975) has found during reading, where the stimulus pattern is more complex and where there is probably more interference from surrounding letters, that subjects obtain lexical or semantic information for words falling on the fovea and do not obtain such information from parafoveal vision. The fact that the normal reader's average saccade length is about 2° (or 8 character spaces) supports this argument (cf., Rayner & McConkie, 1976). Thus, it would appear that during a fixation in reading the reader processes the semantic information around the fixation point. At the same time, visual information from parafoveal vision is stored in the Integrative Visual Buffer and used as a base to which the reader adds new information when his eye moves to that area.

It is important to note that word shape as it was conceptualized in the present studies is more than simply "word outline." The two conditions (*SL* conditions) for which changes were difficult to discriminate at 1° and 3° in Experiment 1 were formed by leaving the terminal letters intact and replacing medial letters with letters that had some visual similarity. Thus, the information that the subjects were able to utilize from the Integrative Visual Buffer apparently involved feature information about the words. In pilot experiments, we have found that more gross types of visual information, such as word length, are available for words beginning as much as 5° from fixation (Rayner, 1976). The finding that word length information is obtained further from fixation than word shape information is consistent with previous results obtained by McConkie and Rayner (1975) in a reading task.

During reading, there must be a certain amount of masking that occurs at the lower perceptual levels. When the eye moves and fixates a new location, the new stimulus pattern overrides the retinal activity produced by the prior fixation. However, as the data from the present experiments suggest, at a higher level in the perceptual processing system the visual information from the two fixations is brought together into a single representation of the stimulus. This integration is possible only because there is sufficient commonality of visual pattern that they can be justified with one another. If the visual patterns from the two fixations are entirely different (as was the case under certain conditions in the present experiments), then masking occurs at the higher level as well as the lower perceptual level. Thus, higher *d'* scores in Experiment 1 and longer naming times in Experiment 2 for the *N-L* and *N-S* alternatives beginning 1° and 3° from fixation can be attributed to masking in the Integrative Visual Buffer leading subjects to respond "different" more frequently and take longer to name the base word. The longer naming times presumably resulted from the fact that the featural information the subject stored in the Buffer about the word prior to his saccade (and began using as a base to which he added new information after the saccade) was inconsistent with the new information that the reader began processing after the eye movement. Thus, processing would have to start anew for that particular word.

In summary, it should be emphasized that subjects in the present experiments were not consciously aware of seeing one stimulus prior to the saccade and then seeing another present after the eye movement. Thus, the results which were obtained were evidently due to preconscious processes. Finally, the results of the experiments presented here begin to place upper bounds on the extent to which certain types of visual information can be integrated over successive fixations by normal, skilled readers.

ACKNOWLEDGMENTS

The research reported in this paper was supported by Grant BNS76-05017 from the National Science Foundation and Grant MH 24241-02 from the National Institute of Mental Health. The author would like to acknowledge the valuable assistance of George W. McConkie and Scott Outlaw and to thank Ralph Norman Haber, George W. McConkie, and Carla J. Posnansky for comments made on an earlier version of this paper.

REFERENCES

Bouma, H. Visual recognition of isolated lower-case letters. *Vision Research,* 1971, *11,* 459–474.

Gibson, E. J. *Principles of perceptual learning and development.* New York: Appleton-Century-Crofts, 1969.

Hochberg, J. Components of literacy: Speculations and exploratory research. In H. Levin & J. P. Williams (Eds.), *Basic studies on reading.* New York: Basic Books, Inc., 1970.

Hodge, D. C. Legibility of a uniform-stroke width alphabet: 1. Relative legibility of upper and lower-case letters. *Journal of Engineering Psychology,* 1961, *1,* 34–36.

Huey, E. G. *The psychology and pedagogy of reading.* New York: Macmillan, 1908.

Kucera, H., & Francis, W. N. *Computational analysis of present-day American English.* Providence, Rhode Island: Brown University Press, 1967.

Mackworth, J. F. Some models of the reading process: Learners and skilled readers. *Reading Research Quarterly,* 1972, *7,* 701–733.

McConkie, G. W., & Rayner, K. The span of the effective stimulus during a fixation in reading. *Perception and Psychophysics,* 1975, *17,* 578–586.

McConkie, G. W., & Rayner, K. Identifying the span of the effective stimulus in reading: Literature review and theories of reading. In H. Singer & R. B. Ruddell (Eds.), *Theoretical models and processes of reading* (2nd ed.), Newark, Del.: International Reading Association, 1976.

Rayner, K. The perceptual span and peripheral cues in reading. *Cognitive Psychology,* 1975, *7,* 65–81.

Rayner, K. *On the integration of information over successive fixations in reading.* Paper presented at the XXI International Congress of Psychology, Paris, France, July 1976.

Rayner, K., & McConkie, G. W. What guides a reader's eye movements? *Vision Research,* 1976, *16,* 829–837.

Smith, F. *Understanding reading.* New York: Holt, Rinehart, & Winston, Inc., 1971.

Woodworth, R. S. *Experimental psychology.* New York: Henry Holt, 1938.

9 Non-Analytic Correspondences and Pattern in Word Pronunciation

Lee R. Brooks

McMaster University
Hamilton, Ontario, Canada

ABSTRACT

In this chapter the claim is made that the presence of an alphabetic spelling system can help a person learn to pronounce a set of words even though the person does not know, in any sense of the word, which letters correspond to which segments of associated sound. This is possible because, on the average, in an alphabetic spelling system words that look alike sound alike. Further, it is possible to increase the effect of this visual similarity by enhancing the patterns formed by words.

I. INTRODUCTION

In this chapter I present some conjectures concerning the development of fluency in reading words aloud and suggest how altering visual patterning might help in the development of this skill. My argument is that there are some possibilities about what is happening in the acquisition of fluent pronunciation that have not received sufficient consideration. I intend to assert only that these possibilities deserve consideration rather than that they are highly probable.

A. The Role of an Alphabet

Discussions of fluent word identification have often been cast in terms of two extreme positions: complete reliance on specific-stimulus learning, or complete reliance on rules (e.g., Huey, 1908; Rozin & Gleitman, 1977). Theories that have claimed that words or morphemes are accessed primarily by nonphonological information, such as visual features or letter groups, have also usually admitted that some amount of specific learning must be done for each word; that is, the reader must learn to specify each word that he knows in terms of nonphonological units as well as in the familiar acoustic features. Although it is not strictly necessary, this position has usually carried the implication that each word must be experienced several times in its visual form in order to allow the learning of the new address.

This specific-stimulus argument typically has allowed the spelling system to affect the rate of learning of new items only by sequential and positional redundancy (e.g., F. Smith, 1971; see also Mason & Katz, 1976, for a recent attempt to analyze the effectiveness of different types of redundancy). Since speech sounds in any natural language do not occur in all possible sequences or posidtions within a word, the symbols in an alphabetic system do not either. One way this redundancy could affect the learning of new items is by allowing the new nonphonological address to be written in terms of letter groups rather than as individual letters. Since it would take fewer letter groups than letters to specify a given word, it is possible that the learning of a nonphonological address would proceed faster for letter groups than for separate letters.

The other extreme position is that the new reader uses either implicit or explicit knowledge of the rules of spelling to convert the visual form of a word into a phonological form so that he can continue to use the old addresses that were acquired when learning speech. A reader who is accomplished at this translation would be able to read rapidly words that were in his spoken vocabulary but that he has not seen before. Indeed, this hypothesized immediate transfer to new items has been one of the leading a priori arguments for the notion that efficient acquisition of reading requires a heavy dependence on phonological translation. Such an argument is particularly clear in discussions of the ease of learning to read English when compared to Chinese (Gleitman & Rozin, 1977) and the disadvantage of English in the early stages of reading when compared to alphabetic systems with simpler phonological correspondences.

The two traditional extremes then, are that the alphabetic spelling system affects the rate of learning to read new words because of stimulus redundancy or because of either explicit or implicit knowledge of the rules of pronunciation. This latter type of knowledge will be referred to in this paper as analytic in the sense that particular segments of the stimulus are associated by the learner with particular segments of the response. What we will entertain in the following section is that there is another, nonanalytic, way in which the spelling system could affect the rate of learning to pronounce new words.

B.   Nonanalytic Correspondence

One of the consequences of an alphabetic system is that within broad limits words that look alike sound alike. Possibly the correspondence between the overall similarity of the stimuli and the overall similarity of the responses is important for the development of fluent word identification. Let us imagine that word stimuli were arrayed in a conceptual space according to their similarity to one another. The more visually similar two words are to one another the closer together they would be. Responses could be arrayed into a space that was scaled according to phonological similarity. In an alphabetic system there should be a general correspondence between the two spaces.

One of the ways that such a correspondence could affect the speed of word identification and the speed of learning a new address is through a more *efficient memory search*. Knowing the location of the stimulus would allow the prediction of the general area in the response space in which the response should be found. With this general location as a retrieval cue, there would presumably be less to learn for each new item before it could be efficiently retrieved. Notice that this does not necessarily mean that the learner directly uses or even knows the spelling rules. In other areas of learning we expect that similarity correspondences between two domains can be exploited without correspondences existing between the components of one domain and the components of another. For example, if all collies had Scottish names and all dachshunds had German names, we would expect that this relation would help learning the names of new collies and dachshunds without there being any relation between parts of the names and parts of the dogs. Words conceivably could be treated in a comparably holistic manner.

A second way in which a correspondence between similarity of stimuli and similarity of responses could be effective is through *indirect component correspondence*. When the general properties of the stimulus indicate the region of the response space in which the desired response would be found, we could imagine that all of the responses in the area would be partially activated. The responses that are close to the desired response will have many components in common with that response and with each other. By some process of summation, the common components of the neighboring responses could cue the components of the desired response without directly using any relation between components of the stimulus and components of the response. As an extreme example, consider the situation shown in Fig. 1. Assume that the stimulus in the box at the top is presented and the task is to identify the word it represents. The unknown word activates the four responses REND, REST, RANT, and BENT as a result of it resembling the stimuli for those four responses in three out of the four elements of each stimulus. Looking only at the four responses that were activated because of stimulus generalization, we could imagine that, because of relative frequency of the response components, an R would be the most activated component in the first position, an E in the second, N in the third, and T in the fourth, for an overall guess of RENT. Notice that the response RENT could be deduced without even knowing which of the stimulus elements corresponded to the first phoneme of the response. By working back from the responses to the stimuli, one could deduce that the first letter of the code must

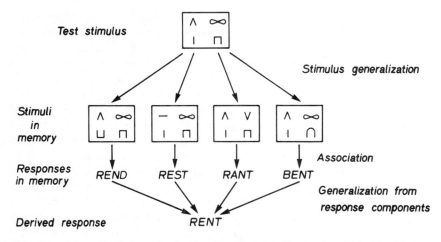

FIG. 1.   A hypothetical mechanism in which an unfamiliar word could be identified non-analytically; that is, without any knowledge of which element of the stimulus signalled which component of the response.

be in the bottom right-hand corner with the remaining letters being read counter-clockwise, but this is not crucial to the operation of this mechanism. Notice also that similarity was assessed by counting the number of stimulus elements that two stimuli have in common. "Holistic" or "nonanalytic" in this case refers to the fact that the stimulus is related to the response on the basis of a single overall similarity measure, rather than by a series of individual correspondences between stimulus components and response components. But the similarity measure itself could be determined by the sum of discrete portions of the stimulus or by some larger feature, such as overall shape. I suspect that this construal of words like "holistic," "global," or "nonanalytic" could be useful in a variety of developmental contexts.

The example in Fig. 1 is meant solely to illustrate the notion that orthographic rules can cue aspects of the response indirectly. Some unlikely assumptions are implied in this example, but they are not crucial to the mechanism. For instance, the response components could also be considered to be two-letter combinations, phonemes, or combinations of phonemes. Further, in this example the desired response was completely deduced by having all of the components of that response activated, and to achieve this it was necessary to assume some form of summation of components. But most of the components would be correct if only one of the four analogous responses was activated. This could still facilitate the retrieval of the desired response if we assume that the cost of the incorrect component was minimal, either because of some limited analytic knowledge (e.g., knowledge of the sounds associated with initial, regular consonants) or because of a concurrent retrieval process based on direct access from visual features.

Because we know the spelling rules of our language, we are tempted to assume that they must be acting analytically; that is, with particular components of the stimulus activating particular components of the response. But this need not be the only way that rules can act either in reading or in concept formation (Brooks, 1978). Instead they could be exerting an effect by insuring the correspondences between overall similarities that were discussed in this section. Although it seems highly unlikely that rules would be acting solely in this nonanalytic fashion even at fluency, we might still consider such a mechanism in at least a supporting role.

II.   A DEMONSTRATION OF IMPLICIT LEARNING

Let us now examine an experiment in which rules exert an effect under conditions in which the subject is unaware of any analytic, component-to-component correspondences. The stimulus materials for this experiment are essentially those used in a previous experiment on fluency upon which Jonathan Baron and I collaborated (Brooks, 1977; Baron, 1977). A quick description of this previous experiment is necessary to provide a background for the current study. Our objective was to compare the rate of learning to pronounce a short list of words for which there was an alphabet with a list for which there was not. As is shown in Fig. 2, we used two short alphabets of artificial symbols that correspond to letters of the English alphabet. Two six-word lists were constructed, one list using the symbols from one of the alphabets and the other list using the symbols from the other alphabet. The responses were then scrambled with respect to the stimuli for one of the lists, which resulted in one of the lists having a functional alphabet and the other list not, but with both lists having matched stimuli and responses. Each subject was taught to translate one of these artificial alphabets into the corresponding English letter name and was then shown the list of six words printed in those letters and asked to read them out loud. After 20 trials of reading these six words presented in various orders, the subject was presented with the other list of six words written in the other set of symbols. The subject was told that there was no alphabet that would work for this list, and that he would be allowed two minutes in which to associate the stimuli in this list with an arbitrary set of responses. After this study period the subject was asked to read out the six words for 20 trials in which the words were presented in various orders. Successive 20-trial blocks alternated between the two lists.

Our interest in this experiment was in whether the paired-associate and the alphabetic conditions would converge to a common rate of word identification or whether there would be a long-term advantage for the alphabet. One might expect convergence either because response execution speed would eventually set a floor on the rate of pronouncing or because with a lot of practice the six words in the alphabetic list would simply be identified as six overall patterns

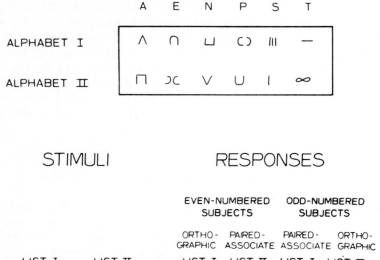

FIG. 2. The stimuli used for an experiment on the effect of an alphabet of which the learners were unaware. In this set of material, the alphabetic responses are related to the stimuli when they are read in reversed order.

or six sets of minimal discriminative features, thus eliminating any effective difference from the paired-associate list. In fact, the alphabetic list was pronounced more rapidly even after 400 trials in this experiment, after 300 trials in a follow-up to this experiment (Brooks, 1977), and after three months of practice in an extension reported by Glenn and Baron (1975). Clearly, the alphabet must have some persistent function in supporting word pronunciation.

For the purpose of this paper, however, my major interest is in whether it was necessary for the subjects to know of the existence of the alphabet in order to get a positive effect from it. In view of the possibilities discussed above, part of the advantage of the alphabetic condition might derive from the fact that in this condition stimuli that look alike would, in general, be paired with responses that sound alike, whereas in the paired-associate condition this would be true only by occasional chance. Consequently, in the experiment that I am about to report, we did not tell the subjects that either of the lists had a functional alphabet, and we printed the letters from right to left, as shown in Fig. 2, in order to prevent them from easily discovering the correspondences. The idea of printing the words from right to left was obtained from a set of studies recently reported by Baron, Alpher, and Hodge (1976). The purpose of their studies was to discover whether people learned component correspondences automatically in the course of learning to name whole items. In their initial experiment subjects made about 11% fewer errors on a list of nonsense syllables that were constructed from an unannounced right-to-left alphabet than they did on a list with no alphabetic correspondences. For their purposes, the possibility that this result was due to overall similarity of the items was an artifact, and they worked hard to eliminate it. However, I believe that the overall similarity just might be an extremely important fact about written languages that deserves separate treatment. As a first step in this direction, the following study is an attempt to obtain the effect of an implicit alphabet using a set of real words and a more varied set of spelling patterns than were used in the Baron, Alpher, and Hodge study.

A.   Method

1.   *Subjects.* The subjects were 16 graduate and undergraduate students at McMaster University. All subjects were paid volunteers and were native English speakers.

2.   *Stimuli.* The stimuli are shown in Fig. 2. As is shown, the stimuli and responses were constant across conditions, with only the assignment of responses to stimuli being varied to produce the implicit alphabetic and the paired-associate conditions. Even-numbered subjects were run with List 1 as implicit alphabetic and List 2 as paired-associate. Odd-numbered subjects were run with the opposite assignment of lists to conditions. The individual stimulus words were drawn with an overall length of 2.5 to 3.5 cm, depending on the letters, and a height of approximately 3/4 cm. The six words for a condition were mounted in a regular 2 x 3 array on cards that were 14 x 21 cm. The stimuli for each condition were arranged in 20 different orders on the cards so that the subjects would not learn a fixed output sequence.

3.   *Procedure.* Half of the subjects were run on the alphabetic condition first and half on the paired-associate condition first. All subjects were given 20 trials on their first condition, then 20 trials on the second, and so on in alternating 20-trial blocks up to a total of 120 trials in each condition.

Subjects were told that they were going to participate in an experiment in which they were to learn to name the words in two paired-associate lists as rapidly and accurately as possible. They were further told that they would be given one minute to study a card on which all of the stimuli were printed with the correct response printed next to each stimulus, and after this one-minute study period they would be shown other cards with only the six stimuli on them. They were to name these stimuli as rapidly and accurately as possible and would be told if they made an incorrect response. Subjects were encouraged not to agonize over any response that they were having difficulty retrieving, but rather to make the best guess that they could and go on. Timing was done by a stopwatch that was started when the stimulus card was placed on the table and stopped with the completion of the sixth response. The study card with the stimuli and associated responses was left next to them throughout all trials, although subjects generally stopped using it at all within the first 20 trials on each condition. A similar study period was also provided before the first 20 trials on the second condition for each subject.

B.   Results and Discussion

The mean times to read six words averaged across 10-trial blocks is shown for both conditions in Table 1. Twelve of the 16 subjects showed a lower total time in the implicit than the paired-associate condition. Eleven of these subjects also showed lower times for the implicit condition in at least 9 of the 12 trial blocks. Twelve subjects made fewer errors in the implicit condition with an average across all subjects of 46.6 errors in the implicit condition and 52.2 errors in the paired-associate condition. All three of these subject statistics are significant at the .05 level by a sign test.

   No subject reported any knowledge that the implicit alphabetic condition had a right-to-left alphabet. On close questioning after the experiment one subject reported noticing that the two words that started with a PA ended with the same two symbols, but he read these two symbols in the order three then four (rather than the correct four then three), and then pointed out how this assignment of symbols to P and A did not work in the remainder of the list. All other subjects expressed surprise that there was an alphabet that read from right to left, although several of them reported looking for an alphabet that scanned in the conventional left-to-right order. Several subjects spontaneously mentioned during the course of the experiment that they were finding it easier to work with the list that unknown to them was alphabetic, but indicated that they did not know why ("For some reason I'm finding this list easier.").

   These results replicate and extend those reported by Baron, Alpher, and Hodge (1976). Subjects were able to perform better on material that was constructed from an implicit alphabet than they are on material that was not.

TABLE 1
Time in Seconds to Pronounce Six-Word Lists Written in Artificial Symbols.
Data Shown are Means for 10-Trial Blocks.

Paired-associate	37.7	20.3	16.5	10.6	9.8	7.5	7.8	6.1	5.7	5.7	5.4	5.2
Implicit alphabet	38.5	20.7	15.2	10.4	8.7	7.0	6.7	5.9	5.5	4.9	5.1	4.9
Difference	−.8	−.4	1.3	.2	1.1	.5	1.1	.2	.2	.8	.3	.3

Before trying to relate this finding to the notions of fluency discussed in the introduction, we must first note that the effect is fairly small. The implicit alphabet condition was only around 7% faster over the last 50 trials and resulted in 11% fewer errors over all trials than did the paired-associate group. However, there is no reason to believe that this procedure and these materials, originally selected for another experiment, are optimal for producing the effect. I believe there is enough reason for interest that it would be worthwhile to nurture it to see if it can be made stronger. Only after we get some control over this effect can we reasonably estimate whether it would be of significance in a natural situation.

But regardless of its size, this effect of an implicit alphabet could be interpreted as being a result of either an analytic or a nonanalytic mechanism. To claim that it was analytic, all we would have to say is that the subjects for some reason were unable to tell us about the component correspondences to which they were, in fact, responding. Our knowledge of the conditions that allow learning without awareness is sufficiently weak that such an explanation cannot be clearly ruled out without much stronger evidence. The possibility that the effect is due to nonanalytic mechanisms follows from the arguments given in the introduction, and for this explanation we would expect that the subjects would not be able to report the alphabetic correspondence.

After having conceded that both explanations are possible, I still must admit that I favor the nonanalytic model. First, although we certainly can point to many everyday instances in which people apparently know rules that they cannot talk about, I think that it is easy to be too facile in attributing implicit analysis to people. Remember that these were adult subjects who reported looking for possible correspondences and giving up; they were surprised that there were any correspondences. We were not trying to interview them on learning that they accomplished as a child or that they did several months ago, so we do not have to contend with some of the extremely poor memory conditions that could affect our everyday reports. When the conditions for reporting any analysis that does take place are as good as they are in this experiment, we should be cautious about assuming implicit analysis lest we miss the possibility that the knowledge is in fact organized in a different, at least partially nonanalytic, manner. The point here, of course, is not that implicit analysis doesn't exist, but rather that we have no license to assume it, given that there is an alternative form of knowledge that can explain our results. The possibility that implicit knowledge in reading is not organized the same way as explicitly given rules is of special interest, given that one of the debates in reading instruction is over what knowledge should be taught explicitly and what knowledge should be left to implicit learning (see, for example, Ruddell, 1974).

The second reason for considering the nonanalytic explanation is that not only can it possibly explain some of these everyday tasks, it is the explanation of choice for a few laboratory studies. For example, in one task that we ran (Brooks, 1977), subjects were given a set of paired-associates to learn in which the stimuli were meaningless strings of letters and the responses were words such as MONTREAL, MOOSE, LION, PARIS, LONDON, POSSUM. After the subjects had completed the memory task, they were told that the strings of letters they had just used as stimuli came from two different complex grammars that determined the order of the letters (finite state grammars, such as those used by Reber, 1976, and Chomsky & Miller, 1958). They were told that all of the stimuli associated with the old world words came from one grammar and the stimuli associated with the new world words came from the other. They were then asked to sort a new set of stimuli that came from these grammars into a new world pile, an old world pile, and a pile that was neither. The subjects performed at 60 to 65% accuracy (where 33% is chance and 45% is the best that was done on the basis of physical similarity alone) despite the fact that the only classification of items that they reported noticing was the orthogonal one between animals and cities. The point of this experiment is that it is hard to imagine analysis (i.e., noticing correspondences between parts of the stimuli and category membership) as occurring either consciously or unconsciously if one does not know what the categories are at the time of learing. On the other hand, if one notices a similarity between a test item and an item previously memorized (e.g., the stimulus associated with CHICAGO) then there is no reason why one could not respond on the basis of this similarity (e.g., this item is from the new world because it looks like the item CHICAGO) without knowing or being able to report analytic rules. The effect of the grammars in this case may have been simply to insure that there would be a greater chance that a physically similar analogy to a new item would occur in the correct category than in the incorrect category.

We can show that an alphabet can have a helpful effect even when the learner does not know about it, and we can find a vaguely related situation in which nonanalytic learning is more probable. This does not prove that nonanalytic learning is taking place in learning to say words fluently, but it does make the possibility more strongly worth considering. That is all that I am arguing for here.

III.   THE MANIPULATION OF VISUAL PATTERNING

The first question that must come to mind in considering nonanalytic fluency is that if it is so easy to learn words, then why does any child ever have trouble? The answer might be that similarity is what the perceiver makes it. If the child compares the similarity of words on the basis of the number of ascenders (b, d, l, etc.) and descenders (g, p, y) in a word, or just its length, then possibly his similarity judgments may not be terribly useful predictors of sound. A skilled reader probably visually organizes a word differently than does a novice reader. This visual organization could have the effect of allowing the operation of any of a variety of analytic mechanisms, but it could also affect the cues used for nonanalytic access to the internal representation of the word and therefore, most important for our purposes, it could affect the effects of stimulus and response generalization. In other words, the training that allows a child to use orthographic rules may also affect the way he perceives the words and because of generalization to phonologically-related words this change in perception may be important to his ability to learn to identify a word rapidly. In the remaining space I will briefly describe two lines of evidence that show that orthographically-relevant patterning can change performance.

A. Vowel Enhancement

One of the important signals for the pronunciation of vowels in English mono-morphemic words is the pattern of vowels and consonants (Venezky, 1970). In general, if two vowels occur together, or are separated by only one *simple* consonant (e.g., not x), then the vowel is pronounced as a glide (the "long" pronunciations of traditional English pedagogy, as in LATE, BITE, BOAT, MEAT). If we emphasized the vowels by making them larger or printing them in a different color, then we would be highlighting this important vowel-consonant contrast. The question is whether such an emphasis would help a subject learn to pronounce unfamiliar words more rapidly.

Tom Anderson has shown that visually emphasizing the contrast between vowels and consonants does help adults learn to pronounce words written in an explicit artificial alphabet (Anderson & Brooks, 1977). Anderson gave his subjects a list of 12 words made up of two examples each of three glided (e.g., TOAD, LEAF, TRADE) and three unglided (TROD, LEFT, TRACT) pronun-ciation patterns. Over a series of 10 presentations his subjects became faster at pronouncing these vowel enhanced words than did subjects who were reading words whose letters were all the same size. This superiority for vowel enhance-ment was not just an effect of distinguishing an arbitrary subset of letters or of producing more distinctive whole-word patterns, as is shown by the fact that the vowel-enhanced group also did better than a group that read words in which a matched arbitrary subset of letters were enhanced.

The superiority of the vowel-enhanced group over the other two was main-tained on a subsequent series of new words comprised of the same artificial letters, all of which were the same size. This shows that whatever the vowel-enhanced group had learned was transferable to a more conventional style of printing. Such a result is crucial if we are to have any hope of using this type of pattern enhancement as a means of instruction. Conceivably, we could use such a variable for training the appropriate visual segmentation of words, as long as the advantage would be maintained after the patterning was faded out.

As with the implicit alphabetic result, this superiority in both training and transfer due to emphasizing the contrast between vowels and consonants in training can be interpreted by both an analytic and a nonanalytic mechanism. The superiority could be because the information necessary for applying rules of pronunciation was made more salient, or it could be because vowel enhancement increased the visual similarities among words that are pronounced similarly. For practical purposes, however, it does not immediately matter which account is correct if it improves learning speed. At least in the case of vowel enhancement, unlike some of the other proposals for transitional alteration of conventional typefaces (e.g., initial teaching alphabet, diacritical marking system, words in color, color phonics), the vowel-consonant pattern that is being emphasized is one that continues to be there in normal printing. Possibly the effect of the vowel-consonant pattern enhancement is to make the word appear different either for the purposes of drawing analogies or for the purpose of applying rules.

B.   Sound-Correlated Patterning

The final bit of evidence that we consider strengthens the case that it is sound-correlated patterning, not just any form of distinctive patterning, that is important in facilitating pronunciation. In the case of vowel enhancement, it is hard to be sure that what is being manipulated is the relevance of the patterning to the orthography rather than some other variable, such as relative discriminability of various letter sequences. But the case is absolutely tight for the material shown in Fig. 3. In this case the pattern that is superimposed on the letters is arbitrary and can either be correlated or uncorrleated with some aspect of phonology. The sound-correlated patterns are correlated in Fig. 3 with the vowel sound and resulted in subjects pronouncing these eight words in an average of 2.3 sec over 100 trials, as opposed to 2.6 sec for the control words and 2.6 sec for the arbitrary patterns. These effects were significant in all eight subjects and showed virtually no interaction between trials and conditions after the first five trials.

The idea for this type of patterning was developed by Amina Miller (Miller & Brooks, 1977). In a series of experiments using artificial alphabets she demonstrated that while both arbitrary and sound-correlated patterns aided word identification for the first few trials, only sound-correlated patterning continued to have an effect. The facilitation due to arbitrary pattern virtually disappeared by about the sixtieth trial.

IV.   SOUND-CORRELATED PATTERNING AND VISUAL SIMILARITY

In the previous two sections we have shown that there is no reason to assume that the only way the alphabet can operate is through analytic knowledge, and that sound-correlated visual distinctiveness is an aid to fluency. One way these two lines of evidence may be related is that readers use sound-correlated visual similarities in a nonanalytic fashion to attain fluency. Another way they may be

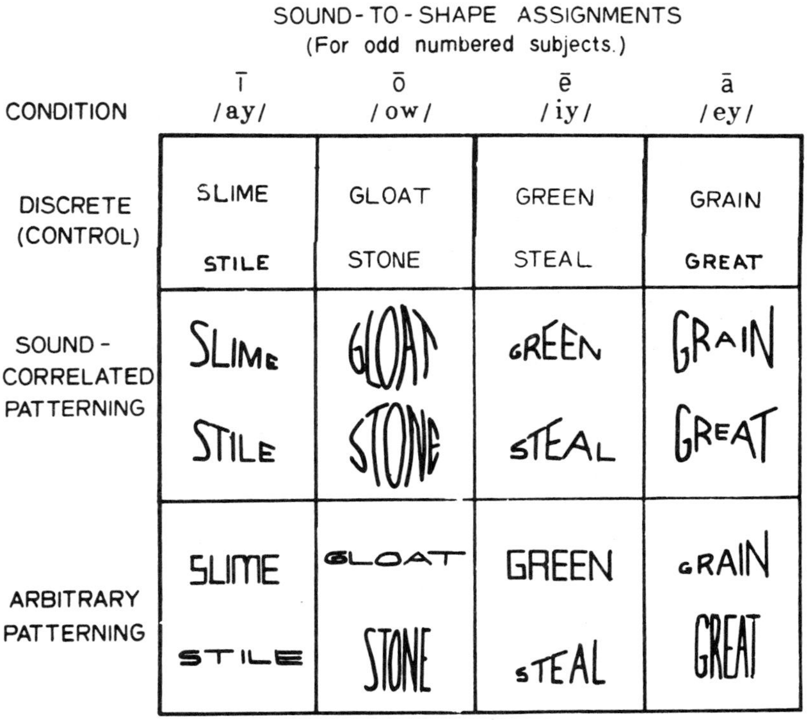

SOUND - TO - SHAPE   ASSIGNMENTS
(For odd numbered subjects.)

CONDITION	$\bar{\imath}$ /ay/	$\bar{o}$ /ow/	$\bar{e}$ /iy/	$\bar{a}$ /ey/
DISCRETE (CONTROL)	SLIME STILE	GLOAT STONE	GREEN STEAL	GRAIN GREAT
SOUND - CORRELATED PATTERNING	SLIME STILE	GLOAT STONE	GREEN STEAL	GRAIN GREAT
ARBITRARY PATTERNING	SLIME STILE	GLOAT STONE	GREEN STEAL	GRAIN GREAT

FIG. 3.   A set of material used to show that patterns that are correlated with the sound of the word facilitate its pronunciation, whereas arbitrarily related patterns do not. The particular patterns that were used in the sound-correlated and the arbitrary conditions were counterbalanced across subjects.

related is that readers can learn to apply implicit, analytic pronunciation rules more rapidly when the relevant information is perceptually salient than when it is not. To separate the roles of explicit analytic knowledge, implicit analytic knowledge, and nonanalytic knowledge, experiments will have to be done that vary both explicit knowledge and visual similarity. For example, we might look for an interaction between the effect of vowel-enhancement with a set of words that group the same items as similar on both the stimulus side and the response side, and its effect with a set of items for which this similarity condition is not true. If high levels of fluency with this material are unaffected by manipulating explicitness of knowledge, we have reason to suspect the importance of explicit instruction. Clearly, explicit instruction should affect adults for the early stages of performance with unknown words, but the effect on later performance is at least in doubt.

But regardless of one's intuitions about the outcome of such experiments, we do not have reason to automatically assume that word identification is a process mainly determined by knowledge of general analytic rules. First of all, there are at least some stimulus-specific effects even with adults learning new words that are printed in traditional English letters. Szumski, for instance (Szumski & Brooks, 1977), has shown that when adults have learned auditorily the meaning of a new word (e.g., PIGHT means coffee, NAWF means gate) they do not assess the meaningfulness of a visually-presented sentence containing that word as rapidly as if they had learned the new word visually. This results despite the fact that the subjects had seen the word previously for the purposes of pronunciation. A similar result was obtained by McClelland (1977) for changes from standard typefaces to script. What is clearly true in both of these cases is that adults have the ability to learn new words rapidly, but that they need at least some specific experience to do so.

A second reason for looking for effects of specific-stimulus knowledge is that we might be more able to understand and accommodate individual differences in the ease with which children respond to explicit instruction in the use of analytic pronunciation rules. If some children are more competent in the use of nonanalytic mechanisms, then varying visual pattern in a way that might increase their success in using these mechanisms is at least worth a try.

ACKNOWLEDGMENTS

I would like to thank Amina Miller for her exceptional assistance in the work reported in this paper. This research was supported by a grant from the National Research Council of Canada.

REFERENCES

Anderson, T. & Brooks, L.R. *The effect of enhancing vowel-consonant patterns on word identification.* Manuscript submitted for publication, 1977.

Baron, J. Mechanisms for pronouncing printed words: Use and acquisition. In D. LaBerge & S.J. Samuels (Eds.), *Basic processes in reading: Perception and comprehension.* Hillsdale, N.J.: Lawrence Erlbaum Associates, 1977.

Baron, J., Alpher, V., & Hodge, J. *Implicit learning of spelling-sound correspondences.* Paper presented to the convention of the Psychonomic Society, 1976.

Brooks, L.R. Visual pattern in fluent word identification. In A. Reber & D. Scarborough (Eds.), *Toward a psychology of reading.* Hillsdale, N.J.: Lawrence Erlbaum Associates, 1977.

Brooks, L. R. Non-analytic concept formation and memory for instances. In E. Rosch & B. Lloyd (Eds.), *Cognition and categorization.* Hillsdale, N.J.: Lawrence Erlbaum Associates, 1978.

Chomsky, N., & Miller, G.A. Finite state languages. *Inform. Cont.*, 1958, *1*, 91–112.

Gleitman, L.R., & Rozin, P. The structure and acquisition of reading II: Relations between orthographies and the structure of language. In A. Reber & D. Scarborough (Eds.), *Toward a psychology of reading.* Hillsdale, N.J.: Lawrence Erlbaum Associates, 1977.

Glenn, F. & Baron, J. *Orthographic factors in reading for pronunciation and reading.* Paper presented to the convention of the Psychonomic Society, 1975.

Huey, E.B. *The psychology and pedagogy of reading.* Cambridge, Massachusetts: MIT Press, 1968. (Original publication, 1908.)

McClelland, J. Letter and configuration information in word identification. *Journal of Verbal Learning and Verbal Behavior,* 1977, *16,* 137–150.

Mason, M., & Katz, L. Visual processing of non-linguistic strings: Redundancy effects and reading ability. *Journal of Experimental Psychology: General,* 1976, *105,* 338–348.

Miller, A. & Brooks, L.R. *The effect of sound-correlated patterning on word identification.* Manuscript submitted for publication, 1977.

Reber, A.S. Implicit learning of synthetic languages: The role of instructional set. *Journal of Experimental Psychology: Human Memory and Learning.* 1976, *2,* 88–94.

Rozin, P., & Gleitman, L.R. The structure and acquisition of reading II: The reading process and the acquisition of the alphabetic principle. In A. Reber & D. Scarborough (Eds.), *Toward a psychology of reading.* Hillsdale, N.J.: Lawrence Erlbaum Associates, 1977.

Ruddell, R. *Reading-language instruction: Innovative practices.* Englewood Cliffs, New Jersey: Prentice-Hall, Inc., 1974.

Smith, F. *Understanding reading: A psycholinguistic analysis of reading and learning to read.* New York: Holt, Rinehart and Winston, 1971.

Szumski, J. & Brooks, L.R. *Word-specific learning in rapid word identification.* Manuscript submitted for publication, 1977.

Venezky, R. L. *The structure of English orthography.* The Hague: Mouton, 1970.

10 Implicit Speech in the Reading of Numbers and Meaningless Syllables

Joël Pynte

Département de Psychologie
Université de Provence
Aix-en-Provence, France

ABSTRACT

According to Klapp, Anderson, and Berrian (1973), response latency in verbal naming experiments is related to a programming mechanism. The first experiment reported in this paper confirmed that in a reading situation (i.e., when several items are presented simultaneously) programming seems to occur at each fixation (cf. Pynte, 1974). Also, overt responses (subjects had to read aloud) seem to be part of one vocal sequence uttered relatively independently from the oculomotor sequence. The second experiment suggested that so-called response programming could be related to perceptual processing in the case of meaningless letter strings.

I. INTRODUCTION

Eriksen, Pollack, and Montague (1970) showed that Verbal Reaction Time (VRT: the interval between the onset of word or number presentation and the moment when the subject starts vocalizing) is a function of the number of syllables required to pronounce the response. This finding was confirmed by Klapp (1971) but was questioned by Henderson, Coltheart, and Woodhouse (1973) in the case of numbers. In an experiment conducted by Klapp (1974), the bias reported by Henderson et al. was removed. These latter findings reveal a "syllabic effect" which is less marked than the one previously observed, but still significant.

Different interpretations of the syllabic effect have been proposed. While Spoehr and Smith (1973) claimed that it parallels a visual processing (according to these authors, a syllabic effect can occur in a tachistoscopic identification task, in the case of words but not in the case of numbers), Klapp et al. (1973)

179

demonstrated that it occurs at the response programming level and not at the perceptual level; they found that it disappears when no verbal response is required but remains present when the verbal response is to be given from a picture instead of from a word. In addition, Klapp (1976) has recently argued that the mechanisms involved in programming the verbal response would also be responsible for memorization: response programming would "lead to the formation of an articulatory Short Term Memory (STM) /p. 724/."

It seemed worthwhile to study such mechanisms in a reading situation, i.e., when several items are presented simultaneously, and recognition is achieved through a sequence of eye fixations. In a previous experiment (Pynte, 1974), we asked the subjects to read a series of three numbers (no pronunciation was allowed during reading, they had to report the whole stimulus upon reading it). We found that Eye Fixation Duration (EFD) on a number depends on the number of syllables necessary to pronounce it. Thus, in such a situation response programming would occur after the identification of *each* item, when the eye would still be fixating the relevant part of the stimulus. This result is consistent with Klapp's theory (1976) that response programming and the formation of STM are the same process. It suggests that a delay may occur between programming and actual pronunciation during reading. Indeed, the overt response corresponding to a given eye fixation may be uttered at the same time that another part of the visual stimulus is being processed. Also, it does not seem the case that the responses corresponding to the various eye fixations are uttered independently from one another. On the contrary, they seem to be part of *one* vocal sequence.

II. EXPERIMENT 1

The aim of the present experiment was to demonstrate the relative independence of programming and pronunciation during a reading-aloud situation. In this connection, we must remember that the Eye-Voice Span (EVS) studied by Buswell (1920) constitutes an overall delay of vocalization with respect to identification. Its value at a given time does not seem to be directly related to the characteristics of the relevant part of the visual stimulus. Woodworth and Schlosberg (1954) noted that measurements such as VRT are "misleading when applied to reading which is a continuous process /p. 508/."

A. Method

1. *Apparatus and Procedure.* Each subject was seated 60 cm from a translucent screen 60 cm wide. His head was held in position by a chin rest. A slide projector placed behind the screen was operated by a pulse generator which determined exposure durations. A photoelectric cell, connected to a second pulse generator, made it possible to record, on one of the tracks of the recorder, the

time interval during which the screen was lighted. Skin electrodes were placed on the subject's temples. The potential differences obtained were amplified and recorded on a second track of the recorder. A microphone was situated a few centimeters from the subject's mouth. A vocal key caused a signal to be recorded on a third track of the recorder as soon as the subject started vocalizing. In addition, the output electric signal of the microphone appeared on the recording sheet after having been amplified and rectified. This last procedure was done for two reasons: to insure that the vocal key worked correctly, and to allow a measure of vocalization duration. Exposure duration was 5 sec. The subject was required to read aloud and was not to report what he had seen upon presentation.

2. *Subjects.*   Twenty-four students of psychology participated in the experiment. They were all paid volunteers and native French speakers.

3. *Stimuli.*   Each stimulus consisted of a series of three two-digit numbers. The visual angle subtended by the series was 45°. Twelve stimuli were used in the experiment. They may be classified in four categories (S1, S2, S3, S4). The numbers constituting these stimuli may themselves be classified in two categories (N1, N2). All the numbers are issued from three digit sets (D1, D2, D3; see Table 1).

4. *Experimental design.*   The digit set from which an item is derived defines the graphic difficulty of this item. There are three levels of graphic difficulty. The order in which the numerals belonging to this set are written defines the verbal difficulty of the item (as well as the number set the item belongs to). There are two levels of verbal difficulty.

The arrangement of the items within each stimulus is such that the three levels of graphic difficulty together with the two levels of verbal difficulty are present at all three possible positions in the series (left, center, and right).

TABLE 1
Stimulus Design

D1	=	(1,	7)							
D2	=	(2,	8)							
D3	=	(3,	9)							
N1	=	(17,	28,	39)						
N2	=	(71,	82,	93)						
S1	=	(17	28	39,	28	39	17,	39	17	28)
S2	=	(17	82	39,	28	93	17,	39	71	28)
S3	=	(71	28	93,	82	39	71,	93	17	82)
S4	=	(71	82	93,	82	93	71,	93	71	82)

Two groups of 12 subjects each were constituted. The first group was assigned the three S1 and the three S2 stimuli, the second group was assigned S3 and S4 stimuli. Thus, each subject saw six stimuli. Six presentation orders were constructed. These six orders were such that after six subjects had completed their task, each of the six stimuli had been presented once and only once at each of the six possible positions and had been once and only once preceded or followed by each of the five other stimuli (and once by no stimulus at all).

5. *Dependent variables.*   Figure 1 shows the typical recording for a stimulus; (1) corresponds to the photoelectric cell, (2) to the electrodes, (3) to the vocal key, (4) to the microphone. The durations labeled "a," "b," and "c" respectively correspond to the three eye fixations realized on a stimulus, whereas "d" is the VRT concerning the first item. (It was not possible to locate with precision the beginning of the responses corresponding to each item). In addition, the duration of vocalization for the whole stimulus (labeled "e") is represented even though it has not been analyzed in detail.

B.   Results

Since each subject saw six stimuli (two sets of three stimuli), and the two groups comprised twelve subjects each, we consequently obtained 144 measures on each Dependent Variable (DV). Figure 2 diagrams these data (with one subfigure per stimulus set). The corresponding values are given in Tables 2 and 3.

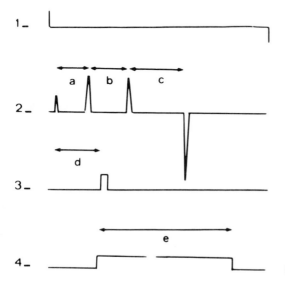

FIG. 1   Typical record.

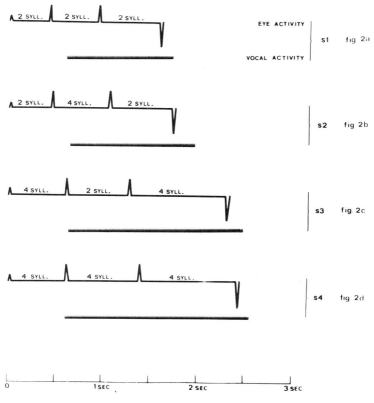

FIG. 2   Results (Experiment 1).

TABLE 2
Mean EFDs (in ms)

	1st fixation	2nd fixation	3rd fixation
S1	413.55 (2 syll.)	472.62 (2 syll.)	680.57 (2 syll.)
S2	461.69 (2 syll.)	624.83 (4 syll.)	684.83 (2 syll.)
S3	631.70 (4 syll.)	682.43 (2 syll.)	1059.85 (4 syll.)
S4	617.96 (4 syll.)	791.17 (4 syll.)	1055.79 (4 syll.)

1. *Eye activity.*   The first eye fixation lasts longer when the first item in the series requires four syllables to be pronounced, than when it requires two syllables ($F(1, 12) = p < .025$). (Moreover, the "graphic difficulty" effect yielded by the first item is not significant). This result supports previous findings (see Pynte, 1974).

A syllabic effect is also observed on the fixation durations realized on the other items in the series: ($F(1, 12) = 50.05, p < .0001$, for the second item, and $F(1, 12) = 13.92, p < .005$, for the third). However, these results have to be considered with caution, since the subject was engaged in the pronunciation of the first item while fixating the second, and in the pronunciation of the second item while fixating the third.

EFDs seem to be longer in the case of the S3 and S4 sets of stimuli than in the case of S1 and S2. This effect may be observed independently from the number of syllables on the second eye fixation. The difference is significant ($F(1, 22) = 7.84, p < .025$). This effect is not due to the number of syllables necessary to pronounce the preceding item since the third fixation is not longer in S2 than in S1 and not longer in S4 than in S3 ($F < 1$). To find an explanation, it must be remembered that S1 and S2 were attributed to a group of subjects, and S3 and S4 to another one. Thus, some subjects were presented stimuli including mainly four-syllable items, and others were presented stimuli including mainly two-syllable items. It may be assumed that, in the course of the session, there progressively arose some expectation as to a certain stimulus type. The presumed verbal difficulty of the whole sequence might have determined the mean duration of the three fixations. Such an interpretation amounts to the assumption that the whole oculomotor sequence was programmed prior to its operation (quite independently from the actual vocal activity). The characteristics of each item would only have had a modulating effect.

2. *Vocal activity.*   Though vocalization duration was recorded, no analysis was performed with respect to this DV. However, it may be seen from the four subfigures of Fig. 2 that this duration differs in length in each case (obviously, the more syllables required to pronounce the stimulus, the longer the vocalization duration).

We are mainly interested in VRTs. It should be noted that the characteristics of the first item in the sequence are the only characteristics likely to have an effect on this VD, for, at the onset of vocalization, this first item is the only one to have been processed by the subject.

In contrast with the strong effect observed on EFD, the VRT remains approximately constant whatever the number of syllables required to pronounce the first item in the sequence. No systematic effect was revealed by the analysis of variance performed on this DV. This result is surprising enough. At least a repercussion of the effect observed on EFD was expected on VRT. The significance of the syllabic effect at the level of EFD should perhaps consequently be recon-

TABLE 3
Mean VRTs and Vocalization Durations (in ms)

	VRT	Vocalization
S1	611.30 (2 syll.)	1133.92 (6 syll.)
S2	654.03 (2 syll.)	1348.40 (8 syll.)
S3	604.83 (4 syll.)	1888.03 (10 syll.)
S4	607.63 (4 syll.)	1969.36 (12 syll.)

sidered. Figure 2 shows that the vocalization is generally initiated before the end of the first eye fixation in the case of the S3 and S4 stimuli sets. On the contrary, the subject is fixating the second item at the onset of vocalization in the case of S1 and S2. It was just as if memorization cannot be completed when too many syllables have to be processed. The subject seems to keep his eyes on such items until the onset of vocalization.

However, this kind of interpretation is not consistent with our previous hypothesis that the whole oculomotor sequence is programmed before its operation. Another possible interpretation is that the syllabic effect on EFD *is not only* related to response programming. It could be involved in the perceptual processing of each item.

C. Disussion

Forster and Chambers (1973) showed that VRT is shorter for words than for meaningless letter strings. This result suggests that response programming occurs *after lexical access.* Klapp (1976) argued that articulatory STM operates "late in the flow of information." Thus, it seems that the feedback of verbal response is not necessary for the identification of words. However, interactions between response programming and perceptual processing have to be considered differently in the case of *nonwords.* Indeed, a meaningless letter string cannot be matched to a lexical entry. The elaboration of a perceptual representation, when such stimuli are presented, probably involves mechanisms closely related to memorization. For example, it could be performed by attempts at pronunciation (or verbal hypotheses).

The idea that encoding is performed according to hypotheses was suggested by the results of a previous experiment (Pynte, 1971). The procedure consisted in measuring tachistoscopic thresholds on CV and VC bigrams. In order to impose a sequential processing, the consonants were larger and thicker than the vowels. The bigrams used (SI, ON, RA, AR) are very frequent in French (they are more frequent than those obtained by replacing the vowels by "U"). However, they are less frequent than those obtained by replacing the vowels by "E" (cf. the transitional probabilities matrix from Ceillier, 1958). Prior to the session, subjects were given the alphabet of letters used in the experiment (A, I, O, N, R, S). One extra letter was included in the alphabet. For the subjects of a first group (G1), it was "U"; for the subjects of a second group (G2), it was "E." Two stimuli were words (ON and SI), and two were nonwords (AR and RA). In the case of words, the bigrams obtained by replacing the vowel by "E" or by "U" were also words (ON gave EN and UN; SI gave SE and SU).

The data showed that for all stimuli, the threshold was lower when the extra letter was "U" than when it was "E." This suggests that a letter recognition threshold does not depend only on its own probability of occurrence but also on the probability of the letters that the subject may expect, given the alphabet presented prior to the session. No lexical inference was involved, for there was no difference between words and nonwords. In addition, perceptual hypotheses concerned units composed of several letters: an additional experiment showed that performance does not depend on the composition of the alphabet when the vowels are presented isolated and not in bigrams.

III. EXPERIMENT 2

The aim of the second experiment reported here was to demonstrate the verbal nature of the hypotheses elaborated during the perceptual processing of meaningless letter strings. A transcoding process (involved in the comparison between an hypothesis and the result of the visual parsing) was also assumed (cf. the model presented by Fig. 3). The perception of a nonword was supposed to be performed through the following steps:

1. preliminary analysis (and storage in a sensory memory);
2. visual parsing (and storage in a visual memory);
3. production of a verbal hypothesis;
4. transcoding (and production of visual features consistent with the hypothesis);
5. comparison between the features and the visual representation.

A. Method

The procedure was similar to the one used in the previous experiment (Pynte, 1971). It consisted in reducing the number of allowed verbal hypotheses and controlling their phonetic characteristics.

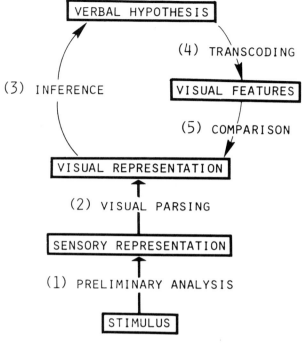

FIG. 3   The model.

1. *Experimental design.*   The perceptual accuracy of a test item (gu) was measured when belonging to three different sets:

1. *gu,* go ga

2. *gu,* go ge

3. *gu,* gi, ge

Three groups, including 5 subjects each, participated in three experimental sessions in three different orders. Prior to each session, each subject was given a different set of letters (e.g., "g, u, o, a").

A session was composed of nine series of nine tachistoscopic presentations. The three syllables belonging to the set were presented three times in a series (cf. Table 4). After each presentation, the subject chose the syllable he felt was the stimulus (he was not obliged to give a response).

Each stimulus consisted of a CV syllable composed of 24 pt. "Pallace Script" Letraset characters. The visual angle subtended by a stimulus was smaller than 1°.

Stimulus duration was constant in a series but diminished with each series. A $\log_{1.26}$ scale was used. The value used in Series 5 corresponded to the recognition

TABLE 4

Experimental Design[a]

	Set 1										Set 2										Set 3									
Series 1	go	*gu*	go	ga	ga	*gu*	*gu*	*gu*	ga	go	ge	*gu*	ge	go	go	ge	*gu*	*gu*	ge	ge	ge	gi	ge	*gu*	*gu*	ge	*gu*	*gu*	ge	ge
Series 2	ga	go	ga	*gu*	*gu*	go	go	*gu*	ga	ga	go	ge	*gu*	go	go	ge	go	ge	gi	gi	gi	*gu*	ge	gi	ge	gi	ge	ge	gi	gi
Series 3	go	*gu*	ga	*gu*	ga	*gu*	ga	ga	go	ga	ge	*gu*	ge	go	go	ge	ge	gi	gi	ge	ge	ge	*gu*	ge	*gu*	gi	*gu*	ge	gi	ge
Series 4	*gu*	ga	go	go	*gu*	*gu*	ga	ga	go	*gu*	*gu*	go	*gu*	ge	*gu*	go	*gu*	*gu*	gi	*gu*	gi	ge	ge	*gu*	gi	ge	gi	*gu*	ge	*gu*
Series 5	ga	go	*gu*	*gu*	*gu*	go	go	go	*gu*	ga	go	ge	ge	*gu*	go	ge	ge	ge	ge	*gu*	ge	*gu*	gi	ge	ge	*gu*	ge	gi	*gu*	gi
Series 6	ga	go	ga	go	*gu*	ga	go	*gu*	ga	ga	go	ge	go	*gu*	*gu*	go	ge	gi	ge	gi	*gu*	ge	gi	*gu*	*gu*	ge	*gu*	ge	ge	*gu*
Series 7	*gu*	ga	go	*gu*	*gu*	*gu*	ga	go	go	*gu*	*gu*	go	ge	go	ge	*gu*	go	ge	gi	ge	*gu*	gi	ge	gi	ge	*gu*	ge	*gu*	gi	ge
Series 8	*gu*	go	go	ga	go	*gu*	*gu*	go	go	ga	*gu*	go	ge	go	ge	*gu*	*gu*	*gu*	gi	*gu*	*gu*	ge	*gu*	ge	gi	gi	gi	go	gi	ge
Series 9	go	*gu*	ga	ga	go	ga	*gu*	ga	ga	go	ge	*gu*	ge	go	go	ge	*gu*	*gu*	ge	ge	ge	gi	*gu*	*gu*	ge	ge	*gu*	*gu*	gi	ge

[a]From a "r-exhaustive" design, cf. Durup, 1968.

threshold (measured independently for each subject during a preexperimental session with the five vowels as stimuli).

2. *Predictions.* In french, "g" is pronounced /g/ when followed by "a," "o," or "u" and pronounced /ʒ/ when followed by "e" or "i." All syllables have a "hard" pronunciation in Set 1; two have a hard pronunciation in Set 2 and only one in Set 3. Therefore, one may assume that:

1. Set 1 ought to facilitate the third step of the model. Indeed, in this case, the subject knows he has to pronounce a hard "g" and may prepare himself.

2. Set 3 ought to facilitate the fourth step of the model. Indeed, when the pronunciation is completed, the subject knows, in the case of Set 3, that the vowel is "u" if the consonant is hard.

3. No facilitating effect ought to occur with Set 2. Indeed, the two pronunciations are possible in this case, and two vowels are consistent with the hard pronunciation.

In addition, the two facilitating effects ought to occur at different stages during the sessions: Set 1 in particular cannot facilitate perception until the subject has learned the pronunciation of the syllables he may construct with the letters given to him prior to the session. The facilitating effect of Set 3, on the contrary, may occur from the beginning of the session; indeed, it is supposed to intervene when an attempt at pronunciation has already been made.

B. Results

Figure 4 shows the number of correct responses to the test item (gu) during each series (i.e., for each stimulus duration) and each session (i.e., for each set).

Performance does not immediately drop when stimulus duration decreases. The learning stage seems to correspond to the first three series. Performance drops below chance level after the fifth series (most of the subjects did not give any response when stimulus duration was below the recognition threshold). During the intermediate stage, the highest performance is obtained with Set 1: a facilitating effect which is presumed to occur at the third step of the model, appears to dominate any other effect during Series 3, 4, and 5. During the learning stage, on the contrary, performance varies as a function of the number of vowels consistent with a "hard" pronunciation of the consonant; the highest performance is obtained with Set 3, and the lowest with Set 1. Set 2 (in which no facilitating effect is assumed to occur) gives a lower performance than the other two sets from the second series up to the sixth (at which point the chance level is reached).

Analysis of variance revealed that the main effect for series was significant ($F(8, 96) = 43.54$, $p < .001$). However, this result is trivial since series are con-

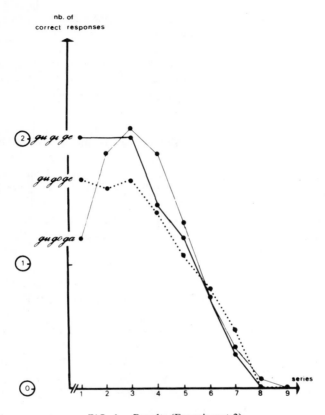

FIG. 4   Results (Experiment 2).

founded with stimulus durations. The main effect of sets was not significant $(F(2, 24) < 1)$, nor the comparison between Set 2 and the two other sets taken together $(F(1, 24) < 1)$. However, this result is not in contradiction with the model, since the superiority of Set 2 in comparison with Set 1 during the first series is consistent with our assumption that Set 1 cannot facilitate perception at the beginning of the session. We were more interested in the interaction of series by sets $(F(16, 192) = 2.10, p < .025)$ and particularly by the difference between the first and the third sets for each series $(F(8, 96) = 4.05, p < .01$ and $F(4, 48) = 6.01, p < .01$ without the last four series).

Thus, the results seem to be consistent with the model. The two predicted effects occurred successively at the beginning of the session in the case of Set 3 and in the middle of the session in the case of Set 1. The perceptual processing of meaningless bigrams could involve attempts at pronunciation (for which consistency with the result of visual parsing would be tested according to a transcoding process).

IV. CONCLUSION

The identification of a verbal stimulus normally ends with naming. In the case of a word this is realized through a lexical inference, and because of phonological rules (cf. Forster & Chamber, 1973). However, in the case of a nonword no rule may specify the phonetic form of the stimulus and the occurrence of several attempts at pronunciation during the perceptual process is not surprising. Also the lack of lexical inference in the case of nonwords makes overt or covert pronunciation more necessary, since naming is confounded with identification when such stimuli are presented.

The syllabic effect observed on numbers could be due to similar mechanisms. The results of a previous experiment in which subjects had to identify numbers pronounced with one, two, three or four syllables seem to be consistent with this view: most of the incorrect responses obtained before identification in such a situation were pronounced in less syllables than the stimulus (Pynte, 1973).

REFERENCES

Buswell, G. T. An experimental study of the eye-voice span in reading. *Supplement Educational Monograph*, 1920, *17*.

Ceillier, R. *La cryptographie*. Paris: Presses Universitaires de France, 1958.

Durup, H. *Plans d'expériences pour mesures répétées fondés sur l'emploi de codes réguliers*. Unpublished manuscript, Institut de Neurophysiologie et de Psychophysiologie, Département du comportement animal, 1968.

Eriksen, C. W., Pollack, M. D., & Montague, W. E. Implicit speech: Mechanism in perceptual encoding? *Journal of Experimental Psychology*, 1970, *84*, 502–507.

Forster, K. I., & Chambers, S. M. Lexical access and naming time. *Journal of Verbal Learning and Verbal Behavior*, 1973, *12*, 627–635.

Henderson, L., Coltheart, M., & Woodhouse, D. Failure to find a syllabic effect in number naming. *Memory & Cognition*, 1973, *1*, 304–306.

Klapp, S. T. Implicit speech inferred from response latencies in same-different decisions. *Journal of Experimental Psychology*, 1971, *91*, 262–267.

Klapp, S. T. Syllable dependent pronunciation latencies in number naming: A replication. *Journal of Experimental Psychology*, 1974, *102*, 1138–1140.

Klapp, S. T. Short-term memory as a response preparation state. *Memory & Cognition*, 1976, *4*, 721–729.

Klapp, S. T., Anderson, W. G., & Berrian, R. W. Implicit speech in reading, reconsidered. *Journal of Experimental Psychology*, 1973, *100*, 308–374.

Pynte, J. Contribution à un modèle de la perception du langage: les hypothèses perceptives au cours de l'identification des lettres. *Cahiers de Psychologie*, 1971, *14*, 187–202.

Pynte, J. Prononciation implicite du stimulus et production d'hypothèses perceptives au cours de la perception visuelle. *L'Année Psychologique*, 1973, *73*, 67–83.

Pynte, J. Readiness for pronunciation during the reading process. *Perception & Psychophysics*, 1974, *16*, 110–112.

Spoehr, K. T., & Smith, E. E. The role of syllables in perceptual processing. *Cognitive Psychology*, 1973, *5*, 71–89.

Woodworth, R. S., & Schlosberg, H. *Experimental psychology*. London: Methuen & Co., 1954.

11
The Origins of Mixed Errors

Tim Shallice
Janina McGill
Psychology Department
The National Hospital for Nervous Diseases
London, England

ABSTRACT

'Mixed errors' are defined as errors that are similar to the correct response on more than one dimension and whose probability of occurrence is greater than a simple stages model would predict. Two examples of them are given: visual–semantic errors in word reading and semantic-phonological errors in spontaneous speech. Alternative models, based on activation and comparator ideas, that maintain aspects of the stages approach and yet predict a high rate of mixed errors are compared in terms of how well they can account for segmentation errors induced by visual masking. It is shown that visual similarity helps to induce segmentation errors, and that semantic cueing can only induce them if the cue is consciously perceived. The results are interpreted within the framework of the activation approach.

I.   INTRODUCTION

Stages analyses of information processing tasks have been very popular in the past ten years. The approach has, however, been almost entirely restricted to reaction time measures. Errors have been relatively little-used, partially because a large amount of data is required for quantitative treatment, but probably because in the standard type of reaction time situation, error analysis necessitates facing the thorny theoretical problems of speed/error tradeoff.

Error analysis is somewhat more promising when stimuli and responses come from a very large set, as in many types of word selection experiments. In such situations error analysis of necessity involves making ancillary assumptions, but such assumptions must also be made when using reaction time measures (see

Sternberg, 1969). On the stages approach an error must be attributable to a failure on a single stage or to a series of independent failures on a number of stages. Certain errors can arise in more than one stage, for the error response is similar to the stimulus in more than one dimension. Thus, in a word reading experiment *seven* is both visually and semantically similar to *several*.

If one assumes that the error transition matrices for different stages do not correlate, the proportion of such errors – mixed errors – can be calculated, given that the rate at which errors arise in each individual stage is known. For a two-stage process, if a type 1 error is one that definitely arises through malfunction in the first stage (e.g., a visual error) and a type 2 error through second stage malfunction (e.g., a semantic error), then

$$M < \frac{a}{1-a}B + \frac{b}{1-b}A$$

where A, B, M are the numbers of type 1, type 2, and mixed errors respectively, and the probability of a randomly selected stimulus-response pair being characterized as a type 1 and type 2 error being a and b, respectively (see Appendix 1). The number of mixed errors found can actually be much greater than the predicted value, which suggests that the relevant stages do not operate independently. Two such situations are semantic/phonological errors in content word selection in spontaneous speech and visual/semantic errors in reading.

In normal spontaneous speech the error rate is relatively low, so the simple equation above should provide a good approximation. Out of a corpus of 63 errors collected over a three month period, in which a single intended word was replaced by an alternative word, 15 word errors had a phonological relation to the intended word (i.e., at least half of the phonemes of each word were present in the other) and 22 had a semantic relation to the intended word or sentence. However, 17 were of the mixed type. Examples included *perpetual hallucinations* emitted as (→) *perceptual hallucinations* and *Finsbury* (a part of London) → Finchley (another part). The appropriate section of Fromkin's (1973) corpus, (Section V) contains 65 errors, of which 7, 27, and 10 were of the phonological, semantic, and mixed type, respectively. It is shown in Appendix 2 that the observed rate of mixed errors is far above the predicted value.

Another situation where the rate of mixed errors is too high is in the production of visual/semantic errors by a phonemic dyslexic patient (Shallice & Warrington, 1975). In reading 2,924 words he made 447 substantive errors, of which 273 were visually related to the stimulus, 19 were nonderivationally and semantically related, and 44 were of the mixed type. Using judges' ratings to estimate the chance of a random stimulus-response pair being rated semantically similar, it can be shown that the equation again produces a gross and significant underestimate for M. (This example should be treated more tentatively than the previous one, as the assumption of independence between the transition matrices is less adequate).

Such analyses of errors have three major disadvantages. Corpora based on observation of naturally occurring errors are, of course, dangerously subject to selection artifacts. Secondly, there is the problem of the criteria used for similarity that in certain cases (e.g., single-word reading errors) can be dealt with by ratings, but in others (e.g., spontaneous speech errors) is more difficult. Thirdly, there is the problem of the nonindependence of the transition probabilities between two stages (due, for instance, to similar effects of word frequency), which is more serious in the word reading case.

However, the effects found are quite strong. More important, the conclusion that follows of nonindependence between the relevant processing stages is supported by more conventional lines of evidence. Motley and Baars (1976) have demonstrated semantic facilitation of Spoonerisms, providing more evidence for the nonindependence of the semantic and phonological stages of content word selection in spontaneous speech. Reaction time analysis provides strong evidence against the independence of visual and semantic stages in word reading (Meyer, Schvaneveldt, & Ruddy, 1975).

It is now standard procedure in simulations of human cognition to distinguish between different domains of processing (see Sutherland, 1973). Thus, a speech comprehension program may differentiate between phonemic, syllabic, lexical, syntactic, and conceptual domains. The rest of the paper will be concerned with situations in which there proves to be an interaction between seemingly distinct domains of processing, the rate of mixed errors providing only one line of evidence. In such situations one could adopt the standard policy, when interactions occur in RT experiments, of arguing that the two variables influence the same stage (e.g., Meyer et al, 1975; Sternberg, 1969). However, this abandons the most basic assumption of the stages approach, that domains of processing are in some sense separable. This assumption is supported from an entirely separate area of knowledge — neuropsychology — in which the separability of microfunctions is increasingly widely accepted. For instance, such a simple task as object-naming can be failed at the cognitive level due to specific neurological damage to any one of at least four systems, namely those that mediate presemantic perceptual classification (Warrington & Taylor, 1973), semantic recognition (Warrington, 1975), name-finding (Newcombe, Oldfield, Ratcliff, & Wingfield, 1971), and phonological ordering of the name (Lecours & Lhermitte, 1969). Moreover, not only can the functional systems be separably damaged, but so can the transmission of information between them at least in the last two cases — optic aphasia (Lhermitte & Beauvois, 1973) and classical conduction asphasia (Benson, Sheremata, Bouchard, Segarra, Price, & Geschwind, 1973), and also probably in the first (see Shallice & Warrington, 1977). In particular, the separability of semantic from nonsemantic domains of processing is supported.

Two simple ways are available for weakening the assumptions of the stages approach while maintaining its essence of separable processing domains, and yet predicting a higher than chance incidence of mixed errors. First one can abandon the assumption that in a stage only one of a number of alternative outputs is selected, and instead assume some form of likelihood function of possible alternatives is transmitted to the next stage. Given its obvious physiological realization, this will be termed the activation approach. Secondly, one could add a comparator stage in which the single output of a later stage is transformed and compared with the stored output of an earlier stage. Only if a match is obtained is the output transmitted to a further stage; otherwise, the process recycles — an obvious incorporation of analysis by synthesis and "editing" ideas. In the former approach the high incidence of mixed errors is explained in terms of evidence summation in the later stage, in the latter by their being less easily failed by the comparator. Two experiments will be described in which attempts were made to assess these two possibilities in a quasi-mixed error situation.

II. SEGMENTATION ERRORS

To avoid the methodological problems relating to the investigation of the sorts of mixed errors described earlier, another class of errors was examined that could be explained by models based on the two approaches just discussed. These are segmentation errors, which were independently discovered in two very different types of situations, namely in reading attempts by two attentional dyslexic patients (Shallice & Warrington, 1977) and in normal recognition of more than one word in visual masking situations (Allport, 1977). In these errors letters from a word in one part of the visual field tend to be perceived in the corresponding part of a word in another part of the visual field. They may be conceived an analogous to one-way visual Spoonerisms, for many of the properties of the two types of error are similar.

The tendency to make segmentation errors is only one aspect of attentional dyslexia. The syndrome can be more abstractly characterized as a difficulty in recognizing an item in the visual field if and only if other items of the same category are also present. Thus, the patients had difficulty in reading single letters only if they were surrounded by other letters, even if they were in a different color. In such cases 35–40% of the errors were other letters present in the visual field (of which there were at most four). When the error matrix derived from all letter recognition experiments on one patient in which a rate of presentation of 2 sec or slower was compared with similarity ratings for upper case letters, there was a highly significant correlation for one subject, although not for the other, for whom much less data were available. It therefore appeared that selection of an item in the visual field for recognition may be deleteriously affected by its similarity to other items in the visual field; this is analogous to the situation with Spoonerisms in which similar phonemes are more likely to transpose (MacKay, 1970; Nooteboom, 1969). If this effect existed, it would support explanations of segmentation effects based on the sort of principles adopted above to explain mixed errors.

A preliminary experiment was performed to confirm that with normal subjects the effect existed. A second experiment was then performed in an attempt to differentiate between the two types of models. In both experiments Allport's (1977) experimental procedure of presenting under pattern masking conditions four words centered at the corners of a rectangle equidistant from the fixation point was used.

III. PRELIMINARY EXPERIMENT

The effect of visual similarity was assessed by comparing the chance of segmentation errors occurring between words that contained two letters in common in the same positions with pairs of words with no letters in common.

A.   Method

1. *Stimulus array.*   Each of the 20 sets of words contained four four-letter words. In any particular stimulus two of the words (either vertically or horizontally spatially arranged) had two letters in common (e.g., *hark, ward*). The other two words had the other two letters appropriately in common (e.g., *live, lone*). The words were selected so that the number of segmentation errors that would be produced by moving one letter to the same position in a word horizontally or vertically adjacent was virtually identical for similar and dissimilar pairs, the dissimilar pairings being obtained by using the other two adjacent relationships available on the rectangular array. Thus, in the example given above *hard* or *line* would be similar errors, *lark* or *word* dissimilar ones. (It should be noted that for similar pairs each possible segmentation error is counted twice, as it can be constructed in two different ways). The three ways in which two complementary letter position pairs could be selected from four letter positions were used as equally as possible. Each set of words appeared once in alternating upper and lower case letters (so that vertically or horizontally adjacent words had a complementary pattern) and once in the same case throughout — that is, equally often upper and lower. The two presentations occurred in corresponding positions in the first and second half of the experiment in an order randomized for case. The two pairs of similar words in a stimulus were equally often vertically and horizontally adjacent, being vertically related on one presentation and horizontally on the other.

2. *Procedure.*   The experiment was performed as a group experiment, so that each subject had a different size of visual array. The font, the relative sizes and positions of the words and of the pattern made were the same as in the main experiment, to be described subsequently. The experiment was run in a single session with a short break halfway through. At the start, an error led to five

extra identical stimuli being presented; these results were not analyzed. Each trial began with a warning signal, succeeded one second later by the stimulus that was exposed for 100 msec, and followed 100 msec later by the pattern mask, which lasted for 1 sec. The stimuli were projected by two identical slide projectors, the fixation point being a faint circle of light.

Subjects, 33 Birkbeck College undergraduates, were instructed that four words would be presented on each trial, and that they were to write down as many of them as they could in appropriate positions during the 15 sec interval between trials. If they were uncertain about a word, they were told still to write it down but to indicate that it was a guess.

B.   Results

Subjects correctly recognized 1.04 words on average for single case stimuli and 0.85 words for mixed case stimuli. There were 1,255 error responses (a mean of 0.96 per stimulus). Of these, 27% were some form of segmentation error. A breakdown of the segmentation errors is given in Table 1. The principal result is that standard horizontal or vertical (H/V) segmentation errors (with letter position maintained) were significantly more likely to occur between similar words than between dissimilar words (Wilcoxon $T = 82.5, N = 28, p < 0.005$ for subjects; $T = 47.5, N = 19, p < 0.05$ for word combinations, amalgamating results over the two presentations of each word combination). By contrast, the number of opportunities for segmentation errors between similar words was very slightly less. Fifty two % of the H/V segmentation errors occurred with single case stimuli, a very similar proportion to the proportion of correct responses.

C.   Discussion

Segmentation errors are considerably more likely to occur if there are identical letters in the same position in the influencing and influenced words. At a gross level, considering determination of figure and of content, this shows that they

TABLE 1
Preliminary Experiment — Segmentation Errors[a]

| | | | Position Preserved | |
| | | | Yes | No |
Word of Origin	H/V Sim.	H/V Dissim.	Diagon.	
% Possibilities	26.0	27.1	7.6	39.4
% Observed	47.8	32.3	6.3	13.6

[a]All errors are included where one letter of a word is replaced by a letter from another word in the stimulus. The Possibilities value is derived by considering the number of words that could be produced by all transpositions of this sort. (The H/V Sim. Possibilities value is *doubled* for reasons given in the text).

can be considered as mixed errors. Logically, determination of content cannot proceed determination of figure. Yet if determination of figure totally precedes determination of content, then errors in ascertaining the figure should not depend upon content, but they do.

However, the explanation of segmentation errors themselves would seem to require a model more complex than the stages one, if only because the interactions of multiple stimuli is under consideration. Yet an explanation of segmentation effects based on either of the types of principle generally used to explain mixed errors can be given. Following the analysis of attentional dyslexia given by Shallice and Warrington (1977), it could be assumed that identification of word components and their position within words occurs in parallel between words, but that the subsequent identification of words is a predominantly sequential process. [This position is related to the one held by Treisman, Sykes, and Gelade (1977) for the processing of disjunctively defined stimuli and indeed would utilize Treisman's (1960) attenuating filter as one type of attentional process.] Segmentation errors would then be presumed to arise in the parallel to serial (spatial) condensation of information, due to inadequate inhibition of the word components analysis of spatially irrelevant information. The partial activation of the word-form units (*visual* logogens) by word components in words other than the one being identified would be analagous to the partial activation of units corresponding to mixed errors in the second stage of one of the processes discussed earlier. That such competition from irrelevant stimuli cannot be prevented is supported by the findings of Eriksen and Eriksen (1974). Moreover, this type of filter account receives neurophysiological support from the work of Gross, Bender, and Rocha-Miranda (1974), if it be assumed that the pulvinar is part of the filter control system — a location that fits well with the lesion site involved in attentional dyslexia. Gross et al. found that pulvinar lesions left the "trigger features" for cells in higher cortical visual areas unaffected, but the cells now responded to all parts of the visual field instead of to a restricted area.

Alternatively, the comparator approach could be used by assuming that if a candidate error response occurs, it is less likely to be rejected by the comparator if its components are actually present in the visual field, even if in an irrelevant stimulus. On this approach it is the comparator that is tricked by spatially erroneous information.

In both models the visual similarity effect is to be predicted. In the former model more components of the error become submaximally activated, and in the latter more components exist in the visual field, so that erroneous acceptance by the comparator is more likely.

The preliminary experiment provides one minor piece of evidence relevant to these alternatives. On the comparator model, if a transform of the candidate is compared with a trace of the input, then it would presumably not be in mixed case. Hence, one would expect that segmentation errors with mixed case stimuli, where the case discrepancy is reduced in relation to that of the correct response, should be relatively more likely to occur than correct responses. No such effect occurs. In fact, the comparator model has difficulty in explaining why the use of mixed case stimuli — which presumably must fail to match — does not lead to complex RT interactions (Meyer & Gutschera, 1975).

IV.   MAIN EXPERIMENT

A standard inadequacy with many versions of the comparator model, particularly analysis-by-synthesis models concerns how the possible outputs are selected for matching. If all possible responses are matched, then the class of models appears indistinguishable from passive models in which input inhibits incorrect candidates, as well as activating the correct candidate. The class of models that can, therefore, be distinguished from activation-type models are those in which only a limited set of possible outputs are matched. On such models, if the candidate error can be made part of the search set, the chance of its occurring as an error will be increased (unless it is always rejected in the matching process). One possible way of attaining this should be by semantic priming. However, if the priming precedes stimulus presentation, then an increase in the appropriate errors would also be predicted on activation theory too. Thresholds for segmentation error candidates would be lowered at the presemantic level, as in Morton's (1969) explanation of context effects. [A similar difficulty in interpretation seems to arise in the recent interesting analogue to this situation with actual Sooonerisms, where Motley and Baars (1976) show experimentally that semantic and phonological factors interact.]

If, however, the cue occurs at the time of presentation, then the lowering of presemantic thresholds cannot occur until well after sufficient information has reached the semantic level for semantic priming to occur. On activation theory, semantic priming should then be at most a very small effect.

A.   Method

1.   *Stimulus array.*   Eight pairs of four-letter words were used, each of which could be expected on grounds of their physical characteristics to give rise to a particular segmentation error (e.g., *leek wear — week*). Pairs occurred in two different combinations. In the experimental stimuli they occurred with another pair of words, one of which was closely related semantically to the candidate segmentation error (e.g., *days*). The other (e.g., *huts*) was selected so that the pair could produce a segmentation error (in this case *hats*) that would itself be primed by one of the original words (i.e., *wear*). In the control stimuli, each pair was placed with another pair so that there was no obvious semantic relation between any of the four words and the two candidate errors.

The four words were arranged so that their ends nearest the fixation point formed a square of side 1.7° centered on the fixation point. The words themselves covered approximately 1.9°. Letters were constructed using Helvetica Medium Letraset, 20 pt. for lower case and 16 pt. for upper case. The pattern mask was composed of letter fragments having the same fonts distributed quasi-randomly; it also contained a fixation point.

Half the words were composed of upper case letters, and half of lower case. All the words on a card were in the same font, and on the two occasions that a particular word appeared, it occured in the same position and in the same font. Half the candidate segmentation errors were produced by the first letter of a word being transposed, and half by one of the other letters. Half of each were produced by vertical transpositions, and half by horizontal. When a semantic cue was present it was always adjacent to the word that contained three of the letters of the candidate segmentation error.

    2. *Procedure.* The subjects were 40 technicians, physiotherapists, nurses, and research workers at the National Hospital. They were tested individually using a Cambridge 2-field tachistoscope, the experiment thus involving both forward and backward masking. The trials were in series of eight with a short break between series; alternate series used SOAs of 60 and 200 msec. Both control and experimental trials involving a particular pair of words occurred in different series, but for a given subject they always involved the same exposure duration. Subjects were assigned on entering the experiment to one of eight conditions varying initial stimulus exposure, order of the series, and order within the series. A practice series of 20 trials initially 200 msec and then 60 msec duration preceded the first trial.

Subjects were instructed that four words would be presented on each trial and that they had to say what the words were and in what position they were presented. They were encouraged to guess but also asked to give confidence ratings for each response — 4 = certain, 3 = very likely, 2 = possible, and 1 = complete guess. They had 80 trials in all.

B. Results

The mean number of words correctly reported on a trial was 1.11 for the 200 msec exposure and 0.35 for the 60 msec exposure. The average number of error responses per trial was 0.74 for the 200 msec exposure and 0.67 for the 60 msec exposure. Of the 1,189 200 msec errors, 23.7% were H/V segmentation errors, compared with 13.4% of the 1,071 60 msec errors.

Two judges assessed all nonsegmentation errors for semantic similarity between the four stimulus words on a trial and the responses. Forty seven response words were assessed by both judges as closely related semantically to one of the stimulus words presented on that trial, and 96 by at least one of the two judges. As a check that this effect was not artifactual, an investigation was conducted to determine whether the responses were produced in the same position in the visual field as the stimulus to which they seemed related. If, as suggested by the

TABLE 2
Confidence Ratings for Different Types of Response[a]

	Duration	
	60 msec	200 msec
Correct	2.75	3.59
Seg. Errors	2.43	3.18
Sem. Errors	1.95	2.67

[a]The Segmentation Error value is derived solely from the planned errors, the Correct one by sampling 25% of each subject's responses, and the Semantic Error one by using all responses either judge considered closely related semantically and not visually related.

findings of Ellis and Marshall (1978), the semantic effect was artifactual, then there should be no relationship between the positions of the stimulus and of the semantically related response. In order to reduce the problem of correlations between form and meaning in the English language, responses with three or more letters in common with one of the stimuli were ignored. Of the remaining mutually agreed more closely related stimulus response pairs, 23 were on the same side of the visual field (of which 15 were in the same position) and 4 were on different sides. The effect of side is significantly different from chance (Wilcoxon: subjects $N = 16$, $T = 17$, $p < 0.005$; words $N = 24$, $T = 44$, $p < 0.005$), suggesting that the semantic relationship is not an artifact in all cases.

Confidence ratings are shown in Table 2. The most surprising finding was that the ratings for segmentation errors in the 200 msec condition were considerably higher than the ratings for correct responses in the 60 msec condition. In the 200 msec condition, subjects frequently rated segmentation errors as "certain." The high confidence ratings given to the segmentation errors strongly suggest that they do not result just from conscious guessing, using the remnants of a fast decaying trace.

Of the segmentation errors, 218 were those that allowed planned comparisons to be made. There was no interaction between the effect of cueing and exposure duration. Amalgamating over exposure duration, there is a significant effect of semantic cueing (Wilcoxon: $T = 133.5$, $N = 29$, $p < 0.05$ for subjects; $T = 411$, $N = 48$, $p < 0.05$ for word pairs). However, as can be seen from Table 3 the effect is not large.

If one separates those trials in which the cue is perceived from those in which it was not, there is no evidence for semantic cueing in the latter situation. Table 4 shows a comparison of the planned segmentation errors made when the cue was and was not perceived. They are compared with the segmentation errors made on the control trials, divided according to whether or not the semantic cue was perceived on the (different) control trial in which it was presented to that

TABLE 3
Semantic Cueing and Segmentation Errors[a]

| | Duration | | |
Semantic Cue	60 msec	200 msec	All
Present %	58.1	54.9	56.0
Not Pres. %	41.9	45.1	44.0
Total No.	74	144	218

[a]The results are derived from planned segmentation errors only.

subject. If the semantic cue is not perceived by the subject, then segmentation errors are no more likely if the candidate error occurs on the same trial as the cue (the experimental condition) than if it occurs on a different trial (the control condition). However, if the cue is perceived, segmentation errors are much more likely to occur if the candidate error and the cue are presented together (Wilcoxon: $T = 48, N = 23, p < 0.005$ for word pairs).

Two additional pieces of evidence support the idea that prior conscious perception of the cue is necessary for semantic facilitation to occur. When both a semantic cue and its primed segmentation error occur, the cue is significantly more confidently perceived, suggesting it is perceived first [Wilcoxon: $T = 29$, $N = 18, p < 0.025$ (2 tail) for trials]; on only two occasions was the subject more confident about the segmentation error. More importantly, if the position of the cue in the stimulus array is considered, there is a tendency for segmentation errors to occur more frequently if the cue is in one of the two lower positions. Yet on these stimuli there is no effect of semantic facilitation (Wilcoxon: $T = 114, N = 22, p > 0.3$ for word pairs). However, if the cue is in one of the two upper positions — the positions in which it is much more likely to be perceived — then there is a significant effect of semantic priming (Wilcoxon: $T = 96, N = 26, p < 0.025$ for word pairs).

TABLE 4
The Effect of Perception of the Cue on Priming[a]

| | Cue Perceived | |
Cue and Error	Yes	No
In Same Stimulus	35	87
In Diff. Stimuli	14	82

[a]The values given are the number of segmentation errors occurring differentiated according to the occurrence of the cue and its perception.

One further, seemingly unrelated, effect should be mentioned. When the word pairs were horizontally adjacent, significantly more first letter transpositions produced segmentation errors (77% of the total), but in the vertically adjacent situation, significantly less first letter transpositions occurred (38% of the total) [Fisher Exact Test: $p < 0.01$ and $p < 0.02$ (2 tail) respectively].

C. Discussion

On initial analysis, there is a weak but significant effect of semantic cueing, a result that does not differentiate very clearly between the two models. However, more detailed analysis suggests that one needs to differentiate between whether the cue is or is not perceived; only in the former case − to be called "conscious priming" − does clear evidence of semantic facilitation occur.

One might attempt to argue that the difference between conscious and subconscious priming is simply that the latter is too weak to produce significant effects. However, there is a considerable amount of literature supporting the existence of sizeable subconscious priming effects (e.g., Lewis, 1972: MacKay, 1972a; Marcel, 1974). Indeed, Allport (1977) showed fairly strong facilitation in tachistoscopic recognition of a pattern-masked word by the presence of a second, semantically related word, of which subjects were unaware, using only 20 msec SOA, a much shorter duration than those used in the present experiment. Moreover, differential positive effects of subconscious and conscious priming have been found in other situations (e.g., Marcel, 1974). Thus, it seems implausible to attribute the lack of a subconscious priming effect to the weakness of the priming stimulus trace.

The positive conscious priming effect is open to various interpretations, of which a comparator process subsequent to conscious perception is one. An alternative is that word components are preserved in a visual short-term memory, and that the "filter" admits word component information from different areas of the visual field sequentially to the word-form unit. Morton's (1969) explanation of context effects could then be applied.

V. GENERAL DISCUSSION

The main experiment provides some evidence supporting a comparator process subsequent to conscious perception. This could be the process on which confidence judgments are based. It could hardly be responsible, however, for segmentation errors. One would need to suppose that subjects *consciously* suppress error responses less when they preserve letter position, do this even less when they are visually similar, and do this when they have been explicitly instructed to guess and yet give high confidence ratings for them.

Moreover, much of the attraction of the comparator approach lies in the assumption that there is relatively unlimited parallel access to the semantic system, and that one becomes conscious only when the construction based on this parallel access can be satisfactorily compared, with the trace of lower levels of processing (see e.g., Allport, 1977 and in essence Turvey, 1974). Such an approach is not supported by the results of the main experiment.

By contrast, the activation approach can explain all the results, provided that one assumes, following Shallice (1972), that in the mapping from phenomenal to information-processing domains of explanation, a necessary (but not sufficient) condition for conscious experience is of a high level of activation within the appropriate system. More specifically, if one assumes after Shallice and Warrington (1975) that at the word-form level there are mutually inhibitory but self-excitatory neural nets for every word-form in the language, then it follows that the activation in a net will rapidly increase if it alone receives input above a certain level. If insufficient input occurs, then some increase in activation will result, but a positive feedback rise will not take place. Moreoever, on a given occasion this rise can take place for at most one net. The system, therefore, tends to select one word-form for every input, provided it is sufficiently strong; it provides a physiological analogue to Morton's (1969) logogen approach to word recognition.

On such a model, the semantic facilitation found by Marcel (1974) and Allport (1977) is explicable, since even for stimuli that produce insufficient activation for conscious perception, some activation is transmitted to the semantic system. Perceptual defense can be explained by an additional negative feedback loop. Semantic errors could occur on the model, if a word-form unit is relatively weakly activated, so that the spread of semantic activation to associated words is not dominated by continuing activation from the graphemic system. As one would expect, subjects produce semantic errors with very low confidence.

Such an activation model deals simply with the physical similarity effects found in the preliminary experiment. However, there does appear to be a major difficulty in accounting for the findings in the main experiment. If the word-form units corresponding to segmentation error candidates are being submaximally activated, why do they not provide sufficient input to the semantic system to allow facilitation from other submaximally activated units? Such facilitation is, after all, the way that Allport's (1977) findings are explained on the model. The difference lies in the way that in the segmentation error case the word-form units corresponding to the segmentation error candidate and the correct response can *both* receive quite strong input. In the model the activation in one will then rise rapidly, and so the activation in the other must be suppressed, so that only a brief effect of it reaches the semantic system. This presupposes that inhibition of competing units primarily occurs when one unit is strongly activated (see also Posner and Snyder, 1975). Empirically, this account is indirectly supported by the way that the number of segmentation errors *increases* with exposure duration and the way that subjects give much higher confidence ratings to segmentation than to semantic errors. Both findings support the idea that when a segmentation error occurs, its unit has been quite strongly activated at the word-form level — which is not necessarily the case when semantic effects occur.

This type of model, based on a set of self-excitatory but mutually inhibitory nets, is a candidate for any system whose function is to select one from a finite number of known continually occurring alternatives integrating both input and context information. (It is a physiologically-plausible realization of the mode of operation of Morton's (1969) logogen units.) A number of subsystems of the speech production system have this sort of function, such as content word selection (discussed earlier), and phoneme selection; a number of phenomena, in addition to mixed errors, support this type of explanation, e.g. the existence of blends (see MacKay, 1972b). Indeed MacKay (1970) has proposed a very closely related explanation to account for the properties of Spoonerisms, to which the segmentation errors are a visuo-spatial analogue. He, however, assumes that "similar programs in the speech production process" inhibit each other. The evidence is, though, much more compatible with the view that the more similar "programs" are, the more they activate each other. The crucial property of selecting only one output can be ensured by all "programs" inhibiting each other, with inhibition being more powerful when the general level of activation rises (see Shallice, 1972).

APPENDIX 1

Consider a process containing two independent stages. Let the probability of a randomly selected response, being characterized as similar to a (different) randomly selected stimulus in the domains corresponding to the first and second stages, be a and b respectively. Let the chance of the first stage operating correctly be p, of it producing no output q, so that the chance of it producing an error output is $(1 - p - q)$. Similarly, let the probabilities of the second stage producing an error output be $(1 - p' - q')$. Let the number of errors similar to the stimulus in the first domain only (type 1), the second domain only (type 2), and in both domains (mixed) be A, B, and M, respectively, and let N be the total number of trials. Type 1 errors can occur whether or not the second stage operates correctly, either through only the first stage producing an error output or through both stages.

Thus, $\quad A/N = (1 - b)(1 - p - q)p' + a(1 - b)(1 - p - q)(1 - p' - q').$

Similarly, $\quad B/N = (1 - a)p(1 - p' - q') + (1 - a)b(1 - p - q)(1 - p' - q')$

and, $\quad M/N = b(1 - p - q)p' + ap(1 - p' - q') + ab(1 - p - q)(1 - p' - q').$

Hence, $\quad M = \dfrac{b}{1 - b}A + \dfrac{a}{1 - a}B - Nab(1 - p - q)(1 - p' - q')$

It should be noted that the independence assumption is used in two ways. First, it occurs in the estimate of the chance probability of a stimulus-response pair being "mixed" as ab. Second, it is assumed that the values of p are not correlated (over stimuli) with those of p'. When, as in the spontaneous speech example, values of p' are close to 1, the second assumption does not need to be made.

APPENDIX 2

Combining one corpus with the other, as they do not differ significantly, produces 22 phonological errors, 49 semantic errors, and 27 mixed errors. To assess whether the rate of mixed errors is too high, it is necessary to know with what probabilities a randomly selected response would be rated as a phonological and as a semantic error. By selecting pairs of words at random from text, a value of 0.03 was obtained for the former. The latter is more difficult to assess. However, if the expected relation is to hold, a lower bound can be obtained for it. Using the normal approximation to the Poisson distribution, there can only be a 5% chance of the probability of a random word being rated semantically similar to the intended sentence being less than 0.45. As the actual value must obviously be an order of magnitude less than this, the relation cannot hold.

ACKNOWLEDGMENTS

We should like to thank Dr. Vernon Gregg for providing the facilities for us to perform the preliminary experiment and Dr. John Morton for his useful comments on an earlier draft.

REFERENCES

Allport, D. A. On knowing the meaning of words we are unable to report: the effects of visual masking. In S. Dornic (Ed.), *Attention and performance VI*. Hillsdale: Lawrence Erlbaum Associates, 1977.

Benson, D. F., Sheremata, W. A., Bouchard, R., Segerra, J. M., Price, D., & Geschwind, N. Conduction asphasia: A clinicopathological study. *Archives of Neurology*, 1973, *28*, 339–346.

Ellis, A. W., & Marshall, J. C. Semantic errors or statistical flukes? A note on Allport's "On knowing the meaning of words we are unable to report." *Quarterly Journal of Experimental Psychology*, in press.

Eriksen, B. A., & Eriksen, C. W. Effects of noise upon the identification of a target letter in a nonsearch task. *Perception and Psychophysics*, 1974, *16*, 143–149.

Fromkin, V. A. *Speech errors as linguistic evidence*. The Hague: Mouton, 1973.

Gross, C. G., Bender, D. B., & Rocha-Miranda, C. E. Inferotemporal cortex: A single-unit analysis. In F. O. Schmitt & F. G. Worden (Eds.), *The Neurosciences: Third study program*. Cambridge: MIT Press, 1974.

Lecours, A. R., & Lhermitte, F. Phonemic paraphasias: Linguistic structures and tentative hypotheses. *Cortex*, 1969, *5*, 193–228.

Lewis, J. L. Semantic processing with bisensory stimulation. *Journal of Experimental Psychology*, 1972, *96*, 455–457.

Lhermitte, F., & Beauvois, M. F. A visuo-speech disconnexion syndrome – Report of a case with optic aphasia, agnosic alexia and colour agnosia. *Brain*, 1973, *96*, 695–714.

Mackay, D. G. Spoonerisms: The structure of errors in the serial order of speech. *Neuropsychologia*, 1970, *8*, 323–350.

Mackay, D. G. Aspects of the theory of comprehension, memory and attention. *Quarterly Journal of Experimental Psychology*, 1972, *25*, 22–40. (a)

Mackay, D. G. The structure of words and syllables: evidence from errors in speech. *Cognitive Psychology*, 1972, *3*, 210–227. (b)

Marcel, A. J. *Perception with and without awareness.* Paper presented to the Experimental Psychology Society, Stirling, 1974.

Meyer, D. E., & Gutschera, K. D. *Orthographic versus phonemic processing of printed words.* Paper presented to the Psychonomics Society, Denver, 1975.

Meyer, D. E., Schvaneveldt, R. W. & Ruddy, M. G. Loci of contextual effects on visual word recognition. In P. M. A. Rabbitt & S. Dornic (Eds.), *Attention and performance V*. London: Academic Press, 1975.

Morton, J. The interaction of information in word recognition. *Psychological Review*, 1969, *76*, 165–178.

Motley, M. T., & Baars, B. J. Semantic bias effects on the outcomes of verbal slips. *Cognition*, 1976, *4*, 177–187.

Newcombe, F., Oldfield, R. C., Ratcliff, G. G., & Wingfield, A. Recognition and naming of object-drawings by men with focal brain wounds. *Journal of Neurology, Neurosurgery and Psychiatry*, 1971, *34*, 329–340.

Nooteboom, S. G. The tongue slips into patterns. In A. G. Sciarone et al. (Eds.), *Nomen: Leyden studies in linguistics and phonetics*. The Hague: Mouton, 1969.

Posner, M. I., & Snyder, C. Facilitation and inhibition in the processing of signals. In P. M. A. Rabbitt & S. Dornic (Eds.), *Attention and performance V*. London: Academic Press, 1975.

Shallice, T. Dual functions of consciousness. *Psychological Review*, 1972, *79*, 383–393.

Shallice, T., & Warrington, E. K. Word recognition in a phonemic dyslexic patient. *Quarterly Journal of Experimental Psychology*, 1975, *27*, 187–199.

Shallice, T., & Warrington, E. K. The possible role of selective attention in acquired dyslexia. *Neuropsychologia*, 1976, *15*, 31–41.

Sternberg, S. The discovery of processing stages: Extensions of Donders' method. In W. G. Koster (Ed.), *Attention and performance II*. Amsterdam: North-Holland, 1969.

Sutherland, N. S. *Intelligent picture processing.* Proceedings of the Conference on the Evolution of the Nervous Sytem and Behaviour, Florida State University, 1973.

Treisman, A. M. Contextual cues in selective listening. *Quarterly Journal of Experimental Psychology*, 1960, *12*, 242–248.

Treisman, A. M., Sykes, M., & Gelade, G. Selective attention and stimulus integration. In S. Dornic (Ed.), *Attention and performance VI*. Hillsdale: Lawrence Erlbaum Associates, 1977.

Turvey, M. T. Constructive theory, perceptual systems and tacit knowledge. In W. B. Weimer & D. S. Palermo (Eds.), *Cognition and symbolic processes*. Hillsdale, N.J.: Lawrence Erlbaum Associates, 1974.

Warrington, E. K. The selective impairment of semantic memory. *Quarterly Journal of Experimental Psychology*, 1975, *27*, 635–658.

Warrington, E. K., & Taylor, A. M. The contribution of the right parietal lobe to object recognition. *Cortex*, 1973, *7*, 152–164.

12 Word Recognition and Production: Reciprocity in Clinical and Normal Studies

Anthony J. Marcel
Karalyn E. Patterson

Medical Research Council
Applied Psychology Unit
Cambridge, England

ABSTRACT

These investigations were based on three aspects of the acquired dyslexia of certain aphasic patients: (1) the inability to read orthographically regular nonwords, (2) semantic errors made in attempting to read single words, and (3) the selective inability to read low imageability words. The first study involved an analysis of patients' attempts to repeat and to read nonwords, and also a lexical decision task in which nonwords varied in their homophony with real words. Patients were able to make lexical decisions adequately, but unlike normal controls, they showed no effect of nonword phonology. This implies that these patients are impaired in a nonlexical route to phonology, but that lexical access is possible via a visual address. The second set of studies, with normal subjects, demonstrates in a variety of tasks that even though a word is pattern-masked such that its presence cannot be detected, its meaning affects subsequent behavior. This implies a dissociation between semantic interpretation of a word and its availability as a response. Pattern-masking interferes not with the visual encoding leading to semantic interpretation, but rather with processes, including consciousness, necessary for response production; in doing so, it may parallel certain clinical phenomena. In the third set of studies, normal subjects' report of single words presented tachistoscopically was suggestive of the patients' behavior in that imageability affected left but not right visual hemifield presentations. This contrasts with the results of a further experiment not involving report, which examined the degree of associative facilitation on a lexical decision task within and across hemifields. The preceding "priming" words were of high and low imageability and were pattern-masked to prevent awareness. Neither imageability nor hemifield affected latency of the size of the associative priming effect. However, contralateral priming was less effective than ipsilateral. These results suggest that (a) lexical and semantic processing of words are carried out in both cerebral hemispheres, (b) the source of word-class effects is in production (the realization of semantics), and (c) it is this process that is laterally asymmetric. The relationships between normal and pathological systems are discussed.

I. INTRODUCTION

This paper has two aims. The first, more general aim is to illustrate the productive interaction between research on clinical and normal populations. The second is to indicate the theoretical direction in which we feel this research impels us, in the area of reading and speech.

Postman, (1975) in his review of work on memory remarked:

> We have not considered the results obtained with brain-damaged patients which continue to be cited as evidence for dual-process theory. The existing data do not impress us as unequivocal; more important, extrapolations from pathological deficits to the structure of normal memory are of uncertain validity (p. 308).

It is certainly reasonable to be cautious in inferring from pathological states to normal ones. However, it is stultifying to fail to make use of such "natural" fractionation of behavior as a cue to relevant investigations of normal populations. The question of the relevance of pathological states for normal research, and vice-versa, is not new. Our response to this issue is to do experiments on each population, where the experimental questions for one are guided by results obtained from the other. What we wish to report is to be viewed as an early stage in such a cumulative process, providing ideas for further work rather than confident theory.

The patients with whom we are concerned are people who have suffered damage to the left cerebral hemisphere resulting in aphasia and a reading impairment that has been termed "deep" or "phonemic" dyslexia. Clinical profiles of several such patients can be found in Marshall and Newcombe (1973), Shallice and Warrington (1975), and Patterson and Marcel (1977). When such patients are asked to read individual words aloud, their performance shows several interesting characteristics reported by others and verified by us (Patterson & Marcel, 1977):

1. Some words, primariily nouns and adjectives, are read correctly.

2. Some words receive no attempt at reading, especially function words and words low in imageability value.

3. Some words evoke paralexic errors, where the relationship between stimulus and response can be classified as visual (e.g., *own* → "now"; *origin* → organ"), derivational (e.g., *courage* → "courageous"), or semantic but non-derivational (e.g., *dream* → "sleep").

4. The patients are almost totally unable to read orthographically regular and pronounceable nonword letter-strings such as *dake*.

At the same time the patients have little difficulty in repeating any of the above when presented aurally, thus ruling out an articulatory explanation of the reading failures. Some process between visual analysis and vocal response has been impaired. Such a syndrome is challenging for us to deal with in terms of our modeling of the reading process. The work which we would like to report is relevant to three of the patients' characteristics mentioned above: (1) the inability to read pronounceable nonwords, (2) semantically related errors to single words, and (3) the selective inability to read low imageability words.

II. FROM GRAPHEME TO PHONEME

It was suggested by both Marshall and Newcombe (1973) and Shallice and Warrington (1975) that one fundamental deficit in phonemic dyslexia is an impairment of the ability to derive a phonological representation of a written word by nonlexical grapheme-to-phoneme rules. Two experiments, testing two phonemic dyslexic patients and a normal control group, were designed to evaluate this hypothesis. The results of this study will be summarized very briefly, as details of the patients and the experiments appear in Patterson and Marcel (1977). Both experiments involved orthographically regular nonwords (e.g., *widge, jub*). The first demonstrated that, although patients performed reasonably well when asked to repeat auditorily presented nonwords, they were essentially incapable of reading aloud such stimuli given visual presentation. Normal subjects performed the reading test without error. The second experiment was a version of the lexical decision task ("Is this written letter-string a word or not?") where we measured the time required to make lexical decisions for a list of items. It is known from previous research (Coltheart, Davelaar, Jonasson, & Besner, 1977; Rubenstein, Lewis, & Rubenstein, 1971) that the "no" decision to a nonword is slower if the nonword is homophonic with a real word (e.g., *brane*) than if it is not (e.g., *brabe*). We replicated this result with normal subjects, who were slower in lexical decision on lists of letter-strings containing homophonic nonwords, and also made more false positive errors to homophonic nonwords than to nonhomophonic nonwords. The two patients, who were able to perform the lexical decision task reasonably well, showed no effect at all of the phonological status of nonwords, either on time or errors. It should also be noted that many words that they were unable to read were correctly classified.

The two experiments from Patterson and Marcel provide convincing support for the notion that the nonlexical route to phonology is essentially inoperative in phonemic dyslexic patients. The experiments also offer an observation of relevance to the process of normal word recognition. Since the phonology of both nonwords and words (Coltheart et al., 1977) affects performance on lexical decisions, it seems that phonological coding normally occurs in the process of

interpreting written language. Yet the patients, impaired in phonological coding, can make word/nonword judgments quite adequately. This suggests that
purely visual or graphic access to the lexical-semantic system is possible and
useable, and that this is the means by which patients achieve what reading they
can. Since it is virtually impossible that they have acquired such a route
subsequent to their injuries, the implication is that a direct graphic route exists
in the normal system. Indeed, with regard to normal people, in addition to our
ability to classify nonwords homophonous with real words, and to recognize
and pronounce words containing ambiguous graphemes (e.g., in English: -ough;
in French: -ent), the experimental evidence reviewed by Bradshaw (1975) suggests that meaning may be accessed from print without any intervening phonological stage. The indication of the papers by Kolers (1970) and Hawkins,
Reicher, Rogers, and Peterson (1976) is that the two routes are tactical alternatives.

At this point, then, we would like to summarize the implications of these first
experiments by the diagram in Fig. 1. There are two routes from print to lexical
representation, one direct graphic, the other indirect via phonology. The patients
are impaired in the latter.

III.   KNOWING THE MEANING BUT NOT THE WORD

The second intriguing aspect of the patients' performance is their paralexic
errors, specifically those responses related to the stimulus in meaning alone.
Obviously some information must be reaching the lexical or semantic system.
Since it is hard to conceive of this without computation of the stimulus word's
specific address, why then could not the word be produced correctly? In the
context of the studies in Section II, lexical access is presumably achievable via
a graphic route; impairment to a nonlexical route to phonology seems largely
irrelevant. This section seeks to answer what sort of model can handle these
data, and what relation they bear to normal processes.

One approach to word recognition and production that attempts to account
for paralexic errors is Morton's (1968, 1970) logogen model. The relevant features of the model are that (a) as a result of visual analysis, graphic information
activates logogens, or lexical entries, maximally activating the one corresponding
to the stimulus; (b) when a first threshold in a logogen is reached, information is
sent to the semantic system, which feeds back to the lexical system activating
semantically related logogens; and (c) when a second threshold of activation is
reached, the corresponding word becomes available as a response, and this
second threshold varies from word to word. According to this model, normal
people essentially never make errors in reading single words because there is
enough visual information to activate the second threshold. The way it might
deal with paralexic errors, particularly derivational and semantic errors, is by

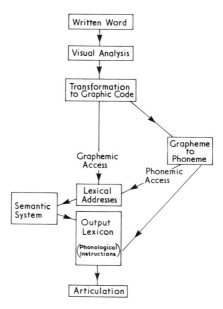

FIG. 1.   Lexical and nonlexical
routes from print to phonology.

assuming that the second threshold is abnormally raised but not equally for all logogens. Thus, the threshold for a particular word may be so high that another word, visually or semantically similar, may be produced instead. We have already concluded that phonemic dyslexia involves an impairment in the grapheme-phoneme route; the logogen model postulates a second departure from normality, an alteration in the functioning of the lexical system.

It is pertinent to examine what relation such errors bear to performance in normal people. To this end will be reported several experiments on pattern-masking prompted by a peculiar observation made several years ago, when the first author was working on an apparently separate topic. That study essentially required children and adults to report what they could see when single words were briefly presented and followed by a pattern mask. Among the errors were responses which bore a striking semantic relationship to the stimulus, but little other similarity (e.g., "king" for *queen*; "red" for *yellow*). The peculiarity lay in the absence of any semantic context, the short delay before a response, and the usual resistance of subjects to violating their visual impressions. These responses were reminiscent of two things: (1) paralexic responses of aphasic subjects, as reported by Marshall and Newcombe (1966), and (2) recent work on the independence of meaning and physical characteristics of words (Wickens, 1972; Worthington, 1964) related to the old issue of subliminal perception.[1] The following experiments were conducted in response to these observations.

[1] Work on this topic, extensively reviewed by Dixon (1971), will not be further discussed here since our principal concerns are with the clinical issue and the pattern-masking effects.

The experiments referred to in this section have been reported as part of a series of studies whose full description and discussion are available elsewhere (Marcel, 1974, 1978). The first experiment was an attempt to examine the availability of different kinds of information under pattern-masking. On each trial either a single word or a blank card was exposed followed by a pattern mask. The subject then had to make one of three decisions: (a) Was there anything before the mask? (b) Given two words, which was more visually similar in meaning to what had been presented? or (c) Given two words, which was more similar in meaning to what had been presented? A large number of trials was given at any one premask exposure duration or Stimulus Onset Asynchrony (SOA), and the (SOA) was then lowered, eventually becoming extremely brief. For most subjects the pattern of results was consistent and quite dramatic. As the exposure duration (SOA) was lowered, the first decision to reach chance (defined as equal to or below 55% correct) was the presence-absence judgment. The next decision to reach chance was that of graphic similarity, and at this point the subjects were still guessing well above chance on semantic similarity.

Before discussing the implications of this result, it is convenient to relate one more experiment. Some subjects felt that they could not reasonably go on making choices after the point at which they could no longer detect anything before the mask. In a sense the experiment was unreasonable, since people were being asked to base a judgment on an event of which they were unaware. In subsequent experiments this problem was overcome by examining the effect of masked words on *other* words, not masked, in a separate task. The following is an example of this. Meyer, Schvaneveldt, and Ruddy (1972) have shown that when two lexical decisions are required in succession, and when both letter-strings are words, the response to the second is faster if it is semantically associated with the first than if it is not (bread-butter vs. nurse-butter). In the present studies the effect of association on decision time was examined when the first word was either pattern-masked or not. Before the experimental session, the SOA at which each subject could no longer detect the presence of a word or judge graphic similarity was individually determined. An SOA just under this was used in the mask condition. Subjects were not required to respond to the first letter-string in either condition. The critical conditions were when both letter strings were words. When the first word was not masked, a semantic relationship between the words shortened reaction time to the second by 62 msec; when the first was masked, the facilitation was 56 msec — equally significant association effects. Incidentally, no subject was aware that anything had preceded the mask during the experimental session.

What these experiments suggest is, first, that visual or graphic information is effective in the absence of phenomenal knowledge of the presence of an event; further, even when graphic information ceases to be usable, one can still show that the stimulus word must have been analyzed to the stage at which it is associated with other words in nonsensory ways, that is, to a lexical or semantic representation. This is clearly reminiscent of semantic paralexias in brain-damaged individuals, and we shall return to this issue shortly. More generally, however, the masking experiments have important implications for perception and consciousness, which we will address now.

To begin with, the role of pattern-masking must be reassessed.[2] The most widely accepted interpretation of masking (Sperling, 1967; Turvey, 1973) is that the masking pattern interferes with a relatively raw representation of visual input (iconic memory) and that only with and after this visual representation can the input be further processed such that stimuli can be identified or coded in phonological or semantic terms. This view is surely mistaken. While stimulus identity, even presence, cannot be recovered by subjects, stimuli have obviously been processed to a "high," semantic level. Pattern-masking, rather than interfering with visual analysis, appears to be preventing access to consciousness. Indeed, the first experiment suggests that a paradigm assumption of the information-processing approach be turned on its head. Decreasing the SOA in pattern-masking seems not to restrict analysis to lower levels. Rather, if the critical process is viewed as one of *recovery* of information, then information is left recoverable from progressively higher levels. The pattern-mask must be having its effect at some stage of visual or graphic representation that supports visual awareness. Yet obviously this cannot be the representation that gives access to the lexical-semantic system. One solution is to propose that consciousness depends on a *record* of the visual analysis, and it is with this that the mask interferes. This is illustrated in Fig. 2.

Obviously, output from this visual-graphic record can reach consciousness without any output from the semantic system; otherwise we would not "see" nonsense words. However, semantic output cannot reach consciousness without the information from the visual record that an event with form and location has occurred to occasion such output.[3] Corroborative evidence for this suggestion comes from another experiment. Words were masked at SOAs beneath detectability and then that combination of word-followed-by-mask (or blank-followed-by-mask) was continuously repeated at fixed interstimulus-intervals. After varying numbers of repetitions, subjects were required either (a) to judge the presence of a word or guess a word, or (b) to perform a lexical decision task where word items were associated or unassociated with the masked word. Repetition increased the effect of the word's meaning on lexical decision time to associated words, but made no difference to the probability of reporting its

[2]None of the associative effects reported here with pattern-masking were obtained if words were energy-masked to the same criterion. This supports Turvey's (1973) notion that pattern-masking operates at a more central processing stage than energy-masking.

[3]This is strikingly reminiscent of the case of "blindsight" reported by Weiskrantz, Warrington, Sanders, and Marshall (1974), where a patient with a visual hemianopia, who was unaware of a stimulus, nonetheless knew its location and other features. This has been interpreted in terms of the "two-visual systems" hypothesis.

216

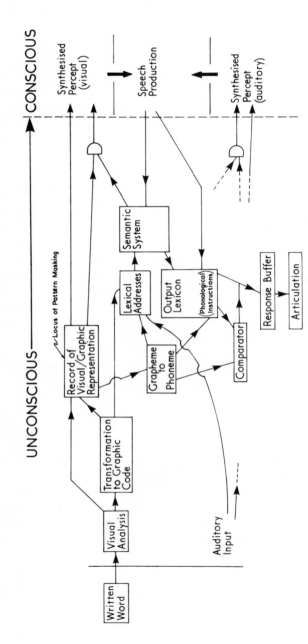

FIG. 2. A tentative model of conscious and unconscious processes in reading.

presence or the ability to produce it. This indicates that increased activation within the lexical-semantic system alone has no effect on availability of the stimulus as a response or awareness of it. Although the semantic system connects directly to the output lexicon (see Fig. 2), a semantic specification per se will not be sufficient to engender vocal production. One behaves rationally and does not attempt to read a word if none is seen (i.e., if there is no synthesized percept). Up to the point of access to the lexical-semantic system, the experiments suggest that stimulus processing is automatic and does not require the involvement of consciousness. Speech production, however, depends upon such involvement.

To return to the aphasic reading impairment, what is the relevance of the foregoing? First, as noted above, it has been shown that under conditions of severe pattern-masking, normal people can have semantic information without being able to identify or produce the specific stimulus word. With less severe pattern-masking (longer SOAs) normal people have been observed by us and by Allport (1977) to produce semantic (as well as) visual paralexias. One possible interpretation of why paralexic errors are not normally produced is that the graphic record that supports conscious awareness of the stimulus, enabling us to produce a response at all, is also the basis of grapheme-phoneme translation. Patterson and Marcel (1977) and Saffran, Schwartz, and Marin (1977), have suggested that nonlexical grapheme-phoneme conversion, while not essential for response production, may function normally to suppress reading errors by providing a representation with which the phonology of any candidate response can be compared. The phonemic dyslexic patient has no way of making such a comparison through a common code[4], since grapheme-phoneme translation is impaired. (In this connection, it has been noted by ourselves and by Werner (1956) that these patients may respond to a written word with a sequence of words containing the correct item and not know it is correct.) Although this is a possible account of both patients' and normals' paralexic responses, it does not rule out the alteration of some process related to lexical-semantic functioning. The latter possibility is indeed appealing in view of the fact that broad syntactic and semantic classes of words show major differences of readability by such patients. For example, nouns and adjectives are read with considerably more success than verbs (Shallice & Warrington, 1975); function words show particular vulnerability (Gardner & Zurif, 1975); and imageability ratings of words provide a good predictor of reading performance (Patterson & Marcel, 1977; Richardson, 1975). In the next section we will focus on imageability. We prefer to postpone further consideration of the mechanisms underlying the reading impairment, particularly additional lexical-semantic involvement, until then.

---

[4]That error-checking requires two sources of information which need a common code for comparison was pointed out by Philip Barnard (personal communication).

IV.   THE LOCUS OF WORD CLASS EFFECTS

The contents of this section have been reported elsewhere (Marcel and Patterson, 1976). A full account of the sequence of experiments and their procedure is in preparation.

The third relevant aspect of the reading performance of phonemic dyslexic patients is their selective inability to read words rated low on imageability (Patterson & Marcel, 1977; Shallice & Warrington, 1975). Our approach to this was once again to see if characteristics of the patients' performance could be produced in normal subjects. Given the context that the patients have damage to their left hemispheres, we decided to look for hemispheric effects. In the first experiment we presented to normal subjects words used with the patients, varying independently on imageability and concreteness (Colorado Concreteness and Imagery Norms, 1973; Paivio, Yuille, & Madigan, 1968). These were presented to either right or left of a fixation point and were followed by a pattern-mask at SOAs determined for each hemifield to yield about 70% correct report (using different words from the same population). The finding was, first, that concreteness had no effect, which accords with our own and Richardson's (1975) finding with patients, and that imageability seems to be the critical variable. Second, imageability interacted with hemifield such that it affected left visual field (LVF) presentations but not those in the right visual field (RVF). In a second experiment, where imageability varied but concreteness, frequency, and word length were held constant, the result was even more clear cut. The percent correct for hemifield and imageability is presented in Table 1.

Clearly, imageability affects left but not right hemifield presentations, a result which appears to mimic the patients' performance. Given these results, we were now able to ask at what stage imageability is having its effect. Various accounts have been proposed, roughly locating the effect at stages of prelexical encoding (Ellis & Shepherd, 1974), lexical (Richardson, 1975), and semantic (Shallice, personal communication) stages. Our strategy was to attempt to eliminate production or report as a factor in order to isolate semantic and preceding stages. We did this by utilizing the pattern-masking technique reported above and examining semantic priming in the lexical decision task. The object was to compare semantic priming by high and low imageability words within and across

TABLE 1
Percentage Correct Report as a Function of Visual Field
and Imageability

		LVF	*RVF*
	Low	38	80
Imageability			
	High	82	82

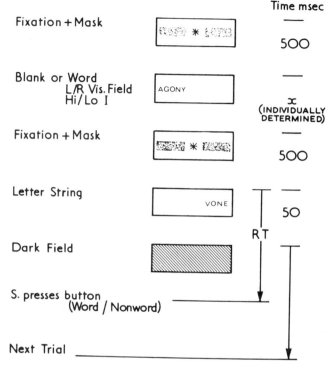

Time msec

Fixation + Mask — 500

Blank or Word
L/R Vis. Field
Hi/Lo I — x (INDIVIDUALLY DETERMINED)

Fixation + Mask — 500

Letter String — 50

RT

Dark Field

S. presses button (Word / Nonword)

Next Trial

FIG. 3.   Sequence of events per trial to assess laterality of semantic and productive contributions to imageability effect.

the two cerebral hemispheres. If report turned out not to be the critical factor, the design could still reveal differential lexical representation or semantic encoding, in the two hemispheres, of high and low imageability words. The procedure is shown in Fig. 3.

The second letter-string, when a word, was preceded by a masked word to which it was either an associate or not, the first word being either high or low imageability. Critical "nondetection" SOAs were individually determined for each hemifield prior to the test session. The first and second stimuli were each unpredictably presented to right or left of fixation. The results of this experiment, shown in Fig. 4, can be summarized as follows: (1) primer imageability produced no difference in latency or in the size of the priming effect; (2) there was no difference in the priming effect between Left → Left and Right → Right presentations; (3) nor was there any difference in the priming effect between Left → Right and Right → Left presentations; however, (4) ipsilateral priming was significantly more effective than contralateral. This is unlikely to be due to retinal location per se, because even if the eye had moved to the location of the undetected first word, subjects refixated before the stimulus for lexical

EXPERIMENTAL   FACTORS

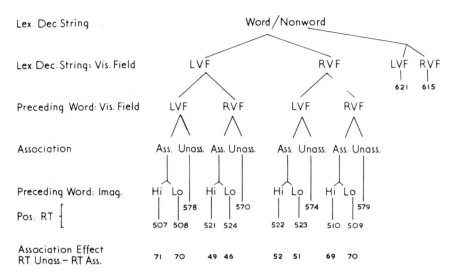

FIG. 4.   Mean lexical decision latency as a function of visual field, semantic association, imageability, and ipsi- versus contralaterality of priming stimulus.

decision, and in any case lexical decision itself was not affected by retinal location.

We would like to interpret these experiments in terms of two contrasts. The first is between the initial hemifield experiments, which required report, and the last one, which did not. When report was required, imageability had an effect, an effect apparently due to the right hemisphere. When report was not involved, imageability had no effect. This seems to be the case right up to the processing stages of lexical access and semantic association, since semantic priming occurred, and without any effect of imageability. Therefore, we propose that imageability has its effect at the stage of production. (Indeed, the patients can sometimes indicate that they understand the meaning of low imageability words that they cannot produce.) The second contrast, within the last experiment, is between the lack of any hemifield or hemispheric effect of side per se and the differential effectiveness of ipsilateral versus contralateral priming. We tentatively interpret this as implying that the recognition and semantic interpretation of single words is carried out in *both* hemispheres (see also Zaidel, 1977), and that what is laterally asymmetrical is access to production. Since this proposal is at variance with most current accounts of hemispheric language functioning, let us point out that all studies known to us that find lateral differences for verbal material require either report or judgments based upon the conscious percept (See Section III). It is noteworthy that in Rayner's paper (this volume), lexical facilitation by a prior parafoveally presented word that was not reportable was not affected by the hemifield of presentation. Evidence from clinical cases suggests some comprehension subserved by the right hemisphere (Gazzaniga & Hillyard, 1971; Kinsbourne, 1975). As opposed to single words, comprehension of sentences (as in the Token Test, De Renzi & Vignolo, 1962) required some short-term memory, and this we would identify with an articulatory buffer component, occurring relatively late in processing (Kleiman, 1975; Morton, 1970), and subserved by the left hemisphere (Zaidel, 1977). This argument finds theoretical support in the recent papers of Kinsbourne (1975) and Moscovitch (1976).

Further discussion of the imageability effect requires some attempt at specifying the origin of the effect and the nature of imageability. Since the effect of imageability on production is hemisphere-specific, it seems reasonable to seek an explanation in terms of lateral specialization. We assume that at an early age the two hemispheres are in some ways equipotential for language, and that roughly between the age of three and puberty one hemisphere specializes in certain subfunctions, specifically production of speech. During the course of language learning, early acquisitions will have roughly equal access to production from their representations in either hemisphere; later ones will not. The relevant time-linked acquisitions can hardly be at the lexical level since several of the high imageability words (e.g., agony, disaster), consistently well-reported irrespective of hemisphere, seem like relatively late lexical acquisitions. Additionally, one of the word classes that suffers most in the patients is function words, many of which are highly frequent and relatively early in appearance. We therefore propose that the critical variable is to be found in semantics, which underlie lexical representation. The instructions to subjects who produce imageability ratings define high imageability words not merely as those with an imageable referent but those which arouse a sensory experience. We would therefore like, tentatively, to divide semantics into those referring to the sensorimotor sphere and those based on logical and linguistic concepts, a separation compatible with distinctions drawn by developmental psychologists. Developmentally, this division would interact with lateralization to yield the following, illustrated in Fig. 5.

From an early stage sensori-motor semantics (Sem_1) are represented in both hemispheres and, as well as being interconnected themselves, both representations have equal access to production (an output lexicon). At a later stage, logical-linguistic semantics (Sem_2) may be also represented in each hemisphere and interconnected; but only Sem_2 in the left hemisphere has access to production, Sem_2 in the right accessing production only via its counterpart in the left.

The left-hemisphere damage sustained by aphasics exhibiting phonemic dyslexia, we propose, impairs access to production from semantics on the left, represented in Fig. 5 by the routes labeled 1L and 2L. The only access to

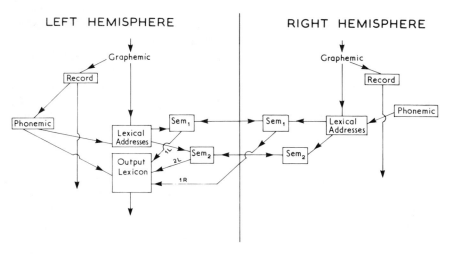

FIG. 5.   Hemispheric differences in semantic and nonsemantic access to phonology.

production that remains is via any existing route from semantics in the right hemisphere, this being route 1R in Fig. 5. The access route is the one by which semantic specifications realize lexical selections, the output of the latter being phonological instructions. Thus, the speech of such patients, both spontaneous and in response to written input, will be biased towards words with "sensori-motor" semantics. In the case of tachistoscopic hemifield presentation to normals, degraded stimulus information will more severely affect recovery of those words whose semantics have only indirect access to production (right hemisphere, low imageability). This follows if we again assume that production requires a good graphic record (c.f. Section III), and that the left hemisphere will lack that requirement with presentations to the right hemisphere, having only the semantic information. This situation will be less detrimental to high imageability words, whose semantics in the right hemisphere have direct access to production. We thus propose that there is indeed an alteration in lexical-semantic functioning in phonemic dyslexia apart from the nonlexical grapheme-phoneme impairment. The formulation offered here locates that impairment in the lexical realization of semantics in the left hemisphere, leaving differential access from semantics in the right hemisphere.

It is to be noted that, according to Fig. 5, grapheme-phoneme conversion does not take place in the right hemisphere. We take this step because of the impairment of the patients whose right hemispheres we assume are intact, and because we associate the development of such a route with oral reading. Note that Cohen and Freeman (this volume) give a further basis, from experimentation with normal subjects, for such a postulation.

V. CONCLUDING DISCUSSION AND COMMENTS

The three sets of studies we have presented illustrate one way in which clinical and normal research interact. Most precarious but most rewarding is the reciprocal feedback that leads to theorizing about one population in terms of the other. Safer and probably of more basic importance is the fact that consideration of both populations has led to the generation of research on one by that on the other. The validity of our inferences and explanations clearly remains to be tested. We doubt, though, whether the experiments would have been done, or the hypotheses generated, if data and theories derived from normals had not been confronted by the pathological behavior.

Let us summarize our notions regarding reading and speech resulting from the work discussed here.

1. The lexical-semantic system can be accessed by both graphemic and phonemic codes.

2. There is a nonlexical route from print to phonology via grapheme-phoneme conversion rules. Phonemic dyslexic patients are impaired in this process.

3. Normal people can have semantic information available without knowing the specific words responsible.

4. Processing of individual words to the level of semantics is automatic and unconscious.

5. Consciousness (and retrieval of specific words for production) requires a record of stimulus information, and it is with this graphic record that pattern masking interferes.

6. One possible account of paralexic errors is that the patients cannot make use of this record to inhibit them, which the normal person does; the patients cannot compare output with input in a common code because they cannot directly convert graphemes to phonemes.

7. Imageability effects are reproducible in normal subjects, but only when consciously based responses are required, and are due to the right hemisphere.

8. Semantic processing of individual content words is carried out in both hemispheres. Production is controlled by the left hemisphere. Sensori-motor semantics have direct access to production from both hemispheres, but derived (logical-linguistically defined) semantics in the right hemisphere can only access production via the equivalent semantics in the left hemisphere. Phonemic dyslexics have impaired access to output phonology from left-hemisphere semantics. These ideas offer a mechanism for the probable involvement of the lexical-semantic system in paralexias.

9. Several of the aspects of phonemic dyslexia are the result of some change in access to or availability of a phonological code. Indeed, given the apparent automaticity of much of reading, it is likely that many observed effects in

normal reading and perception are due to response requirements, including consciousness.

These notions must be treated as speculative hypotheses. Obviously a wealth of experiments is generated by them and needed both for verification and further specification. To take just one example, we have argued that the source of grapheme-to-phoneme translation is the record of the graphic representation, where we are locating the effect of pattern-masking. It might be argued that the apparent automaticity of phonemic translation suggests that it is derived directly from graphic coding of visual input. An experiment that should inform us about this is a lexical decision task, where preceding letter-strings are masked to prevent awareness but to allow semantic access. The question is whether a homophonic nonword like *brane*, when masked and preceding its lexical counterpart *brain*, will have a priming effect on the lexical decision to *brain*. The interpretation offered here predicts that it should not.

Relating pathologies to models of normal function raises several kinds of problems. To start with, to what extent are the various effects noted in a patient explicable in terms of a single factor, possibly in turn influencing others, rather than a number of separate impairments? Faced with several abnormalities, we have proposed two impairments. The one to the nonlexical route to phonology accounts for the inability to read nonwords; the one to the semantic-lexical route to phonology accounts for word-class effects. Either or both may account for paralexic errors. It may of course be possible to treat both of these as a single impairment to the realization of phonology, although in our modeling we have not managed to do so.

A second question is, can one view the syndrome analytically in terms of independent additive impairments to subsystems of normal reading and speech functioning, or does one have to treat the pathological state as a new integrated system? We have attempted an interpretation of aphasic impairments where damage to the left hemisphere affects certain processes in that hemisphere without affecting other processes in the same hemisphere or equivalent processes in the right hemisphere. This is of course a questionable assumption, since unilateral damage or abnormality may well affect sites on the side opposite the source. However, there is no evidence that it does so in cases such as those with which we are concerned here.

Another facet of this problem is that modular theorizing, whereby deletion or impairment of parts of the normal system leaves other parts unaffected is probably inadequate to deal with more general aspects of language in a damaged brain. Given that many patients are aware that they have a language problem, their observed communication probably results in part from strategies for use of an impaired system. This may well be true also of their performance in experimental situations. Indeed, Butterworth has recently (1976) sought to explain jargon aphasia by proposing that the observed behavior is a transformation of the impairment by the attempt to avoid violation of conversational rules. (Thus, some of the paralexic responses in phonemic dyslexia could be due to the patient's desire to say something, even though he knows that he cannot produce the correct word.) However, the same problem confronts us in interpreting normal behavior — the extent to which a functioning system is more than the sum of its parts. Specifically, our model, like many others, as yet contains no real executive functions, without which it will remain fundamentally incomplete.

REFERENCES

Allport, D.A. On knowing the meaning of words we are unable to report: the effects of visual masking. In S. Dornic (Ed.), *Attention and performance VI.* Hillsdale, N.J.: Lawrence Erlbaum Associates, 1977.

Bradshaw, J.L. Three interrelated problems in reading: a review. *Memory and Cognition,* 1975, *3*, 123–134.

Butterworth, B. *Hesitation and the production of neologisms in jargon aphasia.* Unpublished manuscript. Psychological Laboratory, Cambridge University, 1976.

Colorado Concreteness and Imagery Norms. Program on Cognitive Factors in Human Learning and Memory, Report No. 10. Institute for the Study of Intellectual Behavior, University of Colorado, 1973.

Cohen, G., & Freeman, R. H. Individual differences in reading strategies in relation to handedness and cerebral asymmetry. In J. Requin (Ed.), *Attention and performance VII.* Hillsdale, N.J.: Lawrence Erlbaum Associates, 1978.

Coltheart, M., Davelaar, E., Jonasson, J., & Besner, D. Access to the internal lexicon. In S. Dornic (Ed.), *Attention and performance VI.* Hillsdale, N.J.: Lawrence Erlbaum Associates, 1977.

De Renzi, E., & Vignolo, L.A. The token test: A sensitive test to detect receptive disturbances in aphasics. *Brain,* 1962, *85*, 665–678.

Dixon, N.F. *Subliminal Perception: The nature of a controversy.* London : McGraw Hill, 1971.

Ellis, H.D., & Shepherd, J.W. Recognition of abstract and concrete words presented in left and right visual fields. *Journal of Experimental Psychology,* 1974, *103*, 1035–1036.

Gardner, H., & Zurif, E. *Bee* but not *be*: Oral reading of single words in aphasia and alexia. *Neuropsychologia,* 1975, *13*, 181–190.

Gazzaniga, M.S., & Hillyard, S.A. Language and speech capacity of the right hemisphere. *Neuropsychologia,* 1971, *9*, 273–280.

Hawkins, H.L., Reicher, G.M., Rogers, M., & Peterson, L. Flexible coding in word recognition. *Journal of Experimental Psychology: Human Perception and Performance,* 1976, *2*, 380–385.

Kinsbourne, M. Minor hemisphere language and cerebral maturation. In E.H. Lenneberg & E. Lenneberg (Eds.), *Foundations of language development* (Vol. 2). London: Academic Press, 1975.

Kleiman, G.M. Speech recoding in reading. *Journal of Verbal Learning and Verbal Behavior,* 1975, *14*, 323–339.

Kolers, P.A. Three stages of reading. In H. Levin & J.P. Williams (Eds.), *Basic studies on reading.* New York: Basic Books, 1970.

Marcel, A.J. Perception with and without awareness. Paper presented to Experimental Psychology Society, Stirling meeting, July 1974.

Marcel, A. J. *Conscious and unconscious reading: The effects of visual masking on word perception.* Manuscript submitted for publication, 1978.

Marcel, A.J., & Patterson, K.E. Aphasic reading impairment in normal people: The locus of word-class effects. Paper presented to Experimental Psychology Society, Reading meeting, July 1976.

Marshall, J.C., & Newcombe, F. Syntactic and semantic errors in paralexia. *Neuropsychologia*, 1966, *4*, 169–176.

Marshall, J.C., & Newcombe, F. Patterns of paralexia: A psycholinguistic approach. *Journal of Psycholinguistic Research*, 1973, *2*, 175–199.

Meyer, D.E., Schvaneveldt, R.W., & Ruddy, M.G. Activation of lexical memory. Paper presented at the meeting of the Psychonomic Society, St. Louis, November 1972.

Morton, J. Grammar and computation in language behavior. In J.C. Catford (Ed.), *Studies in language and language behavior*. Progress Report No. VI. Ann Arbor: University of Michigan, 1968.

Morton, J. A functional model for memory. In D.A. Norman (Ed.), *Models of human memory*. New York: Academic Press, 1970.

Moscovitch, M. On the representation of language in the right hemisphere of right-handed people. *Brain and Language*, 1976, *3*, 47–71.

Paivio, A., Yuille, J.C., & Madigan, S.A. Concreteness, imagery and meaningfulness values for 925 nouns. *Journal of Experimental Psychology Monograph Supplement*, 1968, *76*, (1).

Patterson, K.E., & Marcel, A.J. Aphasia, dyslexia and the phonological coding of written words. *Quarterly Journal of Experimental Psychology,* 1977, *29,* 307–318.

Postman, L. Verbal learning and memory. *Annual Review of Psychology*, 1975, *26*, 291–335.

Raynor, K. Foveal and parafoveal cues in reading. In J. Requin (Ed.), *Attention and performance VII*. Hillsdale, N.J.: Lawrence Erlbaum Associates, 1978.

Richardson, J.T.E. The effect of word imageability in acquired dyslexia. *Neuropsychologia*, 1975, *13*, 281–288.

Rubenstein, H., Lewis, S.S., & Rubenstein, M.A. Evidence for phonemic recoding in visual word recognition. *Journal of Verbal Learning and Verbal Behavior*, 1971, *10*, 645–657.

Saffran, E.M., Schwartz, M.F., & Marin, O.S.M. Semantic mechanisms in paralexia. *Brain and Language,* 1977, *3,* 255–265.

Shallice, T., & Warrington, E.K. Word recognition in a phonemic dyslexic patient. *Quarterly Journal of Experimental Psychology*, 1975, *27*, 187–199.

Sperling, G. Successive approximations to a model for short-term memory. *Acta Psychologica*, 1967, *27*, 285–292.

Turvey, M.T. Peripheral and central processes in vision. *Psychological Review*, 1973, *80*, 1–52.

Weiskrantz, L., Warrington, E.K., Sanders, M.D., & Marshall, J. Visual capacity in the hemianopic field following a restricted occipital ablation. *Brain*, 1974, *97*, 709–728.

Werner, H. Microgenesis and aphasia. *Journal of Abnormal and Social Psychology*, 1956, *52*, 347–353.

Wickens, D.D. Characteristics of word encoding. In A.W. Melton & E. Martin (Eds.), *Coding processes in human memory*. Washington: Wiley, 1972.

Worthington, A.G. Differential rates of dark adaptation to "taboo" and "neutral" stimuli. *Canadian Journal of Psychology*, 1964, *18*, 257–268.

Zaidel, E. Unilateral auditory language comprehension on the Token Test following cerebral commissurotomy and hemispherectomy. *Neuropsychologia*, 1977, *15*, 1–17.

III SPEECH PERCEPTION AND CODING

13 There May Be Nothing Peculiar to Perceiving in a Speech Mode

James E. Cutting

Wesleyan University
Middletown, Connecticut, United States

ABSTRACT

The speech mode is thought to be a peculiar manner of perceiving, uniquely geared to the extraction of linguistic features from the acoustic signal. Results from several different experimental paradigms were thought to converge on the psychological reality of the speech mode and on the auditory-phonetic distinction. All of these results, however, occur for musical sounds identified as plucked or bowed notes from a stringed instrument. Thus, at present there appears to be no empirical evidence for the existence of a special speech mode for processing linguistic features. The concepts of a speech mode and an auditory-phonetic distinction should be reexamined. This paper takes a small step in that direction.

I. INTRODUCTION

"To speak of 'perception in the speech mode' is to imply, of course, that speech and its perception are somehow special (Liberman, 1970b, p. 238)." To say that there may be no peculiarity to perceiving in a speech mode is to imply that that view may have to be revised, at least with regard to its usual referents. For the past fifteen years many have extolled the singularity of speech perception. Today, however, empirical support for that view seems to be disappearing. This paper tells part of the story why.

Let me preface this account, however, by stating that speech will remain special. Speech perception in the broad sense, as an integral part of language perception, is endemic to humans and a foundation for much that is human—

literature, technology, science, culture. Sign language, its only legitimate con-
tender, is not endemic and has many thousandfold fewer adherents. The perception of sign follows its own rules, and many of those are quite different from
speech (Bellugi & Klima, 1975; Klima & Bellugi, 1976). Moreover, speech has
shaped the vocal tract in a peculiar fashion (Lieberman, 1975); sign, as we know
it, is a recent invention and has not shaped the hand.

Speech perception in the broad sense can be analyzed at many levels: phonetic,
phonological, feeding into morphological, lexical, syntactic, semantic, and
pragmatic tiers of the language heterarchy. It seems a good bet that no other
system, not even that of music, can match it. But the speech mode has been
defined more narrowly: The "concern is not with abstract matters of meaning and syntax, but with the very concrete sounds of speech and their raw perception as the phonetic and phonemic segments that we all know as consonants
and vowels (Liberman, 1970b, p. 238)." Indeed, most effort has been directed
towards the *phonetic level* of perceptual analysis and how it differs from the
auditory level (Cutting, 1974b, 1976; Pisoni, 1973; Studdert-Kennedy, Shankweiler, & Pisoni, 1972; Wood, 1974, 1975a). This distinction was first made in
1969 by Studdert-Kennedy (1974).

Twenty years of research have yielded many results indicative of speech perception at the phonetic level. Many were thought peculiar to perception in the
speech mode. From this collection of results, Wood (1975a, p. 16), for example,
selected six thoughts to converge on the psychological reality of the auditory-
phonetic distinction. Of this list, three appear to converge on the same processes
involved in hemispheric specialization; thus the list reduces to four. These four
results are important because many, including me, had taken them to be the
empirical basis for the peculiarity of perception in the speech mode. They are:
(a) categorical perception; (b) boundary shifts due to selective adaptation;
(c) left-hemisphere effects due to cerebral specialization; and (d) asymmetric
interference with redundancy gain in speeded classification tasks. Although this
list seemed apt just a few years ago, none of these results is peculiar to speech.
In fact, they all occur for a single set of musical sounds. Thus, the empirical base
for a peculiar speech mode has been weakened, and certain aspects of speech
should be assessed anew. What follows is a small step in that direction.

II. CATEGORICAL PERCEPTION

Categorical perception was the first empirical buttress supporting the speech
mode (Liberman, Harris, Hoffman, & Griffith, 1957). Called by Wood (1975a)
the "phoneme boundary effect," categorical perception is a complex concept
involving the intersection of results from identification and discrimination tasks
involving synthetic stimuli generated in equal increments along an acoustic
dimension (Studdert-Kennedy, Liberman, Harris, & Cooper, 1970). Several

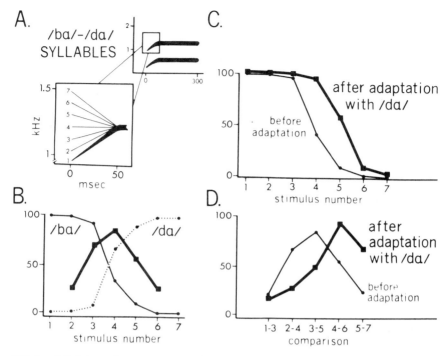

FIG. 1.   (A) Schematic spectrograms of an array of speech syllables synthesized from /ba/ to /da/, (B) schematic identification and discrimination functions for that array, and (C & D) those functions before and after adaptation with Stimulus 7, /da/. (Adapted from Cutting, 1977.)

criteria must be met. First, labeling functions for identified groups must be clear-cut. Second, the discrimination functions must be distinctly nonlinear, with "peaks" (regions of high performance) surrounded by "troughs" (regions of near-chance performance). Third, the location of peaks must occur at identification boundaries and troughs within identified groupings of stimuli. Finally, there should be good agreement between observed discrimination functions and those predicted on the basis of absolute categorization. These four criteria reduce to the notion that the ability to discriminate the sounds is essentially no better than the ability to label them.

Consider a set of seven stimuli, each with two formants, or resonance bands of energy. Such an array can be seen in schematic form in the top left panel of Fig. 1. These particular items were among those used by Mattingly, Liberman, Syrdal, and Halwes (1971). Stimuli 1 through 3 are identified as /ba/ nearly all the time, Stimuli 5 through 7 as /da/, and Stimulus 4 is identified as /ba/ about 40% of the time, and as /da/ 60%. Identification functions for /ba/ and /da/ responses are shown in the lower left panel. A discrimination function is overlaid on the identification functions. Performance for within-category comparisons, such as Stimulus 1/Stimulus 3 and Stimulus 5/Stimulus 7, is relatively poor (the troughs), and performance for the between-category comparison of Stimulus 3/ Stimulus 5 is relatively good (the peak). Performance for other comparisons is intermediate. These patterns reveal the anatomy of categorical perception. The phenomenon is important because "categoricalness is a property of language generally; active-passive and singular-plural, for example, do not admit degree (Mattingly et al., 1971, p. 132)." Thus, the grammars of speech and language share binary features as well as other factors (Liberman, 1970a).

Glottocentrically, many have called all that is not speech by a handy term — nonspeech. There have been several demonstrations that categorical perception does not occur for certain nonspeech sounds. First was a study by Liberman, Harris, Kinney, and Lane (1961), who inverted the spectra of categorically-perceived speech syllables around a center frequency of about 1300 Hz. Categorical perception was not obtained. Similar results were reported by Mattingly et al. (1971). They isolated the second formants and second-formant transitions of the stimuli shown in Fig. 1, and found more continuous perception than for the full syllables from which they were taken. Such results are interesting; they demonstrate that the integrity of the speech signal must not be violated for speech to be perceived as speech. However, there are no appropriate nonspeech control stimuli to be fashioned from the spectral surgery of speech syllables. Not only do such manipulations deny the perceiver a chance to perceive in a speech mode, they also deny the stimulus ecological integrity. It is clear that the notion of modes of perception must be separated from the notion of natural-ness of the stimuli. This distinction is crucial because in vision, for example, Biederman (1972) found that scenes carved up in an arbitrary manner are processed differently from intact scenes, yet his analysis concerned global stimulus properties not perceptual modes. Should the analysis of speech be different?

Mattingly et al. (1971, p. 132) noted categorical perception to be "unusual, if not unique" to speech perception. Recent evidence, however, suggests it is more usual than previously thought. In vision, it has been demonstrated for critical flicker fusion (Pastore, 1976), and to a lesser degree for hue (Bornstein, 1975; Lane, 1967). Elsewhere in audition it has been demonstrated for (a) the perception of onsets in noise-buzz sounds (Miller, Weir, Pastore, Kelly, & Dooling, 1976), (b) the perception of onsets in two-component tones (Pisoni, 1977), (c) the perception of sinusoids varying in intensity before a constant referent (Pastore, 1976), and (d) the perception of musical intervals (Locke & Kellar, 1973).

Rise time is a second musical dimension that is categorically perceived (Cutting, 1977; Cutting & Rosner, 1974, 1976). An array of sawtooth sounds differing in rise time can be identified as *plucked* or *bowed* notes from a stringed musical

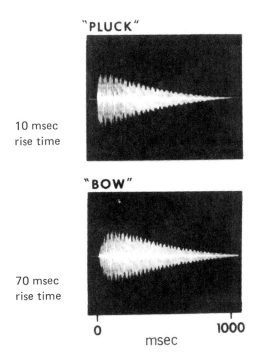

FIG. 2.   Oscillograms of two sawtooth wave stimuli from an array of musical sounds that yield results once thought peculiar to the perception of stop consonants.

instrument. Like the binary oppositions in speech, the plucked versus bowed distinction is natural, at least in the sense that it stems from simple mechanical action of easily fashioned materials. Two stimulus items are shown in oscillographic form in Fig. 2. These 10- and 70-msec rise time musical sounds, along with seven other stimuli, were generated on a Moog synthesizer. They varied only in rise time, by 10-msec increments from 0- through 80-msec. Rapid rising items (with 0- through 30-msec rise times) sound like a plucked string, and more slowly rising items (50- through 80-msec rise times) sound like a bowed string. The item with 40-msec rise time is ambiguous between the two. The perception of these sounds meets all the criteria for categorical perception suggested by Studdert-Kennedy et al. (1970), plus several new criteria. For example, like stop consonants (Pisoni, 1973), plucked and bowed sounds yield no decay of within- and between-category information as a function of delay interval between items in a discrimination pair (Cutting, Rosner, & Foard, 1976). Vowels, on the other hand, yield such decay and also demonstrate a more "continuous" type of perception. These results suggest that the nature of the memory code for stops and for plucked and bowed sounds may be the same, both differing from that for vowels.

Another set of issues in categorical perception centers on the extent to which it is learned (See Lane, 1965; Pisoni, 1976). For example, are the peaks in the discrimination function acquired or innate? Ten years after this question first arose (Liberman et al. 1961), it was answered conclusively by Eimas, Siqueland, Jusczyk, and Vigorito (1971). They demonstrated that one-month-old infants discriminated speech sounds in a manner functionally identical to adults. That is, for example, while infants would discriminate Stimulus 3 from Stimulus 5 of Fig. 1, a /ba/–/da/ comparison, they would not discriminate Stimulus 1 from 3 (both /ba/) or Stimulus 5 from 7 (both /da/) pairs that differ acoustically to the same degree. Thus, the distinctiveness between /ba/ and /da/, and between other such stop consonant pairs, appears not to be acquired; it is already present in the young infant.

One might suppose that the innateness of speech perception separates it from the perception of nonspeech sounds. For example, the young infant might not be able to discriminate between major and minor chords, just as a number of adults cannot. If so, the distinctiveness of the tonal modes would appear to be acquired through learning. While there are no firm data on this dimension as yet, the infant can discriminate between plucked and bowed sounds, but not within plucked or bowed categories, a pattern just like adults (Jusczyk, Rosner, Cutting, Foard, & Smith, 1977). Thus, the perception of this musical distinction is innate to the same degree that the perception of stop consonant distinctions is innate.

One aspect of categorical perception, however, may prove unique to speech: Speech is multidimensionally categorical, whereas all nonspeech sounds examined thus far appear to be categorical along but a single dimension. This factor may be more than a quibble, because the rapid transmission rates of speech may be attributable, in part, to categorical perception along multiple dimensions. For example, the initial phoneme in the syllable /ba/ is /b/ not /d/, a difference in place articulation that is categorical; it is /b/ not /p/, a difference in voicing that is categorical; and it is /b/ not /m/, a difference in manner that is also categorical. Thus, three categorical decisions may be made for the same segment, for an acoustic shape that occurs in less than 100 msec. Liberman, Mattingly, and Turvey (1972) estimated that the transformation of acoustic signal into phonetic message is akin to the reduction of signal load from 40,000 bits/sec to 40 bits/sec, a thousandfold savings for memory. Multidimensional categorical perception may be an important way of achieving such coding rates efficiently.

Nevertheless, simple categorical perception is not peculiar to speech. In fact, it may not be peculiar to humans (Kuhl & Miller, 1975; Morse & Snowden, 1975), although the data are still equivocal (Sinnott, Beecher, Moody, & Stebbins, 1976; Waters & Wilson, 1976) and incomplete. What is unequivocal is that, whereas categorical perception is central to speech perception, it cannot be used to bulwark the speech mode as a peculiar form of auditory perception.

III. BOUNDARY SHIFTS DUE TO SELECTIVE ADAPTATION

A second empirical buttress for the speech mode, at least according to Wood (1975a) and others, dealt with the boundary shift and its underlying mechanisms in selective adaptation. Borrowed and modified from vision research (Blakemore & Campbell, 1969), the adaptation paradigm is built on the foundation of categorical perception. Consider again the /ba/−/da/ array shown in Fig. 1. If Stimulus 7 (/da/) were presented several dozen times in succession, and the listener asked to identify each of the seven members of the stimulus array − and if this procedure were repeated many times − the postadaptation identification function would typically shift towards the /da/ end of the array, as shown in the top right panel of Fig. 1. This shift reflects a change in the tuning of the perceptual apparatus, and it was first reported by Eimas and Corbit (1973). It occurs not only for identification, which could reflect simply a criterion shift in responses, but also for discrimination, as shown in the lower right panel. This second type of shift suggests a change in sensitivity, not simply criterion. The shift in sensitivity is crucial for the argument that opponent-process detectors are differentially fatigued during adaptation.

The perceptual shift was first thought to reflect adaptation of phonetic feature detectors. That view, however, was modified (Cutting & Eimas, 1975), then changed altogether to one that accounted for adaptation in terms of auditory property analyzers (Pisoni & Tash, 1975; Tartter & Eimas, 1975). The latter view seems prudent and more plausible since similar shifts occur for plucked and bowed sounds (Cutting, 1977; Cutting et al., 1976), which are not phonetic in the accepted sense of that term. Thus, in the auditory domain the effects of adaptation are not exclusive to speech.

Wood (1975a), however, did not suggest that adaptation shifts were peculiar to speech. After all, they occur in vision. He stated, rather, that there is a difference in the "relative effectiveness of various speech, speech-like, and nonspeech stimuli in producing systematic phoneme boundary shifts (p. 16)." Thus, whereas shifts might occur for certain speech continua that are categorically perceived, and also for certain nonspeech continua, cross-adaptation effects from nonspeech to speech were thought unlikely. Recently, however, Diehl (1976) demonstrated that a plucked sound produces an adaptation effect on a /ba/− /wa/ continuum, a speech array varying in the duration of formant transitions. This adaptation effect was as potent as that for /da/, a syllable not a member of the adapted array, but one that shares some features with /ba/. Thus, like categorical perception, the boundary shift in a speech array due to selective adaptation is not peculiar to perception in the speech mode.

IV. LEFT-HEMISPHERE EFFECTS DUE
TO CEREBRAL SPECIALIZATION

The left hemisphere of the human brain is specialized to perceive and produce language. The perception of certain speech sounds, particularly the stop conson-ants, is one aspect of language processing for which the left hemisphere has a clear advantage over the right (Studert-Kennedy & Shankweiler, 1970). This was a third result buttressing the existence of a special speech mode. In a typical experimental paradigm a pair of syllables is presented, one to the right ear and one to the left ear at the same time. Most listeners report the item presented to the right ear more easily than the one to the left. This result reflects two facts: the prepotency of the crossed-pathway connections from ear to cortex, and the effect of hemispheric specialization for speech. A second paradigm, used by Springer (1973), is a reaction-time task in which the listener presses a telegraph key when she hears a target syllable. A random ordering of many syllables is presented to one ear, white noise to the other, and the stimulus-to-ear configura-tion counterbalanced over several blocks of trials. Springer found a reliable 14-msec advantage for stimuli presented to the right-ear/left-hemisphere system.

The left hemisphere, however, is specialized for more than speech, and right-ear (Darwin, Howell, & Brady, this volume) and right-side (Morais, this volume) advantages accrue for many different reasons. Certain complex auditory stimuli (Halperin, Nachshon, & Carmon, 1973; Papcun, Krashen, Terbeek, Remington, & Harshman, 1974), certain acoustic properties of speech stimuli (Cutting, 1974a, 1974b), and certain musical stimuli for certain listeners (Bever & Chiarello, 1974; Gordon, 1975) appear to be processed best by the left hemisphere. Recently, Blechner (1977) used the same type of paradigm as Springer did and found that plucked and bowed sounds presented to the right ear, with noise to the left, were responded to more rapidly than those presented in the opposite configura-tion. Interestingly, the magnitude of the right-ear advantage was the same as for speech sounds — a 13-msec significant difference. Thus, the third of four results that I and others thought peculiar to speech perception is also found for the musical sounds. Wood's (1975a) other two measures of laterality — differential ear advantages for temporal-order judgment of dichotically presented stimuli, and unilateral differences in averaged evoked potentials — may or may not occur for the musical sounds. The experiments have not been done.

V. ASYMMETRIC INTERFERENCE WITH
REDUNDANCY GAIN

Wood's (1975a) final converging operation on the auditory-phonetic distinction is the differential interference between auditory and phonetic dimensions of the same stimulus during speeded classification tasks. Since he also found redundancy gain for the same stimuli when they were presented in a perfectly correlated manner (Wood, 1974), that result may be added to bolster this fourth buttress of the speech mode.

Imagine a set of four stimuli: /ba/ at a relatively high fundamental frequency; /ba/ at a low fundamental; /da/ high; and /da/ low. When classifying each item in a random sequence of these stimuli, frequency variation interferes with place decisions, but place variation has no effect on frequency. Moreover, when these dimensions are correlated (such as /ba/ low vs /da/ high) the stimului can be responded to more rapidly than in any other condition. To account for these results, a hybrid parallel-serial model has been proposed (Wood, 1975a, 1975b). These results and others in tasks of speeded classification are developed more fully by Garner (1974, 1976).

The same pattern of results, however, has been found for nonlinguistic stimuli both in vision (Pomerantz & Sager, 1975) and in audition (Pastore, Ahroon, Puleo, Crimmins, Golowner, & Berger, 1976). More importantly, it occurs for plucked and bowed sounds as well (Blechner, Day, & Cutting, 1976). The stimulus set consisted of a plucked sound at a relatively high intensity, a plucked sound at a low intensity, a bowed sound at a high intensity, and a bowed sound at a low intensity. These stimuli yielded not only the same pattern as the speech sounds, but reaction-time differences of the same magnitude. Thus, at least with regard to these four rigorously determined patterns of results, the speech mode now appears to be without empirical support.

VI. THE SPEECH MODE AND THE AUDITORY-PHONETIC DISTINCTION

The notion of a peculiar speech mode is, to a degree, counterintuitive. Why should speech require a special mode of processing and other events not? The answer, of course, is that it seemed a necessary theoretical construct; now these results seem to question its necessity, although the broader observations of Liberman, Cooper, Shankweiler, and Studdert-Kennedy (1967), for example, remain unimpeached. There remains some small chance that all these parallels between the perception of stop consonants and plucked and bowed sounds are without real importance. It may be that underlying the complex of categorical perception, shifts due to selective adaptation, right-ear advantages, and asymmetric interference — all of which are logically, and in many cases empirically demonstrated to be, independent of one another — are two, perhaps more, possible modes of perception. My response to this possibility is twofold. First, the chance of so many parallels occurring by caprice seems vanishingly small, and a single set of mechanisms accounting for both sets of results is more parsimonious than two sets, one for speech and one for music. Second, the results with plucked and bowed sounds are not the only ones that cause one to question the notion of a special speech mode. Other results indicative of speech perception, revealed in certain memory paradigms (Crowder, 1971) and in certain maskinglike paradigms (Dorman, 1974; Dorman, Raphael, Liberman, & Repp, 1975), appear to be accounted for in terms of nonlinguistic processes (Cutting & Dorman, 1976; Darwin & Baddeley, 1974; Pastore, Ahroon, Wolz, Puleo, & Berger, 1976; Remez, 1977). There are still other results in speech perception one could cite in defense of a speech mode, but in my opinion they are irrelevant to the separation of auditory from phonetic processes.

Since certain nonspeech results appear to go against the notion of a peculiar speech mode, they might be considered *counter*-counterintuitive. Counter-counterintuition is, of course, what might have been intuitive all along. The results from the plucked and bowed sounds, in particular, suggest reevaluation of two important concepts: the speech mode and the auditory-phonetic distinction. The second concept must be addressed first, for it has bearing on the first.

A. The Auditory-Phonetic Distinction

As I see it, there are two possible resolutions to the current quandary. The first runs contrary to Wood's (1975a) claim. These four results may not actually converge on the psychological reality of the auditory-phonetic distinction. Instead, they may converge on something else. Perhaps they reflect two different tiers of auditory analysis, or perhaps two different memory codes, one an input and the other an output from short-term memory. Perhaps phonetic processing is more abstract, or simply different, and not tapped by these four experimental situations. The second resolution, on the other hand, is consonant with Wood's analysis. These results may indeed reflect auditory versus phonetic processing. To render this view plausible, however, "phonetic" processing must be said to occur outside of speech as well as within. The Greek word φωνη has at least three translations — voice, sound, and speech — even though linguistic tradition reserves it, *phone,* for a sound of speech. If a definition of the term *phonetic* were expanded to include sounds outside speech, or to include "voices" of musical instruments, we could say that none of these results need be reinterpreted: Many auditory-phonetic differences occur within the speech domain, some outside of speech, but the constellation of results still converges on the distinction. Such a view may be more than whimsy, since the pluck-bow distinction appears to be akin to at least one consonantal-vocalic distinction, that of hard versus soft vocal attack (Hirose & Gay, 1973). This distinction separates /ʔa/ (beginning with a glottal stop) from /a/. In addition, it is allied to that which separates /tʃa/, as in CHOP from /ʃa/ as in SHOP, an affricate-fricative distinction. Finally, like speech, the musical distinction does have articulatory reference, although that reference is extralaryngeal, even extracorporeal.

It seems likely that one of these two interpretations is correct, yet they both have problems. The first appears to have a severe pragmatic constraint: If these four experimental results do not reflect differences between auditory and phonetic processes, I, personally, am at a loss to propose what kind of experiments would properly reveal phonetic processes as different from auditory processes. I think it unlikely that the reality of phonetic processes is so tortuous as to be beyond these already pretzel-shaped paradigms. For this reason I favor the second account — phoneticlike (if not phonetic) distinctions occur for natural events throughout the auditory domain. I realize there are problems in this view. For example, in linguistics the term *phonetic* connotes many meanings not even vaguely touched on (at least thus far) by the plucked and bowed sounds and their results. In addition, the redefinition of a particular type of process is unlikely to solve substantial problems in our understanding of auditory perception in general, and speech perception in particular. However, this new view can guide our thinking. Studdert-Kennedy (1975, p. 14) noted that between the auditory and phonetic processes there lies a gap. In this gap is the none-too-well-understood mapping of acoustic property onto phonetic feature. In my view, the plucked and bowed sounds allow us to peer into the perceptual network and observe one of these mapping processes, and to do so outside the domain of speech. Perhaps because no nonspeech sounds (yet) appear to be multidimensionally categorical, we cannot (yet) peer farther into the system to observe the compilation of a "phonetic" feature matrix and subsequent remappings onto "phonological" processes that might occur for nonlinguistic sounds. I think this line of reasoning and experimentation should be pursued. The observation of speechlike processes outside of speech is important; the more processes shown to be common to the perception of speech and nonspeech sounds, the more unified can be a general theory of the perception of complex, naturally occurring auditory events.

B. The Speech Mode

Both interpretations of the data reported here appear to speak against the pecularity of a speech mode. The first interpretation, that the results have no bearing on the auditory-phonetic distinction and the perception of phonetic features, suggests that speech researchers have simply been unable to gather evidence for a peculiar speech mode. The second interpretation, that phoneticlike processing can occur outside of speech, is almost equally damning. At the same time, however, it seems much more interesting. It suggests that if a speech mode exists, it is not so peculiar as once thought. This is not to say the speech perception is simple. To the contrary, speech perception is just as complex as those at the Haskins Laboratories have reported it to be, if not more so. Although there may be no peculiar speech mode, there remains a complex speech code and all the results discussed in this paper remain indicative of speech perception, and in some cases central to it. Instead, the perception of naturally-occurring, nonlinguistic events appears to have been underestimated and oversimplified. The perception of these sounds may be just as complex as the perception of speech, or if not, its complexity may differ in degree rather than kind. Moreover, to say that the perception of naturally-occurring nonlinguistic events is complex seems to be insufficient. The results discussed in this paper suggest that the perception of these sounds may be complex *in the same way* that the perception of speech is complex.

If this view is correct, one might say that earlier views of auditory perception were out of joint, and that some links in the Great Chain of Being (Tillyard, 1943) can now be realigned to some small degree. In my opinion, speech perception should be welcomed back to join the perception of other natural events. Perhaps we should end one phase of research and begin another (Osherson & Wasow, 1976). Instead of looking for that which is peculiar to speech perception, we might look for commonalities between speech and other systems of events.

ACKNOWLEDGMENTS

Supported by NICHD Grant HD-01994 to the Haskins Laboratories. I thank Mark J. Blechner, Ruth S. Day, Robert E. Remez, and Burton S. Rosner for discussion of issues raised in the paper, and particularly Michael Studdert-Kennedy for trying to keep me from making more errors than I have made. This should be considered a position paper, not necessarily reflecting any views but my own.

REFERENCES

Bellugi, U., & Klima, E. S. Aspects of sign language structure. In J. F. Kavanagh & J. E. Cutting (Eds.), *The role of speech in language.* Cambridge, Mass.: MIT Press, 1975.

Bever, T. G., & Chiarello, R. J. Cerebral dominance in musicians and nonmusicians. *Science,* 1974, *195,* 537–539.

Biederman, I. Perceiving real-world scenes. *Science,* 1972, *177,* 77–80.

Blakemore, C., & Campbell, F. W. On the existence of neurons in the human visual system selectively sensitive to the orientation and size of retinal images. *Journal of Physiology,* 1969, *203,* 237–260.

Blechner, M. J. *Right-ear advantage for musical stimuli differing in rise time.* Unpublished manuscript, 1977.

Blechner, M. J., Day, R. S., & Cutting, J. E. Processing two dimensions of nonspeech stimuli: The auditory-phonetic distinction reconsidered. *Journal of Experimental Psychology: Human Perception and Performance,* 1976, *2,* 257–266.

Bornstein, M. H. Qualities of color vision in infancy. *Journal of Experimental Child Psychology,* 1975, *19,* 401–419.

Crowder, R. G. The sound of vowels and consonants in immediate memory. *Journal of Verbal Learning and Verbal Behavior,* 1971, *10,* 587–596.

Cutting, J. E. Different speech-processing mechanisms can be reflected in the results of discrimination and dichotic listening tasks. *Brain and Language,* 1974, *1,* 363–373. (a)

Cutting, J. E. Two left-hemisphere mechanisms in speech perception. *Perception & Psychophysics,* 1974, *16,* 601–612. (b)

Cutting, J. E. Auditory and linguistic processes in speech perception: Inferences from six fusions in dichotic listening. *Psychological Review,* 1976, *83,* 114–140.

Cutting, J. E. The magical number two and the natural categories of speech and music. In N.S. Sutherland (Ed.), *Tutorial essays in psychology*. Hillsdale, N.J.: Lawrence Erlbaum Associates, 1977.

Cutting, J. E., & Dorman, M. F. Discrimination of intensity differences carried on formant transitions varying in extent and duration. *Perception & Psychophysics, 1976, 20,* 101–107.

Cutting, J. E., & Eimas, P. D. Phonetic feature analyzers and the processing of speech in infants. In J. F. Kavanagh & J. E. Cutting (Eds.), *The role of speech in language*. Cambridge, Mass.: MIT Press, 1975.

Cutting, J. E., & Rosner, B. S. Categories and boundaries in speech and music. *Perception & Psychophysics, 1974, 16,* 564–570.

Cutting, J. E., & Rosner, B. S. Discrimination functions predicted from categories in speech and music. *Perception & Psychophysics, 1976, 20,* 87–88.

Cutting, J. E., & Rosner, B. S., & Foard, C. F. Perceptual categories for musiclike sounds: Implications for theories of speech perception. *Quarterly Journal of Experimental Psychology, 1976, 28,* 361–378.

Darwin, C. J., & Baddeley, A. D. Acoustic memory and the perception of speech. *Cognitive Psychology, 1974, 6,* 41–60.

Diehl, R. Feature analyzers for the phonetic dimension stop vs. continuant. *Perception & Psychophysics, 1976, 19,* 267–272.

Dorman, M. F. Discrimination of intensity differences in formant transitions in and out of syllable context. *Perception & Psychophysics, 1974, 16,* 84–86.

Dorman, M. F., Raphael, L. J., Liberman, A. M., & Repp, B. A. Some maskinglike phenomena in speech perception. *Journal of the Acoustical Society of America, 1975, 57,* p. S58. (Abstract.)

Eimas, P. D., & Corbit, J. D. Selective adaptation of linguistic feature detectors. *Cognitive Psychology, 1973, 4,* 99–109.

Eimas, P. D., Siqueland, E. R., Jusczyk, P. W., & Vigorito, J. M. Speech perception in infants. *Science, 1971, 171,* 303–306.

Garner, W. R. *The processing of information and structure*. Hillsdale, N.J.: Lawrence Erlbaum Associates, 1974.

Garner, W. R. Interaction of stimulus dimensions in concept and choice processes. *Cognitive Psychology, 1976, 8,* 98–123.

Gordon, H. W. Hemispheric asymmetry and musical performance. *Science, 1975, 189,* 68–69.

Halperin, Y., Nachshon, I., & Carmon, A. Shift in ear superiority in dichotic listening to temporal pattern nonverbal stimuli. *Journal of the Acoustical Society of America, 1973, 53,* 46–50.

Hirose, H., & Gay, T. Laryngeal control in vocal attack: An electromyographic study. *Folia Phoniatrica, 1973, 25,* 203–213.

Jusczyk, P. W., Rosner, B. S., Cutting, J. E., Foard, C. F., & Smith, L. Categorical perception of nonlinguistic sounds by two month old infants. *Perception & Psychophysics, 1977, 21,* 50–54.

Klima, E. S., & Bellugi, U. Poetry and song in a language without sound. *Cognition, 1976, 4,* 45–97.

Kuhl, P. A., & Miller, J. D. Speech perception by the chinchilla: Voiced-voiceless distinction in alveolar plosive consonants. *Science, 1975, 190,* 69–72.

Lane, H. Motor theory of speech perception: A critical review. *Psychological Review, 1965, 72,* 275–309.

Lane, H. A behavioral basis for the polarity principle in linguistics. *Language, 1967, 43,* 494–511.

Liberman, A. M. The grammars of speech and language. *Cognitive Psychology, 1970, 1,* 301–323. (a)

Liberman, A. M. Some characteristics of perception in the speech mode. In D. A. Hainburg & K. Pribram (Eds.), *Perception and its disorders.* Baltimore: Williams and Wilkins, 1970. (b)

Liberman, A. M., Cooper, F. S., Shankweiler, D. P., & Studdert-Kennedy, M. Perception of the speech code. *Psychological Review,* 1967, *74,* 431–461.

Liberman, A. M., Harris, K. S., Hoffman, H. S., & Griffith, B. C. The discrimination of speech sounds within and across phoneme boundaries. *Journal of Experimental Psychology,* 1957, *54,* 358–368.

Liberman, A. M., Harris, K. S., Kinney, J., & Lane, H. The discrimination of relative onset time of the components of certain speech and nonspeech patterns. *Journal of Experimental Psychology,* 1961, *61,* 379–388.

Liberman, A. M., Mattingly, I. G., & Turvey, M. T. Language codes and memory codes. In A. W. Melton & E. Martin (Eds.), *Coding processes in human memory.* Washington, D.C.: V. H. Winston & Sons, 1972.

Lieberman, P. *On the origins of language.* New York: Macmillan, 1975.

Locke, S., & Kellar, L. Categorical perception in a nonlinguistic mode. *Cortex,* 1973, *9,* 355–369.

Mattingly, I. G., Liberman, A. M., Syrdal, A., & Halwes, T. Discrimination in speech and nonspeech modes. *Cognitive Psychology,* 1971, *2,* 131–157.

Miller, J. D., Weir, C. C., Pastore, R. E., Kelly, W. J., & Dooling, R. J. Discrimination and labeling of noise-buzz sequences with varying noise-lead times: An example of categorical perception. *Journal of the Acoustical Society of America,* 1976, *60,* 410–417.

Morse, P. A., & Snowden, C. T. An investigation of categorical perception discrimination by rhesus monkeys. *Perception & Psychophysics,* 1975, *17,* 9–16.

Osherson, D. N., & Wasow, T. Task-sepcificity and species-specificity in the study of language: A methodological note. *Cognition,* 1976, *4,* 203–214.

Papcun, G., Krashen, S., Terbeek, D., Remington, R., & Harshman, R. Is the left hemisphere specialized for speech, language, and/or something else? *Journal of the Acoustical Society of America,* 1974, *55,* 319–327.

Pastore, R. E., Ahroon, W. A., Puleo, J. S., Crimmins, D. B., Golowner, L., & Berger, R. S. Processing interaction between two dimensions of nonphonetic auditory signals. *Journal of Experimental Psychology: Human Perception and Performance,* 1976, *2,* 267–276.

Pastore, R. E., Ahroon, W. A., Wolz, J., Puleo, J. S., & Berger, R. S. Discrimination of intensity differences on formant-like transitions. *Perception & Psychophysics,* 1976, *18,* 244–246.

Pastore, R. E. Categorical perception: a critical re-evaluation. In S. K. Hirsh, D. H. Eldredge, I. J. Hirsch, & S. R. Silverman (Eds.), *Hearing and Davis.* St. Louis: Washington University Press, 1976.

Pisoni, D. B. Auditory and phonetic memory codes in the discrimination of consonants and vowels. *Perception & Psychophysics,* 1973, *13,* 253–260.

Pisoni, D. B. Identification and discrimination of relative onset time of two-component tones: Implications for voicing perception in stops. *Journal of the Acoustical Society of America,* 1977, *61,* 1352–1361.

Pisoni, D. B., & Tash, J. Auditory property detectors and processing place features in stop consonants. *Perception & Psychophysics,* 1975, *18,* 401–408.

Pomerantz, J. R., & Sager, L. C. Asymmetric integrality with dimensions of visual patterns. *Perception & Psychophysics,* 1975, *18,* 460–466.

Remez, R. E. *Evidence for a suprasegmental organization in the perception of natural morphemes produced by bass violin.* Manuscript in preparation, 1977.

Sinnott, J. M., Beecher, M. D., Moody, D. B., & Stebbins, W. C. Speech discrimination by monkeys and humans. *Journal of the Acoustical Society of America,* 1976, *60,* 687–695.

Springer, S. P. Hemispheric specialization for speech opposed by contralateral noise. *Perception & Psychophysics,* 1973, *13,* 391–393.

Studdert-Kennedy, M. The perception of speech. In T. A. Sobeok (Ed.), *Current trends in linguistics* (Vol. 12). The Hague: Mouton, 1974.

Studdert-Kennedy, M. The nature and function of phonetic categories. In F. Restle, R. M. Shiffrin, N. J. Castellan, H. Lindman, & D. B. Pisoni (Eds.), *Cognitive theory* (Vol. 1). Hillsdale, N.J.: Lawrence Erlbaum Associates, 1975.

Studdert-Kennedy, M., Liberman, A. M., Harris, K. S., & Cooper, F. S. Motor theory of speech perception: A reply to Lane's critical review. *Psychological Review,* 1970, 77, 234–249.

Studdert-Kennedy, M., & Shankweiler, D. P. Hemispheric specialization for speech perception. *Journal of the Acoustical Society of America,* 1970, *48,* 579–594.

Studdert-Kennedy, M., Shankweiler, D. P., & Pisoni, D. B. Auditory and phonetic processes in speech perception: Evidence from a dichotic study. *Cognitive Psychology,* 1972, *2,* 455–466.

Tartter, V. C., & Eimas, P. D. The role of auditory feature detectors in the perception of speech. *Perception & Psychophysics,* 1975, *18,* 293–298.

Tillyard, E. M. W. *The Elizabethan world picture.* London: Chatto & Windus, 1960. (Originally published, 1943.)

Waters, R. S., & Wilson, W. A. Speech perception by rhesus monkey: The voicing distinction in synthesized labial and velar stop consonants. *Perception & Psychophysics,* 1976, *19,* 285–289.

Wood, C. C. Parrallel processing of auditory and phonetic information in speech perception. *Perception & Psychophysics,* 1974, *15,* 501–508.

Wood, C. C. Auditory and phonetic levels of processing in speech perception: Neurophysiological and information-processing analyses. *Journal of Experimental Psychology: Human Perception and Performance,* 1975, *1,* 3–20. (a)

Wood, C. C. A normative model for redundancy gain in speech perception. In F. Restle, R. M. Shiffrin, N. J. Castellan, H. Lindman, & D. B. Pisoni (Eds.), *Cognitive theory* (Vol. 1). Hillsdale, N.J.: Lawrence Erlbaum Associates, 1975. (b)

14 Spatial Constraints on Attention to Speech

José Morais

Laboratoire de Psychologie Expérimentale
Université libre de Bruxelles
Belgium

ABSTRACT

Evidence for differences in speech recognition performance related to the direction of the speaker is reviewed. First, the ear-of-entry versus spatial-direction characterization of laterality effects observed in dichotic listening situations is discussed. Next, experiments are described that (1) provide a description of the spatial differences in terms of two components, i.e., a decreasing anterior-posterior gradient and lateral asymmetry; and (2) show that these effects are affected by both the posture of the listener and the orientation of his voluntary attention. Last, implications of these findings for a theory of the determinants of the auditory spatial effects are briefly examined.

I. DOES SPEECH PERCEPTION DEPEND ON SPEAKER DIRECTION?

The spatial direction of the auditory sources has been shown by workers on selective attention to be the most effective dimension along which a message can be segregated from others for identification (Broadbent, 1958; Kahneman, 1973; Moray, 1969). Spatial separation of the sound sources was found to be highly helpful in situations in which only one message had to be recognized (Broadbent, 1954; Poulton, 1953; Spieth, Curtis, & Webster, 1954). Little attention has been paid, however, to the possibility of differences in recognition performance specifically related to the direction of the sound source. One exception is a study by Thompson and Webster (1963). Subjects were given the task of identifying CVC words read by a talker in different azimuthal positions, and in the presence of masking noise coming from two loudspeakers situated behind the subject, on either side of the median plane. In one experiment, the 0° listening angle (i.e.,

with the listener facing the talker) yielded better performance than the 180°
angle (i.e., with the listener turning his back to the talker and facing the apparent
origin of noise), about equal to the 90° angle, and worse than the 30° and 60°
angles. In another experiment, there was little difference in performance between
the 0°, 30°, 60°, and 90° angles, but the 180° angle was considerably worse. The
significance of these results is, however, affected by the fact that the masking
effect of the noise may have been stronger in the conditions with the talker in
front or behind the subject than in the other conditions. The two positions are
more likely to be confused when they cannot be distinguished on the basis of
different time or intensity—interaural relationships. Because in the 0° and 180°
conditions the noise was experienced as coming, respectively, from 180° and 0°,
separation of speech and noise may have been more difficult in those conditions
than in the others. As the authors point out, this assumption is supported by data
showing that the threshold for speech opposed by noise at 180° is risen in the
median plane, compared with other planes (Hirsh, 1950; Kock, 1950).

Differences in performance related to the spatial direction of the source have
been mainly discussed in the large literature dealing with laterality effects in
dichotic and monaural listening, but for a long time they were not recognized as
such. Using a paradigm that originated in the study of selective attention, Broadbent's (1954) dichotic span test, Kimura (1961) found that when different verbal
stimuli are presented simultaneously to the two ears of subjects with left hemispheric dominance, the material presented to the right ear was better recognized
than that presented to the left ear. Kimura attributed this "right-ear advantage"
to the predominance of the contralateral auditory pathway over the ipsilateral
one. Later results showing a strong left-ear suppression under dichotic presentation in split-brain patients (Milner, Taylor & Sperry, 1968; Sparks & Geschwind,
1968) have been interpreted as indicating that the ipsilateral input is completely
(or almost completely) suppressed by the contralateral input. It has been assumed
that, in normal people, verbal material presented to the left ear has to be projected in the right hemisphere and transferred across the corpus callosum before
attaining the processing centers in the left hemisphere. This pathway would be
much longer than the contralateral pathway, which directly connects the right
ear and the left hemisphere, thus explaining why sounds entering the right ear
have an advantage over those entering the left ear. Right-ear advantage would be
an ear-of-entry phenomenon, resulting from structural properties of the auditory
system.

In the last ten years, auditory laterality effects have been used by many
authors to study the distribution of mental processes between the two halves of
the brain, and in particular to study processes of speech perception. They have
been commonly considered as ear effects. Curiously, in a different but historically
related line of research, that of selective attention, dichotic presentations have
also been used extensively, but authors have consistently interpreted the results

in terms of apparent spatial origin and not in terms of ears (see Moray, 1969, p. 23).

The ear versus spatial-origin characterization of auditory laterality effects will be the first issue to be examined in the present chapter. Then, an enlarged description of spatial direction effects will be attempted, and some factors that influence these effects will be considered.

II. SPATIAL POSITION VERSUS EAR OF ENTRY

Let us note, first, that the evidence from dichotic and monaural presentations does not differentiate the characterization of laterality effects as ear-of-entry or spatial-origin effects. A message presented to one ear only also appears to originate from the corresponding half of space. Right-ear advantage might thus reflect better processing of messages coming from the right as well as better neural connections of the right ear. The fact that dichotic presentations confound ear of entry with apparent spatial origin was first noted by Bertelson and Tisseyre (1972) in a study of laterality effects in the click-on-sentence task, and it was the starting point for the present experiments.

Morais and Bertelson (1973) have provided a preliminary test of the spatial-origin hypothesis using loudspeakers instead of headphones. On each trial of their experiment, the subject was presented with two simultaneous messages, one over a loudspeaker situated on the left and the other over a loudspeaker situated on the right. Thus, each message reached both ears. If no lateral difference were to be found in that situation, the spatial-origin hypothesis would have become untenable.

Each message consisted of three CV syllables, and the subject was instructed to recall, immediately after presentation, as many syllables as he could, in any order. The percentage of syllables correctly recalled was 39.3 for the right side, and 33.9 for the left side, the difference being significant at $p < 0.005$ ($t = 3.19$, $df = 35$). The data of this experiment have been reanalyzed in order to compute a score of nonhomogeneity, the f score proposed by Marshall, Caplan and Holmes (1975) which takes into account differences in the absolute level of performance. The f score is computed according to the formulae $(A_C - B_C / A_C + B_C) \times 100$, when percentage of correct responses averaged over the two sources is smaller than 50%, and $(A_C - B_C / A_E + B_E) \times 100$, when it is greater ($A$ and B meaning the two sources, C correct responses, and E errors). Here, A means the right-side source and B the left-side source. Therefore, the f score expresses a right-side advantage when greater than 0. The computed mean f score was 7.3 (significantly different from 0 at $p < 0.005$, $t = 2.98$, $df = 35$). About two months later, the same subjects were presented with the same material, delivered this time through headphones in a dichotic listening situation. The mean f score obtained was 10.7, not significantly greater than the preceding one, and there was a positive correlation of 0.57 ($p < 0.0005$) between the two scores.

So when simultaneous verbal messages are delivered through loudspeakers situated to the left and to the right, the message from the right is better reproduced. This result is, of course, consistent with a spatial-direction interpretation of Kimura's effect. However, it does not really refute the ear-of-entry interpretation since, with loudspeakers presentation, intensity and time differences are produced at each ear between messages coming from opposite sides. Time differences could not be relevant because the tape we used was such that the random onset asynchronies between the two messages were much greater than the natural interaural time delay. An effect of the intensity differences at the privileged right ear was, however, a more serious possibility, and right-side advantage could be related to the fact that the right-side message reached the right ear at a higher intensity level than the left-side message. The right-side advantage obtained with loudspeakers could thus still be accounted for in terms of a particular ear-of-entry hypothesis, one based on the intensity of each message at the privileged ear.

The hypothesis that the impression of lateralization is sufficient to produce right-side advantage has been tested by Morais and Bertelson (1975, Experiments 2 and 3). In their Experiment 2, these authors used stereophonic presentations of two simultaneous messages through headphones, in one condition with a 0.7 msec interaural time delay for each message but no intensity difference, and in two other conditions with intensity differences of 9.6 db and 12 db but no time delay.[1] Lateralization of each message was obtained towards the side of the head in which the corresponding ear received that message earlier or at a higher intensity level. One message was lateralized on the left, the other on the right of the median plane. In a fourth condition, dichotic presentation was used. As in Morais and Bertelson (1973), each message consisted of three CV syllables. Before each group of trials the subjects were told which side they should listen to, and they were instructed to reproduce only the syllables on that side, in the order in which they had been presented. Any voluntary attentional bias was thus controlled.

The "time delay" stereophonic condition is the critical one. According to the spatial-direction interpretation, right-side advantage should be observed; according to the ear-of-entry plus intensity differences interpretation, it should not. The mean percentage of correct responses for each side under each condition, the corresponding f scores, and levels of significance for these scores, are shown in Table 1.

[1] In a further experiment, the two messages were presented monaurally to the same ear (by disconnecting one of the earphones) but with an intensity difference of either 9.6 db or 12 db, and these differences produced different degrees of superiority in recall of the louder message.

TABLE 1
Morais and Bertelson (1975, Experiment 2). Mean Percentage of Correct
Responses for Each Side Under Each Condition, the Corresponding
Mean f Scores, and Levels of Significance for These Scores

	L	R	f	$t(df = 31)$	p
Time Delay	49.4	52.6	3.7	2.40	<0.025
9.6. db Intensity Difference	52.0	59.5	10.9	3.95	<0.0005
12 db Intensity Difference	54.1	60.3	7.9	2.46	<0.01
Dichotic	54.0	65.7	16.6	5.05	<0.0005

The fact that right-side advantage was obtained with stereophonic presentations using time delay but no intensity differences shows that apparent lateralization in the auditory space is sufficient to produce lateral asymmetry in performance. The effect was, however, quite small and of marginal significance. Since its demonstration was of prime importance, a new group of subjects was tested under the time delay condition alone (Experiment 3). The mean percentage of correct responses was 45.1 for the apparent left side, and 49.4 for the apparent right side. The mean f score was 5.4 ($t = 2.20$, $df = 15$, $p < 0.025$). It seems, therefore, beyond doubt that spatial direction per se may be a determinant of auditory laterality effects.

One aspect of the results of Experiment 2 remains, however, to be explained. Right-side advantage was greater under the two intensity difference conditions, and particularly under the dichotic condition, then under the time-delay condition. This seems to argue against an interpretation in terms of apparent spatial origin alone and might lead one to consider the possibility of two components being present in lateral asymmetry: one resulting from apparent spatial origin, and one from relative intensity of the two messages at the privileged ear. However, the fact that right-side advantage was not greater in the 12 db intensity difference condition than in the 9.6 db intensity difference condition does not support the two-components explanation. Differences in the size of the effect are probably better explained in terms of differences in the impression of lateralization between the four conditions. In fact, we asked subjects to indicate, on a sheet on which there was a representation of a head, where the train of syllables attended to seemed to come from. The concentration of judgments near the ears was clearly greater in the dichotic condition (90% of the judgments) than in the others (55% to 65%). On the other hand, more judgments were made toward the front in the time delay condition (41%) than in the two intensity difference conditions (15% and 13%) or the dichotic one (7%). Between the two intensity difference conditions there was almost no difference (Morais & Bertelson, 1975, Experiment 5).

After this set of experiments, the spatial-direction interpretation of the right-side advantage observed in diotic listening seems both more adequate to the data and more parsimonious than an hybrid interpretation involving both spatial origin and an effect of intensity differences at a particular ear.[2] Other findings clearly inconsistent with the ear-of-entry interpretation and supporting one in terms of spatial direction alone will be examined later, in connection with the study of the factors that influence auditory spatial effects.

The characterization of laterality effects as spatial effects does not imply, indeed, that the relationship between the direction of the effect and the side of cerebral dominance, which has been firmly established by Kimura (1961), should be questioned. It simply argues against the ear-to-hemisphere wiring interpretation.

III. ENLARGING THE PICTURE OF AUDITORY SPATIAL EFFECTS

The finding that auditory laterality effects are related to the direction of the source in space led us to examine the influence on performance of other directions than those in the midfrontal plane of the head. Morais and Bertelson (1973) had already used, together with the left-right condition, two other conditions in which one of two simultaneous messages was presented over a loudspeaker situated in front of the subject, and the other message over a loudspeaker situated either on the left or on the right. An f score for each of these conditions has been computed, taking A as the frontal loudspeaker and B as the lateral one in the formulae considered above. The f score was 14.4 ($t = 4.62$, $df = 35$, $p < 0.0005$) in the frontal-left condition, and 8.7 ($t = 2.77$, $df = 35$, $p < 0.005$) in the frontal-right condition. Thus, a frontal-direction advantage was observed in both cases.

Hublet, Morais, and Bertelson (1976) and Hublet, Morais, and Bertelson (1977) have provided new data that enlarge the description of auditory spatial

---

[2]In a situation in which the spectrum of the signal was split between the ears, Darwin, Howell, & Brady (this volume) found evidence for both an ear-of-entry and a subjective-location component. More exactly, the authors (in an attempt to reconcile their results with ours) assume that different levels of localization processes may intervene in the determination of laterality effects. In the split-formant situation, sounds presented at the two ears would remain located to the corresponding ear at the cross-correlational or "fuse by frequency band" level, but would be located to one ear only at the later "fuse by pitch" level, and both types of location might determine performance. Since there is no percept of each part of the spectrum in the split-formant situation, and apparent location is a dimension of the percept, the output of the cross-correlational level of localization does not come to consciousness. According to Darwin et al.'s model, the results they have observed do not really dismiss the interpretation of laterality effects in terms of spatial position alone, but argue against an interpretation in terms of *apparent*, *conscious* spatial position alone.

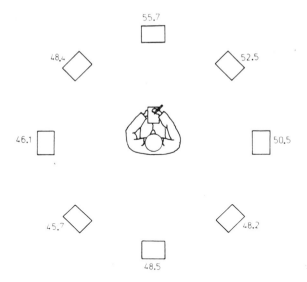

FIG. 1.   Hublet, Morais, & Bertelson (1977). Mean percentage of correct responses for each position.

effects. In the first study, subjects were confronted with two simultaneous messages, one coming from the front and one from a different azimulthal position: 45°, 90°, and 135° from the median plane to the left and to the right, and 180° (i.e., straight behind the subject). On each trial, a single CV syllable was presented through each loudspeaker, and the subjects' task was to identify the syllable from the source that had been previously indicated. Any effect in this situation could then be unequivocally considered as demonstrating a spatial constraint on the focusing of attention to speech. In the second study, two CV syllables differing in pitch were simultaneously presented over one loudspeaker only, which was situated at one of the eight azimuths considered in the former study. The subjects' task was to report the syllable having the high pitch. In addition to revealing a spatial constraint on attention, any effect in this situation would mean that focused attention to speech is constrained by the speaker's spatial direction, not (or not only) at a direction-discriminating level, but at the processing level itself.

As the patterns of performance observed in the two studies were quite similar, the one observed in the second study will be presented here. Mean percentage of correct responses for each position are shown in Fig. 1.

The results may be described in terms of the combination of two components, i.e., a decreasing anterior-posterior gradient and lateral asymmetry. The average of the 0° and the two 45° means was significantly greater than the average of the 180° and the two 135° means ($t = 3.87$, $df = 105$, $p < 0.0005$), thus demonstrating an anterior-posterior asymmetry.[3] For posterior sources there was no significant difference between the 135° and 180° azimuths, but for anterior ones the superiority of the frontal direction over sources at 45° was significant at $p <$ 0.005 ($t = 2.83$, $df = 105$). On the other hand, the average of means for the 45°, 90°, and 135° angles on the right was significantly greater than the average of means for the corresponding angles on the left ($t = 2.97$, $df = 105$, $p < 0.005$), a fact that confirms right-side advantage.

The results of the foregoing experiment provide direct evidence for differences in the accuracy of speech recognition related to the direction of the source, in a situation with no spatial competition. Competition between messages from one direction only proved to be as effective in determining auditory spatial effects as competition between spatially distinct sources. Perhaps all that is needed is simply to make recognition difficult. From a practical point of view, it becomes possible to compare performance for different spatial directions through independent measures.

It must be noted that the present description of auditory spatial effects in speech perception is still partial. Only the direction of the source at head level has been manipulated. Neither the effects of speaker's distance, nor the effects of elevation have been explored. On the other hand, the location of a source is defined with respect to the subject, but the subject has a body made of different segments that can articulate spatially in different ways. The effects of the subject's posture is the topic of the next section.

IV. LISTENING WITH THE EARS OR WITH THE WHOLE BODY?

In the experiments reviewed in the last section, subjects sat on stools with their head, eyes, trunk, and limbs all oriented in the same direction — toward one speaker — a position called "frontal." This posture is probably the most usual in real-life situations where one is listening to speech. One might now ask whether one or several of the different body segments are responsible for the spatial patterns of performance in speech perception observed for subjects in that posture. Regarding, for instance, the advantage of the frontal direction over lateral azimuths, one question might be whether that advantage is related exclusively to the posture of the head, or if the posture of the body below the neck also has some influence. If auditory spatial effects were simply the consequence of some permanent functional feature of the auditory system, such as greater cortical representation of sounds judged by the auditory localization mechanisms as

---

[3]Since this pattern of performance had been revealed in the experiment by Hublet, Morais, & Bertelson (1976), the present results were analyzed using planned comparisons.

coming from certain directions, then head posture would be the only important factor, since it determines the position of the interaural axis.

Morais, Cary, Van Haelen, and Bertelson (in preparation) have run two experiments relevant to this kind of question. The general approach consisted of laterally shifting one or more segments of the subject's body and inspecting the effects this produced on the typical frontal-direction advantage.

In every experimental condition of Experiment 1, two loudspeakers of a set of three — one situated in front of the subject, one at 90° to the left, and one at 90° to the right — were used simultaneously, and each delivered one CV syllable on each trial. In two conditions, the whole body faced the frontal loudspeaker. In one of these conditions sounds came from both the frontal and the left loudspeakers (Condition L), in the other from the frontal loudspeaker and the right one (Condition R). Significant frontal-direction advantage effects were observed in both conditions. In two other conditions, the subject turned his head and eyes, but not the body below the neck, either 90° to the left (with sounds coming from the frontal loudspeaker and the left one), or 90° to the right (with sounds coming from the frontal loudspeaker and the right one).

According to a purely auditory hypothesis of the spatial effects, turning the head to the right by 90° should yield an advantage by the loudspeaker situated on the right of the body as great as the advantage of the frontal loudspeaker over the left one in Condition L. However, the advantage observed for the source at the right in the former condition was small and nonsignificant. According to the same hypothesis, turning the head to the left by 90° should yield an advantage by the loudspeaker situated to the left of the body as great as the advantage of the frontal loudspeaker over the right one in Condition R. However, there was clearly no superiority of any source in that condition.

These results encouraged us to undertake a more detailed analysis of the role of listener's posture in auditory spatial effects. On each trial of Experiment 2, two CV syllables were simultaneously presented, one from a frontal loudspeaker and one from a loudspeaker at 35° to the left. A third loudspeaker at 35° to the right could be seen but remained silent through the entire experiment. In one condition (Condition C) the trunk, the head, and the eyes were oriented towards the frontal loudspeaker. In five other conditions, one or more segments of the subject's body were shifted towards the loudspeaker on the left: head only (eyes remaining oriented towards the frontal source) in Condition H; eyes only in Condition G; trunk and limbs only in Condition T; head and eyes in Condition HG; and all three segments in Condition HGT. The order of the six conditions was varied across subjects according to a latin square design. The six conditions are schematically represented in Fig. 2, together with the results in mean percentage of correct responses for each position and in mean f scores.

As confirmed by statistical analysis, when one of the following segments of the human body, head, eyes, or trunk plus limbs, is oriented laterally, frontal-

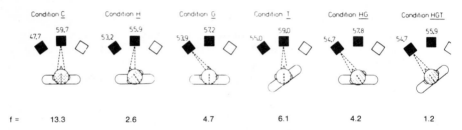

FIG. 2.   Morais, Cary, Van Haelen, & Bertelson (in preparation, Experiment 2). Mean percentage of correct responses for each position under each condition, and mean *f* scores.

direction advantage disappears or is, at least, strongly reduced.[4] The finding that turning the gaze laterally produces about the same effect as turning the interaural axis by the same angle provides a striking demonstration that the latter is not the prime factor.

One possible interpretation of these results is that postural adjustments, generally observed when a listener selectively attends to a source in space, are not simple epiphenomena but are instrumental in improving recognition. Frontal-direction advantage with the whole body towards the frontal speaker would be, at least in part, the result of correct postural adjustments. If one or more of these adjustments are hampered, the frontal-direction advantage falls. An observation by Gopher (1973) on eye movements during selective listening is relevant to this point. Subjects who are exposed to dichotic stimulation and focus attention on one ear tend to make a large saccade at the beginning of the message towards the relevant ear and maintain their fixation in that direction during the entire message. More interestingly, subjects who, in a monitoring task, detect more target words in the right ear than in the left ear produce an even larger effect when they are instructed to fixate 20° to the right of the center, and annul the difference between the ears when they are instructed to fixate to the left of center (Gopher, 1971; reported in Kahneman, 1973, pp. 62–63). In one of our own experiments (Morais, in preparation), employing one source in front of the subject and one behind him, we have observed that subjects looked firmly at the frontal loudspeaker when asked to listen to it, but tried to avoid it and looked at the side, downwards, upwards, or closed their eyes when asked to listen to the source in the rear. It does not seem, however, that closing the eyes is sufficient to alter the typical auditory spatial effects. In an unpublished experiment with Hublet, in which subjects listened to the sources blindfolded, we have obtained the usual frontal-direction advantage. To see the source may be of no help, especially when it does not provide useful information, but this does not rule out

---

[4]Independent planned comparisons for Conditions *C* vs. *H*, *C* vs. *G*, and *C* vs. *T* gave significant levels at, respectively, $p < 0.001$ ($t = 3.37$, $df = 110$), $p < 0.005$ ($t = 2.27$, $df = 110$), and $p < 0.025$ ($t = 2.27$, $df = 110$).

the possibility that keeping the eyes, even if closed, in the direction of the relevant source facilitates selective attention.

A surprising result of Experiment 2 is that in condition *HGT*, the source toward which head, eyes, and trunk plus limbs were oriented did not become the best one. In view of results of earlier experiments (Hublet et al., 1976; Hublet et al., 1977) an advantage of the frontal source over a source on the right side of the subject would be expected. Moreover, the *f* score in condition *HGT* was not significantly different from the scores in conditions in which only one segment was shifted laterally. This suggests that the facilitative effect of postural adjustments cannot account for all the data and, what is more, that the subject's orientation with respect to the sources at the moment of the presentation is not the only determinant of frontal-direction advantage. Factors related to the environment (i.e., the axes of symmetry of the room and the positions occupied by other people or other objects that have a particular role in the experimental situation) and the conditions under which the subject has worked before (the majority of subjects have worked under less ambiguous conditions before being confronted with Condition *HGT*) probably affect the subject's representation of the spatial relationships between himself and the sources. This internal representation of space might combine with postural adjustments in determining the spatial differences in performance.

V. AUDITORY SPATIAL EFFECTS DEPEND ON CORRECT ALLOCATION OF VOLUNTARY ATTENTION

The experiments described to this point give evidence of constraints on attention to speech: in spite of attention-focusing, differences in performance depending on direction of the source arise; in spite of attention focusing, the posture of the subject and characteristics of the environment influence those differences. It would be rather surprising, however, if voluntary attention, generally an agent of active control in the processing of information, takes place only under the action of the determinants of auditory spatial effects without in turn influencing these effects.

Authors who have worked on the right-ear advantage effect in dichotic listening have invariably considered voluntary attention as a possible source of artifact, and so to be controlled, rather than as an experimental variable. The possibility of a voluntary attentional bias has been checked in different ways (analyzing only the first response, asking for unilateral report, comparing free report with prestimulus cued report of one ear) and, at most, voluntary attention was found to contribute only a slight component to lateral asymmetry. However, in order to determine the exact role of voluntary attention in ear differences it is not enough to ensure that the subject listens to a particular ear on each trial, but we have to determine if for observing the ear difference it is not important to attend

TABLE 2
Morais (1975). Mean Percentage of Correct Responses for Each Position
Under Each Condition, Mean f Scores and Corresponding Levels of
Significance

	Left	Right	f	$t(df = 31)$	p
90° R-F	40.6	47.7	10.0	4.04	<0.0005
90° R − 45° F	45.2	44.9	1.8	0.45	N.S.
45° R-F	38.0	39.8	2.9	0.89	N.S.
45° R − 90° F	37.8	40.3	4.6	1.46	N.S.

precisely the left and right ears, not elsewhere. Ear differences have been observed with subjects expecting stimulation to occur in one or two earphones. But let us suppose that with sources on the left and the right sides the subjects pay attention to the front. Would right-side advantage still be observed? Testing the effects of the orientation of voluntary attention involves comparing the spatial-direction effects obtained in a situation in which attention is oriented toward the source delivering the stimuli to be processed with those obtained in a situation in which attention is oriented toward a fictitious source or toward a source delivering stimuli that have to be rejected on the basis of another dimension (pitch, for instance). If sources somewhere on the left and right sides, but not on the midfrontal plane, yield reduced differences in performance in comparison with sources in that plane, then it might be possible to study the role of voluntary attention in lateral asymmetry by comparing lateral asymmetry when the believed and actual positions of sources coincide and when they do not. This requires, of course, that in this situation as well as in the first one subjects believe they are reporting the stimuli from the source to which they are paying attention.

Following a suggestion by Jacques Mehler, Morais (1975) has taken advantage of the ventriloquism effect (the capture of the apparent origin of sound by the sight of a fictitious source) to that purpose. In the experimental room, there were four hidden real loudspeakers situated two at 90° and two at 45° from the median plane to each side, and two visible dummy loudspeakers, which were put either both at 90° or both at 45°. In two conditions (90° real and fictitious; 45° real and fictitious), sound origin and visual cues coincided, and in two conditions (90° real−45° fictitious; 45° real−90° fictitious) they did not. On each trial, there were three CV syllables from each side. Unilateral report, with prestimulus cueing, was requested. Only two out of thirty-four subjects noticed the discordance between sound origin and visual cues, and their data were discarded. Significant right-side advantage was obtained in the 90° real and fictitious condition, but not in the other three (see Table 2). More interestingly, the mean f score for condition 90° real and fictitious was significantly greater than the mean f score for condition 90° real−45° fictitious by planned comparison (t =

1.98, $df = 93$, $p < 0.05$). It seems, therefore, that the false belief of the listener concerning the spatial origin of the messages and the corresponding orientation of his voluntary attention can eliminate, but not create, a lateral asymmetry in performance.

In a similar vein, Morais (in preparation) has taken advantage of the frequent front–back confusions to assess the contribution of voluntary attention to sagittal asymmetry. Two CV syllables, differing in pitch, were delivered simultaneously through two loudspeakers, one situated in front of the subject (0°), the other behind him (180°). The subject's task was to report the high pitch syllable. He was instructed that before each trial he would be told "attention to the front" or "attention to the back," according as to whether the high pitch syllable was to be delivered through the 0° or the 180° loudspeaker. Actually, however, the subject was told the truth in one half of trials and misled in the other half. The different types of trials were randomly presented. As expected, significant frontal-direction advantage was observed in the true information trials ($f = 7.8$, $t = 2.50$, $df = 15$, $p < 0.025$). In the deceptive information trials, however, there was no spatial difference.[5]

It seems, therefore, that both correct allocation of voluntary attention and real origin of the stimulus to be processed in a privileged region of space are necessary components of sagittal asymmetry, as they are of lateral asymmetry. The fact that voluntary attention interacts with the determinants of auditory spatial effects may perhaps bring some light to the nature of these determinants.

VI. IMPLICATIONS OF THE PRECEDING FINDINGS FOR A THEORY OF THE AUDITORY SPATIAL EFFECTS.

In Section II we discussed the fact that a right-side advantage effect may be observed with stereophonic presentations using time differences only, and considered this finding as arguing against an interpretation of lateral asymmetry based exclusively on (1) relative intensity of the two messages at the right ear, and (2) prepotency of the contralateral pathway to the dominant hemisphere (an interpretation that might be derived from Kimura, 1961, 1967). In Section IV we reported that gaze direction and position of the trunk and limbs may, at least, reduce in a significant way the typical frontal-direction advantage effect, these findings showing that frontal-direction advantage cannot be exclusively attributed to the fact that sounds coming from the front reach either ear with no head or pinna shadow. The outcomes of our deception experiments fully agree in providing, both for right-side advantage and frontal-direction advantage, clear

[5]It must be noted, on the other hand, that intrusions (i.e., giving the syllable with the incorrect pitch) were not more frequent in the misleading conditions (in which they came from the source indicated to the subject) than in the nonmisleading conditions.

evidence against interpretations that make strength of input the critical factor in determining spatial effects. There would be no reason, on the basis of such interpretations, for the auditory spatial effects to be affected by misallocation of attention, when the degree of misallocation is the same for the different sources. However, as we have seen, both lateral and sagittal asymmetries disappear when subjects are misled about the spatial origin of the sounds.

A less peripheral interpretation would be that, for some reason related to the auditory projection system, sounds from particular directions in space have a stronger representation in the primary auditory area of the left hemisphere than sounds from other directions. This interpretation differs from the preceding one essentially in that the advantage for sounds from certain directions is not obtained before they are labeled by the auditory system as coming from those directions, but following this labeling and as a consequence of it. A sound that has been decoded as coming from the right side would have a stronger representation on the primary auditory area of the left hemisphere than a sound that has been decoded as coming from the left side. A sound that has been decoded as coming from the front would have the strongest representation of all (see Rosenzweig, 1954, for electrophysiological evidence). If we assume that visual information and knowledge of the situation do not affect the output of the processes of stereophonic fusion, which decode spatial location of the sound (on neurological grounds there is no reason to expect comparison of information from different modalities to occur at such a low level), then differences in the strength of the representation of the sounds in the left-primary auditory area and, as a consequence, differences in performance, should still occur in our deception experiments. In view of the results of these experiments, interpretations of auditory spatial effects based exclusively on the strength of the signal representation at the sole auditory level seem to be as untenable as those based on the strength of the input at the more peripheral level.

The disappearance of the spatial difference when attention is not correctly oriented does not imply, of course, that the input from one side is not mainly conducted by the contralateral pathway, that sounds from the rear are not weakened by the external ear shadow, or that sounds from certain origins do not have greater cortical representations than sounds from other origins. It simply implies that these facts are not sufficient determinants of auditory spatial effects. The phenomenon we are studying undoubtedly has physiological correlates, and one of these may be greater cortical representation for sounds from certain origins (what kind of cortical representation is to be considered below), but to take these correlates as their cause may be a reductionist mistake.

If we choose to speak of the auditory spatial differences as showing up differences in the strength of the cortical representation of the sounds, then we are referring to a representation that is affected not only by the real spatial location of the stimulus, but also by visual suggestion concerning the position of the sources, by posture and direction of gaze. The strength or quality of the input representation has been a concept most frequently used by authors in the laterality effects line of research. Most of them tried to account for poorer performance on one ear on the basis of a loss produced by longer neural pathways, so the "strength/quality" concept was well-adjusted to their model. Now, results have been found that do not point to the role of some neural constraint of the auditory system, but to the role of control processes such as attention, and of postural adjustments. Rather than invoking differences in the strength or in the quality of the cortical representation of the input, it might be more adequate to the data to speak of the spatial differences as revealing differences in the amount of capacity a listener in a particular situation calls upon for the processing of sounds coming from different regions of space. However, it would be paradoxical to propose a conceptual change when we are so far from having a general theory of the auditory spatial differences. We know, indeed, that both lateral asymmetry and the anterior-posterior gradient are (1) affected by the incorrectness of voluntary attention orientation, and (2) influenced by postural adjustments, in apparently the same way. In addition, a significant positive correlation between frontal-direction advantage and right-side advantage has been observed in one of our experiments (Hublet et al., 1977). Yet we still have little idea of what underlies this correlation. The possibility of a relationship between the two spatial effects on an hemispheric basis should, of course, be explored. On the other hand, it is not unlikely that the two effects in part obey different determinants. Particularly, maximum recognition efficiency for sounds coming from the source the listener is facing and looking at may be related to the fact that events in real life frequently carry information on both visual and auditory modalities and draw both visual and auditory forms of attention.

ACKNOWLEDGMENTS

I wish to thank Professor Paul Bertelson for the many fruitful discussions we have had during the preparation of this paper.

REFERENCES

Bertelson, P., & Tisseyre, F. Lateral asymmetry in the perceived sequence of speech and nonspeech stimuli. *Perception and Psychophysics*, 1972, *11*, 356–362.

Broadbent, D. E. The role of auditory localization in attention and memory span. *Journal of Experimental Psychology*, 1954, *47*, 191–196.

Broadbent, D. E. *Perception and communication*. London: Pergamon Press Ltd., 1958.

Gopher, D. *Patterns of eye movement in auditory tasks of selective attention*. Unpublished doctoral dissertation, Hebrew University, Jerusalem, 1971.

Gopher, D. Eye-movement patterns in selective listening tasks of focused attention. *Perception and Psychophysics*, 1973, *14*, 259–264.

Hirsh, I. J. The relation between localization and intelligibility. *Journal of the Acoustical Society of America*, 1950, *22*, 196–200.

Hublet, C., Morais, J. & Bertelson, P. Spatial constraints on focused attention: Beyond the right-side advantage. *Perception*, 1976, *5*, 3–8.

Hublet, C., Morais, J., & Bertelson, P. Spatial effects in speech perception in the absence of spatial competition. *Perception,* 1977, *6,* 461–466.

Kahneman, D. *Attention and effort.* Englewood Cliffs, N.J.: Prentice-Hall Inc. 1973.

Kimura, D. Cerebral dominance and the perception of verbal stimuli. *Canadian Journal of Psychology*, 1961, *15*, 166–171.

Kimura, D. Functional asymmetry of the brain in dichotic listening. *Cortex*, 1967, *3*, 163–178.

Kock, W. E. Binaural localization and masking. *Journal of the Acoustical Society of America*, 1950, *22*, 801–804.

Marshall, J., Caplan, D., & Holmes, J. The measure of laterality. *Neuropsychologia*, 1975, *13*, 315–321.

Milner, B., Taylor, L., & Sperry, R. W. Lateralized suppression of dichotically presented digits after commissural section in man. *Science*, 1968, *161*, 184–185.

Morais, J. The effects of ventriloquism on the right-side advantage for verbal material. *Cognition*, 1975, *3*, 127–139.

Morais, J. *Voluntary attention and auditory asymmetries.* In preparation.

Morais, J., & Bertelson P. Laterality effects in diotic listening. *Perception*, 1973, *2*, 107–111.

Morais, J., & Bertelson, P. Spatial position versus ear of entry as determinant of the auditory laterality effects: A stereophonic test. *Journal of Experimental Psychology: Human Perception and Performance*, 1975, *104*, 253–262.

Morais, J., Cary, L., Van Haelen, H., & Bertelson, P. *The role of the listener's posture in auditory spatial effects.* In preparation.

Moray, N. *Listening and attention.* London: Penguin Books, 1969.

Poulton, E. C. Two–channel listening. *Journal of Experimental Psychology*, 1953, *46*, 91–96.

Rosenzweig, M. R. Cortical correlates of auditory localization and of related perceptual phenomena. *Journal of Comparative and Physiological Psychology*, 1954, *47*, 269–276.

Sparks, R. W., & Geschwind, N. Dichotic listening in man after section of neocortical commissures. *Cortex*, 1968, *4*, 3–16.

Spieth, W., Curtis, J. F., & Webster, J. C. Responding to one of two simultaneous messages. *Journal of the Acoustical Society of America*, 1954, *26*, 391–396.

Thompson, P. O., & Webster, J. C. The effect of talker-listener angle on word intelligibility. *Acustica,* 1963, *13,* 319–323.

15 Laterality and Localization A "Right Ear Advantage" for Speech Heard on the Left

Christopher J. Darwin
Peter Howell
Susan A. Brady

Laboratory of Experimental Psychology
University of Sussex
Brighton, England

ABSTRACT

The question of whether ear differences in the perception of speech are based on the ear of entry of a sound or its subjective location is addressed using a paradigm that dissociates the two. If the first formant of a syllable is played to one ear and the second and third formants to the other ear, the sound is localized to the ear getting the first formant even though the discriminada for a place of articulation judgment are only the second and third formants. A same-different reaction time paradigm showed that there was a reliable, but small, ear difference favoring the right ear when it received the second and third formants, indicating that ear of entry is a significant factor. However, there was an additional advantage for the right ear attributable to the apparent location of the sound. This latter factor was confined to the "different" judgments. A model of the functional organization of the afferent auditory system is offered to account for these and other results and the role of attentional mechanisms in lateral asymmetries for speech is discussed.

I. INTRODUCTION

The existence of auditory perceptual asymmetries in normal human subjects has substantially confirmed the clinically-based hypothesis that man's two hemispheres are complementarily specialized for recognizing verbal and non-verbal sounds (Kimura, 1961a, b, 1964; Luria, 1966; Milner, 1961). The results of these laterality experiments have in addition raised questions about the mechanism that allows cerebral asymmetries to be revealed as differences in performance between the ears. In particular, the following questions have been raised: Is the perceptual asymmetry effect an advantage for a particular ear or for a particular half of space (Morais, 1974/5; Morais & Bertelson, 1973, 1975)? Under what conditions is dichotic competition necessary to reveal the effect (Kimura, 1961a, b; Milner, Taylor, & Sperry, 1968)? Does the effect arise because of a stronger contralateral afferent projection by the auditory system, or because of an attentional bias towards one side (Kinsbourne, 1970; Treisman & Geffen, 1968)? Answers to these questions would be interesting, not merely for the light that they might shed on the origin of the ear difference effect itself, but more generally, for their implications for the functional organization of the auditory perceptual system (see Haggard, in press). This paper uses a recently developed technique for revealing perceptual asymmetries monaurally (Morais, 1975; Morais & Darwin, 1974) to investigate primarily the first of these questions, but with results that have implications for all three.

Kimura's original papers (1961a, b, 1967) on asymmetries in the recall of digit strings emphasized the need for dichotic presentation and described a physiologically-based model to explain the need for dichotic presentation. This proposed that the ear difference effect is due to the slight predominance of the contralateral over the ipsilateral pathway found for monaural stimuli being exaggerated by dichotic competition. Physiological support for this theory is the demonstrably greater cortical evoked potential contralateral to the ear stimulated (Rosenzweig, 1951) and the paucity of single cortical units firing only to the ipsilateral ear (Hall & Goldstein, 1968). Although Kimura's theory explicitly referred to superior contalateral pathways between ears and hemispheres, electrophysiological evidence had also shown greater cortical activity contralateral to the ear receiving the earlier or the louder of two clicks presented one to each ear (Brugge & Merzenich, 1973; Rosenzweig, 1954). This suggests that spatial location might be a more relevant (though less objective) dimension than ears. Morais and Bertelson (1973, 1975) have succeeded in showing effects similar to Kimura's using stereophonic and diotic presentation, where both ears get both stimulus channels. In their most striking example, they find that recall for the digit string subjectively located on the right is superior to that on the left when position is cued only by a difference in time of arrival between the ears. It is difficult to reconcile this result with a model that invokes a stronger contralateral projection between ears (as such) and hemispheres; but as Morais (1974/5) points out, it can be reconciled to Kimura's general model if one assumes that the projection to the hemispheres is based on a spatial location computed at a low level of the auditory system, rather than on actual ear of arrival (see also Haggard, 1975, in press).

What, then, is spatial location: the real position of the sound source with respect to the subject's head, or the apparent position of the sound source to the subject? In an ingenious experiment Morais (1974/5) showed that both of these were important. He misled subjects into thinking that sound came from a pair of visible but mute loudspeakers, when it in fact came from a similar pair of hidden loudspeakers which could be in a different place from the visible ones. Morais found that both the audible and the visible speakers had to be at right angles to the subject to obtain a significant ear difference in the recall of two channels of simultaneously presented syllables.

To explain this result Morais proposed a duplex theory, maintaining that the ear difference effect was determined both by a structural mechanism, such as Kimura's, sensitive to the actual position of the sound source, and also to biased attentional processes, such as those proposed by Treisman and Geffen (1968) and Kinsbourne (1970), sensitive to the apparent position of the source. Although this provides an adequate explanation of Morais' own experiment, other dichotic experiments are more difficult to handle with this duplex theory.

Halwes (1969) played subjects stop-vowel syllables dichotically either on the same pitch or on different pitches. The subjective impression of a dichotic pair of syllables with the same vowel and pitch is of a single midline source, whereas with different pitches it is of two separate sources localized towards their respective ear. Despite this impression of two sources, Halwes found no greater ear advantage when the pitch differed on the two ears. Here, then, subjective localization does not apparently influence the size of the ear difference. In a similar vein, Kirstein (1970) has found that although temporally misaligning syllables makes them easier to attend to selectively, it decreases the ear difference. However, in both these experiments it might be argued that the treatment that made attentional processes easier was also reducing the dichotic competition necessary to reveal ear differences on Kimura's model, leading to no net change in the size of the effect. This objection applies perhaps less strongly to an experiment by Darwin (1969, Experiment 8), who looked at the size of the ear difference for syllable-final stop consonants preceded by different lengths of vowel. The formant transitions cueing the stops were always temporally aligned, but because of the different vowel lengths, the onsets of the sounds were staggered. Subjects reported hearing the same sound in either ear (although they were always different) more often when the vowels were the same length, but this condition also showed the greatest probability of the reported sound being from the right ear. Here, then, the conditions that favor a single percept also favor the larger ear difference.

In the experiment reported here we examine the relative importance for the ear difference effect of the apparent position of sound source and of the actual ear at which the stimulus arrives. We do this by using a paradigm that dissociates the two, allowing subjects to hear on the left, say, a sound that actually came to the right ear. This is made possible because of two previous findings.

First, Rand (1974) has shown, following earlier findings on fusion (Broadbent & Ladefoged, 1957) that when the first formant of a stop consonant-vowel syllable is presented to one ear and the second and third formants to the other, not only do the two sounds fuse into a single subjective percept, but the amplitude of the second and third formants can be reduced by at least 20dB before subjects cease to be able to identify the consonant. With this attenuation the single percept is heard as localized well to the side of the first formant. Since the place of articulation of stop consonants can be cued entirely by changes in the second and third formants it is possible, using Rand's split-formant technique, to produce the impression of a syllable arriving at one ear while allowing the information that determines its place of articulation to enter only the opposite ear. Second, Morais and Darwin (1974) found a reliable ear difference when subjects judged whether the initial consonant of a syllable presented monaurally was the same or different from that of an earlier syllable presented binaurally. Their "different" responses were on average 15 msec faster when the second sound came to the right ear than to the left ear.

If, instead of playing the second syllable monaurally, we play a split-formant sound, will faster reaction times appear in the case where the sound is heard on the right, or in the case where the discriminanda for the perceptual judgment come into the right ear? Kimura's original model predicts that actual ear of entry of the discriminanda should be important; Kinsbourne's attentional model and Morais' modification of Kimura's model predict that apparent location should be important; and Morais's duplex model predicts that both should be important.

II. METHOD

A. General

On each trial of the experiment the subject had to indicate as rapidly as possible whether two consecutively presented syllables had the same or a different initial consonant. The subject did this by moving a lever either away from or towards himself. Each trial started with a binaural warning tone and was followed by the first syllable presented binaurally on a low falling pitch. Half a second after the start of this syllable the second one was played at a higher but also falling pitch. This second syllable could be played either monaurally or with split-formants. In the monaural condition the whole syllable was presented to one ear, whereas in the split-formant condition the first formant was played to one ear simultaneously with the second and third formants being played to the other ear 21 dB lower than they were in the monaural case. The combined level of the second and third formants was approximately 34 dB less than the first formant. The experimental format for a single trial in each of the two conditions is shown in Fig. 1. There was a 3-sec gap between trials. Different pitch contours were used on the two syllables since this arrangement had been used in the earlier experiment of Morais and Darwin (1974).

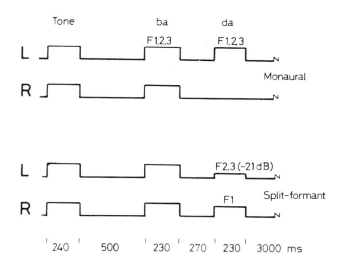

FIG. 1   Format of a single trial in the monaural and split-formant condition.

B. Stimuli

Each syllable lasted 230 msec and was either [ba, da] or [ga], the consonant being cued by 40-msec transitions at the beginning of the syllable (Fig. 2). For all three consonants the first formant rose from 350 Hz to a steady-state of 763 Hz, and the second and third formants had steady-state values of 1618 and 2545 Hz respectively. The starting frequency of the higher two formants, however,

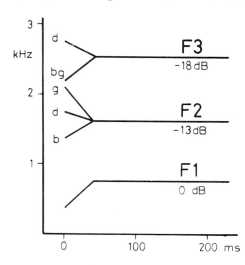

FIG. 2   Stylized spectrograms for the three syllables [ba, da, ga] used in the experiment. The amplitude levels are those used for the binaural and monaural stimuli. The higher formants were attenuated by an additional 21 dB in the split-formant condition.

265

changed with the consonant and were (in the order [b, d, g]) 1373, 1753, 2100 Hz for the second formant and 2200, 1750, 2200 Hz for the third formant. The binaural sounds' pitch fell from 121 to 92 Hz while the monaural and split formant sounds' pitch fell from 151 to 122 Hz.

The synthesis of the speech sounds and the timing and output of the dichotic tape sequence were performed on this laboratory's Elliott 4130 computer. The computed waveforms were stored on a disc, from which they could be retrieved and output simultaneously through a pair of D-A converters at a sampling rate of 7300 Hz. Each channel was low-pass filtered at 3 kHz (48 dB/oct) before recording on a Revox tape recorder. The stimuli were played back over Grason-Stadler TDH-39 headphones in a soundproof booth.

C. Experimental Design

Each of 16 right-handed subjects, ages 19–28, none of whom were known to have any hearing defect, attended for five sessions lasting about two hours each. The sessions were usually held on different days and no subject had more than two on the same day. Each session consisted of a warm-up block of 63 trials followed by four experimental blocks of 126 trials. The entire first session was a practice one whose data were discarded, leaving four scored sessions. Within each session the four experimental blocks consisted of two blocks of the monaural condition and two blocks of the split-formant condition, with each condition using its own fixed trial order. There were equal numbers of same and different trials, and the higher formants went to each replay channel equally often.

As well as the main experimental variable of monaural versus split-formant three other variables were counterbalanced both within and between subjects: which hand held the response lever, headphone orientation, and the order in which the experimental blocks were heard in a session. In addition, the direction of movement to signal "same" was counterbalanced between subjects so that an individual subject always moved the lever the same way throughout the experiment to signal "same," but which hand he held it in varied from block to block.

At the start of a session, subjects took three identification tests; one binaural, one monaural, and one split-formant. Each test started with a demonstration of the three different syllables played twice in the order [ba, da, ga], followed by a random sequence of 24 items which they had to identify. Two subjects were replaced at this stage of the experiment for failing to identify the sounds at better than 90%.

The reaction time experiment was run with the help of a PDP-12 computer, which started and stopped the tape recorder, recorded subjects' responses and reaction times, and gave feedback to the subject via an oscilloscope display. The subject was told that he had to indicate by a rapid lever movement whether the two syllables that he would hear on each trial had the same or different initial consonants and that he would get feedback via an oscilloscope screen, which he could see through the window of the soundproof booth. During the practice block at the beginning of each session, the subjects saw the word "anticipation" on the screen whenever they made a response with a latency of less than 100 msec from the onset of the second syllable, and the word "wrong" whenever they made a mistake. During the experimental blocks (in both the practice and experimental sessions) they were additionally told whether their correct responses were "fast" or "slow," if a response was faster or slower than the mean of the preceding block. In addition to a flat rate of 70 pence per hour, subjects were paid ¼ pence for each "fast" response and penalized ½ pence for each incorrect response; this gave them an average bonus of about 30 pence per session.

After the first and last experimental sessions subjects were asked to write down on which side they heard the split-formant sounds localized during a sequence of 63 trials, as a check that our own impression of these sounds' localization was shared by the subjects. Six of the 16 subjects also took a more elaborate localization test. They were given a diagrammatic head and asked to indicate on it the location of any sound they heard during the presentation of the second syllable. Each subject heard 60 split-formant trials. The instructions specifically emphasized that there might be more than one sound present.

III. RESULTS

A. Identification and Localization Tests

The results of the identification tests confirmed Rand's (1974) finding that the split-formant sounds with extremely attenuated higher formants are readily identifiable. With binaural presentation subjects averaged 98.5% correct, with monaural 98.8%, and with split-formant 97.6%. The 1.2% drop in intelligibility from monaural to split-formant condition was not significant across subjects. In the localization test taken by all subjects, every one reported hearing all the split-formant sounds localized to the side that was in fact getting only the first formant.

In the more elaborate test taken by six subjects, no one indicated more than one sound on any trial, and there were only two occasions of a subject marking a side other than that on which the first formant was presented. The mean apparent position of the sounds in the latter test are shown on the head in Fig. 3. Although dichotic presentation of sounds with the same periodicity but grossly different spectral ranges can give rise to double images, this was not the case in our experiment. We have noticed, however, that if the amplitude of the second and third formants is raised above the considerably attentuated level used here, a double image can be heard (cf. Cutting, 1976; Experiment 5).

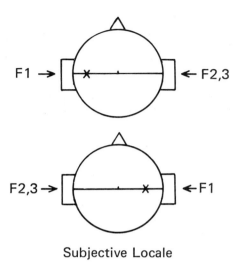

Subjective Locale

Fig. 3   Subjective location of the split-formant sounds for the six subjects who took the more elaborate localization test.

B.   Reaction Times

The raw data for the analysis were the main reaction times for correct trials on each experimental block (of 120 secored trials). Wrong responses ("same" for "different" and the reverse) were counted as errors and, together with anticipations, were not included in the reaction time analysis. Correct responses with a latency of longer than 1 sec were also excluded from the reaction time analysis, although they were not counted as errors.

The mean reaction times for the main experimental variables are shown in Fig. 4. The basic result is that in both the monaural and the split-formant conditions there is an overall advantage for the right ear *when this receives the second and third formants.* With split-formants the faster condition is when the sound is localized to the left, whereas monaurally the faster condition is when the sound is localized to the right. The main statistical analysis was a six-way analysis of variance with factors: (1) experimental condition (monaural vs. split-formant); (2) ear receiving second and third formants (left/right); (3) response (same/different); (4) direction of lever movement (nested under subjects); (5) replications (four sessions); and (6) hand (left/right). Significant main effects were attributable to the right ear being faster than the left ($F_{1, 14} = 17.3$, $p < .001$), same responses being faster than different ($F_{1, 14} = 19.1$, $p < .001$), monaural being faster than split-formant ($F_{1, 14} = 16.9$, $p < .005$) and a general speeding-up over successive sessions ($F_{3, 42} = 9.1$, $p < .001$). No interaction reached significance at the 2.5% level except that between experimental condition, ears and response ($F_{1, 14} = 24.1$, $p < .0005$), that is between the dimensions given in Fig. 4 and more clearly in Fig. 5. This interaction can be described as being due to the following difference between the monaural and the split-formant conditions: in the monaural condition

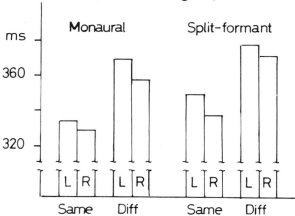

FIG. 4 Mean reaction times for same and for different judgments made in the monaural and the split-formant conditions, displayed according to the ear receiving the second and third formants.

the greater ear difference is seen for the different responses, whereas in the split-formant condition the greater ear difference is for same responses. Separate analyses of variance on the monaural and split-formant conditions confirmed this conclusion. These showed a significant interaction between ears and response, both for monaural ($F_{1, 15}$ = 12.6, p < .005) and split-formant ($F_{1, 15}$ = 8.0, p <

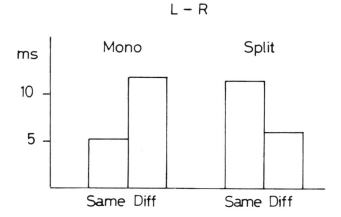

FIG. 5 Mean difference in reaction time between the ears for same and different responses in the monaural and split-formant conditions.

.025) conditions, and also that for both conditions, same judgments were faster than different at the 1% level. Four analyses on the scores on either ear for same and different responses under either monaural or split-formant condition separately showed that in each of these conditions there was a significant advantage for the right ear (monaural–same: $F_{1, 15}$ = 8.3, p < .025; monaural–different: $F_{1, 15}$ = 26.0, p < .001; split-formant–same: $F_{1, 15}$ = 19.2, p < .001; split-formant–different: $F_{1, 15}$ = 5.4, p < .05).

In summary, the reaction time data show that subjects judge the second of two syllables to be the same or different from the first faster when those aspects of the stimulus on which this judgment is based entered the right ear, than when they entered the left. This was true whether subjects heard the sound as being on the left or on the right. The size of this ear advantage was greater monaurally for different than for same responses (replicating Morais & Darwin, 1974), but the opposite was true in the split-formant case. In general, same responses were faster than different (and this did not change with splitting the formants) and reaction times were faster in the monaural condition than in the split-formant.

C. Errors

The number of responses that were errors (i.e., wrong responses and anticipations) was also calculated for each block, and the means for the three main experimental variables are shown in Table 1. An analysis of variance was performed on this data after subjecting it to an arc-sine root transformation. It is important to see whether there are any ear differences in the error data, since if there are, and they are in the opposite direction to the reaction time data, then the interpretation of both error and reaction time data is complicated by the fact that accuracy and speed can be traded-off against each (Swenson & Edwards, 1971).

An analysis of variance showed that there was no main effect involving ear, nor any two-way interaction, but that there was a three-way interaction between ear, experimental condition, and hand ($F_{1, 14}$ = 7.0, p < .025). The interaction

TABLE 1

		Mean Percentage of Errors[a]			
		Monaural		Split-formant	
		Same	Different	Same	Different
Ear receiving	Left	10.2	9.5	11.3	10.8
F2 and F3.	Right	10.7	9.8	11.0	11.0

[a]The only significant effect of errors in this table is that more errors are made in the split-formant than in the monaural condition.

can be described as follows: in the split-formant condition more mistakes are made by a given hand when the higher formants come into the ear on the same side as the hand, whereas for the monaural condition the reverse is true. Put another way, this indicates that for both conditions more mistakes are made by a particular hand when the sound is localized to the opposite side than when it is on the same side. Thus, errors seem to be determined more by the sound's apparent location relative to the responding hand, in contrast to the main reaction time effect, which is determined by the ear of entry of the higher formants irrespective of hand. Higher-order interactions involving these same factors, however, restrict this effect to those subjects who made away-movements for same responses, and within them to the same response. Errors then behave quite differently from the mean reaction times in that they give much less general effects involving ear, which turn out to be based on a sound's apparent location rather than ear per se.

The error analysis also revealed two main effects and a two-way interaction not involving ear: those subjects who moved the lever away to respond "same" were more accurate overall than the other subjects ($F_{1, 14} = 12.1$, $p < .005$), though this effect interacted with whether the correct response should have been same or different ($F_{1, 14} = 6.3$, $p < .025$). In addition, as one might have expected from the identification and the reaction time data, slightly fewer errors were made in the monaural than the split-formant condition ($F_{1, 14} = 8.5$, $p < .025$).

IV. DISCUSSION

This experiment has shown that when subjects have to move a lever to indicate whether the second of two syllables is the same as or different from the first, they make this movement sooner when the discriminanda distinguishing the syllables come into the right ear than if they come into the left. This is true regardless of whether the fused, complete syllable is heard on the left or the right side. In conjunction with the findings of Morais and Bertelson (1975), this poses problems for the three simple models of the origin of the ear difference effect described in the introduction.

The two models that attribute the effect to a contralateral afferent projection either by ears or by spatial location can each handle only one of the results. The ear advantage cannot be simply an *ear* advantage because Morais and Bertelson (1975) found that when both messages were channeled to both ears but with different temporal offsets to produce an impression of different localizations, the sound heard on the right was recalled better than that on the left. Nor can the ear advantage be simply a matter of subjective localization since our experiment shows that when a single sound is split into high and low frequency components the ear advantage is to the side receiving the high frequency sounds whereas the localization is to the side receiving the low frequency sounds. A model attributing the effect to a direction of attention to a contralateral half of space has similar problems. What is being attended? If the contralateral half of subjective space is attended to, then the wrong prediction is made for our experiment; if ears, then the wrong prediction is made for the Morais and Bertelson experiment. How do we resolve the apparent contradiction between these two experiments?

The answer perhaps lies in considering more carefully the sorts of fusion processes that must be taking place in Morais and Bertelson's stereophonic experiment and in our split-formant experiment. In their experiment the two ears receive identical waveforms with a slight difference in relative time of arrival. This imitates, in part, the natural situation in which sound from a source to one side of the head reaches one ear before the other. In the natural situation the higher frequencies will be attenuated somewhat at the ear away from the source because of the acoustic shadow cast by the head. However, in general, all frequencies arriving at one ear from a particular source will be present, albeit at different times and amplitudes, at the other ear. In our split-formant experiment, though, there is virtually no spectral overlap between the two ears. It is possible that different mechanisms are operating to produce "fusion" in these two cases.

Binaural fusion could be achieved for sounds composed of the same spectral frequencies by a cross-correlational process that only compared signals within the same, narrow frequency band (Colburn, 1973; Toole & Sayers, 1965). But such a mechanism cannot be the whole story since sounds with a similar waveform envelope, but with virtually no overlap in their spectra, will still fuse into a single percept (Broadbent & Ladefoged, 1957). Fusion by a common envelope cannot in turn be the prime mechanism because the fusion produced when there is no spectral overlap is less robust than that found when both the envelope and the spectrum are similar (Broadbent & Ladefoged, 1957; Cutting, 1976, Experiment 5; Toole & Sayers, 1965). In addition, Henning (1974) has found that the ability to localize a fused image on the basis of time differences between the envelopes of different sounds at the two ears deteriorates rapidly as the spectral similarity between these signals is reduced.

It is possible, though not compelling, then, that there are two distinct mechanisms responsible for fusion — one that looks only at corresponding spectral frequencies, and one that is concerned with envelope similarities (cf. Toole & Sayers, 1965; Sayers & Cherry, 1957). This distinction has been made in the context of laterality experiments by Haggard (in press), who speculates that "fusion and assignment to localization between and within hemispheres on a spatial basis takes place at a lower level in terms of spectral similarities than it does in terms of shared periodicities (Haggard, 1975)." We will now elaborate this notion and show that it can account for the discrepancy between our experiment and Morais and Bertelson's.

First, let us see how this distinction between different levels of fusion can be applied to Kimura's model and Morais's modification of it. Both these models require some contralateral superiority of the afferent auditory projection; they differ in whether contralateral refers to ears or to spatial location. Let us assume that Morais is correct when he suggests that the contralateral projection is based on the result of some comparison process of the signals at the two ears, rather than being based on each ear alone. But let us now assume, following Haggard (1975), that this comparison process only involves a combination of sounds within the same frequency band. On the basis of such a process, each spectral component of a signal would be projected predominantly to higher anatomical levels contralateral to a position calculated by comparing the two ears for that frequency band. Split-formant sounds would not be fused at this level but would be treated, despite their identical pitches, as two distinct sounds, each projecting predominantly to the side contralateral to their initially calculated position (i.e., contralateral to the side of their respective ear of arrival). Morais and Bertelson's sounds, on the other hand, would at this level be associated with the side at which they were subsequently subjectively localized.

A similar resolution can be achieved for attentional models such as Kinsbourne's by assuming that attention is directed to the initial spatial location, rather than to the apparent subjective location of the sound.

A. Same-different Effects

Splitting the formants of the second syllable in this experiment produced a highly significant change in the interaction between ears and whether the subject responded "same" or "different." In the monaural condition, as in Morais and Darwin (1974), there is a significantly larger ear difference for different than there is for same responses. The present experiment collected more data and the small ear difference for same responses reached significance. For the split-formant sounds, on the other hand, there was a significantly larger ear difference for same judgments than for different, and again both reached significance. The explanation originally offered for the significant ear difference for different judgment by Morais and Darwin took advantage of a model proposed by Bamber (1969) to explain why, for readily categorizable stimuli (Bindra, Donderi, & Nishisato, 1968), same judgments are faster than different. This model maintains that while same judgments can be made solely on the basis of a low level representation of the stimulus, resort must be made to a higher, categorical process to determine that stimuli are categorically different. The need for this categorical processing yields longer reaction times. Morais and Darwin explained their results by assuming that the categorical process involved in different judgments but not required by the same judgments is represented more in the left than the right hemisphere, whereas same judgments can be made on the basis of an unlateralized mechanism. Although at first sight the results of the present experiment appear to be contrary to this model, it does in fact provide the skeleton on which to build an explanation of our results. The important additional postulate is that there are two lateralized mechanisms. The first is responsible for making same judgments and does this faster for sounds that enter the right than the left ear. The second is required, in addition to the first, for different judgments and is faster for sounds subjectively localized on the right side.

Thus for the monaural condition we have a small right-ear advantage for same judgments supplemented by an additional advantage for different judgments based on apparent location. In the split-formant condition, though, the additional ear difference for the different judgments favors the condition where the higher formants come to the left ear. Thus the right-ear advantage is smaller than for same judgments. We have also to explain why the same judgments in the split-formant case show more of a right-ear advantage than in the control case. A related observation is that reaction times generally are slower in the split-formant condition than in the monaural condition. We might put forward the hypothesis, then, that comparing a split-formant sound with a binaural one requires an additional process to simply comparing a binaural with a monaural, and that this process is sensitive to the location, determined on a spectral basis, of the component of the sound relevant to the discrimination. This process, which combines sounds on similar pitches at the two ears, but does not assign them to a new location, is defined in an identical way to Cutting's (1976) "spectral fusion."

Three separate factors then need to be taken into account:

1. A process that can judge sounds with identical formant structure to be the the same, which is faster at handling sounds presented to the right side.

2. A process that can judge sounds fused according to a common periodicity to be the same as binaurally presented sounds, which also handles sounds faster when the component relevant to the discrimination is presented to the right side.

3. A process that can judge speech categories as different, which handles sounds faster when they are subjectively localized to the right side.

Figure 6 illustrates how these processes might be linked together functionally.

Of the three lateralized processes invoked here to explain our results only one, the process for categorizing speech sounds, is one that needs to be expressly linguistic. Retaining and comparing sounds fused either by spectral similarity or common periodicity is not something uniquely useful in verbal classification. Why then should we find that it elicits an advantage for the right ear? This may be a further example of a context effect, similar to the shift in the ear advantage for vowels that can be produced by using all verbal (compared with a mixture of verbal and nonverbal) material on different trials (Spellacy & Blumstein, 1970). A general explanation of such context effects can be made using Kinsbourne s (1970) notion of hemispheric arousal, but in our case it would be perhaps more parsimonious to assume that since the speech categorization process is being performed primarily in the left hemisphere, the results of other bilateral processes are taken from the same hemisphere for a joint decision because of better within- than between-hemisphere connections.

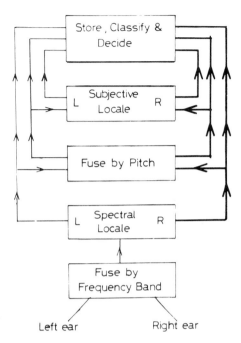

FIG. 6 Model to illustrate how different levels of fusion could interact to give the ear differences observed in this experiment and in those using stereophonic presentation. "Same" judgments can be made on the basis of the output from the lower three boxes, while "different" judgments require, in addition, output from the box labeled "Subjective Locale."

B. Dichotic Competition and Attention

This model has been developed mainly with the results of our split-formant and monaural reaction time experiment in mind. How does the model cater to the results of dichotic experiments, and in particular, what is the relative importance of ear-of-entry and subjective localization under dichotic competition?

With dichotic competition, reliable ear differences can easily be demonstrated in recall errors when subjects only report hearing a single sound source. In our monaural and split-formant experiments (see also Haggard, 1975; Perl & Haggard, 1974), by contrast, there is little indication of any ear difference in the error scores. Thus, the ear difference in recall errors due to the actual, rather than the apparent, sound location is what is enhanced by dichotic competition. Let us suppose, then, that the main effect of dichotic competition is selectively to attenuate the weaker pathway in Fig. 6 leading from the initial spatial representation based on fusion within frequency bands. Errors under dichotic presentation will then depend almost exclusively on a sound's location in this initial spatial representation rather than on its apparent position. Since our split-formant presentation is clearly not equivalent to dichotic presentation, we might also suppose that dichotic competition will only be effective for those frequency regions that are represented for either ear. Simply sharing frequency regions is not a sufficient condition, though, since white noise, although an effective competitor for clicks (Murphy & Venables, 1970) is not an effective competitor for speech (Corsi, 1967; Darwin, 1971).

Since commissurotomized patients show a greatly reduced score on their left ear for recall of dichotically presented speech, but not for recall of monaurally presented speech (Milner, Taylor, & Sperry, 1968; Sparks & Geschwind, 1968), the original Kimura hypothesis of ipsilateral suppression has been supported. Here we are speculating that it is the ipsilateral pathway from the initial spatial representation that is primarily inhibited by dichotic stimulation. The remaining uninhibited pathways would thus reach the ipsilateral hemisphere via the contralateral pathway and the corpus callosum. This organization would thereby imply that fusion by pitch and the determination of apparent location were mainly cortical processes.

This model, as it stands, cannot handle Morais' (1974/5) finding that with loudspeaker presentation the half-space difference for recall of strings of syllables was as much influenced by the real position of the sound source as by its imaginary position. As we have already remarked, this contrasts with Halwes' experiment using sounds on different pitches where the ear difference was found to be no greater under conditions favoring the identification of two sound sources. Morais' experiment differed from Halwes' both in using lists of syllables with different vowels, rather than a single pair of syllables with the same vowel, and real speech, rather than synthetic. Morais' sounds thus differed in pitch and vowel quality at the ears as well as being extended in time. Although this should not result in any greater degree of subjective spatial separation than Halwes' different pitched sounds, it would provide additional dimensions for allowing the subject selectively to attend to one sound rather than the other. We might then agree with Morais (1974/5) that the influence of subjective location which he found under stereophonic competition is indeed the result of an attentional bias, but that this bias can only operate for sounds that are readily selected by being auditorially distinct and extended in time.

This necessary alteration to our original model raises the question of whether the effect of subjective location that we found in our experiment is best attributed to an attentional process or to a more structural difference in the auditory pathways. There is at present no data that allow us to distinguish between these two alternatives.

In summary then the model that we propose retains aspects of all three of the models described in the introduction. The ear difference is in part determined by the ear of entry (or perhaps more precisely by the imaginary location of sound sources based on a comparison across ears within individual spectral regions) and in part by a sound's apparent location. This is true for our reaction time experiment. Recall errors in dichotic experiments appear to be mainly controlled by the ear of entry but may perhaps be influenced by attentional mechanisms based on apparent location if the sounds used allow easy selective attention. We tentatively suggest that the determination of a sound's apparent location is a cortical process, and that the effect of dichotic competition is to inhibit only those ipsilateral pathways whose subsequent projections are based on a sound's ear-of-entry or spectrally-determined spatial location.

ACKNOWLEDGMENTS

The computing facilities used in this experiment were made available through a grant from the Medical Research Council. The two junior authors were supported by a grant from the science Research Council at Haskins Laboratories and at the University of Connecticut by Susan Dutch, whom we thank. We also thank Dr. A. E. Ades for some useful comments.

REFERENCES

Bamber, D. Reaction times and error rates for "same"-"different" judgments of multidimensional stimuli. *Perception and Psychophysics,* 1969, *6,* 169–174.

Bindra, D., Donderi, D. C., & Nishisato, S. Decision latencies of "same" and "different" judgments. *Perception and Psychophysics,* 1968, *3,* 121–130.

Broadbent, D. E., & Ladefoged, P. On the fusion of sounds reaching different sense organs. *Journal of the Acoustical Society of America,* 1957, *29,* 708–710.

Brugge, J. F., & Merzenich, M. M. Responses of neurones in auditory cortex of the macaque monkey to monaural and binaural stimuli. *Journal of Neurophysiology,* 1973, *36,* 1138–1158.

Colburn, H. S. Theory of binaural interaction based on auditory-nerve data I. General strategy and preliminary results on interaural discrimination. *Journal of the Acoustical Society of America,* 1973, *54,* 1458–1470.

Corsi, P. M. The effects of contralateral noise upon the perception and immediate recall of monaurally-presented verbal material. Unpublished masters thesis, McGill University, Montreal, 1967.

Cutting, J. E. Auditory and linguistic processes in speech perception: Inferences from six fusions in dichotic listening. *Psychological Review,* 1976, *83,* 114–140.

Darwin, C. J. Auditory perception and cerebral dominance. Unpublished doctoral dissertation, Cambridge University, 1969.

Darwin, C. J. Dichotic forward and backward masking of speech and non-speech sounds. *Journal of the Acoustical Society of America,* 1971, *50,* 129(A).

Haggard, M. P. Asymmetrical analysis of stimuli with dichotically split-formant information. Speech Perception Series 2 No. 4. Department of Psychology, The Queen's University of Belfast, 1975.

Haggard, M. P. Dichotic listening. In R. Held, D. Leibowitz, & H. L. Teuber, (Eds.), *Handbook of sensory physiology.* New York: Springer-Verlag (in press).

Hall, J. L., & Goldstein, M. H. Representations of binaural stimuli by single units in primary auditory cortex of unanaesthetized cats. *Journal of the Acoustical Society of America,* 1968, *43,* 456–461.

Halwes, T. G. *Effects of dichotic fusion on the perception of speech.* Supplement to Status Report on Speech Research, Haskins Laboratories, September 1969.

Henning, G. B. Detectability of interaural delay in high-frequency complex waveforms. *Journal of the Acoustical Society of America,* 1974, *55,* 84–90.

Kimura, D. Some effects of temporal lobe damage on auditory perception. *Canadian Journal of Psychology,* 1961, *15,* 156–165. (a)

Kimura, C. Cerebral dominance and the perception of verbal stimuli. *Canadian Journal of Psychology,* 1961, *15,* 166–171. (b)

Kimura, D. Left-right differences in the perception of melodies. *Quarterly Journal of Experimental Psychology,* 1964, *14,* 355–358.

Kimura, D. Functional asymmetries of the brain in dichotic listening. *Cortex,* 1967, *3,* 163–178.

Kinsbourne, M. The cerebral basis of lateral asymmetries in attention. In A. F. Sanders (Ed.), *Attention and performance II.* Amsterdam: North-Holland, 1970.

Kirstein, E. *Selective listening for temporally staggered dichotic CV syllables.* Haskins Laboratories Status Report, 1970, *21/22,* 63–70.

Luria, A. R. *Higher Cortical Functions in Man.* London: Tavistock, 1966.

Milner, B. Laterality effects in audition. In V. B. Mountcastle (Ed.), *Interhemispheric relations and cerebral dominance.* Baltimore: Johns Hopkins, 1961.

Milner, B., Taylor, L., & Sperry, R. W. Lateralized suppression of dichotically presented digits after commissural section in man. *Science,* 1968, *161,* 184–186.

Morais, J. The effects of ventriloquism on the right-side advantage for verbal material. *Cognition,* 1974/5, *3,* 127–139.

Morais, J. Monaural ear differences for same-different reaction times to speech with prior knowledge of ear stimulated. *Perceptual and Motor Skills,* 1975, *41,* 829–830.

Morais, J., & Bertelson, P. Laterality effects in diotic listening. *Perception,* 1973, *2,* 107–111.

Morais, J., & Bertelson, P. Spatial position versus ear of entry as determinant of the auditory laterality effects: A stereophonic test. *Journal of Experimental Psychology: Human Perception and Performance,* 1975, *1,* 253–262.

Morais, J., & Darwin, C. J. Ear differences for same-different reactions to monaurally presented speech. *Brain & Language,* 1974, *1,* 383–390.

Murphy, E. H., & Venables, P. H. Ear asymmetry in the threshold of fusion of two clicks: A signal detection analysis. *Quarterly Journal of Experimental Psychology,* 1970, *22,* 288–300.

Perl, N., & Haggard, M. P. *Masking versus hemisphere sharing of processing for speech sounds.* Speech Perception Series 2, No. 3. Department of Psychology, The Queen's University of Belfast, 1974.

Rand, T. C. Dichotic release from masking for speech. *Journal of the Acoustical Society of America,* 1974, *55,* 678–680.

Rosenzweig, M. R. Representations of the two ears at the auditory cortex. *American Journal of Physiology,* 1951, *167,* 147–158.

Rosenzweig, M. R. Cortical correlates of auditory localization and of related perceptual phenomena. *Journal of Comparative and Physiological Psychology,* 1954, *47,* 269–276.

Sayers, B. McA., & Cherry, E. C. Mechanisms of binaural fusion in the hearing of speech. *Journal of the Acoustical Society of America,* 1957, *29,* 973–987.

Sparks, R., & Geschwind, N. Dichotic listening in man after section of neocortical commissures. *Cortex,* 1968, *4,* 3–16.

Spellacy, F., & Blumstein, S. The influence of language set on ear preference in phoneme recognition. *Cortex,* 1970, *6,* 430–439.

Swensson, R. G., & Edwards, W. Response strategies in a two-choice reaction task with continuous cost for time. *Journal of Experimental Psychology,* 1971, *88,* 67–81.

Toole, F. E., & Sayers, B. McA. Inferences of neural activity associated with binaural acoustic images. *Journal of the Acoustical Society of America,* 1965, *38,* 769–779.

Treisman, A. M., & Geffen, G. Selective attention and cerebral dominance in perceiving and responding to speech messages. *Quarterly Journal of Experimental Psychology,* 1968, *20,* 139–150.

16

Speech Timing and Intelligibility [1]

A. W. F. Huggins

Bolt Beranek and Newman Inc.
 and
Massachusetts Institute of Technology
Cambridge, Massachusetts, United States

ABSTRACT

The durations of speech segments are known to be influenced by several factors. The most important of these are probably the intrinsic durations of the component phonemes, the stress on each syllable, and some phrasal effects, such as phrase-final lengthening. Similarities between effects at different linguistic levels suggest that speech timing rules may be hierarchically organized. Despite this fairly detailed knowledge of timing regularities, little is known about how critical correct timing is for intelligibility. An experiment is described that measured the intelligibility of sentences synthesized by rule. The results show that assigning an incorrect fundamental frequency contour reduced intelligibility to about two-thirds of its value with correct fundamental, and that incorrect timing had an even more dramatic effect, reducing intelligibility to about one-third of its "normal" value. There are obvious implications for speech training of the deaf.

I. INTRODUCTION

Speech timing has received much less formal study than have either the spectral or articulatory regularities of speech. No doubt the relative neglect of timing was partly due to the development of instruments for spectral analysis such as the spectrograph, which generate visual displays on which spectral regularities stand out with much more salience than do temporal regularities. Before the advent of the spectrograph, many observations and statements were made about

---

[1] A shorter version of this paper was read at the A. G. Bell Association National Convention, Boston, Massachusetts, June 24–26, 1976.

speech timing, but were rarely supported by measurements, with some notable exceptions, such as Stetson (1951), Hudgins (1934), and Bell (1916), to name a few. These investigators measured durations using a Kymograph (a smoked drum that rotated, on which a needle wrote out the waveform, or intraoral pressure, etc.), a procedure so tedious that few were willing to invest the effort needed to amass the substantial amount of data required by studies of speech timing.

A further set of reasons for neglecting the study of timing are concerned with the difficulty of the task. Speech simply does not consist of a sequence of acoustic beads on a string, with each bead corresponding to a single phoneme. Rather, the phonemes appear in encrypted form in the speech signal (Liberman, Cooper, Shankweiler, & Studdert-Kennedy, 1967). The details of the encryption are affected by speech rate (Kozhevnikov & Chistovich, 1965), which adds to the complication, particularly since speech rate itself is a variable that nobody really knows how to control or measure.

In the last few years, studies of speech timing have begun to proliferate for two separate reasons, both involving computers:

1. Computers produce a very wide range of output by applying an explicit set of rules (the program) to the input data. This idea of a set of explicit rules for relating different descriptions of complex things was quickly adopted in other fields — Chomsky's introduction of it into linguistics has revolutionized the field. The idea is now being applied to speech timing, in an attempt to capture the regularities of timing as a set of rules.

2. Computers have made possible the *testing* of complex theories, which would have been too tedious to check out exhaustively by hand. Computers also raise practical possibilities, such as reading machines for the blind, verbal control of machines, etc.

II. THE MAIN FACTORS AFFECTING SPEECH TIMING

What are the main factors that affect speech timing, as they are known today? We will begin with speech rate, because although it is a basic or fundamental variable, no one yet knows how to incorporate it into a theory. The variability of speech rate raises major problems for those measuring speech timing, since there is no objective way of knowing whether two sentences to be compared were spoken at the same rate. Unfortunately, speech rate is *not* linearly related to segment duration. That is, if you speak a sentence twice as fast, some segments are shortened more than others. In particular, vowels tend to be shortened more than consonants (Kozhevnikov & Chistovich, 1965). Consonant articulations tend to involve targets, or coordinated sequences of targets, that must be *reached,* whereas vowel targets tend to be progressively more undershot as speech rate is increased (Lindblom, 1963). Thus, the reasons for the differential effects of speech

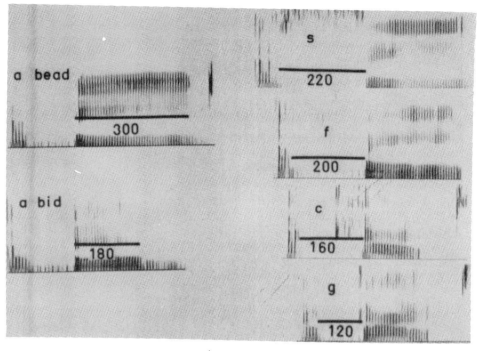

FIG. 1. Differences in intrinsic durations are illustrated for the vowels in *bead* and *bid* (left), and for the initial consonants in *a sea, a fee, a coat,* and *a goat* (right). The heavy line marks the extent of each segment, and the number corresponds to the duration in milliseconds.

rate on vowels and consonants are probably at least partly physiological and mechanical. Since every articulator has finite mass, and is moved by muscles that apply finite forces, there is obviously a maximum rate of articulation, just as there is a maximum rate at which a runner can move his legs.

Speech rate, measured in words per minute, is highly dependent on the speaker's task, and varies over a wide range. However, several recent studies have shown that most of this variability is due to changes in the frequency and duration of pauses. The variability of articulation rate, measured in syllables per second, with pauses excluded, is smaller by an order of magnitude (Goldman-Eisler, 1968). The implications of this for the effect of timing errors on intelligibility are only now being appreciated.

Next we turn to the effects on timing of what is being said. Most of the effects described have been known qualitatively, and in some cases quantitatively, for many years. (Some of these effects are reviewed in more detail, and with more references, in Klatt, 1976.) In looking at the figures remember, as a rule of thumb, that any difference in duration that exceeds 15–20% can probably be perceived (Huggins, 1972). Also, remember that the spectrograms illustrate *acoustic* segments, and that these do not correspond exactly to phonemes. Some acoustic segments, such as the aspiration following release of an initial unvoiced stop and preceding the onset of voicing in the vowel — and, indeed, the formant transition at the start of the vowel — belong to *both* the consonant and the vowel, which makes any definition of a single boundary between them arbitrary (Fant, 1962; Peterson & Lehiste, 1960). Therefore, it is not possible, in general, to segment an acoustic waveform so that each segment corresponds to one and only one phoneme.

Let us consider small units first, and work up to larger units. Figure 1 demonstrates that segments vary in their *intrinsic* durations (House, 1961; Peterson & Lehiste, 1960). On the left are spectrograms of the words *a bead* and *a bid*. The acoustic segments corresponding to the vowels are marked by solid inked lines, and their durations in milliseconds are shown underneath. This large difference between tense and lax vowels must be learned, and not due to physiological factors, since it does not occur in all languages. Consonants as well as vowels vary in their intrinsic durations. On the right of Fig. 1 are shown four consonants in prestress position, in the words: *a Sea, a Fee, a Coat,* and *a Goat.* Note that the break in voicing during the /s/ is nearly twice as long as that during the /g/. Klatt (1976) has estimated that perhaps 50% of the variation in segment duration can be ascribed to differences in their intrinsic durations.

From single segments, let us move on to influences between adjacent segments. These are of two types. First, consonants are shorter when they occur in clusters than when they occur singly; this is illustrated in Fig. 2. The left-hand line in the top three spectrograms shows the progressive shortening of the frication of an /s/ as it occurs in a singleton, in a double cluster, and in a triple cluster, in the words *a say, a stay, a stray.* The right-hand line in the bottom two spectrograms shows the shortening effect of adding an initial /s/ on the unvoiced part of the cluster /tr/.

A second interaction between adjacent segments is the large change in the duration of a vowel segment that results from changing the voicing of the consonant following it (House, 1961). This effect is a major cue for the perception of voicing in the final consonant, yet the cue lies entirely in the vowel. Figure 3 shows two examples of the effect. At the top are spectrograms of the words *dies* and *dice,* and at the bottom those of *a goad* and *a goat.* When spoken in isolation, as here, the vowel segment preceding the voiced consonant is often twice as long as that preceding the unvoiced consonant. The duration of the consonant changes in the opposite direction, but by a smaller amount. In running speech, the combined duration of vowel and following consonant often remains about constant for minimal pairs such as these. It is tempting to look for an explanation of this in terms of articulatory constraints, since the unvoiced consonant requires a deliberate laryngeal gesture to halt vocal cord vibration during the stop closure, whereas in the voiced stop, vibration ceases (if it does cease) only because of the equalization of air pressure above and below the glottis.

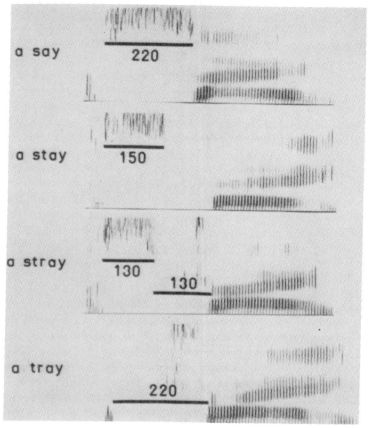

FIG. 2. The shortening effect on a consonant of appearing in a cluster is illustrated. (See text for more detail.)

Although these factors both have an influence, the difference in vowel duration, at least, must be partly deliberate and learned, since it does not occur in all languages. (For example, Danish speakers of English often fail to make the distinction, since it does not occur in Danish, leading errors like "Put another lock on the fire.")

Figure 4 illustrates two syllable-level effects. First, the duration of a consonant is affected by its position within the syllable. A syllable-initial consonant, such as the /s/ in *my seat* shown in the top half of Fig. 4, tends to be 10–20% longer than the same consonant in syllable-final position, as in the words *mice eat* (Klatt, 1974). Differences such as these are one of the ways in which word boundaries are marked (Lehiste, 1960) — the silent intervals formerly believed to occur at every word boundary do not in fact exist!

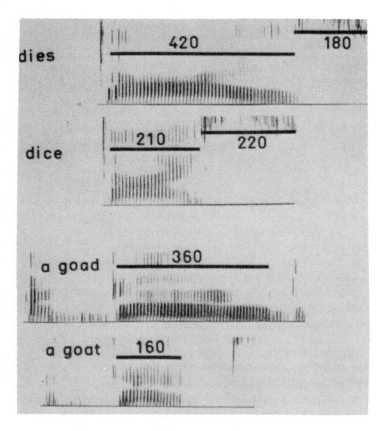

FIG. 3.   The effect of the voicing of a final consonant on the preceding vowel is illustrated in the word pairs *dies, dice,* and *a goad, a goat.* (See text for more detail.)

The bottom half of Fig. 4 shows a second syllable-level effect: the more stress carried by the syllable, the longer all the segments in it tend to become. Note that a change in syllable duration affects all segments in the syllable in the same direction; all are shortened, or all are lengthened, with no change in relative durations (at least to first order). This is in contrast to the effects described above, where the relative durations of adjacent segments changed. Further, note that defining syllable boundaries, which is a prerequisite for measuring syllable duration, faces exactly the same difficulties as defining phoneme boundaries. This problem can be avoided by comparing sentences that are identical except for the syllable in question, or by choosing syllables whose acoustic boundaries coincide with syllable boundaries.

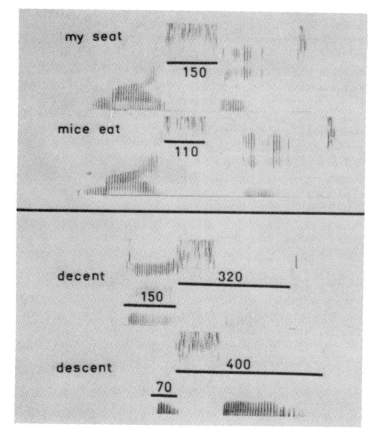

FIG. 4.   Segment duration is affected by its position within the syllable, initial consonants being longer than final consonants, in general (top). The stress carried by a syllable has a large effect on the duration of the segments within it (bottom).

The vowel segment in the initial, stressed syllable in the word *decent* is nearly twice as long as that in the unstressed first syllable in *descent* — although it could also be argued that this is due to the different vowel color, an effect illustrated in Fig. 1. However, it is more likely that the reduced duration causes the change in vowel color than vice versa (Lindblom, 1963). The final syllables show the same effect, the stressed syllable being slightly longer than its unstressed counterpart. The effect is somewhat masked in final syllables due to prepausal lengthening, which is described below.

Two further comments should be made about stress. First, notice the magnitude (6:1) of the ratio of the stressed syllable duration to the unstressed syllable duration in *descent*. Three factors contribute to its size: the longer syllable is

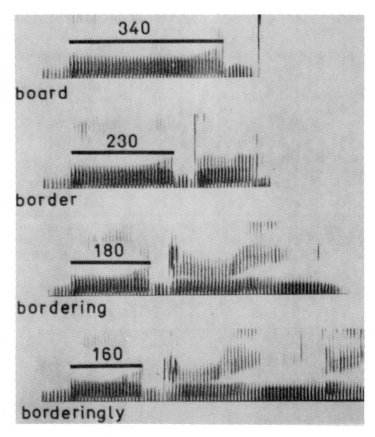

FIG. 5.   A stressed syllable is progressively shortened as the number of unstressed syllables following it is increased.

(1) last, (2) stressed, and (3) contains more segments. If, in addition, the component phonemes were long and voiced, as in *desired,* the ratio would be even larger. Second, the stress we have discussed so far is *word*-level stress. There is also a sentence-level stress, called emphatic or contrastive stress, which has an additional effect. Thus the word *buy* receives emphatic stress, and is longer in "I said *buy* me a cake, not steal one" than it is in "I said buy me a *cake,* not a steak!" Emphatic stress usually has a marked effect on the fundamental frequency (pitch) contour, as well as on durations.

Figure 5 shows the effect of the number of syllables in a word. Adding unstressed syllables to the word *board* causes it to become progressively shorter, with the largest decrease occurring as the first unstressed syllable is added (Lindblom, 1967; Lindblom & Rapp, 1973). As the stressed syllable is shortened, each added syllable has a smaller shortening effect, as if the shortening pressure exerted

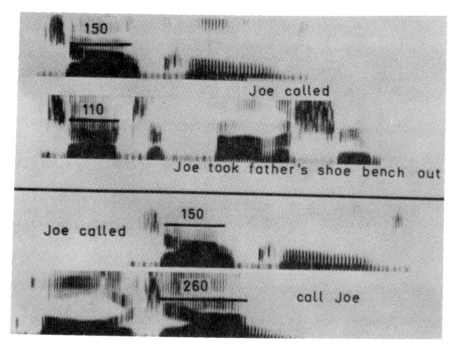

FIG. 6. The more words in a phrase, the shorter the words tend to become (top). The last stressed syllable in a phrase or sentence is often lengthened by a factor as large as 2 (bottom).

by each added syllable was meeting increasing resistance. We will return to this idea of incompressibility later.

With Fig. 6, we finally reach sentence level effects. The more words there are in a sentence, the shorter each word tends to become. Thus, *Joe* is longer in the sentence "Joe called" than it is in the sentence "Joe took father's shoe bench out." Notice the parallel here with the effects due to the number of syllables in the word, and the number of segments in a syllable.

The bottom of Fig. 6 shows an example of prepausal lengthening. The final syllable in an utterance is lengthened often by a factor as large as 2. It has recently been discovered that similar lengthening, though by smaller amounts, occurs *within* sentences, and in the absence of pauses, in syllables at the ends of phrases (Goldhor, 1976; Huggins, 1974; Klatt, 1975). Thus, *Jane* is longer in "Jane married John Kalinski" than it is in "Jane Kalinski married John" because it occurs as the last syllable in the subject noun-phrase in the first example, but not in the second. In his study of timing in an extended passage, Klatt (1975) measured durations of all stressed vowel segments, and found that *all* vowel segments that were more than 40% longer than the median duration occurred immediately before a phrase boundary (except one, which had a single unstressed syllable intervening). Goldhor (1976) has found several other aspects of syntax that affect timing, such as the number of words in a phrase, the position of a phrase in a sentence, and some clausal effects. There are probably other effects that remain to be found and described.

III. A MODEL OF SPEECH TIMING

We have seen how factors at several different levels can affect the duration of individual segments. At the same time, units at all levels consist of strings of these individual segments. Consequently, a change in a single segment affects the duration of the syllable, word, and phrase that contain it.

How can all these effects be integrated into a comprehensive account of speech timing? Or, how do the rules interact? The interesting parallels between rules at different levels suggest a hierarchical organization. For example, the timing of a unit at one level is consistently affected by the number of *other* units at the same level that fall within a single unit at the next higher level. Thus,

1. *segment* duration is affected by the number of other segments within a syllable,
2. *syllable* duration is affected by the number of other syllables within a word, and
3. *word* duration is affected by the number of words in the phrase, clause, or sentence.

Similarly, a *segment's* duration is affected by its position within the syllable, a *syllable's* duration is affected (slightly) by its position within the word, and a *word's* duration is affected by its position within the phrase. It also appears that the duration of a phrase is affected by its position within the sentence (Goldhor, 1976). A further reason for the interest in hierarchically organized rules is that Chomsky and Halle (1968) had considerable success describing regularities of stress patterns in English — which have a strong influence on timing, as we have just seen — by cyclically applying a small set of rules, first to the lowest units on the hierarchy and then successively to higher and higher level units.

In its simplest form, this hierarchical organization of *timing* rules has been found not to work. One failure was described by Klatt (1973). As we saw earlier, the duration of a stressed vowel segment preceding an unvoiced consonant is about two-thirds of its duration before a voiced consonant. Thus, the vowel segment in the word *seat* lasts only about two-thirds as long as the vowel segment in the word *seed*. Additionally, appending an unstressed syllable to a stressed syllable causes a similar reduction of vowel segment duration, to about two-thirds of its monosyllabic length. Thus, the vowel segment in *seedless* is about two-thirds as long as that in *seed*. A strict hierarchical account would predict that when *both* shortening effects apply, as in the word *seatless,* the vowel segment should be shortened to 44% (66% x 66%) of its duration in *seed*. In fact, it is only shortened to 54%. To rescue the hierarchical theory of speech timing (and we should stress that the failure of the hierarchical theory of speech timing does *not* reflect on the correctness of the abstract hierarchies in Chomsky and Halle's *Sound Pattern of English*), Klatt introduced the idea of incompressibility, which is a statement of the law of diminishing returns in speech timing. The more shortening rules that apply, the smaller the effect of each. Each segment has a minimum duration, and *only* that part of its intrinsic duration *in excess* of its minimum is affected by shortening rules. The theory has not been tested in detail, but the concept of incompressibility is reasonable and is supported by other observations. For example, in Fig. 5 (board, boarder, etc.) progressively *less* shortening was caused by each additional syllable.

There are other reasons for questioning the hierarchical principle, however; these are concerned mainly with constraints on performance. If the number of words in the sentence affects the duration of its *first* word, the whole sentence must be planned before the first word is spoken. Although this can be true when the speaker is reading a prepared text, it is less likely for conversational or impromptu speech. There is obviously a memory limit to how much speech can be prepared and stored before production begins. Intuitively, it seems more likely that the units that are fleshed out in detail, one at a time, are about the size of phrases. Further, the idea that the speaker has the whole sentence available before starting to speak would have problems explaining hesitation pauses, in which half a sentence is produced, with appropriate timing, and then suddenly a word is not available when it is needed. This is clearly incompatible with the idea that every word in the sentence is planned before the speaker begins to speak.

There are other timing regularities that appear not to fit into the hierarchical scheme, at least at first sight. An example is isochrony. The principal of iscochrony states that all metrical feet have the same *length* (Abercrombie, 1964). A metrical foot is a sequence of syllables that contains one and only one stressed syllable. Thus, every syllable must fall in some foot. The principal of isochrony is clearly wrong if taken literally, and if by length, *duration* was meant (but see Lehiste, 1973, for more detail). On the other hand, there are some syllable level effects that take place across word boundaries, between different branches of the tree, as it were, which show a tendency towards the effects predicted by isochrony. Thus, an unstressed syllable may cause shortening of a long syllable that precedes it even if it is in a different word — as observed by Bolinger (1963), although without any supporting measurements. The effect does not appear to cross phrase boundaries (Huggins, 1974; 1975), so again it may be possible to save the hierarchical rule structure by redefining the hierarchy on which it operates.

An example of a timing effect of this type is shown in Fig. 7. The top spectrogram is of the sentence "we shout loud." Adding an unstressed syllable to *shout*

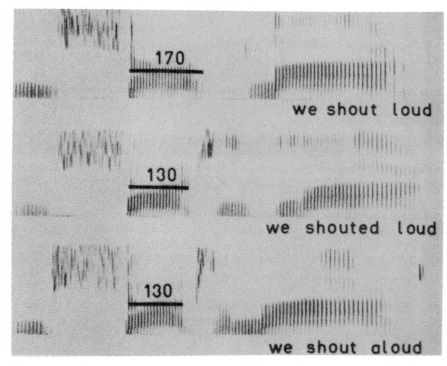

FIG. 7. An unstressed syllable may have a shortening effect on a preceding stressed syllable, even when it falls in a different word. (See text for more detail.)

has the predicted shortening effect, as seen in the middle spectrogram. But a similar shortening effect occurs even when the unstressed syllable is in the following word, as in "we shout *a*loud." This shortening effect of an unstressed syllable does not cross all word boundaries. In particular, it does not seem to cross a phrase boundary. Thus, although the syllable *slave* is shorter in "the slaver faced the wall" than in "the slave faced the wall," the shortening does *not* occur in "the slave defaced the wall," apparently because, in the latter case, a phrase boundary intervenes between the extra syllable and the stressed syllable it could affect.

It may be possible to allow for this effect by adjustment rules at the phrase level, but they remain to be worked out, and it is not known yet where they should and should not apply. In any event, it will be necessary for the adjustment rules to have access to units lower in the hierarchy, for example to know which syllables are stressed and which are not.

Many of the foregoing rules produce much smaller effects in impromptu speech than in citation form, except in phrase-final syllables. This is probably due to the fact that many shortening rules apply simultaneously, which reduces the durations to close to their incompressible minima.

To summarize: the main effects determining segment durations in running speech appear to be:

1. The intrinsic durations of the component segments;
2. The stress on the syllables in the utterance;
3. Phrase-final lengthening, and additional prepausal lengthening.

IV. SPEECH TIMING AND THE DEAF

How are these results relevant to the hearing impaired? Many of the effects mentioned are probably too small to be picked up by the hearing impaired, and it is not likely that technical aids could rectify this. The effects due to intrinsic duration, stress, and phrase-final lengthening probably *are* usable — especially since stress and syntactic boundaries may also be marked by nonspeech body movements.

The stress pattern is of fundamental importance in speech perception. Listeners with normal hearing use a memory coding for speech sounds that reflects the acoustic similarities between the sounds. However, Conrad and Rush (1965) have shown that the memory coding used by the deaf is far less influenced by auditory similarity. Extending this argument slightly, there is no guarantee that the *stress pattern* of a word is a fundamental aspect of its memory representation in the deaf. By contrast, in the hearing the stress-pattern is fundamental, as demonstrated, for example, by Brown and McNeill (1966) in their tip of the tongue experiment.

So far, we have concentrated on timing regularities in speech production. In speech perception, there is a circularity about timing information: it is often important in the identification of a speech sound, yet it is only after the speech sound has been recognized that departures from expected durations, such as those marking word and phrase boundaries, can be detected. From this perspective, it is hard to see how timing information can be very important to perception. On the other hand, one of the most commonly given reasons for the poor intelligibility of the speech of the deaf is its poor timing and rhythm (for extensive reviews of speech of the deaf, see Hudgins & Numbers, 1942; Nickerson, 1975). The rate of deaf speech is usually much too slow — often only half the rate of normal speech. This is partly due to the presence of too many and too long pauses, many of which are inserted in inappropriate places in the speech. The inappropriate pauses may be partly due to problems in breath control. The energy in the air pressure in the lungs is often converted into sound energy with much lower efficiency in the deaf than in the hearing. The deaf commonly produce what is called "breathy" voice, in which the vocal cords never achieve complete closure, allowing air to leak past throughout the glottal cycle. As a result, the air supply is used up rapidly and must be replenished frequently (Nickerson, Stevens, Boothroyd, & Rollins, 1974).

Another major timing deficiency in deaf speech is the lack of contrast between the durations of stressed and unstressed syllables. The range is often 8:1 in normal speech, but is rarely more than 3:1 in speech of the deaf. The problem seems to lie mainly in the unstressed syllables, which the deaf tend to make much too long.

There are also obvious problems for the deaf in articulating the individual speech sounds correctly, and it is on these errors that attempts to improve deaf speech have usually been concentrated. No one really knows how important correct timing is for intelligibility, although there are some suggestive indications. For example, John and Howarth (1965) reported an experiment with some severely deaf children. Recordings were made of the experimenter playing with the child. The experimenter would pick a spontaneous utterance of the child, and would repeat it back to the child with correct timing and rhythm, with the aid of a powerful amplifier. The child would attempt to imitate the correct version, and the child and experimenter would alternate three or four times. The first and last of the child's productions were excised from the recording, and presented, in random order, to college students for identification. The small amount of practice each subject had with his sentence led to a 56% improvement in word intelligibility, and to over 200% improvement in the number of sentence frames correctly identified, in which "put the (noun) in the house" is accepted as correct for "put the man in the house."

V. THE CONTRIBUTION OF SPEECH TIMING
TO INTELLIGIBILITY

The difficulty with studying timing's contribution to intelligibility is that it is hard to separate incorrect timing from incorrect articulation. Speakers who hear sufficiently well to produce normal articulation also have normal timing, so how is one to generate speech with defective timing? The development of computer programs for synthesizing speech by rule has provided a solution. A pilot experiment I have just completed studied directly how speech intelligibility depends on correct timing and fundamental frequency contour.

The synthesis program was developed by Dennis Klatt at the Massachusetts Institute of Technology (Klatt, 1972). It produces fairly high quality speech, at least for single sentences. The input to the synthesizer is a list consisting of the phonetic symbols representing the desired sentence, including word boundaries, together with the digits 1, 2, or 0 preceding each vowel, to mark syllables carrying first and second levels of stress and unstressed (reduced) syllables, respectively. Synthesis of the sentence takes place in three sequential stages. First, timing rules are applied to the input string, and a duration is assigned to each segment.

Second, a parameter track is calculated for each formant frequency and bandwidth, and for the fundamental frequency, as a function of time. Finally, the formant tracks are passed to a simulated terminal analogue synthesizer, which calculates the waveform and stores it. The waveform can then be played out in the normal way through a digital-to-analogue converter.

There are two aspects of this process that are important in the present context. First, segment durations are strongly affected by the stress on the syllable, and second, the fundamental frequency pattern is strongly influenced by the position within the sentence of the "1" stressed syllables, which receive a pitch "bump." Thus, both the segment durations and the pitch contour are independent of each other, except through their common dependence on the digits that specify the stress levels of the vowels. The synthesis program was slightly modified so that the assigned stress levels in the input string could be changed either before or after the timing rules were applied, or both. As a result, either the timing rules, the pitch assignment rules, or both, could be made to operate on incorrect stress assignments without affecting the operation of the rules used for generating the segmental information carried by the other parameter tracks. This latter statement was later confirmed from spectrograms of sentences generated under the four conditions. Also, *knowing what the sentences said,* it was possible to pick out and confirm the presence of each of the component phonemes. The inappropriate time and pitch contour assignments were generated by replacing each "1" stress marker with a "0," and each "0" stress marker with a "1," which effectively misinformed either the timing rules, the fundamental frequency rules, or both, about the stress levels on the syllables. Syllables with "2" stress were not affected.

The speech materials selected for the tests were 25 sentences from a set of 600 developed at the Clarke School for the Deaf (Magner, 1972) for testing the intelligibility of young deaf children's speech. They used a vocabulary appropriate to a seven- or eight-year-old. The subset used here was chosen so that virtually none of the content words occurred in more than one of the sentences. Examples of the sentences are:

1. Seven boys made a long table at school.
2. The water at the farm was very warm.
3. David played in the rain almost all day.
4. Miss Brown put a blanket under a tree.
25. Peter had dinner with the policeman.

Four experimental tapes were made up, in which each of the 25 sentences appeared once, in the same order. The first four sentences and the last were identical on each tape, in that both timing and pitch were assigned while stresses were correctly marked (the five sentences are those given above). Each of the four versions of the twenty remaining sentences occurred on one of the four tapes so that sequence effects due to treatments were counterbalanced. The four

TABLE 1
Intelligibility Scores for the Test Sentences[a]

	Words Correct	Number of Sentences "Correct"			
		"exactly"	"almost"	"half"	"not"
Normal	86%	17 = 43%	30	7	3
Mis-Pitched	63%	12 = 30%	19	12	9
Mis-Timed	52%	4 = 10%	10	16	14
Mis-Pitched and Mis-Timed	48%	4 = 10%	10	14	16

[a]with (1) timing and pitch contour both normal; (2) normal timing but abnormal pitch; (3) abnormal timing but normal pitch; and (4) timing and pitch both abnormal. The left-hand column gives the percentage of words correctly heard, out of the total of 312 words (20 sentences = 156 words, broken into four sets of five, with each set heard by two subjects). The middle column gives the number of whole sentences that were exactly correct for each condition (again, 20 sentences, broken into four sets of five, each heard by two subjects, for a total of 40). The three right-hand columns show, for each condition, how the 40 sentences were distributed among three less-formally defined categories: "almost," "half," and "not correct." (See text for more detail.)

versions will be referred to as "normal," "mis-pitched," "mis-timed," and "mis-pitched mis-timed."

Eight subjects served, each being randomly assigned to one tape. In fact, each tape was heard by one male and one female subject, all of whom were employees at Bolt Beranek and Newman. The subject listened through high quality earphones and controlled the tape recorder, playing each sentence once and then writing down the *words* that were heard. Subjects were told to guess, but not wildly, and that what they wrote did not have to make sense, although all the stimulus sentences were well formed, meaningful English sentences. The first sentence number 1 above) was typed on the response sheet, to give the subjects some idea of what to expect. The experiment took about 20 minutes.

The results were quite dramatic, and are shown in Table 1. The first column of the table gives the percentage of words correctly recognized in the twenty experimental sentences (numbers 5 to 24) for each of the four conditions. It is clear, first of all, that the "normal" sentences were not by any means perfect, since only 86% of the words were correctly heard out of a total of 312. An independent estimate of this figure can be obtained from the four sentences heard in their normal versions by all subjects (numbers 1 to 4, and number 25). Here the percentage of words heard correctly was 84.5% (out of 8 x 30 words). The agreement is remarkably good. The five normal sentences heard by all subjects also provide an opportunity for comparing the subjects. There were quite large differences in their performances, three subjects making no errors at all, and two more missing only two words out of the 30. The worst subject heard only half the words correctly. However, the differences between the four conditions are robust enough to withstand such minor misbalances as were found. Substantially more words were missed when the pitch contour was inappropriate, this condition yielding only 63% correct (out of a total of 312). But when timing was inappropriate, only 52% of the 312 words were heard correctly. With both pitch and timing wrong, scores fell slightly further, to 48%.

The same result is even more strongly present if one considers measures other than percentage of words correct. The second column of the table gives the number of sentences heard exactly correctly, for each condition. Thus, 17 of the 40 sentences (two subjects x 20 sentences) were heard without error in the normal version — almost half — whereas only four of the mistimed sentences were heard correctly, and three of these occurred on two of the easiest sentences, in which only seven out of the total of 104 words were missed (though, of course, the few errors in the mistimed versions of these sentences contributed to the sentences being classified as easy).

The last three columns of Table 1 give scores derived by more subjective criteria, corresponding to "almost," "partly," and "not" understood. Thus, the first column gives the number of sentences in each condition that were substantially correct, allowing minor substitutions, and the missing of one word, as long as the syntactic class of the missing word was clear from the context. The second of the three columns at the right gives the number of sentences "half" correct, in which at least one phrase was heard correctly, but which had more than one major word missing. The last column gives the number of sentences in which the subject had less than one phrase correct. By these criteria, three quarters of the normal sentences and half of the mispitched sentences were correct, but only one quarter of the two mistimed versions were correct.

Thus, it appears that timing information plays a highly important role in speech perception, *at least when the listener does NOT know in advance what is being said.* Subjectively, it is as if inappropriate timing, and to a lesser extent pitch, have a "garden path" effect, misleading the listener so badly that he is unable to pick up the segmental information that is quite clearly present in subsequent listening. The importance of the listener not knowing in advance what is to be said is critical; when making a preliminary demonstration tape of the effects of wrong timing, I was so unimpressed by the magnitude of the effects that I almost abandoned the project. Fortunately, though, I played the tape to some colleagues, and did not tell them what the sentences were. Their difficulties led to the present study.

The foregoing results suggest that timing information plays an even more important role in speech timing than was suspected, and that far more effort should be directed at teaching deaf children correct timing for purposes of improving the intelligibility of their speech.

REFERENCES

Abercrombie, D. Syllable quantity and enclitics in English. In D. Abercrombie, D. B. Fry, P. A. D. MacCarthy, N. C. Scott, & J. L. M. Trim (Eds.), *In Honour of Daniel Jones.* New York: Longmans, Green and Company, 1964.

Bell, A. G. *The mechanism of speech,* New York: Funk and Wagnalls, 1916.

Bolinger, D. L. Length, vowel, juncture. *Linguistics,* 1963, *1,* 5–29.

Brown, R., & McNeill, D. The tip of the tongue phenomenon, *Journal of Verbal Learning and Verbal Behavior,* 1966, *5,* 325–337.

Chomsky, N., & Halle, M. *Sound pattern of English.* New York: Harper and Row, 1968.

Conrad, R., & Rush, M. L. Nature of short-term memory encoding by the deaf. *Journal of Speech and Hearing Disorders,* 1965, *30,* 335–343.

Fant, C. G. M. Descriptive analysis of the acoustic aspects of speech. *Logos,* 1962, *5,* 3–17.

Goldhor, R. S. *Sentential determinants of duration in speech.* Unpublished masters thesis, Massachusetts Institute of Technology, Cambridge, Massachusetts, 1976.

Goldman-Eisler, F. *Psycholinguistics: Experiments in spontaneous speech.* New York: Academic Press, 1968.

House, A. S. On vowel durations in English. *Journal of the Acoustical Society of America,* 1961, *33,* 1174–1178.

Hudgins, C. V. A comparative study of the speech coordination of deaf and normal subjects. *Journal of Genetic Psychology,* 1934, *44,* 3–48.

Hudgins, C. V., & Numbers, F. C. An investigation of intelligibility of speech of the deaf. *Genetic Psychology Monographs,* 1942, *25,* 289–392.

Huggins, A. W. F. Just-noticeable differences for segment duration in natural speech. *Journal of the Acoustical Society of America,* 1972, *51,* 1270–1278.

Huggins, A. W. F. An effect of syntax on syllable timing. Research Laboratory of Electronics (QPR No. 114), Massachusetts Institute of Technology, Cambridge, Massachusetts, 1974.

Huggins, A. W. F. On isochrony and syntax. In G. Fant & M. A. Tatham (Eds.), *Auditory analysis and perception of speech.* New York: Academic Press, 1975.

John, J. E. J., & Howarth, J. N. The effect of time distortions on the intelligibility of deaf children's speech. *Language and Speech,* 1965, *8,* 127–134.

Klatt, D. H. Acoustic theory of terminal analog speech synthesis, in *Proceedings of the 1972 IEEE Conference on Speech Communication and Processing,* 24–26, April 1972, pp. 131–135.

Klatt, D. H. Interaction between two factors that influence vowel duration. *Journal of the Acoustical Society of America,* 1973, *54,* 1102–1104.

Klatt, D. H. The duration of [s] in English words. *Journal of Speech and Hearing Research,* 1974, *17,* 51–63.

Klatt, D. H. Vowel lengthening is syntactically determined in a connected discourse. *Journal of Phonetics,* 1975, *3,* 129–140.

Klatt, D. H. Linguistic uses of segmental duration in English: Acoustic and perceptual evidence. *Journal of the Acoustical Society of America,* 1976, *59,* 1208–1221.

Kozhevnikov, V. A., & Chistovich, L. A. *Speech: Articulation and perception.* Leningrad: Nauka, 1965. (English translation: JPRS 30–543, Washington, D.C.)

Lehiste, I. An acoustic–phonetic study of internal open juncture. *Phonetica (Supplement),* 1960, *5,* 1–54.

Lehiste, I. Rhythmic units and syntactic units in production and perception. *Journal of the Acoustical Society of America,* 1973, *54,* 1228–1234.

Liberman, A. M., Cooper, F. S., Shankweiler, D. P., & Studdert-Kennedy, M. Perception of the speech code. *Psychological Review,* 1967, *74,* 431–461.

Lindblom, B. Spectrographic study of vowel reduction. *Journal of the Acoustical Society of America,* 1963, *35,* 1773–1781.

Lindblom, B. *Vowel duration and a model of lip-mandible coordination.* Speech Transmission Laboratory Progress Status Report 4/1967. Stockholm: Royal Institute of Technology, 1967.

Lindblom, B., & Rapp, K. *Some temporal regularities of spoken Swedish.* Publication No. 21, Institute of Linguistics, University of Stockholm, 1973.

Magner, M. E. *A speech intelligibility test for deaf children.* Clarke School for the Deaf, Northampton, Massachusetts, 1972.

Nickerson, R. S. Characteristics of the speech of deaf persons. *The Volta Review,* 1975, *77,* 342–361.

Nickerson, R. S., Stevens, K. N., Boothroyd, A., & Rollins, A. *Some observations on timing in the speech of deaf and hearing speakers,* BBN Report No. 2905, Cambridge, Massachusetts, 1974.

Peterson, G. E., & Lehiste, I. Duration of syllabic nuclei in English. *Journal of the Acoustical Society of America,* 1960, *32,* 693–703.

Stetson, R. H. *Motor phonetics, a study of speech movements in action,* Amsterdam: North-Holland Publishing Company, 1951.

17

An Experimental Study of Writing, Dictating and Speaking

John D. Gould

IBM Research Center
Yorktown Heights, New York, 10598, United States

ABSTRACT

These experiments (a) studied adult subjects' performance while learning to dictate, and (b) subsequently compared subjects' performance in four methods of composing letters and one-page essays. Subjects were videotaped so that pause times, generate times, and review times could be quantified for each method. Results showed that, as subjects learned to dictate, their pause times and review times decreased in relation to their generate times. In the comparison experiments, the distributions of pause, generate, and review times depended on the method of composition. Planning times, as inferred from the data, however, were equal in the various methods. Of practical significance, subjects required the same time to compose dictated and written letters. The resultant quality was equal, even though subjects were just learning to dictate.

I. INTRODUCTION

The experiments reported here are the first four in an ongoing series. The intent is to study psychological processes during composition and to contrast these in various methods of composing. The goals are to understand composing and to provide evidence about the best methods to use for various tasks and conditions. Composing methods studied include Writing (W), Dictating (D), and Speaking (S). Speaking differs from dictating in that the author (a) need not give secretarial or typing instructions and (b) assumes the recipient will listen to the composition rather than read it, which thus may allow him to use a different grammar. In addition, a condition in which authors cannot see what they write (WNS) was also included. This tests the conventional wisdom that writing is superior to dictating, in part because, with writing, authors have an external record that they can easily review.

Generation tasks have not received the research attention from psychologists that reception tasks have. For example, hearing, seeing, smelling have been studied more than speaking, debating, playing musical instruments, singing, writing letters, writing computer programs. Consequently, available research methodology to study composing is limited and prior work is scarce. Document composition is an important task. Children, from the time they enter school until leaving 10–25 years later, are regularly taught writing, and sometimes speaking, skills. In business, professionals spend 10–15% of their time writing (Klemmer & Snyder, 1972).

I know of few prior experiments or theories on document composition involving adults. Work on motor programs (e.g., Stelmach, 1976), speech production (e.g., Liberman, 1970), linguistics (e.g., Chomsky, 1965), mental plans (Miller, Galanter, & Pribram, 1960), and how skills are learned (LaBerge & Samuels, 1974) is relevant but not directly to the point. Deese's recent work (1975) provides some insights into the role of memory in speaking. He suggests that the same short-term memory mechanisms that limit perception may not limit production. The work on pauses as a method of detecting planning times in oral composition (Henderson, Goldman-Eisler, & Skarbeck, 1966) is interesting, but subject to criticism (cf. Rochester, 1973). Studies of abnormalities in speech and writing (aphasia and agraphia) provide little insight into general

DOCUMENT CREATION – A PROCESS MODEL

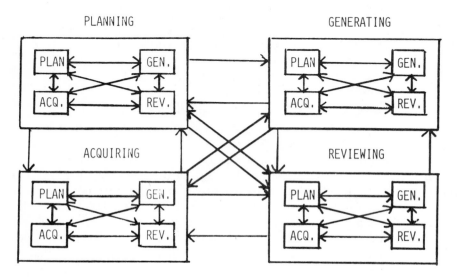

FIG. 1.   A descriptive model of document composition.

processes in composition. Autobiographies and biographical sketches of famous authors reveal great differences in their general approach to composition. For example, whereas some authors often dictate, Sartre, who is going blind, refuses to switch from handwriting to dictating even though he realizes he will no longer be able to write (Sartre & Contat, 1975).

Figure 1 shows a simple, intuitive model of document composition used to guide the present experiments. Four processes are assumed: *Planning, Generating, Reviewing,* and *Acquiring* external information. Clearly, the model must

1. be multi-level, (e.g., planning occurs when the author prepares an outline and, at a microlevel, in the nervous system where the pronunciation of one phoneme is influenced by the plan to say a subsequent phoneme);
2. be iterative, (e.g., an author may plan, then generate, and, on the basis of feedback, re-plan and re-generate);
3. involve feedback;
4. be recursive, (e.g., a high-level planning function can "call" a low level planning function); and
5. allow for overlapping processes and automatic processes.

The model is global, descriptive, and imprecise, and indicates that a sufficient model of composition must be complex, and not, for example, a simple stage model.

The intent was to learn more about document composition than could be ascertained from measures such as total time to compose, changes made during and after composing, and the resulting linguistic characteristics. Consequently, a subject was given specific types of letters to compose, and he was videotaped while composing. *Generating* was the actual time spent writing, dictating, or speaking. *Planning* was inferred from a combination of pause times and generating rates. *Reviewing* was the time spent replaying dictation or re-reading writing. *Acquiring* external information was the time spent reading other materials.

Subjects first had to be trained to use a dictation machine. Because learning this skill is a process of some interest in itself, following a brief training program subjects were videotaped as they dictated a series of ten similar, simple letters (Experiment 1) and then a series of six somewhat more difficult letters (Experiment 2). Of particular interest was how the processes of generating, planning, reviewing, and accessing change with practice. On the next day, W, WNS, D, and S were compared for letters of information reply (Experiment 3) and for brief essays (Experiment 4).

II. TRAINING

A. Method

1. Subjects.   Eight subjects, four males and four females, were obtained through a local temporary manpower agency. Three were undergraduates, about twenty-years-old. One was about 30, had two years of college, and had done some office work since then. Another was about 45–50, a college graduate, and substitute teacher. Another was about 30, with an advanced degree in music. The other two were recent college graduates looking for permanent jobs. These subjects served in all four experiments.

2. Procedure.   Subjects were trained to dictate, using an IBM Executary Model 211 machine. In the half-hour self-paced audiovisual training program, a subject first read some instructions about proper dictating, then listened to a letter being dictated, and then read the typed version of that dictated letter. Following this the subject simultaneously re-listened to that dictation while reading the proof-edited typed version (typed on another page and marked up in red pencil). This marked-up version demonstrated a variety of potential dictation errors (e.g., failure to spell out proper names or give punctuation instructions). Seemingly incidental to all of this, a subject learned to use the dictation equipment. He then received further printed and aural instructions about how to make changes in what he said and some general principles of good dictating. Then he practiced dictating and changing individual sentences. Last, he dictated a letter of his own.

B. Results and Discussion

Subjects required about 20–30 min to go through the training program, and they practiced with the equipment in composing a letter of their own for another 15–30 min. No one dropped out, a result that was not completely anticipated given the general observation that many people in real-life try dictating and then soon give it up.

III. EXPERIMENT 1

The purposes were to give subjects practice at dictating, and to learn how performance changes as the subject learns to dictate. Of particular interest were any changes in the sequences and time courses of planning, generating, reviewing, and acquiring information, and the effectiveness of various subject-selected dictating strategies.

A. Method

1. Apparatus and experimental design.   A television camera was placed above the shoulder of a seated subject who was given a table of student information, i.e., the names, ages, home states, college majors, class ranks, etc., of 25 students. The subject then dictated ten letters, each in response to a similar request for the names of students who had certain characteristics, e.g., living in Damon Hall, age 19 or less, from New York, etc. Each inquiry was from the same person and place, and differed only in the details of the request. Thus, each letter the subject dictated could be similar. In this experiment, as well as in the others, subjects were required to compose formal letters, i.e., with return address, inside address, salutation, body, complementary closing, and signature.

Procedurally, subjects started a time clock, read the letter of inquiry in front of them, dictated a letter of reply using the student information tables, and then stopped the clock. While composing, subjects were allowed to make written notes if they chose. After a subject dictated his first letter, it was typed and he then proofread and edited it. There was only one "re-do" (or proof-editing), of a letter once it was typed. The subject then dictated a second letter, it was typed, and he proofread and edited it. After that a subject dictated successive letters and there was a delay of two, three, sometimes four letters before he proof-edited any particular one. This delay also occurred in the remaining three experiments. Subjects were told to assume that all changes they made at each single re-do stage would be accurately incorporated into the "final" version.

Each subject received a different order of the ten letters-tasks, according to eight rows of a 10 x 10 Latin square design.

A secretary, experienced at typing dictation, was a permanent part of this and the other three experiments. She was instructed to be a "good secretary," to type as accurately as possible, but not to do any "editing" (e.g., re-wording) for subjects. Two different women served as secretaries, and inspection indicated they followed instructions.

Strategies available to authors range from (a) the "spew strategy" of quickly dictating an initial draft and, after receiving it back from a typist, beginning the serious editing of it, to (b) the "first-time-final" strategy of attempting to compose a final draft on the first draft. In all experiments, subjects were encouraged to adopt the latter strategy, minimizing the number of corrections required during proof-editing.

2. Analysis of videotapes. Each subject was videotaped in Experiments 1–4. Mirrors located in front of the subject formed images of his or her face and hands, which provided a picture of him or her while writing, dictating, pausing, or reading. An overhead microphone provided an audio record. A clock in the system revolved every 6 sec, and the videotapes were analyzed to this accuracy.

In videotape analysis, a 6-sec interval was assigned to pause time if a subject was not generating or reviewing. A 6-sec interval was assigned to generate time if a subject was talking in D or S or writing in W or WNS. A 6-sec interval was assigned to review in D or S if a subject was replaying his oral composition. It was not always possible to be sure from the eye movements of subjects when they were reviewing their written material in W, so those review times (which appeared to be infrequent) were included in pause time for W letters. Acquiring times are not included as a separate category in the results. Frequently, subjects generated while they acquired (i.e., read) material; sometimes, during pauses, it was difficult to determine when subjects were reading.

Subjects were also instructed (a) to assume that a secretary would listen to their entire letter before beginning to type it; (b) how to change something they had said earlier; (c) that they would be evaluated on composition time and quality (defined below) of the *typed* version of their dictation; and (d) not to assume that the secretary was familiar with letters that they had already dictated.

The quality of the 80 dictated letters was determined after the experiment by having four college students and the experimenter rate them in three areas: (a) syntax, grammar, punctuation, spelling, and general format; (b) the degree to which the letter conveyed the relevant information clearly and correctly; and (c) the general appropriateness, responsiveness, and persuasiveness of the content. Prior to these ratings, letters with significant revisions were retyped. In the others, raters assumed handwritten proof-editing changes were incorporated correctly. Incorrect information was identified for the raters in colored pencil. A 5-point scale was used, with 1 = unacceptable, 2 = minimally acceptable, 3 = acceptable, 4 = more than acceptable, and 5 = excellent.

B. Results and Discussion

Mean time was 3.1 min, and subjects always reported the correct names. Mean quality rating was 3.1. Mean words per min (words in typed version divided by time to compose) were 24.5.

1. General style. On the first several letters most subjects generally paused once in a major way (e.g., .5—.8 min) to plan their response, either prior to beginning dictation or after dictating the salutation of their letter. They gave many typing instructions (mean = 15; range per subject = 9—24). Aside from "letter to . . . . " and "letter from . . . . ," these were mainly spelling and punctuation instructions. Subjects made few changes while they were dictating (about one change per letter). These changes were generally "local," i.e., changes made on words just dictated, rather than "global," e.g., changes made on earlier material through general instructions to the secretary. Forty-five of them followed a review, 20 were local instructions to the secretary (e.g., "insert a colon after . . . "), and the remaining 20 were immediate corrections of something just said (e.g., "check that").

It was possible that subjects would compose very deep and locally, e.g., dictate a phrase, change it, and then change the change. The videotapes showed, however, that subjects generally operated at a single level (e.g., plan, generate a phrase, plan, generate another phrase, review the last phrase, change the last phrase, generate a third phrase). They rarely dropped more than one level deep (a three-level example is generate a phrase, review it, change it, review the change, change the change, review this, change the changed change).

Whereas dictation proceeded smoothly, it appeared from the videotapes to be a fragile skill; a mistake seemed to be bothersome and disrupting, especially early in practice. Perhaps in real-life, subjects, as a result of such mistakes, would have given up and switched to writing.

Four subjects almost never wrote notes, whereas three subjects almost always wrote notes of a few words. Aside from the one long initial pause while the note-makers searched the table and jotted notes, their dictating behavior became similar to the other group's. Both required about 2.4 min on their last five letters. The note-makers used about two-thirds of this time to get started, whereas the non-note-makers used about one-third of this time to get started.

In the quality ratings, syntax, grammar, format, and spelling had the lowest rating (2.9), $F(2, 14) = 19.16; p < .001$. Clarity and correctness had a rating of 3.1, and general appropriateness had a rating of 3.2. On the quality ratings, the variance among the five raters was about twice that of the eight authors, mainly because most of the letters were similar and, consequently, the inter-rater reliability was low (all $r < = .29$; 2 of 10 rater intercorrelations were significant at the .01 level).

Subjects made few changes when proofreading the typed versions of their dictation: 37 letters were not changed at all; on 32 letters 1–3 individual words, typos, or punctuations were changed; 3 letters were reformatted, and 8 letters were changed extensively.

2. Learning to dictate.   Dictating performance improved with practice. Mean time on the first two letters was 4.5 min and mean time on the last two letters was 2.5 min, $F(9,72) = 5.11; p < .01$. Average quality rating was 2.8 on the first two letters and 3.2 on the last two letters, $F(9,63) = 3.14; p < .01$.

It was predicted on intuitive grounds that, with practice, subjects' generating times would be reduced (they would speak faster), review times would be reduced (there would be fewer reviews and fewer changes), pause times would be reduced (less need for new planning), and acquiring times would be reduced (they would remember the place and nature of some information).

As skill developed, generating times became shorter, decreasing from 1.6 min on the first two letters to 1.2 min on the last two letters ($F(1,7) = 6.70; p < .05$), because subjects spoke more rapidly. Pause times became shorter, decreasing from 1.6 min to .6 min ($F(1,7) = 9.90; p < .05$), because planning was sometimes overlapped with generation or review. Review times, which occurred on only 10 of the first 16 letters, occurred on only 4 of the last 16 letters. The key point, however, is that pauses and reviews began to drop out as separate events. That is, the ratio of pause times to generate times was reduced from .98 to .54, and the ratio of review times to generate times was reduced from .59 to .16. At first some subjects generated, paused, and searched the table for an appropriate name, generated it, then paused and searched again. But with practice subjects began to overlap searching and reading the table while generating the body of the letter. With practice, pauses and reviews were purposive (e.g., an author reviewed with a specific purpose of changing two predetermined words), rather than curious (e.g., an author reviewed to learn whether what he or she said was actually recorded). The inside address and the return address became fairly automatic. The body of the letter showed the most decrease, from 2.3 min to 1.1 min. On 23 of the last 40 letters, during proofreading, subjects either made no changes (18) or corrected only typos (5).

3. Author differences.   Differences among the authors' mean times ranged from 2.0 to 4.5 min, and differences among the authors' mean quality ratings ranged from 2.6 to 3.3. These time differences are large relative to simple generation tasks, e.g., oral reading by comparable subjects (informal evidence), but small relative to other generation tasks, e.g., computer programming (Grant & Sackman, 1967). There was no significant correlation, across authors, between time and quality of compositions.

Aside from notes, the strategies subjects used varied considerably at first. For example, one subject alternated between dictating and pausing, almost never reviewing and always speaking very deliberately. Another subject did much local reviewing, alternating among dictating, pausing, and reviewing. Another subject initially dictated her letter quite fast and then did a complete review of it, occasionally modifying a word or two. With practice, these differences dropped out and no obvious relation between quality and strategy was found.

IV. EXPERIMENT 2

The purposes were to give subjects practice at dictating letters that involved more original composition, and to measure their performance while they did this. Subjects were instructed to assume they were on the staff of the president of a major furniture company, and dictate answers to six letters he had received. These included a request for support from a political candidate, letters of complaint about the company's products, and a letter of condolence. On each letter to be answered, there were some hand-written notes by the president indicating his desired reply.

A. Method

Each subject received a different order of these six letters, according to six rows of one 6 x 6 Latin square and two rows of another square. Other instructions were the same as in Experiment 1. Quality of the proof-edited letters was rated after the experiment by four college student judges and the experimenter.

B. Results and Discussion

Subjects dictated these letters competently. Mean composition time was 6.0 min, and mean quality rating was "Acceptable" (3.0). There was no relation between composition time and quality.

Composition time showed marginal improvement with practice, decreasing from 7.2 to 4.9 min ($F(5,35) = 2.1$; $.10 > p > .05$). This was due mainly to a reduction in the number of reviews from 4.9 on the first letter to 1.9 on the sixth letter, $F(5,30) = 4.11$; $p < .05$). In comparison to the previous experiment, subjects now had an hour or two of dictation experience, and the letter-tasks were not as similar.

Generally, subjects alternated frequently between periods of generating (mean number generations of per letter = 6.7), pausing (5.9 per letter), and reviewing (3.3 per letter). Mean generation period was .3 min, mean pause period was .4 min, and mean review period was .4 min. It was evident from the facial expressions and lip movements recorded on videotape that planning was the main activity during pauses and a significant activity during reviewing. Subjects simultaneously generated the inside address (and return address) while they acquired the necessary information. Regarding memory load, as in the previous experiment, subjects rarely forgot what they had already said, i.e., after a long pause to plan or write notes they generally did not review to remind themselves of what they had previously said.

As in all the experiments, subjects were serious about composing good quality letters. For example, the videotapes showed sober reflection when subjects composed a letter of condolence.

Mean generation time per letter (2.2 min), pause time (2.6 min), and review time (1.4 min) did not vary with practice or the particular letter-task. The ratio of pause times to generate times remained constant at about 1.2, whereas the ratio of review times to generate times decreased from 1.0 to .53 with practice. These ratios, in comparison with those of Experiment 1, indicate that more planning and reviewing occurred in these letters requiring more composition. Mean words per min (wpm) was 16, and mean wpm of generation time were 44.7. These rates are much less than the 200–250 wpm rate (informal evidence) at which subjects speak memorized material. This implies that additional planning also occurred during generation. Subjects gave an average of 13 typing instructions per letter, but varied widely from 1.2 for one subject to 25.3 for another. These instructions were similar to those of Experiment 1.

As in the first experiment, the letters were rated somewhat higher on clarity and correctness (3.1) than on general appropriateness (3.0), or on syntax, grammar, format, and spelling (2.8), ($F(2,14) = 4.50$; $p < .05$). There was low reliability among the 5 raters (all $r < = .40$; 4 of 10 rater intercorrelations were significant at .01 level), and the mean ratings from one rater to another ranged from 2.8 to 3.3. There was no strong indication that some authors appealed to some raters more than to other raters.

Subjects almost always operated on "one-level." Generally, subjects made about two changes while dictating each letter. These usually followed a brief review, and ranged from inserting a punctuation mark to starting the body of the letter over. However, they generally were of a few words. Some "reviewing ' was essentially only backing up to locate the section that subjects already intended to change.

In proofreading, subjects made few changes. On 24 of 48 letters, subjects changed 1–3 punctuation marks, spellings, or words. Eighteen letters were not changed at all or merely corrected for typos. Six letters were changed in major ways.

Some characteristics of dictating styles varied among subjects. One subject, comparatively nervous, wrote extensive notes and then dictated very fast. The other subjects made notes (brief ones) on only 7 of 42 letters. Two subjects hardly ever changed their dictation during composition.

V. EXPERIMENT 3

The purpose was to compare four methods of composing brief business letters: W, WNS, D, and S. This was possible now that subjects had demonstrated facility at dictating acceptable letters.

A. Method

Subjects composed two formal letters with each method in response to letters of inquiry. Each letter of inquiry was from the same person and requested information about events in a school situation, e.g., for textbooks, for schedules of teachers, for lists and location of audiovisual equipment. (School situations provide a task to which a variety of potential subjects can relate.) In real-life, such requests would require a person to retrieve information from a file memo. Thus, a subject was also provided an appropriate file memo for each request. The file memo always contained a superset of the information requested, and subjects had to compose replies by selecting the appropriate subset. These replies frequently involved formatting information into columns.

In WNS, subjects wrote on a paper tablet with a sharp wooden stylus. Carbon paper was placed beneath the top sheet of the tablet so that a permanent imprint was obtained. Prior to starting the experiment, subjects wrote one WNS letter for practice, which also served as a check to make sure they knew the proper written format for formal letters.

The instructions for W, WNS, and S were similar to those in the earlier experiments for D. However, in S, subjects were told (a) that judges would listen to their letters rather than read them, (b) they should not give any typing instructions, and (c) unlike with the other methods, they would not have a subsequent proofreading stage.

The order of the four composition methods and the order of eight letters themselves was different for each subject, being balanced across subjects with a modified 8 x 8 Graeco-Latin square.

The quality of the final (i.e., corrected for changes made during proof-editing) typed versions of W, WNS, and D letters was rated after the experiment by four college student judges on the areas used in Experiment 1. The initial versions of S letters were listened to and also rated by these judges. In addition, three of these college students were given a stack of eight letters, two W, two WNS, two D, and two S. Each letter was composed by a different subject, but all were in response to the same letter of request. First, they rank-ordered the eight letters in the stack on the basis of overall quality. They listened to the S letters, and read the others. They did this for eight successive stacks of letters. Following this, two of them were given stacks of six letters, the S letters being excluded. From each stack they were asked to pick out the two dictated letters, and they were given correct answer feedback after every stack.

B. Results and Discussion

1. Method differences.   Table 1 shows the key results for each method. Time to compose depended upon method, $F(3,35) = 34.62; p < .001$. Speaking was significantly faster than the other three methods (Duncan range test, p < .01). Following procedures outlined by Clark (1973), the difference among methods generalizes both to people similar to these subjects and also to letters of this general type, $F'(3,42) = 6.95, p < .001$. The average quality rating was the same on all four methods ($p > .10$), being acceptable (3.0). Rank order judgments did show some significant quality differences, however. The median rank of S letters (6th) was worse than the median ranks of at least seven of eight subjects' W, WNS, and D letters ($p < .07$, at least). The median ranks of D (4.5th) and WNS (4th) letters were worse than the ranks of seven of the eight subjects' W (3rd) letters ($p < .07$, at least).

Dictated letters and written letters were surprisingly similar. The two college student judges correctly selected, on the average, 8 of the 16 dictated letters, when each should have selected 5.3 of them by chance alone.

Subjects composed W and WNS letters very similarly. They did not appear to do much re-reading of their composition in W (and, of course, none in WNS). There were about one less generate-pause alteration in WNS than in W (cf. Table 1). Subjects frequently used a finger on their nonwriting hand to keep their place in WNS. Still, they occasionally lost their place and would try to find it by looking for indentations in the top sheet of paper. Their handwriting was legible enough for secretaries to type.

TABLE 1
Results from Experiment 3

	Method of Composing				
	Write	Write/No See	Dictate	Speak	Significance Level
Mean total time (min)	6.4	6.8	5.7	3.6	p < .001
Mean generate time (min)	4.9	4.9	2.7	1.7	p < .001
Mean pause time (min)	1.5	1.7	2.1	1.7	p > .10
Mean review time (min)	—	—	0.8	0.2	—
Mean no. generation periods	5.8	4.8	6.7	3.6	p < .05
Mean no. pauses	5.9	4.6	5.5	3.2	p < .05
Mean no. reviews	—	—	2.6	0.4	—
Mean no. words	87.5	83.8	95.6	95.1	p > .10
Words/min	14.1	13.0	17.4	29.2	p < .001
Words/min. of generation	18.6	17.3	36.5	61.6	p < .001
Quality rating of syntax, spelling, grammar, format	3.1	3.0	2.6	2.9	p < .10
Quality rating on clarity and correctness of information	3.2	3.0	3.0	2.9	p > .10
Quality rating on appropriateness	3.4	3.4	3.1	3.1	p > .10
Median quality rank (out of 8)	3rd	4th	4.5th	6th	—

The fact that W and WNS did not differ on these letters (or on the more complex ones of Experiment 4) indicates that the presence of an easily reviewed external record of what one has already composed may not be a major advantage of writing over dictating. The act itself of generating provides a feedback that gives some structure and memory to one's thoughts.

In general, a particular subject showed about the same style of composing from method to method. There was usually a major pause (e.g., .5–1.5 min) either before beginning to compose or prior to the body of the letter. While planning clearly occurred during this and other pauses, the lip movements, facial expressions, and occasional overt comments of subjects shown on the videotapes demonstrated that it occurred during reviewing also. Only a small amount of pause time was due to acquiring information (reading). Subjects overlapped acquiring the information required for the return address and inside address with generating this information in their own letters. Subjects generally did not make notes prior to composing. They made relatively few changes in their letters during composition. When they did, they almost always made them just after the "mistake" was written or dictated.

Proofreading proceeded rapidly for all methods, and there were relatively few changes made here also. Between 9 and 11 of the 16 W, 16 WNS, and 16 D letters were not changed. With the exception of 2 D letters, only minor changes were made.

Total composition time was broken into generate time, pause time, and review time (Table 1). Generate times were significantly longer on W and WNS than on D and S ($F(3,21) = 135.63$; $p < .001$; Duncan range $p < .01$). The longer generate times on D than on S were due in part to subjects giving an average of 20 typing instructions per dictated letter, which were similar to those in the earlier experiments. Words, when spelled out, were often done so slowly and deliberately. The somewhat shorter pause times and higher word production rate in S than in D suggest that subjects struggled for the appropriate way to express themselves in D compared to S. Review times occurred in 12 of 16 D letters and 7 of 16 S letters, which also suggests that subjects were more concerned about the exact wording of D letters. Most of these reviews occurred in the body of the letter. Subjects alternated among generate, plan, and review more in D than in the other conditions. In S, once subjects reached the body of their letter, they spoke fairly continuously, generally with only one or two pauses intervening. They "simultaneously" acquired information while they spoke.

Over all methods, the letters were rated somewhat better on appropriateness than on syntax, format, grammar, and spelling. Following procedures outlined by Winer (1971, p. 377), this result generalizes to people similar to these subjects, and to letters of this general type, $F'(19,14) = 9.03$; $p < .001$. There was no significant interaction between composition method and quality areas.

2. Author differences.   On time scores, differences among authors were small compared with differences among composition methods (Table 2). Authors

TABLE 2
Analysis of Variance of Time Scores (Min) in Experiment 3

Source	df	Mean Square	F	p Value
Authors	7	8.91	—	—
Methods	3	32.54	34.62	p < .001
Trials	1	7.09	7.54	p < .01
Meth. × Tr.	3	7.19	7.65	p < .001
Order	7	2.57	2.73	p < .05
Letters	7	8.67	9.22	p < .001
Error	35	.94		

accounted for about the same amount of variance as did differences among the eight letter-tasks, and they accounted for about 3.5 times as much variance as did overall practice effects. On mean quality ratings, the range of author differences was 2.7 to 3.4, which is relatively small for many generation tasks. Mean square author variance was 4.37, mean square composition method variance was 3.83, mean square letter-task variance was 2.49, and mean square overall practice variance was 1.96.

Are some authors relatively good at oral composition and other authors relatively good at written composition? No, not in the small sample studied. The better authors were relatively good in all methods and the poorer authors were relatively poor in all methods. A related question is whether some authors appeal to some "recipients," i.e., raters, and other authors to other raters. No evidence was found for this either.

VI. EXPERIMENT 4

The purpose was to compare the four methods of composition on documents requiring more creativity. Subjects composed formal letters on eight prescribed topics (e.g., a letter to their congressman on capital punishment, a letter applying for a sales clerk's job, a letter describing the significance of the U.S. Bicentennial, a letter describing one's daily activities).

A. Method

The design of Experiment 3 was used, except that each subject was given a different row of the design, i.e., order of conditions. The instructions were the same as in Experiment 3. Subjects were told to compose letters of about one type-written page. The rating, ranking, and selection tasks were performed after the experiment by three college students.

B. Results and Discussion

In general, the results on these more complicated letters were similar to those of the simpler letters of the previous experiment. Table 3 shows some key results. Mean times to compose in the four methods, which seemed intuitively fast for letters of this complexity, did not differ significantly (Table 4, $p > .10$). However, Duncan range tests on individual pairs of means showed that S was faster than W (Duncan range test, $p < .05$). The average quality rating was the same for all four methods ($p > .20$), being roughly "acceptable." The median rank of W, WNS, and D letters was 4th (out of 8) and the median rank of S letters was 5th. It was nearly impossible to pick out the dictated letters from the written ones, when three college students attempted to do this blindly after the experiment. On the average, they correctly selected 5.7 of the 16 dictated letters, when they should have selected 5.3 of them by chance alone. Average sentence length, one of two important indicants of readability (see Kintsch, Kozminsky, Streby, McKoon, & Keenan, 1975) was not significantly different in the four methods. Word frequency, the other useful measure of readability, is presently being analyzed. The type-token ratio, conventionally defined as the ratio of the total number of words (tokens) to the number of different words (types) was W = 3.06, WNS = 2.71, D = 3.24, and S = 3.37.

There were many similarities in the way subjects composed using the different methods. They overlapped their generating with acquiring external information needed for the return address and the inside address. They took a long pause, either prior to writing or after the salutation. Some of their pauses in W and WNS were to rest their hand and arm. Occasionally, they lost their place in WNS. Sometimes in D, following a pause, they would then review because (it appeared from facial expressions in the videotapes) they forgot what they had last said. In W, subjects did not do much re-reading of their writing. With the exception of one subject, subjects generally did not make notes in any method. Subjects made few changes while composing. These changes were generally minor. Subjects almost never reviewed their letters after generating them. Proofreading was done rapidly, and subjects made few changes. Eleven of the 16 W, 11 of the 16 WNS, and 7 of the 16 D letters were not changed at all. The majority of proofreading changes, when they did occur, were minor, i.e., typos, punctuation, and one-word changes. Only three of 48 W, WNS, and D letters were changed in a major way. Thus, instead of a great amount of editing and changes of already generated material, subjects generally composed a letter straightaway, and left it that way after proofreading it.

Interestingly, about the same amount of planning time was required in W and in D. Using the data of Table 3, the amount of planning during generation time can be estimated from <Generate time − (mean number words/maximum possible wpm)>, where maximum possible wpm is estimated as 40 for W and as 200 for

TABLE 3
Results from Experiment 4

	Method of Composing				
	Write	Write/No See	Dictate	Speak	Significance Level
Mean total time (min)	11.2	9.8	10.2	8.8	$p > .10$
Mean generate time (min)	8.4	7.7	3.9	3.2	$p < .001$
Mean pause time (min)	2.8	2.0	5.0	5.1	$p < .01$
Mean review time (min)	–	–	1.0	0.4	–
Mean no. generation periods	9.2	6.3	11.6	10.0	$p < .05$
Mean no. pauses	9.0	6.5	10.9	9.9	$p < .05$
Mean no. reviews	–	–	2.4	1.0	–
Mean no. words	166.0	153.8	208.4	219.3	$p < .01$
Words/min	15.1	16.3	22.5	29.3	$p < .001$
Words/min of generation	20.3	20.3	59.5	78.1	$p < .001$
Mean sentence length	17.9	16.5	19.2	19.4	$p > .10$
Quality rating on syntax, spelling, grammar, format	2.9	2.9	2.6	2.8	$p > .10$
Quality rating on clarity and correctness of information	3.3	3.1	3.4	3.3	$p > .10$
Quality rating on appropriateness	3.3	3.0	3.4	3.3	$p > .10$
Median quality rank (out of 8)	4th	4th	4th	5th	–

TABLE 4
Analysis of Volume of Time Scores (Min.) in Experiment IV

Source	df	Mean Square	F	p Value
Authors	7	62.92	–	–
Methods	3	15.28	2.16	p > .10
Trials	1	.05	–	
Meth. x Tr.	3	18.58	2.62	p > .10
Order	7	6.11	–	
Letters	7	16.37	2.31	p > .10
Error	35	7.08	–	
Total	63			

D (informal evidence). Adding this result to the observed pause times in Table 3 indicates a total plan time of 7.1 min in W and 7.9 min in D. Results on the simpler letters (Table 1) also showed that W and D required the same amount of planning time: 4.2 min for W and 4.3 min for D. (The slightly larger D than W values may be due to the inclusion of time to give typing instructions in generate time, although these did not add any additional words to the text.) Speaking required 2.9 min planning time in Experiment 3 and 7.2 min in Experiment 4, using 200 as the estimate of maximum possible WPM.

Based upon gestures and facial expressions on the videotapes, subjects seemed to have had less confidence in their dictation than in their writing. Dictating still lacked the "automatocity" (LaBerge & Samuels, 1974) of writing. Sometimes speaking seemed to proceed somewhat more smoothly than dictating. Occasionally, subjects started the body of the letter over in dictation.

Unlike Experiment 3 (Table 2), the results on these more complex letters showed that variation among subjects was greater than variation among different composing methods (see Table 4). In addition, author variance was now about three times that of rater variance.

Generate times (Table 3) were at least twice as long in W and WNS as in D and S, $F(3,21) = 33.43$; $p < .001$; Duncan range $p < .01$. On the other hand, pause times in D and S were about twice as long as in W and WNS, $F(3,21) = 6.37$; $p < .01$; Duncan Range $p < .05$. This difference could be due to (a) the faster output rates in D and S than in W and WNS, which may have prevented planning during generating, and/or (b) inexperience at dictating or speaking formal letters.

Mean wpm differed across the four composition methods (Table 3), $F(3,21) = 6.35$; $p < .01$. These composing rates are substantially less than the upper limits for generation rates, estimated as follows. Adults write memorized material at about 30–40 wpm and copy printed material at 40 wpm. They speak memorized material at 200–250 wpm and read aloud printed material at 200 –250 wpm (informal evidence). Thus, written composing rates were about

316 GOULD   PART III

one-third of their maximum, and oral composing rates were about a ninth to an eighth of their maximum.

Whereas the length of the letters was greater in D and S than in W and WNS, $F(3,21) = 5.53$; $p < .01$, these additional words conveyed no additional information, since the quality ratings were the same for all four methods. Reviews occurred on 10 of the 16 dictated letters and on 5 of the 16 spoken letters. Mean review time was 2.5 times as much in D as in S, perhaps because subjects had little experience or feedback on how their spoken words are read but much on how their spoken words are heard.

The quality of the letters (Table 3) was rated somewhat higher on clarity and correctness than on syntax, format, grammar, and spelling. Although this result generalizes to other people similar to these subjects, $F(2,14) = 14.5$; $p < .001$, following the procedures of Winer (1971, p. 377), it falls short of generalizing to *both* other samples of subjects *and* other raters, $F'(2,4) = 6.37$, $.10 < p < .05$. Quality ratings showed no significant difference with practice or with the particular letter task. It was relatively unpleasant to listen to letters spoken at these slow rates (30–75 wpm); clearly, a mechanism for the listener to speed up speech is required in any real-world application of spoken letters.

VII. GENERAL DISCUSSION

These experiments have taken a broad swipe at a large area rather than a deep thrust into a small area. They are part of an ongoing research program, as indicated below, and not a stand-alone set of experiments. It was anticipated that written letters would be superior to dictated letters, and thus the plan was to identify the causes of these differences, including the role of limited capacity memory, different composing strategies, and the effects of "secondary" tasks, such as giving secretarial instructions. Dictating seemed to be a not-much-used alternative to writing, a potentially important one because of potentially faster output rates that, among other advantages, might allow an author to get momentary thoughts out of his mental working memory before they are forgotten. However, with less than one day's practice people were as competent in their dictating as in their writing.

One might have thought, assuming a short-term memory limited by capacity, by depth of processing, or due to some other mechanism, that spoken sentences would have been longer than written sentences because of their potentially faster output rate. However, in both cases average sentence length was about twice the classic seven or so unrelated words that one can hold in short-term memory. How much author variables rather than consideration for the recipient determines sentence length is unclear.

It was initially thought that speaking letters would have a speed advantage over writing them, and would be easier and more natural than dictating them, because the author knows the recipient will listen to rather than read the letter. Although this speed advantage for authors did occur, judges sometimes found it tedious to listen to letters. The letters were spoken too slowly for preferred listening rates. This mismatch, the fact that subjects' speaking behavior was influenced by their recent training in dictating, and the fact that the first version of S letters was rated compared with the second version of the other letters, may have led to somewhat lower ratings for S letters than would have otherwise occurred.

Good authors were good authors, regardless of method. Thus, in composing letters to be read, compositional factors are more important than output modality factors.

Developing conclusions from negative results is always tenuous. From a practical point of view, however, the standard errors of the means are already small enough to suggest that no major differences will occur even if more subjects were run.

Compositions were under 225 words, and these studies were carried out in an uninterrupted environment. In real-life, people are frequently interrupted in their work, and they sometimes compose longer compositions. These two factors presently limit the generalization of the results.

There were some weaknesses with the rating scales. First, one or more of the areas were probably not unidimensional. In such cases it is not clear whether ratings were made to the average, worst, or best dimension in that area. Second, and perhaps partially due to this, inter-rater reliabilities were low. Third, it is not certain whether raters used, as a reference point for an acceptable letter, the average letter in the set under evaluation or what, in their own past experience, constituted an acceptable letter. Several lines of evidence, however, suggest the latter. These include chats with the raters, the fact that they did not change their earlier ratings after seeing additional letters, and the finding that when other similar raters compared the letters of Experiment 3 with those composed by experienced businessmen (Gould, 1979), they ranked the businessmen's letters as slightly better (median rank out of 8 was 4th vs. 5th). In any case, these problems do not seriously affect the comparisons among different composition methods. The 3,264 ratings in the four experiments were spread over the 5-point scale as follows: 1 = 8%, 2 = 14%, 3 = 49%, 4 = 23%, and 5 = 6%.

Why don't we and other people in real-life dictate, if in fact we can quickly learn to do so? The very many possible reasons can be divided into five categories: *actual performance* reasons, *perceived performance* reasons, *actual operational* reasons, *perceived operational* reasons, and *preference* reasons. *Actual perform-ance* reasons should not be the cause for not dictating letters of this general type, as the present results and a replication (Gould & Boies, 1978) show. Based upon the mouth being 5–6 times faster than the hand, one might expect that dictating would eventually become much faster than writing. However, with many years more experience in dictating, authors' dictation becomes only about

20–35% faster than their writing, depending upon the complexity of the one-page documents studied (Gould, 1979).

Novice dictators may not know that their performance in writing and dictating is equivalent, and so their *perceived performance* differs (see Gould & Boies, 1978). The non-intuitiveness of the present findings is thus partially explained in that method of composition is more a matter of preference than of performance. *Operational* reasons mainly involve actual or perceived interactions with secretaries and, secondarily, with equipment. These are likely candidates to affect whether one dictates or writes. We have begun developing some general methodology to study these reasons experimentally.

Some authors may simply *prefer* a particular method of composition, independent of performance and operational reasons. Implicit in the analyses of performance reasons and operational reasons is that an author is goal-directed to do his or her work efficiently and with excellence. This may not, however, always be the case.

ACKNOWLEDGMENTS

This work benefited greatly and throughout from cooperation and discussion with Stephen J. Boies. I thank him, Evon Greanias, Don Lyon, Don Nix, and Martin Chodorow for their comments on this manuscript.

REFERENCES

Chomsky, N. *Aspects of the theory of syntax*. Cambridge, Mass.: MIT Press, 1965.

Clark, H. H. The language-as-fixed-effect fallacy: A critique of language statistics in psychological research. *Journal of Verbal Learning and Verbal Behavior*, 1973, *12*, 335–359.

Deese, J. *Thought into speech: Preliminary data*. Paper presented at 1975 Psychonomic Society meetings, Denver, Colorado.

Gould, J. D. How experts dictate. *Journal of Experimental Psychology: Human Perception and Performance,* 1979, in press.

Gould, J. D., & Boies, S. J. How authors perceive their written and dictated letters. *Human Factors,* 1978 (in press).

Grant, E. E., & Sackman, H. An exploratory investigation of programmer performance under on-line and off-line conditions. *IEEE Trans. Human Factors*, 1967, *HFE-8*, 33–48.

Henderson, A., Goldman-Eisler, F., & Skarbeck, A. Sequential temporal patterns in spontaneous speech. *Language and Speech*, 1966, *9*, 207–216.

Kintsch, W., Kotminsky, E., Streby, W. J., McKoon, G., & Keenan, J. M. Comprehension and recall of text as a function of content variables. *Journal of Verbal Learning and Verbal Behavior*, 1975, *14*, 196–214.

Klemmer, E. T., & Snyder, F. W. Measurement of time spent communicating. *Journal of Communication*, 1972, *22*, 142–158.

LaBerge, D., & Samuels, S. J. Toward a theory of automatic information processing in reading. *Cognitive Psychology*, 1974, *6*, 293–333.

Liberman, A. M. The grammars of speech and language. *Cognitive Psychology*, 1970, *1*, 301–323.

Miller, G. A., Galanter, E., & Pribram, K. H. *Plans and structure of behavior*. New York: Holt, 1960.

Rochester, S. R. The significance of pauses in spontaneous speech. *Journal of Psycholinguistic Research*. 1973, *2*, 51–81.

Sartre, J. P., & Contat, M. Sartre at seventy: An interview. *The New York Review, 22(13)*, August 7, 1975, 10–17.

Stelmach, G. E. (Ed.) *Motor control: Issues and trends*. New York: Academic Press, 1976.

Winer, B. J. *Statistical principles in experimental design* (2nd ed.). New York: McGraw-Hill, 1971.

18

Audition and Speech Coding in Short-Term Memory: A Tutorial Review

Robert G. Crowder

Department of Psychology
Yale University
New Haven, Connecticut United States

ABSTRACT

This review covers phonological coding in short-term memory, the properties of echoic memory, and the distinction between these. Conrad's discovery of phonologically-based confusions errors in visual memory tests, and the correlation of these confusions with confusions derived from tests of listening acuity, were the initial stimulus for hypotheses about relating speech and short-term memory. Studies of EMG responses and articulatory suppression tie these effects to the production side of speech behavior. Four recent lines of evidence show that phonological coding is not necessarily the major agent of short-term retention: (a) evidence for visual coding in "operating memory," (b) evidence for short-term retention of phonologically identical stimulus lists, (c) evidence restricting the confusion effect to situations requiring memory for temporal order, and (d) evidence that phonological coding appears as a result of the re-hearsal of information, rather than as a result of simply encoding it.

Echoic memory is reserved for occasions in which stimulus information persists as sound, rather than as abstract phonological categories. Of techniques for demonstrating echoic memory, the most important are the comparison of visual and auditory presentation and the stimulus suffix effect. Whereas other interpretations for each of these two phenomena have been advanced, the fact that they depend in exactly the same way on the phonetic categories being remembered by the subjects reinforces their association with echoic memory.

Even though there is imperfect closure on the properties of echoic memory and of phonological coding, the distinction between them is crucial and well-supported. In all cases, evidence for the phonological code appears independently of sequential position, whereas evidence for echoic memory is specific to recent positions.

I. INTRODUCTION

As a society we communicate with the past and future through pictures as well as words and although cave paintings are the common ancestor for both art and writing, the direction of evolution is toward more and more reliance on the linguistic mode, first through oral chronicles, and then through written history. The individual child's communication with his past and future — his memory — evolves in a similar way, from a prelinguistic (perhaps visual) mode to increasing use of the linguistic mode. The achievement of literacy by either the individual or the society is a difficult step and it greatly reduces the burden upon memory; however, it does not change the reliance of social and individual memory upon language. Of course this evolution towards linguistic memory does not result in a discarding of the pictorial mode: Cultures have an elite memory mode in works of visual art, just as individuals have a parallel storage mode based on visual imagery. But the verbal mode predominates in carrying memory in the service of the rational processes. This may be related to the unique, multilevel, hierarchical structure of the language, which permits a variety of paraphrase operations that release the user from a verbatim reliance on the exact input. In any case, one has only to compare the difficulties encountered by the congenitally blind with those encountered by the congenitally deaf (Furth, 1966) in order to appreciate the primacy of language in cognition.

Aristotle and Locke would not have been surprised by these arguments for associating memory with language. They would have been shocked, in contrast, by the extent to which we are now tying memory to certain of the actual bodily functions that subserve language, particularly to speech and hearing. This survey is intended to cover just that domain, the set of theoretical and research conclusions that have placed speech and hearing into our process models for short-term memory. The three sections will cover phonological (speech) coding in short-term memory, echoic memory, and the distinction between these two coding modalities.

II. PHONOLOGICAL CODING

Following on earlier, informal, reports by Conrad (1962) and by Sperling (1960), it was undoubtedly Conrad's (1964) systematic demonstration that errors of substitution in visual memory closely matched hearing errors that forced all serious students of memory to come to grips with the relation between speech and memory. Basically, this *confusion effect* is a high conditional probability that, given that an error has been made substituting a wrong letter for the correct one, the intrusion will be phonologically similar to the correct response. Conrad and Hull (1964) reported the related observation that the unconditional probability of recalling letters correctly was reduced if the material to be recalled contained a high density of phonologically similar items, a finding we may call the *similarity decrement.*

There is one main issue that will pervade my survey of evidence on phonological coding: Whether the transform that underlies the confusion effect and similarity decrement is an active or a passive process. It was Estes (1973) who more or less defined this opposition. He referred to the passive alternative as the central-recoding hypothesis, which holds that information initially registered visually is recoded into a speech format by an automatic central process. What I am calling the active alternative was described by Estes (1973) as the *multiple-trace hypothesis,* which holds that the process of deliberately subvocalizing the stimulus information results in an auditory—articulatory residue, or feedback. The multiple-trace hypothesis requires active participation of some relatively peripheral part of the speech system, whereas the former hypothesis does not.

Morton's *logogen model* (Morton, 1969) partly resolves this opposition between the active and passive hypotheses, because in it, even the most central level of the system (the logogens) is inherently connected to articulatory gestures. Still, a part of Estes' opposition remains provocative: Is the phonological code a structural necessity in the visual processing system, or is it a byproduct of some strategy applied by the subject? Our survey will suggest that the latter position is correct, and it will further help to clarify another vexing issue: whether the phonological code arises during the acquisition, retention, or retrieval stage.

A. The Effects of Delay

We begin with the last issue first. If the evidence for phonological coding came entirely from retrieval processes, then the effects ought to be just as strong after a long retention interval as after a short retention interval. Perhaps the level of recall would have declined during this delay, but the size of the confusion effect or of the similarity decrement should not have changed. On this matter the evidence is mixed. Studies employing the confusion effect as the measure of phonological coding have consistently shown that phonology plays a smaller and smaller role during a period with interpolated distractor activity. Conrad (1967) first showed this in a study in which a short list of letters was presented in a window, followed immediately by a continuing stream of digits. The entire series, letters and digits, had to be shadowed at a challenging rate until, after a sequence of digits varying in length, the process was interrupted for a recall test of the letters. Conrad found that at intervals of less than three seconds of digit-shadowing there was a strong confusion effect, whereas after only 7.2 sec there was none. Estes (1973) and Healy (1975) have obtained essentially the same result over comparable intervals.

When we look at the effects of delay upon the similarity decrement, a less consistent picture emerges. Baddeley (1968) presented series of several words to be retained, and then an interpolated stream of digits that had to be copied before recall. In cases free of initial ceiling or subsequent floor effects, Baddeley found no particularly high rate of forgetting for lists high in phonological similarity (MAN, CAB, CAT, MAX, and so on.) There was indeed a similarity decrement, but its size did not change out to retention intervals of about 10 sec. Posner and Konick (1966) looked at the similarity decrement in a Brown-Peterson situation as a function of whether the interpolated information-processing load was difficult or easy. The size of the similarity decrement increased as a function of retention interval, but it was independent of the difficulty of the task occupying that interval. (This was the critical observation on which the *acid bath* model of Posner & Konick was based.) Finally, Liberman, Shankweiler, Liberman, Fowler, and Fischer (1977) tested five-letter series either high or low in phonological similarity at either an immediate test or after a completely unfilled 15-sec interval. The subjects were first-grade students grouped according to reading ability. Like Posner and Konick's subjects, the good readers showed an increase in the size of the similarity decrement with the longer interpolated period; however, for the poorer readers, the effect was not a function of delay.

This empirical confusion may be resolved by adoption of the active hypothesis in preference to the passive hypothesis. The active hypothesis makes the prediction that phonological coding symptoms should appear to the extent the task allows for subvocal rehearsal of the stimulus material. The two studies that show an increased similarity decrement are those allowing the freest rehearsal. The good readers in the Liberman et al. experiment may be assumed to be the best rehearsers and, given that there was no interpolated task, they had plenty of time for it. In the Posner and Konick study, the interpolated task was nonverbal (mental arithmetic) and thus possibly compatible with rehearsal. On the other hand, the most effective inhibitors of rehearsal should have been the rapid shadowing used by Conrad, Estes, and Healy, who all obtained a decreasing confusion effect over filled retention intervals. Baddeley's study gave a constant effect over time, even though his subjects were also obliged to shadow; however, the rate at which his subjects shadowed was considerably slower (one per second) than in the studies of Conrad, Healy, and Estes (over two per second). This evidence all supports the conclusion that phonological coding will be evident to the extent subjects have had a recent opportunity for rehearsal, not that phonological coding is an inherent part of the system for encoding visual information. This conclusion also denies the notion that phonological coding is located in the retrieval stage.

B. The Suppression of Articulation

On the supposition that the rehearsal involved in phonological coding employs some part of the articulatory system, several studies have contrived to prevent, or suppress, articulatory movements during processing of visual memory stimuli.

Such suppression is generally sufficient to remove the confusion effect. Conrad (1972) and Estes (1973) required subjects to make some dummy vocal response just as each stimulus letter appeared on the screen; in Conrad's study the subjects said *the* in unison with the presentation, and in Estes' study they classified each stimulus letter as being *high* or *low* in the alphabet. In both experiments performance remained above chance, although it was damaged by the suppression activity and the errors that occurred could not be traced to phonological features. In a second experiment (Estes, 1973, Experiment 2) subjects were discouraged from phonlogical coding by a speeding up of the presentation rate from 400 msec per item to 200 msec. Free rehearal periods were inserted early, midway, or late in the stream of digit-shadowing that occupied the retention interval; these 1.6 sec periods were intended to determine whether rehearsal of the items, based on some transitory memory trace, could restore the phonological code abolished by the rapid presentation. The confusion effect was found to occur under these conditions only if the rehearsal pause was introduced within about 1 sec of the original presentation. An important and unresolved issue for theory is what the storage modality was that held the information during this second. In any case, the Estes study clearly ties the occurrence of the confusion effect to the opportunity for rehearsal. It also shows, as did Conrad's (1972) experiment, that performance is better than chance when the confusion effect has been made to disappear.

There will be more to say on articulatory suppression in the last section of this review, which contrasts echoic memory with phonological coding. We shall not take the time here to cover two related experiments that employed a biofeed-back-training routine to teach subjects to suppress their own covert articulatory responses during encoding (Cole & Young, 1975; Glassman, 1972; these two experiments have turned in directly contradictory conclusions on important issues. For the moment, the main result is that a highly peripheral concurrent vocalization task, and in the case of Conrad's study a "thoughtless" task, can eliminate evidence for speech coding in memory. This argues, in conformity with the active hypothesis, that the speech code does not result from an automatic central recoding operation (Sperling, 1967).

C. The Limited Scope of Phonological Coding

In this section I want to discount a point of view that I subscribed to far longer than I care to admit: that the phonological code is so important in short-term storage that the two may nearly be equated. For this discussion I have to leave aside the difficult issue that primary memory, or short-term storage, is not necessarily well represented in some of the short-term memory tasks here under consideration (see Crowder, 1976, Chapter 6). I trust it goes without saying that by trying to lay out boundary conditions on the phenomena discovered by Conrad, I am not in the least denigrating their importance, which, in the modern experimental study of memory, is second to none.

1. *Visual coding in short-term memory.*   The separation of a functional from a structural memory store becomes blurred as we draw closer to James's (1890/1950) original ideas about primary memory — that it represents the width, in time, of the conscious present, and that information in it never really left the conscious present. Broadbent's (1971) desk-top metaphor and the concept of working memory (Baddeley & Hitch, 1974) are both efforts to formalize the intuition that primary memory "contains" what the person is concentrating on at the moment, or that it is that very process of concentration. From this, it is then a short step to the appreciation that subjects surely can concentrate on aspects of stimulus material that are not phonological. This process is best documented in the visual modality.

The experiments on visual rotation reviewed by Metzler and Shepard (1974) indicate an active working memory system filled with visual content. Tversky's (1969) experiment on mental transformations between verbal and pictorial representations of the same stimulus object also reveals a nonphonological working-memory process going on in real time. Posner, Boies, Eichelman, and Taylor (1969) showed that the generation and maintenance of visual images was more disrupted by mental arithmetic than by visual distraction; their evidence makes the most convincing case that visual transformations and the sort of mental operations used in conventional short-term memory studies are, at least in part, drawing on the same resource. In the section to follow, we shall see one reason subjects might usually be disposed to concentrate on phonological attributes in most language and memory experiments. Still, the fact that there is the possibility of attending to visual attributes instead lends credibility to the active hypothesis.

2. *Order information and phonological coding.*   There is no fundamental difference between order information and item information in memory. In both cases it must be retained that a particular verbal item — long a part of the subject's permanent memory store — occurred in a particular time and place. We use the term "item information" when only a loose approximation to the time of occurrence must be retained, such as that an item occurred somewhere in a group of items presented together as a list. We use the term "order information" when there is a more strict criterion of time of occurrence, such as that an item occurred just after FIRECRACKER and just before FLYSWATTER within a group of items presented as a list. With this point of logic and terminology aside, however, there is evidence that phonological coding is selectively involved in the retention of fine-grained order information, where an item occurred within a list, rather than where or whether it occurred within the experimental session.

Watkins, Watkins, and Crowder (1974) compared phonologically distinctive lists (TUB, CAB, DOCK, and so on) with phonologically similar lists (TAB,

BACK, CAT, and so on) under conditions of both free recall (12 items per list) and serial recall (7 items per list). With serial recall they observed the usual similarity decrement, but they found that similarity actually improved performance in free recall. When the serial task was scored by a free recall criterion, furthermore, similarity again enhanced performance. The cause of the facilitation of retention for so-called item information by phonological similarity is not known. There could be a guessing artifact with high phonological similarity in free recall: The subject could encode the prevailing vowel sound and then simply generate all of the single-syllable words that rhyme. However, Watkins et al. took the precaution of always leaving out two words that would otherwise qualify under such a criterion, and these words seldom appeared as intrusions. A sophisticated guessing strategy, however, may prove to be the explanation. What is important for present purposes is that a similarity-based facilitation in free recall denies that there is a wholesale destruction of memory traces under high phonological similarity (as Posner's acid bath model would maintain, for example). Instead, it is only a component of performance that suffers from phonological similarity.

Healy (1975) has shown that phonological coding is not just restricted to memory for within-list order (as opposed to memory for whether items occurred on a particular list), but that it is further restricted to the dimension of temporal order and not spatial order. She developed two tasks in which subjects always saw the same four letters on each trial of the experimental session. In the *temporal order task* the spatial locations of these four letters were permanently fixed to four side-by-side windows of a visual display unit (B always left, K next, P next, and M on the far right). What changed on each trial, and what was therefore the target of performance, was the temporal sequence in which these four letters occurred in these four positions. In Healy's *spatial order task* the four letters were always exposed in the same temporal order (B first, K second, P third, and M last) and what changed from trial to trial was the spatial location of the letters on the horizontal array of four windows. The main outcome was that there was a strong phonological confusion effect at short retention intervals for the temporal order task, but not for the spatial order task. The phonologically rich distractor task of digit-shadowing, furthermore, had a strong inhibitory effect on performance in the temporal task, but not in the spatial task. Finally, a manipulation of articulatory suppression, saying ONE, TWO, THREE, FOUR during presentation, had a strong negative effect on temporal order memory but no clear effect on spatial order memory. From these observations Healy concluded that phonological coding is a specialized device operating for the retention of temporal order information.

3. *Experimental subversion of phonological coding.*   I have recently been conducting experiments with materials that are designed to make phonological coding an impossible vehicle of retention: lists constructed from phonologically identical words — PEAR PAIR PEAR PARE PAIR PARE PARE. This research

indicates that subjects can remember even temporal order information without a phonological code. In one experiment subjects saw lists of several words from either a three-word vocabulary without phonological distinctiveness (PEAR PAIR PARE), or from a three-word vocabulary with some minimal phonological distinctiveness (PAIR PORE POOR). Some subjects were asked to pronounce the words out loud as they appeared on the screen, and others were told to mouth them vigorously but to emit no sound. The result of this simple two-by-two comparison is shown in Fig. 1, which is a plot of error proportions at each position for the four conditions. In the phonologically distinctive condition there was a conventional modality effect (Crowder & Morton, 1969), a terminal advantage for the condition in which the stimuli came through the ears as well as through the eyes, even though in both conditions there was involvement of the articulatory musculature (either in mouthing silently or in vocalizing overtly). The modality effect was reversed in the condition with phonologically constant stimulus vocabularies. The main point is not what caused the reversal (which occurs in several experiments and is always of borderline reliability), but rather that subjects were, after all, able to retain lists of phonologically identical items.

In this experiment, it is impossible to refute categorically the claim that subjects resorted to some concealed phonological code. The requirement of conspicuous articulatory responding, speaking, or mouthing would have made such a covert code quite a difficult affair, however, for the subjects would have had to

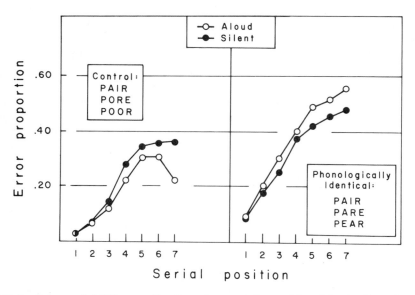

FIG. 1 Error probabilities as a function of presentation serial position for lists of seven words from phonologically distinct vocabularies of three words (left panel) or from phonologically identical vocabularies (right panel). The parameter is whether vocalization of visual presentation was silent or overt.

be internally vocalizing something discrepant from their concurrent mouthing or overt vocalization, and at just the same time. Also, in another experiment with the same design as this one, there was no tendency for performance to improve over successive runs with the same three-word vocabularies, as there should have been if subjects were working out a secret phonologically-distinctive code.

These stimulus materials are, of course, grotesquely artificial, but the message they allow us to infer is the same one we have been repeatedly encountering in this chapter: that the phonological code is a supplementary agency, not a primary agency, for recall in these short-term memory tasks. Thus, Estes (1973) found that his subjects still remained well above chance performance when deprived of a phonological code by a suppression technique. My subjects suffered about a 20% decrement from phonological identity of stimulus vocabularies, not a total breakdown.

III.   ECHOIC MEMORY

At an earlier session of this conference (Crowder, 1975) I reviewed the various experimental techniques that have been used to determine the properties of sensory memory within the auditory system (see also Crowder, in press). I shall not try to summarize that coverage here. Instead, I intend to recall briefly the main findings arising from my own work in echoic memory, and to give some idea of where the newer experiments are leading.

A.   The Suffix Effect

Morton and I (Crowder & Morton, 1969) maintained that the operation of a stimulus suffix could be assigned to a process of masking within the auditory analysis system. In a suffix experiment a list of eight or nine items is read aloud for the subject to recall immediately; Roediger and Crowder (1976) have shown that it does not matter whether the stimulus items are characters or words, nor whether instructions call for ordered or free recall. In the control condition there is either silence following the last item or an innocuous cue such as a bell. In the experimental condition, however, an extra word, called the stimulus suffix, is presented after the last memory item in time with the prevailing rate of presentation. The subject knows fully that the suffix will be occurring, what word will be used as the suffix, and that he is not responsible for recalling it. Whereas the buzzer and the suffix have exactly the same informational value, they lead to quite different outcomes. With the nonverbal cue there are both large primacy and recency effects, whereas with the suffix, the recency effect is completely or largely removed.

Crowder and Morton assumed that, ordinarily, in auditory presentation, echoic memory provides a source of extra information concerning the last item (or items). The echoic store, which we termed *precategorical acoustic storage,* was assumed to be vulnerable to interference from subsequent auditory input. Since the echoic store was supposed to be precategorical, it would not matter whether that subsequent input were relevant memory information or a redundant suffix, insofar as its effect on prior entries in the system. Thus, as each list item arrives, there is a masking operation upon the echoic trace of the previous item. In the auditory control condition, nothing arrives after the last memory item and the echoic information can be translated into a performance advantage; when the suffix is the last item in the series, and thus the only one free of masking, it does not help the subject's performance.

It should be emphasized that the main component of performance in immediate memory is conventional, postcategorical, short-term memory. The contribution of echoic memory is parallel and supplementary. It is parallel because information about the last item is held simultaneously in echoic form and in processed, verbal form. It is supplementary because the echoic information is just used to correct discrepancies with the verbal trace and is not in any sense a primary agency for performance. Thus, it is an error to consider the last item as being "in" echoic memory at the time the suffix arrives. It, like all the other items, was identified immediately upon presentation; unlike the other items it has a redundant sensory representation, unless the latter is removed by the suffix.

In the suffix experiment there is considerable delay between the occurrence of the last memory and its recall, because recall in this task is usually constrained to being with the first item and to proceed through in order. Although the suffix effect occurs whether or not this is the case (Roediger & Crowder, 1976), there remains an obligation to explain how the echoic information assists performance over so long a time span. One possibility is that the echoic trace simply persists for several seconds in raw form. A second possibility is that the subject reviews the last three or four items within a second or so of the occurrence of the last item, comparing his verbal memory of these items with whatever sensory information he might have of the last sound or sounds heard. When he later begins his public recall effort, all performance would then be based on conventional verbal memory processes. The suffix would alter the scenario only by depriving the subject of an echoic cross-check during his review of the last few list items.

A number of experiments on the suffix effect have produced results that are entirely consistent with the echoic memory hypothesis, but not conclusive in proving it (Crowder, 1976, Chapter 3). I shall limit myself to referring to one set of results that clearly does favor the echoic hypothesis in preference to other hypotheses for the suffix effect. Then, I shall conclude with new experiments designed to clarify the exact type of masking mechanism at work.

B.   Relation of the Echoic Store to Speech Sounds

A strength of the Crowder and Morton explanation of the suffix effect, a strength that recommends it over other explanations that are equally suitable for the suffix effect itself (Kahneman, 1973), is that it easily accommodates a second finding, the modality effect, whereas the alternative hypotheses do not. When visual and auditory presentation are compared, there is generally equivalent performance, except on the last few items, which are recalled better following auditory than following visual presentation. Both the suffix effect and the modality effect are contrasts between two otherwise identical serial position curves, one with and the other without a strong recency effect. According to the Crowder and Morton model, they are both consequences of echoic memory. Such alternative accounts as Kahneman's (1973) of the suffix effect must (a) maintain that the two empirical phenomena are related only by coincidence, and (b) remain silent as to why there is a modality effect at all.

The theoretical unity of the modality and suffix effects has been greatly reinforced by evidence (Crowder, 1971) that the occurrence of both depend identically upon the classes of speech sounds being remembered by the subject. When subjects were asked to remember series whose items were distinguished only by the feature of place of articulation (BAH GAH GAH BAH DAH BAH DAH) there was neither a suffix effect nor a difference between auditory and visual stimulus presentation. However, when a distinction between vowel sounds was the critical memory dimension (BAH BEE BAH BOO BAH BEE BOO), the suffix and modality effects were again obtained in their usual form (Crowder, 1975). Although this pattern of dependence of the modality and suffix effects on the phonetic features being retained must remain a complete mystery to alternative accounts of the suffix effect, it is readily understandable from the viewpoint of an echoic memory system that is crucial in subserving the perception of speech (Darwin & Baddeley, 1974).

C. Mechanisms of Backward Masking by the Suffix

The term *backward masking* is just a shorthand expression for an experimental result, no more specific theoretically than the term *retroactive inhibition.* Having made the case that the suffix effect is a true masking phenomenon, the next responsibility is to work out what type of masking is operating in it. There are at least four such masking mechanisms that may be distinguished: Masking by *erasure* occurs when the subsequent mask displaces the prior target from some fixed-capacity storage area, such as in buffer models of short-term memory. Once the target information is so displaced it is gone for good. Masking by *integration* occurs when the target and mask are received together by some higher-order processor. For this to happen when the mask is presented at a delay relative to the target, it is assumed that the mask catches up with the target along the transmission line. Performance suffers with integration masking because the configuration formed by the target and mask has a smaller signal-to-noise ratio than that of the target alone. In audition, it would be as if the subject heard the last memory item and the suffix pronounced at the same time.

There are two varieties of masking by *interruption, attentional interruption* and *nonattentional interruption.* In the first of these, there is a stage of processing dependent on some limited-capacity attention resource. Before the work of the limited resource is complete, in respect to a given target item, the mask arrives and diverts the attentional system to itself, depriving the target of its full share of processing. In nonattentional interruption there is unlimited capacity on the receiving end of the readout process; however, the activity generated by each stimulus event is inhibited by any other stimulus events in the same temporal region. According to this model, each event begins feeding information into an unlimited central processor as soon as it occurs, but each event also exerts inhibition on its neighbors' output of information into the central processor. When a mask follows closely on a target it degrades readout of the target, not by diverting attention to itself, but by inhibiting what the target can supply to the central processor.

The predictions of these four masking mechanisms may now be compared with the results of some recent suffix experiments I have performed. For example, what should be the effect of presenting more than one suffix item, as opposed to presenting only a single suffix? If the erasure hypothesis were correct, the multiple suffixes should have at least as large an effect as the single suffix, and possibly a larger effect. In independent experiments, Morton (1976) and I have shown that, in fact, two or three suffixes have a smaller effect on performance than a single one. My own data, previously unpublished, are shown in Fig. 2. There were separate control conditions for the two experimental conditions, one involving a single nonverbal (buzzer) cue after the last memory item, and a second involving three such nonverbal cues. The two experimental conditions were

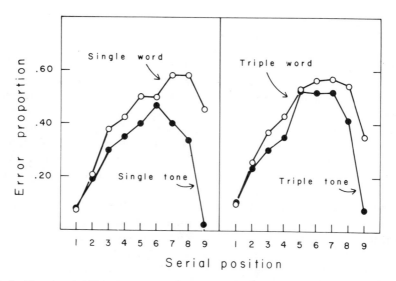

FIG. 2   Error probabilities as a function of presentation serial position for lists of nine digits followed by a single tone or suffix (left panel), or by three tones or three suffixes (right panel).

identical to these control conditions, except that verbal suffixes were substituted for the nonverbal cues. The multiple cues, control or experimental, were presented in time with the stimulus presentation rate. It is clear from the figure that a smaller effect was obtained with the multiple suffixes than with the single one. Morton obtained the same result. On this evidence we may rule out masking by erasure as the operating model for the suffix effect.

The multiple suffix experiment also eliminates the integration hypothesis for, at most, a subsequent suffix can only leave the target item unaffected if it does not additionally combine with it. Nor does the attentional interruption hypothesis predict the relief produced by additional suffix items. If the original mask diverts attention from the target to itself, there is no reason why a second mask should restore processing to the target; rather, the subsequent mask would divert attention from the first mask to itself. By elimination we may conclude that only the nonattentional interruption hypothesis remains intact against the evidence on multiple suffixes. According to this model, the first mask exerts an inhibitory effect on generation of information from the target to the central processor. When the second mask arrives it begins to exert an inhibitory influence on the first mask. Inhibition of the first mask by the second mask means the first mask can no longer be inhibiting the target as well as otherwise, which explains the relief observed in performance. It is thus a case of disinhibition and, indeed, the nonattentional interruption model is formally equivalent, logically, to all explanations of the phenomenon of disinhibition based on lateral inhibition.

Converging support for the nonattentional model comes from additional experiments I have been doing, comparing a suffix arriving simultaneously with the last item to one delayed slightly after the last item. If the integration model is correct, then presenting the suffix and last item simultaneously is the worst possible arrangement, because it guarantees the kind of overwriting believed to occur only probabilistically in backward masking — the mask overtaking the target during transmission and combining with it at the central processor. On the other hand, the interruption hypotheses, with or without an attentional limitation, predict that if the target and mask are fed together into the system, they should be processed together without either's interrupting the processing of the other. In three independent experiments, I have found that presenting the suffix simultaneously with the last memory item leads to a smaller performance decrement than presenting it after a slight delay.

Of course, common sense tells us that the simultaneous condition could be a mixed blessing if the suffix item itself were extremely loud; a shouted suffix would overwhelm a whispered memory item. I have verified this prediction also in a study where a moderate suffix shows increased masking with slight delays, but a loud suffix shows the biggest effect with simultaneous presentation.

Finally, we must recognize that if a suffix is delayed too long, it will not matter what masking effect occurs, because the subject will, by then, already have been able to complete the readout process for the target item. There is only so much information that can be gleaned from the echoic trace of the target item, and once this information has been processed, it no longer matters whether masking occurs as far as performance is concerned.

Thus, the complete model of the situation begins with an increasing gradient of nonattentional interruption (to account for disinhibition), supplemented with a decreasing gradient of integration masking (to account for a loud suffix), and additionally supplemented with a gradient of readout for the reason just mentioned. These three gradients relate the observed masking influence to the time delay separating the suffix and the last item. The complete model implied by these three assumptions is shown in Fig. 3. The components are represented in terms of what supports good performance on the last (target) item. Remember also that this treatment is concerned only with the small echoic memory component of performance in this situation, not with the conventional short-term verbal memory responsible for the overwhelming majority of correct recalls of items. Although every assumption represented here is supported by the studies I have just cited, further experiments are now being conducted to test more subtle predictions of the model.

IV. PHONOLOGICAL CODING AND ECHOIC
MEMORY DISTINGUISHED

It is natural to expect that phonological coding and echoic memory are related to one another, given the known connections between audition and articulation

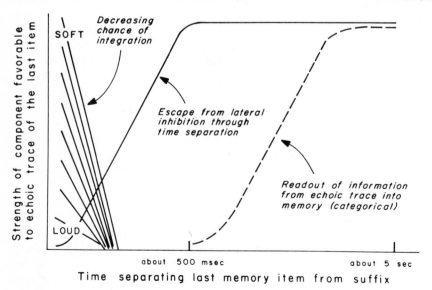

FIG. 3   Theoretical gradients relating sources of effective use of echoic memory for the last item to the delay between the occurrence of the last item and the suffix item. See text for explanation.

in the speech chain. Why not, as some have suggested (Tell, 1972; Thompson & Clayton, 1974) simplify matters by defining a single system responsible for both the echoic effects (modality effect, suffix effect) and the phonological coding effects (similarity decrement, confusion effect)? The formal distinction proposed by Crowder and Morton — that phonological coding comes from either auditory or visual presentation whereas echoic memory comes only from true auditory presentation — is no help because it is circular. But there are several lines of empirical support for the distinction we made and they will be reviewed in this last section.

A. Structural Similarity of Suffix to List Items

There is evidence that structural similarity or phonological similarity between the suffix and the list items has effects that are functionally distinct from the suffix effect itself. By structural similarity, here, I intend a level of similarity more abstract than the physical channel (Crowder, 1972; Morton, Crowder, & Prussin, 1971) yet less abstract than the semantic level (Crowder, 1972; Morton et al., 1971).

1. *Phonological similarity.* Crowder and Cheng (1973) had subjects remember lists of seven synthetic syllables from a vocabulary of three items, /gi, gI, gu/. In a control condition there was a tone following the last item, but main interest was in two suffix conditions. In one of these the suffix was the syllable /bI/, and in the other it was /ba/. The former was chosen because it comes from the same neighborhood, as it were, of vowel space, as do the three memory items; indeed /bI/ matches one of them in its vowel. The /ba/ suffix was chosen to be as far away as possible from the memory vocabulary in vowel space. We expected this manipulation of phonological similarity between the memory items and interpolated items to have at least some performance effect (Wickelgren, 1965), but the question was whether there would be an interaction with the suffix manipulation.

Figure 4 shows the result of the Crowder and Cheng (1973) experiment. Both experimental conditions had a large suffix effect, as compared with the control condition, but there was no larger suffix effect per se in one than in the other. That is, the extent to which the suffix removed, or reversed, the recency effect in the control condition was not different for the two experimental conditions. One might object that the contrast in phonological similarity was not potent enough to show the interaction. However, examining performance across all list positions, we found reliably worse performance overall in the /bI/ condition than in the /ba/ condition. If phonological similarity effects and suffix effects had a similar locus, they should have interacted rather than been additive.

2. *Structural similarity.* Another recent, unpublished, experiment of mine makes the same point. It was a two-by-two comparison of whether the suffix

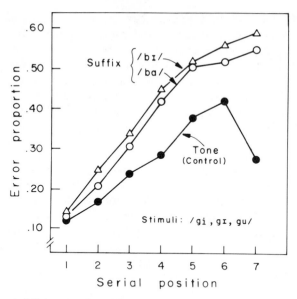

FIG. 4 Error probabilities as a function of presentation serial position for lists of seven syllables followed by either a tone, or one of two suffix items. (After Crowder & Cheng, 1973).

was a buzzer or the word GO, and whether the memory list items were unbounded vowel sounds or consonant-vowel syllables, /a, i, u/ or /ba, bi, bu/, respectively. All items were synthesized on the Haskins parallel resonance synthesizer and were presented at a 2 per sec rate. Although this was not the original purpose of the experiment, notice that when the stimuli were consonant-vowel syllables, their structure matched that of the suffix word, GO, which was also a consonant-vowel syllable, but when the stimuli were unbounded vowels the suffix was less similar to the memory items.

Figure 5 shows the result of this experiment. The first thing to notice is that the size of the suffix effect, defined as that portion of the suffix-control discrepancy that is selective at the end of the list, did not differ between the two stimulus vocabularies. However, performance on the early and middle positions showed interference when there was structural similarity (consonant-vowel) between the suffix and memory items, but not when there was a mismatch between them. As in the Crowder and Cheng study, similaity between the stimulus items and the suffix did not change the size of the suffix effect, although it did reliably affect performance of the list as a whole, just as we should expect if the echoic system were functionally distinct from the system responsible for phonological and structural similarity effects.

The Cheng study, and those considered just before it, remind us that, across experiments, we have already seen this same dissociation: The echoic memory phenomena always occur on the last few positions, whereas the speech-coding effects show up across the whole list (Baddeley, 1968; Watkins, et al., 1974).

Two further remarks on the data of Fig. 5: I have been bothered for years as to why the suffix effect sometimes seems located entirely in the last serial position and other times in the last few or even most items except the first one or two (though always there has been an increasing, selective, effect the further towards the final position one looks). It now appears that at least some of this variation in the extent of the suffix effect may be assigned to fortuitous variation in the structural similarity between the suffix item and the stimulus items. Second, notice performance in the early positions of the buzzer control conditions, showing an early advantage for the consonant-vowel syllables over the unbounded vowel sounds. It is possible that this superiority demonstrates a phenomenon noted by Shankweiler, Strange, and Verbrugge (1977) in vowel perception. They showed that the coarticulational junctures between consonants and vowels provide important phonemic information about the vowels; when the vowels are in isolation, the subject needs to rely on formant-frequency calculations, which Shankweiler et al. suggest are more difficult cues to interpret than consonant-vowel transitions.

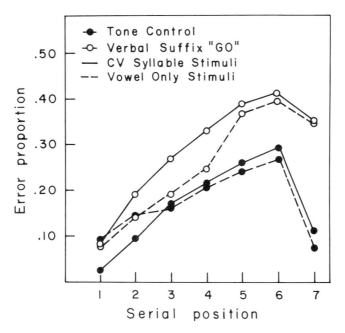

FIG. 5   Error probabilities as a function of presentation serial position for lists of seven syllables followed either by the suffix word GO or by a nonverbal cue. The stimulus items were either CV syllables or unbounded vowel sounds.

B. Articulatory Coding

Other experiments have tried to involve the articulatory apparatus more directly in manipulations of the phonological code. Cheng (1974) developed a mixed-modality presentation procedure for lists of seven consonant letters. One mode was visual/articulatory; written syllables appeared on a screen, and the subject had to articulate them covertly when they occurred. The second mode was auditory; through a loudspeaker the subject heard the seven items pronounced. On each trial the subject received a new permutation of the seven letters, FRGKMVY. The same permutation occurred in the two channels. These particular letters were chosen because when given their conventional letter names, each has a distinctive vowel sound /ef, keI/ and so on. However, the same letters can also be presented as the initial segment of consonant-vowel syllables ending in a uniform vowel sound /a/. In this latter condition they are, naturally, much more similar phonologically than in the first. Cheng thus had at his disposal two input modes — visual/articulatory and auditory. And he had two phonological similarity conditions — low-similarity letter names and high-similarity consonant-vowel syllables ending in /a/. Similarity was manipulated orthogonally on the two modes to produce four conditions, distinctive-distinctive, distinctive-similar, similar-distinctive, and similar-similar, where the first term refers to the visual/articulatory mode and the second to the auditory mode. But recall that the same item was always occurring on both modes at the same time; if the second letter on a particular trial were K, in the distinctive-similar condition, for example, the subject would have been asked to read and articulate the syllable KAY on the screen, and he would have heard through earphones the syllable /ka/. If the next letter were F, he would have read from the screen the syllable EF, and he would have heard the syllable /fa/.

The question was whether distinctiveness, which we should expect would improve performance, would have qualitatively similar or different effects in the two modalities. The finding in Fig. 6 indicates that there was a qualitative difference. This figure shows the net advantage of distinctiveness (letter names) over similarity (syllables uniformly ending in /a/) in the two modalities. The similarity decrement obtained here was roughly independent of serial position within the auditory mode. Once again, therefore, a manipulation that Crowder and Morton (1969) would have relegated to articulatory coding, receptive to both visual and auditory input, was shown to be functionally distinct from a manipulation they would have assigned to the echoic memory system (precategorical acoustic storage).

Levy (1975) showed much the same thing with an entirely different technique. She found a modality effect favoring auditory input of lists of three sentences, as opposed to visual input. She also found that articulatory suppression, counting from 1 to 10 softly during presentation of the sentences, was harmful to recall. The observation of interest here was that these two effects were functionally

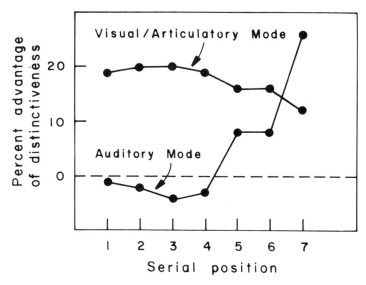

FIG. 6   The net advantage of distinctiveness (better names rather than syllables paired with /a/) in the visual/articulatory and auditory modalities in recall of seven consonant lists. (After Cheng, 1974).

distinct. The modality effect appeared only for the last of the three sentences presented, while the effect of articulatory suppression extended across all three sentences equally.

C. A Difficulty with the Present Argument

A potential difficulty with the present argument, which stresses functional dissociation of phonological coding and echoic memory, is raised by a set of studies that purport to show functional equivalence between them. It will be recalled that studies of articulatory supression during visual input were seen, earlier in this review, to prevent the confusion effect in experiments of Estes (1973) and others. This was taken to indicate that keeping the speech machinery occupied had prevented the strategy of phonological recoding. Four studies have been reported (Murray, 1968; Peterson & Johnson, 1971; Tell, 1972; Thompson & Clayton, 1974) in which either the confusion effect or the similarity decrement was likewise removed by articulatory suppression, but then restored, in another condition, by switching from visual to auditory presentation. That is, these studies show that, whereas suppression removes evidence for speech coding in visual presentation, such evidence is still obtained, even in the presence of suppression at presentation, by using auditory input. The authors of these experiments concluded that either the speech musculature or, alternatively, the auditory sensory system were equivalent means of setting up a unitary audition-speech code. Such a unitary code is just what I have been at pains to discredit in this section of the review — namely an auditory-type representation that may be achieved equivalently through subvocal speech or through hearing (see Sperling, 1967).

But there is a way out, without recourse to new theoretical assumptions. It has already been asserted here that the auditory system is capable of holding information that was received through the ears for a second or two in precategorical form. The solution to our problem is to put this storage system to work during application of the suppression technique to auditory stimulus presentation. When input is visual, the subject is out of luck if he must pronounce some dummy item during occurrence of the memory stimuli, because no buffer memory will hold the stimulus until he has time to make a speech response to it. However, when there has been auditory presentation, the subject can rely on echoic memory for a second or two later. When at last he has finished pronouncing the suppression, or dummy, item, he still has the echoic trace of the stimulus and can subvocalize it, setting up the occasion for a similarity decrement and a confusion effect. The auditory presentation modality is, thus, not an equivalent way of producing a phonological code; it is, rather, a way of holding information until a busy subject can translate it into the phonological code himself.

ACKNOWLEDGMENTS

Some of the research reported here was supported by USPHS Grant 1 R01 MH 26623-01. The assistance of Guinevere Butterfield in preparing stimulus materials, and of Virginia Walters in collecting and tabulating data, is warmly acknowledged.

REFERENCES

Baddeley, A. D. How does acoustic similarity influence short-term memory? *Quarterly Journal of Experimental Psychology,* 1968, *20,* 249–264.

Baddeley, A. D., & Hitch, G. Working memory. In G. H. Bower (Ed.), *The psychology of learning and motivation* (Vol. 8). New York: Academic Press, 1974.

Broadbent, D. E. *Decision and stress.* London and New York: Academic Press, 1971.

Cheng, C. —M. Different roles of acoustic and articulatory information in short-term memory. *Journal of Experimental Psychology,* 1974, *103,* 614–618.

Cole, R. A., & Young, M. Effect of subvocalization on memory for speech sounds. *Journal of Experimental Psychology: Human Learning and Memory,* 1975, *1,* 772–779.

Conrad, R. An association between memory errors and errors due to acoustic masking of speech. *Nature,* 1962, *193,* 1314–1315.

Conrad, R. Acoustic confusions in immediate memory. *British Journal of Psychology,* 1964, *55,* 75–84.

Conrad, R. Interference or decay over short retention intervals? *Journal of Verbal Learning & Verbal Behavior,* 1967, *6,* 49–54.

Conrad, R. Speech and reading. In J. F. Kavanagh & I. Mattingly (Eds.), *Language by ear and by eye.* Cambridge: MIT Press, 1972.

Conrad, R., & Hull, A. J. Information, acoustic confusions, and memory span. *British Journal of Psychology,* 1964, *55,* 429–432.

Crowder, R. G. The sound of vowels and consonants in immediate memory. *Journal of Verbal Learning & Verbal Behavior,* 1971, *10,* 587–596.

Crowder, R. G. Visual and auditory memory. In J. F. Kavanagh & I. G. Mattingly (Eds.), *Language by ear and by eye.* Cambridge: MIT Press, 1972.

Crowder, R. G. Inferential problems in echoic memory. In P. M. A. Rabbitt & S. Dornic (Eds.), *Attention and performance V.* London and New York: Academic Press, 1975.

Crowder, R. G. *Principles of learning and memory.* Hillsdale, N.J.: Lawrence Erlbaum, Associates, 1976.

Crowder, R. G. Sensory memory mechanisms. In E. C. Carterette & M. Freidman (Eds.), *Handbook of perception,* (Vol. 9). New York: Academic Press. In press.

Crowder, R. G., & Cheng, C. –M. Phonemic confusability, precategorical acoustic storage, and the suffix effect. *Perception & Psychophysics,* 1973, *15,* 145–148.

Crowder, R. G., & Morton, J. Precategorical acoustic storage (PAS). *Perception & Psychophysics,* 1969, *5,* 365–371.

Darwin, C. J., & Baddeley, A. D. Acoustic memory and the perception of speech. *Cognitive Psychology,* 1974, *6,* 41–60.

Estes, W. K. Phonemic encoding and rehearsal in short-term memory for letter strings. *Journal of Verbal Learning & Verbal Behavior,* 1973, *12,* 360–372.

Furth, H. G. *Thinking without language: Psychological implications of deafness.* New York: Free Press, 1966.

Glassman, W. E. Subvocal activity and acoustic confusions in short-term memory. *Journal of Experimental Psychology,* 1972, *96,* 164–169.

Healy, A. F. Temporal-spatial patterns in short-term memory. *Journal of Verbal Learning & Verbal Behavior,* 1975, *14,* 481–495.

James, W. *The principles of psychology.* New York: Dover, 1950. (Originally published, 1890).

Kahneman, D. *Attention and effort.* Englewood Cliffs, N.J.: Prentice-Hall, 1973.

Levy, B. A. Vocalization and suppression effects in sentence memory. *Journal of Verbal Learning and Verbal Behavior,* 1975, *14,* 304–316.

Liberman, I., Shankweiler, D., Liberman, A. M., Fowler, C., & Fischer, F. W. Phonetic segmentation and recoding in the beginning reader. In A. S. Reber & D. Scarborough (Eds.), *Toward a psychology of reading: Proceedings of the CUNY conferences.* Hillsdale, New Jersey: Lawrence Erlbaum, Associates, 1977.

Metzler, J., & Shepard, R. N. Transformational studies of internal representation of three-dimension objects. In R. Solso (Ed.), *Theories of cognitive psychology: The Loyola symposium.* Hillsdale, New Jersey: Lawrence Erlbaum Associates, 1974.

Morton, J. Interaction of information in word recognition. *Psychological Review,* 1969, *76,* 165–178.

Morton, J. Two mechanisms in the suffix effect. *Memory & Cognition,* 1976, *4,* 150–160.

Morton, J., Crowder, R. G., & Prussin, H. A. Experiments with the stimulus suffix effect. *Journal of Experimental Psychology,* 1971, *91,* 169–190.

Murray, D. J. Articulation and acoustic confusability in short-term memory. *Journal of Experimental Psychology,* 1968, *78,* 679–684.

Peterson, L. R., & Johnson, S. T. Some effects of minimizing articulation on short-term retention. *Journal of Verbal Learning and Verbal Behavior,* 1971, *10,* 346–354.

Posner, M. I., Boies, S. J., Eichelman, E. H., & Taylor, R. L. Retention of visual and name codes of single letters. *Journal of Experimental Psychology Monographs,* 1969, *79,* 1–17.

Posner, M. I., & Konick, A. W. On the role of interference in short-term retention. *Journal of Experimental Psychology,* 1966, *72,* 221–231.

Roediger, H. L. III, & Crowder, R. G. Recall instructions and the suffix effect. *American Journal of Psychology,* 1976, *89,* 115–125.

Shankweiler, D., Strange, W., & Verbugge, R. Speech and the problem of perceptual constancy. In R. Shaw & J. Bransford (Eds.), *Perceiving, acting, and knowing.* Hillsdale, N.J.: Lawrence Erlbaum Associates, 1977.

Sperling, G. The information available in brief visual presentations. *Psychological Monographs,* 1960, *74*(Whole No. 498).

Sperling, G. A. Successive approximations to a model for short-term memory. *Acta Psychologica,* 1967, *27,* 285–292.

Tell, P. M. The role of certain acoustic and semantic factors at short and long retention intervals. *Journal of Verbal Learning and Verbal Behavior,* 1972, *11,* 455–464.

Thompson, J. T., & Clayton, K. N. Presentation modality, rehearsal-prevention conditions, and auditory confusions in tests of short-term memory. *Memory & Cognition,* 1974, *2,* 426–430.

Tversky, B. G. Pictorial and verbal encoding in a short-term memory task. *Perception & Psychophysics,* 1969, *6,* 225–233.

Watkins, M. J., Watkins, O. C., & Crowder, R. G. The modality effect in free and serial recall as a function of phonological similarity. *Journal of Verbal Learning and Verbal Behavior,* 1974, *13,* 430–447.

Wickelgren, W. A. Acoustic similarity and retroactive interference in short-term memory. *Journal of Verbal Learning and Verbal Behavior,* 1965, *4,* 53–61.

IV HEMISPHERE DIFFERENCES

19

Functional Cerebral Space: a Model for Overflow, Transfer and Interference Effects in Human Performance: A Tutorial Review

Marcel Kinsbourne
Robert E. Hicks
Neuropsychology Research Unit
The Hospital for Sick Children, Toronto, Canada

ABSTRACT

Limitations on dual-task performance differ systematically depending on the cerebral localization of the control centers involved. Computer-based single-channel and multichannel models seem insufficient to account for these differences. An alternative notion, the functional cerebral distance concept, seems to account for the data at hand. This states that the limitations on dual-task performance are due to intertask interference within a single highly linked "cerebral space." The degree of interference is an inverse function of the "functional distance" between the cerebral control centers. The more neuronally interconnected they are, the more mutually interfering cross-talk they generate when orthogonally active. But, conversely, motor overflow and transfer of training is greater between functionally close (highly interconnected) cerebral control centers.

I. INTRODUCTION

When the human operator, while fully engaged in an attention-demanding task, is required simultaneously to perform a second such task, he typically loses efficiency on the main task. This generalization holds for all attention-consuming tasks except for those where time-sharing can be accomplished by switching attention between the tasks. Only when one of the tasks is so highly practiced as to be defined as "automatized" does its simultaneous performance not compromise performance on the main task. A notable exception was described by Allport, Antonis & Reynolds in 1972. These phenomena have been considered under the general heading of the single-channel limited capacity model of the human operator (Broadbent, 1958; Kerr, 1973; Welford, 1968), which assumes that a finite amount of energy or capability for effort powers the human organism. This capacity may be invested into a single activity or shared out between multiple simultaneous performances. Kahneman (1973) has made this explicit: "There is a limitation in general processing capacity, and that capacity, or effort, can be allocated interchangeably to various activities." Similarly, Moray (1967) describes the mind as analogous to a general purpose computer, which can apply its limited capacity interchangeably to widely different classes of processing. Some would regard the sharing out ingredient of multiple task performance as itself an activity that draws upon the same limited store of capacity (Taylor, Lindsay, & Forbes, 1967).

Many investigators no longer adhere to strict single-channel theory. Treisman (1969), reviewing pertinent literature, drew a distinction between dividing attention between two inputs presented to a single "analyzer," which is difficult to do, and dividing attention between inputs bound for two different analyzers, which is easier. Allport, Antonis, & Reynolds (1972) demonstrated minimal interference between word-shadowing and picture recognition and no interference at all between word-shadowing and sight reading of music. Their "multichannel hypothesis" envisages a number of independent, special purpose computers (processors and stores) operating in parallel "without mutual interference." Treisman & Davies (1973) showed that the limits of divided attention become less stringent when stimuli are presented to eye and ear, rather than both to eye or both to ear. Thus, not only sharing a particular cognitive processor, but also sharing modality of input, makes dual task performance more difficult. A model calling for a finite number of independent analyzers becomes more difficult to sustain in view of such results, and as Treisman & Davies point out, in order to avoid circularity, one needs other than behavioral criteria for deciding whether one or two analyzers were involved in any given paradigm. The functional cerebral distance concept, which departs from computer analogy, offers such external criteria, derived from known characteristics of localization of function in the brain.

The single- and multichannel concepts are metaphors derived from the perspective of the communications engineer and do not necessarily do justice to the organization of biological systems. We will propose an alternative approach. To each human operator is available a limited amount of functional cerebral space. This space consists of a highly linked neural network. The programming of a particular continuous activity involves not only the cerebral locus at which the programming is accomplished, but also involves, by spread of activation, a large proportion of the total cerebral space, the amount occupied being greater the more closely the operator's performance approximates the maximum of which he is capable. In the dual-task paradigm a second focus of unrelated activity has to be set up within the confines of the same space. Whether that second focus is close or relatively distant from the first in functional terms depends upon the specifics of localization of function in the brain. The closer the foci are to each other, the more apt is the motor program generated by each to be perturbed by overflow from the other one. The greater the functional distance between them, the less likely or less severe is such contamination and therefore, the better able the operator is to perform both simultaneously with a relatively high level of efficiency. Thus, according to this model, if a single cerebral program is being developed, then comparable programs are facilitated to a greater extent at functionally closer loci than at functionally distant loci and, successively, transfer of training is greater to the closer locus. In contradistinction, unrelated motor programs can be run concurrently most effectively if based on neural activity in loci functionally remote from each other.

In order to operationalize the model, it must be made clear when programs are considered to be comparable, and when they are unrelated.

Comparable programs are not only ones that utilize identical patterns of muscular contraction. Indeed, such a restrictive definition would limit the concept to mirror symmetric limbs. Rather, they are comparable in action pattern. Tapping a rhythm with hand and with foot would be comparably programmed, if the rhythm is the same. Humming the same rhythm is again comparable, in spite of the totally different effector system involved. Unrelated motor programs are ones that generate disparate action melodies — regardless of whether the concurrent acts are orthogonal (e.g., steering and accelerating a car) or co-ordinated.

The total available amount of functional cerebral space is regarded as increasing during normal maturation and decreasing in the course of the neuronal depletion that often accompanies aging. Focal lesions within the brain increase the functional distance between loci disconnected by the lesion.

Finally, one may note that it is logically possible for the operator, depending on the relative pay-off of the two tasks, to favor the performance of one task over the other. When two unrelated tasks are in competition there is also the option of either permitting them to proceed at an undiminished rate, though contaminated by error due to overflow from the other center of activation or of reducing rate of information transmission to reduce the extent of activated cortex to protect each from error-inducing cross-talk.

II. THE NEUROLOGICAL BASIS OF DIFFERENCES IN FUNCTIONAL DISTANCE

It would be possible to construct a functional space based entirely on findings at the behavioral level. Operationally, concurrent activities that maximally coordinate when correlated, and maximally conflict when unrelated, would be closely adjacent within that topological space, and vice versa. Naturally, the enterprise would exclude what Kahneman (1973) has termed "structural interference" when two action programs compete for the same output channel. The behavioral space could then be superimposed on the real brain, in an effort to establish the relevant brain–behavior correspondences. In fact, we need not restrict ourselves in this fashion, as enough is known about the degree of functional interconnectedness between the processors under discussion for us to generate behavioral predictions, against which the validity of the functional space model for revealing neural relationships can be tested right away. In other words, we can determine whether our topological functional space represents functional cerebral space.

The output channels considered in this discussion are the two hands, the two feet, rightward gaze, leftward gaze, and the voice. A wealth of evidence supports the view that rightward gaze is controlled from the left cerebral hemisphere, and leftward gaze from the right (summarized by Kinsbourne, 1974a). Thus, the control center for rightward gaze is within the same hemisphere as the language control facility for most right-handed and about half of nonright-handed individuals, as well as in the same hemisphere as the control center for right-hand and right foot movements. The leftward gaze control center shares a hemisphere with the control center for the left hand and foot, as well as for certain spatio-temporal processes. We will assume that control centers within a hemisphere are functionally closer than control centers between hemispheres, with one important exception.

It is a general principle in the bisymmetric vertebrate nervous system that mirror image loci in the two halves of the neuraxis are closely connected by commissures at all levels of the nervous system (Kinsbourne, 1974a). This closeness of connection may be deduced from the wealth of commissural fibers, notoriously those crossing in the corpus callosum in mammals. There is also a scattering of physiological evidence in favor of the concept that mirror image loci are better connected functionally than are loci representing different bodily parts on the same side. It is a striking general rule that motor overflow (as revealed in the presence of associative movements, but particularly in children) is primarily to the mirror image limb and to a lesser extent to the other two limbs (e.g., Stern, Gold, Hoin, & Barocas, 1976). An electromyographic study of this was performed by Davis (1942a, b). He measured the EMG and response amplitude of all four limbs when only one limb was instructed to act. Expressed as a percentage of the amplitude of the electromyogram of the responding limb, he found 7.9% activity in the contralateral homologous limb, 3.6% in the ipsilateral limb and 3.1% in the diagonally opposite limb. So closely related are mirror image loci that Anrep (1923) found that the conditioned salivary reflex to tactile stimuli of a particular point on a dog's skin may be obtained from stimulating the symmetrical point on the other side of the dog's body. Dawson (1947, 1954) found that when sensory nerves were unilaterally stimulated, evoked potentials could be recorded from both the homologous and the opposite sensory regions of the cerebral cortex. Gibson and Hudson (1935) found bilateral transfer of the conditioned knee-jerk. Gibson (1939), testing the generalization of verbal conditioning to a particular locus on the back of human subjects to one side of midline, found a generalization decrement with increasing distance from that point, except for an upturn of the amount of conditioned response at the mirror image locus on the other side from the one initially stimulated. Thus we conclude that paired limbs may with validity be regarded as more highly interconnected than homolateral limbs. With respect to diagonally paired limbs, it is clear that these must be less well connected than either of the other types of pairings because callosal connections are strictly homologous, and there is therefore no direct connection between the hand area on one side and the foot area on the other. Communication between those two areas has to involve more synaptic crossing than does communication between paired limbs or limbs that are on the same side of the body.

The functional distance model therefore would regard paired limbs as more highly interconnected than homolateral limbs, and these in turn more highly interconnected than diagonally-paired limbs. Control of the right hand, right foot, rightward gaze, and voice form one functionally close cluster, and left arm, left leg, and leftward gaze form another. With respect to cognitive operations, verbal processing would be more closely related to the left hemispheric cluster and spatiotemporal to the right hemispheric cluster.

With respect to the four limbs and to right and left lateral gaze, these relationships would be maintained in nonright-handers. But they would not necessarily be maintained with respect to voice control and the two alternate modes of cognitive processing.

We now proposed to consider to consider the experimental evidence.

III. SIMULTANEOUS IMITATIVE EFFECTS

A. Between Limbs

It is well established that a movement sequence carried out by one limb may overflow into similar movement of lesser amplitude in the contralateral limb (Cernacek, 1961; Clare & Bishop, 1949; Lundervold, 1951). The probability and amplitude of a "mirror movement" increases as a function of the force with which the primary movement is performed and as the duration of the primary movement pattern increases (Lundervold, 1951). Associated movement in the homolateral and the diagonally-paired limb also occurs, but is less frequent, less conspicuous and most easily observed in young children.

Also, a movement sequence is often altered when another movement sequence has to be carried out by the mirror image limb (Cohen, 1970). Again, these interactions occur, though less prominently, within other limb pairings.

B.   Vocal-Manual Overflow

Kimura (1973a) has recently reported an excess of right over left free hand gestures while subjects are speaking. Insofar as these gestures were not performed with conscious intent, they could be regarded as overflow phenomena. Their asymmetry is predictable from the shorter functional distance between the vocal and right arm control centers than between the vocal and left arm control centers. Kimura (1973b) found no such asymmetry for nonright-handers. This is predictable from the more variable lateralization of voice control in this group.

It is noteworthy that verbal behavior, even in right-handers, does not invariably elicit a preponderance of right hand gestures. If the verbalizations are based on imaginative thought that seems likely to involve the opposite hemisphere or both hemispheres, then the gesture might involve the right hand, or the left hand, or be predominantly bimanual (Kinsbourne & Sewitch, 1975). Nevertheless, the findings remain compatible with the notion that motor overflow from thought processes is preferentially channeled to the functionally most closely related effector.

IV.   SEQUENTIAL TRANSFER EFFECTS

A.   Reaction Time

A response is faster if it constitutes a repetition of the response made just previous to it than if it follows a different response (Bertelson, 1963, 1965). However, even if the two sequential responses are different, the second response is faster if it follows another response made with the same hand than if it follows a response made with the other hand (Rabbitt, 1965). This result is predicted by the functional distance model, insofar as the motor representation of fingers of the same hand are in closer proximity than are the representations of fingers of the two hands.

A similar result was obtained by Blyth (1962). He examined the 12 possible ways in which two sequential responses can be made with different limbs. He found that the second response was faster where the two responses required the successive movement of mirror-image-paired or ipsilateral limbs than of diagonally-paired limbs.

B.   Transfer of Training

Cook (1933a) had subjects practice mirror tracing a star-shaped maze with the right hand for 100 trials under visual guidance. Then the left hand, left foot, and the right hand were tested on the same task. Another group was given original training with the left foot, and then the other three limbs were tested for transfer. Cook found 89%, 81%, and 74% transfer for mirror-image-paired, ipsilateral and diagonally-paired limbs respectively. When only 10 training trials were given, the amount of transfer in absolute terms was less, but the rank order of transfer of two or three remaining limbs was the same as before (Cook, 1933b). With an irregular maze without visual guidance, the pattern of transfer was again identical (Cook, 1934).

Ammons and Ammons (1970) measured the correlation over two successive 8 min periods of performance on a pursuit rotor task. Sixteen groups were formed by the various possible pairings of limbs across the two sessions. The correlation between sessions was highest for the four groups that used the same limb in both sessions (.85), intermediate for the four groups using mirror image limbs for the two sessions (.76), less for the four groups using homolateral limbs (.64), and least for the four groups using diagonally paired limbs (.56).

V.   SIMULTANEOUS INTERFERENCE EFFECTS

So far we have considered empirical data in the literature consistent with the functional distance model, when viewed retrospectively. In this section, we refer to a series of experiments in which the functional distance model was put to an explicit test. These experiments all relate to the predicted relative degree of interference between concurrently active output mechanisms depending on the functional distance between them.

A.   Between-Limb Interference

Briggs and Kinsbourne (1978) engaged subjects in a two-limb step-tracking task, using a device known as the complex coordinator. This incorporates four display panels, one for each limb, and four levers, each responsive to the movement of one limb. Each display panel is partitioned into two sections, and on each section there are five locations, any one, but only one, of which may be illuminated at a given time. The device is so programmed that it unpredictably varies the location of the lighted element in one section of each display panel. The subject is then required to align the light on the alternative sections with the test light. This he can do by moving the appropriate lever in the right direction and to the right extent. At each trial, then, subjects were required to move two limbs in such a ways as to align the lights under their control with the location of the test light on that trial. Once that alignment was achieved, the program moved on to the next item. The test lights changed location, and another set of movements by the two limbs was required. The setting of the lights for the two limbs varied orthogonally, so that in most cases the two limbs would have to move to a different extent and half the time in opposite directions. The output of the 750 trials was a total time score for the set of problems as a whole, as well as an error score for each of the two limbs separately. The error score was a count of the number of times on which the appropriate location was overshot. Incidentally, "undershooting" was hard to define in a discontinuous way in this experiment, as subjects, when exhibiting difficulty, would not so much stop short as rather slowly reach the correct location. These tendencies to undershoot would contribute to the total time taken, but were not in themselves measurable.

The functional space model predicts that when limbs are orthogonally occupied in this manner, there will be interference between them in inverse relationship to the functional distance between them. Thus, in terms of both dependent variables, it was expected that the most efficient combination would be the diagonally-paired, the next most efficient the ipsilateral and the least efficient the mirror-image-paired. This expectation was fulfilled by the findings of the experiment.

B. Vocal-Manual and Verbal-Manual Interference

The functional distance model predicts that when the voice and one hand are concurrently active, and not engaged in unrelated activities, there will be greater interference between the voice and the right hand than between the voice and the left hand. This excess interference could be expressed either by the relatively greater decrement in the efficiency of right hand performance, or more loss in efficiency of vocal performance when paired with the right hand, or both. Kinsbourne and Cook (1971) tested this hypothesis by having subjects balance a dowel rod on the tip either of the right or the left index finger. After half an hour of practice in each of the two conditions, subjects were given a set of such (control) trials interspersed in a counterbalanced fashion with a set of trials during which they were asked to perform a concurrent verbal task. During verbalization there was a decrement in right hand performance (in terms of the average length of time the rod could be balanced before it fell). There was no such decrement on the left. Hicks (1975) replicated this result and found it also to hold for humming (as for speaking). This suggests that it is the motor control of vocalization rather than verbal or musical programming per se that has this effect. Hicks, Bradshaw, Kinsbourne, and Feigin (1978) used finger-sequencing tasks in a similar manner and also found that the greater the response-response incompatibility of the finger ring sequence was, the greater was the amount of observed lateralized interference. The lateralized effect on finger movements of the right hand holds for covert as well as for overt activity. Hicks, Provenzano, and Rybstein (1975) found that concurrent verbal rehearsal produced more interference with finger movements of the right than left hand (when rehearsal was silent, as well as when it was vocalized).

Briggs (1975), using the complex coordinator, found that the right hand made more errors than the left hand when the subject was given the concurrent task of shadowing a verbal message under conditions of delayed auditory feedback. This was in contrast to control trials in which the right hand was superior.

Bowers, Heilman, Satz, and Altman (1975) had subjects finger-tap while performing each of three verbal tasks — a verbal fluency task, listening to stories, and reading stories. In each case, right hand tapping performance was more disrupted than left. But a visuospatial task — scanning an array of faces — equally interfered with the performance of both hands.

Kinsbourne, Hicks, and LaCasse had trained musicians practice playing two orthogonal tunes simultaneously on the piano. When they could do so without error, they were then, on some trials, asked to hum along with the tune played by the right hand and on other trials with the tune played by the left hand. Half the time they played the low notes with the left hand and the high notes with the right hand. Half the time they crossed hands and played the high notes with the left hand and the low notes with the right hand. They found that accuracy of playing, as well as of humming, was greatest when humming accompanied the right hand. This was predicted by the functional distance model. If the vocal control center and the functionally neighboring right hand control center are engaged in unrelated activities, this engenders more interfering crosstalk than when the two left-sided control centers are both turning out action programs that correspond to each other in rhythm and pattern (of positional and pitch change, respectively). The interference became manifest when the nature of playing errors was ascertained. More than 90% of playing errors by the hand engaged in playing the tune that was not accompanied by voice consisted in the temporary switching of the pattern of playing so as to conform with that of the accompanied hand. It appeared that the action pattern had temporarily assumed control of both hands.

C. Developmental Studies

Insofar as the above noted interference effects represent an imperfection in insulation between concurrently active control centers close to each other in functional space, it will be expected that the less mature nervous system would be particularly subject to such effects. An initial demonstration that these effects hold for five-year-old children was offered by Kinsbourne and McMurray (1975), using rate of tapping with the index finger as a dependent variable. They found that given verbal recitation to do while finger tapping, there was a greater decrement of right than of left finger-tapping speed. This was in contrast to a baseline condition in which right finger-tapping was faster than left. More recently we have applied this on a cross-sectional basis to children aged 3–11 (Hiscock & Kinsbourne, in press; Kinsbourne & Hiscock, 1977). We confirm the existence of the effect in children and show that the degree of interference is proportionately greater the younger the child (as might be expected within the restricted cerebral space of the immature individual).

D. Anomalous Cerebral Organization

Several of the studies listed used nonright-handed as well as right-handed subjects. In each case, the selective lateralization of the interference effect was not found among nonright-handers. This is to be expected, because among left-handers there are substantial groups of individuals with right hemisphere language, and ones in whom language is bilateral. Rather, the effects were spread more evenly across the two sides. Hicks (1975) found this outcome both for left-handers and for right-handers with nonright-handed relatives. With a finger-sequencing task, comparable to that used by Hicks, Provenzano, & Rybstein (1975), Lomas & Kimura (1976) replicated the greater interference of verbal activities with the right hand performance of right-handers, but found interference with both hands in left-handers. Given that left-handers are so miscellaneous in cerebral organization, the present paradigms offer an opportunity for determining the details of that organization with respect to verbal processes in the individual case.

Anomalies in cerebral organization can also be induced by sectioning of connecting pathways. Such disconnection increases effective functional distance between the disconnected loci. Thus, the irradiation of conditioned reflex from one side of the body to mirror-symmetrical loci on the other side, reported by Anrep (1923), is completely abolished by corpus callosum section (Bykoff, 1924). In terms of the model, the callosal section increases to infinity the functional distance between the central representations of somatic sensation for the two sides of the body.

Kreuter, Kinsbourne, and Trevarthen (1972) had a subject with complete callosal section finger-tap with both hands while speaking. They were able to demonstrate a dramatic interference within the left hemisphere (i.e., between vocalizing and right-sided tapping). Interference was greater the harder the verbal task. The right hemisphere, functionally remote from the left-sided verbal processor on account of the callosal section, continued to program uncontaminated finger-tapping. A retarding effect on left finger-tapping only occurred when the subject made an error and halted all performance to recoup and start again.

VI. PERCEPTUAL INTERFERENCE

This difficult topic will be addressed only briefly at this time. Certainly the functional distance model is potentially applicable to the identification of simultaneous stimuli, of the same or different category, and within the same or in different modalities (Treisman, 1969). Thus, it is well-known that, whereas dichotic presentation of words can challenge a subject's perceptual abilities, and dichotic presentation of tonal patterns can do likewise, a mixed presentation of words to one ear and tones to the other presents no difficulty at all. This type of outcome could be attributed to the relatively great functional separation of cerebral areas responsible for the recognition of words and of tones. However, it is confounded by the greater potential for masking between sound patterns of the same category. Again, in the visual modality, two simultaneous presentations, however distinct in categorical nature, must necessarily be separately located in the visual field, calling for shifts of attention between them. The effect of such shifts of attention on performance are unknown. The area awaits further study.

VII. FACILITATION EFFECTS AND THE BIASING OF DIVIDED ATTENTION

Whereas the human operator typically loses efficiency on either or both of two tasks when he has to perform them simultaneously, occasionally the addition of a secondary task actually facilitates performance. This is particularly apt to happen when the primary task is very easy, and is then attributable to the beneficial effect on performance of increase in arousal when this is moderate in degree (cf. the discussion of the Yerkes-Dodson function in Kahneman, 1970). A facilitation effect selective to one hemisphere was described by Hellige & Cox (1976) using the very light concurrent load of rehearsal of two words. In an attempt at replication, Boles (1977) obtained only a nonsignificant trend in this direction. Both investigators used gap detection as the primary task. Such facilitation should probably be viewed in the context of shifts induced in the relative efficiency of recognition of right- versus left-sided displays of visual features induced by lateralized concurrent tasks, as described by Kinsbourne (1970, 1973, 1975), Bowers et al. (1975) and Chow, Swanson, Kinsbourne, and Hicks (1978). We shall now explain how these orientational shift paradigms also illustrate the functional distance principle.

In bisymmetrically structured and innervated organisms, each half of the neuraxis subserves orientation of the animal toward the opposite side of space. The rightward and leftward orienting facilities are in dynamic balance at various levels of central nervous organization, including the cerebral level (Kinsbourne, 1974a). We now apply the concept of functional distance to the effect of selective activation of one cerebral hemisphere on the state of the balance between the ipsilateral and contralateral orienting control centers. The activation of the hemisphere primarily responsible for whatever is the existing cognitive state leads to some spread of activity into the homolateral orienting control center and therefore tips the balance of orienting tendencies such that the vector resultant orientation is swung contralateral to the more active hemisphere. Any spread of activiation to the opposing orientor on the other side of the brain is naturally more limited because of the functionally greater distance to be traversed and therefore insufficient to offset this asymmetrical effect. It follows that when a hemispherically specialized cognitive set is adopted, and the direction of orientation of the person not specified by the experimenter, there will be observable orienting biases contralateral to the active hemisphere. This has been experimentally demonstrated in terms of eye and head deviations by Kinsbourne (1972) and also shown for lateral gaze by Kocel, Galin, Ornstein, and Merrin

(1972), Gur, Gur & Harris (1975), Schwartz, Davidson, and Maer (1975), and Hiscock (1977). Submotor orienting biases due to lateralized concurrent activity have also been demonstrated by Kinsbourne (1970, 1973, 1975), Bowers et al. (1975), Chow et al. (submitted, 1978), and a wide range of perceptual asymmetries could be based on such a mechanism (cf. Kinsbourne, 1974b). A further illustration of the explanatory power of the functional distance model resides in its clarification of the empirical data of Treisman & Geffen (1968). They showed that it was easier to maintain attention to the right than to the left of two concurrent verbal messages while at the same time attempting to divide attention between both channels to detect secondary nonverbal signals. The functional distance between the left sided verbal processor and the left lateralized rightward orienting control center makes the rightward attention during verbal processing compatible with functional brain organization and therefore efficiently achieveable. But the combination of verbal processing with leftward orientation involves the two neighboring control centers in the left hemisphere in opposing states. The verbal control center is in a state of excitation and the orienting control center is in a state of inhibition. The resulting interference impairs either the verbal processing or the consistency of leftward orientation, or both.

A final illustration of the functional distance principle as it affects the relationship between lateralized processor and lateralized orientor derives from the logical prediction that orienting in one direction should favor the immediately subsequent specialized cognitive processing of the hemisphere that programmed the orienting, rather than of the alternate hemisphere. Kinsbourne (1975) and Casey (1977) report studies that test and lend support to this model, and an early finding by Gopher, reported in Kahneman (1973), lends itself to a similar interpretation.

VIII. IS FUNCTIONAL DISTANCE NECESSARILY TRANSITIVE?

The question arises: Is spread of activation between any two loci in the brain equiprobable in either direction? There is experimental evidence for exceptions to any such rule though the neuronal basis of the deviations from complete transitivity are quite unknown. The exceptions arise from two sets of phenomena: motor overflow from locally applied muscular effort and transfer of training from locally performed skilled movement sequences.

A voluntary movement, however discrete it is intended to be, is not necessarily accompanied by total inactivity of other bodily parts, movement of which serves no adaptive function with respect to the operator's intention. Rather, there is typically some overflow movement, overt or covert (e.g., detectable by electromyography) to other muscle groups. The extent of this overflow decreases with progressive maturation of the nervous system and increases as a function of the amount of muscular effort invested in the intentional movement.

In the course of studies of motor overflow (cf. Stern et al., 1976) it has become apparent that overflow between the action of the nonpreferred and preferred hand is not symmetrical. The left hand action generates more uncalled-for right hand overflow movement than vice versa. When the left hand flexes rhythmically, its rhythm punctuates steady pressure by the right hand more than vice versa (Welch, 1898). With respect to transfer of training, a similar phenomenon occurs. Training of the left hand transfers more effectively in terms of subsequent savings in the training of the right hand than vice versa (Hicks, 1974). This leads one to the paradoxical proposition that the functional distance from the control center of the right hand to that of the left hand is greater than that from the control center of the left hand to that of the right hand. Perhaps these phenomena are expressions of the fact that the human organism has a species-specific preprogrammed rightward response bias. Thus newborn infants both turn to the right for positively valenced stimuli and withdraw toward the right from negatively valenced stimuli more often than to the left (Liederman and Kinsbourne, 1977). Also, in double simultaneous stimulation, children often fail to respond to one of the stimuli. The younger the child (down to age 4), the greater the probability is that the single response will be to the right (Schulman and Satz, 1977). Finally, there is solid neuropsychological evidence that motor control for movement sequences is largely lateralized to the left hemisphere (Roy, 1975).

IX. IMPLICATION OF THE FUNCTIONAL SPACE MODEL FOR THE POSSIBLE ADAPTIVE VALUE OF HEMISPHERIC SPECIALIZATION OF FUNCTION

The functional distance model casts a new perspective on the question of what might possibly be the adaptive value of hemispheric specialization.

The basic facts of cerebral lateralization of function are well known (e.g., Kinsbourne, 1978). In most people the left cerebral hemisphere subserves language function; perhaps in a more general sense those cognitive processes that can be described as analytic or specific. The right hemisphere is credited with spatio-temporal specialization, perhaps in a more general sense the establishing of relationships between coexisting specific features. Thus, the right hemisphere supplies context for the left hemisphere's specific action. The specializations of the hemispheres are thus complementary rather than alternate or in conflict. Contrary to claims that each hemisphere mediates an in-itself complete and self-sufficient alternate processing mode or "consciousness" (Ornstein, 1972), we regard the two hemispheres as typically concurrently in action, except in situations (more prevalent in the laboratory than in the real world) in which the demand characteristics of the task draw upon one cognitive mode only. It, therefore, follows that cerebral organization should be adapted so as to permit the frequent and efficient concurrent functioning of two very disparate types of neuronal activity, the analytic, or specifying, and the relational. Naturally, at some stage, the output of each program has to be synchronized with that of the other in order to integrate and implement the total act. However, the generating of each program would proceed more efficiently if minimally inconvenienced by cross-talk from the other program concurrently being elaborated. The maximal available functional distance between the complementary action control centers is thus necessary. Such distance is conveniently achieved by lateralizing these two types of activity in separate cerebral hemispheres.

This model departs from the more current view that each hemisphere is in terms of its neuronal hardware more specialized for performing in a particular cognitive mode (Semmes, 1968) and conforms better to the by now well established fact that early loss of one hemisphere permits the other one to assume the specialized function of the damaged hemisphere to a high level of excellence (Kinsbourne & Smith, 1974). Also, the present model explains why it, apparently, is just as efficient to have the reversed specialization frequently found in non nonright-handers of language on the right and spatiotemporal function on the left side of the brain. There would, on the basis of this model, be an important disadvantage in having both verbal and spatio-temporal function represented within the same hemisphere, be it left or right. The difficulty would arise if the characteristics of a relatively difficult task called for the simultaneous exertion of both specific and relational functions. We therefore predict that hemispherectomized subjects, and to a lesser extent those nonright-handers who apparently lack hemispheric specialization of function, would be dramatically disadvantaged only in those test situations so designed as to call for the combined exertion of the alternate modes of processing that in most people are lateralized in opposite sides of the brain.

These predictions remain to be tested. Among promising paradigms for such a test is that of Brooks (1967, 1970). He showed that subjects find it easier to visualize (perform mental rotation) in conjunction with listening to verbal inmation, than reading the same information. In terms of functional distance, the listening-visualizing combination should indeed be more efficient, because it involves opposite hemispheres, whereas the visuospatial component of reading would be more likely to involve right hemispheric processes, and thus cross-talk with right hemispheric visualization. According to the model, the distinction between these two conditions should be less marked in nonright-handers, insofar as some of them would be expected to have more diffusely represented verbal and/or spatial functions.

The paradigms used by Allport, Antonis and Reynolds (1972) could similarly be applied to this problem. They found little or no interference between shadowing of words and picture recognition or sight-reading of piano music (probably because the concurrent tasks are controlled from opposite hemispheres). A nonright-handed subject sample might, on account of the presumed presence of individuals with relatively diffuse cerebral alerting during cognitive functioning, manifest significant interference even between tasks such as these.

X. OVERVIEW

The functional distance principle, using the concept of a highly-linked neuronal space of limited extent, has greater explanatory value than the straightforward single channel limited capacity model of the human operator. In a strictly compartmentalized system, "cross-talk" between compartments would be incapable of limiting concurrent performance. Any limitations on the concurrent performance of two tasks would then arise from some limited resource of "energy" or "effort" available for cognitive processing of any kind at any time. In the highly-linked mammalian brain, this concept is unnecessary. The notion of a limited functional cerebral space, in contrast to the computer-based notion of limited capacity, takes cognizance of known properties of biological control systems, which function in ways quite dissimilar from computers. It has proven its heuristic value by generating studies (and accounting for previously unexplained empirical findings) that show that capacity is by no means invariant, and that there is no uniform ceiling on "effort." Rather, the extent to which an operator may perform concurrently depends on the functional organization of the relevant cerebral control centers. There is always some limitation on dual task performance (other than automatized) because functional cerebral space is finite. If we conceive of highly automatized performance as involving only a very limited cortical area, if any at all, then we can, using the same model, accommodate the corollary finding that the limitation on capacity is lifted when one or both of the concurrent performances is highly automatized (Fitts & Posner, 1967).

ACKNOWLEDGMENTS

This work was supported in part by a grant from the Connaught Foundation.

REFERENCES

Allport, D. A., Antonis, B., & Reynolds, P. On the division of attention: A disproof of the single channel hypothesis. *Quarterly Journal of Experimental Psychology,* 1972, *24,* 225–235.

Ammons, R. B., & Ammons, C. H. Decremental and related processes in skilled performance. In L. E. Smith (Ed.), *Psychology of motor learning.* Proceedings of C.I.C. Symposium on Psychology of Motor Learning. University of Iowa, 1970.

Anrep, G. V. The irradiation of conditioned reflexes. *Proceedings of the Royal Society,* 1923, *96B,* 604–626.

Bertelson, P. S–R relationships and reaction-times to new versus repeated signals in a serial task. *Journal of Experimental Psychology,* 1963, *65,* 478–484.

Bertelson, P. Serial choice reaction-time as a function of response versus signal-and-response repetition. *Nature,* 1965, *206,* 217–218.

Blyth, K. W. Experiments on choice reactions with the hands and feet. Doctoral dissertation, University of Cambridge, 1962.

Boles, D. B. Laterally biased attention with concurrent verbal load: A failure to replicate. Master of Science dissertation, University of Oregon, 1977.

Bowers, D., Heilman, K. M., Satz, P., & Altman, A. Intrahemispheric competition. Simultaneous performance on motor, verbal, and nonverbal tasks by right-handed adults. Paper to the International Neuropsychology Society Annual Meeting, Toronto, 1975.

Briggs, G. G. A comparison of attentional and control shift models of the performance of concurrent tasks. *Acta Psychologica,* 1975, *39,* 183–191.

Briggs, G. G., & Kinsbourne, M. Cerebral organization revealed by multilimb tracking performance. Submitted for publication, 1978.

Broadbent, D. E. *Perception and communication.* Oxford: Pergamon, 1958.

Brooks, L. R. The suppression of visualization by reading. *The Quarterly Journal of Experimental Psychology,* 1967, *19,* 289–299.

Brooks, L. R. An extension of the conflict between visualization and reading. *The Quarterly Journal of Experimental Psychology,* 1970, *39,* 199.

Bykoff, K. Versuche an Hunden mit Durchschneiden des Corpus Callosum. *Zentralblatt der gesamten Neurologie und Psychiatrie,* 1924, *39,* 199.

Casey, M. C. The effect of lateral eye positioning on information processing efficiency. In Ergonomics Program Report, North Carolina State University, Raleigh, N. C., 1977.

Cernacek, J. Contralateral motor irradiation-cerebral dominance: Its changes in hemiparesis. *Archives of Neurology,* 1961, *4,* 165–172.

Chow, S. L., Swanson, J. M., Kinsbourne, M., & Hicks, R. E. The effect of a concurrent verbal task on visual sensitivity in the two half-fields: A signal detection analysis. Submitted for publication, 1978.

Clare, M. H., & Bishop, G. H. Electromyographic analysis of the physiologic component of tremor. *Archives of Physical Medicine,* 1949, *30,* 559–566.

Cohen, L. Interaction between limbs during bimanual activity. *Brain,* 1970, *93,* 259–272.

Cook, T. W. Studies in cross education. Mirror tracing the star-shaped maze. *Journal of Experimental Psychology,* 1933, *16,* 144–160. (a)

Cook, T. W. Studies in cross education. II. Further experiments in mirror tracing the star-shaped maze. *Journal of Experimental Psychology,* 1933, *16,* 679–700. (b)

Cook, T. W. Studies in cross education. III. Kinesthetic learning of an irregular pattern. *Journal of Experimental Psychology,* 1934, *17,* 749–762.

Davis, R. C. The pattern of response in a tendon reflex. *Journal of Experimental Psychology,* 1942, *30,* 452–463. (a)

Davis, R. C. The pattern of muscular action in simple voluntary movements. *Journal of Experimental Psychology,* 1942, *31,* 347–366. (b)

Dawson, G. D. Investigations on a patient subject to myoclonic seizures after sensory stimulation. *Journal of Neurology, Neurosurgery and Psychiatry,* 1947, *10,* 141–162.

Dawson, G. D. A summation technique for detection of small evoked potentials. *Electroencephalography, Clinical Neurophysiology,* 1954, *6,* 65–84.

Fitts, P. M., & Posner, M. I. *Human performance.* Belmont, Calif.: Cole Publishing Co., 1967.

Gibson, E. J. Sensory generalization with voluntary reactions. *Journal of Experimental Psychology,* 1939, *24,* 237–253.

Gibson, J. J., & Hudson, J. Bilateral transfer of the conditioned knee-jerk. *Journal of Experimental Psychology,* 1935, *18,* 774–783.

Gur, R. E., Gur, R. C., & Harris, L. J. Cerebral activation, as measured by subjects' lateral eye movements, is influenced by experimenter location. *Neuropsychologia,* 1975, *13,* 35–44.

Hellige, J. B., & Cox, P. J. Effects of concurrent verbal memory on recognition of stimuli from the left and right visual fields. *Journal of Experimental Psychology*, 1976, *2*, 210–221.

Hicks, R. E. Asymmetry of bilateral transfer. *American Journal of Psychology*, 1974, *87*, 667–674.

Hicks, R. E. Intrahemispheric response competition between vocal and unimanual performance in normal adult human males. *Journal of Comparative and Physiological Psychology*, 1975, *89*, 50–60.

Hicks, R. E., Bradshaw, G. J., Kinsbourne, M., & Feigin, D. S. Vocal–manual trade-offs in hemispheric sharing of performance control in normal adult humans. *Journal of Motor Behavior*, 1978, *10*, 1–6.

Hicks, R. E., Provenzano, F. J., & Rybstein, E. D. Generalized and lateralized effects of concurrent verbal rehearsal upon performance of sequential movements of the fingers by the left and right hands. *Acta Psychologica*, 1975, *39*, 119–130.

Hiscock, M. Effects of examiner's location and subject's anxiety on gaze laterality. *Neuropsychologia*, 1977, *15*, 409–416.

Hiscock, M., & Kinsbourne, M. Ontogeny of cerebral dominance: Evidence from time-sharing asymmetry in children. *Developmental Psychology*, in press.

Kahneman, D. Remarks on attention control. *Acta Psychologica*, 1970, *33*, 119–131.

Kahneman, D. *Attention and effort*. Englewood Cliffs, N.J.: Prentice-Hall, 1973.

Kerr, B. Processing demands during mental operations. *Memory & Cognition*, 1973, *1*, 401–412.

Kimura, D. Manual activity during speaking. I. Right-handers. *Neuropsychologia*, 1973, *11*, 45–50. (a)

Kimura, D. Manual activity during speaking. II. Left-handers. *Neuropsychologia*, 1973, *11*, 51–55. (b)

Kinsbourne, M. The cerebral basis of lateral asymmetries in attention. *Acta Psychologica*, 1970, *33*, 193–201.

Kinsbourne, M. Eye and head turning indicate cerebral lateralization. *Science*, 1972, *176*, 539–541.

Kinsbourne, M. The control of attention by interaction between the cerebral hemispheres. In S. Kornblum (Ed.), *Attention and performance IV*. New York: Academic Press, 1973.

Kinsbourne, M. Lateral interactions in the brain. In M. Kinsbourne and W. L. Smith (Eds.), *Hemispheric disconnection and cerebral function*. Springfield, Ill.: Thomas, 1974. (a)

Kinsbourne, M. Mechanisms of hemispheric interaction in man. In M. Kinsbourne and W. L. Smith (Eds.), *Hemispheric disconnection and cerebral function*. Springfield, Ill.: Thomas, 1974. (b)

Kinsbourne, M. The mechanism of hemispheric control of the lateral gradient of attention. In P. M. A. Rabbitt and S. Dornic (Eds.), *Attention and performance V*. London: Academic Press, 1975.

Kinsbourne, M. *The asymmetrical function of the brain*. New York: Cambridge University Press, 1978.

Kinsbourne, M., & Cook, J. Generalized and lateralized effects of concurrent verbalization on a unimanual skill. *Quarterly Journal of Experimental Psychology*, 1971, *23*, 341–345.

Kinsbourne, M., Hicks, R. E., & LaCasse, P. Dual task performance by musicians: A demonstration of the functional distance principle. In preparation.

Kinsbourne, M., & Hiscock, M. The development of cerebral dominance. In S. Segalowitz and E. A. Gruber (Eds.), *Language development and neurological theory*. New York: Academic Press. In press.

Kinsbourne, M., & McMurray, J. The effect of cerebral dominance on time sharing between speaking and tapping in preschool children. *Child Development*, 1975, *46*, 240–241.

Kinsbourne, M., & Sewitch, D. Gaze and gesture during mental activity. Paper to the International Neuropsychology Annual Meeting, Tampa, Florida, 1975.

Kinsbourne, M., & Smith, W. L. (Eds.) *Hemispheric disconnection and cerebral function.* Springfield, Ill.: Thomas, 1974.

Kocel, K., Galin, D., Ornstein, R., & Merrin, E. Lateral eye movement and cognitive mode. *Psychonomic Science,* 1972, *27,* 223–224.

Kreuter, C., Kinsbourne, M., & Trevarthen, C. Are deconnected hemispheres independent channels? A preliminary study of the effect of unilateral loading on bilateral finger tapping. *Neuropsychologia,* 1972, *10,* 453–461.

Liederman, J., & Kinsbourne, M. Neonatal behavioral asymmetries: State or trait? Paper presented at the Soceity for Research in Child Development, Biannual Meeting, New Orleans, 1977.

Lomas, J., & Kimura, D. Intrahemispheric interaction between speaking and sequential manual activity. *Neuropsychologia,* 1976, *14,* 23–33.

Lundervold, A. Electromyographic investigations during sedentary work, especially typewriting. *British Journal of Physical Medicine,* 1951, *14,* 32–36.

Moray, N. Where is capacity limited? A survey and a model. *Acta Psychologica,* 1967, *27,* 84–92.

Ornstein, R. E. *The psychology of consciousness.* San Francisco: W. H. Freeman & Co., 1972.

Rabbitt, P. M. A. Response facilitation on repetition of a limb movement. *British Journal of Psychology,* 1965, *56,* 303–304.

Roy, E. A. Toward a typology of apraxia. *Mouvement,* 1975, 29–44.

Schulman, H. M., & Satz, P. Response patterns of children to homologous bilateral simultaneous stimulation. Unpublished manuscript (1977), University of Florida at Gainesville.

Schwartz, G. E., Davidson, R., & Maer, F. Right hemisphere lateralization for emotion in the human brain: Interactions with cognition. *Science,* 1975, *190,* 286–288.

Semmes, J. Hemispheric specialization: A possible clue to mechanism. *Neuropsychologia,* 1968, *6,* 11–26.

Stern, J. A., Gold, S., Hoin, H., Barocas, V. S. Toward a more refined analysis of the "overflow" or "associated movement" phenomenon. In D. V. S. Sankar (Ed.), *Mental health in children.* Westbury, N.Y.: PJD Publications Ltd., 1976.

Taylor, M. M., Lindsay, P. R., & Forbes, S. M. Quantification of shared capacity processing. *Acta Psychologica,* 1967, *27,* 223–229.

Treisman, A., & Geffen, G. Selective attention and cerebral dominance in perceiving and responding to speech messages. *Quarterly Journal of Experimental Psychology,* 1968, *20,* 139–150.

Treisman, A. Strategies and models of selective attention. *Psychological Review,* 1969, *76,* 282–299.

Treisman, A., & Davies, A. Divided attention to ear and eye. In S. Kornblum (Ed.), *Attention and Performance IV.* New York: Academic, 1973, 101–117.

Welch, J. C. On the measurement of mental activity through muscular activity and the determination of a constant of attention. *American Journal of Physiology,* 1898, *1,* 283–306.

Welford, A. T. *Fundamentals of skill.* London: Methuen, 1968.

20 Factors Affecting Face Recognition in the Cerebral Hemispheres: Familiarity and Naming

Carlo Umiltà
Istituto di Psicologia
Università di Padova, Italy

Daniela Brizzolara
Patrizia Tabossi
Hugh Fairweather
Istituto di Psicologia,
Università di Bologna, Italy

ABSTRACT

Recognition of unknown faces was investigated using discrimination reaction times (RTs) to stimuli presented tachistoscopically in the right or left visual field. The stimuli were either named or unnamed, familiar or unfamiliar. The two factors of familiarity and naming were varied orthogonally. For male subjects, familiarity precipitated a shift in laterality from a right to a left hemisphere dominance. Naming reduced overall RT. Laterality effects were less clear-cut in females. The results are discussed in relation to current notions concerning differences in information processing modes across the cerebral hemispheres.

INTRODUCTION

A considerable number of studies have used the reaction time technique to assess the relative share of right and left hemisphere components in analyzing visual information. If the identification of certain visual stimuli depends either predominantly or exclusively on the activity of neural mechanisms lateralized to one hemisphere, then reactions to stimuli presented initially in the corresponding (contralateral) visual field should occur quicker and/or more accurately than those following presentation in the alternate visual field (see Milner, 1971).

Face recognition may be counted among that increasing number of potentially hybrid processes that generally yield advantages for left visual field presentation, sometimes parity between the fields, and on occasion a right visual field advantage. Left visual field superiorities have been demonstrated for normal adults in a variety of paradigms, using either actual photographs or "Identikit" faces, Berlucchi, Brizzolara, Marzi, Rizzolatti, and Umiltà (1974); Geffen, Bradshaw, and Wallace (1971); Hilliard, (1973); Moscovitch, Scullion, and Christie (1976); Perez, Mazzucchi, and Rizzolatti (1975); and Rizzolatti, Umiltà, and Berlucchi (1971). Parity has been induced when matching is simultaneous rather than to a memorized target (Moscovitch et al., 1976, Experiment 1); when a series of face recognitions is preceded by a series of word *namings* (but not *recognitions*; see Klein, Moscovitch, & Vigna, 1976, Experiment 1); and for a mixed words/faces series when the words are to be reported first (Klein et al., 1976, Experiment 3). A right visual field advantage has been demonstrated for both discrimination RT's to, and recognition accuracy for, photographs of famous personalities (Marzi, Brizzolara, Rizzolatti, Umiltà, & Berlucchi, 1974). Whereas simultaneous matching of caricatures to photographs of the Beatles yielded faster RT's in the *left* visual field, there were no differences for the two corresponding homogeneous conditions (Moscovitch et al., 1976, Experiment 5).

Using a delayed matching paradigm Buffery (1974) found that cartoon faces were matched more accurately if the match stimulus was presented in the left visual field, independently of target location. Performance approached chance level at the longest delay (16 sec). In replication, Patterson and Bradshaw (1975, Experiment 1) failed to find an overall field difference for geometric patterns arranged in clearly facelike configurations, though at an interstimulus interval (1060 msec) shorter than any Buffery used. Facelike configurations differing from a single memorized target on all three features (eyes, nose, mouth) were matched faster when presented in the left hemifield (Patterson & Bradshaw, 1975, Experiment 2); but if differing on only one feature, this superiority reversed (Patterson & Bradshaw, 1975, Experiment 3). The features used in this last experiment were, it may be noted, also much less discriminable than previously.

Clinical evidence, based on studies of patients with unilateral lesions, has long favored a right hemisphere location for face recognition, though not without some reservations. De Renzi and Spinnler (1966) found greater impairment with right-sided lesions for immediate memory for faces as tested by recognition of a single memorized face among an array of twenty. Correlation with a similar test using abstract figures tempted consideration of the deficit as an essentially perceptual one, restricted to subtle discriminations. Benton and Van Allen (1968) have also demonstrated clear deficits in right hemisphere patients for a simultaneous matching task involving one target, and a match array of six faces of which either one (front views only) or three (array faces differing in either angle of view or lighting) were correct matches. Warrington and James (1967) additionally find that parietal as opposed to temporal lesions compound the deficit. With faces of well-known public personalities, however, this within-hemisphere relation is clearly reversed, whereas the between-hemisphere relation remains. Further, asking patients to name the personalities (as opposed to indicating recognition by profession, etc.) not surprisingly reveals extremely poor performance on the part of left temporal patients.

Milner (1968) required her patients to remember 12 faces subsequently to be recognized from among an array of 25. If the memorizing and test phases were separated by either a filled or unfilled interval of 1.5 min, the group of right temporal patients performed worse than all other lesion groups. With no delay between phases, however, the performances of right temporals, left temporals, and normal controls could not be statistically distinguished. It would appear from these findings that right temporal patients specifically fail to consolidate or rehearse (a number of) memory traces when given the opportunity.

For four split-brain patients, half-faces presented tachistoscopically in the left visual field took perceptual precedence over those presented simultaneously on the right, for recognition-by-pointing; but this laterality effect was reversed for the more difficult recognition-by-naming condition (Levy, Trevarthen, & Sperry, 1972). A somewhat stranger parameter of left hemisphere involvement has been provided by Yin (1970), who found that patients with right hemisphere lesions in fact performed better than those with left-sided lesions, if the faces were inverted.

Superior performance in the left visual field for face recognition tasks, or corresponding deficits with damage to the right hemisphere, is usually referred to a predominance on the part of the right hemisphere for analysis of visuospatial material. Independent substantiation of this predominance for the intact brain, notably in the case of form perception, is uncertain (Kimura & Durnford, 1974). Bryden (1973, 1976) has for instance failed to replicate earlier findings of left field advantages for both dot location and form recognition. Superior recognition of random forms following tachistoscopic left field presentation may only appear with increased complexity (Fontenot, 1973; *contra* Hannay, Rogers, & Durant, 1976, using lagged recognition). Thus, Buffery (1974) found an advantage for left field presentation of the match stimulus in a difficult delayed matching task involving inverted cartoon faces, or scrambled features of those faces.

Inconsistencies elsewhere may be partly due to technique: a left visual field advantage is found for *speed* of simultaneous matching of checkerboard patterns (Gross, 1972), but not for *accuracy* in the identification of such patterns (Kimura & Durnford, 1974). Again, line slants are more accurately identified in the left visual field (Fontenot & Benton, 1972; Kimura & Durnford, 1974), whereas easy line discriminations are performed faster in the right visual field, although this superiority reverses as difficulty increases (Umiltà, Rizzolatti, Marzi, Zamboni, Franzini, Camarda, & Berlucchi, 1974). An explanation in terms of verbal coding for the easier orientations (horizontals, verticals, and $45°$ diagonals, as opposed to mixtures of different diagonals) in this last experiment would not, however, verify the finding that a spatial task (telling the time from an unnumbered clock-face) is more efficiently performed in the left visual field, even with a verbal response (Brizzolara, Umiltà, Marzi, Berlucchi, & Rizzolatti, 1975).

The availability of verbal mediators is indeed a recurrent item on a checklist of parameters promoting right field superiorities in face recognition. In some instances, for example, response mode (Geffen et al., 1971) or instructed priming of verbal processing (Klein et al., 1976) it is fairly clear how this mediation may operate; in others it is not. Do, for instance, famous faces achieve their right field dominance by virtue of their verbal labels (i.e., names) or by virtue of an ease of processing mediated by familiarity? (It may be contended, for instance, that a feature-by-feature analysis, at which the left hemisphere has been claimed to excel [see Cohen, 1973] is, at least logically, only possible when those features have been identified, which identification would surely be assisted by familiarity). The present series of experiments sought to disentangle these factors in four groups of subjects in which the two factors of familiarity and namedness were varied orthogonally.

II.   METHOD

A.   Subjects

A total of 48 males and 48 female students at the University of Bologna took part in the experiment.

All subjects were right-handed, as gauged from a questionnaire on hand usage for twenty activities. Each subject was run individually in one practice session lasting about 45 min, and four experimental sessions lasting about 30 min, on five consecutive days.

B.   Materials

Stimuli were black and white photographic slides of the four male faces used in the Rizzolatti et al. (1971) study, chosen on the basis of their physiognomical similarity, and photographed in a white cap to obscure differences in hair color or style.

C.   Experimental conditions

In condition 1 ("Unfamiliar") subjects began the first practice session without any previous exposure to the stimuli, which were unnamed. In condition 2 ("Named unfamiliar") each stimulus was allotted a name (Carlo, Franco, Mario, Paolo), and subjects had to learn the four names during the practice session. In condition 3 ("Familiar") subjects had been given photographs of the four faces four days prior to the first test session, and instructed to consult the photographs daily in order to learn to recognize them. In condition 4 ("Named familiar") subjects received the same photographs and instructions as for condition 3, but in this case each photograph was named on the reverse side. In order to qualify for the experiment proper, at the first test session, subjects in condition 3 had to recognize the four test faces from among 24 other different faces randomly arranged on a single display card; those subjects in condition 4 additionally had to name the faces correctly.

D. Procedure

Each subject attended for five consecutive daily test sessions, during which he was seated inside a sound-proof room and positioned in a head and chin rest 50 cm in front of a translucent screen. The stimuli were back-projected onto this screen between 5–10° to the right or left of a clearly-marked central fixation point, thereby subtending an angle of 7° 30′ from fixation to the geometric center of the stimulus. Stimuli measured 5 cm in length and 3 cm in width.

Each trial consisted of: an acoustic warning signal for 1 sec, followed 2 sec later by a stimulus tachistoscopically exposed for 100 msec. Intersignal interval was 7 sec. The task was one of discriminative reaction time (RT): the subject held a button in each hand, and to each button two faces were assigned. The hand-to-faces correspondence was balanced over subjects.

During the first practice session, subjects were acquainted with the experimental situation. They were informed of the necessity to fixate the central point after each warning signal, and to respond as quickly and accurately as possible following each stimulus presentation. Subjects then performed blocks of practice trials in each visual field, with feedback regarding accuracy, until they achieved a sequence of 9 out of 10 correct responses (never more than 160 trials in all, usually much less).

Each subsequent test session consisted of four blocks of 40 trials each, of which the first five were practice trials in which the subject was informed of errors. Blocks alternated in visual fields in an ABBA fashion, balanced across subjects within groups.

Median RTs to each stimulus within each block excluding errors, and RTs > 2 sec were computed. These medians were also averaged across sessions to give an overall RT measure for each visual field. Errors were also scored within each field.

III. RESULTS

Two analyses of variance, one for correct RTs and one for numbers of errors, were performed using a five factor mixed design. The three between-subjects factors were: naming (named vs. unnamed stimuli); familiarity (familiar vs.

unfamiliar stimuli); and sex. The two within-subjects factors were: session (first, second, third, and fourth days) and visual field (left vs. right).

For RTs, only two main factors attained significance. RTs improved over test session, $F(3,264) = 81.28$, $p < 0.001$: 890.3 msec in the first, 814.6 msec in the second, 761.8 msec in the third, and 731.5 msec in the fourth. RTs to named stimuli were faster than to unnamed stimuli $F(1,88) = 5.23$, $p < 0.025$: 762.4 msec vs. 836.7 msec. RTs to unfamiliar stimuli were slightly but not significantly faster than to familiar stimuli (793.2 msec vs. 805.9 msec).

Familiarity did, however, interact significantly with visual field, $F(1,88) = 9.11$, $p < 0.005$ (see Fig. 1). The left visual field had an 11.1 msec advantage over the right in the case of unfamiliar faces (787.7 msec vs. 798.8 msec), whereas the right visual field had an 11.8 msec advantage in the case of familiar faces (800.0 msec vs. 811.8 msec). On the other hand there was not the slightest hint of a corresponding interaction between naming and visual field: unnamed stimuli produced RTs of 837.1 msec in the right field and 836.2 msec in the left; whereas for named stimuli the figures were 761.1 msec and 761.6 msec.

Familiarity also intereacted strongly with sex and test session in a three-way interaction: $F(3,264) = 5.86$, $p < 0.001$ (see Fig. 2). RTs for males were marginally faster overall to familiar rather than to unfamiliar stimuli (an effect entirely contributed by scores on day 1); whereas for females the opposite was consistently the case (the contrast appearing most notably again on day 1).

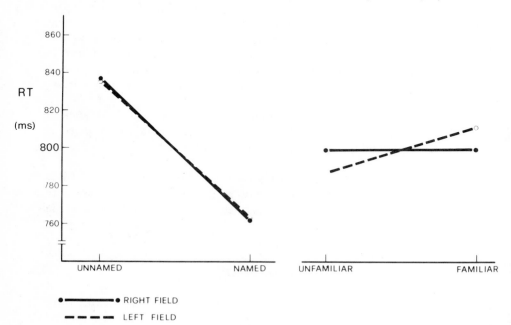

FIG. 1   Effect of naming and familiarity with respect to right and left visual field.

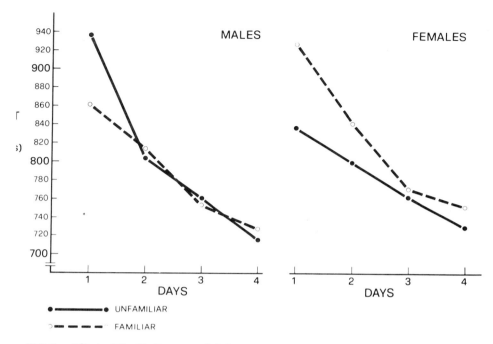

FIG. 2   Effect of familiarity across 4 daily test sessions for males and females separately.

The second order interaction between familiarity, sex, and visual field marginally fails to reach significance: $F(1,88) = 3.63$, $p < 0.1$. Separate t-tests for each of the eight sex x condition groups revealed a slight tendency for significant laterality effects to be found more often among males than females (see Table 1).

TABLE 1
Overall RTs Within Each Field,
for Each Condition

Condition	Males		Females	
Field	R	L	R	L
Unnamed unfamiliar	877	850	820	814
	($p < .05$)		(N.S.)	
Unnamed familiar	828	857	825	824
	($p < .01$)		(N.S.)	
Named unfamiliar	743	748	755	739
	(N.S.)		($p < .05$)	
Named familiar	725	746	824	819
	(N.S.)		(N.S.)	

For males, for unnamed unfamiliar faces, RTs were faster in the left visual field ($t = 2.42$, $p < 0.05$); whereas for unnamed but familiar faces, this reversed to a right visual field advantage ($t = 3.40$, $p < 0.01$). A similar absolute right field advantage for named familiar faces failed to reach significance ($t = 1.68$, NS) although a further six subjects run in this condition later all revealed right field superiorities (of 7, 13, 14, 29, 46, and 62 msec), which would elevate the statistics considerably ($t = 2.55$, $p < 0.05$). For females, only for the named unfamiliar group was there a significant (left) field superiority ($t = 2.20$, $p < 0.05$), no other group remotely approaching conventional levels of significance (ts of 0.42, 0.17, and 0.54). It is perhaps also worth noting that of 32 t-test comparisons of RTs across visual fields (i.e., day-by-day rather than of overall means) only one reached significance.

In the case of the analysis of variance for errors, one must be aware of the possible heterogeneity of variance and covariance of the percentage data. The F statistics for this analysis were assessed against the F required for significance assuming the worst possible degree of heterogeneity of variance and covariance (see Myers, 1966). Thus, conservatively, only the main effect of daily test sessions attained significance: $F(3,264) = 78.46$, $p < 0.001$. The mean percentage of errors was 15.9 on the first day, 11.6 on the second, 9.0 on the third, and 7.4 on the fourth. No other source of variance in the error analysis attained significance.

IV.   DISCUSSION

As already noted, previous experiments using RTs for the discrimination of either actual photographs or facelike designs have generally demonstrated a left visual field (i.e., right hemisphere) advantage (Geffen et al., 1971; Moscovitch et al., 1976; Rizzolatti et al., 1971). One earlier study (Marzi et al., 1974) had, however, suggested that this advantage might switch to the right field, left hemisphere, if the faces were of well-known personalities, indicating possibly a discrimination mediated verbally, i.e. by the relevant name. A similar explanation had been earlier proposed to account for a right field advantage for easy line discriminations (Umiltà et al., 1974). Such an explanation would not by itself suffice in the case of human faces, since those faces to which names may be easily attached tend invariably to be the most familiar. The aim of the present research was to unconfound these two factors of naming and familiarity in the reversibility of the laterality effect for face recognition. The results appear to give a fairly clear answer.

Familiarity is the determining factor for the laterality effect: for unfamiliar faces there is a left field advantage, for familiar faces a right field advantage (see Fig. 1). The opportunity for explicit verbal mediation, i.e. whether or not the stimulus is named, plays no part in this functional localization, neither alone nor in interaction with the factor of familiarity. Whereas one might have expected that the effect of familiarity would have diminished with practice, i.e. that faces initially unfamiliar would become familiar and, consequently, that the left field advantage would reduce or reverse, the relevant interaction — familiarity x visual field x test session — failed to reach significance. It might be noted that the total stimulus exposure over all test sessions was, in real terms, slight (64 sec).

How does familiarity effect this transfer to a right field, left hemisphere advantage? Experiments with human split-brain patients have suggested that the two cerebral hemispheres process faces differently (Levy et al., 1972; Sperry, 1974). According to Sperry (1974), the right hemisphere appears to respond directly to the whole face as a perceptual unit, whereas the left looks for individual characteristics upon which to base its discrimination. Briefly presented familiar stimuli might be recognized on the basis of only one or two characteristics, thereby endowing a left hemisphere advantage. Such a duality of processing modes in the case of human faces, one holistic (right hemisphere), the other analytic (left hemisphere), may be construed in terms of the more general duality of information processing modes: in parallel for the right hemisphere, in series for the left (Cohen, 1973), while noting that the former, in fact, differs from the strictly holistic notion in that it too involves individual features.

Naming, while failing to interact with laterality, is not without an overall effect — witness the clear superiority of those subjects who had to learn to name the stiumulus faces. But why is this overall effect independent of visual field of presentation? One may recall a perhaps similar failure on the part of an explicitly verbal response to deny a right hemisphere advantage for telling the time from an unnumbered clockface (Brizzolara et al., 1975). It would seem from these two results that verbal mediation enters only at the stage of response selection, and not earlier at the stimulus processing stage, thus speeding overall RT independently of initial stimulus location.

The failure to generate laterality effects in females for the unnamed unfamiliar condition (see Table 1) was unexpected, though not without parallel. Recently, for example, Perez et al. (1975), using the same stimuli as in the present study but with go—no go responding for the unnamed unfamiliar condition, also found a right hemisphere advantage limited to males. Of other laterality studies mentioned in the Introduction only Patterson and Bradshaw (1975) included sex as a factor in their statistics, and they found no sex x field interaction. Two other studies (Buffery, 1974; Hilliard, 1973) used only female subjects and did find hemifield effects. However, when significant sex x field interactions have been reported elsewhere in the literature, they have almost always indicated less clear-cut laterality effects in females, for both verbal and nonverbal stimuli (for review see Fairweather, 1976).

Examples of the facilitating effect of familiarity are numerous, the most apposite perhaps being that supplied by Hock (1973) for simultaneous same-different judgments of dot patterns. Rotation and symmetry were also factors in this experiment, and their respective effects correlated. On the basis of this correlation, Hock subsequently divided his subjects into those exhibiting either larger or smaller symmetry effects, dubbing the resultant groups as emphasizing either "structural" or "analytic" modes of processing, respectively. The familiarity factor operated for both groups of subjects, though apparently in different ways. Thus, for the "structural" group, for instance, unfamiliar stimuli were treated as equivalent to rotated familiar stimuli, whereas for the "analytic" group the latter were processed just as fast as unrotated familiar stimuli, in turn inferior only to the unfamiliar. In other words, only for the "analytic" groups had familiarity apparently operated to isolate features. One must, however, be very wary of terminologies. Hock (1973) uses the term "structural" to denote a process by which a whole is *built from parts* (using, for instance, symmetry to achieve this). This use is thus analogous to that of "synthetic" by Cohen (1975) in describing a *left* hemisphere advantage in the use of prior information (name, orientation) for the classification of rotated/unrotated alphanumeric stimuli. The tandem use of "analytic" in both cases denotes a process by which complex visual stimuli are *broken down into parts*, and for which Cohen (1975) claims a *right* hemisphere predominance (for further discussion of individual differences in relation to laterality see Hock, Kronseder, and Corcoran, in preparation).

One may conclude on two methodological notes, one of dilemma and one of caution.

First, the present subject population divided into those who consistently made considerable numbers of errors (albeit within limits acceptable to most laterality researchers), and those for whom an error was comparatively rare. This division is sufficiently balanced for the jettisoning of either group to render the results unrepresentative. Current work in our laboratory indicates that tailoring a task to avoid this division risks failure to generate laterality effects at all. Sophisticated signal detection analysis, and/or of error types, suggest themselves as possible resolutions.

Second, the day-to-day hemifield comparisons almost totally failed to espouse statistical significances. Many of the "failures to replicate," by now legion in the laterality literature, may be explicable in terms of chance findings based on a minimum of trials. It is fast becoming clear that laterality effects ebb and flow, very probably in important ways, with continued practice (see, for example, Kallman & Corballis, 1975; Perl & Haggard, 1975) and serious theoretical advance is likely to be impeded without such consideration.

ACKNOWLEDGMENTS

The writing of this paper was supported in part by a fellowship from the Royal Society of Great Britain (H.F.)

REFERENCES

Benton, A. L., & Van Allen, M. W. Impairment in facial recognition in patients with cerebral disease. *Cortex*, 1968, *4*, 344–358.

Berlucchi, G., Brizzolara, D., Marzi , C. A., Rizzolatti, G., & Umiltà, C. Can lateral asymmetries in attention explain interfield differences in visual perception? *Cortex*, 1974, *10*, 177–185.

Brizzolara, D., Umiltà, C., Marzi, C. A., Berlucchi, G., & Rizzolatti, G. A verbal response in a discriminative reaction time task with lateralised visual stimuli is compatible with a right-hemispheric superiority. *Brain Research*, 1975, *85*, 185.

Bryden, M. P. Perceptual asymmetry in vision: Relation to handedness, eyedness, and speech lateralisation. *Cortex*, 1973, *9*, 418–432.

Bryden, M. P. Response bias and hemispheric differences in dot location. *Perception and Psychophysics,* 1976, *19,* 23–28.

Buffery, A. W. H. Asymmetric lateralisation of cerebral functions and the effects of unilateral brain surgery in epileptic patients. In S. J. Dimond & J. G. Beaumont (Eds.), *Hemisphere function in the human brain*. London: Elek Science, 1974.

Cohen, G. Hemispheric differences in serial versus parallel processing. *Journal of Experimental Psychology*, 1973, *97*, 349–356.

Cohen, G. Hemispheric differences in the utilization of advance information. In P. M. A. Rabbitt & S. Dornic (Eds.), *Attention and performance V*. London: Academic Press, 1975.

De Renzi, E., & Spinnler, H. Facial recognition in brain damaged patients. An experimental approach. *Neurology*, 1966, *16*, 145–152.

Fairweather, H. Sex differences in cognition. *Cognition*, 1976, *4*, 231–280.

Fontenot, D. J. Visual field differences in the recognition of verbal and nonverbal stimuli in man. *Journal of Comparative and Physiological Psychology*, 1973, *85*, 564–569.

Fontenot, D. J., & Benton, A. L. Perception of direction in the right and left visual fields. *Neuropsychologia*, 1972, *10*, 447–452.

Geffen, G., Bradshaw, J. L., & Wallace, G. Interhemispheric effects on reaction time to verbal and nonverbal visual stimuli. *Journal of Experimental Psychology*, 1971, *87*, 415–422.

Gross, M. M. Hemispheric specialisation for processing of visually presented verbal and spatial stimuli. *Perception and Psychophysics*, 1972, *12*, 357–363.

Hannay, H. J., Rogers, J. P., & Durant, R. F. Complexity as a determinant of visual field effects for random forms. *Acta Psychologica*, 1976, *40*, 29–34.

Hilliard, R. D. Hemispheric laterality effects on a facial recognition task in normal subjects. *Cortex*, 1973, *9*, 246–258.

Hock, H. S. The effects of stimulus structure and familiarity on same-different comparison. *Perception and Psychophysics*, 1973, *14*, 413–420.

Hock, S., Kronseder, C., & Corcoran, S. K. Hemispheric asymmetry and individual differences in perceptual processing. (In preparation.)

Kallman, H. J., & Corballis, M. C. Ear asymmetry in reaction time to musical sounds. *Perception and Psychophysics*, 1975, *17*, 368–370.

Kimura, D., & Durnford, M. Normal studies on the function of the right hemisphere in vision. In S. J. Dimond & J. G. Beaumont (Eds.), *Hemisphere function in the human brain*. London: Elek Science, 1974.

Klein, D., Moscovitch, M., & Vigna, C. Attentional mechanisms and perceptual asymmetries in tachistoscopic recognition of words and faces. *Neuropsychologia*, 1976, *14*, 55–66.

Levy, J., Trevarthen, C., & Sperry, R. W. Perception of bilateral chimeric figures following hemispheric deconnexion. *Brain*, 1972, *95*, 61–78.

Marzi, C. A., Brizzolara, D., Rizzolatti, G., Umiltà, C., & Berlucchi, G. Left hemisphere superiority for the recognition of well known faces. *Brain Research,* 1974, *66,* 358.

Milner, B. Visual recognition and recall after right temporal lobe excision in man. *Neuropsychologia*, 1968, *6*, 191–209.

Milner, B. Interhemispheric differences in the localisation of psychological processes. *British Medical Bulletin*, 1971, *27*, 272–277.

Moscovitch, M., Scullion, D., & Christie, D. Early versus late stages of processing and their relation to functional hemispheric asymmetries in face recognition. *Journal of Experimental Psychology: Human Perception and Performance*, 1976, *2*, 401–416.

Myers, J. L. *Fundamental of experimental design.* Boston: Allyn and Bacon, 1966.

Patterson, K., & Bradshaw, J. Differential hemispheric mediation of non-verbal visual stimuli. *Journal of Experimental Psychology: Human Perception and Performance*, 1975, *1*, 246–252.

Perez, E., Mazzucchi, A., & Rizzolatti, G. Tempi di reazione discriminativi alla presentazione di materiale fisiognomico in soggetti maschili e femminili normali. *Bollettino della Società Italiana di Biologia Sperimentale*, 1975, *51*, 1445–1450.

Perl, N., & Haggard, M. Practice and strategy in a measure of cerebral dominance. *Neuropsychologia*, 1975, *13*, 347–352.

Rizzolatti, G., Umiltà, C., & Berlucchi, G. Opposite superiorities of the right and left cerebral hemispheres in discriminative reaction time to physiognomical and alphabetical material. *Brain*, 1971, *94*, 431–442.

Sperry, R. W. Lateral specialisation in the surgically separated hemispheres. In F. O. Schmitt & F. G. Worden (Eds.), *The neurosciences: Third study program*. Cambridge, Mass.: M.I.T. Press, 1974.

Umiltà, C., Rizzolatti, G., Marzi, C. A., Zamboni, G., Franzini, C., Camarda, R., & Berlucchi, G. Hemispheric differences in the discrimination of line orientation. *Neuropsychologia*, 1974, *12*, 165–174.

Warrington, E., & James, M. An experimental investigation of facial recognition in patients with unilateral cerebral lesions. *Cortex*, 1967, *3*, 317–326.

Yin, R. K. Face recognition by brain-injured patients: A dissociable disability? *Neuropsychologia*, 1970, *8*, 395–402.

21

Verbal and Pictorial Processing by Hemisphere as a Function of the Subject's Verbal Scholastic Aptitude Test Score

Neal E. A. Kroll
David J. Madden

Department of Psychology, University of California
Davis, California, United States

ABSTRACT

Visual field differences in a recognition memory task were investigated. A pair of letters (the "memory stimulus," or MS) was presented to the center of the subject's visual field. After various retention intervals, a test stimulus (TS) was presented to either of the visual fields. The subjects decided as rapidly as possible if the two letters in the TS had the same names as the two letters in the MS. The relationship between visual field of presentation and decision time wa was correlated with the subject's Verbal Scholastic Aptitude Test (VSAT) score. This correlation was strongest when the MS and TS had the same names, but different cases. Under these conditions, subjects with low VSAT scores (below 500) tended to respond faster to the TS if it were presented to the right visual field, whereas subjects with high VSAT scores tended to respond faster if it were presented to the left. In a subsequent experiment, subjects were evaluated on various subtests of verbal abilities, and the vocabulary sub-score was found to be the best predictor of the type of visual field effects found both in a letter matching task, as above, and in a similar task using nonsense figures.

I. INTRODUCTION: VISUAL FIELD DIFFERENCES AND INFORMATION PROCESSING

Among the host of psychological questions associated with the development of the tachistoscope are those concerning visual field (VF) differences. Initially, these differences were thought to represent aspects of fundamental perceptual processes, such as scanning habits associated with reading. However, alternative explanations have grown out of the clinical neuropsychological evidence favoring the notion that the cerebral hemispheres play different roles in human cognition (Luria, 1966). Since the arrangement of the visual pathways allows relatively selective stimulus presentation to each cerebral hemisphere, tasks involving tachistoscopic recognition can be employed to differentiate the cognitive functioning of each hemisphere. On the whole, tachistoscipic studies have supported the notions of hemispheric differences arising from neurological data — such as verbal material being best processed by the left hemisphere (e.g., MacKavery, Curcio, & Rosen, 1975) and some types of nonverbal information being best processed by the right hemisphere (e.g., Fontenot, 1973; Kimura, 1969).

The experimental studies have also attempted to specify just what the specialization entails. Whereas early theories held that each hemisphere is specialized for a particular *type of stimulus*, more recent evidence favors specialization based on the *type of analyses* required by the task. For example, Cohen (1973) has concluded that the left hemisphere may be more efficient at processing events in a serial mode, but only when namable events are involved; with nonverbal symbols, both hemispheres apparently employ a parallel mode of analysis. Another dimension that appears both to be important and to interact with the verbal/spatial processing of the information might best be described as the easy/difficult dimension. When comparing faces, subjects make easier comparisons (several features changed) faster when the test-face is presented in the LVF, but make difficult comparisons (a single feature changed) when the test-face is presented in the RVF (Patterson & Bradshaw, 1975). However, when the visual complexity of single letters increases, identification accuracy tends to shift from the RVF to the LVF (Bryden & Allard, 1976). Thus, the processing of information is at least as important in determining VF differences as is the type of information presented. One method of distinguishing some different forms of cognitive processing, and establishing their relation to VF differences, has been the use of the Posner paradigm.

A.   Visual Field Differences in the Posner Paradigm

In the Posner paradigm (e.g., Posner, Boies, Eichelman, & Taylor, 1969), subjects are required to judge if two stimuli (e.g., two alphabetic letters) have the same name ("True") or not ("False"), ignoring transformations of the sensory properties (e.g., changes in the case of the letter). Several researchers have seen the Posner paradigm as an ideal method to approach the study of hemispheric differences in visual information processing, since the same type of stimuli (e.g., letters) are compared either in a mode that allows direct visual comparisons (the Physically Identical, or Same Case [SC] stimuli), or in a mode that apparently requires the subjects to name the stimuli and to compare these names (the Name Identical, or Different Case [DC] stimuli; see Parks & Kroll [1975] for a different interpretation).

1. *Comparison stimuli presented simultaneously to the same VF.*   Experiments using simultaneous presentation have typically found that, in right-handed

subjects, the Physically Identical comparisons can be made more rapidly when the stimuli are both presented to the right hemisphere via the LVF, than if both are presented to the left hemisphere via the RVF. This has been found when SC and DC letter combinations are mixed randomly (Cohen, 1972; Geffen, Bradshaw, & Nettleton, 1972); when only SC letter comparisons are presented, so that any physical change also represents a name change (Geffen, et al., 1972; but see Egeth & Epstein, 1972); when irregular polygons are compared rather than letters (Hellige, 1975); and when subjects are instructed to classify only Physically Identical letters as True (Davis & Schmit, 1973). These experiments also typically find that Name Identical comparisons are made more rapidly when the stimuli are both presented to the RVF, than if both are presented to the LVF. Again, this appears to be true whether SC and DC letter comparisons are mixed randomly (Cohen, 1972; Geffen, et al., 1972) or only DC comparisons are being presented (Davis & Schmit, 1973; Geffen, et al., 1972; but see Hellige, 1975, and his "V-form" subjects). The explanation usually given for the above pattern of results is that the right hemisphere is more efficient at comparing the Physically Identical stimuli along a visuospatial dimension, while the verbal abilities of the left hemisphere render it more efficient with the Name Identical stimuli.

2. *Comparison stimuli presented sequentially.* Experiments presenting comparison stimuli sequentially have had much less success in obtaining clear-cut hemispheric differences. Klatzky (1972) used drawings of familiar objects as stimuli, with different drawings of the same object (and hence having the same name) being analogous to DC letters. She varied the Inter-Stimulus Interval (ISI) among 0.1, 0.5, 1, and 4 seconds and found an association between the response hand and the VF of presentation, but she did not find a relationship between type of comparison (Physical vs. Name Identical) and VF. Wilkins and Stewart (1974), using letter stimuli and ISIs of 50 and 990 msec, also found no evidence in their latency measures for a relationship between the type of comparison and the VF of the second letter (the first letter was always presented centrally). They did report an interaction of VF, Case, and ISI, but only in the error data analysis of what was nearly an error-free task. Thus, though the results from simultaneous presentation have been relatively consistent and easy to interpret, the results from successive presentation have been disappointing, especially since hemispheric differences have been reported in other memory tasks (e.g., Cohen, 1976; Dee, & Fontenot, 1973; Hannay & Malone, 1976; Hines, Satz, & Clementino, 1973; McKeever & Suberi, 1974).

3. *Presenting the comparison stimuli to different VFs.* While most experiments have presented both stimuli to the same VF, two of the above studies (Davis & Schmit, 1973; Klatzky, 1972) allowed the VFs of the two stimuli to vary independently. Both studies found that subjects could respond faster when the stimuli were presented to opposite VFs than when they were both presented to the same VF.

B.   Verbal Abilities and the Posner Paradigm

Hunt (e.g., Hunt, Lunneborg, & Lewis, 1975) has noted that subjects with low
scores on tests of verbal ability tend to show a greater difference between their
decision times for DC and SC matches than do subjects with high verbal scores.
In the Hunt experiments, the subjects compared pairs of single letters that were
presented simultaneously. Kroll and Parks (1978) have recently completed an
experiment in which they were able to obtain Verbal and Quantitative Scholastic Achievement Test (VSAT and QSAT) scores on 90 of their subjects. In
this experiment, double letters were used for memory and test stimuli (MS
and TS), and these MS and TS were separated in time by 8 sec of (a) "Nothing,"
i.e., a blank screen indicated that the subject should sit passively during the retention interval; (b) "Chanting," i.e., a small white dot appearing on the screen
indicated that the subject should repeat aloud the MS letters during the retention
interval (see Parks & Kroll, 1975); or (c) "Arithmetic," i.e., a subtraction task
appeared on the screen (three digits followed by a dash followed by two digits,
all appearing simultaneously in a row with no "carrying" required, e.g., "565–
31") indicated that the subject was required to say the correct answer during
the retention interval.

A significant Posner Effect was found under all three conditions, and the size
of the effect correlated significantly with the subject's VSAT scores under the
Nothing and Chanting conditions, and just missed being significant under the
Arithmetic condition ($t(88) = 1.93$). Table 1 presents these correlations along
with (a) correlations between QSAT scores and Posner Effects under each condition, (b) correlations between the Posner Effect averaged over all three conditions
for each subject and the SAT scores, and (c) the magnitude of the Posner Effect
under each condition for those 28 subjects with VSAT scores that equaled or exceeded 600 and for those 20 subjects with VSAT scores not exceeding 500.

The aspect of the data summarized in Table 1 that is most relevant to the
present discussion is that the relation between Verbal Ability and the Posner
Effect holds up in a memory task as well as it did for Hunt in a simultaneous
comparison task. Thus the VSAT score is a potentially valuable independent
variable that can be studied in conjunction with hemispheric effects, and that
might improve the chances of discovering a hemispheric effect in the Posner
paradigm with successive comparison.

II. EXPERIMENT 1: VERBAL TEST STIMULI PROJECTED
TO LEFT OR RIGHT VF

The first experiment measured the Posner Effect of highly right-handed college
students as a function of their verbal abilities under the following conditions:
(a) Double letters were used as MS and TS. Double letters have been shown to
result in longer lasting Posner Effects than single letters (e.g., Parks & Kroll,

TABLE 1
Correlations Between VSAT and QSAT Scores and the Posner Effect as a
Function of Distractor Task, and the Magnitude of the Posner Effect for Those
Subjects With Highest and Lowest VSAT Scores[a]

*Correlations Between SAT Scores and Posner Effect as a Function
of Distractor Task*

Task:		Nothing	Chanting	Arithmetic	Average
R_{VP}	=	−0.270	−0.305	−0.201	−0.384
R_{QP}	=	−0.186	−0.187	−0.270	−0.331

Magnitude of Posner Effect as a Function of Distractor Task (msec.)

Task:	Nothing	Chanting	Arithmetic
Top 28:	45	40	25
Bottom 20:	91	98	54

[a] P = Posner Effect = (RT for Same Name, Diff Case) − (RT for Same
Name, Same Case)
   V = Verbal SAT score
   Q = Quantitative SAT score
   R_{VQ} = 0.623; N = 90; R required for $a < 0.05 = 0.209$.

1975) and thus seem more appropriate when the relationship between memory
and hemispheric effects is under investigation. (b) Only the TS were presented to
the sides, and the MS were always presented to the center, to reduce the possibility of encoding and processing interactions. (c) Retention intervals of 0.5, 1,
2, and 4 sec were used to see if any effects found were stable or changing over
time. (d) Subjects responded via a yoked double lever (one for each hand) to
reduce field by hand interactions.

A. Method

1. *Subjects.* Seventy-two undergraduates (visual acuity 20/20 ±10, corrected) participated in the experiment and were given credit in their introductory psychology courses as compensation. At the end of the experimental session
subjects completed the 20-item form of the Edinburgh Handedness Inventory
(Oldfield, 1971). Only those 38 demonstrating a right-handed laterality quotient
at the fifth decile or higher were included in the present report. These 38 subjects
were divided by their scores on the VSAT, obtained from college entrance
records. The 23 subjects (7 males, 16 females) who scored 500 or higher on the
VSAT were designated as High Verbal (12 in the 0.5-2 second intervals and 11 in
the 1–4 intervals). The remaining 15 subjects (3 males, 12 females) who scored
below 500 were designated Low Verbal (7 in the 0.5-2 and 8 in the 1–4 intervals).

2. *Stimuli.*   The MS and TS were the 12 possible paired combinations of the upper and lower case forms of the letters J, N, and R. Each letter pair contained an upper and a lower case letter, and letters were not repeated within pairs. On each trial, the subject decided as rapidly as possible whether the TS letter pair had the same names as the previously presented MS letter pair (a true match) or different names (a False match). The MS and TS letter pairs could either be the same or different in case and this relationship was orthogonal to, and logically independent of, the True/False classification. Case changes always involved both letters. On False trials, only one letter of the MS was changed in the TS, left and right letters were replaced equally often.

3. *Design.*   The MS were presented to the center of the subject's VF and the TS were presented to either the LVF or the RVF. The letter pairs were rear-projected onto a plexiglass screen at a viewing distance of 191 cm from the subject. The TS appeared at a point displaced 10 cm (3°) to the left or right of the midline of the viewing screen and were 5 cm (1.5°) in width. Duration of both the MS and TS was 150 msec. Viewing was binocular and subjects used a chinrest to reduce head movement.

The two values of each of the independent variables of TS VF (LVF, RVF), Name Match (True, False), Case (SC, DC), and Retention Interval (Short, Long) were factorially combined to form 16 different trial types. There were two instances of each trial type in each block of 32 trials and, within each block, the order of the trial types was random, with the constraint that no runs greater than three were allowed for a particular VF or a True/False match.

4. *Procedure.*   Each subject was given a written description of the stimuli, possible case changes, and instructions indicating that the task was to decide as rapidly and accurately as possible whether the MS and TS had same or different names. They were also instructed that the TS would appear randomly to the left or right, so that the best strategy was to fixate on the center of the screen at all times. A 500 msec dot appeared prior to the onset of the TS to help fixation. The subject simultaneously moved two levers, one in each hand, to indicate the decision. Half of the original 72 subjects moved both levers toward themselves for True and away for False; the other half used the opposite arrangement. These response levers were yoked, and their displacement from a resting position stopped a clock that had started running at the termination of the TS. The true/false decision time was recorded to an upper limit of 1500 msec. Errors were discarded from the reaction time analysis. Each subject was tested in two half-hour sessions on different days – the first session consisting of a practice block of 32 trials, plus three blocks of experimental trials; the second consisting of eight practice trials, plus another three blocks of experimental trials – a total of 192 experimental trials.

In summary, the sequence of events in each trial was: (1) a 150 msec MS in the center of the screen, (2) a variable retention interval of 0.5, 1, 2, or 4 sec,

including a fixation dot during the last 500 msec, (3) a 150 msec TS presented 3°
to the left or right of center, and (4) the subject's response.

B. Results

Since the error rate was less than 5% in any of the conditions, only the reaction
time data were analyzed. A mean reaction time was computed for each subject
for each of the 16 trial types. An inspection of the data indicated that, with the
exception of the shortest interval (see the Discussion section below), the hemispheric effects were more closely related to a subject's VSAT score than they
were to the retention interval. Therefore, new averages were computed, collapsing
over retention intervals, and subjects were separated by their VSAT scores. A
VSAT score of 495 was used as the dividing point between Low and High Verbals, since that was approximately the intercept of the line of best fit relating
VSAT and the magnitude of the difference in reaction times between RVF and
LVF conditions of the True, DC trials [RT_d = 0.226(VSAT) $-$ 111.60, r =
$-0.366, p < 0.05$].

Since Low and High Verbals did not differ in their True, SC performance, the
comparison between RVF and LVF was treated as if there were one group of 38
subjects. This comparison found that RVF presentation results in significantly
faster decision times than does LVF presentation under true, SC conditions
($t(37)$ = $-2.85, p < 0.01$). To test the different VF effect on Low and High Verbals under True, DC conditions, a reaction time difference score was found for

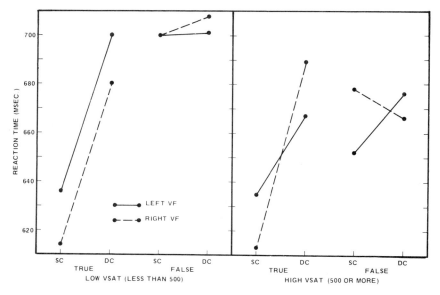

FIG. 1.   Average reaction times for correct decisions as a function of the subject's VSAT
score, the correct classification, the case relationship, and the visual field of presentation.

each subject ($RT_{RVF} - RT_{LVF}$) and a between groups test was performed and found to be significant ($t(36) = 3.01$, $p < 0.01$). Since both the sizes of the two groups (23 highs, 15 lows) and their standard deviations (41.63, 59.64) differed, this latter analysis was recomputed using a Behrens distribution instead of a student-t (Phillips, 1973), and was still found to be significant ($d(14, 22) = 2.84$, $p < 0.01$).

In comparing High and Low Verbals on the size of their Posner Effects (True, DC − True, SC), the difference between these groups was not significant, either when averaged over visual fields ($t(36) = 1.24$) or when compared on LVF only ($t(36) = 1.74$). The correlations between Posner Effect and VSAT also lacked significance (Averaged over VF, $r = -0.231$; LVF, $r = -0.244$). This lack of a significant difference in size of Posner Effect between High and Low Verbals might be due to the task differences (i.e., the present use of hemifield presentation) or simply to the smaller number of subjects in the present study, since the correlations are not much lower than they were in the Kroll and Parks (1978) study (-0.231 here vs. -0.270 in their "Nothing" condition).

C. Discussion

Unlike earlier Posner paradigm experiments using successive comparisons, Experiment 1 did find significant VF effects related to type of processing required (i.e., SC/DC stimuli). Surprisingly, these effects are not very similar to those previously found with simultaneous comparisons. In fact, the results from the High Verbal subjects over the three longer retention intervals are exactly the opposite from the expectations based on the simultaneous comparisons. At the 0.5 sec retention interval, both High and Low Verbal subjects performed faster with RVF presentation under both SC and DC conditions. This RVF superiority for even Physical Identical comparisons for all subjects at the shortest retention interval, and for Low Verbal subjects at all retention intervals, might be related to the increased difficulty of comparing pairs of letters over the more usual task of comparing single letters. (See the introduction for a discussion of the effects of increasing task difficulty.) Of more concern to us, however, was the difference between High and Low Verbal subjects at the longer retention intervals. Since subjects were differentiated on their verbal abilities, we were curious as to the importance of the use of verbal stimuli (letters) and to the precise verbal ability relevant to the observed effect.

III. EXPERIMENT 2: PICTORIAL TS PROJECTED TO LVF OR RVF

The second experiment differed from the first in the following ways: (a) Only half of the subjects were run with the letter stimuli, the other half were presented with pictorial stimuli (Gibson figures) for MS and TS. As with the letter stimuli, one transformation between MS and TS was irrelevant to the subject's classification. With letters, the irrelevant transformation was "case"; with figures, it was "orientation." (b) In addition to choosing subjects on the basis of their VSAT scores on record, they were given another examination of their verbal abilities. (c) The exposure duration of the TS was reduced to decrease the possibility of eye movements during exposure. (d) All trials were run at the same (1 sec) retention interval.

A. Method

1. *Subjects.*   Forty-eight subjects survived the screening for right-handedness and visual acuity, and were allowed to choose either class credit or five dollars as compensation. Twenty-four subjects (7 males, 17 females) with VSAT scores of 510 or higher were designated High Verbal; 24 (5 males, 19 females) with VSAT scores of 490 or lower were designated Low Verbal. Since one High Verbal and eight Low Verbal subjects did not complete the experiment, the data on only 39 subjects are presented.

2. *Stimuli.*   The same combinations of MS and TS letter-pairs used in Experiment 1 were also used with the Letter Group (5 males, 15 females). For the Figure Group (4 males, 15 females), three items were chosen from a series of letter-like figures developed by Gibson, Gibson, Pick, and Osser (1962). A nonverbal analogy to upper and lower cases was developed by presenting each of these new items in both an upright and 180° rotation orientation. Each normally-oriented figure and its rotated counterpart was combined into 12 figure-pairs that allowed for the same type of counterbalancing that had been applied to the letter-pairs. As with the letters, only one figure of the MS pair was replaced to form a False TS. Figure 2 illustrates these figure-pairs and the possible relations between MS and TS.

3. *Design.*   The two values of each of the independent variables of TS VF (LVF, RVF) Match Decision (True, False), and Orientation or Case (Same, Different) were factorially combined to form eight different trial types. There were four examples of each trial type in each block of 32 trials, and each block was randomized as in Experiment 1. The size of the new figure stimuli and TS position in the LVF and RVF were identical to those of the letter-pairs.

4. *Procedure.*   Subjects completed the recognition memory test in a single session in which they received instructions, 16 practice trials, and three experimental blocks of letter or figure stimuli. The original 24 subjects in each VSAT group were counterbalanced with regard to their order of appearance in the laboratory, with their receiving letter or figure stimuli, and with response lever direction. The sequence of events in a particular trial, except for the retention interval (now a constant 1 second) and TS duration (now only 100 msec), was identical to that of Experiment 1.

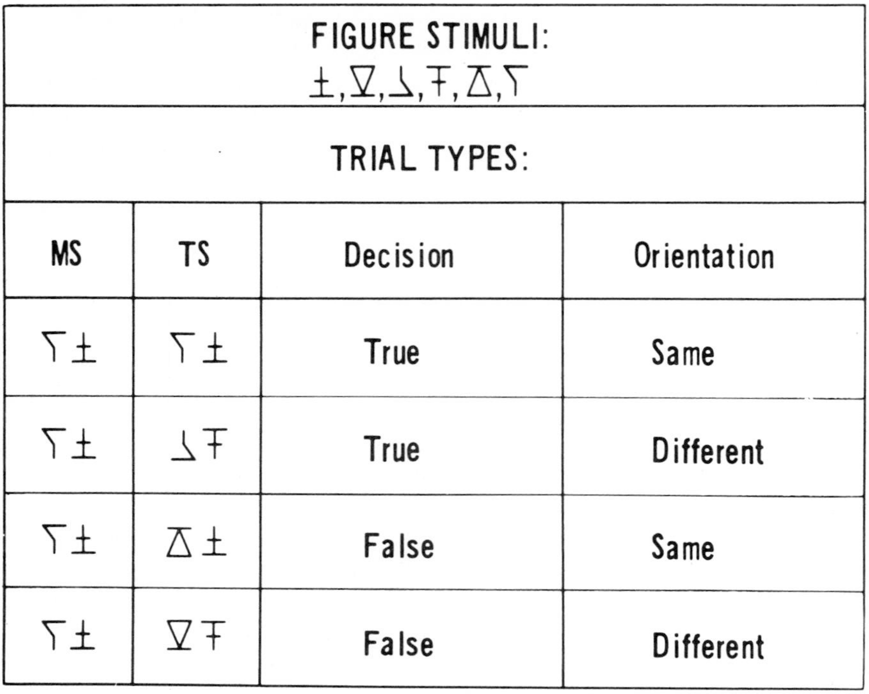

FIGURE STIMULI: ±,▽,⅃,Ŧ,△,⅂			
TRIAL TYPES:			
MS	**TS**	Decision	Orientation
⅂±	⅂±	True	Same
⅂±	⅃Ŧ	True	Different
⅂±	△±	False	Same
⅂±	▽Ŧ	False	Different

FIG. 2.   Example of trial types for Figure stimuli.

In addition to the recognition memory task, each subject subsequently completed a 90 minute battery of three tests constructed on the basis of questions in a manual sold to prepare students for taking the SAT. The tests were designed to evaluate vocabulary, reading comprehension, and English usage.

B. Results

The assumption underlying the plan of Experiment 2 was that one of the VSAT subtests would be more highly predictive of the experimental effects than would the overall test. In looking at those effects appearing to be the most important in Experiment 1 (True, DC, LVF/RVF; True, LVF, DC/SC; and True, Case x VF), a consistently higher correlation was found between these effects and the subjects' vocabulary scores than between these effects and any other set of test scores. This was true both within groups and combined over groups (see Table 2). The correlation between Vocabulary and (1) True, DC, LVF/RVF was −0.380 in the Letter Groups and −0.422 in the Figure Group, (2) True, LVF, DC/SC was −0.405 and −0.460, and (3) True, Case x VF was 0.326 and 0.396. Since the Vocabulary scores seem to be the best predictors of the effects of interest, subjects in both Letter and Figure groups were separated into High and

TABLE 2
Correlations Between Selected Experimental Effects and Test Scores

	Experiment 2 (Combined Sample, N = 39)					Experiment 1
	Vocab.	Read.	English	VSAT	QSAT	VSAT (N = 38)
True, Diff Case (Left-Right VF)	−0.414	−0.273	−0.080	−0.260	−0.323	−0.366
True, Left VF (Diff-Same Case)	−0.427	−0.155	−0.052	−0.225	−0.300	−0.244
Case X VF	0.367	0.304	0.097	0.323	0.316	0.261

Low Vocabulary groups, with subjects having a score higher than 50 being placed in the High Vocabulary Group. (Over all 39 subjects, the mean Vocabulary score was 51.23, with a standard deviation of 9.79 and a range from 27 to 70.) This division resulted in 11 High and 9 Low subjects in the Letter Group, and 9 High and 10 Low subjects in the Figure Group. The average reaction times for High and Low Vocabulary subjects is presented in Figure 3.

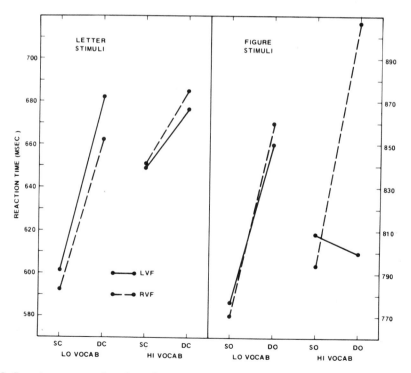

FIG. 3. Average reaction times for correct True decisions as a function of the type of stimuli, the subject's Vocabulary score, the case or orientation relationship, and the visual field of presentation.

The results of the Letter Group, plotted as a function of vocabulary instead of VSAT, do not resemble the results of thef first experiment as much as one would like. These differences might be attributable to the decreased duration of the TS which resulted in an increased error rate and possibly different speed/ accuracy tradeoffs in the different conditions (see the discussion following).[1] In the presentation of the results, effects are analyzed both by each stimulus condition separately (i.e., Letters and Figures) and combined. The analyses on combined groups are to demonstrate the robustness of the effects — not an attempt to ignore the possible differences in processing that might be required by the two types of stimuli, or by the two types of transformations used. It should be emphasized that the Different Orientation condition of the Figure Group allows for a very different sort of transformation (i.e., rotation) than that which is generally assumed to be required by the Different Case condition of the Letter Group (i.e., naming). However, there is also the possibility that *both* groups are doing the same thing — comparing the TS with both possible visual representations of the MS — and that neither rotation nor naming is really involved in the decision-making process. This possibility fits in quite well with some of the current theories concerning the Posner Effect (e.g., Parks & Kroll, 1975). Another possibility is that one hemisphere can make the required transformation, whereas the other hemisphere must retrieve the possible representations and make comparisons. Yet another possibility is that the Low Verbal subjects fit one of the above explanations, and the High Verbal subjects fit another. Unfortunately, the current results do not allow a decision among these possibilities. However, since those aspects of the first experiment that replicate show up more strongly in the Figure Group, one is tempted to say that these data are most in agreement with the notion that letters and figures are processed similarly, at least by High Verbal subjects.

The superiority of RVF presentation, seen in both SC and DC conditions for Low VSAT subjects and in the SC condition for the High VSAT subjects of Experiment 1, is much less evident in this second experiment. The RVF superiority seen with the Low Vocabulary subjects in the Letter Group is not significant ($t(8) = 1.13$). However, the interaction between Group and VF on True, DC and DO trials remains. This tendency for Highs to respond faster to LVF than RVF is significantly greater than is the tendency for Lows to do so, for both overall subjects ($t(37) = 2.14$, $p < 0.05$) and for the Figure Group alone ($t(18) = 1.11$).

Looking at the Posner Effect (DC/SC) averaged over VF as a function of test scores, we find that this also correlates most highly with the Vocabulary scores,

---

[1]We are currently working on a series of experiments designed to answer some of the questions raised by these experiments. As of this writing, only High Vocabulary subjects have been run with Verbal stimuli. Under conditions that lower the error rate, the pattern of results being obtained is nearly identical with that found in the first experiment for High VSAT subjects.

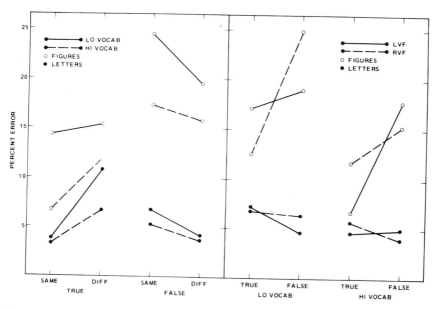

FIG. 4.   Average percentage of error in Experiment 2, collapsing over visual field in the left panel, and collapsing over case and orientation relationships in the right panel.

both overall (−0.233 for Vocabulary vs. −0.008 for VSAT) and for the Verbal (−0.334 vs. −0.260) and Figure (−0.222 vs. + 0.145) groups. In terms of the High and Low Vocabulary groups, the Lows had a significantly greater Posner Effect with Letters ($t(18) = 2.14, p < 0.05$) and overall ($t(37) = 2.19, p < 0.05$), but not with Figures alone ($t(17) = 1.09$). However, even in the Figure Group, the Posner Effect is significantly greater for the Lows with LVF presentation ($t(17) = 2.68, p < 0.02$).

Subjects obviously had a great deal more difficulty dealing with the unfamiliar figures than with the letters. This difficulty shows up both in the longer reaction times and in the number of errors. Figure 4 presents the error data for Experiment 2 and, since the False errors tend to be more stable across subjects than the False reaction times, the errors are given for False as well as True trials.

The most striking effect evident in the error data is the interaction of True/False by VF by Low/High Vocabulary score. In the Figure Groups, this effect seems to be caused by the Low subjects being relatively unbiased when the TS is presented to the LVF, but being heavily biased toward True when the TS is presented to the RVF. The Highs, on the other hand, appear to be just the opposite, showing a stronger true bias with the LVF presentation. This three-way interaction was significant with the Figure Group ($t(17) = 2.31, p < 0.05$) and with all subjects combined ($t(37) = 2.63, p < 0.02$), but not with the Letter Group alone ($t(18) = 1.25$).

IV. DISCUSSION

Although the second experiment did not completely replicate the pattern of results found in the first, possibly because of the increased error rate, several important findings did replicate and several interesting conclusions appear warranted.

The verbal abilities of the subject, as measured by the VSAT or apparently more accurately by the Vocabulary test, can be used as a partial predictor of not only the magnitude of the Posner Effect (Hunt et al., 1975; Kroll & Parks, 1978), but also the difference in Posner Effect between hemispheres. High Verbals are more likely to show a LVF-RH superiority on DC comparisons and Low Verbals are more likely to show a RVF-LH superiority. Since Hellige (1975) found a LVF and RVF difference in superiority on DC trials as a function of the subject's performance on an eyelid conditioning task, one wonders if "V-form responders" are likely to also score higher on vocabulary tests than "C-form responders."

The High Verbals tend to show the strongest hemispheric differences in that they show different patterns for the left and right VF presentations on same and different case (orientation) comparisons, and they maintain their hemispheric differences across stimulus conditions. There are at least two possible explanations for the High Verbals showing a stronger hemispheric effect: (1) they are more likely to have hemispheric specialization with regard to processes involved in performing the Posner Task, and (2) the Posner Task and the vocabulary test are both speed-comparison tasks that tax the Low Verbal subject's ability to use retrieval and comparison processes in the most efficient manner. In either case, the data of the present experiments suggest that the Low Verbals carry out the same type of processing with both hemispheres, although the RVF-LH might be somewhat more efficient when the stimuli are verbal (letters). However, the High Verbals, at least with these relatively simple stimuli separated by a retention interval of at least 0.5 seconds, are apparently doing different kinds of processing in the two different hemispheres, with the RVF-LH more efficient in making Physically Identical comparisons and with the LVF-RH more efficient in making Formally Equivalent comparisons. If we assume that, when both MS and TS are shown to the center, High Verbals have each Hemisphere processing the information in its most efficient manner, and further assume that subjects can respond on the basis of the first comparison completed, we would predict that High Verbals would show a smaller Posner Effect than Low Verbals — which they do.

The next question would be: How are the hemispheres of the High Verbals processing the information to give us this pattern? The present data gives no clues concerning the answers to this question, but one possibility will be suggested that seems in line with what is known about both the Posner Effect and about hemispheric differences. Since the left hemisphere appears to process information serially (Cohen, 1973), one might assume that the left hemisphere first compares the TS against the memory image of the MS, and only if this comparison fails does the left hemisphere try other possibilities (either a transformation or a comparison with alternatives that must be retrieved or generated). The right hemisphere, however, has a preference for parallel processing (Cohen, 1973), which in this case might mean that both alternative representations of the MS are retrieved or generated, and the TS is compared with both representations more-or-less simultaneously (Parks & Kroll, 1975). However, the representation presented as the MS might still be expected to be compared somewhat faster.

In conclusion, the present experiments find that, when MS and TS are more complex than single letters (i.e., pairs of letters or Gibson figures) and when the data from Low Vocabulary subjects are removed from the analysis, hemispheric effects can be observed in a Posner task with successive presentation. The pattern of results, however, are the opposite from those expected by theory and found with simultaneous presentation. Future work must be done to ferret out the effects from stimulus complexity and role of memory processes before we will be able to fully understand what this result pattern is telling us about the possible differential processing of information by the two hemispheres.

ACKNOWLEDGMENTS

This research was supported by a grant from The University of California to the first author. Mr. Dean Malley provided technical assistance.

REFERENCES

Bryden, M., & Allard, F. Visual hemifield differences depend on typeface. *Brain and Language, 1976, 3,* 191–200.

Cohen, G. Hemispheric differences in a letter classification task. *Perception & Psychophysics, 1972, 11,* 139–142.

Cohen, G. Hemispheric differences in serial versus parallel processing. *Journal of Experimental Psychology, 1973, 97,* 349–356.

Cohen, G. Components of the laterality effect in letter recognition: Asymmetries in iconic storage. *Quarterly Journal of Experimental Psychology, 1976, 28,* 105–114.

Davis, R., & Schmit, V. Visual and verbal coding in the interhemispheric transfer of information. *Acta Psychologica, 1973, 37,* 229–240.

Dee, H., & Fontenot, H. Cerebral dominance and lateral differences in perception and memory. *Neuropsychologia, 1973, 11,* 167–173.

Egeth, H., & Epstein, J. Differential specialization of the cerebral hemispheres for the perception of sameness and difference. *Perception & Psychophysics, 1972, 12,* 218–220.

Fontenot, D. Visual field differences in the recognition of verbal and nonverbal stimuli in man. *Journal of Comparative and Physiological Psychology, 1973, 85,* 564–569.

Geffen, G., Bradshaw, J., & Nettleton, N. Hemispheric asymmetry; verbal and spatial encoding of visual stimuli. *Journal of Experimental Psychology, 1972, 95,* 25–31.

Gibson, E. J., Gibson, J. J., Pick, A. D., & Osser, H. A. A developmental study of the discrimination of letter-like forms. *Journal of Comparative and Physiological Psychology, 1962, 55,* 897–906.

Hannay, H., & Malone, D. Visual field effects and short-term memory for verbal material. *Neuropsychologia,* 1976, *14,* 203–209.

Hellige, J. Hemispheric processing differences revealed by differential conditioning and reaction time performance. *Journal of Experimental Psychology: General,* 1975, *104,* 309–326.

Hines, D., Satz, P., & Clementino, T. Perceptual and memory components of the superior recall of letters from the right visual half-fields. *Neuropsychologia,* 1973, *11,* 175–180.

Hunt, E., Lunneborg, C., & Lewis, J. What does it mean to be high verbal? *Cognitive Psychology,* 1975, *7,* 194–227.

Kimura, D. Spatial localization in the left and right visual fields. *Canadian Journal of Psychology,* 1969, *23,* 445–458.

Klatzky, R. Visual and verbal coding of laterally presented pictures. *Journal of Experimental Psychology,* 1972, *96,* 439–448.

Kroll, N. E. A., & Parks, T. E. Interference with short-term visual memory produced by concurrent central processing. *Journal of Experimental Psychology: Human Learning and Memory,* 1978, *4,* No. 2, 111–120.

Luria, A. *Higher cortical functions in man.* New York: Basic Books, 1966.

Mackavery, W., Curcio, F., & Rosen, J. Tachistoscopic word recognition performance under conditions of simultaneous bilateral presentation. *Neuropsychologia,* 1975, *13,* 27–33.

McKeever, M., & Suberi, M. Parallel but temporally displaced visual half-field metacontrast functions. *Quarterly Journal of Experimental Psychology,* 1974, *26,* 258–265.

Oldfield, R. C. The assessment of handedness: The Edinburgh inventory. *Neuropsychologia,* 1971, *9,* 97–111.

Patterson, K., & Bradshaw, J. Differential hemispheric mediation of nonverbal visual stimuli. *Journal of Experimental Psychology: Human Perception and Performance,* 1975, *1,* 246–252.

Parks, T. E., & Kroll, N. E. A. Enduring visual memory despite forced verbal rehearsal. *Journal of Experimental Psychology: Human Learning and Memory,* 1975, *1,* 648–654.

Phillips, L. D. *Bayesian statistics for social scientists.* New York: Crowell, 1973.

Posner, M. I., Boies, S. J., Eichelman, W. H., & Taylor, R. Retention of visual and name codes of single letters. *Journal of Experimental Psychology Monographs,* 1969, *79,* No. 1, Part 2.

Wilkins, A., & Stewart, A. The time course of lateral asymmetries in visual perception of letters. *Journal of Experimental Psychology,* 1974, *102,* 905–908.

22 Between-Hand vs. Within-Hand Choice-RT: A Single Channel of Reduced Capacity in the Split-Brain Monkey

Yves Guiard
Jean Requin
Institut de Neurophysiologie et Psychophysiologie C.N.R.S.
Marseille, France

ABSTRACT

The present work, using two intact-brain and two split-brain baboons, investigated the role of forebrain commissures in the performance of a choice-RT task, in which one of two equiprobable left and right visual dots served as stimulus, and the response consisted of a binary choice between hands.

In *Experiment 1,* it was found that the two split-brain monkeys were unable to carry out the choice task, whereas the two control monkeys reached fairly high accuracy scores.

In *Experiment 2,* conducted in the two split-brain monkeys, it was shown that their choice inability resulted not from a deficit in some input stage, but clearly from a deficit in the ability to select the response from a bimanual motor repertoire.

A double channel interpretation of this result, which assumed that the deficit was due to the inability of the stimulated hemisphere to prevent its irrelevant competitor from making the erroneous response, was not supported by the results of *Experiment 3.* In this experiment, while one go signal was dispatched to one hemisphere, one no-go signal was simultaneously dispatched to the other hemisphere. Such additional information left the accuracy scores unimproved in both split-brain monkeys.

Finally, an alternative model was proposed, based on the general assumption that the two cerebral hemispheres are alternately activated in bilateral tasks. This model accounted for the dramatic choice deficit observed in the split-brain monkeys by hypothesizing that commissurotomy critically reduces the speed of the attentional interhemispheric switching mechanism, thereby prohibiting the fast correction of erroneous lateralized motor set.

Preliminary tests, through the analysis of sequential effects and of latencies of correct and incorrect responses in both operated and control animals, yielded reasonable support of this model. In turn, the model may provide a new look at some classical results in the field of split-brain studies.

I. INTRODUCTION

One of the most significant issues of the last quarter of century in the field of experimental psychology has been the finding that the central nervous system behaves in an intermittent way (Craik, 1947, 1948) when responding to a continuously changing environment. This discovery led to the Single Channel Model of the brain (Welford, 1952, 1967), which received considerable support in studies of the so-called psychological refractory period (see Bertelson, 1966, for a review). Since then, and particularly with the development of work on selective attention, the single channel concept has remained a core tool, both for generating experiments and conceiving interpretive models (Kahneman, 1973; Moray, 1969).

During the same period the problem of the neuroanatomical substrate of attentional capacity was approached in a large body of clinical and experimental studies on the bisected brain, starting with the work of Myers and Sperry (Myers, 1956; Myers & Sperry, 1953; Sperry, 1961). But this research trend developed with the purpose of demonstrating that splitting cerebral structures led to a splitting of cerebral functions. This double channel model of the split-brain was not always assumed in its crude version, according to which the split-brain patient has a duplex conscious activity (Dimond, 1972; Gazzaniga, 1970; Sperry, 1968). As a rule, nonetheless, the model appears implicit in the split-brain literature.

A critical evaluation of the double channel theory leads to two principal observations: first, this theory is not unique in being able to explain the basic finding of split-brain research, that is, a deficit in the cross integration of the two sensorimotor half-fields. For example, such a deficit might just as easily be accounted for in terms of one hemisphere being suppressed, or inactive during the testing.

Second, until now, this theory has not been supported by any direct experimental evidence. Gazzaniga and Sperry (1966) and Gazzaniga and Young (1967) made critical tests of the ability of split-brain patients and monkeys to carry out two simultaneous independent visuomotor tasks involving the hemispheres separately. Although the authors interpreted the outcome as evidence for the double channel view, claiming that "splitting the brain increases the information capacity (...) for tasks not requiring integration of the two hemispheres" (Gazzaniga & Young, 1967, p. 371), their results were largely held as inconclusive, and in fact, could never be replicated. Kreuter, Kinsbourne, and Trevarthen (1972), on the other hand, found that "the attention mechanism in commissurotomy patients is of less capacity than prior to operation, rather than double" in a bilateral tapping task. Moreover, a number of consistent findings in the split-brain literature, such as unilateral neglects (Teng & Sperry, 1974) ear suppressions in dichotic listening tasks (Milner, Taylor & Sperry, 1968; Sparks & Geschwind, 1968; Springer & Gazzaniga, 1975), or the lack of recall interference in animals after a reversed learning with different hemispheres of a binary discrimination (Myers, 1965; Trevarthen, 1962), provide strong evidence against any double channel model. Finally, one finds it difficult to believe that commissurotomy creates two separate mental realms, when the behavioral innocuousness of this surgery has been repeatedly emphasized in epileptic patients, and regularly confirmed in experimental animals.

Thus, the double channel model of the split-brain appears somewhat arbitrary. Why, then, has it been so widely accepted, particularly in the field of neuropsychological research? One possible reason could be that this model conforms strictly to the classical notion of a hierarchical nevraxial organization linking "higher" attentional functions to recent structures and "lower" automatic functions with ancient structures. If applied in a simplistic way to the bisected brain, this notion generates, quite naturally, the double channel view. More than a century ago, Fechner (1860) conceived that, if it were possible to divide the brain longitudinally in the midline, a divided stream of consciousness would result (quoted by Zangwill, 1976). As far as the attentional function is held as a neocortical secretion, the discrepancy between unity of conscious experience and duplicity of cortical structures must be solved with the assumption that the forebrain commissures subserve a concerting function, because of which two potentially autonomous cortices behave in harmony.

But another way of reconciling the notion of two cortices with a unitary attentional process is to hypothesize that some attention-distribution center, located in a subcortical unitary structure (for example, the reticular formation of the brain-stem), shares the attentional energy, conceived of as limited in amount, between two cortices, viewed as peripheral computers (Trevarthen, 1974). According to this alternative model, the commissural bridge would no longer be a unifying structure but rather an assisting device, serving a stabilizing function in the interhemispheric distribution of attentional energy (Kinsbourne, 1974). With sectioned commissures, the model would still predict a single channel of attention, but one of decreased capacity due to some impairment of the distribution function.

The present experiments investigate the ability of split-brain monkeys to perform an interhemispheric choice-RT task, one involving a fast choice between two equiprobable left and right manual responses. These experiments provide the opportunity of discussing alternative models of an increased vs. decreased capacity in the split-brain. The former model would predict no deficit in the split-brain animals, neither in terms of speed nor in terms of accuracy, since such a task should require no cross-talk between hemispheres, and might then be properly achieved through a parallel functioning of the isolated hemispheres.

The latter model, assuming that the control of both left and right sensorimotor half-spaces requires a fast sequential scanning (i.e. fast changes in the sharing of attention between left and right sides of space) would predict a consistent impairment of performance if the commissural switching device is destroyed.[1]

II. PROCEDURE

In the monkey, learning of a choice-RT task involves long and delicate periods of training, precluding the use of large samples. Indeed, a serious difficulty was encountered by the monkeys in having to comply with both speed and accuracy requirements. This typical difficulty may possibly explain why most of the behavioral experiments involving animals distinguish between speed and accuracy requirements into separate training programs. Nevertheless, inasmuch as the present study was concerned with the temporal and spatial distribution of processing capacity, choice-RT procedures appeared particularly suitable; since an RT task may be assumed as requiring the whole subject's capacity, variations in RT or in error rate may be reasonably interpreted in terms of variations in the distribution along time or between events of some constant attentional amount.

A. Subjects

Four adult baboons (*Papio papio*) were used in the experiments. Two of them had undergone split-brain surgery, i.e. complete midsagittal division of Corpus Callosum, Anterior Commissure, and a midsagittal division of the optic chiasm. The two others were intact-brain controls; one of these had undergone the chiasm division only, and therefore served as a secondary control. All the surgery was performed before training.

B. Apparatus

The experiments were performed in a sound isolated and dimly illuminated cubicle. The monkey was free-moving in a Trevarthen's working cage equipped in its front side with two arm apertures and a mask supporting a pair of spectacles fitted with polaroid filters of opposed orientations (Trevarthen, 1972). A work-panel 20 cm away from the cage consisted of two light-emitting diodes, red in color, located at eye level 5 cm apart horizontally, and 16 cm below, two response levers with a 13 cm distance between them. In front of each diode was a polaroid filter that could be rotated, thus allowing one or the other eye to perceive the diode onset (see Fig. 1). A reward cup was located between the levers.

---

[1]To our knowledge, no split-brain patients or animals have been tested in such an ordinary RT task as one involving a choice between hands. This may be due to the negative prediction that results from the classical view in regard to the performance of the split-brain on this kind of task.

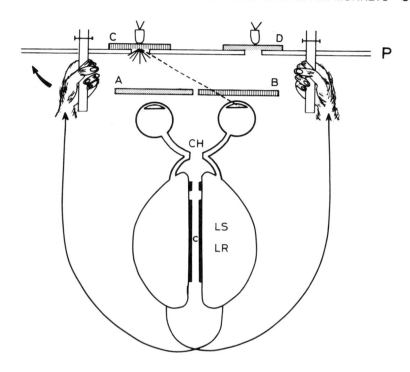

FIG. 1.   Schema of the situation in Experiment 1, in the case of a split-brain monkey presented with a left signal. The polaroid filters A and B fixed on the mask are of opposed
orientations. In this experiment, the adjustable filters C and D, mounted against the diodes
on the panel (P), are so oriented that each signal can be perceived with the opposite eye
only. The present example shows that the left signal is visible for the right eye only, through
filter B. Since transection of the optic chiasm (CH) prevents the projection of a monocular
input to the contralateral (left) hemisphere, only the right hemisphere receives specific information from the left signal (LS) through the geniculo-striate pathway. As to the left response (LR), the picture is similar, since control of the distal effectors (hand, wrist) should
depend exclusively on the contralateral motor cortex. Note the high S−R spatial compatibility, and the preservation of the critical connections allowing each hemisphere to control the whole S−R chain on the opposite side. Thus, no interhemispheric transmission of
information through commissures (C, here sectioned) should be necessary for the production
of a fast and correct reaction.

Stimulus and reward delivery was automatically controlled from outside the
cubicle by an electronic device[2] dependent on a high speed paper tape reader.
All temporal intervals separating significant events were automatically recorded
on a paper tape by way of a multichannel sequential chronometer.

[2]We are indebted to A. Zenatti, who designed the electronic programming and rewarding device.

C. Behavioral Shaping

The monkey was first trained to produce fast RTs in a *simple-RT* paradigm either with the left or right diode-lever device. The experimenter selected one side by keeping only one arm aperture open, and by making use only of the spatially corresponding diode. By pressing with his free hand on the available lever, the monkey spontaneously started an unpredictable foreperiod (in most cases four FPs, ranging from 0.6 to 1.2 sec), and waited for the signal. If a release occurred before the FP completion, no signal was presented, and the monkey had to start again the trial with a new manual pressure. If the release occurred within the response signal duration, it triggered with no delay a reward sound, followed by the relatively slow mechanical delivery of a peanut. Shorter RTs were obtained by gradually reducing the duration of the stimulus, i.e. of the reward availability.

A press-then-release, instead of a wait-then-press, behavioral sequence was chosen in our experiments in order to make sure that the occurrence of the response signal coincided with a proper attentive set in the monkey. In addition, any no-go response in these conditions has a clear overt significance, since it involves the active maintenance of pressure on the lever(s).

After the monkey had learned the simple-RT task equally well on both sides, he was taught a binary *choice-RT* task, with both levers being required to start the FP, and one or the other response signal occurring during a trial. Left and right signal occurrences were randomized according to the principles of the "exhaustive" series designed by Durup (1967), allowing the counterbalancing of sequential effects. The monkey was trained to respond to the signal by releasing the lever on the same side as the signal within the signal duration (see Fig. 2).

Since a bimanual pressure was required for starting a trial, a bimanual release also had to be allowed on each trial. It therefore appeared necessary to consider the first nonanticipatory release in a trial as the relevant choice response, then to reinforce it with no delay if correct, and to hold any subsequent lever manipulations as irrelevant events. Therefore all the latency and accuracy data that are reported for the choice tasks are first releases. In order to reinforce the first release specifically, the electronic rewarding device was designed to take only the first release in a trial into account, and — if correct — to emit the reward sound in synchrony with its occurrence. Thus, the reward was definitely lost in a trial where the wrong lever was released in first order, even if the correct but second release occurred within the signal duration.

D. Subsidiary Control Experiment

In a choice-RT task, the use of a regular FP procedure is legitimate as far as the subject performs the task with no or very few errors. But this happened not to be the case in our two split-brain monkeys (see Experiment 1). As far as their error scores may be identified as chance scores, the possibility arises that, with

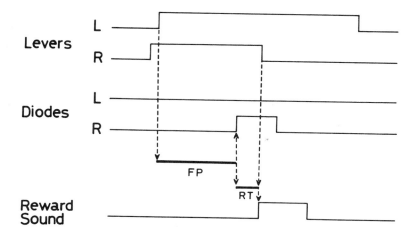

FIG. 2.   Chronology of events on a rewarded trial in the between-hand choice-RT task of Experiment 1. With a spontaneous pressure on both left (L) and right (R) levers, the monkey starts the trial that begins with a regular 1 sec foreperiod (FP) followed with an equal probability by the onset of the left or right diode. In this example, the response signal is delivered on the right side, calling for the release of the right lever. The monkey releases the right lever before signal offset, thus triggering a reward sound shortly preceding delivery of a peanut.

the regular 1 sec FP they merely learned a time estimating performance without attending to the response signal. Such a strategy could be worthwhile, since the monkey may compensate the relatively high reward uncertainty with an increased working tempo, i.e. a larger trial sample per time unit.

This possibility was tested in the two unskilled operated monkeys, in a few control sessions where the FP was randomly varied, without any transitional training between the regular and irregular procedures. Whereas their error-scores remained very close to chance, results clearly showed that both animals actually attended to the response signal and processed it, since their responses were performed around the various times corresponding to the signal occurrences (see Fig. 3, for an example).

III.   EXPERIMENT 1

A.   Methods

The monkeys were engaged in a binary choice-RT task that involved the hemispheres separately, both for signal reception and response production, as described in Figs. 1 and 2. The purpose of this experiment was to provide an esti-

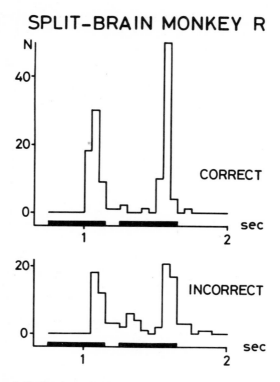

FIG. 3.   Temporal distribution of the response in a between-hand choice-RT task using two equifrequent unpredictable foreperiods 750 and 1,250 msec in duration: example in split-brain monkey R for the right response, computed over three sessions, where the monkey performed 85% of right responses with an overall 40% error rate. The data have been dichotomized according to response correctness. The abscissae represent time elapsing from the onset of the bimanual pressure. Overlined parts indicate the two possible occurrences of the response signal 400 msec in duration.

mation of the performance plateau that each monkey could reach after an appropriate training. Therefore, training was continued in each animal up to a level where no further improvement could be obtained. Since this choice task appeared to be of considerable difficulty for the two split-brain monkeys, these animals received much more training than the controls. Then, the experimental data that are presented in the following were collected in a series of daily sessions, each consisting of about 100 self-paced trials. Fourteen and 20 experimental sessions given to the controls and to the split-brain monkeys, respectively, appeared to be sufficient for demonstrating that, in each animal, the performance plateau had been attained.

B.   Results and Discussion

Figure 4 presents the results of each control animal. Two differences are found between the controls: first, monkey W reveals a large and highly consistent position bias favoring right RTs, whereas no such bias is found in monkey M. Second, mean speed and accuracy of responses appreciably improved in monkey M during the first half of the sessions, whereas the overall performance level of monkey W appears fairly stable over sessions.

Apart from these differences, which do not preclude the validity of the control results as such, the first point to be noted is that both control monkeys performed true choice-RTs, with an RT plateau located, on the average, around 300

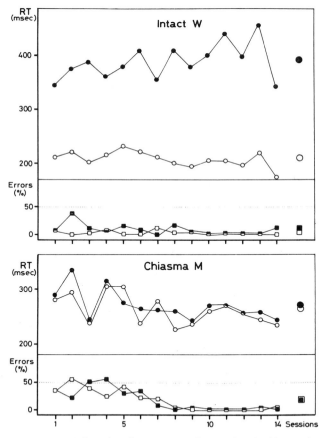

FIG. 4.   Mean correct RT (msec) and percentage of errors for the 14 experimental sessions of Experiment 1, for each of the two intact-brain monkeys. RT as well as error data are plotted for the left and right sides, with filled and unfilled symbols, respectively. Isolated symbols represent the data averaged over all sessions.

msec in monkey W, and around 250 msec in monkey M. On the other hand, both animals made practically no more errors in the second half of the sessions: while the overall error rates in monkeys W and M are 5.8% and 16.7%, respectively, their error rates calculated over the last 7 sessions become 3.3% and 0.6%, respectively.

Thus, the two intact-brain baboons were found capable of performing the choice-RT task with fairly high speed and accuracy scores, comparable to those commonly found in human subjects placed in analogous situations. Note in addition that splitting the chiasm does not seem to alter performance.

In contrast, the data in Fig. 5 show a dramatic impairment in the efficiency of both split-brain monkeys. These two animals provide very similar results: neither displays any consistent lateral bias and neither tends to improve performance over sessions.

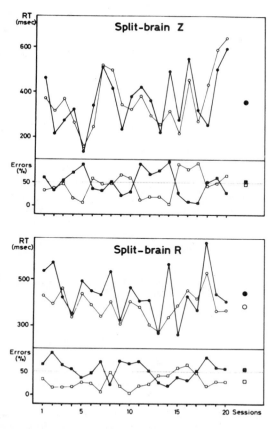

FIG. 5.　　Mean correct RT (msec) and percentage of errors for the 20 experimental sessions of Experiment 1, for each of the two split-brain monkeys. RT as well as error data are plotted for the left and right sides with filled and unfilled symbols respectively. Isolated symbols represent the data averaged over all sessions.

First, their mean RT is about 100 msec longer than that of the controls, around 350 msec in monkey Z and around 400 msec in monkey R. This result seems uneasily conciliable with the double channel view: with the assumption that the two separated hemispheres function in parallel in tasks not requiring an interhemispheric cross-talk, one would have hypothesized the division of the present choice-task into a couple of parallel go/no-go tasks, and therefore could not have predicted such an effect of surgery upon RT.

Second, we find a very striking accuracy deficit in each split-brain monkey, with the overall error rate located around chance at the 50% mark, which indicates that both operated animals were practically unable to perform the choice task. Analysis of the error rates across the sessions shows that when the monkeys reached a lower error rate on one side, this was always compensated for by an increased error rate on the other side; the mean error rate over the two sides thus remained close to 50%. Very asymmetrical error rates indicate a rigid repetition of one response on one side throughout the session, irrespective of the side of signal presentation. If such a pattern is related to some hemispheric dominance phenomenon, then it is worth noting that it clearly appears reversible in both monkeys, thus providing evidence against any hypothesis of unilateral brain damage caused by surgery.

An analysis of the interrelease interval (IRI), i.e. the time interval between the first-relevant and the second-irrelevant-hand releases, was performed in each of the four animals. Although this analysis led to a rather complicated picture due to large intragroup and intraindividual variances, it turned out that the split-brain animals separated their two hand releases with shorter and more variable IRIs than did the controls.

The finding of an inability to choose, in the context of an abnormal motor sequence in the two monkeys that had their commissures sectioned, was clearly suggesting that some critical functional relation between the two hemispheres had been impaired by this surgery. Since in the choice situation of Experiment 1 both the input and the output alternatives were dichotomized between the separated hemispheres, the results raised the question of whether the former or the latter separation, or both, was responsible for the deficit. In other words, would the choice deficit disappear if the processing of the two signal alternatives, or the selection between the two response alternatives, was achieved by a single hemisphere? This point was investigated in a further experiment involving the two split-brain monkeys, with an experiemntal design crossing these two factors.

IV. EXPERIMENT 2

A. Methods

By rotating the polaroid filters mounted on the diodes, the experimenter could either separate the two input alternatives by hemispheres (each signal being sent to the opposite eye, as in Experiment 1), or not (either signal being sent to the same eye for a block of trials). In an analogous way, the experimenter could either make the monkey perform a choice reaction involving the two hemispheres (a between-hand choice, as in Experiment 1) or a single hemisphere (a one handed go/no-go choice). Under the latter condition, the monkey was rewarded both for releasing the lever within the limits of the signal duration when the signal occurred on the working side, and for keeping the lever pressed down for one additional sec if the signal occurred on the opposite side (see the diagrammatic representation of this experimental design in Fig. 6).

The experiment was performed with each split-brain monkey in a balanced design that included an equal number of experimental blocks in each of the four treatments defined by the crossing of the two separation factors. The monocular input condition, as well as the unimanual output condition, were balanced with respect to the left and right sides. Each monkey would normally receive 74 trials per block; two blocks of different conditions were performed each day. Monkeys Z and R completed 12 and 16 sessions respectively.

Before performing the experiment, preliminary training was given to the animals for the unimanual go/no-go task, alternating left and right responses. The acquisition of that new task was readily achieved, but a transfer transient

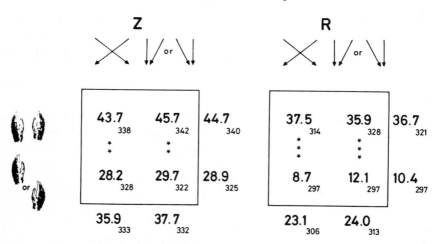

FIG. 6.   Mean percentage of errors and mean correct RT (msec) in each of the two split-brain monkeys for each condition of Experiment 2. The left column refers to the interhemispheric separation of the input alternatives, with each signal dispatched to the contralateral eye, and the right column to the dispatching of either input alternative to the same hemisphere, either left or right. The upper line corresponds to the between-hand choice-RT task, and the lower line to the one-handed go/no-go task, either performed with the left or right hand. Percentages and RTs were averaged over 6 blocks in monkey Z and over 8 blocks in monkey R. A Chi Square test ($df = 1$) was performed on overall error frequencies for each vertical and horizontal comparison. * = $p < .05$; ** = $p < .01$; *** = $p < .001$.

between blocks for which the instructions alternated was regularly observed in both animals. This transient consisted of a systematic inverted response to go and no-go signals during the trials following the side changes. In spite of appropriate training with frequent side alternation, this difficulty was never entirely overcome. During the experimental testing, the side alternations thus caused the unimanual error rates to be appreciably inflated, especially in monkey Z.

B. Results and Discussion

Figure 6 indicates the error rates and the RTs in monkeys Z and R for each experimental condition. There were no systematic differences related to laterality of input or output; data regarding left and right sides were therefore collapsed.

Inspection of the error rates leads to the same clear conclusions in both animals. The input separation is not responsible for the choice deficit in these animals, since the suppression of the stimulus separation between eyes produces negligible differences. This finding appears consistent with the double visual system theory (Schneider, 1969; Trevarthen, 1968), which assumes that the processing of mere spatial cues is achieved at a subcortical level in structures that are not divided by the neocortical commissurotomy.

However, the results also show that the use of two hands as competitors for the response is a critical factor in each of the two split-brain monkeys. The error rates are consistently reduced when a within-hand, instead of a between-hand choice is to be performed. This finding seems to be a robust one, if the lower familiarity, as well as the particular transfer difficulty of the unimanual condition are taken into account.

The RT data in Fig. 6 confirm that the input mode had no effect on performance. The RTs are no more affected by the separation of the signal alternatives than are the error rates. Turning to the more critical comparison between the output conditions, one may note the lack of any consistent differences in terms of speed of reactions between the between-hand task and the one-handed task. This result indicates that the remarkable accuracy improvement observed in the split-brain animals under the latter condition was not due to any substantial change in a speed/accuracy tradeoff.[3]

This experiment strongly suggests that the response ordering deficit observed in Experiment 1 in the surgical group performing the between-hand task was not

---

[3]Nevertheless, it would not be legitimate to make too strict vertical comparisons in the figure, because the RT distributions were not dealt with identically in the two conditions. In the between-hand choice condition, all correct RTs shorter than 1000 msec were taken into account. On the contrary, in the case of the one-handed go/no-go choice, in which the distribution of RTs to the go signal could show a second well separated mode, the RTs belonging to the slower RT group were discarded from the RT distribution, and held as errors. Therefore the RT estimation in the between-hand condition could have been slightly disfavored.

a secondary effect that expressed the subject's uncertainty about what to do, but a primary motor deficit related to commissurotomy. Such a finding appears discrepant with that of Ettlinger and his collaborators who found no impairment in the bilateral coordination of split-brain monkeys (Elliott, Ettlinger, Maccabe, & Richardson, 1976; Ettlinger & Morton, 1963). Nevertheless, whereas the present bimanual task required a simultaneous control of the phasic activity of both hands, it is not clear whether the tasks they used, involving mainly slow and tonic movements, did so. On the contrary, our data seem consistent with those reported by Preilowski (1972). This author, studying the acquisition of a tracking task requiring continuous bimanual coordination, showed that split-brain patients could never reach the final stage, in which tracking normally becomes fast and smooth and ceases to rely on slow proprioceptive and visual feed-back mechanisms. This deficit, he proposed, could result from the suppression of some motor corollary outflow from one cortex to the other.

Our data might be interpreted along analogous lines: whereas responding in a bimanual tracking task implies a continuous graded control of both effectors, responding in a between-hand choice RT task implies a discrete, all-or-none control of both effectors. Preilowski's interpretation, which supposes that bilateral motor coordination is achieved through direct cross-talk between two simultaneously acting response generators, would lead to the hypothesis that the critical interhemispheric information to be transmitted in the present case should be a mere inhibitory signal from the relevant hemisphere to its irrelevant competitor. According to this hypothesis, a reduction or a suppression of the response deficit should be observed if the lacking transcommissural information was replaced by some external inhibitory cue dispatched from the panel to the irrelevant hemisphere. This prediction was tested in each split-brain animal in a further experiment using two redundant signals, one calling for a go response, the other for a no-go response, simultaneously dispatched in each trial to different hemispheres.

V. EXPERIMENT 3

A. Methods

The apparatus was identical to that of Experiment 1, with filters making each red diode visible to the contralateral eye only. A pair of yellow diodes was added and located 2 cm under the red pair. Each yellow diode was covered with a polaroid filter making its onset visible with the contralateral eye only. In Experiment 3, the diodes were so connected that the onset of the upper red signal on one side was rigidly associated with the onset of the lower yellow signal on the other side. The subject was required, as in Experiment 1, to release the lever located on the same side as the red signal.

Prior to undergoing the present experiment, the two monkeys were trained to perform a unilateral go/no-go choice-RT task, involving the use of one lever and of the ipsilateral red-yellow signal couple, alternately on the left and right sides. Both go and no-go responses were rewarded if correct. This preliminary training was aimed at teaching the animals the inhibitory instruction related to the new yellow diodes, and it was continued until a high accuracy level was reached. Monkey R succeeded in the task with less than 10% errors on either side. Unfortunately, monkey Z could not do better than 30% errors on the left side, even though he made fewer than 15% errors on the right side.

Each monkey underwent 10 sessions over which the previous choice condition presenting one signal out of two, used as a control condition, was balanced with the present testing condition presenting two signals out of four.

B. Results and Discussion

The results, which are presented in Table 1, do not provide evidence for any double channel interpretation.

On the one hand, in neither animal is accuracy improved by the redundant signal. In other words, the error scores in this new bimanual testing condition remain very much higher than those recorded in unimanual go/no-go tasks during the preliminary training to Experiment 3. This indicates that no functional division of the task into a couple of parallel subtasks occurred.

Whereas the finding of an unchanged error rate in monkey Z may be somewhat inconclusive owing to his poor preliminary learning of the left unimanual

TABLE 1
RTs and Error Rates With and Without a Simultanoeus No-Go Signal[a]

		Condition				
		Control			Testing	
	RT	(sd)	%	RT	(sd)	%
Z	289.3	(48.4)		275.0	(32.1)	
Monkey			44.4			45.2
R	319.6	(43.9)		333.9	(53.5)	
			39.2			43.0***

[a]Note: Mean and standard deviation of RTs, and mean of error rates in each split-brain monkey, for each condition of Experiment 3. One RT value, irrespective of response correctness, as well as one error rate value was calculated for each session. One value in the present table was obtained by averaging 5 values. For each animal, a t test was performed on RTs ($df = 8$), and a Chi square test on error frequencies. *** = $p < .001$.

task, the finding of an increased error rate in monkey R clearly runs counter the double channel hypothesis, suggesting some confusing effect of the additional information. If a doubling of attentional processes had been made possible by the split-brain surgery, then it should have occurred in the present testing condition, where it would have provided better accuracy scores, and therefore higher reward frequencies.

On the other hand, inspection of RTs in Table 1 shows that the use of two simultaneous signals instead of one, in either monkey, did not produce faster reactions. These negative results thus remain consistent with a single channel model of the split-brain.

VI. GENERAL DISCUSSION

The results of the present experiments, and especially those of Experiment 3, provide evidence against the double channel model of the split-brain, and appear consistent with those of Kreuter et al. (1972). Clearly enough, they show that the two split-brain monkeys were not able to do two things at once. The most reasonable working hypothesis remains that performance of the split-brain primate is underlaid by the ordinary basic mechanisms of a limited attentional capacity shared between two structurally distinct but functionally nonautonomous cortical channels.

On the other hand, the outcome of Experiment 2 shows that the dramatic choice deficit observed in the split-brain monkeys performing the between-hand choice-RT task resulted from their inability to choose the correct response, without any noticeable impairment in the input function. This result may be readily interpreted in terms of an attentional capacity basically devoted to the nonautomatic input-decoding and output-coding functions. Along these lines, the low attentional requirements of the input-decoding in a binary choice-RT task using simple dots as stimuli contrasts with the high attentional requirement of the output production. Whereas a rough localization of a dot stimulus may be carried out by an inattentive subject, and even by a cortically blind patient (Pöppel, Held, & Frost, 1973), the fast triggering of a disjunctive motor reaction appears of much greater attentional demand.

One particular feature of an RT task, in which the subject's task terminates as soon as the overt act is begun, is that it requires all the subject's attention *before* the triggering of the response. If preparing for a response implies an accurate control of its availability, then preparation must depend on the general constraints of the selective attention process. The notion of specificity of preparatory processes appears to be confirmed by a large amount of work (see Requin, in press, for a review).

The arguments presented above provide the first assumption of a tentative model explaining the deficit observed in the surgical group performing the between-hand choice-RT task: in a binary choice-RT task, preparation is an asymmetrical process leading, at the time of the response signal, to unequally prepared competitive responses. Such a preselection mechanism, which is assumed both in normal and split-brain subjects, may be merely conceived of in terms of one response being favored with respect to the other response, and thus not necessarily in terms of an all-or-none mechanism.

Whatever may be the depth, as well as the steadiness of such a preselection mechanism during FP, a second assumption follows: on about half of the trials, i.e., those trials in which the preselection turned out to be disconfirmed by the response signal, a fast corrective process is required, aimed at inhibiting the response favored with a higher preparation, and activating the response disfavored with a lower preparation. As far as a between-hand paradigm is used, such a high speed switching mechanism is assumed to require commissural integrity.

Therefore, the model will explain the low error rates of the controls with the assumption that they successfully achieved the correcting operations; conversely, it will explain the quasi-chance error rates of the split-brain monkeys with the assumption that they failed in the performance of the correcting operations, owing to their inability to achieve fast interhemispheric attentional switchings.

This *ad hoc* explanatory model was tested on the available data through predictions of its two main assumptions. First, the possibility of a response preselection process during FP was indirectly tested in each of the four animals, through analysis of first order sequential effects related to left and right signal presentations. The results, presented in Table 2, show in all monkeys significant sequential effects on error probability. According to what happened in the very last trial (either signal or response), the probability of observing a given response was modulated. Such recency effects validate the view that in each animal, preparation was an asymmetrical process, with one response being more likely to occur than the other before delivery of the response signal. Therefore they support the first assumption of the model.

Second, the assumption that low error rates were reached by the controls due to successful corrective switchings, whereas high error rates in split-brain animals resulted from their inability to perform such corrective operations, was tested through its different predictions, for the control and surgical groups, in terms of the difference between mean correct and mean erroneous RTs. Although in the former group one should expect mean correct RT to be longer than mean erroneous RT, because the time loss due to the switching operation should presumably affect mainly, or only, the correct RT distribution, one should not expect such a difference to appear in the latter group, because neither RT distribution should be affected by such a time loss.

The calculation was performed for each session, on the data of the four animals. Unfortunately, no satisfactory estimates of mean erroneous RT could be obtained in the case of the controls, because the relatively small number of trials within a session and the time constraints actually used in Experiment 1 generated

TABLE 2
First Order Sequential Effects Upon Error Probability[a]

Monkey		Signal Alternation		Response Alternation	
		L	R	L	R
	W	53.3	52.0	67.9*	82.8**
	M	77.5***	74.7***	63.5*	58.2
	Z	35.8*	48.2	73.1***	63.8
	R	60.7*	47.5	60.0*	50.2

[a]Note: Percentages of errors on alternations calculated under the between-hand choice condition for each of the four monkeys and for each side of signal presentation on the present trial. The two columns on the left refer to percentage of errors on trials with a signal alternation, irrespective of which response was made on the last trial; the two columns on the right refer to percentage of errors on trials where a response alternation was required, irrespective of which signal occurred on the last trial. The scores were calculated according to the formula:

$$\frac{\text{errors on alternations} \times 100}{\text{errors on alternations} + \text{errors on repetitions}}$$

Chi Square tests were performed on error frequencies ($df = 1$).

$* = p < .05; ** = p < .01; *** = p < .001$. L, R = left, right response signal on the present trial.

very few or no errors. Nonetheless, inspection of the available data suggested that both control monkeys performed slower correct than erroneous RTs, which is consistent with the classical findings in choice-RT experiments using skilled human subjects (Rabbitt & Vyas, 1970). Because of appreciably higher frequencies of erroneous responses, more reliable estimates of the difference between correct and erroneous RTs for each experimental session were obtained in the split-brain monkeys. The mean of the *correct minus erroneous RT* differences, calculated in the blocks of Experiment 2 that involved a between-hand choice task, was −3 msec in monkey Z ($df = 11; t = 0.2, p > .10$) and −56 msec in monkey R ($df = 15; t = 4.2, p < .001$).

Thus, as predicted by the model, the data show that the two split-brain monkeys did *not* take more time, on the average, to perform a correct response than to make an error. Moreover, they show, in the case of monkey R, a significantly *slower* erroneous than correct RT. Though no unequivocal interpretation may be proposed for the latter result, it may be accounted for in terms of the model by hypothesizing two nonexclusive phenomena.

On the one hand, longer erroneous RTs could merely be due to a retinal eccentricity effect. It has been known since Poffenberger (1912) that the foveal reception of a stimulus produces shorter RTs than an extrafoveal reception. If preselection of one side, during FP, is assumed to involve not only preparation for one response, but also a visual fixation of the expected stimulus, it follows that the *a posteriori* probability of a foveal reception of the response signal is lower in the case of an erroneous than in the case of a correct response. Therefore one should expect mean erroneous RT to be disfavored in this respect, as compared with mean correct RT. Such an effect must concern the normal subject too. If so, the finding of faster erroneous than correct RTs in normal subjects, in spite of such an error disadvantage, will appear of increased significance.

On the other hand, longer erroneous RTs in split-brain monkeys could result from unsuccessful attempts to achieve the corrective switchings. Taking into account the finding of Experiment 2 that these animals were able to discriminate the signals, such attempts seem likely.

Thus, the results collected in the present series of experiments, while militating against a double channel model of the split-brain, appear in agreement with Kinsbourne's (1974) and Trevarthen's (1974) general views, and consistent with a model that assumes that splitting the brain impairs its ability to involve both cortical machineries through a fast alternation, thereby prohibiting cross integration functions in situations where heavy time constraints are imposed. Indeed, further testings of the model are needed in the split-brain, and an investigation of the relationship between temporal constraints and accuracy of responses in the between-hand choice paradigm should provide valuable data.

The present study also calls for a reinterpretation of some classical findings in the field of split-brain studies, and suggests the possibility of accounting for a large amount of empirical data within a common theoretical framework.

REFERENCES

Bertelson, P. Central intermittency twenty years later. *Quarterly Journal of Experimental Psychology*, 1966, *18*, 153–163.

Craik, K. J. W. Theory of the human operator in control systems. I. The operator as an engineering system. *British Journal of Psychology*, 1947, *38*, 56–61.

Craik, K. J. W. Theory of the human operator in control systems. II. Man as an element in a control system. *British Journal of Psychology*, 1948, *38*, 142–148.

Dimond, S. J. *The double brain*. Edinburgh and London: Churchill Livingstone, 1972.

Durup, H. Recherche de plans d'expérience temporels à transitions exhaustives simples ou multiples. *Bulletin du C.E.R.P.*, 1967, *16*, 21–39.

Elliott, R. C., Ettlinger, G., Maccabe, J. J., & Richardson, N. Bimanual motor performance in the monkey: Successive division of the forebrain and of the cerebellum. *Experimental Neurology*, 1976, *50*, 48–59.

Ettlinger, G., & Morton, H. B. Callosal section: Its effect on performance of a bimanual skill. *Science*, 1963, *139*, 485–486.

Fechner, G. T. *Elemente der psychophysik* (vol. 2). Leipzig: Breitkopf & Härtel, 1860.

Gazzaniga, M. S. *The bisected brain*. New York: Appleton-Century-Crofts, 1970.

Gazzaniga, M. S., & Sperry, R. W. Simultaneous double discrimination responses following brain bisection. *Psychonomic Science*, 1966, *4*, 261–262.

Gazzaniga, M. S., & Young, E. D. Effects of commissurotomy on the processing of increasing visual information. *Experimental Brain Research,* 1967, *3,* 368–371.

Kahneman, D. *Attention and effort.* Englewood Cliffs, N.J.: Prentice-Hall, 1973.

Kinsbourne, M. Mechanisms of hemispheric interaction in man. In M. Kinsbourne & W. L. Smith (Eds.), *Hemispheric disconnection and cerebral function.* Springfield, Ill.: C. C. Thomas, 1974.

Kreuter, C., Kinsbourne, M., & Trevarthen, C. Are deconnected cerebral hemispheres independent channels? A preliminary study of the effect of unilateral loading on bilateral finger tapping. *Neuropsychologia,* 1972, *10,* 453–461.

Milner, B., Taylor, L., & Sperry, R. W. Lateralized suppression of dichotically presented digits after commissural section in man. *Science,* 1968, *161,* 184–186.

Moray, N. *Attention: Selective processes in vision and hearing.* London: Hutchinson, 1969.

Myers, R. E. Function of corpus callosum in interocular transfer. *Brain,* 1956, *79,* 358–363.

Myers, R. E. The neocortical commissures and interhemispheric transmission of information. In G. Ettlinger (Ed.), *Function of the corpus callosum.* Boston: Little, Brown & Co., 1965.

Myers, R. E., & Sperry, R. W. Interocular transfer of a visual form discrimination habit in cats after section of the optic chiasma and corpus callosum. *Anatomical Records,* 1953, *115,* 351–352.

Poffenberger, A. T. Reaction time to retinal stimulation with special reference to the time lost in conduction through nerve centers. *Archives of Psychology,* 1912, *23,* 17–25.

Pöppel, E., Held, R., & Frost, D. Residual visual function after brain wounds involving the central visual pathways in man. *Nature,* 1973, *243,* 295–296.

Preilowski, B. Possible contribution of the anterior forebrain commissures to bilateral motor coordination. *Neuropsychologia,* 1972, *10,* 267–277.

Rabbitt, P. M. A., & Vyas, S. M. An elementary preliminary taxonomy for some errors in laboratory choice RT tasks. *Acta Psychologica,* 1970, *33,* 56–76.

Requin, J. Spécificité des ajustements préparatoires à l'exécution du programme moteur. In H. Hécaen (Ed.), *Du contrôle de la motricité à l'organisation du geste.* Paris: Masson, in press.

Schneider, G. E. Two visual systems. *Science,* 1969, *163,* 895–902.

Sparks, R., & Geschwind, N. Dichotic listening in man after section of neocortical commissures. *Cortex,* 1968, *4,* 3–16.

Sperry, R. W. Cerebral organization and behavior. *Science,* 1961, *133,* 1749–1757.

Sperry, R. W. Hemisphere deconnection and unity in conscious awareness. *American Psychologist,* 1968, *23,* 723–733.

Springer, S. P., & Gazzaniga, M. S. Dichotic testing of partial and complete split-brain subjects. *Neuropsychologia,* 1975, *13,* 341–346.

Teng, E. L., & Sperry, R. W. Interhemispheric rivalry during simultaneous bilateral task presentation in commissurotomized patients. *Cortex,* 1974, *10,* 111–120.

Trevarthen, C. Double visual learning in split-brain monkeys. *Science,* 1962, *136,* 258–259.

Trevarthen, C. Two mechanisms of vision in primates. *Psychologische Forschung,* 1968, *31,* 299–337.

Trevarthen, C. The split-brain technique. In R. D. Myers (Ed.), *Methods in psychobiology.* London and New York: Academic Press, 1972.

Trevarthen, C. Functional relations of disconnected hemispheres with the brain stem, and with each other: Monkey and man. In M. Kinsbourne & W. L. Smith (Eds.), *Hemispheric disconnection and cerebral function.* Springfield, Ill.: C. C. Thomas, 1974.

Welford, A. T. The "psychological refractory period" and the timing of high speed performance: A review and a theory. *British Journal of Psychology,* 1952, *43,* 2–19.

Welford, A. T. Single channel operation in the brain. *Acta Psychologica,* 1967, *27,* 5–22.

Zangwill, O. L. Thought and the brain. *British Journal of Psychology,* 1976, *67,* 301–314.

23

Individual Differences in Reading Strategies in Relation to Cerebral Asymmetry

Gillian Cohen
Roger Freeman

Department of Experimental Psychology
University of Oxford
Oxford, England

ABSTRACT

Performance of left- and right-handed subjects was compared over a battery of reading tests. When speed of silent reading with adequate comprehension was used as an index of reading proficiency, left-handers were significantly poorer readers than right-handers. Oral reading speed was compared for normal texts, and for texts that were visually distorted by case alternation, or syntactically and semantically distorted by a type of fourth order approximation. Left-handers showed relatively more decrement as a result of visual distortion, whereas right-handers were relatively more impaired by linguistic distortion. Left-handers therefore appear to rely more heavily on visual analysis during reading, and to make less use of contextual constraints. Left-handed subjects were recalled for a follow-up study, and given a dichotic listening test. Eight showed a left-ear advantage for recognition of monosyllabic words, and were significantly slower readers than those with a right-ear advantage. A further experiment explored hemisphere differences in a lexical decision task. Words and nonwords were presented in left and right visual fields. Stimuli were in either case-alternated or non-case-alternated forms. Nonwords were further divided into homophones and nonhomophones. These manipulations were used to probe for hemisphere differences in access to the internal lexicon by a visual look-up, or by phonological recoding. Reaction times (RTs) to homophonic nonwords were slower in the right visual field than in the left, but RTs to words and nonhomophonic nonwords were faster. Phonologically mediated access to the internal lexicon appears to be a left hemisphere based strategy.

I. INTRODUCTION

Current models of the reading process suggest that the fluent reader samples the visual information present in the graphic representation but does not analyze it exhaustively. He employs his knowledge of linguistic and semantic constraints to construct and predict the message, so that visual analysis is minimized (Goodman, 1972). Kolers (1970) has noted that more highly skilled readers make fewer fixations, and thus appear to sample the text less frequently than poor readers. It seems likely, therefore, that good readers rely more on contextual (linguistic and semantic) constraints, and less on visual information. Some evidence in support of this conclusion comes from a study by Marcel (1974), which showed faster readers extracted more words from tachistoscopically presented material, and benefited more from increasing contextual constraint. These findings, however, do not provide wholly adequate confirmation of the hypothesis that the proportion of visual analysis and contextual information employed in reading varies with the skill of the reader. The number of fixations is only a fairly crude indication of how far the reader is relying on visual analysis, since the amount of information gained by the visual system from each fixation is variable. The skilled readers in Kolers' study might make fewer fixations but gain more information. While Marcel's work demonstrates a superior use of context by the faster readers, it is important to remember that the strategies employed in tachistoscopic recognition are not necessarily the same as those employed in normal self-paced reading of text. The first study is therefore designed to examine the relationship between reading skill and the extent to which the reader depends on visual or contextual information, in a paradigm more closely resembling normal reading. This investigation was also designed to explore possible differences in reading skill relating to handedness in adult readers. A relationship between handedness and reading ability has been suggested by various studies. An association between reading disability and left- or mixed-handedness in children has been reported by Naidoo (1961), Zangwill (1960), and others, and it has been suggested that inconsistent hand preference reflects weakly established hemispheric lateralization of linguistic and visuospatial functions. In line with this suggestion, Marcel and Rajan (1975) found that the more proficient child readers showed greater right visual field superiority for word recognition. Zurif and Carson (1970) noted that at fourth grade, good readers showed a right ear advantage for dichotically presented digits, whereas poor readers had a left-ear advantage. Similarly, Bakker, Smink, and Reitsma (1973) found a positive correlation between reading skill and right ear dominance in older children, although this was not evident in younger children.

Although Buffery and Gray (1972) have claimed that there are sex differences in verbal ability — the superiority of females, resulting from a stronger lateralization of the language function — there is no experimental evidence that adult females are superior in reading skill. It has often been noted that girls are more advanced than boys in learning to read, and that the incidence of reading difficulty is higher in boys (Critchley, 1970) but tests of reading performance in older children show that sex differences have disappeared by the early teens (Thompson, 1975). While there are therefore some results linking sex, handedness, and cerebral lateralization with reading skill in children, these relationships have not been established for adult readers.

The first experiment compares the performance of right- and left-handed normal adult readers in a series of reading tasks designed to provide a measure of reading skill, and to test how far reading performance is sensitive to (a) visual distortion, and (b) contextual distortion of the text.

II. EXPERIMENT 1

A. Method

1. *Subjects.* Two groups of subjects, 24 right-handers and 24 left-handers were tested. Each group consisted of 12 males and 12 females. The groups were matched for age and educational level; they were all students or graduates. Handedness was assessed by means of a questionnaire that queried hand preference for a variety of tasks. The average scores for right hand preference were 90% for the right-handed group and 30% for the left-handed group. Eye dominance, foot dominance, hand preference in early childhood, and the handedness of close relatives were also recorded.

2. *Materials.* Eighteen passages of text varying in length between 115 and 130 words were typed with an electric typewriter on separate cards. Spacing and alignment was standardized. Three passages were allotted to each of six conditions. Except in the Silent Difficult condition, all the passages were extracts from modern short stories selected so as to be approximately similar in style and equally intelligible. In the Silent Difficult condition, three technical passages were employed, selected from textbooks on philosophy, computer technology, and literary criticism.

3. *Procedure.* Subjects were tested individually. Each card was presented to the subject face down. He was instructed to turn over the card, press a button that started an Advance TC11 timer as his eyes fell on the first word, and press a second button that stopped the timer as he finished reading the last word. The subject sat facing a microphone, and in the oral conditions reading was recorded. Reading speed, expressed as the number of words per minute (WPM) was measured for each passage. Three passages were read in each condition, and a mean WPM score averaged over the three passages was calculated.

Subjects were instructed to read as fast as possible, and to maintain understanding so that they would be able to answer questions about the passage. Comprehension was tested immediately after each passage had been read, and the total number of correct answers recorded for each condition.

The six conditions were presented in the same order for all subjects as follows:

1. Normal Oral (NO): the subject read aloud, instructed as mentioned.
2. Silent Easy (SE): the subject read silently through the story extracts.
3. Silent Difficult (SD): the subject read silently through the technical passages.
4. Case Alternation (CA): the subject read aloud passages that were visually distorted by being typed with alternating upper and lower case letters, a manipulation that has been shown to cause a decrement in reading speed (Fisher, 1975).
5. Cloze Task (CT): the subject read aloud passages from which 10% of the words had been deleted. He was instructed to supply words that would be grammatically and semantically acceptable in place of the missing words while reading aloud as fast as possible.
6. Fourth Order Approximation (4OA): the subject read aloud passages constructed using only every fourth word of the original, so that the linguistic and semantic constraints were weakened. An example sentence of the resulting text was "Sweat and hand off seemed eyes the and trees early fresh drawing dial tarmac like his from minute to an side he pickings gave known dream enough a had indecision." In this condition comprehension was not tested by questions, but the subject was asked to say what he thought the passage was about in as much detail as possible. Text of this kind has been shown to reduce reading speed and increase errors (Morton, 1964).

It was predicted that, if good readers rely more on contextual information than on visual information, the 4OA condition would impair their reading more seriously, whereas the decrement produced by the visually distorting CA condition would be relatively slight. Poor readers might be expected to show the opposite pattern of results.

B. Results

The mean WPM for each group is shown in Tables 1 and 2. Reading speeds are shown in WPM, and as a percentage difference from the Normal Oral speed in brackets.

TABLE 1
Mean WPM Scores for Left- and Right-Handers in Normal Oral,
Silent Easy, and Silent Difficult, and the Reading
Proficiency Score

	N.O.	S.E.	S.D.	R.P.
Right	230	349 (+ 52%)	281 (+ 22%)	315
Left	219.5	303.5 (+ 38%)	248.5 (+ 13%)	276

TABLE 2
Mean WPM Scores for Right- and Left-Handers and the
Percentage Decrement from Normal Oral Caused by Case
Alternation and Fourth Order Approximation

	N.O.	C.A.	4OA
Right	230	217 (−5%)	167 (−27%)
Left	219.5	201.5 (−8%)	166 (−24%)

1. *Differences in reading proficiency.*   The scores in the SE and SD conditions were averaged and taken as an index of reading proficiency (RP). Comparison of the reading proficiency of the four groups (RM = right-handed males, LM = left-handed males, RF = right-handed females, LF = left-handed females) by the Kruskal Wallis test showed a significant difference ($H = 14.3, df = 3, p < 0.01$). Post hoc application of Nemenyi's test showed RM = RF > LM = LF. The poorer performance of the left-handers was also confirmed in a X^2 test. Figure 1 suggests

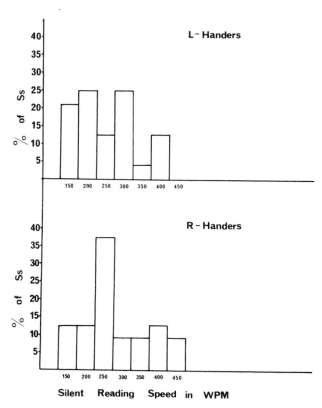

FIG. 1   Left- and right-handed subjects distributed according to reading speed.

TABLE 3
Comprehension Scores (Percentage Correct),
and the Mean Number of Reading Errors Per
Subject in the 4OA Condition

	Comprehension	Mean No. of errors in 4OA
Right	86%	8.3
Left	84%	7.3

that left- and right-handed readers were differently distributed with respect to R.P. Accordingly, subjects were divided into three categories, poor readers (below 250 WPM), middle-grade readers (150-350 WPM), and good readers (above 350 WPM). Left- and right-handed readers were differently distributed between these categories with $X^2 = 6.88$, $df = 2$, $p < 0.05$. When all the subjects had been ranked according to reading proficiency, the 10 poorest readers consisted of 6 left-handers and 4 right-handers, while the 10 best readers consisted of 7 right-handers and 3 left-handers. There was no significant sex difference in reading proficiency.

The comprehension scores for the four groups are shown in Table 3. By the Kruskal Wallis test ($H = 1.8$, n.s.) there was no difference between the groups. Reading errors occurred too rarely for analysis except in 4OA. Analysis of the 4OA errors also revealed no significant difference between groups $H = 2.0$, n.s.).

2. *Differences in reading strategy.*   Comparison of the percentage decrement in reading speed produced by the CA and the 4OA conditions was used to examine differences in reading strategy. The Cloze task was not analyzed for reasons discussed below. Table 4 shows the scores for the 10 best and 10 worst readers in all conditions. For poor readers 4OA produces a decrement 17% larger than the decrement caused by CA. For good readers, 4OA is slower by 23%. This difference is significant by t test, ($t = 2.86$, $n = 18$, $p < 0.01$). As predicted, the decrement caused by 4OA exceeds the decrement produced by CA by a larger amount in the best readers than in the poorest readers.

TABLE 4
Mean WPM Scores for the 10 Best and 10 Poorest Readers,
With Percentage Differences from Normal Oral for Each Condition

	N.O.	S.E.	S.D.	C.A.	4OA
10 Best Readers	263	468 (+ 72%)	404 (+ 54%)	257 (−2%)	198 (−25%)
10 Poorest Readers	200	202 (+ 1%)	174 (−13%)	178 (−11%)	144 (−28%)

The same analysis was applied to the scores of the left- and right-handed subjects. The mean differences between CA and 4OA were 16% for the left-handers
and 22% for the right-handers (t = 3.33, n = 46, $p < 0.01$).

C. Discussion

1. *The difference between good and poor readers.* As predicted, the good
readers are much less impaired than poor readers by visual distortion (CA), and
relatively more impaired by contextual distortion (4OA), but this latter effect
is quite small. The most marked finding is that good readers can read silently
very much faster than they read orally, whereas the poor readers' silent reading
is no faster than their oral reading. This suggests that poor readers are employing
the same strategy in both conditions and forming a complete subvocal phonemic
representation during silent reading. The extent of this difference between the
good and poor readers is more surprising in view of the fact that all the subjects
in this study were of a university standard of education. It does not seem likely
that the slow silent reading of the poor readers was due to comprehension difficulties, since the two groups show a larger difference on the Silent Easy passages
than on the Silent Difficult passages.

It was noted that there was a qualitative difference in the performance of
good and poor readers on the 4OA material. Good readers struggled to impose an
intonation pattern on the material, segmenting in into phrase-like units. Poor
readers read in a monotone as if it were a word list. When asked what they
thought these passages were about, good readers gave a remarkably complete
reconstruction of the original text. Poor readers typically responded "Don't
know," or "Something about a man." These unanticipated observations were
not scored, but serve to suggest that the good readers were processing semantically,
while the poor readers 'switched off' at the semantic level.

The Cloze task was not successful in differentiating between readers. It was
predicted that good readers would have greater awareness of the contextual
constraints within the text, and so do better at supplying the missing words.
In fact, those who performed this task rapidly filled the gaps with words that
were barely acceptable; others took longer because they adopted a higher standard
of acceptability, often backtracking to revise an earlier choice, or hesitating
between two possibilities. This tradeoff between speed and degree of aptness
made it impossible to score this task effectively, and it was therefore not included
in the analyses.

2. *The difference between left- and right-handed subjects.* The overall difference in reading proficiency has several interesting aspects. Whereas right-handed
readers appear to be normally distributed about the mean, the left-handers tend
to cluster at the bottom end of the scale. Although the scores on the handedness
questionnaire fail to differentiate between good and poor left-handers (i.e., there

is no correlation between reading proficiency and strength of hand preference) there is a tendency for familial left-handers to be slower readers than nonfamilial left-handers. Of the 8 familials in this study, 5 fall into the poor reader category. It is possible that a difference in cerebral lateralization of the language function underlies the performance differences among left-handers. The finding that left-handers were less impaired by contextual distortion and more by visual distortion, relative to right-handers, suggests that a difference in the use of visual versus contextual information might be related to handedness. But the largest left-right differences occur in the silent reading conditions where the slower reading of the left-handers may well be caused by the inclusion of a phonemic processing stage.

III. EXPERIMENT 2

The distribution of left-handed subjects' scores in reading proficiency (see Fig. 1) appears to have two peaks, as opposed to the more normal distribution of the right-handed subjects. This suggests the possibility that the left-handers are of two different kinds, and that the distribution might reflect differences in cerebral lateralization. Evidence of the effects of brain lesions, intracarotid amytal injections, and dichotic listening experiments indicates that, whereas in the majority of right-handers the left hemisphere is specialized for language processing, only about two-thirds of left-handers conform to this pattern. The remaining one-third appear to have a reversed lateralization, with language represented in the right hemisphere, or show little lateral asymmetry of language function. While differences in the methods of assessing handedness, and of testing cerebral lateralization, have contributed some variability to estimates of the exact proportions of left, right and mixed dominance, there is ample evidence for differences in the pattern of language lateralization within the left-handed population.

In order to examine the possibility that differences in reading proficiency were related to differences in cerebral asymmetry, the left-handed subjects were recalled for a dichotic listening test. When verbal material is simultaneously presented to both ears, recognition is superior for items presented to the ear contralateral to the hemisphere specialized for language processing. (A right ear advantage indicates left hemisphere dominance for language; a left ear advantage indicates right hemisphere dominance.) Although ear differences may also reflect attentional strategies and the order in which items are reported, the correlation between the results of dichotic listening studies, and amytal injections (Kimura, 1961) suggests that ear advantage is a reliable indicator of cerebral asymmetry.

A. Method

Eighteen of the original 24 left-handed subjects responded to the recall, and a dichotic listening test was administered. Pairs of monosyllabic words were presented simultaneously to the two ears of the subject over headphones connected to a Sony stereophonic tape recorder. Monaural presentations of practice words were adjusted to give subjectively equal intensity in each ear for each subject individually. The tape (constructed by Lishman and McMeekan[1]) delivered groups of three pairs of words with half a second between each pair.[1] Following each group, the subject was instructed to write down what he had heard in any order, and to try to report as many words as possible. There were 20 groups of 3 pairs in the series, making 120 words in all. The headphones were interchanged halfway through the series. Half the subjects started with channel one played to the right ear, and channel two the left ear, and half had the opposite arrangement.

The number of words correctly reported from each ear was recorded, and the score for right ear presentation was expressed as a percentage of the total number of words correctly reported.

B. Results

Eight of the subjects showed a left ear advantage (LEA), and 6 of these had been classified in Experiment 1 as poor readers, with reading proficiency scores below 250 WPM. The mean R.P. score for the subjects with an LEA was 217 WPM; for the subjects with an REA it was 314 WPM ($t = 3.72, n = 16, p < 0.001$). The correlation between reading proficiency and REA was tested by a Spearman Rank Correlation Coefficient, and yielded $r_s = 0.68, p < 0.01$. The difference in ear advantage accounts quite well for the distribution of left-handers' R.P. scores in Fig. 2.

C. Discussion

The finding is consistent with the results of Zurif and Carson (1970), and shows that the relationship between a right ear advantage and reading proficiency persists in adulthood. Marcel and Rajan (1975) reported a similar association between reading ability and right visual field superiority for word recognition in young children. However, it is still not clear how these findings should be interpreted. Ear and visual field asymmetries may reflect lateralization of attention and of memory as well as that of language processing. Whatever the functional differences that underlie the observed asymmetries, it is still difficult to understand why right hemisphere dominance should be disadvantageous for reading. One possibility is that a processing mechanism that favors material on the right of the fixation point is optimal for left to right reading, in that it enables the reader to anticipate more effectively. Right hemisphere dominance, favoring material behind the fixation point, might make forward anticipation more difficult. This possibility could be tested, since it follows that the association between right hemisphere

[1]Thanks are due to Dr. W. A. Lishman of the Institute of Psychiatry, University of London, for his kindness in making available a copy of his dichotic listening tape, and details of his own results.

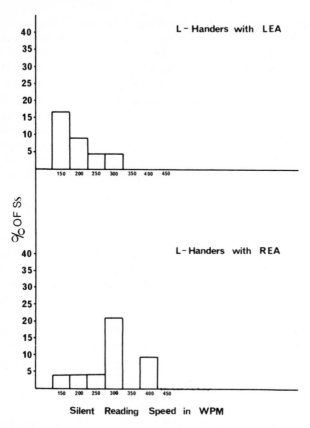

FIG. 2   Left-handers with left ear advantage, and with right ear advantage, distributed accordint to reading speed.

dominance and slower reading should not hold good for Hebrew readers, who read from right to left.

IV. EXPERIMENT 3

This experiment was undertaken to test the hypothesis that the two cerebral hemispheres have different roles in word recognition. Recently, Bradshaw (1975) reviewed the evidence relating to the problem of whether silent reading or word recognition necessarily involves a stage of phonological recoding that succeeds visual analysis and mediates access to the meaning, or whether the skilled reader can access meaning directly from the visual representation without forming a phonological representation. Since there is experimental support for both possibilities, a reasonable conclusion is that both strategies can be employed. They might operate in parallel, or one particular strategy might be selected depending on the skill of the reader and the nature of the task. Phonological recoding seems to be most evident in the early stages of learning to read, and, in adults when material is unfamiliar or difficult. Coltheart, Hull, and Slater (1975) also report that phonological recoding is more prevalent in females.

In addition to the clinical evidence showing that, in right-handed people, speech is lateralized in the left hemisphere, there is some evidence suggesting that covert phonological recoding is also a left hemisphere function. Cohen (1972) found reaction times to judge pairs of letters to be nominally identical were faster when the letters were presented to the left hemisphere. Recently, Levy and Trevarthen (1977) have compared the linguistic abilities of the two isolated hemispheres in split-brain patients. They found that the right hemisphere could carry out a visual word matching task. That is, when a word was presented to the left visual field (LVF), and so to the right hemisphere, the patient could point to the corresponding word in a list of alternatives. The left hemisphere, but not the right, could carry out a phonological word matching task. When a word was presented to the right visual field (RVF, i.e., left hemisphere), the patient could then point to a rhyming word in a list of alternatives, but when the word was presented to the LVF (right hemisphere), performance on phonological matching was at chance level.

Experiment 3 was a lexical decision task (LDT) with words and nonwords presented in the LVF and RVF. In LDTs it is assumed that the stimulus is "looked up" in an internal lexicon, accepted as a word if a match is found, and rejected as a nonword if no match is found. Logically, look-up can be carried out either by visually matching the stimulus to a stored visual representation, or by phonologically recoding the stimulus and matching to a stored phonological representation. When the nonwords are homophonic with real words (e.g., *shert*) they generally take longer to reject than when they are nonhomophonic (e.g., *trep*) (Rubenstein, Lewis, & Rubenstein, 1971). This homophone effect indicates that phonological recoding occurs, and that the phonological match interferes with the judgment. If phonological recoding is a left hemisphere function, homophonic nonwords should cause more difficulty when presented in the RVF.

In the first part of this experiment both words and non words appeared in case-alternated and noncase-alternated forms. On the assumption that case-alternation makes the visual pattern unfamiliar, it should induce a phonological matching strategy and increase the homophone effect in the left hemisphere.

A. Method

1. *Subjects.* Ten subjects who were all strongly right-handed young adults were tested.

2. *Stimulus materials.* A list of 248 stimuli was compiled, consisting of 120 words and 128 nonwords. Nonwords were subdivided into homophones and

nonhomophones. Half of the items in each of these categories were case-alternated and half were noncase-alternated. Case-alternated stimuli began with a lower case letter. Half of the items in each of these categories were case-alternated and half were noncase-alternated. Case-alternated stimuli began with a lower case letter. Half the noncase-alternated stimuli were printed in upper case, and half were printed in lower case. All the stimuli were either four or five letters long, word length being equated between conditions. Words were all high frequency, and nonwords were all pronounceable. The word-likeness of the homophones and nonhomophones was equated in terms of the number and position of the letters by which they differed from real words.

Half of the stimuli in each category were presented in the LVF, and half in the RVF. In order to ensure that asymmetries between the visual fields should be due to processing differences and not to unequal difficulty of particular items, two separate versions of the stimulus list were created, Pack A and Pack B. These were identical, except that every item that appeared in the LVF in Pack A appeared in the RVF in Pack B, and vice versa. Half the subjects were tested on Pack A, and half on Pack B. Categories of stimuli and LVF and RVF presentations were pseudorandomized throughout the list with constraint that not more than 4 words or 4 nonwords be consecutive.

The stimuli were stencilled in black on 6 x 4" white cards, with 3° of visual angle between the central fixation point and the edge of the nearest letter (the terminal letter of LVF stimuli, the initial letter of RVF stimuli). Each stimulus subtended approximately 4° horizontally and 1° vertically.

3. *Procedure.* Stimuli were presented in a three field tachistoscope (Electronic Developments Ltd.). On each trial a field containing a central fixation cross was displayed. Following a verbal warning signal, the stimulus was exposed for 200 msec. Subjects were instructed to fixate the cross, and to judge each stimulus as "word" or "nonword," signaling their decision by pressing one of two response buttons as fast as possible without making errors. Half the subjects pressed the right hand button for responses of "word," and the left for "nonword"; half had the opposite arrangement. Testing was divided into 2 sessions, trials 1–124 and 125–248. Practice trials preceded each session, and continued until improvement leveled off. Reaction times were measured from the stimulus onset to the response, and errors were recorded. Reaction times for error trials were not scored.

B. Results

Median RTs were calculated for individual subjects. Table 5 shows the means of these medians for each stimulus category, for the noncase-alternated forms only. The case-alternated stimuli were excluded from the analysis because those visual field differences that appeared for Pack A were reversed for Pack B. It was there-

TABLE 5

RTs (Means of Medians) in msecs for Left and Right Visual Fields in Each
Stimulus Category in Experiment 3, Part 1 (Means are for
Noncase-Alternated Stimuli; Case-Alternated Forms Were Present
In the List, but not Included in the Medians)

Words		Homophonic Nonwords		Nonhomophonic Nonwords	
LVF	RVF	LVF	RVF	LVF	RVF
628	609	686	721	723	691

fore clear that the effects were due to unequal difficulty of particular stimuli.
Case alternation appears to produce more difficulty when it breaks grapheme
clusters or causes radical changes in overall word shape, and these factors had
not been adequately controlled.

Analysis of variance of the RTs for noncase-alternated stimuli was carried out
[subjects x stimulus category (words, homophones, nonhomophones) x visual
fields (left, right)]. The effect of stimulus category was significant $F(2, 18) =$
$13.02, p < 0.01$, and the interaction of visual field with stimulus category was
also significant $F(2, 18) = 4.2, p < 0.05$. Following the procedure advocated by
Clark (1973), min F' was calculated [(9, 15) 5.3], and was significant at $p <$
0.01, so that it can be concluded that the results have generality beyond the
language sample used in the experiment. As can be seen in Fig. 3, error percentages follow the same trend as the RTs. Post hoc testing by the Newman Keuls
method showed that the RVF was significantly slower than the LVF for homophonic nonwords, and significantly faster for nonhomophonic nonwords, $p <$
0.05. Although in the RVF RTs for homophonic nonwords are significantly
slower than for nonhomophonic nonwords, in the LVF they are actually faster.
It is possible that, visually or orthographically, homophonic nonwords are less
wordlike than nonhomophones, since constructing a homophonic nonword
necessarily entails using a spelling pattern that is a less common alternative, and
the digram and trigram frequencies for the two kinds of nonwords may therefore
differ, as well as the positional frequency of single letters, which Mason (1975)
has shown to be an important factor in word recognition.

The fact that the homophone effect is evident when nonwords are presented
to the left hemisphere, and not when they are presented to the right hemisphere,
supports the conclusion of Levy and Trevarthen that phonological matching is a
left hemisphere function. The possibility that it is a strategy that mediates
lexical decision only in specific conditions, and is dictated by the nature of the
task, was tested in a modified version of Experiment 3. The presence of 50%
case-alternated items in the list, and the difficulty of judging these by visual
matching, might have induced subjects to employ a phonological look-up. To
test this possibility the case-alternated items were removed from the list in Part 2.

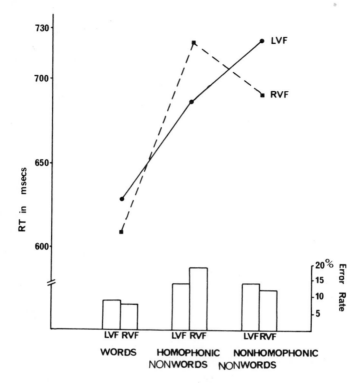

FIG. 3   Reaction times to make word/nonword judgments in the left and right visual fields in Experiment 3, Part 1.

Six new subjects were selected as before. The experimental method was exactly the same, except that the stimulus list was reduced to 124 items by the removal of the case-alternated stimuli, and testing was carried out in a single session. Again half the subjects worked with Pack A, and half with Pack B. The results are shown in Table 6. There was no significant difference between homophones and nonhomophones, and no significant interaction with visual fields.

TABLE 6

RTs (Means of Medians) in msecs for Left and Right Visual Fields in Each Stimulus Category in Experiment 3, Part 2 (Case-Alternated Stimuli Having Been Removed from the List).

Words		Homophonic Nonwords		Nonhomophonic Nonwords	
LVF	RVF	LVF	RVF	LVF	RVF
578	572	689	673	678	650

C. Discussion

The reduction of the homophone effect in Part 2 confirms that phonological matching is a strategy that may characterize left hemisphere processing, but not right hemisphere processing, and that it mediates lexical access in conditions in which visual matching is hampered by specific features of the task. However, the results are consistent with two interpretations. The left hemisphere may employ phonological and visual strategies on an either/or basis. Baron and McKillop (1975) noted that fast readers, when asked to classify sentences as sense or nonsense, used a visual strategy, but shifted to a phonological one if homophonic nonwords were presented in the list. Alternatively, both kinds of matching may operate in parallel, with judgment being mediated by the fastest match. In this case, conditions that favor visual matches would produce visually mediated judgments, and conditions that impede visual matches would produce phonologically mediated matches. This latter possibility is compatible with the conclusion reached by Forster and Chambers (1973) that phonological representations are normally formed after lexical access.

The hemispheric differences evident in the operation of visual and phonological strategies in word recognition may also obtain in reading text. Whether any link exists between individual differences in reading proficiency, the ability to shift flexibly between visual and phonological strategies, and patterns of cerebral lateralization is at present only a speculation, but one that would be worth further investigation.

ACKNOWLEDGMENTS

This research was supported by a grant from the Mental Health Research Fund to the first author, and an SRC research studenship to the second author.

REFERENCES

Bakker, D. J., Smink, T., & Reitsma, P. Ear dominance and reading ability. *Cortex,* 1973, *X,* 301–312.

Baron, J., & McKillop, B. J. Individual differences in speed of phonemic analysis, visual analysis and reading. *Acta Psychologica,* 1975, *39,* 91–96.

Bradshaw, J. L. Three interrelated problems in reading: a review. *Memory and Cognition,* 1975, *3,* 123–134.

Buffery, A. W. H., & Gray, J. A. Sex differences in the development of spatial and linguistic skills. In C. Ounsted & D. C. Taylor (Eds.), *Gender differences, their ontogeny and significance.* London: Churchill, 1972.

Clark, H. H. The language-as-fixed-effect fallacy: A critique of language statistics in psychological research. *Journal of Verbal Learning and Verbal Behaviour,* 1973, *12,* 335–359.

Cohen, G. Hemispheric differences in a letter classification task. *Perception and Psychophysics,* 1972, *11,* 139–142.

Coltheart, M., Hull, E., & Slater, D. Sex differences in imagery and reading. *Nature*, 1975, *253*, 438–440.

Critchley, M. *The dyslexic child.* London: Heinemann, 1970.

Fisher, D. F. Reading and visual search. *Memory and Cognition*, 1975, *3*, 188–196.

Forster, K. I., & Chambers, S. M. Lexical access and naming time. *Journal of Verbal Learning and Verbal Behaviour*, 1973, *12*, 627–635.

Goodman, K. S. Psycholinguistic universals in reading. In F. Smith (Ed.), *Psycholinguistic and reading.* New York: Holt, Rinehart and Winston, 1972.

Kimura, D. Cerebral dominance and the perception of verbal stimuli. *Canadian Journal of Psychology*, 1961, *15*, 166–171.

Kolers, P. A. Three stages of reading. In H. Levin & J. P. Williams (Eds.), *Basic studies on reading.* New York: Basic Books, 1970.

Levy, J. & Trevarthen, C. Perceptual, semantic and phonetic aspects of elementary language processes in split-brain patients. *Brain*, 1977, *100*, 105–118.

Marcel, T. The effective visual field and the use of context in fast and slow readers of two ages. *British Journal of Psychology*, 1974, *65*, 479–492.

Marcel, T., & Rajan, P. Lateral specialization for recognition of words and faces in good and poor readers. *Neuropsychologia*, 1975, *13*, 489–497.

Mason, M. Reading ability and letter search time: Effects of orthographic structure defined by single letter positional frequency. *Journal of Experimental Psychology*, 1975, *104*, 146–166.

Morton, J. The effects of context upon speed of reading, eye movements and the eye-voice span. *Quarterly Journal of Experimental Psychology*, 1964, *16*, 340–351.

Naidoo, S. *An investigation into some aspects of ambiguous handedness.* M.A. Thesis. University of London, 1961.

Rubinstein, H., Lewis, S. S., & Rubinstein, M. A. Evidence for phonemic recoding in visual word recognition. *Journal of Verbal Learning and Verbal Behavior*, 1971, *10*, 645–657.

Thompson, G. B. Sex differences in reading attainment. *Education Research*, 1975, *18*, 16–23.

Zangwill, O. L. *Cerebral dominance and its relation to psychological function.* Edinburgh: Oliver and Boyd, 1960.

Zurif, E. B., & Carson, G. Dyslexia in relation to cerebral dominance and temporal analysis. *Neuropsychologia*, 1970, *8*, 351–361.

V RESPONSE AND PHYSIOLOGICAL PROCESSES

24

The Neurophysiology of Human Attention: A Tutorial Review

Terence W. Picton
Kenneth B. Campbell
Jacinthe Baribeau-Braun
Guy B. Proulx
Departments of Medicine and Experimental Psychology
University of Ottawa
Canada

ABSTRACT

The study of the event-related potentials recorded from the human scalp provides evidence about the neurophysiology of selective information processing that can improve our understanding of human attention. The early components of the sensory evoked potential are unaffected by changes in attention, suggesting an initial stable registration and analysis of incoming information. When attention is directed toward a particular sensory channel, there is enhancement of a negative component in the evoked potential with a peak latency of around 100 msec $- N_{\overline{100}}$. This effect is based on the simple stimulus attributes that define the selected channel, and it occurs irrespective of the significance of the stimuli within that channel. It reflects a "stimulus set" selection process. The evoked potential to an important signal or target stimulus within an attended channel contains, as well as the enhanced $N_{\overline{100}}$ component, a large late positive wave with a peak latency of near 350 msec $- P_{\overline{350}}$. This component reflects a "response set" selection process. The $P_{\overline{350}}$ amplitude varies with the amount of meaningful information processed from the signal to appropriate perceptual or motor response. During attention there are long-lasting negative shifts recorded mainly from frontal regions. This negativity possibly represents the exertion of effort in the active organization and control of selective information processing.

429

I. INTRODUCTION

Attention is the process underlying the selection and organization of available information for appropriate response. Information can be provided by both memory and sensory environment. Responsiveness may involve both overt behavior and conscious awareness, in the latter case there being a connotation of attention related to perceptual clarity. Attention is intimately related to general arousal, which controls the availability of both information and response. Attention is directed and maintained by the exertion of mental effort in order to optimize a necessarily selective responsiveness to large amounts of incoming information.

At the present time the psychological evaluation of human selective attention has amassed a large amount of experimental data, and has produced several definite yet disparate theories concerning the mechanisms of selection. Psychological processes such as attention can perhaps only be properly understood at the intersection of converging lines of evidence originating from different experimental approaches (Garner, Hake, & Eriksen, 1956). A promising source of correlative and convergent information derives from human neurophysiology, particularly from the study of event-related potentials during various attentive tasks (Näätänen, 1975; Picton, Hillyard, and Galambos, 1976; Hillyard & Picton, in press; Tueting, in press).

The *event-related potential* is a series of electrical changes recorded in temporal association with a physical or mental event. *Sensory evoked potentials* are elicited in response to physical stimuli, particularly any rapid change in environment. These potentials are designated by their polarity and usual latency in milliseconds. Event-related potentials may also occur in relation to mental activity, independent of sensory input. Such *emitted potentials* (Weinberg, Walter, Cooper, & Aldridge, 1974) may occur at the time of an expected but omitted stimulus, or may possibly occur in conjunction with the purely sensory evoked potentials in response to significant incoming stimuli. Event-related potentials may also occur prior to some anticipated perceptual or motor activity, and such waveforms may be considered *preparatory potentials*.

The event-related potentials recorded from the human scalp are usually too small to observe in the ongoing background electroencephalogram, and averaging techniques are necessary for their evaluation. Averaging carries with it a set of experimental and recording requirements that should be mentioned, partly in way of apology for the simplicity of some of the evoked potential paradigms, and partly to explain some of the limitations of the recording technique. The evoked potential being averaged must be constant in morphology and must occur in unrelated background activity. Often, these requirements are not fully met and the average evoked potential must, therefore, be considered a somewhat distorted version of the response to any individual event. Averaging enhances the signal-to-noise ratio only by the square root of the number of trials averaged and, therefore, thousands of stimuli may have to be presented in order to evaluate very small evoked potentials.

Human event-related potentials are recorded from the scalp at some distance from their generation, and this can cause immense difficulties in their interpretation. At any particular latency, multiple areas of the brain may be simultaneously responding to an incoming stimulus. At the scalp the field-transmitted potentials from these many areas may overlap in simple or intricate fashion. Scalp distribution studies (Picton, Woods, Stuss, & Campbell, in press) provide one approach to the differentiation of underlying generators, but even the most accurate and extensive mapping of a distant electrical field cannot indicate the sources of that field with certainty. The scalp-recorded evoked potentials derive mainly from the brain systems that can create large and distinct electrical fields, and more amorphous neural areas, such as the reticular formation, may not create electrical fields that can be observed at the scalp. Scalp recordings can also pick up extracranial potentials that might occur in relation to incoming stimuli or their responses. The eyeball, scalp musculature, tongue, and skin all generate contaminating potentials that may obscure or distort the underlying brain events, and such artifacts must be rigorously controlled (Picton & Hink, 1974).

II. EVOKED POTENTIAL DURING AUDITORY VIGILANCE

The neurophysiological examination of human vigilance will serve to introduce the evoked potentials, to illustrate their use in the study of attention, and to provide a reasonable starting-point for later discussions. Vigilance involves the detection of infrequent stimulus changes over a prolonged period of time. Such a paradigm, with its presentation of large numbers of stimuli, is admirably suited to the recording of the small early auditory evoked potentials deriving from the cochlear nerve and brainstem.

There are no changes in the early and midlatency auditory evoked potentials between a condition of auditory vigilance and a condition wherein subjects read a book and ignore the auditory stimuli. There is, however, as shown in Fig. 1, a definite attentional enhancement of the late negative–positive complex occurring with mean peak latencies of 90 and 160 msec $- N_{\overline{90}} - P_{\overline{160}}$. This complex is probably generated in cortex and is best recorded over frontocentral regions of the scalp. The response to the detected infrequent signal stimuli shows, as well as the enhanced $N_{\overline{90}} - P_{\overline{160}}$ components, a large late negative–positive complex $N_{\overline{250}} - P_{\overline{450}}$ (Fig. 2). The late positive wave has a more posterior scalp distribution than the earlier components of the auditory evoked potential. This late negative–positive complex is stimulus–independent and can be recorded in response to a stimulus omission, if such is the signal event to be detected. Figure 3 illustrates on the left event-related potential recordings taken while a

IGNORE   ATTEND

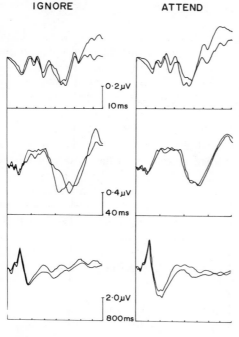

FIG. 1. Auditory evoked potentials following a 60 dBSL click presented every second. In the "ignore" condition the subject read a book, and in the "attend" he carefully listened to the clicks in order to detect an occasional faint signal. Evoked potentials were averaged with three different time bases and amplifer sensitivities. Each tracing represents the average of 2048 responses. Recording was made between vertex and right mastoid with relative negativity of the vertex showing as an upward deflection. There are no significant differences between the two conditions in the early or midlatency potentials. The late $N_{\overline{90}} - P_{\overline{160}}$ components are markedly enhanced during attention. Unpublished data from Picton and Hillyard (1974). Subject V.S.

IGNORE   ATTEND

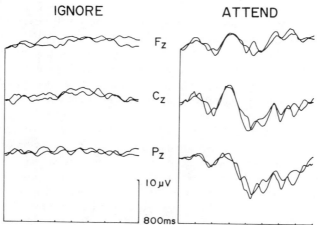

FIG. 2 Evoked potentials to occasional fainter "signal" stimuli occurring during a long train of clicks, when the subject read a book or detected and counted the number of signals. Evoked potentials were obtained from frontal, central, and parietal scalp locations, each referred to the left mastoid. Negativity of the scalp relative to the mastoid is shown by an upward deflection. Each tracing represents the average of 80 responses. The evoked potentials in the "ignore" condition are so small as to be almost unrecognizable in the residual unaveraged noise, but a small $N_{\overline{90}}$ wave is just visible in frontal and central recordings. Unpublished data from Picton and Hillyard (1974). Subject R. H.

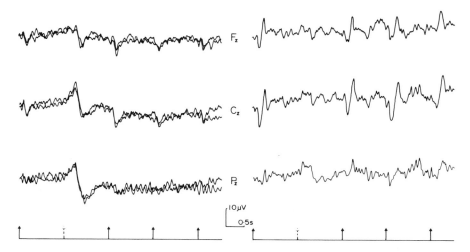

FIG. 3. Evoked potentials to omitted stimuli. Fifty-five dBSL clicks were presented regularly every 1.1 sec and every 4–20 sec one click was omitted. The subject was asked to keep a running count of the number of omissions. On the left are shown the evoked potentials to the clicks and the omitted stimulus when the subject was actively counting. Averaging was synchronized to the click immediately preceding the omission. Each tracing presents the average of 32 responses. Recordings were taken from midfrontal, vertex, and midparietal scalp regions referred to the left mastoid with relative negativity of the scalp electrode represented by an upward deflection. During the recordings on the left the subject was accurately detecting the stimulus omissions. A large late negative–positive complex is noted following the stimulus omission. The negativity of the complex is maximal at the vertex, whereas the positivity is largest at the parietal electrode. The task was extremely boring and during one portion of the recording, as evidenced by the tracings on the right, the subject was drowsy and occasionally asleep. Only about one third of the stimulus omissions were counted, and a large late frontocentral negative wave appears in the click evoked potential. Unpublished data from Picton et al. (1974a). Subject S.H.

subject was actively detecting and keeping a running mental count of stimulus omissions in a regular train of clicks.

These results suggest three neurophysiological processes associated with auditory perception. There is an early processing of incoming auditory information that is relatively constant regardless of whether the auditory stimuli are attended or ignored. The amplitudes of the late evoked potential components vary with changes in attention. Directing attention toward auditory stimuli is associated with an enhancement of the $N_{\overline{90}} - P_{\overline{160}}$ evoked potential components. A large $N_{\overline{250}} - P_{\overline{450}}$ complex occurs in response to detected signals within the attended train of auditory stimuli. The precise relationships between these neurophysiological events and the processes of selective attention is the subject of the succeeding sections of this paper.

III. PROBLEMS OF GENERAL AROUSAL

The enhancement of the cortical evoked potentials noted in these experiments might be related more to nonselective arousal mechanisms than to specific auditory attention. During the auditory vigilance tasks the subject might be in a more heightened arousal state than during the more relaxing reading condition, and the changes in the $N_{\overline{90}} - P_{\overline{160}}$ components might therefore reflect a generalized increase in cortical excitability, rather than a specific change in the auditory system.

There are definite changes in the evoked potential associated with obvious changes in general arousal. As a subject becomes drowsy and falls asleep, a large late negative wave $N_{\overline{350}}$ occurs in the evoked potential, often followed by a later positive wave $P_{\overline{650}}$ (Weitzman & Kremen, 1965). The effect of drowsiness on the evoked potentials is demonstrated in the right half of Fig. 3. The source and functional significance of the $N_{\overline{350}}$ wave is unknown. It might possibly represent an excitatory phenomenon associated with an unsuccessful attempt at awakening, or it might just as easily be an inhibitory wave preventing awareness or memory of the incoming information.

Despite these striking effects of drowsiness and sleep upon the evoked potential, little is known about the effects of varying levels of arousal within the waking non-drowsy state. Indeed, arousal in the waking state is difficult to define and harder to measure. Increased arousal is usually associated with behavioral activation as evidenced by increased muscle tension and speed of response, autonomic changes such as an increased heart rate and wider pupillary dilation, and alterations in the electroencephalogram resulting in desynchronization of rhythmic activity and increased cortical negativity. There are, however, many specific situational determinants of such physiological response patterns that often obscure any relationship to a hypothetical general arousal level (Lacey, 1967).

Several experiments have considered the possible effects of general arousal on the sensory evoked potential during the waking state. Studies that have attempted to manipulate general arousal independently of selective attention have found that attention and arousal have similar effects on the evoked potential (Eason & Dudley, 1971; Eason, Harter, & White, 1969). However, it is probably impossible to change levels of arousal in the waking state independently of any attentional change. Indeed, arousal can reflect the effort involved in the expansion of attentional capacity (Kahneman, 1973). It is therefore difficult to be sure that there are arousal-mediated evoked potential changes independent of attention.

Evoked potential changes with arousal are possible, however, and to control for possible different levels of general arousal between conditions, several early experiments used alternating stimuli of different modalities, with attention directed to one modality or the other during different recording periods (Satterfield, 1965; Spong, Haider, & Lindsley, 1965). The specific enhancement of the response to the attended stimuli relative to the response to the ignored stimuli showed that the evoked potential effects were not due to changes in the general level of arousal between recording blocks. There might, however, have been some phasic expectancy process related to the stimuli in the attended modality. Since the stimuli were regularly alternated, the subjects could have easily cycled between brief periods of arousal immediately prior to the relevant stimuli and relaxation during the irrelevant stimuli. If this occurred, the enhancement of the $N_{90} - P_{160}$ potentials to the attended stimuli could still reflect heightened generalized cortical activation, rather than a purely selective attention. Indeed, the examination of the electroencephalogram prior to the relevant stimuli in an alternating sequence showed increased cortical negativity and flattening of background activity, both suggestive of heightened cortical activation (Näätänen, 1967, 1970). Moreover, one could hypothesize that the late positive wave noted in response to detected signal stimuli might represent a transient fall off of the ongoing cortical negativity (Wilkinson & Spence, 1973). The psychological concomitant of this wave might therefore not be related to cognitive information processing, but to a *reactive change of state* following the detection of an expected signal (Karlin, 1970).

To control for such cycles of activation prior to relevant stimuli, one can present the relevant and irrelevant stimuli in a random manner. When visual and auditory stimuli were randomly presented, no attention-related differences in evoked potentials were noted in several studies (Hartley, 1970; Näätänen, 1967; Wilkinson & Ashby, 1974; Wilkinson & Lee, 1972). Other studies, however, reported increases in the 50–200 msec evoked potentials to relevant — as opposed to irrelevant — stimuli when using random presentation methods (Eason, et al., 1969; Picton, Hillyard, Galambos, & Schiff, 1971; Velasco, Velasco, Machado, & Olvera, 1973). Even with no change in the preceding evoked potential components with such random stimulus presentation schedules, there usually remains a late positive component in the evoked potential to signal stimuli (Donchin & Cohen, 1967; Smith, Donchin, Cohen, & Starr, 1970).

The stimuli in these latter experiments were, however, partially predictable in their time of occurrence. Usually there were two separate sequences of stimuli, each sequence being determined by specific rules governing the timing of the stimuli and the probability of the signals. Under such conditions, subjects can predict to some degree the occurrence of the relevant stimuli for which they might, therefore, be able to be relatively more prepared (Näätänen, 1975). Consequently, it is still possible that any evoked potential changes recorded in these paradigms may reflect heightened generalized cortical excitability, selectively timed to coincide more often with the relevant than with the irrelevant stimuli.

IV. CORTICAL NEGATIVE SHIFTS

One possible correlate of this heightened cortical excitability is a negative shift in the resting potential of the cortex. This section will therefore discuss the relationship between such negative shifts and arousal or attention. In 1964

Walter and his colleagues reported that following a warning stimulus and prior to an "imperative" stimulus requiring a motor response there was a negative baseline shift that could be recorded from the scalp using direct-coupled recording techniques. They postulated that this "contingent negative variation" might be the "electric sign of cortical 'priming' whereby responses to associated stimuli are economically accelerated and synchronized" (Walter, Cooper, Aldridge, McCallum, & Winter, 1964).

This negative baseline shift is widely recorded from the frontocentral areas of the scalp. There are, however, specific differences in this scalp distribution, depending on the nature of the anticipated response (Butler & Glass, 1974; Järvilehto & Fruhstorfer, 1970; McAdam & Whitaker, 1971; Syndulko & Lindsley, 1977; Vaughan, Costa, & Ritter, 1969). As a result, Hillyard (1973) suggested that each kind of contingent negative variation contains both a nonspecific diffuse negative baseline shift and a process-specific negativity distributed over those areas of cortex particularly relevant to the anticipated task.

Recently, Loveless and Sanford (1973) and Weerts and Lang (1973) have suggested that there are two distinct phases to the contingent negative variation. The first phase occurs in relation to the warning stimulus and is possibly related to an orienting response. The second phase occurs prior to and in anticipation of the second stimulus and is related to some preparatory activity. The early phase of the contingent negative variation can be differentiated from the later phase by its scalp distribution, the early waves being more anterior (Gaillard, 1976; Syndulko & Lindsley, in press). The early phase is also unaffected by such experimental manipulations as the adoption of a sensory rather than a motor set, which reduces the later phase (Loveless & Sanford, 1974), or the hemispheric asymmetries associated with hand of motor response (Rohrbaugh, Syndulko, & Lindsley, 1976). The different phases of the contingent negative variation are also associated with different autonomic concomitants (Lang, Ohman, & Simons, this volume). The early phase has been variously described as habituating (Weerts & Lang, 1973), constant (Gaillard, 1976), or increasing in amplitude (Rohrbaugh et al., 1976) with repetition of the eliciting paradigm. This early negativity is larger when the warning stimulus is auditory rather than visual (Gaillard, 1976), but it is difficult to know whether this is related to modality—specific sensory processing or to the inherently greater alerting quality of auditory stimuli.

These considerations suggest that the contingent negative variation might represent a combination of three different neurophysiological processes. Immediately after the warning stimulus there is a negativity that might be related either to orientation to the warning or to initiation of the response preparation. Immediately before the imperative stimulus there is a preparatory negativity in those areas of cortex necessary for the perceptual or motor response. Throughout the preparatory interval, depending upon the intentional engagement of the subject, there might also be a more general negativity associated with the organization of behavior.

The contingent negative variation has been related to attention through several experiments. Distraction from the anticipated task causes attenuation of the preceding negativity (McCallum & Walter, 1968; Tecce & Scheff, 1969). Several experiments have found a general correlation between the negativity preceding motor response and the speed of reaction time (Besrest & Requin, 1969; Hillyard, 1969) but others have not (Näätänen & Gaillard, 1974; Rebert & Teece, 1973). One obvious dissociation between the two phenomena is seen in the experiments of Naitoh and his colleagues (Naitoh, Johnson, & Lubin, 1971), who found that in sleep-deprived subjects there was little contingent negative variation, although reaction time was unchanged from that of normal well-rested subjects with normal contingent negative variations. Some experiments have correlated the negativity preceding a perceptual task with perceptual accuracy (Hillyard, Squires, Bauer, and Lindsay, 1971; Wilkinson & Haines, 1970) and others have not (Järvilehto & Fruhstorfer, 1970; Paul & Sutton, 1972). Thus the contingent negative variation seems less closely related to motor or perceptual performance than would be presumed for a specific attentional process.

There has also been a great deal of consideration given to the relationship between the state of arousal and the contingent negative variation. Subjects who are anxious and who are exposed to a stressful experimental situation tend to show smaller amplitude contingent negative variations (Low & Swift, 1971), especially if the subjects are female (Knott & Peters, 1974). Such findings might possibly be related to changes in the general level of cortical negativity upon which the phasic negativity of the contingent negative variation is superimposed. If the resting baseline is quite high, it is possible that no further increase in negativity can occur during the preparatory interval — a "ceiling" hypothesis (Knott, 1972). Unfortunately, variations in cortical baseline are extremely difficult to evaluate because of the problems of electrode and amplifier drift, and the difficulties in controlling noncerebral sustained potentials from the eye, skin, and scalp musculature.

Tecce (1972) has proposed that the contingent negative variation might actually be directly related to attention, attention itself being related to general arousal by an "inverted-U" relationship. Thus, during distracting tasks, there is increased arousal and a decreased ability to attend to the specific task in the CNV paradigm. Certainly, distraction from a specific task causes decreased performance of that task, a decreased contingent negative variation, and evidence of increased general arousal in the heart rate and eye blink rate (Tecce, Savignano-Bowman, & Meinbresse, 1976). However, as discussed in the preceding paragraph, there is little definite evidence linking the contingent negative variation to such behavioral measures of attention as reaction time and accuracy of perception. Also, the inverted-U relationship between activation and performance has recently been critically reviewed by Näätänen (1973), who pointed out that high levels of activation under experimental conditions often involve strong emotional reactions that might interfere with performance independently of the effect of activation.

The relationship between prestimulus negative shifts and the poststimulus components of the evoked potential, especially the late positive component, has recently been reviewed by Tueting and Sutton (1973). The late positive component of the evoked potential is independently affected by the stimulus relevance (Donald & Goff, 1971) and probability (Friedman, Hakarem, Sutton, & Fleiss, 1973) and has a more posterior scalp distribution than the usual contingent negative variation (Hillyard, Courchesne, Krausz, & Picton, 1976). These findings suggest functionally distinct underlying mechanisms (Donchin, Tueting, Ritter, Kutas, & Heffley, 1975). Such studies do not, however, rule out the possibility of a longer-lasting "resident" cortical negativity that is set up by the subject at the beginning of the experimental situation and transiently discharged with the detection of relevant signal stimuli (Wilkinson & Ashby, 1974; Wilkinson & Spence, 1973). On close examination of the left hand portion of Fig. 3, one can see a very small falloff in the baseline after the detection of the omitted stimulus possibly associated with some increased alpha activity, but this seems quite distinct from the parietally dominant positive component associated with the detection of the stimulus omission.

A slow negative baseline shift associated with attention is demonstrated in Fig. 4. This shows the recordings from a modal subject during an experiment requiring intermittent attention to brief trains of auditory stimuli in order to detect which one is of slightly higher frequency. With attention, a slow negativity develops after an initial stimulus and persists for a variable time during the train of tonebursts, usually lasting several seconds after the signal detection. This negativity is greater in amplitude over the frontal regions, where it is half-again as large as in the parietal areas. Attention to the stimuli caused enhancement of the N_{100} component to the first stimulus in all conditions of attention when compared to the control condition, but the evoked potentials to the following stimuli showed little change in this component. It is probable that the first stimulus was particularly attended as a pitch standard for later comparisons. Late positive waves occurred in response to the informative stimuli, particularly the actual signal stimuli. This late positive component was maximally recorded from the parietal region. There was no significant correlation between the N_{100} component and the preceding negativity. There was a small correlation (+0.48 for the mean data from nine subjects) between the P_{350} component and the preceding cortical negativity, suggesting a definite but certainly not determinant relationship. In this experiment attention therefore seems evidenced by three distinct electrophysiological phenomona. There is enhancement of the N_{100} component to the initial stimulus in the attended train. There is a distinct late positive component in the evoked potential to the informative and signal stimuli.

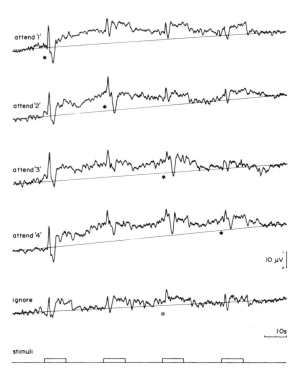

FIG. 4. Evoked potentials during intermittent attention. Blocks of four 500 Hz 75 dBSL 1 sec tones occurring every 2.5 sec were presented every 20–30 sec. The subject was asked to detect which of the stimuli had a slightly higher frequency (520 Hz). The subject was instructed to relax as much as possible during the interval between the blocks at which time he was also able to blink and write down the number of the signal location in the previous block. A control trial was performed while the subject read a book and ignored the auditory stimuli completely. In the control trial the third stimulus was always the signal, whereas in the active attending trials the signal was randomly located at any one of the four positions. Evoked potential averaging was carried out by grouping together those blocks in which the stimulus occurred at the same location. Averaging commenced 2 sec before the initial stimulus and continued over a period of 12 sec. Each of these tracings represents the average of 32 responses recorded between midfrontal and earlobe electrodes with increasing negativity of the midfrontal electrode being represented by an upward deflection. Recordings were done with a frequency bandpass of 0–30 Hz. No eye movements occurred during the trials utilized for the averaging. The slight negative drift noted in the tracings was common to all subjects and might have been related to a small temperature differential between the different electrode positions. With attention there is a negative baseline shift during the train of stimuli, an enhancement of the $N_{\overline{100}}$ response to the initial stimulus and a late positive component in response to the informative and signal stimuli. These recordings also demonstrate the sustained negative shift occurring during the one second toneburst. Subject D.S.

439

Finally, there is a sustained cortical negativity persisting throughout the stimulus presentation and subsiding slowly after the signal detection.

The precise physiological mechanisms underlying the generation of such slow cortical negative waves are little known (Rebert, in press). In general, sustained negativity in animal recording has been associated with increased neuronal activity, and it is therefore probable that the scalp-recorded negative shifts we have been discussing might reflect an increase in underlying cortical activity initiated through thalamocortical (Skinner, 1971) or corticocortical (Zappoli, Papini, Denoth, Pasquinelli, Rossi, Martinetti, & Guerri, in press) connections. Sustained surface negativity and increased unit firing have been noted in the prefrontal cortex of monkeys during delayed response performance (Fuster, 1973; Stamm & Rosen, 1972). Fuster has suggested that this activity might be related to the "sensorial and mnemonic attention" required for correct task performance, but the exact nature of this relationship is not well understood.

The function of the human scalp-recorded negative shifts recorded during attention or as the nonspecific component of the contingent negative variation is even less understood. They might be related to such variables as "conation" (Low, Borda, Frost, & Kellaway, 1966), "motivation" (Rebert, McAdam, Knott, & Irwin, 1967), "intentional engagement" (Deecke, Scheid, & Kornhuber, 1969), or "conscious effort" (Näätänen, in press). Cooper, McCallum, and Papakostopoulos (in press) have suggested that the contingent negative variation might be characteristic of a "scopeutic" state wherein a subject is actively engaged in his environment, as opposed to a "categoric" state wherein a subject responds automatically or unthinkingly. All of these formulations are somewhat similar. They are characterized by the exertion of some sort of mental effort directed towards an anticipated task, and by some particular organization of expectancies and preparedness.

The frontal regions of the human cortex have been related to the ability to maintain attention and to direct behavior (Luria, 1973). These anterior frontal regions are an area of the brain where interoceptive and exteroceptive information can be integrated into perception and behavioral programming (Nauta, 1971). In patients who are surgically or pathologically without frontal cortex, the behavior is characteristically unselective, inappropriate, impulsive, and unsustained. It might be possible, therefore, to hypothesize that the more general component of the contingent negative variation — the component that is more frontal in origin — is related to activity in the frontal regions that programs, directs, and energizes the mechanisms of attention. Such activity in a way reflects the mental effort exerted in the organization of selective information processing (cf. Kahneman, 1973). This can occur both before and during the processing of task-relevant information (cf. Donald, 1970). This negativity need not correlate highly with performance, since such would depend on the efficiency and not the amount of effort exerted. In its selectivity and goal-directedness, this hypothesized frontal activity shows some of the characteristics of consciousness (Posner and Klein, 1973; Shallice, 1972).

The efferent connections of the anterior frontal region are to the association areas of the parietal, temporal, and limbic cortex, to the hypothalamus, and to the reticular areas of the thalamus and mesencephalon (Nauta, 1971). Skinner (in press) has proposed that the outflow from the frontal regions to the reticular nuclei of the thalamus might reflect the programming of a selective gating of information in the precortical sensory pathways. Such efferent activity might thus underlie the selection of sensory channels for attention. The corticocortical connections may serve in part to activate those areas of cortex necessary to the analysis of and response to important incoming information. Such corticocortical activation might be evidenced by the more specific preparatory portions of the contingent negative variation. Such preparatory activity will in effect determine the context in which incoming information is processed (cf. Pribram, 1971, p. 344; Pribram & McGuiness, 1975). These two frontal efferent connections may therefore function to determine where to attend and what to attend for.

V. LEVELS OF SELECTION

Returning now to the study of evoked potentials during selective attention, we find there is one major criticism that can be levied against the paradigms with random stimulus presentation that found no attention-related change in the evoked potential. These experiments were carried out at a sufficiently slow rate of stimulus presentation that it was possible, and indeed introspectively probable, that attention could have been switched between channels in order to process all of the information from all channels. Channel selection was consequently unnecessary and may or may not have been used depending upon the strategy of the subject.

Hillyard, Hink, Schwent, and Picton (1973) used stimuli presented at a rapid rate and in completely unpredictable sequence. Both ear of delivery and pitch were used to differentiate the stimuli to be attended from those to be ignored. The baseline to $N_{\overline{100}}$ peak amplitude of the auditory evoked potential was on average a third again as large when the stimuli were attended as when they were ignored, this difference being highly significant. Thus, there is in this study clear evidence that selective attention to an auditory channel defined by ear and tonal frequency is associated with enhancement of the $N_{\overline{100}}$ component of the auditory evoked potential. It is impossible to explain this result by any phasic expectancy or arousal process associated with the attended stimuli. Figure 5 shows recordings from a similar experiment, with clicks presented to one ear and brief tonebursts to the other.

An additional experiment reported by Schwent, Hillyard, and Galambos (1976a) verified that the initial assumption concerning the effects of stimulus rate was indeed correct. At fast stimulus presentation rates there was a definite effect of attention upon the $N_{\overline{100}}$ component of the auditory evoked potential, but at interstimulus intervals of 960 msec or more no change could be recognized. Another interesting aspect of the selective mechanism is that it is more efficient

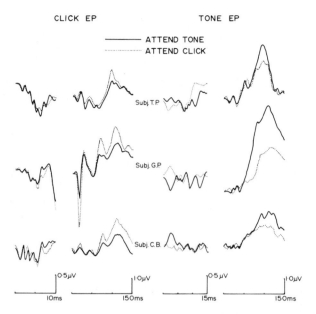

FIG.5. Auditory evoked potentials during a binaural listening task. Tonepips of 45 dBSL intensity of 7.5 ms duration and of 500 Hz frequency were presented to the left ear and equally loud 100 μs clicks were presented to the right ear according to a randomized time schedule with interstimulus intervals between 150 and 800 ms, and in a moderate level general background noise. Subjects were instructed to attend to one ear in order to detect and count a random infrequent signal stimulus, and to ignore the other ear as much as possible. Evoked potentials were recorded from vertex to right mastoid using different time bases in order to examine the early and late evoked potential components. Each tracing represents the average of 2048 responses. Data from three subjects are shown. Although the responses are somewhat variable, there is no consistent change in the early evoked potential components with attention. The late negative component at 100 ms shows, however, consistent and significant enhancement with attention. Subject G.P. also shows an attention-related enhancement of the click evoked post-auricular muscle response at 10–15 ms.

when the stimuli are of lower intensity (Schwent, Hillyard, & Galambos 1976b). When the intensity of the stimuli reaches more than 60 dB above threshold, the attentional change is much smaller. It is difficult to evaluate whether this intensity-related effect is due to saturation of the generator mechanism for the $N_{\overline{100}}$ component at the higher intensities (Picton, Goodman, & Bryce, 1970), or due to some overriding effect of intensity upon any selective mechanism making loud stimuli impossible to ignore.

The stimulus selection mechanism underlying these experiments seems to be based upon such simple attributes of the stimuli as pitch and spatial location. Schwent and Hillyard (1975) showed that there was an enhancement of the N_{100} component of the auditory evoked potential related to the selective allocation of attention to any one of four channels defined by four different pitches and spatial locations. A further experiment by Schwent, Snyder, and

Hillyard (1976c) showed that such selective mechanisms can be based singly on pitch or spatial location, although the effect on the N_{100} component is larger if both cues are available.

The task in most of these studies involved the detection of an occasional signal stimulus in the attended channel. The response to such signal stimuli contained, in addition to an enhanced N_{100} component, a large late positive wave peaking between 300 and 400 msec. Such a positive component was not seen in the response to the nonsignal stimuli in the attended channel. Similar results are illustrated in Fig. 6. These findings suggest two separate levels of selective attention similar to those described by Broadbent (1971, p. 177) as "stimulus set" and "response set." Stimulus set involves the selection of incoming information for analysis and evaluation based upon simple physical characteristics irrespective of meaning; response set involves the selection of perceptual and motor responses judged as important and appropriate after complete evaluation of incoming information.

It is, nevertheless, still possible to propose a single selective mechanism based upon full evaluation of incoming data and final selection of the appropriate and

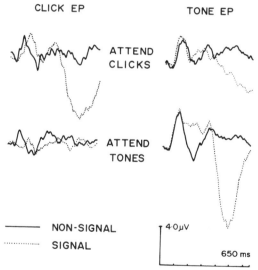

FIG. 6. Late components of the auditory evoked potential during a binaural listening task. Evoked potentials to the signal stimuli (580 Hz tones and 10 dB fainter clicks) are compared to the responses to the nonsignal stimuli under the different conditions of attention, as described in the legend for Fig. 5. There is enhancement of the N_{100} response to both signals and nonsignals with attention to that stimulus channel, and there is a large late positive wave in response to the detected signal stimuli. The latency of the N_{100} response to the click signal is longer than that to the nonsignal clicks because of its lesser intensity. This subject found the signal tonepips difficult to disregard, and there is a small late positive wave in response to these even when they were ignored. Each tracing represents the average of 200 responses. Recordings were taken from vertex to right mastoid. The frequency response (−3 dB) of the recording system was 0.45–25 Hz. Subject K.C.

important responses. One might, for example, propose that in the binaural listening task there is a response set maintained for the nonsignal stimuli in the attended ear, the activation of which results in changes in the $N_{\overline{100}}$ component of the evoked potential, and a different response set for the signal stimuli, the activation of which causes both an enhanced $N_{\overline{100}}$ component and a later positive component. The differences in the evoked potentials to signal and nonsignal stimuli thus may merely reflect the differences in their required responses. There are two experiments that provide evidence against such a proposal. Hink and Hillyard (1976) used a binaural listening experiment in which different passages of prose were spoken to each ear, one by a male voice and one by a female voice. Into each discourse were introduced random irrelevant probe stimuli having the same formant structure as the speaker's vowel "a" but otherwise quite meaningless. Examination of the evoked potential to these completely irrelevant probe stimuli showed a channel-specific attentional effect. Thus, the $N_{\overline{100}}$ changes seem to reflect an early selective mechanism based upon simple pitch and spatial cues without attribution of significance. A further experiment by Hink, Hillyard, and Benson (1978) used four computer-generated syllables delivered in random order either to the left ear (spoken in a male voice) or to the right ear (female voice). The subject was requested to detect and count one of the syllables in one of the ears. There was an increased $N_{\overline{100}}$ component in the evoked potential to all syllables in the attended ear, both targets and nontargets. The late positive wave of the evoked potential occurred only to the signal syllable in the attended ear and did not occur to the same signal delivered to the other sensory channel. This experiment, therefore, gives evidence of hierarchy of selection with response set (as evidenced by the late positive component of the evoked potential) occurring only after stimulus set selection (as evidenced by the enhanced $N_{\overline{100}}$ component). If there was a unitary response set selection, one would have presumed that the signal in the unattended ear would have been differentiated from the nonsignal in that ear by the occurrence of a late positive wave. The hierarchy of stimulus set and response set in this experiment was probably necessary because of the rapidity of the stimulus presentation. At slower stimulus presentation rates one might have been able to use a response set mode of attention without the necessity of a preceding stimulus set. In the experiment of Smith, Donchin, Cohen, and Starr (1970), this probably occurred. When instructed to detect the click stimuli in one ear occurring in a series of letters and numbers and to ignore all the stimuli in the other ear, the subject has a large late positive wave associated with the click stimuli to either ear, and there was no consistent change in the earlier evoked potential components.

VI. THE EARLY PROCESSING OF SENSORY INFORMATION

The selective binaural listening experiments described in the previous paragraphs can provide the possibility of examining the very early components of the auditory evoked potential under conditions with demanding attentional requirements and without possible contaminating effects of arousal. Recording the early components in such experiments is, however, quite difficult because of the increased muscle tension occurring during the experiment and increasing the variability of the small amplitude early components. Such variability is even more problematical if tonepip stimuli are used instead of click stimuli to enhance the channel separation of stimulus set attention, because such tonal stimuli elicit smaller and less distinct early components. Woods and Hillyard (in press) presented random bursts of click stimuli to each ear while the subject attended to a spoken prose passage in one of the ears and ignored a similar prose passage in the other. The rapid presentation of such click stimuli allowed large numbers of responses to be averaged. There were no attention-related changes in the brainstem-evoked potential components to the click stimuli. Unfortunately, the later evoked potential components were too small to be reliably measured, probably because of the very short interstimulus intervals used. Thus there was no definite electrophysiological evidence of a stimulus set selection occurring. The authors also point out that there might have been a frequency-specific stimulus set attention mechanism focused on the lower speech frequencies of the acoustic input as well as on the ear of delivery. Such a possible mechanism would have resulted in the clicks to both ears being similarly ignored.

We performed a selective binaural listening experiment using somewhat longer interstimulus intervals, using stimuli that were the focus of attention rather than irrelevant probes. The stimuli were programmed to occur at random interstimulus intervals of between 150 and 800 msec, with a rectangular distribution of interval probability. These stimuli were randomly allocated to the right ear as 55 dBSL 500 Hz 7.5 msec tones, or to the left ear as 50 dBSL clicks. One in 20 stimuli were randomly converted to "signals" — 580 Hz tones or 45 dBSL slicks. The evoked potentials were recorded from vertex to right mastoid using different time bases in order to evaluate both early and late components of the evoked potential. The subjects were instructed to focus attention on one ear in order to detect and keep a running count of the number of signals in that ear — a task that was performed at between 60 and 95% accuracy, and was subjectively associated with intermittent blocking of the unattended channel from perception. Illustrative responses to the nonsignal stimuli are shown in Fig. 5. There were no significant attentional changes in the evoked potential prior to the N_{100} component. Attended stimuli showed a definite enhancement of this component relative to when the stimulus was ignored. The attended signal stimuli showed both an enhancement of the N_{100} component and a large late positive wave with a peak latency of between 350 and 550 msec (Fig. 6). The results of these experiments therefore again suggest an early analysis of incoming sensory information that is relatively stable irrespective of the direction of attention, a stimulus set selection evidenced by changes in the N_{100} component, and a response set selection indexed by the late positive component of the evoked potential.

This stability of the early evoked potential components must, however, be interpreted cautiously. The early components are small in amplitude and relatively variable in the residual unaveraged background activity. It is possible that small changes could have been missed, confidence levels for the amplitude differences being fairly wide. The statistical evaluation of these components was based on the average across subjects, and could not consider the possibility of individual-specific changes. Changes in the overall pattern of neural responsiveness could also be missed in the scalp-recorded evoked potentials, which derive mainly from those neurons that fire synchronously at stimulus onset (Donald, in press).

These findings are, nevertheless, compatible with animal research demonstrating the great stability of the evoked potentials at the initial levels of the primary sensory pathways during behavioral changes (reviewed in Picton, et al., 1976). There certainly exist efferent pathways in the primary sensory system capable of changing the responsivity of early sensory neurons, but such efferent activity could serve a stimulus-dependent tuning process rather than result from a central selective process controlling sensory input. This relative stability at the early levels of the primary sensory system contrasts with the tremendous plasticity of neural responsiveness in the reticular information and association areas of thalamus and cortex. We therefore postulated (Picton & Hillyard, 1974) a dual auditory sensory system: a primary system that performs a stable and consistent analysis of incoming information irrespective of the direction of attention; and a secondary system (involving such areas as the brainstem reticular formation and association cortex) that is variably involved in sensory processing depending upon current perceptual requirements.

Recent animal experiments using multiple-unit recordings rather than evoked potential recordings have, however, shown definite changes in the activity of early sensory nuclei during habituation (Buchwald & Humphrey, 1972; Weinberger, Oleson, & Ashe, 1975) and classical conditioning (Oleson, Ashe, & Weinberger, 1975). Plasticity therefore can exist to some degree in the primary sensory system. The simple distinction of primary and secondary sensory pathways, although still valid in a relative sense, is not as clear cut as originally postulated. The behavioral significance of primary pathway plasticity is, however, difficult to interpret. This plasticity could be more related to changes in simple brainstem reflexes than to any attentional selection of incoming information for higher processing.

The most reasonable hypothesis about human attention that remains is that there is an initial registration and analysis of sensory information occurring prior to and independently of attentional selection. Attention has its most definite neurophysiological correlates in the evoked potential components that occur later than 50 msec after stimulus onset. It is to the nature and functional significance of these various components that our discussion now turns.

VII. THE NATURE OF THE $N_{\overline{100}}$ COMPONENT OF THE EVOKED POTENTIAL

The $N_{\overline{100}}$ component of the evoked potential is determined more by the characteristics of the onset of a stimulus than by any aspect of its continuance (Clynes, 1969; Onishi & Davis, 1968). This is not so important when evaluating the response to brief clicks or tonepips. However, if one wished to examine those events occurring during the perception of a more prolonged sensory stimulus, one should evaluate the sustained evoked potential occurring during the stimulus rather than the onset evoked potential occurring at its beginning. Auditory stimuli may elicit sustained negative shifts lasting the duration of the stimulus, as can be seen from Fig. 4. This negativity, like the $N_{\overline{100}}$ component, may be enhanced by attention, but such a change occurs only when attention is necessary throughout the stimulus, rather than merely at its onset — for example, in the detection of stimulus duration changes rather than stimulus intensity changes (Picton & Woods, 1975). The transient nature of the $N_{\overline{100}}$ component suggests that it reflects some changes in brain activity, and might be more related to the activation rather than the activity of cerebral processes.

The refractory period of the $N_{\overline{100}}$ component is fairly prolonged, extending approximately 10 seconds (Davis, Mast, Yoshie, & Zerlin, 1966). This refractory period can be examined by measuring the amplitude of the evoked potential at various stimulus presentation rates, as illustrated in the left portion of Fig. 7. The refractory period is specific to the nature of the repeating stimulus, and changing the pitch of a repeating toneburst enhances the amplitude of the evoked potential (Butler, 1968), as shown in the right portion of Fig. 7. The rather prolonged refractory period of the $N_{\overline{100}}$ response poses problems in psychophysiological correlation, since the second of the two stimuli, although perceived and responded to in a similar manner to the first, may have a markedly smaller evoked potential. If the $N_{\overline{100}}$ does, however, represent the activation of cerebral processes necessary to the processing of incoming sensory information, its attenuation with decreasing interstimulus intervals might indicate the persistence of previously activated neural processes that need not be further reactivated. The change in the response caused by changing the nature of the repeating stimulus would index the additional neural processing that must be activated to process the different information. The refractory period of the $N_{\overline{100}}$ might therefore represent one way of evaluating the temporal span of primary memory processes, or the duration of the "conscious present" as discussed by Michon (this volume).

At the present time there is some controversy as to the cerebral origin of the $N_{\overline{100}}$ component of the scalp-recorded evoked potential. In the general latency range of this component there is activity occurring in the primary auditory

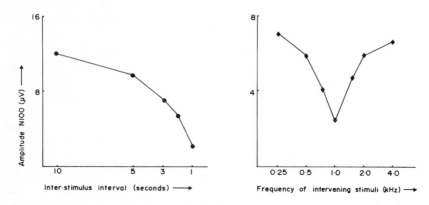

FIG. 7. Refractory periods of the auditory $N_{\overline{100}}$ component. Left: amplitude of the $N_{\overline{100}}$ component to the onset of an 80 dBSL 1kHz 600 ms toneburst presented at different rates. Interstimulus intervals were measured between the points of onset of each stimulus. The mean data from four subjects is presented. Right: the amplitude of the $N_{\overline{100}}$ component to the onset of an 80 dBSL 1kHz toneburst presented once every 4 sec. Three equally loud stimuli of 1kHz or a different frequency were presented in the interval between these tonebursts, so that the overall stimulus rate was once a second. The amplitude of the evoked potential to the 1 kHz toneburst varied with the tonal frequency of the intervening stimuli showing the specificity of the refractory period. Mean data for eight subjects is presented.

cortex, in the auditory association areas of the temporal lobe, and in frontal association cortex. When recording the scalp distribution of this potential a frontocentral maximum can be obtained. This might indicate an origin in frontal association cortex (Picton, Hillyard, Krausz, & Galambos, 1974), but it is also possible to obtain such a scalp distribution from volume conducted potentials originating in the primary auditory cortex of the supratemporal plane (Vaughan & Ritter, 1970). The animal evidence suggests that both may contribute to the scalp-recorded waveform (Arezzo, Pickoff, & Vaughan, 1975). There is also evidence of activity in the lateral temporal regions occurring in the same general latency range as the vertex $N_{\overline{100}}$ response (Wolpaw & Penry, 1975). It has been recently proposed that in the visual and somatosensory modalities there are "parallel late waves" arising from the primary sensory cortex and from the association cortex (Donald, 1976), and it is probable that the principle of such parallel late waves extends to the auditory system.

There is some evidence from human intracranial recordings that one can record from the frontal cortex, in the first 200 msec after an expected but absent stimulus, potentials similar in morphology to those evoked by the stimulus when it is present (Weinberg, Walter, & Crow, 1970). These potentials are often followed by a later positive wave. In averaged scalp recordings the earlier components of the emitted potential are difficult to evaluate because of variability in timing and only the later positivity is definitely recognized. Thus, the $N_{\overline{100}}$ component to an attended stimulus might be composed of both sensory evoked activity and emitted cerebral processes related to perceptual expectancies. This differentiation of the human event-related potentials into evoked and emitted components is similar to the distinction between the exogenous and endogenous components of the animal's sensory evoked potential made by John and his colleagues (John, 1976; John, Bartlett, Shimokochi, & Kleinman, 1975), the exogenous process representing the analysis of the physical stimulus, and the endogenous process reflecting the release of memory information relevant to its evaluation.

There are two possible relations between endogenous and exogenous components of the event-related potential. The endogenous component may be elicited in some manner by the exogenous response, and represent the actual perception of the stimulus; or the two components may be related in a comparison process, the exogenous component of the evoked potential representing the analyzed incoming sensory information, and the endogenous component representing the relevant memories to which exogenous activity may be compared. In the comparison concept the endogenous components of the evoked potential do not represent the interpretation of the incoming sensory information, but rather supply the context for that interpretation.

A possible mechanism underlying the attentional enhancement of the $N_{\overline{100}}$ component of the evoked potential involves the reticular nuclei of the thalamus. Extensive work over the last few years has led Skinner and his colleagues (Skinner, in press; Skinner & Yingling, 1977; Yingling & Skinner, 1976) to conclude that this area of thalamus subserves an inhibitory gating function for activity being relayed to the cortex. There are two control systems affecting this inhibitory function. The thalamic reticular nucleus is inhibited by activity in the mesencephalic reticular formation and selectively activated by the frontal cortex. General arousal, mediated by midbrain reticular activity, can therefore cause widespread increase in the thalamocortical response to incoming sensory information. Through its connections to the thalamic reticular formation it is quite possible that the frontal cortex can selectively program the access of sensory information to cortex. Skinner therefore suggests that negative shifts in the frontal cortex are not related to general arousal, but rather to higher cerebral processes through which the frontal cortex exerts its influence on the reticular nuclei of the thalamus.

In summary, the general possible hypotheses about the $N_{\overline{100}}$ component should perhaps be delineated. It would seem that the $N_{\overline{100}}$ component represents the activation or reactivation of processes in short-term memory relevant to the analysis of attended incoming information. Access to such processes is determined by the organization of stimulus set selective attention, deriving from activity in the frontal cortex and effected by the gating mechanisms of the thalamic reticular nuclei. The general accessibility of cortex to incoming information is controlled by the mesencepahalic reticular formation and probably correlated to levels of general arousal. The mode of action of the short-term memory processes is that of a comparison between incoming information and subjective expectancies and memories (cf. Neisser, 1976). Perception and response result subsequent to and dependent upon such a comparative process.

VIII. THE LATE COMPONENTS OF THE EVOKED POTENTIALS

The pattern of the evoked potential after the $N_{\overline{100}}$ component becomes quite complex. It is probable that at this latency there are many possible responses available to the subject, and the complexity of the recording merely reflects the variable choice of appropriate responses. What follows is a brief catalogue of the late evoked potential components.

There are several late negative waves. Two of these have already been discussed: a large late frontocentral negativity associated with sleep, and a late frontal wave occurring in response to a warning stimulus to form the initial portion of the contingent negative variation. Another late negative wave usually occurs with the detection of a signal stimulus in association with a later larger positive component. Klinke, Fruhstorfer, and Finkenzeller (1968) showed that the response to an omitted somatosensory stimulus was a negative–positive complex. In their evaluation of the relationship of the late positive wave to reaction time, Ritter, Simson, and Vaughan (1972) suggested that this negative wave might index the actual decision processes that had already proceeded to response by the time of the late positivity. Picton, Hillyard, and Galambos (1974) demonstrated that the negative wave differed in scalp distribution from the following positivity. Two elegant scalp distribution studies (Simson, Vaughan, & Ritter, 1976, 1977) have recently shown that the late negative wave $N_{\overline{200}}$ is modality-specific in its scalp distribution, whereas the following positivity has a field distribution that is similar across modalities in which the signals are presented. The late negative wave seems to occur in response to improbable stimuli, irrespective of whether they are attended or not (Ford, Roth, & Kopell, 1976a; Squires, Donchin, Herning, & McCarthy, 1977). Its amplitude is less, however, when attention is directed toward another modality (Ford, Roth, Dirks, & Kopell, 1973), and it has thus been suggested that the negative wave might represent neural processes underlying the discrimination of targets within a specific sensory modality (Ritter, in press).

Many late positive components have been described in the event-related potential. A positive wave in the evoked potential almost inevitably follows the $N_{\overline{100}}$ wave by 60–100 msec. Its scalp distribution is less frontal in extent than that of the preceding negative component (Picton, Hillyard, Krausz, & Galambos, 1974; Roth, Krainz, Ford, Tinklenberg, Rothbart, & Kopell, 1976). This positive component is often increased in size in conditions resulting in enhancement of the later positive waves, probably because this later positivity begins during or even before the peak of the $P_{\overline{180}}$ component. It has, therefore, been suggested that there is associated with the detection of relevant stimuli one large late long-lasting positivity (Wilkinson & Ashby, 1974), the duration of which varies with the amount of processing required, and the morphology of which is interrupted by the superimposition of two negative waves at 100 and 220 msec (Näätänen, 1975). However, the $P_{\overline{180}}$ component has a very distinct scalp distribution from the later positive wave (Hillyard et al., 1976) suggesting different underlying generator mechanisms.

The most frequently recorded late positive wave is a large positivity occurring at the peak latency of 300 msec or more, that is often termed the P_3 or $P_{\overline{300}}$ component. This positive wave is recorded in response to many kinds of attended stimuli presenting task-relevant information (Tueting, in press). Scalp distribution studies (Simson et al, 1976, 1977; Vaughan & Ritter, 1970) show that this component is largely recorded from centroparietal areas, except in certain conditions such as the inhibition of a motor response ("no–go") when the scalp distribution is more frontal (Hillyard et al., 1976).

Improbable stimuli can occasionally elicit a late positive wave even when irrelevant and unattended (Roth, 1973). Squires, Squires, and Hillyard (1975b) have shown that this positivity is somewhat earlier in latency and somewhat more frontal than the positivity associated with an attended detected signal, and suggested that it might be termed the P_{3_a} to differentiate it from the later and larger P_{3_b}. This differentiation has been upheld in several later studies (Ford, Roth, & Kopell, 1976b; Snyder & Hillyard, 1976). In a principal component analysis of evoked potential data under ignore and attend conditions, there is a small early positivity associated with improbability, independent of attention and accounting for a small portion of the variance, although a larger portion is related to the negative wave of similar latency (Squires, Donchin, Herning, & McCarthy, 1977). Such an early P_{3_a} is not recognizable in the control data for the many attentional experiments that we have been discussing, probably because the differentiation and recognition of unattended improbable stimuli must be fairly easy and not require any attentional effort. It has been suggested that this small positive wave might represent the activity of a "mismatch" detector (Snyder & Hillyard, 1976; Squires et al., 1975b). Roth (in press) and Ford (in press) raise the possibility that the early positive wave might effect the initial processing of an improbable stimulus, whereas the later continuation of the positivity only occurs if further processing of that improbable stimulus is deemed relevant. In general, a reasonable hypothesis is that the early positive wave occurring in response to an improbable irrelevant signal might be the psychological correlate of "noticing but not paying much attention."

Courchesne, Hillyard, and Galambos (1975) found that highly novel stimuli occurring during a visual vigilance task elicited large late positive waves with a very frontal scalp distribution. These waves were of similar latency to the parietal late positivity occurring in response to the detected signal in the vigilance task. Such frontal late positive waves are perhaps related to that part of the orienting response concerned with the modification of behavioral expectancies.

A slow positive-going baseline shift has also been reported in association with the detection of signal stimuli (Hillyard et al., 1976; Squires et al., 1975b; Squires et al., 1977). At the present time it is difficult to tell whether this represents a return to baseline of a preceding cortical negativity, or whether it represents the continuation of stimulus information processing. A possibly distinct late positivity ("P_4") occurring after the P_{300} has been recognized by several researchers, but at the present time the psychological determinants of this wave are not well-understood. Picton, Woods, Stuss, and Campbell (in press) have hypothesized that it might represent the utilization of information in perceptual readjustment.

IX. THE NATURE OF THE PARIETOCENTRAL LATE POSITIVE WAVE

Certainly one of the most important determinants of the amplitude of this late positive component is stimulus improbability. Sutton, Braren, Zubin, and John (1965) reported that a low probability stimulus elicited a larger late positive component than a highly probable stimulus when the subject was requested to guess the type of stimulus prior to its occurrence. This, and a second series of experiments showing that the late positive wave occurred at the time of stimulus uncertainty resolution, suggested that this late positive component might be related to the "effective information content of the stimulus" (Sutton, Tueting, Zubin, & John, 1967).

Several studies have shown that the major determining variable of the late positive component is the probability of the response to the stimulus rather than the actual stimulus probability itself. In the guessing paradigm, the late positive component is not simply determined by the probability of occurrence of the feedback stimuli but by the relative probability of their confirming or discon-firming meaning — the "outcome probability" (Friedman et al., 1973; Tueting, Sutton, & Zubin, 1971). Karlin and Martz (1973) showed that the late positive wave in a reaction time task was determined by the probability of the motor response rather than the probability of the stimulus eliciting that response. Friedman, Ritter, and Simson (in press) have shown that in a vigilance task the amplitude of the late positive component to the nonsignal stimulus is determined by the probability of all the nonsignals taken together, rather than the individual probability of any given nonsignal. It is therefore not the amount of information present in the stimulus but the amount of information actually transmitted to response (cf. Keele, 1973, Chapter 4) that seems to determine the amplitude of the late positive wave.

We have investigated this dependence of the late positive component on the amount of task-relevant information in an experiment evaluating the evoked potentials to feedback stimuli following a time-estimation task. One of three light-emitting diodes denoted that the response had been within a time interval considered correct, and two other diodes denoted whether the response had been too fast or too slow. The probability and therefore the information content of the feedback stimuli could be altered by varying the duration of the time interval wherein responses were judged correct. A control condition, in which the feedback stimuli were not related to performance, was also included. Results from these experiments are illustrated to the left and to the upper right of Fig. 8. The amplitude of the late positive component of the feedback evoked potential ($P_{\overline{375}}$) is largely determined by the amount of task-relevant information in the stimuli, measured in bits as $-\log_2$ (feedback probability). The correlation coefficients between the $P_{\overline{375}}$ component and the information content of the stimuli varied from +0.32 to +0.90 for the eight individual subjects, and for the mean data was +0.92. Another way of manipulating the information content in this experiment is to use qualitative feedback (correct and incorrect) rather than quantitative feedback (correct, too fast, too slow). The effects of such a manipulation are shown in the lower right of Fig. 8

The amplitude of the late positive component is more closely related to the subjective expectancy rather than the objective probability of the upcoming response. This is elegantly shown in the recent experiment of Squires, Wickens, Squires, and Donchin (1976) evaluating the effects of stimulus sequence on the late positive component. Even though a signal is at all times equally improbable, the late positive component to a signal stimulus occurring after a long train of nonsignals is larger than if it occurs after many signals. This could be related to a local subjective probability estimate for response, which differs from the objective global probability of stimulus occurrence (cf. Remington, 1969). The signal stimulus occurring after a train of nonsignals would therefore be experienced as more immediately improbable than it really was.

Another major determinant of the late positive component is the confidence of the subject in his perception of the signal. Hillyard et al. (1971) demonstrated that greater confidence in a threshold signal detection task was associated with larger amplitudes of the $P_{\overline{300}}$ component of the evoked potential. Squires, Squires, and Hillyard (1975a) demonstrated that this effect held true even if the confident response was actually a false alarm, but was not true for correct rejections. This was attributed to the greater confidence in or distinctness of the detection as opposed to the rejection. When the task was made easier, probability began to play an increasing role in the amplitude of the $P_{\overline{300}}$ and at high signal probabilities the confident correct rejection elicited a larger $P_{\overline{300}}$ than the hit. They therefore proposed two factors controlling the $P_{\overline{300}}$ amplitude: at lower intensity levels, confidence was most important, and at higher levels signal improbability became predominant. Increasing difficulty of signal discrimination also decreases the amplitude of this late positive wave (Adams & Benson, 1973; Ford et al., 1976b).

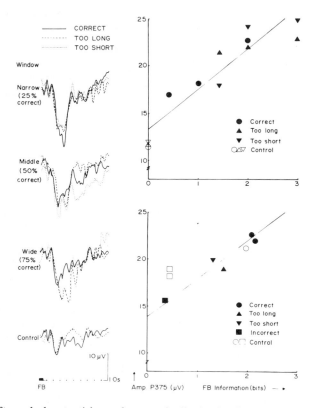

FIG. 8. Left: evoked potential waveforms to feedback stimuli following a time estimation task. The percentage of correct responses was manipulated by altering the duration of the time window wherein a response was judged correct. In the control condition feedback was presented without meaning to the task and with individual stimulus probabilities of 50%, 25%, and 25%. Each tracing represents the average of 32 responses. The recordings were taken from the vertex to linked mastoids with relative negativity of the vertex represented by an upward deflection. Subject M.H. Upper right: mean data from eight subjects in the experiment illustrated on the left. Baseline to peak amplitude of the $P_{\overline{375}}$ wave is plotted against the amount of information presented by the feedback stimuli. The regression line (correlation coefficient 0.92) is drawn using both control and experimental data. Lower right: amplitude of the $P_{\overline{375}}$ component of the evoked potential in a series of experiments manipulating the information content of the feedback stimuli. The window for correct time estimation was adjusted so that the subjects performed at approximately 25% correct level. In one block of trials (qualitative feedback) information as to the incorrect responses was simply "incorrect," and in another block (quantitative feedback) the information was either "too short" or "too long." The mean data from 14 subjects is plotted. The regression line (correlation coefficient 0.97) was based on the two experimental conditions. In a control condition two different equiprobable stimuli were both used to provide a qualitative disconfirming feedback ("incorrect") with no evidence as to whether the response was too fast or too slow. It was presumed that the late positivity to the control stimuli would be similar to that of the single incorrect feedback stimulus. The amplitude of the late positivity elicited by these stimuli was, however, between that of the quantitative and the qualitative incorrect feedback, possibly because the subjects considered the stimuli more informative than they really were.

454

These effects of stimulus discriminability and perceptual confidence have recently been elegantly evaluated in terms of the underlying information processing by Ruchkin and Sutton (in press b). They propose that the late positive component of the evoked potential indexes the amount of information received by a subject, this being equal to the information provided by an event less the information loss related to the subject's uncertainty as to whether his perception of that event was correct, such a loss being termed "equivocation."

Information may be redundant to task performance. Squires, Donchin, Squires, and Grossberg (1977) presented a train of combined visual–auditory stimuli, with infrequent and easily discriminable signal stimuli occurring randomly in either modality. When instructed to count the number of signals in one modality, the amplitude of the P_{300} wave was unaffected if the signal in the other modality occurred simultaneously, since the information presented by such an event was redundant to the task. If, however, the discriminability of the signals was made more difficult, the information in the double signal stimulus became less redundant and was associated with a larger P_{300} than the simple signal stimuli, this late positive wave being equally prominent whether the instructions were to count the signals in one or the other modality or in both.

The information provided by a stimulus can be varied by changing the predictability of that stimulus. Donchin, Kubovy, Kutas, Johnson, and Herning (1973) showed that the more predictable a stimulus was, the smaller the P_{300} amplitude in its evoked potential. In the previously described experiment, in which a subject had to determine which of four stimuli in a train was the signal stimulus (Fig. 4), the amount of information provided by the different stimuli varied with the location of the signals in the train. The probability of the first stimulus being a signal was 0.25 and the probability of it being a nonsignal was 0.75. If it did actually turn out to be a signal it would have provided two bits of information and the following stimuli would present no further information. If the second stimulus was a signal, the information in the stimuli would be divided into 0.42 bits for the first stimulus and 1.58 bits for the second. If the last stimulus was a signal, this would be completely predictable on the basis of the other three being nonsignals; in such a case the information would be divided as 0.42 bits for the first stimulus, 0.58 bits for the second stimulus, and 1.0 bit for the third. As can be seen in Fig. 4, the amplitude of the P_{350} component evoked by the nonsignal stimuli varied with the information content of the stimuli.

Completely predictable stimuli can, however, elicit late positive components in the evoked potential. This is especially true if the stimuli elicit some finalization of response to a set of stimuli. Friedman, Simson, Ritter, and Rapin (1975) showed that when words were presented in sentence structure, the word at the end of the sentence was associated with a large P_{300} even when it was completely predictable. They therefore suggested that in this case the P_{300} was related to "syntactic closure." It is possible that these types of late positive components might be related to the final resolution of temporal uncertainty. Ford et al. (1976a) presented suggestive evidence that under certain conditions temporal rather than stimulus improbability might be the determinant of the $P_{\overline{300}}$ amplitude. Temporal equivocation may perhaps be one reason why the $P_{\overline{300}}$ to an omitted stimulus remains smaller despite computer analysis to compensate for the latency variability (Ruchkin and Sutton, in press a). In our experiment, in which a subject had to detect which of the four stimuli in a train was the signal stimulus, the evoked potential to the signal contained a large late positivity irrespective of the signal location (and therefore its predictability) in the train. When the signal occurred in the fourth position it was by then completely predictable, but still elicited a definite late positive wave.

A final aspect of information processing involves the attribution of meaning. This meaning of a stimulus varies with the context in which it is perceived. This is also true of the late positive component of the evoked potential. Figure 9 shows evoked potentials to stimuli occurring with similar probabilities (and therefore similar information contents) in three different contexts. In one condition the subject merely kept a running count of the number of both stimuli and there was a small $P_{\overline{300}}$ in the evoked potential that was somewhat larger for the less probable stimulus. In another condition the stimuli provided feedback about performance on a preceding sensory discrimination task. A much larger late positive wave was elicited by these stimuli although their improbability (and therefore their objective information content) remained the same. The range of possible perceptual responses to the stimuli as feedback − the context of their evaluation − was far wider than in the simple counting task. The stimuli were thus more meaningful. A final condition, in which the subject read a book and ignored the stimuli, served as control.

Thus the parietocentral late positive component of the evoked potential seems in some way associated with the passage of unequivocable task-relevant information to its appropriate response in the context of the range of possible responses to that information.

There is as yet little knowledge of the functional significance of this relationship. Karlin (1970) postulated that the late positive wave might represent a reactive change in the state occurring in association with but not as an integral part of sensory information processing. Squires, Hillyard, and Lindsay (1973) suggested that the $P_{\overline{300}}$ might represent the output of a comparator mechanism that functions to match incoming sensory information to expectancies, this output being determined by the closeness of the match and the unexpectedness of the outcome. Donchin and his colleagues have postulated that the $P_{\overline{300}}$ might reflect the activity of a general-purpose processing system invoked when necessary for the evaluation of significant stimuli in relation to general contextual hypotheses (Donchin et al., 1973; Squires et al., 1976). Picton and Hillyard (1974) conceived that the $P_{\overline{300}}$ might reflect the general activation of the necessary perceptual and motor responses to a significant event. Donald (in press) has

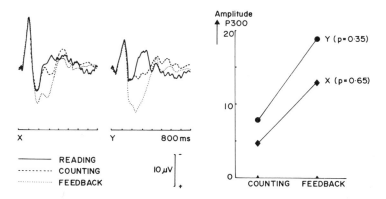

FIG. 9.   Stimulus meaning and the late positive component of the evoked potential. In this experiment an initial pair of tonepips followed by a faint light preceded a final 70 dBSL 800 ms toneburst of 1kHz (X) or 8 kHz (Y). In the first condition the subject read a book and ignored all stimuli. In the second condition the subject ignored the initial stimuli but kept a running count of the number of final tonebursts at each frequency — the 1 kHz toneburst being approximately twice as frequent as the 8 kHz toneburst. In the last condition the subject performed a difficult pitch discrimination to decide whether the two tonepips were the same or different, and responded during the light stimulus. The final toneburst then served as feedback as to whether the response was correct (X) or incorrect (Y). The subjects performed with an accuracy of 60–70%. Waveforms from subject F.X. are shown on the left, and the mean data for four subjects is shown on the right. Evoked potentials were recorded between the vertex and the left mastoid and each tracing represents the average of 200 (X) or 100 (Y) responses.

suggested that the late positive component of the evoked potential is a non-specific signal of a changeover in the content of short-term memory processing, rather than the information processing itself, and possibly reflecting an "erase" function occurring at the completion or initiation of such association cortex processing.

The parietal lobe is an area of polysensory association cortex that is highly developed in primates, especially in man. Patients with lesions of this pareital cortex display complex symptomatology (Critchley, 1953). They are unable to attribute meaning to incoming stimuli (agnosia) and have difficulty in the initiation of simple behavioral activity (apraxia). They are particularly unable to process information in the context of language, spatial constructs, or body image. Their disability seems to involve an inability to process incoming information to its necessary perceptual or motor response. Their defect has been described as a sensory "neglect" or "inattention."

The neural activity of such polysensory association cortex is difficult to study in animals. Mountcastle (1976) has described the activity of neurons in the parietal lobe of primates. There are sets of neurons that are active "when the animal emits a particular behavioural act under a specific motivational drive." The parietal lobe combines the information available from the senses into the context of the immediate goals of the animal in order to generate "directives for action." Kornhuber (1974) has suggested that the parietotemporal association cortex is concerned with the "tactics" of response, based upon immediate sensory input, with the global "strategy" for action being proposed by frontal and limbic cortex. Deecke, Becker, Grözinger, Scheid, and Kornhuber (1973) have indeed shown that motor activity may be preceded by a premotor positivity arising from the parietal regions.

In this respect it is appropriate to consider the relationship of the human late positive wave to behavioral responses, the simplest of which is a reaction time response. The difficulties involved in such a seemingly simple correlation are, however, immense (Ritter, in press; Tueting, in press). If both reaction time and the $P_{\overline{300}}$ are measured at the same time, the motor potentials associated with the reaction interact with the scalp recording of the $P_{\overline{300}}$. If they are measured at different times, there is no certainty that the psychological processes are similar under each condition. Another problem is whether the peak latency should be the definitive timing measurement for the $P_{\overline{300}}$, since the late positivity begins much earlier than its peak, at times as early as 105 msec (Chapman, 1973). Certain studies have suggested a similarity between reaction time and the $P_{\overline{300}}$ peak latency (Kutas & Donchin, in press; Picton et al., 1974a; Ritter et al., 1972). Other studies have shown, however, that in certain conditions the $P_{\overline{300}}$ peak latency could precede the usual reaction time by 100 msec or more (Squires et al., 1977; and in the figures of Donald, 1970, and Roth, Kopell, Tinklenberg, Darley, Sikora, & Vesecky, 1975). It is possible that in these difficult perceptual judgments a multiple observation process occurs with accumulation of evidence for different response options (cf. Vickers, this volume). The $P_{\overline{300}}$ might occur with the initiation of such an observing process. In overview of these many experiments, it seems that the late positive component of the evoked potential is associated with responsiveness, but the exact temporal relationships are unclear. Thus it is possible to conceive of the $P_{\overline{300}}$ as representing the initiation of many possible appropriate responses, only some of which need be related to motor activity. Spatiotemporal mapping of the late positive waves indicates a changing of scalp distribution from the beginning to the end of the process, suggesting possible changes in the underlying generators (Lesevre & Renault, in press). The responses intitiated during the late positive component might be related to the fixation of information into memory, the initiation of appropriate behavior, the activation of further perceptual observation, or the modification of the general strategy of behavior. All of these responses can be initiated in the parietal region, but may secondarily involve other regions of the brain for the final completion of the response.

Several researchers (e.g., Posner, 1975; Simson et al., 1976) have suggested a possible relationship between the late positive wave and conscious awareness. The late positive component of the evoked potential probably occurs at about the same time as conscious awareness might occur. At the present time, however, it is difficult to say whether there is a particular response of the brain that is by nature "conscious" or whether, more probably, consciousness is an emergent property of total brain responsiveness (Sperry, 1969). Consciousness has many aspects. As well as passive awareness, there is also an active intentional component to consciousness, as mentioned in the earlier discussion of the frontal activity, that might underly the organization of perception. At the present time, however, the actual requirements for and electrophysiological concomitants of consciousness are almost completely unknown. Our research remains with the overwhelming question as to the nature of "the substrata of consciousness," the most complex of all sensori-motor processes, "by which physiologically speaking the organism is adjusted to its environment, and psychologically speaking, the subject to the object" (Jackson, 1875/1958).

X. TENTATIVE CONCLUSIONS

This paper has reviewed the use of human event-related potentials in evaluating the processes of selective attention. The present state of knowledge is such that we have pretended to no final understanding and have therefore included many postulates that are by nature hypothetical and in intent heuristic. The following is a brief summary of a general theoretical position that can be revised and extended by future experiment.

When attention is directed toward an incoming stimulus there is no observable change in the early components of the evoked potential that reflects activity in the primary sensory pathways. This suggests a relatively stable registration and analysis of incoming information. A major selective process involves stimulus set attention and is indexed by the enhancement of a late negative wave in the evoked potential beginning around 50 msec after the stimulus and peaking at around 100 msec. This selection of incoming information is determined by simple physical characteristics of the stimuli. Such a selection is probably mediated by means of a thalamic gating system centered in the reticular nuclei of the thalamus and susceptible to both specific organization by the frontal cortex, and general inhibition by the mesencephalic reticular formation concerned with arousal. Thus the mechanims of selective attention and general arousal are similar, the one resulting from a selective organization of thalamic gating mechanisms, and the other resulting from a nonspecific opening of all of the thalamic gates. The processes that are evidenced by the scalp-recorded $N_{\overline{100}}$ wave are poorly understood, but it is possible they involve a comparison between incoming information and endogenous memories and expectancies. As a result of such a comparative evaluation, significant stimuli are selected as requiring necessary perceptuomotor responses. This type of selection involves response set attention. Such response sets can in part be primed by activation of the cortical regions that evaluate stimulus—response contingencies, this activation being recorded as a localized negativity over the cortex specific to the response. The late positive wave of the evoked potential occurs in relation to the final response selection and in general reflects the amount of unequivocal information processed from stimulus to response. The negativity recorded mainly from the frontal regions of the brain during attention probably reflects the neural processes underlying the organization of attention and the allocation of effort to those aspects of sensory information processing that are significant to the underlying goals and needs of the subject. Such processes select the source of incoming information and set the context of its processing.

ACKNOWLEDGMENTS

The senior author would like to express his appreciation for the many discussions about evoked potentials that he has had with his colleagues. In particular he would like to thank Dr. Steven Hillyard with whom much of the conceptualization of the levels of selective attention was done; Dr. Walter Ritter, for extensive discussions on the functional significance of the late positive component; and Dr. Donald Stuss, for long conversations about the frontal lobe. He would also like to thank Doctors Merlin Donald, Judy Ford, Bob Hink, Tom Roth, Dan Ruchkin, Skip Skinner, and Sam Sutton, who allowed him to refer to papers that are still in press. Previous reviews of the field by Näätänen (1975) and by Tueting (in press) were immensely helpful in the preparation of this present paper. The three new experiments referred to in this paper were performed with the assistance of the Medical Research Council of Canada, and the Ontario Mental Health Foundation. The secretarial assistance of Mrs. Barbara Reynolds in preparing this paper is gratefully appreciated.

REFERENCES

Adams, J. C., & Benson, D. A. Task-contingent enhancement of the auditory evoked response. *Electroencephalography and Clinical Neurophysiology,* 1973, *35,* 249—257.
Arezzo, J., Pickoff, A., & Vaughan, H. G. The sources and intracerebral distribution of auditory potentials in the alert rhesus monkey. *Brain Research,* 1975, *90,* 57—73.
Besrest, A., & Requin, J. Onde d'expectative et niveau de performance dans une situation de temps de réaction. *Comptes Rendus des Séances de la Société de Biologie,* 1969, *163,* 1875—1879.
Broadbent, D. E. *Decision and stress.* London: Academic Press, 1971.
Buchwald, J. A., & Humphrey, G. L. Response plasticity in cochlear nucleus of decerebrate cats during acoustic habituation procedures. *Journal of Neurophysiology,* 1972, *35,* 864—878.
Butler, R. A. The effect of changes in stimulus frequency and intensity on habituation of the human vertex potential. *Journal of the Acoustic Society of America,* 1968, *44,* 945—950.
Butler, S. R., & Glass, A. Asymmetries in the CNV over left and right hemispheres while subjects await numeric information. *Biological Psychology,* 1974, *2,* 1—16.
Chapman, R. M. Evoked potentials of the brain related to thinking. In F. J. McGuinan and R. Schoonover (Eds.), *Psychophysiology of thinking.* New York: Academic Press, 1973.

Clynes, M. Dynamics of vertex evoked potentials: The R-M brain function. In E. Donchin and D. B. Lindsley (Eds.), *Average evoked potentials: Methods, results and evaluations* Washington: NASA, 1969.

Cooper, R., McCallum, W.C., & Papakostopoulos, D. A bimodal slow potential theory of cerebral processing. In J. E. Desmedt (Ed.), *Progress in clinical neurophysiology, Volume 6: Cognitive components in cerebral event related potentials and selective attention.* Basel: Karger, in press.

Courchesne, E., Hillyard, S. A., & Galambos, R. Stimulus novelty, task relevance and the visual evoked potential in man. *Electroencephalography and Clinical Neurophysiology,* 1975, *39,* 131–143.

Critchley, M. *The parietal lobes.* London: Edward Arnold, 1953.

Davis, H., Mast, T., Yoshie, N., & Zerlin, S. The slow response of the human cortex to auditory stimuli: recovery process. *Electroencephalography and Clinical Neurophysiology,* 1966, *21,* 105–113.

Deecke, L., Becker, W., Grözinger, B., Scheid, P., & Kornhuber, H. H. Human brain potentials preceding voluntary limb movements. *Electroencephalography and Clinical Neurophysiology,* 1973, (Supplement) *33,* 87–94.

Deecke, L., Scheid, P., & Kornhuber, H. H. Distribution of readiness potential, pre-motion positivity and motor potential of the human cerebral cortex preceding voluntary finger movements. *Experimental Brain Research,* 1969, *7,* 158–168.

Donald, M. W. Direct-current potentials in the human brain during timed cognitive performance. *Nature,* 1970, *227,* 1057–1058.

Donald, M. W. Topography of evoked potential amplitude fluctuations. In W. C. McCallum & J. R. Knott (Eds.), *The responsive brain.* Bristol: John Wright, 1976.

Donald, M. W. Current theories of transient evoked potentials: limits and alternative approaches. In J. E. Desmedt (Ed), *Progress in clinical neurophysiology. Volume 6: Cognitive components in cerebral event-related potentials and selective attention.* Basel: Karger, in press.

Donald, M. W., & Goff, W. R. Attention-related increases in cortical responsivity dissociated from the contingent negative variation. *Science,* 1971, *172,* 1163–1166.

Donchin, E., & Cohen, L. Averaged evoked potentials and intramodality selective attention. *Electroencephalography and Clinical Neurophysiology,* 1967, *22,* 537–546.

Donchin, E., Kubovy, M., Kutas, M., Johnson, R., & Herning, R. I. Graded changes in evoked response (P300) amplitude as a function of cognitive activity. *Perception and Psychophysics,* 1973, *14,* 319–324.

Donchin, E., Tueting, P., Ritter, W., Kutas, M., & Heffley, E. On the independence of the CNV and the P300 components of the human agated evoked potential. *Electroencephalography and Clinical Neurophysiology,* 1975, *38,* 449–461.

Eason, R. G., & Dudley, L. M. Physiological and behavioural indicants of activation. *Psychophysiology,* 1971, *7,* 223–232.

Eason, R. G., Harter, M. R., & White, C. T. Effects of attention and arousal on visually evoked cortical potentials and reaction time in man. *Physiology and Behaviour,* 1969, *4,* 283–289.

Ford, J. M. Does P300 reflect template match/mismatch? In D. Otto (Ed.), *Proceedings of the Fourth International Congress on Event Related Slow Potentials of the Brain,* U.S. Government, in press.

Ford, J. M., Roth, W. T., Dirks, S. J., & Kopell, B. S. Evoked potential correlates of signal recognition between and within modalities. *Science,* 1973, *181,* 465–466.

Ford, J. M., Roth, W. T., & Kopell, B. S. Auditory evoked potentials to unpredictable shifts in pitch. *Psychophysiology,* 1976, *13,* 32–39. (a)

Ford, J. M., Roth, W. T., & Kopell, B. S. Attention effects on auditory evoked potentials to infrequent events. *Biological Psychology,* 1976, *4,* 65–77. (b)

Friedman, D. G., Hakarem, G., Sutton, S., & Fleiss, J. L. Effect of stimulus uncertainty on the pupillary dilation response and the vertex evoked potential. *Electroencephalography and Clinical Neurophysiology*, 1973, *34*, 475–484.

Friedman, D., Ritter, W., & Simson, R. Analysis of non-signal evoked cortical potentials in two kinds of vigilance tasks. In D. Otto (Ed.), *Multidisciplinary perspectives in event-related brain potential research*. U. S. Government, in press.

Friedman, D., Simson, R., Ritter, W., & Rapin, I. The late positive component (P300) and information processing in sentences. *Electroencephalography and Clinical Neurophysiology*, 1975, *38*, 255–262.

Fuster, J. M. Unit activity in prefrontal cortex during delayed-response performance: neuronal correlates of transient memory. *Journal of Neurophysiology*, 1973, *36*, 61–78.

Gaillard, A. W. K. Effects of warning-signal modality on the contingent negative variation. *Biological Psychology*, 1976, *4*, 139–154.

Garner, W. R., Hake, H. W., & Eriksen, C. W. Operationism and the concept of perception. *Psychological Review*, 1956, *63*, 149–159.

Hartley, L. R. The effect of stimulus relevance on the cortical evoked potentials. *Quarterly Journal of Experimental Psychology*, 1970, *22*, 531–546.

Hillyard, S. A. Relationships between the contingent negative variation (CNV) and reaction time. *Physiology and Behaviour*, 1969, *4*, 351–357.

Hillyard, S. A. The CNV and human behaviour: A review. *Electroencephalography and Clinical Neurophysiology*, 1973, (Supplement) *33*, 161–171.

Hillyard, S. A., Courchesne, E., Krausz, H. I., & Picton, T. W. Scalp topography of the "P3" wave in different auditory decision tasks. In W. C. McCallum & J. R. Knott (Eds.), *The responsive brain*. Bristo: John Wright and Sons, 1976.

Hillyard, S. A., Hink, R. F., Schwent, V. L., & Picton, T. W. Electrical signs of selective attention in the human brain. *Science*, 1973, *182*, 177–180.

Hillyard, S. A., & Picton, T. W. Event-related brain potentials and selective information processing in man. In J. E. Desmedt (Ed.), *Progress in clinical neurophysiology, Volume 6: Cognitive components in cerebral event-related potentials and selective attention*. Basel: Karger, in press.

Hillyard, S. A., Squires, K. C., Bauer, J. W., & Lindsay, P. H. Evoked potential correlates of auditory signal detection. *Science*, 1971, *172*, 1357–1360.

Hink, R. F., & Hillyard, S. A. Auditory evoked potentials during selective listening to dichotic speech messages. *Perception and Psychophysics*, 1976, *20*, 236–242.

Hink, R. F., Hillyard, S. A., & Benson, P. J. Event-related brain potentials and selective attention to acoustic and phonetic cues. *Biological Psychology*, 1978, *6*, 1–16.

Jackson, J. H. On the anatomical and physiological localization of movements in the brain. In J. Taylor (Ed.), *Selected writings of John Hughlings Jackson*. London: Staples Press, 1958. (Originally published, 1875.)

Järvilehto, T., & Fruhstorfer, H. Differentiation between slow cortical potentials associated with motor and mental acts in man. *Experimental Brain Research*, 1970, *11*, 309–317.

John, E. R. A model of consciousness. In G. E. Schwartz & D. Shapiro (Eds.), *Consciousness and self-regulation. Advances in research* (Vol. I). New York: Plenum, 1976.

John, E. R., Bartlett, F., Shimokochi, M., & Kleinman, D. Electrophysiological signs of readout from memory. I, Raw data observations. *Journal of Behavioural Biology*, 1975, *14*, 247–282.

Kahneman, D. *Attention and Effort*. Englewood Cliffs, N.J.: Prentice-Hall, 1973.

Karlin, L. Cognition, preparation and sensory-evoked potentials. *Psychological Bulletin*, 1970, *73*, 122–136.

Karlin, L., & Martz, M. J. Response probability and sensory-evoked potentials. In S. Kornblum (Ed.), *Attention and performance IV*. New York: Academic Press, 1973.

Keele, S. W. *Attention and human performance.* Pacific Palisades, Ca.: Goodyear, 1973.

Klinke, R. Fruhstorfer, H., & Finkenzeller, P. Evoked potentials as a function of external and stored information. *Electroencephalography and Clinical Neurophysiology,* 1968, *25,* 119–122.

Knott, J. R. Central and peripheral measures of motivational states. *Electroencephalography and Clinical Neurophysiology,* 1972, *Supplement 31,* 131–137.

Knott, J. R. & Peters, J. F. Changes in CNV amplitude with progressive induction of stress as a function of sex. *Electroencephalography and Clinical Neurophysiology,* 1974, *36,* 47–51.

Kornhuber, H. H. Cerebral cortex, cerebellum and basal ganglia: An introduction to their motor functions. In F. O. Schmitt & F. G. Worden (Eds.), *The neurosciences: Third study program.* Cambridge, Mass.: MIT Press, 1974.

Kutas, M., & Donchin, E. Variations in the latency of P300 as a function of variations in semantic categorizations. In D. Otto (Ed.), *Multidisciplinary perspectives in event-related brain potential research.* U.S. Government, in press.

Lacey, J. I. Somatic response patterning and stress. Some revisions of activation theory. In M. H. Appley & R. Trumbull (Eds.), *Psychological stress: Issues in research.* New York: Appleton-Century-Crofts, 1967.

Lesevre, N., & Renault, H. B. Chronotopographical study of the P300 wave and of the motor potential obtained during visual pattern stimulation in a simple reaction task. In D. Otto (Ed.), *Multidisciplinary perspectives in event-related brain potential research.* U.S. Government, in press.

Loveless, N. E., & Sanford, A. J. The CNV baseline: Considerations of internal consistency of data. *Electroencephalography and Clinical Neurophysiology,* 1973, (Supplement) *33,* 29–33.

Loveless, N. E., & Sanford, A. J. Slow potential correlates of preparatory set. *Biological Psychology,* 1974, *1,* 303–314.

Low, M. D., Borda, R. P., Frost, J. D., & Kellaway, P. Surface-negative slow potential shift associated with conditioning in man. *Neurology,* 1966, *16,* 771–782.

Low, N. D., & Swift, S. J. The contingent negative variation and the "resting" DC potential of the human brain: Effects of situational anxiety. *Neuropsychologia,* 1971, *9,* 203–208.

Luria, A. R. The frontal lobes and the regulation of behaviour. In K. H. Pribram & A. R. Luria (Eds.), *The psychophysiology of the frontal lobes.* New York: Academic Press, 1973.

McAdam, D. W., & Whitaker, H. A. Language production: Electroencephalographic localization in the normal human brain. *Science,* 1971, *172,* 499–502.

McCallum, W. C., & Walter, W. G. The effects of attention and distraction on the contingent negative variation in normal and neurotic subjects. *Electroencephalography and Clinical Neurophysiology,* 1968, *25,* 319–329.

Mountcastle, V. B. The world around us: Neural command functions for selective attention. *Neurosciences Research Program Bulletin,* 1976, *14,* April supplement.

Näätänen, R. Selective attention and evoked potentials. *Annales Academiae Scientiarum Fennicae,* 1967, B151, *1,* 1–226.

Näätänen, R. Evoked potential, EEG, and slow potential correlates of selective attention. In A. F. Sanders (Ed.), *Attention and performance III.* Amsterdam: North-Holland, 1970. (Reprinted from *Acta Psychologica,* 1970, *33.*)

Näätänen, R. The inverted-U relationship between activation and performance: a critical review. In S. Kornblum (Ed.), *Attention and performance IV.* New York: Academic Press, 1973.

Näätänen, R. Selective attention and evoked potentials in humans – a critical review. *Biological Psychology,* 1975, *2,* 237–307.

Näätänen, R. Significance of CNV-kinds of slow shifts during preparation for, and performance of, different tasks. In D. Otto (Ed.), *Multidisciplinary perspectives in event-related brain potential research*. U.S. Government, in press.

Näätänen, R., & Gaillard, A. W. The relationship between the contingent negative variation and the reaction time under prolonged experimental conditions. *Biological Psychology*, 1974, *1*, 277–291.

Naitoh, P., Johnson, L. C., & Lubin, A. Modification of surface negative slow potential (CNV) in the human brain after total sleep loss. *Electrocencephalography and Clinical Neurophysiology*, 1971, *30*, 17–22.

Nauta, W. J. H. The problem of the frontal lobe: A reinterpretation. *Journal of Psychiatric Research*, 1971, *8*, 167–187.

Neisser, U. *Cognition and reality* San Francisco: Freeman, 1976.

Oleson, T. D., Ashe, J. H., & Weinberger, N. M. Modification of auditory and somatosensory system activity during pupillary conditioning in the paralyzed cat. *Journal of Neurophysiology*, 1975, *38*, 1114–1139.

Onishi, S., & Davis, H. Effects of duration and rise time of tonebursts on evoked V-potentials. *Journal of the Acoustic Society of America*, 1968, *44*, 582–591.

Paul, D. D., & Sutton, S. Evoked potential correlates of response criterion in auditory signal detection. *Science*, 1972, *177*, 362–364.

Picton, T. W., Goodman, W. S., & Bryce, D. P. Amplitude of evoked responses to tones of high intensity. *Acta Otolaryngologica*, 1970, *70*, 77–82.

Picton, T. W., & Hillyard, S. A. Human auditory evoked potentials II. Effects of attention. *Electroencephalography and Clinical Neurophysiology*, 1974, *36*, 191–200.

Picton, T. W., Hillyard, S. A., & Galambos, R. Evoked responses to omitted stimuli. In M. N. Livanov (Ed.), *Major problems of brain electrophysiology*. Moscow: USSR Academy of Sciences, 1974. (a)

Picton, T. W., Hillyard, S. A., & Galambos, R. Habituation and attention in the auditory system. In W. D. Keidel & W. D. Neff, (Eds.), *Handbook of Sensory Physiology Volume V, Auditory System. Part 3: Clinical and Special Topics*. Berlin: Springer-Verlag, 1976.

Picton, T. W., Hillyard, S. A., Galambos, R., & Schiff, M. Human auditory attention: A central or peripheral process? *Science*, 1971, *173*, 351–353.

Picton, T. W., Hillyard, S. A., Krausz, H. I., & Galambos, R. Human auditory evoked potentials: I, Evaluation of components. *Electroencephalography and Clinical Neurophysiology*, 1974, *36*, 179–190. (b)

Picton, T. W., & Hink, R. F. Evoked potentials: How? what? and why? *American Journal of EEG Technology*, 1974, *14*, 9–44.

Picton, T. W., & Woods, D. L. Human auditory evoked sustained potentials. *Electroencephalography and Clinical Neurophysiology*, 1975, *38*, 543.

Picton, T. W., Woods, D. L., Stuss, D. T., & Campbell, K. B. Methodology and meaning of human evoked potential scalp distribution studies. In D. Otto (Ed.), *Multidisciplinary perspectives in event-related brain potential research*. U.S. Government, in press.

Posner, M. I. Psychobiology of attention. In M. S. Gazzaniga & C. Blakemore (Eds.), *Handbook of Psychobiology*. New York: Academic, 1975.

Posner, M. I., & Klein, R. M. On the functions of consciousness. In S. Kornblum (Ed.), *Attention and performance IV*. New York: Academic Press, 1973.

Pribram, K. H. *Languages of the brain: Experimental paradoxes and principles in neuropsychology*. Englewood Cliffs, N.J.: Prentice-Hall, 1971.

Pribram, K. H., & McGuiness, D. Arousal, activation, and effort in the control of attention. *Psychological Review*, 1975, *82*, 116–149.

Rebert, C. S. Issues pertaining to the electrogenesis of slow potential changes in the central nervous system. In D. Otto (Ed.), *Multidisciplinary perspectives in event-related brain potential research*. U.S. Government, in press.

Rebert, C. S., McAdam, D. W., Knott, J. R., & Irwin, D. A. Slow potential change in human brain related to level of motivation. *Journal of Comparative and Physiological Psychology*, 1967, *63*, 20–23.

Rebert, C. S., & Tecce, J. J. A summary of CNV and reaction time. *Electroencephalography and Clinical Neurophysiology*, 1973, (Supplement) *33*, 173–178.

Remington, R. J. Analysis of sequential effects in choice reaction times. *Journal of Experimental Psychology*, 1969, *82*, 250–257.

Ritter, W. Latency of event-related potentials and reaction time. In D. Otto (Ed.), *Multidisciplinary perspectives in event-related brain potential research.* U.S. Government, in press.

Ritter, W., Simson, R., & Vaughan, H. G. Association cortex potentials and reaction time in auditory discriminations. *Electroencephalography and Clinical Neurophysiology*, 1972, *33*, 547–555.

Rohrbaugh, J. W., Syndulko, K., & Lindsley, D. B. Brain wave components of the contingent negative variation in humans. *Science*, 1976, *191*, 1055–1057.

Roth, W. T. Auditory evoked responses to unpredictable stimuli. *Psychophsiology*, 1973, *10*, 125–137.

Roth, W. T. How many late positive waves are there? In D. Otto (Ed.), *Multidisciplinary perspectives in event-related brain potential research.* U.S. Government, in press.

Roth, W. T., Kopell, B. S., Tinklenberg, J. R., Darley, C. F., Sikora, R., & Vesecky, T. B. The contingent negative variation during memory retrieval task. *Electroencephalography and Clinical Neurophysiology*, 1975, *38*, 171–174.

Roth, W. T., Krainz, P. L., Ford, J. M., Tinklenberg, J. R., Rothbart, R. M., & Kopell, B. S. Parameters of temporal recovery of the human auditory evoked potential. *Electroencephalography and Clinical Neurophysiology*, 1976, *40*, 623–632.

Ruchkin, S. S., & Sutton, S. Latency characteristics and trial by trial variation of emitted potentials. In J. E. Desmedt (Ed.), *Progress in clinical neurophysiology. Volume 6: Cognitive components in cerebral event-related potentials and selective attention.* Basel: Karger, in press. (a)

Ruchkin, D. S., & Sutton, S. Equivocation and P300 amplitude. In D. Otto (Ed.), *Progress in clinical neurophysiology. Volume 6: Cognitive components in cerebral event-related potentials and selective attention.* Basel: Karger, in press (b)

Satterfield, J. H. Evoked cortical response enhancement and attention in man. A study of responses to auditory and shock stimuli. *Electroencephalography and Clinical Neurophysiology*, 1965, *19*, 470–475.

Schwent, V. L., & Hillyard, S. A. Evoked potential correlates of selective attention with multichannel auditory inputs. *Electroencephalography and Clinical Neurophysiology*, 1975, *38*, 131–138.

Schwent, V. L., Hillyard, S. A., & Galambos, R. Selective attention and the auditory vertex potential: I Effects of stimulus delivery rate. *Electroencephalography and Clinical Neurophysiology*, 1976, *40*, 604–614. (a)

Schwent, V. L., Hillyard, S. A., & Galambos, R. Selective attention and the auditory vertex potential: II Effects of signal intensity and masking noise. *Electroencephalography and Clinical Neurophysiology*, 1976, *40*, 615–622. (b)

Schwent, V. L., Snyder, E., & Hillyard, S. A. Auditory evoked potentials during multichannel selective listening: Role of pitch and localization cues. *Journal of Experimental Psychology: Human Perception and Performance*, 1976, *2*, 313–325. (c)

Shallice, T. Dual functions of consciousness. *Psychological Review*, 1972, *79*, 383–393.

Simson, R., Vaughan, H. G., & Ritter, W. The scalp topography of potentials associated with missing visual or auditory stimuli. *Electroencephalography and Clinical Neurophysiology*, 1976, *40*, 33–43.

Simson, R., Vaughan, H. G., & Ritter, W. The scalp topography of potentials in auditory and visual discrimination tasks. *Electroencephalography and Clinical Neurophysiology*, 1977, *42*, 528–535.

Skinner, J. E. Abolition of a conditioned, surface-negative, cortical potential during cryogenic blockade of the non-specific thalamocortical system. *Electroencephalography and Clinical Neurophysiology*, 1971, *31*, 197–209.

Skinner, J. E. A neurophysiological model for the regulation of sensory input to cerebral cortex. In Otto, D. (Ed.), *Multidisciplinary perspectives in event-related brain potential research*. U.S. Government, in press.

Skinner, J. E., & Yingling, C. D. Central grating mechanisms that regulate event-related potentials and behaviour. A neural model for attention. In J. E. Desmedt (Ed.), *Progress in neurophysiology. Volume 1: Attention, voluntary contraction and event-related cerebral potentials*. Basel: Karger, 1977.

Smith, D. B. D., Donchin, E., Cohen, L., & Starr, A. Auditory averaged evoked potentials in man during selective binaural listening. *Electroencephalography and Clinical Neurophysiology*, 1970, *28*, 146–152.

Snyder, E., & Hillyard, S. A. Long-latency evoked potentials to irrelevant, deviant stimuli. *Behavioural Biology*, 1976, *16*, 319–331.

Sperry, R. W. A modified concept of consciousness. *Psychological Review*, 1969, *76*, 532–536.

Spong, P., Haider, M., & Lindsley, D. B. Selective attentiveness and cortical evoked responses to visual and auditory stimuli. *Science*, 1965, *148*, 395–397.

Squires, K. C., Donchin, E., Herning, R. I., & McCarthy, G. On the influence of task relevance and stimulus probability of ERP components. *Electroencephalography and Clinical Neurophysiology*, 1977, *42*, 1–14.

Squires, N. K., Donchin, E., Squires, K. C., & Grossberg, S. Bisensory stimulation: Inferring decision-related processes from the P300 component. *Journal of Experimental Psychology: Human Perception and Performance*, 1977, *3*, 299–315.

Squires, K. C., Hillyard, S. A., & Lindsay, P. H. Cortical potentials evoked by confirming and disconfirming feedback following an auditory discrimination. *Perception and Psychophysics*, 1973, *13*, 25–31.

Squires, K. C., Squires, N. K., & Hillyard, S. A. Decision-related cortical potentials during an auditory signal detection task with cued observation intervals. *Journal of Experimental Psychology: Human Perception and Performance*, 1975, *104*, 268–279. (a)

Squires, N. K., Squires, K. C., & Hillyard, S. A. Two varieties of long-latency positive waves cvoked by unpredictable auditory stimuli in man. *Electrocencphalography and Clinical Neurophysiology*, 1975, *38*, 387–401. (b)

Squires, K. C., Wickens, C., Squires, N. K., & Donchin, E. The effect of stimulus sequence on the waveform of the cortical event-related potential. *Science*, 1976, *193*, 1142–1145

Stamm, J. S., & Rosen, S. C. Cortical steady potential shifts and anodal polarization during delayed response performance. *Acta Neurobiologiae Experimentalis*, 1972, *32*, 193–209.

Sutton, S., Braren, M., Zubin, J., & John, E. R. Evoked potential correlates of stimulus uncertainty. *Science*, 1965, *150*, 1187–1188.

Sutton, S., Tueting, P., Zubin, J., & John, E. R. Information delivery and the sensory evoked potential. *Science*, 1967, *155*, 1436–1439.

Syndulko, K., & Lindsley, D. B. Motor and sensory determinants of cortical slow potential shifts in man. In J. E. Desmedt (Ed.), *Progress in clinical neurophysiology. Volume 1: Attention, voluntary contraction and event-related cerebral potentials*. Basel: Karger, 1977.

Tecce, J. J. Contingent negative variation (CNV) and psychological processes in man. *Psychological Bulletin*, 1972, *77*, 73–286.*FIG. 1.*

Tecce, J. J., Savignano-Bowman, J., & Meinbresse, D. Contingent negative variation and the distraction-arousal hypothesis. *Electroencephalography and Clinical Neurophysiology*, 1976, *41*, 277–286.

Tecce, J. J., & Scheff, N. M. Attention reduction and suppressed direct-current potentials in the human brain. *Science*, 1969, *164*, 331–333.

Tueting, P. Event-related potentials, cognitive events, and information processing. In D. Otto (Ed.), *Multidisciplinary perspectives in event-related brain potential research*. U.S. Government, in press.

Tueting, P., & Sutton, S. The relationship between pre-stimulus negative shifts and post-stimulus components of the averaged evoked potential. In S. Kornblum (Ed.), *Attention and performance IV*. New York: Academic Press, 1973.

Tueting, P., Sutton, S., & Zubin, J. Quantitative evoked potential correlates of the probability of events. *Psychophysiology*, 1971, *7*, 385–394.

Vaughan, H. G., Costa, L. D., & Ritter, W. Topography of the human motor potential. *Electroencephalography and Clinical Neurophysiology*, 1969, *25*, 1–10.

Vaughan, H. G., & Ritter, W. The sources of auditory evoked responses recorded from the human scalp. *Electroencephalography and Clinical Neurophysiology*, 1970, *28*, 360–367.

Velasco, M., Velasco, F., Machado, J., & Olvera, A. Effects of novelty, habituation, attention and distraction on the amplitude of the various components of the somatic evoked responses. *International Journal of Neuroscience*, 1973, *5*, 101–111.

Walter, W. G., Cooper, R., Aldridge, V. J., McCallum, W. C., & Winter, A. L. Contingent negative variation: An electric sign of sensori-motor association and expectancy in the human brain. *Nature*, 1964, *203*, 380–384.

Weerts, T. C., & Lang, P. J. The effect of eye fixation and stimulus and response location on the contingent negative variation (CNV). *Biological Psychology*, 1973, *1*, 1–19.

Weinberg, H., Walter, W. G., Cooper, R., & Aldridge, V. J. Emitted cerebral events. *Electroencephalography and Clinical Neurophysiology*, 1974, *36*, 449–456.

Weinberg, H., Walter, W. G., & Crow, H. J. Intracerebral events in humans related to real and imaginary stimuli. *Electroencephalography and Clinical Neurophysiology*, 1970, *29*, 1–9.

Weinberger, N. M., Oleson, T. D., & Ashe, J. H. Sensory system neural activity during habituation of the pupillary orienting reflex. *Behavioral Biology*, 1975, *15*, 283–301.

Weitzman, E. D., & Kremen, H. Auditory evoked responses during different stages of sleep in man. *Electroencephalography and Clinical Neurophysiology*, 1965, *18*, 65–70.

Wilkinson, R. T., & Ashby, S. M. Selective attention, contingent negative variation and the evoked potential. *Biological Psychology*, 1974, *1*, 167–179.

Wilkinson, R. T., & Haines, E. Evoked response correlates of expectancy during vigilance. *Acta Psychologica*, 1970, (Supplement) *33*, 402–413.

Wilkinson, R. T., & Lee, M. V. Auditory evoked potentials and selective attention. *Electroencephalography and Clinical Neurophysiology*, 1972, *33*, 411–418.

Wilkinson, R. T., & Spence, M. T. Determinants of the post-stimulus resolution of the contingent negative variation (CNV). *Electroencephalography and Clinical Neurophysiology*, 1973, *35*, 503–509.

Wolpaw, J. R., & Penry, J. K. A temporal component of the auditory evoked response. *Electroencephalography and Clinical Neurophysiology*, 1975, *39*, 609–620.

Woods, D. L., & Hillyard, S. A. Attention at the cocktail party: Brainstem evoked responses reveal no peripheral gating. In D. Otto (Ed.), *Multidisciplinary perspectives in event-related brain potential research*. U.S. Government, in press.

Yingling, C. D., & Skinner, J. E. Selective regulation of thalamic sensory relay nuclei by nucleus reticularis thalami. *Electroencephalography and Clinical Neurophysiology*, 1976, *41*, 476–482.

Zappoli, R., Papini, M., Denoth, F., Pasquinelli, A., Rossi, L., Martinetti, M. G., & Guerri, S. CNV in patients treated by different psychosurgical procedures. In D. Otto (Ed.), *Multidisciplinary perspectives in event-related brain potential research*. U.S. Government, in press.

25 The Psychophysiology of Anticipation

Peter J. Lang
Arne Öhman[1]
Robert F. Simons

Department of Psychology
University of Wisconsin
Madison, Wisconsin, United States

ABSTRACT

Three experiments, investigating cortical and visceral responding during a two-stimulus anticipation paradigm, are discussed. In each experiment, subjects received auditory warning stimuli signaling the presentation of either high or low interest color slides at the end of a six-second foreperiod. Slide duration, subject control of exposure time, and a reaction time (RT) requirement served as independent variables during the experimental series. Results of the present investigations revealed that both cortical and visceral response systems may reflect the degree of "anticipated interest." Specific expression of this variable, however, may be largely determined by the context in which it occurs. A discussion of motor expression and its modulation of physiological responding is presented.

I. INTRODUCTION

The experience of anticipation precedes meaningful events that are in some way predictable. Phenomenological analysis suggests that such states of expectation permit us to deal more effectively with subsequent stimuli, facilitating information intake as well as prompting more efficient and appropriate responding. Observation of expectant subjects reveals characteristic behaviors such as specific sense organ orientation (Sokolov, 1963) and the inhibition of irrelevant motor

---

[1] Present address: Institute of Psychology, University of Bergen, Postbox 25, N-5014 Bergen, Norway.

activity (Obrist, 1968), around which an objective description of anticipation may be organized. Workers in the field of human information processing have made extensive use of "anticipation" paradigms (e.g., reaction time) in an effort to elucidate internal processing stages that may underly an anticipatory set (Massaro, 1975; Sternberg, 1969). Recently, physiological recording techniques have been introduced into the information processing field (e.g., Posner, 1975). It is assumed that physiological events will covary with cognitive mechanisms, previously defined only by performance indices. This approach should permit the delineation of a "psychophysiology of anticipation." The present paper describes a series of experiments that are consistent with this purpose.

A two-stimulus paradigm was employed in this research. Physiological activity was recorded between the onset of the warning signal and the occurrence of the second stimulus. Specifically, we wished to determine whether physiological processes that precede the delivery of a significant stimulus differ from those preceding a less important or less interesting event. In addition, we assessed the contribution to the anticipatory psychophysiology of relevant and irrelevant overt motor responding. Finally, the studies investigated the covariation between visceral and cortical activity in the foreperiod to determine whether they are related to the same psychological processes or whether each may be differentially sensitive to specific subprocesses of the anticipatory state.

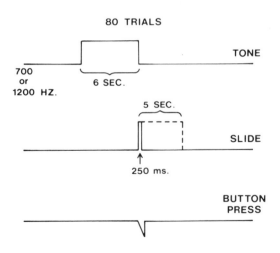

FIG. 1.   Sequence and timing of events comprising the two stimulus anticipation paradigm utilized in the present series of experiments. Two six-second tones (700 or 1200 Hz) signaled the occurrence of either high or low interest slides immediately at tone offset. Subjects performing the reaction time task depressed a microswitch as soon as possible following tone offset. Slide duration was contingent upon RT latency in Experiment 1, and unrelated to performance in Experiment 2.

II. TWO-STIMULUS ANTICIPATION PARADIGM

In the three experiments described here all subjects were male college students. At the outset of each anticipation trial subjects were presented one of two auditory tones (either 700 or 1200 Hz) for a 6-sec period. As can be seen in Fig. 1, tone offset was simultaneous with the presentation of a projected slide. For each subject one frequency always preceded the high interest slides (varying photographs of attractive, nude females); the other tone preceded a low interest slide (a repeated photograph of some common household object, such as a box of hand tissues).

It was expected that the different slide types would modify subjects' motivation to attend and differentially influence their preparatory set. Set was also manipulated in the first experiment by making the slide viewing time contingent on the latency of a motor response to tone offset. In this procedure the subject held a small microswitch in his hand. He was under instructions to press the switch as quickly as possible at the termination of the tone. If his response latency was less than 250 msec, the slide was projected for a full 5 sec. Failure to meet this criterion (achieved readily by attentive college students) resulted in a very brief slide presentation (less than 500 msec), which permitted little scanning of the content.

III. THE HEART RATE RESPONSE

The assessment of organ systems mediated by the autonomic nervous system (ANS) has proved useful in explorations of the anticipatory state. The cardiovascular system has been of particular interest to investigators, and a great number of studies of preparatory set report heart rate data. This cardiac response has been broadly interpreted as an index of energy mobilization or arousal (Duffy, 1962), a summary of concomitant motor activity (Obrist, Webb, & Sutterer, 1968), and as a feedback system that modulates cortical and subsequent motor responding (Lacey & Lacey, 1970).

Figure 2 illustrates the changes in heart rate normally observed in a two-stimulus anticipation paradigm of 4–8 sec duration. Curves of this sort are rarely obtained on single trials. A host of paradigm irrelevant factors (mechanical, neural, and humoral) continuously modulate heart rate, constituting a kind of biological "noise" in which the psychologically relevant heart rate signal is buried. Waveforms of the type presented here are produced by averaging successive interpulse intervals over repeated trials, time locked to preparatory stimulus onset. This generates a kind of cardiac rate evoked potential, analogous to the cortical evoked potential studied in electroencephalography (see Picton, et al. Chapter V. 24). The morphology of this response is both distinctive and reliable. With the onset of the preparatory period the heart decelerates briefly. This is followed by an acceleratory hump, which in turn gives way to a precipitous and

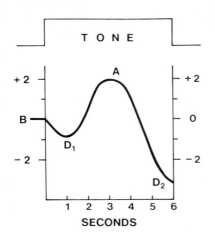

EVOKED HEART RATE RESPONSE

FIG. 2.   Idealized representation of the evoked cardiac waveform. This response is triphasic in form, involving a brief initial deceleration (D_1), an accelerative phase (A_1), and a final deceleration (D_2) lasting until the end of the stimulus interval. Scoring of this response is described by Gatchel and Lang (1973).

progressive deceleration until the end of the preparatory interval and/or the subject's response.

The three phases of the typical heart rate response are often scored separately, and interpreted as independent components that reflect different psychological processes.[2] The initial deceleration (D_1) is observed even when single, pure tones are presented, unaccompanied by other stimuli. This deceleration is held by Graham and Clifton (1966) to be part of an unconditioned orienting response. It has been shown to habituate over trials to nonsignal stimuli (Graham & Slaby, 1973), to be diminished when intertrial intervals are short, and to be increased when the time between stimuli is long (Gatchel & Lang, 1974).

The acceleratory phase (A. Fig. 2) is obtained in response to single stimuli when they are abrupt (startle) or when their intensity approaches the range of discomfort. Such cardiac acceleration has been interpreted as an index of Sokolov's (1963) defensive reflex. However, acceleration in the two-stimulus paradigm has been evoked in the absence of aversive stimuli, e.g., when increased effort is required in a subsequent response (Chase, Graham, & Graham, 1968). Acceleration has also been held to index active problem solving or mentation, as contrasted with perceptual processing (Lacey & Lacey, 1970).

Nearly all investigators report late deceleration (D_2) in anticipation of an overt response (Connor & Lang, 1969; Lacey & Lacey, 1970). However, Schwartz and Higgins (1971) also obtained decelerations from subjects instructed only to *think* they were making a response. Furthermore, deceleration appears as a

---

[2]For a more detailed description of the procedures utilized when a components analysis of the heart rate response is undertaken, see Gatchel and Lang (1973).

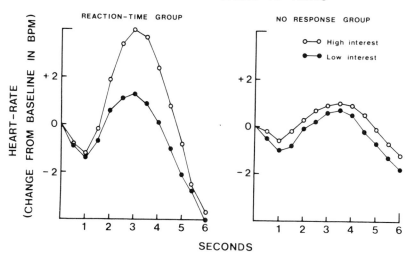

FIG. 3.   Average evoked heart rate response elicited in anticipation of high and low interest slide presentations in the reaction time and no-response groups of Experiment 1.

conditioned event in classical conditioning even though no motor response may be required (Geer, 1964). Finally, Lacey and Lacey (1970) view the late deceleration as an index of an attentive set and point to correlations between deceleration and reaction time (RT) latency as evidence for this view.

IV. EXPERIMENTAL STUDIES ON HEART RATE RESPONSE

In the first experiment to be reported here, the heart rate responses of two groups of subjects were examined.[3] Both groups received 80 presentations of the two-stimulus anticipation paradigm described earlier. A slide contingency group pressed a microswitch at tone offset and their response latency controlled the duration of the slide. A no-response group received exactly the same stimuli without instructions to respond, with slide duration for each subject determined by the performance of a yokemate in the contingency group.

Figure 3 depicts the evoked heart rate response of both groups to the tones signaling the high and low interest slides. The expected triphasic response waveform is clearly illustrated. It is also clear that the amplitudes of specific response components are affected, both by the response contingency and the slide content manipulations. The requirement to perform a reaction time task prompted a

[3]For a detailed description of the procedure and methods of data reduction and analysis, see Simons, Öhman, and Lang.

large, statistically significant secondary deceleration, independent of slide content. As we have already noted, this has been the finding of several investigators. Less predictably, the interest manipulation influenced only the acceleratory phase of the response, with a faster heart rate preceding the high interest slides. Furthermore, this effect is apparent in Fig. 3 only under response conditions – an impression confirmed by a statistically significant interaction between response and interest value for this acceleratory component. Thus, the simple anticipation of a motivationally significant event did not generate a differential heart rate response, but anticipation of the same slides under RT conditions prompted a significant discriminating acceleration.

Consideration of these data suggested two plausible alternative hypotheses:

1. The amplitude of anticipatory heart rate acceleration is determined by the interest value of the second stimulus *only* when subjects are preparing for a *functionally relevant response*. This presumes that subjects were differentially motivated to view the two slide types. Furthermore, when a response actually determines the exposure of an anticipated stimulus – when the response directly determines a contingency with the attendant feedback – only then does the amplitude of visceral preparatory responses covary with differential interest.

2. The alternative explanation does not assume the importance of the contingency. The notion is borrowed from Sperry (1952) that "perception and ideas are found, upon analysis, to have their factual significance and meaning in terms ultimately of overt operation." This might suggest that the preparation for overt

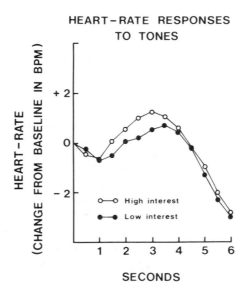

FIG. 4.   Average evoked heart rate response curves as a function of anticipated high and low interest slides in Experiment 2.

responding would, in itself, serve as a vehicle for the expression of interest differences. That is, the motor preparation need not be relevant to the anticipated stimulus. It is assumed that differential visceral arousal may be activated by any motor program designed to terminate at the end of the preparatory interval.

To test these alternative hypotheses, the laboratory procedure was modified in a way that dissociated response latency from slide duration. In a second experiment, a single group of subjects was administered the two-stimulus anticipation paradigm. They were assigned the task of pressing a key rapidly at tone termination. However, the latency of their motor response in no way related to the slide stimuli. In fact, for all 80 trials, regardless of performance, the slide stimuli were exposed for a full 5 sec.

Resulting heart rate data for these subjects is illustrated in Fig. 4. The basic waveform is again triphasic, with the pronounced secondary deceleration already noted to be characteristic of the reaction time task. In this experiment, however, the interest effect is markedly attenuated. Heart rate accelerations in anticipation of high and low interest slides were statistically indistinguishable. The results support the hypothesis that the differential heart rates seen in Experiment 1 depended on the presence of a response latency-slide duration contingency. More generally, they suggest that heart rate differences will not appear simply because subjects are waiting for stimuli of different interest value; they occur only if the subject has to do something about the stimuli to insure the anticipated perception.

Despite their apparent clarity, these results do not exclude the possibility that differential cardiovascular activity can occur in the absence of overt responses. Preparation to process stimuli is not restricted to gross overt behaviors, and their importance in this case may be an artifact of the experimental task. Thus, it may be argued that an assured 5-sec exposure places few attentional demands on the subject. He does not need to prepare to scan the material. Preparation can wait until the slide actually appears. Nevertheless, psychological preparation alone might place a differential load on the cardiovascular system if the perceptual task were more difficult. Under these conditions, the value of the percept to the subject might indeed be indexed by cardiac acceleration.

In order to explore this issue, the basic experimental paradigm was modified once again. Twelve additional subjects were administered a new no-response procedure in which three readily discriminable tones were randomly presented. One frequency was always followed by a high interest slide of 500 msec duration. A second frequency preceded a half-second exposure of the low interest slide. The third tone had no slide sequel. The short duration of the slides made it important for the subject to be "ready" at the point of slide exposure or scanning and stimulus intake would be minimal.

The results of this procedure are presented in Fig. 5. As for the other subjects who were not required to perform a RT task, there is no pronounced late deceleration descending below base line values. However, a significantly larger acceleratory component has appeared in anticipation of the high interest slide.

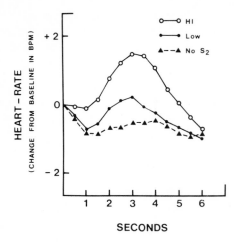

FIG. 5. Average evoked heart rate responses to each of the three different warning stimuli presented in Experiment 3.

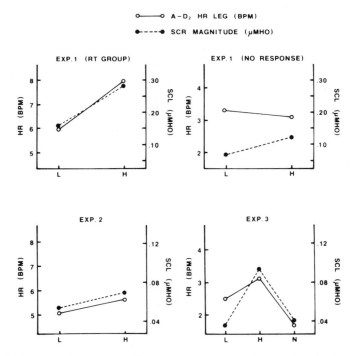

FIG. 6. The covariation between heart rate response amplitude (A-D$_2$ component) and magnitude of skin conductance responding obtained during all three experiments. Both measures significantly differentiated high from low interest stimuli during Experiment 1 (RT condition) and Experiment 3. No significant differences on either measure were obtained in Experiment 2 or under no-response conditions in Experiment 1.

476

Furthermore, acceleration is negligible when there is nothing to be viewed. Our hypothesis appeared to be confirmed: overt responding is not necessary to evoke cardiovascular changes that characterize aspects of the anticipatory state. However, processing of the anticipated stimulus clearly demands some preparatory activity — if not overt response control, then sensory orientation, or perhaps simply an organization of cognitive structures to receive input. It is also clear that these phasic heart rate changes are not part of a general state of excitement or emotional arousal that precedes interesting or important events. They appear to be components of specific preparatory activity.

While our discussion of visceral data has focused on the pattern of cardiac activity, it should be pointed out that other organs innervated by the ANS react similarly in this experimental paradigm. In all experiments, skin conductance was monitored. Though not as readily divisible into discrete psychophysiological components, the amplitude of skin conductance provided a kind of summary response, adding together in this single measure the impact of both the response and interest variables manipulated here. This is illustrated in Fig. 6. The heart rate measure is the difference between maximum acceleration (A) and minimum secondary deceleration (D_2), a rough estimate of the total waveform (Lang & Hnatiow, 1962). The parallel is readily apparent between this measure and the skin conductance response under all experimental conditions.

V. THE CORTICAL SLOW WAVE

In addition to heart rate and skin conductance, electrocortical activity was recorded continuously during all the experiments previously described. Electrodes were placed at the vertex and earlobe with potential differences between these sites monitored with long (30 sec) time constant amplifiers. The primary response under investigation was the cortical slow potential.[4] The significance of slow cortical changes for a situation in which a subject expects a second stimulus was first described by W. Grey Walter and his associates (Walter, Cooper, Aldridge, McCallum, & Winter, 1964). Exploring reaction time preparatory periods of .5—1.0 sec, he noted that a slow surface negative wave developed across the interval, peaking at the onset of the response signal. He first called this phenomenon the E-wave or expectancy wave, but later changed the nomenclature to the more descriptive "contingent negative variation" (CNV). Since Grey Walter's discovery, a host of researchers have studied this phenomenon, noting, for example, that negativity is related to reaction time latency (Lacey & Lacey,

[4]Fast evoked potentials were averaged for a 1750 msec epoch starting 250 msec before stimulus onset. A typical waveform leaving a negative peak around 100 msec, and positive peaks around 200 and 300 msec was observed (see, e,g., Simons & Lang, 1976, Fig. 3). However, no aspect of the evoked potential proved sensitive to the experimental manipulations and, therefore, these data will not be discussed further.

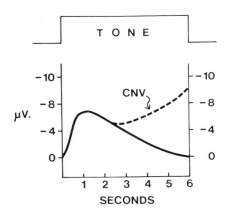

CORTICAL SLOW WAVE RESPONSE

FIG. 7.   Idealized representation of the slow cortical response obtained under response or no-response conditions. Procedures for obtaining the average curves and scoring the two components may be found in Simons, Öhman, and Lang.

1970; Rebert & Tecce, 1973) and precipitating a continuing controversy as to whether it is best considered as an index of motivation or attention (Rebert, McAdam, Knott, & Irwin, 1967; Tecce, 1972; Tecce & Scheff, 1969). Recently, investigators have begun to explore such cortical potentials during preparatory periods of longer duration similar to those in which the slower developing visceral responses are usually studied (Loveless & Sanford, 1974; Weerts & Lang, 1973). A product of this work was the discovery that the cortical activity during the preparatory interval actually includes two phases of negativity, which may have been confounded in earlier short interval experiments.

The morphology of the cortical slow wave in the context of our two-stimulus anticipation paradigm is illustrated in Fig. 7. The significant events occur after the short-lived cortical evoked potential described by Picton (See Chapter V. 24), and consist of a first negative peak about one second after stimulus onset and a maximal subsequent negativity at the onset of the second event. The CNV is presumed to be this later process, described in the figure by a dotted line. Recent studies suggest that the first phase of negativity has a primary origin in the frontal areas of the brain (Rohrbaugh, Syndulko, & Lindsley, 1976) and that it is part of an orienting response to the first stimulus. This first phase was not differentially responsive to the experimental variables under investigation here.

VI. EXPERIMENTAL STUDIES ON CORTICAL SLOW WAVE

It is not clear from previous work if the long-interval CNV is dependent on the occurrence of a response, or whether it is a true expectancy wave that would be seen whenever subjects anticipate a significant or interesting second event. Several investigators, using much shorter ISIs have demonstrated a shift in the

SLOW CORTICAL POTENTIAL

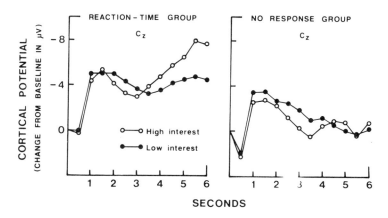

FIG. 8.   Average cortical slow-wave response curves recorded from a vertex (C_z) electrode placement as a function of response requirement (reaction-time vs. no-response group) and slide content (high vs. low interest) in Experiment 1.

cortical potential prior to delivery of a second event in the absence of overt responding (Cohen & Walter, 1966; Costell, 1972; Gullickson, 1970). As mentioned above, however, this may have reflected primarily the early orienting activity. Experiments utilizing longer interstimulus intervals have, in the main, been unable to produce a clear second (CNV) component without a motor response requirement (Lacey & Lacey, 1974; Loveless, 1975). In terms of the heart rate response that was previously examined, we may wonder to what extent does the CNV parallel late deceleration. Does it differentiate high and low interest stimuli in the same manner as acceleration? Does it combine these functions in the same way as skin conductance, or is its relationship to the experimental variables unique?

The slow cortical potentials obtained from the vertex in the first experiment are presented in Fig. 8. It will be recalled that two groups of subjects were observed, one of which had a reaction time task in which slide duration was contingent on response latency and another that had no RT task, but whose slide durations were yoked to the first group. There is a clear and significant effect of response group. That is to say, in anticipation of responding a second negative potential develops, one not readily apparent in the no-response condition. To this extent, the CNV is analogous to late cardiac deceleration. However, this late negativity appears to be significantly larger in the response group when a high interest slide is anticipated — an impression confirmed by a significant group × slide interaction. Thus, the CNV is also consonant with cardiac acceleration. At this point late negativity seemed to sum variables in the manner of skin conductance.

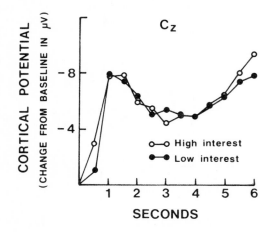

SLOW CORTICAL POTENTIAL

FIG. 9.   The average cortical slow-wave response in anticipation of high and low interest slides obtained at the vertex (C_z) during Experiment 2.

In the second experiment of this series subjects performed a reaction time task that was unrelated to slide duration, and all subjects observed both high and low interest slides for 5 sec. This condition generated interesting similarities and differences between visceral responding and the cortical potentials, which are illustrated in Fig. 9. Paralleling the autonomic data, a late negative component accompanies the reaction time task. Furthermore, dissociating the reaction time from slide duration attenuates the effect of slide content. However, unlike the visceral response, the effect of interest does not altogether disappear and a significant difference in anticipatory negativity was still found for the two slide types. This effect cannot be easily assigned to some difference in the sensitivity or reliability of measurement. If anything, the heart rate response is assessed more accurately, and the error terms for heart rate analyses are generally lower than those for the cortical potentials.

It is interesting to consider that the vertex electrodes are just above the motor strip, and to speculate that this late negativity may be measuring neural activity which is a part of the motor program that leads to a response. If so, these results suggest that response mobilization involves the coding of many meaningful discriminations, even when they do not relate to the task or result in differential responding. In fact, the reaction time latencies occasioned by the different tones in these experiments were never significantly different, even when reaction time controlled slide duration.

The third experiment generated further inconsistencies between cortical and visceral responses. In this procedure, brief slide exposure (500 msec) prompted a distinct preparatory set in our subjects without any overt response requirement. Heart rate acceleration was greatest to high interest slides and absent in the no-slide condition. As may be seen in Fig. 10, a parallel result was not obtained for

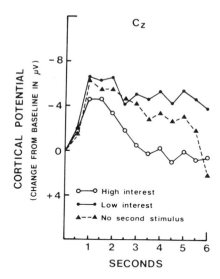

FIG. 10. Average cortical slow-wave responding elicited by each of the three different warning stimuli presented in Experiment 3.

the cortical CNV. Under these no-response conditions there is no obvious development of the late negativity through which the interest effect was previously expressed. This suggests that motor preparation is quite important to the development of the CNV and that variables that modulate this cortical event are in some way mediated by a somatomotor program.

VII. CONCLUSIONS

In agreement with Lacey and Lacey (1974), we conclude that the CNV is not a process that is completely parallel to the heart rate response. Both deceleration *and* acceleration may covary with the CNV (Connor & Lang, 1969); however, these visceral and cortical responses showed differential sensitivity to the various independent variables studied in our experimental series. It now seems clear that neither cardiac acceleration nor deceleration are inevitably linked to motor expression. Although Chase et al. (1968) found greater acceleration associated with subsequent response effort, in this research acceleration was clearly influenced more by "interest value" and brevity of exposure than by the presence of a motor response requirement. Similarly, we observed cardiac deceleration prior to a motor response, but others have often noted deceleration when no such response is forthcoming (Geer, 1964; Lacey & Lacey, 1974; Obrist, 1968). Examination of the cortical data indicates a more consistent physiomotor covariation. The weight of evidence suggests that the second component of the slow potential (CNV) occurs mainly prior to motor responding. This is consistent with the findings of a signal detection experiment by Loveless (1975), and the observations of Lacey and Lacey (1974) in studying a timing task with delayed feedback.

The Lacey and Lacey (1974) experiment illustrates other conditions in which cortical and cardiac systems may be either parallel or completely independent. In their experiment, subjects were required to time an interval by pressing a response key when they perceived 30 sec had elapsed. Each response was followed 4.5 sec later by a visual feedback display indicating the accuracy of the response. Preceding the key press, a substantial cardiac deceleration occurred. In addition, there developed a vertex negative slow cortical potential. However, following the motor response, and prior to feedback, the heart showed a second highly significant deceleration, while the vertex potential returned to and remained at base level. Similar to our results, these data indicate an association between heart rate and the presence of a motor response. However, they also suggest that anticipatory deceleration can occur in the absence of a motor event, and in this circumstance there is no CNV.

Both visceral and cortical measures reflected degree of "anticipated interest," but not always in the same experimental context. Thus, heart rate acceleration and skin conductance indexed differential interest under *contingent* response conditions and prior to brief slide presentations; the CNV covaried with interest value under *all* response conditions, even when RT was irrelevant to slide presentation, but disappeared when there was no overt response requirement.

These results suggest that autonomic measures reflect "interest" to the extent that perception of the relevant event is uncertain. Subjects performing the contingent reaction time task continually faced the possibility that a temporally short slide rather than a long slide would be presented, while subjects in the third experiment always received brief exposures that could be missed if they were unprepared. Higgins (1971) systematically manipulated the probability that the foreperiod stimulus actually predicted a second event. One group was simply asked to detect second stimulus occurrence; another group was instructed to perform an RT task. He found greatest acceleration for both groups when the second event was most uncertain (i.e., 50% probability). A similar result was recently reported by Lawler, Obrist, and Lawler (1976). Thus, we are led to conclude that foreperiod acceleration is a function of the significance of the preparatory stimulus (Coles & Duncan-Johnson, 1975), and that such significance is enhanced by the uncertainty as well as by the interest value of the predicted stimulus.

Our data suggest that visceral responses covary with most cognitive and motor events occurring in the preparatory interval. This seems reasonable if we take the autonomic nervous system to be active in all the housekeeping functions of the organism. Any response or preparation for response requires some redistribution of energy, a compensatory adjustment of the visceral system, and we should expect to find the footprints of purposeful mentation and behavior in many vegetative organs of the body. In contrast, the brain is an organ differentially specialized for explicit behaviors and specific kinds of information processing. As mentioned above, the vertex is located very near the motor strip. From this perspective it is not surprising that the vertex CNV would be closely allied to motor preparation. However, highly localized brain events may have little significance for the vegetative system. We presume that much of the brain's discrete activity (which is not linked to overt responses or broad response preparation) may not be differentiated from "biological noise" at the level of the viscera. The one instance in which the brain discriminated an independent variable, and the autonomic responses failed to do so, was the greater negativity in anticipation of high interest slides under noncontingency response conditions. Our experimental analysis suggests that a differential set to intake the two slides was not prompted by this paradigm. The fact that CNV differences were still obtained may relate to the neural coding of a motor program, which could include a potential for differential responding, unrealized at the level of effectors or visceral support systems.

Although we may speculate as to the specific meaning of specific organ responses, it is important not to neglect more general conclusions: these results clearly show that physiological events are not gross correlates of phenomenological states. As the CNV is not subjective expectancy, so heart rate changes do not index an experience of anticipatory excitement. Both visceral and cortical measures appear to be related to specific components of cognitive and motor preparation for stimulus processing. However, it is also true that visceral events, particularly, must always be interpreted as part of specific transactions between the subject and the environment (Lacey & Lacey, 1970). As we have seen here, the psychological "meanings" of most physiological responses are not constant across all laboratory paradigms. The significance of a physiological data set must be evaluated in terms of the stimulus context in which it is obtained.

ACKNOWLEDGMENTS

This research was supported in part by grants to the first author from the National Institute of Mental Health (MH10993) and the Wisconsin Alumni Research Foundation. The research was conducted while the second author was a Visiting Scientist supported by the University of Wisconsin Graduate School and a Visiting Research Scholar under the Fulbright-Hays program. The third author was a National Institute of Mental Health trainee (MH 5 TO1 MH-05363-27). The assistance of Michael Falconer in development of computer software for experimental control and data analysis, Paul Peterson in statistical analysis, and Jean Holland in drawing the graphs is gratefully acknowledged. Statistical analyses were accomplished at the Academic Computing Center, University of Wisconsin, Madison.

REFERENCES

Chase, W. G., Graham, F. K., & Graham, D. T. Components of the HR response in anticipation of reaction time and exercise tasks. *Journal of Experimental Psychology,* 1968, *76,* 642–648.

Cohen, J., & Walter, W. G. The interaction and responses in the brain to semantic stimuli. *Psychophysiology*, 1966, *2*, 187–196.

Coles, M. G. H., & Duncan-Johnson, C. C. Cardiac activity and information processing: The Effects of stimulus significance, detection, and response requirements. *Journal of Experimental Psychology: Human Perception and Performance*, 1975, *1*, 418–428.

Connor, W. H., & Lang, P. J. Cortical slow wave and cardiac rate responses in stimulus orientation and reaction time conditions. *Journal of Experimental Psychology*, 1969, *82*, 310–320.

Costell, R. M. Contingent negative variation as an indicator of sexual object preference. *Science*, 1972, *177*, 718–720.

Duffy, E. *Activation and behavior*. New York: Wiley, 1962.

Gatchel, R. J., & Lang, P. J. Accuracy of psychophysical judgments and physiological response amplitude. *Journal of Experimental Psychology*, 1973, *98*, 175–183.

Gatchel, R. J., & Lang, P. J. Effects of interstimulus interval length and variability on habituation of autonomic components of the orienting response. *Journal of Experimental Psychology*, 1974, *103*, 802–804.

Geer, J. H. Measurement of the conditioned cardiac response. *Journal of Comparative and Physiological Psychology*, 1964, *57*, 426–433.

Graham, F. K., & Clifton, R. K. Heart rate change as a component of the orienting response. *Psychological Bulletin*, 1966, *65*, 305–320.

Graham, F. K., & Slaby, D. A. Differential heart rate changes to equally intense white noise and tone. *Psychophysiology*, 1973, *10*, 347–362.

Gullickson, G. R. The contingent negative variation in the pre-school child. *Dissertation Abstracts*, 1970, *31*, 3022B.

Higgins, J. D. Set and uncertainty as factors influencing anticipatory cardiovascular responding in humans. *Journal of Comparative and Physiological Psychology*, 1971, *74*, 272–283.

Lacey, B. C., & Lacey, J. I. Studies of heart rate and other bodily processes in sensorimotor behavior. In P. A. Obrist, A. H. Black, J. Brener, and L. V. DiCara (Eds.), *Cardiovascular psychophysiology*. Chicago: Aldine Publishing Co., 1974.

Lacey, J. I., & Lacey, B. C. Some autonomic–central nervous system relationships. In P. Black (Ed.), *Physiological correlates of emotion*. New York: Academic Press, 1970.

Lang, P. J., & Hnatiow, M. Stimulus repetition and the heart rate response. *Journal of Comparative and Physiological Psychology*, 1962, *55*, 781–785.

Lawler, K. A., Obrist, P. A., & Lawler, J. E. Cardiac and somatic response patterns during a reaction time task in children and adults. *Psychophysiology*, 1976, *13*, 448–455.

Loveless, N. E. The effect of warning interval on signal detection and event-related slow potentials of the brain. *Perception and Psychophysics*, 1975, *17*, 565–570.

Loveless, N. E., & Sanford, A. J. Slow potential correlates of preparatory set. *Biological Psychology*, 1974, *1*, 303–314.

Massaro, D. W. *Experimental psychology and information processing*. Chicago: Rand McNally, 1975.

Obrist, P. A. Heart rate and somatic-motor coupling during classical aversive conditioning in humans. *Journal of Experimental Psychology*, 1968, *77*, 180–193.

Obrist, P. A., Webb, R. A., & Sutterer, J. R. Heart rate and somatic changes during aversive conditioning in a simple reaction time task. *Psychophysiology*, 1968, *5*, 696–723.

Posner, M. I. *Psychobiology of attention. Handbook of psychobiology*. New York: Academic Press, 1975.

Rebert, C. S., McAdam, D. W., Knott, J. R., & Irwin, D. A. Slow potential change in human brain related to level of motivation. *Journal of Comparative and Physiological Psychology*, 1967, *63*, 20–23.

Rebert, C. S., & Tecce, J. J. A summary of CNV and reaction time. *Electroencephalography and Clinical Neurophysiology*, 1973, *Supplement 33*, 173–178.

Rohrbaugh, J. W., Syndulko, K., & Lindsley, D. B. Brain wave components of the contingent negative variation in humans. *Science*, 1976, *191*, 1055–1057.

Schwartz, G. E., & Huggins, J. D. Cardiac activity preparatory to overt and covert behavior. *Science*, 1971, *173*, 1144–1146.

Simons, R. F., & Lang, P. J. Psychophysical judgment: Electro-cortical and heart rate correlates of accuracy and uncertainty. *Biological Psychology*, 1976, *4*, 51–64.

Simons, R. F., Öhman, A., & Lang, P. J. *The effects of response requirement and anticipated interest on cortical slow potentials, heart rate, and skin conductance.* (Manuscript available from P. J. Lang.)

Sperry, R. W. Neurology and the mind-brain problem. *American Scientist*, 1952, *40*, 291–312.

Sokolov, E. N. *Perception and the conditioned reflex*. New York: Macmillan, 1963.

Sternberg, S. The discovery of processing stages: Extension of Donders' method. In W. G. Koster (Ed.), *Attention and performance II*. Amsterdam: North Holland, 1969.

Tecce, J. J. Contingent negative variation (CNV) and psychological processes in man. *Psychological Bulletin*, 1972, *77*, 73–108.

Tecce, J. J., & Scheff, N. M. Attention reduction and suppressed direct-current potentials in the human brain. *Science*, 1969, *164*, 331–333.

Walter, W. G., Cooper, R., Aldridge, V. J., McCallum, W. C., & Winter, A. L. Contingent negative variation: An electric sign of sensorimotor association and expectancy in the human brain. *Nature*, 1964, *203*, 380–384.

Weerts, T. C., & Lang, P. J. The effect of eye fixation and stimulus and response location on the contingent negative variation (CNV). *Biological Psychology*, 1973, *1*, 1–19.

26 Sequential Effects of Distracting Stimuli in a Selective Attention Reaction Time Task

Anthony G. Greenwald
Karl E. Rosenberg

Department of Psychology
The Ohio State University
Columbus, Ohio, United States

ABSTRACT

The processing mechanisms employed in a task can sometimes be inferred by determining which sequential relationships between trials increase or decrease reaction time. In three selective attention reaction time (SART) experiments, we have examined sequential effects involving events that occurred simultaneously in both a focal channel of stimulation (to which the subject had to respond) and a distractor channel (which had to be rejected by attentional mechanisms). Our findings for 2-trial sequences demonstrated that, on the trial just after one on which the distractor and focal channels had conflicting content, subjects exhibited two levels of rejection of the distractor channel, both (a) being less affected generally by information in the distractor channel, and (b) inhibiting the response associated with the last distractor stimulus. Analysis of 3-trial sequences showed effects on reaction times due to the distractor event from the second preceding trial. This unanticipated finding indicated the existence of previously unsuspected residual (i.e., memorial) effects of unattended information. In discussing these results, we offer a taxonomy of 2-trial sequential SART effects and note gaps in the currently available data.

I. INTRODUCTION

In a selective attention reaction time (SART) task the experimenter presents a *distractor* that must be ignored, simultaneously with the presentation of a *focal* stimulus to which the subject must respond rapidly. "Standard" choice reaction time tasks also have distracting stimuli that must be ignored; these distractors include general cues from the laboratory room or extraneous stimulation from experimental equipment used for stimulus presentation. The SART procedure is distinctive, however, in that the distractor is typically difficult to ignore and also tends to select a response that conflicts with the one the subject must make to the focal stimulus.

The Stroop (1935) color naming task is the prototype of SART tasks. In the Stroop task the focal stimuli are colors that are to be named rapidly, while the distractors are conflicting color-name words that are difficult to ignore because they are the shapes that bear the focal color stimuli. A SART task that has been used in earlier research by Greenwald (1970a, 1970b, 1972) is that of rapidly naming digits that are presented at regular intervals on a visual display device, with simultaneous distractors consisting of auditorily presented names of the same or other digits. In the digit-naming task reaction times are delayed by an average of about 40 msec if the distractor is the name of a digit that conflicts with the focal one, compared to its being the name of the same digit. This reliably obtained difference will be referred to as a "conflict effect." As documented in Dyer's (1973) review of the Stroop and related selective attention phenomena, conflict effects are obtained in a variety of SART tasks in addition to the Stroop color-naming task and Greenwald's digit-naming task.

II. LOGIC OF USING SART DATA TO INFER MEMORY FOR THE CONTENT OF THE UNATTENDED CHANNEL

If reaction time on Trial n varies as a function of events that occurred on a prior trial (Trial $n-1$, $n-2$, etc.), then the prior event(s) must have altered structure or activity in the nervous system in a fashion that influenced processing on the current trial. By definition, such an alteration can be classed as a memory effect. If the prior event(s) that influenced Trial n's reaction time occurred in the distractor channel then the demonstrated memory is for unattended information. This use of the SART procedure has some advantages over memory tests based on recall or recognition of information received in an unattended channel (cf. Moray, 1970, Chapter 4). One advantage is the likelihood that RT measures may be more sensitive to residual effects of prior events than are recall or recognition measures. More important, however, the subject is never given any task for the distractor channel other than the general instruction to ignore it. By contrast, when memory for unattended information is tested by a recall or recognition query, the subject comes to expect such tests and may therefore attempt to monitor the distractor channel in order to perform well. Recall or recognition procedures are thus open to the criticism that the distractor channel is not truly an unattended channel.

III. EFFECT OF PROPORTION OF CONFLICT TRIALS IN AN EXTENDED SEQUENCE

The first study to be presented here (Rosenberg, 1976, Experiment 1) was an attempt to demonstrate residual effects of distractors occurring over an extended series of trials. An earlier SART study (Greenwald, 1972) had established that the very last event to occur in a distractor channel (that is, on Trial $n-1$) leaves a memorial residue (see summary of this evidence in Table 3, below). This conclusion of memory for the distractor event from Trial $n-1$ was nicely consistent with data from a study using recall measures in a dichotic listening task (Norman, 1969). The attempt to extend the demonstration of residual effects to Trials $n-2$ and beyond was an important test, in that the effect of the very last $(n-1)$ distractor event could be interpreted as requiring only a sensory buffer type of memory. In contrast, residual effects of more remote distractor events would implicate a more durable form of memory.

Rosenberg's first experiment employed a set of 10 relatively nonconfusable letters of the alphabet (A, D, E, J, K, M, O, P, Q, and R) both for the focal visual stimuli and for the simultaneous auditory distractors. Subjects encountered these stimuli in blocks of 50 trials, presented at a regular 4-sec intertrial interval with no warning signal other than the preceding periodic stimuli. The only variable that differentiated blocks of trials from one another was the probability of occurrence of distractor-focal stimulus agreement on each trial. Probability treatment levels of .1, .3, .5, .7 and .9 were each used in two blocks, one in the

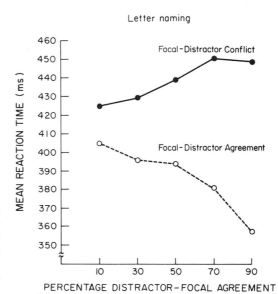

FIG. 1. Effects of distractor-focal stimulus agreement vs. conflict and proportion of agreeing trials on SART performance in a letter-naming task. (Data from Rosenberg, 1976, Experiment 1, $N = 14$.)

first half and the other in the second half of the session, with order of treatments and selection of stimuli randomized independently for each of 14 adult subjects.

The analysis focused on the magnitude of the conflict effect — that is, the difference in reaction time between agreement and conflict trials — as a function of the agreement probability independent variable. If the magnitude of the conflict effect varied with the overall proportion of agreements in a block of trials, we would (or so we thought) have demonstrated memory for distant events in the unattended channel.

The results were as shown in Fig. 1.[1] It may be seen there that the magnitude of the conflict effect increased directly with the proportion of agreements in blocks of trials; the more agreement trials there were in a series, the greater was the superiority of reaction times on agreement trials relative to conflict trials.

IV. EFFECTS OF SEQUENCES OF AGREEMENTS AND CONFLICTS

There is a potential flaw in the interpretation of the Fig. 1 results as indicating memory for distant events in the unattended channel. Consider that, as the proportion of agreement trials in a block increases, so also does the proportion of trials that directly follow upon an agreement trial. Therefore, the results displayed in Fig. 1 might be obtained just as a consequence of a strong dependence of the magnitude of the conflict effect on whether or not the immediately preceding $(n-1)$ trial was an agreement trial.

This alternative interpretation was tested on 27 adult subjects (Rosenberg, 1976, Experiment 2) using the letter-naming SART task with blocks of trials, in all of which the overall probability of agreement was maintained at .5. The sequence of agreement and conflict trials was recorded for use in analyses. The effects of sequential patterns of agreements and conflicts were then examined with an analysis of variance in which four main effect factors were defined in terms of occurrence of agreement vs. conflict on, respectively, Trial n, $n-1$, $n-2$, and $n-3$. This analysis is shown in Table 1. If the occurrence of agreement on any of the three preceding trials affected the overall reaction time (collapsed over agreement and conflict) on Trial n, this would appear as a main effect of the factor for that prior trial. On the other hand, if the occurrence of agreement vs. conflict on a prior trial influenced the magnitude of the conflict effect on Trial n, this would appear as a two-way or higher-way interaction effect involving the factor for the prior trial and that for Trial n.

The Table 1 analysis shows two strong effects and three weak ones. The strong effects are easier to deal with. One was the main effect of agreement vs. conflict on Trial n — the expected conflict effect. The second strong effect was the interaction effect involving Trials n and $n-1$. The conflict effect was greater

---

[1] Throughout this report we do not consider error data. In our experiments errors were too infrequent to provide hypothesis testing data. In tests of sequential effects, the four trials following any error were omitted from analyses.

TABLE 1
Analysis of Variance for Sequential Effects
in a Letter-Naming SART Task
(Data from Rosenberg, 1976, Experiment 2)

Source	F^a	$p <$
Main Effects		
A (Trial n)	144.16	0.001
B (Trial $n-1$)	4.16	0.06
C (Trial $n-2$)	1.0	ns
D (Trial $n-3$)	6.82	0.02
Interaction effects for which $F > 1.0$		
A × B	26.36	0.001
C × D	3.33	0.09
A × C × D	1.50	ns

[a]Degrees of freedom for all F ratios are 1/26.

Note: Each design factor has two levels — agreement or con-flict. Thus the main effects test whether distractor-focal stimulus agreement vs. conflict on the current trial (Trial n) or on one of the three preceding trials affects current-trial reaction time.

when the immediately preceding trial was an agreement trial than when it was a conflict trial.[2] This is just the effect that was of concern, since a very strong effect of this type could account for the Fig. 1 results without any involvement of memory for remote events in the unattended channel.

One of the weak effects was a main effect of Trial $n-1$, indicating that reaction times were a bit faster following agreement trials than following conflict trials. The other two weak effects introduced an element of disarray to the overall picture. These were a main effect and an interaction effect involving Trial $n-3$. In the absence of any such effects involving Trial $n-2$, these last two effects are difficult to account for.

The pattern of results is shown in Fig. 2, which presents the sequential effects in this experiment to varying depths. The main effect of Trial n (the conflict effect) appears as the separation of the two points over the position for the current trial (n) on the abscissa. The interaction effect involving the current and preceding trials is to be found in the points over $n-1$. There it may be seen that the occurrence of agreement on the preceding trial facilitated performance on a current agreement trial, but hampered performance on a current conflict trial. The weak main effect for the third preceding trial is shown in the fact that the unfilled circles over $n-3$ in Fig. 2 represent slower reaction times than do the filled circles.

---

[2] Another way to describe this finding is that reaction time on Trial n was facilitated when Trial $n-1$ was of the same type (conflict vs. agreement).

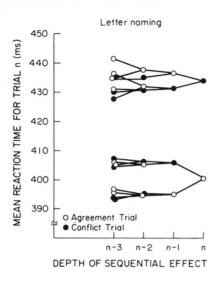

FIG. 2 Analysis of sequences of agreement and conflict trials in an SART letter-naming task with overall probability of agreement = .5. (Each point plotted over abscissa value $n-i$ indicates the mean reaction time for the $(i + 1)$th trial in a sequence of agreements and conflicts coded in order by the connected filled or unfilled dots starting at that point and proceeding to the terminal node at the right. Data from Rosenberg, 1976, Experiment 2, $N = 27$.)

Do these data allow a conclusion about memory for unattended information? If we ignore the weak effect of Trial $n-3$ in Fig. 2, it appears that the only clear evidence is for a residue of just the most recent unattended event. This would be a very desirable conclusion in some respects. It would be consistent with the idea that unattended information is received into a sensory buffer — then processed to the point necessary to cause the interference manifest in the conflict effect — but not processed sufficiently for its effects to survive overwriting of the sensory buffer by the next occurring unattended event.

This conclusion is so neat and attractive, indeed so consistent with previous theorization about the processing fate of unattended information (Deutsch & Deutsch, 1963; Moray, 1970; Treisman, 1969), that one is tempted to ignore the minor lack of fit of Fig. 2 to this conception. However there was another troublesome problem that emerged in comparison of the data of Figs. 1 and 2. The magnitude of the effect of Trial $n-1$ on Trial n's conflict effect in Fig. 2 was *much* smaller than was needed to explain the wide range of conflict effects shown in Fig. 1. This left two plausible conclusions: either (a) the subject sample was drastically different between Rosenberg's two letter-naming experiments, or (b) the effect of Trial $n-1$ varies as a function of the overall probability of agreement in the series. The former explanation cannot be ruled out even though the subjects in both studies were recruited in the same fashion and even though their mean levels of reaction time were about equal. The latter explanation obviously has the greater potential interest. If the impact of the preceding trial's distractor-focal stimulus configuration on the current trial's conflict effect does vary as a function of overall probability of agreement in an extended series, we are returned to the possible conclusion that distant events in the distractor channel do leave memory residues.

V. FURTHER STUDY OF
AGREEMENT-CONFLICT SEQUENCES

In the last experiment to be presented here, we extended the range of tasks to be employed in the SART paradigm. A group of 18 subjects provided data for both visual and auditory variations of a position-naming task. In the visual stimulus replication, subjects saw the distracting word "left" or "right" presented randomly on the left or right side of a display monitor. Position was the focal stimulus. The task was therefore to ignore the word, while naming the side (left or right) on which the word appeared. In the auditory stimulus replication, the same distracting words were heard in the left or right ear of the subject's headset. Again, the task was to name the position of the word while ignoring the word itself.

Intertrial interval (ITI) of 1.5, 3.0, or 4.5 sec was an independent variable in this experiment. Our intention was in part to determine whether the magnitude or depth of sequential effects would increase as the ITI decreased. If these effects remained constant with variations in ITI, it would be plausible to interpret them as being dependent on the sequence of events rather than on the timing of the events. The 2-trial sequential effect found previously (the A x B interaction of Table 1) was in fact found for both the visual and auditory position-naming tasks and was *not* affected by ITI. We proceeded, then, to collapse the data across levels of ITI and to search for sequential effects involving more than just the most recent trial. Results of these analyses, conducted to a depth of two preceding trials, are shown in Figs. 3 and 4. The visual task (Fig. 3) showed a main effect of the type of trial (conflict vs. agreement) that occurred two trials preceding, this being an effect that was found neither in the earlier letter-naming experiment (Fig. 2), nor in the auditory position-naming replication of the current experiment (Fig. 4). The auditory task showed several significant effects that were traceable to the second preceding trial. The most substantial of these was the triple interaction involving the current trial and both preceding trials. The fact that this interaction effect occurred neither for the visual position-naming task, nor in the earlier letter-naming experiment, renders its significance unclear.[3]

Beyond the inconsistency of analysis of variance effects across experiments, there is a more subtle and pervasive problem in attempting to interpret the sequential effects shown in the position-naming task. Consider a sequence in which a conflict trial is followed by another conflict trial. In a 2-choice task there are two quite different ways in which this can occur. One is for both the focal

---

[3]An additional analysis to a depth of three preceding trials was conducted for the position-naming tasks. Although no effects involving the third preceding trial were found in the auditory replication, two interaction effects involving Trial *n−3* were found for the visual replication. Again, the lack of support for these interaction effects in the earlier experiment and in the paired auditory replication causes us to defer any attempt to interpret them.

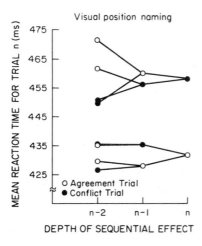

FIG. 3. Analysis of sequences of agreement and conflict trials in a visual SART position-naming task. (See Fig. 2 caption for explanation of method of coding sequences. Previously unpublished data, $N = 18$.)

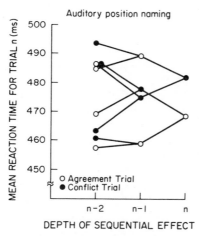

FIG. 4. Analysis of sequences of agreement and conflict trials in an auditory SART position-naming task. (See Fig. 2 caption for explanation of method of coding sequences. Previously unpublished data, $N = 18$.)

stimulus and distractor to be *repeated* on consecutive trials, such as the word "left" occurring twice consecutively in the right side position. A quite different conflict → conflict sequence involves *nonrepetition* in both the distractor and focal channels, such as "left" on the right side followed by "right" on the left side. In the analyses of Figs. 3 and 4, these possibilities were not treated as distinct. Similarly, a conflict trial following an agreement trial could occur in the position-naming task by repetition of either the distractor or the focal stimulus, but not both. Another way to analyze this same transition is to observe that when a conflict trial follows an agreement trial either the distractor of Trial *n−1* becomes the focal stimulus of Trial *n*, or vice versa, but not both. In general, for a 2-choice SART task it is possible to analyze any 2-trial transition alternatively in terms of (a) the sequence of occurrence of conflict and agreement,

TABLE 2

Analysis of Selected 3-Trial $(n-2, n-1, n)$ Sequential Effects
Involving both Distractors (D) and Focal (F) Stimuli in a 2-Choice SART Task
(Stimuli Were Positioned Visual (Vis) or Auditory (Aud) Words)

| | | | Relation of Trial $(n-2) \rightarrow (n-1)$ transitions for D and F to their $(n-1) \rightarrow (n)$ transitions | | | | |
			Same for both D & F	Same for F only	Same for D only	Same for neither	Average
lature of	Both D & F repeat	Vis	420	430	460	465	444
		Aud	452	460	480	468	465
·ansition	Only F repeats	Vis	430	446	476	474	457
		Aud	471	497	496	500	491
etween	Only D repeats	Vis	432	437	455	433	439
		Aud	471	474	474	484	476
·rial $n-1$ nd	Neither repeats	Vis	433	443	444	442	441
		Aud	458	480	473	463	469
·rial n	Average	Vis	429	439	459	454	
		Aud	463	478	481	479	

Jote: Data from 16 subjects. (Two who had cells with few observations were dropped.) The first olumn averages for each stimulus condition (vis or aud) were highly reliably different from the verages of other columns, indicating the capacity of subjects to prepare selectively after Trial $n-1$ or the same pattern of transitions in the distractor and focal channels that characterized the relaionship between Trials $n-2$ and $n-1$.

(b) the sequence with respect to repetition or nonrepetition in the focal and distractor channels, and (c) the relationship of a distractor to the last focal stimulus or of a focal stimulus to the last distractor.

Given the multiple possibilities for classifying the position-naming SART data, how should one choose among them? We had already tried the first of the above-mentioned classifications and had some reason for dissatisfaction with it, because the auditory and visual data showed different patterns of significant effects. Although it could be that the auditory and visual tasks were qualitatively different insofar as selective attention processes were concerned, it seemed worth exploring the alternative bases of classification to see if they would reveal a pattern that did not vary across stimulus modalities.

We tried the various possibilities and discovered that one seemed more successful than the others. It is shown in Table 2. This analysis is based on repetition considered separately in the distractor and focal channels for the Trial $n-1 \rightarrow$ Trial n transition. However, for the Trial $n-2 \rightarrow n-1$ transition the classification scheme considers not repetition in each channel but, rather, whether or not the transition in each channel is of the same type as for Trials $n-1 \to n$. To repeat, the only justification for presentation of the position-naming data according to this scheme for analyzing to depth $n-2$ is that it yields more similar findings for the visual and auditory task variations than did any of the several others schemes that were tried.

Before considering the details of Table 2, let us review typical findings of sequential effect analyses in standard choice reaction time experiments. The established findings are: (a) repetition of the stimulus on successive trials results in decreased reaction times — the repetition effect is likely to increase as the number of consecutive repetitions increases to at least 3 or 4; (b) response to a given stimulus is likely to be slower the more trials that have intervened since the stimulus' last occurrence (see Falmagne, Cohen, & Dwivedi, 1975; Kornblum, 1973).

Consider, in the light of these established findings, the results in Table 2. Perhaps most surprising was the comparison of sequences involving repetitions of the focal stimulus from Trial $n-1$ to Trial n versus sequences involving non-repetition. Remarkably, the data of the position-naming experiment showed that (a) reaction times tended to be *slower* for focal stimulus repetition than non-repetition (but not significantly so), and (b) reaction times for the case when both the focal and distractor stimulus repeated on consecutive trials (first row of Table 2) were virtually the same as for the case when neither repeated (fourth row of Table 2). A second SART finding that contrasts with standard sequential effects is for the case in which the same response was required on two successive trials, but the stimulus changed (i.e., the distractor was different). For this case (second row of Table 2), reaction times were worse than for any other transition represented by rows of Table 2. In sum, the sequential effects obtained in the position-naming SART task were not at all those to be expected from standard choice reaction time studies of repetition and other sequential effects.[4]

Let us consider now the columns of Table 2, representing the relation of the Trial $n-2 \to n-1$ to the Trial $n-2 \to n$ transitions. Here a clear pattern emerges in which reaction times are relatively rapid on Trial n if the two transitions for both channels *jointly* are of the same type over the span of three trials. This effect can be seen in two ways: First, it may be noted that the first column means are lower than those for any of the other columns. More precisely, the importance of events in the distractor channel on Trial $n-2$ is shown by a com-

---

[4]We wish to emphasize that the lack of standard repetition effects in the Table 2 data may in part be a consequence of some characteristics peculiar to a 2-choice SART task. Consider that (a) if the exact stimulus (both focal and distractor components) repeats, the correct response stays the same; but (b) for two of the three ways in which the stimulus can change from one trial to the next, the response also must change in order to be correct (the response is to be repeated only if just the distractor component changes); (c) therefore, subjects may have been predisposed to change response whenever any stimulus change occurred; (d) this last strategy is one that may be peculiar to a 2-choice task and is also one that would tend to obliterate facilitating effects due to focal component repetition.

parison between the first two columns of Table 2. Both of these columns concern sequences for which two successive transitions in the focal channel are of the same type. In the second column, however, the $n-2 \rightarrow n-1$ transition in the distractor channel is of a different type from the $n-1 \rightarrow n$ transition, and reaction times are consistently slower in this case. The Column 1 vs. Column 2 comparison was highly significant in the analysis combined across the visual and auditory tasks ($F = 37.95$, $df = 1/15$, $p < .001$), and was not significantly different for the two tasks ($F < 1$).

In summary, the data of the position-naming experiments require interpretations that could not have been anticipated from standard choice reaction time sequential-effect studies. Repetition of the exact stimulus (focal + distractor) was relatively unimportant in the SART procedure, and requirement of the same response on consecutive trials on which the distractor was changed turned out to be more difficult than transitions that didn't involve response repetition. Although evidence for sequential effects involving distractors to depth $n-2$ (or beyond) was equivocal in the earlier 10-choice letter naming task (Rosenberg, 1976), nonetheless such effects were clearly apparent in the Table 2 data for the 2-choice position-naming task.

VI. MEMORY FOR UNATTENDED INFORMATION

The letter-naming and position-naming findings have indicated that unattended events can influence performance not only on the current trial (e.g., the conflict effect), and the following trial (e.g., the Fig. 2 effect of preceding conflict vs. agreement), but also on the second following trial (the repetition-of-transition effect of Table 2). The last of these findings strongly suggests that processing of unattended information can exceed the limits suggested by most existing conceptions. That is, since a sensory buffer form of memory does not explain sequential effects beyond the $n-1$ depth, our depth $n-2$ effects suggest that unattended information must be stored in some form more durable than the hypothesized sensory buffer.

VII. RELATION BETWEEN SART AND INFORMATION REDUCTION TASKS

In information reduction tasks each choice response is mapped onto two or more stimuli. Such tasks are useful in sequential effect studies, since they permit separation of effects due to response repetition from those due to signal repetition. SART tasks can be interpreted as a special class of information reduction tasks, ones in which each response is mapped onto two or more compound stimuli, each such compound consisting of a focal stimulus and one of the possible distractors with which it can be paired. In SART tasks subjects are, by instruction, freer to ignore the differences among the equivalent stimuli than in other information reduction tasks. However, because the distracting stimulus component is usually difficult to ignore in SART tasks, this difference may be more an apparent than a real distinction. Thus, the important distinction between SART and other information reduction tasks may be that, in SART, the surplus stimulus information has a highly compatible mapping onto the set of response alternatives (e.g., auditory letters onto letter vocalizations), whereas the surplus stimulus information in other information reduction tasks is usually irrelevant to the required response. If we ignore these (possibly very important) differences between SART and information reduction, we may see the similarity between our analyses of effects of distracting information from the second preceding trial in SART, and analyses of 3-trial sequential effects in information reduction. Until further research has been done in the SART paradigm, it may be premature to claim that our observation of an effect of distracting information at depth $n-2$ has significance beyond that of previous findings of 3-trial sequential effects in information reduction (Smith, Chase, & Smith, 1973; Rabbitt & Vyas, 1974).

VIII. TAXONOMY OF 2-TRIAL SEQUENTIAL
EFFECTS IN SART

The need to refine theoretical accounts of sequential effects involving unattended information has led us to develop a taxonomy of 2-trial sequential effects for SART experiments. The taxonomy, presented in Table 3, employs as classification dimensions the various procedures that may need to be distinguished in order to test alternative theoretical interpretations. The dimensions of classification include:

1. the occurrence of conflict vs. agreement on the current trial;
2. conflict vs. agreement on the preceding trial;
3. repetition vs. nonrepetition of the stimulus in the focal channel;
4. repetition vs. nonrepetition of the stimulus in the distractor channel;
5. focal stimulus identical to vs. different from prior distractor; and
6. distractor identical to vs. different from prior focal stimulus.

Although the taxonomy of 2-trial SART sequences is based on the six dichotomous dimensions here listed, these dimensions are not independent and there turn out to be, not 64 ($=2^6$), but only 15 possible different types of sequences in the taxonomy. Additional observations about the taxonomy are that:

1. seven of the 15 2-trial sequences are impossible in a 2-choice SART task;
2. one of the 15 sequences is impossible in a 3-choice SART task;

3. four is the minimum number of stimulus and distractor alternatives needed in order to permit all 15 sequences; and

4. thirteen of the 14 possible types of sequences in the 3-stimulus SART task are equiprobable under random selection of focal and distractor stimuli, making it a desirable situation for comparative investigation of these sequences.

The results that we have presented to this point provide data about 11 of the 15 2-trial sequences of Table 3. In reexamining some earlier data collected by Greenwald (1972) we discovered that that study included five of the 15 sequences, two of which were among the four that were missing from our other studies noted in Table 3. (Needless to say, we are in the process of filling the remaining gaps in our classification scheme with 3-stimulus and 4-stimulus tasks.) The data given in Table 3 provide a convenient basis for summarizing the theory-relevant sequential effects that have been demonstrated in one or another of the SART experiments. We shall conclude by summarizing the inferences about information processing that are afforded by the existing SART data.

A. Modulation of Distractor Channel Processing as a Function of Prior Trial Type (Conflict vs. Agreement)

Several aspects of the data indicated that the absolute level of processing of the distractor channel is less on the trial after a conflict trial than after an agreement trial. Specifically, the interfering effect of a conflicting distractor was greater after an agreement trial than after a conflict trial (cf. Row 1 vs. Row 8 of Table 3, or Rows 6 and 7 vs. Row 9, but note the exception in Row 10, which will be considered later); and the facilitating effect of an agreeing distractor was greater after an agreement trial than after a conflict trial (cf. Row 11 vs. Row 14, or Rows 12 and 13 vs. Rows 14 and 15). It appears that the distractor-processing apparatus adjusts rapidly to each indication that the distractor information is helpful or harmful.

B. Inhibition of Response Associated With the Distractor on a Preceding Conflict Trial

Several lines of evidence converge on the interpretation that after a conflict trial there is a residual tendency to inhibit the response associated with that trial's distractor. Comparison of Row 1 vs. Row 3 of Table 3 shows that less interference results when the distractor on a conflict trial is the same as the one on the preceding conflict trial than when a new distractor is employed. Comparison of Row 1 vs. Row 5 shows that the subject has special difficulty when

TABLE 3

Taxonomy of 2-Trial Sequences in Selective Attention Reaction Time (SART)

Type of sequence with respect to distractor-focal stimulus conflict	Focal stim. repeats	Distractor repeats	Focal → distractor	Distractor → focal	Trial n−1	Trial n	Digit-naming Greenwald (1972)	Letter-naming Rosenberg (1976)	Position-naming auditory	Position-naming visual	2-stimulus task	3-stimulus task	4-stimulus task	6-stimulus task	k-stimulus task
1					C-d	A-b	395	461			--	--	24	360	$k(k-1) \times (k-2)(k-3)$
2	✓				A-c	A-b					--	6	24	120	$k(k-1)(k-2)$
3		✓			C-b	A-b	377				--	6	24	120	$k(k-1)(k-2)$
4 (Conflict →)			✓		B-c	A-b					--	6	24	120	$k(k-1)(k-2)$
5				✓	C-a	A-b	415				--	6	24	120	$k(k-1)(k-2)$
6	✓	✓			A-b	A-b			472	455	2	6	12	30	$k(k-1)$
7 (Conflict →)			✓	✓	B-a	A-b			477	458	2	6	12	30	$k(k-1)$

Example (focal stimulus in capital)

Illustrative data (Mean reaction times in msec)

Relative frequencies of various types of trials under random stimulus selection

500

	#														
Agreement	8				C-c	A-b		472			--	6	24	120	k(k-1)(k-2)
→	9			✓	A-a	A-b			497	476	2	6	12	30	k(k-1)
Conflict	10		✓	✓	B-b	A-b	375		481	445	2	6	12	30	k(k-1)
Conflict	11				B-c	A-a		436			--	6	24	120	k(k-1)(k-2)
→	12	✓		✓	A-c	A-a			485	437	2	6	12	30	k(k-1)
Agreement	13		✓	✓	C-a	A-a	377		470	433	2	6	12	30	k(k-1)
Agreement	14				B-b	A-a		423	460	424	2	6	12	30	k(k-1)
→ Agreement	15	✓	✓	✓	A-a	A-a			458	432	2	3	4	6	k

the focal stimulus on a conflict trial calls for the response associated with the distractor that occurred on the just-preceding conflict trial. Rows 9 and 10 show an interesting difference that was noted above; however, because of the confoundings indicated by the multiple check marks in Rows 9 and 10, it is not possible to declare which aspect of the 2-trial sequences is responsible for this difference. One possibility is that the difference is due to the tendency to inhibit the response to the prior distractor.[5]

C. Facilitation Due to Repetition of Distractor and Focal n—2 → n—1 Transitions

This effect (see Table 2) is not represented in Table 3 because it is one that involves 3-trial sequences. If we wish to assume that this effect is in the general category of a facilitation on one trial of the processes that were employed on a previous one, then we must conclude that, after Trial $n-1$, the processor (our pseudonym for the central nervous system) must record the nature of transformations of the stimulus from Trial $n-2$ that could have been used to predict the stimulus on Trial $n-1$. Since the transformation information that must be recorded includes the transformation in the distractor channel, this 3-trial sequential effect provides an important indication of memory for information received in an unattended channel.

IX. CONCLUSIONS

We shall use the generic term "priming" to designate effects in which the reuse of a just-used mechanism is facilitated. In previous research by others using single-stimulus choice reaction time tasks, priming has been demonstrated for mechanisms associated with (a) the particular stimulus that last occurred, (b) the particular response that last occurred, and (c) the particular rule for mapping responses to stimuli that was last used (Rabbitt & Vyas, 1973). A remarkable aspect of our findings for SART tasks has been that the first of these standard priming effects was weak and the second was absent. The processes that were found to manifest priming in the SART tasks were ones associated with (d) the distractor-focal relationship (conflict vs. agreement) that last occurred, (e) the specific distracting stimulus that last occurred, and (f) the specific combination of transitions between trials (either repetition or nonrepetition) in both the distractor and focal channels that last occurred.

The significance of our findings is partly in their implication of inhibitory processes that operate at both perceptual and response levels in SART per-

---

[5]Evidence for a tendency to inhibit the response associated with the just-preceding distractor has been obtained also in research using the Stroop color-naming task (Dalrymple-Alford & Budayr, 1966; Sichel & Chandler, 1969).

formance. That is, part of the ability to respond rapidly and selectively to one of two sources of stimulation has been shown to consist of the capacity to inhibit tendencies to process and to respond to potential distractors.

Another significant aspect of our findings is their bearing on theories of the level of processing accorded to unattended information. Our results have indicated that the processor retains information derived from the second preceding event in the distractor channel and, possibly, from even more remote distractor events.

ACKNOWLEDGMENTS

This research was supported in large part by National Institute of Mental Health Grant MH-20527 (*Mechanisms of Voluntary Action and Voluntary Attention*) to The Ohio State University.

REFERENCES

Dalrymple-Alford, E. C., & Budayr, B. Examination of some aspects of the Stroop color-word test. *Perceptual and Motor Skills,* 1966, *23,* 1211–1214.

Deutsch, H. A., & Deutsch, D. Attention: Some theoretical considerations. *Psychological Review,* 1963, *70,* 80–90.

Dyer, F. N. The Stroop phenomenon and its use in the study of perceptual, cognitive, and response processes. *Memory and Cognition,* 1973, *1,* 106–120.

Falmagne, F. C., Cohen, S. P., & Dwivedi, A. Two-choice reactions as an ordered memory scanning process. In P. M. A. Rabbitt & S. Dornic, (Eds.), *Attention and performance V.* New York: Academic Press, 1975.

Greenwald, A. G. A double-stimulation test of ideo-motor theory with implications for selective attention. *Journal of Experimental Psychology,* 1970, *84,* 392–398. (a)

Greenwald, A. G. Selective attention as a function of signal rate. *Journal of Experimental Psychology,* 1970, *86,* 48–52. (b)

Greenwald, A. G. Evidence of both perceptual filtering and response suppression for rejected messages in selective attention. *Journal of Experimental Psychology,* 1972, *94,* 58–67.

Kornblum, S. Sequential effects in choice reaction time: A tutorial review. In S. Kornblum (Ed.), *Attention and performance IV.* New York: Academic Press, 1973.

Moray, N. *Attention: Selective processes in vision and hearing.* New York: Academic Press, 1970.

Norman, D. A. Memory while shadowing. *The Quarterly Journal of Experimental Psychology,* Vol. *XXI,* Part 1, February, 1969.

Rabbitt, P. M. A., & Vyas, S. What is repeated in the "repetition effect"? In S. Kornblum (Ed.), *Attention and performance IV.* New York: Academic Press, 1973.

Rabbitt, P. M. A., & Vyas, S. M. Interference between binary classification judgments and some repetition effects in a serial choice reaction time task. *Journal of Experimental Psychology,* 1974, *103,* 1181–1190.

Rosenberg, K. E. *Selective attention as a function of the cue relevance of distracting stimuli.* Unpublished masters thesis, The Ohio State University, 1976.

Sichel, J. L., & Chandler, K. A. The color-word interference test: The effects of varied color-word combinations upon verbal response latency. *The Journal of Psychology,* 1969, *72,* 219–231.

Smith, E. E., Chase, W. G., & Smith, P. G. Stimulus and response repetition effects in retrieval from short-term memory: Trace decay and memory search. *Journal of Experimental Psychology,* 1973, *98,* 413–422.

Stroop, J. R. Studies of interference in serial verbal reactions. *Journal of Experimental Psychology,* 1935, *18,* 643–662.

Treisman, A. M. Strategies and models of selective attention. *Psychological Review,* 1969, *76,* 282–299.

27

Selective Attention as a Motor Program

Jean-Marie Coquery

Laboratoire de Psychophysiologie
Université de Lille I
France

ABSTRACT

Selective attention and motor commands are both considered as central efferent programs acting upon specific restricted motor and sensory neuronal pools. Descending efferent activity controls either motor neurons or interneurons mediating segmental and ascending sensory flow; motor commands thus influence sensory relays, and efferences directed toward sensory channels modulate motor reactivity.

If selective attention uses similar efferent mechanisms as those involved in motor commands, it becomes of interest for the study of attention to examine the influence of limited active movements upon the sensory information carried over the pathways involving the actively moved limb. The first part of this chapter reports results from experiments on cats showing that during movement somatic volleys are reduced at the first lemniscal relay and possibly reamplified at the specific thalamic relay.

The second part reports experiments in man linking attention to orienting reaction, and hence to efferent programs. During *passive* attention, unexpected stimuli induce late cortical waves (N2 and P3), considered as components of the generalized orienting response and possibly reflecting the release of stimulus identification programs. Attention to expected stimuli has the same effects as the repetition of an unexpected stimulus: the generalized orienting reaction habituates and focuses on structures involved in the processing of attended stimuli. Further habituation of this localized orientation reaction is prevented during *active* attention.

The third part presents data from an experiment on man using cutaneous reflexes of the lower limbs. The results show that the nociceptive reflexes are indeed specifically enhanced in the leg to which the subjects pay attention as compared to the reflexes in the leg that is nonattended.

I. INTRODUCTION

The title of this contribution refers to selective attention as motor program. Perhaps I should say right away that the term *motor* may be somewhat restrictive. One might better use a concept with broader meaning. With respect to attentive behavior, the expression "efferent" or "emitted" program is perhaps more appropriate. In effect, the targets of higher commands are not limited to the motoneurons. Although I do not intend to review here the literature on sensory control (see Coquery, 1972; Towe, 1973), I take for example the sensorimotor cortex, which in addition to influencing the motor neurons also controls, through collaterals of the corticospinal tracts, the somato-sensory relays in the spinal cord (Fetz, 1968; Wall, 1967), the medulla (Harris, Jabbur, Horse, & Towe, 1965; Jabbur & Towe, 1960) and the thalamus (Andersen, Junge, & Sveen, 1967; Iwama & Yamamoto, 1961; Shimazu, Yanagisawa, & Garoutte, 1965). Some of its efferences end up on the dorsal column nuclei (Gordon & Miller, 1969).

Another important motor pathway, the reticulospinal system, has been shown to control interneurons mediating the transmission of cutaneous afferents to the motoneurons and, at the same time, to ascending spinoreticular tracts (Carpenter, Engberg, & Lundberg, 1965).

It seems legitimate, therefore, not to distinguish too sharply between motor programs resulting in muscle activity and programs aimed at the different levels of sensory integration, which we may call programs of analysis. This extension of the notion of motor programs seems all the more necessary as there is a permanent and structural interaction between input and output control. An efficient way to regulate motor activity is to act upon the sensory afferents by which such an activity can be released, adjusted, or disturbed. This type of output regulation does not take place without repercussion on discriminative and cognitive functions since sensory information, in addition to its role in motor adjustment, has evolved into a powerful tool for cognitive regulation, allowing especially anticipatory behavior. On the other hand, any program of analysis directed toward a specific sensory channel is also likely to involve specific motor effects.

I shall first briefly review some data on the control of sensory transmission during movement. Next, I shall report experiments linking attention to the orienting reaction and hence to efferent programs. Finally, I shall present results from a preliminary experiment showing that selective attention involves a specific modulation of motor reactivity.

II. MODIFICATIONS OF SENSORY TRANSMISSION DURING MOVEMENT

Attention and movement may both be considered as products of efferent programs. And, as motor commands are usually directed toward restricted pools of neurons, programs of analysis also exhibit some specificity in their effects on

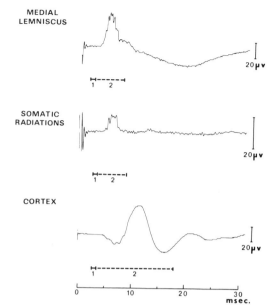

FIG. 1. Evoked potentials recorded in the medial lemniscus,
in the somatic radiations, and
over the S1 cortex of the cat.
Each trace represents an average
of 100 responses to an electrical stimulation of the paw.
After A/D conversion, the potentials were integrated over an
epoch (2) indicated by the dotted
line, taking as a baseline the mean
value during epoch (1) indicated
by the solid line.

ascending and segmental sensory flow. Let's then take motor behavior as a
model of attentive behavior and see how it influences transmission of somatic
sensory messages. I shall focus here on the modifications of transmission in the
lemniscal system of the cat during conditioned movements.

Ghez and Lenzi (1971) and Ghez and Pisa (1972) have shown that volleys
evoked in the medial lemniscus by stimulation of the superficial radial nerve are
reduced when the cat uses the stimulated forelimb for pressing on a lever. Such
a depression starts more than 100 msec before the actual displacement of the
limb and is thus ascribed to central influences. Coulter (1974), using a similar
procedure, also found a depression of the lemniscal volley and pointed out that
it only involved pathways from the actively moved limb.

I performed a similar experiment on seven cats trained to press a lever in order
to get milk, recording with gross electrodes volleys elicited in the medial lemniscus,
in the somatic radiations, and over the primary cortex. Electrical stimulation was
applied to the skin of the forelimb when the cats stayed still or at the time they
touched the lever. Records were taken during a maximum of ten sessions (7.6
sessions on the average). During each session the animals got about 100 stimulations during movement, and the same number while keeping still. The area of the
potentials was measured by numerical integration (Fig. 1). For each session, the
median value of the potentials recorded at each level was computed for movement and no movement and, for each animal, the medians were averaged over
the sessions.

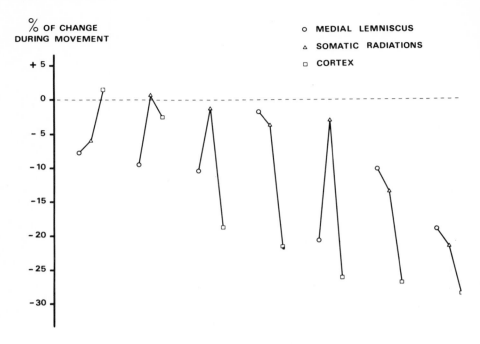

%
**OF CHANGE
DURING MOVEMENT**

o **MEDIAL LEMNISCUS**

△ **SOMATIC RADIATIONS**

□ **CORTEX**

FIG. 2.   Variations during a conditioned movement of evoked potentials recorded in the medial lemniscus, in the somatic radiation, and over the S1 cortex. For seven cats, the mean values of the potentials recorded at the three sites during a lever pressing movement are plotted as a percentage difference from values during rest.

The first thing to note is that cutaneous volleys undergo considerable modulation along the lemniscal pathway. Correlation between potentials recorded at the three levels is indeed very low. In absence of movement the median product —moment correlation between potentials recorded in the lemniscus and in the somatic radiations is only +.17, +.17 also between lemniscus and cortex and +.15 between somatic radiations and cortex. During movement these values become respectively +.12, +.14 and +.11.

Second, the results show that across animals the lemniscal volley is depressed during movement by 11.2% on the average (range: −1.7% and −20.6%). Beyond the thalamic relay, the recorded potential still present a slight depression (−6.8% on the average; range +.8% and −21.6%). The diminution is less than after the first relay, but the difference is not satistically significant. Potentials recorded over the primary cortex are more deeply depressed, by 17.4% on the average (range: +1.5% and −28.6%). Figure 2 gives the individual results of the seven cats.

The modifications of sensory transmission during movement do not appear to be identical at the different levels of the lemniscal pathway. On the average, they are more pronounced at the first relay and at the cortical level than at the thalamus. Although not significant in this small sample, these differences are in agreement with results from a previous experiment (Coquery & Vitton, 1972) showing that cortical potentials elicited by stimulation of the moving limb (thus before the first relay) are always diminished during movement, whereas they show a smaller decrease and sometimes an increase when stimulation is applied directly to the thalamic relay.

This might indicate the motor commands have differential effects on the different sensory relays, reducing the volleys transmitted by the first relay and possibly reamplifying them as they pass through the thalamus.

It would be risky to draw precise inferences from these results: obviously, more data are needed and other pathways such as the extralemniscal ones should be investigated. However, I would like to raise a few questions concerning the significance of these modulations. For many investigators, the depression of sensory volleys at the first relay is to be looked at as an improvement of the signal to noise ratio. Indeed, if the emission of efferent programs resulted in widespread facilitation of sensory transmission, there would be, as a consequence, a tremendous increase of noise in the sensory channels. A reduction of trans-mittive capacity benefits the most concentrated and intense afferents. It is only after such a first stage filtering that a possible thalamic facilitation may be useful for sensory integration.

But should we consider the ascending sensory volley as a message? In a ballistic movement, such as pressing a lever or a key for a reaction time experiment, the whole movement is programmed beforehand and its completion does not require much, if any, information about the conditions of its performance. Therefore, we may consider the motor command as the signal, and any afference occurring while it is carried out as noise. This is another way of looking at the significance of the sensory reduction during movement as improving the execution of the intended movement.

Would it be the same for skilled movements or for movements of exploration in which the motor program must continuously be adjusted to the consequences of the movement itself? This would be worth investigating especially as this situation is closer to what goes on during discriminative attention.

Some insight about the significance of the modulation of the lemniscal relays during movement and attention may also be given by looking at the role the lemniscal pathway is supposed to play in behavior. Wall (1970) has put forth the idea that the role of impulses traveling in the dorsal columns is not to provide detailed sensory information but rather to release and to control response pro-grams, either motor programs or programs of analysis. The sensory information to be acted upon by these programs of analysis travels in the extralemniscal pathways, which have very little specificity and show a great deal of convergence from different places and different submodalities. But their convergence can be reduced, their specificity increased or even shifted, by means of central influences from the cerebral cortex or the brain stem. If we follow Wall's hypothesis, then a selection of information that focuses on smaller receptive fields and on specific submodalities could be reflected by a reduction of the size of the volleys transmitted by the extralemniscal pathways. As for the reduction of transmission at the first relay of the lemniscal system, it could reflect an additional selective control or shaping of the information involved in the building up or in the resetting of efferent programs.

III. ATTENTION AND ORIENTING REACTIONS

Let us now turn to a second set of data that again leads to the consideration of attention as an efferent program. Although similar data have been reported by others, especially by Ford, Roth, Dirks, and Kopell (1973) and by Courchesne, Hillyard, and Galambos (1975), I shall first briefly report an experiment we conducted in man, looking at the evoked potentials in two conditions of attention, or, to be more specific, in two conditions of passive expectancy.

We recorded vertex and specific cortical evoked potentials elicited by an expected or an unexpected stimulation in six subjects. In this experiment, the only task the subjects had to perform was to select, by pressing either one of two pedals, the stimulus they would be given two seconds later, which was either a mild electrical shock to the forefinger or a flash. They were instructed to deliver about the same number of shocks and flashes but to avoid any alternate or regular sequence of stimuli. After one or two training sessions, the subjects paced themselves (one choice every 6 sec, on the average) and got a roughly equal number of cutaneous and visual stimuli during the experimental session.

Nine stimuli out of 10 were given in accordance with the subject's choice; one out of 10, in a random order, did not match the subject's selection. Subjects had been warned during the training session about possible errors in the delivery of stimuli due to the unreliability of the programming device, and they were told to ignore them.

The situation then became one in which each time the subject expected the stimulus he chose his attention or expectancy was oriented toward either the cutaneous or the visual modality. Stimuli from either modality have about the same frequency and include no task to be performed. The subject's attention may be said to be *passive attention:* a passive expectancy as opposed to an active readiness.

If we now compare the vertex evoked potentials elicited by expected and unexpected stimuli, we see that *unexpected* stimuli are followed by characteristic late waves (Fig. 3), namely a negative wave (N2) peaking around 260 msec after the stimulus, and a positive wave (P3), usually merging with the end limb of N2. For some subjects, N2 is seen only in the potentials elicited by unexpected stimuli; for the group as a whole, it is significantly higher (at .05 with a two-tailed sign test) in the responses to unexpected stimuli. P3 is usually more pronounced in responses to unexpected stimuli, but its merging with the end of N2 precludes a precise and independent measurement.

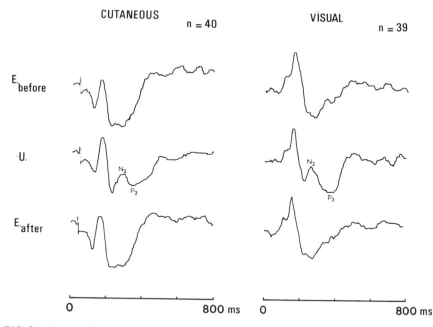

FIG. 3. Averaged vertex evoked responses to expected and unexpected visual or cutaneous stimuli. E.before: responses to expected stimuli immediately preceding an unexpected stimulus from the same modality. U.: responses to unexpected stimuli; note the presence of N2 and P3 waves. E.after: responses to expected stimuli immediately following an unexpected stimulus from the same modality.

These components of the evoked response are well known and have already been shown to vary with different conditions of attention. In the present experiment, the procedure we used makes it certain that their occurrence or their increase was due only to the selective attention to a given modality. Moreover, these cortical events cannot represent a passive direct response to the afferent sensory volley, but rather an active processing of the information carried over a given input channel. It would otherwise be difficult to explain why they arise in the absence of an expected stimulus as reported by Picton and Hillyard (1974) or by Ruchkin, Sutton, and Tueting (1975).

These waves can be and have been considered as a reaction to an unexpected stimulus, that is to say, as components of the generalized orienting reaction. They could reflect a process of investigation, of analysis of the unexpected stimulus together with the beginning of a response. We know that if a sudden stimulus is repeated, the orienting reaction habituates and at first (from generalized) becomes localized. Sokolov (1960) interprets this phenomenon by reference to a neural model progressively built by the repetition of the stimulus, one to which each incoming stimulus is compared. If the stimulus fits the model, the orienting reaction is reduced or suppressed. This interpretation of the habituation of the orienting reaction can easily be transposed to our situation. In this case, however, the neural model of the stimulus is not built up by repetition but set up by the subject's own choice. In this condition, the expected stimulus matches the model and either does not elicit any orienting reaction or only a weaker one, as reflected in the N2 and P3 waves.

On the whole, an unexpected event brings about the emission of a rather stereotyped response, the orienting reaction. This response has the characteristics of an efferent program acting upon the effectors as well as upon the sensory channels, as shown by the various muscular, autonomic, and sensory expressions of arousal. It is also the first element of attentive behavior: attention is caught but is still diffuse, not yet focused on the arousing stimulus. In my opinion, selective or focused attention corresponds to differential habituation or a progressive concentration on a few relevant components, of the orienting response. A stimulus that is repeated identically in a regular fashion becomes subjectively probable and is easily anticipated. In selective attention the expected stimulus is also anticipated, its characteristics foreseen; this is very similar to what takes place during habituation. Why then, have so many investigators shown that some components of the evoked potentials, especially the N1 and P3 waves, are increased if the stimuli are expected? Moreover, why does paying attention to a repeating stimulus make habituation slower?

These discrepancies may be explained if we recall that in most cases attention is not only a passive expectancy of the stimulus but involves readiness to perform a task on the occurrence of the expected signal. It is likewise well known that, when a stimulus calls for a response or for a decision not to respond habituation slows down, especially when the task is more complex or difficult. This leads one to think that active attention, involving the performance of a task, reduces the habituation of only the localized orienting reaction and that arousal concentrates on the structures involved in the decoding of the afferent message that allows the maintainance of a program of analysis specific for this message while efferences directed toward other information channels are attenuated. In other words, there would be no difference in nature between the arousal induced by an *unexpected* stimulus and the arousal by a signal to which we pay attention, except that in the latter case arousal is concentrated on the structures involved in the decoding of the attended message.

IV. EFFECTS OF SELECTIVE ATTENTION ON SPINAL REFLEXES

The whole problem is essentially one of showing effects of this concentration of activation. Some evidence has already been provided, for instance by Eason, Harter, and White (1969) with visual evoked potentials. I have attempted to demonstrate these selective effects by using as a criterion the size of polysynaptic reflexes elicited by attended or unattended stimuli. The test reflex is a flexion reflex of the short femoral biceps; it is elicited by electrical stimulation of the sural nerve at the ankle. The stimulation is a train of 10 pulses which, at the reflex threshold, are usually felt as unpleasant or even slightly painful.

Attention was set by asking the subjects to estimate the strength of the shocks to one leg. Five intensities were used; the highest intensity was set slightly above the reflex threshold; the median one served as a reference with a value of 100. After two training sessions, subjects were told that the aim of the experiment was to determine how well they could estimate stimulus intensity despite disturbing stimulations.

The experimental session was divided into four blocks, and each block into four sequences. During one sequence the subjects paid attention to one leg; attention was paid to the other leg during the next sequence. Each sequence included, in a random order, 16 shocks, 12 to the attended leg, four of them eliciting a reflex, and four to the other leg, also eliciting a reflex. Subjects had to estimate the shocks to the attended leg only. The reference stimulation was given three times at the beginning of each sequence, 2 sec before each stimulation a warning click was given over a loudspeaker.

Seven subjects were run. For each leg we compared the reflexes elicited by the relevant and by the not relevant shocks. The mean difference was expressed in z score, taking as a reference the distribution of the reflexes to unattended stimuli. This made it possible to pool all the data for a same condition of attention.

The results show that the polysynaptic reflexes are slightly higher when elicited by attended stimuli. The difference is modest, .21 σ on the average but, with a t test, significant at the .001 level.

Whatever physiological mechanism is responsible for these effects, it is likely that selective attention has a specific influence on spinal reflex pathways. It is impossible to tell with certainty whether it facilitates the attended pathways or depresses the reactivity of the unattended ones. However, the fact that a previously noneffective stimulus may become potent when carefully attended makes it probable that selective attention has a positive effect on the attended pathways.

The limited number of estimations and their restricted range of variation did not enable us to correlate perception with motor reactivity. However, we know from Hugon (1973) that when the reflex increases, subjects report a more painful sensation. It is then very likely that, just as in motor programs, the programs of analysis at work in selective attention are responsible for a specific modulation of both motor and sensory functions.

REFERENCES

Andersen, P., Junge, K., & Sveen, O. Corticothalamic facilitation of somatosensory impulses. *Nature*, 1967, *214*, 1011–1012.

Carpenter, D., Engberg, I., & Lundberg, A. Differential supraspinal control of inhibitory and excitatory actions from the FRA to ascending supraspinal pathways. *Acta Physiologica Scandinavica*, 1965, *63*, 103–110.

Coquery, J. M., Fonctions motrices et contrôle des messages sensoriels d'origine somatique. *Journal de Physiologie*, Paris, 1972, *64*, 533–560.

Coquery, J. M., & Vitton, N. Altérations des potentiels évoqués sur le cortex somesthésique du Chat durant un mouvement conditionné. *Physiology & Behavior*, 1972, *8*, 963–967.

Coulter, J. D. Sensory transmission through lemniscal pathway during voluntary movement in the cat. *Journal of Neurophysiology*, 1974, *37*, 831–845.

Courchesne, E., Hillyard, S. A., & Galambos, R. Stimulus novelty, task relevance and the visual evoked potential in man. *Electroencephalography and Clinical Neurophysiology*, 1975, *39*, 131–143.

Eason, R. G., Harter, M. R., & White, C. T. Effects of attention and arousal on visually evoked cortical potentials and reaction time in man. *Physiology & Behavior*, 1969, *4*, 283–289.

Fetz, E. E. Pyramidal tract effects on interneurons in the cat lumbar dorsal horn. *Journal of Neurophysiology*, 1968, *31*, 69–80.

Ford, J. M., Roth, W. T., Dirks, S. J., & Kopell, B. S. Evoked potential correlates of signal recognition between and within modalities. *Science*, 1973, *181*, 465–466.

Ghez, C., & Lenzi, G. L. Modulation of sensory transmission in cat lemniscal system during voluntary movement. *Pflügers Archiv*, 1971, *323*, 273–278.

Ghez, C., & Pisa, M. Inhibition of afferent transmission in cuneate nucleus during voluntary movement in the cat. *Brain Research*, 1972, *40*, 145–161.

Gordon, G., & Miller, R. Identification of cortical cells projecting to the dorsal column nuclei of the cat. *Quarterly Journal of Experimental Physiology*, 1969, *54*, 85–98.

Harris, F., Jabbur, S. J., Horse, R. W., & Towe, A. L. Influence of the cerebral cortex on the cuneate nucleus of the monkey. *Nature*, 1965, *208*, 1215–1216.

Hugon, M. Exteroceptive reflexes to stimulation of the sural nerve in normal man. In J. E. Desmedt (Ed.), *New developments in electromyography and clinical neurophysiology* (Vol. 3). Basel: Karger, 1973.

Iwama, K., & Yamamoto, C. Impulse transmission of thalamic somatosensory relay nuclei as modified by electrical stimulation of the cerebral cortex. *Japanese Journal of Physiology*, 1961, *11*, 169–182.

Jabbur, S. J., & Towe, A. L. Effect of pyramidal tract activity on dorsal column nuclei. *Science*, 1960, *132*, 547–548.

Picton, T. W., & Hillyard, S. A. Human auditory evoked potentials. II: Effects of attention. *Electroencephalography and Clinical Neurophysiology*, 1974, *36*, 191–199.

Ruchkin, D. S., Sutton, S., & Tueting, P. Emitted and evoked P_{300} potentials and variation in stimulus probability. *Psychophysiology*, 1975, *12*, 591–595.

Shimazu, H., Yanagisawa, N., & Garoutte, B. Cortico-pyramidal influences on thalamic somatosensory transmission in the cat. *Japanese Journal of Physiology*, 1965, *15*, 101–124.

Sokolov, E. N. Neuronal models and the orienting reflex. In M. A. Brazier (Ed.), *The central nervous system and behaviour*. New York: J. Macy, 1960.

Towe, A. L. Somatosensory cortex: Descending influences on ascending systems. In A. Iggo (Ed.), *Handbook of sensory physiology, Volume II: Somato-sensory system*. Berlin: Springer, 1973.

Wall, P. D. The laminar organization of dorsal horn and effects of descending impulses. *Journal of Physiology*, London, 1967, *188*, 403–423.

Wall, P. D. The sensory and motor role of impulses travelling in the dorsal columns towards cerebral cortex. *Brain*, 1970, *93*, 505–524.

28 Storage Codes for Movement Information

George E. Stelmach
Hugh D. McCracken

Motor Behavior Laboratory
University of Wisconsin
Madison, Wisconsin, United States

ABSTRACT

In a series of experiments designed to examine the separate storage of distance and location cues, the avilability of movement information was manipulated in a distance reproduction paradigm. Location information was altered by varying the time spent at the movement endpoints, and distance information was manipulated by either omitting, disrupting, or augmenting the dynamic phase of the movement. Experiment 1 supported the hypothesis that distance representation was dependent on location cues, as distance representation was altered by interpolated information processing activity when the location cues were minimal. Since providing only movement endpoint information reduced distance reproduction accuracy, Experiment 2 showed that location extrapolation was not the sole determiner of distance representation. In Experiments 3 and 4, distance representation was found to be enhanced by repetition and disrupted by movement reversals, whereas augmented location information stabilized accuracy across movement amplitude. Although the findings of the latter experiments suggested a separate storage code for distance information, there was a consistent interaction of movement-starting positions with distance accuracy. These results, taken together, emphasize the interdependence of the two movement cues, and argue that distance memory representation is dependent upon the relative amount of distance and location information present in the criterion movement. The findings militate against a dual storage mode concept for movement cues.

I. INTRODUCTION

An important part of the processing of movement information is the monitoring of incoming sensory inputs and their subsequent contact with items in memory. In movement feedback situations where there are no visual or auditory cues, intrinsic information is derived from the movement itself. Such sensory information is based on proprioception, which is thought to provide a variety of useful movement cues such as acceleration, amplitude, direction, location, and velocity (Stelmach, 1976). While these cues have been discussed by psychologists for a long time (Hollingsworth, 1909; Woodworth, 1899), only within the last two decades have the sensory cues subserving kinesthetic perception been systematically investigated (Laabs, 1973; Posner, 1967; Stelmach, Kelso, & Wallace, 1975).

A wide array of information is available to aid in blind movement reproduction, but little attention has been given to the specific cue(s) used to aid movement reproduction. It is apparent that, relative to the understanding of the visual and auditory modalities, the state of knowledge on how proprioceptive (movement) information is coded in memory is not well developed. While Leuba (1909) and Woodworth (1899) discussed the separation of distance and location information, Laabs (1973) was the first modern-day investigator to use a paradigm that separated these cues. Laabs proposed that there are different storage modes for distance and location information, and that these cues exhibit different retention characteristics.

Early studies that examined retention characteristics utilized invariant starting and reproduction location positions, which allowed both location and distance cues to be reliable. In contrast, Laabs (1973) used a procedure that forced reliance on either distance or location cues by making the opposing cue unreliable. This procedure found location information to be well retained, unless a rehearsal prevention task was present, while distance information decayed and was unaffected by interpolated information processing activity. Based on this finding, Laabs advocated separate storage modes for these cues; location information was centrally stored, whereas distance information was stored in a kinesthetic mode and had no access to central processing. Though the dual storage mode concept has been well received, there are several kinds of data that question the independence of the two movement cues. Inspection of Laabs' (1973) distance data indicates that short distance errors follow a retention function similar to that of location cues. Similarly, Posner and Keele (1969) found that short movements behaved more like visual codes. Further, studies by Marteniuk (1973), Moxley (1974), and Stelmach and Kelso (1975) have supported the view that distance information is susceptible to interpolated processing activity and, in Laabs' terms, has access to central processing. In addition, starting position effects found in distance reproduction suggest that the initial location of the reproduction movement influences the directionality of reproduction errors (Stelmach & Kelso, 1973). In a later study, Laabs (1974) found that both the end location and movement amplitude shifted distance reproduction errors in the direction of the interpolated movement. These foregoing findings question the independence of distance and location cues by suggesting that location information influences distance representation, and that both cues are processed similarly, but perhaps at different levels.

To postulate a separate storage mode for distance seems tenuous, for there are no known physiological receptors that provide extent information (Skoglund, 1973). It seems intuitive that distance information may be derived from other sources of movement information: for example, extrapolation from the start and finish locations of the criterion movement (Keele & Ells, 1972), retaining a copy of the motor outflow (Jones, 1974), or making a movement at a fixed rate for a certain time period (Laabs, 1973; Leuba, 1909; Woodworth, 1899).

The present series of experiments chose to examine the extrapolation hypothesis (Keele & Ells, 1972) by augmenting position cues and by altering distance information. The assumption underlying Experiments 1 and 4 was that resting on the movement endpoints for longer time periods would make the start and finish locations more distinct, thereby facilitating distance reproduction. In Experiment 2 it was argued that if distance was obtained primarily from movement endpoints, there was little need to make the actual movement. Experiment 3 attempted to strengthen the distance code by having the subject repeat the criterion distance several times prior to reproduction. In addition to the location augmentation assumption, Experiment 4 sought to disrupt any distance code by having subjects perform several movement reversals while moving between the endpoints. Support for the extrapolation hypothesis would cast doubt on the cue-separation technique and question the theoretical utility of separating movement cues.

II. EXPERIMENT 1

A. Method.

1. *Subjects.*   Thirty-six right-handed male freshman volunteers from the University of Wisconsin, were randomly assigned to three distance conditions ($n = 12$). All were paid for their services.

2. *Apparatus.*   A lever positioning task described in Stelmach and Walsh (1973) was used. Briefly, the apparatus consisted of a lever that moved freely from right to left through a 180° arc in the vertical plane. The lever could be positioned throughout the arc in degree intervals (1 deg = 4 mm). A chin-rest fixed the subject's head while he was seated facing the apparatus. The lever was completely shielded from the subject's view throughout the experiment and a Lafayette eight-bank timer was used to sequence experimental events.

3. *Procedures and Instructions.*   The experiment took place in a dimly lit sound-proof chamber, with the subject seated facing the apparatus surrounded by a black curtained area that prevented visual cues. After a brief instructional period, subjects grasped the lever palm up and actively explored the full range of move-

ment for familiarization purposes. In addition, standardized instructions were read to each subject, with emphasis placed on remembering the distance during the criterion movement and clarifying that reproduction would always be from a different starting position, either backwards or forwards from the criterion starting position.

There were three location duration manipulations (immediate, 2, and 5 sec). In the immediate condition the command was always to "Grasp the handle and move." In the 2 and 5 sec conditions, the experimenter timed from the moment the subject's fingers touched the handle for either 2 or 5 secs. The "Move" command was issued so that the subject's initial loss of contact with the starting position coincided with either 2 or 5 secs. Likewise, at the finishing locations, the command to "Release" was issued just prior to the expiration of the experimental time for all three conditions (immediate, 2, and 5 sec). Subjects in all conditions always placed their hand in their lap after releasing the lever and the experimenter returned the lever to the new starting position.

After the criterion movement presentation, one of the three retention interval conditions followed. In the immediate retention interval the subject grasped the lever in the new starting position and immediately estimated the criterion movement. During the 15 sec delay retention interval, subjects had been told to concentrate on the criterion distance to be reproduced. In the 15 sec interpolated processing activity (IPA) retention interval, the subject was read a randomly chosen three-digit number that was always above three hundred; and the subjects were instructed to count backwards from that number by threes as quickly and as accurately as possible. The commands "Grasp the handle" and "Recall" instructed the subject to stop counting and to reproduce the criterion distance.

4. *Criterion Responses.* Five different distances (26°, 52°, 78°, 104°, and 130°) were used from two criterion starting positions (15° and 25°). Each criterion distance was reproduced ± 10° from each criterion starting position. Thus, there were five distances replicated from the four reproduction starting positions; two were forward from the criterion starting positions and two were backward. These criterion responses constituted blocks of twenty trials performed, once in each retention interval condition. The presentation order of criterion distances and retention intervals was randomized, with the constraint that no repetition of retention interval condition occur, and subjects were rotated through different random orders of trials.

5. *Design.* The design was thus a 3 x 3 x 5 x 2 x 2 (location duration x retention interval x distance reproduction x starting position direction x replicates, analysis of variance for constant error (CE) and absolute error (AE). Variable error (VE) was calculated as the standard deviation of the constant errors for the four replicates of each target.

B. Results and Discussion

The means and standard deviations of durations, retention intervals and distances are presented in Table 1. The duration main effect was not significant for any dependent variable (F's < 1). The retention interval main effect was significant for VE and AE, F's $(2, 66)$ = 22.9 and 47.64, p's $< .05$, respectively (see Fig. 1). For both dependent measures, there was a significant increase in error over the delayed interval, and a further significant increase in error under interpolated processing, p's $< .05$ (Tukey's HSD, Kirk, 1968). Further, distance was a potent source of variance for VE, AE, and CE, F's $(4, 132)$ = 17.81, 3.04, and 28.84, p's $< .05$, respectively. For VE and AE, this meant significant increases in error with increasing distance. For CE, short movements were overshot, while long movements were undershot, the customary range effect (Ellson & Wheeler, 1947).

The durations x retention intervals interaction was significant for AE, $F(4,66)$ = 4.03, $p < .05$. A simple main effect analysis showed that the immediate location duration error was significantly larger than the 2 or 5 sec durations under the IPA condition $p < .05$. Further analysis revealed that no simple combination of differences accounted for the interaction.

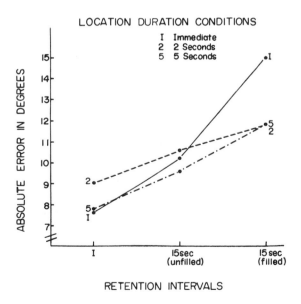

FIG. 1 Mean absolute error of location duration conditions as a function of retention intervals.

TABLE 1
Means and Standard Deviations of Duration, Retention Intervals, and Distances[a]

Main Effects		Immediate			Two Seconds			Five Seconds		
		CE	AE	VE	CE	AE	VE	CE	AE	VE
Duration	M	.15	10.99	11.18	2.58	10.51	11.05	2.98	9.90	10.07
	SD	5.44	3.54	6.19	4.65	3.66	6.87	4.95	3.37	6.92
Retention Intervals										
Immed.	M	−.66	7.74	8.26	2.17	9.07	10.14	2.12	7.90	8.34
	SD	4.27	1.30	4.53	4.44	3.19	4.97	2.96	1.57	3.57
15 sec.	M	−.12	10.28	11.02	2.88	10.56	10.59	2.36	9.85	9.84
	SD	3.89	1.35	5.65	6.06	3.66	6.06	5.04	2.15	4.71
Filled	M	1.24	14.95	14.27	2.68	11.90	12.42	4.46	11.93	12.32
	SD	7.65	2.68	6.73	3.47	3.81	8.87	6.34	4.49	10.13
Distances										
26°	M	6.77	9.29	7.41	7.16	8.62	6.39	7.68	9.27	7.26
	SD	9.84	8.26	5.05	6.08	5.28	4.07	9.19	8.00	8.00
52°	M	2.38	10.68	10.95	4.42	10.20	10.55	3.96	9.39	9.34
	SD	9.34	5.50	6.21	7.07	5.68	6.65	7.41	4.20	3.59
78°	M	−.78	11.29	12.32	3.67	10.82	11.55	1.04	9.54	10.19
	SD	8.29	5.02	6.08	8.07	5.15	5.60	6.95	4.58	5.65
104°	M	−4.86	11.79	12.25	−1.63	11.19	12.84	1.29	10.39	11.88
	SD	7.73	5.51	6.15	7.85	5.54	6.08	7.24	4.12	4.72
130°	M	−2.75	11.90	12.98	−.72	11.74	13.93	.93	10.90	12.17
	SD	9.46	4.80	6.11	8.04	6.88	8.81	8.19	7.12	9.94

[a]Means and standard deviations are expressed in degrees. CE is constant error. AE is absolute error. VE is variable error.

The durations x retention intervals x distances interaction was significant for CE only $F(16, 264) = 1.72, p < .05$. Again no simple combination of differences could account for the interaction (Levin & Marascuilo, 1970). There was, however, a tendency for the extreme distance errors to shrink towards zero under interpolated processing conditions as location duration increased, with the two longest distances being most affected at the 5 sec location duration.

The greater absolute errors of the immediate duration condition (see Fig. 1) in the filled retention interval suggest that reducing location information hinders distance reproduction. Caution needs to be taken in interpreting any effect of forcing the subject to release the lever quickly, as in the immediate durations condition; this action may cause interference rather than manipulate encoding. However, since there was no increased error at the immediate and 15 sec retention interval conditions, this possibility seems remote and focuses attention on the increases in error with information processing activity. Further, the fact that the range effect in the filled retention interval was less pronounced in the 2 and 5 sec duration conditions suggests the importance of location information.

Since the previous experiment only gave marginal support for the extrapolation hypothesis through manipulating the endpoints of the movement, a different experimental approach was taken in Experiment 2. This experiment differed from the previous one in that it removed the dynamic movement phase between the endpoints. Thus, distance reproduction was examined when only endpoint information was provided, the rationale being that if distance information was derived primarily from the endpoints, it should make little difference whether the subject actively traverses the isomorphic distance.

III. EXPERIMENT 2

A. Method

1. *Subjects.* Eight right-handed female subjects were recruited from the University of Wisconsin. Each subject was paid for her service.

2. *Apparatus.* The apparatus was the same as in the previous experiment. In addition, to aid the subject in finding the lever's handle, an elastic lead line was attached from the lever handle to the table top. To aid in controlling time intervals, a switch was built into the lever handle, and connections were made to the apparatus stops. By wiring through a relay and an eight-bank timer, a tone command could be sounded at various times after the subjects grasped the handle.

3. *Procedures and Design.* There were two conditions in the experiment, a distance plus location and a location only condition. In the distance plus location condition, a 250 msec tone signaled the subject to quickly find the handle using the lead line and grasp it. After 3 sec at the starting location, a second tone

signaled the subject to move from the start to the end-location where she maintained her grasp for 3 sec until the release tone sounded. The presentation of the
criterion movement took approximately 9 sec. The experimenter then altered
the starting position of the lever and sounded another tone for reproduction.
Within approximately 2 sec, the subject again grasped the handle, and at the
tone reproduced her estimate of the criterion distance.

In the location only condition the subject grasped the handle for 3 sec, as in
the other condition; however, instead of moving directly to the endpoint of the
criterion movement, the subject released the handle and placed her hand to the
right of the lead line. The experimenter then moved the lever to the end-location
and signaled the subject to grasp the handle at this position using the lead line.
After 3 sec on the end location, the tone was again sounded requiring the subject
to release the handle. As in the other condition, the presentation time of the
criterion movement was 9 sec. Any response taking longer than 9 sec in either
condition was omitted and repeated later. The reproduction movement was performed in the same manner as the distance plus location condition.

Four subjects performed the distance plus location condition first, while the
second four subjects performed the location only condition first. The criterion
target distances were 26°, 78°, and 104°, each of which was presented from 15°,
25°, or 35°, and reproduced 15° forward or backward from these starting locations. These procedures ensured that the location cues were unreliable. Each
subject twice performed a random order of the eighteen possible combinations
creating a total of 36 trials for each condition. The design was a 2 x 2 x 3 x 2
(order x conditions x distances x direction of reproduction starting position)
arrangement, with order as the only between subject variable. The six raw scores
from each starting position were averaged to determine CE, AE, and VE.

B. Results and Discussion

The means and standard deviations of reproduction errors for conditions are presented in Table 2.

The clear superiority of the location plus distance condition over the location
only condition was revealed in the significant main effect for AE, $F(1, 6) = 7.98$,
$p. < .05$, and marginally so for VE, $F(1,6) = 4.5$, $p < .10$. No CE main effect
was found. The distance main effects were significant for CE and VE, F's$(2, 12) =$
7.32, and 9.44, p's $< .05$, respectively, but not for AE. Error increased significantly as distance increased. Direction of reproduction starting position (forwards
or backwards from the original criterion starting position) was significant for CE,
$F(1,6) = 6.34$, $p < .05$ but not for AE or VE. Backward shifts produced undershooting while forward shifts produced overshooting.

Of the two-way interactions distance interacted with reproduction direction
in both VE and AE, F's $(2,12) = 6.58$ and 3.91, p's $< .05$, respectively. Forward

TABLE 2
Means and Standard Deviations
of Groups, Distances and Mode of Reproduction[a]

		Locations only			Location plus distance		
		CE	AE	VE	CE	AE	VE
Movement							
Conditions	M	−.24	10.84	8.58	1.53	7.84	7.25
	SD	8.96	2.95	1.06	4.52	1.49	1.41
Distance x Modes							
52° Back	M	.95	8.16	5.55	−1.14	6.14	6.10
	SD	9.02	3.62	1.11	4.98	1.68	2.02
52° Forward	M	8.37	12.16	8.60	4.50	8.33	6.43
	SD	9.92	6.56	2.72	7.07	4.77	2.13
78° Back	M	−3.68	12.64	9.42	−.81	7.77	8.06
	SD	12.72	6.40	2.91	4.95	2.39	3.07
78° Forward	M	1.83	7.95	6.59	2.89	8.39	6.39
	SD	8.58	4.96	2.63	7.28	3.16	1.72
104° Back	M	−5.02	11.52	10.47	1.93	7.52	6.99
	SD	10.87	6.26	4.71	6.70	2.70	1.83
104° Forward	M	−3.93	12.60	10.87	1.83	8.91	9.50
	SD	9.65	5.43	4.28	4.45	2.67	3.65

[a]Means and standard deviations are expressed in degrees. CE is constant error, AE is absolute error and VE is variable error.

error exceeded backward error at 52° and 104°, while backward error exceeded forward error at 78°. A significant condition by distance interaction was found in CE, $F(2, 12) = 11.66, p < .05$, which revealed the effect of removing distance information. The effect dramatically increased the range effect for the location condition, whereas error for the distance plus location condition remained constant across distance (see Fig. 2).

The conditions x distance x direction of reproduction interaction was the only other significant interaction effect $F(2,12) = 8.27, p < .05$ for AE. This interaction superceded the distance x direction of reproduction interaction previously mentioned for absolute error and showed it to be caused by the locations only condition. The location plus distance means showed equal increments in error across distance for each direction of reproduction starting position, whereas the location only group interacted with direction of reproduction across distances.

The implication of the superiority of the distance plus location condition is that useful information is derived from the dynamics of the movement. Distance information thus appears to be codeable and is maintained in memory. To

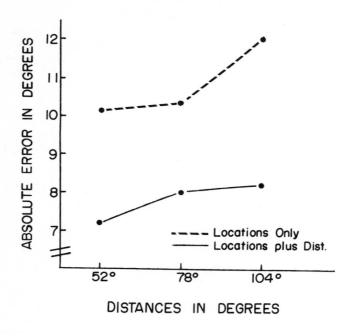

DISTANCES IN DEGREES

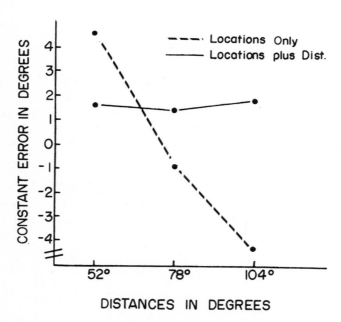

DISTANCES IN DEGREES

FIG. 2 The Locations Only and the Locations plus Distance conditions as a function of movement distance for both absolute and constant errors.

expand on the problem by using a converging operations approach (Garner, Hake, & Erikson, 1956), the next experiment attempted to augment distance information by using a repetition technique. Thus, experiment 3 strengthened the distance information by having the subject repeat the distance moved between endpoints (Adams & Dijkstra, 1966). A repetition effect would extend to the previous findings and indicate that distance information is a relevant movement cue that is processed and stored.

IV. EXPERIMENT 3

A. Method

1. *Subjects.* Twenty-four subjects, both male and female, were paid to take part in the experiment. All subjects were right-handed and ranged in age from 17 to 32 years. Five female and three male subjects were tested in each of the three between subject groups in the design.

2. *Procedure and Design.* The experiment began once the subject's body position was standardized and the procedures explained and practiced. Procedures differed with respect to the presentation of the movement to be reproduced. In the 6 repetions group, subjects were verbally cued to grasp the handle by the command "Grasp." One second after the handle was grasped a tone sounded, indicating that the subject should move to a stop; one second later the tone sounded again, cueing release of the handle. This procedure was repeated 6 times from random starting positions of 0°, 10°, 20°, 30°, 40°, and 50°. The stops were altered on each repetition, so that the length moved remained constant with only starting positions varying. After the 6 repetitions were completed, reproduction was initiated from 15°, 25°, or 35° selected at random. Again the subject was given the "Grasp" command, and 1 sec later the tone sounded cueing reproduction. The subject moved to what he thought was the criterion length, held that position for approximately 1 sec, and then released the handle. In the 6 sec endpoint group there was only 1 movement of the criterion length. The procedure was identical to one of the 6 repetitions, except that the subject held the handle for 6 sec at both the start and end of the single criterion movement. The 1 sec endpoint group was identical to the 6 sec endpoint group, except that the subject only held the handle for 1 sec at the start and end of the standard movement. For both endpoint groups, cirterion movement starting positions were identical to the repetitions group.

The design was a 3 x 8 x 4 x 3 (groups x subjects x distances x reproduction starting position) factorial with repeated measures on the last two factors. The groups factor consisted of 6 repetitions, 6 sec endpoint duration, and a 1 sec endpoint group. Movement distances tested were 30°, 54°, 78°, and 102°, and reproduction always began at 15°, 25°, or 35°.

TABLE 3

Means and Standard Deviations
of Groups, Distances and Starting Positions[a]

		6 Repetitions			6 Sec End Points			1 Sec End Points		
		CE	AE	VE	CE	AE	VE	CE	AE	VE
GROUPS	M	1.37	5.00	4.41	3.32	11.80	9.94	2.61	11.09	8.82
	SD	4.02	2.14	2.85	10.33	5.36	5.60	9.49	5.31	5.45
DISTANCES										
30°	M	1.54	4.09	2.87	2.01	8.65	7.40	9.29	12.9	8.24
	SD	3.70	1.78	2.32	7.38	4.46	4.86	11.21	7.21	4.29
54°	M	1.90	4.73	3.76	3.43	12.20	10.94	3.72	9.19	7.61
	SD	3.90	1.94	2.46	9.24	4.35	5.84	7.67	4.12	4.72
78°	M	1.31	5.18	5.50	5.80	12.36	12.34	.45	11.34	9.12
	SD	3.49	2.06	3.09	9.18	5.73	5.84	9.87	4.75	7.09
104°	M	.73	6.01	5.49	2.06	13.98	9.09	-3.02	10.86	10.31
	SD	4.85	2.49	3.40	14.24	6.53	5.83	8.87	4.62	5.31
STARTING POSITIONS										
15°	M	.63	4.57	4.04	4.91	11.87	10.49	5.19	10.90	9.43
	SD	3.86	2.16	2.93	9.81	6.53	7.38	8.64	5.68	5.92
25°	M	2.34	5.63	4.62	4.81	12.29	10.35	1.29	11.93	9.73
	SD	4.06	2.13	3.43	9.94	5.19	4.96	11.62	5.97	5.68
35°	M	1.14	4.81	4.56	.26	11.23	8.99	1.34	10.42	7.30
	SD	3.86	2.13	2.71	10.19	5.13	4.83	10.55	4.49	4.54

[a]Means and standard deviations are expressed in degrees. CE is constant error, AE is absolute error, VE is variable error.

B. Results and Discussion

The means and standard deviations of groups distances and starting positions are presented in Table 3. The main effect for groups was significant in AE and VE, F's $(2, 21) = 24.85$ and 28.3, p's $< .001$, respectively, and clearly showed the superiority of the 6 repetition group over the other two groups. The only other main effect was for distances in VE, $F(3, 63) = 4.77$, $p < .05$. Simple effects revealed the two longer distances were significantly different from the shortest. No other differences were significant.

Of the two way interactions in Fig. 3, the groups by distance interaction was significant for CE and AE, F's $(6, 63) = 3.27$ and 2.48, p's $< .05$, respectively. In addition, the distances interacted with starting positions in CE, $F(4, 126) = 4.21$, $p < .05$. The only significant three-way interaction occurred in AE and involved groups, distances and starting positions producing an $F(12, 126) = 2.38$, $p < .05$. With the marked effects of eliminating and augmenting distance information in the previous experiments (see Fig. 2 and 3), the real possibility of a separate distance code appeared viable. Experiment 4 therefore sought to interfere with this distance code information by having subjects perform four reversals while traversing the distance between endpoints, and varying the location durations.

V. EXPERIMENT 4

A. Method

1. *Subjects.* Sixteen female subjects were randomly assigned to either a distance control or a reversals group. Each was paid for her service.

2. *Apparatus.* The apparatus was the same as was used in the three previous experiments.

3. *Procedure and Design.* Standardized instructions were read to each subject to ensure that they understood what the experiment entailed. The distance control group performed straightforward distance reproduction, as in all the previous experiments. The four reversals group grasped the handle at a tone command. Grasping the handle activated a relay connected to the Hunter eight-bank programmer, which generated a 100 msec tone after an appropriate location duration delay (100 msec or 3 sec). Following the start of the movement, four 250 msec tones signaled reversals in direction. During the second reversal period, subjects always went past the final location of the criterion movement. To equate total time of 11 sec for each group, the distance groups moved slowly and smoothly during criterion presentation. The distance group procedures were identical to the reversals groups, except for the movement reversals. Reproduction starting position duration was held constant at 100 msec for both groups.

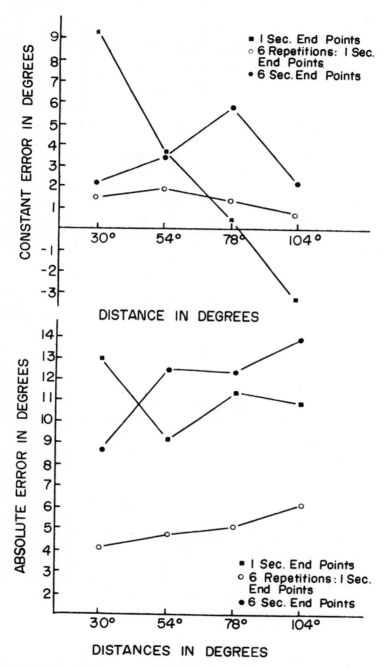

FIG. 3 The 1 Sec. Endpoint, 6 Sec. Endpoint, and the 6 repetitions conditon as a function of movement distance for both absolute and constant errors.

4. *Design and Conditions.* There were 3 criterion distances, 52°, 78°, and 104°. In addition each distance was initiated ±15° from 3 starting positions as in Experiment 2. Location duration, distances, and reproduction starting positions were all within subject factors, whereas distance versus reversals was the between group factor. The design was thus a 2 x 8 x 2 x 3 x 2 (groups x subjects x location duration x distances x starting position direction) factorial with 3 dependent variables AE, VE, and CE. Raw scores for analysis were produced by averaging the three forward and three backward starting position reproduction scores at each distance.

B. Results and Discussion

The means and standard deviations for groups, location durations, distances and starting positions are shown in Table 4.

The clear superiority of distance over reversals occurred in a group main effect for AE and VE, F's $(1, 14)$ = 5.69 and 17.18, p's $< .05$, respectively. In addition, the location duration main effect showed less error and decreased variability as location duration increased, F's $(1, 14)$ = 4.66 and 5.01, p's $< .05$ for AE and VE, respectively. The only other main effect was a direction effect for CE, $F(1, 14)$ = 35.8, $p < .05$.

Of the two-way interactions, location durations interacted significantly with backward and forward starting positions for AE, $F(1, 14)$ = 7.26 and VE, F

TABLE 4
Means and Standard Deviations
of Groups, Location Durations, Distances and Starting Positions[a]

		Distance Only			4 Reversals		
		CE	AE	VE	CE	AE	VE
GROUPS	*M*	.42	8.05	5.91	−.01	10.32	8.04
	SD	4.87	1.71	1.08	3.62	2.57	.96
LOCATION DURATIONS							
0 sec	M	−.43	8.18	6.05	−.43	11.25	8.95
	SD	5.47	1.59	1.07	4.14	2.51	0.75
3 sec	M	1.28	7.92	5.78	.40	9.40	7.13
	SD	4.85	1.92	1.69	4.10	2.43	1.74
DISTANCES							
52°	M	1.76	7.48	5.83	1.68	11.45	9.22
	SD	5.57	3.07	2.09	6.58	3.00	2.65
78°	M	−1.05	7.67	6.04	.72	10.02	7.50
	SD	5.13	1.63	2.05	2.53	2.40	1.94
104°	M	.57	8.98	5.87	−2.45	9.49	7.40
	SD	6.27	1.50	1.29	4.77	2.90	2.69

(continued)

TABLE 4 *(continued)*

		Distance Only			4 Reversals		
		CE	AE	VE	CE	AE	VE
STARTING POSITIONS							
Backwards	*M*	−2.49	7.77	6.07	−5.24	9.92	8.49
	SD	4.61	2.45	1.66	3.93	1.99	1.75
Forwards	*M*	3.34	8.33	5.76	5.21	10.72	7.59
	SD	6.10	2.47	1.27	5.41	3.70	1.56
LOCATION DURATION x							
STARTING POSITIONS							
0 sec.	*M*	−2.69	8.41	6.58	−7.40	12.26	10.81
Backward	*SD*	6.14	3.38	2.49	5.33	3.25	2.19
0 secs.	*M*	1.83	7.94	5.52	6.54	10.23	7.08
Forward	*SD*	6.97	2.38	.75	6.88	3.83	.95
3 sec.	*M*	−2.29	7.12	5.56	−3.08	7.58	6.16
Backward	*SD*	4.80	3.07	1.93	2.74	1.57	2.31
3 sec.	*M*	4.86	8.72	6.00	3.88	11.22	8.11
Forward	*SD*	5.77	2.71	1.80	6.75	4.69	2.94

[a]Means and standard deviations are expressed in degrees. CE is constant error, VE is variable error, AE is absolute error.

$(1, 14) = 12.26$, p's $< .05$. The differences between backwards and forwards reproduction starting positions reduced (as time increased) and no difference was present at 3 sec. Groups, location durations, and reproduction starting positions also interacted significantly for CE, $F(1, 14) = 4.8$; and location duration, distance and reproduction starting position interacted significantly for AE, $F(2, 28) = 9.95$ and for VE, $F(2, 28) = 8.5$, both p's $< .05$. No other result was significant.

VI. GENERAL DISCUSSION

How distance information is derived from a movement has puzzled investigators for many years. There are no known distance receptors in the joint capsule, though the pacinian corpuscles are known movement transducers that provide information about acceleration, direction, and velocity (Skoglund, 1973). Thus, some have thought that distance information may be obtained from joint receptors (Keele & Ells, 1972; Skoglund, 1973). In this regard, these experiments sought to examine the importance of location information in distance reproduction by increasing the time spent at the beginning and endpoints of the criterion movement, and by manipulating the availability of distance information. The logic was that if location information from the movement endpoints was used to derive distance, reproduction should be enhanced with increased endpoint exposure, and remain unaffected by the availability of distance information.

Support for the extrapolation hypothesis was found in Experiments 1, 3, and 4. In Experiment 1, reproduction of the 2 and 5 sec duration conditions suffered the least after interpolated processing activity. Smaller absolute errors and reduced range effects were evident in both of these duration conditions. These findings suggested that less central capacity was required to maintain distance representation when location information was augmented. Further evidence came from the retention intervals by distance interaction in CE, where the range effect was reduced under information processing conditions as a function of location duration. The two other experiments in which location duration was varied (Experiments 3 and 4) provided some support to the extrapolation hypothesis in each of the dependent error measures. The strongest duration effects were observed in Experiments 3 and 4. In Experiment 3, there was a pronounced group by distance interaction, indicating that location duration reduced the range effect across the movement amplitude. In addition, in Experiment 4, strong location duration effects were observed in AE and VE, and a strong location duration groups x direction interaction again supported the idea of information increasing as time increased. These findings support the proposition that location information can be utilized in distance representation, and extend the notion first advanced by Wallace and Stelmach (1975), that increasing time spent at a location increases reproduction accuracy.

Experiments 2, 3, and 4 found that when distance information was altered, it produced marked effects on reproduction accuracy. The omission of the movement phase between endpoints in Experiment 2 disrupted performance, as reflected by AE and CE. The dynamic phase of the movement provided codeable information which was used to improve distance accuracy (see Fig. 2). Conversely, Experiment 3 showed that augmenting distance representation by repetitions reduced AE and CE compared to the duration conditions. It is interesting to note that when movement information is kept to a minimum, either by minimizing location of excluding distance cues, pronounced range effects are observed in both experiments. In Experiment 4, in which reversals were assumed to disrupt distance information but not location information, reversals increased error to the same level as when the distance travelled was absent in Experiment 2. These facts argue against the extrapolation hypothesis and suggest that distance information is a separate movement code; however, close scrutiny of the data, particularly the interactions in Experiments 2, 3, and 4, suggests an interdependence between the two movement cues. Although there are differences in distances, these experiments show that increased exposure to location information increases the stability of distance representation. On the other hand, these same experiments show that providing or augmenting distance produces the same stabilizing effect on constant error via a different information source. It appears that distance representation can be improved from either location or distance information.

It seems intuitive that if distance representation can be obtained from two sources (distance and/or location), and if the code is derived from location, distance cues will likely interact with movement information coded similarly. Reproduction starting position information is probably in such a location code. Under this assumption, starting position information should interact with the representation of distance derived from location information. Such an interaction is observed for CE in Experiments 2, 3, and 4, and for VE in Experiment 4. In Experiments 2 and 4, CE shows a clear interaction of the "location only" code with starting positions and distance moved, whereas the "location plus distance" code does not interact. For example, as location information increased in a situation where distance information was weak, starting position effects disappeared. Overall, these findings suggest an interdependence of distance and location codes and indicates they can be differentiated by the relative amounts of distance versus location information present. If the former is enhanced, it is resistant to starting position effects, whereas if the latter is primary, it is more susceptible to starting position interactions. Thus, the movement phase between endpoints provides information that reduces distance reproduction dependence on anchor points.

Interdependence is also supported across experiments by using AE as the dependent measure. When location information is kept to a minimum, distance information is not accurately reproduced (Experiments 1, 2, 3). Further, if location information can be used in conjunction with distance information, as in the locations with distance group (Experiment 2) and the repetitions group (Experiment 3), reproduction accuracy is improved. Thus, using a variety of dependent error measures, it is possible to explicate a role for location in distance reproduction; however, the data are far from solely supporting location-extrapolation as the only source of distance reproduction information.

The interdependence of distance and location cues observed in the present experiments cast doubt on the theoretical utility of thinking of the two cues as separate storage cues. Such an idea seems rather intuitive, since the cue-separation technique itself only forces reliance on different subsets of cues and can never completely isolate location from distance. Both cues can be utilized together, and their interaction seriously questions Laabs (1973) dual storage concept as originally conceived, in which distance information has no access to central processing. Experiments 1, 2, and 3 clearly show that distance information is enhanced, stored and maintained in memory. Therefore, some modifications in Laabs' model seem warranted. Although the cue-separation technique may yield different accuracy and decay characteristics (for movement cues), this may be nothing more than a reflection of different levels of the same code. Nevertheless, there appears to be little gained by retaining the concept of dual storage of distance and location information in its postulated form. The resting assumptions of storage independence, rapid distance decay, and distance information's presumed imperviousness to information processing activity have all been assaulted. A more useful approach appears to lie presently in the empirical quantification of location and distance information contributions to movement representation.

ACKNOWLEDGMENTS

This research was supported by Grant MH22081-01 from the National Institute of Mental Health, and by Grant NE-G-3-0009 from the National Institute of Education, awarded to the first author. The opinions expressed herein do not necessarily reflect the position or policy of either agency, and no official endorsement should be inferred.

REFERENCES

Adams, J. A. & Dijkstra, S. Short-term memory for motor responses. *Journal of Experimental Psychology,* 1966, *71,* 314–318.

Ellson, D. G., & Wheeler, L. *The range effect.* (Tech. Rep. 4) Dayton, Ohio: Wright Patterson Air Force Base, U.S. Air Force Material Command, 1947.

Garner, W. R., Hake, H. W., & Eriksen, C. W. Operationism and the concept of perception. *Psychological Review,* 1956, *63,* 149–161.

Hollingsworth, H. L. The inaccuracy of movement. *Archives of Psychology,* 1909, *2,* 1–87.

Jones, B. Role of central monitoring of efference in short-term memory for movements. *Journal of Experimental Psychology,* 1974, *102,* 37–43.

Keele, S. W. & Ells, J. C. Memory characteristics of kinesthetic information. *Journal of Motor Behavior,* 1972, *4,* 127–134.

Kirk, R. E. *Experimental design: Procedures for the behavioral sciences.* Wadsworth Publishing Co., 1968.

Laabs, G. E. Retention characteristics of different reproduction cues in motor short-terms memory. *Journal of Experimental Psychology,* 1973, *100,* 168–177.

Laabs, G. T. The effect of interpolated motor activity on the short-term retention of movement distance and end-location. *Journal of Motor Behavior,* 1974, *6,* 279–288.

Leuba, J. H. Influence of the duration and rate of arm movements upon judgment of their length. *American Journal of Psychology,* 1909, *20,* 374–385.

Levin, J. R. & Marascuilo, L. A. Where the interaction is: An Introduction to Type IV Errors. *American Educational Research Journal,* 1970, *7,* 397–421.

Marteniuk, R. G. Retention characteristics of short-term memory cues. *Journal of Motor Behavior,* 1973, *5,* 312–317.

Moxley, S. E. L. Attention demand in short-term kinesthetic memory (Doctoral dissertation, University of Michigan, 1974). *Dissertation Abstracts International,* 1974, 75–10240.

Posner, M. I. Characteristics of visual and kinesthetic memory codes. *Journal of Experimental Psychology,* 1967, *75,* 103–107.

Posner, M. I. & Keele, S. W. Attention demands of movements. Paper presented at the 16th Int. Congress of Applied Psychology Symposium on Work and Fatigue. Amsterdam: Swetts & Zeitlinger, 1969.

Skoglund, S. Joint receptors and kinesthesis. In: Iggo, (Ed.), *Handbook of sensory physiology: Somatosensory system* (Vol. 2). Berlin, Heidelberg, New York: Springer-Verlag, 1973.

Stelmach, G. E. (Ed.) *Motor control: Issues and trends.* New York: Academic Press, 1976.

Stelmach, G. E. & Kelso, J. A. S. Distance and location cues in short-term motor memory. *Perceptual and Motor Skills,* 1973, *37,* 403–406.

Stelmach, G. E. & Kelso, J. A. S. Memory processes in motor control. A paper presented at Attention and Performance VI Symposium, Stockholm, Sweden, July 28 – August 2, 1975.

Stelmach, G. E., Kelso, J. A. S., Wallace, S. W. Preselection in short-term motor memory. *Journal of Experimental Psychology, Human Learning and Memory,* 1975, *1,* 745–755.

Stelmach, G. E. & Walsh, M. F. The temporal placement of interpolated movements in short-term motor memory. *Journal of Motor Behavior,* 1973, *5,* 165–173.

Wallace, S. A. & Stelmach, G. E. Proprioceptive encoding in preselected and constrained movement, *Movement,* 1975, *7,* 147–152.

Woodworth, R. S. Accuaracy of voluntary movement. *Psychological Review Monograph Supplement,* 3, *13,* 1899.

29

On the Temporal Control of Rhythmic Performance

Dirk Vorberg
Rolf Hambuch

Fachbereich Psychologie/Soziologie
Universität Konstanz
Konstanz, Germany

ABSTRACT

The model proposed by Wing (1973) for the timing of interresponse intervals is tested on data from a Morse key tapping task, which required subjects to group their responses by twos, threes, or fours. Under these conditions, the serial covariance function of the interresponse intervals is found to differ systematically from that predicted by the model, demonstrating the existence of higher-order rhythmic groups in the underlying timing structure. Alternative extensions of the basic Wing model are presented that differ in the assumptions concerning the organization of the postulated timekeepers. Several tests of these models support a model assuming sequentially organized timekeepers, and give no evidence for hierarchic assumptions. To reconcile these findings with current views about the organization of complex behavior, it is suggested that serial ordering and timing of behavior are performed by different mechanisms.

I. INTRODUCTION

Two problems are basic to an understanding of the control of complex, temporally structured behavior like speech or musical performance. One is the problem of serial order of behavior, outlined by Lashley in his famous 1951 paper; the other one is that of timing of segments in the behavior flow. For example, strong constraints on the order of words within phrases, and phonemes within words, have to be obeyed for speech to be acceptable. However, as the work of Noteboom (1974) and Huggins (this volume) demonstrates, utterances that are well formed with regard to serial order are not understandable unless additional constraints on the duration of the individual phonemes hold. Similarly, musical performance without accurate temporal control is deficient, even if perfect with respect to the intended serial order of pitch, loudness, phrasing and so on, since it lacks an essential element of music: rhythm.

Lashley's paper is still influential today, as witnessed by the recent theoretical papers on serial order by Estes (1972), Martin (1972), Jones (1974, 1976), and Shaffer (1976). There is now ample evidence showing that the assumption of sequential, chain-like organization of behavior is inadequate as an explanation of the phenomena of serial order in speech, memory, perception, and motor performance. All the authors cited above agree with Lashley in postulating hierarchic representations that control serially ordered behavior. Much less is known about the structure of the mechanisms responsible for the timing of behavior. In particular, it is not clear whether both serial order and timing are achieved by the same mechanisms. In this chapter, we shall focus on the timing of simple rhythmic behavior. Our main concern will be whether hierarchic structures that are ubiquitous in the serial order of music (e.g., Martin, 1972; Michon, 1974; Restle, 1970) are reflected by the temporal properties of rhythmic performance as well, or whether timing can be adequately accounted for by sequentially organized temporal mechanisms.

The growing interest in the temporal properties of performed music is documented by a number of recent empirical papers (Gabrielson, 1974; Michon, 1974; Povel, 1976; Wagner, 1968, 1971; Wagner, Piontek, & Teckhaus, 1973). However, with the exception of Michon's paper, this research has been largely descriptive and does not provide direct insight into the structure of the underlying timing mechanisms. What is missing is a unifying theoretical framework that directs the data analysis and helps to focus attention on the informative aspects of the data. To us, the work of Wing (Wing, 1973; Wing & Kristofferson, 1973a, 1973b) on the timing of interresponse intervals in periodic tapping seems to be a promising first step in this direction. Following a suggestion of Voillaume (Voillaume, 1971; Fraisse & Voillaume, 1971), Wing has developed a simple quantitative model which is based on the idea that the temporal inaccuracy in periodic tapping may be partitioned into parts which are due to the lack of precision of a hypothetical internal timekeeper, and to temporal "noise" in the executing motor system, respectively. Closely related models have been proposed by Kozhevnikov and Chistovich (1965) for speech timing, by McGill (1962) and Ten Hoopen and Reuver (1967) for the study of biological rhythms, and by Nelson and Williams (1970) for certain queuing problems.

Our purpose in this chapter is to test and extend Wing's model, so that it is applicable to rhythmic performance. In the following, we first sketch Wing's basic model. Then, an experiment investigating the temporal properties of rhythmic grouping is described and analyzed in terms of this model. To account for the observed discrepancies between model and data, several alternative extensions of the basic model are presented, which are then tested by more elaborated analyses of the data.

II. WING'S MODEL

The model proposed by Wing (1973) for self-paced periodic tapping is shown in Fig. 1. Two processes are assumed. At time intervals, A_i, a timekeeper generates trigger pulses each of which initiates a motor response. Upon execution of these commands, the motor system introduces variable delays, M_i, between the trigger pulses and the occurrence of the overt responses. If the ordering of the trigger pulses is maintained in the ordering of the overt responses, the ith interresponse interval, I_i, which is bounded by the ith and the $i + 1^{th}$ response, can be expressed in terms of the timekeeper and motor delay variables:

$$I_i = A_i + M_{i+1} - M_i, \qquad i = 1, 2, ... \qquad (1)$$

as can be verified from Fig. 1. Additional assumptions of the basic model, which will also be employed in all its extensions to be discussed later, are that the time-keeper intervals, A_i, and the motor delays, M_i, are sequences of independent random variables with respective variances var(A_i) = var(A) and var(M_i) = var(M), which are constant, and with cov(A_i, M_j) = 0 for all i and j.

These assumptions imply that the covariance between any two successive interresponse intervals (IRIs) is negative, whereas nonadjacent IRIs do not covary. This means that IRIs that happen to be smaller than average will tend to be followed by ones that are larger, and vice versa. Note, however, that this prediction is not due to any error-correcting mechanism built into the model, as all time-keeper and motor delay intervals are assumed to be mutually independent.

According to the assumptions, the IRI sequences must be samples from a stationary process. Therefore, the model can be tested by estimating the *serial* or *autocovariance* function, $\gamma(m) = $ cov(I_i, I_{i+m}), $m = 0, 1, 2, ..$ (Kendall & Stewart, 1968, p. 404) from the data and comparing it to the model's predic-

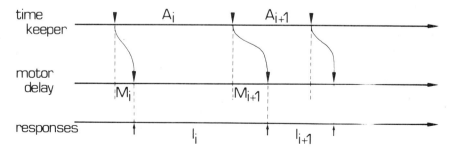

FIG. 1. The timing model proposed by Wing (1973).

tions. In the following, we use this model, which has been successfully tested by Wing and Kristofferson (1973a, 1973b) as a starting point for more complex models for rhythmic performance. Our strategy is to compare the model against data from an experiment investigating rhythmic tapping to see where it fails, and to replace or add assumptions when this turns out to be necessary. First, we describe the experiment and the results of a preliminary analysis in terms of the basic model. Then, we present alternative extensions of the model and test them against the data.

III. EXPERIMENT

A simple rhythmic task that offers some chance for the basic model to hold is rhythmic grouping. Much as in Wing's experiments, we had our subjects tap as evenly as possible at prescribed rates, but at the same time induced them to group their responses by twos, threes, or fours. This was achieved by presenting only every second, third, or fourth tone during the synchronisation phase of a trial. Although grouped tapping may seem a trivial rhythmic activity, we shall demonstrate empirically that it is hierarchically organized in the sense that low-level units, the responses within groups, combine to make up higher level units, the rhythmic groups. Hierarchical organization is often seen as the essential feature of rhythm (e.g., Martin, 1972). The main problem to be investigated with the aid of the extended models is whether hierarchical structures can also be found in the underlying timing mechanisms.

As controls, the experiment also contained ungrouped as well as synchronized tapping conditions. The number of responses per rhythmic group will be symbolized by r, $r = 1, 2, 3$ or 4.

A. Method

1. *Task.* The subject's task was to depress a morse key periodically at a given rate. Every trial began with a synchronization phase, during which a train of 40 ms duration tones (1000 Hz, ca. 70 db SPL, square wave) was presented over loudspeakers. The subject was to tap evenly in such a way that, depending on conditions, either every response, or every second, third, or fourth response coincided with a synchronization tone (see Fig. 2). One of four numbered lights indicated to the subject how many responses to produce per group. On synchronization trials, the synchronization phase lasted for $(20r + 1)$ responses; on continuation trials, the synchronization tones were withheld after four groups, and the subject was to continue at the established rate for another $(16r + 1)$ responses. Under either condition, a 1 sec tone following the last response indicated to the subject that he should stop.

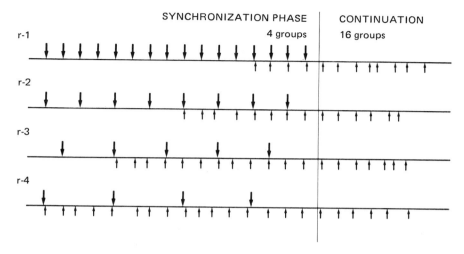

FIG. 2.   Illustration of experimental event sequences under continuation conditions. Arrows above a line represent experimenter-controlled synchronization tones, those below responses.

2. *Procedure.* The morse key was placed on a table in front of the subject. He was free to respond in a manner convenient to him, but was encouraged to adopt a habitual mode of responding. On every trial, he could listen as long as he wanted before starting to respond; a second, disconnected morse key was provided for trial responding. The subject was instructed to place his first response on a synchronization tone.

The experiments were run in a sound-attenuated room. From an adjacent room, an on-line computer (Dietz-Mincal 621) controlled the stimulus events and recorded the IRIs to the nearest 0.1 msec.

3. *Conditions.* Two rates (3.33 or 2 beats/sec, corresponding to IRIs of 300 or 500 ms, respectively), four values of r, (r = 1, 2, 3, 4), and two response modes (continuation or synchronization) were orthogonally combined to yield 16 different conditions. Within successive blocks of 16 trials, all conditions occurred once in random order. Whether continuation or synchronization responding would be required was not known to the subject until the end of the first four groups of the synchronization phase. A session consisted of four blocks of 16 trials, and lasted about 60 min. Between blocks of trials, there were 5 min rest, during which the subjects were informed about the means and variances of the IRIs.

4. *Subjects.* Three musically experienced subjects were run (Subject RH is the coauthor). Data from a fourth subject without musical experience were discarded, as he was unable to keep the prescribed tempos. After two or three practice sessions, eight experimental sessions were run per subject on successive days, giving 32 response sequences per subject per experimental condition.

IV. RESULTS

For each response sequence, the data from the initial synchronization phase were discarded, leaving $16r$ analyzable IRIs per sequence. Several checks for deviations from stationarity did not reveal any systematic changes in the means or the variances within sequences. However, subjects occasionally had difficulties in keeping the correct tempo. Therefore, all sequences were eliminated from the analysis in which the mean IRI differed by more than 10 msec from the prescribed value. This amounted to 9.4, 10.7, and 5.9% of the sequences for subjects HL, RH, and GS, respectively.

The serial covariance functions with lags from zero to four were computed separately for each sequence by

$$G(m) = \frac{1}{n-m-1}\left[\sum_{i=1}^{n-m} I_i I_{i+m} - \frac{\sum_{i=1}^{n-m} I_i \sum_{i=1}^{n-m} I_{i+m}}{n-m}\right] \tag{2}$$

where $G(m)$ is the estimator of the serial covariance with lag m, and n denotes the number of IRIs in the sequence.[1] These statistics were averaged over all replications under a given condition. For all statistics, standard errors were estimated from the corresponding standard deviations computed over replications.

With no grouping instructions ($r = 1$), the continuation data essentially support the Wing model. At the high tapping rate (300 ms), all lag one covariances were signficantly less than zero, whereas those at lags two, three, and four did not differ systematically from chance. Although not statistically significant, the pattern of results was the same at the rate of 500 for subjects HL and GS;

---

[1] The estimates are biased. The expectation of $G(m)$ computed from samples of size n is given by

$$E[G(m)] = \gamma(m) - \frac{1}{(n-m)(n-m-1)} \sum_{i=1}^{n-m-1} (n-m-i)[\gamma(m-i) + \gamma(m+i)]$$

where $\gamma(m)$ denotes the theoretical serial covariance with lag m of the underlying stationary process. Unless very long sequences are used, the bias in these estimates is quite large. A bias correction was employed for $G(0)$ and $G(1)$, assuming that $\gamma(m) = 0$ for $m > 1$. To test covariances with lags greater than one, the uncorrected estimates were compared against the respective biased expectation predicted from the equation above after insertion of the obtained estimates $\hat{\gamma}(0)$ and $\hat{\gamma}(1)$.

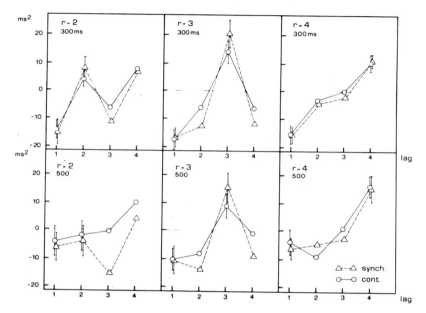

FIG. 3. Serial covariance functions obtained under grouping conditions. The vertical bars indicate the size of the standard error of the covariance estimates.

for RH, however, significant positive covariances were obtained at lag two. Since this subject had difficulties in keeping a constant tempo, these conflicting findings at the low rate might be due to undetected deviations from stationarity.[2] Similar results were obtained under the synchronization condition, except that some of the higher order covariances were significantly negative, probably indicating some feedback from previous responses.

When subjects are instructed to group their responses by twos, threes, or fours, serial covariance functions are obtained which differ strikingly from the pattern predicted by the Wing model (see Fig. 3). As expected, all serial covariances are negative at lag one. However, at lags greater than one, significant positive dependencies between IRIs are found. The important point to note is that the positive peaks in the serial covariance functions occur at lags that equal

[2]It is straightforward to derive the expectation of the lag m covariance estimator, $G(m)$, if the process is not stationary in the means. Assuming that $\text{cov}(I_i, I_{i+m})$ still depends on m only, $E[G(m)]$ can be shown to be inflated by the sample lag m covariance of the means,

$$\frac{1}{n-m-1}\left[\sum_{i=1}^{n-m}\mu_i\mu_{i+m} - \frac{\sum_{i=1}^{n-m}\mu_i\sum_{i=1}^{n-m}\mu_{i+m}}{n-m}\right]$$

where $\mu_i = E(I_i)$. This is positive for monotonic trends in the means.

the number of responses to be grouped under a given experimental condition. With the exception of grouping by twos at the low rate (500 ms), this holds under all conditions. The reliability of these findings can be seen from the vertical bars around the data points which indicate the size of the estimated standard errors. The same pattern of results was obtained for all individual subjects, and it holds for both the continuation and the synchronization conditions.

These results demonstrate the behavioral reality of higher-order units in grouped tapping. As the sequential dependencies in the IRIs reveal, low-level units, that is, the observable responses, are organized into higher-level units the size of which is expressed in the serial covariance functions. It is clear that the timing structure underlying grouped tapping is more complex than that postulated by the Wing model for ungrouped tapping. To account for these data, the basic model has to be modified in such a way that the higher-order rhythmic groups are represented in the postulated timing mechanism. In the following, we will assume that the IRIs that separate the r responses in a group are not generated by the same timekeeper, but a group of r timekeepers. Unless this collection of r timekeepers produces intervals which are all equal in mean, predicted lag r serial covariance can be shown to be positive even if the timekeepers are independent of each other; more precisely, it will equal the variance of the means of the IRIs within a group.

To check this explanation of our results, we examined the obtained means of the different IRIs within groups. For almost all conditions, slight but significant differences between the means were observed, thus supporting the notion of separate timekeepers that generate the time-intervals within groups. However, the patterns of the means were not consistent over conditions, but turned out to be highly idiosyncratic; therefore, we do not present the data in detail. Note that similar idiosyncratic patterns of mean IRIs were observed by Povel (1976), who analyzed the temporal structure of recorded music.

In the next section, we present alternative extensions of the Wing model which are all based on the assumption that timekeepers are organized into groups. The main interest will concern how the separate timekeepers are coordinated; in particular, we shall investigate whether a hierarchical organization of the timekeepers has to be assumed, or whether a simple chaining assumption can adequately account for the data. Note that the results to be reported in the following section cannot be due to differences in the means of the different IRIs within groups, since − contrary to the analysis described in this section − the IRIs within groups will always be treated separately.

V.   EXTENSIONS OF THE BASIC MODEL

Because of lack of space, models for the timing of rhythms with four responses per group only will be presented in detail. However, their extension to an arbitrary number of responses per group should be obvious. Although the models will be applied to rhythmic grouping only, it should be noted that they can be applied to the production of any rhythm containing unequal temporal intervals as well. Application of these models to the synchronization data will not be considered in this chapter.

Figure 4 presents three possible models for the timing of tapping responses grouped by fours. All the models agree in postulating that four timekeepers determine the timing of the overt responses up to additional delays introduced during the execution of the commands by the motor system. The models differ from each other with regard to assumptions concerning the interaction between the timekeepers.

Model I uses a simple sequential or chaining assumption where each timekeeper triggers the next one after a delay. The last timekeeper in the chain restarts the first one, and the cycle is repeated. In this model, higher-order units, i.e., the rhythmic groups, are formed by simply combining lower-order units. Therefore, the precision with which higher-order units can be timed depends on the timing precision of all the constituent lower-order units. Model I corresponds to the "comb" or "preplanning" model proposed for speech timing by Kozhevnikov and Chistovich (1965).[3]

Model II illustrates a simple hierarchical organization of the timekeepers. Here, timekeeper 1 controls the duration of the higher-order rhythmic group, whereas the remaining timekeepers control the timing of the responses within groups. Note that low-level timekeepers exert no influence on the high-level timekeeper, which implies that temporal irregularities within a rhythmic group do not affect the group's total duration.

Model III represents a fully hierarchical organization. Timekeeper 1 controls the onset of each rhythmic group, timekeeper 3 subdivides the group and determines the onset of the second half, and timekeepers 2 and 4 subdivide the halves still further. As before, lower-order timekeepers are triggered by higher-order ones, but not vice versa. In this model, the hierarchical structure which is usually found in the accent pattern of four beat bars, and which is incorporated in Martin's (1972) rhythmic stress rule for speech, is reflected in the structure of the timekeepers.

Which testable predictions can be derived to distinguish the models from each other? It turns out that the serial covariance function is not the most appropriate tool to analyze the statistical structure of sequences of IRIs that differ systemati-

---

[3]In the speech timing literature, this model is usually contrasted with a "chaining" model, in which the chaining of the timekeepers and the motor delay is assumed in the sense that the next timekeeper in the rpogram is started only after the occurrence of the previous overt response has been signaled (see Ohala, 1975, for a discussion). Except for measurement error in the determination of the overt responses, the model predicts independent IRIs (Ohala & Lyberg, 1976) and is therefore rejected for periodic tapping (Wing, 1973) as well as for rhythmic grouping. All the models discussed in this paper can be considered as "preplanning" models, which differ in their assumptions concerning the organization within the level of the timekeepers.

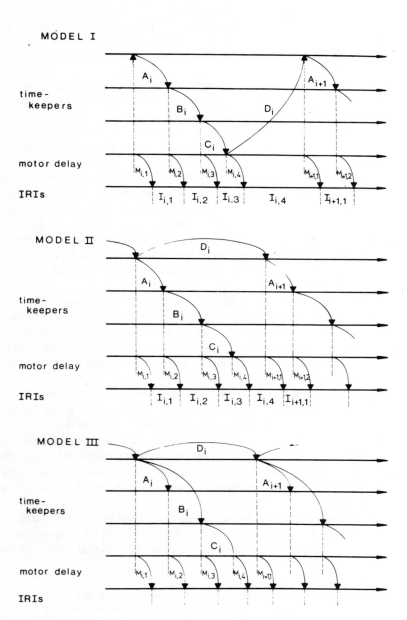

FIG. 4. Schematic of three alternative models for the timing of responses grouped by fours.

TABLE 1
IRIs Expressed in Terms of Time Keeper and Motor Delay Random Variables

	Model I	Model II	Model III
$I_{i,1}$	$A_i + M_{i,2} - M_{i,1}$	$A_i + M_{i,2} - M_{i,1}$	$A_i + M_{i,2} - M_{i,1}$
$I_{i,1}$	$B_i + M_{i,3} - M_{i,2}$	$B_i + M_{i,3} - M_{i,2}$	$B_i - A_i + M_{i,3} - M_{i,2}$
$I_{i,3}$	$C_i + M_{i,4} - M_{i,3}$	$C_i + M_{i,4} - M_{i,3}$	$C_i + M_{i,4} - M_{i,3}$
$I_{i,4}$	$D_i + M_{i+1,1} - M_{i,4}$	$D_i - A_i - B_i - C_i + M_{i+1,1} - M_{i,4}$	$D_i - B_i - C_i + M_{i+1,1} - M_{i,4}$

cally in means, as they eventually do in rhythmic grouping or in the production of more complex uneven rhythms. Rather, it is both mathematically more convenient and more informative to distinguish the different IRIs within rhythmic groups and to analyze their variance-covariance structure within as well as between groups. In this way, the underlying timekeeper organization can be revealed unambiguously.

As seen in Fig. 4, we label the successive IRIs within the ith group by $I_{i,1}$, $I_{i,2}$, $I_{i,3}$, and $I_{i,4}$. The timekeeper random variables that determine the end points of the first, second, third, and fourth IRI are denoted by A_i, B_i, C_i, and D_i, respectively. The motor delay preceding the jth response within the ith group is denoted by $M_{i,j}$. To derive the variances and covariances of the IRIs, we first express them in terms of the underlying timekeeper and motor delay random variables. This is done for Models I, II and III in Table 1.

As an example, consider the last interval, $I_{i,4}$, in group i. By inspection from Fig. 3, this is seen to equal $D_i + M_{i+1,1} - M_{i,4}$ given the chaining assumption of the timekeepers (Model I), whereas it equals $D_i - A_i - B_i - C_i + M_{i+1,1} - M_{i,4}$ and $D_i - B_i - C_i + M_{i+1,1} - M_{i,4}$ for the hierarchical Models II and III, respectively.

Once these defining equations of the IRIs are given for a model, their variances and covariances can be derived in a straightforward fashion by using the distributive property of covariances, and by noting that the covariance of a random variable with itself equals its variance, i.e., $\text{cov}(X, X) = \text{var}(X)$:

Let $X = sA + tB$, and $Y = vC + wD$, where A, B, C, and D are random variables and s, t, v, and w are arbitrary constants. Then

$$\text{cov}(X, Y) = \text{cov}(sA + tB, vC + wD) = sv \cdot \text{cov}(A, C) + sw \cdot \text{cov}(A, D) + tv \cdot \text{cov}(B, C) + tw \cdot \text{cov}(B, D). \quad (3)$$

Consider the derivation of the covariance between the second and the fourth interresponse interval within the ith group, $I_{i,2}$ and $I_{i,4}$, respectively, for Model III:

$$\text{cov}(I_{i,2}, I_{i,4}) = \text{cov}(B_i - A_i + M_{i,3} - M_{i,2}, D_i - B_i - C_i + M_{i+1,1} - M_{i,4})$$

$$= \text{cov}(B_i, D_i) - \text{cov}(B_i, B_i) - \text{cov}(B_i, C_i) + \dots$$

$$\dots + \text{cov}(M_{i,2}, M_{i,4})$$

By the independence assumption all these covariances equal zero except $\text{cov}(B_i, B_i)$. Therefore the result is

$$\text{cov}(I_{i,2}, I_{i,4}) = -\text{cov}(B_i, B_i)$$

$$= -\text{var}(B_i).$$

In the same way, the remaining variances and covariances for the interresponse intervals within a group can be derived. The results are given in Table 2. To simplify the notation, lower case letters are used to denote the variances of the corresponding upper-case random variables, e.g., $a = \text{var}(A) = \text{var}(A_i)$. Since the structures are symmetric, only the upper triangles of the matrices are given.

All the models predict zero covariances between IRIs from different groups except for the last and the first IRI in adjacent groups, $I_{i,4}$ and $I_{i+1,1}$, respectively, which is

$$\text{cov}(I_{i,4}, I_{i+1,1}) = -\text{var}(M) = -m. \tag{4}$$

Inspection of the variance-covariance structures within groups in Table 2 reveals predictions which are characteristic of the alternative models. All the models generate covariances between IRIs that are either zero or negative. The chaining assumption incorporated in Model I seems the natural generalization of the Wing model, as it predicts covariances between adjacent IRIs equaling the variance of the motor delays and zero covariances between all nonadjacent IRIs. In contrast, the hierarchical models predict some additional negative covariances within groups. Another prediction typical of the hierarchical models is the ordering of the variances of IRIs within groups. For Model II to hold, the last IRI in a group must have a variance which is not less than that of the others. Similarly, Model III predicts that the variance of the second and the fourth IRI cannot be less than that of the first and the third, respectively.

Clearly, the alternative models are distinguishable by the variance-covariance structures they predict, unless the timekeeper variances are zero. This identifiability result can be shown to hold in general, not just for the specific models considered here. In fact, for the timing of rhythmic groups with r responses, there are $r!$ different timekeeper structures, all of which are identifiable by the variance-covariance structures they generate. Thus, except for statistical problems, the organization of the postulated timekeepers can be inferred by an analysis of the variance-covariance structure of observed IRIs.

An important problem is to distinguish a sequential or chaining timekeeper organization from hierarchical organizations. Although this can be done by comparing the predicted variance-covariance structures against the data and deter-

TABLE 2
Variance-covariance Structures of IRIs Within Groups
Predicted by Alternative Models

Model I

	$I_{i,1}$	$I_{i,2}$	$I_{i,3}$	$I_{i,4}$
$I_{i,1}$	$a + 2m$	$-m$	0	0
$I_{i,2}$		$b + 2m$	$-m$	0
$I_{i,3}$			$c + 2m$	$-m$
$I_{i,4}$				$d + 2m$

Model II

	$I_{i,1}$	$I_{i,2}$	$I_{i,3}$	$I_{i,4}$
$I_{i,1}$	$a + 2m$	$-m$	0	$-a$
$I_{i,2}$		$b + 2m$	$-m$	$-b$
$I_{i,3}$			$c + 2m$	$-c-m$
$I_{i,4}$				$a + b + c + d + 2m$

Model III

	$I_{i,1}$	$I_{i,2}$	$I_{i,3}$	$I_{i,4}$
$I_{i,1}$	$a + 2m$	$-a-m$	0	0
$I_{i,2}$		$a + b + 2m$	$-m$	$-b$
$I_{i,3}$			$c + 2m$	$-c-m$
$I_{i,4}$				$b + c + d + 2m$

mining which model gives the closest fit, we derive an intuitively more appealing test. Instead of directly analyzing the variability of the IRIs, we look at the precision with which the higher-order units are timed.

For repeating rhythms consisting of r responses per rhythmic group, the sum of any r successive IRIs will be the same on the average, if the process is stationary. With regard to the variances, however, the situation is different, since the IRIs are not statistically independent. Given the hierarchical assumption, with a high-level timekeeper directly controlling the duration of the rhythmic groups, the variance of the sum of r successive IRIs will be smaller if they form a group than if j of them are taken from group i and the remaining $r-j$ from group $i + 1$, $1 \leqslant j < r$. In the latter case, the timing precisions of both groups contribute to the variance, whereas in the former case it is only that of a single group. In contrast, the sequential timekeeper assumption implies that the variance of the sum of r adjacent IRIs should not depend on how they are chosen, since the be-

TABLE 3
Variances of Group Durations Predicted by Alternative Models

	Model I	Model II	Model III
$\text{var}(T_{i,1})$	$a + b + c + d + 2m$	$d + 2m$	$d + 2m$
$\text{var}(T_{i,2})$	$a + b + c + d + 2m$	$d + 2a + 2m$	$d + 2a + 2m$
$\text{var}(T_{i,3})$	$a + b + c + d + 2m$	$d + 2a + 2b + 2m$	$d + 2b + 2m$
$\text{var}(T_{i,4})$	$a + b + c + d + 2m$	$d + 2a + 2b + 2c + 2m$	$d + 2b + 2c + 2m$

ginning of the rhythmic groups is not directly represented in the assumed time-keeper structure.

We formalize these ideas by defining variables $T_{i,j}, j = 1, r$, by

$$T_{i,j} = \sum_{k=j}^{r} I_{i,k} + \sum_{k=1}^{j-1} I_{i+1,k} \tag{5}$$

For example, with four responses per group, we have

$$T_{i,1} = I_{i,1} + I_{i,2} + I_{i,3} + I_{i,4}$$
$$T_{i,2} = I_{i,2} + I_{i,3} + I_{i,4} + I_{i+1,1}$$
$$T_{i,3} = I_{i,3} + I_{i,4} + I_{i+1,1} + I_{i+1,2}$$
$$T_{i,4} = I_{i,4} + I_{i+1,1} + I_{i+1,2} + I_{i+1,3}.$$

The variances of these variables as predicted by the alternative models are presented in Table 3. As stated above, under Model I, all the variances are equal, whereas both Model II and III predict the inequality $\text{var}(T_{i,1}) < \text{var}(T_{i,j}), j \neq 1$ unless all timkeeper variances except d equal zero.

If Model I holds, the variance of the motor delay, $m = \text{var}(M)$, can be estimated by comparing the sum of all the variances of the IRIs within a group to the variance of the group's total duration, $T_{i,1}$. By combining the equations in Tables 2 and 3, we find

$$\sum_{j=1}^{r} \text{var}(I_{i,j}) - \text{var}(T_{i,1}) = 6m.$$

Of course, analogous equations hold for r responses per group. Thus, a reasonable estimator of the motor delay variance is

$$m = \left[\sum_{j=1}^{r} \text{var}(I_{i,j}) - \text{var}(T_{i,1}) \right] / 2(r - 1). \tag{6}$$

Obtained estimates of m, $\hat{m}$, may be used to test the consistency of Model I. First, they must be positive except for sampling error; this is also true for Models II and III.[4] Provided Model I holds, an upper bound for $\hat{m}$ is given by

$$0 \leqslant 2\hat{m} \leqslant \min_{j} [\text{var}(I_{i,j})], \tag{7}$$

since the variance of any IRI equals the variance of the corresponding time-keeper plus twice the motor delay variance.

VI. TESTS OF THE MODELS

From each response sequence obtained under grouping instructions, all variances and covariances of the IRIs within and between successive rhythmic groups were estimated by the serial cross-covariances

$$G_{jk}(m) = \frac{\displaystyle\sum_{i=1}^{n-m} I_{i,j} I_{i+m,k} - \dfrac{\displaystyle\sum_{i=1}^{n-m} I_{i,j} \sum_{i=1}^{n-m} I_{i+m,k}}{n-m}}{n-m-1}, m = 0, 1, \tag{8}$$

where $G_{jk}(m)$ is the estimator of the covariance between the jth IRI in a group and the kth IRI in the mth group later.[5] As before, these statistics were averaged over all replications, and tested statistically by using the standard errors estimated from the observed standard deviations.

Figure 5 summarizes the obtained covariances. For each condition with r responses per group, a $r \times 2r$ rectangle is shown, the left half of which represents the covariances between the IRIs within groups, and the right half those from successive groups. An asterisk indicates that the corresponding estimate was significantly less than zero by a one-tailed t-test ($p = .05$). Covariances predicted

---

[4]This corresponds to the test for the "preplanning" model proposed by Kozhevnikov and Chistovich (1965).

[5]Under all three models, the resulting estimates of the variances and covariances within rhythmic groups, i.e., with $m = 0$, are unbiased, except $G_{1r}(0)$, where r is the number of responses in a group. Under any model, the bias in an estimate based on a sequence comprising n groups can be computed from

$$E[G_{jk}(m)] = \gamma_{jk}(m) - \frac{1}{(n-m)(n-m-1)} \sum_{i} [\gamma_{jk}(m-i) + \gamma_{jk}(m+i)] (n-m-i)$$

where $\gamma_{jk}(m)$ is the theoretical cross-covariance predicted by the model under consideration.

SUBJECTS

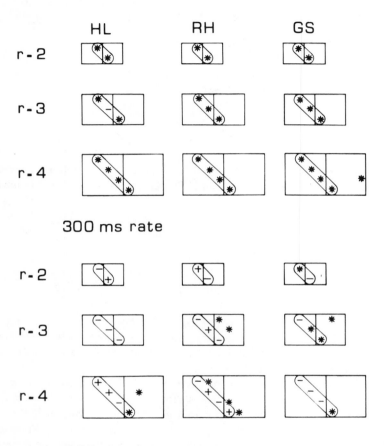

FIG. 5.   Variance-covariance structures within and between adjacent groups obtained under the different experimental conditions. (See text for explanation.)

to be negative by Model I are encircled. Within these are as, the sign of non-significant observed covariances is given by a + or a −.

At the 300 ms tapping rate, the results unequivocally support Model I. As the sequential timekeeper assumption implies, all adjacent IRIs are found to covary negatively with each other, both within and between groups, whereas covariances between nonadjacent IRIs are close to zero. Combining over subjects and conditions, 26 out of the 27 covariances predicted were significantly smaller than zero, whereas only one of the remaining 90 covariances differed significantly from chance. Thus, there is no evidence in favor of the hierarchical timekeeper assumption.

At the 500 msec rate, the data of subject GS are in moderate agreement with the predictions from Model I; those of the remaining subjects, however, are consistent with neither model. We tentatively attribute this to fluctuations of the timekeeper rates at the slow tempo, which are too slight to be detected by our rough checks for stationarity, but nevertheless tend to raise the serial covariances (cf. footnote 2). Evidence for this argument is found in the number of significant positive covariances between nonadjacent IRIs: 20 out of a total of 90 exceeded the critical value $t_{.95}$, without forming a consistent pattern. To check the ad hoc explanation further, we examined the sequential dependencies between the durations of successive rhythmic groups. As expected, at the 500 ms rate, large positive serial covariances were observed at most of the lags from one to four rhythmic groups, whereas for the 300 ms rate, most covariances at lag one were negative and those at greater lags close to zero. We therefore conclude that the discrepant results at the slow tempo are due to the subjects' inability to keep their timekeeper rates constant, rather than to a basic shortcoming of the model.

Inspection of the variances of the IRIs within rhythmic groups shows that they do not support the hierarchical models either. If any systematic ordering of the variances can be discerned at all, there is a slight tendency for the first IRI in a group to show the largest variability, whereas the existence of a timekeeper that directly controls the duration of the groups would imply the last one to be the most variable.

Analyses of the timing precision of different concatenations of r adjacent IRIs (cf. Equation 5 and Table 3) provided results by which the hierarchical timekeeper assumption has to be rejected. Table 4 shows the obtained variances, pooled over subjects. There is no tendency of the variance of "natural" groups, $\text{var}(T_{i,1})$, to be less than that of groups which are defined in a way that overlaps the natural group boundaries; if any, a slight tendency in the opposite direction is noted. None of the differences was significant by Wilcoxon matched-pairs tests ($r = 2$) or Friedman analyses of ranks ($r = 3, 4$) of the individual sub-

TABLE 4
Variance Estimates (in ms^2) of the Duration of Rhythmic Groups

Rate	r	$\text{var}(T_{i,1})$	$\text{var}(T_{i,2})$	$\text{var}(T_{i,3})$	$\text{var}(T_{i,4})$
300 msec	2	79.2	73.3		
	3	119.5	116.3	110.5	
	4	146.2	139.0	138.7	147.2
500 msec	2	213.7	218.0		
	3	284.3	284.2	281.3	
	4	459.9	443.3	417.5	445.9

TABLE 5
Estimates of Motor Delay Standard Deviation (in msec)
Obtained at the 300 msec Rate

	Responses per Group, r			
Subject	1	2	3	4
HL	2.3	2.1	1.5	1.8
RH	3.9	3.1	3.5	3.1
GL	3.9	3.6	3.9	4.4

jects' data. Thus, it must be concluded that the beginning of a group has no particular representation in the timing structure underlying rhythmic tapping, which eliminates all but the sequential Model I from consideration.

The standard deviation of the motor delays, m given Model I, was estimated by equation 6. At the 500 msec, where the model was already found to fail, several of the estimates turned out to be negative, and none was significantly greater than zero. Of course, the explanation offered above for the failure of Model I under these conditions accounts for these results as well. The estimates obtained at the 300 msec rate are given in Table 5. Ten of the 12 standard deviations were significantly greater than zero by one-tailed t-tests ($p = .05$). The inequality (Equation 7) that compares the motor delay variance to the minimum IRI variance in a group held in every instance, giving further support to Model I. The variability of the motor delays does not seem to be systematically related to the number of responses per group; no differences were found by a Friedman analysis of ranks. It should be noted that the order of magnitude of the motor delay standard deviation observed here agrees well with that reported by Wing (1973) for periodic tapping.

In summary, all the analyses of the 300 msec data give evidence for a simple sequential timekeeper structure controlling rhythmic grouping, and argue against hierarchical assumptions. At the slow tempo, the data agree with neither model. This seems to be due to imperfect stability of the timekeepers, which lies outside the present range of the models.

VII. DISCUSSION

Our results seem to leave us with a paradox. On one hand, the obtained serial co-variance functions clearly indicate the existence of higher-order rhythmic units in grouped tapping, which can be taken as evidence for hierarchical organization of behavior. On the other hand, however, all the data analyses support the assumption of sequentially organized timekeepers, and reject hierarchical time-keeper assumptions.

One way of solving the paradox is to distinguish between the control of serial order of behavior and that of timing of behavior, as was proposed in the introduction. If separate mechanisms are responsible for these different aspects of behavior control, evidence for hierarchical organization obtained from the serial order of behavior does not necessarily contradict evidence for sequential timing of behavior. To reconcile our findings with current views about the organization of complex behavior (Estes, 1972; Jones, 1974, 1976; Martin, 1972; Shaffer, 1976), we propose the following tentative theory.

Underlying rhythmic performance, there is a motor program by which appropriately ordered behavior is generated. The program contains both the information necessary to specify the identity of the individual movements and their succession, as well as the relevant timing information. To account for the complexities of serial order, e.g. in music, the program's structure is likely to be hierarchic. However, when the program is executed, it ultimately has to be translated into a sequence of individual steps, the duration of which is controlled by the hypothetical timekeeper mechanisms after being supplied with the appropriate timing information from the program. Thus, hierarchical organization inferred from observations about the ordering of behavior relates to the *structure* of the underlying motor program, whereas the sequential timing observed in our data relates to its *execution*.

In applying these ideas to the control of rhythmic performance, we have to be aware of the fact that temporal properties of behavior may reflect the working of both serial order and timing mechanisms. For example, in the production of rhythm, the regular succession of temporal intervals within rhythmic groups is achieved by the joint operation of the program generating the order and the timekeepers controlling the duration of the intervals. To a first approximation, we may assume that the means of the intervals are diagnostic of the serial order mechansims, whereas the statistical structure of behavior as reflected in the variances and covariances of the interresponse intervals is diagnostic of the timing controls. In this sense, we are justified in interpreting the obtained serial covariance functions as indicating hierarchic serial order mechanisms, since their shape was seen to be mainly due to systematic differences in the mean intervals within rhythmic groups. The observed variance-covariance structures, however, which are uneffected by differences in the means, may be taken as evidence for sequential timekeeper organization. Note that this interpretation is also consistent with the work of Martin (1972) and Michon (1974) who inferred hierarchical organization underlying serial order in speech and musical rhythm from the succession of mean intervals.

Although our theory is highly speculative, it should be noted that an analogous theory of the control of rapid movement sequences has been proposed by Kornhuber (1974) on the basis of physiological data. According to Kornhuber's theory, the cerebral cortex does not set up an exact temporal program of the whole movement sequence, but provides only a sequential program, which is then executed in a step-by-step fashion under timing control of the cerebellum. A possible reason why the hierarchical organization inherent in the motor program is not preserved during its execution may be economy: Hierarchical timekeeper organizations would require the simultaneous monitoring of several overlapping intervals, which are much longer than those to be generated by sequentially organized timekeepers. More importantly, sequential timekeeper structures have the property of leaving the serial order provided by the motor program unchanged, whereas elaborate feedback mechanisms are necessary for hierarchical timekeepers not to disturb the intended serial order (see Fig. 4).

As yet, our theory concerning the temporal control of rhythmic performance is based on highly limited data. It remains to be seen whether similar results obtain over a larger range of tempo with better control for deviations from stationarity, and in the production of more complex rhythms. Another problem is the obvious oversimplification of the basic model, which does not assume any interaction between the motor system and the postulated timekeepers, nor feedback of perceived temporal irregularities on later timekeeper intervals. Experimental work as well as extensions of the model to take care of these limitations are under way.

ACKNOWLEDGMENTS

This research was supported by Grant No. 17/76 provided by the University of Konstanz. We are grateful to Günter Schäfer for help in carrying out the experiment, and to Uwe Mortensen for a critical reading of a first draft of this paper.

REFERENCES

Estes, W. K. An associative basis for coding and organization in memory. In A. W. Melton & E. Martin (Eds.), *Coding processes in human memory*. New York: Halstead, 1972.

Fraisse, P., & Voillaume, C. Les repères du subject dans la synchronisation et dans la pseudo-synchronisation. *Année Psychologique*, 1971, *71*, 359–369.

Gabrielson, A. Performance of rhythm patterns. *Scandinavian Journal of Psychology*, 1974, *15*, 63–72.

Jones, M. R. Cognitive representations of serial patterns. In B. H. Kantowitz (Ed.), *Human information processing: Tutorials in performance and cognition*. Potomac, Md.: Lawrence Erlbaum Associates, 1974.

Jones, M. R. Time, our lost dimension: Toward a new theory of perception, attention, and memory. *Psychological Review*, 1976, *83*, 323–355.

Kendall, M. G., & Stewart, A. *The advanced theory of statistics* (Vol. *3*), (2nd ed.). London: Griffin, 1968.

Kornhuber, H. H. Cerebral cortex, cerebellum, and basal ganglia: An introduction to their motor functions. In F. O. Schmitt & F. G. Worden (Eds.), *The neurosciences. Third study program*. Cambridge: MIT Press, 1974.

Kozhevnikov, V. A., & Chistovich, L. A. *Speech: Articulation and perception*. (Joint Public Research Service No. 30543). Washington, D. C.: U.S. Department of Commerce, 1965.

Lashley, K. S. The problem of serial order in behavior. In L. A. Jeffress (Ed.), *Cerebral mechanisms in behavior.* New York: Wiley, 1951.

Martin, J. G. Rhythmic (hierarchical) versus serial structure in speech and other behavior. *Psychological Review,* 1972, *79,* 487–509.

McGill, W. J. Random fluctuations of response rate. *Psychometrika,* 1962, *27,* 3–17.

Michon, J. A. Programs and "programs" for sequential patterns in motor behavior. *Brain Research,* 1974, *71,* 413–424.

Nelson, R. B., & Williams, T. Random displacements of regularly spaced events. *Journal of Applied Probability,* 1970, *7,* 183–195.

Noteboom, S. G. Some effects on phonemic categorization of vowel duration. *I.P.O. Annual Progress Report,* 1974, *9,* 47–55.

Ohala, J. J. The temporal regulation of speech. In G. Gant & M. A. A. Tatham (Eds.), *Articulatory analysis and perception of speech.* London: Academic Press, 1975.

Ohala, J. J., & Lyberg, L. Comments on "Temporal interactions within a phrase and sentence context". *Journal of the Acoustical Society of America,* 1976, *59,* 990–992.

Povel, D. J. L. *Temporal structure of performed music. Some preliminary observations.* Report 75FU05, Department of Psychology University of Nijmegen, Nijmegen, 1976.

Restle, F. Theory of serial pattern learning: Structural trees. *Psychological Review,* 1970, *77,* 481–495.

Shaffer, L. H. Intention and performance. *Psychological Review,* 1976, *83,* 375–393.

Ten Hoopen, M., & Reuver, H. A. Analysis of sequences of events with random displacements applied to biological systems. *Mathematical Biosciences,* 1967, *1,* 599–617.

Voillaume, C. Modèles pour l'étude de la régulation des mouvements cadencés. *Année Psychologique,* 1971, *71,* 347–358.

Wagner, C. Untersuchungen zur Ergonomie des Klavierspiels. In *Biomechanics* I, Basel: Karger, 1968.

Wagner, C. The influence of the tempo of playing on the rhythmic structure studied at pianist's playing scales. In *Biomechanics* II, Basel: Karger, 1971.

Wagner, C. Experimentelle Untersuchungen über das Tempo. *Österreichische Musikzeitschrift,* 1974, *29,* 589–604.

Wagner, C., Piontek, E., & Teckhaus, L. Piano learning and programed instruction. *Journal of Research in Music Education,* 1973, *21,* 106–122.

Wing, A. M. *The timing of interresponse intervals.* Technical Report No. 56, Department of Psychology, McMaster University, Hamilton, 1973.

Wing, A. M., & Kristofferson, A. B. The timing of interresponse intervals. *Perception and Psychophysics,* 1973, *13,* 455–460. (a)

Wing, A. M., & Kristofferson, A. B. Response delays and the timing of discrete motor responses. *Perception and Psychophysics,* 1973, *14,* 5–12. (b)

30

Issues in the Theory of Action: Degrees of Freedom, Coordinative Structures and Coalitions

Michael T. Turvey
University of Connecticut
Storrs, Connecticut
    and
Haskins Laboratories
New Haven, Connecticut

Robert E. Shaw
University of Connecticut
Storrs, Connecticut

William Mace
Trinity College
Hartford, Connecticut
United States

ABSTRACT

Two major problems for a theory of coordinated movement are considered: The context-conditioned variability in the terminal variables of the motor apparatus, and the management of the large number of degrees of freedom that the motor apparatus attains. One approach to these problems argues that, in general, the free-variables of the motor apparatus are not controlled individually, but are partitioned into a smaller number of collectives, where each collective regulates internally and relatively autonomously a number of degrees of freedom. Another and closely related approach seeks to identify a system in which the responsibility for planning and executing an act is optimally distributed across the components of the system. This paper develops the concept of coordinative structure in concert with the first approach. Using the second approach, the paper lays the ground for showing that the perception and action systems participate in a style of organization in which the operational component and the context of constraint are wedded together into a single, relatively closed system. Such a system is referred to as a coalition, and it is claimed that a coalition is the minimum organization required to solve the problems of context-conditioned variability and degrees of freedom.

THE PROBLEMS OF CONTEXT-CONDITIONED
VARIABILITY AND DEGREES OF FREEDOM

A. Two Kinds of Machine

There are two quite dissimilar approaches that might be taken toward designing a machine that acts within and upon an environment (cf. Greene, in press, a). In one approach, the mechanical variables of the machine are programmed so that a desired action is achieved by virtue of a single computation, which in a single instance specifies all the necessary details, including those needed to immunize the machine against perturbing influences. In the other, one begins with the construction of autonomous systems designed, in part, to preserve the stability of the machine in its intended environment. Then, given these systems that perform as they wish, the problem is to organize them in such a fashion that the systems, and thus the machine, perform as we wish.

In the first kind of machine executive procedures are called upon to control individually each mechanical variable, whereas in the second they are called upon to control the autonomous systems, with each system regulating internally a subset of the mechanical variables. Let us elaborate: Where the total number of mechanical variables is quite small, the first design is obviously felicitous; but where that number is large, then it is roughly apparent that the first design will prove to be overly cumbersome and costly. By contrast, a machine of the second kind would be inelegant where few mechanical variables were concerned, since any arbitrary configuration of those variables could not be achieved directly, but only indirectly through the modulation and interaction of the autonomous subsystems. The advantage of the second kind of machine, however, is that, given the right organization, it may achieve an approximation to a desired configuration of a very large number of mechanical variables through the regulation of the relatively few variables of the autonomous subsystems.

B. The Keyboard Metaphor: Address-Specific
(Individualized) Control

One nineteenth century view of the coordination of voluntary movement (see Luria, 1966) was that it was exclusively a function of efference, specifically of the giant pyramidal cells of the cortical motor strip. The corticospinal projection was thought to contain all the details relating to the spatial and temporal patterning of commands to muscles. The motor area of the cortex was regarded as a kind of keyboard on which an executor's "hand" could play out the score for a movement. "Pressing" (exciting) one key brought about a determinate degree of extension at a given joint, pressing another brought about a determinate degree of flexion, and so on. This classical view promotes a machine of the first kind since it assumes that a coordination of movements can result from a single stage of exact computation. It allows that a motor program can be written as machine language instructions, that is, in terms of the innervational states of individual muscles. Insofar as this view assumes that control proceeds from the top down to a specific address — the individual muscle or the individual motoneuron — we will refer to the style of control as address-specific (individualized) control. Let us examine the keyboard metaphor and its associated style of control from the orientation of two major problems that any theory of coordinated movement — of action — must resolve.

The joints and the permissible motions of the complex biokinematic chains that compose the skeletomuscular hardware of animals, comprise a large number of degrees of freedom [Bernstein (1967) suggests that it may reach three figures.] For each coordinated act, therefore, the values for each individual degree of freedom would have to be prescribed. To be more precise, the executive at the keyboard would have to specify from the set of all possible combinations of muscle contractions the particular combination that would achieve the desired objective. The executive problem in this case is analogous to that of finding the optimum of a function of many variables. Algorithms that theoretically allow the solution to such problems prove to be infeasible in practice. Thus one could differentiate the function with respect to each of its variables and equate the derivatives thereby obtained. But the solution of the resultant system of equations is no simpler a problem than the direct search for an optimum. Gel'fand and Tsetlin (1962) remark that even where the number of variables (degrees of freedom) is relatively small, say, four or five, the computation of an extremum or optimum is exacting and often impossible for contemporary computational procedures (see also Sivazlian & Stanfel, 1975). An algorithm may exist, but only with respect to an abstract machine. A physically realizable machine brings with it extra-logical or extra-algorithmic principles (cf. Shaw & McIntyre, 1974) best understood as cost variables, such as how much heat the components of the machine can tolerate, and how much time the machine can spare for computation. An animal that must react adaptively to the contingencies of its environment does not have infinite time to select the right combination of biokinematic variables; its best policy, argue Gel'fand and Tsetlin (1962) and Greene (1972, in press, a), is to aim for a rough approximation through the use of "quick and dirty" procedures. At all events, we will refer to the problem described above as the problem of *degrees of freedom.*

The second major but related problem is posed by *context-conditioned variability.* The keyboard variables — the individual muscles and their innervational states — do not have fixed movement consequences. On the contrary, these variables relate to movement in a way that is dependent on contextual contingencies. If the nineteenth century executive were truly indifferent to context (as the notion of control solely through efference suggests) and wrote his movement score as a function, with the states of individual muscles (m) as its arguments, that is, as $f(m_1 m_2 \ldots m_n)$, then the function would be indeterminate in that for given ms and for given values of these ms the resultant act would not be fixed. In short, the specified function and the resultant behavior would relate equivocally. The reason, in part, is that other variables that affect the biokinematic chains are not specified, are not taken into account, in the function. To develop this point let us consider various forms of context-conditioned variability as delineated by Bernstein (1967).

C. Sources of Context-Condition Variability

In the first place, there is the anatomical source of context conditioned variability: The muscles can vary in their roles with regard to joint movement. Consider, by way of example, the upper pectoralis major, which inserts proximally in the clavicle and distally in the upper shaft of the humerus. With the arm in an approximately horizontal position, in which the axis of the humerus is just below the horizontal axis of the shoulder joint, contraction of the pectoralis will adduct the arm in the horizontal plane. But from an approximately horizontal position, in which the axis of the humerus is slightly *above* the horizontal axis of the shoulder joint, contraction will adduct the arm in the *vertical* plane (Wells, 1961). The moral (for a brain as well as for a student of kinesiology) is that a muscle's role cannot be taken for granted; at each phase of a movement, an individual muscle's action is contingent on (among other things) the muscle's line of pull to the joint's axis of motion.

Cognate with this class of equivocalities is the realization that the role a muscle plays depends not only on the disposition of limb segments but also on the external force contingencies. Lowering the arm from a horizontal side position against a resistance requires the use of the adductors of the arm, notably, the lattisimus dorsi; but in lowering slowly (that is, against gravity) the adductors are palpably soft, for the responsibility of the movement befalls the adductors, the deltoids, which perform their task by lengthening or, as Hubbard (1960) prefers to call it, pliometric contraction

Ideally, agonists and antagonists are paired in the keyboard arrangement so that an executive might simply excite alternatively one and then the other. If the machine being instructed was composed of hinge joints, each of one degree of freedom, then a fixed mechanical arrangement could be assumed between an agonist-antagonist pair, and the ideal keyboard arrangement would be realizable. But where ball joints are concerned, such as at a hip or a shoulder, the collection of muscles that is instrumental in moving the limb and the collection opposing the movement vary with each trajectory. Rather than there being a fixed anatomical relation between agonist and antagonist, there is, on the contrary, a problem of having to choose the muscles to be employed in a given movement (Weiss, 1941).

In the second place, there is the context-conditional variability resulting from mechanical sources. Most notable among these is the fact that, depending on the dynamic and static conditions of the limb segment, the same innervational state of a muscle may give rise to a variety of motions of the segment differing in displacement and velocity, and different innervational states may produce identical motions. The lesson here is a simple one: The innervational states of an individual muscle and the movements they entail relate equivocally.

A closely related source of variability is indigenous to multilink kinematic chains of which a whole arm, a whole leg, or the whole body are examples. Quite simply, the movement of any one link will result in a displacement of the links attached. The consequence of this is that the attached, or "light" links, passively carried by the agonist, or "heavy" link (in the terminology of Eshkol and Wachman, 1958), will induce forces and moments as reactions to the "heavy" links trajectory and thereby complicate its control. From the perspective of the keyboard metaphor and exclusively efferent control, multilink biokinematic chains look capricious. Closer examination, from a different perspective, reveals, however, that facility with a gross body skill is synonymous with exploiting these reactive consequences to the fullest (Bernstein, 1967). One characterization of the skilled performer is that, of the changes in forces at the joints necessary for a given movement, the performer provides (economically) only those changes in forces that are not provided reactively.

Most evidently, the two mechanical sources of context-conditioned variability go hand-in-hand. Thus, because the links have mass, once impelled, they gather momentum and develop kinetic energy. A given degree of muscle activity acting against a movement may stop it, simply retard it, or even reverse it; the same degree of activity, in concert with the movement, may induce marked acceleration. What follows from a given degree of muscle activity depends on the kinetic conditions of the links. While the significance and ubiquity of this principle was ignored by proponents of the keyboard metaphor (see Bernstein, 1967), it is also given short shrift in contemporary theories of coordinated movement (see Stelmach, 1976). In part, this negligence seems to be due to the assumption that the innervational states of muscles are in phase or concurrent with the movements of biokinematic links (Hubbard, 1960), an assumption that deserves our attention, if only briefly.

The "in-phase" assumption is a most convenient one because, as Hubbard (1960) elegantly points out, it permits the luxury of inferring muscle events from movement events. For example, as the elbow flexes, the biceps shortens and the triceps lengthens, from which we might infer that there was continuous graded stimulation contracting the one muscle and relaxing the other.

Fast movements, often referred to as ballistic, are anomalous from the perspective of the "in-phase" assumption. Their control is characteristically "bang-bang" (Arbib, 1972): an initial burst of acceleration as the agonist contracts, an intervening period of inactivity and then a burst of deceleration as the antagonist acts to degenerate the kinetic energy of the link. In fast movements muscle activity is simultaneous with only a small portion of the movement. But perhaps the "in-phase" assumption does hold for movements conducted at a more leisurely pace, movements that we might refer to as nonballistic. Hubbard has argued and demonstrated that even here, the "in-phase" assumption is found wanting (Hubbard, 1960); as far as he can discern, the basis of slow movements is the same as that of fast movements — that is, discrete bursts of muscle activity that alternately act to accelerate and decelerate the link. The control of slow movements, in this perspective, is characteristically "bang-bang-bang," and so on. There is some support for this characterization (e.g., Aizerman & Andreeva, 1968; Chernov, 1968; Litvintsev, 1968). It appears that the slow movement of a link, say, wrist extension or elbow flexion, is the result of pulls by both opposing muscles, where each muscle pulls ten times per second (Aizerman & Andreeva, 1968; Hubbard, 1960), first one and then the other.

In the third and final place we may recognize the context-conditioned variability that arises by virtue of the physiology. We can relate here only a small part of what is, most obviously, a very lengthy story.

The motor unit, conventionally defined as an alphamotoneuron together with the bundle of extrafusal muscle fibers that it innervates, may be considered as the functional final common path. Alphamotoneurons sometimes have monosynaptic connections with several descending systems. However, these monosynaptic projections to alphamotoneurons represent but a small part of the total neural projection to these cells, and of themselves probably do not bring about motoneuron firing (Evarts, Bizzi, Burke, DeLong, & Thach, 1971). In very large part, the major influences ultimately exerted on motor units occur via the segmental interneurons so that their modulation of motoneuron activity is highly flexible. Significantly, the same descending "instruction" might at different times encounter quite different "states" in the segmental interneurons; its affect, therefore, on a target motoneuron, is open to considerable variation.

The point is that the segmental apparatus of the spinal cord is an active apparatus that does not passively reproduce supraspinal instructions (Paillard, 1960). On the contrary, it appears that supraspinal and spinal influences relate in a free-dominance fashion (see below) in the coordination of acts. There is evidence that the state of the segmental apparatus can (among other things) convert a flexion reflex into one of extension (Lisin, Frankstein, & Rechtmann, 1973), enhance or inhibit contractile states evoked by cortical stimulation (e.g., Gellhorn, 1948), and affect the latency of voluntary movment (Gurfinkel' & Pal'tsev, 1965).

The implication of context-conditioned variability is simple enough: The motor apparatus cannot be regulated solely by efferent impulses arising in the cells of the motor strip. The contemporary perspective on coordinated activity contrasts with the nineteenth century perspective in recognizing that a continuous afferent flow of exteroceptive and proprioceptive information is the backdrop against which acts are constructed. Indeed, for Bernstein (1967) the decisive factor in coordinated activity is not the efferent impulses but the complex system of afferentation that tailors the components of the activity to the prevailing contingencies.

Patently, the problem of context-conditioned variability could be solved for the first kind of machine we described above by making available to it detailed information about the current states of the muscles and joints. It is commonly understood that signals to the sensorimotor cortex refer to muscle tension, muscle length, joint angle changes, and their time derivatives (Granit, 1970). It follows, therefore, that the flavor of the nineteenth century keyboard metaphor might be preserved by allowing that the specifications of individual muscle variables be guided by detailed information on the muscles and the positions and motions of the individual biokinematic links. A fine-grain description of afference might be coupled to the fine-grain description of efference, and all the details of the act − all the individual degrees of freedom − computed in a single step. It is our impression that a hybrid perspective much like this characterizes a number of current accounts of coordinated movements and motor programs (e.g., Keele & Summers, 1976; Schmidt, 1976). Unfortunately, this perspective, while proposing a resolution to the problem of context-conditioned variability, does not address the problem of degrees of freedom. We might even claim that it compounds the latter problem by requiring that the values of the large number of degrees of freedom on the input side be mapped by the executive onto values for the large number of degrees of freedom on the output side.

II. THE CONCEPT OF COORDINATIVE STRUCTURE

There are two closely intertwined and popular approaches to solving the related action problems of degrees of freedom and context-condition variability. Both approaches are evidenced to a degree in the second kind of machine described above. One approach seeks an optimal grain-size for describing the skeletomuscular units that serve as the vocabulary for acts. The other approach seeks to describe and understand an organizational format in which the responsibility for planning and executing an act is optimally distributed across the various computational components of the acting system.

In this section we will consider the first approach. In particular, we will examine and elaborate on the point of view that the free-variables of biokinematic chains are able to be partitioned into collectives (Gel'fand, Gurfinkel', Tsetlin, & Shik, 1971), where the variables within a collective change relatedly; and that the action vocabulary is these collectives, rather than the individual degrees of freedom.

In the literature, collectives of biokinematic variables take a variety of forms and are given a variety of labels. Our choice is *coordinative structure* (Easton, 1972; Turvey, 1977), which we will define generally as *a group of muscles, often spanning several joints that is constrained to act as a unit*. A coordinative structure is a relatively autonomous system: It regulates internally a number of biokinematic degrees of freedom, but is itself to be regarded as a single degree of

freedom. There are grounds for distinguishing between marshalling of such auto-
matisms and their modulation or tuning (see Boylls, 1975; Greene, 1972, in press,
a; Turvey, 1977). Marshalling a coordinative structure may be characterized as
defining the "ballpark" of a component activity, whereas tuning a coordinative
structure may be characterized as tailoring the component activity to current
contingencies, that is, making appropriate adjustments within the "ballpark"
(Greene, 1972, in press, a).

Notable sources of tuning are movements of parts of the body, in particular
the head and the eyes (Easton, 1972; Turvey, 1977), and memory (Boylls, 1975).
But the primary source of tuning, in most natural circumstances, must be the
detection of information about the relations among the body parts (propriospecific information), information about the properties and layout of the environment (exterospecific information), and information about the relation of
the body to the layout of the environment (expropriospecific information) (see
Lee, 1978). The informational support for tuning (and for coordinated movement in general) is amodal. The three kinds of information described above are
secured through the partially overlapping sensitivities of the various perceptual
systems (Gibson, 1966), although vision is the most bountiful and oftentimes
the most reliable supplier (Lee, 1978).

A brief examination of the guidance system of an airplane follows. It illustrates
the conception of a coordinative structure and provides a framework for understanding tuning.

A. The Guidance System of an Airplane as an Illustration

The kinematic state-set of an airplane consists of all the configurations into
which its movable parts can enter; for purposes of illustration, only those
movable parts that must be coordinated in order to guide the airplane in flight
are considered.

An airplane typically has a control system with a minimum of five hinged
parts: two ailerons on the rear edge of the wings that can be moved up or down
to control roll; two elevators on the horizontal portion of the tail section that
can also be moved up or down to control pitch; and finally, the rudder on the
vertical tail fin that can be moved left or right to control the yaw of the aircraft.
Construed as a *freely-linked* kinematic chain, the airplanes guidance control system has five degrees of freedom, one degree of freedom for each hinged part.
Each degree of freedom provides a coordinate dimension for the state-space
comprising all possible configurations of the five movable components. Or, put
differently, each possible configuration of the five control components can be
represented by a point in a hyperdimensional kinematic space of five dimensions.
Such a space of possible configurations is clearly too complex to be imagined,
much less mastered, for manually controlled flight. It is instructive to compute

the information load placed on a pilot in the above situation, where each aileron, elevator, or rudder has to be independently controlled; that is, where the style of control is address-specific with each kinematic degree of freedom individually controlled.

Assume that although each hinged part can move continuously, only k number of discrete positions are truly effective because of the inertia of the aircraft in flight. Thus, the total number of possible discrete configurations of a system with five free kinematic links is k^5. However, for the sake of simplicity, let k take on only eight values — a conservative estimate, since most airplanes have considerably more sensitive guidance control systems. This system's total kinematic state-space would consist of $k^5 = 8^5 = 32,768$ independent states. Thus, the information load on a pilot who must manually select a particular configuration of the guidance control system in order to select a desired flight pattern is $\log_2 n$, where n is the total number of independent choices. For our particular example, $n = 8^5 = (2^3)^5 = 2^{15} = 32,768$ and $\log_2 n = 15$ bits.

To grasp how complicated this task would be, consider a more familiar case: If we assume a comparably sensitive manual control system for an automobile (i.e., $k = 8$) with three degrees of freedom (accelerating, steering, and braking), then only 9 bits of information must be processed by the driver for each guidance decision $[\log_2 8^3 = \log_2 (2^3)^3 = 9$ bits]. However, even here we are stretching the limits of human information processing (Miller, 1957).

In the case of the 15 bit information load demanded of the pilot of the airplane with the crude guidance system described above, we are dangerously in excess of the average load believed permissible. Clearly, a safe aircraft requires a guidance system with more manageable degrees of freedom, so as to reduce the information processing load on the pilot. This can be accomplished by imposing constraints on the guidance control system.

The kinematic links of the airplane can be constrained in the following way: Let the ailerons of each wing be inversely yoked so that one moves up as the other moves down, and vice-versa; yoke the rudder on the vertical fin of the tail section to the ailerons, so that it moves left when the right aileron is depressed, and vice-versa; and yoke the elevators on the horizontal portions of the tail section so that they move in unison, going up and down together. With its movable guidance components so constrained, the airplane has a greatly reduced kinematic state-set and can be controlled more simply. The guidance system now has but two degrees of freedom, namely, the aileron-rudder sybsystem, where the inverse up-down movement of the ailerons is mechanically coordinated with the left-right movement of the rudder (a *macro* with one degree of freedom). Assuming that this coordinated guidance system is at least as sensitive as the cruder version, then we may note that its state-set is $k^2 = 8^2 = 64$. The latter number represents a dramatic reduction of 32,704 from the original state-set, consisting of 32,768 possible unconstrained configurations. More importantly, however, these constraints on the design of the guidance control system achieve a 500 fold reduction in the information processing load placed on the pilot (that is, $2^{15} - 2^6 = 2^9$ or 512).

The joystick, through which the pilot exerts his control of the airplane, links the two subsystems so that they are mutually constrained to act as a unit. It follows from the immediately preceding paragraph that the significant feature of the guidance system so produced is that the joystick represents for the pilot but two degrees of freedom, each defined over eight values — an information processing load of six bits (that is, where $n = 8^2 = (2^3)^2 = 2^6 = 64$; and $\log_2 n = \log_2 64 = 6$ bits). By moving the joystick left or right (one degree of freedom), the plane banks or turns in either direction; by moving the joystick forward or backward (a second degree of freedom), the plane's angle of ascent or descent is controlled.

Patently, the two-dimensional space of the joystick is the control space for the coordinative structure formed by constraining the freely moving parts of the airplane in the manner described. (With the free-variables left unconstrained, the control space was five-dimensional.) Furthermore, we may note that the two-dimensional control space represented by the joystick's movements is synonymous with the coordinative structure defined over the freely moving parts; the two concepts — control space and coordinate structure — are formally equivalent.

Finally, we recognize that the airplane's guidance system provides a good illustration of the radical difference in efficiency that exists between a system in which the free-variables are controlled individually, and a system in which it is collectives of free-variables that are controlled.

B. Examples of Coordinative Structures

Let us now take a look at some of the biokinematic events that have been (or may be) promoted as instances of the concept of coordinative structure.

The activity of a single limb during locomotion consists of two broadly defined phases: support and transfer. The support phase, during which the fact is in contact with the ground, is composed of extensor activity over the limb joints; the transfer phase, carrying the foot from one support to the next, is composed essentially of flexion. In an ingenious experiment (Orlovskii & Shik, 1965) conducted with dogs locomoting freely on a treadmill, a very brief impedance was applied at the elbow during transfer-flexion. In consequence, the movement at the elbow was slowed but so was the movement at the shoulder and wrist. However, a similar impedance delivered during support-extension did not retard the movement at the other joints. It is arguable that the link motions during flexion are constrained to act as a unit by means of spinally-mediated afferentation (cf. Boylls, 1975). But what of the extensors? They, apparently, are not linked by shared afference, but they do appear to be linked — that is, they do behave as a unit during locomotion. Witness to this claim is the observation that, across various gaits, the timing of limb extensor EMGs is nearly invariant with respect to step cycle and, further, that the activity periods of extensor muscles relative to each other change little as speed of locomotion changes (Engberg & Lundberg, 1969). The implication, perhaps, is that in locomotion the limb extensors are constrained to act as a unit by means of common *efference* (Boylls, 1975).

A unitary arrangement of joint changes that has been investigated quite thoroughly and that, therefore, provides an exemplary case, is that which preserves the stability of the head during respiration (Gurfinkel', Kots, Pal'tsev & Fel'dman, 1971). With inspiration and expiration, the torso (in both its upper and middle parts) deflects backwards and forwards, respectively. The displacement is of sufficient magnitude such that, if left unchecked, marked excursion would occur in the overall center of gravity. However, the respiratory-induced oscillations in the torso are balanced by antiphasic oscillations at the hip and at the cervix. Changes in the angle of the hip and of the cervix are simultaneous with changes in the angle of the torso, and the relation among these changes in invariant with frequency of respiration. This constraint on the biokinematic chain is wrought neither by means of mechanical conspiracy nor by spinally-mediated afferentation (Gurfinkel', Kots, Pal'tsev & Fel'dman, 1971); as with the extensors during locomotion, the coupling source is probably efferent.

Controlling two joints of the arm provides a further case in point. When a person is requested to simultaneously flex or extend his wrist and flex or extend his elbow, the joints are moved mainly in a coupled fashion (Kots & Syrovegin, 1966), although this synchrony is achieved with less practice in the case of changes of the same type (e.g., flexion-flexion) than in changes of the opposite type (e.g., extension-flexion) (Kots, Krinskiy, Naydin, & Shik, 1971). Significantly, the two rates of change of joint angle preserve one or another invariant ratio that is not attributable to mechanical coupling. Individuals differ in the ratios they use and they tend to have three to seven such ratios. Furthermore, they use a different subset of these ratios (usually three or four of them) for each of the four combinations of flexion and extension (Kots & Syrovegin, 1966).

Finally, let us take note of observations on the production of speech that suggest that oftentimes movements of the tongue, lips, velum, and jaw may be constrained as a unit (Kent, Carney, & Severeid, 1974).[2] To illustrate, in uttering the word *contract* lowering the velum is initiated with the release of oral closure for /k/, and elevating the velum begins with the tongue tip movement for alveolar closure (Kent et al., 1974). In uttering the word *we,* the transitions from the glide /w/ to the vowel /i/ is mediated by the contemporaneity of a forward gesture of the tongue body, and a release of lip protrusion. With increase in emphatic stress, there is an increase in the displacement and velocity of the tongue body and in the displacement and velocity of the upper lip. However, the relation

[1]We thank Carol Fowler for bringing these particular observations to our attention.

between the lingual and labial displacements and velocities remains invariant over variations in stress (Kent & Netsell, 1971). Apparently, for utterances like /wi/, the stress contrast modulates *both articulators or neither articulator.*

It is dimly apparent from these examples that where several muscles are constrained as a unit, whatever the mechanism, the activities of the individual muscles covary in terms of a ratio that is relatively fixed and indifferent to overall magnitude changes in these activities. In reaching this tentative conclusion we are somewhat guilty of the "in-phase" assumption, for our examples have crossed the muscle state-link movement boundary and, glibly, we are treating the two as isomorphic. Nevertheless, we believe the conclusion has heuristic merit and, following Boylls (1975), we proceed to identify two prescriptions for a ccordinative structure.

C. Structural and Metrical Prescriptions

A "structural prescription" refers to the ratios of activities in the muscles composing a coordinative structure that are invariant with respect to absolute activity level. As Boylls (1975) remarks, a metrical prescription is like a "scalar" quanitity, which multiplies by the same amount the activities of each muscle in a coordinative structure. In the example just given, of uttering /wi/, emphatic stress is analogous to a metrical prescription, for it magnifies the lingual and labial activities to the same degree; the ratio between the two activities that is preserved over stress is the structural prescription.

The specification of structural and metrical prescriptions for coordinative structures is, in part, what is meant by tuning. A change in structural prescription changes the dynamic topography of a biokinematic chain whose links have been constrained to act as a unit; a change in the metrical prescription changes, among other things, the speed with which the dynamic topography is realized. Our guess is that metrical prescriptions can be modulated more rapidly and with greater facility than structural, and there are a few experiments in favor of this view.

From the work of Asatryan and Fel'dman (1965) and Fel'dman (1966) we learn that where the muscles at a joint have been constrained to act as a unit — either for the preservation of a particular posture against opposing moments of force, or for the purpose of moving, on signal, to a new prescribed position, again against opposing moments of force — the muscle complex is describable as a nonlinear spring with definite stiffness and damping parameters. In the case where a posture is to be maintained, if the opposing moments of force are changed unexpectedly, the limb segment moves initially to a posture that is in accord with the original parameters, and only then does it move to a posture that is in accord with the new parameters relevant to the new moments. In the case of moving to a prescribed position, if the moments are changed subsequent to the signal to move but prior to movement, the limb will move initially, but erroneously, to a position that would be predicted for the "spring" parameters present at the time of the signal. One might interpret these observations to mean that once a coordinative structure has been activated, the parameters of that structure cannot be modified until the task, for which it was set, is complete. But a more prudent interpretation is that the temporal scale over which changes wrought through tuning can occur does not always overlap the temporal scale over which can occur changes wrought through generated kinetic energy. Where the scales do overlap, the personality of a coordinative structure can change — in flight, as it were.

It can be shown by experiment (Vince & Welford, 1967) that a movement by a hand begun slowly in response to a signal for a "slow movement" can be accelerated in response to a further signal, one that is for a "fast movement," in very much the same time that it would take to initiate a fast movement from rest. And this is so even if the second signal arrives during the latent period of the first. On this experiment and another (Megaw, 1970), in which the second signal called for a slightly different movement from the first signal, it appears that the form of an "initiated" movement is less rapidly altered than the vigor with which it is conducted. In our terms, structural prescriptions are less rapidly alterable than metrical prescriptions.

An especially interesting illustration of metrical modulation is to be found in the activity of the baseball batter (Hubbard & Seng, 1954). In this illustration we can point to the derivative properties of the optical flow field at the eyes as the information for metrical prescription. As with all batting skills, it is mechanically advisable to move in the direction of the ball. The right-handed baseball batter does so by lifting his left and leading foot, moving it forward and parallel to the ball's line of flight, to finally place the foot some distance in front of, and probably slightly to the side of, the foot's initial position. The start of this step is synchronized with the release of the ball from the pitcher's hand. The duration of the step, however, and the start of the swing (which more often than not coincides with the completion of the step) are inversely related to the speed of the ball, to which the speed and duration of the swing remain relatively indifferent (Hubbard & Seng, 1954).

We may consider the act of batting as supported by a function defined over a small number of coordinative structures, which for present purposes suffices as our definition of an action plan (Turvey, 1977). It can be hypothesized that the batter's stepping pattern arises primarily from the activities of knee extensors and hip abductors and flexors constrained to act as a unit. A structural prescription on this coordinative structure defines the dynamic topography of the stepping movement. On release of the ball the batting plan is initiated; during its unfolding, the plan is tailored to the current contingencies by the optically specified metrical prescription: The duration of the step (and hence the initiation of the swing) is functionally related to the speed of the ball.

In this last example we catch a glimpse of a central problem for the theory of how acting and perceiving conflate: In the performance of acts exterospecific, propriospecific, and expropriospecific information must be selectively percolated through the action structures at the right time. Conventional theories of selective attention do not address the question of how the selection of information is temporally constrained so as to be compatible with the dynamical requirements of the system it serves.

An interesting observation of Orlovskii's (1972) may have some bearing on this problem. Given supraspinal stimulation of the spinal cord known to enhance flexor and extensor contraction in the inert animal, it was shown that when this stimulation was continuous with locomotion, the effects of the stimulation were manifest only at select points in the locomotory cycle. One might interpret this result as saying that the interaction of coordinative structures created "holes" or "slots" through which the continuously present supraspinal influences could "flow" (cf. Boylls, 1975. Is this an instance of a general principle? In that the visual information that supports activity is not characterizable as momentary signals or stimuli but as continuous optical flow fields (Gibson, 1958; Lee, 1974), may we conjecture that the "introjection" of information into an act is constrained by the interaction among coordinative structures mediating the act? That selective percolation at the right time is defined, in very large part, by the act itself?

D. The Concepts of a Control Space and a Moving Point of Control

Consider once again the airplane guidance system described earlier. The concept of a control space is instanced by the two-dimensional space describing the joystick's movements, and it provides an elegant way of characterizing the two tuning functions of metrical and structural prescriptions. The two subsystems of the airplane's guidance system and the control space are depicted in Fig. 1. In

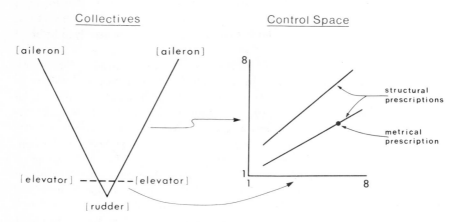

FIGURE   1.

reference to a task such as that of Kots and Syrovegin (1966), one of the subsystems can be likened to the collective of muscles regulating the change at the elbow, and the other can be likened to the collective of muscles regulating the change at the wrist. As Fig. 1 shows, any point in the control space is a metrical prescription, since it defined values for the variables of the collectives; a line in the control space is a structural prescription, since the slope of a line in the space defines a particular relation holding between the kinematic values of the two subsystems, that is, a ratio that is preserved invariant over metrical change.

The potential usefulness of the concept of a control space suggests that we should seek a way of determining such spaces for the biokinematic variables of natural systems. Consider a kinematic analog to animals and humans: A robot with the capability of locomoting across a room and opening a door. We restrict ourselves to considering simply the control of a single limb of the robot. Let the robot's limb consist of two rigid segments of unequal length, connected together by a joint (an "elbow") that permits 360° rotation in the plane, with this articulated limb connected by a similar circular joint to the main body of the robot (a "shoulder"). What is the structure of the control space of this two-joint system, and what is the minimal number of degrees of freedom needed to describe it?

The robot arm described above is, essentially, a compound planar pendulum with two kinematic degrees of freedom. In general, a precise representation of the total kinematic state-set of a mechanical system of l degrees of freedom can be provided by a control space defined over l parameters. The sturcture of the control space of the limb can be determined by taking the (topological) product over the unrestricted motions of the multiple linkages of its freely jointed kinematic chains. In the case of our *idealized* robot, the segment extending from the shoulder can rotate through a 360° planar angle around the shoulder joint; a similar rotation is permissible for the lower segment connected to the elbow joint. Furthermore, since these two segments are independent, for each angle that one of them assumes, the other is free to assume any one of its continuous angular positions. Thus, all possible positions of this articulated limb may be represented as the topological product of the angular positions of two circles. This topological product determines a manifold with two degrees of freedom known as a *torus* — a closed surface of two dimensions resembling the outside of a bagel.

Intuitively, one can conceive of the topological product of two circles as that surface (a torus) generated by stringing a small circle on a large circle and then moving the small circle in such a way that the larger circle consistently penetrates its center. All the points on the surface of this object specify possible kinematic states, or configurations, of the articulated limb of the robot. To locate a specific kinematic state on this surface requires imposing a coordinate system on the surface. Such a coordinate system is readily provided by dividing the circumference of the torus into degrees and, similarly, by dividing the circumference of the small circle into degrees. These two coordinate dimensions — two degrees of freedom — can then be used to locate every possible combination of circular joint values permitted by the kinematic linkages of the robot's limbs. If the values assumed by the two joints are truly independent of one another, then the torus provides a natural model of the control space of the robot's arm because it represents every possible kinematic state and no impossible ones. A person might have thought that a surface like a sphere or an ellipsoid would have done just as well, but neither of these is the product of variable-sized circles. The sphere is a product of equal circles and the ellipsoid is generated by a circle and an ellipse. The torus is the only closed surface that can be generated as the topological product of two *variable* circles.

Of course, the control space described is too idealized even for our robot. Neither of its joints will really allow a full 360° of rotation because we restricted the joints to the same plane. Thus, like the human arm, the robot's segmented limb will be restricted in its freedom of rotation. In general, the individual kinematic links of an animal or a human are anatomically constrained as to restrict free variation — a fact that must be expressed in their control spaces. In illustration, suppose that the shoulder joint of the robot permits free variation of its kinematic link through an angle limited to 180°, whereas the elbow joint permits free variation of its kinematic link through only 90°. Then the restricted control space that represents these natural anatomical constraints is but one quarter of the surface area of a half torus (cut in the way one would halve a bagel). In general, the natural, anatomical constraint placed on the degrees of freedom of ideal kinematic systems can be represented as bounded portions of the ideal topological manifold, corresponding to the control space of that system.

It is worth noting that the method of taking topological products over kinematic chains with more liberal joints will produce higher dimensional manifolds that represent control spaces of such systems. For instance, an articulated limb consisting of a ball joint and a 360° hinge-joint yields a topological product specifying a closed manifold of points — a control space — of three degrees of freedom, namely, the part of the space lying between two concentric spheres.

In the preceding we have demonstrated how the kinematic state set of a collection of biokinematic free-variables can be reduced to a minimal representation as a control space. This reduction has the virtue of providing an ideal solution to the problem of determining the minimal degrees of freedom required for the control of a coordinative structure by tuning.

To summarize: The concept of a control space is formally equivalent to that of a coordinative structure; and tuning a coordinative structure is formally equivalent to *a moving point of control* in the control space. The position of the point of control defines the metrical prescription and the direction of movement (a line, a plane, or a hyperplane) through the space identifies the structural prescription.

Let us now return to the airplane guidance system. By linking together the parts of the guidance system in the manner described, a system of five degrees of freedom is reduced to a system of two degrees of freedom. Put in a slightly different way, the linkage constrains three degrees of freedom and leaves unconstrained two degrees of freedom. Consequently, to complement the constraint supplied by the linkage, the source of control of the joystick must possess at least two degrees of freedom. In the course of piloting the plane, the pilot supplies the requisite constraint not supplied by the linkage. If for some reason the pilot could move only his right arm, and then only in a plane parallel to the sagittal plane — that is, forward or backward — then the pilot would not be able to control the plane. The single degree of freedom at the pilot's disposal is not the complement of the guidance system.

What does the moving point in the control space represent in natural systems such as animals and humans? After all, unlike the case of the airplane control space, there is neither joystick nor pilot to guide the moving point in a literal sense.

As suggested earlier, it is reasonable to assume that in animals and humans the constraints that complement the available degrees of freedom of the coordinative structures and tune them to their precise parametric values, originate primarily in the environment, and are picked up through perceptual activities. If this is so, then it strongly suggests that the unit of analysis for action must be of a grain sufficiently coarse to include, in addition to the anatomical and physiological aspects of the actor, certain relevant portions of the perceptual environment. In other words, the theoretical analysis must be at a grain that is truly ecological and not just psychological or physiological on the one hand, nor just physical or informational on the other (see Fowler & Turvey, in press; Shaw & McIntyre, 1974).

III. TOWARD A DEFINITION OF COALITIONS

Later in this section we will present a quasi-formal analysis of different organizational styles as models of control systems. This analysis carries us toward a formal definition of a coalition and a potential resolution to the problems of context-conditioned variability and degrees of freedom.

To set the stage for this analysis, we must make some prefatory comments on major principles of organization in complex systems; we do this through a brief comparison of a hierarchy and a heterarchy. In addition, we will present an example of one principle — that of free dominance — as manifest in the relation between preserving balance and performing acts that create imbalance.

A. Preliminary Remarks on Organizational Principles

A familiar form of organization is the hierarchy: The burden of computation on higher stages is alleviated by apportioning minor computation and processing to lower stages. We (Shaw, 1971; Shaw & McIntyre, 1974; Turvey, 1977) and others (e.g., Minsky & Papert, 1972) have claimed, however, that the hierarchy does not do justice to the organizational style manifest by complex dynamical (biological) systems. A hierarchy does not appear to provide the necessary computational power (see Sutherland, 1973); and significant biological events, such as remodeling or aging, are not easily defined over a hierarchy (cf. Shaw & McIntyre, 1974). Let us consider, therefore, in these preliminary remarks, the distinction between a hierarchy and a style of organization that, in theory, approximates more closely the biological form, namely, a heterarchy.

A pure hierarchy is characterized by the unidirectionality of commands or information flow. Given two structures or systems that are at different levels of the hierarchy then A, the higher system, always commands B; B never commands A. In a pure hierarchy, therefore, the relationship between any two levels of the hierarchy is immutable. In less pure forms, this unidirectionality feature is relaxed slightly to allow some flow of command from the lower to the higher level; in this case we say, more properly, that there is a fixed asymmetry in the command flow between structures of different levels. Significantly, where A and B are systems at the same level of the hierarchy, there is no conversation between them at all.

A second hierarchical feature is that for any given system the role that it plays is singular and immutable. The corollary of this feature is no less important; namely, that for every function to be computed (or role to be played) there is a specific system in which that function is invested. Collecting these two features, it is evident that a principle characteristic of a hierarchy is the centralization of control, the investment of decision making in one executive system.

A heterarchy is distinguished from a hierarchy in that "free-dominance" defines the relation between any two systems. Partitioning the systems into agents and instruments is arbitrary in that the extant relations depend on context, on the task being performed. The hierarchical unidirectionality of command is replaced by reciprocity in the flow of information. Further, the hierarchical fixedness of roles is replaced in a heterarchy by "functional pluripotentialism" (Filimonov, 1954 cited by Luria, 1966) meaning that no system is responsible for solely a single function, and that any system can assume a (limited) variety of roles as situation and task demand. It follows from this redundancy of function that any inventory of basic constituent elements will be equivocal. Relatedly, management of a heterarchy is not the prerogative of any one system. Many systems would function cooperatively in decision making, although not all systems need participate in all decisions. Collecting these features, it is evident that a principal characteristic of a heterarchy is decentralization of control.

B.   Reciprocity of Control Between Transport and
      Postural Activities

We may distinguish two classes of activity in gross motor tasks: transport and postural (cf. Smith & Smith, 1962). Both classes may be regarded as transformations of posture; that is, configurations of trajectories as the limbs move from one relatively stable arrangement to the next, although transport transformations are oftentimes more intricate and sometimes more arbitrary than postural. The principal distinction between the two is that transport activities are oriented to the local conditions of stimulation, for example, the flight of the ball, or the motions of an opponent, whereas postural activities are oriented to the global conditions or terrestrial stimulation, the global physical invariants (Shaw & McIntyre, 1974), such as the horizon, gravity, and the ground plane. It goes without saying that most gross motor acts — as manifest in tennis, soccer, etc. —·involve a tight confluence between the two classes. Our question is: How is this confluence realized?

1. Constraining the selection of transport activities. Fomin and Shtil'kind (1972) have introduced the term "pedate system" for any system with legs such that the system's normal contact with the surface of support is by means of the plantar parts of the feet. For nature's pedate systems, surface contact through the feet, intertial contact through the vestibular system, and optical contact through the ocular appraratus are the three sources of information about the system's orientation and movement relative to the environment (Lee, 1978). Of the three, vision is the more informative and influential; the vestibular system is not sensitive enough for fine balance control (Lee & Lishman, 1975), and surface contact through the feet is ambiguous about the body's relation to the environment when the feet move relative to the environment, such as when the surface is compliant, unsteady, or narrow (Lee, 1978).

From Gibson (1966) and others (Lee, 1974; Warren, 1976) we have learned that the optical flow patterns at the eye are specific to one's movements with respect to the layout of environmental surfaces. To illustrate, a person attempting to maintain an upright steady stance is perturbed by transformations of the total optic array: a form of inclusive optical expansion induces backward body sway, and a form of inclusive optical contraction induces forward body sway (Lee & Aaronson, 1974). Witness to the human pedate system's sensitivity to this visual source of expropriospecific information is the observation that body sway can be driven phasically by extremely small oscillations in optical expansion and contraction (Lee, 1978).

We can claim, therefore, that while standing or locomoting, the maintenance of an upright posture is an active process (cf. Aggashyan, Gurfinkel', & Fomin, 1973) oriented principally (but not solely) to preserving the *absence of certain kinds of inclusive optical change.* Patently, any transport activity is, in the final analysis, a disturbance of the body's relation to the global invariants which, on the above, is specified primarily by the optical flow pattern. But for a great many transport activities, the activity is possible only if, during the movement, a relatively stable relation is preserved between the body as a unit and the global invariants. Could this be achieved by a simple feedback system, that is, by a process in which the perturbation is corrected subsequent to the activity or, better still, subsequent to phases of the activity? The problem with any feedback solution is that oftentimes the specified compensatory changes are for states that are no longer current. It is evidently the case that while some form of feedback (e.g., velocity or acceleration feedback) is necessary to the integrity of the transport activity postural activity relations, it is not sufficient. Let us consider in this regard the concept of "region of reversibility" as it relates to the concept of pedate system.

The set of all transformations of the biokinematic chains defines a phase space of which a subset is the region of *controllable* transformations. Within the latter there is defined a particular subset such that for any two points in the subset, there is a control process by which either point can be attained from the other; in short, for any movement defined within the subset there is an inverse. This subset is the "region of reversibility," and by the use of the term "equilibrium" for a pedate system, Fomin and Shtil'kind (1972) mean that the kinematic state of the system is within this region. Significantly, the region of reversibility for a particular pedate system is not constant, and among possible sources of variation, we may recognize the conditions of the support surface (compare ice skating to running on the road) and the speed at which the body is moving relative to the surface supporting its locomotion. Now it follows that a major constraint on the planning and executing of many transport activities is that they conserve the pedate system within the region of reversibility. More precisely, and more practically, the constraint is that transport activities do not carry the system *too closely to the boundaries* of the region. Proximity to the boundary is costly in that coordinative effort would have to be disproportionately allocated to postural activities at the expense of transport activities.

By way of summary, it is proposed that preserving a relatively invariant relation to the global invariants in the course of transport activities is partially achieved by an *equilibrium-oriented constraint on the selection of transport activities.* Let us consider a further possible factor.

2. *Anticipatory postural activities are transport-specific.*   As alluded to above, preserving balance through feedback alone would often be too late and too slow. This tardiness, however, can be circumvented. When a cat detects an incipient stumble, approximations to the proper muscular response are rapidly generated to preserve the upright posture of the cat long enough for relatively low-level feedback mechanisms to take charge (Roberts, 1967). A particularly sophisticated version of this style of control is suggested by the observations of Belen'kii, Gurfinkel' and Pal'tsev (1967).

On receipt of an auditory signal, a participant is requested to raise his arm rapidly forward to the horizontal position. In the interval prior to the first signs of activity in the deltoid muscles of the shoulder, the muscles most responsible for the movement, there is evidence for considerable modification in the muscle states of the trunk and lower limbs. If it is the right arm that is raised, activity in the biceps femoris of the right leg and the sacrolumbar muscles of the left side precede activity in the deltoids. In addition, a definite anticipatory relaxation occurs in the left biceps femoris. We see, in short, an orderly pattern of change — of fixing and relaxing links in the kinematic chain of the body — preceding the transport activity of raising the arm. This pattern is both stable and *specific to the transport activity:* The pattern is constant over repetition and the pattern anticipatory to lowering the arm is distinctively different from that anticipatory to raising the arm (Belen'kii et al., 1967; Pal'tsev & El'ner, 1967).

We may interpret these anticipatory changes as intended to minimize the perturbations of the pedate system that would result from the movement of the arm. But insofar as these changes do occur *prior* to the movement and are specific to the moment, we may recognize the larger implication that, at least for this limiting case, the specification of a particular transformation of a kinematic chain, which is a particular transport activity, is concurrently the specification of a particular transformation of other kinematic chains, which is the cognate, postural activity.

If these anticipatory postural adjustments are absent or impaired (owing to brain injury), then pronounced excursions in the center of gravity accompany the arm movement (Pal'tsev & El'ner, 1967). Nevertheless, the anticipatory adjustments are not the whole story, for in the normal case other postural adjustments, presumably of a more precise nature, accompany and follow the movement of the arm (Pal'tsev & El'ner, 1967). It seems as if the anticipatory adjustments put the pedate system into the *ballpark* (see Greene, 1972, in press, b) of postural arrangements apropos the dynamics of moving the arm and apropos the disposition of the limb subsequent to the movement. We may state, therefore, the larger implication, noted above, more simply and somewhat differently: The plan for a transport activity, such as an arm motion, specifies the ballpark of necessary postural activity or, relatedly, a transport plan "pied-pipes"[2] an approximate, postural plan.

The preceding statement, in both its simple and more complicated forms, must be qualified on two counts. First, the relations between transport and postural activity is not a fixed-dominance relation, as pied-piping would seem to imply. The weight of the evidence (Belen'kii et al., 1967; El'ner, 1973; Pal'tsev & El'ner, 1967) favors a free-dominance relation. Second, there is the question of the generality of this form of control. There is the possibility of course, that the balance-oriented fixing and relaxing of biokinematic links, preparatory to and *specific to* a transport activity, is manifest only in simple motor tasks such as studied by Belen'kii et al. (1967). It can be argued, however, on rational grounds, that the form of control described above would be apt for many forms of transport activity; as a general principle, approximating a desired state through feedforward makes the task of feedback regulation considerably more simple and more efficient (cf. Greene, 1972, in press, a).

---

[2]This term was suggested to us by Robert Remez, with all due respect to John Robert Ross.

In the general case, then, the intended transport activity can be the basis for specifying an anticipatory but approximate feedforward adjustment of postural control structures. In the acquisition of a skill (say, a gymnastics routine) it would be beneficial for the performer to become sensitive to the postural activity implications of intended transport activities (see Belen'kii et al., 1967, for a modest demonstration). An advantage of this sensitivity is that by approximating postural controls ahead of time the performer can devote more coordinative effort to the intricacies of the skill.

In sum, we recognize that the confluence between the transport and postural activities is mediated by a reciprocal, free-dominance relation. Activities oriented to local conditions of stimulation are constrained by information about the actor in relation to the global invariants; and, in turn, activities oriented to the global invariants are attuned to the emerging transport activities. On this limited analysis it would appear that the subsystems supporting transport and postural activities are components of a heterarchical organization.

C. Coalitions: Systems with Functional Integrity

We turn now to distinguishing among control systems as they are modeled by the placing or relaxing of certain restrictions on nets of states. In very large part, our intention is to show that a solution to the problem of degrees of freedom must emerge *pari passu* with a solution to the problem of degrees of constraint — a problem that was introduced in the concluding remarks of Section II. When taken together, the overarching problem becomes that of how a (biological) system and its environment mutually constrain one another. The reciprocity of animal and environment is captured by the term ecosystem; a special system that exhibits *functional integrity* (defined below) and that will be said by us to be a coalition. Our strategy, in a nutshell, will be to develop the concept of a coalition by contrasting it with systems whose control principles are both simpler and less abstract — systems such as aggregates, chains, complex-chains (e.g., hierarchies), and heterarchies.[3]

In order to delineate clearly how one type of control system necessarily differs from another, only *pure* cases of each type will be considered. The reader, therefore, should be cautioned against confusing the labels for control systems as used here with the way these labels are often used in the literature. As remarked earlier, pure hierarchies are defined as possessing no mutability among levels of control, that is, no free-dominance relations. Many theorists, however, are primarily interested in hierarchical organizations where the principle of immutable, superordinate control is not sacrosanct, and where inversion of dominance relations is allowed. By out taxonomy, the latter would define a mixed case more aptly described as heterarchical organization of a hierarchy.

---

[3]Elsewhere we have treated the concepts of heterarchy and coalition as synonymous (e.g. Turvey, 1977); here they are distinguished.

It is our belief (although it should be proven) that any system of a mixed-type can be defined as a logical product of a proper subset of pure systems. Hence, the analysis to be given should introduce the set of minimal contrasts required to characterize exhaustively all the subcategories of *pure* control systems.

The above assumption that only pure cases are needed for complete logical characterization of control systems allows the following conjecture to be made (again, a proof would be desirable): *All control systems are properly included as special cases in the category of structures that we shall call coalitions.* In other words, by placing appropriate restrictions on the properties of coalitions, each of the other type of control system can be defined. This inclusion relationship can be represented as follows:

aggregates $\supset$ chains $\supset$ hierarchies $\supset$ chain-complexes $\supset$ heterarchies $\supset$ coalitions

Each structure on the left of the inclusion sign is a special case of that structure on the right under which it is included. There are many different ways to distinguish these structures from one another; for our purposes we will consider only how they differ with respect to their inherent principles of organizational control — what we shall call their dominance of control principles. It will prove to be the case that such an analysis has important implications for *what* such systems can do as well as *how* they might do it. The goal is to show how the concept of a coalition provides a more adequate control system model for living systems than any of the lesser models because it alone is sufficiently well-structured to offer a potential solution to the degrees of freedom problem and the problem of context-conditioned variability.

1. *Nets.*   Nets of states provide the medium or structural support for defining control principles. Four primitives comprise a control net: first, a set S of elements called "states"; second, a set R of elements called "dominance relations"; third, a function DOM whose domain is S and whose range is contained in R; and fourth, a function $\overline{\text{DOM}}$ whose domain is R and whose range is contained in S. The first and second primitives are self-explanatory. The third primitive asserts that a function DOM exists such that DOM $(a, b) = a$ DOM $b = a \rightarrow b$ (read as "a dominates b"). The fourth primitive asserts the inverse, namely, $\overline{\text{DOM}}(a, b) = a$ $\overline{\text{DOM}}$ $b = b \rightarrow a$ (read as "a is dominated by b" or "b dominates a").

All possible control nets may be constructed from the intuitive elements given in Fig. 2.

From inspection of Fig. 2 it follows that nets may or may not possess feedback control loops. One also sees that dominance loops may be defined on a single state, a pair of states, a triplet of states, etc. Hence, the circuit of the dominance relation may be monadic, dyadic, triadic, tetradic or, in general, n-adic, where n is the number of states in the loop.

The properties depicted in Fig. 2 can be used to distinguish several classes of control systems. A strongly connected system is one that has the maximum number of n-adic loops; that is, where there are k states, n (the number of loops)

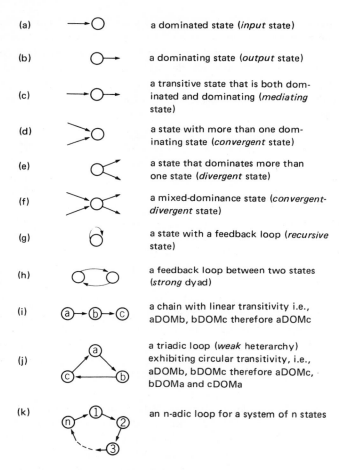

(a)   a dominated state (*input* state)

(b)   a dominating state (*output* state)

(c)   a transitive state that is both dom-
      inated and dominating (*mediating*
      state)

(d)   a state with more than one dom-
      inating state (*convergent* state)

(e)   a state that dominates more than
      one state (*divergent* state)

(f)   a mixed-dominance state (*convergent-
      divergent* state)

(g)   a state with a feedback loop (*recursive*
      state)

(h)   a feedback loop between two states
      (*strong* dyad)

(i)   a chain with linear transitivity i.e.,
      aDOMb, bDOMc therefore aDOMc

(j)   a triadic loop (*weak* heterarchy)
      exhibiting circular transitivity, i.e.,
      aDOMb, bDOMc therefore aDOMc,
      bDOMa and cDOMa

(k)   an n-adic loop for a system of n states

FIGURE 2.

equals k. Control systems, therefore, are potentially distinguishable on a connec-
tedness dimension.

It is also possible to distinguish control nets in terms of their "spread" of
control, that is, the extent to which every state participates equally in the functions computed by the net. The greater the number of divergent states, or divergent branches from single states, the more centralized the control of the system.
Conversely, the greater the number of convergent states, or convergent branches
onto single states, the more focused the effect of the control. Moreover, the
more strongly connected the net, then the greater the decentralization or spread
of control. These two properties, *strength* of connectivity among states, and
spread of control (or of the effect of control) provide useful dimensions by
which the diverse varieties of control nets may be distinguished. Indeed, the

logical product of the fundamental net elements [Fig. 2 $(a) - (k)$] yields all structural models needed to support the descriptions of all possible control systems differing along these two dimensions. Some of the types of control systems that have enjoyed popularity among systems theorists are presented in Fig. 3. Let us now survey the range of control systems typically discussed. For the sake of completeness, we start with the most trivial of "systems" — the lowly aggregate.

2. *Aggregates.*   Aggregates consist of collections of isolated states that exhibit free-variation. In *free-variation,* each state behaves in a manner unconstrained by the behavior of any other state in the collection. *By control of a given state, we mean a relationship among states of a collection that reduces the degrees of freedom that the given state posses in free-variation.* Hence, the control principle for an aggregate is trivial, since such a collection of k-states exhibits a maximum of k-degrees of freedom and requires a separate source of constraint

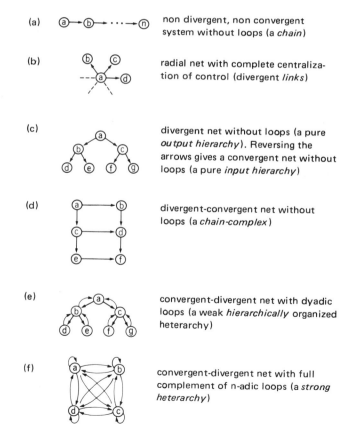

(a)   non divergent, non convergent system without loops (a *chain*)

(b)   radial net with complete centralization of control (divergent *links*)

(c)   divergent net without loops (a pure *output hierarchy*). Reversing the arrows gives a convergent net without loops (a pure *input hierarchy*)

(d)   divergent-convergent net without loops (a *chain-complex*)

(e)   convergent-divergent net with dyadic loops (a weak *hierarchically* organized heterarchy)

(f)   convergent-divergent net with full complement of n-adic loops (a *strong heterarchy*)

FIGURE 3.

for each state, that is, k-degrees of constraint. Clearly, a perfectly controlled system is one in which for each degree of freedom exhibited there exists a degree of constraint; or put differently, a perfectly controllable system is one in which for each dominating state, there exists a reciprocal state that dominates it. Such reciprocal states will be said to be *dominance-duals.*

An example of an aggregate is a gas consisting of randomly excited particles. Although such kinetic structures may be stochastically described (the gas laws), they do not consist of states that are jointly controllable. (Only an ideal gas would qualify as a perfect aggregate.) Therefore, let us reserve the concept of a controllable system for those collections of states that can be constrained as a whole in such a way as to exhibit fewer degrees of freedom than permitted under free-variation. Collections of states exhibiting such constraints will be said to be *structured.* Put differently, a *structure* is a system of states possessing fewer degrees of freedom than a collection of free-varying, unconstrained states.

The concept of *control* refers to either a *dynamic* process or a *syntactic* procedure that acts to bring about structuralization of a system. Typically, however, the concept of control is reserved for *transient,* rather than permanent, structuralization of a collection of states achieved by time-invariant rule, rather than time-variant law (Pattee, 1973). For instance, although it is appropriate to say that a population (an aggregate) of molecules is *dynamically* controlled in accord with the gas laws, we shall for the most part be concerned with systems (e.g., biological systems) that are *syntactically* controlled in accord with a program of constraints (e.g., DNA, perceptual information, or remembered rules).

Since, by definition, aggregates are syntactically uncontrollable systems, their study offers little help toward a solution to the problem of how coordinative structures (a syntactic concept!) may become attuned to the environment.

3. *Chains.*   The simplest nets possessing nontrivial principles of control are chains. A chain is a concatenation of states that obeys the linear transivity principle of dominance, namely, if a DOM b and b DOM $c,$ then a DOM c (Figs. 2i and 3a). To see why collections of chained states are controllable systems in the above sense, consider a collection of seven states $[a, b, c, d, e, f, g]$ partitioned into the following pair of chains: $a \rightarrow b \rightarrow c; d \rightarrow e \rightarrow f \rightarrow g.$ A control signal with but two degrees of freedom can provide impetus to activate each chain by stimulating states a and $d,$ respectively. This represents a savings of five degrees of freedom over the seven degrees of freedom the states would exhibit as a free-varying aggregate of states.

But notice that to control the system, the signal must be specifically addressed to enter each chain at the start-state, the extreme left state. For this reason we call such structures address-specific systems. As weak as such structures are, they nevertheless have the virtue of allowing a partition of several states (a chain) to be controlled as if it possessed but a single degree of freedom (form the perspective of some executive). Traditional examples of such systems are "stimulus-response" chains or reflex-arcs. As argued earlier, the shortcomings of such models for action control systems is that (a) they require a system with total centralization of control (an executor or homunculus) to orchestrate the chains; this means that the degrees of freedom problem is left unresolved; and (b) chains are rigid, undirectional structures, and therefore offer no way in which the action system of an animal or human might become appropriately tuned to environmental exigencies.

4. *The concept of pluripotentiality.* A network of chains can be constructed by concatenating chains by means of divergent and convergent net modules (see Fig. 2). For instance, a planar net of five states comprising two chains can be constructed as depicted in Fig. 4. With the use of divergent or convergent states to build chain-complexes, an important new property is introduced into control systems that is not found in simple chains. Figure 4 represents two dominance functions: DOM(a, b, c) and DOM(a', b, c'). Notice that these two chain-functions have a state in common, b. This means that b, unlike the other four states in the complex, plays a *functionally equivocal* role in two distinct functions. Furthermore, as more complex nets are built from divergent and/or convergent states, a greater number of states like b will lie at the intersections of chains. The number of such functionally equivocal states in a system will be said to provide a measure of the system's *pluripotentiality.*

Thus, a system with great pluripotentiality is one whose states are likely to be engaged in a large variety of functions — a measure of the richness of the system's multipurposiveness. Thus, unlike aggregates and isolated chains, chain-complexes (networks) are necessarily systems with some degree of pluripotentiality, where certain states assume a degree of universality, or nonspecificity, of function. By generalizing this property, it is reasonable to ask whether there might not be a continuum of controllable systems ranging from those with functionally univocal (unique) states through those with states that have lesser or greater functional equivocality to those remarkable systems (like the human brain?) that appear to have essentially functionally universal states. (A universal Turing machine being such a system.) Indeed, as will become evident, such a continuum of functional plasticity does seem to exist — ranging from simple chain-complexes to coalitions.

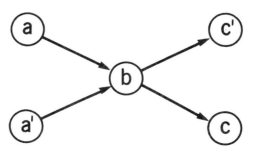

FIGURE 4.

5. *Hierarchies: Nets without control loops.*   Many interesting properties of control systems, in addition to pluripotentiality, can be modeled by chain-complexes. A very special and extremely popular property is that of being hier-archically organized. As we shall see, such systems allow for the introduction of a degree of generality into control systems not permitted in systems organized at but a single level of control

Control nets may be constructed from two kinds of elements distinguished by what they dominate. A *terminal-state* takes some dynamic aspects of the environment as its value, such as being "on" or "off," conducting or not con-ducting. Thus, we say a terminal state dominates values in the *execution* mode, i.e. aDOM $[1, 0]$. On the other hand, a *state-variable* is a state that takes another state, or a partition of states, as its value. Thus, we say a state variable dominates values (other states) in the *control* mode, that is, A DOM $[B, C, . . ., N]$ or A DOM $[b, c, . . . n]$ (where lowercase letters represent terminal-states). By *levels* of control, we mean an ordering of dominance relations among state-variables, states, and values. Every physically realizable control net by definition must have a minimum of two levels — a control level and an execution level. Hence, a control system necessarily exists simultaneously in two modes: the control (syn-tactic) mode, and the execution (dynamic) mode. We can now make explicit the intuitive notion of a hierarchically organized control system.

A *hierarchy* is a net with two or more levels of control constructed solely from divergent elements (see Figs. 2 and 3). Notice that a hierarchy can only be composed from divergent (or convergent) state modules (see Fig. 3c). A chain of state-variables constitutes a degenerate hierarchy but can still have levels of con-trol (see Fig. 3a). Significantly, the notion of the levels of control in a net should not be confused with that of *pure* hierarchy. Not all structures organized at multiple levels of control are hierarchies in the strict sense defined above. Con-sider Fig. 5. It depicts a chain-complex with two levels of control — a primary level that consists of links (a, d), (b, e), and (c, f) and a secondary level that consists of state-variables A, B, C. Despite the fact of more than one level of control, the system depicted in Fig. 5 is *not* a hierarchy; it is constructed from components other than divergent (or convergent) state modules.

Recall that the dominance of control principle for chains (which are based on linear transitivity) is too inflexible to account for context-conditioned variability. A linearly transitive structure can not be tuned to the many contingencies of the environment in which it operates. A similar argument can be levied against chain complexes such as hierarchies, in spite of the introduction of higher levels of control. On the other hand, hierarchies or other nets with more abstract levels of organization have the important advantage over chains and chain-complexes with but a single level of control. The advantage is that state-variables may be used to represent collections of nonspatially contiguous substructures (e.g., states, chains, or subcomplexes of chains) that can be treated as if they possess but a single controllable degree of freedom. In this way, a complex collection of biokinematic chains might be optimally organized under relatively simple control

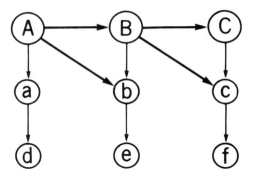

FIGURE 5.

principles. Thus, the advantage of hierarchical organization is a certain degree of economy of control.

Unfortunately, such economy of control is not gained without a loss of a desirable property. The loss is in the lessening of the "spread" of control by which the functional plasticity of natural systems might be modeled. Because of its divergent organization, a hierarchy necessarily has a high degree of centralization of control centered around a single state-variable — sometimes called a "pontifical" state or "executive" state. Notice also that the spread of control is inversely related to the degree of pluripotentiality in the system: The farther the states are from the topmost level of the executive state-variable, the less functional equivocality enjoyed by the states. In Fig. 3c, A has the greatest functional equivocality, B and C next, with d, e, f, g bringing up the rear. This follows from the fact that A DOM (B, C) while B DOM (d, e) and C DOM (f, g); hence A DOM (d, e, f, g). Therefore, A plays a role in four functions (chains), B and C in two chains each, while d, e, f, g are terminal (and in this sense functionally univocal). Thus, we might say that the spread of control (or, inversely, of pluripotentiality) is *anisotropic* in hierarchies.

While systems with such gradients of control may exhibit a certain economy, they suffer from the defect of being too easily infirmed by localized insults. If a superordinate node of control is lost (say, by injury or destruction to neural tissue in a living system), then all subordinate portions of the structure dominated by it will be left syntactically uncontrolled (e.g., paralysis or spasms). This shortcoming is a direct result of the fact that hierarchically organized control nets, no less than chains, are governed by a linear principle of transitivity of dominance. Removal of a mediating state (or state-variable) necessarily disconnects portions of the control net.

To summarize: pure hierarchies therefore provide no means for explaining the functional plasticity observed in natural systems whose functioning often remains intact under a variety of insults. Similarly, because the gradient of the flow of control is ever descending in a pure hierarchy, such control systems are not responsive to environmental fluctuations to which natural systems are observed to adapt. But what type of control principle, and what type of structural organization, is required to model the adaptive, pluripotential, functionally resilient systems observed in nature?

6. *Heterarchies: Nets with control loops.*   There is but one way in which a system might maintain a stable level of functioning under insults that destroy connectivities among subordinate states or state-variables, and that is to have in reserve redundant or backup structures that may be conscripted in case of an emergency. But clearly this requires that dominating nodes in a control net be able to receive information from below regarding the nature and extent of the insult to the system; for how else might the executive nodes know which reserve states to recruit? However, since this is but a species of the context-conditioned varibility problem, no pure hierarchy without control loops could know, even in principle, which reserve structures to conscript. Indeed, strictly speaking, without feedback from below, the higher nodes would not even know there was an insult to the net.

McCulloch (1945), recognizing the need for a solution to this problem, suggested that natural control systems function as reliably as they do primarily because they seem to violate the principle of linear transitivity of dominance at will — exhibiting what we earlier called "free dominance." For this reason, he argued, if for no other, natural systems must be organized as "heterarchies" rather than as pure chain-complexes, hierarchies, or other networks without control loops.

A *heterarchy* is a net characterized by reciprocity in dominance of control relationships, namely, if A DOM B, B DOM C, then not only does A DOM C hold, but C DOM A and B DOM A as well. (Recall Fig. 3e, f). Therefore, heterarchies exhibit control governed by a principle of *circular* dominance which is manifested as loops that follow dyadic, triadic, or n-adic circuits through the system.

This control principle of circular transitivity offers a potential solution to the problem of context-conditioned variability. Circular transitivity of dominance relations makes it possible to introduce feedback into the system so that subordinate nodes (terminal states) that experience insult or constraint, due to environmental vicissitudes, can inform the superordinate nodes of the prevailing state of affairs. In this way, the virtue of heterarchies over hierarchies, or other nets limited to unidirectional flows of control, is the capacity to be sensitive to perturbations in contextual constraints. Such "context-sensitivity" is a necessary condition for any system that is capable of adaptive behavior in a changing environment — an indispensable property for all living systems. A minimal heterarchy with this adaptive property can be modelled as shown in Fig. 6.

Let us assume that at some time t_1 A DOM B, B DOM (C, D) and hence A DOM (C, D) (the solid arrows). In addition, let us also assume the existence of feedback loops C DOM A and D DOM A, such that if state B is compromised by insult, such that the linear transitivity of control from A cannot be received by C or D, then C and D can so inform A of the quiescence of B. In other words, if

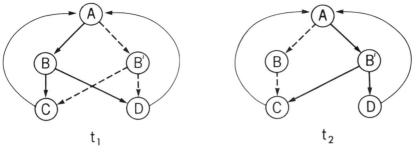

FIGURE 6.

at some later time t_2 A does not receive continuous confirmation that B has conveyed the appropriate control signal to C and D, then A will know to disconnect B and recruit the backup structure B' in its place (Fig. 6 at time t_2).

Unfortunately, the above solution to the context-conditioned variability problem is far from optimal, since it increases the anisotropic pluripotentiality of the system. This means that the highest node not only is burdened with the planning and execution of the downward-flow of control, but must now take on the added burden of processing information fed back to it from every subordinate level of control. Recall that the fundamental fallacy of too much central control is that insult to the top-most node renders the system completely inoperable.

For extremely complex hierarchically organized heterarchical systems, where the "node-to-terminal ratio" (number of levels of control) is quite high, an attempt is often made to reduce the dependence of the system on central control by introducing a greater spread of control in the form of an optimization assumption. An example of such an optimization assumption is the *Province of Ignorance Principle* (cf. Turvey, 1977). This principle asserts the condition that no level in a hierarchical-heterarchy is permitted to dominate, nor to be dominated, by any level not immediately adjacent to it. Thus, in a system such as the one depicted above (Fig. 6), it is permitted that A DOM (B) and B DOM (C, D), but not A DOM (C, D). Similarly, no feedback would be permitted to "leapfrog" over intermediate levels of control; for instance (C, D) DOM A would not be allowed. This means that superordinate nodes can activate, but cannot tune, nodes immediately inferior to it. Moreover, whatever tuning takes place from the environment must be passed upward to the higher nodes following a "domino" principle.

We can now illustrate how the Province of Ignorance Principle can be used to reduce the unequal spread (anisotropy) of pluripotentiality in a hierarchically organized net. This is accomplished by allowing only dyadic feedback loops. This system with optimized control loops can be compared with a system possessing both dyadic and triadic control loops. Consider Fig. 7a depicting a system in which the Province of Ignorance condition holds: Here we see that no state-variable either dominates or received feedback from more than two other states, regardless of how high a level it may occupy. Hence, although node A is

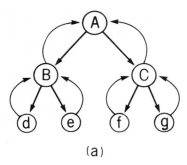
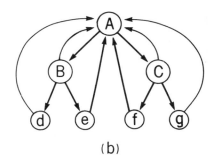

(a)   (b)

System satisfying Province   System violating Province
of Ignorance assumption   of Ignorance assumption

FIGURE   7.

structurally central, it is not really functionally central. Moreover, it is also conceivable that once node *B* or *C* has been activated by *A,* they may continue to
function independently of *A,* since their control for tuning emanates from below
rather than from above.

By contrast, Fig. 7b depicts a system in which the most superordinate node is
both structurally and functionally central. Here subordinate nodes can only be
tuned to fluctuations in the lower level context by control from above. Consequently, without information from central control they can not operate at all.
Thus, we see how the Province of Ignorance Principle can optimize control by
introducing more homogeneous distribution of pluripotentiality. Furthermore,
this property has an important byproduct, namely, the creation of relative
autonomy among the functional components of the system.

The system represented in Fig. 7, however, is still a mixed case consisting of
heterarchical control principles superimposed over a hierarchical structure. Let
us consider a pure heterarchy, in which pluripotentiality is perfectly homogeneous, and in which every state or state-variable is functionally central.

Notice in Fig. 3f that each state has the same number of input and output
arrows, indicating that no state is functionally more central than any other. Such
a pure heterarchy is a strongly connected feedback control system. In principle,
such a system is formally capable of computing any well-defined function whatsoever. This follows from the fact that if we allow the heterarchy to consist of
an arbitrary number of appropriately selected states, each able to compute a
certain primitive function, then the system can be programmed to simulate the
computational power of a universal Turing machine — a device for which it has
been shown there exists no computational limitations.

Does this mean that heterarchies necessarily provide an ideal model for any
natural system? We think not, for natural systems, unlike purely mathematical
ones, do much more than just compute functions. Rather as von Neumann (1966)
observed, the truly remarkable thing about living systems is that they exhibit
actions or goal-directed behaviors — what he called their *effectivities.* Effectivities

are manifested by animals in two fundamental ways: as *appetitive drives,* such as seeking food, mates, and shelter, and as nonconsumatory, or *conative* activities involving planning, such as sorting food, building nests, and shelters before they are actually required, seeking tools, pursuing an education, etc.

Even more remarkable is the fact that animals or other living systems do not express such effectivities in an unsystematic way, but seem to have them integrated into an organized whole. For this reason it is accurate to say that the goal-directed activities of living systems possess a *functional integrity.*

It is precisely this property of functional integrity, that is, of having an organized system of effectivities, that distinguishes pure heterarchies from what we shall call pure coalitions (again we admit the possibility of nonpure or mixed cases). In the last section we explore the concept of control systems that exhibit functional integrity and attempt to demonstrate why such structures are functionally distinct, at least in terms of their dominance of control principles, from heterarchies.

7. *From heterarchies to coalitions.*

To motivate the next class of control systems (coalitions), we would do well to pause and consider carefully the fundamental limitations of heterarchically organized control systems. Let us examine a simple control system — a room with a thermostatically controlled heater.

The system has three sources of *internal* control and three sources of *external* control. Let us consider the three internal sources of constraint first: Assume that the thermostat has been set to a criterion of 72°F. As the room cools down below this set-point, the thermocouple in the thermostat expands and closes the circuit, thereby activating the heater. However, when the temperature of the room reaches 72°, the thermocouple in the thermostat contracts and breaks the electrical circuit, thereby deactivating the heater. We can schematize these control functions as follows: *Rm* DOM *th, th* DOM *ht, ht* DOM *rm* and therefore, *th* DOM *rm* — a clear case of circular transitivity of control.

The beauty of this simple heterarchical control system is that under *normal* circumstances (i.e., those for which the system was designed), it possesses functional integrity: It is capable of achieving a goal-directed function, or effectivity. The effectivity achieved by the "room-thermostat-heater" system is obviously that of keeping the temperature of the room at 72°F.

The system also has three potential sources of external control, only one of which it was designed to handle. These potential sources of external control are represented by the arrows on each of the three states from the environment. Inputs to a system from the outside (that is, from states not within the closed feedback system) are called *feedforward* relations. Every *simple* feedback system is designed to control but one dimension of feedforward relations with its environment, although such relations may be indeterminately rich. Our simple system has the effectivity of being able to control only the thermal dimension of its environment. This is represented by the input arrow to the room, construed as a thermal niche in the broader environment.

This feedforward relation to the room indicates that, as a compartment, it is not completely insulated form the broader thermal environment. Indeed, it is this fact that allows perturbations in temperature and that, therefore, makes necessary the effectivity of the control system in question. By contrast to the controllable thermal dimension of variability, the other two arrows represent feedforward relations to dimensions of the broader environmental context that are uncontrollable by the system as it now stands. To control the potentially perturbing effects on the system from nonthermal aspects of the environment, this thermal control system with but one effectivity (i.e., to control heat of room) would have to be expanded to include at least two other effectivities. For instance, the feedforward relation to the heater might represent the way in which the quality or quantity of fuel delivered to the heater might vary below standard, thereby rendering the system incapable of achieving its goal of maintaining the room at 72°F. A control system that is unable to satisfy its effectivity thereby experiences a loss of functional integrity.

Similarly, the functional integrity of the thermal control system might be violated by a feedforward relation from the environment to the thermostat, say by sunlight (a nonthermal dimension) falling upon it. Since the air of the room is relatively transparent, and the thermostat is opaque, light energy falling upon it would be converted to heat, thereby constraining the thermostat to give a spuriously high reading of the actual temperature of the room. Again, such a feedforward relation between the system and its environment would be uncontrollable by the feedback dimension of the system and would mitigate its effectivity, thus compromising the functional integrity of the system.

One is tempted to ask, however, whether simple control systems, such as the one above, might not simply be enlarged so as to subsume the offending feedforward dimensions of the extended environment? Unfortunately, this strategy of subsumption leads to a potentially infinite regress, for any new states brought in to enlarge the system are "Trojan horse" states, in which new uncontrollable feedforward relations are necessarily hidden. Indeed, it is inevitable that the more one tires to close a heterarchical system by subsuming more and more dimensions of variability from its environment under its state-set, then the greater will be the number of feedforward relations smuggled in by this process. Therefore, the technique of creating ever more encompassing heterarchical systems has the unfortunate consequence of increasing, rather than decreasing, the distance between the proposed system and a viable solution to the problem of context-conditioned variability for that system.

The above argument can be generalized to heterarchically organized, "psychological" control systems in the following way: Every control system has a logically irreducible triad of components — a component in which the dimension of variability to be controlled is defined (an *environmental* "niche"); a component capable of measuring, or sensing, values along the dimension of information in

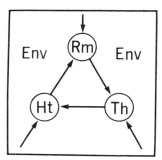

Rm = temperature of room
Th = thermostat
Ht = heater
Env = environment

(a)

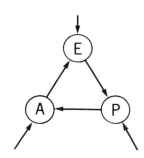

E = environmental niche
P = perceptual system
A = action system

(b)

FIGURE 8.

question (a *perceptual* system); and a component capable of modulating the information dimension (an *action* system). (Notice the similiarity of Fig. 8b, a "psychological" control system, to the thermal control system discussed above.)

The argument regarding the regress of feedforward-control applies *a fortiori* to complex psychological control systems that must retain their functional integrity. In complex environments, the sources of uncontrollable variability are greatly multiplied. Indeed, the above argument can be generalized to show that any naturally instantiated control system will be victimized by uncontrollable feedforward inputs from the environment, unless certain very strong assumptions regarding the "fit" of the system to the extended environment are made.

In other words, to avoid this problem of context-conditioned variability, and to achieve functional integrity, the control system must somehow be initially designed with the *whole* of the environment in mind. It is not adequate merely to design a system to operate adaptively with respect to a narrow environmental niche, unless a guarantee can be given *a priori* that all the variables of the system, taken within the context of the larger environment, are somehow logically *closed.* This is tantamount to demanding that the system must qualify as an *ecosystem.* Consequently, the concept of functional integrity will have to apply to the *whole* ecosystem and not just to the operational component (e.g., the animal or human) alone.

It is our contention that an ecosystem is not merely a very large heterarchy composed of an organism coupled to an environment of potentially perturbing influences. An environment that is sufficient to support a functioning organism must itself be thoroughly organized. If one were to think of the organism as a heterarchy, one could also think of the environment as a heterarchy. This step gives more credit to the environment and acknowledges its order, but is not sufficient to capture the idea of an ecosystem. The interaction of two complicated heterarchies otherwise indifferent to one another would result in an immensely complicated heterarchy. Suppose that one heterarchy had K degrees of freedom and the other had L degrees of freedom. The new system would have KL degrees of freedom, and we would have magnified, not solved, the degrees of freedom problem.

What must be added to the heterarchical property of circular transitivity is a symmetry relation (cf. Shaw, McIntyre, & Mace, 1974), which binds the organism to its environment. If we hold to the image of an organism-environment relation as one of two interacting heterarchies, we would add the requirement that each heterarchy be tailored to the other. They cannot be indifferent to one another; rather, one must complement the other. Recall the example of the airplane guidance system in which sufficient degrees of constraint had to be provided to correspond to the degrees of freedom. This was an example of mutual tailoring of systems. Our candidate for the symmetry relation binding the heterarchies is *dual complementation.* To say that an organism is the dual complement of its environment is also to assert than an environment is the dual complement of its organism, i.e. that the environment is just as thoroughly organized as its organism *and is specific to it* (cf. Gibson, 1977). The relation of dual complementation also carries with it the idea that it is the overarching whole formed by the duals, that is the proper unit. Neither member of a dual pair is properly constrained without the other, or without the whole being defined by their closure. Although defined at a coarser grain than circular transitivity, dual complementation is no less a control principle. An organization that can be characterized as having this style of control is what we call a coalition; and we take a coalition to be the minimum sufficient organization to capture the intuitive notion of an ecosystem. A coalition is not a system-plus-context. It is the minimal system that carries its own context. Finally, a coalition is, for us, the minimal organization that can properly be said to have functional integrity. An organism, perhaps as a heterarchy, is not enough.

In conclusion, we doubt that any approach to the problem of degrees of freedom, or the problem of context-conditioned variability, will be adequate if treated as any style of organization less than a coalition.

ACKNOWLEDGMENTS

The writing of this paper was supported, in part, by Grant HD-01994 from the National Institute of Child Health and Human Development, and Grant RR⁻5596 from the National Institutes of Health, both awarded to the Haskins Laboratories. The authors wish to acknowledge Carol Fowler, Robert Remez, and James Todd for their contributions to the authors' appreciation of the problems approached by this paper.

REFERENCES

Aggashyan, R. V., Gurfinkel', V. S., & Fomin, S. V. Correlation and spectral analysis of fluctuations of the human body during standing. *Biophysics,* 1973, *18,* 1173–1177.

Aizerman, M. A., & Andreeva, F. A. Simple search mechanisms for control of skeletal muscles. *Automation and Remote Control,* 1968, *29,* 452–463.

Arbib, M. A. *The metaphorical brain: An introduction to cybernetics as artificial intelligence and brain theory.* New York: Wiley, 1972.

Asatryan, D. G., & Fel'dman, A. G. Functional tuning of the nervous system with control of movement or maintenance of a steady posture – 1. Mechanographic analysis of the work on the joint on execution of a postural task. *Biophysics,* 1965, *10,* 925–935.

Belen'kii, V. Ye., Gurfinkel', V. S., & Pal'tsev, Ye. I. Elements of control of voluntary movements. *Biophysics,* 1967, *12,* 154–161.

Bernstein, N. *The corrdination and regulation of movements.* Oxford: Pergamon Press, 1967.

Boylls, C. C. A theory of cerebellar function with applications to locomotion. II. The relation of anterior lobe climbing fiber function to locomotor behavior in the cat. *COINS Technical Report 76-1,* Department of Computer and Information Science, University of Massachusetts, 1975.

Chernov, V. I. Control over single muscles or a pair of muscle antagonists under conditions of precision search. *Automation and Remote Control,* 1968, *29,* 1090–1101.

Easton, T. A. On the normal use of reflexes. *American Scientist,* 1972, *60,* 591–599.

El'ner, A. N. Possibilities of correcting the urgent voluntary movements and the associated postural activity of human muscles. *Biophysics,* 1973, *18,* 966–971.

Engberg, I., & Lundberg, A. An electromyographic analysis of muscular activity in the hindlimb of the cat during unrestrained locomotion. *Acta Physiologica Scandinavia,* 1969, *75,* 614–630.

Eshkol, N., & Wachman, A. *Movement notation.* London: Weidenfeld and Nicholson, 1958.

Evarts, E. V., Bizzi, E., Burke, R. E., DeLong, M., & Thach, W. T. Central control of movement. *Neurosciences Research Program Bulletin,* 1971, *9,* No. 1.

Fel'dman, A. G. Functional tuning of the nervous system with control of movement or maintenance of a steady posture – III. Mechanographic analysis of the execution by man of the simplest motor tasks. *Biophysics,* 1966, *11,* 766–775.

Fomin, S. V., & Shtil'kind, T. I. The concept of equilibrium of systems having legs. *Biophysics,* 1972, *17,* 137–141.

Fowler, C. A., & Turvey, M. T. Skill acquisition: An event approach with special reference to searching for the optimum of a function of several variables. In G. Stelmach (Ed.), *Information processing in motor control and learning.* New York: Academic Press, in press.

Gel'fand, I. M., Gurfinkel', V. S., Tsetlin, M. L., & Shik, M. L. Some problems in the analysis of movements. In I. M. Gel'fand, V. S. Gurfinkel', S. V. Fomin, & M. L. Tsetlin (Eds.), *Models of the structural-functional organization of certain biological systems.* Cambridge, Mass.: MIT Press, 1971.

Gel'fand, I. M., & Tsetlin, M. L. Some methods of control for complex systems. *Russian Mathematical Surveys,* 1962, *17,* 95–116.

Gellhorn, E. The influence of alterations in posture of the limb on cortically induced movements. *Brain,* 1948, *71,* 26–33.

Gibson, J. J. Visually controlled locomotion and visual orientation in animals. *British Journal of Psychology,* 1958, *44,* 182–194.

Gibson, J. J. *The senses considered as perceptual systems.* Boston: Houghton Mifflin, 1966.

Gibson, J. J. The theory of affordances. In R. Shaw & J. Bransford (Eds.), *Perceiving, acting and knowing: Toward an ecological psychology.* Hillsdale, N.J.: Lawrence Erlbaum Associates, 1977.

Granit, R. *The basis of motor control.* New York: Academic Press, 1970.

Greene, P. H. Problems of organization of motor systems. In R. Rosen & F. M. Snell (Eds.), *Progress in theoretical biology* (vol. 2). New York: Academic Press, 1972.

Greene, P. H. Strategies for heterarchical control — an essay. I. A style of controlling complex systems. *International Journal of Man-Machine Studies,* in press. (a)

Greene, P. H. Strategies for heterarchical control — an essay. II. Theoretical exploration of a style of control. *International Journal of Man-Machine Studies,* in press. (b)

Grillner, S. Locomotion in vertebrates: Central mechanisms and reflex interaction. *Physiological Review,* 1975, *55,* 247–304.

Gurfinkel', V. S., & Kots, Ya. M., Pal'tsev, Ye. I., & Fel'dman, A. G. The compensation of respiratory disturbances of the erect posture of man as an example of the organization of interarticular interaction. In I. M. Gel'fand et al. (Eds.), *Models of the structural-functional organization of certain biological systems.* Cambridge, Mass.: MIT Press, 1971.

Gurfinkel', V. S., & Pal'tsev, Ye. I. Effect of the state of the segmental apparatus of the spinal cord on the execution of a simple motor reaction. *Biophysics,* 1965, *10,* 944–951.

Hubbard, A. W. Homokinetics: Muscular function in human movement. In W. R. Johnson (Ed.), *Science and medicine of exercise and sport.* New York: Harper, 1960.

Hubbard, A. W., & Seng, C. N. Visual movements of batters. *Research Quarterly,* 1954, *25,* 42–57.

Keele, S. W., & Summers, J. J. The structure of motor programs. In G. Stelmach (Ed.), *Motor Control: Issues and trends.* New York: Academic Press, 1976.

Kent, R. D., Carney, P. J., & Severeid, L. R. Velar movement and timing evaluation of a model for binary control. *Journal of Speech and Hearing,* 1974, *17,* 470–488.

Kent, R. D., & Netsell, R. Effects of stress contrasts on certain articulatory parameters. *Phonetica,* 1971, *24,* 23–44.

Kots, Ya. M., Krinskiy, V. I., Naydin, V. L., & Shik, M. L. The control of movements of the joints and kinesthetic afferentation. In I. M. Gel'fand, V. S. Gurfinkel', S. V. Fomin, & M. T. Tsetlin (Eds.), *Models of the structural-functional organization of certain biological systems.* Cambridge, Mass.: MIT Press, 1971.

Kots, Ya. M., & Syrovegin, A. V. Fixed set of variants of interaction of the muscles of two joints used in the execution of simple voluntary movements. *Biophysics,* 1966, *11,* 1212–1219.

Lee, D. N. Visual information during locomotion. In R. B. MacLeod & H. L. Pick, Jr. (Eds.), *Perception: Essays in honor of James J. Gibson.* Ithaca, N. Y.: Cornell University Press, 1974.

Lee, D. N. On the functions of vision. In H. L. Pick, Jr. & E. Saltzman (Eds.), *Modes of perceiving and processing of information.* Hillsdale, N.J.: Lawrence Erlbaum Associates, 1978.

Lee, D. N., & Aronson, E. Visual proprioceptive control of standing in human infants. *Perception & Psychophysics,* 1974, *15,* 529–532.

Lee, D. N., & Lishman, J. R. Visual proprioceptive control of stance. *Journal of Human Movement Studies,* 1975, *1,* 87–95.

Lisin, V. V., Frankstein, S. I., & Rechtmann, M. B. The influence of locomotion on flexor reflex of the hind limb in cat and man. *Experimental Neurology,* 1973, *38,* 180–183.

Litvintsev, A. I. Search activity of muscles in the presence of an artificial feedback loop enclosing several muscles simultaneously. *Automation and Remote Control,* 1968, *29,* 464–472.

Luria, A. R. *Higher cortical functions in man.* New York: Basic Books, 1966.

McCulloch, W. S. A heterarchy of values determined by the topology of nervous nets. *Bulletin of Mathematical Biophysics,* 1945, *7,* 89–93.

Megaw, E. D. Response factors and the psychological refractory period. Unpublished thesis, University of Birmingham, England, 1970.

Miller, G. A. The magical number seven, plus or minus two: Some limits on our capacity for processing information. *Psychological Review*, 1956, *63*, 81–97.

Minsky, M., & Papert, S. Artificial Intelligence. *Artificial Intelligence Memo, 252*. Artificial Intelligence Laboratory, MIT, Cambridge, Mass., 1972.

Orlovskii, G. N. The effect of different descending systems on flexor and extensor activity during locomotion. *Brain Research, 1972, 40,* 359–371.

Orlovskii, G. N., & Shik, M. L. Standard elements of cyclic movement. *Biophysics,* 1965, *10,* 935–944.

Paillard, J. The patterning of skilled movements. In J. Field, H. W. Magoun, & V. E. Hall (Eds.), *Handbook of physiology: Neurophysiology,* (vol. 3). Washington, D. C.: American Physiological Society, 1960.

Pal'tsev, Ye. I., & El'ner, A. M. Preparatory and compensatory period during voluntary movement in patients with involvement of the brain of different localization. *Biophysics, 1967, 12,* 161–168.

Pattee, H. H. The physical basis and origin of hierarchical control. In H. H. Pattee (Ed.), *Hierarchy theory: The challenge of complex systems.* New York: Braziller, 1973.

Roberts, T. D. M. *Neurophysiology of postural mechanisms.* New York: Plenum Press, 1967.

Schmidt, R. A. The schema as a solution to some persistent problems in motor learning theory. In G. Stelmach (Ed.), *Motor control: Issues and trends.* New York: Academic Press, 1976.

Shaw, R. E. Cognition, simulation and the problem of complexity. *Journal of Structural Learning.* 1971, *2,* 31–44.

Shaw, R. E., McIntyre, M., & Mace, W. The role of symmetry in event perception. In R. B. MacLeod and H. L. Pick, Jr. (Eds.), *Perception: Essays in Honor of James J. Gibson.* Ithaca, N. Y.: Cornell University Press, 1974.

Shaw, R. E., & McIntyre, M. Algoristic foundations to cognitive psychology. In W. Weimer and D. Palermo (Eds.), *Cognition and the symbolic processes.* Hillsdale, N. J.: Lawrence Erlbaum Associates, 1974.

Sivazlian, B. D., & Stanfel, L. E. *Optimization techniques in operations research.* Englewood Cliffs, N. J.: Prentice-Hall, 1975.

Smith, K. U., & Smith, W. H. *Perception and motion.* Philadelphia: W. G. Saunders, 1962.

Stelmach, G. (Ed.). *Motor control: Issues and trends.* New York: Academic Press, 1976.

Sutherland, N. S. Intelligent picture processing. Paper presented at Conference on the Evolution of the Nervous System and Behavior, Florida State University, Tallahassee, 1973.

Turvey, M. T. Preliminaries to a theory of action with reference to vision. In R. Shaw & J. Bransford (Eds.), *Perceiving, acting and knowing: Toward an ecological psychology.* Hillsdale, N. J.: Lawrence Erlbaum Associates, 1977.

Vince, M. A., & Welford, A. T. Time taken to change the speed of a response. *Nature,* 1967, *213,* 532–533.

von Neumann, J. *Theory of self-reproducing automata.* A. W. Burks (Ed.), Urbana, Ill.: University of Illinois Press, 1966.

Warren, R. The perception of egomotion. *Journal of Experimental Psychology: Human perception and performance,* 1976, *2,* 448–456.

Weiss, P. Self-differentiation of the basic pattern of coordination. *Comparative Psychology Monograph,* 1941, *17,* 21–96.

Wells, K. F. *Kinesiology.* Philadelphia: Saunders, 1961.

VI THEORIES AND MODELS

31 An Adaptive Module for Simple Judgment

Douglas Vickers
Department of Psychology
University of Adelaide
South Australia

ABSTRACT

A number of studies suggest that the observer in a two-category discrimination task reaches his decision by making a series of inspections of the sensory input, and then accumulating evidence independently for each alternative until he has achieved a criterion amount in favor of one. By postulating a third accumulator, which registers the sum of the evidence totals, minus their modulus, this process can also be applied to the main features of three-category tasks, judgments of sameness and difference, and signal detection. Besides describing response times and errors, the general decision module can also account for subjective confidence by supposing this to be determined by the difference (or average difference) between the evidence total for one response and the total(s) accumulated for the other(s).

In order to extend such an approach to account for adaptive responses to variations in the stimulus series, it has been customary to make use of plausible, but ad hoc, assumptions about the manipulation of the criterion amounts of evidence. The present paper attempts to overcome this limitation by suggesting a mechanism for the control of the primary decision process, in which the confidence associated with each response is compared with a preset target. By assuming that positive and negative deviations from the target for each response are accumulated independently by a secondary decision process exactly like the primary one, appropriate increases or reductions in the primary criterion levels can be initiated, based on a statistical evaluation of the performance of the primary process.

Computer simulations of this adaptive decision module show it to be a stable system, capable of responding appropriately to a wide variety of constraints in the range, distribution, and sequence of stimuli, and of successfully simulating human performance in several different judgmental tasks.

I. A GENERAL DECISION MODULE FOR RESPONSE
FREQUENCY AND TIME IN SIMPLE JUDGMENTS

A. An Accumulator Model for Two-Category Discrimination

One of the most elementary judgments we make is to decide which of two stimuli is the greater or lesser along some dimension, such as length or brightness. Since Jastrow (1888), it has been traditionally supposed that errors resulted from random disturbances in the sensory effect produced by a stimulus, and that, over time, the distribution of sensory effect should be approximately normal (Boring, 1917; Cartwright & Festinger, 1943; Cattell, 1893; Tanner & Swets, 1954; Thurstone, 1927a, 1927b). When the objective difference $(v - s)$ between a variable stimulus v and a standard s is near threshold, it can be assumed that the difference between the means $\overline{V}$ and $\overline{S}$ of the distributions of sensory effect is linearly related to $(v - s)$, and that their variances σ_V^2 and σ_S^2 are equal (Treisman & Watts, 1966).

According to Thurstone (1927a), fluctuations in sensory effect occurred from one trial to the next, and each judgment was a function of the "discriminal difference' $(V - S)$ on that trial. However, in order to account for the generally observed tradeoff between speed and accuracy, it has come to be generally assumed that fluctuations in $(V - S)$ occur from moment to moment within each trial, with a mean $(\overline{V - S}) = \overline{V} - \overline{S}$, and a standard deviation $\sigma_{(V-S)} = (\sigma_V^2 + \sigma_S^2)^{1/2}$ (Audley & Pike, 1965; Cartwright & Festinger, 1943; Crossman, 1955; Pike, 1973; Thomson, 1920). On a particular trial, the task for an observer is to decide whether the stream of $(V - S)$ differences, inspected at a steady rate, arises from the situation where v is objectively greater than s, or from its converse. In order to account for the fact that both errors and response times remain inversely related to $(v - s)$, even when this varies unpredictably from trial to trial, many theorists have supposed that the observer follows an 'optional-stopping' procedure of inspecting this stream until he has achieved a critical amount of evidence in favor of one alternative or the other (Audley, 1973; Pike, 1973).

There is a variety of decision rules that might be applied in this situation, as exemplified by the "runs" hypothesis of Audley (1960), the "random walk" models of Stone (1960), Edwards (1965), Laming (1968), and Link and Heath (1975), or the "counting" processes suggested by La Berge (1962) and McGill (1963). In order to account for the relation between the overall caution exercised by an observer and the relative times for correct and incorrect responses, Vickers (1970) proposed an *accumulator* model, in which the observer accumulates positive and negative $(V - S)$ differences separately until he attains a total k_g or k_l in favor of a response of the form "$V > S$" or "$V < S$," respectively. On the basis of detailed studies of changes in response time distributions, and an extensive review of the literature, this author has argued that the properties of an accumulator model match the empirical characteristics of discrimination performance more closely than those of alternative decision processes (Vickers, 1970, 1972a, 1972b; Vickers, Caudrey, & Willson, 1971).

Although this may be so, it remains true that most of the stochastic models give a reasonable first approximation to the data, and a number of writers have questioned whether further exercises in curve-fitting are profitable at this stage (e.g., Pike, 1968; Wilding, 1974). One alternative, suggested by Wilding (1974), is to examine effects of other variables on the pattern of results; another, implied by Rabbitt (1971), is to consider how these models might be adapted to account for performance in other related tasks. The strategy followed by the author, on which the organization of this chapter is based, is to consider how a model might be developed that would apply to a number of tasks, that would account for other aspects of performance besides response frequency and time, and that would be sensitive to the effects of other factors than those usually investigated. This procedure resembles a process of improving pattern recognition through feature testing over a wider sample of instances, rather than through greater precision in matching against a template.

B. Three-Category Decisions

One of the simplest modifications of the two-category discrimination task occurs when an *intermediate* response is allowed to indicate that the stimuli appear equal (Guilford, 1954; Thurstone, 1948; Woodworth & Schlosberg, 1954). Although a number of models have been proposed to account for the observed pattern of response frequencies (e.g., Greenberg, 1965; Olson & Ogilvie, 1972; Treisman & Watts, 1966; Urban, 1910), none of these is designed to explain the pattern of response times. However, two ways in which this might be done are outlined by Pike (1973). Both assume that an observer establishes lower and upper cutoffs x_l and x_g on the dimension of $(V - S)$ differences. The first *latency function* hypothesis assumes that observations falling below x_l give rise to $V < S$ responses, those above x_g to $V > S$ responses, and those between x_l and x_g to judgments of the form $V = S$. Variations in response time are explained by supposing that the closer an observation is to a particular cutoff, the longer it takes to classify. The second *multiple observations* model proposes that observations in each category are counted until a critical total r_l, r_g, or r_e is reached, whereupon the observer responds $V < S$, $V > S$, or $V = S$, respectively. As argued by Vickers (1975), an immediate disadvantage of these proposals is their complexity. In addition to the "sensory bias," determined by x_l and x_g, the multiple observations model postulates a "decision bias," reflected in values of r_l, r_g, and r_e. A similar complexity characterizes the latency function model, which leaves the classification process unspecified, and must therefore presuppose particular forms of the latency function.

A simpler alternative, also considered by Vickers (1975), is provided by a *counter and clock* process, based on the notion of a "neural clock" proposed by McGill (1963), Sekuler (1965), Bindra, Williams, and Wise (1965), and Nickerson (1969). A model of this kind can be realized by using any one of a variety of optional-stopping processes to control the two extreme responses, with the added condition that, if a response has not eventuated by a preset deadline, a decision is made that $V = S$. Unfortunately, such a model predicts that the mean time taken to make an intermediate response should always be longer than that for an extreme response, which is contradicted by the finding that the relation between these times appears to depend upon the relative bias towards the intermediate response (Carlson, Driver, & Preston, 1934; Cartwright, 1941; Fernberger, Glass, Hoffman & Willig, 1934; Kellogg, 1931). Even when the model is complicated by the supposition of a "noisy" clock, the pattern of times for intermediate responses differs from that of the empirical data (Vickers, 1975); in addition, a number of findings suggest that observers are incapable of deadline responding, and must accumulate a predetermined amount of evidence before reaching a decision (Vickers, Nettelbeck, and Willson, 1972).

In the light of these difficulties, Vickers (1975) suggested a model in which evidence for each response is accumulated separately in three accumulators (one for each alternative), with the amount in each accumulator being zero at the start of a trial. On each trial the observer makes a series of inspections, at a steady rate, of the momentary $(V - S)$ differences. The amount of each positive difference is added to a total t_g, and that of each negative difference (after a reversal of sign) is added to a separate total t_l. Meanwhile, an inverse function of each difference (ignoring its sign) is added to a third total t_e. As soon as either t_g, t_l, or t_e reaches or exceeds a corresponding critical amount k_g, k_l, or k_e, a response is made of the form $V > S$, $V < S$, or $V = S$, respectively. This model gave a good account of the pattern of response times and frequencies obtained by Vickers (1975) in a series of four experiments.

However, although this model yielded predictions that were consistent with the data, it too suffers from some disadvantages. In the first place, the choice of inverting function remains undesirably arbitrary. Secondly, even if a long series of inspected differences are of the same sign, it adds as much evidence to the intermediate accumulator as when the differences are equally balanced between positive and negative; this seems implausibly inefficient. Finally, the quantities accumulated in the various accumulators are not commensurate, and this, as will become clear later, poses some difficulty for further development of the model.

One solution, which avoids these difficulties, and which also appears to be consistent with the available data, is to suppose that the evidence tested in the intermediate accumulator is given by the sum of the evidence totals in the two extreme accumulators, minus their modulus. Where t_g represents the total of positive differences accumulated (i.e., the evidence favoring a response of the form $V > S$), and t_l represents the total of negative differences (the evidence

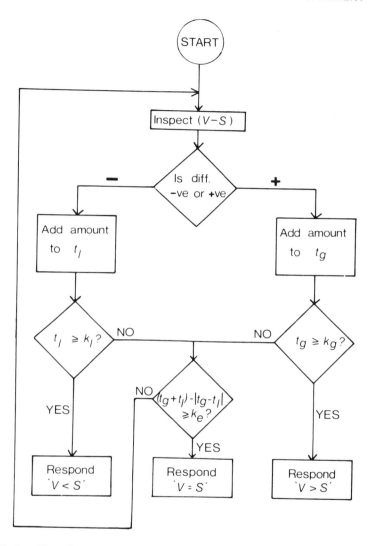

FIG. 1.   Flow diagram of revised accumulator model of three-category judgment.

favoring the response $V < S$), then this model proposes that a response is made when $t_g \geq k_l$ or $[(t_g + t_l) - |t_g - t_l|] \geq k_e$, where k_g, k_l, and k_e are predetermined critical amounts of evidence for a response of the form $V > S$, $V < S$, or $V = S$, respectively. A flow diagram of the proposed process is shown in Fig. 1. As can be seen from the diagram, each inspected difference will add an amount to either t_g or t_l, but not to both at the same time. On the other hand, the value

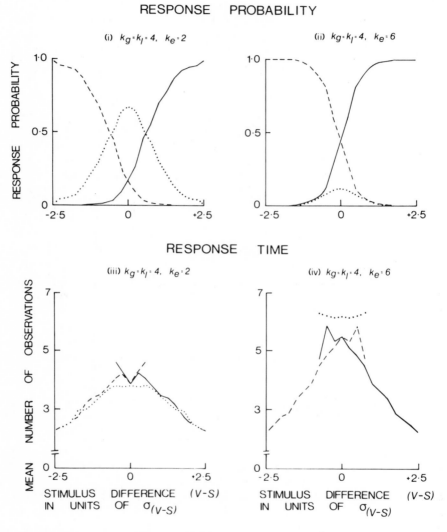

RESPONSE   PROBABILITY

(i) $k_g = k_l = 4$, $k_e = 2$

(ii) $k_g = k_l = 4$, $k_e = 6$

RESPONSE   TIME

(iii) $k_g = k_l = 4$, $k_e = 2$

(iv) $k_g = k_l = 4$, $k_e = 6$

STIMULUS   DIFFERENCE   (V-S)
IN   UNITS   OF $\sigma_{(V-S)}$

STIMULUS   DIFFERENCE   (V-S)
IN   UNITS   OF $\sigma_{(V-S)}$

FIG. 2.   Patterns of response probabilities and times (i.e., mean number of $V - S$ differences inspected), as predicted by the revised accumulator model of three-category judgment for different values of the intermediate criterion k_e and the extreme criteria $k_g = k_l$. The solid line represents probabilities and times for responses of the form $V > S$, dashed lines those for $V < S$, and dotted curves those for $V = S$.

of $[(t_g + t_l) - |t_g - t_l|]$ will increase whenever the effect of an inspected differ-
ence is to reduce the value of $|t_g - t_l|$, and will remain stationary whenever $|t_g - t_l|$ is increased.

Figure 2 shows some examples of the general pattern of response probabilites
and times predicted by a computer simulation of 4000 trials of the proposed
process, operating on a normal distribution of $(V - S)$ differences, with mean
$\overline{(V - S)}$, and standard deviation $\sigma_{(V-S)}$. Twenty-one mean values of this distribution, varying from -2.5 to 2.5 $\sigma_{(V-S)}$, were presented in random order to
the process, following the method of constant stimuli. In Fig. 2, parts i and iii
exemplify the situation in which there is a relatively low value for the intermediate criterion k_e, and a consequent bias in favor of the "equals" response.
In contrast, parts ii and iv give typical predictions where there is a bias against
the intermediate response.

Comparison with the data obtained by Kellogg (1931) and Vickers (1975)
shows that the model predicts appropriately shaped functions relating response
frequency and time to stimulus difference. In particular, the relative times predicted by the model for extreme and intermediate responses depend upon the
bias toward making intermediate judgments, as evidenced by the data of Kellogg
(1931), Carlson et al. (1934), Fernberger et al. (1934), Cartwright (1941), and
Vickers (1975). However, given the current paucity of data, any complete
evaluation of the model is impossible, and would in any case be beyond the
scope of the present chapter. What seems significant at this stage is that, of all
the optional-stopping processes considered for two-category discrimination, only
an accumulator process in which evidence for each alternative is simply totalled
appears to be capable of such a natural and satisfactory extension to the three-
category situation. The question arises whether this advantage continues to hold
for other related judgments.

C. Judgments of Sameness and Difference

A judgment with close affinities to the three-category task is involved in deciding
whether two stimuli are the same or different. Where stimuli differ along one dimension, the three-category task can be converted into a same-different one by
asking the observer to respond "different" whenever the variable stimulus appears
either greater or less than the standard, and to respond "same" when the two
stimuli appear to be equal. The simplest way of adapting the three-category
model just outlined to a same-different task is to relabel its responses in a similar
way, i.e. to attach the response "same" to the decision outcome $V = S$, and the
response "different" to both the outcomes $V > S$ and $V < S$.

Figure 3 gives some examples of the pattern of predictions generated for this
model by a computer simulation of 4000 trials of the proposed process, operating
on a normal distribution of $V - S$ differences, with mean $\overline{V - S}$, and standard
deviation $\sigma_{(V-S)}$. As with the three-category version, 21 mean values of this
distribution, varying from -2.5 to 2.5 $\sigma_{(V-S)}$, were presented in random order

to the hypothesized process. Figure 3, parts i and iii again exemplify the situation in which the criterion k_e is relatively low, and there is a bias in favor of a "same" response. Meanwhile, parts ii and iv show the general pattern of probabilities and times when k_e is set higher, and there is a consequent bias against the "same" judgment.

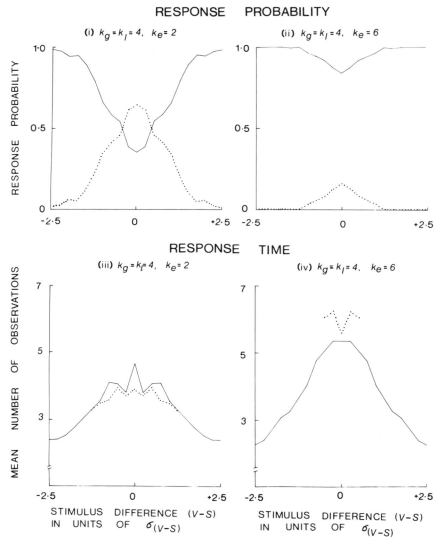

FIG. 3. Patterns of response probabilities and times (i.e., mean number of $V - S$ differences inspected), as predicted by an accumulator model of same-different judgment for different values of the intermediate (same) criterion k_e and the extreme (different) criteria $k_g = k_l$. The solid line represents probabilities and times for "different" responses, and the dotted curve those for "same" judgments.

The predictions shown in Fig. 3 have obviously close relationships to those for the three-category version shown in Fig. 2. As with three-category decisions, the proposed model predicts that the relative times to make "same" and "different" judgments of unidimensional stimuli should depend upon the relative bias towards "same" responses, and what evidence there is seems consistent with this. Times for "same" judgments may be longer than those for all "different" responses (Bindra et al., 1965; Nickerson, 1969), or intermediate between those for "different" judgments of large stimulus differences and those for small differences (Bindra, Donderi, & Nishisato, 1968). In each of two experiments, Nickerson (1971) found that the times for correct "same" responses by one of his two observers were longer than those for her correct "different" responses at all stimulus differences. On the other hand, times for correct "same" responses by the other observer, who showed a greater relative tendency to make incorrect "same" responses, were intermediate between those for correct "different" responses to large and to small stimulus differences. Although the evidence is hardly abundant, the consistency of the pattern would seem to justify an attempt to develop the model further.

D. Signal Detection

A further task, which closely resembles the same-different judgment, is that of signal detection. The similarity is illustrated by two experiments by Bindra et al. (1965), in which observers were required to decide whether pairs of successively presented tones were of the same or different pitch. In the first experiment one response key was labeled "same" and the other "different," whereas in the second one key was labeled "yes" and the other "no," and observers were asked to press the appropriate key in answer either to the question, "Are the tones the same, yes or no?" or "Are the tones different, yes or no?" Most, if not all experiments on signal detection can be similarly construed as an attempt by the observer to decide whether some target stimulus is the same as, or different than, a background stimulus. Empirical support for this view has been obtained by Ryder, Pike, & Dalgleish (1974), who also present evidence from a number of other studies suggesting that observers in detection tasks appear to base their decisions on some difference between the quantity sampled in the observation interval and that sampled from some background activity, rather than solely on the sensory effect produced by the stimulus presented in the observation interval. The main distinguishing feature of the signal detection paradigm appears to be that, unlike same-different tasks, which typically present both increments and decrements, the former usually employs increments only. To apply the proposed accumulator model to a situation of this kind, it is necessary only to attach a response of the form "signal" to the decision $V > S$ (where V represents the perceived target, and S the perceived background stimulus), and another of the form "nonsignal" to each of the other two logically possible decision outcomes.

Examples of the patterns of response probabilities and times predicted by an accumulator model of signal detection are shown in Fig. 4. The patterns are

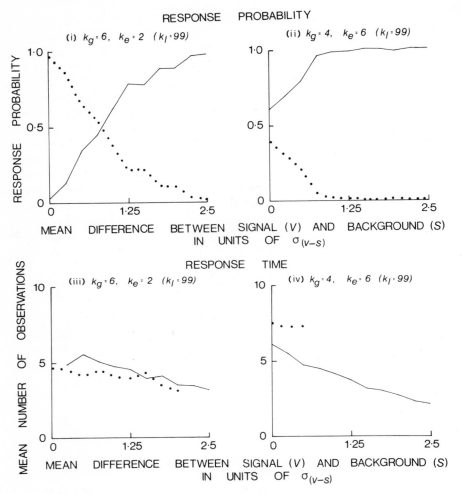

FIG. 4. Patterns of response probabilities and times (i.e., mean number of $V - S$ differences inspected), as predicted by an accumulator model of signal detection, for different values of the intermediate (nonsignal) criterion k_e and the extreme (signal) criterion k_g. (Since decrements were not used, the other extreme criterion has been given an arbitrary high value of $k_l = 99$). Data for "signal response are represented by solid lines, and those for "nonsignal" by dotted curves.

based on a computer simulation of 2000 trials of the proposed process, again operating on a normal distribution of $V - S$ differences, with mean $\overline{V - S}$ and standard deviation $\sigma_{(V-S)}$. In this instance, 11 values of the mean, varying from 0 up to 2.5 $\sigma_{(V-S)}$ were presented in random order to the hypothesized process. Since negative values of $\overline{V - S}$ were not used, the criterion k_l for the $V < S$ outcome has been set to an arbitrary high value of 99, thereby reducing the probability of a $V < S$ outcome virtually to zero. Figure 4, parts i and iii give typical predictions where the criterion k_e is low, and there is a consequent bias in favor of the "nonsignal" response. Conversely, parts ii and iv show typical patterns where the value of k_e is high, and there is a bias against the "nonsignal" response. (The fact that "noise" times appear to peter out in part iv is due to there being an insufficient number of "noise" responses (less than 5) for values of $\overline{V-S}$ greater than 0.5). As would be expected, the model exhibits a similar relation between the relative times for "signal" and "nonsignal" responses, and the bias towards detecting a signal to that predicted above for the two main classes of response (i.e., extreme and intermediate) in three-category tasks, as well as in judgments of sameness and difference.

Although no published data are known with which these predictions may be directly compared, Fig. 5 shows response frequencies and mean times for two observers from an unpublished study by the author and M. Johnson. In this experiment, six observers were required to indicate on each trial whether the average height of an array of vertical line segments of randomly varying length, randomly positioned within a central area, had been slightly increased (i.e., whether or not a signal had been added to the noise). Contrary to the predictions of a simple clock process, the mean time for correct rejections was faster than that for false alarms, and was intermediate between the time for hits at small signal magnitudes (differences between the average height of the central lines v and that of the surrounding lines s) and that for large signal magnitudes. Evidence that the relative time for correct rejections and hits depends on the bias towards making 'signal' or 'nonsignal' responses is provided by the finding (shown in Fig. 5, parts i and iii) that the observer who showed the strongest bias towards making "nonsignal" responses (207 "signal" and 293 "nonsignal" responses over an objective series of 250 signal and 250 nonsignal trials) took less time to make "nonsignal" than "signal" responses at each of the three signal magnitudes for which data were available for comparison. In contrast, the observer who displayed least bias towards making "nonsignal" responses (325 "signal," as opposed to 175 "nonsignal" responses) took longer to make "nonsignal" than "signal" responses (as shown in Fig. 5, parts ii and iv).

Results similar to these have been obtained by Pike and Ryder (1973) using near-threshold auditory signals. In one experiment, in which signals occurred with a probability of only 0.25, and in which there is likely to have been a bias, similar to that of observer 1 in Fig. 5, parts i and iii, towards making "nonsignal" responses, false alarms took less time than hits, and more time than correct rejections. In a second experiment, in which signal and nonsignal events were equiprobable, and bias towards signal events stronger (though perhaps not quite as strong as that of observer 6 in Fig. 5, parts ii and iv), false alarms took longer than hits, and about the same time as correct rejections.

It would be clearly desirable to confirm this pattern, and instructive to linger on some inviting comparisons between data and predictions from the model about effects of varying signal intensity [with which Grice (1968) and Murray (1970) have been concerned]. However, perhaps sufficient evidence has been

RESPONSE PROBABILITY

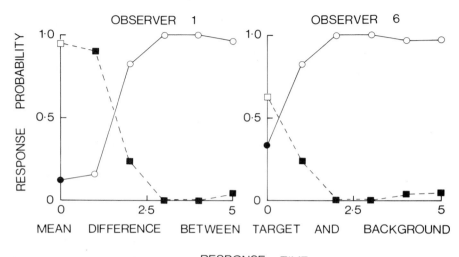

RESPONSE TIME

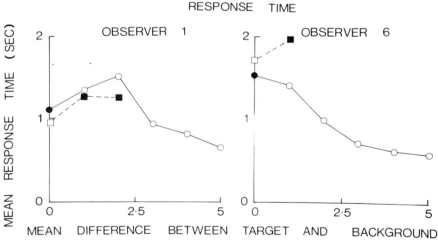

FIG. 5. Empirical response probabilities and times from an unpublished experiment by Vickers and Johnson. Squares joined by broken lines denote "nonsignal" responses, and circles joined by solid lines represent "signal" responses. Empty symbols indicate responses made correctly, and filled symbols those made incorrectly. Observer 1 showed the greatest relative bias towards making "nonsignal" responses, and observer 6 showed the smallest relative bias in that direction. (The mean difference between the target and the background line segments is expressed in terms of the smallest unit increments on the Tektronix 611 display on which they were generated. Photographed stimuli were then projected so that each display unit corresponded to a difference of about 1 mm, and were viewed from a distance of about 2 m).

presented to indicate that the extension of the accumulator model of two-category judgment to three-category decisions, judgments of sameness and difference, and signal detection possesses considerable explanatory potential. There seem at present to be good grounds for believing that these, and other, simple judgments may all be mediated by a single decision mechanism, which can be applied to different tasks by suppressing one or more responses, or by varying the attachment of responses to decision outcomes. Such a mechanism would have obvious usefulness as *a general purpose decision module*, capable of performing the basic computations for a more complex information-processing network. Before pursuing this possibility, however, it is pertinent to ask whether this general decision module can account for the behavior of other response variables, besides time and frequency.

II.   CONFIDENCE IN SIMPLE JUDGMENTS

Among the response variables so far left out of account, that of reported confidence has some practical interest, as well as carrying a considerable theoretical burden in applications of the theory of signal detection outlined by Green and Swets (1966). However, the convenience, stability, and orderliness of the confidence measure appears to have blunted curiosity concerning possible underlying mechanisms. The only hypothesis, directly applicable to optional-stopping mechanisms of the kind suggested above for simple judgments, appears to be that of Audley (1960), who suggests that confidence is an inverse function of the number of observations taken before reaching a decision.

This hypothesis gives a good account of the direct relation between stimulus difference and confidence, reported by Garrett (1922), Johnson (1939), Festinger (1943), and Pierrel and Murray (1963), and the inverse relation between response time and confidence, found by Henmon (1911), Seward (1928), Volkmann (1934), Pierrel and Murray (1963), Audley (1964), Katz (1970), and Emmerich, Gray, Watson, and Tanis (1972). Unfortunately, although confidence appears to be an inverse function of the number of observations taken by an observer to reach a final decision concerning the sensory input, the opposite relation appears to hold when confidence is recorded after the opportunity for taking further observations has been terminated independently of the observer. For example, Irwin, Smith, and Mayfield (1956) found that, when observers were shown different numbers of cards, each with a randomly varying positive or negative number printed on it, and were asked to judge whether the mean of the total pack was greater or less than zero, mean confidence ratings were greater after 20 cards had been inspected than after only 10.

Vickers (1978) has argued that the important difference between the two situations is that, when observations are taken until a critical amount has been attained, then a decision will require few observations only when most of the evidence accumulates in favor of one response, with the result that there is a large discrepancy between the totals t_g and t_l at the moment of decision, while a decision will require many observations only when t_g and t_l accumulate at more similar rates, so that the discrepancy between them at the moment of decision is small. In contrast, a comparison of the difference between t_g and t_l after arbitrarily different numbers of observations implies nothing about the statistical quality of the observations. If t_g is construed as the evidence for a response of the form $V > S$, and t_l as the evidence for the converse $V < S$, then, according to Vickers (1972a, 1978), a neat resolution of the conflicting results can be achieved in the two-category case by supposing that subjective confidence is determined by the *balance of evidence*, i.e.,the difference between t_g and t_l. Thus confidence in a response of the form $V > S$ would be determined by the difference $(t_g - t_l)$, which, at the moment a decision is reached, would be equivalent to $(k_g - t_l)$. Conversely, confidence in a response of the form $V < S$ would be determined by the difference $(t_l - t_g)$. Where there are three responses, the confidence in any one alternative, rather than the other two, may be supposed to be determined by the average of the two differences between the evidence total for that response and the total for each of the two alternatives.

The hypothesis that subjective confidence in simple judgments is a linear function of the difference(s) between the amounts of evidence accumulated in favor of the various response alternatives has a number of interesting implications, which are presented in detail by Vickers (1978). Unfortunately, it is not within the scope of the present chapter to illustrate the patterns of confidence measures predicted for each task, which, in any case, frequently outrun the experimental evidence needed to evaluate them. What seems important at present is that the *balance of evidence* hypothesis can be extended beyond two-category discriminations, with the result that the general decision module outlined in the first section becomes capable of providing a closely integrated account of response frequency, time, and confidence in a number of simple judgments. We may now turn to consider what other *independent* variables might be accounted for by this approach.

III.   THE PROBLEM OF ADAPTATION

The general decision model outlined so far appears to have considerable flexibility, scope, and economy. As it stands, however, it remains impossible to account for a variety of adaptive responses to changes in the range, distribution, or sequence of stimulus differences without supposing that the observer manipulates the values of k_g, k_l, or k_e according to some plausible but *ad hoc* hypothesis. For example, if a stimulus difference of size m were embedded within a series of very small differences, we should in general expect an observer to make a slower, more careful judgment of m than if it were embedded in a series of very large differences, and we should explain this by arguing that the observer may raise the value of k when the task becomes more difficult.

One strategy for explaining such changes in performance is to suppose that there is some internal level, standard, or reference variable that the process is designed to maintain (Jones, 1973; Kalmus, 1966; Milsum, 1966; McFarland, 1971). Since variations in instructions and task difficulty lead to large, orderly variations in response time and in the proportion of errors made, but appear to have little effect on confidence (Festinger, 1943; Garrett, 1922; Johnson, 1939), it seems reasonable to suggest that an observer may try to make judgments with *on average* a certain *target level of confidence,* although he cannot guarantee this for any particular judgment. The negative feedback for a stable control system can be generated by subtracting the target level of confidence from the actual level each time a response is made, with positive discrepancies giving rise to reductions in criterion level, and any negative mismatch to an increase. The hypothesis that confidence functions as a reference variable for the correction and control of performance has some resemblance to the view that a major factor governing the behavior and development of higher animals is the achievement and maintenance of a certain level of competence in their interactions with the environment (Conolly & Bruner, 1974; White, 1959).

In order that only established trends in the stimulus sequence should reliably produce a corrective adjustment, the most economical hypothesis seems to be that amounts of "overconfidence" and "underconfidence" should be accumulated (in exactly the same way as the original positive and negative stimulus differences) until a preset amount K has been attained. For the present, there seems to be no reason to suppose that K is variable (although different observers may operate with different values of K). The main effect of K is to determine the average frequency of adjustments by specifying the amount of evidence required.

A further detail concerns the amounts by which k_g and k_l should be increased or decreased. Since we should expect observers to have some awareness of the abruptness of any change in the sequence of stimuli, and to react accordingly, it may be supposed that a measure of "confidence in the adjustment" is used to determine the amount of each correction. That is, the observer increases or decreases the primary criterion by an amount proportional to the difference between the totals accumulated in the pair of control accumulators associated with that criterion. Like K, the coefficient x, which determines the proportionality of each adjustment, may be supposed to remain quite stable, although varying from one observer to another. Its main effect appears to be analogous to that of the gearing in a physical control system.

Figure 6 shows a simple way of embodying these considerations in a control system capable of regulating the behavior of an accumulator process for two-category discrimination. It consists of an additional two-category accumulator process attached to each of the responses by the primary decision process, and operating independently. Values of target confidence for each response may be

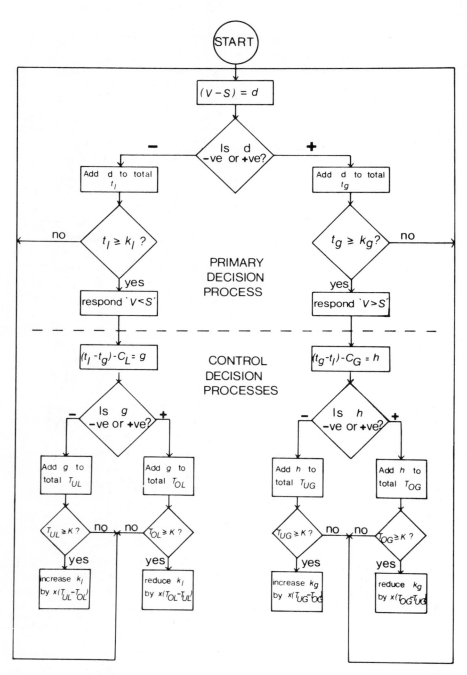

FIG. 6

614

thought of as susceptible to change by experimental instructions, by manipulation of some payoff matrix, by other motivational determinants, or perhaps by other control processes. The model can be extended to deal with three-category decisions, same-different judgments, or signal detection simply by adding a third control accumulator process for the intermediate response, into which is fed each positive or negative discrepancy between the target level and the appropriate expression for confidence in the intermediate response.

Although limitations of space preclude any attempt to characterize its behavior, it appears from extensive simulation that this adaptive model constitutes a stable control system, capable of responding to a number of constraints in the stimulus sequence, including variations in the range of stimulus differences, the distribution of differences, the *a priori* probabilities of alternative responses, and the sequence in which stimuli are presented. A full treatment of these properties is given by Vickers (1978), and shows the general adaptive module to be an explanatory mechanism of considerable power. Although it remains mathematically intractable, the process is conceptually simple, and its behavior is not difficult to simulate on a digital computer. It seems eminently capable of a neurophysiological realization, embodying only the well-established properties of excitation, inhibition, temporal summation, and threshold discharge. Because of its iterative, modular nature, there seem to be no obvious limits to its use in more complex information-processing configurations.

Meanwhile, the notion that confidence functions as a reference variable for the control of performance remains to be explored. If it does, it seems likely that this will be in conjunction with, or under the control of, other reference variables. For example, the possibility that expectation may fulfil a similar role appears to be implied by the finding that the relation between the local and the cumulative probability of a response is important in an observer's adjustment to changes in the *a priori* probability of that response, becoming inoperative once that probability has stabilized (Vickers, Leary, & Barnes, 1977). Just as liver cells regulate a large variety of physiological processes, while a single function, such as respiration, may in turn be controlled by a number of different systems, so we may expect to find a similar complexity in the control of information processing. Despite this potential complexity, however, the behavior of higher level control systems may well turn out to show more constancy and generality

---

FIG. 6.   Flow diagram of an adaptive accumulator model of two-category discrimination. The primary decision process, situated above the broken line, accumulates positive and negative ($V - S$) differences separately until the total t_g or t_l reaches or exceeds a criterion amount k_g or k_l, whereupon a response is triggered of the form $V > S$ or $V < S$, respectively. Whenever a primary decision is reached, its associated confidence [$(t_l - t_g)$ or $(t_g - t_l)$] is compared with its corresponding target level C_L or C_G. For each primary response, positive and negative discrepancies from target are then accumulated separately until a criterion amount of overconfidence or underconfidence is reached, whereupon the primary criterion levels are reduced or increased, respectively.

than the systems regulated by them, and to be more useful for the characterization and understanding of changes and individual differences in human performance.

ACKNOWLEDGMENTS

I should like to express my gratitude to R. J. Willson and P. Barnes for carrying out the extensive programming required for the simulation of the adaptive process. The work was supported by a grant (A67/16419) from the Australian Research Grants Committee.

REFERENCES

Audley, R. J. A stochastic model for individual choice behaviour. *Psychological Review,* 1960, *67,* 1–15.

Audley, R. J. Decision-making. *British Medical Bulletin,* 1964, *20,* 27–31.

Audley, R. J. Some observations on theories of choice reaction time: Tutorial review. In S. Kornblum (Ed.), *Attention and performance IV.* New York: Academic Press, 1973.

Audley, R. J., & Pike, A. R. Some alternative stochastic models of choice. *British Journal of Mathematical and Statistical Psychology,* 1965, *18,* 207–225.

Bindra, D., Williams, J. A., & Wise, J. S. Judgments of sameness and difference: Experiments on decision time. *Science,* 1965, *150,* 1625–1627.

Bindra, D., Donderi, D. C., & Nishisato, S. Decision latencies of "same" and "different" judgments. *Perception and Psychophysics,* 1968, *3,* 121–130.

Boring, E. G. A chart of the psychometric function. *American Journal of Psychology,* 1917, *28,* 465–470.

Carlson, W. R., Driver, R. C., & Preston, M. G. Judgment times for the method of constant stimuli. *Journal of Experimental Psychology,* 1934, *17,* 113–118.

Cartwright, D. Relation of decision-time to the categories of response. *American Journal of Psychology,* 1941, *54,* 174–196.

Cartwright, D., & Festinger, L. A. A quantitative theory of decision. *Psychological Review,* 1943, *50,* 595–621.

Cattell, J. M. On errors of observation. *American Journal of Psychology,* 1893, *5,* 285–293.

Conolly, K. J., & Bruner, J. S. *The growth of competence.* London: Academic Press, 1974.

Crossman, E. R. F. W. The measurement of discriminability. *Quarterly Journal of Experimental Psychology,* 1955, *7,* 176–195.

Edwards, W. Optimal strategies for seeking information: Models for statistics, choice reaction times, and human information processing. *Journal of Mathematical Psychology,* 1965, *2,* 312–329.

Emmerich, D. S., Gray, J. L., Watson, C. S., & Tanis, D. C. Response latency, confidence and ROCs in auditory signal detection. *Perception and Psychophysics,* 1972, *11,* 65–72.

Fernberger, S. W., Glass, E., Hoffman, I., & Willig, M. Judgment times of different psychological categories. *Journal of Experimental Psychology,* 1934, *17,* 286–293.

Festinger, L. Studies in decision: I. Decision-time, relative frequency of judgment, and subjective confidence as related to physical stimulus difference. *Journal of Experimental Psychology,* 1943, *32,* 291–306.

Garrett, H. E. A study of the relation of accuracy to speed. *Archives of Psychology,* 1922, *56,* 1–105.

Green, D. M., & Swets, J. A. *Signal detection theory and psychophysics.* New York: Wiley, 1966.

Greenberg, M. G. A modification of Thurstone's law of comparative judgment to accommodate a judgment category of "equal" or no difference. *Psychological Bulletin*, 1965, *64*, 108–112.

Grice, G. R. Stimulus intensity and response evocation. *Psychological Review*, 1968, *75*, 359–373.

Guilford, J. P. *Psychometric methods* (2nd ed.). New York: McGraw-Hill, 1936/1954.

Henmon, V. A. C. The relation of the time of a judgment to its accuracy. *Psychological Review*, 1911, *18*, 186–201.

Irwin, F. W., Smith, W. A. S., & Mayfield, J. F. Tests of two theories of decision in an "expanded judgment" situation. *Journal of Experimental Psychology*, 1956, *51*, 261–268.

Jastrow, J. A. A critique of psycho-physic methods. *American Journal of Psychology*, 1888, *1*, 271–309.

Johnson, D. M. Confidence and speed in the two-category judgment. *Archives of Psychology*, 1939, *34*, 1–53.

Jones, R. W. *Principles of biological regulation: An introduction to feedback systems*. New York: Academic Press, 1973.

Kalmus, H. *Regulation and control in living systems*. London: Wiley, 1966.

Katz, L. A comparison of type II operating characteristics derived from confidence ratings and from latencies. *Perception and Psychophysics*, 1970, *8*, 65–88.

Kellogg, W. N. Time of judgment in psychometric measures. *American Journal of Psychology*, 1931, *43*, 65–86.

La Berge, D. A recruitment theory of simple behavior. *Psychometrika*, 1962, *27*, 375–396.

Laming, D. R. J. *Information theory of choice-reaction times*. London: Academic Press, 1968.

Link, S. W., & Heath, R. A. A sequential theory of psychological discrimination. *Psychometrika*, 1975, *40*, 77–105.

McFarland, D. J. *Feedback mechanisms in animal behaviour*. London: Academic Press, 1971.

McGill, W. J. Stochastic latency mechanisms. In R. D. Luce, R. R. Bush, & E. Galanter (Eds.), *Handbook of mathematical psychology* (Vol. 1). New York: Wiley, 1963.

Milsum, J. H. *Biological control systems analysis*. New York: McGraw-Hill, 1966.

Murray, H. G. Stimulus intensity and reaction time: Evaluation of a decision theory model. *Journal of Experimental Psychology*, 1970, *84*, 383–391.

Nickerson, R. S. "Same-different" response times: A model and a preliminary test. In W. G. Koster (Ed.), *Attention and performance II. Acta Psychologica*, 1969, *30*, 257–275.

Nickerson, R. S. "Same-different" response times: A further test of a "counter and clock" model. *Acta Psychologica*, 1971, *35*, 112–127.

Olson, C. L., & Ogilvie, J. C. The method of constant stimuli with two or more categories of response. *Journal of Mathematical Psychology*, 1972, *9*, 320–338.

Pierrel, R., & Murray, C. S. Some relationships between comparative judgment confidence and decision-time in weight lifting. *American Journal of Psychology*, 1963, *76*, 28–38.

Pike, A. R. Latency and relative frequency of response in psychophysical discrimination. *British Journal of Mathematical and Statistical Psychology*, 1968, *21*, 161–182.

Pike, R. Response latency models for signal detection. *Psychological Review*, 1973, *80*, 53–68.

Pike, R., & Ryder, P. Response latencies in the yes/no detection task: An assessment of two basic models. *Perception and Psychophysics*, 1973, *13*, 224–232.

Rabbitt, P. M. A. Times for the analysis of stimuli and for the selection of responses. In A. Summerfield (Ed.), *Cognitive psychology. British Medical Bulletin*, 1971, *27*, 259–265.

Ryder, P., & Pike, R., & Dalgleish, L. What is the Signal in signal detection? *Perception and Psychophysics,* 1974, *15,* 479–482.

Sekuler, R. W. Signal detection, choice response times, and visual backward masking. *Canadian Journal of Psychology,* 1965, *19,* 118–132.

Seward, G. H. Recognition time as a measure of confidence. *Archives of Psychology,* 1928, n° 99, pp. 59.

Stone, M. Models for reaction time. *Psychometrika,* 1960, *25,* 251–260.

Tanner, W. P., & Swets, J. A. A decision-making theory of visual detection. *Psychological Review,* 1954, *61,* 401–409.

Thomson, G. H. A new point of view in the interpretation of threshold measurements in psychophysics. *Psychological Review,* 1920, *27,* 300–307.

Thurstone, L. L. Psychophysical analysis. *American Journal of Psychology,* 1927, *38,* 368–389.   (a)

Thurstone, L. L. A law of comparative judgment. *Psychological Review,* 1927, *34,* 273–286.   (b)

Thurstone, L. L. Psychophysical methods. In T. G. Andrews (Ed.), *Methods of psychology.* New York: Wiley, 1948.

Triesman, M., & Watts, T. R. Relation between signal detectability theory and the traditional procedures for measuring sensory thresholds: Estimating d' from results given by the method of constant stimuli. *Psychological Bulletin,* 1966, *66,* 438–454.

Urban, F. M. The method of constant stimuli and its generalizations. *Psychological Review,* 1910, *17,* 229–259.

Vickers, D. Evidence for an accumulator model of psychophysical discrimination. In A. T. Welford & L. Houssiadas (Eds.), *Current problems in perception. Ergonomics,* 1970, *13,* 37–58.

Vickers, D. Some general features of perceptual discrimination. In E. L. Asmussen (Ed.), *Psychological Aspects of Driver Behavior.* Institute for Road Safety Research, S.W.O.V., Voorburg, The Netherlands, 1972.   (a)

Vickers, D. Decision processes in perceptual organisation. In J. F. O'Callaghan (Ed.), *Pictorial organisation and shape.* Division of Computing Research, C.S.I.R.O., Canberra, A.C.T., 1972.   (b)

Vickers, D. Where Angell feared to tread: Response time and frequency in three-category discrimination. In P. M. A. Rabbitt & S. Dornic (Eds.), *Attention and performance V.* London: Academic Press, 1975.

Vickers, D. *Decision processes in visual perception* (in preparation, 1978).

Vickers, D., Caudrey, D., & Willson, R. J. Discriminating between the frequency of occurrence of two alternative events. *Acta Psychologica,* 1971, *35,* 151–172.

Vickers, D., & Johnson, M. *Times for signal detection with noisy visual signals* (unpublished research report).

Vickers, D., Nettelbeck, T., & Willson, R. J. Perceptual indices performance: The measurement of "inspection time" and "noise" in the visual system. *Perception,* 1972, *1,* 263–295.

Vickers, D., Leary, J., & Barnes, P. Adaptation to decreasing signal probability. In R. R. Mackie (Ed.), *Vigilance: Theory, operational performance, and physiological correlates.* New York: Plenum Press, 1977.

Volkmann, J. The relation of time of judgment to certainty of judgment. *Psychological Bulletin,* 1934, *31,* 672–673.

White, R. W. Motivation reconsidered: The concept of competence. *Psychological Review,* 1959, *66,* 297–333.

Wilding, J. M. Effects of stimulus discriminability on the latency distribution of identification responses. *Acta Psychologica,* 1974, *38,* 483–500.

Woodworth, R., & Schlosberg, H. *Experimental psychology.* New York: Holt, 1954.

32

The Relative Judgment Theory of the Psychometric Function

Stephen W. Link

Department of Psychology
McMaster University, Hamilton, Canada

ABSTRACT

The theory of relative judgment is based upon sequential comparisons between a presented stimulus and a mental psychophysical standard. The process of comparison continues until either of two response thresholds is first exceeded; then a response is emitted. This sequential theory of judgment provides predictions for both response probability (RP) and response time (RT), and a fundamental relationship between RP and RT. The application of the theory to the psychometric function rests on the assumption that a single mental standard, not necessarily identical to the experimenter's standard, provides the referent against which individual stimuli are compared. To confirm the predicted relation between RP and RT, three experiments are examined. In all cases the theoretically predicted relationship is supported by the data. As a bonus, it is now possible to estimate the expected value of the mental standard from either RP or RT results, compare the estimates, and relate the estimated value to units of the physical stimulus.

I. INTRODUCTION

History is replete with examples of replicable scientific observations that eventually obtain the status of empirical laws. The psychometric function which Urban (1910) defined as "A mathematical expression which gives the probability of a judgment as function of the comparison stimulus [sic] " is an example. Over a wide range of experimental conditions, methods, and stimuli, psychologists have discovered that as the difference between a comparison stimulus and a standard increases, the probability of judging the comparison stimulus to be greater than the standard also increases. The empirical fact is that this rather smoothly increasing function of stimulus difference appears to have the form of a cumulative probability function.

The existence of such a widely found result has tempted statisticians to discover the "best" mathematical description of its form. For the psychometric function the best description has been claimed to be (Bock & Jones, 1968) (1) the normal distribution, (2) the log normal, (3) the angular, and (4) the logistic. Of course, each of these proposals has merit, but as Feller (1940) pointed out, poor fit will not permit great discrimination among these, as well as many other, functional forms because each will provide a reasonably close fit to empirical results. Nevertheless the pursuit of a mathematical form for the psychometric function has led many statisticians to favor the logistic distribution (c.f. Berkson, 1953; Cox, 1970).

In spite of the arguments in favor of the logistic, there is little agreement concerning the reason for its frequent appearance in psychological research. A major impediment to providing a theory consistent with the assumed logistic form of the psychometric function is raised by the fact that the probabilities that appear to follow this cumulative probability distribution so nicely are not cumulative probabilities at all. Rather, they are probabilities obtained from formal choice experiments (Bush, Luce, & Galanter, 1963) and should be considered as choice probabilities. Thus a theory that accounts for the empirical result must predict that choice probabilities, when viewed as an increasing function of stimulus difference should "appear" to match the cumulative logistic distribution.

The many difficulties in finding the best form for the psychometric function assume less importance if we shed our empirical cloaks, don our theoretical caps, and view the psychometric function as only one manifestation of discriminative performance. As a start, we might suspect that if both response probabilities and response times are measured then response probability and correct and error response times should vary as a function of stimulus difference. Moreover, these variables should be related by predictions from a theory of discrimination. A theory of psychophysical discrimination that predicts all of these response measures will then permit experimental verification of relations between response probability and response time. The predictions and experimental analyses of such a theory are the focus of this chapter.

II. THE THEORY OF RELATIVE JUDGMENT

Relative Judgment Theory (RJT) (Link, 1975; Link & Heath, 1975) provides a new theoretical basis for two choice discrimination experiments, and as we will see, a new basis for the psychometric function. The theory postulates that through experience, such as training or preexposure, a mental standard is established. When the experimenter presents a stimulus to the subject, a psychological value of the stimulus is compared against the mental standard by subtraction.

During a single trial these differences are accumulated over time until one or the other of two fixed response thresholds is first exceeded; a response is then emitted. Because the theory is sequential, immediate relations between choice probability and response time result. These theoretical relations provide a quite reasonable account of choice probability and response time for a number of experiments.

We will assume that in a multistimulus, two-choice experiment the presentation of a stimulus results in a comparison between random variables representing psychological values X_i for stimulus $S_i (i = 1, 2, \ldots n)$ and X_r for the subject's mental standard. The process of comparison occurs during a time unit of size Δt, for which we define the stationary difference random variable $d_i = X_i - X_r$ to characterize the result of the comparison process. For the first k time units, we let the sum of all such differences be $D_{ik} = \Sigma_{j=1}^{k} d_{ij}$. The random variable D_{ik} we will take to be a sum of independent identically distributed random variables that performs a random walk on a psychological dimension of comparative difference.

As shown in Fig. 1 the random walk performed by D_{ik} is bounded by two response thresholds equidistant from a zero value for comparative difference. If the random walk first exceeds the response threshold at A, then response R_A, let us say the "greater than" response, occurs; otherwise the response R_B must occur first because the random walk must eventually terminate at either A or $-A$ (Wald, 1947). The distance between response thresholds is assumed to be constant during a trial, and equals the total amount of comparative difference

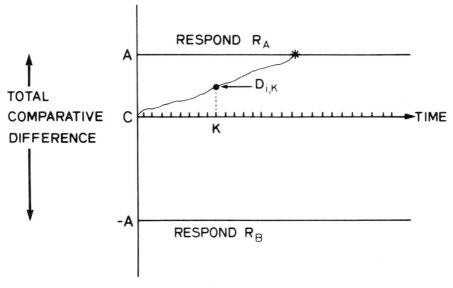

FIG. 1.

needed by the subject to meet the experimenter's speed and accuracy instructions. The starting value of the random walk, that is, D_{i0}, is labelled C and may be shifted positively to bias responding toward response R_A, or shifted negatively producing bias toward response R_B.

The mathematical development of this theory of sequential discrimination rests on the well known Wald Identity:

$$E(e^{-D_{iN}} M_i(\theta)^{-N}) = 1,$$

where N is the value of k when the random walk stops (at either A or $-A$) and $M_i(\theta)$ is the moment generating function for d_i. From Wald's Identity it follows that the probability of first responding R_A given stimulus S_i is

$$P_{Ai} = \frac{e^{\theta_i(A+C)} - 1}{e^{\theta_i(A+C)} - e^{-\theta_i(A-C)}} \qquad (i = 1, 2, \ldots n)$$

where θ_i is a nonzero solution to $M_i(\theta) = 1$. Algebraic manipulation then gives

$$P_{Ai} = \frac{e^{\theta_i A} - 1}{e^{\theta_i A} - e^{-\theta_i A}} + \frac{1 - e^{-\theta_i C}}{e^{\theta_i A} - e^{-\theta_i A}} \qquad (1)$$

When there is no response bias, a recognized criterion for symmetry of the psychometric function (Green & Swets, 1966, p. 125), then $C = 0$ and Equation 1 becomes

$$P_{Ai} = (e^{\theta_i A} - 1)/(e^{\theta_i A} - e^{-\theta_i A}).$$

Rewriting this equation yields

$$P_{Ai} = (1 + e^{-\theta_i A})^{-1} \qquad (2)$$

which is the defining equation of the distribution function of a standard logistic variable (evaluated at the point $\theta_i A$).

Maximum likelihood estimates of $\theta_i A$ can be obtained by computing $\ln (P_{Ai}/1 - P_{Ai}) = \theta_i A$. When the value of P_{Ai} is not too near 0 or 1, a useful estimate of $\theta_i A$ can be obtained from the (Anscombe, 1956) transform $\theta_i A = \ln [(n_{Ai} + \frac{1}{2})/(n_i - n_{Ai} + \frac{1}{2})]$ where n_{Ai} is the number of greater than responses, and n_i is the total number of responses, to stimulus S_i. Whether the values of P_{Ai} appear to generate a psychometric function consistent with a cumulative logistic distribution is largely a matter of whether estimates of $\theta_i A$ are a linear function of the stimulus magnitudes employed by the experimenter. It is, however, precisely this empirical fact that has led to the adoption of logistic distribution as a basis for the psychometric function.

To determine whether the psychometric function results from the accumulation of comparative difference as postulated by RJT, we examine the predicted relationship between response probability and response time. In general, the mean decision time equals the average distance to the response thresholds divided by the rate of drift, that is,

$$EDT_i = [P_{Ai}(A - C) - (1 - P_{Ai})(A + C)] / \mu_i$$

$$= [A(2P_{Ai} - 1) - C] / \mu_i$$

where $\mu_i = E(X_i - X_r)$ is the expected discrepancy between the psychological values of S_i and the subject's mental standard. Collecting together all nondecision components of response time into an average value K yields a predicted mean RT to stimulus S_i of $ERT_i = EDT_i + K$. For experiments in which response bias is negligible we find that

$$ERT_i = \frac{A}{\mu_i}(2P_{Ai} - 1) + K. \tag{3}$$

Thus, for fixed response thresholds at A and $-A$, the mean response time depends upon a probability that can be estimated from choice response data and upon an unknown value μ_i. When μ_i is known, ERT_i is a linear function of $(2P_{Ai} - 1)/\mu_i$ having slope A and intercept K.

While a set of $\mu_i (i = 1, 2, ... n)$ that provide a best fit for Equation 3 may be found by least squares, there are other procedures that are preferable and that involve the selection of fewer than n parameters. For example, it is known that when $\theta_i = 0$, then necessarily $\mu_i = 0$. Therefore, when estimates of $\theta_i A$ are a linear function of stimulus difference, as in the case of a logistic psychometric function, the position on the abscissa where $\theta_i A = 0$ provides an estimate of the value of a subject's average mental standard in terms of stimulus magnitude. Thus, when a stimulus magnitude, say S_r, generates psychological values having expected value equal to the expected value of the subject's mental standard, $E(X_r)$, then $\mu_i = 0$.

For the rather small range of stimulus magnitudes characteristic of psychometric function experiments an appealing assumption concerning μ_i is that the drift rate is a similarity transformation of the difference between S_i and S_r. Specifically, let $\mu_i = m(S_i - S_r)$, where m is a constant, S_i is a stimulus magnitude, and S_r is the value of the subject's mental standard defined in units of the stimulus. Equation (3) may then be written as

$$ERT_i = \frac{A}{m}\left(\frac{2P_{Ai} - 1}{S_i - S_r}\right) + K \tag{4}$$

where A/m is an unknown slope, and K is the mean nondecision time. One advantage of Equation 4 over Equation 3 is that only the stimulus magnitude corresponding to the subject's mental standard need be estimated, and this value can often be determined from the psychometric function. A second advantage is that only the relative differences between stimulus magnitudes and S_r need be known in order to assess the least squares fit of Equation 4. The three experiments examined below use Equation 4 to provide evidence that RJT provides an excellent account of data.

III. KELLOGG'S EXPERIMENT

In a now classic study of split disk brightness discrimination, Kellogg (1931) required subjects to determine which side of a split disk was brighter. Four luminances were used to create seven stimuli with the property that the difference in luminance between the left and right sides of the disc was an arithmetic progression having a step size of one and ranging from -3 to 3 Δs units. After 4,000 trials Kellogg began recording response times without the subject's knowledge, and obtained 240 observations for each value of S_i.

Kellogg's careful balancing of the stimuli, his attempt to minimize response bias, and the large number of observations suggest that $\theta_i A$ be estimated using the maximum likelihood calculation, $\theta_i A = \ln (P_{Ai}/1 - P_{Ai})$. These estimates are shown in Fig. 2 as a function of the luminance difference between the two sides of the disc. A least squares fit yielded the equation $\theta A = 1.14 \, \Delta s + .31$ with a standard error of .15. Solving this equation for the value of Δs at which $\theta A = 0$

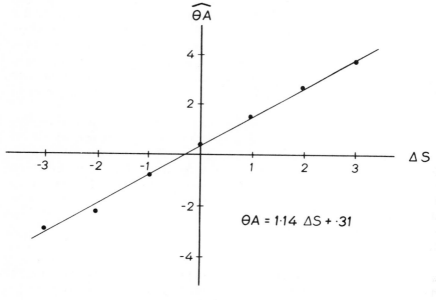

FIG. 2.

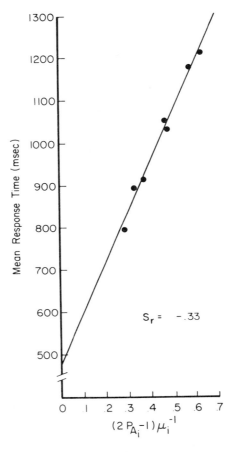

FIG. 3.

gives $\Delta s = -.27$. Thus, given the standard error, we would expect the average value of the subject's mental standard to lie in the region $-.40$ to $-.13$ Δs.

To examine the predicted relation between response time and response probability given in Equation 4, values of S_i were taken to equal values of the visually presented stimulus difference, i.e., -3, -2 ... $3\Delta s$. Values of S_r ranging from -3 to 3 in steps of .01 were defined and for each value the agreement between Equation 4 and the actual data points was assessed by calculating average squared deviation. A minimum squared deviation occurred when S_r assumed the value $-.33$ Δs, a value in good agreement with that obtained from the estimated position of the mental standard by using the psychometric function.

Figure 3 shows the result of plotting the mean RTs according to Equation 4 and taking $S_r = -.33$. The linear fit is quite good with slope 1186 and intercept 475 msec. At the minimum the standard error proved to be only 18 msec. The descent to this minimum was quite steep as revealed by standard errors of 50 at

$S_r = -.40$ and 56 at $S_r = -.27$. Thus the best fit at $S_r = -.33$ is considerably better than assuming, from calculations employing the psychometric function, that $S_r = -.27$. The difference between the two estimates of S_r is well within sampling error, and therefore the theory appears to provide a quite respectable account of Kellogg's results.

The relationship between mean RT and choice probability given in Equation 4 can be examined without reference to the psychometric function. Even in experiments in which the error rate is rather small, changes in the value of μ_i can have a significant effect upon response time. To illustrate the application of Equation 4 without first examining the psychometric function, data from a well known card sorting experiment were examined.

IV.   THE SHALLICE AND VICKERS EXPERIMENTS

Seven subjects sorted eight card packs containing 40 cards each.

> Each card contained two lines, one of 4.5 cm. The other line took eight difference values ranging from 3.4 to 4.4 cm depending upon the pack it was in. Their positions were varied along the top of the card, being a constant distance of 1.0 cm apart. In each pack 20 cards had the longer line on the left and 20 on the right. . . . Each subject sorted the pack into two piles depending on whether the long line was on the left or the right. (Shallice & Vickers, 1964, p. 45)

Let us suppose that subjects consistently compare the line on one side of the card to the line opposite. If the comparison is from left to right, then whenever the 4.5 cm line appears on the left, a positive difference results; otherwise, the difference is negative. The discrepancy obtained is a visual discrepancy which generates a psychological value that is compared to the subject's mental standard. In the present experiment, the 4.5 cm line appeared equally often on the left or right-hand sides of the cards and, therefore, the discrepancies are as often positive as negative. Thus the subject would do well to maintain a mental standard for the difference equal to zero.

The data reported by Shallice and Vickers were not partitioned according to whether the long line actually occurred on the left or right hand side. However, for the eight values of physical difference between lines, corresponding to the eight decks, we do have available the number of errors and the mean response time. The data, then, may be considered as defining the positive side of a perfectly balanced psychometric function experiment. The psychometric function itself is not of immediate concern, for the error rates varied from .037 to only .007 for the 11 mm difference. However, the predicted relationship between choice probability and response time may still be examined.

The lowest panel in Fig. 4 shows the result obtained by applying Equation 4 to the average data for the experiment described earlier (Experiment 3). The

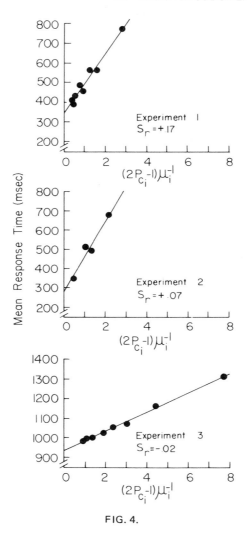

FIG. 4.

least squares fit yielded an estimate of the subject's mental standard for physical difference equal to −.02 mm, a value quite near zero. The slope and intercept values were 48 and 939 msec, respectively, and the standard error was only 8.3 msec. The rate of convergence to the minimum was quite fast, with the standard error having values of 15 msec and 18 msec when the subject's standard was taken to be −.07 or .03 mm, respectively. The quite close fit gives additional evidence in favor of Equation 4, as do the additional results shown for Shallice and Vickers' Experiments 1 and 2 which were similar to Experiment 3.

In each of these experiments a balanced experimental method has provided estimates of the mental standard as having a value near zero. It might be assumed then that subjects simply compare one component of the stimulus to the other, and the discrepancy so obtained is used to drive the decision process. That is, the subject uses as a standard the value of a standard established by the experimenter. This assumption would be in accord with the many theories of discrimination based upon Thurstonian psychophysical models. However, the estimated value of a subject's mental standard is generally zero only in "balanced" discrimination experiments. The next experiment illustrates this point.

V.   THE LINK (1971) EXPERIMENT

Four very well practiced subjects were required to respond "same" or "different" depending upon whether a line presented 200 msec after a fixed standard, S_0, was of the same or a different length from S_0. If a comparison line was different from S_0, it was always either longer or shorter depending upon the subject. On 50% of the trials S_0 was followed by a re-presentation of S_0; the remaining trials were equally divided among lines which varied from the standard by 1, 2, 3, or 4 mm. If the subject adops as a mental standard the experimenter's standard, then whenever the comparison is of the same length as the experimenter's standard, the value of μ will be zero. This would result in long response times and chance performance. Adopting such a standard would, in this case, lead to rather odd performances. Alternatively, the mental standard may be displaced from the experimenter's standard and result in a nonzero value for μ when S_0 is the comparison stimulus.

In addition to varying the stimulus differences, RT deadlines were imposed on the task. Subjects were instructed at the beginning of each trial to respond faster than either 260 or 460 msec, or were to be as accurate as possible. Each of these instructions was presented equally often, and in all respects the experiment was completely randomized within each block of 240 experimental trials. Theoretically the effect of the RT deadline instruction should be to force the subjects to vary the total comparative difference used in the decision process. With a 260 msec deadline there should be little if any discrimination, because in order to produce such rapid responses the value of A must be near zero. When a moderate deadline is in force then the value of A should increase, and when accuracy is required, the value of A should be still greater. The effect on Equation 4 is to increase the slope of the function relating RT and choice performance. But the subject's mental standard should be found to be identical across the various RT deadline conditions.

The results shown in Fig. 5 were obtained by a least squares method analogous to that used in the preceding experiments. It can be seen that for the 260 msec RT deadline the slope was zero, indicating that performance was rather poor. When the RT deadline was relaxed, the slope of Equation 4 increased, and when the subjects were to be accurate, the slope increased again. Within each deadline condition the least squares fit was quite good with standard errors of 1.9 and 1.3 msec for the 460 msec and accuracy conditions respectively. The estimated position of the average mental standard, labelled S_r in Fig. 5, equalled $S_0 + .74$ for the 460 msec, and $S_0 + .78$ for the accuracy condition.

The conclusion to be drawn is that the subject's mental standard was not the same as the experimenter's standard but was instead about .75 mm distant from the experimenter's standard. The adoption of the standard may be an automatic, learned feature of human discrimination that depends upon the frequency of presenting various stimuli, but the important fact is that the comparison process is not accurately characterized in terms of differences from the experimenter's standard.

It appears that in experiments in which the comparison stimuli are balanced on either side of the experimenter's standard, both the subject's and experimenter's standards match quite nicely. This result would give support to Thurstone's assumption that the value zero is a standard for comparative judgment. However, when the balancing is changed, as in Link (1971), we observe a shift of the subject's mental standard away from the physical standard established by the experimenter.

In summary, we have shown how the well-known psychometric function can be derived from relative judgment theory and how the theory relates response time and response probability. Whereas our analysis has assumed unbiasedness

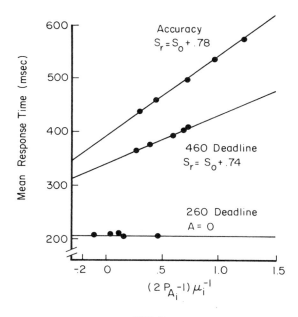

FIG. 5.

with respect to response thresholds, future experiments will report results in which response bias is manipulated in order to promote changes in the response times and in the psychometric function.

ACKNOWLEDGMENTS

This project is supported by the National Research Council of Canada and by the Science and Engineering Research Board of McMaster University. Mr. Norman Wintrip and Miss Julia Cox have assisted in the collection and analysis of data for this project.

REFERENCES

Anscombe, F. J. On estimating binomial response relations. *Biometrika,* 1956, *43,* 461–464.

Berkson, J. A statistically precise and relatively simple method of estimating the bio-assay with quantal response, based on the logistic function. *Journal of the American Statistical Association,* 1953, *48,* 565–599.

Bock, D. R., & Jones, L. V. *The measurement and prediction of judgment and choice.* San Francisco: Holden-Day, 1968.

Bush, R. R., Galanter, E., & Luce, R. D. Characterization and classification of choice experiments. In R. D. Luce, R. R. Bush, & E. Galanter (Eds.), *Handbook of mathematical psychology.* (Vol. 1). New York: Wiley, 1963.

Cox, D. R. *The analysis of binary data.* London: Methuen, 1970.

Feller, W. On the logistic law of growth and its empirical verifications in Biology. *Acta Biotheoretica,* 1940, *4,* 51–66.

Green, D. M., & Swets, J. A. *Signal detection theory and psychophysics.* New York: Wiley, 1966.

Kellogg, W. N. The time of judgment in psychometric measures. *American Journal of Psychology,* 1931, *43,* 65–86.

Link, S. W. Applying RT deadlines to discrimination reaction time, *Psychonomic Science,* 1971, *25,* 355–358.

Link, S. W. The relative judgment theory of two choice response time. *Journal of Mathematical Psychology,* 1975, *12,* 114–135.

Link, S. W., & Heath, R. A. A sequential theory of psychological discrimination. *Psychometrika,* 1975, *40,* 77–105.

Shallice, T., & Vickers, D. Theories and experiments on discrimination times. *Ergonomics,* 1964, *7,* 37–49.

Urban, F. M. The method of constant stimuli and its generalizations. *Psychological Review,* 1910, *27,* 229–259.

Wald, A. *Sequential analysis.* New York: Wiley, 1947.

33 A Model for the Visual Recognition of Words of Three Letters

Don Bouwhuis
Institute for Perception Research
Eindhoven, The Netherlands

ABSTRACT

The model to be presented predicts recognition performance in a situation where subjects respond to Dutch words consisting of three letters presented at different eccentricities in the visual field.

As basic features of the word stimulus the constituent letters were chosen, being about midway between elementary visual properties and global word-shape. This choice is empirically supported by a strong relation between letter recognition in words and in meaningless strings.

The perception of letters in such a case is taken to be position-specific, as letters in words are subject to interaction by neighboring letters dependent on eccentricity. By means of a probabilistic rule, letter recognition, given a stimulus word, leads to a set of letter strings as viable alternatives. From these strings only the real words are retained by means of a matching procedure for which the final response probabilities are predicted with the Constant Ratio Rule. Thus word frequency effects are not separately incorporated in the model.

All parameters of the model are supplied by earlier results on letter recognition. Though the reliability of these data is not optimal, predictions of the model compare favorably with responses obtained in a word recognition experiment. Tests of the model are described for correct and incorrect responses to words presented at four different eccentric positions.

I. INTRODUCTION

If one considers that reading involves word recognition, and word recognition involves recognition of simpler elements, word recognition is therefore important for both the study of reading and the study of elementary recognition. Emphasis on the latter approach leads to experiments with more tightly controlled condi-

631

tions than are possible in a reading situation and, of course, need not be concerned with words at all. Even if words are studied, the aspects under investigation may require the elimination of the typical reading setting. Eliminating the conditions favoring correct recognition one by one reveals more clearly the properties of the recognition function but can in itself not produce a clear insight in what happens in reading.

In this paper a word recognition paradigm was modified to more closely resemble a normal reading situation. However, in order to have adequate experimental control over the stimuli, the stimuli used were single words. This situation must, of course, somewhat depart from reading. Nevertheless, the present approach accounts for one important step in reading: the perception of words from a string of letters somewhere within a line. Specifically, responses to briefly presented words were predicted by means of letter recognition data and word knowledge. Much is already known about letter recognition; by including word knowledge a model has been developed that predicts not just changes in word response probabilities as a function of conditions, but these probabilities themselves. The present approach, therefore, contrasts with studies on factors influencing recognition accuracy or recognition time.

In the next section stimulus aspects used in recognition studies will be compared with those in reading studies. The model itself will then be presented, followed by a test using data from experiments by Bouma (1973). In the discussion, some properties and limitations, as well as possible extensions of the model, will be elaborated.

II.   READING VERSUS RECOGNITION

A.   Word Contour

In the early days of experimental psychology, research on reading was more intensive than it has been during the first half of the twentieth century. Starting around 1880, most research workers then employed fragments of actual text. Huey (1908/1968) worked with lines cut from the American Journal of Psychology and was able to demonstrate a number of phenomena of prime importance with this material. The quality of his observations, which have been corroborated in recent times, makes up for his lack of statistical evidence. Experimental deviation from reading situations started, however, quite soon afterward. Snellen, who was the successor of Donders, introduced a visual screening test, consisting of single capital letters with progressively reduced size.

Now small size has not found wide application in recognition studies, but single presentation either as letter, letter string, or word has. Likewise, the use of capital letters has been pervasive in word recognition experiments, although it is not entirely clear why. The word contour is eliminated, but though vertical letter size is standardized, letter width is not, which is only partially compensated by equal spacing in some type faces. Similarity is not controlled either, but in any case perception is more difficult, because "dominant parts," as Huey (1968) called them, are eliminated. Dominant parts are provided, among other ways, by word contour, as determined by the succession of short letters, ascenders and descenders (Table 1).

The function of word contour is one of the basic issues in the early investigations on reading. It was supposed, by Cattell, Erdmann, and Dodge, Dearborn, and others, and still is, that the perception of words is mediated more by their total outline than by their constituent letters. A more detailed view was expressed by Zeitler, Goldscheider and Müller, and Messmer (Huey, 1968) stating that dominant parts of words alone could trigger their recognition. Huey (1968) noted that "Total form is not perceived separately, but that, in one act of projection, the total form and the parts to fill it are placed . . ." This scheme closely resembles the Gestalt view to be introduced some twenty years later, which has only rarely, if ever, resorted to words as illustrations for the unitary forces in perception.

It is true that word perception undoubtedly entails more acquired components than figure ground segregation, but this does not dispel the notion of Gestaltlike properties of words. In order to experimentally impair word perception it should therefore be quite effective to obliterate word contour. While printing in capital letters just standardizes contour, a reader should be expected to have even more trouble with modified contours. These have been produced by mixing upper and lower case letters within a word.

Another drastically altered word contour is arrived at by printing the letters vertically aligned; apart from being unfamiliar for the reader, it forces him to change scanning direction. Without any formal theory related to the perception of the constituent parts of words, detailed predictions of recognition responses with these procedures are beyond reach.

similarity groups of letters

short letters	a s z x
	e o c
	n m u
	r v w
ascenders	t i l f
	d h k b
descenders	g p j y q

TABLE 1.   Classification of letter types. Similarity has been established in a range of recognition experiments.

B. Luminance

The most straightforward way to reduce visibility is to decrease luminance. For an effective degradation, however, the luminance level must be much lower than 30 cd/m^2, below which the contrast sensitivity is also impaired, leading to reduced resolving power. Therefore, a luminance level exceeding 30 cd/m^2 is generally acceptable for reading, but reduced luminance essentially requires stimulus size increments to compensate for the lower contrast sensitivity.

The highest liminance that is usually reported in the literature seems to be about 10 fL, corresponding to 34 cd/m^2. Characters are usually presented at lower levels, and thus are viewed under lighting conditions that are suboptimal for reading.

C. Duration

Increases in stimulus duration beyond 30 msec seem to increase word recognizability very little provided poststimulus masking does not occur within 100–200 milliseconds from stimulus offset.

Normally we find eye fixations in reading pauses to be minimally of the order of 100 msec, with an average of 200 msec. (Andriessen & de Voogd, 1973). It is not clear, however, whether the processing of the visual mechanism going on in the extremely short presentations of 2–3 msec sometimes applied, can be directly related to that during the much longer regular eye fixation pauses.

D. Type Font

In order to be sure that the visual attributes of the stimulus presented for short durations can be optimally processed, the word or letters are often made up in a large and simple type face. This is especially the case in so called lexical decision tasks in which no visual errors or confusions are allowed. In both tasks, recognition and decision, the word or letter string extends over a large area of the fovea by which visual interference relative to a smaller word in a regular typefont is reduced.

III. EYE POSITION AND VISUAL INTERFERENCE

As was noted already, single stimulus presentation is practically the rule in recognition tasks that do not imply search. In printed text the reader is scanning one line at a time, which is completely filled with words, whereas there are non-attended lines above and below the one under consideration. With eye position fixed, only the small portion of the letters or words surrounding the fixation point can be perceived clearly. Huey (1968) cites results of Erdmann and Dodge, and of Cattell, who found that from a short eye fixation on a line of connected text, a maximum of about five words could be reported. The words ranged in length from two to ten letters with five letters on the average. However, only four or five letters could be reported when letters were presented in a random arrangement, which is of course the same result as that found by Sperling (1960). Sperling was also able to show that, during a short time after presentation, more letters were actually available than were reported. This might partially explain the fact that, when the stimuli were unconnected words, two words could be reported (Cattell, cited by Woodworth & Schlosberg, 1956). This is twice the number of reportable unconnected letters; apparently the subject is able to organize the available letters into word structures under these conditions. However, connected words are even better recognized, and in this case it is clear that not all details could have been perceived. Figure 1, derived from data of an experiment by Bouma (1973), shows the probability of correct report of words averaging four to five letters as a function of eccentricity.

At eccentricities exceeding 1° visual angle the probability of correct recognition decreases sharply. This result is only valid for singly presented words. Assuming that if there are more words in the display, they do not influence the perception of each other (which is not true), the average number of words having four—five letters that can be perceived in one line in one eye fixation is about five. This number can be estimated from the curve in Fig. 1 yielding three words on the right side and two on the left. Visual interference, however, would limit this number considerably but apparently context makes up for that part of a meaningful line that has not been perceived sufficiently well.

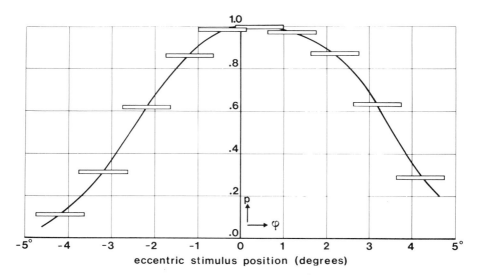

eccentric stimulus position (degrees)

FIG. 1   Recognition scores of words, ranging in length from 3-6 letters (average 4.5 letters) as a function of eccentricity of presentation for 100 ms. Note the right-field superiority. One degree comprises four letters. Data from Bouma (1973).

The relevance of the eccentric position of words during reading is made clear by the fact that eye saccades average about eight letter positions, whereas 1° visual angle comprises four letter spaces. In as much as the extent distribution of left to right saccadic movements is positively skewed, much larger jumps of up to 20 letters (5° visual angle) can occur. For an account of the visual interference effects of this saccade based eccentricity, the reader is referred to the chapter by Bouma on the functional visual field in this volume.

At this point we may elaborate somewhat more fully on the concept of global wordshape. Aside from being vague, global wordshape is an unstable property of a word, because of the widely varying interference over the visual field, which will continuously modify it.

Wordshape is conveyed by the constituent letters of the word. Figure 2 shows the perception of separate letters, initial and final ones only, in words and meaningless strings. Apparently there is a close correspondence between letter perception in both cases, though performance is better on words. So the problem of global wordshape could possibly be restated in terms of the contribution of the constituent letters and their mutual interference effects.

That letters are more accurately reported in words may be based on the fact that readers do not need to perceive all letters correctly in order to recognize the word, and therefore may sometimes be able to infer a letter that has not actually been seen. This of course cannot hold for strings, which is why the superior performance in words has been called completion (Bouma, 1973). Word recognition therefore minimally requires letter perception and word knowledge. Both factors have been incorporated in the model to be presented.

IV. THE RECOGNITION MODEL

We will take the situation in which the subject tries to recognize real words which he knows to have three letters. It is supposed that he perceives a letter for any of the three positions of the word; that is, the internal representation is a string of three letters. Which letters will be perceived depends on the position in the word and on the eccentricity of the word. It should be noted that the dependence is not stated in terms of the adjacent letters, but just taken to be position-specific. In this way interference is in a sense a stable property within words. For any position in the word, a confusion probability can be defined that a letter belonging to the stimulus word, l_i, is perceived as λ_j, which can be written for the middle position as:

$$P_\phi(-\lambda_j - | - l_i -) \tag{1}$$

The subscript ϕ denotes the eccentricity of the stimulus word. Clearly, probability 1 defines a confusion matrix. Furthermore, the simplest way in which these

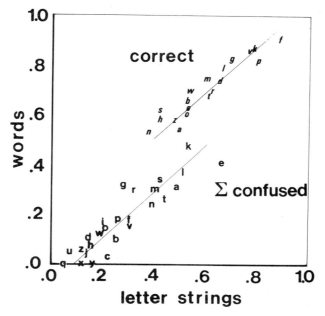

FIG. 2 Comparison of letter scores in words and meaningless strings. Upper right data points represent fractions correct. The lower left points represent the fractions of incorrectly reported letters: the response probability minus the fraction correct. Data from Bouma (1973).

probabilities can be combined is by taking them independent of each other. Then the probability of the activation of any string $\lambda_h\lambda_i\lambda_j$ can be written as:

$$P_\phi(\lambda_h\lambda_i\lambda_j|l_pl_ql_r) = P_\phi(\lambda_h--|l_p--)\,P_\phi(-\lambda_i-|-l_q-)\,P_\phi(--\lambda_j|--l_r) \quad (2)$$

For one eccentricity ϕ the probability of a letter string perceived for the presented stimulus word can be obtained by multiplying the appropriate terms of three confusion matrices, one for each letter position. Other ways of combination are conceiveable, and generally desirable, and a consideration of some aspects of the independence assumption will be postponed until the discussion.

The second stage in the model represents the effect of word knowledge. It has been assumed that on every trial a large number of strings is activated; most of them will be meaningless, but some will be real words. It appears, however, that observers faced with the task of recognizing words only rarely report nonsense strings. When not pressed for an answer, they may sometimes state not to have seen the stimulus at all. For the final choice of the word response, then, it is supposed that all meaningless strings are rejected, whereas all activated words are retained. With regard to the reported words, it is generally found that visual factors are much more important than effects owing to frequency of occurrence of words (Morton, 1969; Rumelhart & Siple, 1974). Since in normal reading context as well as visual factors are operative, the role of word frequency would be expected to be even smaller there. So the basic issue here is how much of word recognition can be accounted for by visual factors and word knowledge. Consequently, in the model the response is chosen from among the real words activated by the letters of the stimulus word according to the Constant Ratio Rule (Clarke, 1957). This can be formally expressed as:

$$P(r_k \mid w_s) = \frac{P(r_k)}{\sum_l P(r_l)} \tag{3}$$

where the r_l are the words among the activated strings $\lambda_h \lambda_i \lambda_j$, and w_s is the presented stimulus word corresponding to $l_p l_q l_r$ in probability 2.

In this way, the word recognition process is completely covered in a minimal fashion, by activation of letter strings dependent on the stimulus, selection of words, and the prediction of response probabilities by the Constant Ratio Rule. In the form the model is stated there are some mathematical correspondences with the earlier formulations of Morton (1969) and of Rumelhart and Siple (1974). However, in Morton's model there is no account of the processes going on before the triggering of the logogens or word alternatives. In Rumelhart and Siple's model (1974), letter confusions are predicted theoretically and there is no letter position effect; additionally, the choice rule works already on the level of individual letters.

V. AN EXPERIMENTAL TEST

For a test of the model two different kinds of data are needed. First, letter confusions that occur for letters in different positions of words themselves, presented at various eccentricities. Second, the set of all known Dutch words of three letters is required to specify which of the perceived letter strings are words.

Experimental data relevant to the letter confusions were collected by Bouma (1973). His experiments were directed at the contribution of initial and final letters of words to their recognition in the eccentric visual field. In order to obtain pure estimates of the recognition of these letters, they could not be presented in words because letter completion would occur. Words were therefore transformed into unpronounceable strings by exchanging all letters not asked for with visually similar letters as established by Bouma (1971). In this way the visual characteristics of the words were maintained as closely as possible (Table 2). Subjects reported the initial and final letter of the string presented randomly to the right or the left of the fixation point. In this way letter confusions of the first and last letters of the three-letter words used by Bouma (1973)

WORD TRANSFORMATION

word		string	report
gas	→	gzs	initial and
lip	→	lfp	final letters
arm	→	sru	
fee	→	ieo	middle letter

TABLE 2. Illustrations of how words are changed into meaningless strings to be employed for letter recognition. For the recognition of the middle letter in /arm/ the letters *a* and *m* are replaced by similar letters (Table 1) in order to obtain a visually similar string. The subject is then asked to report the middle letter.

were obtained. In order to obtain letter confusions for the middle letters, a supplementary experiment was run, in which the words were again transformed with respect to the first and last letter. The words themselves were also presented in a recognition task, in which the subjects reported whole words. The model should predict these word responses. In both the original experiment of Bouma (1973) and the supplementary one, there were 100 words of three letters, each one presented twice, once right, and once left of the fixation point, for 100 msec at a background luminance of 100 cd/m². For the typeface see Table 2. The 100 words were split up in two groups for presentation eccentricities ±3° and ±2°. The same eleven subjects took part in all experiments; for further technical details the reader should consult Bouma (1973). For the second stage of the model, which involves a selection of words from activated strings, a word vocabulary was needed. This vocabulary was composed of words appearing in two word counts: De la Court, as published by Linschoten (1963) and Uit den Boogaart (1975), making a total of 409 words of three letters. Later the list was found to be incomplete and a number of commonly known words from several sources were added to it, extending it to 541 entries. It was established experimentally afterwards that words that did not appear in this list are not generally known.

VI. RESULTS

A. Correct Responses

Figure 3 shows the predicted and experimentally obtained proportions of words correctly identified at the four eccentricities employed. One set of predictions was made for the 409-word list, another for the 541-word list. Both sets of predictions follow closely the experimental values, but there is an underestimate. This amounts to 3% for the 409 entry list and 8% for the 541 entry list. Whatever

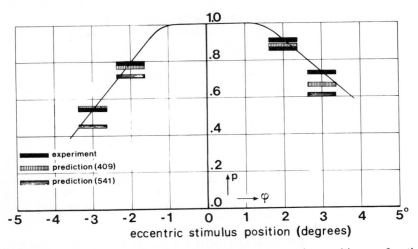

FIG. 3   Experimental and predicted probabilities of correct word recognition as a function of eccentricity. Two sets of predictions by the model are shown: one with a list of 409 words, the other with a list of 541 words.

other causes there may be for the underestimation, this difference is to be expected on the basis of the applied Constant Ratio Rule. When more word alternatives exist for a stimulus word, the probability of the correct response will decrease relative to a situation with fewer alternatives. An important point to notice is the superior right field performance, which is also present in the predictions. It has been assumed that the left hemisphere of the brain, corresponding to the right visual field, is engaged specifically in the processing of language material.

Apparently, since the model is based on the recognition of constituent letters, the specialization might well be limited to letters or even less complex features of the word. An explanation in terms of less visual interference in the right field is definitely simpler than language specialization on the level of words.

B.   Letter Recognition and Completion

In addition to correct responses, the model predicts incorrect responses. An incorrect word may still have one or two letters in common with the stimulus word. This is relevant to the present model, if the letters appear in the same place as in the stimulus word. Thus an analysis of the correctness of letters in the responses includes both the correct and the greater part of the incorrect responses. In Fig. 4 the proportions of correct letters predicted by the model are compared with the proportions appearing in the responses of the subjects. Proportions are averaged over the letters appearing in the stimulus words. Also shown are the probabilities that these letters are correctly recognized in their position

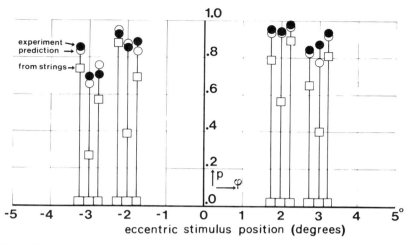

FIG. 4 Experimental and predicted probabilities of correct letter recognition in the words presented as a function of position in the word and eccentricity. The lower squares represent averages of letter scores in meaningless strings as used in the model.

in an unpronounceable string. Completion is defined as the difference between the letter recognition probability in words and the one in meaningless strings. Evidently, most completion takes place in the middle positions of words where letter recognition is weak.

VII. DISCUSSION

A model is proposed predicting single word recognition and letter recognition under conditions relevant for reading situations. The only factors taken into account were the recognition of letters in specific word positions, combined with an independence assumption, and word knowledge. The results of a test of the model have provided evidence that a substantial part of word recognition under the conditions stated can be explained without reference to general word shape, dominant parts, or frequency effects. Actually, the concept of general or global word shape has been shown to be amenable to specification because its properties can be explained in terms of interference-dependent letter recognition. Recognition of letters flanked on both sides by other letters is severely impaired in the eccentric visual field which results in a word shape different from that on fixation. Word knowledge in the observer enables him to complete the missed features of the word, leading to apparently good letter scores. Though letter recognizability in meaningless strings is much lower than that in words, the model can successfully predict scores for letters in words from that in strings.

A. Word Frequency

The experiments reported by Goldiamond and Hawkins (1958) showed that word frequency may influence responses under quite difficult perception conditions. Recent experiments by Richards (1973a, 1973b) replicating the original Goldiamond and Hawkins experiments demonstrated that the frequency effect is strongly influenced by the demand characteristic of the task. It is very improbable that the demand characteristics stimulating the frequency effect were present in the experiments, considering the recognizability of the words and the lenient instructions. Neither would reading seem to be so demanding. Apart from this, frequency data could only have been used in a very crude way, since for at least one-third of the Dutch three-letter words, frequency of occurrence is unknown, being less than 10^{-6}.

B. Interaction and Independence

It is often mistakenly thought that mutually interacting processes should also be stochastically dependent. Interacting processes occur in the perception of a number of adjacent letters, where the presence of one letter interferes with the perception of another. In such a situation the probability of perceiving a letter may still be independent of the probability of perceiving one of the neighboring letters. This may be true even though the recognition probabilities may be decreased relative to a situation without interference by other letters. Imposing this independence condition on letter perception considerably simplifies the recognition theory, because there is no need to estimate probabilities of parameters specifying the dependence relation.

The present approach was intended to study how much of word recognition can be accounted for with such an independence assumption. There are, however, also practical reasons for such an approach. Experimental support for dependency parameters must be unreliable in view of the relatively small number of observations on all possible different letters, letter positions, and positions in the visual field.

Some sources of letter recognition dependence will now be considered in detail. Without loss of generality, the effect of dependence can be shown here by considering two letters of the word.

Let P_1 be the probability that a letter, not necessarily the correct one, has been perceived for a presented letter, and P_2 an analogous probability for an adjacent letter. The covariance expresses the degree of dependence between these two variables as follows:

$$Cov\, P_1 P_2 = EP_1 P_2 - EP_1 \cdot EP_2$$

From this it follows immediately:

$$EP_1 P_2 = EP_1 \cdot EP_2 + Cov\, P_1 P_2 \tag{4}$$

Except for the covariance term, equation 4 is analogous to the letter combination rule 2 of the present model. The left term gives the letter perception in words, which is predicted by the product on the right, implying the independence condition, whereas the covariance is assumed to be near zero. However, when there is a positive covariance between the recognition probabilities, the independence based prediction will underestimate the probability of correct word recognition. This could be a second explanation of the underestimation of the correct responses by the model.

Letter recognition will covary when the subject looks to the left or right of the fixation mark during presentation. The letters on the fixated side will be perceived more clearly than those on the other side. Considering the fairly low recognizability of some letters and the absence of visually unexplainable guesses, the occurrence of this behavior would seem improbable. In general, observers — certainly when they are experienced — fixate quite accurately. It can further be shown that positive covariance can be induced by variation in the recognition probabilities (Bouwhuis, 1973). One source of variation is that observers differ in recognition performance. Since recognition performance is distributed over several letters and letter positions, the small number of comparable observations would lead to unreliable individual predictions. Another source could be that some letters interfere more with the perception of adjacent letters than others. The number of possible combinations of three letters, or even two for that matter, renders the experimental study of differential interference unrealistic.

Finally, negative covariance would arise if subjects attend to only one letter position at the expense of others. Since subjects can report up to four or five letters from a larger display, and even more in words or text, this strategy would seem improbable in the experiments under consideration. Experiments are in progress to obviate some of these limitations, though apparently not all of them can be overcome simultaneously. Theoretical developments could be useful too, because an explicit formulation of interference effects over the visual field and within words would greatly reduce experimental effort connected with the letter confusions. Contribution to the close fit of the model by any of these factors could of course still only be moderate, but might be required in a more accurate prediction for individual words.

C. Extension of the Model

As regards developments of the model, the first extension seems to lie in the direction of longer words. This will imply that the model itself must be modified with respect to middle letters. It is hardly feasible for subjects to report, or even see, middle letters of longer words in the eccentric field. Besides, length confusions tend to occur in these cases, which cannot be accounted for by the present position-based approach.

Since the number of words in those cases is appreciably larger, it is questionable whether the Constant Ratio Rule will suffice any longer. More complicated choice theories will then probably be required. As a first step, this very simple model has the advantage of needing no free parameters, which probably cannot be avoided in more rigid formulations for more complicated perception processes. The simplicity of the present version of the model indicates that it could be profitable to test formal recognition models in reading situations.

REFERENCES

Andriessen, J. J., & de Voogd, A. H. Analysis of eye movement patterns in silent reading. *IPO Annual Progress Report,* 1973, *8,* 29–34.

Bouma, H. Visual recognition of isolated lower-case letters. *Vision Research,* 1971, *11,* 459–474.

Bouma, H. Visual interference in the parafoveal recognition of initial and final letters of words. *Vision Research,* 1973, *13,* 767–782.

Bouwhuis, D. *Het Klemtoonoordeel, persoonlijk of eenstemmig?* 1973, IPO Report no. 253.

Clarke, F. R. Constant-ratio rule for confusion matrices in speech communication. *Journal of the Acoustical Society of America,* 1957, *29,* 715–720.

Goldiamond, I., & Hawkins, W. F. Vexierversuch: The log relationship between word-frequency and recognition obtained in the absence of stimulus words. *Journal of Experimental Psychology,* 1958, *56,* 457–463.

Huey, E. M. *The Psychology and Pedagogy of reading.* Cambridge: The MIT Press, 1968. (Originally published , 1908).

Linschoten, J. *De la Court's frequentietelling van Nederlandse woorden.* Utrecht: Psychological Laboratory, Rep. no. 6301, 1963.

Morton, J. Interaction of information in word recognition. *Psychological Review,* 1969, *76,* 165–178.

Richards, L. G. "Vexierversuch" revisited: A reexamination of Goldiamond and Hawkins' experiment. *American Journal of Psychology,* 1973, *86,* 707–715. (a)

Richards, L. G. On perceptual and memory processes in the word-frequency effect. *American Journal of Psychology,* 1973, *86,* 717–728. (b)

Rumelhart, D. E., & Siple, P. Process of recognizing tachistoscopically presented words. *Psychological Review,* 1974, *81,* 99–118.

Sperling, G. The information available in brief visual presentations. *Psychological Monographs,* 1960, *74,* no. 11, Whole No. 498.

Uit den Boogaart, P. C. *Woordfrequenties in gesproken en geschreven Nederlands.* Utrecht: Oosthoek/Scheltema en Holkema, 1975.

Woodworth, R. S., & Schlosberg, H. *Experimental psychology.* New York: Henry Holt and Company, 1956.

34

The Word Frequency Effect: A New Theory

Michel Treisman
Peter A. Parker
Department of Experimental Psychology
University of Oxford
Oxford, England

ABSTRACT

The finding that it is easier to recognize common words than rare words has been explained by two types of theory. On the one hand, it has been proposed that when a word is not fully recognized, a response may be chosen by guessing from a restricted set of possibilities. Broadbent (1967) and Catlin (1969) have discussed competing versions of this theory. Alternatively, it has been suggested that the stimulus provides greater or less evidence for each word in the listener's vocabulary, and that that word is selected for which the evidence is greatest.

An alternative theory of the identification of complex stimuli is outlined here, and results of a computer simulation are presented. An experiment on the recognition of spoken letters of the alphabet is described, and the predictions of the different theories are compared with data from this experiment and with other data from the literature. It appears that the data best support the present theory.

I. INTRODUCTION

Words that occur commonly in speech are more easily recognized than those that are rare. This is the word frequency effect. It is an intriguing finding, first because it presents in quantified form an interaction or combination of the effects of past experience and the present stimulus on perception, and so may offer a basis for investigating this. Second, because the statistical structure of words is better understood than that of any other large class of complex stimuli we might wish to study.

A response bias explanation for the word frequency effect was put forward by Pollack, Rubenstein, and Decker (1960). They proposed that listeners are

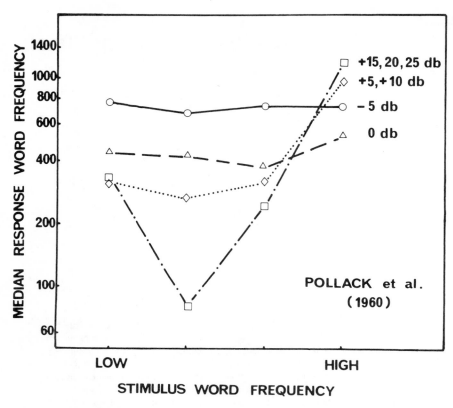

FIG. 1 Data obtained by Pollack, Rubenstein, and Decker (1960) for the auditory detection of words in white noise. The median frequency of incorrect response words is shown as a function of stimulus word frequency for the S/N ratios shown as parameters.

equipped with a hierarchy of response biases, reflecting their experience of the language, and thus are more likely to emit frequent than infrequent words. The acoustic information provided by an imperfectly recognized stimulus defines a set of alternative responses from which the listener chooses one. They also made what is now known as the assumption of acoustical equivalence: "that the acoustical characteristics of high and low frequency words are the same," from which it follows that the response sets defined by high or low stimulus words are equivalent random samples. The results of an experiment on the auditory detection of words are illustrated in Fig. 1. From these they concluded that "the median frequency of the distribution of meaningful word responses is independent of the stimulus word frequency" (Pollack et al., 1960).

There are two difficulties with this conclusion. First, although the prediction that error response frequency will be independent of stimulus frequency is intuitively appealing, it is not derived rigorously from the model. Second, the conclusion that their data support this prediction requires that four of the 36 high frequency stimulus words be disregarded. The unrevised data (shown in Pollack et al.'s Fig. 2 and replotted in Fig. 1 above) appear to show an increasing predominance of high frequency errors as the frequency of the stimulus word increases, at the higher signal intensities. This raises a problem. Neither the main effect nor the interaction follow from their model, nor from any other so far proposed, and they require to be explained.

Before returning to this question we shall briefly review the main theories that have been put forward to explain the word frequency effect. An alternative theory will then be proposed and a crucial test of the theories presented. The main measures that will be used in analyzing the data are the probabilities of correct responses or of errors of high or low frequency, given a high or low frequency stimulus word: $P(C \mid H)$, $P(C \mid L)$, $P(HE \mid H)$, $P(LE \mid H)$, and so on. If response word frequencies can be regarded as falling into two classes only, a convenient index of the distribution of frequency for incorrect responses is given by the ratio of high to low frequency error responses, given high or low stimulus words: the high stimulus error ratio, $HSER = P(HE|H)/P(LE|H)$, and the low stimulus error ratio, $LSER = P(HE|L)/P(LE|L)$. (A glossary of symbols is provided at the end of the paper.)

Theories of the type put forward by Pollack et al. (1960) may be called "restricted response set" theories. They are sometimes known as "fragment" theories. Broadbent (1967) named them "sophisticated guessing" theories and this name has become popular. Broadbent assumes that if the stimulus is not recognized, the fragmentary information received defines a set of possible responses consisting of h high-frequency and l low-frequency words. A response is generated by guessing from this set with guessing probabilities determined by word frequencies. He derives a prediction for the effect of stimulus word frequency on error response frequency in the following way: Consider the errors that may occur when a given set is selected by a high frequency stimulus word (HS). If the response generated by guessing is the stimulus it will not count as an error. There are then $(h - 1)$ words, each with the high frequency bias f_H, which may occur as an error, and l low-frequency words each with bias $f_L < f_H$. Then the ratio of the probabilities of high to low errors will be $HSER = (h - 1)f_H/lf_L$. But if the same set is selected by a low frequency stimulus (LS), the ratio will be $LSER = hf_H/(l - 1)f_L$ and thus $HSER < LSER$.

Catlin (1969) criticized Broadbent's version of sophisticated guessing theory. The set of words selected by a stimulus may be considered as consisting of the stimulus itself and a residual set of potential errors. Catlin argued that if words have frequencies assigned them without regard to their acoustical neighbors — which is what "independence" implies — then the ratio of high to low potential errors in the residual set cannot depend on the frequency of the stimulus word. Thus, Catlin's version of sophisticated guessing theory reinstates Pollack's prediction, i.e. $HSER = LSER$.

Broadbent (1967) also developed an alternative to restricted response set theories (see also Morton, 1968). Green and Birdsall (1958) presented a statistical decision model for the discrimination of words in noise. They assumed that for each possible response word there is a decision axis: presentation of a stimulus produces an effect on each axis that can be represented as a normally distributed variable with mean d' for the signal and zero for any other word. The axis with the largest input on a given trial determines the response. This model is analogous to the signal detection model for spatial or temporal forced choice. It differs in that here the subject is forced to choose from a set of possible responses.

Broadbent (1967) applied this model to the discrimination of words in noise with the set of possible choices taken to include any word in the language. To make the model more tractable, he employed Luce's (1959) choice theory as an approximation to the signal detection formulations based on normal distributions. This version of Luce's theory has two parameters, a and V: log a corresponds to d' and V is a measure of bias. In order to apply this formulation to word recognition, Broadbent defined a as the response strength accruing to the stimulus word as a result of presenting the signal, and assigned high frequency words a bias V, and low frequency words a bias 1. We may represent the response strength of a high frequency stimulus word by a_H, and that of a low frequency word by a_L. If the vocabulary contains N_H high and N_L low frequency words, they will have the response strengths shown in Table 1.

This model will be referred to as the Universal Forced Choice Model (UFCM) for word recognition, since the forced choice is assumed to involve every word in the vocabulary. Broadbent distinguished two versions of the UFCM, depending on the parameter values. In the first, an "observing response theory," which assumes that the subject "tunes" the auditory apparatus to detect more likely stimuli, the word frequency effect is due to a_H being greater than a_L. The second is a "criterion bias theory" in which $a_H = a_L$ but V, the bias in favor of high frequency words, is greater than 1.

Since N_H and N_L are large for natural language, the UFCM predicts that the *HS* and *LS* error ratios will be approximately equal. Broadbent (1967) presented data which he regarded as supporting this prediction and therefore allowing him to reject sophisticated guessing theory in favor of the universal forced choice model. This conclusion is not accepted by supporters of sophisticated guessing theory, such as Catlin (1969), who argues that the latter also predicts *HSER = LSER*.

TABLE 1
Response Strengths in the Universal Forced Choice Model

Stimulus	Correct	HF Errors	LF Errors	Error Ratio
HS	$a_H V$	$(N_H - 1)V$	N_L	$(N_H - 1)V/N_L$
LS	a_L	$N_H V$	$N_L - 1$	$N_H V/(N_L - 1)$

We see that there are difficulties with the theories reviewed. Restricted response set theories have not clearly specified how the discrimination processes select the response set. On the other hand, the universal forced choice model does not adequately explain why error responses are often similar to the stimulus (Savin, 1963). Broadbent and Broadbent (1975) attempted to assimilate this observation by assuming that a stimulus presentation may increase not only the magnitude of the decision variable corresponding to the word presented but also, to a lesser extent, the decision variables for words similar to it. However, this modification has not been quantitatively integrated into the theory. Another difficulty is the disagreement about what prediction restricted response set theory should make with regard to the effect of stimulus word frequency on error response frequencies. There is the unexplained increase in error frequency as a function of stimulus frequency which can be seen in Pollack et al.'s (1960) data, and is illustrated in Fig. 1. Broadbent (1967) presented *HS* and *LS* error ratios for two experiments. In the second, on disyllables, the *HSER* is 2.30 times greater than the *LSER*. Although this may be incompatible with the prediction that *HSER* $<$ *LSER,* it also casts doubt on his alternative, that the error ratios are equal. It appears that some further development of theory may be needed.

II. A THEORY OF THE PERCEPTUAL IDENTIFICATION OF COMPLEX STIMULI

A theory of word recognition can be developed from assumptions that although related to ideas discussed above are sufficiently different to generate alternative predictions. The theory deals with the processes of discrimination that restrict the set of alternatives; the mechanism that generates a response from this set; and includes a theory of the constitution of such sets. It rests on the following assumptions.

1. The word recognition system can be regarded as containing a universe of U word-images distributed in a multidimensional acoustic space whose dimensions are acoustic parameters. Thus, words that sound similar will be closely associated in the space. Some points in this space will be determined by combinations of acoustic parameters which do not constitute a word. These will be referred to as "holes." If the auditory presentation of a stimulus word selects the corresponding word-image alone this word-image will determine the response: this would constitute complete recognition.

2. It is convenient, at least in the first instance, to assume that acoustical equivalence holds, i.e. that the probability distribution of frequency f_i over the space is independent of the location of the point i in the acoustic space.

For the most part it is also a convenient simplification to assume that there are only two levels of frequency, f_H and f_L, with $f_H > f_L$. N_H high frequency and $N_L = U - N_H$ low frequency words are represented in the space. The expected proportion of high frequency word-images in any part of the space will then be $p_H = N_H/U$, and $N_H f_H + N_L f_L = 1$.

3. When a complex signal such as a word is presented, the acoustic parameters defining it are decoded with greater or less success. It is convenient to assume, though not essential to the model, that these dimensions are decoded categorically (Liberman, 1957), so that either a point (category) on a dimension is located or a residual range of uncertainty is left. The ranges of uncertainty on the different dimensions defining a complex stimulus will determine an acoustic subspace or subvolume a containing a subset s of word-images.[1] It may also contain holes. On the assumption that mishearing results from loss of information rather than distortion the subset will include the word-image corresponding to the presented stimulus. The acoustic space is illustrated in Fig. 2. The expected size of an acoustic subspace will get smaller as signal intensity increases. If the density of word images in the space is constant, the expected magnitude of the subset, s, will decrease with intensity in the same way.

The decoding process postulated here implies that the information in the stimulus is wholly exhausted in decoding the dimensions: all points within the subspace so selected will have the same standing in relation to generation of a response. No one of them, including the stimulus word-image, is more strongly indicated than any other by the stimulus, because the information in it has been wholly utilized in delimiting the subspace.

4. A response is selected by forced choice restricted to the points in the subspace, in accordance with a signal detection model. Each point in the space has a corresponding decision axis z, which will have the value $z(t)$ at time t. On any trial the perceptual system selects the word-image that has the highest value of this evidence variable. The effect of presenting a stimulus is to add to the value on each axis in the selected subspace a quantity δ. This is the same for each location. The value of $z(t)$ will also be affected by two other additive components, $\epsilon(t)$, the momentary effect of noise, and ϕ, an effect of word frequency.

The addition of δ restricts the forced choice to the subspace since it is assumed that δ is sufficiently large to make the effect of other distributions negligible. The probability that a given stimulus will be selected is then given by the appropriate integral defined over the subspace. Since the value of δ is constant, the result will be determined by the effects of ϕ and of noise. The restricted forced choice envisaged is illustrated in Fig. 3. The figure shows one "hole", w_{i+7}, a nonword that has little or no frequency increment. Although a nonword may be emitted as an error when it lies in the subspace, this should be rare.

5. It is assumed that there are only two frequency classes, high and low, and the value at each location has a corresponding component ϕ_H or ϕ_L. We assume that each time a word is perceived a small increment is added to the axis, and

[1] The word "subspace" as used here is not to be understood as a linear or vector subspace but as a subvolume of restricted dimensions. Note also that the term "partial identification theory" is replaced by "perceptual identification theory" in later publications (Treisman, 1978a).

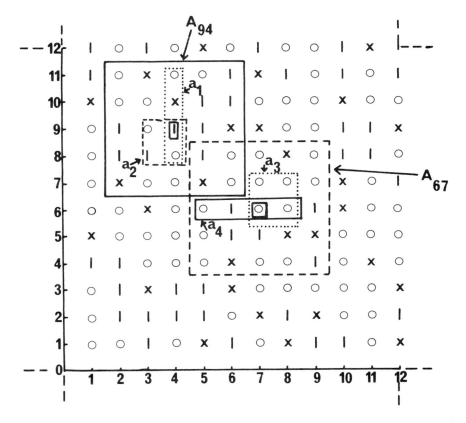

FIG. 2 Part of a schematic two-dimensional acoustic space is shown, containing word images, w_{ij}, where i refers to position on the ordinate, j on the abscissa. The number "1" indicates a high frequency word, "O" a low frequency word, "X" a hole. A high frequency (HF) and a low frequency (LF) stimulus word have been presented, and the corresponding word-images w_{94} and w_{67} are shown boxed. The first is surrounded by the acoustic neighborhood A_{94}, the second by the acoustic neighborhood A_{67}. On Trials 1 and 2 the stimulus word corresponding to w_{94} was presented and delimited the acoustic subspaces a_1 and a_2, each of four points, and containing word-image subsets of magnitude $s = 3$ and $s = 4$, respectively. On Trials 3 and 4 the LS corresponding to w_{67} was presented and selected a_3 and a_4, each with $s = 4$ word-images. 115 word-images are shown, giving a local density of .80, and $p_H = .34$.

this takes time to decay. The higher the prior value on the axis, the less scope there is for adding a further increment, and so the smaller it will tend to be. Thus a curve showing ϕ, which is the sum of the residues of such previous increments, as a function of the number of previous presentations of the word within a relevant period, would tend to be negatively accelerated. Since this function is unknown, it is convenient and plausible to approximate it by a logarithmic function. Thus, $\phi_L = \ln f_L$ and $\phi_H = \ln f_H$.

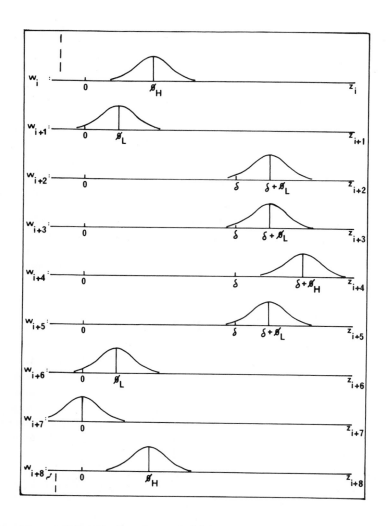

FIG. 3 Perceptual identification theory: decision axes are shown for locations w_i to w_{i+8} in the acoustic space. On each axis the distribution is shown that might result from repeated presentations of a stimulus word that each time happened to select the subspace containing the locations w_{i+2} to w_{i+5}. The momentary value on any decision axis in the subspace on trial t is given by $z_{i+j}(t) = \delta + \phi_{i+j} + \epsilon_{i+j}(t)$, where ϕ_L and ϕ_H are the low and high frequency increments respecitvely, δ is the component added by the stimulus word, and $\epsilon_{i+j}(t)$ is the effect of noise. The mean of the corresponding distribution is $\delta + \phi_{i+j}$.

Following Broadbent (1967), Luce's (1959) choice theory can be used to approximate the signal detection integral, in which case the probability of selecting the word-image w_i from a set containing s word-images of which h are high frequency becomes

$$P(w_i) = \frac{f_i}{h f_H + (s - h) f_L}$$

6. This expression is the same as that given by the restricted response set theories. But the present theory departs from earlier ones in that selection from a restricted subset in proportion to frequency (or some monotonic increasing function of frequency) here leads to consequences different from those proposed by either Catlin (1969) or Broadbent (1967). Catlin (1969, 1973) argued that if the frequencies of words in the residual set are independent of the stimulus word, the frequencies of error responses should not vary with the word presented. Broadbent (1967) argued that all words, including the stimulus word, should be taken into account in predicting error frequencies. Both views can be supported, but only if extreme assumptions are made. The first theory rests on the implicit assumption that the vocabulary is infinite. But language, though large, is finite. In the second case, the conclusions would follow if the language were restricted to a single subset of words. But language, though finite, is large.

To allow for the fact that the vocabulary is not so large that a given subset will never be sampled more than once, and that it cannot be arranged that any set will be equally often sampled by high and low frequency stimuli, it is necessary to develop a theory of sampling for this situation. This must take account of the probability of generating responses of a given type — correct responses, high frequency errors, or low frequency errors — from a defined subset, the probability that a subset of that constitution will be selected by a given stimulus word, the prevalence of such subsets in the acoustic space for a prescribed value of s, and the distribution of s for a particular signal intensity. This argument, when developed (Treisman, 1978a), leads to the expressions

$$P(C|H) = F \sum_{h=1}^{s} H(U - 1, N_H - 1, s - 1; h - 1) / [h(F - 1) + s], \tag{1}$$

$$P(HE|H) = \frac{(N_H - 1)(s - 1) F}{U - 1} \sum_{h=2}^{s} H(U - 2, N_H - 2, s - 2; h - 2) / [h(F - 1) + s], \tag{2}$$

$$P(LE|H) = \frac{(U - N_H)(s - 1)}{U - 1} \sum_{h=1}^{s-1} H(U - 2, N_H - 1, s - 2; h - 1) / [h(F - 1) + s], \tag{3}$$

$$P(C|L) = \sum_{h=0}^{s-1} H(U-1, N_H, s-1; h)/ [h(F-1)+s], \qquad (4)$$

$$P(HE|L) = \frac{N_H (s-1) F}{U-1} \sum_{h=1}^{s-1} H(U-2, N_H-1, s-2; h-1)/$$
$$[h(F-1)+s], \qquad (5)$$

and

$$P(LE|L) = \frac{(U-N_H-1)(s-1)}{U-1} \sum_{h=0}^{s-2} H(U-2, N_H, s-2; h)/$$
$$[h(F-1)+s], \qquad (6)$$

where $F = f_H/f_L$ and $H(a, b, c; d)$ is the hypergeometric distribution. The expected probabilities should also be taken over the distribution of values of s, but this is not known. In applying the model, s is assumed to take two or three neighboring values, and its distribution is then estimated from the data.

III.   A COMPUTER SIMULATION OF THE MODEL

The expressions given by the present theory differ from those given by the various versions of restricted response set theory. But it might seem that we simply have differing combinatorial intuitions in conflict, and such conflicts are notoriously difficult to resolve. To confirm the argument, it seemed that it might be useful to simulate the processes envisaged by the present theory and compare the results given by a computer with the expectations generated by the different theories. For the simulation, a one-dimensional array was set up containing U locations, of which $p_H U$ were randomly designated as high frequency and the remainder as low frequency. The presentation of 500 *HF* stimulus words and 500 *LF* words was then simulated. When the universe contained less than this number of *HF* or *LF* words sampling was with replacement, each word being sampled as near as possible equally often. For each presentation of a stimulus word a set of s contiguous locations including that word was randomly selected from the s possible subsets of this constitution. (Each such set had the same probability of being selected on any trial, that is, the distribution was rectangular.) One of the locations in this set was then selected as the response, the probability of a given location being chosen being proportional to the (high or low) frequency previously assigned to it. The response was then classified as correct (C), a high frequency error (HE), or LF error (LE), and the result stored. This whole sequence, commencing with the setting up of the universe, was repeated 100 times, and the mean of the 100 estimates of each of the measures taken was calculated. Thus, the results are based on 100,000 simulated trials for each set of parameters.

The model assumes that the volume of the acoustic subspace a will be lower the higher the intensity of the signal. For a given signal intensity we would expect a to have some variance, since noise will affect decoding of the signal. For a given value of a we would also expect s, the number of word images contained in the subspace, to have some variance, since holes are randomly distributed. However, the equations given earlier were derived for parametric values of s and accordingly, the simulation was performed for fixed values of s. For this reason, no locations in the unidimensional array were designated as holes. To do so would have been effectively equivalent to adding variance to s, since holes, being assigned frequency zero, would not generate responses.

Figure 4 compares simulated and calculated values of the different probabilities for various parameter values. Close agreement is shown between the two,

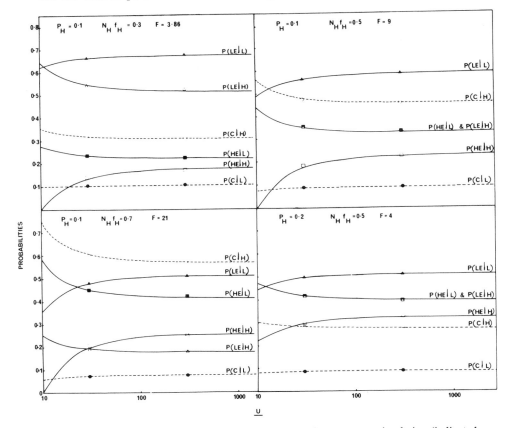

FIG. 4   Perceptual identification theory: The results of a computer simulation (indicated by the filled and empty symbols) are compared with curves given by the theory for the same parameters. For all the curves $s = 8$.

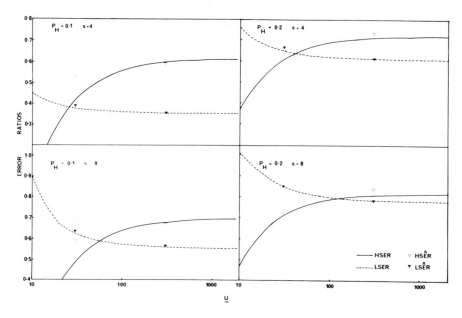

FIG. 5   Perceptual identification theory: Error ratios given by a computer simulation and curves calculated from the theory are plotted against U for the parameters shown. $N_H f_H = .5$ for all the curves.

indicating that the equations generated by perceptual identification theory provide an adequate description of the model simulated. Figure 5 compares simulated and calculated error ratio values. The fit is not quite so good, as would be expected in view of the much larger confidence intervals attaching to these measures. A main finding is that, for a wide range of parameter values, partial identification theory predicts a crossover from $HSER < LSER$ at low values of U to $HSER > LSER$ at high values. Above $U = 1000$ all the curves become asymptotic.

Figure 5 illustrates that for a wide range of parameter values and for sufficiently large values of U neither the prediction that $HSER = LSER$ (Catlin, 1969; Pollack et al., 1960) nor that $HSER < LSER$ (Broadbent, 1967) is made by the present theory. Instead we have $HSER > LSER$. This is the effect shown, at the higher stimulus intensities, in Fig. 1. Moreover, the difference between the two error ratios is greater for the smaller value of s. (s decreases as stimulus intensity rises). Thus, the form of the data found by Pollack et al. (1960) matches the implications of the present model. It appears that the different predictions for the relation between $HSER$ and $LSER$ could provide the basis for a crucial experiment to test between the theories.

IV. AN EXPERIMENTAL TEST OF PERCEPTUAL
IDENTIFICATION THEORY

A straightforward way to proceed might be to run word identification experiments with stimuli of two frequencies and calculate the *HS* and *LS* error ratios. A difficulty with this approach is that each such experiment gives only a single comparison between a value of *HSER* and a value of *LSER*. It is difficult to analyze this statistically, and so unless the results of a number of experiments are available, the final conclusion is problematic.

An alternative that may be more informative is to conduct an experiment that will predict not a point but a curve. This may be done as follows. The UFCM prediction that the *HSER* is less than the *LSER* does not depend on there being only two frequency classes. For any number of classes, if these are ordered and a cut made at any point, classifying those above the cut as "high" and the rest as "low," then the "high" error ratio will be less than the "low." The difference will be negligible if U is large but not if it is small.

A familiar, well-defined, small set of words whose frequencies have been well studied is that of letters of the alphabet. If we rank the letters in order of frequency of occurrence, there are 25 ways in which they can be divided into N_H "high" and N_L "low" letters. If their frequencies, from high to low, are represented by $f_1 > f_2 \ldots f_i \ldots f_{26}$, then the *HSER* and *LSER*, as predicted by the UFCM, can be calculated as a function of N_H, for given frequencies of presentation p_i of the individual letters. If stimulus letters are presented in the experiment with the same frequencies with which they occur in normal experience, then the relative frequency of presentation of a given high frequency letter, H_i, on high frequency trials (i.e., those trials on which a high frequency stimulus is presented) will be given by

$$p_i = f_i / S_H(N_H),$$

where

$$S_H(N_H) = \sum_{j=1}^{N_H} f_j .$$

Similarly, the relative frequency with which a given low frequency letter, L_k, will be presented on low frequency trials will be given by

$$p_k = f_k / S_L(N_H),$$

where

$$S_L(N_H) = \sum_{m=N_H+1}^{U} f_m .$$

While p_i and p_k will vary as a function of N_H, the frequencies of presentation of the stimuli, taken over the experiment as a whole, will of course be constant, at f_i and f_k.

It follows that for a given value of N_H the probability of a high frequency error when the *HF* stimulus letter H_i is presented will be $[S_H(N_H) - f_i]/[1 + (a - 1)f_i]$ and the probability of a low frequency error will be $[S_L(N_H)/[1 + (a - 1)f_i]$. Then the high stimulus error ratio predicted by the UFCM will be

$$HSER(N_H) = P(HE|H)/P(LE|H)$$

$$= \sum_{i=1}^{N_H} \frac{p_i [S_H(N_H) - f_i]}{1 + (a - 1)f_i} \Bigg/ \sum_{j=1}^{N_H} \frac{p_j S_L(N_H)}{1 + (a-1)f_j}$$

$$= \frac{S_H(N_H) \displaystyle\sum_{i=1}^{N_H} \frac{(f_i - f_i^{\,2}/S_H(N_H))}{1 + (a - 1)f_i}}{S_L(N_H) \displaystyle\sum_{j=1}^{N_H} \frac{f_j}{1 + (a - 1)f_j}} \tag{7}$$

Similarly

$$LSER(N_H) = \frac{S_H(N_H) \displaystyle\sum_{i=N_H +1}^{U} \frac{f_i}{1 + (a - 1)f_i}}{S_L(N_H) \displaystyle\sum_{j=N_H + 1}^{U} \frac{(f_j - f_j^{\,2}/S_L(N_H))}{1 + (a - 1)f_j}} \tag{8}$$

It is immediately evident that whatever the value of N_H, the *HSER* will be less than the *LSER*. The curves given by these expressions when $a = 1$ are shown in the right-hand panel of Fig. 6, for N_H ranging from 2–18. These were calculated using the frequencies of occurrence of letters of the alphabet reported by Underwood and Schulz (1960). The curves show that the ratios rise, as would be expected, as more letters are included in the "high" category, but that at each point *HSER* is clearly less than *LSER*. It is also evident that the curves diverge, the difference $(LSER(N_H) - HSER(N_H))$ becoming larger as N_H increases. This effect is not negligible: the difference between the two curves at $N_H = 18$ is 26.4 times greater than the difference at $N_H = 5$.

The effect of a on the shape of these curves is minor. For $a = 1$, *HSER* (5) $= .623$, *LSER* (5) $= .855$, *HSER* (18) $= 15.117$ and *LSER* (18) $= 21.237$. For a high value, $a = 5$, these points become $.625$, $.852$, 15.138, and 21.118. The divergence at $N_H = 18$ is now 26.3 times as great as at $N_H = 5$. Therefore, the curve for $a = 1$ will be taken as the standard prediction.

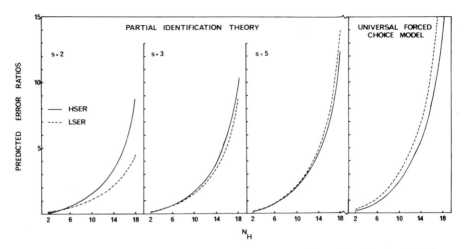

FIG. 6   Error ratios for the recognition of letters of the alphabet in noise predicted by partial identification theory and by the universal forced choice model. These are shown as a function of the number of letters categorized as "high," when this ranges from 2 to 18. For partial identification theory, the predictions depend on the value of s and curves are shown for 3 values of s. The UFCM predictions are shown for $a = 1$.

This prediction makes the usual assumption that the bias determining the probability of a response, V, is identical with its frequency of occurrence f. However, it might be argued that the universal forced choice model does not require to assume more than that this bias is a positive monotonic increasing function of f. If so, is it possible that there might be some plausible monotonic transformation of f that would give $HSER(N_H)$ and $LSER(N_H)$ curves that converged, instead of diverging, as N_H gets larger?

We examine this by defining the bias in the universal forced choice model as $V = f(f)$ and determining the predictions that would result for various forms of this function. We then define

$$T_H(N_H) = \sum_{j=1}^{N_H} V_j, \; T_L(N_H) = \sum_{m=N_H+1}^{U} V_m \text{ and } T_U = \sum_{n=1}^{U} V_n.$$

Proceeding as before we obtain

$$HSER(N_H) = \frac{\displaystyle\sum_{i=1}^{N_H} \frac{f_i(T_H(N_H) - V_i)}{T_U + (a-1)V_i}}{T_L(N_H)\displaystyle\sum_{j=1}^{N_H} \frac{f_j}{T_U + (a-1)V_j}} \tag{9}$$

and

$$LSER(N_H) = \frac{T_H(N_H) \sum_{i=N_H + 1}^{U} \dfrac{f_i}{T_U + (a - 1) V_i}}{\sum_{j=N_H + 1}^{U} \dfrac{f_j(T_L (N_H) - V_j)}{T_U + (a - 1)V_j}} \tag{10}$$

Evidently $HSER(N_H)$ will be less than $LSER(N_H)$ if V is any positive increasing function of f. If we let $V = f^k$, then when k is high, V will vary rapidly with f; if k is low, the bias will vary more slowly with f. In fact, if we let $V = f^3$, the divergence between the curves as N_H gets larger is greatly increased: applying Equations 9 and 10 with $a = 1$, $LSER(18) - HSER(18)$ is 184.5 times greater than $LSER(5) - HSER(5)$. If we reduce k to 1/3, the curves still show a large degree of divergence: $LSER(18) - HSER(18)$ is 12.0 times greater than the difference at $N_H = 5$. Even if k is reduced to 0.1, the divergence is still considerable: the difference between the two curves at $N_H = 18$ is 8.6 times as great as at $N_H = 5$. For $k = 0.1$ and $a = 10$ this ratio is 10:1.

Lyregaard (1976) has suggested a way in which $V = f(f)$ can be estimated. Expressed in terms of the present description of the universal forced choice model, the argument would run as follows: if the response to a stimulus must be chosen from two words for each of which a has the same value, then the relative probabilities of the two responses will be determined by their biases alone. This situation can be achieved by presenting homophones (such as BARE-BEAR) at intensities sufficiently high for one of the two correct responses to be almost always reported. (The subjects respond in writing.) Then the ratio of the frequency with which the first form is reported to the frequency of the second form, $P(Word_1)/P(Word_2)$, will estimate the ratio of their biases, V_1/V_2. From data of this sort Lyregaard (1976) finds that V is proportional to $f^{.67}$. However, his estimation procedure involves the assumption that intelligibility is independent of frequency for high frequency words. This can be avoided and an estimate obtained more simply by writing $P(Word_1)/P(Word_2) = V_1/V_2 = (f_1/f_2)^k$, and solving for k for each pair of homophones. If this is done, the mean value of k for these data is .59, with standard error .090. Since error in estimating word frequencies will reduce the slope of the relation between V and f, .59 can be taken as a lower limit for k. For $V = f^{.6}$, $LSER (18) - HSER (18)$ would be 16.8 times greater than $LSER (5) - HSER (5)$.

(While this procedure provides an estimate of $V = f (f)$ for the universal forced choice model, since we can suppose that there is a signal detection axis for each of the two homophones, each having its own bias but receiving the same increment when the stimulus word is presented, this is not true for partial identification theory. The latter assumes that when the presented stimulus is decoded, this selects a set of word images of which only one will correspond to the homophone. Selection between two meanings will take place at a later stage, and it is the effect of frequency at this later stage that may be estimated from Lyregaard's (1976) data.)

The prediction made by Broadbent's (1967) version of sophisticated guessing theory would also be that $HSER < LSER$ throughout, the difference between the curves being generally greater as the response set is smaller than the whole alphabet. It does not seem that Catlin's (1969) version of this theory would apply to a small vocabulary, as it implicitly assumes an infinite universe. It appears that it would converge with Broadbent's approach when the vocabulary is restricted.

The prediction given by perceptual identification theory is shown in the first three panels of Fig. 6, for three values of s. This parameter will increase as signal intensity decreases. The predictions were derived from Equations 2, 3, 5, and 6 taking

$$f_H = \sum_{i=1}^{N_H} f_i/N_H \text{ and } f_L = \sum_{i=N_H+1}^{U} f_i/N_L$$

for each value of N_H. For each curve s is constant, and all that varies is the proportion of letters classified as "high" or "low." These curves differ from those predicted by the other theories in that in some cases (when s is low, i.e., signal intensity is high) a crossover is shown, $HSER$ being less than $LSER$ for a small N_H, but the relation reversing when N_H is large. However, this effect decreases as s increases, the prediction becoming similar to that given by the UFCM when s is large. Thus, the present theory predicts that at least some of the curves should show a crossover, whereas other theories do not predict this.

Figure 7 shows word frequency effect curves predicted by perceptual identification theory (Equations 1 and 4) and the UFCM. The latter are given by

$$P(C|H) = \frac{af_H}{af_H + (N_H - 1)f_H + N_L f_L} \tag{11}$$

and

$$P(C|L) = \frac{af_L}{af_L + N_H f_H + (N_L - 1)f_L} \tag{12}$$

It is evident that both theories predict a word frequency effect and that the predictions are indistinguishable.

There are two difficulties in conducting a word recognition experiment with letters of the alphabet. The first is that this constitutes a small, known, message set, and previous work with such sets has shown that they do not give the word

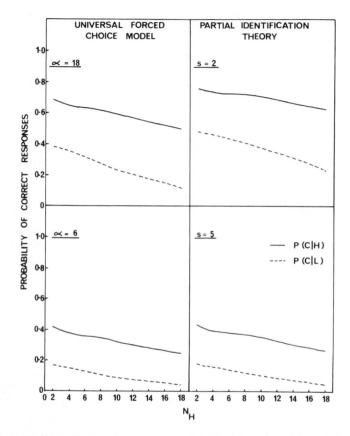

FIG. 7   Probabilities of correct responses predicted by the universal forced choice model (Equations 11 and 12) and perceptual identification theory (Equations 1 and 4), for the values of a and s shown as parameters.

frequency effect (Broadbent, 1976; Pollack et al., 1960). A possible reason is that rapid learning of new, equal frequencies for members of the message set might occur, either during prior familiarization or during the actual conduct of the experiment. This would be supported by Goldiamond and Hawkins' (1958) finding that a training session in which nonsense syllables were presented with unequal frequencies produced marked effects in a subsequent experiment, and by the effects of immediate stimulus context on detectability.

The second difficulty is that the frequencies of letters of the alphabet tabulated by Underwood and Schulz (1960) refer to written material, whereas we are concerned with an auditory discrimination experiment. Experience of spoken letters may differ from that of written material, even though much of it may come from spelling aloud.

It was thought that both these difficulties might be avoided by departing from the usual procedure in which stimuli are presented with equal frequency, and instead presenting the stimulus letters with the same relative frequencies with which they are assumed to have occurred in the subjects' prior experience. This should prevent the subjects coming to assign equal frequencies to them during the course of the experiment, and so diluting the word frequency effect, if this is what happens. Serving in the experiment would also tend to increase the correlation of subjects' expected frequencies with those found in the Underwood and Schulz (1960) count, if they differ.

A. Apparatus and Procedure

The letters were prerecorded by a single male speaker and presented on a Ferrograph tape recorder whose output passed through a step attenuator and was then mixed with white noise. The latter passed through a high-pass filter used to reduce a 50 Hz hum. The output then went to a loudspeaker. Subjects sat at tables at the far end of the laboratory with their backs to the loudspeaker. The center of the row of tables was 6.5m from the loudspeaker.

A session lasted one hour. Four blocks were presented in a session, each lasting 12.5 min and consisting of 125 trials. Each trial began with the trial number. After 2 sec (from onset to onset) the letter was given, and after 4 sec, during which the subject wrote his response on a numbered answer sheet, the next trial commenced. Thus, letters were separated by 6 sec. Subjects had a short rest between each block of trials.

The white noise was adjusted to 60 db SPL as measured with a Dawe noise level meter (scale C) at the mid-position of the subjects. The intensity of a sample of tape-recorded speech was set at the same level, and the letters were adjusted to match the speech. This gave a S/N ratio of 0 db; lower levels were obtained by attenuating the letters. In Experiment 1 the S/N ratios were 0 db and -8 db, and in Experiment 2, 0db and -16 db.

The letters were presented with frequencies derived from data given by Underwood and Schulz (1960). These frequencies and the corresponding numbers of "high" and "low" presentations in a 1000 as a function of N_H are shown in Table 2. The letters were presented in random order with no constraints on sequence and were pronounced as spoken in England. Thus "W" was "double-u" and "Z" was "zed."

In Experiment 1 six subjects attended for one practice and four experimental sessions. Not more than one session was given on a single day. Subjects attended in pairs for the first experimental session, but all six subjects were tested together for the last three sessions. In the first two sessions they received 1000 presentations at 0 db, in the final two sessions 1000 presentations at -8 db.

Two subjects were male and four female, and their ages ranged from 18 to 23. They were paid for their services.

TABLE 2
Letters of the Alphabet:
Frequencies (Underwood and Schulz, 1960)
and Presentations (in a 1000).

Letters	Frequency	Presentations	HS	LS
E	0.1257	126	–	–
T	0.0882	88	214	786
A	0.0798	80	294	706
I	0.0736	74	368	632
O	0.0734	73	441	559
N	0.0710	71	512	488
S	0.0675	67	579	421
R	0.0621	62	641	359
H	0.0530	53	694	306
L	0.0407	41	735	265
D	0.0397	40	775	225
U	0.0307	31	806	194
C	0.0279	28	834	166
M	0.0258	26	860	140
F	0.0220	22	882	118
G	0.0211	21	903	97
W	0.0203	20	923	77
Y	0.0196	20	943	57
P	0.0193	19	–	–
B	0.0155	15	–	–
V	0.0101	10	–	–
K	0.0073	7	–	–
X	0.0019	2	–	–
J	0.0018	2	–	–
Z	0.0010	1	–	–
Q	0.0009	1	–	–

Experiment 2 was similar. Five of the subjects had served in Experiment 1, the sixth was new and received two sessions of practice before the experiment. Three were male, three female, and the age range was 19 to 23. Each subject was tested singly for four experimental sessions. In each session there were two blocks at 0 db and two blocks at −16 db. Thus, there were 1000 trials at each intensity for each subject.

B. Results

Figures 8 and 9 illustrate that the word frequency effect is present. In Experiment 2 this is more marked at the higher intensity, as would be expected. In Experiment 1 signal intensity is confounded with practice, as the lower intensity was given in the second two sessions. The tendency for the effect to reverse for small values of N_H may be linked with a tendency for the letter "A" to be more

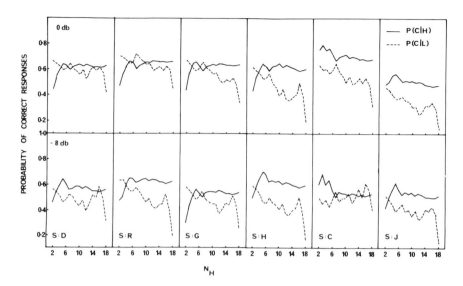

FIG. 8   Experiment 1: Probabilities of correct responses for a high frequency or low frequency stimulus word are shown separately for 6 subjects at two intensity levels. The data are analyzed for N_H varying from 2 to 18.

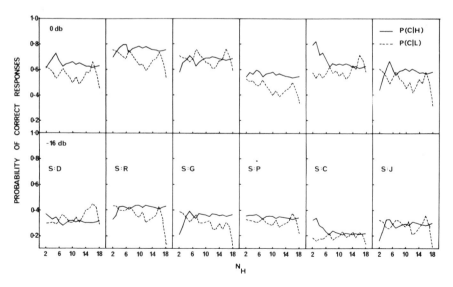

FIG. 9   Experiment 2: Probabilities of correct responses for 6 subjects at two intensity levels.

frequent than "E" in the responses. In 24 cases (6 subjects x 4 conditions), "A" occurred more frequently as a response than "E" in 17, and equally often in two.

Figure 10 gives the error ratios for Experiment 1 and Fig. 11 for Experiment 2. The curves are not highly regular, but the irregularities are not simply noise. For example, in Fig. 10 every low stimulus error ratio curve shows a dip at 10 (L added to N_H) and a peak at 13 or 14 (C and M added), suggesting that these fluctuations reflect constant features of the alphabet. The similarities might have arisen from subjects' hearing the same white noise, since they were tested together for 3 sessions. But the irregularities are similar for the 0 db and −8 db conditions, although these curves were determined in different sessions, and similar irregularities are shown in Fig. 11, although in Experiment 2 subjects were tested individually. Repeated and reliable irregularities such as these are difficult for the UFCM to account for, since it requires that the response is selected by forced choice from the entire vocabulary, whatever stimulus is presented. They present no difficulty for any version of restricted response set theory, including partial identification theory, since different letters would be expected to have different proportions of high and low frequency word-images in their acoustic neighborhoods, and so to produce differing effects on the error ratio, as they transfer from the low to high categories.

Both sophisticated guessing theory and the UFCM predicted that *HSER* would be less than *LSER* for all values of N_H. Partial identification theory predicted that a crossover would be shown in some at least of the curves. Inspec-

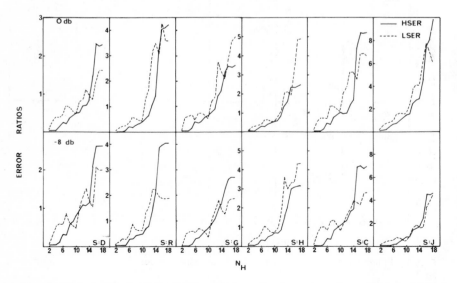

FIG. 10   Experiment 1: High stimulus and low stimulus error ratios with 2 to 18 high frequency letters placed in the "high" category, and the remainder classified as "low."

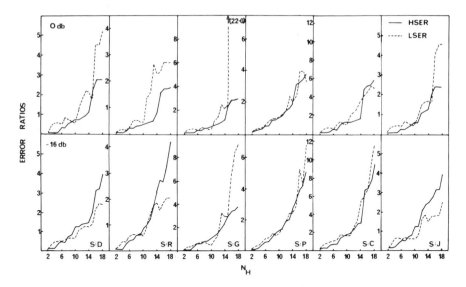

FIG. 11   Experiment 2: *HS* and *LS* error ratios for 6 subjects and two S/N ratios. Three points not shown (Subject G at 0 db) each had an error ratio of 22.

tion of Figs. 10 and 11 suggests that the expected crossovers do occur. All theories predicted *HSER* < *LSER* for low values of N_H. If we consider this to be shown when at least 3 of the points from N_H = 2 to N_H = 6 have *HSER* < *LSER*, then all 24 curves in Figs 10 and 11 confirm this common prediction. The theories differ for N_H large. If we take *HSER* > *LSER* at the upper end of the curve when this is the direction of the difference at at least 3 of the last five points plotted, then 8 of the 12 curves in Fig. 10 and 4 of those in Fig. 11 show this relation.

The signs test may be used to examine whether this constitutes significant evidence for the occurrence of crossovers. The null hypothesis would be that the relationship between *HSER* and *LSER* is independent of N_H. Then the true relationship between the curves will be the same, for example, *HSER* < *LSER*, whether we consider the lower or the upper ends of the curves. But random factors may contrive to reverse this relationship at one or the other or both ends of the curves in a proportion of cases. If so, the null hypothesis implies that the number of cases in which *HSER* < *LSER* for N_H small but the relation apparently reverses to give *HSER* > *LSER* for N_H large should be approximately the same as the number of changes in the reverse direction. In fact, the curves show 12 cases of the first type of change and none of the second. Applying the signs test, the probability of this occurring by chance if the null hypothesis is true is p = 0.0002, one-tailed. This is highly significant evidence against the universal forced choice and sophisticated guessing theories. Partial identification theory predicted that in a proportion of cases, those in which the stimulus intensity and the subject's sensitivity combined to determine a small value of s, crossovers would occur in the direction found. The evidence is wholly compatible with this prediction.

Partial identification theory also predicted that crossovers should be more common at the higher stimulus intensities. This is not fully confirmed. Although this pattern is shown by 3 of 6 curves at -16 db, and 5 of 6 at -8 db, it is present in only 4 of 12 at 0 db. This may be due to the confounding of signal intensity and practice in Experiment 1 but is also found in Experiment 2, in which this was avoided.

A second feature of the curves shown in Fig. 6 is different for the two theories and can be checked against the data. The UFCM gives numerically larger error ratios than does partial identification theory. For the latter the high stimulus and low stimulus error ratios at $N_H = 18$ are for $s = 2$, 8.75 and 4.52; for $s = 3$, 10.38 and 8.75; and for $s = 5$, 12.39 and 13.98. Accuracy of recognition falls as s gets larger. But in 23 of the 24 sets of curves (6 subjects x 4 conditions) provided by these experiments, the subject was more accurate than would be predicted for $s = 5$, so the latter value can be taken as an upper limit to s for these data.

The UFCM predicts high and low stimulus error ratios of 15.12 and 21.24 at $N_H = 18$, for $a = 1$. Variation in a has little effect on these figures.

Thus, we have a second differentiating prediction. Partial identification theory implies that the observed values of the error ratios at $N_H = 18$ should fall below the values predicted for $s = 5$ (12.39 and 13.98). Universal forced choice predicts that they will not differ significantly from 15.12 ($HSER$) and 21.24 ($LSER$).

The 24 values of $HSER(18)$ have a mean of 4.07 (median 3.83) and in all cases are less than 12.39. The mean is significantly less than 12.39 ($t = 20.38$, 23 df, $p < .0005$, one-tailed) and significantly less than 15.12 ($t = 27.07$, 23 df, $p < .0005$). Twenty-three values of $LSER(18)$ fall below 13.98 (the exception is an outlier of 22.00). The mean is 4.93 (median 3.88) and is significantly less than 13.98 ($t = 10.21$, $p < .0005$) and significantly less than 21.24 ($t = 18.41$, $p < .0005$).

Thus, the values tend to be in the range predicted by partial identification theory, but are markedly smaller than is required by the universal forced choice model. However, the values predicted by the latter were calculated on the assumption that bias is directly proportional to frequency, and they could be reduced by modifying the bias function, $V = f(f)$. Lyregaard's (1976) data suggested that the universal forced choice bias function might be represented by $V_i = f_i^k$, with k not less than about .6. If we substitute this function into Equations 9 and 10, the UFCM predictions for $a = 1$ fall to $HSER(18) = 7.50$ and $LSER(18) = 10.06$. But the means obtained in the experiment are significantly below both these values ($t = 8.40$, $p < .0005$ and $t = 5.79$, $p < .0005$). For $a = 10$ and $k = .60$ the predicted error ratios are 7.52 and 9.97, with similar implications.

C. Further Evidence

Partial identification theory predicts that for large vocabularies $HSER > LSER$ (see Fig. 5). This prediction has been examined for six sets of data from the literature in which words from large vocabularies have been presented for recognition. These are (1) Broadbent's (1967) monosyllable experiment, in which subjects listened to monosyllables selected from two ranges of frequency, and (2) Broadbent's (1967) disyllable experiment. This was similar except that disyllables were employed.

An extensive series of data has been collected by Brown and Rubenstein (1961) and is reported more fully by Morton (1968). The vocabulary consisted of the approximately 6500 monosyllabic content words in the Lorge Magazine Count. These were divided into 13 frequency categories, and 1300 words were presented to 6 observers at 0 db S/N ratio, and the experiment repeated at 10 db. It is possible to reduce the results at each intensity to two frequency classes for each of which C, HE, and LE response measures can be derived, either by defining the 500 words in the highest category as "high" and the 6000 others as "low," or by classifying the highest 6000 as "high" and the remainder as low. These will be referred to as (3) the H-500/0, (4) H-500/10, (5) H-6000/0, and (6) H-6000/10 analyses. In each case the values of the high stimulus and low stimulus error ratios have been calculated, and these are plotted in Fig. 12. Further details of these analyses will be given elsewhere (Treisman, 1978a).

The error ratios for these sets of data were also predicted from the UFCM and partial identification theory, using parameters, a and s, estimated from the data. The observed values are plotted against the predicted values in Fig. 13.

In Fig. 12, in five of the six cases $HSER$ exceeds $LSER$, as predicted by partial identification theory, but not by any of the competing theories. The fit of observed to predict values in Fig. 13 is obviously better for partial identification theory than for the UFCM.

D. Discussion and Conclusion

A theory of the identification of complex stimuli has been presented whose assumptions are, first, that decoding sensory information selects a restricted set of possible responses and excludes the remainder. In this respect it is a form of restricted response set theory. Second, a response is selected by a forced choice over the restricted set, in accordance with signal detection theory, but stimulus information makes no contribution to determining the result of this choice. Third, this forced choice can be approximated by random selection over the subset, with biases proportional to word frequency. Fourth, the probabilities of different types of responses are given by a theory of subset sampling developed for the acoustical space envisaged by the model.

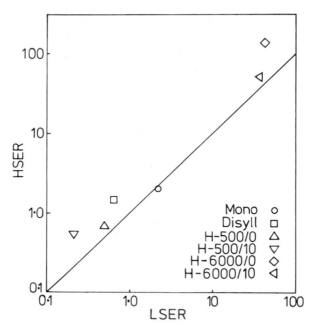

FIG. 12 High stimulus error ratios are plotted against the corresponding low stimulus error ratios on logarithmic coordinates for data obtained by Broadbent (1967) and Brown and Rubenstein (1961). The straight line represents *HSER = LSER*.

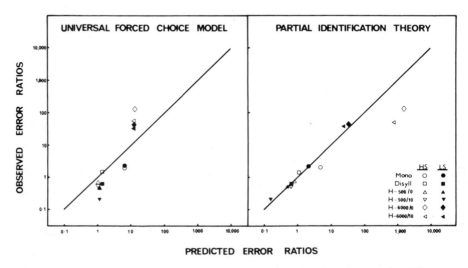

FIG. 13 Observed *HS* and *LS* error ratios are plotted against the values predicted by the UFCM and partial identification theory for the data of Broadbent (1967) and Brown and Rubenstein (1961).

Different types of evidence supporting the theory are reported. The agreement between the results of the computer simulation and the curves calculated from Equations 1 through 6 provides strong justification for accepting the logic leading to the latter. The occurrence of the crossover pattern in half the cases in Fig. 10 and 11 confirms the predictions made by partial identification theory in Fig. 6. The theory is further supported by confirmation of crucial predictions by an analysis of data obtained by Broadbent (1967) and Brown and Rubenstein (1961), which will be reviewed more fully elsewhere (Treisman, 1978a).

The theory contains a number of postulates and is fairly complex. However, the task the subject performs is complex, and too simple a theory may fail to match the complexity of the data. Some of the postulates are essential, and others, such as the relation between ϕ and f, could readily be modified but have been made precise in order to provide a quantifiable and testable formulation. Thus, it can be seen that the prediction that under some conditions high frequency errors will be relatively more common when a high frequency stimulus is presented than when a low frequency stimulus is given would follow from the general consideration that random factors would cause some areas of the acoustic space to have a preponderance of high frequency word images and other areas to be mainly low frequency. If high and low stimuli are chosen with equal frequency from all words of the appropriate frequency class, then high frequency stimuli will more often sample areas of the former type and low stimuli areas of the latter type. But a qualitative consideration of this sort would not very readily predict the effect of parameters such as p_H or U on the error ratios, or the effect of s or N_H on the relation between $HSER(N_H)$ and $LSER(N_H)$ when letters of the alphabet are presented. Here the equations derived from the exact postulates are essential.

Two assumptions may deserve further comment. The model implies that acoustic loci may occur that do not correspond to any word. The belief that such "holes" exist is not necessary for any of the predictions tested in the present paper. These depend on the theory of sampling from the acoustic space. But the assumption that holes occur finds a place in applying the theory to provide a full analysis of the Brown and Rubenstein (1961) data (Treisman, 1978a) and is specifically tested elsewhere (Treisman, 1978b).

It is also assumed that the information in the stimulus is exhausted in defining the subset selected, so that the decision variable for the correct response does not receive any greater increment than those for the other words in the subset. This is the simplest assumption, and it is included in the model since it has not so far been necessary to depart from it in order to fit data or offer explanations. Any alternative would require additional postulates and would make the equations derived more complex. If data did oblige us to proceed in this direction, the simplest way to extend the model might be to assume that decoding the stimulus produces a "subjective probability density function" on each dimension of the acoustic space. The assumption made heretofore is equivalent to postulating that this function is rectangular on each dimension, and that a is the product of these densities for those word images for which they are all non-zero. If instead we were to assume, say, that these distributions are normal, then δ would be continuously variable and would have its greatest magnitude at or near the word-image corresponding to the stimulus presented.

The theory developed here is sufficiently general to apply not only to auditory word recognition but to any vocabulary of complex stimuli, such as gestures or written words, and it will be of interest to explore its further application.

GLOSSARY OF SYMBOLS

a	The acoustic subvolume selected when a stimulus word is presented.
a	The choice theory parameter representing the increase in the response strength for the stimulus word resulting from presentation of the signal.
a_H	The response strength for a high frequency stimulus word.
a_L	The response strength for a low frequency stimulus word.
d'	The signal detection theory parameter representing the difference between the means of the signal + noise and noise distributions, divided by the standard deviation of the noise distribution.
δ	The increment added to the decision variables for each word image in a selected subvolume.
ϵ	The noise component of the decision variable for a word image in the acoustic subvolume.
f	The frequency of occurrence of a word in the language.
f_H	The frequency of occurrence in the language of a high frequency word, assuming that there are two levels of frequency.
f_L	The frequency of occurrence in the language of a low frequency word, assuming that there are two levels of frequency.
F	f_H/f_L
ϕ_i	A component added to the decision variable for a word of frequency i.
HS	A high frequency stimulus word.
$HSER$	The error ratio, given that a high frequency stimulus is presented: $P(HE|H)/P(LE|H)$.
LS	A low frequency stimulus word.
$LSER$	The error ratio given that a low frequency stimulus is presented: $P(HE|L)/P(LE|L)$.
N_H	The number of high frequency words in the vocabulary.
N_L	The number of low frequency words in the vocabulary.
p_i	The relative frequency with which the $HF(LF)$ letter i is presented in an experiment, on trials on which a $HF(LF)$ letter is presented.

$P(C\|H)$	The probability of a correct response, given that a high frequency stimulus is presented.
$P(C\|L)$	The probability of a correct response, given that a low frequency stimulus is presented.
$P(HE\|H)$	The probability of a high frequency error, given that a high frequency stimulus is presented.
$P(HE\|L)$	The probability of a high frequency error, given that a low frequency stimulus is presented.
$P(LE\|H)$	The probability of a low frequency error, given that a high frequency stimulus is presented.
$P(LE\|L)$	The probability of a low frequency error, given that a low frequency stimulus is presented.
s	The subset of word-images contained in the acoustic subvolume selected by the stimulus word.
$S_H(N_H)$	$\displaystyle\sum_{i=1}^{N_H} f_i$
$S_L(N_H)$	$\displaystyle\sum_{i=N_H+1}^{U} f_i$
$T_H(N_H)$	$\displaystyle\sum_{i=1}^{N_H} V_i$
$T_L(N_H)$	$\displaystyle\sum_{i=N_H+1}^{U} V_i$
T_U	$\displaystyle\sum_{i=1}^{U} V_i$
U	The total number of words in the vocabulary.
$UFCM$	The universal forced choice model.
V	The choice theory parameter representing the bias in favor of a given response.
w	A location in the acoustic space.
z	The signal detection decision axis corresponding to a point in the acoustic space.

ACKNOWLEDGMENTS

This work was done while in receipt of support from the Medical Research Council of Great Britian. We would like to thank Dr. S. Sternberg for stimulating us to take up this problem again. Reprint requests should be addressed to: Dr. Michel Treisman, Department of Ex-

perimental Psychology, University of Oxford, South Parks Road, Oxford, OX1 3UD,
ENGLAND.

REFERENCES

Broadbent, D. E. Word-frequency effect and response bias. *Psychological Review,* 1967,
  74, 1–15.
Broadbent, D. E., & Broadbent, M. P. H. Some further data concerning the word frequency
  effect. *Journal of Experimental Psychology: General.* 1975, *104,* 297–308.
Brown, C. R., & Rubenstein, H. Test of response bias explanation of word-frequency effect.
  Science, 1961, *133,* 280–281.
Catlin, J. On the word-frequency effect. *Psychological Review,* 1969, *76,* 504–506.
Catlin, J. In defense of sophisticated-guessing theory. *Psychological Review,* 1973, *80,*
  412–416.
Goldiamond, I., & Hawkins, W. F. Vexierversuch: The log relationship between word-
  frequency and recognition obtained in the absence of stimulus words. *Journal of Ex-
  perimental Psychology,* 1958, *56,* 457–463.
Green, D. M., & Birdsall, T. G. The effect of vocabulary size on articulation score. Tech.
  Memo. No. 81, University of Michigan, Electronic Defense Group, 1958. Reprinted in
  J. A. Swets (Ed.), *Signal detection and recognition by human observers.* New York: Wiley,
  1964.
Liberman, A. M. Some results of research on speech perception. *Journal of the Acoustical
  Society of America,* 1957, *29,* 117–123.
Luce, R. D. *Individual choice behavior.* New York: Wiley, 1959.
Lyregaard, P. E. On the relation between recognition and familiarity of words. *National
  Physical Laboratory Acoustics Report Ac 78,* 1976.
Morton, J. A. A retest of the response-bias explanation of the word-frequency effect. *British
  Journal of Mathematical and Statistical Psychology,* 1968, *21,* 21–33.
Pollack, I., Rubenstein, H., & Decker, L. Analysis of incorrect responses to an unknown
  message set. *Journal of the Acoustical Society of America,* 1960, *32,* 454–457.
Savin, H. B. Word-frequency effect and errors in the perception of speech. *Journal of the
  Acoustical Society of America,* 1963, *35,* 200–206.
Treisman, M. A. A theory of the identification of complex stimuli with an application to
  word recognition. *Psychological Review,* 1978, in press. (a)
Treisman, M. Space or lexicon? The word frequency effect and the error response frequency
  effect. *Journal of Verbal Learning and Verbal Behavior,* 1978, *17,* 37–59. (b)
Underwood, B. J., & Schulz, R. W. *Meaningfulness and verbal learning,* Philadelphia: Lip-
  pincott, 1960.

35

Visual Search, Visual Attention, and the Attention Operating Characteristic

George Sperling
Melvin J. Melchner

Bell Laboratories
Murray Hill, New Jersey, United States

ABSTRACT

Visual search experiments, in which subjects search an array of background objects for a target, are difficult to interpret because eye movements occur that are not under experimental control. The present experiments eliminated eye movements by presenting arrays of alphanumeric characters in brief flashes on a cathode ray oscilloscope. In previous experiments of this type we found that subjects searching for a numeral target in a background of letters could search simultaneously for an unknown one-of-ten numeral almost as well as for a single known numeral, and they could scan in parallel 15 to 25 characters in an array. The efficiency of this search was shown to be limited by the local density of characters.

In the attention experiments reported here, two different targets appeared in each sequence of character arrays. When the subject's task was to search simultaneously for an unknown large-size and an unknown small-size numeral, there was considerable interference between the two tasks. Instructions to attend primarily to the large or primarily to the small numeral were highly effective. Two other pairs of visual search tasks also were studied, and data from the three experiments were used to trace out Attention Operating Characteristic (AOC) curves. An AOC is defined as the locus of points on a graph plotting performance on search task 1 against performance on search task 2; it is analogous to the Receiver Operating Characteristic (ROC) of signal detection theory. Using an AOC, it is possible to measure the compatibility of two tasks between which attention is divided. In order to do this one cannot use just one condition of attention for each pair of tasks, for this would be comparing one point from each of two curves instead of comparing two curves. (A similar problem occurs in signal detection with ROC curves).

Attention-switching and attention-sharing models of two-task performance are defined. Our data enabled us to show that, in these experiments, movement along the AOC was primarily due to switching between two attention states, although some sharing of attention also occurred.

I. VISUAL SEARCH UNDER A SINGLE ATTENTIONAL STATE

The primary mechanisms of visual attention are overt: eye movements and body orientation. But even within a single eye fixation, as we will demonstrate, attentive processes determine what particular kinds of signals are analyzed and from what parts of the visual field they are accepted.

Consider normal visual search. The subject searches an array of objects (background objects) for a critical object (target) by moving his eyes over the array. While the pattern of eye movements is interesting in itself, it complicates the analysis of attention because the eye movements are not under experimental control. Therefore, we eliminate eye movements in our experiments by having the subject keep his eyes fixated on the center of a display, and presenting new stimuli to him every t msec. This method gives the experimenter precise control over the flow of information to the visual system. When t is 240 msec, this display sequence approximates the sequence that the eyes produce for themselves in natural visual search.

A typical paradigm is illustrated in Fig. 1. The subject first sees a fixation field presented for one second, and then a sequence of alphanumeric character arrays. Each character array is presented as a brief flash lasting a fraction of a millisecond. The briefly flashed arrays are clearly visible; in other experiments (Sperling, 1973)[1] we have found no difference in performance between brief flashes and arrays presented continuously for 200 msec. One of the character arrays, the critical array, contains the target character. It is preceded by a random number (from 7 to 12) of noncritical arrays and followed by at least 12 noncritical arrays. The subject does not know which array contains the target character, nor what the particular target will be, nor where in the array it is located. His task is to report the identity and location of the target character, and his degree of confidence in the correctness of his report.

The great advantage in collecting reports of confidence and location — even when we are interested primarily in identification — is that confidence and location enable us to "purify" the data by indicating when the subject is guessing. We have established the following: (1) when our subjects do make location confusions, they nearly always are confusions of two adjacent locations; and (2) when subjects use the lowest confidence category ("guessing"), their responses are, in fact, statistically independent of the stimulus (guessing!). Therefore, most of the effects of guessing are eliminated simply by scoring responses as wrong whenever a location is in error by more than one position, or whenever the lowest confidence category is used (cf. Sperling & Melchner, 1976b).

The data (probability of a correct response) are analyzed in terms of $\hat{l}$, the average number of characters the subject scans in each array, and $\hat{t}$, the average time it takes to scan one character. In previous studies (Sperling, Budiansky,

[1] In this experiment, the arrays tested were those illustrated in Fig. 2 of text, and onset-to-onset times tested were 240 msec and 480 msec.

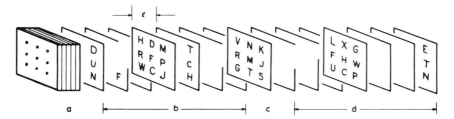

FIG. 1.   Sequence of consecutive displays in the search experiment. (a) Fixation field; (b) 7 to 12 noncritical displays; (c) critical display with single target numeral; (d) 12 noncritical displays; (*t*) interval from the onset of one stimulus to the onset of the next. The subject attempts to identify the target numeral (e.g., "5"), its location, and he gives his confidence in the correctness of his reports. (From Sperling, et al., 1971. Copyright 1971 by the American Association for the Advancement of Science.)

Spivak, & Johnson, 1971) we studied the ability of a subject to search for a single target numeral when the background characters were letters. Some salient results and conclusions were:

1. Telling the subject in advance which particular numeral (e.g., "5") will be presented on each one of a long series of trials does not improve the detectability of that numeral, relative to its detectability when the subject is searching for an unknown one-of-ten numerals. A related observation is that when the subject detects a target, he detects both its location and its identity. That is, he does not report seeing an unknown numeral in a particular location, or seeing a particular number in an unknown location. Detection of a numeral among letters implies both identity and location information.

2. The maximum number of characters a subject can scan in an array (max $\hat{l}$, his "span") is about 15–25 characters. Increasing the number of characters in the array beyond a subject's span does not improve his performance.

3. In viewing letters whose size is greater than about .5 deg, subjects approach their asymptotic performance when arrays are presented every 120 msec; increasing t to 240 msec improves performance only slightly; increases in t beyond 240 msec are of no benefit whatsoever. A corollary conclusion is that when a subject searches arrays of many letters naturally by means of eye movements (i.e., corresponding to a new input about every 240 msec), his processing capacity is unused for almost half of the time (between 120 and 240 msec after each eye movement).

4. The most efficient search (min $\hat{t}$) occurs when new arrays occur every 40 to 50 msec (corresponding to 20 to 25 fresh arrays per sec). In these presentations, most subjects achieve a $\hat{t}$ of less than 10 msec, corresponding to scan rates in excess of 100 characters per sec. When arrays are more closely spaced than every 40 msec, performance deteriorates rapidly.

5. The conclusion from these and related studies is that subjects scan in parallel 15 to 25 characters in an array.

| (a) | (b) | (7 x 7) | (a + b − 1) − (7 x 7) |

(a)

.78	.60	.68	.70	.50
.82	1.00	.97	.91	.56
.80	.97	.97	.92	.82
.92	.96	.92	.93	.56
.67	.73	.80	.79	.56

20.05

(b)

.50	.31	.59	.62	.60	.26	.20
.49						.43
.65						.56
1.00			1.00			.70
.77						.66
.32						.55
.50	.30	.69	.75	.74	.26	.28

13.60

(7 x 7)

.46	.13	.24	.24	.11	.08	.04
.43	.57	.48	.59	.77	.13	.16
.54	.39	.96	.96	.91	.52	.32
.88	.74	1.00	.95	1.00	.79	.50
.70	.68	.92	.83	.96	.79	.23
.32	.38	.65	.65	.74	.20	.20
.26	.29	.50	.56	.57	.21	.15

25.43

(a + b − 1) − (7 x 7)

.04	.18	.35	.38	.49	.18	.16
.06	.21	.12	.09	−.07	.37	.27
.11	.43	.04	.01	0	.04	.24
.12	.06	−.03	.02	−.08	.03	.20
.07	.24	.04	.09	−.03	−.23	43
0	.29	.08	.15	.05	.36	.35
.24	.01	.19	.19	.17	.05	.13

7.22

FIG. 2.   Three display configurations tested in the search paradigm: 5 x 5, 7 x 7 frame plus one center location, and 7 x 7. The subject's task was to identify the target, an unknown one-of-ten numeral, that occurred at a random location among the letter background characters. The proportion of correct target identifications at each location is indicated at the location itself. The proportion of correct identifications (over all locations and all trials) times the number of stimulus letters ($\hat{l}$) is indicated under each display. The right-most panel indicates the location-by-location superiority of the sum of the parts (a + b − 1) over the whole (7 x 7).

At Attention and Performance V we reported on one reason for the limited capacity: local sharing of processing capacity between nearby locations of the same array. We compared the performance (number of locations scanned, $\hat{l}$) in separate experiments. Each experiment involved identification of an unknown one-of-ten numeral in one of the three arrays shown in Fig. 2: (a) a 5 x 5 array, (b) a 7 x 7 array, and (c), the sum of (a) and (b), a 7 x 7 array. Performance on the whole (c) is clearly less than the sum of performances on the component parts (minus the duplicated central location); c < a + b − 1. From a location-by-location analysis of the deficit we can characterize it as follows: The probability of correct identification at a location in (c) will be lower than at the corresponding location in (a) or (b) to the extent that the location in (c) has more neighbors. Thus, the drop in performance is most obvious at the locations that correspond to the corners of the 5 x 5 array. This is local interference (cf. Estes, 1972, 1975).

II.   VISUAL SEARCH UNDER MULTIPLE ATTENTIONAL STATES

In contrast to the local interference by neighbors, there is a global effect of attention in visual search we shall report here. In an attempt to produce an optimum array of characters for visual search, we constructed an array in which we made a modest attempt to match the number of characters in each local area to the density of information-processing capacity in that area. This array consisted of very small characters in the center, surrounded by larger and larger characters in each successively larger ring around the center. To our surprise, we found that performance was not improved. This led us to investigate the question of whether subjects can search in parallel for targets of different sizes. This question has been posed by Kinchla (1977) in a somewhat different paradigm. Kinchla found that instructions to attend to stimuli of a particular size influenced his subjects' decision criteria but not the quality of information they obtained from the stimuli. Nothing in his results would suggest the difficulty our subject had.

A. Procedure

The experimental paradigm was the same as before except that the critical array now contained two target numerals, a large one and a small one, chosen independently, and the subject's task was to report both numerals, both locations, and both confidences. The spatial arrangement of the small characters in the *inside* and the large characters in the *outside* of an array is illustrated in Fig. 3. The size and number of the *inside* and *outside* characters were chosen so that in control experiments, in which the task of the subject was to report only *inside* or only *outside* numerals, the probability of a correct report was approximately the same for *inside* and *outside* targets.

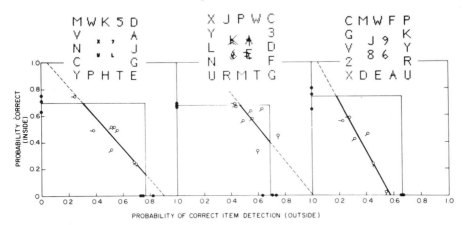

FIG. 3.   Data from divided attention experiments. Typical stimuli, each with two targets, are illustrated at top. Each open circle represents data from one block of 30 to 60 trials (report of both targets); each filled circle represents data from a control session (report of only the designated class of targets). The direction of the "tail" on a data point represents the attention instruction: down indicates "give 90% of your attention to the outside," left indicates "90% to inside," diagonal indicates "equal attention." The vertical and the horizontal lines are best-fits to the control data; the diagonal lines are best-fits to the multiple detection data; the darkened portion is the estimated Attention Operating Characteristic (AOC).

In addition to the *Small* condition described above, two other conditions were investigated, *Noise* and *Reversal.* In the *Noise* condition, the *inside* was composed of large characters (the same size as the *outside*), but detection of a critical numeral was made comparably difficult by superimposing a randomly-chosen, squiggly line segment ("noise" segment) on each *inside* character. In the *Reversal* condition, background characters in the *inside* were numbers and the target was a letter.

In all conditions, the *outside* was the same. The background characters were all the letters of English except that the letters B, S, Z, Q, O, and I were omitted because of their similarity, respectively, to the numerals 8, 5, 2, 0, 0, and 1. In the *Reversal* condition, which was studied separately after the others, the numerals 0 and 1 also were omitted.

B. Results

Some data from a typical subject viewing the display with *Small* characters are illustrated in the leftmost section of Fig. 3 (Sperling & Melchner, 1975, 1976a). The ordinate indicates the probability of correctly identifying the small target numeral (from the *inside*); the abscissa indicates the probability of correctly identifying the large target numeral (from the *outside*). In these experiments both numerals always occurred in the same array.

Each point in Fig. 3 represents data from a different block of trials. In some blocks the subject was instructed to give 90% of his attention to the large *outside* characters, and 10% to the small *inside* characters. In other blocks the percentages were reversed, and in still others he was told to pay equal attention to both. Figure 3 indicates that he was indeed able to follow these instructions, and that he was able to trade off performance on one class of targets against the other. The range of performances of which he is capable, as he varies his attention from being concentrated entirely on the small targets to entirely on the large targets, defines his "Attention Operating Characteristic" (AOC) for this task. In this task, the AOC is approximately a straight line with slope of -1, indicating that the subject can exchange a certain amount of probability on one task (ΔP_1) for an equal amount on the other (ΔP_2).

In control conditions, the subject was told to report just one kind of target (e.g., the *outside* target) for an entire block of trials. These data are graphed directly on the axes of Fig. 3. A vertical line is drawn through the mean of the *outside* control data, and a horizontal line through the *inside* mean. The intersection of these two points defines the "independence point," the point at which the subject would operate if he could perform both search tasks simultaneously without any interference, i.e., independently of each other. Insofar as the AOC lies inside the independence point, it represents some degree of interference between the two tasks.

The middle section of Fig. 3 illustrates performance in the *Noise* condition. The *outside* search task was the same as in the *Small* condition; the *inside* search task was matched to be of equal difficulty. Nonetheless, we see here that the AOC curve is closer to the independence point. This subject can carry out these two search tasks (with targets of equal size) with very little mutual interference.

The righthand section of Fig. 3 illustrates performance in the *Reversal* condition, in which the subject searches for a letter target among numerals on the *inside*, and for a numeral target among letters on the *outside*. The data show that the mutual incompatability of these two search tasks is nearly total.

C. Controls and Further Experiments

Interference between two search tasks does not occur because of any memory deficit. To prove this, the display was altered so that the targets remained the same but each background character was replaced with just a single dot. In this case, subjects gave errorless reports of both targets. Thus, the subject's inability to report both targets in the experimental condition is due to the mutual interference of the two search tasks.

By occasionally putting the inside and outside targets into different arrays (instead of always in the same array) we can determine how long it takes the subject to switch attention from one to the other class of stimuli. We tested one subject extensively on the reversal task with intervals from the letter to the number target of ±480, ±240, and 0 msec. The results indicate that this subject could switch from one task to the other in from 0.24–0.48 sec.

In a quite different paradigm, Adam Reeves and the senior author (1976) had been able to measure the reaction time distribution for an attention shift, and found it to be similar to the distribution of reaction times for motor responses. The mean attentional RT is typically between 0.3–0.5 sec for the discrimination of one of a set of three target letters from a background of letters. These direct measurements of attention-switching latency are consistent with the indirect inferences from the search task.

In summary, we found that our various instructions to subjects profoundly influenced *what kind* of targets were detected, and *where* they were located. Shaw, Kohn, and Nemeth (1976) recently demonstrated that "the probability of a target being at a spatial location has a dramatic effect on how subjects distribute their attention or processing capacity over the visual field." Previously, Sperling (1960) observed that when attention was directed by a poststimulus cue to one row of a briefly-flashed three-row display, the cue exerted a profound effect on which letters were processed for recall — provided the cue occurred while there were still more letters visually available to the subject than he could ultimately report. The physically unobservable distribution of attention during (and immediately after) a brief exposure largely determines what will be detected and what will be recalled.[2]

---

[2] For a provocative, molecular analysis of some factors that might limit performance see Norman and Bobrow (1975).

III.   THE ATTENTION OPERATING CHARACTERISTIC (AOC)

The best way we know of quantitatively describing the effects of attention is the Attention Operating Characteristic (AOC). The AOC is quite analogous to the Receiver Operating Characteristic (ROC) in discrimination tasks. Consider two density functions $f_1(t)$ and $f_2(t)$, and a criterion, c. In a discrimination task, f_1 and f_2 could represent the density function of the noise (f_1) and of the signal plus noise (f_2) on a sensory continuum. As the subject varies his criterion c, he defines his Receiver Operating Characteristic (ROC) or preferably, his Discrimination Operating Characteristic (DOC), as we believe it should be called. The graph of a DOC is a mirror image of the ROC graph. The DOC graph is preferable because it represents better performance on each task (correct identification of signal when it occurs; correct identification of noise when it occurs) by increasing coordinate values (upward and rightward). All of the representations, ROC (or DOC) and AOC, have the useful property that the mixture of two strategies is represented along a straight line joining the two strategies, and that *any* mixture of strategies is represented at the center of gravity of the probability-weighted component strategies.

In attention tasks, let f_1 and f_2 represent the attention demands of two tasks. A good example is that of a student who wished to attend two courses offered at overlapping times in different classrooms on the same day. At the end of the day, he is given two test questions, once chosen from course 1, the other from course 2. The probability that the information needed to answer the test question is offered at any instant of the class period is given by f_1 and f_2 respectively for the two classes (we assume there is no repetition or redundancy in the classroom lectures.) The student is allowed to switch classrooms just once, by quickly running from classroom 1 to classroom 2 at time c. For each switching criterion c, his performance on questions about course 1 and course 2 defines his *Attending* Operating Characteristic (Fig. 4). Two AOCs are shown in Fig. 4 — one in which it is assumed that if the student were present in Class n at the critical moment, his probability p_n of correctly answering the subsequent test questions is 1.0, and another AOC for which p_n is assumed to be 0.7. Note the similarity of Fig. 4c to Fig. 3.

The classroom analogy leads to a quite general formulation. The coordinate axes (arguments) of f_1 and f_2 need not be interpreted as time. For example, arranging "feature detectors" on a continuum according to the ratio t of their utilities for task 1 and task 2 would yield a feature-detector utility interpretation for t. This is a mathematically equivalent basis and, in fact, corresponds closely to the likelihood ratio of signal to noise, which is an appropriate axis for ROC tasks. Moreover, the AOC method of analyzing and interpreting data from visual attention is equally applicable to other attention tasks, such as the sharing — or switching — of auditory attention between two ears.

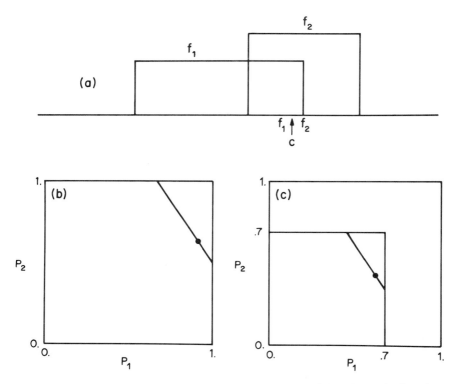

FIG. 4.   Criterion Model of the Attention Operating Characteristic. (a) Density functions f_1, f_2 and the criterion. The abscissa represents time. In this example, f_1 and f_2 represent the density of information in two classrooms as a function of time, and c represents the time of switching from classroom 1 to classroom 2. (b) Attending Operating Characteristic (AOC) for a student as a function of his switching time, c. The abscissa represents the probability p_1 of correctly answering a test question from classroom 1; the ordinate represents the probability p_2 of correctly answering a test question from classroom 2. The data point represents performance for the particular criterion c shown in (a). (c) Same, but with the assumption that the student has only a probability p ($p = .7$) of answering the test question correctly even if he was in the classroom during the instant the relevant information was presented. (See text.)

A.   Moving Along an AOC: Sharing or Switching?

In order to examine in more detail the mechanism by which the subject moves along the AOC curve, that is, the mechanism by which attention is shifted from one search task to the other, consider the 2 x 2 contingency table (Table 1) in which the joint occurrences of correct reports on the two tasks are tabulated for a single instructional condition. This table has three degrees of freedom; two of these, the marginals P_1 and P_2, are used to make the AOC. The third degree of

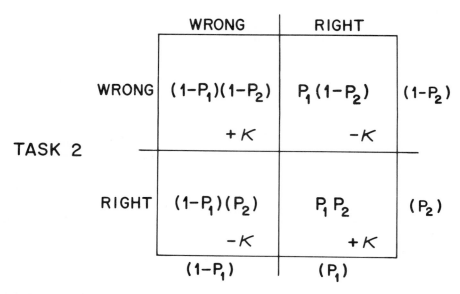

TASK 1

TABLE 1. Contingency table for the joint probability of correct responses in a divided-attention experiment. When $k = 0$, the algebraic expressions represent the predictions of ideal shared attention (statistical independence of the two tasks); when $k < 0$, there is negative correlation representing some degree of attention-switching between different states, i.e., more than one criterion in the AOC model.

freedom (correlation) provides information about the mechanism of attention. We consider here two (of many) possible mechanisms: *sharing* and *switching*. The mechanisms are outlined below without formal derivations.

In sharing, attention is assumed to be divided between the two tasks in some fixed proportion, which does not vary from trial to trial within a single instructional condition. Insofar as there is less attention available for each task than in a control condition, performance suffers relative to the control. Here, shared attention corresponds to having a fixed criterion c in Fig. 4a, and the probabilities of correct responses are directly proportional to the areas under f_1 and f_2 to the left and to the right, respectively, of c. The 2 x 2 contingency table is assumed to show statistical independence. By definition, in shared attention the probability of a correct response on one task is the same whether the response on the other task (for that trial) was correct or incorrect.

In two-state attention switching, two different component attention states (S_1, S_2) are assumed to occur randomly, from trial to trial, in the search task. In the ideal case, the two component states (S_1, S_2) are states of shared attention; each component state corresponds exactly to one of two criteria c_1, c_2 in the model. (However, the following analysis also applies to the case where the component states S_1, S_2 are themselves mixtures of yet other states.) To move along the AOC curve by switching attention, the subject is assumed to vary the proportion of trials he is in S_1 by switching between c_1 and c_2 from trial to trial. Two interesting properties of two-state attention switching are (1) mixtures of S_1 and S_2 produce a straight line AOC curve connecting S_1 and S_2; and (2) the contingency table for a mixed state is the mixture of the two separate contingency tables (from states S_1 and S_2).[3] From (2) it can be shown that, under the conditions of the experiment, we expect any contingency table produced by switching between states to have a negative correlation and to show nonindependence by the Chi-square test. By assuming the ideal case (i.e., two-state switching in which each component state is a state of shared attention), one can estimate the particular two states between which attention is being switched.

When this analysis is applied to the data described above, we discover that the major mechanism of altering attention is switching — i.e., altering the proportion of times the subject is in S_1 or S_2. On the other hand, we can also reject the hypothesis, at least for some of the data, that the subject manifests only two attentional states (i.e., only the two extreme states determined by the intersections of the AOC curve with the control condition lines). Thus, attention *sharing* is not merely the operative mechanism at the end points of the AOC, but is also a mechanism for moving along an AOC.[4]

B.   Conclusion

In a more general vein, the AOC is a useful way of studying attention, and particularly of describing the compatibility of two tasks. A pair of tasks to be performed simultaneously determines an AOC. To compare two pairs of tasks, one cannot use just one condition of attention for each pair, for this would be comparing one point from each of two curves and not comparing two curves. (An analogous problem occurs in signal detection theory with ROC curves.)

In conclusion, we see that subjects cannot simultaneously search two areas for a large and a small target as well as they can search for two different equal-sized targets. The instruction to search simultaneously with equal attention for a large and a small sized target causes the subject to switch his attention from trial to trial between searching primarily for large and searching primarily for small

---

[3]The *mixture* S_3 of two contingency tables S_1 and S_2 is defined as follows. Let the proportion of S_1 in the mixture be a, $0 \leqslant a \leqslant 1$. For any triple p_1, p_2, and p_3 of corresponding elements in S_1, S_2, and S_3, we define $p_3 = ap_1 + (1 - a)p_2$.

[4]In this simplified theory, when a negative contingency is observed at the endpoint of an empirically determined AOC, the negative contingency is assumed to be generated by switch-between two states, one of which lies beyond the observable endpoint, at the "true" endpoint of the AOC.

targets. Although the mechanism by which a subject varied his performance along an AOC in our visual search tasks was primarily by switching attention between extreme states, some sharing of attention also occurred.

ACKNOWLEDGMENTS

The authors wish to acknowledge the helpful suggestions of Judith Harris.

REFERENCES

Estes, W. K. Interaction of signal and background variables in visual processing. *Perception and Psychophysics, 1972, 12,* 278–286.

Estes, W. K. The locus of inferential and perceptual processes in letter identification. *Journal of Experimental Psychology: General, 1975, 104,* 122–145.

Kinchla, R. A. The role of structural redundancy in the perception of visual targets. *Perception and Psychophysics, 1977, 22,* 19–30.

Norman, D. A., & Bobrow, D. G. On data-limited and resource-limited processes. *Cognitive Psychology, 1975, 7,* 44–64.

Shaw, M. L., Kohn, B., & Nemeth, R. Optimal allocation of information processing resources. Paper read at the Psychonomic Society, St. Louis Missouri, November, 1976.

Sperling, G. The information available in brief visual presentations. *Psychological Monographs, 1960, 74,* No. 11 (Whole No. 498).

Sperling, G. Paper presented at Attention and Performance V, Stockholm, 1973.

Sperling, G., Budiansky, J., Spivak, J. G., & Johnson, M. C. Extremely rapid visual search: The maximum rate of scanning letters for the presence of a numeral. *Science, 1971, 174,* 307–311.

Sperling, G., & Melchner, M. J. Multiple detections in a visual search task: The sharing and switching of attention. Paper read at the Psychonomic Society, Denver, Colorado, November, 1975.

Sperling, G., & Melchner, M. J. Visual search and visual attention. In V. D. Glezer (Ed.), *Information Processing in Visual System. Proceedings of the Fourth Symposium of Sensory System Physiology.* Leningrad, U.S.S.R.: Academy of Sciences, Pavlov Institute of Physiology, 1976. (a)

Sperling, G., & Melchner, M. J. Estimating item and order information. *Journal of Mathematical Psychology, 1976, 2,* 192–213. (b)

Sperling, G., & Reeves, A. Reaction time without observable response. Paper read at the Psychonomic Society, St. Louis, Missouri, November, 1976.

36

Model Acceptability and the Use of Bayes-Fiducial Methods for Validating Models

Henry Rouanet
Dominique Lépine
Université René Descartes
Paris, France

Daniel Holender
Université Libre de Bruxelles
Belgium

ABSTRACT

The use of significance tests for validating models is basically inadequate, since nonsignificant results only pertain to the compatibility of the data with the model. In this paper an alternative form of data analysis is proposed, whose objective is to assess the acceptability of the model given the data. The use of Bayes-fiducial inference is suggested in this connection; the approach is exemplified through the analysis of an experiment planned for investigating a model of successive stages of information processing in binary choice reaction.

I. INADEQUACY OF SIGNIFICANCE TESTS FOR VALIDATING MODELS

The research presented in this chapter was motivated by the acknowledged fact that today most branches of experimental psychology make use of numerous and often very refined information processing models, which in turn have been matched by an equally large and elaborate amount of experimental work. However, there is generally a wide gap between the numerical indications furnished by the statistical analyses of the data and the conclusions about the model's validity formulated by the experimenter. Statistical procedures of validation have remained rudimentary or stereotyped, and in any case they have not given rise to the specific developments that might have been anticipated. This is surprising, especially since refined conclusions drawn from experimentation may depend crucially on the statistical procedures employed — a state of affairs that certainly merits serious investigation.

By way of an example, we shall take the experimental paradigm so widely used after Sternberg (1969): The method of additive factors for analyzing processing stages in reaction time situations. In order to illustrate what we have in mind, it will suffice to consider a situation involving two experimental factors that can influence mean reaction time (RT); we shall consider one of the experiments reported by Holender and Bertelson (1975). By adopting a theoretical framework in which RT is decomposed into successive stages of information processing, one can interpret in terms of an *additive mechanism* (i.e, the experimental factors act on distinct stages) the *additive model* of analysis of variance (i.e., there is no interaction between the factors). Postulating the additive mechanism for a given individual henceforth amounts to testing the statistical hypothesis: $\zeta = 0$, where ζ denotes the "interaction effect" parameter between the two factors for the individual under consideration (see Appendix).

What is the usual practice for comparing model and data? Essentially, direct inspection of average results, together with the calculation of some significance tests. In the present situation one would typically start out with $\bar{z}$, the average of the observed individual interaction effects z, and test the null hypothesis $H_o : \bar{\zeta} = 0$, where $\bar{\zeta}$ denotes the population mean of the individual interaction effects ζ. (Notice that H_o amounts to the hypothesis of no interaction between the two experimental factors in the sampled population of subjects.) Then if the absolute value of the test-statistic does not exceed the order of magnitude of its expectation under the given null hypothesis (i.e., when the result is nonsignificant, especially "largely nonsignificant," the F-ratio being close to, or less than, 1), one would typically conclude that the "experimental evidence is in favor of the model." Albeit cautiously formulated, such a conclusion is somewhat adventurous in terms of the consequences it entails, since as soon as one argues further using this conclusion, the model's validity is *actually taken for granted*.

Such practices are certainly quite widespread, yet they raise at least two fundamental difficulties. First, $\bar{\zeta}$ is merely an average parameter, and one might easily have $\bar{\zeta} = 0$ without all or even most of the individual parameters ζ equaling or approaching zero. To overcome this difficulty, some experimenters may suggest testing, in addition, the null hypothesis of the homogeneity of individual effects, whenever technically feasible — i.e. testing $H_o' : \tau = 0$, where τ denotes the population standard deviation of the individual effects ζ. (H_o' amounts to the hypothesis of no double interaction between the "subjects" factor and the two experimental factors.)

In what follows we will take this suggestion and concentrate on the second main difficulty, namely the basic inadequacy of significance tests for the purpose of validating models. Others have drawn attention to this inadequacy, and it can be viewed as a version of the "fallacy of the null hypothesis significance test" already denounced by Rozeboom (1960), among many other statisticians or methodologists [for the method of additive factors, see Sternberg's (1969) own reservations and suggestions]. There is no doubt that experienced searchers are aware that the use of significance tests can be misleading, but the specific inadequacy of tests as tools for validating models is often lost among general "warnings," so the full consequences of this inadequacy are not always appreciated. We will therefore address this criticism in connection with an experiment chosen to illustrate these issues.

In experiment 4 of the series reported by Holender and Bertelson (1975), the two experimental factors in a RT situation of binary choice (two signals and two responses) were: (1) the relative frequencies of the signals (frequent: .75, and rare: .25) and (2) the duration of the foreperiod within blocks of trials (short: .5 sec, and long: 5 sec). In each of the two conditions of foreperiod duration, each subject carried out 144 trials with the frequent signal and 48 trials with the rare signal, in two experimental sessions.

Here the interaction effect (observed) can be defined as the difference of the differences between mean RT in the four combinations of the two experimental factors (hence, averaged over the two sessions): for the group of 12 subjects involved in the experiment, the average interaction effect $\bar{z}$ was found to be: $(434 - 401) - (382 - 343) = -7$ msec (accurate values rounded off). Such an effect is fairly small, a result which is "in favor" of the additive model, especially in view of the large main effects of the two experimental factors (the half-sum of which is about 45 msec) as well as the sizeable variances of RT within subjects and conditions [averaging these variances across subjects, conditions, and sessions yields the value of $(75 \text{ msec})^2$, henceforth called the group *intravariance*].

If we now test H_o: $\bar{\zeta} = 0$, the outcome is far from significant, thus furnishing at first glance one more argument "in favor" of the additive model. However, upon closer examination, it becomes clear that this "nonsignificant" result arises not only from the weak value of the observed mean effect $\bar{z}$, but also from the large variance of the observed individual effects z [about $(20 \text{ msec})^2$] — henceforth called the *intervariance* — as well as from the restricted number of subjects (12). The ratio of the intervariance to the number of subjects characterizes what we call the *interprecision* (see Appendix). Now suppose the interprecision is increased four times — say, by halving the intervariance (14^2 instead of 20^2) and doubling the number of subjects (24 instead of 12) — then the F-ratio will quadruple and become significant at usual levels (assuming an identical observed effect $\bar{z} = -7$ msec). Here we see the seemingly paradoxical consequences of using significance tests for validating models: the more conscientiously a searcher attempts to improve experimental precision, the greater the risk he runs of finding a significant result. Thus, he must conclude that the experimental evidence points to the rejection of the model, although this model might actually provide a quite reasonable approximation of the data!

For another illustration, consider the problem of the homogeneity of the individual effects ζ. The observed individual effects z range in absolute value from $|z| = 3$ msec to $|z| = 35$ msec; their variance (intervariance) is large (20^2). However, testing H_o': $\tau = 0$ yields a result largely nonsignficant; this is now due to the magnitude of the group intravariance. The number of trials and the intravariance make up the two components of what we call the group *intraprecision* (see Appendix). Here, in spite of the relatively elevated number of trials per subject and condition, the intravariance is so large in itself as to make the intraprecision quite poor and render the data compatible with the hypothesis that the true effects ζ are all equal to each other ($\tau = 0$).

The same difficulty would arise if we were to proceed to a series of individual analyses. Testing the null hypothesis of no interaction between the two experimental factors, separately for each of the 12 subjects ($H_o: \zeta = 0$, for each individual) can be done along the following lines. Under the usual sampling model, the observed effect z of a subject comes from a normal distribution whose mean is ζ and whose variance is estimated by s^2/k, where s^2 is the intravariance (of the subject) and k is a coefficient determined by the numbers of observations under conditions and sessions. The ratio s^2/k characterizes the intraprecision (for the subject; see Appendix). For instance, in the case of Subject 1 it was found that $s^2 = 65^2$ and $k = 17.7$; thus for this subject $s^2/k = 15^2$. Then under $H_o: \zeta = 0$, the ratio $z/s\sqrt{k}$ is a Student's t-statistic. For instance, for Subject 1, the observed effect is $z = 3$ and the t-statistic is 0.19 (largely nonsignificant). As it turns out, none of the values of these individual t-statistics is significant (see Table 1). For the "extreme" subject 12, whose observed mean interaction effect is $z = -35$ msec, the t-statistic in absolute value comes to only 1.44. All these nonsignificant results can again be clearly ascribed to the weakness of intraprecision, which renders each individual data compatible with the hypothesis that the observed effect z is the reflection of a real effect ζ zero.

In summary, the fact that data-model compatibility hinges so crucially on experimental precision should disqualify the use of significance tests in examining the validity of models. A genuine criterion for validity, even a crude and imperfect one, should never allow the lack of experimental precision to intervene in favor of the model. Investigating a model under poor precision conditions amounts to trying to reach a conclusion in the presence of "noise"; if some conclusion can be reached, it must be *in spite of* the noise, not *because* of it. As already pointed out, there is nothing new in this criticism of significance testing, although it becomes crucial in the context of models. The remainder of this chapter will be devoted to the procedures that we propose as alternatives to significance tests. These procedures and their methodological motivations are based on some of our work on Analysis of Variance and its Bayes-fiducial extensions (see Rouanet, Lépine, and Pelnard-Considère (1976) for another illustration of this approach).

II. FIDUCIAL INFERENCE AND THE NOTION
OF ACCEPTABILITY

As an alternative to the idea of *data compatibility with the model,* we would like to propose the notion of *model acceptability by the data.* To grasp this notion intuitively, imagine the chain of reasoning an experimenter might use to assess the validity of the additive model for the individual data of Subject 1 (see Table 1): the observed mean interaction effect $z = 3$ msec is quite negligible, and if it happened to be the accurate reflection of the true effect ζ, then the additive model (for this subject) would be acceptable as a first approximation. Yet this reflection may well be considerably distorted, due to the lack of experimental precision. The point is, therefore, to try to prove that the true effect is also likely to be negligible. Either this can be done, and the additive model is acceptable — that is, the descriptive assessment "observed effect negligible" extends to the inferential conclusion "true effect negligible." Or this cannot be done, and no inferential conclusion can be reached about the model's acceptability.

The above formulation of the model validity problem will certainly be considered realistic by experimenters; we will now show that it leads naturally to a simple solution, in the case of the individual parameters ζ. Using again the individual notations z (observed effect), s^2 (intravariance) and s^2/k (intraprecision), let us now consider the normal distribution with mean z and variance s^2/k (see Fig. 1 for Subject 1). This distribution is completely determined by the data and the sampling model, being centered around the observed mean effect and dispersed according to the experimental precision. Therefore, by a natural convention, this distribution can serve to represent the uncertainty about the parameter ζ that arises from experimental data.

Following R. A. Fisher's (1959) usage, distributions constructed in this fashion will be called *fiducial*, since — unlike sampling distributions — their status depends on a "trust" element (see III for a more general discussion of the fiducial approach).

With the help of the fiducial distribution about parameter ζ, we can formulate the idea of model acceptability more precisely: to the extent that the fiducial distribution covers values near zero, the additive model becomes more or less acceptable. In practice, in order to evaluate the degree of acceptability, we can fix a probability value γ close to unity, and look for the absolute value l such that the proportion of values between $-l$ and $+l$ of the distribution is equal to γ. This limit l will be called an *absolute fiducial limit*.[1] Clearly, as l increases, the model becomes less acceptable. If we fix γ at .90, we find for Subject 1 the limit l to be about 26 msec, and we may state: "with the fiducial guarantee $\gamma = .90$, the parameter ζ lies between -26 and $+26$ msec."

In the sequel, we will express fiducial statements by means of an auxiliary variable ζ^* (associated with the parameter ζ) whose distribution is by definition the fiducial distribution about ζ. The proportion of ζ-values between $-l$ and $+l$ will be expressed as the fiducial probability (denoted P^*) that the variable ζ^* is less than l in absolute value, that is $P^*(|\zeta^*| < l) = \gamma$.

---

[1]Other kinds of fiducial limits can naturally be defined from the fiducial distribution, for instance upper and lower limits of an interval centered on the observed value z (see Section III).

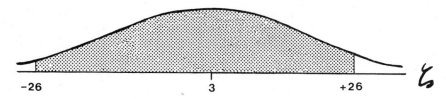

FIG. 1.   Fiducial distribution for the parameter ζ (interaction effect) of Subject 1. The shaded area, between −26 and +26, represent 90% of the distribution, that is: $P*(|\zeta*| < 26) = .90$.

The absolute fiducial limit l is based on the observed effect z and the intra-precision s^2/k, just like the test-statistic t, which is equal to $z/s/\sqrt{k}$. As the two components are combined in another way, however, the resulting properties are quite different:

1. For a fixed value of z, when the precision is very poor, the limit l will be very high, indicating that the model is least acceptable.

2. With growing precision, provided z is sufficiently close to zero, the decreasing of l will mean an increasing degree of acceptability.

3. In the limiting case where $z = 0$, l becomes smaller as the precision improves, thus acceptability is an increasing function of precision.

The data of Subject 1 may serve to illustrate case (2): with $z = 3$ and $s^2/k = 15^2$, the limit l is 26 msec. Assuming the same small value of z, but s^2/k four times smaller, the limit l would come out as 14 msec, which means a great improvement in acceptability. However, in both cases, the compatibility with H_o, as appreciated by the t-statistic, is high because z is close to zero.

In general, whenever the experimental precision is improved and the observed effect remains negligible, using fiducial methods to assess the model's acceptability will never lead to the absurd situation mentioned in the first section in connection with significance tests; on the contrary, the experimenter will be provided with better arguments for the model's acceptability.

Table 1 presents the main results of individual analyses in Holender and Bertelson's experiment 4.

Discrepancies will be noticed between the rankings of the 12 subjects in the three rows; they stem from the heterogeneity of the individual intravariances. For example, the observed effect for Subject 7 is more favorable to the model than that of Subject 12 ($|z|$ = 22 and 35, respectively). The intravariances are respectively 53^2 and 101^2. Consequently (1) the additive model is *more acceptable* for Subject 7 than for Subject 12 (l = 38 and 66, respectively), whereas (2) the data are *less compatible* with H_o for Subject 7 than for Subject 12 ($|t|$ = 1.72 and 1.44, respectively). Such results should prevent any temptation of using significance tests when assessing acceptability, even on a merely comparative basis.

TABLE 1

Individual analyses (Holender and Bertelson's data). First row: observed interaction effects z for each of the 12 subjects, who are ranked according to the absolute magnitude of these effects. Second row: values of the t-test statistic. Third row: values of the absolute fiducial limit l at the guarantee .90

Subject	1	2	3	4	5	6	7	8	9	10	11	12
z	+3	+6	+7	+9	+11	−12	−22	−24	+25	−29	−29	−35
t	+.19	+.36	+.33	+.55	+.61	−.63	−1.72	−1.44	+1.53	−1.55	−1.50	−1.44
l	26	31	35	32	34	36	38	45	46	52	53	66

693

III. FIDUCIAL (OR BAYES-FIDUCIAL) INFERENCE; FIDUCIAL AND CONFIDENCE METHODS

Procedures for constructing distributions of parameter values based on experimental data and sampling models have come a long way since "Bayes' postulate" (1763). In the 1930s of this century many statisticians began to use such procedures systematically. Some of them, following Fisher, employed direct reasoning along the line of his "pivotal argument." Others, like Jeffreys, reasoned within the classical Bayesian framework; that is, they used prior distributions. However, they did this not to bring in extraexperimental knowledge or opinions, as was the case for the subjective Bayesian school, but on the contrary, to express an initial "state of ignorance" about parameters.[2] Such prior distributions are called *noninformative* by present-day Bayesian statisticians [see especially Lindley (1970) and Box & Tiao (1973)]. From the point of view of data analysis, with which we are concerned here, the foregoing differences in derivation processes are immaterial; therefore, we will indifferently call *fiducial* or *Bayes-fiducial* all procedures based uniquely on experimental data and a sampling model.[3] What is crucial is that, since those procedures deliberately discard extraexperimental factors, the distributions that come out are genuinely suitable to serve as references for expressing "what the data have to say about the parameter."

To attain the objective of validating models, we will suggest as a proper basis the systematic use of fiducial distributions. The approach will be presented by means of further examples more complex than the individual analyses described above, but will remain focused on the investigation of the additive model.

Meanwhile, we think it necessary to clarify the important distinction between fiducial and confidence methods. Confusion arises not only from the semantic closeness of the two terms, but also because the two methods in some cases yield similar, or even identical, results. For example, consider a confidence interval calculated for an individual parameter ζ, say for Subject 1, at the confidence level .95. Applying the familiar procedure, the limits are found to be $3 \pm 1.96 \times 15 = -27$ and $+33$. Now, from the very construction of the fiducial distribution we have:

$$P^*(-27 < \zeta^* < +33) = .95 \tag{1}$$

that is, the interval $(-27, +33)$ is simultaneously a confidence interval at the level .95 and a fiducial interval at the guarantee .95. However, two points need to be noted: (1) the coincidence expressed by Relation 1 is *not* logically related to the frequency interpretation that stems from the theory of confidence meth-

---

[2]Comprehensive accounts of these approaches can be found in Fisher (1959) and Jeffreys (1961).

[3]Thus we include among fiducial procedures a good many recently developed under the heading of "Bayesian statistics."

od and that excludes any idea of a probability over a parameter space. Standard statistical textbooks rightly draw attention to this fundamental point. Despite that, observed confidence intervals are often — even though informally — interpreted in terms of probability statements over parameter values, but this interpretation is supported only when the confidence interval happens to coincide (as in the above example) with a fiducial interval.[4] (2) As soon as one leaves elementary situations, coincidences like Relation 1 no longer happen; then the probabilistic interpretation of observed confidence intervals is unsupported and may become unreasonable (see the case of the parameter ζ in the next section).

It is an unquestionable fact that confidence methods in experimental data analysis are confined practically to elementary situations. Indeed, it is to be suspected that confidence methods, when correctly reduced to the frequency interpretation, cannot adequately cope with most situations that require going beyond significance tests. For instance, the *absolute* fiducial limit l defined earlier was naturally introduced to go beyond the test of the model $\zeta = 0$, and the point is that this absolute fiducial limit does *not* coincide with any absolute confidence limit.

IV. FIDUCIAL ANALYSIS OF HOLENDER AND BERTELSON'S DATA; INFERENCES ON POPULATION PARAMETERS

We will now apply the fiducial approach to the data of Holender and Bertelson's experiment 4 in order to make inferences about the population parameters. The derivations and computations are more complex than in the case of the individual parameters; they have all been made using noninformative prior distributions, as has become standard practice in the Bayesian analysis of random-effects models (see Box & Tiao, 1973, chapters 5 and 6). We will comment on the main results and present graphs of fiducial distributions. As for circumstances in which these procedures are valid, a rule of thumb is that a fiducial distribution is valid whenever the corresponding significance test is itself valid.

A. Population Mean $\bar{\zeta}$ of the Individual Parameters

The fiducial distribution relative to the population mean is shown in Fig. 2. The mean of this distribution is the average observed effect of interaction $\bar{z} = -7$ msec; its dispersion depends mainly on the interprecision, with a correction term con-

---

[4]A. W. F. Edwards (1976) puts it nicely: "Ironically, a major reason for the success of the confidence approach was that many basic problems . . . do enable a valid fiducial argument to be used, and the confidence argument then gives, numerically speaking, the fiducial answers."

tingent on the intraprecision. Its shape is symmetrical and resembles that of a Student's distribution with few degrees of freedom.

From this distribution, statements about $\bar{\zeta}$ can be derived, as was made earlier for each of the individual parameters ζ. We thus find $P^*(|\bar{\zeta}^*|<16) = .90$, meaning that "with a fiducial guarantee of .90, the parameter $\bar{\zeta}$ lies between -16 and $+16$ msec." Thus, the absolute fiducial limit for $\bar{\zeta}$ is markedly lower than the limits found for any of the individual parameters ζ (recall the limit of 26 for Subject 1). This is because the interprecision is not as poor as the intraprecision. Yet it is far from being good, and the observed effect $\bar{z}$ is not quite near zero; therefore the absolute fiducial limit for $\bar{\zeta}$ is still far from zero. To appreciate the influence of experimental precision alone, assume that $\bar{z}$ becomes zero, the precision being the same; then the center of the fiducial distribution would shift to zero and the limit would decrease to 10 msec: $P^*(|\zeta^*| < 10) = .90$.

B.   Population Standard Deviation τ of individual Parameters: Examination of Interindividual Homogeneity

Assuming that individual parameters ζ are normally distributed in the population, we can derive a fiducial distribution relative to the standard deviation τ of these effects. This distribution is shown in Fig. 3.

Fiducial statements based on this distribution furnish judgments about the homogeneity of the individual effects. Setting the guarantee γ, the upper fiducial limit l' may be sought such that $P^*(\tau^* < l') = \gamma$. For instance it is found that:

$$P^*(\tau^* < 23) = .90$$

This is an objective indication about the "homogeneous model" for individual parameters: $\tau = 0$. If the upper limit 23 msec is *not* deemed too high as a standard

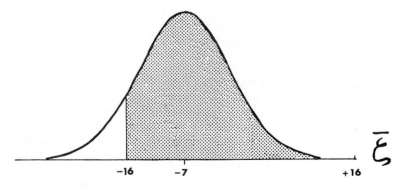

FIG. 2.   Fiducial distribution for the mean interaction effect $\bar{\zeta}$ in the subject's population;

$P^*(|\bar{\zeta}^*|<16) = .90$.

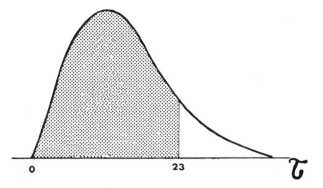

FIG. 3.   Fiducial distribution for the standard deviation τ of the individual parameters of interaction; $P^*(\tau^* < 23) = .90$.

deviation of individual effects, then it may be concluded that the homogeneous model is acceptable as a first approximation. Otherwise, no such conclusion is possible. The problem can then be reversed to examine whether the homogeneity model can be rejected by seeking the lower fiducial limit l'' such that $P^*(\tau^* > l'') = \gamma$. Thus, we find:

$$P^*(\tau^* > 5) = .90$$

If then this lower limit 5 msec is *not* too low, the homogeneous model can be rejected (as a first approximation). If, however, the lower limit is considered too low, the preceding two analyses taken together will prevent any inferential conclusion from being reached at the guarantee .90, with respect to either homogeneity or heterogeneity.

Remark.   The inference about parameter τ (or rather τ^2) provides a simple illustration of a situation where fiducial and confidence methods lead to divergent results. Confidence limits for τ^2 are readily obtained by using classical procedures (see, for instance Scheffé, 1959, chapter 6). The lower limit at the confidence level .90 is found here equal to -74, a value that not only differs from that of the lower fiducial limit for τ^2 (i.e. 5^2), but that is negative in sign — a rather awkward outcome for a positive parameter! (By way of contrast, fiducial limits for positive parameters will always be positive.)

C. Overall Statement about the Additive Model's Acceptability

In addition to the statements already made relative to parameters $\bar{\zeta}$ and τ, an overall statement about the additive model's acceptability may be needed. This can be done in the following way: for any positive real number ϵ, let φ_ϵ denote the proportion of individual parameters ζ lying between $-\epsilon$ and $+\epsilon$. Still assuming normality for the distribution of individual effects ζ, the parameter φ_ϵ is given by the formula:

$$\varphi_\epsilon = F\left(\frac{\bar{\zeta} + \epsilon}{\tau}\right) - F\left(\frac{\bar{\zeta} - \epsilon}{\tau}\right)$$

where F denotes the cumulative standard normal distribution function. Let φ_ϵ^* denote the fiducial variable associated to the parameter φ_ϵ; then for any given proportion $\omega (0 \leqslant \omega \leqslant 1)$ there is a well-defined fiducial probability $P^*(\varphi_\epsilon^* > \omega)$. Now, regarding the proportion ω as fixed, let us consider the function which associates the value $P^*(\varphi_\epsilon^* > \omega)$ to each number ϵ. As ϵ increases from 0 to $+\infty$, this function increases from 0 to 1. Consequently, for any given guarantee γ, there exists a value of ϵ, denoted $\epsilon(\omega, \gamma)$, for which the preceding fiducial probability is equal to γ, i.e.:

$$P^*(\varphi_{\epsilon(\omega,\gamma)}^* > \omega) = \gamma.$$

Suppose we choose the proportion ω close to unity. The smaller the value $\epsilon(\omega, \gamma)$, the more globally acceptable the additive model, since with the guarantee γ, the proportion of individuals whose absolute effects ζ are less than $\epsilon(\omega, \gamma)$ is at least equal to ω.

In the present case, setting $\omega = .90$ and $\gamma = .90$ yields the value $\epsilon(\omega, \gamma) = 43$ msec. This means that with the guarantee .90, at least 90% of the individual interaction effects lie between −43 and +43 msec.

This limit of 43 msec may seem high at first sight. However, a still higher value might have been anticipated if we recall that 90% of the observed effects z lie between −35 and +35. The increase from 35 to 43 is in a sense the price to pay for transforming a descriptive statement about the *observed* effects for the subjects *examined* into an inferential statement about the *true* effects in the subjects' *population*. Taking into account the relative closeness of the two values 35 and 43, we may appreciate that this price, due to the lack of statistical precision, is not excessive.

The judgment $P^*(\varphi_{43}^* > .90) = .90$ can be viewed as an overall appraisal of the additive model. Naturally, it can be felt that the fiducial limit 43 msec (or even already the descriptive limit 35 msec) is too high for the additive model to be considered acceptable. If so, one can again reverse the problem and seek to reject an approximate version of the additive model. This will be done by looking for a new ϵ-value such that, given ω and γ both close to unity, with the guarantee γ, the proportion of individual whose absolute effects $|\zeta|$ are greater than ϵ is at least equal to ω. In the present case, the value $\epsilon = 1.3$ ms is found. If this value is not deemed too low, the approximate additive model can be rejected. If however, this value $\epsilon = 1.3$ msec is judged too low, the conclusion of rejection cannot be reached. In such a case, one will be led, along the line of sequential analysis, to increase the experimental precision by collecting further observations until a conclusion is reached.

V. COMMENTS AND CONCLUSIONS

In the previous sections we have applied a number of fiducial procedures to a set of typical data, and tried to substantiate our claim that fiducial methods are far better suited to the process of model validation than the usual practices. The use of fiducial methods should also help an experimenter to clearly delineate the following two issues that inevitably arise during the validation process of a model: (1) which level of analysis is best appropriate for the investigation of the model (mean parameter, or overall parameters taking individual differences into account, etc.) and (2) which degree of approximation one is ready to tolerate in order to pronounce upon the model's acceptability.

A related issue is about combining the results of several sets of data. For instance, Experiment 4 of Holender and Bertelson belonged to a series whose overall objective was to examine the additive model with respect to the variables temporal uncertainty and selective preparation, the latter being manipulated in several ways each requiring a separate experiment. The appraisal of the results arising from a series of experiments is usually made in a merely qualitative manner, and experimenters often wish there were more quantitative evaluation procedures. Now the use of Bayes-fiducial analyses for each of the experiments in a series lends itself naturally to such a quantitative approach, since each fiducial analysis can be viewed as a Bayesian analysis, and the essence of the Bayesian approach is to combine information arising from several sources.

Final comment. Developing fiducial methods for a number of current models in experimental psychology appears to be feasible because the necessary computing power is now available. However, the technical complexities of computations should not be exaggerated, especially if only approximate results are sought. The numerical values presented in this paper are all attainable (at least approximately) by hand computations, with one exception: the value $\epsilon(\omega, \gamma)$.

Naturally, in order to take full advantage of Bayes-fiducial methods, a reserved attitude toward ready-made statistical packages will be recommendable. Adapting a new statistical method to experimental psychology may take some pains, just as does the adaptation of a new mathematical model.

ACKNOWLEDGMENTS

This research benefited from a grant made available by DGRST (Délégation Générale à la Recherche Scientifique et Technique) within the Project (ACC) "Informatique et Sciences humaines," contract n° 75−7−0454. Computer programs have been written by M. −O. Lebeaux, to whom we are most grateful.

APPENDIX

We index the 2 × 2 conditions by $jk(j = 1, 2; k = 1, 2)$ and the 2 sessions by $l(l = 1, 2)$.

Consider first a given subject; for condition jk and session (l), let $x^{jk(l)}$ be the observed mean (average of observations) and $n_{jk(l)}$ the number of observations. We define the *individual observed effect* as the following contrast between the 8 observed means:

$$z = \frac{1}{2}[x^{11(1)} - x^{21(1)} - x^{12(1)} + x^{22(1)} + x^{11(2)} - x^{21(2)} - x^{12(2)} + x^{22(2)}]$$

(This contrast is essentially — up to a factor of 4 — the "individual one degree of freedom interaction contrast" considered by Sternberg, 1969, p. 298).

We then associate to each of the 8 $jk(l)$ combinations a "true" mean (for the given subject) $\mu^{jk(l)}$. Then, under the usual sampling model, the observed mean $x^{jk(l)}$ comes from a distribution with mean $\mu^{jk(l)}$ and variance $\sigma^2/n_{jk(l)}$, where σ^2 is the "true" variance — assumed homogeneous — within conditions and sessions (for the given subject).

Assuming independence between the 8 samples, the observed effect z comes from a distribution with mean ζ and variance σ^2/k, where

$$\zeta = \frac{1}{2}[\mu^{11(1)} - \mu^{21(1)} - \mu^{12(1)} - \mu^{22(1)} - \mu^{11(2)} - \mu^{21(2)} - \mu^{12(2)} - \mu^{22(2)}]$$

and

$$\frac{4}{k} = \frac{1}{n_{11(1)}} + \frac{1}{n_{21(1)}} + \frac{1}{n_{12(1)}} + \frac{1}{n_{22(1)}} + \frac{1}{n_{11(2)}} + \frac{1}{n_{21(2)}} + \frac{1}{n_{12(2)}} + \frac{1}{n_{22(2)}}$$

Let now s^2 be the observed variance within conditions and sessions; s^2 is an estimate of σ^2 and will be called the *intravariance* (for the given subject). The ratio s^2/k is the estimate of σ^2/k. This ratio (or its inverse) will be defined as the *intraprecision* (for the given subject).

Consider now the group of subjects; we index the n subjects by $i(i = 1, 2, ..., n)$. We assume that both the variances σ_i^2 and the k_i coefficients are homogeneous among subjects, and henceforth denote σ^2/k the common value of the σ_i^2/k_i. The average of the individual observed variances s_i^2 will henceforth be denoted s^2 and called the *intravariance* (for the group), and the ratio s^2/k (or its inverse) will be defined as the *intraprecision* (for the group). The average of the individual observed effect z_i is $\bar{z} = 1/n\Sigma z_i$. Let the "true" effects ζ have a (population) mean $\bar{\zeta}$ and variance τ^2. Then the average observed effect $\bar{z}$ comes from a distribution with mean $\bar{\zeta}$ and variance $1/n(\tau^2 + \sigma^2/k)$. The observed variance $\Sigma(z_i - \bar{z})^2/n - 1$ is an estimate of $\zeta^2 + \sigma^2/k$ and will be called the *intervariance*.

The ratio

$$\Sigma(z_i - \bar{z})^2/n(n - 1)$$

is an estimate of $(1/n)(\tau^2 + \sigma^2/k)$. This ratio (or its inverse) will be defined as the *interprecision*.

REFERENCES

Box, G. E. P., & Tiao, G. C. *Bayesian inference in statistical analysis.* Reading: Addison-Wesley, 1973.

Edwards, A. W. F. Fiducial probability. *The Statistician,* 1976, *25,* 15–35.

Fisher, R. A. *Statistical method and scientific inference.* Edinburgh: Oliver & Boyd (2nd ed.), 1959.

Jeffreys, H. *Theory of probability.* Oxford: Clarendon (3rd ed.), 1961.

Holender, D., & Bertelson, P. Selective preparation and time uncertainty. *Acta Psychologica,* 1975, *39,* 193–203.

Lindley, D. V. *Introduction to probability and statistics from a Bayesian viewpoint (part 2: Inference).* Cambridge: Cambridge University Press, 1970.

Rouanet, H., Lépine, D., & Pelnard-Considère, J. Bayes-fiducial procedures as practical substitutes for misplaced significance testing: An application to educational data. In D. N. M. de Gruijter & L. J. T. Van der Kamp (Eds.), *Advances in psychological and educational measurement.* New York: Wiley, 1976.

Rozeboom, W. W. The fallacy of the null-hypothesis significance test. *Psychological Bulletin,* 1960, *57,* 416–428.

Scheffé, H. *The analysis of variance.* New York: Wiley, 1959.

Sternberg, S. The discovery of processing stages: Extension of Donder's method. In W. G. Koster, Attention and Performance II, *Acta Psychologica,* 1969, *30,* 276–315.

Author Index

Numbers in *italics* refer to pages on which the complete references are listed.

A

Abercrombie, D., 289, *296*
Abrams, S. G., 135, *143*
Adams, J. A., 525, *533*
Adams, J. C., 453, *460*
Aggashyan, R. V., 575, *593*
Ahroon, W. A., 237, 238, *242*
Aizerman, M. A., 562, *593*
Aldridge, V. J., 430, 436, *467*, 477, *485*
Allan, L. G., 28, *40*
Allard, F., 376, *389*
Allmeyer, D. H., 45, *62*, 126, 129, *144, 146*
Allport, D. A., 11, *23*, 45, *61*, 93, *107*, 196, 204, 205, *207*, 217, *225*, 345, 346, 358, *359*
Alper, V., 169, 170, *176*
Altman, A., 352, 356, *360*
Ambler, B. A., 84, *86*
Ammons, C. H., 351, *359*
Ammons, R. B., 351, *359*
Andersen, P., 506, *513*
Anderson, T., 173, *176*
Anderson, W. G., 179, *191*
Andreeva, F. A., 562, *593*
Andriessen, J. J., 120, 129, 131, 137, *143*, 634, *644*
Anrep, G. V., 348, 354, *359*
Anscombe, F. J., 622, *630*
Antes, J. R., 132, *143*

Antonis, B., 45, *61*, 345, 346, 358, *359*
Arbib, M. A., 561, *593*
Arezzo, J., 448, *460*
Aronson, E., 575, *594*
Asatryan, D. G., 568, *593*
Ashby, S. M., 435, 438, 451, *467*
Ashe, J. H., 446, *464, 467*
Atkinson, R. C., 78, *86*
Audley, R. J., 600, 611, *616*
Averbach, E., 8, 11, 14, *20*, 94, *107*, 138, *143*

B

Baars, B. J., 195, 200, *208*
Baddeley, A. D., 238, *241*, 323, 326, 331, 337, *340, 341*
Baker, M. A., 135, *143*
Bakker, D. J., 412, *425*
Bamber, D., 78 79, 83, *86*, 273, *277*
Barenfeld, M., 135, *146*
Barlow, H. B., 26, 33, *39*
Barnes, P., 615, *618*
Barocas, V. S., 348, 357, *362*
Baron, J., 167, 168, 170, *176, 177*, 425, *425*
Bartlett, F., 449, *462*
Bartlett, N. R., 103, *107*
Battersby, W. S., 16, *21*
Bauer, J. W., 437, 453, *462*

Beauvois, M. F., 195, *208*
Becker, W., 134, *144, 458, 461*
Beecher, M. D., 234, *242*
Belen'kii, V. Ye., 576, 577, 578, *593*
Bell, A. G., 280, *296*
Beller, H. K., 79, 83, 84, *86*
Bellugi, U., 230, *240, 241*
Bender, D. B., 199, *207*
Benson, D. A., 453, *460*
Benson, D. F., 195, *207*
Benson, P. J., 444, *462*
Benton, A. L., 364, 365, *373*
Berger, R. S., 237, 238, *242*
Berkson, J., 620, *630*
Berlucchi, G., 364, 365, 366, 370, 371, *373, 374*
Bernstein, N., 559, 560, 561, 562, *593*
Berrian, R. W., 179, *191*
Bertelson, P., 80, *86,* 247, 248, 249, 250, 251, 252, 253, 254, 255, 259, *259, 260,* 262, 271, *278,* 350, *359, 360,* 392, *409,* 688, 689, *701*
Besner, D., 211, *225*
Besrest, A., 437, *460*
Best, P. R., 103, *107*
Bever, T. G., 97, 98, *108,* 236, *240*
Biederman, I., 232, *240*
Bindra, D., 81, *86,* 273, 277, 602, 607, *616*
Birdsall, T. G., 648, *674*
Bishop, G. H., 349, *360*
Bizzi, E., 131, *144,* 562, *593*
Bjork, E., 6, *21,* 122, *144*
Blaha, J., 78, *86*
Blakemore, C., 25, 29, 35, *39,* 235, *240*
Blechner, M. J., 236, 237, *240*
Blecker, D., 84, *87*
Bloomfield, J. R., 129, *144*
Blumstein, S., 274, *278*
Blyth, K. W., 350, *360*
Bobrow, D. G., 129, *145,* 681, *686*
Bock, D. R., 620, *630*
Boies, S. J., 78, 80, *88,* 105, 106, *109, 110,* 317, 318, *318,* 326, *341,* 376, *390*
Boles, D. B., 355, *360*
Bolinger, D. L., 289, *296*
Bongartz, W., 12, 15, *21*
Bonnet, C., 26, 27, 28, 29, 32, 34, *39, 40*
Boomer, D. S., 98, *107*
Boothroyd, A., 292, *297*
Borda, R. P., 440, *463*
Boring, E. G., 600, *616*
Bornstein, M. H., 232, *240*

Bouchard, R., 195, *207*
Bouma, H., 94, *107,* 120, 122, 123, 124, 125, 126, 129, 139, 140, *143, 144,* 152, *161,* 632, 635, 636, 638, 639, *644*
Bouman, M. A., 30, *41*
Bouvier, A., 34, *39*
Bouwhuis, D., 124, *144,* 643, *644*
Bower, G. H., 97, 98, *107*
Bowers, D., 352, 355, 356, *360*
Box, G. E. P., 694, 695, *701*
Boylls, C. C., 564, 566, 567, 568, 570, *593*
Boynton, R. M., 132, *146*
Bradshaw, G. J., 352, *361*
Bradshaw, J. L., 125, *144,* 212, *225,* 364, 366, 370, 371, *373, 374,* 376, 377, *389, 390,* 420, *425*
Brandt, T., 30, *40*
Braren, M., 452, *466*
Bregman, A. S., 65, 66, 67, 68, 69, *74, 75*
Breitmeyer, B. G., 30, *39*
Briggs, G. E., 78, 82, *86*
Briggs, G., 45, 46, 56, *61*
Briggs, G. G., 351, 352, *360*
Brizzolara, D., 364, 366, 370, 371, *373, 374*
Broadbent, D. E., 44, 45, *61,* 95, *109,* 245, 246, *259,* 263, 272, *277,* 326, *340,* 345, *360,* 443, *460,* 645, 647, 648, 649, 653, 656, 662, 669, 670, 671, *674*
Broadbent, M. P. H., 649, *674*
Brooks, L. R., 167, 168, 171, 173, 174, 176, *176, 177,* 358, *360*
Brown, C. R., 669, 670, 671, *674*
Brown, D. R., 122, *146*
Brown, E. R., 102, *110*
Brown, I., 44, 51, 58, *62,* 107, *110*
Brown, J. F., 30, *39*
Brown, R., 291, *296*
Brown, R. H., 27, 28, *40*
Brownell, H. H., 85, *86*
Brugge, J. F., 262, *277*
Bruner, J. S., 613, *616*
Bryce, D. P., 442, *464*
Bryden, M. P., 365, *373, 376, 389*
Buchwald, J. A., 446, *460*
Budayr, B., 502, *503*
Budiansky, J., 677, *686*
Buffardi, L., 44, *61*
Buffery, A. W. H., 364, 365, 371, *373,* 412, *425*
Burke, R. E., 562, *593*
Burks, A. W., 588, *595*
Burrows, D., 82, *86*

Bush, R. R., 620, *630*
Buswell, G. T., 136, 140, 141, *144,* 180, *191*
Butler, R. A., 447, *460*
Butler, S. R., 436, *460*
Butterworth, B., 224, *225*
Bykoff, K., 354, *360*

C

Camarda, R., 365, 370, *374*
Campbell, F. W., 29, 35, *39, 40,* 235, *240*
Campbell, J., 65, 66, *74*
Campbell, K. B., 431, 452, *464*
Cantor, N. E., 44, 51, 56, 60, *61, 62,* 107, *110*
Caplan, D., 97, *108,* 247, *260*
Carlson, W. R., 602, 605, *616*
Carmon, A., 236, *241*
Carn, R., 137, *144*
Carney, P. J., 567, *594*
Carpenter, D., 506, *513*
Carpenter, P. A., 85, *86, 87*
Carroll, F. S., 95, *110*
Carroll, J. M., 97, 98, *108*
Carso, G., 412, 419, *426*
Cartwright, D., 600, 602, 605, *616*
Cary, L., 253, 254, *260*
Case, B., 79, *87*
Casey, M. C., 356, *360*
Catlin, J., 645, 647, 648, 653, 656, 661, *674*
Cattell, J. M., 600, *616*
Caudrey, D., 601, *618*
Cavanagh, J. P., 93, 94, *108*
Ceillier, R., 186, *191*
Cernacek, J., 349, *360*
Chambers, S. M., 185, 191, *191,* 425, *426*
Chandler, J. P., 55, *61*
Chandler, K. A., 502, *504*
Chao-Ming Cheng, 95, *108*
Chapman, R. M., 458, *460*
Chase, W. G., 10, *22,* 85, *86,* 472, 481, *483,* 498, *504*
Cheng, C-M., 335, 336, 338, 339, *340, 341*
Chernov, V. I., 562, *593*
Cherry, E. C., 272, *278*
Chiarello, R. J., 236, *240*
Chistovich, L. A., 280, *296,* 536, 543, 549, *554*
Chomsky, N., 172, *176,* 288, *296,* 300, *318*
Chow, S. L., 355, *360*
Christie, D., 364, 370, *374*

Clare, M. H., 349, *360*
Clark, H. H., 85, *86,* 309, *318,* 423, *425*
Clarke, F. R., 638 *644*
Clayton, K. N., 335, 339, *342*
Clementino, T., 377, *390*
Clifton, R. K., 472, *484*
Clynes, M., 447, *461*
Cohen, A., 143, *145*
Cohen, G., 78, *86,* 366, 371, 372, *373,* 376, 377, 388, 389, *389,* 421, *425*
Cohen, G. H., 132, *146*
Cohen, J., 479, *484*
Cohen, L., 349, *360,* 435, 444, *461, 466*
Cohen, R. L., 28, 30, *40*
Cohen, S. P., 496, *503*
Colburn, H. S., 272, *277*
Cole, R. A., 325, *340*
Colegate, R., 14, *21*
Coles, M. G. H., 482, *484*
Collins, J. F., 9, 10, 12, *21*
Coltheart, M., 138, *144,* 179, *191,* 211, *225,* 421, *426*
Connor, W. H., 472, 481, *484*
Conolly, K. J., 613, *616*
Conrad, R., 291, *296,* 322, 323, 325, *340, 341*
Contat, M., 301, *319*
Cook, J., 350 352, *360 361*
Cook, T. W., 350, 351, *360*
Cooper, F. S., 230, 233, 237, *242, 243,* 280, *296*
Cooper, R., 430, 436, 440, *461, 467,* 477, *485*
Coquery, J. M., 506, 509, *514*
Corballis, M. C., 372, *373*
Corbit, J. D., 235, *241*
Corcoran, S. K., 372, *373*
Coriell, A. S., 8, 14, *20,* 94, *107,* 138, *143*
Corsi, P. M., 276, *277*
Costa, L. D., 436, *467*
Costell, R. M., 479, *484*
Coulter, J. D., 507, *514*
Courchesne, E., 438, 451, 452, *461, 462,* 510, *514*
Cox, D. R., 620, *630*
Cox, P. J., 355, *361*
Craik, K. J. W., 392, *409*
Crimmins, D. B., 237, *242*
Critchley, M., 413, *426,* 457, *461*
Crook, M. N., 30, *40*
Crossman, E. R. F. W., 600, *616*
Crow, H. J., 448, *467*

Crowder, R. G., 95, *108,* 237, *240,* 325, 326, 328, 329, 330, 331, 335, 336, 337, 338, *341, 342*
Curcio, F., 376, *390*
Curtis, J. F., 245, *260*
Cutting, J. E., 230, 231, 232, 233, 234, 235, 236, 237, 238, *240, 241,* 267, 272, 274, *277*

D

Dalgleish, L., 607, *618*
Dalrymple-Alford, E. C., 502, *503*
Dannenbring, G. L., 65, 68, *74, 75*
Darley, C. F., 458, *465*
Darwin, C. J., 238, *241,* 262, 263, 264, 270, 273, 276, *277, 278,* 331, *341*
Davelaar, E., 211, *225*
Davidson, R., 356, *362*
Davies, A., 45, *62,* 346, *362*
Davis, H., 447, *461, 464*
Davis, R., 377, *389*
Davis, R. C., 348, *360*
Dawson, G. D., 348, *360*
Day, R. S., 237, *240*
Decker, L., 645, 646, 647, 649, 656, 662, *674*
Dee, H., 377, *389*
Deecke, L., 440, 458, *461*
Deese, J., 300, *318*
DeLong, M., 562, *593*
Denoth, F., 440, *467*
DeRenzi, E., 221, *225,* 364, *373*
Deutsch, D., 492, *503*
Deutsch, H. A., 492, *503*
deVoogd, A. H., 126, 131, 137, 139, 140, *143, 144,* 634, *644*
Dichgans, J., 30, *40,* 131, *144*
Dick, A. O., 10, *21*
Diehl, R., 235, *241*
Diener, H. C., 30, *40*
Dijkstra, S., 525, *533*
Dill, A. B., 137, *144*
Dimmick, F. L., 28, *40*
Dimond, S. J., 392, *409*
Dirks, S. J., 450, *461,* 510, *514*
Disch, K., 5, *22*
Dixon, N. F., 213, *225*
Do, P., 107, *110*
Donald, M. W., 438, 440, 446, 448, 456, 458, *461*

Donchin, E., 435, 438, 444, 450, 451, 452, 453, 455, 456, 458, *461, 463, 466*
Donderi, D. C., 79, 80, *87,* 273, *277,* 607, *616*
Dooling, D. J., 97, 102, *108*
Dooling, R. J., 232, *242*
Dorman, M. F., 237, 238, *241*
Doty, R. W., 7, *21*
Draguns, J., 4, *21*
Driver, R. C., 602, 605, *616*
Dudley, L. M., 434, *461*
Duffy, E., 471, *484*
Duncan-Johnson, C. C., 482, *484*
Durant, R. F., 365, *373*
Durnford, M., 365, *373*
Durup, H., 188, *191,* 396, *409*
Dwivedi, A., 496, *503*
Dyer, F. N., 488, *503*

E

Eason, R. G., 434, 435, *461,* 512, *514*
Easton, T. A., 563, *593*
Edwards, A. W. F., 695, *701*
Edwards, W., 270, *278,* 600, *616*
Efron, R., 94, *108*
Egeth, H., 6, *21,* 377, *389*
Egeth, H. E., 78, 82, 84, *87*
Eichelman, E. H., 326, *341*
Eichelman, W. H., 376, *390*
Eijkman, G., 45, 46, 53, 59, *61*
Eijkman, E. G. J., 138, *146*
Eimas, P. D., 234, 235, *241, 243*
Eisler, H., 94, *108*
Elfner, L. F., 71, *75*
Elliott, R. C., 404, *409*
Ellis, A. W., 202, *207*
Ellis, H. D., 218, *225*
Ells, J. C., 517, 530, *533*
Ellson, D. G., 519, *533*
El'ner, A. N., 577, *593, 595*
Emmerich, D. S., 611, *616*
Engberg, I., 506, *513,* 567, *593*
Engel, F. L., 127, 128, 129, 130, *144*
Epstein, J., 377, *389*
Eriksen, B. A., 9, 17, 18, *21,* 122, *144,* 199, *207*
Eriksen, C. W., 6, 9, 10, 12, 13, 14, 17, 18, 19, *21,* 122, *144,* 179, *191,* 199, 430, *462,* 525, *533*
Eshkol, N., 561, *593*

Estes, W. K., 5, 6, *21,* 45, *61,* 122, 126, 130, *144,* 323, 325, 329, 339, *341,* 536, 553, *554,* 678, *686*
Ettlinger, G., 404, *409*
Evarts, E. V., 131, *144,* 262, *593*

F

Fairweather, H., 371, *373*
Falmagne, F. C., 496, *503*
Fant, C. G. M., 282, *296*
Farmer, R. M., 95, *111*
Fechner, G. T., 393, *409*
Feigin, D. S., 352, *361*
Fel'dman, A. G., 567, 568, *593, 594*
Feller, W., 620, *630*
Fernberger, S. W., 602, 605, *616*
Festinger, L. A., 600, 611, 613, *616*
Fetz, E. E., 506, *514*
Finkenzeller, P., 450, *463*
Fischer, F. W., 324, *341*
Fisher, D. F., 5, *22,* 414, *426*
Fisher, P., 45, 46, 56, *61*
Fisher, R. A., 691, 694, *701*
Fitts, P. M., 5, *21,* 359, *360*
Flavell, J. H., 4, *21*
Fleiss, J. L., 438, 452, *462*
Flom, M. C., 17, *21*
Foard, C. F., 232, 233, 234, 235, *241*
Fodor, J. A., 98, *108*
Fomin, S. V., 575, 576, *593*
Fontenot, D. J., 365, *373,* 376, *390*
Fontenot, H., 377, *389*
Forbes, S. M., 45, *62,* 346, *362*
Ford, J. M., 450, 451, 453, 456, *461, 465,* 510, *514*
Forgays, D. G., 125, *145*
Forster, K. I., 185, 191, *191,* 425, *426*
Fowler, C., 324, *341*
Fowler, C. A., 573, *593*
Fraisse, P., 78, *87,* 91, 94, 95, 98, 100, 102, 103, 106, *108,* 536, *554*
Francis, W. N., 151, 156, *161*
Frankstein, S. I., 562, *594*
Franzini, C., 365, 370, *374*
Freeman, R. B., Jr., 32, *39*
Friedman, D., 452, 455, *462*
Friedman, D. G., 438, 452, *462*
Fromkin, V. A., 194, *207*
Frost, D., 406, *410*
Frost, J. D., 440, *463*

Fruhstorfer, H., 436, 437, 450, *462, 463*
Furth, H. G., 322, *341*
Fuster, J. M., 440, *462*

G

Gabrielson, A., 536, *554*
Gaillard, A. W. K., 436, 437, *462, 464*
Galambos, R., 430, 433, 435, 441, 442, 446, 448, 450, 451, *461, 464, 465,* 510, *514*
Galanter, E., 300, *319,* 620, *630*
Galin, D., 355, *362*
Ganz, L., 3, 4, 9, 12, 13, *21,* 26, 28, 30, 39, 40
Garcia, B., 95, *110*
Gardner, G. T., 45, *62,* 129, *146*
Gardner, H., 217, *225*
Garner, W. R., 98, 100, *108,* 237, *241,* 430, *462,* 525, *533*
Garoutte, B., 506, *514*
Garrett, H. E., 611, 613, *616*
Garrett, M. F., 98, *108*
Gatchel, R. J., 472, *484*
Gates, A., 125, *144*
Gay, T., 238, *241*
Gazzaniga, M. S., 221, *225,* 392, 393, *409, 410*
Geer, J. H., 473, 481, *484*
Geffen, G., 262, 263, *278,* 356, *362,* 364, 366, 370, *373,* 377, *389*
Gelade, G., 199, *208*
Gel'fand, I. M., 559, 563, *593*
Gellhorn, E., 562, *593*
Geschwind, N., 195, *207,* 246, *260,* 276, *278,* 392, *410*
Ghez, C., 507, *514*
Gibson, E. J., 150, *161,* 348, *360,* 383, *389*
Gibson, J. J., 348, *360,* 383, *389,* 564, 570, 575, 592, *593*
Glass, A., 436, *460*
Glass, E., 602, 605, *616*
Glassman, W. E., 325, *341*
Gleitman, L. R., 163, 164, *176, 177*
Glenn, F., 168, *177*
Goff, W. R., 438, *461*
Gold, S., 348, 357, *362*
Goldhor, R. S., 287, 288, *296*
Goldiamond, I., 642, *644,* 662, *674*
Goldman-Eisler, F., 98, *108,* 281, *296,* 300, *318*
Goldstein, A. G., 32, *40*

Goldstein, M. H., 262, *277*
Golowner, L., 237, *242*
Goodman, K. S., 412, *426*
Goodman, W. S., 442, *464*
Gopher, D., 135, *144,* 254, *259*
Gordon, G., 506, *514*
Gordon, H. W., 236, *241*
Gorea, A., 35, *40*
Gough, P. B., 85, *87*
Gould, J. D., 132, 134, 137, *144,* 317, 318, *318*
Graham, D. T., 472, 481, *483*
Grahman, F. K., 472, 481, *483, 484*
le Grand, Y., 119, 120, *145*
Granit, R., 563, *593*
Grant, E. E., 306, *318*
Grantham, D. W., 45, *62*
Gray, J. A., 412, *425*
Gray, J. L., 611, *616*
Green, D. M., 94, *109, 611, 616,* 622, *630,* 648, *674*
Greenberg, M. G., 601, *617*
Greene, P. H., 558, 559, 564, 577, *594*
Greeno, J. F., 99, *108*
Greenwald, A. G., 488, 489, 499, *503*
Grice, G. R., 609, *617*
Griffith, B. C., 230, *242*
Grillner, S., *594*
Grindley, G. C., 127, 129, *145*
Gross, C. G., 199, *207*
Gross, M. M., 365, *373*
Grossberg, S., 455, 458, *466*
Grözinger, B., 458, *461*
Guerri, S., 440, *467*
Guilford, J. P., 601, *617*
Gullickson, G. R., 479, *484*
Gur, R. E., 356, *360*
Gur, R. C., 356, *360*
Gurfinkel', V. S., 562, 563, 567, 575, 576, 577, 578, *593, 594*
Gutschera, M. W., 200, *208*

H

Haber, R. N., 6, 7, 11, *22*
Haggard, M., 372, *374*
Haggard, M. P., 262, 272, 273, 275, *277*
Haider, M., 434, *466*
Haines, E., 437, *467*
Hakarem, G., 438, 452, *462*
Hake, H. W., 430, *462, 525, 533*
Hall, G. S., 6, *22*

Hall, J. L., 262, *277*
Halle, M., 288, *296*
Halperin, Y., 236, *241*
Halwes, T., 231, 232, *242*
Halwes, T. G., 263, *277*
Hamilton, P., 103, 104, 105, *108*
Hanes, L. F., 28, *40*
Hannay, H., 377, *390*
Hannay, H. J., 365, **373**
Harris, F., 506, *514*
Harris, K. S., 230, 232, 233, 234, *242, 243*
Harris, L. J., 356, *360*
Harshman, R., 236, *242*
Hart, G., 29, *41*
Harter, M. R., 434, 435, *461,* 512, *514*
Hartley, L. R., 435, *462*
Hawkins, H. L., 78, *87,* 212, *225*
Hawkins, W. F., 642, *644,* 662, *674*
Healy, A. F., 323, 327, *341*
Heath, R. A., 53, *61,* 600, *617,* 620, *630*
Heffley, E., 438, *461*
Heilman, K. M., 352, 355, 356, *360*
Held, R., 406, *410*
Hellige, J. B., 355, *361,* 377, 388, *390*
Henderson, A., 300, *318*
Henderson, L., 179, *191*
Henmon, V. A. C., 611, *617*
Henning, G. B., 272, *277*
Herder, J., 83, *86*
Herning, R. I., 450, 451, 455, 456, *461, 466*
Hicks, R. E., 106, 108, 352, 353, 354, 355, 357, *360, 361*
Hill, P. B., 95, *110*
Hill, R. M., 26, 33, *39*
Hlliard, R. D., 364, 371, *373*
Hillyard, S. A., 221, *225,* 430, 432, 433, 435, 436, 437, 438, 441, 442, 444, 445, 446, 448, 450, 451, 452, 453, 456, 458, *461, 462, 464, 465, 466, 467,* 510, 511, *514*
Hines, D., 377, *390*
Hink, R. F., 431, 441, 444, *462, 464*
Hirose, H., 238, *241*
Hirsh, I. J., 93, *108,* 246, *260*
Hiscock, M., 353, 356, *361*
Hitch, G., 326, *340*
Hiwatashi, K., 39, *41*
Hnatiow, M., 477, *484*
Hochberg, J., 132, 135, *145,* 150, *161*
Hock, H. S., 84, *87,* 371, 372, *373*
Hock, S., 372, *373*
Hockey, R., 103, 104, 105, *108*
Hodge, D. C., 152, *161*

Hodge, J., 169, 170, *176*
Hoffman, H. S., 230, *242*
Hoffman, I., 602, 605, *616*
Hoffman, J. E., 14, 18, 19, *21*
Hoffman, M., 12, *21*
Hoin, H., 348, 357, *362*
Holding, D. H., 138, *145*
Holender, D., 688, 689, *701*
Hollingsworth, H. L., 516, *533*
Hollingsworth, S., 122, *147*
Holmes, J., 247, *260*
Holmgren, J. E., 78, *86*
Homick, J. L., 71, *75*
Horse, R. W., 506, *514*
House, A. S., 282, 283, *296*
Howarth, J. N., 292, *296*
Howell, P., 82, *87*
Hubbard, A. W., 560, 561, 562, 569, *594*
Hublet, C., 250, 251, 252, 255, 259, *260*
Hudgins, C. V., 280, 291, *296*
Hudson, J., 348, *360*
Huey, E. B., 163, *177*
Huey, E. G., 149, *161*
Huey, E. M., 632, 634, *644*
Huggins, A. W. F., 94, 95, 103, *108*, 281, 287, 289, *296*
Huggins, J. D., 472, 482, *485*
Hugon, 513, *514*
Hull, A. J., 322, *341*
Hull, E., 421, *426*
Humphrey, G. L., 446, *460*
Hunt, E., 378, *390*
Husserl, E., 92, *108*

I

Idson, W. L., 59, *61*
Ikeda, H., 35, *40*
Ikeda, M., 129, *145*
Irwin, D. A., 440, *465*, 478, *485*
Irwin, F. W., 611, *617*
Iwama, K., 506, *514*

J

Jabbur, S. J., 506, *514*
Jackson, J. H., 459, *462*
James, M., 364, *374*
James, W., 90, 91, *108*, 326, *341*
Jannssen, W. H., 106, *108*
Jarvella, R. J., 97, *108*

Järvilehto, T., 436, 437, *462*
Jastrow, J. A., 600, *617*
Jeffreys, H., 694, *701*
Jennerod, C., 134, *146*
John, E. R., 449, 452, *462, 466*
John, J. E. J., 292, *296*
Johnsen, A. M., 82, *86*
Johnson, C. A., 28, *40, 119, 145*
Johnson, D. M., 611, 613, *617*
Johnson, L. C., 437, *464*
Johnson, M., 609, *618*
Johnson, M. C., 677, *686*
Johnson, N. F., 78, 79, *87*
Johnson, R., 455, 456, *461*
Johnson, S. T., 339, *341*
Johnston, D. M., 127, *145*
Johnston, J. C., 11, *22*
Jonasson, J., 211, *225*
Jones, B., 517, *533*
Jones, L. V., 620, *630*
Jones, M. R., 99, *108, 536, 553, 554*
Jones, R. W., 613, *617*
Jones, S., 85, *88*
Jonides, J., 6, *21*, 82, *87*
Junge, K., 566, *513*
Juola, J. F., 78, *86*
Jusczyk, P. W., 234, *241*
Just, M. A., 85, *86, 87*

K

Kahn, B. J., 45, 46, 59, *61*
Kahneman, D., 4, 12, 17, *21, 22, 94, 99, 109,* 245, 254, *260,* 346, 347, 355, 356, *361,* 392, *410,* 434, 440, *462*
Kallman, H. J., 372, *373*
Kalmus, H., 613, *617*
Kaplan, E. L., 140, *145*
Kappauf, W. E., 7, *22*
Karl, J. C., 28, *40*
Karlin, L., 435, 452, 456, *462*
Katwijk, A. van, 97, 103, *109*
Katz, L., 164, *177, 611, 617*
Kaufman, L., 134, *145*
Kellaway, P., 440, *463*
Keele, S. W., 10, 11, *22, 106, 109, 452, 463,* 516, 517, 530, *533, 563, 594*
Keenan, J. M., 313, *318*
Kellar, L., 232, *242*
Kellogg, W. N., 602, 605, *617, 624, 630*
Kelly, D. H., 30, *40*
Kelly, W. J., 232, *242*

Kelso, J. A. S., 516, *534*
Kendall, M. G., 537, *554*
Kent, R. D., 567, 568, *594*
Kerr, B., 345, *361*
Killeen, P., 99, 105, *109*
Kimura, D., 246, 250, 257, *260*, 261, 262, *278*, 350, 354, *361, 362*, 365, *373*, 376, *390*, 418, *426*
Kinchla, R. A., 28, *40*, 679, *686*
Kinney, J., 232, 234, *242*
Kinsbourne, M., 12, 16, *22*, 106, *108*, 221, *225*, 262, 263, *278*, 348, 350, 351, 352, 353, 354, 355, 356, 357, 358, *360, 361, 362*, 392, 393, 406, 409, *410*
Kintsch, W., 313, *318*
Kirk, R. E., 519, *533*
Kirstein, E., 263, *278*
Klapp, S. T., 179, 180, 185, *191*
Klatt, D. H., 94, *109*, 281, 283, 287, 288, 292, *296*
Klatzky, R. L., 83, *87*, 377, *390*
Kleiman, G. M., 221, *225*
Klein, D., 364, 366, *373*
Klein, R. M., 440, *464*
Kleinman, D., 449, *462*
Klemmer, E. T., 300, *318*
Klima, E. S., 230, *240, 241*
Klinke, R., 450, *463*
Knoll, R. L., 51, *62*
Knott, J. R., 437, 440, *463, 465*, 478, *485*
Kocel, K., 355, *362*
Kock, W. E., 246, *260*
Koenderink, J. J., 30, *41*
Kohn, B., 681, *686*
Kolers, P. A., 212, *225*, 412, *426*
Konick, A. W., 324, *341*
Kopell, B. S., 450, 451, 453, 456, 458, *461, 465*, 510, *514*
Kornblum, S., 80, *87*, 496, *503*
Kornhuber, H. H., 440, 458, *461, 463*, 553, *554*
Korte, A., 28, *40*
Kotovsky, K., 102, *110*
Kots, Ya. M., 567, 570, *594*
Kozhevnikov, V. A., 280, *296*, 536, 543, 549, *554*
Kozminsky, E., 313, *318*
Krainz, P. L., 450, *465*
Krashen, S., 236, *242*
Krausz, H. I., 433, 438, 448, 450, 451, 452, *462, 464*

Kremen, H., 434, *467*
Krendel, E. S., 129, *145*
Kreuter, C., 354, *362*, 392, 406, *410*
Krinskiy, V. I., 567, *594*
Kristofferson, A. B., 93, 94, 103, *109, 111*, 536, 538, *555*
Kroll, N. E. A., 376, 378, 386, 389, *390*
Kronseder, C., 372, *373*
Krueger, L. E., 79, 81, 84, *87*
Kubovy, M., 4, 12, *22*, 455, 456, *461*
Kucera, H., 151, 156, *161*
Kuhl, P. A., 234, *241*
Kulikowski, J. J., 29, *40*
Kutas, M., 438, 455, 456, 458, *461, 463*

L

Laabs, G. E., 516, 517, 532, *533*
LaBerge, D., 45, *61, 91, 109*, 300, 315, *318*, 600, *617*
LaCasse, P., 353, *361*
Lacey, B. C., 471, 472, 473, 477, 479, 481, 482, 483, *484*
Lacey, J. I., 434, *463*, 471, 472, 473, 477, 479, 481, 482, 483, *484*
Ladefoged, P., 95, *109*, 263, 272, *277*
Laming, D. R. J., 53, *61*, 600, *617*
Lamont, A., 119, *145*
Lane, H., 232, 234, *241, 242*
Lang, P. J., 436, *467*, 472, 473, 477, 478, 481, *484, 485*
Lappin, J. S., 5, *22*
Lashley, K. S., 102, *109*, 535, *555*
Lawler, J. E., 482, *484*
Lawler, K. A., 482, *484*
Leary, J., 615, *618*
Lecours, A. R., 195, *208*
Lee, D. N., 564, 570, 575, *594*
Lee, M. V., 435, *467*
Leeuwenberg, E. L., 99, *109*
Lefton, L., 6, 7, *22*
Lehiste, I., 282, 283, 289, *296, 297*
Leibowitz, H. W., 27, 28, *40*, 119, *145*
Lenzi, G. L., 507, *514*
Lépine, D., 690, *701*
Lesevre, N., 458, *463*
Leuba, J. H., 516, 517, *533*
Levelt, W. J. M., 16, *22*
Levin, H., 140, *145*
Levin, J. R., 519, *533*

Levy, B. A., 338, *341*
Levy, E. J., 10, *23*
Levy, J., 365, 371, *373,* 421, *426*
Lévy-Schoen, A., 132, 134, *145*
Lewis, J., 378, *390*
Lewis, J. L., 204, *208*
Lewis, S. S., 211, *226,* 421, *426*
Lhermitte, F., 195, *208*
Liberman, A. M., 229, 230, 231, 232, 233, 234, 237, *241, 242, 243,* 280, *296,* 300, *319,* 324, *341,* 650, *674*
Liberman, I., 324, *341*
Lieberman, P., 230, *242*
Liederman, J., 356, 357 *362*
Lindblom, B., 280, 285, 286, *296, 297*
Lindley, D. V., 694, *701*
Lindsay, P. H., 45, *62,* 437, 453, 456, *462, 466*
Lindsay, P. R., 346, *362*
Lindsey, P. H., 11, *22*
Lindsley, D. B., 434, 436, *465, 466,* 478, *485*
Link, S. W., 53, *61,* 600, *617,* 620, 629, *630*
Linschoten, J., 639, *644*
Lishman, J. R., 575, *594*
Lisin, V. V., 562, *594*
Litvintsev, A. I., 562, *594*
Locher, P. J., 135, *145*
Locke, S., 232, *242*
Lockhead, G. R., 83, *87*
Loeb, M., 135, *143*
Loftus, G. R., 136, *145*
Lomas, J., 354, *362*
Loveless, N. E., 436, *463,* 478, 479, 481, *484*
Low, M. D., 440, *463*
Low, N. D., 437, *463*
Lubin, A., 437, *464*
Luce, R. D., 94, *109,* 620, *630,* 648, 653, *674*
Lundberg, A., 506, *513,* 567, *593*
Lundervold, A., 349, *362*
Lunneborg, C., 378, *390*
Luria, A. R., 261, *278,* 376, *390,* 440, *463,* 558, 574, *594*
Lyberg, L., 543, *555*
Lyregaard, P. E., 660, 661, 668, *674*

M

Maccabe, J. J., 404, *409*
Mace, W., 592, *595*

Machado, J., 435, *467*
Mackavery, W., 376, *390*
Mackay, D. G., 196, 204, 206, *208*
MacKay, D. M., 26, *40*
Mackworth, J. F., 150, *161*
Mackworth, N. H., 116, 122, 124, 132, *145*
Madigan, S. A., 218, *226*
Maer, F., 356, *362*
Magner, M. E., 293, *297*
Malone, D., 377, *390*
Mandler, G., 91, *109*
Marascuilo, L. A., 519, *533*
Marcel, A. J., 204, 205, *208,* 210, 211, 213, 217, 218, *225, 226*
Marcel, T., 412, 419, *426*
Marin, O. S. M., 217, *226*
Marks, L. E., 32, 33, 35, *40*
Marshall, J., 216, *226,* 247, *260*
Marshall, J. C., 202, *207,* 210, 211, 214, *225, 226*
Marteniuk, R. G., 516, *533*
Martin, J. G., 97, 98, 99, 102, *109,* 536, 538, 543, 553, *555*
Martinetti, M. G., 440, *467*
Martz, M. J., 452, *462*
Marzi, C. A., 364, 365, 366, 370, 371, *373, 374*
Mashhour, M., 32, 33, *40*
Mason, M., 164, *177,* 423, *426*
Massaro, D. W., 44, 45, 46, 59, *61,* 94, *109,* 126, *145,* 470, 483
Mast, T., 447, *461*
Matsuda, F., 32, 33, *40*
Mattingly, I. G., 231, 232, 234, *242*
Mayfield, J. F., 611, *617*
Mazzucchi, A., 364, 371, *374*
McAdam, D. W., 436, 440, *463, 465,* 478, *485*
McCallum, W. C., 436, 437, 440, *461, 463, 467,* 477, *485*
McCarthy, G., 450, 451, *466*
McClelland, J., 176, *177*
McClelland, J. L., 11, *22*
McConkie, G. W., 126, 137, 140, *145, 146,* 150, 156, 160, *161*
McCullock, W. S., 586, *594*
McDougall, R., 98, *109*
McFarland, D. J., 613, *617*
McGill, W. J., 536, *555,* 600, 602, *617*
McGuiness, D., 441, *464*
McIntyre, M., 559, 573, 574, 575, 592, *595*

McKay, D. P., 129, *146*
McKeever, M., 377, *390*
McKillip, B. J., 425, *425*
McKoon, G., 313, *318*
McMurray, J., 353, *361*
McNeill, D., 291, *296*
Megaw, E. D., 569, *595*
Meinbresse, D., 437, *466*
Melchner, M. J., 676, 680, *686*
Merrin, E., 355, *362*
Merzenich, M. M., 262, *277*
Metzler, J., 326, *341*
Meyer, D. E., 195, 200, *208, 214, 226*
Michels, K. M., 134, *147*
Michon, J. A., 94, 98, 99, 103, 106, 107,
    109, 110, 536, 553, *555*
Miller, A., 174, *177*
Miller, G. A., 172, *176,* 300, *319*
Miller, G. W., 106, *108*
Miller, J. D., 232, 234, *241, 242*
Miller, J. O., 83, 84, *88*
Miller, R., 506, *514*
Millodot, M., 119, *145*
Milner, B., 246, *260,* 261, 262, 276, *278,*
    363, 365, *374, 392, 410*
Milsum, J. H., 613, *617*
Minsky, M., 573, *595*
Mishkin, M., 125, *145*
Mo, S. S., 107, *110*
Montague, W. E., 179, *191*
Moody, D. B., 234, *242*
Moore, J. J., 44, 45, *61*
Morais, J., 247, 248, 249, 250, 251, 252,
    254, 255, 256, 257, 259, *260,* 262, 264,
    270, 271, 273, 276, *278*
Morandi, A. J., 132, *145*
Moray, N., 44, 45, *62,* 245, 247, *260,* 346,
    362, 392, *410,* 488, 492, *503*
Mori, T., 39, *41*
Morse, P. A., 234, *242*
Morton, H. B., 404, *409*
Morton, J., 140, 145, 200, 204, 205, 206,
    208, 212, 221, *226,* 323, 328, 329, 332,
    335, 338, *341,* 414, *426,* 638, *644*
Morton, J. A., 648, *674*
Moscovitch, M., 221, *226,* 364, 366, 370,
    373, 374
Motley, M. T., 195, 200, *208*
Mountcastle, V. B., 457, *463*
Moxley, S. E. L., 516, *533*
Murdock, B. B., 82, *87*
Murphy, E. H., 276, *278*

Murray, C. S., 611, *617*
Murray, D. J., 339, *341*
Murray, H. G., 609, *617*
Myers, J. L., 52, *62,* 370, *374*
Myers, R. E., 392, 393, *410*

N

Näätänen, R., 430, 435, 437, 438, 440, 451,
    460, *463, 464*
Nachshon, I., 236, *241*
Nagata, S., 39, *41*
Naidoo, S., 412, *426*
Naitoh, P., 437, *464*
Nas, H., 30, *41*
Nauta, W. J. H., 440, 441, *464*
Naydin, V. L., 567, *594*
Neisser, U., 8, *22,* 119, 130, *145,* 450, *464*
Nelson, R. B., 536, *555*
Nemeth, R., 681, *686*
Netsell, R., 568, *594*
Nettelbeck, T., 602, *618*
Nettleton, N., 377, *389*
Neuhaus, W., 28, 29, *40*
Newcombe, F., 195, *208,* 210, 211, 213, *225,
    226*
Newell, A., 5, *22*
Nickerson, R. S., 78, 79, 80, 81, 82, 83, *87,
    88,* 291, 292, *297,* 602, 607, *617*
Nishisato, S., 273, *277,* 607, *616*
Nodine, C. F., 135, *145*
Noizet, G., 107, *110*
Noland, J. H., 34, 36, *41*
Noorden, L. P. A. S., van, 95, *110*
Nooteboom, S. G., 94, *110,* 143, *145,*
    196, *208,* 535, *555*
Norman, D. A., 11, *22,* 95, *111,* 129, *145,*
    129, *145,* 489, *503,* 681, *686*
Norman, J., 4, 12, *22*
Noton, D., 132, 135, *146*
Numbers, F. C., 291, *296*

O

Obonai, T., 35, *40*
Obrist, P. A., 481, *470,* 482, *484*
Obusek, C. J., 95, *111*
Ogilvie, J. C., 601, *617*
Ohala, J. J., 543, *555*
Öhman, A., 473, 478, *484*

Oldfield, R. C., 195, *208, 379, 390*
Oleson, T. D., 446, *464, 467*
Ollman, R. T., 5, *22*
Olson, C. L., 601, *617*
Olvera, A., 435, *467*
Onishi, S., 447, *464*
Orban, G., 26, *40*
O'Regan, J. K., 132, 137, *146*
Orlovskii, G. N., 566, 570, *595*
Ornstein, R., 44, *62*, 355, *362*
Ornstein, R. E., *110*, 357, *362*
Osherson, D. N., 240, *242*
Osser, H. A., 383, *389*

P

Pachella, R. G., 5, *22*, 83, 84, *88*
Paillard, J., 562, *595*
Paivio, A., 218, *226*
Pal'tsev, Ye., I., 562, 567, 576, 577, 578, *593, 594, 595*
Pantle, A., 29, 34, 36, 38, *40, 41*
Papakostopoulos, D., 440, *461*
Papcun, G., 236, *242*
Papert, S., 573, *595*
Papini, M., 440, *467*
Parks, T. E., 376, 378, 386, 389, *390*
Pasquinelli, A., 440, *467*
Pastore, R. E., 232, 237, 238, *242*
Pastore, R. G., 44, 46, 54, *62*
Pattee, H. H., 582, *595*
Patterson, K., 125, *144*, 364, 371, *374*, 376, *390*
Patterson, K. E., 210, 211, 217, 218, *225, 226*
Paul, D. D., 437, *464*
Peeples, D. R., 132, 134, *145*
Pelnard-Considère, J., 690, *701*
Perez, E., 364, 371, *374*
Perkins, D. N., 95, 100, *110*
Perl, N., 275, *278*, 372, *374*
Perry, J. K., 448, *467*
Peters, G., 45, 46, 56, *61*
Peters, J. F., 437, *463*
Peterson, G. E., 282, *297*
Peterson, L., 212, *225*
Peterson, L. R., 339, *341*
Petiteau, H., 34, *39*
Pew, R., 83, *88*
Pew, R. W., 5, *23*
Phillips, L. D., 382, *390*
Pick, A. D., 383, *389*

Pickoff, A., 448, *460*
Picton, T. W., 430, 431, 432, 433, 435, 438, 441, 442, 446, 447, 448, 450, 451, 452, 456, *462, 464,* 511, *214*
Pierrel, R., 611, *617*
Pike, A. R., 600, 601, *616, 617*
Pike, R., 600, 601, 607, 609, *617, 618*
Piontek, E., 536, *555*
Pisa, M., 507, *514*
Pisoni, D. B., 230, 232, 233, 234, 235, *242, 243*
Plomp, R., 94, *110*
Poffenberger, A. T., 6, *23*, 408, *410*
Pohlmann, L. D., 44, 46, 54, *62*
Pollack, I., 645, 646, 647, 649, 656, 662, *674*
Pollack, M. D., 179, *191*
Pomerantz, J. R., 237, *242*
Poppel, E., 93, 106, *110*, 406, *410*
Posner, M. I., 11, *23*, 78, 80, *88*, 91, 94, 99, 105, *110*, 205, *208*, 324, 326, *341*, 359, *360*, 376, *390*, 440, 458, *464*, 470, *484*, 516, *533*
Postman, L., 210, *226*
Potter, M. C., 10, *23*
Poulton, E. C., 245, *260*
Povel, D. J. L., 536, 542, *555*
Prablanc, C., 134, *146*
Preilowski, B., 404, *410*
Preston, M. G., 602, 605, *616*
Pribram, K. H., 300, *319,* 441, *464*
Price, D., 195, *207*
Proctor, J. D., 84, *86*
Provenzano, F. J., 352, 354, *361*
Prussin, H. A., 335, *341*
Puleo, J. S., 237, 238, *242*
Pynte, J., 179, 180, 185, 186, 191, *191*

R

Rabbitt, P. M. A., 350, *362,* 408, *410,* 498, 502, *503,* 601, *617*
Rajan, P., 412, 419, *426*
Rand, T. C., 263, 267, *278*
Raphael, L. J., 237, *241*
Rapin, I., 455, *462*
Rapp, K., 286, *297*
Ratcliff, G. G., 195, *208*
Rayner, K., 126, 137, 140, *145, 146,* 150, 156, 159, 160, *161*
Reber, A. S., 172, *177*
Rebert, C. S., 437, 440, *464, 465,* 478, *485*

Rechtmann, M. B., 562, *594*
Reder, S. M., 126, *144*
Reed, C., 78, 79, *88*
Reeves, A., 681, *686*
Reicher, G., 11, *23*
Reicher, G. M., 212, *225*
Reitsma, P., 412, *425*
Remez, R. E., 238, *242*
Remington, R., 236, *242*
Remington, R. J., 453, *465*
Renard, C., 27, 28, 32, *39*
Renault, H. B., 458, *463*
Repp, B. A., 237, *241*
Requin, J., 406, *410, 437, 460*
Restle, F., 99, 102, *110, 536, 555*
Reuver, H. A., 536, *555*
Reynolds, P., 45, *61, 345, 346, 358, 359*
Richards, L. G., 642, *644*
Richards, W., 36, 37, 39, *41,* 134, *145*
Richardson, J. T. E., 217, 218, *226*
Richardson, N., 404, *409*
Riggs, L. A., 6, *23*
Ritter, W., 436, 438, 448, 450, 451, 452, 455, 458, *461, 465, 467*
Rizzolatti, G., 364, 365, 366, 370, 371, *373, 374*
Roberts, T. D. M., 576, *595*
Robinson, D. A., 131, 132, 134, *146*
Robinson, J. S., 84, *88*
Robson, J. G., 29, 30, *40, 41*
Rocha-Miranda, C. E., 199, *207*
Rochester, S. R., 300, *319*
Roediger, H. L., III, 329, 330, *341*
Rogers, J. P., 365, *373*
Rogers, M., 212, *225*
Rohrbaugh, J. W., 10, 13, *21, 436, 465, 478, 485*
Rollins, A., 292, *297*
Rollins, H., 85, *88*
Rosen, J., 376, *390*
Rosen, S. C., 440, *466*
Rosenberg, K. E., 489, 490, 491, 492, 497, *503*
Rosenzweig, M. R., 258, *260, 262, 278*
Rosner, B. S., 232, 233, 234, 235, *241*
Rossi, L., 400, *467*
Roth, W. T., 450, 451, 453, 456, 458, *461, 465, 510, 514*
Rothbart, R. M., 450, *465*
Rouanet, H., 690, *701*
Roufs, J. A. J., 117, 132, *146*
Roy, E. A., 357, *362*

Rozeboom, W. W., 688, *701*
Rozin, P., 163, 164, *176, 177*
Rubenstein, H., 211, *226, 421, 426,* 645, 646, 647, 649, 656, 662, 664, 670, 671, *674*
Rubenstein, M. A., 211, *226,* 421, *426*
Ruchkin, D. S., 511, *514*
Ruchkin, S. S., 455, 456, *465*
Ruddell, R., 171, *177*
Ruddy, M. G., 195, *208,* 214, *226*
Rudnicky, A. I., 69, *74*
Rumelhart, D. E., 638, *644*
Rush, M. L., 291, *296*
Rybstein, E. D., 352, 354, *361*
Ryder, P., 607, 609, *617, 618*

S

Sackman, H., 306, *318*
Saffran, E. M., 217, *226*
Sager, L. C., 237, *242*
Samuels, S. J., 300, 315, *318*
Sanders, A. F., 95, *110,* 117, *146*
Sanders, M. D., 216, *226*
Sanford, A. J., 436, *463, 478, 484*
Sartre, J. P., 301, *319*
Satterfield, J. H., 434, *465*
Satz, P., 352, 355, 356, 357, *360, 362,* 377, *390*
Savignano-Bowman, J., 437, *466*
Savin, H. B., 649, *674*
Sayers, B. McA., 272, *278*
Scheerer, E., 12, 13, 15, *21, 23*
Scheff, N. M., 437, *467, 478, 485*
Scheffé, H., 697, *701*
Scheid, P., 440, 458, *461*
Schiepers, C. W. J., 120, 142, 143, *146*
Schiff, M., 435, *464*
Schiller, P. H., 16, *23*
Schlosberg, H., 122, 124, *147,* 180, *191,* 601, *618,* 635, *644*
Schmidt, R. A., 563, *595*
Schmit, V., 377, *389*
Schneider, G. E., 403, *410*
Schulman, H. M., 357, *362*
Schultz, D. W., 6, *21*
Schultz, R. W., 658, 662, 663, *674*
Schvaneveldt, R. W., 195, *208,* 214, *226*
Schwartz, G. E., 356, *362, 472, 485*
Schwartz, M. F., 217, *226*
Schwent, V. L., 441, 442, *462, 465*

Scott, T. R., 34, 36, *41*
Scullion, D., 364, 370, *374*
Segerra, J. M., 195, *207*
Sekuler, R., 26, 29, 32, 34, 35, 38, 39, *41*
Sekuler, R. W., 602, *618*
Semmes, J., 358, *362*
Seng, C. N., 569, *594*
Severeid, L. R., 567, *594*
Seward, G. H., 611, *618*
Sewitch, D., 350, *361*
Shaffer, L. H., 536, 553, *555*
Shaffer, W. O., 129, *146*
Shallice, T., 91, *110*, 194, 195, 196, 199, 205, 206, *208*, 210, 211, 217, 218, *226*, 440, *465*, 626, *630*
Shankweiler, D. P., 230, 236, 237, *242, 243*, 280, *296*, 324, *341*
Sharpe, C. R., 29, *41*
Shaughnessy, E., 85, *88*
Shaw, M. L., 681, *686*
Shaw, P., 6, *23*
Shaw, R. E., 559, 573, 574, 575, 592, *595*
Shebilske, W., 136, *146*
Shepard, R. N., 326, *341*
Shepherd, J. W., 218, *225*
Sheremata, W. A., 195, *207*
Sherlock, L., 30, *41*
Sherrick, Jr., C. E., 93, *108*
Shiffrin, R. M., 45, *62*, 129, *146*
Shiina, K., 32, *39*
Shik, M. L., 563, 566, 567, *593, 594, 595*
Shimokochi, M., 449, *462*
Shtil'kind, T. I., 575, 576, *593*
Shimzau, H., 506, *514*
Shuntich, R., 12, 13, 14, 15, *23*
Sichel, J. L., 502, *504*
Sikora, R., 458, *465*
Simon, H., 5, *22*
Simon, H. A., 90, 99, 100, 102, *108, 110*, 135, *146*
Simons, R. F., 473, 477, 478, *484, 485*
Simson, R., 450, 451, 452, 455, 458, *462, 465*
Sinnott, J. M., 234, *242*
Siple, P., 638, *644*
Siqueland, E. R., 234, *241*
Sivazlian, B. D., 559, *595*
Skarbeck, A., 300, *318*
Skinner, J. E., 440, 441, 449, *466, 467*
Skoglund, S., 517, 530, *534*
Slaby, D. A., 472, *484*
Slater, D., 421, *426*

Sloan, L. L., 120, *146*
Slobin, D. I., 85, *88*
Sloboda, J. A., 78, *88*
Smink, T., 412, *425*
Smith, D. B. D., 435, 444, *466*
Smith, E. E., 78, *88*, 126, *146*, 179, *191*, 498, *504*
Smith, F., 150, *161*, 164, *177*
Smith, K. U., 574, *595*
Smith, L., 234, *241*
Smith, M. C., 16, *23*
Smith, O. W., 30, *41*
Smith, P. G., 498, *504*
Smith, W. A. S., 611, *617*
Smith, W. H., 574, *595*
Smith, W. L., 358, *361*
Snowden, C. T., 234, *242*
Snyder, C., 205, *208*
Snyder, E., 442, 451, *465, 466*
Snyder, F. W., 300, *318*
Sokolov, E. N., 469, 472, *485*, 511, *514*
Sorkin, R. D., 44, 46, 54, *62*
Sparks, R. W., 246, *260, 276, 278*, 392, *410*
Spellacy, F., 274, *278*
Spence, M. T., 435, 438, *467*
Spencer, T., 12, 13, 14, 15, *23*
Sperling, G. A., 8, 10, 11, *23*, 215, *226*, 322, 325, 340, *342*, 635, *644*, 676, 677, 680, 681, *686*
Sperry, R. W., 246, *260*, 262, 276, *278*, 365, 371, *373, 374*, 392, *409, 410*, 459, *466*, 474, *485*
Spieth, W., 245, *260*
Spinnler, H., 364, *373*
Spivak, J. G., 677, *686*
Spoehr, K. T., 126, *146*, 179, *191*
Spong, P., 434, *466*
Springer, S. P., 236, *242*, 393, *410*
Springston, F., 97, 98, *107*
Squires, K. C., 437, 450, 451, 452, 453, 455, 456, 458, *462, 466*
Squires, N. K., 451, 452, 453, 455, 456, 458, *466*
Stamm, J. S., 440, *466*
Standing, L. G., 11, *22*
Stanfel, L. E., 559, *595*
Stark, L., 132, 135, *146*
Starr, A., 435, 444, *466*
Stebbins, W. C., 234, *242*
Steffy, R. A., 10, *21*
Stelmach, G. E., 300, *319*, 516, 517, 531, *533*, 561, *595*

Stern, J. A., 348, 357, *362*
Sternberg, S., 6, *23,* 51, *62,* 78, *88,* 93, *110,* 194, 195, *208,* 470, *485,* 688, 700, *701*
Stetson, R. H., 280, *297*
Stevens, K. N., 292, *297*
Stewart, A., 377, *390, 537, 554*
Stockdale, J. E., 82, *87*
Stone, M., 5, *23, 600, 618*
Strange, W., 98, *109,* 337, *342*
Streby, W. J., 313, *318*
Stroop, J. R., 488, *504*
Studdert-Kennedy, M., 230, 233, 236, 237, 239, *242, 243,* 280, *296*
Stuss, D. T., 431, 452, *464*
Suberi, M., 337, *390*
Summers, J. J., 563, *594*
Sutherland, N. S., 195, *208,* 574, *595*
Sutterer, J. R., 471, *484*
Sutton, S., 437, 438, 452, 455, 456, *462, 464, 465, 466, 467,* 511, *514*
Sveen, O., 506, *513*
Swanson, J. M., 355, 356, *360*
Sweet, A. L., 7, *23*
Swensson, R. G., 5, *23,* 270, *278*
Swets, J. A., 600, 611, *616, 618,* 622, *630*
Swift, S. J., 437, *463*
Sykes, M., 199, *208*
Syndulko, K., 436, *465, 466,* 478, *485*
Syrdal, A., 231, 232, *242*
Syrovegin, A. V., 567, 570, *594*
Szumski, J., 176, *177*

T

Takeuchi, T., 129, *145*
Tanis, D. C., 611, *616*
Tanner, W. P., 600, *618*
Tartter, V. C., 235, *243*
Tash, J., 235, *242*
Taylor, A. M., 195, *208*
Taylor, H. A., 45, *61*
Taylor, L., 246, *260,* 262, 276, *278,* 392, *410*
Taylor, M. M., 32, 34, *41,* 45, *62,* 346, *362*
Taylor, R. L., 326, *341,* 376, *390*
Taylor, S. G., 122, *146*
Tecce, J. J., 437, *465, 466, 467,* 478, *485*
Teckhaus, L., 536, *555*
Tell, P. M., 335, 339, *342*
Teng, E. L., 392, *410*
Ten Hoopen, M., 536, *555*
Terbeek, D., 236, *242*
Thach, W. T., 562, *593*

Thomas, E. A. C., 44, 51, 52, 56, 58, 59, 60, *61, 62,* 79, 84, *88,* 106, 107, *110*
Thomas, I. B., 95, *110*
Thompson, A., 83, *87*
Thompson, G. B., 413, *426*
Thompson, J. T., 335, 339, *342*
Thompson, P. O., 245, *260*
Thomson, G. H., 600, *618*
Thurston, L. L., 600, 601, *618*
Tiao, G. C., 694, 695, *701*
Tidd, K., 83, *86*
Tillyard, E. M. W., 240, *243*
Tinklenberg, J. R., 450, 458, *465*
Tisseyre, F., 247, *259*
Todd, I. C., 99, 102, *110*
Tolhurst, D. J., 29, *40, 41*
Toole, F. E., 272, *278*
Towe, A. L., 506, *514*
Townsend, J. T., 122, *146*
Townsend, V., 127, 129, *145*
Trabasso, T., 85, *88*
Treisman, A. M., 45, 59, *62,* 199, *208,* 262, 263, *278,* 346, 354, 356, *362,* 492, *504,* 600, 601, *618,* 653, 669, 671, *674*
Trevarthen, C., 354, 365, 371, *362,* 392, 393, 394, 403, 406, 409, *410,* 421, *426*
Tsetlin, M. L., 559, 563, *593*
Tueting, P., 430, 438, 451, 452, 458, 460, 461, *466, 467,* 511, *514*
Turvey, M. T., 12, 15, *23,* 205, *208,* 215, *226,* 234, *242,* 563, 564, 569, 573, 578, 587, *593, 595*
Tversky, B., 78, 82, 83, *88,* 135, 136, *146,* 326, *342*

U

Uit den Boogaart, P. C., 639, *644*
Umiltà, C., 364, 365, 366, 370, 371, *373, 374*
Underwood, B. J., 658, 662, 663, *674*
Urban, F. M., 601, *618,* 619, *630*

V

Van Allen, M. W., 364, *373*
Van Borselen, J. W., 95, *110*
Van Haelen, H., 253, 254, *260*
van Nes, F. L., 30, *41*
van Noorden, L. P. A. S., 67, 74, *75*
Vanthoor, F. L. J., 138, *146*

Vaughan, H. G., 436, 448, 450, 451, 458, 460, 465, 467
Velasco, F., 435, 467
Velasco, M., 435, 467
Venables, P. H., 276, 278
Vendrik, A. J. H., 45, 46, 53, 59, 61
Vesecky, T. B., 458, 465
Vickers, D., 600, 601, 602, 605, 611, 612, 615, 618, 626, 630
Vigna, C., 364, 366, 373
Vignolo, L. A., 221, 225
Vigorito, J. M., 234, 241
Vince, M. A., 569, 595
Vitton, N., 509, 514
Vitz, P. C., 99, 102, 110
Voillaume, C., 536, 555
Volkmann, J., 611, 618
Von Kries, J., 6, 22
Von Neumann, J., 588, 595
Vos, P. G. M. M., 95, 98, 100, 102, 110
Vroon, P. A., 93, 94, 106, 110, 111
Vyas, S. M., 408, 410, 498, 502, 503

W

Wachman, A., 561, 593
Wagman, I. H., 16, 21
Wagner, C., 536, 555
Wald, S., 621, 630
Wall, P. D., 506, 509, 514
Wall, S., 6, 21, 82, 87
Wallace, G., 364, 366, 370, 373
Wallace, S. A., 531, 534
Wallace, S. W., 516, 534
Walsh, M. F., 517, 534
Walter, W. G., 430, 436, 437, 448, 463, 467, 477, 479, 484, 485
Warren, R., 575, 595
Warren, R. M., 71, 75, 95, 111
Warren, R. P., 95, 111
Warrington, E. K., 12, 16, 22, 194, 195, 196, 199, 205, 208, 210, 211, 216, 217, 218, 226, 364, 374
Wason, P. C., 85, 88
Wasow, T., 240, 242
Watanabe, A., 39, 41
Waters, R. S., 234, 243
Watkins, M. J., 326, 337, 342
Watkins, O. C., 326, 337, 342
Watson, C. S., 611, 616
Watts, T. R., 600, 601, 618

Waugh, N. C., 95, 111
Weaver, W. B., 44, 51, 59, 62, 106, 110
Webb, R. A., 471, 484
Webster, J. C., 245, 260
Weerts, T. C., 436, 467, 478, 485
Weigel, G., 6, 23
Weinberg, H., 430, 448, 467
Weinberger, N. M., 446, 464, 467
Weir, C. C., 232, 242
Weiskrantz, L., 216, 226
Weiss, P., 560, 595
Weitzman, E. D., 434, 467
Welch, J. C., 357, 362
Welford, A. T., 345, 362, 392, 410, 569, 595
Wells, K. F., 560, 595
Werner, H., 217, 226
Wertheim, A. H., 106, 111
Weymouth, F. W., 17, 21
Wheeler, D. D., 11, 23
Wheeler, L., 519, 533
Wheeless, L. L., 132, 146
Whitaker, H. A., 436, 463
White, C. T., 434, 435, 461, 512, 514
White, R. W., 613, 618
Wickelgren, W., 60, 62
Wickelgren, W. A., 335, 342
Wickens, C., 453, 456, 466
Wickens, C. D., 45, 62
Wickens, D. D., 213, 226
Wilding, J. M., 601, 618
Wilkins, A., 377, 390
Wilkinson, R. T., 435, 437, 438, 451, 467
Williams, J. A., 81, 86, 602, 607, 616
Williams, J. D., 79, 88
Williams, L. G., 134, 146
Williams, T., 536, 555
Willig, M., 602, 605, 616
Willson, R. J., 601, 602, 618
Wilson, W. A., 234, 243
Winer, B. J., 311, 316, 319
Wing, A., 11, 23
Wing, A. M., 107, 111, 535, 536, 537, 538, 543, 552, 555
Wingfield, A., 195, 208
Winston, P. H., 63, 75
Winter, A. L., 436, 467, 477, 485
Winzenz, D., 98, 107
Wise, J. S., 81, 86, 602, 607, 616
Wist, E. R., 30, 40
Wodinsky, J., 129, 145
Wohlgemuth, A., 34, 36, 41
Wolford, G., 122, 147

Wolpaw, J. R., 448, *467*
Wolz, J., 238, *242*
Wood, C. C., 230, 235, 236, 237, 238, *243*
Woodhouse, D., 179, *191*
Woods, D. L., 431, 445, 447, 452, *464, 467*
Woodworth, R. S., 122, 124, *147,* 149, *161,*
    180, 191, 516, *534,* 601, *618,* 635, *644*
Worthington, A. G., 213, *226*

Y, Z

Yamamoto, C., 506, *514*
Yanagisawa, N., 506, *514*
Yarbus, A. L., 132, 133, 134, *147*
Yin, R. K., 365, *374*

Yingling, C. D., 449, *466, 467*
Yoshie, N., 447, *461*
Young, E. D., 392, *410*
Young, M., 325, *340*
Yuille, J. C., 218, *226*
Zaidel, E., 220, 221, *226*
Zamboni, G., 365, 370, *374*
Zangwill, O. L., 393, *409, 412, 426*
Zappoli, R., 440, *467*
Zelnicker, D., 80, *87*
Zerlin, S., 447, *461*
Zuber, B. L., 135, *143*
Zubin, J., 452, *466, 467*
Zurif, E. B., 217, *225,* 412, 419 *426*
Zusne, L., 134, *147*

Subject Index

A

Acquisition stage, 323
Action plan, *see* motor program
Activation, *see also* arousal
  cortical evoked potentials and, 434–435, 447
  selective attention and, 513
  in word perception, 205
Acoustic masking, 70–71
Acoustic spectrum, 64–67
Adaptation process, 26, 32–35
  time constant in, 35
Additive factor method, 688
After-effect
  movement and, 26–27, 32–35
  spatial frequency and, 35
Alpha activity
  contingent negative variation and, 438
Anterior commissure, *see* neocortical commissures
Anticipation
  contingent negative variation and, 436, 479, 482
  heart rate and, 469–470, 472, 475, 477
  in motor control, 576–578
  selective attention and, 512
  sensory information and, 506
Anticipatory behavior, postural adjustments, set, *see* anticipation
Aphasia, 210, 214, 221, 224

Arousal, *see also* activation
  cortical evoked potentials and, 490, 494–495, 441, 445, 449
  heart rate and, 471
  orienting reaction and, 512
  selective attention and, 512
Articulatory system, 323–328, 334–339
  articulation rate, 281
  auditory articulatory procedure, 323, 338
  visual articulatory procedure, 338
Asymmetric interference, 230, 236–237
Attention, *see also* selective attention
  contingent negative variation and, 437–438
  cortical evoked potentials and, 430, 435, 442, 445, 510–511
  direction of, 91
  division of, 44, 59–60
  heart rate and, 473
  mechanisms of, 682–686
  orienting reaction and, 512
  to speech, 245, 255, *see also* speech perception
  sharing of, 648
  switching of, 684–685
  temporal dimension of, 106
Attention operating characteristic, 675–686
  compatibility of tasks and, 685
Attentive behavior, set, *see* attention and selective attention

Attenuation hypothesis, *see* single channel theory
Auditory laterality effect, 246–262, 271–274, *see also* auditory spatial effect
  advantage for a particular half of space, 262, 272
  contralateral afferent projections and, 262, 271–273
  dichotic and monaural situation, 245–250, 255, 262–276
  ear-of-entry phenomenon, 246–248, 250, 264, 271, 275–276
  right ear advantage, 236–237, 246–250, 254–255, 262, 276
  selective attention and, 246–248, 255, 262, 276
  in split-brain, 246
Auditory perception, *see* auditory stream organization
Auditory perceptual asymmetry, *see* auditory laterality effect
Auditory-phonetic distinction, 230, 236, 238–239, *see also* asymmetric interference
Auditory spatial effect, *see also* auditory laterality effect
  anterior posterior gradient in, 251–252, 259
  cerebral dominance and, 250, 257–258
  cortical representation and, 252, 258–259
  direction-discriminating level, 251
  frontal-direction advantage, 250, 252–259
  right-side advantage, 247–259
  time delay stereophonic condition, 248–249
  ventriloquium effect, 256
  voluntary attention and, 248, 251, 254–259
Auditory stream organization, 65–74
  belongingness in, 70–71
  common fate in, 71–72
  competition of, 69–70
  continuity in, 68–71
  frequency similarity in, 66–67
  masking in, 70–71
  perceptual closure in, 71
  simplicity in, 67–68
Auditory vigilance
  cortical evoked potentials and, 431–433
Autonomic changes
  contingent negative variation and, 480–483
  cortical evoked potentials and, 436–437

B

Binaural fusion, 263, 272, 275
Biokinematic variables, 559–560, 563, 566–568, 571–572
Biological control systems, 579–581
  aggregates as, 581
  chains as, 582
  coalitions as, 589–592
  heterarchies as, 589–592
  hierarchies as, 584
  nets as, 579–580
Bloch's law, 4, 12–13, 26, 28, 30
Brainstem evoked potentials, 445
Brainstem reticular formation, *see* mesencephalic reticular formation

C

Categorical perception, *see also* speech perception
  age and, 234
  discrimination function, 231, 234–235
  identification function, 231–232, 235, 245
  labeling function, 231
  multidimensional, 234, 239
  plucked and bowed sounds and, 232–239
Cerebellum,
  timing control of movement and, 554
Cerebral asymmetry, dominance, specialization, *see* laterality effects
Commissurotomy, *see* neocortical commissures
Comparison judgment,
  analytic process in, 78–79
  confirmation checking in, 82, 84–85
  exhaustive analysis in, 83
  priming effect in, 80, 85
  stimulus familiarity in, 84
  stimulus probability in, 84
  stimulus sampling artefact in, 79–80, 85
  response bias in, 81–82, 85
  trace strength in, 80–81, 85
  two-processes model in, 83–85
Composing,
  memory and, 300, 307, 315–316
  practice effects and, 301–302, 305–307
  strategies in, 302–303, 306, 316
  subject differences in, 306, 308, 312, 315
Conation,
  contingent negative variation and, 440
Consciousness, 91, 204–205, 224, *see also*

Consciousness (*contd.*)
present, experience of
in perception, 204–205
priming and, 204
cortical evoked potentials and, 459
cortical motor potentials and, 459
in the split-brain, 392–393
Contextual information
in reading, 412, 416–418
Contingent negative variation,
alpha activity and, 438
anticipation and, 436, 479, 482
arousal and, 437–438
attention and, 437–438
autonomic changes and, 480–482
conation and, 440
cortical areas and, 478
emotional reactions and, 438
expectancy and, 441
hemispheric asymmetry and, 436
interstimulus interval and, 437, 441, 478
mental effort and, 440
motivation and, 440
motor program and, 480, 483
neurophysiological mechanisms of,
440–441
orienting response and, 436, 478
perceptual accuracy and, 437
preparation and, 437, 440–441, 480–483
reaction time and, 437, 477–480
sensory systems and, 446–448
signal detection and, 438, 481
stimulus vs response set and, 436
"Control space" concept in motor system,
570–572
"Coalition" concept in biological control
systems, 578–579
"Coordinative structure" concept in motor
system, 563–569, 572–573, 582
Corpus callosum, *see* neocortical
commissures
Cortical evoked potentials
activation and, 434–435, 447
arousal and, 430, 434–435,441, 445, 449
attention and, 430, 435, 437–438, 442,
445, 510–511
auditory vigilance and, 431–433
autonomic changes and, 434–437
consciousness and, 459
decision process and, 450
early components of, 444–448
expectancy and, 434, 450, 452–453, 456,
459, 510

Cortical Evoked Potentials (*contd.*)
habituation and, 446
late postive component of, 435, 438,
443–446, 450–460, 510–512
late negative-positive complex of, 431,
450
memory processes and, 434, 447–448, 450,
458–459
mental effort and, 430
muscle tension and, 434, 445
N 1 component of, 431, 433–434,
438–450, 459
N 2 component of, 510–512
neurophysiological mechanisms of, 436,
438, 446–449, 451, 459
orienting response and, 436, 452
preparation and, 436, 510
reaction time and, 458
response probability and, 452
responsiveness and, 430, 446, 458–459
selective attention and, 430, 433–434, 440,
443, 449, 458
sensory transmission and, 506–510
short-term memory and, 449, 457
stimulus discriminability and, 455
stimulus meaning and, 456
stimulus presentation rate and, 447
stimulation probability and, 452–455
stimulus vs response set and, 436,
442, 443–445, 459
temporal uncertainty and, 436
time estimation and, 453
Cortical motor potentials, 459
Cortical negativity, *see* contingent negative
variation
Cortical representation
auditory spatial effect and, 252, 258–259
Corticospinal tract, 506, 558
Cutaneous afferents
reticulo-spinal system and, 506

D

Decision, *see also* discrimination
cortical evoked potentials and, 450
three-category decision, 601–605
Degrees of freedom
in motor system, 558–592
Detection accuracy, 44–61
reaction time and, 47–60
Dichotic listening, 44–45, 489

Dictating, 313, 315–318
  creativity and, 306, 312
  typing instructions and, 299, 303–304, 307–311
Digit-naming task, 488
Discrimination, see also decision
  speed-accuracy trade off and, 600
  two-category discrimination, 600–601
  of word in noise, 648
Discrimination operating characteristic, 682
Displacement analyzing system, 27–30, 36–39
Distracting stimuli, 487–488, 499
  choice reaction time and, 487
  selective attention and, 487
Divided attention
  between inputs, 346
  hemispheric biasing, 355–356
Document composition, model of, 301–316, see also composing
Dorsal column nuclei, 506
Double visual system, 403, 406
Dual task
  the "functional distance" model and, 349–355
  in the split-brain, 392, 404–406
Duration, see temporal processing
Dynamics of movement, 523
Dyslexia, 194, 196, 199, 210–213, 217, 221, 224

E

Ear-of-entry phenomenon, see auditory laterality effect
Eccentric vision, 117, 119–120, 127, 132, 134, 138, 143
Echoic memory
  attentional interruption, 331–353
  erasure, 331–333
  integrative model, 331–354
  limited-capacity attention, 332–333
  masking effect, 329–334
  modality effect, 331, 335, 338–339
  recency effect, 329–331, 335
  retroactive inhibition, see masking
  structural similarity, 335–337
  suffix effect, 329–333, 335–337
Efferent program, see motor program
Emitted potentials, 430, 448–449
Emotional reactions and contingent negative variation, 438

Energy summation, 4–5, 7–8, 12–13, 20
Error-correcting mechanism in tapping task 537
Event–related potentials, see cortical evoked potentials, contingent negative variation and motor potentials
Expectancy, see also preparation
  contingent negative variation and, 441
  cortical evoked potentials and, 434, 450, 452–453, 456, 459, 510
  selective attention and, 512
Expectancy wave, see contingent negative variation
Exteroceptive information, 562
Extralemniscal pathways
  sensory information and, 509–510
Eye guidance, 117, 134–135
Eye movement
  monitoring of, 156
Eye saccades
  control of, 117, 131, 132, 134
  direction of, 132
  extent of, 132
  eye pause duration, 132, 134
  fixation duration, 132, 180, 186
  fixation pause, 137
  latency, 137
  length of, 160
  moment of occurence of, 132
  regressive eye saccade, 137, 140
  successive eye pause, 143
  timing and direction of, 134
Eye voice span, 140
Face recognition
  as a function of visual field, naming familiarity and sex, 363–372
Facilitation in information processing and the cerebral space model
  motor effects, 349–350
  perceptual effects, 355–356
Familiarity
  laterality effects in face recognition and, 363–372
Feature
  analysing system, 25–29
  detection of, 26, 682
Feedback mechanisms
  in motor control, 575–576
  proprioceptive information and, 516
  time keepers and, 554
Feedforward mechanisms
  in motor control, 578–579, 589–591
Fluency in word identification, 163–165

Foreperiod, *see* interstimulus interval
Foveal vision, 117–119, 121, 126, 138, 143, 149
Frequency
  in auditory perception, 66–67
  in movement perception, 29–31, 36–39
Functional cerebral space
  the adaptive value of hemispheric specialization and, 357–358
Functional distance
  intra versus interhemispheric, 348
  paired limbs and, 348–349
Functional plasticity
  in biological systems, 583

G

Gaze deviations
  as an index of motor overflow, 355–356
Gestalt psychology, 64, 73, 99
  in auditory perception, *see* auditory stream organization
Gibson figures
  recognition of, as a function of visual half field and verbal activity, 382–387
Grapheme-phoneme translation, 213, 216–217, 224
Graphemic unit, 204–205
Graphic information, 215
Grating
  in movement perception, 29–30

H

Habituation
  cortical evoked potentials and, 446
  orienting reaction and, 510–512
Handedness
  reading ability and, 411–426
  cerebral lateralization of language and, 418
Head deviations
  as an index of motor overflow, 355–356
Hearing, *see* audition
Heart rate,
  anticipation and, 469–472, 475–477
  arousal and, 471
  attention and, 473
  conditioning and, 473
  interstimulus interval and, 470–472
  motivation and, 474–475

Heart Rate (*contd.*)
  motor program and, 475
  orienting response and, 459, 472
  preparation and, 471, 475, 477
  reaction time and, 473
  skin conductance and, 479
Hemispheric asymmetry, specialization, *see* laterality effects
Hierarchy vs heterarchy in biological control systems, 574, 578–579, 584–589
Homophone effect
  as a function of visual half-field, 420–425

I

Icon, 4, 8, 20
Iconic memory, 138, 215
Identification process, 649–654, 660–663, 667–672
Imageability, 218, 220–221
Information-reduction task, 497
Information processing, *see also* parallel processing and serial processing capacity, 345–346, 391–409
  parallel versus serial, 346, 376, 388–389, 401
  visual perception and, 3–5
Intelligibility
  speech timing and, 281, 291–293, 295
Interference
  in information processing and the cerebral space model, 351–355
  structural interference, 347
  visual interference, *see* visual masking
Internal clock, 93
Interresponse intervals (IRI)
  in tapping tasks, 537–553
Interstimulus interval (ISI)
  contingent negative variation and, 437, 441, 478
  heart rate and, 470–472
Intertrial interval
  in position-naming task, 493

J

Joints, 559–562, 566–567, 571–572
Joint receptors, 517, 530
  movement information and, 530
  movement reproduction and, 517

K

Kinesthetic perception
  storage mode of, 516
Knowledge in reading, 171–173
  analytic vs non analytic mechanism in, 173–175
  explicit vs implicit analytic mechanism in, 171–172, 175

L

Language, 232, 236, see also phonological coding
Language perception, see also reading ability and speech perception
  laterality effects in, 411–426
Laterality effects
  in audition, 246, 258
  auditory spatial effect and, 250, 257–258
  contingent negative variation and, 436
  in face recognition, 363–372
  in Gibson figure recognition, 382–389
  in letter recognition, 375–382
  in perception of musical sounds, 236
  in speech perception, 236, 246, 261, 262
  in word perception, 411–426
Left-hemispheric effects, see laterality effects
Lemniscal pathways
  sensory information and, 507–509
Letter-naming tasks, 489, 491–492
  sequential effects in, 491–492
Letter recognition, 121, 126, see also recognition and word perception
  completion and, 640–641
  dependence, 642–643
  as a function of visual half-field, 375–382
  Posner effect and, 378
  threshold, 186
  verbal ability and, 375–389
Lexical access, 195, 212
Lexical decision, 211, 214, 216, 218, 224
  as a function of visual half-field, 420–425
Lexical inference, 191
Lexical information, 156, 159
Lexical level, 221
Lexical representation, 212, 215
Lexical system, 212–216
Locomotion, 566–571, 576
Logogen, 199, 205, 212–213, 638

M

Masking, see visual masking
Masking noise,
  spatial direction and, 245–246
Medulla
  sensorimotor cortex and, 506
Memory, see also echoic memory, iconic memory and short–term memory
  auditory information and, 329–330, 340
  composing and, 300, 307, 315–316
  cortical evoked potentials and, 434, 447–448, 450, 458–459
  sensory information and, 329
  unattended information and, 488–489, 492, 502
  verbal information and, 322, 330, 334
  visual information and, 322, 324, 326
Mental effort
  contingent negative variation and, 440
  cortical evoked potentials and, 430
Mesencephalic reticular formation, 431, 446, 449, 459
Mixed errors in word reading and speech, 193–206
Model acceptability, see model validation
Model validation, 687–701
  experimental precision and, 690
  significance tests and, 687–690
Motivation
  contingent negative variation and, 440
  heart rate and, 474–475
Motoneurons, 506, 562
Motor activity
  sensory transmission and, 506–509
Motor adjustment
  sensory information and, 506
Motor command, 509
  temporal patterning of, 558
Motor control
  anticipation in, 576–578
  feedback mechanisms and, 575–576, 585–588
  feedforward mechanisms and, 578–579, 583–591
  motor cortex and, 558
  vestibular system and, 575
  visual information in, 569–570, 575
Motor coordination, 558–592
  in the split-brain, 404
Motor cortex
  in motor control, 558

Motor delay interval
  in tapping task, 597
Motor outflow copy, 517
Motor overflow
  between limbs, 349
  eye and head deviations with asymmetric
    cognitive processing, 355–356
  as a function of "functional distance"
    between cerebral centers, 345–347
  as a function of maturation, 356
  vocal-manual overflow, 350
Motor program, 505–513
  contingent negative variation and, 480, 483
  heart rate and, 475
  motor control and, 559, 563, 569
  muscle activity and, 506
  in rhythmic performance, 553–554
  sensory control and, 506
  sensory integration and, 506
  in vocal activity, 180, 185
Motor reactivity, see spinal reflexes
Motor system, 536, 543, 554
  "control space" concept in, 570–572
  "coordinative structure" concept in,
    563–569, 572–573, 582
  degrees of freedom in, 558–592
  time keeper and, 554
  variability in 559–563, 573, 579
Motor unit, 562
Movement
  acceleration of, 526
  amplitude of, 526–533
  coordination of, 558–592
  fast vs slow, 561
  temporal structure of, 553
  velocity of, 526
Movement cue, see movement information
Movement information,
  joint receptors and, 530
  storage modes of, 515–533
Movement perception
  movingness analyzing system in, 27–30,
    34–39
  sinusoidal grating and, 29–30
  spatial frequency and, 29–32, 36–38
  square-wave grating and, 30
  temporal frequency and, 29–31, 36–39
  velocity and, 29–32, 35–38
  visual perception and, 25–29
Movement reproduction, 526–533
  extrapolation hypothesis and, 517, 531
  joint receptors and, 517

Movement reproduction (contd.)
  retention interval in, 518
Movingness analyzing system, 27–30, 34–39
Muscle activity, 506, 561, 568
  motor program and, 506

N

Naming
  and laterality effects in face recognition,
    363–372
Negative shift, see contingent negative
    variation
Neocortical commissures
  accuracy of choice-RT in monkey and,
    397–401
  in bilateral attention tasks, 393, 407–409
  "functional distance" principle and, 348
  processing capacity in man and, 392, 404
  verbal manual interference, 354
Neurophysiological mechanisms
  contingent negative variation and,
    440–441
  control evoked potentials and, 436, 438,
    446–449, 451–459
Nonphonological information, 163–164
Nonspeech sounds, 232, 234–235, 238–239
Nonwords, 210–211

O

Optic chiasma
  section in the monkey, 391–409
Order perception, 93–95
Orienting response,
  arousal and, 512
  attention and, 510–512
  contingent negative variation and, 436,
    478
  cortical evoked potentials and, 436, 452
  habituation and, 511–512
  selective attention and, 510–512
Orthographic rules, 166, 173

P

P_3 component, $P_{\overline{300}}$ component see late
  component of cortical evoked
  potentials

Pacinian corpuscles, *see* joint receptors
Parafoveal vision, 140, 149–151
Paralexia, 210, 212–217, 224
Parallel processing, 5, 20, 53–54, 58, *see also* information processing.
Pattern, *see* sequential pattern
Perceptual accuracy,
  contingent negative variation and, 437
Perceptual defense, 205
Phoneme boundary effect, *see* categorical perception
Phonological coding
  auditory presentation and, 335, 338–340
  central recording hypothesis in, 323–325
  confusion effect, 323–325, 327, 335, 339–340
  delay and, 323, 324
  interpolated information processing load and, 323–324, 327
  logogen model in, 323
  multiple-trace hypothesis in, 323–326
  representation, 211
  similarity, 265, 322–324, 327, 335–336, 338–340
  stage, 195
  translation, 264
  visual presentation and, 324, 335, 338–340
Phonology, 212, 224
Pluripotentiality, *see* plasticity
Position-naming tasks
  intertrial interval and, 493
  sequential effects in, 493–497
Posner effect
  as a function of visual half–field, 376–382
  verbal abiity and, 378–382
Postural adjustments,
  auditory spatial effect and, 252–255, 257–259
Practice,
  method of composing in, 301–302, 305–307, 312, 316–317
Precategorical acoustic system, *see* echoic memory
Precategorical storage,
  temporal processing and, 94–95
Preconscious process, 161
Preparation, *see also* expectancy
  contingent negative variation and, 437, 440–448, 480–483
  cortical evoked potentials and, 436, 510
  heart rate and, 471, 475, 477
  of responses in the split–brain monkey, 406–408

Preparatory activity, set, *see* preparation and expectancy
Preparatory interval, period, *see* interstimulus interval, preparation and expectancy
Preparatory potentials, *see* contingent negative variation and motor potentials
Preparedness, *see* preparation and expectancy
Present experience of, *see also* simultaneity
  information availability and, 91, 96–97
  properties of, 92–93
  segmentation of, 91–92, 96–98
Primary cortex
  sensory information and, 507
Priming effect, 219
  semantic, 220
  conscious vs subconscious, 204
Primary memory, *see* short-term memory
Probability over a parameter space, 694–695
Processing capacity
  in temporal processing, 56
Prononciation rules, 164
Proprioception, *see* proprioceptive information
Proprioceptive information
  in feedback mechanisms, 516
  as movement information, 516
  sensory motor cortex and, 563
  storage mode of, 516
Psychometric function, 619–630
  logistic psychometric function, 623, *see also* relative judgment theory
  response probabilities and, 620
  response times and, 620
Pyramidal cells, 558

R

Reaction time
  contingent negative variation and, 437, 447, 478–480
  cortical evoked potentials and, 458
  detection accuracy and, 47–60
  distracting stimuli and, 487–504
  in face recognition, 363–372
  heart rate and, 473
  in lexical decision, 420–425
  perception of duration and, 47–60
  in Posner same-different paradigm, 268–274, 376–382, 388–389
  selective attention and, 487–503
  in split-brain monkey, 391–409
  verbal, 179

Reaction time (*contd.*)
in word reading, 195
Readiness, *see* preparation and expectancy
Reading,
ability and handedness, 411–421
eye control in, 136
foveal and parafoveal cues in, 149–161
impairment, 210
perceptual processes in, 190
peripheral, 150
of syllables, 179–191
theories of, 150
visual interference in, 121
visual search and, 115–143
visual semantic errors in, 194
of words, 193–207
Recall, 247, 262–263, 322–323, 327, 329–331, 334, 338, 488
Receiver operating characteristic, 682
Recognition, *see also* letter recognition and word perception of faces as a function of visual field, naming, familiarity and Sex, 363–372
of Gibson figures, 383–389
of letters, 121, 126, 186, 375–389, 640–643
vs reading, 632–634
of words, 631–644
Rehearsal, 324–325
Relative judgement, theory of, 620–630
choice probability and, 621
comparison process and, 621
random walk and, 621–622
response time and, 621
Repetition effect, *see* reaction time and sequential effects
Residual effects, *see* sequential effects and reaction time
Respiratory-induced oscillations, 567
Response frequency, *see* response probability
Response inhibition, 499
Response probability, 626–630
cortical evoked potentials and, 452
in simple judgement, 600–611
Response programming, *see* motor program
Response time, 626–630
in simple judgement, 600–611
Responsiveness,
cortical evoked potentials and, 430, 446, 458–459
Retention interval,
movement reproduction and, 518

Retention stage, 323–326, 326–327
Reticulo-spinal system,
spinal interneurons and, 506
cutaneous afferents and, 506
Retinal image, 116–119, 138, 140
Retrieval stage, 323–325
Rhythmic activity, 95, *see also* temporal processing
motor program in, 553–554
in musical performance, 536, 553
in tapping task, 538, 543
Right-ear advantage, *see* laterality effects
Right-side advantage, *see* laterality effects

S

Same-different judgment, 264–274, 605–607, 628–630, *see also* Posner effect
comparison judgement and errors in, 270–271
reaction time and, 270–271, 274
Scene analysis, 63
Segmentation errors in word perception, 196–206
Selective adaptation, boundary shift and, 235–237
Selective attention, *see also* attention
activation and, 513
anticipation and, 512
arousal and, 513
auditory laterality effect and, 246–276
auditory spatial effect and, 248–251, 254–259
cortical evoked potentials and, 430, 433–434, 440, 443, 449, 458
expectancy and, 512
in movement control, 570
orienting reaction and, 510–512
reaction time and, 487–503
speech perception and, 245–246, 251, 254–255
spinal reflexes and, 506, 512–513
in split-brain monkey, 391–409
Semantic access, 224
Semantic context, 214
Semantic cueing, 202, 204
Semantic errors, 194–195, 205
Semantic facilitation, 203
Semantic information, 159–160, 217
Semantic paralexia, 215
Semantic priming, 200, 218–220
Semantic representation, 215
Semantic stage, 195

Semantic system, 215
Sensorimotor cortex
    dorsal column nuclei and, 506
    medulla and, 506
    proprioceptive information and, 563
    spinal cord and, 506
    thalamus and, 506
Sensory buffer, *see* memory
Sensory control
    motor program and, 506
Sensory evoked potentials, *see* cortical
    evoked potentials
Sensory information
    anticipation and, 506
    extralemniscal pathways and, 509–510
    lemniscal pathways and, 507–509
    motor adjustment and, 506
    primary cortex and, 507
Sensory integration
    motor program and, 506
Sensory system
    contingent negative variation and,
        446–448
Sensory transmission,
    cortical evoked potentials and, 509
    motor activity and, 506–508
Sequential effects, *see also* reaction time
    as a function of "functional distance", 390
    in letter naming tasks, 491–492
    as a memory process, 488–489
    in the monkey, 407–408
    in position naming tasks, 493–497
    priming and, 502
    taxonomy in selection task, 498–499
Sequential pattern, 90, 95, *see also* temporal
    processing
Sequential priming in behavior, 553
Serial processing,
    in temporal processing, 54
    in visual perception, 5, 20
Serially-ordered behavior, 535, 553
Sex,
    laterality effects in face recognition and,
        363–372
Short-term memory, *see also* memory.
    in articulation, 180, 185
    cortical evoked potentials and, 449, 457
    functional memory, 326
    order information and, 326–327
    primary memory, 325–326
spatial order task and, 327
    specious present and, 95–96
    structural memory, 326

Short-term memory (contd.)
    temporal order task and, 327–328
    visual icon and, 8
Signal detection, 607–611
    contingent negative variation and, 438,
        481
Simple judgment
    adaptation and, 612–616
    confidence in, 611
    decision mechanism and, 611
Simultaneity, 91, 93–94, *see also* present,
    experience of.
SingleChannel theory, 45–46
    dual tasks and, 345
    split-brain and, 391–409
Skilled vs novice readers, 172
Skin conductance
    heart rate and, 479
Slow cortical potentials, *see* contingent
    negative variation
Somatic radiations
    sensory information and, 507
Spatial direction
    apparent spatial origin, 246–249, 256,
        262–267, 271–276
    of auditory source, 245–252, 255–258, 262,
        271–273
    masking noise and, 245–246
    real position, 262–263, 275–276
Spatial information processing, 117
Speaking, 299–300, 308–309, 315–317
Specious present, *see* present experience of
Speech coding, *see* phonological coding
Speech mode, *see* speech perception
Speech perception, *see also* categorical
    perception
    auditory laterality effects in, 246, 252
    auditory level and, 230
    boundary shift in, 235, 237
    phonetic level and, 230
    selective attention and, 245–246, 251,
        254–255
Speech production, *see also* speech timing
    and deafness, 291–292
Speech rate, *see* speech timing
Speech timing, 163–207, 535–568
    articulation rate and, 281
    deafness and, 291–292, 295
    hierarchical theory of, 289–291
    intelligibility and, 281, 291–293, 295
    phonemes and, 280, 282, 286
    sentence level effect in, 287
    stressed pattern and, 284–286, 288–293

Speech timing (*contd.*)
  syllable duration and, 284–285, 288
  syllable level effect in, 283–284, 289
  temporal segmentation and, 98, 103,
    280–293
  word duration and, 288
Speed-accuracy trade off, 5, 60
Spelling rules, 164–167
Spelling system, 163–164
Spinal cord, 506, 562, 570
Spinal interneurons
  reticulo spinal system and, 506, 562
Spinal reflexes,
  selective attention and, 506, 512–513
Split-brain, *see* laterality effects and
    neocortical commissures
  Split-formant sound, 264, 266–275
Spoonerisms, 195–196, 200, 206
Stimulus onset asynchrony, 214
Stimulus vs response set
  contingent negative variation and, 436
  cortical evoked potentials and, 436,
    443–445, 449, 459
Stimulus response mapping, 502
Storage mode of movement information,
    515–533
Strategies, method of composing and,
    302–303, 306, 316
Stroop color naming task, 488
Subliminal perception, 214
Succession, *see* order perception
Supraspinal influences, 562, 570
Syllabic effect, 179, 181, 184
Synchronization, 94, 538–542, *see* also
    simultaneity

                    T

Tachistoscopic detection, 127
Tachistoscopic recognition, 129
Tapping,
  error-correcting mechanism in, 537
  interresponse interval in, 537–553
  motor delay interval in, 537
  rhythmic grouping in, 538, 543
  Wing's timing model of, 537
Tempo, *see* rhythmic activity
Temporal control, *see* timing control
Temporal patterning of motor commands,
    558
Temporal processing, *see also* time,
  experience of

Temporal processing (*contd.*)
  experience of duration and, 90, 94
  filled-duration illusion and, 44
  nontemporal information in, 43–45, 51,
    56–60
  precategorical storage and, 94–95
  processing capacity in, 56
  serial processing in, 54
  sequential information in, 93–99
  temporal conditioning and, 105
  temporal orientation and, 96
  temporal pattern and, 90, 99–103, *see also*
    sequential pattern
  temporal summation constant in, 38–39
  temporal summation process in, 26–39
Temporal uncertainty
  cortical evoked potentials and, 456
Thalamus
  sensori motor cortex and, 506
Time estimation
  cortical evoked potentials and, 453
Time, experience of, *see also* temporal
    processing
  subjective speed of time in, 106–107
  time constant in, 93
  time estimation paradigm and, 106–107
  time quantum in, 93
Time keeper,
  feedback mechanisms and, 554
  motor system and, 554
  in tapping, 536–537, 542–543, 546–554
Timer, 51–52, 56, 59
Timing control of behavior
  cerebellum and, 554
  cerebral cortex and, 535
Transfer of training between limbs, 350–351
Transitions between trials, *see* sequential
    effects
Transport vs postural activities, 574–578
Tuning, 99, 101–106

                    U

Unattended information
  memory and, 488–502
Universal forced choice model, 648–649,
    657–663, 666–672

                    V

Variability in motor system, 559–563, 573,
    579

Velocity
  movement perception and, 29–32, 35–38
Ventriloquium effect, 256, *see also* auditory
    spatial effect
Verbal ability
  laterality effects and, 375–389
Verbal scholastic aptitude, *see* verbal ability
Vestibular system
  in motor control, 575
Visual analysis in reading, 412, 416–418
Visual buffer, 150–151, 159–160, *see also*
    memory and short-term memory
Visual exploration, *see* visual search
Visual feature, 163
Visual field, 117–134, *see also* visual
    perception
  limitation of, 131
  in reading, 125
Visual information processing, 117, 126, 129,
    see also visual perception
  model of, 3–5
  in motor control, 569–570, 575
  serial, 5, 20
Visual interference, *see* visual masking
Visual masking, 634–636
  backward, 138, 140, 143, 201
  cognitive factors in, 16–20
  forward, 138–201
  lateral, 122
  pattern-masking, 214–218, 224
  visual buffer and, 160
Visual perception, *see also* visual
    information processing
  acuity in, 3–20, 120–121, 125, 127
  attention in, 675–686
  awareness in, 215
  critical duration in, 4
  decay in, 8–11, 14–15, 20
  integration of, 150
  interruption (erasure) in, 13–16, 20

Visual perception (*contd.*)
  isolation and, 123, 127
  movement information in, 25–39
  persistence in, *see* decay in
  retinal locus and, 6–7, *see also* visual field
  temporal resolution in, 4–13
Visual record, 215–216
Visual search, 116, 120, 127, 675–686
Vocal activity, 180, 185, *see also* speech
    production and speech timing
Vowel consonant contrast, 173, 175
Vowel enhancement, 173–174

W

Word frequency effect, *see also* word
    perception
  response bias explanation of, 645–649
  restricted response set and, 645–649,
    653–654
Word length information, 160
Word perception, 126, 160, 163–177,
    193–207, 209–225
  duration effect on, 634
  eye position and, 634–636
  fluency in, 163, 165
  gestaltlike properties of words and, 633
  luminance effect on, 634
  non analytic correspondance in, 163–164
  recognition model, 636–638
  type font effect on, 634
  visual angle effect on, 635–636
  word contour and, 632–633
Word pronunciation, 163–177
Word reading, 193–207
Word shape information, 160
Word superiority effect, 126
Writing, 299–318

AN INQUIRY CONCERNING
THE POPULATION OF NATIONS

AN

INQUIRY

CONCERNING

THE POPULATION
OF NATIONS

CONTAINING

A REFUTATION OF MR. MALTHUS'S
ESSAY ON POPULATION

BY

GEORGE ENSOR

[1818]

REPRINTS OF ECONOMIC CLASSICS

AUGUSTUS M. KELLEY · PUBLISHERS
NEW YORK · 1967

FIRST EDITION 1818

(London: Effingham Wilson, *Royal Exchange*, 1818)

Reprinted 1967 by

Augustus M. Kelley · Publishers

Library of Congress Catalogue Card Number

67-16339

PRINTED IN THE UNITED STATES OF AMERICA
by SENTRY PRESS, NEW YORK, N. Y. 10019

AN INQUIRY

CONCERNING

The Population of Nations:

CONTAINING

A REFUTATION OF MR. MALTHUS'S

ESSAY ON POPULATION.

By GEORGE ENSOR, Esq.

LONDON:

PRINTED FOR EFFINGHAM WILSON, ROYAL EXCHANGE.

1818.

CONTENTS.

PART I.

CHAPTER I.

Introduction.—Populousness encouraged and enforced by Athenian, Lacedemonian, Roman, Jewish, Persian, Mahometan, Chinese, Hindoo, Gaulish legislators - *p.* 1

CHAPTER II.

Philosophers favoured populousness - - *p.* 8

CHAPTER III.

Legislators and authors unfriendly to population - *p.* 10

CHAPTER IV.

Contradictions of states and writers respecting population.—Spain, England.—Mr. Malthus, &c. - - *p.* 12

CHAPTER V.

Contradictions and exaggerations of writers principally in consequence of ignorance of facts.—Ancient estimates of different countries and people - - - *p.* 20

CHAPTER VI.

Attempts of authors, from want of facts, to ascertain the population of states by hearths, families, taxation, houses, marriages, baptisms, births, burials; by fuel consumed; by food eaten; by churches, by cobwebs - - *p.* 30

CHAPTER VII.

Actual census at Rome—at Athens. Ignorance and errors of Mr. Mitford, in consequence of his hatred of Republics, exposed. Errors of Mr. Hume respecting the Athenian census - - - - - *p.* 50

Chapter VIII.

Confusion and contradictions respecting population from want of census in European nations, particularly in England and Ireland.—Census of 1801 and 1811.—Domesday book a model.—Though census have been made for wasteful or ambitious purposes, necessary ;—should be frequent and elaborate, including land in tillage, &c.— Guesses of writers concerning territorial extent of Great Britain, the cultivated land, horses, their consumption, &c. - - - - - - *p.* 61

Chapter IX.

Opposition to Mr. Malthus—do not oppose him on the grounds of other writers. Mr. Malthus, though not superstitious, dogmatizes on Nature—Nature's mighty feast, according to Mr. Malthus—his abuse of the people—iniquitous governments and the truly idle, silently or openly supported by him.—The true cause of the distress of the people. Origin of the doctrines of Mr. Malthus—his confusion respecting checks, and the great deficiency of those mentioned by him ;—might have added the natural check—the celestial, or religious—the precocious, or fiscal —the philosophical—the magnanimous—the athletic—the proprietary check :—his direct contradictions on this particular—his argument for the increase of the Jews in Egypt miraculous, and contradicts his own theory—his geometrical and arithmetical ratios exposed. That population presses against food, disproved ;—the cause of the mistake explained by the situation of Sweden, by the situation of the British.—The poor man's labour far more surcharged than the rich man's property by taxes. Plenty in Britain, but iniquitously divided—given to idle dogs, horses, &c.— Mr. Malthus's tendency to increase beyond food, false.— The argument and examples of Mr. Malthus for the pressure of population against subsistence—from war, in the savage state—his *eat a village* ridiculed :—he supposes want of subsistence is an inducement to war—disproved by all great events ancient and modern.—Emigration, not from want of food and room, proved by various facts and arguments, and from his own reasoning and assertions— his monstrous contradictions—his contradictions concerning population following the natural order. Mr. Malthus

subjects the seasons to man's disposition to inordinate
breeding—considers plague, pestilence, famine, as corrective of redundant population. Man's happiness, accôrd-
ing to Mr. Malthus, depends on the abundance of his
food.—His false and unpopular remarks respecting Siberians and Russia—respecting food, &c.—abuses the people.—People will not breed if fed—even the rich and prerogative orders perish. *p.* 77

PART II.

CHAPTER I.

Means adopted to increase the people—promiscuous intercourse—polygamy—fining bachelors—compulsory measures—parish marriages. Mr. Malthus—bounties—exemptions—lying-in and foundling hospitals. Mr. Malthus.
Hospitals for health. England deficient in some respects
—greatly improved in others. Mr. Malthus supposes that
inoculation has not increased population, and that all remedies against plagues, &c. have also been ineffectual.—
On the contrary, health promotes population; and every
life saved is so much stock saved—the people riches *p.* 149

CHAPTER II.

Further means that have been adopted to increase the people
by tributes of men and women—by total transfers of people. Catharine of Russia's ruinous projects—Mr. Malthus's projects—Sir John Sinclair's, &c.—Agriculture—
pasture—manufactures—colonial policy, as means of increasing population. Spence's—Southey's—Preston's, &c.
—to feed the people with fish. Count Rumford's cookery.
—Mr. Gray proposes eating-houses, &c.   -   *p.* 179

CHAPTER III.

Modes of checking or destroying population—emasculation
—absolute celibacy. Mr. Malthus—Tibet—celibacy of
priests, &c.—protracted celibacy by law—custom. Mr.
Malthus and Swiss political peasant. Mr. Malthus advises late marriages—praise of the Norwegians, that they
are better off than the English, exposed—his sermon on
marrying, &c. Polyandry. Abstinence of married people

from cohabiting—total separation—protracting the time of
suckling children—abortion—infanticide—exposing children—infants employed in manufactures—selling children
—Spartan Cryptia. Persecutions—depopulation by Highland proprietors unparalleled—monopolies tend to depopulate—bad government—civil war—foreign war—conquests. Slavery injurious—destroyed the population at
Rome—Servile wars. Mistake of Mons. Say respecting
the cheapness of slaves' work. Mr. Malthus supposes in
all countries, except West Indies, slaves will support their
population—False—by different examples—as slavery destroys, liberty restores population - - - *p.* 193

CHAPTER IV.

Some writers superciliously indifferent respecting the possibility of increasing population.—Dr. Jarrold's *mind-check.*
—Surgeon Birch.—Mr. Malthus.—Mr. Weyland *p.* 255

CHAPTER V.

Dissertation on Population in Ireland.—Mr. Malthus's—Mr.
Weyland's—Mr. Ricardo's—Mr. Grahame's opinions, &c.
exposed.—The poverty and populousness of Ireland truly
explained - - - - - - - *p.* 260

CHAPTER VI.

No free nation distressed by excess of people.—Ill-governed
nations distressed, whether having few or many people.—
Population declining and misery increasing with the viciousness of the government;—and the reverse—population increasing and comfort with liberty.—Examples—
Egypt—Crete—Rhodes—Cyprus—Sparta—Athens—
Italy - - - - - - - - *p.* 297

PART III.

CHAPTER I.

Various considerations respecting what should determine the
meaning of Populousness—or the contrary—as different
states of society—situation—climate—soil—unhealthiness
—salubrity—aridity—commodities—customary food—habits—intemperance—abstemiousness—luxury—government - - - - - - - - *p.* 308

CHAPTER II.

The considerations in the preceding chapter considered by a review of the population in China—perhaps no sufficient reasons for disbelieving its immense imputed population. —The Chinese never advanced beyond the second or middle state - - - - - - - *p.* 316

CHAPTER III.

On populous cities - - - - - - *p.* 334

CHAPTER IV.

Population neither forced nor defrauded not alarming—population to be encouraged—how—natives and foreigners admitted absolute liberty of entry and egress.—Iniquitous conduct of the English government.—Error of Gibbon on the policy of some ancient states, Roman, Athenian, &c. respecting their increasing their population from abroad. —All not criminals to have the same right to labour, and trade, and sojourn—foreigners not to possess civil authority, except in extraordinary cases - - - *p.* 355

CHAPTER V.

No cause of fearing over-populousness.—Should people exceed, why not migrate?—Mr. Malthus.—Colonizing.— India,—the effects of that country on the commerce and opulence of Great Britain.—The British in India, and on their return.—The monstrous and confused government of British India.—Its ruinous effects in India.—The remedy suggested to convert the Hindoos to Christianity.—The government despotic; yet considered, particularly by Sir W. Jones, as necessary, and appointed by Providence.— The vices of the Asiatics referable to their governments. —The Asiatics equal to the Europeans proved, by examples from ancient and modern times.—The Hindoos no way peculiar—yet they must be treated as no other people ever were;—exemplified.—No colonization; no community of interest, language, &c.—What should be done in respect to India.—I no advocate for colonizing.—Colonies seldom succeed.—Losses by West Indian colonies to Great Britain.—If colonies be planted, to be treated with the utmost liberality.—Ancient opinions on that subject - - - - - - - - *p.* 370

CHAPTER VI.

Corn laws.—Bounties.—Prohibition to import foreign corn,
&c.   -   -   -   -   -   -   -   -   *p.* 420

CHAPTER VII.

Principal causes of poverty in England—the expense of the
monarchy—namely, many courts, the nobility, the ecclesiastical establishment, the House of Commons, the national debt, subsidies, wars, military establishments, pensioners, sinecurists,—which are contrary to custom and
precedents, to common sense and common honesty. The
circumstances of England and America contrasted.—
REFORM   -   -   -   -   -   -   *p.* 441

CHAPTER VIII.

Conclusion.—Summary view   -   -   -   -   *p.* 487

THE POPULATION
OF NATIONS.

PART I.

CHAPTER I.

Introduction.—Populousness encouraged and enforced by Athenian, Lacedemonian, Roman, Jewish, Persian, Mahometan, Chinese, Hindoo, Gaulish legislators.

THE anxiety which population has excited; its increasing interest; the new and accumulating assemblage of facts; the various views of writers; their advances towards truth; their errors; their incongruities; the importance and difficulty of the subject,—have induced me to investigate population in its most interesting relations.

Let me state, that though I have briefly noticed some particulars connected with the main topic of discussion; as marriage, property, poverty, subsistence—reserving them for a future treatise;—I have not omitted any particular which seemed to me necessarily associated with population. My object has been, in treating this subject, to preserve unity of design with ampleness and despatch in the execution.

Let me also premise, that I hope my opinion will not be hastily assumed : I may deny an author's statement, yet believe him honest; I may disregard his argument, yet admit his positions; I may acquiesce in the course of his reasoning, yet resist his inference. Right and wrong should both be exhibited at once, to win the erroneous from their misconceptions, and to confirm the intelligent in the rectitude of their views, reasonings, and sentiments. Besides, the thoughts and projects of writers and legislators should be displayed in favor of opposite systems, in order that the sincere and unsophisticated may possess the whole subject :— thus only can they be enabled to attain an adequate and satisfactory conclusion; for thus the mind is purified from prejudices, and conviction attains the dignity of science.

A numerous population has been generally esteemed a positive good ; some have qualified their expressions respecting it, while a few repute populousness a positive evil. The latter doctrine, which appears paradoxical, I shall hereafter investigate : at present I proceed to specify some of the statesmen and philosophers who have favored by their authority and institutions the increase of mankind. First, of legislators; and first among these, the Athenians, who rank chief among the nations of antiquity.

Among the Athenians parentage gave a distinguishing prerogative. According to Dinarchus[1], fathers of legitimate children were alone eligible to the ministry and to military command; lawful offspring

---

[1] Adversus Demosthenem : Opera Demosth. p. 99.

were also necessary to enable orators to address the people[1]. Parents recruited the democracy, and they were in consequence considered by those who framed the law[2], more interested in the execution of their office. The Athenians also enacted compulsory laws to induce population, and bachelors were subjected to penalties[3].

The Lacedemonians were equally intent with the Athenians, by rewards and penalties, by honors and infamy, to encourage population; indeed Plutarch[4] couples Lycurgus and Solon as zealously promoting the same object. By the laws of Sparta, those citizens who had three children were free from watch and ward; and those who had four, according to Aristotle[5], or five, according to Ælian[6], were exempted from all public employments : while those who abstained from marriage were oppressed[7], discredited[8], fined, and the fine reiterated : they were also excluded from the schools of exercise, particularly from those in which the naked virgins exhibited their prowess. *Incorrigible* bachelors were also at certain festivals dragged round the altars and beaten by the women[9]; and to consummate their misery, they sunk into the grave hated and disgraced. An old bachelor at Sparta was reputed an outcast, selfish and sterile; while

[1] Petit, Leges Atticæ, p. 262.   [2] Thucydides, lib. 2. p. 128.
[3] Julius Pollux, lib. 3, Περι Αγαμων.   [4] Moralia, p. 259.
[5] De Repub. lib. 2. c. 9.   [6] Historia Varia, lib. 6. c. 6.
[7] Apud Stobæum, sermo 64. p. 412.
[8] Plutarch. in Lysandro et in Lycurgo.
[9] Athenæus, lib. 13. p. 555.

the father of a family was distinguished in manhood, reverenced in age, and honored as a public benefactor and a common parent. By his children he enjoyed the prerogative of representing the dignity of the state, and by them the desperate valor of Spartan patriots obtained a double crown of glory. Of the three hundred chosen Spartans who sacrificed themselves for the liberty of Greece at Thermopylæ with Leonidas, all, says the historian[1], had children.

The statesmen at Rome pursued the same policy, and by more various expedients than those adopted by Athens or Lacedemon. The *jus trium liberorum* was inserted in the Roman code; which *equity*[2] (such is the language of the law) was enlarged for those who had four children, and which again was amplified when the family increased to five[3]. Children were the most powerful intercessors for an offending parent, and criminals as they enumerated their offspring reduced the customary inflictions of the law. Children relieved the dependent from subjection : even women, who have been degraded in most nations, at Rome were taught to regard their children as their sureties for emancipation. Mothers who had three children escaped tutelage[4], and a freed woman who had four attained unconditional liberty[5].

In aid of these inducements, Julius Cæsar con-

---

[1] Herodotus, lib. 7. c. 205.　　[2] Suetonius, lib. 5. c. 21.

[3] Domat, Civil Law, p. 271. Gravina says, "Concessa fuit immunitas onerum personalium." De Jur. Civ. p. 348.

[4] Taylor's Civil Law, p. 120.

[5] Columella, lib. i. c. 8.

ferred presents on those who had many children[1], and
Augustus increased their amount[2]. At Rome also
the married had a distinct place in the theatre[3], an
honor not unimportant among a people so fond of
public exhibitions. Married persons were preferred
to public employments, and by the *lex Papia Poppæa*
their pretensions were advanced by one year for each
of their children[4]. Beside rewards and prerogatives
to bribe individuals to marriage, the Romans enacted
penalties and disabilities against those who abstained
from that contract:—a legatee forfeited his bequest,
if in a hundred days after the death of the testator he
was not married[5]; and in order that marriages might
be contracted for the purpose of population, a married man without children could only receive half of
the sum bequeathed to him[6]. Furius Camillus obliged
the unmarried with threats and fines to espouse those
widowed by the wars[7]. Julius and Augustus Cæsar
sanctioned by laws the acts of the censors, and inflicted on bachelors the fine *uxorium*[8]. To all these in-
stigations by pain and pleasure, superstition added its
sanction, and a marvellous story was related[9] of the
destruction of the Fabii who neglected to obey the
ordinance of marriage.

[1] Dion Cassius, lib. 43. c. 25.   [2] Ibid. lib. 56. c. 10.
[3] Gravina, p. 348.   [4] " Ut annum adderent singuli
ad ætatem parentis, &c. is candidatus præferretur qui plures liberos
haberet, quamvis ætate esset inferior." Gravina, p. 347 et seq.
[5] Gravina, p. 352.   [6] Taylor, Civil Law, p. 145.
[7] Plutarch. in Camillum.   [8] Valerius Maximus, lib. 2. c. 9.
[9] Dion. Halicarnass. lib. 9. c. 22.

Nor should the Jews be omitted in this summary. To "increase and multiply," they reputed a divine command. Under this impression some have argued that the longevity of the antediluvians was a means adopted by Providence for this purpose [1]. Whatever occasioned the procrastinated being of those people, there can be no doubt of their anxiety to enlarge their population : a new married man was exonerated from all civil business, and he was freed from the paramount duties of war for one year [2]. The Jews also held, that to satisfy the law a man should be married at twenty years of age [3], and that he who neglected the precept of " Increase and multiply" was a homicide [4].

The Persians were not less attentive than other nations to the populousness of their empire. Herodotus [5] says that a Persian was respected according to the number of his children, and that the king sent annual presents to those who were so fortunate and so serviceable. Nor were the women of Persia without their public rewards on such occasions. Plutarch [6]

---

[1] The Rev. Dr. Millar, late fellow of Trinity-college Dublin, in what he entitled " Philosophy of History " doubts this, as Noah's progeny was not more numerous than that of many existing families as favorably circumstanced : vol. 1. p. 119. He supposes that their longevity was intended to maintain the principle of patriarchal government. p. 123.—Why ?   [2] Deut. chap. 24.

[3] Selden De J. Nat. &c. lib. 5. c. 3. p. 545.

[4] " Quicunque negligit præceptum de multiplicatione humani generis, habendum esse veluti homicidam." Ibid. p. 549.

[5] lib. 1. c. 136. Strabo, lib. 15. t. 2. p. 491,

[6] Moralia, p. 146,

relates that Alexander doubled the gifts to pregnant women, which had been instituted by Cyrus.

Mahomet and his followers have been equally zealous for marriage and population. Thornton [1] says, that at Constantinople no unmarried man, or, what is esteemed the same, who has not a female in his family, —would be permitted to keep an independent establishment. " The women of this religion," says Lady W. Montague, " are taught to believe that they best ensure their future happiness by employing themselves in making young mussulmans, while those who die unproductive perish in a reprobate state."

The laws and writings of the Chinese, ancient and modern, abound with the most exalted expressions in favor of marriage and children.

The civil and religious code of the Hindoo [2] considers marriage an indispensable duty : in consequence, Moor [3] states that " so universal is matrimony among the Hindoos, that it would be difficult to find an unhusbanded female of a respectable family arrived at puberty—that is of the age of eleven or twelve."

The ancient Gauls [4] considered their countrymen disgraced who were unmarried at twenty years of age: yet the penalty for celibacy was not inflicted among the Romans [5], before the bachelor attained his twenty-

[1] State of Turkey, vol. 2. p. 252. This may also proceed from jealousy of married men.

[2] Orme's History : Dissertation, &c. p. 6.

[3] Hindoo Infanticide, p. 2.

[4] Pastoret des Loix, partie 4. p. 88.   [5] Gravina, p. 352.

fifth year. The modern French have their inducements to marriage; and almost all European nations distinguish by honors, prerogatives, exemptions, privations, pains, or disgraces, (which I shall hereafter particularize,) the different states of celibacy and marriage.

If we turn from civilized society to rude life, the savage tribes appear still more interested for the sufficiency of their people by the frequent incorporation of their enemies. Heriot[1] mentions the Miamacs, Iroquois and Albinaquis among the Indians, who elect their chiefs on account of their numerous offspring.

CHAPTER II.

Philosophers favored populousness.

PHILOSOPHERS succeed legislators in their admiration and recommendations of marriage and children. Pythagoras[2], agreeably to his habit of associating earth and heaven, said that men should marry in order to leave new adorers of God. Clemens of Alexandria[3], a fit commentator of such doctrine, insisted that Pythagoras rejected beans because they occasioned sterility in women. Plato adopted his master's fantastic expressions, adding[4], that women divorced should repeat their marriage until they had produced children for themselves and the state. Hierocles[5] considered the procreation of children an act of gratitude to pa-

[1] Travels in Canada, p. 551. [2] Iamblichus, Pythag. Vita, c. 18.
[3] Stromata, lib. 3. p. 435. [4] De Legibus, lib. 11. p. 974.
[5] Apud Stobæum, sermo 73. p. 449.

rents : and Epaminondas, the only general whom antiquity has classed with philosophers, on being asked
what one unmarried and childless should do to serve
his country, replied, " Die for it [1]."
Authors of the last and present century have also
been decisive in their praise of population. Vauban [2]
assumes that " the abundance of people is the means of
all things:"—Mirabeau[3], that "population is the first of
social goods." In the *Elémens de la Politique*[4] it is
stated that the people should be as numerous as possible.
Germans and Spaniards have enforced the same theme:
so have the Italians, and none more than Filangieri [5],
who reputes *populazione et richezze* equivalent.
The English have added their voice to the great
majority for the multiplication of mankind. Sir William Temple [6] proposed a tax on bachelors when
they were twenty-five years old, " since the late custom among us of marrying late or never." Bolingbroke[7]
insisted " that the increase of people must be always
an advantage, and can never be hurtful to any state."
Swift [8] as vehemently said, that " it is an undoubted
maxim that the people are the riches of a country."
Sir James Steuart[9] affirmed that " the increase of
numbers in a state shews youth and vigour." The *En-
cyclopedia Britannica* concludes, " As the strength and

[1] Apud Stobæum. sermo 66. p. 421.   [2] Dixme Royale, p. 22.
[3] "Lepremierdesbiensdelasociété." L'AmidesHommes,t.1.c.2.
[4] " Aussi nombreux qu'il soit possible," t. 1. c. 14. p. 205.
[5] Della Legislazione, lib. 2. c. 1.   [6] Works, folio, vol. 1. p. 268.
[7] Philosophical Works, vol. 4. p. 112.
[8] Works, vol. 9. p. 396.   [9] Polit. Œcon, b. 1. c. 12.

glory of a kingdom or state consist in the multitude of its subjects, celibacy above all things should be discouraged." Dagge [1], "that the strength of every commonwealth chiefly consists in the number of its inhabitants." Paley [2] speaks of " the importance of population, and the superiority of it above every other national advantage—that it is the true and absolute interest of a country." And Mr. Bentham, in the language of Mons. Dumont, considers " *la force et la richesse d'une nation—le nombre des hommes* [3]."

CHAPTER III.

Legislators and authors unfriendly to population.

SOME legislators and writers have, on the contrary, been unfriendly to the birth of children and the increase of mankind. The Thracians mourned when a child was born, and rejoiced at its decease [4]. So did the Causini [5],—so did those who lived in the neighbourhood of Caucasus [6]. Heraclides [7] says the same of the Locri, and Mela [8] of the Essedones :—the Siks [9] are equally perverse in their expressions of joy and sorrow.

[1] Criminal Law, &c. p. 272.   [2] Essays on Population, vol. 2. p. 370.
[3] Théorie, &c. t. 1. p. 238. This list might be enlarged indefinitely to the same purpose. Dr. Burn in his Observations on an equal Land Tax argues this opinion with great judgement.
[4] Herodotus, lib. 5. c. 4.   Sextus Empiricus, p. 158.
[5] Nicolaus Damascenus, p. 570. Apud Stobæum, sermo 119. p. 603.
[6] Strabo, lib. 11. t. 2. p. 135.   [7] Ibid. p. 532.
[8] lib. 2. c. i.   [9] History of Dekkan, vol. 2. p. 143.

Puffendorf[1] speaks timorously of an excessive population—that thus a nation may sink under the weight of its own people. The same was afterwards repeated in France, which induced an English writer sneeringly to say, " The discovery is attributed to Mirabeau." In our own island similar terrors have been occasionally expressed. Harrison quaintly observed, "Some do grudge at the increase of the people in these days, thinking a necessary brood of cattle far better than a superfluous augmentation of mankind." Cock[2], in a pamphlet published in 1658, asserted that the increase of the people was so much dreaded that a poor man was not permitted to marry till the age of thirty, nor a poor woman till she was twenty-five. Mr. Ricardo, who published his Essay on Political Economy last year, advises that government should make some effort to restrain the improvident marriages of the lower orders[3]. Dr. Whitaker, in the year preceding, lamented the numbers and sturdiness of the people : " Under the Gascoignes and the Nevils the features of Hunslet were a great manor-house, a park, a slender and obsequious population[4];" and " I need not expose the contrast." But of all writers, Mr. Malthus is most deranged by the prospect of an excessive population. It is in him a dread, an alarm, a horror, a sin unsatisfied, a constitutional malady, which truth and error, knowledge and ignorance, cruelly feed and

[1] lib. 6. c. 1. He also speaks of a legal prohibition of the marriage of the poor, p. 331.
[2] Barrington's Ancient Statutes, p. 395.   [3] p. 112.
[4] Topography of Leeds. He repeats this precious sentiment.

inflame: for while he insists that men cannot multiply
without corresponding, or rather anticipated, subsistence[1], he talks as if somehow they could attain a multitudinous increase without food, and then perish superlatively even beyond the excess of their mysterious
augmentation.

CHAPTER IV.

*Contradictions of states and writers respecting population.—Spain,
England.—Mr. Malthus, &c.*

HAVING stated some opinions and authorities for
and against populousness, I shall add some of the
direct contradictions and by inference made on this
subject by the same nations and the same writers. In
1548 the French government published an ordinance
absolutely hostile to the multiplication of the people ;
and in 1572 the Hugonots were massacred, and " the
king himself in person led the way to these assàssi-
nations[2]." Yet in this depopulating monarchy it was
a maxim that women were not to be expatriated, " sur
le prétexte qu'elles porteront ailleurs les germes de la

---

[1] This is so flagrantly his position, that Mr. Ricardo, the eulogist
of Mr. Malthus, says : " Mr. Malthus appears to me to be too much
inclined to think that population is only increased by the previous
provision of food ;—that it is food that creates its own demand, that
it is first by providing food that encouragement is given to marriage,
—instead of considering that the general progress of population is affected by the increase of capital, the consequent demand for labour,
and the rise of wages ; and that the production of food is but the
effect of that demand." Political Economy, p. 561.

[2] Hume, vol. 6. p. 205.

population et de la fécondité [1]." What contradictions did not Louis the Fourteenth exhibit! He revoked the edict of Nantz, while he exempted for five years from severe charges all those who were married at twenty [2]. His Christian majesty has been exceeded by his Catholic majesty in the opposition of his ordinances to each other. Philip the Fourth [3] in 1623 granted to new married men the privilege of nobility for four years, and the exemptions of the same class to those who had six children. The municipal regulations of Castile promoted the same effects by the same provisions :—yet Jews and Moors were swept off by the same government; and as these transferred with their persons—capital, industry and art, the loss of numbers in their expulsion became a permanent deficiency.

The English government has few pretensions either to better principles or to a more consistent policy. Many laws have been made for the preservation of the people. In the reign of Henry the Seventh, much land passed from tillage to pasture ; it was then enacted that houses of husbandry with twenty acres of land should be upheld : and by the 25th of Henry the Eighth no one was permited to have more than two thousand sheep. Barrington [4] says the statute is still in force. Again, how dolorous were the reflections respecting inclosures, which Hume [5] admits depopulated the country! Lord keeper Coventry directed the judges

---

[1] Pastoret des Loix, partie 2. p. 115.
[2] Voltaire, L'Histoire, &c. chapitre "Gouvernement intérieur."
[3] Townsend's Travels in Spain, vol. 2. p. 34.
[4] Ancient Statutes, &c. p. 412.   [5] History, vol. 6. p. 44.

of assize to " make strict inquiry after depopulations, inclosures—a crime of a crying nature, that barreth God of his honour, and the king of his subjects; church and houses go down together [1]." Yet the system of England in many ways advanced pasturing at the expense of tillage, and thus by necessity men were displaced by sheep.

Consider the hostility of the laws in the same code in other particulars. He who killed another, *se defendendo*, forfeited his goods; " because thereby a true man was killed [2];" yet for centuries thousands were annually executed by the law, and the value of a true man's life was about a shilling. As to the judicial law [3] of the same period, that Heretics, Jews and Turks should not have their clergy; this was common to all Europe, when faith was strong and priests despotic.

In England, many laws have been made in favor of marriage; by one [4] in the reign of Edward the First, it was ordained that lords should not keep possession of female wards if they did not marry them when they were sixteen. The 5th of Elizabeth, c. 12. s. 4. enacts that " every badger lader, kidder carrier, buyer and transporter of butter, cheese, corn or grain, shall be licensed, unless he is a married man." Yet bonds for procuring the marriage of persons are declared void [5]; and marriages [6] and births were assessed;—for a duke's marriage fifty pounds, which was reduced as the indi-

---

[1] State Trials, (Irish edit.) vol. 1. p. 566.
[2] Law Dictionary, vol. 2. p. 228.   [3] Ibid. vol. 1. p. 500.
[4] Reeves's History of the Engl. Law, vol. 2. p. 111.
[5] L. Dict. vol. 2. p. 411.   [6] Ibid. vol. 1. p. 398.

viduals declined in dignity. Thus Acbar favored marriages and taxed them [1] ; and thus the government of Tonquin was at once friendly and hostile to the marriage of its people [2]. Blackstone also remarks the contradictions of the English code, by favoring, if not compelling, the marriage of the father of a natural child with its mother [3]; and the numerous restraints, especially to the union of the lower classes [4], which he says is evidently detrimental to the public by hindering the increase of the people.

The laws of England are self-destructive on this as on various subjects:—they fix the wages of labor, tax the necessaries of the industrious, impose the same law on the ingenious and enterprising, and on the inexpert and doltish, localize individual exertion ;—all these are inimical to the increase and comforts of society: yet if we should believe British rulers, they have been most anxious for the populousness of the country, and the greater population of a village, town, or district, has often been proclaimed by them as the triumph of their own ability and virtue. I must observe, however, that their conduct is not peculiar :

[1] Ayeen Akberry, p. 248.

[2] According to Hamilton, "the greatest nobles thought it no shame or disgrace to marry their daughters to English or Dutch seamen for the time they were to stay at Tonquin." Pinkerton's Voyages, &c. vol. 8. p. 484. Yet the tax which legalizes marriage at Tonquin amounts to twenty-three crowns. Exposé Statistique du Tunquin &c. par M. M—n.   [3] Commentaries, vol. 1. p. 455.

[4] Ibid. p. 438. Dr. Halley lamented the difficulties the people encountered in entering the marriage state.

Colbert [1] endeavoured by recompenses to increase the people, but he prevented the commerce of grain; which is not much less incongruous than the English law of settlements, which limits the commerce of labor and the intercourse of mankind. Thus legislators have not merely controverted by their practice sound policy, but traversed their own projects and wishes. So have authors, whose errors of contradiction are infinite, and none certainly in this respect has exceeded Mr. Malthus: he says [2], " It is an utter misconception of my argument to infer that I am an enemy to population,—I am only an enemy to vice and misery." In what region, in what state, in what age does he not exhibit the misery of mankind? What is the burthen of his theme?—That population " presses so hard against the limits of their food [3], that their population pressed so hard against the limits of their means of subsistence [4]," which he frequently repeats [5]. Does he not involve all savage and civilized societies, all states ancient and modern, every European nation now existing, "except perhaps Russia [6]," as laboring under this pressure? Distress so clings to mankind in his system, that the sum of his philosophy is, Man and misery,— no matter whether many or few, whether thronged in cities, united in towns, cultivating the earth, pasturing herds of cattle, hunting nature's commoners,—in every variety of life, in every shade of being, mankind exceeds the subsistence which the earth affords:

[1] Eloges de Mons. Thomas, t. 3. p. 286.   [2] vol. 2. p. 432.
[3] vol. 1. p. 155. [4] vol. 1. p. 165. [5] as v. i. p. 231. [6] vol. 2. p. 69.

No living thing, whate'er its food, feasts there,
But the chameleon, who can feast on air.

In the same disregard of his principles and argument he says, *an increase of population is a great positive good, when it follows its natural order* [1];—and he considers the natural order, contrary to sir James Steuart, multiplication of people in consequence of extended agriculture. Yet what is more broadly advanced by him;—is it not his primary position; is it not the aim of his argument; does it not intervene in his details—that man by nature tends to increase beyond the increase of subsistence, and this with accelerated progression? He states in the beginning of his treatise [2], that *population has a constant tendency to increase beyond the means of subsistence.* To the same effect he says, " the *tendency* [3] to early marriages is so strong that we want every possible help that we can get to counteract it." Here this natural tendency is so strong that it requires, according to him, a double check. Is this tendency natural or not? Will he say it is unnatural?—Yet it is to be counteracted by every possible means, he says, because it is pernicious. And yet Mr. Malthus also says [4], " We cannot but conceive that it is an object of the Creator that the earth should be replenished; and it appears to me clear that this would not be effected without a tendency in population to increase faster than food: and as without the present law of increase the peopling of the earth does not proceed very rapidly, we have undoubtedly some reason to believe that this law is not

[1] vol. 2. p. 212. [2] vol. 1. p. 4.
[3] vol. 2. p. 55 [4] vol. 2. p. 239.

too powerful for its apparent object. The desire of the means of subsistence would be comparatively confined in its effects, and would fail of producing that general activity so necessary to the improvement of the human faculties, were it not for the strong universal effort of population to increase with greater rapidity than its supplies."

Mark this passage. What becomes of his praise of population when *it follows its natural order?* which order in the last quotation he insists is not the order of God's providence; for God impressed *a tendency to population faster than food;* and that this advance of population was necessary to improve the human faculties and people the earth.

Hanc deus et melior litem natura diremit.

The contradictions of Mr. Malthus multiply on every separate topic. He talks of the wisdom of the author of nature, "which is apparent in all his works[1];" and again[2], "the laws of nature which are the laws of God." Yet how grievously he charges with evil these same laws in the following words[3], that "though human institutions appear to be, and indeed often are, the obvious and obtrusive causes of much mischief to mankind, they are in reality light and superficial in comparison with the deep-rooted causes of evil which result from the *laws of nature* and the passions of mankind :"

Est operæ pretium duplicis pernoscere juris
Naturam.

This is truly a new way of reasoning from nature's laws to nature's God. But it certainly proves one po-

[1] vol. 2. p. 447.   [2] vol. 2. p. 452, Appendix.   [3] vol. 2. p. 24.

sition of the Professor of Political Economy in the East India College,—that the subject of population *is yet in its infancy* [1], if he be the master of the art. These contradictions and repugnances of Mr. Malthus I here mention to justify for the present a passing observation on his defects; for I shall hereafter, when I investigate his theory, exhibit numerous inconsistencies in his Essay. The reason of this sad deficiency in this writer has proceeded from different causes. Having originally, as appears to me, no very commanding mind, with moderate learning, and, by his own avowal in respect to this particular subject, very limited knowledge; he fastened a theory on a dispute, and thus advanced opinions which he had not ingenuousness to retract, and dared not defend. Finding on consideration that his original doctrine was narrow and false and hideous—for what could be more false and monstrous than that population was only controlled by vice and misery?—he attempted to restore its credit by adding moral restraint to the insolvent firm of his philosophy. And in order to keep these partners in tolerable society, he laboured to reconcile antipathies and harmonize discord. Thus his contradictions have increased with every new edition [2]; till in some instances, as in that already noticed, of increase and supplies, tendency and natural, and nature and God; they resemble a certain glorious creed. I know no-

[1] vol. 1. p. 25.

[2] Mr. Malthus has lately published a fifth edition, in three volumes. The advertisement speaks of additions, (they may be had in a separate volume,) not corrections. I always quote the fourth edition unless I specify another.

thing on this side the Limbo of vanity to which his
antitheses in error may be more aptly compared, than
that puzzle in legerdemain by which liquors of different flavours and different colours are drawn from the
same vessel and the same orifice.

CHAPTER V.

*Contradictions and exaggerations of writers principally in conse-
quence of ignorance of facts.—Ancient estimates of different countries and people.*

THE causes of the errors and exaggerations of writers respecting population, though no doubt depending in some measure on laxity of mind and a passion
for extravagance, are mainly referable to their ignorance of facts. Who with any acquaintance of actual
surveys could believe or relate the reputed forces of
the Persian army? I do not say with Richardson,
that no such expedition to Greece was ever undertaken; nor that the forces of Xerxes were inconsiderable :—his dominions were extensive, and his people
obedient. But who can believe the versifier [1], who
stated that at Thermopylæ four thousand men encountered three millions! or the historian [2] himself,

[1] In Herodotus, lib. 7. c. 228.
[2] Herodotus, lib. 7. c. 60. He states the ships at 1,207. c. 89.
This is not impossible. Herodotus says that the Greek king ascertained the number of his forces thus, 10,000 men were comprehended in a certain space, which was repeatedly filled, &c. lib. 9. c. 60.
How much this tends to corroborate the amount, I leave to the
reader. It is not much worse than calculating a nation by its fighting
men, or an army by its regiments; even though we should not credit that Tyrconnel's regiment was composed of one man.

who sums the Persian's land army at 1,700,000? This number might not have been enrolled; they might possibly have been embodied in parties through the territories of the great king. Yet why should we suppose that Xerxes was more cordially followed than a modern sultan, whose captains of a thousand men seldom command five hundred, which for many reasons soon decline to a tenth of their titular amount? Such dashing statements I should not stop to expose, if they did not reappear in modern authors to justify their enormities. Chateaubriand in his *Essai Historique*, &c. states that the Persians killed at Platæa amounted to two hundred thousand; adding, "*mon calcul est modéré.*" If so, every Persian was destroyed; for Herodotus [1] says that the whole number of Persians, Greeks, and confederates, who fought for the barbarians, did not exceed three hundred thousand men; and certainly one-third of that army was not Persians. Yet are the multitudinous combatants of Xerxes, considering the mighty success of his power, an ordinary array in comparison to the innumerable throng of warriors which limited districts and towns armed against each other. Sibaris sent three hundred thousand men against Crotona, which rival city met the assailants with one hundred thousand [2].

The same superlative enumeration is not unfrequent in other particulars connected with population. Homer says that Crete had a hundred cities (ἑκατομπολιν); in the Odyssey they amount only to ninety; and as it is a religious duty to preserve a great poet's veracity inviolate, Strabo [3] accommodates

[1] lib. 9. c. 32.　　[2] Diodorus Siculus.　　[3] lib. 10. v. 2. p. 69.

the variation by saying that Homer spoke of Crete at different periods. Stephanus [1] ascribes to Laconia a hundred cities: and it is remarkable that Crete and Lacedæmon, which had so many traits of actual resemblance, concurred in this casualty. As tracts of land had a hundred cities—cities had a hundred gates. Messene [2] seems to have had innumerable gates. Let this be true or fictitious, Wallace, in his endeavours to prove the populousness of ancient states, refers absolutely, as to a notorious fact, to the account of ancient Thebes; saying [3], "it is celebrated by Homer for its hundred gates, out of each of which marched two hundred men with horses and chariots." Nor does he stop till he affirms that Thebes was "more than twice and a half or perhaps thrice as populous as London."

Wallace should have known that Diodorus Siculus [4] says expressly that a *hundred* gates meant many gates [5]. Nor is it uncommon to use a definite number in order to excite an hyperbolical conception. Thus we read of the hundred islands [6]; of the cistern at Constantinople of a *thousand columns*;—yet long since the thousand columns have been reduced by

[1] De Urbibus, p. 76.

[2] Εστι Πυλος, προ Πυλοιο, Πυλος γε μεν εστι και αλλος. Plutarch. Moral. p. 404.

[3] Pages 43, 44. 2d edit.

[4] lib. 1. Mela says that the gates of Thebes were differently interpreted;—Sive, ut alii ajunt, centum aulas habent, totidem olim principum domos. lib 1. c. 9.

[5] This definite number sometimes regards a particular sum, as the days in the year. Thus Balbi speaks of a great city near Sora which he was told had 366 gates. Pinkerton's Travels, vol. 9. p. 395.

[6] Herodotus, lib. 1. c. 151. It is said "Maledives" signify a thousand islands.

counting them to three hundred and thirty-six. Thus we read of the building in Java of a thousand temples. And so of ten thousand others.

Herodotus [1] relates that wonder-working Egypt had in the time of Amasis twenty thousand cities. Yet according to Theocritus [2], when Ptolemy reigned, Egypt contained thirty-three thousand three hundred and thirty-nine cities. Had the poet described their population and extent, these no doubt would have been as extravagant as their number. Babylon of course enjoyed its wonders—walls three hundred feet high, and a hundred massy gates of brass: yet it is not the least extravagance in the story, that this city when besieged by Cyrus [3] contained provisions for all its people for twenty years duration.

Among the vast and populous cities on record is Nineveh. God said to Jonah, " Should not I spare Nineveh, that great city, in which there are more than six score thousand persons that cannot discern their right hand from their left?" On this text Wallace writes [4] : " According to the Book of Jonah there were one hundred and twenty thousand children in Nineveh, who could not discern between their right hand and their left hand. Now computing according to the proportion, which is, from the most accurate observations, found to be most consistent with truth, and reckoning such as were too young to discern between their right hand and their left to be all those who were below two years of age complete, the inhabitants of Nineveh were two millions two hundred thousand;

[1] lib. 2. c. 177.   [2] Idyl. 17.
[3] Xenophon Instit. Cyri, lib. 7. p. 190.   [4] p. 332.

if they were below three, the inhabitants of Nineveh were more than one million five hundred thousand; and if below four, above one million one hundred thousand; and if all below five, they were more than nine hundred thousand : thus populous was this exceeding great city." So spoke Wallace, a man not unlearned. Yet this statement enforces another conclusion,—that this exceeding great city was inhabited by an exceedingly insensate people : it contained, as we cannot doubt the authority, one hundred and twenty thousand persons who could not discern their right hand from their left. Yet it is mentioned as a circumstance lamentable and astonishing, that in London [1] one hundred thousand individuals are without the means of education.

Yet this account of Nineveh is moderate, when compared to the numerous Jews who according to Josephus [2] assembled at Jerusalem at the feast of the passover, amounting to twenty-seven millions. If so, there were twenty-seven times more Jews at Jerusalem than there were individuals in the Champ de Mars, near Paris, at the confederation,—the greatest assemblage of people that Europe probably ever exhibited. I saw it.

Nor is this the only relation concerning the Jewish people and their astonishing numbers. The Jews, exclusive of the tribes of Benjamin and Levi, sent forth one million five hundred and seventy thousand men : if so, the fighting men of all the tribes

[1] On the authority of Mr. Allen, stated in the Report of the Committee of the House of Commons on Public Education.

De Bello Judaico, lib. 7. c. 18.

amounted to one million six hundred and ninety-one thousand men [1]; which enumeration is only less by nine thousand men than the host composed of many commanded by the great king; and this population was contained on an area of one hundred and fifty miles long by about fifty broad ; that is, on a territory, not the most fertile, whose superficies was about one sixth part of the extent of England. Wallace, referring to this topic, concludes : "As we cannot but admit that Palestine was of a very small extent, and the accounts of its numerous armies are taken from Scripture itself, and their numbers are expressly asserted in several different parts of it, all concurring in that particular with each other; this fact will have a peculiar force, and almost determine this question with such as acknowledge the authority of Scripture."

The populousness of other nations, but in rather a mitigated tone, has also been glorified. Milton speaks of the " populous North," and Scythia and many people were associated notions through all ages, even to the present time, when sir W. Jones, under its new title of Tartary, by a miserable and tenth-told simile repeats the vulgar error [2]. Yet Herodotus [3], whom some treat as a romancer, questioned the populousness of Scythia; and Aristides [4] called it a solitude.

[1] 1 Chronicl. 21. See Wallace, p. 53.

[2] He compares the many warriors it sent forth, to those who issued from the Trojan horse. Asiatic Researches, Preliminary Discourse, p. 12. Giannone uses the same figure of the academy of Pontanus, lib. 28. p. 426. Storia di Napoli. Tiraboschi employs it also in his History of Italian Literature:—In short, it is common property among the Della Cruscans. [3] lib. 4. c. 81.

[4] Των Σκυθων ερημιαν. Orationes, t. 2. p. 225.

Germany has also been reputed the *officina gentium*; yet the Germans had neither cities nor villages : their houses were dispersed and insulated ; a circumstance which Tacitus, a resident of Rome, where fires were common and destructive, conjectured, might have been adopted as a remedy against such casualties. And as this surmise was not amply absurd, Mr. Malthus [1] having stated it, adds with confidence from his own fancy, that this dissocial mode of raising their dwellings "is strongly calculated to prevent the generation and check the ravages of epidemics." If so, we might conclude that a *chancery of health* was an appendage of the shifting savage state. Tacitus to his supposition for the singleness of their houses—"*sive adversus casus ignis remedium*," adds, "*sive inscitia ædificandi*." Thus it is questionable if the inhabitants of this populous country had talents to build two houses under one roof. Nor does it appear that this *populous* country was more advanced in the time of Marcellinus [2].

The Gauls also were *tremendously numerous.* Cicero [3] speaks of their immanity and multitude, and immediately interrogates " *Quid illis terris asperius, quid incultius oppidis* [4] *?* " Their cities had no resemblance to existing cities, if Strabo [5] is an authority. And yet Montesquieu [6] considered that in the time of

[1] vol. 1. p. 130.

[2] Eorum urbes sunt nemora; latissimos enim circos dejectis obstruunt arboribus, ubi constructis tuguriis. &c. lib. 4. p. 364.

[3] Opera Omnia, t. 2. p. 512.   [4] p. 511.

[5] Oppida ut circumdata retiis busta declinant. lib. 16. c. 2.

[6] Lettres Persannes. Lettre 108.

Julius Cæsar the world was fifty times more populous than when he wrote ; from which even Wallace [1] recoils.

Nor was Great Britain without its claims to populousness. We have no definite account of its towns and cities and people when king Bladud reigned, but he was a great philosopher, and lived about nine centuries before our æra. Julius Cæsar, however, speaks of the *infinite multitude* of men in this island. The facility with which rude tribes collect, their hideousness and disorder [2], might excuse his falsehood, if we did not know that Cæsar assailed Britain in order to forward his schemes at Rome, and that the same policy directed his narrative. How could Britain then have been populous, when some of its inhabitants were as barbarous as the Agathirsi ? Maitland will not admit that his countrymen painted their bodies ; and perhaps he would also have denied Herodian's [3] testimony concerning the iron hoops about their necks and waists, which Herodian says they consider ornamental, and display as other barbarians do gold— to signify their opulence. Yet Whitaker [4] says, *Caledonia* means a wood ; and I doubt if southern Britain was much better than a wilderness also. They had neither cities nor tillage [5]. How could Britain be populous? One barbarous country may be populous

---

[1] p. 35.

[2] Thus Cicero speaks of the immanity of barbarians and their innumerable multitude. t. 2. p. 567. [3] lib. 3. p. 200.

[4] History of Manchester, p. 439.

[5] Μητε πολεις μητε γεωργιας εχοντες. Dion Cassius, lib. 76. c. 12.

in respect to another ; but in reference to an agricultural nation it must be unoccupied. Yet such is the effect of confident assertions repeated, that sir W. Temple, a scholar, a philosopher, and a statesman, however incongruous the union may appear, affirmed that ancient Britain "was filled with infinite numbers of people[1] :" adding, "they lived most upon milk, and flesh which they got by hunting : little upon corn, which was not in much esteem or plenty among them. In short, they resembled the Germans[2] and other barbarians in their mode of living; and were of course few in numbers, because their means of living was scanty, half-naked, and ill lodged. I cannot refrain from noticing the mass of absurdities which the respect and adoration of the oak has occasioned. Jewish[3] patriarchs, druids of Germany and Britain, have honoured that tree. Why? conjectures are infinite. The reason probably is, it sheltered them, it fed them :— those then who held that men sprang from oaks, only erred by inferring that what supported life caused it, merely mistaking the nurse for the mother.

Spain also has been reputed as swarming with inhabitants. Cicero[4] characterizes Spain by its numbers. I. F. Rehfues, librarian to the late king of Wurtemburg, in a work published in 1809 computes the population of that peninsula when inhabited by the

[1] Works, vol.2. p.530. Shaftesbury, a man very inferior to Temple, speaks very irreverently of our barbarous ancestry. Miscel. 3. c. 1.

[2] Agriculturæ non student; majorque pars victûs eorum in lacte, caseo, carne consistit. Cæsar de Bello Gallico, lib. 6. c. 21.

[3] Genesis 35. 4. Joshua, 24. 26, &c.

[4] Nec numero Hispanos, nec robore Gallos, nec calliditate Pœnos, &c. De Harusp. t. 2. p. 431.

Moors at seventy-eight millions. Mons. Say [1] thinks it formerly contained twenty-four millions, and that now it contains only eight. I do not believe it ever contained twenty-four millions, and it is more probable that at present its people are eight than ten or eleven millions, according to other estimates [2]. The population attributed to towns is still more exaggerated than that ascribed to countries. Mons. Laborde says Taragon contained two millions of people. Isaac Vossius, who only allowed to all ancient Europe thirty millions of inhabitants, insisted that Nankin formerly contained twenty millions. And Wernerus Rolefinchius [3] computed ancient Rome at twenty-seven millions. Thus enormities proceeded, as I have said in the beginning of this chapter, principally from ignorance of facts. As investigation detects lies, surveys reduce numbers. The Helvetii, by the census found in their camps, amounted only to 368,000 persons, men, women, and children ; which is not thrice more than the present population of the Pays de Vaud [4] ;— yet what multitudes would have been fancied, had there been no enumeration, or had the census merely stated their twelve towns and four hundred villages !

[1] t. 2. p. 155.
Jacob in his Travels mentions a census which states the population at 10,351,075, in 1803.
[3] This brave calculator I only know through Keysler. Travels, letter 47.
[4] They were 112,951 when Price wrote on Annuities, &c. p. 286.

CHAPTER VI.

Attempts of authors, from want of facts, to ascertain the population of states by hearths, families, taxation, houses, marriages, baptisms, births, burials; by fuel consumed; by food eaten; by churches, by cobwebs.

As most rulers have been remiss in improving the science of government, and as many have considered that their dominion was secured by the ignorance of the people, and even by their exclusion from political topics ; no direct means of ascertaining the resources of nations, their opulence and population, existed ; nor was a knowledge of these circumstances attainable. Curious and patriotic individuals, therefore, adopted by necessity such expedients and substitutes as presented themselves. The first political œconomists in this country resorted to the taxes as some basis for their theories and calculations.

Sir W. Petty, who deserves to be first mentioned on account of the extent of his inquiries and his disposition to establish principles, was obliged [1] to resort to the hearth-money returns, in order to estimate the wealth, stock, trade, consumption : and having ascertained these as well as his opportunities afforded, he calculated the population. Taxation, however, can never determine the number of families ; and supposing the families enumerated, this could not establish the amount of the people ; for the individuals composing families vary in different nations, provinces, districts, even in the same town. In the Reports [2] of

---

[1] Sir W. Davenant's Works, vol. 1. p. 128.   [2] vol. 2. p. 49.

the Society for bettering the Condition of the Poor,
referring to the distressed in Hamburg, it is said:
" The whole number consisted of 7391 individuals,
and composed 3903 families." Here each family did
not contain two individuals. I may observe that this
mode of estimating the people by the hearths in far-
famed England is inferior to the Tartar census mentioned by Marco Polo whe [1], who says he had inspected the amount of the revenues and of the people of
the Great Khan,—that there were 160 toman of fires ;
that reckoning a family for each fire, every toman contained ten thousand families; that is, altogether,
1,600,000 families. He adds, that every household-
er had written on his door the names of all the inmates, the number of horses, &c. and that this was
the practice in all the cities of Mangi and Cathay.

Sir W. Petty was followed by Davenant, who [2] considered the Excise and the number of houses *no ill
measures* to form a judgement of the trade, wealth,
and abilities of a country. The supposition would
prove the infancy of the science, had he not stated [3]
that " the matters we have hitherto handled have been
in a manner entirely new, and such wherein very little
help could be had from books." It appears that this
political writer was also precluded from obtaining any
official information : he complains repeatedly [4] that
the commissioners of Excise refused him the inspection of authentic documents. In consequence, his

---

[1] Travels. Pinkerton's Travels, vol. 7. p. 156.
[2] Works, vol. 1. p. 40. [3] Ibid. vol. 2. p. 168.
[4] Ibid. vol. 1. p. 149. 293. vol. 2. p. 85—168.

conjectures were frequently erroneous. He says[1] himself, that by a computation founded on sir W. Petty's calculation, he estimated that the malt duty at sixpence a bushel would produce 1,050,000*l.*; but by another, and what he considers an improved computation, he rates it at 650,000*l.* Thus erred sir W. Petty and sir W. Davenant; the best computers, according to some[2], that England has produced—and so egregiously were they mistaken by their substituted and conjectural estimates.

It may be thought that, however authors might have erred respecting their conclusions on other topics of political œconomy, they must have approximated the truth when they calculated the population after having established the amount of the taxed houses in the country. On this assumption Davenant inferred[3] that the people from 1600 to the period when he wrote, increased nine hundred thousand. He states[4], that in 1685 there were 1,300,000 houses in the whole kingdom, of which those having one chimney amounted to 554,631. He states also that in 1795 there were in England 1,300,000 families, which he concludes comprehended seven millions of individuals.

The increase of houses being reputed a proof of an increased population, a decrease of houses has been assumed as proving the decline of the people. Under this apprehension Dr. Price[5] complains, "What a me-

---

[1] Works, vol. 1. p. 197.

[2] Price (on Annuities) said so of Davenant. p. 299. Davenant said the same of Petty. Works, vol. 1. p. 40.

[3] vol. 2. p. 3.   [4] vol. 1. p. 203.

[5] On Annuities : Supplement, &c. p. 299.

lancholy reverse has taken place since [the Restoration]! In 1759 the number of houses in England and Wales was 986,482, of which not more than 330,000 were cottages having less than seven windows. In 1766, notwithstanding the increase of buildings in London, the number of houses was reduced to 980,692. According to these accounts, then, our people have since the year 1690 decreased near a million and a half." The inadequacy of such modes of calculation is manifold. First, it is taken for granted that the taxed houses are all the houses : yet Price [1] himself noticed an enormous disparity between two surveys of London ; one making the amount of the houses of this metropolis 85,805, and the other 95,968. In the first the houses and the landlords assessed were assumed to be the same in amount; but many landlords held more than one house:—this is one of the many evils of indirect estimates.

Suppose, however, the number of houses ascertained, still this could afford only a progress towards the knowledge of the population of the state. By what number are the houses to be multiplied ? Decker [2] says seven ; for, having mentioned 1,200,000 houses, he computes the population at 8,400,000. Brakenridge says, six [3]; Scipione Mazzella [4], between five and six. Many authors state five, which is the catholic

[1] Note on Expectation of lives, &c. p. 142.
[2] On Trade, p. 11. Appendix.
[3] This was the ordinary computation in Davenant's time. Works, vol. 1. p. 19
[4] He says that the Neapolitan territories contain 2,600,000, and that the *fires* of all the provinces amount to 483,468. Storia de Napoli, p. 324.

multiplier at present. Gregory King[1] and Davenant, between four and five. What can be expected from such guessing, but impertinent authorities for transient dogmatism or continued error?

The number of houses affords no surety even for estimating the population of districts or towns of the same nation. Townsend[2] says, Barcelona has 10,267 houses, 20,128 families, and 94,880 persons : but he also mentions a town in Spain, and there are probably others, which has fewer people than houses. Houses are insufficient, considering them in reference to the same city : Who would calculate the inhabitants of the old town of Edinburgh by the inhabited houses of the new one? The houses of parishes or streets are insufficient premises for estimating adjoining parishes or contiguous streets. In Calmet's Buildings, in Mary le Bone, by a late report made to the House of Commons, it appeared that twenty-four small houses lodged nightly seven hundred persons. What disparity between these and the palaces in their neighbourhood, where half the year they are empty, or haunted by an old butler or a decayed waiting-woman!

Houses may increase without any equivalent increase of people. When the citizens of London added a house in the west part of the town to their city residence, London was not populated according to the increased ratio of the houses built. Houses may decrease without any proportional decrease of the people. When landlords destroyed many cottages in or-

[1] He supposed that a million of houses contained between four and five millions. Davenant's Works, vol. 2. p. 176.

[2] Travels in Spain, vol. 1. p. 86.

der to enlarge their domains, or to lessen the poor rates as they thought, they filled the poor houses, one of which contained the inmates of many cottages. Again, noble mansions have sunk under accumulated taxation, and smaller houses are decaying: yet this declension does not define the reduced population; for many householders have only moved into boarding houses:—the reduction of houses then is to be considered a wasting disease, not a mortality accomplished.

Houses may continue the same, and the people increase rapidly. In the Western Islands and in the Highlands, the inhabitants have increased from five to six and seven to each house; nor should I be surprised if the same now occurred in France. How many more people would the houses of the count of Blois and Chartres have lodged under a better government than the ancient monarchy?—It is said he had a house for every day in the year. Under equal laws, these with their territories, which were lost on one, would have been enjoyed by many. On the contrary, houses may continue undiminished, and the people disappear. When the French seized Holland, though no houses were beaten down, the population of Amsterdam fell from 220,000 to 190,000. In Megara[1], containing above a thousand houses, little more than one half of them are inhabited. Yet travellers and theorists argue from houses to population, when there may be more houses than families or even than individuals. The Jews at least guarded against this ab-

[1] Hobhouse, Travels, p. 479.

surdity in some measure, by limiting its extent, a habitation [1] being restricted at least to the dwelling of three persons.

Yet notwithstanding the disparity between houses and people, and their relative fluctuation according to times and seasons [2] in the same country, writers assume the amount of the population of foreign states by some loose conjecture concerning their houses. Van Egmont [3] said that Florence contained 8,800 houses, or 60,000 inhabitants. Boswell [4] stated that in 1729 there were in Corsica 40,000 families which paid a tax to the Genoese; thence he rates the people at 200,000 individuals. Eton [5] supposes that Constantinople never contained much more than 300,000 inhabitants. Mr. Hobhouse [6], assuming that the registry of the houses in 1796 was exact, concludes that 88,185 houses must have contained 500,000 inmates. Laressa says, Holland, by computation, contains 4000 houses and 20,000 inhabitants. Salt [7] computes the houses of Adowa to be 800, and their inhabitants 8000. Passing easterly, the same varying estimates are assumed. In Le Nouveau Voyage à Bassora [8], Ismid (Nicomedia) is said to have 50,000 houses and 300,000 inhabitants. Buchanan [9] says that the census from the Cutwal made the houses of Seringapatam

---

[1] Habitatio non est dicenda nisi tres simul inhabitaverint. Selden de J. G. &c. lib. 2. c. 5. p. 182.

[2] In Paris there is little emigration in summer; much more from London; and still more from Moscow.

[3] Travels, vol. 1. p. 32.　　　　　　[4] Travels, p. 164.

[5] Survey of the Turkish Empire, c. 7.

[6] Travels, p 889.　　　[7] Travels, p. 424.　　　[8] p. 9.

[9] Pinkerton, Travels, vol. 8. p. 605.

4,163, the families contained in them 5,499, and he multiplies the houses by five.

Thus, in this summary, we perceive the calculation by houses varies, without any sufficient grounds, from four to a house to ten; and these random calculations are sometimes made without attention or memory. I am pretty secure in this reproof; for it has happened that the same author in different parts of the same work varies his own calculations. Wallace[1] states, "Xenophon says that Athens contained about ten thousand houses, which on an average of five inhabitants to a house amounts to 50,000:" yet subsequently he writes[2], "According to Xenophon there were 10,000 houses or families in Athens; allowing therefore seven to each family, there were 70,000 Athenians who dwelt in the city:"—this is to calculate as Falstaff fought.

To assume the number of a people by the amount of their houses, is conjecture; but to infer the number of a people in one country by conjecturing the amount of their houses, and then to use this diluted guess to resolve the amount of the population of another country, is worse than romance. In some countries, a great portion of the people live without houses. Buchanan[3] speaks of a tribe in India who have neither houses nor cultivation, who catch birds and game which they barter for rice. Bruce speaks of a people who live one part of the year under trees, and in another on them. At Naples many sleep abroad. Even in London, according to Mr. Colquhoun, not a few are houseless.

[1] Note on page 55.　[2] p. 298.　[3] Pinkerton, vol. 8. p. 576.

Again, some houses are confined, as those of the Bös-
jesmans, which consist of a mat of rushes thrown over
two cross sticks; the houses of the Crim Tartars [1]
consist of a single room, as do those for the most part
at Nanking [2] and Pekin; yet these confined habitations frequently contain more inmates than large
dwellings. Again, in some towns houses are of one
story, in others of many. Bernier [3] remarks that the
houses of Delhi and Agra are low, and that at Lahore
they are lofty. Houses are also in some places piled
aloft; those at Rome were often seventy feet high [4],
yet those of Tyre were still more elevated [5]. Houses
of many stories are also differently appointed : in some
places each story contains a family or more, while at
Jonnina [6] the lower chambers are occupied by the
cattle; and perhaps for some such reason, at Messina [7]
the higher the lodging the more fashionable the residence. The houses even of Paris and London afford
no knowledge interchangeably of the population of
these cities [8].

To all these and many more considerations are to
be added the state of society and the habits and peculiarities of cities and states. Supposing that Olympio-

---

[1] Chardin : Pinkerton, vol. 9. p. 144.
[2] Nieuhoff: Pinkerton, vol. 7. p. 248. [3] Pinkerton, vol. 8. p. 208.
[4] Strabo says they were by law not to exceed this height. lib. 5.
p. 429.
[5] Domos altiores fieri quam Romæ. ibid. p. 530.
[6] Hobhouse, Travels, p. 68. [7] Cockburn's Travels, vol. i. p. 269.
[8] When Maitland wrote, the houses in London were 95,968,
when the population of London was not greater than that of Paris
at present. Yet by a new census the houses in Paris are 27,371,—
families, 227,252,—individuals, 715,595.

dorus and Publius Victor assigned a tolerable conjecture concerning the number of houses of ancient Rome, —what city now in Europe is so circumstanced as to afford any basis for a thinking man to estimate its population, when according to Herodian [1], Nero's palace reached the length of the city, and that some householders had many hundred [2] slaves? Yet authors have calculated the amount of the Roman people, and they have succeeded accordingly :—So they have the population of other towns. Erivan, says Chardin [3], is divided into nine wards, and has fifteen thousand houses, and as many shops in the market places, among which are three hundred inns, some so large as to lodge three hundred people : the inhabitants were formerly computed at 550,000. There is a peculiarity also which has not been sufficiently noted:—in some countries the marriage of children causes a separation of the family; while in others, as in Hindostan and China, two and even three generations sometimes continue to occupy the same dwelling :—these variations are extreme. Meares mentions a single house near Nootka Sound in which 800 persons ate and slept.

Population has been assumed not only by general taxation, but by poll or personal taxes. Josephus [4] says that he learned the amount of the people in Egypt by inspecting the books of the publicans who levied the tax. Davenant [5] used the same means, saying that the poll tax in the reign of William and Mary shows *something near the truth* the numbers

[1] lib. 4. p. 208.　　[2] Tacitus speaks of one who had 400.
[3] Pinkerton, vol. 9. p. 156.　　[4] De Bello Jud. lib. 2. c. 16.
[5] Works, vol. 1. p. 137.

and classes of society. Arthur Young [1] remarks on the mode of estimation by taxes, " that all computations by taxes must be erroneous; they may be below, but cannot be above the truth." This observation is only so far false, that in some oppressed countries taxes are anticipated and sometimes repeated in the same year. Besides, the return of the poll tax or any other tax in a fraudulent government will be accommodated to the service of the passing administration. It has been so in Russia; and the enumerations in 1723, 1743, 1783, are now abandoned as defective. Yet existing English writers adopt the extravagancies of Russian statements. Sir R. Wilson, who noticed that Suwarrow *officially* commanded 70,000 men when he led only 35,000 [2], estimates the population of Russia at fifty millions [3]. Tooke also exaggerates, though he admits that the returns are suspicious, from the small comparative mortality they assign; the deaths being to the living as 1 to 58, though in England they are as 1 to 40. Mr. Tooke's politics, however, harmonize with his philosophy; for among the felicities of this good and great domination, he says [4], " Another striking object is, the uncommonly favourable propor-

[1] Tour in Ireland, vol. 2. p. 199.

[2] Anderson, who wrote between Sir Robert's first and second pamphlet, states the population of the empire at 37,000,000. Were I not afraid of compromising the safety in some measure of some persons, I could relate an extraordinary instance of the passion of *one* Russian minister to swell the supposed numbers of the Russian people, by wishing to influence an historian to belie his narrative. The author communicated the anecdote to me at St. Petersburg, the day the proposal was made to him.

[3] This he has done in two pamphlets.

[4] History of Russia, vol. 1. p. 532.

tion which the males bear to the females, and which seems intended by *nature* as the foundation of the military grandeur of the Russian empire." Thus does this Christian minister use nature, that gadding queen, as loosely as Mr. Malthus. Before I quit this point, let me ask what causes this disproportion,—is it that more males are born? No, but more female children perish. Mr. Malthus [1] has noticed this in the registers of St. Petersburg, adding, " which is directly contrary to what has been observed in all other countries." Not so positively, for Salt makes the same remark relative to the children at the Cape of Good Hope. I should suppose that it was by no means so peculiar as these writers imagine; for though females may be less liable to death than males when treated with equal kindness, it seems probable that they should in every stage of life be less able to resist equal severity. What is the state of many Russian families? The landlord divorces the husband, and forces him from his home to towns, in order to earn the capitation tax; which accounts for the extraordinary male population of St. Petersburg. This capital counts two males for one female. Thus lordly rapacity renders families fatherless:—and may we not conclude that, in a common misery, the weaker, that is the female infants, are the greatest sufferers?

Population has been confidently estimated by marriages: but the proportion of the married and unmarried varies in every country; there is also the greatest difference respecting the ages at which parties unite in

[1] vol. 1. p. 357

different states; and this and other circumstances render great inequality in their productiveness. Marriages may increase, and do often increase, after a great mortality, as in Prussia in 1811; and it sometimes occurs that many marriages infer increased deaths. In Holland, when the marriages were 1 to 64 individuals, the deaths were 1 in 22 annually, according to the tables of Susmilch.

Those who calculate by marriages disregard numerous disturbances to their theory, even if the registry of marriages were accurate. They seem to think that a marriage is tantamount to so many animals *in esse.* Yet in countries where divorces are common, and widows and widowers repeat their connexions, many marriages are contracted by the same individuals, and comparatively few births, perhaps fewer than where divorces are not permitted: besides, marriages between old persons, when two crutches go to make one staff, are not more productive than the marriages mentioned by Marco Polo [1]: "If the son of a Tartar die before he has been married, and the daughter of another die also unmarried, the parents of the deceased meet together and celebrate a marriage between the dead."

To calculate people by their marriages infers extreme regularity in the intercourse of the sexes: yet it appears by the Annual Register [2], that in 1759 there were in London more foundlings than marriages, the former being 4969, the latter only 4089; and in ten years after, the foundlings in Paris were still more nu-

[1] Pinkerton, Travels, &c. vol. 7. p. 124.
[2] Annual Register 1759, p. 165.

merous than in London, being as 6426 to 4860. In
France also, the children of unmarried mothers before the revolution were 1 to 47, subsequently they
were 1 to 11. There may be a population without
marriages, and also without any connexion between
the sexes; as the Essenes, who recruited their numbers
by adoption; as the Dunkards [1], who, though consisting
of males and females, and having common property,
admit no sexual intimacy in their society : should any
of their body choose to marry, they are provided with
necessaries and dismissed. Corresponding to these
partly in their consequences are the unmarrying towns
and countries, whose stock of people is upheld by
drafts from places where men are more prolific or
breeding cheaper.

Many have calculated the number of individuals by
baptisms : yet in some cases this might prove the burials, as in China, where the missionaries performed
this pious office to perishing and abandoned infants,
as they said, "*pour leur sauver l'ame.*" And who could
now calculate the South Americans, except an adept
in the geometrical theory of Mr. Malthus, when the
Franciscan friars boasted they had baptized in Mexico
and the adjoining provinces in sixteen years six milli
ons of Indians? There are no grounds from this ce
remony to draw any conclusion. In Devonshire there is
1 marriage to 113 persons ; yet this does not produce
more baptisms than Derbyshire, which has not more
than 1 marriage to 137 persons: and it produces fewer
baptisms than Cornwall, which has only 1 marriage

---

[1] Annual Register 1759, p. 342.

to 141 persons. Rickman accounts for this by the marriages of the sailors in Plymouth and Portsmouth. So imperfect are baptisms for this purpose, that in the Population Abstracts [1] it has been thought necessary, in consequence of their supposed deficiency, to increase their number by introducing a prerogative arithmetic, and counting seven baptisms as eight children.

Calculations by births are much superior to the conjectures already mentioned. There were such registries at Athens and at Rome. In 1538 Cromwell [2], when he was vicar-general to Henry the Eighth, issued directions for framing such lists. In 1539 Francis the First [3] directed an ordinance to the curates of the several parishes of his kingdom for the same purpose, and registries soon became general throughout Europe. On these the most extensive and positive conclusions have been founded. Muret, on the decline of the births in Swisserland, insisted on the depopulation of that country; and hundreds have assumed that population has increased, because births had become more numerous. Nor is this the whole of the assumption: the decrease and increase have been calculated by guesses. This is the mode adopted by Monsieur Necker [4] in estimating the population of France: he first considered the registries of births as facts extensive as the births; he then multiplied them by 25 and three-quarters, which produced 24,802,580. Yet

[1] p. 24.
[2] Law Dictionary, vol. 2. p. 586.
[3] Causes Celèbres, t. 5. p. 89.
[4] Bibliothèque de l'Homme Publique.

Monsieur de Calonne at the same period [1], and a prime minister also, stated that the population of France exceeded this number by more than three millions. But why calculate by births only? To decide on this partial view, supposes that all who are born in different times or periods live generally to the same age. Yet it is ascertained as accurately as the births and deaths in France, that the chance of living has greatly increased since the revolution;—those who died under the old monarchy being to the living as 1 to 30, and after the revolution as 1 to 40, a fact pregnant with conclusions.

Is it not also obvious that a people may not increase, though the births increase? Catharine of Russia in her *Instructions*, &c. says, " The boors have generally speaking twelve, fifteen, and to twenty children at one marriage; but it rarely happens that the fourth part of them reach maturity." Even should they reach maturity, this would not ascertain a population equivalent to the births; for in some nations life is greatly prolonged, and in others abbreviated after the attainment of manhood, and this abbreviation may proceed from opposite causes. Young men are remarkably subjected to death in St. Petersburg, which is referred to the excessive use of ardent spirits. Life is also comparatively short, according to Turreau and Beaujour,

[1] Le calcul vérifié en 1787 est environ 28 millions. Tableau de l'Europe, p. 10. Mr. Malthus in his chapter on France, &c. perplexes himself and his readers by putting cases and arguing on them. How did it happen that he did not see the work just quoted, which would have decided the question at once?

in the United Provinces of America; which, if true, may arise from the higher premium for increased exertion, and in consequence the greater wear and tear of the laborious. It is, however, contradicted.

A double registry of births and deaths is more likely to afford exact information. Plato [1] recommended this; and he proposed that the names of the individuals should be erased from the registry as they died. It is obvious that the ground for any just conclusion must rest on the accuracy of the documents. Davenant [2] insists on the validity of the present duty (speaking of course of his own time) on marriages, births, and burials; yet he admits the imperfectness of the returns; and he adds, that " Mr. Gregory King, from his general knowledge of political arithmetic, has so corrected them as to form a more distinct and regular scheme of the inhabitants in England, than peradventure was ever made concerning the people of any country." This is extravagant, though Mr. G. King possessed considerable sagacity, and drew admirable results from scanty and imperfect materials.

Suppose the births and deaths minutely specified; these could only express the amount of the population of a town or country which neither received recruits nor admitted emigration, or which received in return people equivalent to its issues. A country or district the emigrants from which were many, as from the Spanish provinces which principally supplied South America with Spaniards, would appear to have more people by the registry of births than it really possess-

[1] De Legibus, lib. 6. p. 877.　　　[2] Works, vol. 1. p. 137.

ed; as a country the people of which was supported by the introduction of foreigners, would appear by the deaths to have fewer inhabitants than in truth it contained: and these errors would increase with the comparative excess. How weak then is Gibbon's lamentation—that no one had left an account of the deaths and births at Rome, as by them, he inferred, the population of Rome might be explained! Rome was so peculiarly situated when it became the metropolis of the world, that these particulars could not have afforded any reasonable approach to a vague generality;—the perpetual resort from the provinces; the many domiciliated foreigners; the multitude of slaves who did not breed, and of freemen who abstained from marriage—utterly excluded the population of this city from being illustrated by any records of births and deaths. In all cases the double entry of births and deaths must prove imperfect; their deficiency is enormously exhibited by a relation from Thucydides[1]. The Athenians, in order to hallow Delos, passed a law that no one should be permitted to bring forth or to die in Delos, but that the parturient and perishing should be removed to Rhenea. It is clear that a registry in Delos would during the continuance of this custom exhibit neither births nor deaths; and of course were such accounts the only authority for estimating population, Delos would be reputed entirely depopulated, while the people of Rhenea, as the births or deaths of the transferred Delians were alternately more or less, would appear to have increased or decreased, though in fact

---

[1] lib. 3. p. 242.

neither the births nor deaths of the Delians could have altered its population.

Writers have indulged their genius in many other modes of estimating the numbers of people in countries and cities. To the quantity of coal consumed in London some have resorted. If so, the population of the capital doubled from the beginning to the middle of the eighteenth century; for in 1762, 570,774 chaldrons of coals were imported into London [1], and only half as much fifty years preceding. If the comsumption of coals be a criterion, no one existed when timber was the only fuel; which opinion probably would be little more absurd than the terrors of government concerning the deleterious quality of smoke, which induced the ministry of the reign of Edward the First to forbid by proclamation the burning of coals [2].

Some calculate the progress of London population by the oxen, cows, calves, sheep, lambs, pigs, slaughtered for its support: others by the grain consumed; as if there was no difference in the use or abuse of grain in different periods. An Indian political œconomist insisted that formerly Seringapatam contained 500,000 inhabitants in the time of Tippoo, from the consumption of grain in that city. Buchanan [3] treats the estimate contemptuously—yet how much more accurate is his own?

Things the most remote, the most absurd, and the most opposite, have been used in surmising the amount of population—the increase of gin-shops and the decrease of churches have been mentioned. Smith in

---

[1] Annual Register 1763, p. 64. [2] Stowe's London, vol. 1. p. 2.
[3] Pinkerton, &c. vol. 8. p. 605.

the Ancient and Present State of Kerry[1], infers that the inhabitants of Ireland have greatly diminished, because the barony of Corkagenny contained formerly twenty parish churches, and that at present there only remain nine places of worship. If churches are to direct to similar estimates, how sadly has London become depopulated! When Fitzstephen wrote, London contained thirteen great churches beside one hundred and twenty-six parish churches; yet it is questionable if Mr. Vansittart, in order that "his memory may outlive his life half a year," could raise as many churches for the existing people of London, as, proportionably to its population, consecrated this metropolis in the time of Fitzstephen. If churches direct population estimates, how lamentably has Paris declined since the revolution! Eustace sighs over the churches which sympathized with the fall of the old monarchy; for from 222 they declined to 39,—which I may remark is the exact amount of the churches in modern Athens, where the people are scarcely ten thousand souls. Indeed there is not a more wretched mode of estimating mankind, or their morality[2], than by these buildings. Moses, according to Josephus[3], considered that the chosen people had but one temple and one altar;—yet how miraculous their multitudes! while in Nepaul, according to Colonel Kirkpatrick, "there are nearly as many temples as houses, and as many idols as inhabitants." Such are the estimates on theo-

[1] p. 172.   [2] The Abyssinians are the most church-building people, individually, existing. Bruce's Travels, vol. 3. p. 642.—Their virtues are few.   [3] lib. 4. c. 8.

logical principles:—while Heliogabalus [1] inferred the
magnitude of Rome from ten thousand weight of cobwebs which had been collected in that capital.

CHAPTER VII.

Actual census at Rome—at Athens. Ignorance and errors of Mr.
Mitford in consequence of his hatred of Republics, exposed. Er-
rors of Mr. Hume respecting the Athenian census.

YET all countries have not been destitute of actual
enumerations of their people. Servius Tullius made
a very accurate census. He divided the classes of
citizens according to their age[2]. *Pueritia* included all
under seventeen years; *Juventus*, those from seventeen
to forty-six; and *Senectus*, all those more advanced in
life. By this census the people amounted to 85,300[3].
It was extensive, minute, and so accurate that it was a
document of great authority at Rome[4]. The census was
repeated when Valerius was a second time consul; then
the people amounted to 130,000[5]. The same number comprehended the population under Appius Claudius[6]. A census was taken at each lustrum; and
Dion of Halicarnassus mentions successively 313,823
390,736—394,336—450,000 : such was the progression of Roman people, who however afterwards declined to 137,000, the historian says, in consequence
of their repeated defeats by Hannibal. Beside the enu-

---

[1] Lampridius in Vitam Heliogabali, c. 26.
[2] Taylor, Civil Law, p. 121.
[3] Dion of Halicarnassus, lib. 4. c. 22.   [4] Ibid. lib. 4. c. 5.
[5] Ibid. lib. 5. c. 20.   [6] lib. 6. c. 63.

meration at the lustrum, it appears from Polybius [1] that there was an annual enrolment of all those who attained the military age. Perhaps I should observe that the census did not comprehend children or women: for though Dion of Halicarnassus specifies the number of Sabine women who were ravished, and though the first census of the people under Romulus comprised every individual,—the colony consisting probably of fighting men only,—yet the same expressions are used respecting the population of Rome, after the Romans had families, and refer solely to those able to bear arms [2]. The colony under Romulus, says the historian [3], consisted of 3000 foot and 300 horse; and he speaks of the people at his decease amounting also to 46,000 foot and 1000 horse.

I now proceed to make some observations on the population of Athens. It is interesting in itself, for the Athenians are most interesting in all their relations; it suits the subject; and he who writes on man prospectively to his advancement, and does not aid modern experience by ancient knowledge, fails in half his duty. Besides, the errors entertained respecting the population of Athens are many. It has been frequently said that there had been only two census of the Athenian people: they were numerous, and it is remarkable that in various circumstances the population continued nearly the same. Philochorus [4] in the scholia on Pin-

---

[1] Ποιωσι δε τατο καθ' εκαϛον ενιαυτον. lib. 6. c. 17. p. 641.

[2] As Εν ηϐη. Dion Halicarnassus, lib. 5. c. 20.—πολιται και τας εν ηϐη παιδας. Ibid. lib. 9. c. 36.—των εχοντων την ϛρατευσιμον ηλικιαν, lib. 11. c. ult.   [3] lib. 2. c. 16.

[4] Petit, Leges Att. p. 551.

dar mentions a census in the ninth Olympiad, in the time of Cecrops, amounting to 20,000 citizens. When Demetrius Phalereus ruled [1], the Athenians amounted to 21,000, the μετοικοι to 10,000, and both possessing 400,000 slaves. Herodotus [2] states the Athenians at 30,000; in which he probably includes the μετοικοι and citizens: if so, the Athenians were equally numerous during all these periods. Mr. Mitford, however, insists that in the age of Pericles the Athenians were only 14,040. Unfortunately, however, for this historian [3],—the enemy of the people and the eulogist of tyrants and the Pisistratidæ,—this deficiency was not a depopulation. It is true, the people in the time of Pericles were stated to be 19,000 [4], and at the same period it is also stated that they were 14,040: but though the latter enumeration succeeded a pestilence, it does not appear that the people suffered considerably,—so active is freedom to recruit its losses: for the apparent reduction of the people arose from enforcing a law against foreigners and interlopers at a time of suspicion and danger. On this occasion five thousand persons, who were not born of Athenian citizens by father and mother, were disfranchised. Exactness and impartiality were so sacredly observed, that even Lysias was degraded to the class of μετοικοι because, though he had been naturalized by six thousand citizens, he was not accepted by the senate previously to his admission by the people [5]. Twenty thousand, or nearly that number, seem to have been the amount

---

[1] Athenæus Deipnos. lib. 6. p. 272.   [2] lib. 5. c. 97.
[3] History of Greece, vol. 1. p. 248. first edit.
[4] Plutarch. in Periclem.   [5] See Auger, Discours Prelim. p. 8.

of the Athenians at the death of the orator Lycurgus[1], who bequeathed fifty drachmæ to every citizen. His fortune at his decease amounted to 160 talents :—estimating the talent at 60 minæ, and the mina at 100 drachmæ, and 50 drachmæ to every citizen,—160 talents would afford legacies to 19,200 individuals. Demosthenes also, in his Oration against Aristogiton, sums the Athenians at 20,000.

Mr. Mitford is not only in error, but, in his dread of democracies, he slanders the Athenian people and their republic. He says, " of all forms of government democracy is not only the most capricious but the most selfish." And his reason for this dogma is, that Athens "consisting of less than 30,000 citizens should hold extensive and populous territories under subjection[2]." Now this same number 30,000 is the estimate of the British who govern India, and these 30,000 hold 60,000,000 not as tributaries but as serfs and vassals. What does he mean by the selfishness of democracies? Consider the financial arrangements of Athens. Here the poorer classes were wholly exempted from taxation; the burthen fell on the rich, or rather on the richest[3]: while in monarchies, as in France before the revolution, the Athenian policy was reversed, for the nobles were exempted from contributing to the state. At Athens it was esteemed honourable, not onerous, to officiate for a free people. At Athens there were no sinecurists, no pluralists ; no one could even hold twice the same magistracy[4], nor two offices in the same

[1] Plutarch. Moral. p. 453. Vitæ Orator.　　[2] vol. 2. p. 102.
[3] Demosthenes adv. Phœnippum, p. 1023.
[4] Petit, Leg. Att. p. 221.

year. Never did it occur to them that state officers should possess salaries in order to live in splendour: on the contrary, chief magistrates and ministers were ordered to abstain from distinctions in dress, equipage, and entertainment[1]. Archons, judges, treasurers, tax-gatherers, generals or ambassadors, all in every responsible and exalted situation were paid moderately when they officiated, and when they retired from office of course they ceased to receive the public money.

Mr. Mitford says that democracies are most selfish and capricious. Yet the Athenians twice abandoned Athens and Attica, and beheld the ruin of their delightful city, sooner than acknowledge Hippias[2] and the great king. This historian may dwell on popular caprice; yet the Athenians under unexampled difficulties were ruled by Pericles during fifteen years: for the people, said Xenophon[3], will freely obey those, of whose virtue and ability they are assured. Mr. Mitford also descants on *democratical extravagance:* yet the common theme of reproach by the English court critics is the parsimony of the American government. The Athenians were neither parsimonious nor prodi-

---

[1] Αλλ' ισος και ομαλος εσθητι και διαιτη και τροφαις. Plutarch. Moral. p. 40.

[2] This Hippias was not selfish, forsooth; yet he exasperated the Persians, conducted them to Marathon, and in order to resume tyranny under Xerxes desolated his country. In Xerxes we see the magnanimous allies;—in Hippias, Louis XVIII. I may here state an error of Mitford respecting the taking of Athens. He says that all the Athenians that were taken at the assault were put to the sword, vol. 1. p. 393. They were not; and 500 of them were afterwards redeemed from slavery by the Samians. Herod. lib. 9. c. 99.

[3] Opera, p. 764.

gal. Could they be prodigal who adorned the world with eternal monuments of their genius? The fragments of their artists are the models, the admiration and despair, of modern genius :—such were their expenses. For all useful purposes, till a king trespassed on their dominion, they austerely husbanded and appropriated the public treasure :—this people, this sovereign people, resigned their special revenues from the mines of Laurium to equip a fleet. Mr. Mitford speaks of Athenian extravagance, while he details the vast sums stored in their treasury ;—six thousand talents in money [1], 1,200,000 pounds sterling. Thus he declaims to the British, whose government is most lavish even while it labours with insolvency. Mr. Mitford, in his aversion to freedom, blunders against all sufferance :—he reviles Athens for the sin of democracy, while he perverts facts to prove that it was not a democracy; for he suggests that the active citizens must have attained the age of thirty, " before which," he says, " they seem not to have been legally competent to vote in the assemblies of the people." On this occasion he praises Dr. Gillies for having " avoided the important question,—at what age the Athenians became competent to vote in the assembly of the people." An author's merit in avoiding an important question implicated with his subject, is rather more doubtful than the paint-

[1] Vol. 2. p. 169. Mr. Mitford has laboured successfully, in the opinion of those who have introduced his History to students, to prove that a tyrant was a bon homme. Yet this author is enraged that the king of Sparta should be obliged to submit to the *tyrannical authority* of the Ephori. (vol. 2. p. 500.) Therefore pre-eminence is odious in five persons elected by the people, but legitimate and good if exercised by an hereditary officer.

er's skill, who, unable to express a passion, concealed the head of the most afflicted character on his canvass.

The mystery seems to me not very involved. The Athenians enjoyed privileges according to their years. At twenty years old, to use an English term, Athenian citizens were *of age*, they were freed from guardianship[1], they might will and even adopt[2]; at twenty they were liable to be enrolled for foreign wars. At this age also they were, I suppose, enabled to vote; for their names were inserted εις τον ληξιαρχικον γραμματειον[3]—and the ληξιαρχοι especially superintended the assemblies of the people, they directed the scrutiny of those entitled to vote, fined those who did not attend, *atque funiculum minio tangentes, per lictores, eos qui in foro erant ad concionem pellebant*[4].

The disparity between the Athenian citizens and those domiciliated at Athens was not by any means so extreme as Mr. Mitford imagines: 30,000 were not the ruling population, supposing the citizens 30,000; for those included only, as I have said, those of the military age, who were not the fourth of the citizens. Dion of Halicarnassus[5], having mentioned a census of the Romans των εν ηδη πολιτων which amounted to 110,000, added, that the females, boys, domestic servants, &c. were three times greater. The free Athenians of a military age represented families which contained, according to the ordinary estimate, 120,000;

---

[1] Petit, Leg. Att. p. 493.   [2] Ibid. p. 140.
[3] Æschines in Timarchum, p. 275. Lycurgus adversus Leocratem, p. 157. Oratores Vet. Græci.
[4] Julius Pollux, Onomasticon, lib. 8. c. 9. p. 401.
[5] lib. 9. c. 25.

and surely they were not less: for Thucydides speaks
of the Athenians having 13,000 heavy-armed soldiers;
and that the light-armed, the young, and the old able
to bear arms, with the μετοιωκν to guard the city,
amounted to 16,000 more; beside 1,200 cavalry and
1,600 archers [1]. If, then, the military citizens were
30,000, the Athenian citizens (multiplying 30,000 by
4) were one-fourth of the whole population.

As Mr. Mitford would reduce the free Athenians
to a tenth, in his detestation of democracies; Mr.
Hume, in opposition to Mr. Wallace, who rested his
argument in favour of the populousness of ancient nations mainly on the multitude of slaves in ancient
times, insisted that the census which rated the slaves
at 400,000 was faulty by a cypher, and that 400,000
should have been 40,000 [2]; but the Greeks did not
count by cyphers. The words of Athenæus, to whose re-

---

[1] lib. 2. p. 109. And he afterwards says that the Athenians had
10,000 heavy armed foot and 3000 at Potidæa (p. 119). These were
Athenians. We read also of their having two hundred and fifty
galleys at sea. Thucydides, lib. 2. p. 182. Suppose each of them
had 200 men, this would give a population of 50,000. The ship
manned by Cleomenes carried exactly 200 men. Herodotus, lib.
8. c. 17. There is another mode of conjecturing the crew of an
Athenian galley, by the pay of a *Lacedemonian* galley. Persia granted 30 minæ to each trireme, and this was three oboli a man. Xenophon, Helen. lib. 1. p. 441. This would give, at 6 oboli to a drach-
ma and 100 drachmæ to a mina, three oboli to 200 men for thirty
days. In the time of Homer, ships carried from 120 to 50 men at
least :—these are the highest and lowest, and, if I mistake not, the
only numbers assigned to ships in his *catalogue*.

[2] Mr. Hume should have recollected that, when the affairs of
the Athenians became disastrous in Sicily, Thucydides says more
than twenty thousand slaves passed over to the enemy, the greater

port both writers allude, are οικετων δε μυριαδας τεσσα-
ρακοντα.

Hume's reasoning is still more erroneous than his
emendatory criticism : indeed it is a combination of
inadvertencies, of false reasoning and direct contradiction. Having assumed, after Athenæus, that the Athenians consisted of 21,000 citizens, and 10,000 μετοικοι or denizens, and having reduced the 400,000
slaves to 40,000, he argues, " Now these being but the
fourth of the inhabitants, the free Athenians were by
this account 84,000, the strangers 40,000, and the
slaves (calculating by the smaller number, and allowing that *they married and propagated at the same rate
with freemen*") were 160,000, and the whole of the inhabitants 284,000 :"—a number surely large enough.
The other number, 1,720,000, makes Athens larger
than London and Paris united. In this passage,
Hume assumes, first, that those ancient authors who
discoursed on the population of Athens spoke of the
city or town only ; but in ancient language *city* was
synonymous with state. Bryant [1] remarked that Troy
in Homer is used occasionally as a town or a district.
This narrow and enlarged mode of speaking was customary in all the Grecian commonwealths ; and this
partially accounts for those errors respecting the population of towns and their extent, so frequent among
authors. I may add, it is the cause of the blunders
and supposed hopeless difficulties of travellers and

part of whom were manufacturers, και ανδραποδων πλεον η δυω
μυριαδες ηυτομολιηκεσαν, και τουτων πολυ μερος χειροτεχναι. lib. 7.
p. 507.

[1] Dissertation, &c. p. 132.

critics respecting the extent of Babylon : they cannot understand how Babylon could extend to an area of eighty square miles, according to Strabo : but Babylon signified a city and a district, it was rated as one third of the Persian empire— supplying the great king and his army for four months [1]. Aristotle's observation in his Republic [2] is explanatory : he says, " City has different interpretations :—a city is not comprised in the same walls, for Peloponnesus might be so surrounded as perhaps was Babylon, which was rather a nation than a city, some of its inhabitants not having heard of the surrender of the city till the third day." Besides, What is more common than to use the name of a town for the state, when (as Venice) the name of the chief city and the country is synonymous ? Athens in the census meant Attica.

Hume, in the passage just quoted, also assumes that *the slaves married and propagated at the same rate with freemen.* Yet this acute and considerate author, in the ardour of his attack on Wallace, argues effectually in the same essay [3], that slaves neither married nor propagated : his words are, " The ancients talk so frequently of a fixed, stated portion of provisions assigned to each slave, that we are naturally led to conclude that slaves lived almost all single." He says again, " Xenophon in his Œconomics, where he gives directions for the management of a farm, recommends a strict care and attention of laying the male and female slaves at a distance from each other ; he seems not to suppose that they are ever married." There is

[1] Herodotus, lib. 1. c. 192, 193.   [2] lib. 3. c. 3.
[3] Populousness of Ancient Nations.

then no reason, from these objections, to impeach the census of Athens inserted in Athenæus, which, with the breeding citizens and denizens and the comparatively barren slaves, gave a population to Attica of five or six hundred thousand persons. Athens abounded with artisans, was commercial, eminently maritime. Herodotus [1] mentions that at the battle of Salamis the Athenians had 127 ships, which were reinforced by 53. Thucydides [2] also speaks of their fleet at another period, which consisted of 250 vessels. Attica formed nearly a triangle, whose sides were sixty miles long, with a base of forty miles; it was also peninsular [3]. These circumstances justify the amount of the population assigned to it by the ancient census.

Beside the census alluded to, there were accurate registries of the years and pretensions of the people from infancy onward. The seven ages are of Grecian origin [4]; and these divisions in some measure directed the periods of each man's special registry or enrolment. Children were registered in infancy, they were inserted in the *fratria* from the third to the seventh year of their age, according to Petit's reading [5]. At

[1] lib. 8. c. 1. A very few of the sailors were Platæans, who soon left the fleet. c. 34.　　　　　　　　　　　　[2] lib. 2. p. 182.

[3] Strabo says it was called ακτη, i. e. *littus*, because much of the land stretched along the sea. lib. 9. p. 713. Apollodorus said nearly the same. Stephanus de Urbibus, p. 55.

[4] They were thus distinguished by the Greek interpreter of Ptolemy de Judiciis, p. 166. Βρεφος, παις, μειρακιον, νεος, ανηρ, πρεσβυτης, γερων. Or according to Julius Pollux, Παιδιον, παις, μειρακιον, νεανισκος, ανηρ, γερων, πρεσβυτης. Onomasticon, lib. 2. c. 1.

[5] Leg. Attic. p. 150. Perhaps the registry by the κηφυκης mentioned by Andocides (Oratores Veteres, t. 2. p. 16.) referred to this.

18 there was another registry [1], when the youth began to learn the rudiments of war within the frontiers. At 20, as I have stated, they were registered by the λεξ-ιαρχοι. They were also distinguished at different periods of their age by repeated inscriptions.

But it was not merely the population of the state of Athens, but also the property of the state in its mass and subdivisions, that was ascertained. Solon [2] calculated the amount, and distributed the people into classes, who supported the commonwealth according to their opulence. There was also a continued registry of patrimonial property [3]. All these things enabled their writers and orators to form just estimates; as they possessed a summary of the stock and numbers of this consummate people, whose institutions are a perpetual inheritance to all nations who dare love liberty, eloquence, and the arts.

CHAPTER VIII.

Confusion and contradictions from want of census in European nations, particularly in England and Ireland.—Census of 1801 and 1811.—Domesday book a model.—Though census have been made for wasteful or ambitious purposes, necessary ;—should be frequent and elaborate, including land, in tillage, &c.—Guesses of writers concerning territorial extent of Great Britain, the cultivated land, horses, their consumption, &c.

IMPERFECT as generally are the traditional notices of classical antiquity respecting population, and other

---

[1] Julius Pollux, lib. 8. c. 9.
[2] Scholia in Thucydid., lib. 3. p. 181. Plutarch. Solon.
[3] Patrimonium et ληξις appellatur. Julius Pollux, lib. 8. c. 9. p 401.

greatquestions connected with political œconomy, they
are elaborate and exact in comparison to subsequent
accounts of many European nations. When Hume
wrote those Essays which. with few exceptions, exhibit such rare exactness and sagacity, he was authorized
in saying, " We know not the number of any European
state, or even city, at present." Hence the most extraordinary positions, and the utmost absurdity and confusion, assailed the political student. Let us state
some of these in respect to London and England.

In 604, according to Bede, London was very populous, and the emporium of many nations coming by
sea and land. In the reign of Stephen, the historian
Fitzstephen mentions, that at a muster of the Londoners there were 20,000 horsemen armed, and 60,000
footmen. In 1606, Coke [1] in his prosecution of Gar-
net stated that " London had more than 500,000
souls within her liberties." Yet in 1631, according to
a survey made by order of the privy-council, the inhabitants of London were 130,178, which Price [2] says
was taken a few years after a plague that had swept
off a *quarter* of the people. Sir John Treby [3] in his
speech for the city of London, on a quo warranto, in
1683, stated, " The city of London is the metropolis of
the kingdom, and consists of about fifty thousand citizens and inhabitants."

With regard to the population of England, the difficulties and contradictions are equally confounding.
Coke said in the house of commons, that when he
was in commission with chief-justice Popham, there

---

[1] State Trials, vol. 1. p. 286. Irish edit.
[2] Annuities, &c. p. 146.   [3] State Trials, vol. 3. p. 622.

was a survey made of all the people of England, and that there were 900,000 of all sorts. This account, Hume [1] seems to think, obtains some credit from Murdens statement, taken from the Salisbury collections of the military force of the nation when Britain was menaced by the Spanish armada; in which the able-bodied men are rated at 111,513, who with those armed and trained amount to 236,603. He also adds, " Harrison says, that in the musters taken in the years 1574 and 1575, the men fit for service amounted to 1,172,674 [2]; yet it is believed that a full third was omitted. Such uncertainty and contradiction are there in all these accounts." This is true: yet I imagine Hume has in part increased the inconsistencies of which he complains. When Coke spoke of 900,000 of all sorts, he meant men of all sorts able to bear arms; and the estimate alluded to respecting the forces to oppose the Spanish armada, were men actually serving; which Hume indirectly admits. Besides, the 236,603 were only a portion of those who were serving [3]; for the document omitted the whole array of some counties, and also the forces raised on the borders and in Yorkshire, which were reserved for the north. Coke's and Harrison's accounts, then, seem not materially to differ in their gross amount.

[1] History, vol. 5. p. 482.

[2] This number corresponds with that given by Sir W. Raleigh. In 1583, he says, on a view of all the men in England, 1,172,000 were capable of bearing arms. Invention of Shipping.

[3] There is an abstract of numbers of the armed men in the counties through the kingdom, taken in the year 1588, in the Annual Register for 1760, p. 179; but it is so erroneous in parts, that it is unintelligible for any just opinion.

If the government of Great Britain has acted so indifferently towards its people, as to be ignorant and heedless of their amount, it might be instructive, perhaps, to inquire the motive of the omission. Some have hinted that, with so religious a ministry, the curse on king David for numbering the people must have had a considerable influence; which curse, by the by, Bodin[1] says, God inflicted on David, because the king neglected to pay to God (that is the clergy) two drachmas of silver for each person numbered. It may be so; but I rather suppose the British ministry were withheld not so much by the Jewish as the Egyptian theology. The Egyptians, says Plutarch[2], adore the blind mouse, because their priests hold that darkness preceded light.

To these remarks there are very gratifying exceptions. In 1801 a return was made of all the people in Great Britain, who according to the survey amounted to 10,942,646. In 1811 the census was repeated, according to which the people had increased to 12,596,803: and apportioning the increase to the divisions of the island, it appears that in the interval from 1801 to 1811 England's population had increased in ten years fourteen and a half per cent., and Wales and Scotland thirteen per cent. Those who believed, or seemed to believe, that increase of people proves an amelioration of their circumstances, (which is generally true, except, as in Ireland, where the introduction of a cheaper food supplies more with the means of a mere existence; or as in England, where capital was

---

[1] De la République, liv. 5. p. 504.   [2] Moralia, p. 541.

expended as income,) assumed or laboured to confirm the veracity of the two returns. Mr. Rose [1] spoke of the whole imputed increase as demonstrated. But the falsehood of the imputed multiplication of the people between the two periods is proved by Mr. Rickman, who digested the population returns. He says, " the population of Great Britain must exceed the number of persons in the above summary, (of 1801) inasmuch as there are some parishes from which no returns have been received." There are other acknowledged deficiencies. I imagine also that there was some apparent increase of numbers in consequence of the ability acquired by a repetition of the survey, and by an abatement of the people's reserve in communicating the amount of their families. These causes operated in parts of Ireland ; in the county of Armagh [2] there was an apparent increase in less than one year (from 1813 to 1814) of twenty per cent. That the people in Great Britain did increase considerably in the interval stated, is manifest : I only object to the amount of the difference between the first and second returns as deciding the measure of that increase.

[1] Speech in parliament, January 17. 1816.

[2] In 1813, barony of Armagh

	1813		1814
barony of Armagh	29,958	in 1814	32,708.
Upper Fews	17,979	———	19,617.
Lower Fews	16,699	———	17,294.
Upper Orien	23,358	———	24,104.
Lower Orien	19,437	———	19,864.
	107,431		113,587.

The other three baronies made no second return, they having complied *formally* with the act of parliament ; so that the appa-

The British government, having been so long inconsiderate respecting its population, has of course been still more careless concerning that of its dependencies; and the consequences have corresponded with this neglect;—calculations and estimates and houses and taxes and births and marriages and deaths have fluttered in every direction. Read the following summary of guesses: Sir William Petty in 1641 calculated the inhabitants of Ireland at 1,460,000 : and that by the rebellion in 1652 they were reduced to 850,000, "an awful lesson," says Dr. Ledwich [1], " to the disturbers of publick tranquillity." This gentleman should have improved the innuendo, and added, that this lesson was forgotten occasionally by some of the Irish, and perpetually by the British administration in that country. Sir William Petty [2], in the sequel of his calculations, stated that the population of Ireland in 1672 was 1,100,000, and that in 1688 it was 1,200,000. Captain South in 1695 fixed the numbers of the Irish at 1,034,102. In 1740 an abstract was made of the Protestant population by the supervisors of hearth-money, for then the Catholics were accounted naught: and as this abstract was formed from the houses, and these houses were calculated to contain six persons each, I may omit the sequel. Dr. Brakenridge [3] supposed that, when he wrote (the middle of the last century), Ireland contained a whole million, and that hereafter it might possibly contain two millions

rent increase of 6,156 persons in less than twelve months, proceeded from five of the eight portions which compose this county.

[1] Survey of Aghaboe, p. 73.　　　　　[2] Political Arithmetic.
[3] Philosophical Transactions, vol. 49.

more. Mr. Bush, from various enumerations of houses, and multiplying each by 6½, drew what conclusions he pleased [1]. Adam Smith[2], who wrote about this time, said generally : Ireland contains more than two millions. Chalmers, author of the *Estimate*, states the Irish (in 1791) at 4,193,000. Dr. Beauford, in his *Memoir* in 1792, fixes them at 3,733,320; and Barrow [3], in his remarks on Chinese population, talks of three millions and a half. Authors who have written still later are equally discordant on this subject. Mr. Newenham calculates the Irish at 5,400,000 [4]; Mr. Rickman,[5] at 4,000,000; Colquhoun, at 4,500,000; while the orthodox Dr. Duigenan, (the representative of the Irish Protestant church in parliament, and the champion of Protestant ascendancy,) calculating by houses and persons and fractions, insisted in one of his anticatholic effusions, that Ireland did only contain, and could only contain, 3,060,000 [6]. Mr. Gray, the last writer on this subject[7], sums the people of Ire-

---

[1] I shall state the years and houses ; they may serve the reader.

Houses in 1754	395,439
1767	424,646
1777	448,426
1785	474,322
1788	621,484

[2] Wealth of Nations, b. 5. c. 3. p. 465.   [3] p. 578.

[4] His calculation is nearest the truth : yet from my own knowledge of the census of some of the counties, and from a communication which Sir John Newport favoured me with, the population is probably above six millions.

[5] He says, at the beginning of the last century the population of Ireland was 1,500,000, and that in 111 years it increased to 4,000,000.

[6] Of whom, he said, 1,500,000 were not Roman Catholics.

[7] Since that, Lord Donoughmore, in his speech on Catholic affairs

land roundly at 4,000,000. Amidst all this confusion, a bill was passed for an actual census of the inhabitants in Ireland, and returns were made in 1813. The Irish minister said these were not sufficiently accurate to be presented to parliament. In consequence, the returns were renewed the year following : since that time no questions, I believe, have been asked in parliament respecting the result of these surveys ; and certainly no authentic publication has been made to that effect. Thus the government of Ireland, which had been hitherto barren, at last *felt unusual throes* ; but, unlike its great prototype in Milton, its first effort was abortive, and its only offspring was still-born.

All this is strange, in a country proud of its liberty and knowledge, and under administrations who pretended (for we must speak in the past tense) to direct the tone of thinking in Europe. Some governments no doubt have countenanced their inertness; as in Tonquin [1], where it is said the numbering a populous nation is considered impracticable ; and other kings have equalled our executive in the difficult and indirect methods to divine the amount of their subjects. As Arianthus, who, wishing to ascertain the number of the Scythians [2], ordered every one of his subjects to bring him the point of an arrow, of which he made a vessel so large that it contained 600 amphoræ.

All the Asiatic nations have not been so stupid as the Tonquiners. China has possessed from time immemo-

in 1817, stated the Catholics at 4,000,000, Dissenters, 500,000, Established Church, 500,000.

[1] Pinkerton, Travels, &c. vol. 9. p. 754.

[2] Herodotus, lib. 4. c. 81.

rial an elaborate census; it is specified in Duhalde. Turpin[1] says that there is a census in Siam every year; and the moderate amount of the people taken by him from such documents, favours their accuracy. The Mahometans also, when they conquered Persia, made a very accurate census of that country ; so did the Romans of their provinces, and Hearne[2] likens their Itineraries to Domesday-book.

With Domesday-book before the king and the hereditary counsellors of the crown, (and the representatives of the people, as they are called,) England and its dependencies continued without a general census. Yet the government could direct a census of the Protestants in Ireland in 1740, and of the Catholics[3] in England in 1746. An enlarged or liberal census, however, they could not entertain. Yet the Earl of Clarendon[4], when viceroy in Ireland in the reign of James the Second, solicited that the number of tenements in Ireland should be ascertained by application to the clergy through the bishops. Yet this was resisted. Then why should Mr. Hobhouse affect surprise that " the Mahometans never make any efforts to ascertain the exact number of inhabitants in any town or district?" Until lately, the British government in this respect was as unenterprising as the Turks, and very inferior to modern Christian despotism. Howard says that there is annually a census of the population of Na-

---

[1] Pinkerton, Travels, vol. 9. p. 575. [2] Discourses, &c. p. 123.

[3] In the Annual Register 1767, p. 107, it is said, this was done by the clerk of the house. There was another direction to the same effect from the bishops to the clergy.

[4] Annual Register 1763, p. 253.

ples[1] : yet it has happened that the British government was less alive to the amount of the people of the British empire than his Neapolitan majesty was to the number of his subjects, or a Russian lord to the poll of his boors. At last, an accurate and laborious survey of the population of Dublin was made by the Rev. Mr. Whitelaw[2] in 1798 : this suggested the possibility and propriety of a general survey of the people of England. To this public-spirited clergyman, unpaid and unpensioned, we are obliged for executing the least imperfect survey of a considerable population perhaps existing.

Yet were the population as positively ascertained as the individuals of a family, many other particulars should be known and minuted :—the ages of the parties marrying, the periods of greatest mortality, the rela-

[1] On Prisons, p. 117, he quotes one of them in 1777 as follows :

Males	170,574
Females	165,642
Priests	3,303
Monks	4,231
Nuns	6,311
	350,061 ;

exclusive of soldiers and mariners.

[2] This is far superior to Maitland's of London in 1737, which regarded the houses. The amount of people in Dublin in 1798, including the garrison and hospitals, amounted to 182,370. I may observe that I have now before me *An account of the population of Dublin, by order of government in* 1813, *since completed, arranged and revised by William Gregory,* which makes the total of those within the jurisdiction of the lord-mayor, 165,360. The population of Dublin was calculated by the hearth-money when Clarendon was viceroy : it was of course erroneous : in 1752 the population of Dublin was *estimated* at 200,000.

tive proportion of deformed children [1] to those well-made, &c. Sir James Stewart [2] requires that the state of the different classes should be kept separate, in order to exhibit those which increased and those which declined ;—these and many other particulars would be highly instructive. Yet were all this executed, much would remain undone ; Domesday-book happily exists, which in many respects affords a model for perfecting a complete census.

Formerly such a record was deemed essential to government. Alfred began a work of this kind about the year 900 ; William commenced that which exists in 1080, and in six years it was executed : it refers to Edward the Confessor's time, as Alfred's did to Ethelred's. In this the nation is divided into counties, rapes, laths, hundreds, cities, towns, vills ; the arable pasture and woodland possessed by each man is valued ; the condition of each town, its population, &c. is specified, with the exception of the four northern counties. Yet so little were the British rulers and legislators disposed to follow the Conqueror in his attention to facts, that in laying a tax on each parish, they calculated the parishes in England at 50,000 [3]. And so little were the successors of these legislators disposed to accuracy, that few years have elapsed since Domesday-book was printed by order of the House of Commons;

[1] Those born in Paris are 23,293, of which 132 have some external obvious defect.

[2] Political Œconomy, vol. 1. p. 73.

[3] Hearne supposes the House of Commons was deceived by Holinshed, who quoted Ranulf. Discourses, p. 46.

Parishes and parochial chapelries in England and Wales, 10,674; parishes in Scotland, 921. Population Abstract, p. 15.

and under their auspices it appeared as no reprint of an ancient book ever passed the press [1].

Though I lament these neglects and omissions, it is almost doubtful whether the surveys which have been executed have not been rather injurious than useful; for almost all political estimates and surveys and census, except those in 1801 and 1811 in Great Britain, have been undertaken either from sordid or ambitious purposes. In the Roman state the census was a muster-roll, by which the patricians under honourable terms supplied those armies which conquered and cursed the world. Nor do I see why the registry of children by Servius [2] had any nobler view, or those during the consulate or under the empire [3]. The census of citizens according to their estates, by Servius Tullius, in effect added a prerogative to property beyond its intrinsic influence, and under the show of regulation disfranchised the mass of the people. A Roman Itinerary was a book of rates, to enable the *publicans* to exact tribute of men and money and grain. The same remarks apply to other nations:—the births and deaths in ancient India [4] were registered on account of the tax imposed on each: and we probably are indebted for our more accurate approaches towards

[1] See Reeves's History of the English Law, vol. 1. p. 220, for the particulars of this parliamentary publication.

[2] Dion of Halicarnassus, lib. 4. c. 15.

[3] Capitolinus is wrong in saying, "Inter hæc liberales causas ita meruit, ut primus juberet apud præfectos Ærarii Saturni unumquemque civium natos liberos profiteri intra trigessimum diem nomine imposito"—in M. Antonio.

[4] Idque tributorum gratia et ne bonæ malæve nativitates et mortes lateant. Strabo, lib. 15. t. 2. p. 449.

a knowledge of population, to the taxes or duties on marriages, births and burials, mentioned by Davenant[1]. And what was Domesday-book? Camden styles it *Gulielmi librum censualem*; for its main object was to facilitate the levy of the king's casualties. Such were the Extents in Scotland; as one professedly in the reign of Alexander[2], as another respecting a contribution of 28,000 pounds[3]. That called the *new extent*, in 1365, was effected in order to raise the ransom of David[4]. Kames speaks of another extent, by which 3000 pounds were to be levied to defray an embassy to Denmark. A knowledge of the people's numbers, or of their property, did not proceed from a generous care or becoming curiosity; but from rapacity, which lavished the people's lives and fortunes in vain expense, or childish projects, or ruinous ambition. Such was Domesday-book, such was the Down survey which Sir W. Petty executed by order of government;—the prominent object of which work was to exonerate government from its debts to those adventurers who had assisted in the subjugation of Ireland in 1654.—Considering then the causes which have introduced us to the knowledge of many facts relative to political œconomy,—reflecting that they originated through escheats, forfeitures, duties, taxes, tithes, ballotings, conscriptions,—the advantage of knowledge so acquired is questionable; and certainly most inauspicious have been the forerunners of political œconomy, the last-born of all the sciences.

[1] Works, vol. 1. p. 137.
[2] Chalmers says there was one before this. Caledonia, vol. 1. p. 745. There were many. Kames's Law Tracts, vol. 2. p. 211. Mackenzie's Institutions, p. 123.
[3] Kames's Law Tracts, vol. 2. p. 195.   [4] Chalmers, p. 746.

Yet without a survey, general and minute, this science cannot be entertained as it deserves. Occasional embarrassments, temporary success, abundance or scarcity, the folly of one government, the selfishness of another— will make the councils of nations and the opinions of the people fluctuate, or even rush from one extreme to its opposite. With little authentic knowledge principles must be imperfect; and thence the interests of the community are subjected to narrow views of policy, to factions in trade and commerce, to splenetic orders in council, to corn laws, and the like. Is it not wretched that the domain of the empire is unknown, and that of its cultivated land, of its stock, &c., there is not a caballa for mystagogues to guess by? Read their conjectures. Sir John Sinclair[1] computes the acres of Great Britain at 67 millions; Mr. Cary computes them at 55,193,060. In the Bath Society Papers[2] they are computed at 73,258,471; and that of these, 22 millions are uncultivated. Davenant[3] estimated the land in England and Wales at 39 millions of acres. Middleton[4] estimated them as containing 46,916,000. Potts[5] says, decisively, that they contain 32,150,000 square statute acres. Colquhoun in his Essay on Indigence[6] states the acres of England and Wales at 37,334,400; and in a work on the *Wealth, Power,* &c., he calculates the cultivated land at 30,620,000. Mr. Brooke, a fellow of the Royal Society, computes the tillage land of England and Wales at ten millions and a half of acres. Mr. Playfair, an editor of Adam Smith[7],

[1] Communications to the Board of Agriculture, vol. 6. part 1.
[2] vol. 12. p. 197.   [3] Works, vol. 1. p. 197.
[4] Survey of Middlesex.   [5] Gazetteer of England and Wales.
[6] p. 27 and 58.   [7] vol. 2. p. 141.

dogmatizes that "the whole arable land in England does not exceed 5,000,000 of acres, which is not above one tenth of the good land in the country." Sir John Sinclair[1] makes the same computation. Yet Gregory King[2] and Davenant[3] computed the arable land at 9,000,000 acres. Middleton says there are 26,000,000 acres in aration. Mr. Pitt of Wolverhampton computes the cultivated land at 26,000,000, and that six millions of acres are waste. The same variations are made respecting the area of Ireland. Templeman computes that its acres amount to 27,457,000; Dr. Grey[4] to 25,000,000; Mr. Grey[5] to 21,000,000; Cruttwell to 19,000,000; Gerard Malines, in his *Lex Mercatoria*, to 18,000,000; Newenham to $13\frac{1}{2}$ millions of square acres; and Dr. Beauford to 11,943,100.

So of other calculations which depend on guessing. One writer calculates the sheep of Britain at 40,000,000; another at six millions; Mr. Lawrence at 26,000,000:— not that Mr. Lawrence who about a century since, in his State of Ireland[6], calculated three wine bibbers to a parish, five ale topers to the same; and that Ireland lost by men who married whores and who lived above their income five thousand pounds annually. In like manner Mr. W. Pitt calculated the horses of Britain at 1,000,000; Mr. Jacob, at 2,200,000. Mr. W. Pitt[7] also computes the consumption of horses at five millions of acres; Mr. Bell computes the same at 16,000,000 of acres. Why are not these particulars brought within the region of facts by actual computation:

[1] Dixon's Introduction, vol. 1. p. 1.
[2] Davenant's Works, vol. 2. p. 216.   [3] Ibid. vol. 1. p. 219.
[4] Young's Tour in Ireland, vol. 2. p. 72.   [5] On Population.
[6] p. 47 and 54.   [7] Board of Agriculture, vol. 5.

Yet England is not more dull and darkling than other monarchies in Europe. The ignorance of the French government of France before the revolution was hideous : some efforts were made during the republic towards political knowledge ; and Bonaparte began in 1807 a metrical survey of each *commune*, with a census of the property of each individual. Six thousand communes were so surveyed, thirty-four thousand communes still remain unnoticed. To be sure, a reporter in the French Institution expects from the increasing taste for *Geodesia*, that sovereigns will know the extent of their territories more accurately than landlords the extent of their domains. If they do, they will employ better artists than those who laid down the charts which are furnished at enormous expense to the British navy. General Cockburn says [1] that Cape St. Vincent, as marked in them, is thirty miles displaced ; Cape St. Vincent might have challenged more accuracy. I now conclude this chapter, having endeavoured to impress the necessity of actual surveys and specific enumeration. Sir James Stewart[2] long since insisted, "that every plan proposed for this purpose, which does not proceed upon an exact recapitulation of the inhabitants of a country, parish by parish, will prove nothing more than an expedient for walking in the dark." Vauban, who preceded Stewart many years, and who felt and expressed pity for the people and indignation at their oppressors, spoke to the same purpose [3]. He also proposed that there should be every year a survey of the people [4], and every ten years a census of their property.

[1] Travels, vol. 2. p. 131.   [2] Political Œconomy, vol. 1. p. 73.
[3] Dixme Royale, p. 216.   [4] Ibid. p. 184. He exhibits a table for marking the population, stock, &c. p. 221 et seq.

CHAPTER IX.

*Opposition to Mr. Malthus—do not oppose him on the grounds of
other writers. Mr. Malthus, though not superstitious, dogmatizes
on Nature—Nature's mighty feast, according to Mr. Malthus—
his abuse of the people—iniquitous governments and the truly
idle, silently or openly supported by him.—The true cause of the
distress of the people. Origin of the doctrines of Mr. Malthus—
his confusion respecting checks, and the great deficiency of those
mentioned by him ;—might have added the natural check—the celestial, or religious—the precocious, or fiscal—the philosophical—
the magnanimous—the athletic—the proprietary check :— his direct
contradictions on this particular—his argument for the increase of
the Jews in Egypt miraculous, and contradicts his own theory—
his geometrical and arithmetical ratios exposed. That population
presses against food, disproved ;—the cause of the mistake explained
by the situation of Sweden, by the situation of the British.—The
poor man's labour far more surcharged than the rich man's property by taxes. Plenty in Britain, but iniquitously divided—given
to idle dogs, horses, &c. Mr. Malthus's tendency to increase beyond food, false.—The argument and examples of Mr. Malthus
for the pressure of population against subsistence—from war, in the
savage state—his eat a village ridiculed :—he supposes want of subsistence is an inducement to war—disproved by all great events
ancient and modern.—Emigration, not from want of food and room,
proved by various facts and arguments, and from his own reasoning and assertions—his monstrous contradictions—his contradictions concerning population following the natural order. Mr.
Malthus subjects the seasons to man's disposition to inordinate
breeding—considers plague, pestilence, famine, as corrective
of redundant population. Man's happiness, according to Mr.
Malthus, depends on the abundance of his food.—His false and unpopular remarks respecting Siberians and Russia—respecting
food, &c.—abuses the people.—People will not breed if fed—even
the rich and prerogative orders perish.*

In this chapter I shall expose some of the many errors and contradictions of Mr. Malthus. I have already

noticed more than one, and in the sequel others will occasionally force themselves on our consideration.

This writer has had many panegyrists, and some oppugners. I have professed myself of the latter class ; yet I desire not to be mixed with them in respect to the reasons of their opposition. Dr. Jarrold [1] published a Dissertation against Mr. Malthus, in which he says, " of Providence Mr. Malthus seems to have a very vague and imperfect idea :"—and in a less mysterious strain he says, " very few persons have such an opinion of the Deity as to suppose that he would endow with life without providing the means of its support; yet this is the idea that Mr. Malthus holds out[2]." Did Dr. Jarrold ever read of a famine, or drought, or hurricane, or locusts, &c., occasioned by excessive rain ?

But the dogma which has been hurled at him a thousand times is, " Increase and multiply, and replenish the earth." These ghostly assailants consider that all are bound to marry and procreate. Had not Mr. Malthus been sheathed in celestial panoply, this weapon from the armoury of Heaven had long since trans-

[1] Dissertations on Man, &c. p. 327. Dr. Jarrold has of course made great advances into the science of Providence :—he finds that *it was never designed* that the inferior animals should die of old age, but be fatted for man's table, p. 231.—*He believes that those places where no vegetables grow, no animals breathe, are useful in giving repose and in restoring the salubrity of the atmosphere*, &c. p. 230: that is, where the atmosphere may *take the air*, and the air of the cities rusticate a little. Dr. Jarrold insists that the religion of Christ and the doctrine of Mr. Malthus *both cannot be true* : p. 252. This is the old artifice ; and would have suited Dr. Jarrold better as D.D. than as M.D.

[2] p. 362.

pierced him. I may observe in his favour, that Cumberland[1], in illustrating indifferent from necessary duties, says, " as it is free, now that the earth is well peopled, for a man to live single or married." Neither can I condemn Mr. Malthus, because Mr. Heron and the author of *l'Examen de l'Esclavage* defend the slave trade on the supposed principles of the Essay on the Principle of Population. My objections to him arise from his want of science; his infinite contradictions; his inhumanity; his loud abuse of the people; his silence respecting the hard-heartedness of the opulent; his general indemnity for kings and ministers. His observations are a never-ending dilemma ; and though not sick with superstition, he often employs as highly doctrinal a tone as the most devout mystic. For instance: he says, " the laws of *nature,* which are the laws of God, had doomed him and his family to suffer for disobeying their repeated admonitions." From this, one would suppose that man was warned not to breed, by a voice equal to Virgil's Fame. Yet on the contrary, it is a dogma of Mr. Malthus, that there is a tendency in *nature* to increase beyond the means of subsistence. Nor is this the whole ; for the denouncement in the Decalogue, of visiting the sins of the fathers on the children, he applies to sinners against his theory ; as if breeding were condemned and not commanded. He says[2], " in the moral government of the world it seems evidently necessary that the sins of the fathers should be visited upon their children." I do not perceive the evident necessity of any punishment undeserved. We are, however, obliged to Mr.

[1] Law of Nature, &c. c. 6. and 9.   [2] vol. 2. p. 329.

Malthus for discovering that " Increase and multiply "
is original sin and its punishment also.

This is among the rare inventions of Mr. Malthus :
and it appears in an edition in which, he says, *he endeavoured to soften some of the harshest conclusions
of the first essay.* In the first, he considered neither
children nor parents, but full-grown men met at *nature's mighty feast,* at which a straggler obtruded, who
is thrust out, for *there is no cover for him* [1]. A mighty
feast truly, which could not afford food for one casual
visitor. Yet here he holds to his text : for even at
nature's feast, to which Mr. Malthus is the purveyor,
population presses against the means of subsistence,
and the banquet of nature shrinks into a short allowance ministered by a miser. Reduce this figurative
language to intelligible prose. By what law of nature
do some feast, and many want necessaries—nay want
necessaries, that others may feast in spite of nature ?
By what view of nature, or God, or man, do some rejoice in all the *delicacies of the season*—that is, all un-
seasonable things ;—and others suffer the privations
of grain and roots planted in due time and gathered
accordingly ? There are questions on this subject that
have escaped Mr. Malthus. Paley's Philosophy, which

[1] Mariner, in his Account of the Tonga Islands, having told the
manner in which, in England, men provided themselves with food
—they " laughed at what he called the ill-nature and selfishness of
the white people ; and told Mr. Mariner that the Tonga custom
was far better, and that he had nothing to do when he felt himself
hungry, but to go into any house where eating and drinking was
going forward, sit himself down without invitation, and partake
with the company," &c.; and he acted so, and was treated with
the utmost hospitality.

is the text book in our university, and of course not jacobinical, speaks of another *feast* [1], from which, he says, " you would hardly permit any one to fill his pockets or his wallet, or carry off with him a quantity of provision to hoard up, or waste, or give his dogs, or stew down in sauces, or convert into articles of superfluous luxury; especially if by so doing he pinched the guests at the lower end of the table." Yet this is permitted by Mr. Malthus; and the guest so pinched is reviled for not obeying the repeated admonitions of God and nature.

Mr. Malthus says [2] no one has a right to subsistence when his labour will not fairly purchase it. If so, a portion of this man's property is more sacred that that man's life. But suppose the position true, and that a right to subsistence depends on the labour of the individual :—who labour? the rich, the aristocracy, the proprietors of land, the holders of stock, heirs in their own right, and princes by right divine? Here again Paley interposes : " It is a mistake to suppose that the rich man maintains his servants, tradesmen, tenants, and labourers : the truth is, they maintain him." Mr. Malthus may have heard that the strongest spirit is drawn from the poorest grape ; but he has not heard that the greatest wealth is produced by the poorest men.

[1] vol. 1. b.   c. 4. p. 137.
[2] vol. ii. p. 206. In the sequel, p. 456, he says, " The sole reason why I say the poor have no claim of right to support, is, the physical impossibility of relieving a progressive population." O, most impotent conclusion ! Then the poor who exist have no right to subsistence, because by possibility they may greatly increase — then *posse* and *esse* are the same. This was not his reason ; it is the subterfuge of afterthought.

Nor God, nor nature, nor law, nor gospel, can divert him from calumniating the people. He quotes [1] St. Paul—"If a man will not work, neither shall he eat;" which he applies to the poor. As if they eat in idleness; as if Paul applied it to the poor, and not to those professed teachers of the gospel who presumed to be fed, and who did not labour in their vocation. By this perversion of the text of the apostle, we should conclude that the poor are non-residents, pluralists, sinecurists, and the like.

Mr. Malthus [2] considers that attributing in any way the distress of the poor to the higher classes of society is a vulgar error, and asserting that they suffer by the mismanagement and prodigality of rulers, is the greatest wickedness [3] : nay, that those who impeach human institutions, for numerous evils to society, are the most successful supporters of despotism ;—to which he adds something about *revolutionary horrors*. These are astounding dogmas. He thinks that governments are comparatively inoperative respecting the want and unhappiness of the people [4], and *that it depends upon the conduct of the poor themselves*. Does slavery depend on the slaves themselves? Did it depend on the people in France that the nobles were exonerated from taxes? Does it depend on the Irish peasantry that the proprietors are absentees? or on the catholics of Ireland that they pay tithes to the protestant clergy? Does it depend on the poor of England that they pay for salt a tax thirty times the original cost of the article? Did the British people war on France in

[1] b. 3. part 2. c. 1. p. 266.
[2] vol. 2. p. 215.
[3] vol. 2. p. 297, et seq.
[4] vol. 2. p. 315.

defence of the old monarchy and of its priests and nobles? Do the people who pay the taxes incurred in that war understand *legitimacy?*

Mr. Malthus abuses the people; and against none has he been more unmeasured in his slanders than against the British people. He says of them, " Even when they have an opportunity of saving, they seldom exercise it[1]." Yet amidst aggravated taxation and distress, eight hundred thousand labouring Britons are now enrolled in benefit societies. The fact is, the poor have increased, because the wages of labour have not at all advanced proportionably to the enhancement of the articles of subsistence, and that much capital has been extinguished. As taxes augmented, the necessaries of the people,—their bread, beer, cheese, tobacco, soap, salt, &c.,—were surcharged: and as the taxes pressed unequally, some had their comforts curtailed, others were reduced to a stint; and many, from the crowd forced down into the lowest order of labourers, have been rendered miserable. The poor rates (I speak of course generally) simply return in alms part of those sums which unfeeling landlords, griping priests, the state money-changers, and a rapacious prodigal government have wrested from the pittance of the laborious.

It is necessary to say a few words on the origin of the new school in this branch of political œconomy. When the French monarchy, after centuries of misrule and frequent acts of insolvency, had perished miserably,—and before the league of despots had forced the revolutionary leaders to follow the outrageous ex-

[1] vol. 2. p. 98.

ample of the sovereigns of Europe,—many vain notions
concerning government and humanity were fondly
taught: the Cumæan song was resung; *Magnus ab
integro sæclorum nascitur ordo;* and the perfectibility of man counted some enthusiastic advocates. We
were told that men might outlive the patriarchs, and
women exceed in longevity the daughters of ægis-
bearing Jove, who according to Hesiod enjoyed life
nine times longer than the phœnix. These notions,—
whether from devotees or not, whether shaded by superstition or enlightened by philosophy,—arise from a
contempt of facts, from self-presumption and conceit,
and should be reprehended and repressed. Mr. Godwin
indulged in some extravagancies of this kind, in which
he was partly countenanced by experimental philosophers [1]. He suggested that mind might obtain absolute mastery over matter [2]; that man might be so

[1] Franklin in his letter to Priestley says, (Feb. 8, 1780,) "We may
perhaps learn to deprive large masses of their gravity, and give
them absolute levity, for the sake of easy transport. Agriculture
may diminish its labour, and double its produce : all diseases may,
by sure means, be prevented or cured, (not excepting even that of
old age,) and our lives lengthened at pleasure, even beyond the antediluvian standard."

[2] He said that it should happen " that ploughs when turned into
a field, will perform their office without the need of superintend-
ence." This is not much more than the *travelling* steam-engines
mentioned by Mons. Say with such admiration.

So many extraordinary things have actually been effected by man,
that it is almost dangerous to say what he may not effect. Sir W.
Temple spoke as the height of phrensy in projectors, the transfusion
of young blood into old men's veins, which will make them game-
some. Works, vol. 1. p. 303. Yet blood has been transfused from
an old dog into a young lamb, and inversely :—by this process the
old dog became vigorous, and the lamb inert and senseless.

spiritualized as to become purely intellectual; that he might increase at will, and be in a great measure freed from distress. These doctrines Mr. Malthus esteemed not only visionary but pernicious: and he, like other doctors, recommended a directly contrary regimen to that hitherto prescribed. If Mr. Godwin, like Dante, presumed to ascend to the sun's orbit by the sole strength of his desires, Mr. Malthus determined to plant him in his mother earth: and what Mr. Godwin considered an emanation of the great spirit, Mr. Malthus reputed a *sloth* in nature, and first and last a merely eating animal. This doctrine affected novelty; and rushing in with the flood of fearful opinions, when the French people had exerted their power, a great population was easily proved a tremendous evil; while the listless and unreforming temper of the great was gratified, when a sage told them that the amelioration of society was contravened by *deep-seated causes of nature;* that men would overbreed, and that this excess could only be repressed by vice and misery[1]. All these things, to be sure, had been stated at large by Wallace in his " Various Prospects," &c.: but these not being assisted, when Wallace wrote, with the terrors and difficulties which prepared them a reception when republished by Mr. Malthus, excited, when first announced, little noise and no apprehension.

Mr. Malthus undertook the subject of population in consequence of Mr. Godwin's " Inquirer." He commenced author not from mature thought, or after profound investigation, but confessedly *on the impulse of*

---

[1] It is not to be forgotten, that these two were one and the only cause in his first essay.

the occasion [1]. His first essay having a success which might well surprise him, he read, and he enlarged his work. He read, however, not to correct his first loose conceptions, but to support his prejudices. Thence one volume increased in size ; it then became two; and two became three volumes, with appendixes and prefaces and notes. Mr. Malthus, however, affirms that he is a corrector of prevailing opinions [2]. He also says [3], " If the principles which I have endeavoured to establish be false, I most sincerely hope to see them completely refuted." Let him be gratified.

In the first edition of his work in 1798, he acknowledged only one check to equalize population and subsistence—" which check can only be found in vice and misery." This was a discovery, no doubt. In his preface to the second edition he says, " throughout the whole of the present work I have so far differed in principle from the former, as to *suppose* another check *possible*, which does not strictly come under the head either of vice or misery." In the subsequent editions, the check " vice and misery" is divided into two checks; and moral restraint [4]—the unknown, the *possible*,—springs into being; and this last-born of his sagacity ranks the first in his system. Yet in this repeatedly improved edition the defects are many. He calls moral restraint the inducement of the dignitary who would rather live a bachelor, than marry and not possess the establishment, and the parade, and the retinue of a certain cast,

[1] Preface to second edition.
[2] b. 4. c. 8.   Observe again, I always quote the 4th edition, unless I specify another.
[3] vol. 2. p. 420.   [4] vol. 1. p. 16, et seq.

If this be moral, all the incumbrances of a monstrous fortune are attributes of morality. If this be tiew, we must forget Mandeville's doctrine of "Vice shaking hands with Virtue." To call a man moral, because if he married he should graduate a minute lower according to the scale of expense and fashion, and therefore abstains from matrimony,—is monstrous. He says he uses moral in its *most confined sense*[1]: I should say rather, indefinitely. It is also remarkable, that *misery*, which is a cause and a co-ordinate check in page 19, is subordinate and an effect in page 20. He has a note on this, which adds to the confusion. The evil of a total change in the machinery of an hypothesis, without altering the sequel, is evinced in this instance: indeed the whole work exemplifies the absurdity of placing three heads on shoulders moulded for one.— To proceed:

Mr. Malthus insists that plants and irrational animals procreate without any regard to the support of their offspring[2]: that is, the moral check does not affect them. As he did not allow this check to man in his original essay, we should not despair but in due time he will extend it hereafter to the humbler tenants of the earth[3]. Who does he mean by irrational animals? or in his philosophy are all animals, except man, irrational?

[1] vol. 1. p. 19. [2] vol. 1. p. 3.

[3] I offer the following instance to his attention; and, if true, it is the most effectual check of which I have read:—" But it happens when they [vipers or winged insects in Arabia] are incited by lust to copulate, at the very instant of emission the female seizes the male by the neck, and does not quit her hold till she has devoured him." Beloe's Herodotus, b. 3. c. 109.

Passing by this large exclusion, I imagine that his three checks, even with his interpretation of the moral check, will not comprehend all the obstructions to the increase of mankind.

·Mr. Malthus notices the want of ardour in man in the savage state[1] : and as he affirms that the passion between the sexes is so equal, that it may be considered in algebraic language a given character, there is a corresponding want of ardour in the women of that state. Here then is a mighty and an original check to population omitted, as not included in his checks ; for this deficiency of passion is not referable to morality, or vice, or misery. Mr. Malthus might call this the *natural* check,—the term is his own.

Under which of the three checks does he place the following ? A person in India having become a *guru* " when he pleases may marry ; but he is thereby degraded from becoming a portion of the divinity, and from his power : and no one has yet been found so desirous of marriage as to relinquish these pre-eminencies[2]." Should not this be called the *celestial* check ? And I doubt if Origen (who according to Eusebius[3] emasculated himself because he read in the gospel, " There be some which make themselves eunuchs of men for the kingdom of heaven's sake,") should not be classed under the same exalted designation. Origen's situation was not singular : The priests of Cybele[4] in Phrygia were actually castrated. In modern times

[1] vol. 1. p. 44.
[2] Buchanan. Pinkerton, Travels &c., vol. 8. p. 634.
[3] Præparatio Evangelica, lib. 6. c. 8.
[4] Herodian, lib. 1. c. 40.

priests of certain religions are equally abstinent, though they do not by such absolute proofs ensure their virtue.

Mr. Malthus says that " a rich and commercial nation is by the *natural* course of things, led more to pasture than tillage." Now tillage supports more people than pasture [1]. Shall we call this the natural, or pastoral check, or both? It cannot be referred to moral restraint, or vice, or misery.

Under what check shall we class the very early marriages of females in some countries ; which anticipating the females' vigour, rapidly exhaust their powers. Travellers have observed [2], that in such circumstances women soon cease to bear children. Shall we call it the precocious check?

Under what check are we to range those marriages which are deferred by the operation of duties, taxes, &c., not moral restraint, nor vice, nor misery?—perhaps the *fiscal* check. Swift said, " No wise man ever married." Is this the *philosophical?* Joseph Scaliger refrained from marriage, lest he should have a child that would disgrace his family. This at least should be called the magnanimous. Aristotle says [3], the athletic habit is injurious to generation. Were exercises in Greece immoral, or vicious, or miserable? The conquerors in the games memorialed the year by their names ; their glory was a sort of descendible nobility . and Gorgus of Messene [4] by such feats attained the government of his country. Under which head stands

[1] vol. 2. p. 191.   [2] Pinkerton, Travels, vol. 11. p. 103.
[3] De Republica, lib. 7. c. 16.
[4] Polyb. Exerp. &c. lib. 7. p. 1368.

emigration? Men emigrate for various causes: but
certainly they are not always induced by morality, or
forced by vice and misery.

Mr. Malthus says, "It is not enough that a country should have the power of producing food in abundance; but the state of society must be such as to afford the means of its proper distribution: and the
reason why population goes on so slowly in these
countries (Siberia, &c.) is, that the small demand for
labour prevents the distribution of the produce of the
soil; which, while the divisions of land remain the
same, can alone make the lower classes of society par-
takers of the plenty which it affords [1]." Here is a check
enormous in its operation. Can Mr. Malthus force
it under any one of his special checks, with any truth
or consistency? In the countries referred to there is
confessedly abundance of food; yet the increase of
the people is checked by the *small demand of labour*,
which he attributes to the disproportionate divisions
of the land.—Here, then, this production of food and
men is obstructed by the vast inequality of property.
To what compartment of his checks is this check
adapted? And mark his contradictions. He states [2]
that "the principal and most permanent cause of
poverty has little or no direct relation to forms of government *or the unequal division of property;* and
that as the rich do not in reality possess the power of
finding employment and maintenance for the poor,
the poor cannot, in the *nature* of things, possess the
right to demand them." I tell you again, from Paley,
that it is the poor who support the rich; and it is con-

[1] vol. 1. p. 199—200.   [2] vol. 2. p. 422.

trary to *the nature of things* for the rich to demand more from the poor than they can conveniently grant. The question between the rich and poor is not wheher the rich should give or maintain, but whether hey should take and impoverish. The unequal division of property, in one of the last passages quoted, he says, prevents the produce of the soil and the increase of the people: and yet in the last passage he holds a contrary opinion. And so much does the state of property enter into his œconomical views, that he insists that the specific cause of the poverty and misery of the lower classes of people in France is the extreme subdivision of property in that country [1].

Mark again the effect of the unequal division of property in respect to this subject, and his confusions. He says [2], " In countries where, from the operation of particular causes, property in land is divided into very large shares, there arts and manufactures are absolutely necessary to the existence of a considerable population. Without these, modern Europe would be unpeopled." Here, again, the forms of government and the unequal division of property, which he treated as nought respecting the comforts of the lower orders, are so mighty, that if their perniciousness were not counteracted by arts and manufactures, Europe, he says, would be a desert. So much for his consistency. And under what head of morality, of vice, or misery, are we to class the check of large shares of property, which without arts and manufactures would have left Europe unpeopled?

I have now stated some particular restraints to po-

[1] vol. 2. p. 374.   [2] vol. 2. p. 273.

puation, which the science of Mr. Malthus has not embraced. I proceed to other particulars of his philosophy.

We come now to his arguments for the disposition of mankind to increase and multiply exceedingly. He says[1], " Population when unchecked (—when did that happen?) goes on doubling every twenty-five years." Yet this rate of increase does not satisfy him : he asserts, " It is calculated that the Israelites, though they increased very slowly while they were wandering in the land of Canaan, on settling in a fertile district of Egypt doubled their numbers every fifteen years during the whole period of their stay[2]." I must ask, is it not alarming to introduce an incident of the adventures of a miraculous people into a political inquiry? What should we think of a Roman who, to prove or elucidate any question, should state that the eight great deities did not multiply beyond twelve[3] for a long time ; but when the gods were adopted by all-conquering Rome, they multiplied so surprisingly, that the population of heaven, according to Pliny[4], outnumbered the people of the earth?—should we not think that he spoke pontifically? What has Jewish increase to do with this subject? Suppose that Aristotle, when he said, that in Syria above Phœnicia mules brought forth[5], signified the wondrous fecundity of Palestine,—this would be marvellous, but certainly no

---

[1] vol. 1. p. 8.   [2] p. 556.   [3] Herodotus, lib. 2. c. 46.
[4] " Quamobrem major cœlitum populus, etiam quam hominum intelligi potest." Plin. Hist. Nat. lib. 1. c. 6.
[5] Animalium Hist. lib. 6. c. 24. t. 1. p. 882. He also says that in Cappadocia mules are fruitful, p. 1157.

proof of ordinary generation. Yet is the imputed increase of the Jews in Egypt so multiplying and doubling their numbers every fifteen years, that about
seventy persons in 230 years increased to 2,500,000[1],
a miracle little inferior to the productiveness of mules.
That a few slaves, whose pregnant women Pharaoh
willed should miscarry, whose men were worked to
their destruction[2],—that these in a narrow district
of Egypt should increase with a rapidity unknown
in any extensive favored country;—nay, that these
slaves should equal the whole present population of
Egypt, if Volney's[3] calculation be near the truth,—
is an exaggerated miracle. Truly Mr. Malthus might
as well have proved his argument for bounties on the
export of corn by the supply of quails and manna in
the wilderness[4]. The multiplication of these *miserable*
slaves in Egypt (I use misery as Mr. Malthus does)
is so mighty a miracle, that Mr. Robert Atkins, in his
Compendious History of the Israelites lately published, endeavours to explain it with the help of the Tal-
mud, by a surplus produce of females among them,
and thus assigning eighteen women to each man : if

[1] Josephus says it was not easy to count them, but that the
fighting men were 600,000, lib. 2. c. 14, 15.

[2] They complain in the Old Testament of making bricks without straw. Josephus says they were employed in cutting canals,
building walls round the cities, and ramparts and embattlements
and pyramids.

[3] His estimate is 2,300,000.

[4] Mr. Malthus insists that population cannot be very rapid, except where the price of labour is very high (vol. 1. p. 288.) It would
be satisfactory to learn the wages of these slaves—surely none ever
obtained so much !

so, they resembled the herds of Augeas [1], who became more prolific every succeeding year, and fortunately produced many heifers, Θηλυτοκοι τε. Such is one of the proofs or illustrations afforded by Mr. Malthus of the disposition of man to increase most rapidly, and who chooses to be pleasant on Mr. Anderson, by an innuendo on the *well-known infidelity of the age.* Besides, Mr. Malthus forgets that this increase in Egypt, if considered historically, must impugn his theory respecting the pressure of population against the means of subsistence, and that population runs an accelerated course, while food follows step by step. All this shows little depth of management in the author: this is not merely to fly a paper kite, but when it is aloft to cut the string of the toy. It would much more have consorted with Mr. Malthus's repeated terrors, to have inserted, instead of this generative wonder, another document from the same source, " And it came to pass, when men began to *multiply* on the face of the earth, and daughters were born unto them, that *wickedness* became great on the earth [2]."

He says, " population has this constant tendency to increase beyond the means of subsistence [3]." To make this statement very imposing, he avers that population increases in a geometrical, and food in an arithmetical ratio, which might be summarily denied by the oracular answer ουτ' εν αριθμω. This perversion of the terms of an abstract science has deceived many. He proceeds [4], " The rate according to which the productions of the earth may be supposed to increase, it

---

[1] Theocritus, Idyl. 25. v. 125.   [2] Genesis 6.
[3] vol. 1. p. 4.   [4] vol. 1. p. 9.

will not be easy to determine. Of this, however, we may be perfectly certain ; that the ratio of their increase must be totally of a different nature from the ratio of the increase of population. A thousand millions are just as easily doubled every twenty-five years by the power of population as a thousand ; but the food to support the increase from the greater number will by no means be obtained with the same facility." Suppose so ; what fact is told, what truth is taught, what conclusion is realized or approached, in consequence?—I can perceive no good in any such supposes. Wallace indulged himself in exhibiting the geometric increase of mankind in the antediluvian world, amounting to 206,158,430,208 : " Thus we see," said Wallace [1], " to what a prodigious multitude mankind must have increased in 1200 years :" yet he continues that there was no such increase, nor could it be ; adding, " it is easy to institute a calculation according to any assumed hypothesis." Should we follow Mr. Malthus in *supposing*, we might invert the terms, and assume that food increased beyond the people by a transcendental geometry. If Mr. Malthus supposes that a thousand millions may be doubled every twenty-five years by the power of population, I may suppose that the food of man may be doubled a thousand times in the same period: a herring has 40,000 eggs, [2] a cod fish ten times that number [3]. But without re-

[1] Populousness of Ancient Nations, p. 8.

[2] There are lakes, *peuplés d'enormes poissons,* and which are equally productive as sea fish. Yet a project was offered to the academy of Berlin to increase the fecundity of salmon trout.

[3] To this the following verse might be applied :

Φυλον αμουσον αγουσα πολυσπερεω καμασηνων.

Plutarch. Moral. p. 550.

sorting to the ichthyophagi or going beyond the earth[1], it appears that in 1788 two bulls and three cows strayed away in New South Wales, who in seven years increased to a herd of a thousand :—Now men live on fish, and flesh, and grain. As to " the incredible increase of a barley-corn," I refer the reader to the treatise of M. P. Knetczmer, counsellor of state to his Prussian majesty. Suppose the power of generation in men equal to the increase of the Jews in their sad captivity, or greater still, we may suppose that the animals which they eat are more disposed to generate[2] as is the food of inferior animals, who live on shrubs, plants[3], grain, &c. more apt to increase than the animals themselves. I say, I may suppose on these suppositions, that the food of man may multiply far beyond the possible multiplication of man ; that is, one extravagance may rebut another; or rather, that two puerile hypotheses may perish together.

" The constant tendency of population to increase beyond the means of subsistence." What is meant by tendency ? Is it the disposition of the sexes to each other ? Is this the signification of the term ? Yet this tendency is countervailed by other tendencies as pow-

[1] Reaumur proved that an aphis may have twenty generations in one year, and that in five it may be the parent of 5,904,900,000.

[2] " Bestiæ hominum causa generatæ sunt, nedum bestiarum causa arborum fructus, et terræ fruges, et tot rerum copiæ comparatæ sunt." Cicero, t. 4. p. 238. Herodotus says that animals which serve for the purposes of food, to prevent their total consumption, are always very prolific. Thalia, c. 108. Derham might use this in the chapter on the balance of animals in his Physico-Theology.

[3] Mr. Malthus does not seem to have advanced far in the science of natural history when he stated, " No one can say why such a plant is annual." vol. 2. p. 17.

erful. This tendency in some is felt and repressed, or suffered, and is unproductive :—the connexion of the sexes in London, for instance ; where Mr. Wallace seems at least to have had no faith in his geometrical increase of mankind, which he derived perhaps from the descent tables of lawyers. It may here be remarked, not only how these two authors differed from each other, but how Mr. Malthus differs from those who originally estimated man's increase; Sir William Petty[1], Davenant, &c. the first of whom supposed a doubling possible in ten years. Yet Davenant calculated the actual increase in England at 9000 a year, or a million a century ; and this Sir James Stewart[2] considered preferable to a more rapid multiplication. Gregory King[3] supposed that in 1260 the people of England was 2,750,000, and that these doubled in 435 years ; that is, at the close of the 17th century they amounted to 5,500,000, which are the exact numbers assigned by Davenant[4] to England at that period. Gregory King supposed the next doubling would be in 2300. Sir William Petty[5] conjectured that Ireland in 1169 contained 300,000 inhabitants, who he fancied in the ordinary course of increase became in 500 years 1,200,000[6]. These inven-

---

[1] Polit. Arithmetic.   [2] Polit. Œconomy, vol. 1. p. 75.
[3] Davenant's Works, vol. 2. p. 176.
[4] Works, vol. 1. p. 197.   [5] Polit. Arithmetic, p. 14 or 24.
[6] Mr. Grahame says " that the population of every country has a tendency to increase beyond the quantity of food with which the country actually supplies its inhabitants, appears to be a position which his (Malthus) adversaries should be as little willing as they can be able to controvert." Inquiry into the Principle of Population, p. 102.

tors or original supposers of the greatest possible increase in a few years, never speculated, never talked
of a continuation of this increase ;—that was reserved
for Mr. Malthus, who attempts to dignify with great
practical importance his geometrical increase and
arithmetical supply. I marvel he did not invoke nature on the occasion,—nature and arithmetic are ancient allies : Ενιοι γαρ την φυσιν εξ αριθμων συνιςασιν.

Had Mr. Malthus amused himself by mooting a
vexatious question or a mere paradox, he should not
have been disturbed by me: but his argument is instigated by something more than a mere scholastic pru-
riency. If the propensity to increase be so predominant, how happens it that any portion of land is uncultivated ? If the infusive force (to use Thompson's
language) be so irresistible, if its potentiality be so
enormous, and that while we breed like giants we
must feed like pigmies ;—what could prevent the land
from sudden and universal cultivation ? Or, viewing
the question in another light, how does it happen
that the same people grow rich as they grow more populous, and live better as they increase in numbers ?
There is an account of Harmony in the Philanthro-
pist : the colony so called consisted at first of a few
who fled from Germany : they began with 20,000
dollars; yet they have increased immensely by generation and by new settlers, and yet their capital is now
thirty times greater than their original stock.

It is strange that Mr. Malthus could have persisted
in maintaining his ratio of increase of food and population, as in the beginning of the series they are directly the reverse. Suppose the population doubled

in 15 years; as this doubling implies a new country, the land brought into cultivation [1] might have been quadrupled or more in the same time; and this increased cultivation might have continued until population began to thicken in the land. This has happened in the United Provinces of America; the population has increased extremely, yet the food and all the comforts of life have outrun the population.

Yet Mr. Malthus persists in his ratios; and he is so far consistent, that he reaffirms the general pressure of population against subsistence: so intently does he enforce this point, that we may rejoice we are not declining daily in stature and in all our animal functions, as lowland horses on being mountain fed, from heavy cattle dwindle to ponies. I really wonder he did not help his argument for the immemorial pressure, by some accounts of man's gigantic paternity. St. Augustine determined that the antediluvians were of colossal magnitude, on the credit of some fossil bones of the larger beasts, which his want of knowledge of comparative anatomy ascribed to man before the flood. Hakewell would also strengthen the theme by his remarks on triple births in olden time. While the great

[1] Turnbull says, " It is easy for agriculturists in England to ask why the Brazilians, or why the Americans on the Ohio or the Mississippi, do not pay more attention to their crops ; why they do not break up more land, or endeavour by the methods used in Europe to procure larger returns : the reason is, because there are no markets. Why, for example, should a colonist trouble himself with ploughing or digging ten acres, when he gets as much from five, as himself, his family, and his pigs and cattle require, and there is no market for what remains, all his neighbours being in the same situation ?" Voyage &c. p. 49.

Linné would add irresistible weight to the pressure of Mr. Malthus. Linnæus[1] believed " that Adam and Eve were giants; and that mankind from one generation to another, owing to poverty and other causes, have diminished in size."

Let us investigate the truth of this pressure; let us consider its amount in the country of Linnæus. Sweden makes a considerable topic in the review of nations by Mr. Malthus: he says[2] it does not produce food for its population. First let me observe, that hitherto Sweden has been in what Mr. Malthus would call an *unnatural* state; it possessed Livonia, and it depended on that province for large supplies of grain[3]. This country became annexed to Russia, and thus the farm of the state was reduced. Sweden also possessed Pomerania, and it monopolized all the corn exported from that country. But suppose Sweden had never commanded either Livonia or Pomerania, the import of grain is no proof of want of food: Venice before she possessed *terra firma* did not raise a stalk of grain, yet her own people had plenty of provisions; and even the refugees from Apuleia, when that city was besieged by Attila, were hospitably entertained by the Venetians.

No country could be more favourable for the theory of Mr. Malthus than Sweden; the land is sterile, the climate austere, and subject to occasional excesses. Yet what is here the amount of this pressure? According to Cantzlaer, Sweden uses 440,000 tons more grain on an average than she grows[4]; but by the same

[1] Lachesis Laponica, translated by Sir J. E. Smith. [2] vol. 1. p. 329.
[3] Annual Register, 1769, p. 10. [4] Malthus, vol. 1. p. 329.

account 400,000 tons of grain are consumed in distillation. If then the spirits procured from these 400,000 tons be unnecessary, the pressure is only equivalent to 100,000 men, four Swedish tons of grain being the apportioned food for one man. This deficiency is not alarming. Suppose, however, that every pint of spirits is to be considered as so much food; suppose also, that Sweden exported no fish [1], we can abate the pressure by other considerations. The burthensome *corvées* which the possessors of certain crown lands are obliged to perform, are so pernicious, that the obligation to supply post-horses [2] only, occasions a waste of labour to the farmer, both of men and horses, annually, equal to 300,000 tons of grain. If the loss, then, by these *corvées* were prevented by a better administration, the deficit of grain by this single improvement would be reduced to 100,000 tons, equivalent to the pressure of 35,000 individuals. Could not Mr. Malthus have made a further advance into politics, and transferred this diminished pressure by charging it on government rather than on geometry and propagation?

Could he not have conjectured that the disproportion between the food and the people of Sweden might be as truly referred to the love of dominion in their kings and nobles, as to man's love of the sex? Have not the Swedish kings pressed on national subsistence beyond the pressure of 35,000 individuals? and yet the burthen of the Swedish nobles was still more intolerable;

---

[1] It is said the fisheries produce 300,000 tons. Much of this is exported.

[2] Malthus, vol. 1 p. 340,

for in 1682 an extraordinary diet of the clergy, bourgeois, and peasants, in order to humble the despotic
nobility, conferred on Charles XI. absolute power [1].   Who can calculate the pressure against subsistence by the perversion of labour and the immense
impositions of Charles XII.? Would Mr. Malthus
estimate the pressure of this sovereign at less than
100,000 men, considering the men raised and the
funds exacted for their support? At what mark on the
political barometer shall we graduate the incumbency
of Gustavus III., the most hypocritical, *politic*
young king on record? From his progress a greater
arithmetician than Mr. Malthus could with difficulty
reckon how many lies go to make one despot [2]. What
was the pressure of his successor, our applauded ally;
his civil misrule, his endless wars, his perpetual failure? Yet Mr. Malthus while this man ruled, lamented [3]
—what? that the people of Sweden are continually
going beyond the average increase of food. This is the
view of Sweden by a collegiate professor of political
œconomy. The people overbreed, and they press against
subsistence; when these people (I have also been in
Sweden) endured a pressure, of which a detail of the
peine fort et dure can alone afford some intimation.

Strange as it may appear to Mr. Malthus, man may
be made miserable not only by overbreeding, but by
forcing the vigorous into armies, by exacting provisions, by endless taxation, by rapacity and waste, by
wars, by court pageants, by castle building, by sup-

[1] Mably, Droit Publique, t. 2. p. 235.
[2] His deeds and words are stated in the Annual Register.
[3] vol. 1. p. 334.

porting grand operas and the like,—all these were inflicted on the poor inhabitants of this cold and barren country. When these miseries are considered, Mr. Malthus might as well declare against the overbreeding of a ship's crew, men only being aboard, who being robbed by pirates endured short allowance during the remainder of the voyage.

Let us consider the question of pressure under another view: let us dismiss the operation of misgovernment entirely from the argument, and let us make England the groundwork of this study. First, I must state, that I do not say there is no misery in England; on the contrary, I am satisfied that it is urgent and extensive. Yet I say, there is no grievous pressure by population against subsistence. When we talk of population and subsistence, we should consider all the people and all the food. Then, if the sum of one does not exceed the sum of the other, there is no deficiency. If, however, one-fifth of the people take five portions of food, leaving the other four parts of the population short by so much of their proportion, this is not properly a pressure of population against food. In like manner, if one part of the community force another part to labour while they themselves are indolent, this is not the pressure of labour on population : and supposing we spoke of such tyranny in Egypt or Palestine, we would say; the Jews were oppressed in one country, and the Canaanites in the other.

Without meaning that all men should equally labour or feed alike, though all should be occupied and temperate ; without any reference to or apprehension of such rigid equality, I say ; the English people do not receive their share of the public provisions: and however it may shock the arrogance of self-instituted legislators, they do not obtain their rights in the article of food. Man has a paramount right to his property, man has also an equal right at least to the produce of his labour, for labour originally determined property. If so, the law should not assess labour more than property. Yet what is the case in England? Mr. Preston calculates that the taxes deduct ten from eighteen shillings of the labourer's wages. Suppose they were less onerous.—How would the nobles and members of parliament rage and declaim at the mention of a fifty per cent property tax? How did they rave when the ministry wished to impose a five per cent property tax on them? and how did they glorify their patriotic exertions in resisting them? Excellent men! followers of Poplicola and the Gracchi,—you would not pay five per cent, but you were satisfied others should pay much more; for while you negatived the ways and means, you passed the estimates. Who can doubt the valour and purity of our house of commons!

If labour and property were equally regarded, property should pay as much as labour; if the labourer paid 10 shillings out of 18, the proprietor or stockholder should pay 1000 pounds out of 1800. This may seem tremendous; yet the terror is not that so much should be deducted from the proprietor, but that so much should be subtracted from the labourer: because what in this case would be taken from the rich man would but end some superfluity; while every shilling taken from the poor one would restrict his necessaries, and cut his means of living to the quick. This is no fantastic doctrine, it has actually directed the policy of many nations. Under the aristocracy of Rome, property was not merely assessed proportionably to labour; but the laborious were entirely exempted from contributing, and even from war; they were considered as having acquitted themselves to the state by being fathers of families: and in Athens the whole taxation was answered by the rich, and sometimes by the richest [1].

I have therefore stated the question less favourably for the poor than they have been actually treated in some countries. And I am authorized to infer from that statement, that the misery of the poor in England is not of their own making (or breeding, as Mr. Malthus would say); and I also conclude, that if the wants of the poor are overbalanced by the superfluities of the rich, there is no pressure of population against subsistence. Consider the city of London last year. Dreadful accounts of starving manufacturers were commonly confronted in the opposite columns of the same newspaper by grand entertainments, splendid fetes, routs: nor were the East and West ends of the town so distant in that sad year as North and South. The lord-mayor proposed to the *city* that the sum of 1000 pounds, usually expended in a dinner on Easter Monday, should be applied to charitable purposes; on which the Court *resolved unanimously in favor of the ancient custom and dignity*

---

[1] In times of great difficulty they formed a part of the Roman *levy en masse.* " Asperis reipublicæ temporibus cum juventutis inopia esset,—proletarii (a prole creanda) in militiam tumultuariam legebantur." A. Gellius.

of the city of London!! *Sic inde huc omnes tanquam ad vivaria currunt*; and thus a sum that would have dined 20,000 persons who wanted both dinner and supper, was wasted on a few plethoric citizens. Nor are these propensities confined to either end of London. It may be said of the richer English, what Pelloutier[1] said of the Celts: "No national or provincial assembly was held, no civil or religious festival observed, no birth-day, marriage, or funeral solemnized no treaty of alliance or friendship confirmed, without a feasting." How in this country it can be said that population presses against subsistence, I cannot understand, when so much is destroyed; for one half of the food on such occasions is burned, exhausted, evaporated—divided between the fire and the air; and then of that which escapes culinary consumption, twice as much is eaten as health requires. Compare then in England those who waste and eat and drink inordinately, with those who live sordidly through necessity, and the pressure on subsistence will be greatly relieved: nor have I any doubt but many more die by satiety than privation. The poor man has complaints, but they are limited by his means; while the retinue of a rich man's disorders equals the extent of his fortune.

> "———Some by violent stroke shall die,
> By fire, flood, famine, by intemp'rance more
> In meats and drinks, which on the earth shall bring
> Diseases dire."

I think I might rest the argument here against the pressure of population on subsistence in Britain; and

[1] t. 1. lib. 2. c. 12.

if I could only strengthen the refutation, I should not increase the proof. But I must ask, How can the pressure be entertained for an instant by any one who has noticed the beasts which the rich support, for jollity, for whim, for I know not what, by the labour of man, that is at the expense of the comforts of the poor? What shall we say of their dogs? Julius Cæsar was to blame, who, seeing some foreigners at Rome with dogs and monkeys in their arms, asked sarcastically if the women of their country had no children. And it may be thought by those who still call Cæsar god, that he prophetically rebuked Frederic the Great, who honoured dogs and not man with monuments. Mr. Malthus has not abused the dog-fancier: no, it is the man, who, being poor, is so *unnatural* as to dote on women and increase his kind :—had he become a beggar by rearing blind puppies, he had passed uncensured by him. But what are lapdogs and the sportsman's dogs—from king Charles's spaniel to the king's buckhounds led by the duke of Montrose—to the studs of hunters and racers, and the rabble of pampered idle horses which swarm through the land? Do these not press on subsistence? How much do the savage animals corrode and consume of man's food? I speak of those creatures shot and hunted, yet preserved by those who claim a descent from the chiefs of William the Conqueror, and who exhibit the game laws as the title deeds of their inheritance. Nothing is said of this compound pressure against subsistence, which in respect to the effects of population on human food presses or compresses as the vice and screw. One idle horse will consume the food of two men, and he must be attended also. Mr. Colquhoun has computed that inferior animals consume in Great Britain eleven millions of quarters of grain, and men eighteen millions. Would there be a pressure, if what is wasted on useless beasts was left in the hands of the labourer? I do not say given to the poor, but not wrested from the industrious ;—the grain imported is a trifle in comparison to the food of man consumed by useless brutes.

Nothing, however, is said by Mr. Malthus on these topics ;—a lady's pug dog, or a hound, or a pointer is unnoticed ; but a child too many obtrudes on *nature's feast.* The philosophy of Mr. Malthus, his pressure of population against food, is a new reading of a celebrated parable ; it is a tale of Lazarus, omitting Dives and his dogs.

The inordinate propensity of man to breed Mr. Malthus has affirmed in various ways, and with an affected latitude of language. If Mr. Colquhoun calculates the prostitutes at all near the truth, it may exhibit *this tendency* of population to increase, while it does not add one to their actual number; indeed so far is it from adding to the stock of people, that it impairs the powers of generation and the multiplication of the people. There is misery in the world, and poverty; and in many instances children are produced heedlessly and viciously : this, however, does not prove the constant tendency of population to increase beyond the means of subsistence ; it evinces at most the improvidence of some individuals; and for one man or woman who produces a child that he or she had not a fair prospect of supporting—many become incapable of supporting their families by ambitious projects, by prodigality in equipage, buildings, horses; by gambling, by neglect of business, by ignorance of its details, by drunkenness, by company-keeping, by taxes which consume the means of employment and the profits of labour; by wars which fundamentally derange society and its concerns. Yet all these do not amount to an *item* in the philosophy of Mr. Malthus; for to his imputed *tendency of population* the unprovided, the unemployed, the miserable, the poor, are wholly ascribed. This word tendency is so loose and unphilosophical, that it might be applied to the hanging tower of Pisa, or to a weathercock out of order; yet it is an accredited term with writers on population, and they use it much as Mr. Wordsworth does in his Excursion :

> " To hear the mighty stream of *tendency*
> Uttering, for elevation of our thought,
> A clear sonorous voice, inaudible
> To the vast multitude whose doom it is
> To run the giddy round of vain delight."

I am surprised that these philosophers, who can advance into the regions of fancy and apply the terms of the abstract sciences to man and matter, did not, beside over-populousness, meet in their vagrancy with other tendencies. There is a tendency in water to attain its level; yet water will ascend rapidly in certain tubes, but beyond some inches the liquid proceeds no higher. Again : profit is often inversely as the supply, and the profits of a capital decrease with the accumulation of wealth. Thus abundance fixes its own limits, in direct opposition to the misery of Mr. Malthus, and the geometric and arithmetic whimsies of him and his followers ; who, full of nature and wisdom, place man and his means of living in most artificial opposition. There is a boundary to the advance of population, which is common to men and all things : and though I am neither atomist nor necessarian, this common principle operates on man (with others conformable to his constitution), as he is a portion of the universe. Adam Smith and David Hume were not lynx-eyed to see *the stream of tendency.* Hume favoured the populousness of nations as presumptive proof of improved circumstances: and Smith said, that " the demand for men, like that of every other commodity, necessarily regulates the production of man ; quickens it when it goes too slowly, and stops when it advances too fast [1]." This, I admit, is stating the question in mercantile phraseology ; but it is intelligible and true, where man and industry are not oppressed.

The arithmetical and geometrical ratios are jargon. Where property is equitably divided, and labour free, there will be no tendency but to supply what is wanting. Mr. Malthus pleads for discord : yet where there is neither force nor injustice, all things will repose when rest is necessary, and all will move with the general impulse. This order the ancients called the harmonical.

Yet Mr. Malthus advances far beyond the doctrine of tendency and its presumed consequences : he insists that " population presses against the limits of the means of subsistence [2] :" a mode of expression not

---

[1] Wealth of Nations, vol. 1. b. 1 c. 8. p. 122.

[2] This he reiterates, vol. 1. pp. 106. 231. 377.

unusual with him. This pressure, he says, has affected mankind in every country, and in all stages of society. In short, it has been so great, so compulsory and desperate, that, advancing beyond Hobbes, who taught that a state of nature was a state of war, he insists, " one of its (war's) first causes and most powerful impulses was, *undoubtedly,* an insufficiency of room and food." This is dogmatism which requires strength and energy to support or even to excuse.—Let us examine the assertion. The first war, we may conclude, began among the pastoral and savage tribes, as they commenced the gradation of society. What could a savage obtain as sustenance by fighting another savage, or by tribe assaulting tribe? The answer of Mr. Malthus is they prosecuted hostilities to eat each other. This approaches the Hibernian story of two game cats, who fought and ate each other, so that the ends of their tails only remained. Now for his documentary proof of this surmise [1]. " The chief of the Amolakis (when they enter into an enemy's country) says to each, To you is given a hamlet to *eat ;* to you, such a village.——These expressions remain in the language of some tribes in which the custom of eating their prisoners taken in war no longer exists. Cannibalism [2],

[1] vol. 1. p. 66.

[2] The kindness of Mr. Malthus towards man in insisting on cannibalism, seems doubtful. That there were and are cannibals, I neither affirm nor deny: but it is observable that Herodotus, among all his wonders, confines this act to one people: lib. 4. c. 107. D'Azora denies that the Indians of South America are cannibals. Porter thought that the people of the island of Nukaheevah ate their enemies ; he however found he was mistaken. The Samoits were thought cannibals. Pinkerton, Travels, vol. 1. p. 64;—this is contradicted. Ibid. p. 529.

however, undoubtedly prevailed in many parts of the
new world : and, contrary to the opinion of Dr. Robertson, I cannot but think that it must have had its
origin in extreme want." He therefore presumes that he
favours human nature in ascribing this practice rather to
hunger than revenge. I wonder he did not advance man
to the poetic character of the lion ; " for t'is the royal
disposition of that beast", &c. His kindness to man
equals his ingenuity. Why did he not quote the tale of
Saturn eating his children ; and of the Essedones [1]
eating their parents? But the great god of the pagans
was not hungry ; and the Essedones ate their parents
through piety [2].   Mr. Malthus might have increased
the obligation of humanity to him, by noticing the
abstinence of the two Sicilians, who after the Sicilian
vespers deferred eating the Frenchman's heart to the
next flesh-meat day.   The story is as well authenticated as Robinson Crusoe and Friday firing in *the
name of God* at the *affrighted savages*.   Thus Mr.
Malthus proves an excessive population among the
Indians ; and he founds one of his arguments on a
word which he supposes has outlived the practice of
cannibalism : as if these barbarians abstained from
metaphors, who in fact speak only in exaggerated
figures.   What might not be related of the Hungri,
with the solitary instance mentioned by Gibbon of the
Hun who squatted on the field of battle and sucked
the reeking blood from an expiring enemy? What
gourmands are the French? *Il mangait tout son bien* is
a common expression for prodigality. What a voracious Swiss parson was that, of whom the peasant told

---

[1] Herodotus, lib. 4. c. 26. Polyhistor. lib. 1. c. 20.
[2] " Hæc sunt apud eos ipsos pietatis ultima officia": lib. 2. c. 1.

Dr. Moore, *Il mange tout notre bled!* At this rate of interpretation the Romans fed on words[1], and the Athenians enjoyed a repast on their own heart[2]. What does the expression of the chief of the Amalekis differ from that of Louis XIV, who directed his generals to make a vigorous impression at first, and subsist his armies on his enemies?

Mr. Malthus is not satisfied with supposing that want of food and room occasioned savage warfare; he infers that the same causes induce the wars in the advanced stages of society : that is, as hunger moved barbarians to war, a good appetite now promotes the hostility of nations. His words are, " And greatly as the circumstances of mankind have changed since it first began, the same cause still continues to operate, and to produce (though in a small degree) the same effects." This opinion truly harmonizes with the chieftain's question to Sir John Malcolm, " How, if there is no plundering, do you support your numerous warlike population?" That piracy was common in ancient Greece, as gang robbery is in modern Greece and in British India ; that there were mercenaries who fought on any side in all times, Carians and Cretans and Goths and Brabançons and Switzes and Hessians and Hanoverians—I doubt not : but even of these it does not appear that want of room and food obliged them to adopt so unprincipled and flagitious a profession. Those who were free to choose, embraced this profession through presumption and vice and idleness ; choosing rather an excessive exertion than

---

[1] Edi tuum verbum, says Plautus.

[2] In the Plutus of Aristophanes, ταυτον θυμον φαγοντες.

regulated labour. Neither the regular nor irregular wars, called also [1] *la petite guerre*, of barons against barons [2], afford any supposition that they fought for want of room and food. I know plundering excursions were common in barbarous Europe; and they were at that period, agreeable to the *law of nature and nations*. Thus I have read that Mary Scott was married to Giddy, who " besought his father-in-law to maintain her for some time : with this request he complied, upon condition that he was to receive for her board the plunder of the next harvest moon." Does this exhibit a want of room and food? No: merely licentiousness of life. And what were such plunderings to the feuds and deadly feuds which some thought were peculiar to Scotland, but which, unhappily, have been the effects of enmity and revenge, I might say of disinterested malignity, through all the uncivilized nations of the earth?

Look to Africa: Park [3] speaks of two kinds of wars which resemble the great and less wars of Europe : those resembling the latter, called tegria, " are very common ; particularly about the beginning of the dry season, when the labours of the harvest are over, and provisions are plentiful. These plundering excursions always produce speedy retaliation." This statement proves that they arise not from want but wantonness [4] ; at least, not because one party has little, but because

---

[1] Martens, Droit des Gens, t. 2. p. 361.   [2] Joinville, p. 342.
[3] Travels, p. 292.
[4] Golberry says, " a thatched hut, the building of which costs nothing, some ells of common linen, and six pounds of millet or rice, every day, are sufficient for lodging, feeding, and clothing a

another has much. Bruce[5], speaking of the Arabs, says that it is customary for them to *destroy* each other's harvests; and that the matamores are granaries under ground, where the inhabitants provide a store eventually to support themselves.

Want is not the cause of war—wars do not originate in order to serve self,—for most wars are injurious, and many fatal ;—they are undertaken from some ancient grudge or present vexation : they are instigated by malice, or passion, or envy : and it commonly happens that those nations which confine on each other are the least friendly. Scotland was in alliance with France, and in enmity with England. The lowlanders and highlanders of Scotland were equally offensive to each other. Thus Humboldt remarks, " in all parts of Spanish America there is a decided antipathy between the inhabitants of the plains or warm regions, and the inhabitants of the table land of the Cordilleras." It is melancholy that a hill or a valley will mark the bounds of hatred and affection ; and that a river or rivulet will be at once the waters of memory or forgetfulness : even a space which fluctuates with the sea's ebb, or which hitherto has existed within the air-drawn lines of longitude or latitude, shall become the object of hostilities, and ultimately involve the universe in war.

family consisting of a father, mother, and four children—Twenty days labour per year are sufficient to ensure an abundant supply of food ; so that the existence of a negro family may be said to be a gratuitous gift of nature, granted without expense or fatigue: hence celibacy is scarcely known in Africa: indeed it is so rare that it attaches a sort of shame to those who adopt it."

[1] Travels, vol. 5. p. 229.

War is still less instigated by want of room and food in civilized than in savage and pastoral societies; yet Mr. Malthus suggests that in them also want of food and room have had a predisposing influence. Every mighty achievement of ancient and modern arms disproves the imputation. Was it for want of room and food that Semiramis made war on the Hyperboreans? that Crœsus, the richest of princes, assailed Persia[1], notoriously poor? that Cyrus[2] sought the miserable Massagetæ, or Darius the Scythians, whose inhospitable country proved his ruin? Was it the want of room and food which induced in any degree Cambyses[3] to make war on three nations at once? Did these causes move Xerxes to collect all the disposable forces of Asia in order to conquer Greece, which Demaratus[4] told him was the child of poverty? or to change the place of onset, did Philip of Macedon make war on the Scythians, impelled or moved by these causes? Ateas their general addressed him: "You rule over the warlike Macedonians, and conquer man; but I and the Scythians conquer hunger and thirst[5]." Did Alexander turn the current from Greece against Asia, through want of room and food? No; this man called *Great*, this oracular brood of Jupiter, fought for glory. " What do I not suffer," said the raging man as he toiled on in destruction, " what do I not suffer to be praised by you, O Athenians?" And oratory by the tongue of Demosthenes crowed Philip and royalty

---

[1] Herodotus, lib. 1. c. 71.　　[2] Ibid. lib. 1. c. 207.

[3] Ibid. lib. 3. c. 17.　　[4] Ibid. lib. 7. c. 102.

[5] Plutarch. Moral. p. 105.

as they deserved. Was Pyrrhus stinted in room and food? or is the unanswered question of his minister Cyneas forgotten[1]? Pyrrhus was a hero; peace was insufferably tedious to him:

" For quiet to quick bosoms is a hell."

How is the absurdity of this supposition evinced by the all-conquering Romans! They fought to gratify the patricians, but surely not for want of room; for every effort was made to support the population of Italy by draughts from the provinces; and the land, from being once a garden, became sterile and uncropped: and such, let it be remembered, were the room and food the Romans gained by war and conquest,—the most successful nation that ever existed. War was so entirely the business of the Romans, that Florus[2] should rather have attributed this barbarity to them than to the Dacians.

The motives of conquerors, who are by far the most flagitious of the human race, are not and were not want of room and food. When vengeance or envy did not instigate them, the cause was infuriate ambition, or madder fanaticism. Want of room or food operated neither formerly nor now. Did they move Louis the Fifteenth to make war on Paoli and the Corsicans; or the Corsican to trample over Europe; or Austria to seize a third of Poland; or Russia, while it quarters the world, to add wilderness to wil-

[1] " What hinders you now from not beginning the enjoyment?" Apud Stobæum, Sermo 10, p. 131.

[2] Daci tanta barbaries est ut pacem non intelligant. lib. 4. p. 269.

derness, and Caucasus to Kamtchatka, and California to Finland? Did such motives induce England to war in the West? She fought America that she might lose 3*d*. a pound on tea; for while she charged 3*d*. a pound *duty* in America, she took off 6*d*. a pound on the export of the same article from England. Is she moved by want of food and room to war in the East? She prevents the import of food from the East, and will not admit one of her people to reside liberally in that vast continent. Men do not make war for its supposed advantages [1] : they are not so absurd. Wars are made to excite or gratify the passions.

Mr. Malthus refers emigrations to want of food and room. Emigrations are either of individuals or the multitude; in few cases is want of food and room the motive to emigrate. I do not say that they are inoperative; but that in respect to other causes they are unimportant in the dispersion of mankind. Those who emigrate from Europe to America are not the miserable. Those who cross the Atlantic must possess funds to pay their passage, and supply themselves with necessaries during their voyage. They go abroad, not to escape poverty, but to advance their fortune. Thus the provinces supply London, and the Irish resort to England; or if it should be said, with truth, that some are forced abroad through distress, how many Irish emigrate through ambition, pleasure, fashion, from any cause rather than poverty !

The authenticated emigrations from want are few,

---

[1] The Scythian, in Justin, says truly, Belli certamina anceps, præmia victoriæ nulla, damna manifesta. lib. 2. c. 3.

these few proceeded in consequence of famines, and not from any continued surcharge of people exceeding the means of subsistence. Of emigrations from political violence and fanatic tyranny, and despotism and conquest, history is crowded with their relations. In the Grecian states, many alternately emigrated from their respective states, as factions or forms of government failed or triumphed[1]. Italy during its republics exhibited the same scenes. The duke of Alva filled Europe with the industrious Netherlanders, and Louis XIV forced abroad his best subjects by the same conduct. When Louis XV seized Corsica, the shores of the Mediterranean were filled with its refugees. The treatment of European governments to their people first planted America, and the same violations of humanity and equity continued and continue to swell the population.

If there are comparatively few instances of emigration in such circumstances, there are still fewer of the movement of great bodies of men simultaneously through want of the means of living. The Hebrews fled (if the account be received) from Egypt, not through want of food, but oppression; they fled from the lamented flesh pots of Egypt to *enjoy* hunger in the Desert. Thus it is said that 240,000[2] Egyptians revolted from Psammeticus to the Ethiopians, not through hunger but ill treatment. So in Greece, Evander[3] conducted a colony of the defeated party from Palantum in Arcadia to Italy. Thus the Syracusans who fled from the tyranny of Dionysius found-

[1] Paruta, p. 141.   [2] Herodotus, lib. 2. c. 30.
[3] Dion Halicarnassus, lib. 1. c. 31.

ed Ancona[1]. Thus the people of the colonies founded by Dorieus[2] and by Demaratus of Corinth had aban‑doned their country in consequence of domestic out‑rage. Seven hundred Athenian families were forced abroad by Cleomenes ; and the thirty tyrants actually expelled the strength of the city, who accumulating without, assailed their enemies and restored both them‑selves and their country[3]. Thus at Rome, in the time of Appius Claudius[4], a seventh part of the peo‑ple emigrated, and the retreat of the citizens to mount Aventine was a preparation for a still further seces‑sion. In all these and a thousand other instances we hear nothing of the pressure of population against sub‑sistence, except the apologue of the Belly and its members, which Mr. Malthus will hardly pervert to serve his theory. In all these we read of the violence of factions, the tyranny of princes, the monopoly of patrician or of particular families ; in short, the rape and ruin of liberty and property the common inheri‑tance of the people.

Mr. Malthus[5] dares not positively say that the nor‑thern nations never undertook any expedition unless forced by the want of room and food; he is obliged to admit with Mallet, that annually they held a meet‑ing to consider whom they should assail. Yet amidst all these battles and expeditions by land and water, by the northern and by all barbarians, he insists "a state of sloth and not of restlessness and activity seems evidently to be the *natural* state of man[6],"

[1] Strabo, lib. 5. p. 439.　　　[2] Herodotus, lib. 5. c. 41.
[3] Herodotus, lib. 5. c. 72.　[4] Dion Halicarnassus, lib. 6. c. 63.
[5] vol. 1. p. 140.　　　　　　　[6] vol. 1. p. 110.

Mobilis et varia est fermè natura malorum.

What is nature or natural, which may be called the caballa of Mr. Malthus, the Stoics reputed the natural the rational state. Mr. Burke says " art is man's nature "—but Mr. Malthus applies it to all those and a hundred other varieties and contradictions. What can he mean in the just quoted passage by the *natural* state? Is it not the simplest state of life and society? Are children slothful, or are they not most imitative and rather vertiginous in their activity? Look to the first societies of men; we do not read of their dispersion in consequence of want of room and food. Thucydides [1] speaks of the perpetual migrations in Hellas. The Huns [2] had no home; and the Scots, whether their name is derived from their erratic disposition as was that of the Pelasgi, were notorious vagabonds, *per diversa vagantes.*

Suppose the savage the natural state, how can this be called a state of sloth and inactivity, where man, to subsist, must rival the swiftest by despatch, the craftiest by artifice, and the strongest by confederate exertions? The pastoral state supposes a roaming life. The shepherd must at least change his abode with his flocks, even though no beasts threatened the fold. Those who combine two modes of living are necessitated to exert a double energy. So much for man being nature's *sloth.* It is astonishing how any one who marked the spirit of adventure—the mighty toil

[1] lib. 1. p. 2.

[2] Nullusque apud eos interrogatus, respondere unde oritur potest, alibi conceptus, natusque procul et longius educatus. Marcellinus, lib. 31. c. 2.

frequently encountered for no profit, could so characterize mankind. Mr. Malthus has probably been deceived into this remark by accounts of savages—that having hunted down a beast, they sleep and eat till the brute has been consumed; hungry and jaded they sink under fatigue and repletion. Yet at another time these same men would exhibit a state of pure vitality. The savage knows but two situations, and they are the extremes of hunger and gluttony—of a frame wrenched by exertion, and again dissolved by intolerable lassitude.

It might have been supposed that Mr. Malthus would have had some misgiving of his philosophy, when he adverted to total emigrations. When Orgetorix, one of the heroic tribe, wished to conquer Gaul, he thought it convenient to persuade the Helvetians that their country was confined for their numbers. Orgetorix died, but his successors in power pursued the same policy. The people believed as they were taught; they destroyed their towns, villages, and private buildings, and all the corn which they were unable to carry with them, determined to conquer or perish[1]. Here I cannot perceive the imputed pressure of population against subsistence, or the people's want of room and food. They assailed Gaul as Cæsar had, and as the same general had advanced into Britain. Cæsar, who seems to have been jealous that the Helvetians should interfere with the theatre of his glory, met and repelled them; and those people who could not live at home with their whole stores, contrived to sub-

---

[1] He says they did so, ut domum reditionis spe sublata, paratiores ad omnia pericula subeunda essent.

sist on their diminished means within their former frontier. But these are not the entire consequences deducible from this fact—their wants were not so very pressing, when they destroyed their superfluous grain preparatory to the expedition. Observe also, the emigration was total. And Mr. Malthus is obliged to admit that entire emigrations were not uncommon. What is his answer? That these evinced " the unwillingness of the society to divide, but by no means that they were straitened for room." Wonderful love! We are then to conclude, that in a world in which, according to Mr. Malthus, all are stinted for room and food, whole nations, which could not subsist at home, passed in a mass abroad through a refined sensibility—nay, though their own country could not support them singly, another country, though straitened, did support them and its former population. Does this prove a pressure of people against food in the country supporting so increased a population? Nor is this half the wonder of this prodigious pressure. Mr. Malthus admits, "that after a great emigration the countries often remained quite deserted and unoccupied for a long time[1]." How could this happen if the pressure of population was general? Would not the vacuum be instantly replenished? Would not the land be instantly overrun and possessed, as on the emigration of the Ionians the Achæans divided their land and cities by lots among themselves[2]? Many countries have been deserted, and have remained so ; Mallet[3] speaks of 20,000 men who accompanied the

[1] vol. 1. p. 137.   [2] Pausanias, lib. 7. c. 6.
[3] History of Denmark, vol. 1. p. 137.

Lombards into Italy, whose emigration so depopulated the country, that the king of France sent Swabians to occupy it; and Sybaris[1], being conquered, remained, according to Strabo, 58 years unoccupied.

I find nothing, generally, in modern or ancient authors, to justify the conclusions of Mr. Malthus respecting the causes of war and emigration. I do not say that misery has had no influence. I intimate that the want of food and room has been the least urgent of all their inducements. The Gauls envied the Romans their cultivated lands, and they won the Capitol. But though the Romans lived better than the Gauls, are we to conclude the Gauls were pinched with poverty at home? If so, all unsatisfied desires are physical wants. Florus[2] attributes the assaults of the Cimbri, Theutoni, and Tigurini on the Roman empire to the overflow of the ocean pushing them from their seats: and just as truly as Malthus attributes to the flood of life, and the ebb of subsistence, the movements and removals of mankind. Rome had carried her power beyond her moral means :

––––––Then the spirits of the north swept
Rome from the earth where in her pomp she slept.

She had advanced on all sides, and was in her turn repelled, and again circumscribed within her seven hills, long before the Arimaspians[3] drove out the Issedones : these forced forward the Scythians, the Scythians expelled the Cimmerians ; these in the course of time overspread Asia[4], occupied Lydia, seized Sar-

[1] Strabo, lib. 6. p. 263.   [2] lib. 3. c. 3.
[3] Herodotus, lib. 4. c. 13.   [4] Herodotus, lib. 1. c. 15.

dis. The Cimmerians again reflowed. If these advances and retreats were effected by want of food, we must call impulse a consuming power, and hunger shall become a generic term for every passion, every folly, and all the extravagances of the human heart. Mr. Malthus, unobserving the damning documents of all history, which confirm that wars and emigrations have been the effects of restlessness, tyranny, and ambition, in the utmost confusion of ideas and figures, says, " These combined causes soon produce (in the pastoral state) their *natural* and invariable effect—an extended population. A more frequent and rapid change of place then becomes necessary; a wider and more extensive territory is successively occupied; a broader desolation extends all around them; want pinches the less fortunate members of society; and at length the impossibility of supporting such a number together becomes too evident to be resisted. Young *scions* are then pushed out from the parent stock, and instructed to explore fresh regions, and to gain happier seats for themselves by their *swords.* The world is all before them, 'where to choose[1].'" Really, Mr. Malthus, this is against all the prerogatives of bad writing. A country, he insists, as it becomes occupied with herds and shepherds, suffers aggravated desolation; and the less fortunate members of this pastoral society reverse the happy prospect proposed by Isaiah, for it seems they, that is, the young scions, beat their crooks into rapiers! Why? against whom? for Mr. Malthus says " the world is all before them, where to choose." Then these valo-

[1] vol. 1. p. 113.

rous young scions must, like the immortal Getæ, war on the welkin. After this Mr. Malthus should have dwelt on the emigration from the East to Shinar, and the subsequent dispersion from Babel; and though these could not have helped his argument, for in neither case is any hint given of population pressing against the means of subsistence, part of the account would have countenanced his rhetoric, while his language affords some proof of this ancient story; as it appears that even in our days the sin of attempting to build *castles in the air* will be visited on the projectors by broken metaphors, and every confusion of language and discourse.

If this passage does not exhibit of itself the extreme incompetence of Mr. Malthus to lead the public opinion, I quote the following from the same chapter, entitled *Of the checks to population amongst the ancient inhabitants of the north of Europe:* " We are told that Abram and Lot had so great substance in cattle that the land would not bear them both, that they might dwell together. There was strife between their herdsmen; and Abram proposed to Lot to separate, and said, Is not the whole land before thee? If thou wilt take the left hand, then I will go to the right; if thou depart to the right hand, then I will go to the left. This simple observation and proposal is [are] a striking illustration of that great spring of action which overspread the whole earth with people; and in the progress of time drove some of the less fortunate inhabitants of the globe, yielding to irresistible pressure, to seek a scanty subsistence in the burning deserts of Asia and Africa, and the frozen regions of

Siberia and North America." From the proposal of Abram to Lot Mr. Malthus draws an argument for the general pressure of population against food, though, confessedly, the pressure was of abundance, *so great substance of cattle*; their inconvenience was superfluity, and they could relieve this by turning to the right or to the left. It is almost discreditable to lose time in exposing such contradictions.

In his chapter on *Emigration* we are assailed with various absurdities:—indeed they are not few, nor casual, nor shadowy; but general and decided. He says, " Every resource however from emigration, if used effectually, as this would be, must be of short duration. There is scarcely a state in Europe, *except perhaps Russia*, the inhabitants of which do not often endeavour to better their condition by removing to other countries. As these states, *therefore*, have nearly all rather a redundant than deficient population [1]," &c. Yet these Russians, the favoured among the nations of Europe, are not permitted to emigrate. Mr. Malthus has been at St. Petersburg. Does he imagine that the Russians are better fed than the British? Why, the people of Britain would consider Russian fare little better than famine; and by the by they are forced occasionally to eat the rind of the pine [2]. But his absurdity is monstrous when he accounts for the redundancy of European population, " *except perhaps in Russia*," that the inhabitants of the different states of Europe *endeavour to better their condition by removing to other countries*. This is rare induction, particularly by Mr. Malthus, who

[1] vol. 2. p. 69.   [2] Tooke's History of Russia, vol. 1. p. 615.

says, " It is the hope of bettering our condition, and
the fear of want, rather than want itself, that is the
best stimulus to industry." And to the same purport,
" The desire of bettering our condition, and the fear
of making it worse, like the *vis mediatrix naturæ* in
physic, is the *vis mediatrix reipublicæ* in politics [1]:"
and thus we reach a conclusion, that a redundant population and a desire to better our condition are synonymous. The redundancy of population is not confined to Europe : he hints that it operates in America,
and in all states and nations ; the savage, the pastoral,
the agricultural, and all orders and gradations of social life. This being his text and commentary, let
him reconcile the following dogmas with his general
reasoning. The savage state, without forecast or retro-
spect [2], is so beneath all our views and prospects, that
I abandon it to his dominion. Respecting the others,
I feel myself intimately interested. I ask him, how
does his ten-times repeated assertion, that population
presses against the means of subsistence, coincide with
the following positions? " It is the *nature* of pasturage to produce food for a much greater number of
people than it can employ [3]." Population, then, does
not press in this state of society on subsistence.
Again, he says, " It is the *nature* of agriculture,

[1] vol. 2. p. 106.

[2] Savages want food from improvidence. Lichtenstein says, " The
Caffres, who have no idea but of living from day to day, without
any regard to the future, consider the breeding of cattle kept by
the colonists as wholly superfluous." Park also speaks of the pro-
crastinating temper of the Negroes : present pleasure is their only
object ; futurity gives them little or no concern. p. 321.

[3] vol. 1. p. 415.

particularly when well conducted, to produce support for a considerable number above that which it employs[1]." Neither, then, does population press on subsistence in this state of society. I have already quoted what he says of *arts and manufactures, that without these modern Europe would be unpeopled[2].* Those, then, who follow arts and manufactures must of course be deducted from his pressure on subsistence. One state only remains to be considered, the commercial, of which he says, " if things had been left to take their *natural* course, there is no reason to think that the commercial part of the society would have increased beyond the surplus produce of the cultivators; but the high profits of commerce, from monopolies and other peculiar encouragements, have altered this *natural* course of things, and the body politic is in an artificial and, in some degree, diseased state, with one of its principal members out of proportion to the rest[3]." Here then we have three *natures* expressly stated; by which three conditions of society, two of which, he says, by their *nature* would produce more food than those who exercise them could consume, and a third, which would not have consumed more, *naturally,* than the surplus of the cultivators : these, with artists and manufacturers just mentioned, embrace all the great component parts of civilized and social life. How, then, does he reconcile the grand dogma of population pressing against the means of subsistence, and these statements ? for there is no dogma in any writer more enforced, more variously and unremittingly pursued, than the pressure

[1] vol. 2. p. 203.   [2] vol. 2. p. 273.   [3] vol. 2. p. 159.

of population against subsistence, arising from an inordinate propensity or tendency of man to multiply [1]. To such extent are these opinions inculcated, that we might imagine we were reading Adrian Beverland, who held that original sin was Adam's connexion with his wife; or Paracelsus, who, among his fancies in chemistry, propounded that sin and the propagation of mankind were necessary associates.

Yet Mr. Malthus, who fatigues, yet is never weary of contradictions and repugnancies, insists that he is not unfriendly to population; and requires the reader to attend to the *bent and spirit* [2] of his book. Why should an author, and in the fourth edition of his work, appeal from his language, to the reader's gross guess at his meaning, to the bent and spirit of his theory? What critical alembic shall make the extract, and what new mechanism shall preserve the essence? For myself, most conscientiously I declare, that the straight and crooked parts of this essay, all that is right-forward and involved in his doctrine, both in substance and spirit, are averse to populousness. I remember he says, probably to divert animadversion, " That an increase of population, when it follows its *natural* order, is both a great positive good in itself, and absolutely necessary to a further increase in the animal produce of the land and labour of any country, I should be the last to deny. The only question is, what is the *natural* order of its progress [3]?" This order is, he insists, contrary to Sir James Stewart, when agriculture precedes multiplication; that is, when food exceeds population.

[1] vol. 2. p. 239.　　[2] vol. 2. p. 441.　　[3] vol. 2. p. 213.

Even on this reconsidered statement, I repeat, he is unfavourable to population; for he repeatedly affirms that there is a redundancy of people in all European states, " except perhaps in Russia." He also frequently mentions that population is kept up to the level of the means of subsistence. And a fundamental maxim of his science is: " the constant effort towards population, which is found to act even in the most vicious societies, increases the number of people before the means of subsistence[1]." Then what becomes of his verbal patronage for population when it *follows its natural order,* which never occurs, the surplus being always on the side of population?

Yet Mr. Malthus, in order to crown the whole series of contradictions, says, " he can *easily* conceive that this country, with a proper direction of the national industry, might, in the course of some centuries, contain two or three times its present population, and yet every man in the kingdom be much better fed and clothed than he is at present[2]." Who would not think that this was a passage purloined from Mr. Godwin and the Perfectibles? Few extravagances in authors have more surprised me than this flourish. Swift said of an imaginary people;—they are buried on their head, for they hold all things will be turned upside down. I leave the application to the reader.

Mr. Malthus may appeal to the *bent and spirit* of his work, having uttered a saving insulated extravagance amidst a throng of contrary assertions; he may for the instant make votive offerings to Pan, and expect that after centuries dead men on their crowns

[1] vol. 1. p. 22.　　　　[2] vol. 2. p. 274.

will be live men afoot : he may use *nature* and *natu-ral*, which perform more offices than the good and evil principles in the Persian theology, with all the subinfeudation of their agents and satellites ; he may talk of the *natural* order, and that he favours multipli-cation. Yet his manifest opinions, his direct language, his selections from historians and travellers, his rea-soning, his sophistication, his surmises ; the propensi-ties he attributes to man, the order he confers on his great agent *nature*, declare the contrary. One would suppose, from his account of wars and cannibalism, that mankind were all descendants of Thyestes. Man in his philosophy is an eating creature, rife to generate, who increases and hungers and ravens and famishes; even a plentiful season is ominous, and successive years of prosperity, a demonstration that famine and dearth advance. His words are[1], " Among the signs of an approaching dearth, Dr. Short mentions one or more years of luxuriant crops together; and this obser-vation is probably just, as we know that the general effect of years of cheapness and abundance, is to dis-pose a greater number of persons to marry, and under such circumstances the return of a year merely of an average crop might produce a scarcity." Dr. Short's guess means, in vulgar language, " long fair, long foul." Suppose an average year after a plentiful year; suppose many marriages, still nine months must succeed be-fore the hypothetical plenty added one individual to the original stock. What would be the amount of the consumption of all the babes for the first and se-cond years? Could their sucking one year, or eating

[1] vol. 1. p. 567.

panada the second, or a slice from a quartern loaf the third, produce a scarcity? And,'I ask, was the surplus of the abundant years all wasted at the marriage-feasts and at the christenings? Dr. Short talks of more years than one of luxuriant crops. What, have Pharaoh and his alien minister again been busy to convert abundance and want to the subjugation of the people?

Mr. Malthus far surpasses Dr. Short in his commentary on the Doctor's *signs of an approaching dearth.* He says[1], " that contemplating the *plagues and sickly seasons* which occur in these tables (of Sussmilch), after a period of rapid increase, it is impossible not to be impressed with an idea that the number of inhabitants had in these instances exceeded the food, and the accommodations necessary to preserve health." Here *accommodations* appear in aid of food, and truly an aggregate ally of large pretensions. No matter. It is enough that Mr. Malthus proves his theory[2] of the unabated disposition to increase in man, by imputing the plagues and sickly seasons to " increase and multiply." When Adam and Eve ate the forbidden fruit,

Th' inclement seasons, rain, ice, hail, and snow,

changed the face of heaven. But now, when original sin has become inveterate iniquity, the badness of the seasons is aggravated; what was inclement then, is now superlatively sickly; and thus plagues, pestilences and famines, Mr. Malthus states and restates, are

[1] vol. 1. p. 553.

[2] I know nothing superior to this, except the British ministers' referring the destruction of Bonaparte's army by the frost, to their ability. Yet Bonaparte had rather a better set-off in his favour in the expedition to Walcheren.

the terrible correctives of the redundance of mankind[1].

This is not a casual conjecture; for Mr. Malthus, with little power to act the dogmatist, insists it is *impossible* not to be impressed with an idea that sickly seasons arise from a rapid population. If so, and these are induced by overbreeding, ultra-population rules the highest destiny. According to this arrangement, astrology, instead of sovereign on earth, is subject in heaven. Admirable discovery! Now we have only to ascertain the excess beyond the average deaths under different heads of disease, with the casual increase of the people, and prepare for a catarrh, or the natural small-pox, or the typhus fever from Ireland, or for the plague coming post haste in a bill of parcels from Smyrna.

Mr. Malthus has made another advance toward this anticipated knowledge. Sickly seasons, and of course excess of people, he says are periodical. " It appears[2] clearly from the very valuable tables of mortality which Sussmilch has collected, and which include periods of fifty or sixty years, that all the countries of Europe are subject to periodical sickly seasons, and very few are exempt from those great and wasting plagues which once or twice perhaps in a century sweep off the third or fourth part of the inhabitants[3]."

[1] vol. 1. p. 564, 565.

[2] vol. 1. p. 537.

[3] Of the 254 great famines and dearths enumerated in the table, 15 were before the Christian æra, beginning with that which occurred in Palestine in the time of Abraham. If, subtracting these 15, we divide the years of the present æra by the remainder, it will appear that the average interval between the visits of this dreadful scourge has been only about $7\frac{1}{2}$ years. vol. 1. p. 564.

Here then their recurrence, and of course overbreeding, appear comet-like twice a century : in a more extended period, he says they follow at intervals of seven and eight years. Yet unfortunately for this strong alliance and necessary connexion between increasing populousness and seasonable mortalities, Mr. Malthus states, " Epidemics have their seldomer or frequenter returns, according to their sundry soils, situations, air, &c. Hence some have their yearly, as Egypt and Constantinople ; others, once in four or five years, as about Tripoli and Aleppo; others, scarce once in ten, twelve, or thirteen years, as England ; others not in less than twenty years, as Norway and the northern islands [1]."

There is no end to the absurdities and contradictions of Mr. Malthus. Nor are his fantastic views harmless, or amusing, or grateful. No: they have nothing cheering; on the contrary, want, and pressure, and distress, and sickness, and disease, from *deep-rooted causes, from the laws of nature*, from an increase of people, from an increase of food, no matter whether we contemplate earth or heaven, laws or their infraction, all form one labyrinth leading to one sad extremity.—And if you hearken to Mr. Malthus, all this is irremediable: for he says[2], " in a country which keeps its population at a certain standard—if the average number of marriages and births be given, it is evident that the average number of deaths will also be given : and to use Dr. Heberden's metaphor, the channels through which the great stream of mortality is constantly flowing, will always convey off a given quantity. Now if we stop up any of these channels, it is most perfectly

[1] vol. 1. p. 139, note.　　　[2] vol. 2. p. 286.

clear, that the stream of mortality must run with greater force through some of the other channels ; that is, if we eradicate some diseases, others will become proportionably more fatal." We have then the satisfaction to hear that a country may not be able to prolong the life of those whom it has rescued from disease and death; that if we cure the gouty, we kill the paralytic ; and that if we redeem the infant from the grave by the vaccinating lancet, we place a sword in the soldier's hand, or sharpen the axe of the executioner !

Mr. Malthus may insist on his love of the poor, and his love of population: I have heard he is a good man ; yet is he an indifferent author. Having read one extreme in Godwin, he threw himself into the opposite extravagance : and having obtained a reputation, he cannot abandon the cause of his glory. Like other heroes, his honour requires him to defend his acqu:-sitions. I do not doubt but he is a good man : would he were a poet! and then we might repeat that he is the best *natured* man with the worst *natured* muse. He says, among a hundred similar expressions, " corn countries are more populous than pasture countries, and rice countries more populous than corn countries. But their happiness does not depend either upon their being thinly or fully inhabited ; upon their poverty or their riches, their youth or their age, but on the proportion which the population and the food bear to each other[1]." Really, then, the island Rodriguez[2], eighteen miles long and six broad, abounding in wood, water, land turtles, &c. and containing only three families, is more happy than Great Britain or all Eu-

[1] vol. 1. p. 577.   [2] Grant's History of the Mauritius, p. 103.

rope together [1]; where the people, according to Mr. Malthus, are disproportioned to their food. And Rodriguez is three or thirty times less happy, if each family contained ten persons, than Juan Fernandez. Alexander Selkirk lived on it alone; for Friday was a fancied obtruder by De Foe, who so far was ignorant of this new and only felicity of mankind. Selkirk lived on this island for four years at nature's mighty feast, and none to interrupt his board or lessen his store, the happiest man on record, except perhaps Philoctetes. Admirable philosopher! The power of satiating the coarsest animal appetite

> " Is all in all, and I in thee,
> For ever : and in me all whom thou lov'st."

Were he to write a commentary on the Iliad, he would praise the genius of the poet who imagined the *perpetual chime:* and if he recounted the defeat of Hector, it would begin and end with the mal-administration of the commissariat. Mr. Malthus's man is all mouth. Yet he who might assume the motto,

> " Man delights not me, nor woman neither,"

assures us he favours population when it follows the *natural* order.

If Mr. Malthus affixed any meaning to the last quotation, and that the proportion which food bears to the population is first and last and midst, the criterion of happiness, and happiness alone—how happy is Otaheite amidst its Eareeoie societies, and infanticides, and wars! for Mr. Malthus admits [2] that *its population is considerably below the average means of*

---

[1] vol. 2. p. 273.　　　　　　[2] vol. 1. p. 97.

subsistence. How blessed is Russia, which, as I have before quoted from him, is the only country that perhaps has not a redundant population! How paradisaical must be Siberia; and particularly that part of it in the neighbourhood of Krasnoyarsh; for Pallas says, a pood or forty pounds of wheaten flour was sold for about twopence halfpenny, an ox for five shillings, and a cow for about four!—Yet what is Mr. Malthus's remark on this account? Does he rejoice? No: he calls this an *unnatural cheapness* [1]; and refers it to a want of vent for the products of the soil :— this, says he, will soon arise: indeed he *concludes* it must have already happened; and that population now proceeds with rapid strides. I cannot understand what he means by unnatural cheapness on this occasion, nor on any other, except that the article sold did not pay the cost of production. But how little must have been that expense in a country of vast extent, thinly peopled, inland, and so circumstanced that Pallas [2] speaks in admiration of the facility of its cultivation and the abundance of its returns!

There is another circumstance which Mr. Malthus seldom mentions, and then so tenderly and generally, which, with the silence of his opponents on his reserve, is a sad sign of the spirit of the times. He talks of no vent, but nothing of misrule—of unnatural cheapness, but nothing of despotism. Is this the mode for freemen and citizens to treat the principle of population, or any other principle? Yet has this baseness (in honesty and truth I cannot lessen the term) excited little resentment. Mr. Malthus, when he escapes

[1] vol. 1. p. 206.   [2] Travels, t. 1. p. 261.

from *nature* and *its great purposes,* condemns the people and reviles *the indolent* [1] *inhabitants of the plains of Siberia*—reviles them while he praises their government. " And though the Russian government has been incessant in its endeavours to convert the pastoral tribes of Siberia to agriculture, yet many obstinately persist in bidding defiance to any attempts that can be made to wean them from their injurious sloth [2]." Why should they labour? does he not say there is no sufficient vent for the produce of their labour? If there were a vent, would increased labour improve the labourer's condition? Mr. Malthus assures us the people are slothful and indolent; and that the Russian government is incessant in its endeavours to promote agriculture. What have been its attempts to wean the people from their sloth? Has it made them free? A Tartar's curse is, May you live in one place, and work like a Russian [3]!

Wonderful have been the exertions of this government, for mighty are the pretensions of its rulers. Catharine was prodigiously solicitous even for the Poles, when amidst the massacres of the people, and the devastations of the country, she called herself their *tender mother,* (*mater Eumenidum*)*:* and who can doubt her humility and patriotism, when in her *Instructions* [4], &c., she says, " We think and esteem it our glory to declare that we are created for our people." And an

[1] vol. 1. p. 200. [2] vol. 1. p. 207.
[3] Bell's Travels. Pinkerton, vol. 7. p. 281. Lesseps says, " that the vicinity of the Russian settlements has hitherto produced no change in the mode of life of the resident Cossacs." Travels, vol. 2. p. 87. Why should it?
[4] p. 194.

English writer informs us that the Russians are the happiest people on earth, "because the peasantry look upon the monarch as a divinity; styling him god of the earth—*Zemnoi Bog:* ignorant of any government but a despotic sceptre, and of any condition but vassalage; happily deprived of all means of evil information." These are not the words of Mr. Malthus [1]; he praises the government and condemns the people; and refers their indolence to any cause but the true one; to no cause—to *unnatural cheapness.*—The same unnatural cheapness is observable in South America [2], where an ox is not worth one shilling, or one penny; and there the people have had their Zemnoi Bog; and there to kneel on a carpet was a prerogative of the white people. At present they begin to disbelieve that Ferdinand is a divinity on earth; that he can do no

[1] They are the words of Mr. Eton. Mr. Thornton quotes and condemns them: yet Mr. Thornton speaks of a rival government —the Porte, thus: " Only the koran and books treating of the law and the doctrines of the Prophet were forbidden to be printed ; a useful and salutary prohibition, which at the same time preserves religion in its purity," &c. vol. 1. p. 65. The religion that such conduct induces is much like that of the Russians, who enjoy religion in its purity. Thornton says, a Russian would suffer martyrdom sooner than smoke tobacco, because the Scripture says, That which enters into the mouth does not defile a man, but that which comes out of his mouth. vol. 2. p. 94.

[2] Semple's Sketches of the Carraccas. Mawe speaking of Barriza Negro, near Monte Video, says, " here are numbers of great breeding estates, many of which are stocked with from 60,000 to 200,000 head of cattle ; those are guarded principally by men of Paraguay, called peons. 10,000 head are allotted to four or five peons, whose business is to collect them every morning and evening."

wrong; and that ministers are always right : in short, they begin to think that freedom is better than slavery. Nor is it improbable that, should they conquer their liberty, this will be as efficient in promoting agriculture and population, as the egotism of an empress, or the impotent ukases of her successors.

He who seeks for the causes of the people's sloth, and their paucity, and the wilderness which surrounds them, except in their government when it is despotic, is a contemptible theorist. Ehrenmalm, pursuing a scale of superlative misery, considered the life of the Laplander more easy than that of the Greenlander; and the Greenlander's life, which admits no choice but the ice of the sea or the ice of the land, as " better than the life of the people of Siberia, who only see the arrival of soldiers or disgraced courtiers [1]." What signify the wishes or the exertions of a despotic prince? And it has been long remarked [2], that a reward offered in a Russian proclamation is always clogged by a threat :—they avail not. Suppose them as rational as they are absurd : what did Catharine's village-building scheme produce in Russia? The money was absorbed by the courtiers; and Zemnoi Bog, the tender mother, was entertained on her tour with visions of distant towns and a population multiplied to the eye of her godship—just as a company of strollers represent a drama in a barn, " one man playing many parts." What signify the good laws of a despot? Catharine states unconsciously [3], that the cause of the non-execution of the ordinance of 1722, which en-

[1] Pinkerton, Travels, vol. 1. p. 370.
[2] Annual Register, 1770, p. 30.   [3] Instructions, p. 135.

joined that persons who tortured their vassals should be submitted to guardians, is *unknown*. The imperial ordinance was waste paper; and the counterparts of Huggins and Hodges flogged their vassals to death in contempt of the mandate. Not only the laws but the individual orders of the despot are contemned. Colonel Thespy de Belcourt, a Polish officer, was sent with others to Siberia. They were ill treated on the road, contrary to the express injunctions of the Empress. The colonel relates in his memoirs, that when he signified to his conductors the command of the Empress, they answered, *Le bon Dieu est bien haut, et l'Impératrice est bien loin; nous ferons ce qu'il nous plaira.*

What! could not Russia, or even Siberia, win from Mr. Malthus one innuendo respecting the effects of despotism aggravated unnaturally by distance from the point of its concentration? No: the sum and substance of his sagacity discovered that the people were incorrigibly slothful; and that population was restrained by the unnatural cheapness of cattle and grain. Catharine[1] draws a better conclusion. Speaking of the Russians, she says " that not one fourth of the children of one marriage attains maturity: and she assigns as the cause of this premature mortality, that the lords never reside in the villages—and that they tax the people by the poll from one to five rubles, [she might have added, to five hundred] without regarding their ability to pay them. This, she adds, " often obliges husbandmen to quit their homes sometimes for fifteen years, in order to acquire means to satisfy their lords." Mr. Malthus

[1] Instructions, p. 138.

will call this a pressure of population against the
means of subsistence; and I doubt if he would be
restrained, though he were reminded that more than
once he has distinguished Russia from those nations
of Europe which suffer a redundant population. I
say that these children die through despotism, through
a subinfeudation of tyranny. Who can believe that
there is a stint of subsistence in Siberia? Yet the abbé
Chappe d'Auteroche[1] affirmed that two-thirds of the
children of Siberia die in infancy, though, he subjoins,
their parents are robust. He also speaks of the depopulation of villages. The same is observed respecting the people of the Cape of Good Hope.
Lord Valentia says, the Dutch debilitated the Hotten-
tots by supplying them with spirits to excess, and
thus they enslaved them. So far both governments
pursued the same objects, but by different means;—
the consequences are similar. Lichtenstein, speaking of the colonists at the Cape, who abound with
provisions, observes, " it is very moderate to reckon
ten children to each family[2]." The mortality, however, is extreme. Salt says of this country, " nothing
seems wanting except an increase of population,
which an extraordinary fatality among children seems
to render hopeless without some external assistance;
but every attempt of this nature has not been attended
hitherto with the expected advantages[3]." Humboldt
also speaks of the mortality of infants in parts of
South America. What is the cause of this? The
pressure of population? No; but the pressure of bad
government, of intolerable masters, just as overworked

[1] Annual Register, 1764, p. 93.　　[2] p. 113.　　[3] Travels, p. 9.

negresses in the West Indies miscarry:—it is the abuse of human life and human comforts.

Mr. Malthus, having mentioned a mortality, cries, Here is a proof of the great tendency, the universal pressure;—*nature* is at work to check redundances. Then they who torture, they who divorce the husband and wife, and thus expose whole families to premature death, that they may raise a few rubles on the husband's head, are accredited agents in the prime ministry of all-reconciling nature; and the chief of this huge despotism, who meditated, even in his escape from ruin and desolation, new wars and a new crusade, is nature's self. The people are dispersed, or they are destroyed in the armies, and their families are reduced. "Aye," says Mr. Malthus, "we always find nature faithful to her great object; at every false step we commit, ready to admonish us of our errors [1]:" that is, the people overbreed. Neither here nor any where that Russian affairs are discussed, does the despotism of chiefs and nobles interrupt the tenour of his theme. If the children perish excessively, reference is made to an unnatural overbreeding people [2]; much in the style of Colonel Keating, who, " in his

---

[1] vol. 2. p. 287. In the next page promiscuous intercourse appears " admonishing us severely of our error; would point to the only line of conduct approved by nature, reason, and religion; abstinence from marriage till we can support our children; a chastity till that period arrives."

[2] So far as Mr. Malthus may be exculpated by a single incidental passage *contradicting* a hundred others, I quote the following: " Sir Francis d'Ivernois very justly observes, that if the various states of Europe kept and published annually an exact account of their population, noting carefully, in a second column, the exact

balances and harmonies of nature," says, " though the lioness have three whelps, two always die." Mr. Malthus might as well attribute the mortality of the Russians in the field and at their sieges, and when they stormed Ishmael or Oczakow, to the pressure of population against food, as the great mortality of infant children to their overbreeding parents. A bad government will destroy the children ; a worse will destroy the men ; and the worst will mortify even the passion of the sexes, and obliterate the human race.

This may be thought a dread heresy by Mr. Malthus and the votaries of the new system,—those who hold that if men be fed they will breed, and that government has little influence in restricting the population of mankind.

Yet does tyranny consume and extinguish the people; nay, hereditary honours have frequently worn away the prerogative classes. The bourgeoisie of the town of Berne, that is, the aristocracy of the canton of Berne, for the government of the canton is possessed by the municipality[1], declined ; and in order to recruit its numbers from 1583 to 1654, 487 families were made

age at which the children die, this second column would show the relative merit of the governments, and the comparative happiness of their subjects." vol. 1. p. 471. Yet so little influence had government on population, in his conviction, that eight lines preceding this quotation he couples America and Russia, the freest and most despotic governments. His words are : " In countries circumstanced like America or Russia, or in other countries after a great mortality, a large proportion of births may be a favourable symptom."

[1] In all the aristocratical cantons, those who are not born in the city are subjects. Bibliothèque de l'Homme Publique, vol. 5. partie 2. p. 30.

bourgeois. In two centuries 379 of these became extinct; and in 1783 little more than one-fifth of those were in existence. In a century, from 1684 to 1784, 207 Bernoise families became extinct. Le Statistique de la Suisse specifies other incorporations of families, and their repeated extinction; yet to be eligible to the highest offices[1] marriage is requisite. Mr. Malthus[2] has noticed the failure of the Bernoise families; and the whole account is stated by him with seeming gratification, as a proof of the discreet reserve of the people, and the benefit which must result in consequence to society. Truly, the annihilation of an order of people, with their repeated recruits, happily illustrates the excellence of the preventive check. But Mr. Malthus forgets that all this sadly interferes with another cardinal position of his *craft*, that population will always keep itself up to the level of the means of subsistence. Must we suppose that all those who were chosen for their character and circumstances, and who from their situation were among the favoured, perished through distress?

This event is no peculiarity. The same occurred at Rome among the patricians, and afterward among the Venetian nobles. Shakespear hit their character when Petruchio says that he went to Padua " to wive wealthily, and therefore happily." For it was not their vice to marry before they could provide for a family. Such was the prudence of the nobility, so cautious were they that population should not press on the means of subsistence, that a law[3] was passed

[1] That is, senators, &c. Bibliothèque de l'Homme, tome 5. p. 56.
[2] vol. 1. p. 411.   [3] De Statutis Venetis, p. 185.

in 1535, prohibiting any Venetian from giving more than 5000 ducats as a portion with his daughter; and in 1550 the sum was reduced to 4000 ducats. What was the result of this mighty circumspection? The citizens who became the noble in respect to the new citizens gradually declined. Bodin[1] speaks of their being reduced to 4 or 5000. Amelot says they had fallen to 2500; and when Addison wrote they were only 1500, "notwithstanding the addition of many new families since that time. It is very strange that with this advantage they are not able to keep up their numbers, considering that the nobility spreads equally through all the brothers, and that so very few of them are destroyed by the wars of the republic[2]." Here those who possessed the good things of the state could not support their order, though repeatedly recruited from the people;—with all their wealth and honours, and privileges and prerogatives, they perished.

> " ——————'Tis the plague of great ones,
> Prerogatived are they less than the base:
> 'Tis destiny unshunnable: 'Tis death."

The prerogative order dissolved, though the most wretched of mankind; the Roman Catholics of Ireland, the Pariars of Hindostan, the Jews every where, support their race; yet the patricians of Rome, the burghers of Berne, the noble Venetians, perish among honours and opulence. So in England, even in the present reign, 48 titles conferred by former kings have become extinct; and not a few peerages have also ceased even during the life of him who conferred

[1] De la République, liv. 2. p. 225.
[2] Remarks on Italy, Works, vol. 5. p. 186.

them. Therefore Josephus[1] and after him Eusebius[2] are greatly mistaken in considering the extinction of Herod's race within a century miraculous. It is not uncommon; it is customary to all those who would respire on commanding heights, contemning the people and the plains. The *effeminate disease* mentioned by Hippocrates[3] was confined to the higher orders. The inability to continue the race is confined to the noble Scythians. The nobleman can scarcely be a father, the lady cannot be a nurse should she be a mother[4]. The child even by sucking the strength of a woman is hardly reared. How shall this thing, which barely lives, communicate life? Generation by such parents is like a spring in the desert;—it has no stream. Nobles are exotics in a conservatory adorned with a double flower; while the people are the wild plants of the field, which quicken in every joint and root and berry, and though cropped, and trodden, live and luxuriate.

---

[1] Antiq. lib. 18. c. 11.   [2] Præparat. Evang. lib. 2. c. 10.

[3] Περι αερων.

[4] Interea tormentum ingens nubentibus hæret
Quod nequeunt parere, &c.   Juvenal. Sat. 2. v. 136.

PART II.

CHAPTER I.

Means adopted to increase the people—promiscuous intercourse—polygamy—fining bachelors—compulsory measures—parish marriages. Mr. Malthus — bounties— exemptions — lying-in and foundling hospitals. Mr. Malthus. Hospitals for health. England deficient in some respects—greatly improved in others. Mr. Malthus supposes that inoculation has not increased population, and that all remedies against plagues, &c. have also been ineffectual.—On the contrary, health promotes population ; and every life saved is so much stock saved—the people riches.

THOSE who have favoured the multiplication of mankind have suggested different modes to promote this object. Some have proposed a promiscuous intercourse between the sexes. According to Strabo[1], the Spartans having made a vow that they would not cohabit with their wives during the siege of Messene, which unexpectedly lasted nineteen years, and fearing that their country might be depopulated, directed the young of both sexes, who were children at the commencement of this war, to live promiscuously, *ut cuncti virginibus cunctis commiscerentur, rati hoc pacto copiosiorem procreatum in subolem.* To a similar state of society Sir John Davies attributes the population of Ireland : " living by the milk of the cow, without husbandry or tillage ; there they in-

[1] lib. 6. p. 510.

creased and multiplied into infinite numbers by promiscuous generation among themselves[1]."

On the contrary, some writers consider promiscuous
cohabitation injurious to population ; but they employ
this expression defectively. Mr. Mallet, in the reign
of Charles the Second, introduced a bill to repeal one
which had been passed in that of James, which enacted
that it was felony to marry a second husband or wife,
the former being living." He pressed the repeal as a
measure " for peopling the nation, and preventing the
promiscuous use of women[2]." Mr. Malthus also considers a promiscuous connexion a great check ; but
in no instance does he employ the expression accurately, though he uses it, as is usual with him, in a variety of senses. The Eareeoie societies approach this
unlimited profligacy, I admit ; but he employs the term
prostitution and promiscuous intercourse[3] respecting
these societies generally, and in his language these expressions are synonymous. But they are not inter-
changeable. Graunt, in his Bills of mortality, applies
it with more propriety. He says, " when it is found
how many ewes, suppose twenty, one ram will serve,
we may geld nineteen or thereabouts ; for if you emas-
culate but ten, you shall by promiscuous copulation
hinder the increase." This question I submit to the
curious in sheep.

After promiscuous intercourse we ascend to concubinage and polygamy. Sir James Stewart seems to

---

[1] On Ireland, p. 162.   [2] Annual Register, 1763, p. 265.
[3] The following numbers will lead to some passages exhibiting
his loose phraseology in this particular : vol. 1. p. 18, 88, 90, 93,
96, 99, 101, 102, 184, 186, &c.

have acquiesced in the ability of such connexions to increase the people: he says, " I have not proposed plans of multiplication, &c., principally because I believe it will be found a sufficient abundance of children are born already, and that we have neither occasion for concubinage nor polygamy to increase their numbers[1]."

Those who favour concubinage resort necessarily to patriarchal times. According to Selden[2], before the law, marriage conferred no distinction in the intercourse of the sexes. Mahomet followed the early habits of the Jews, which suited the rude people he commanded, and his own temperament. There is a curious sort of concubinage in Russia: " in many families the father marries his son, while a boy of eight or nine years old, to a girl of a more advanced age, in order, as it is said, to procure an ablebodied woman for the domestic service. He cohabits with this person, now become his daughter-in-law, and frequently has several children by her." So says Coxe[3], and Ker Porter confirms it; yet the Russians will not eat a cock because he is a polygamist.

To polygamy an extensive population has often been attributed. Strabo[4] says the Persians had many wives and concubines; *propaganda subolis gratia.* Suetonius[5] says it was the intention of Julius Cæsar to introduce this practice for the same purpose. Diodorus Siculus[6] accounts for the populous-

---

[1] vol. 1. p. 74.

[2] Coitus cum scorto—sicut coitus cum uxore sua et de jure, &c. lib. 7. c. 5. p. 808.

[3] book 4, c. 1.   [4] lib. 15. t. 2. p. 491.   [5] lib. 1. c. 52.

[6] lib. 1. The priests had but one wife.

ness of Egypt by polygamy, as Duhalde [1] does for the multitudes in China. So does Bolingbroke for the *prodigious number* of the Jews; " if we believe them to have been real, to that prodigious and constant increase of people which a well-ordered polygamy caused [2]."

> " In pious times, ere priestcraft did begin,
> Before polygamy was made a sin;
> When man on many multiplied his kind,
> Ere one to one was cursedly confin'd."

Such doctrines we should not expect from Bolingbroke. He adds, " this sort of polygamy is quite conformable to the law of nature, and provides the most effectual means for the generation and education of children." Why did not Bolingbroke consummate this rhapsody by introducing Solomon, the wisest of men, in all his glory amidst his many hundred wives and concubines?

> " Thus Israel's monarch after heaven's own heart,
> His vigorous warmth did variously impart
> To slaves and wives."

Lastly, Bolingbroke defends polygamy by the authority of Moses against Cecrops.

Barbeyrac [3] imagines that polygamy caused an overflowing population.

Bruce [4] supports polygamy and Mahomet. He says it was established by him " for the welfare of

[1] vol. 2. p. 10.

[2] Philosophical Works, vol. 4. p. 112. Madan, in Thelypthora, endeavours to honour the Jewish institutions as greatly tending to population. chap. 10.

[3] Notes on Puffendorff, lib. 6. c. 1. p. 19.

[4] Travels, vol. 1. p. 291.

his people. He did not permit a man to marry two or three or four wives, unless he could maintain them: then he was interested for the rights and ranks of the women. In Jedda, the people almost destitute for the necessaries of life can only marry one wife: from this arises the want of people." He adds, that in Arabia Felix, where there are plenty of provisions, men may marry four wives: " hence people are increased in a four-fold ratio by polygamy." How this exhibits Mahomet's solicitude for the rights or ranks of women, when one man is estimated as equivalent to four women, I do not understand. It may be observed that he reduced the value of woman to one half of the cheapened calculation of the Sikhs [1]. Surely that enterprising traveller might as fairly have attributed the scantiness of the population at Jedda to the acknowledged poverty of the country, and the populousness of Arabia Felix to the abundance of the land, as to any difference in the customary marriages of the two countries.

Suppose that polygamy did increase the children of particular fathers, it would remain to be proved that this increased the population of the state, or even the number of births. Chardin says [2], the Mahometan Tartars have many wives, because, say they, these bring us many children, which we may sell or exchange for necessaries. To the same purpose Captain Beaver says [3], among the Naloos " a man's wealth is

---

[1] The Adi-Grant'h, the Bible of the Sikhs, is said to have been enlarged by twelve men and a half—that is, twelve men and one woman. Sketch of the Sikhs, note, p. 31.

[2] Harris's Collection, b. 3. c. 2. p. 865.

[3] African Memoranda, p. 327.

calculated from the number of his wives." But this
only refers to the advantage of particular families;
and unless it be proved that there are many more
women than men in the ordinary course of generation, (which in another publication I shall show is contrary to fact,) or that those who are wived to polygamists would otherwise have been unmated and sterile,
these statements, though true, are nugatory as to the
main question. They only prove that the powerful
appropriated the rights of others—and that the richest,
by taking many wives, reduced the less rich to live
bachelors.

Suppose that the polygamist has many children,
how does this advance population? Niebuhr states [1]
the increase of families by polygamy—but he says that
the mortality is excessive among the children, and that
the number of children sinks many parents into great
misery. The present king of Persia is reported to have
had fifty sons when he was twenty-five years old. These,
if they should escape the suspicion of a brother's vengeance, will probably add nothing to the numbers of
the state; nor will the brood of his courtiers be more
lasting;—who no doubt, in their generation, imitate
his majesty. We may, however, discuss this subject
in a higher tone, and deny that polygamy promotes
population even in the appropriating families. Eton
states [2] that Christian parents have more children than
the Mahometans who adopt polygamy. Nor can this
be attributed to the general decline of the Turkish institutions and government; for Ricaut [3], who admired

[1] t. 2. c. 5.   [2] Survey of the Turkish Empire, p. 275.
[3] Turkish Empire, b. 2. c. 21.

Mahomet and the Porte and polygamy, wrote long ago: "his [Mahomet's] main consideration was the increase of his people; knowing that the greatness of empire and princes consists more in the numbers and multitude of the people than in the extent of their dominions:" and having descanted on the beginning of the world, and the increase of mankind, and polygamy among the Jews, he concludes, "Through sorcery and witchcraft these marriages [the Turkish] are now observed not to be so fruitful and numerous as is the marriage bed of a single wife." Every moral reason, that is in this case every reason, opposes the probable increase of people by polygamy. When the discipline of Turkey was pre-eminent, and the Mahometans triumphed, their success justified all their institutions to uninquiring minds. Their fortune has been for some time checked; and men now begin to learn that the Mahometans were numerous not because they were polygamists, but in spite of this evil. Volney [1] sanctions the opinion of Montesquieu, whom in general he does not favour, that polygamy is one cause of the depopulation of Turkey.

To promote marriage, various schemes have been proposed: and I repeat, that in giving a brief history of opinions, I trust my own may not be prejudged. Honours and rewards, pains and penalties, prerogatives and exceptions have been multiplied, to quicken the disposition of men to matrimony. The penal parts of legislature are generally esteemed the most operative, and I shall begin with them. Plato proposed to fine bachelors;

[1] Il a eu raison de dire que la polygamie étoit une cause de dépopulation en Turquie. Voyage en Syrie, t. 2. p. 327.

and agreeably to the usual affluence of his language, he varies the penal age from 35 in one book[1] to 37 in another[2]. I shall not here add instances from Grecian politics, having already noticed them: and I shall only, for the same reason, subjoin one from the Roman institutions, on account of its peculiarity. I allude to that law admired by Montesquieu[3], which prohibited unmarried women from the use of certain ornaments.

Nor has modern Europe wanted politicians who would inflict on recreant bachelors the vengeance of the law. Dr. Short proposed that fines should be imposed on bachelors, and that their amount should be applied to support the married poor. Decker[4] proposed fines also; but not, he says, to encourage marriages, but because the expenses of bachelors in respect to their fortunes admit of it. How is that discovered? At least it is as plausible that those who marry are equal to the charges of the connexion as those who do not are incompetent: for the improvident marriages of some, or the licentious or unsocial lives of others, are extrinsic to general legislation. In other countries of modern Europe similar laws have been recommended. Montesquieu[5] laments that Europe still wants laws to promote the propagation of the species: and Valazé[6] would supply his intimation by fixing the penal age of bachelors at thirty years.

---

[1] de Legib. lib. 4. p. 835. [2] Ibid. lib. 6. p. 860.

[3] L'Esprit des Loix, liv. 23. c. 26.

[4] On Trade, p. 88. Dr. Price talked of a tax on celibacy paying off the national debt, p. 115. Great effects from little causes. If he were not the reviver of the sinking fund, this would appear a joke. But an enthusiast never wanted an expedient.

[5] L'Esprit des Loix, liv. 23. c. 21. [6] Loix Penales, p. 207.

To the penal may follow the compulsory. Frederic the *great* [1] carried off a number of young Saxon women and married them to Prussians provided by the crown. A lunatic king [2] said,

> "——————————Let copulation thrive:
> To't luxury, pell mell, for I lack soldiers."

Yet probably these truly royal weddings were as little productive as Mons. Beausobre's advice, who recommended Frederic, in order to assist population, to decree *que les hommes n'épousent des femmes très-désagréables.*

Under the head of compassion may be classed parish marriages: and as some consider that the poor-laws increase the people, they may be here mentioned. A girl is pregnant; the parish officers, finding that the woman will be chargeable, pursue the reputed father. If taken, he is menaced by magistrates and churchwardens. Crabbe exhibits this judicial achievement and happy consummation:

> "Near her the swain, about to bear for life
> One certain evil, doubts 'twixt war and wife:
> But while the falt'ring damsel takes her oath,
> Consents to wed, and so secures them both."

How magistrates and parish officers, who must be supposed good protestants and to know the liturgy of the established church, can oblige such parties to marry, is strange, if indeed all orders did not prove that they are religious by rote, or rather in the abstract. But it is still stranger that they do not see, that eventually this must increase the evil; and that the alternative penalty of a wife, if the man should not

---

[1] Wraxall's Memoirs, vol. 1. p. 214.　　　[2] Lear.

divorce himself by sudden flight, must increase the number of the poor. They may think with Margaret[1], " Is not marriage honourable in a beggar ?" but they cannot say with Priuli, " Get brats and starve with them :" for the brats and their parents must be supported by those persons whose officers promoted such marriages.

Bounties on marriages have been numerous and not unknown to many countries: in 1767 a number of young maidens were portioned in Florence on account of the happy delivery of the grand duchess[2]. For every reason it would have been better to have made the donation to women lately delivered. At Naples, in the year following[3], 20,000 ducats given by that city to the new queen were apportioned among 200 young women. In 1767 the queen of Denmark[4] ordered 30 rix dollars to each of twenty-five women, in order to enable them to marry : yet two years preceding, in 1765, the king of Denmark[5] forbade first and second lieutenants in the army to marry, unless they had 150 crowns exclusive of their pay.

The court and crown of France have been great populators. Madame de Pompadour says in her memoirs, that she prevailed on the king to apply 600,000 livres designed for a *fête* on account of the duke of Burgundy's marriage, towards the marrying young women. She adds, that M. de Billeuse, who was fond of calculating every thing, (the precursor of Mr. Colquhoun,) estimated that the marriages would yield annually 20,000 citizens to the monarchy. Louis XV.

[1] Much Ado about Nothing. [2] Annual Register, 1767, p. 66. [3] Ibid. 1768, p. 147. [4] Ibid. 1767, p. 151. [5] Ibid. 1765, p. 75.

patronized population ; and, following the policy of his predecessors, ordained that marriage should exempt his subjects from military conscription[1] ; for this mode of recruiting is not of consular or imperial, but of royal origin. Thus he reduced premature marriages; which of course had no effect but making the poor poorer, and deaths more numerous. This great monarch was consequential throughout; while he afforded bounties for marriages, he exhausted the sources of the ordinary revenue, and effected a national bankruptcy : and while he invited foreigners to France[2] by assigning them lands rent-free for fifteen years, he repelled their entry by misrule ; nay expelled his people by violations of personal liberty, and by breaking those fundamental laws by which, in the language of the parliament of Paris, *he had himself ascended the throne*[3]. This language preceded the revolution twenty years.

Some governments of Europe have distinguished their costly mismanagement by a bounty on soldiers' marriages. Observe the conduct of the Romans, who were eminent for their military science. Soldiers and wives they held incompatible : and it is remarked among the extraordinary means adopted under a declining population, after the state had long merged

[1] Les mariages prematurés étoient multipliés par la crainte des loix militaires. Depere.

[2] Annual Register, 1766, p. 132.

[3] In 1768 the parliament in a remonstrance told the king, " there are two sorts of laws ; those of the king and those of the kingdom : and that by the latter he ascended the throne," &c. Yet we must suppose that the legitimate government ought to be supported at any expense, &c.

into a monarchy, that Pertinax [1] admitted women to associate with the soldiers. Modern sovereigns have improved on this feeble effort to recruit a consuming people. The empress queen Theresa first suffered the troops to marry [2]. In the year following [3] she enjoined them to marry; helping her ordonnance by increasing the pay of all serjeants and corporals by three kreutzers a day for each child.—Thus, she stated, she intended to supply the loss of men in the wars.

The empress Catharine of Russia, among her other maternal achievements, was a great friend to population. Beside lessening the punishment for adultery, and portioning damsels, while she squandered forty millions on her own sterile amours [4], she encouraged the marriages of her soldiers. Mr. Tooke informs us [5], " according to an estimate made some years ago, it was reckoned that in the field regiments alone, and a few garrisons, about eighteen thousand sons of soldiers are taught and maintained at the expense of the state in schools appointed for that purpose.—Similar institutions are kept up for all the regiments of the guards." And how much more does every child so educated cost than a peasant's son? and just so many does this institution deduct from the whole population. In 1765 [6], orders were read in England at the head of the regiments of foot guards and troops of horse, signifying that those who were lawfully married

---

[1] Herodian, lib. 3. p. 172. Libanius, Orat. Funeb. Opera, p. 284.
[2] Annual Register, 1767, p. 4.   [3] Ibid. 1768, p. 35.
[4] Anderson's Sketches of Russia, p. 371. The author is loyal also.
[5] History of the Russian Empire, vol. 1. p. 619.
  Annual Register, 1765, p. 149.

might send their wives to the lying-in hospitals, and have their children supported: yet every child so reared cost the price of five children reared in the ordinary way. But what signifies the waste of property or the ruin of the people?—One soldier's son is more valuable in a military monarchy, and in those which depend on standing armies, than many peasants. Military schools, military colleges, serve to promote the separation of soldier and citizen, and with the barrack system determine the caste of arms. Such bounties are ruinous and absurd. As specimens of sentimentality in courts, they are like Xerxes' tears—he wept, because in a hundred years not one should be alive of all his military array: yet was he driving them with many myriads more to swift destruction. They resemble the same Catharine's deeds in Poland; who while she massacred the people, endowed an orphan-house [1].

Legislators having called maids and youths together by proclamations and bounties, and having thus far exculpated themselves from the senseless censure of their indifference to the great command;—the state wives being pregnant, their parturition became a subject of national solicitude. The cantons of Switzerland sympathized with the kingdoms of Europe—they dreaded depopulation: to counteract this calamity, it was proposed to stop emigration—introduce strangers—particularly midwives;—portion maidens, and erect foundling hospitals. Here we behold a display of great vigour: but these oligarchies entirely omitted to reform their governments. Tweddell saw the aristocrats of Switzerland as they were and are.

[1] Annual Register, 1765, p. 95.

Their politics at home and abroad are abominable. They hire out their citizens to be the body guards of tyrants, to assist them in their flagitious conquests. Remember, when you revile the French for their outrages in Switzerland, (and they were hideous,) that the Swiss hired their citizens to Louis XV; and that they were eminently active in subjecting the brave Corsicans to the French crown[1]. The Swiss oligarchies, while they dreaded depopulation, did not withdraw their troops from supporting tyrants and conquerors; nor did Berne reduce the taxation of the Pays de Vaud[2]: nor did this overruling canton liberate its own people; and they fell before the French. Had Switzerland been free, the French would not have conquered Switzerland: without giving them any credit for forbearance, they would not have attempted the conquest. Enough of this. *La Société Economique de Berne* saw, or thought they saw, depopulation; and like all such societies in Europe, which subsist by overlooking the causes of public evil, they proposed breeding by bounty, and nurturing by artifice.

The same course, but much more flagitiously, the Swedish king Gustavus III. pursued. This man, who blossomed a hypocrite, having by his agents imposed a belief that an accidental scarcity was the act of the senate; and having by the remaining friends of the old tyranny, who conspired in 1756[3] to massacre in

[1] See Annual Register, 1768, p. 60.

[2] In Bibliothèque de l'Homme Publique, t. 5. p. 47, it is said the inhabitants paid 30 per cent. thus:

le lods	16
la dime	10
encense	2
droits de patrage, &c.	2

[3] Mably, Droit Publique, t. 2. p. 284.

the diet all the senators and ministers who were attached to their country and the republic, gained the army; he attained despotism, and he exercised it even while he spoke of tyrants, as if his actions rivalled the deeds of Harmodius. This Gustavus was a populator also: he established medicine-shops, lying-in hospitals, foundling-hospitals, and the like.

England of course could not resist the common impulse: yet I should be unjust in omitting that here such institutions have not originated with royalty. Sir W. Harper [1] in Queen Elizabeth's reign left a property to be applied to the marrying young maidens; and the Earl of Buckinghamshire [2] contributed to the same purpose. London possessed a lying-in hospital of some standing, as may be learned by the oath required of the midwives who might have baptized infants *in extremis.*—They were sworn, that in performing this sacrament, " ye shall not in any wise use or exercyse any manner of wychecraft, charmes, sorcerye," &c. We now come to foundling hospitals.

Addison in the Guardian, No. 105, recommended foundling hospitals: and he urged the English by stating that " there are at Paris, Madrid, Lisbon, Rome, and many other large towns, great hospitals built like our colleges." He might have displayed various coincidences between foundling hospitals and our colleges. Twenty-six years after this intimation by Addison, Captain Thomas Coram after seventeen years exertion effected the establishment of a foundling hospital. I think we may lament his success; at least I may here say that men and states should well consider

[1] Annual Register, 1762, p. 84. [2] Ibid. 1762, p. 71.

not only the good that may be done and the evil that
may be prevented, but the good which cannot be done,
and the evil which must result from all establishments :
for it seems that as men grow old, establishments grow
worse.

Foundling hospitals, as a means of increasing the
people, are among the least rational of human institutions. For the facts.—In the Gazette of Deux Ponts,
April 9, 1771, it is stated, that of 108 children received in the foundling hospital of Normandy, 104
died.   In Valencia [1], about the year 1786, of 332
159 died. And Swinburne says [2] that in Cordova 500
chidren are annually lost in the foundling hospital of
that city. Tooke states [3] that from the establishment
of foundling hospitals in Russia in 1786, during a
period of twenty years, of 37,607 children received,
only 7,100 survived, or four fifths perished. In Ireland
also, up to the half-year ending the 8th of July, 1797,
the mortality amounted to three fourths of the number
of children received. This is to sacrifice to Juno and
Moloch on the same altar.   What a mighty destruction ! how much more excessive than the ruin of slaves
in their swiftest state of decline ! for not more than a
fourth of them perished during the first four years after their arrival in our West India islands. The deaths
in the foundling hospital of Dublin, and which exceeded the waste of life in similar institutions in the
despotism of Russia, are referable to the aggravated

[1] Townsend's Travels in Spain, vol. 2. p. 322.

[2] Travels in Spain, p. 305.

[3] History of Russia, vol. 1. p. 585 : and those of St. Petersburg
the same, p. 586.

misrule and total disregard of the higher orders of Ireland, to every national concern in that insulted degraded country, except when some sectarian or sordid interest quickens their attention. The eighth report of the Board of Education justifies this observation by the following statement, " that except when offices of emolument were to be disposed of, it was difficult out of nearly two hundred governors to procure the attendance of five once a quarter." A year or two ago the mortality was so great, that a bill was brought into parliament to restrain the reception of children during the winter: and I believe no child is now admitted without a certificate ascertaining its parents. If so, it is no longer a foundling hospital.

Though it is not easy to understand how so many deaths could be effected, except by a determination to destroy in those who should preserve, yet no care, no anxiety could prevent in such institutions a great mortality. The mere transfer of an infant child from its mother's bed to the hospital must be pernicious. Besides, infants require the utmost solicitude: any casual claim on a mother's attention often proves fatal to the child. A proverb at Montpellier [1] is explanatory: " The season of rearing silk-worms sends many children to paradise:" meaning that this office divides the mother's care with her children. There are other causes of neglect; a foundling is reputed a beggar's bastard; the nurses are not the most select; they are paid little and worked much. Tooke, with a design to eulogize, says that in the foundling hospitals in Russia

[1] Morgue in the National Institute on the population of Montpellier.

each nurse suckles two babes: and this may be praised;
for Boisgelin, speaking of Copenhagen, says that each
nurse suckles two, and never more than three children.
What must be the consequence, when a single stranger
must perform the part of three mothers? Musæussays [1]
the eagle brings forth three—two live, and one is reared:
—the reason assigned for this mortality is the difficulty of providing for the eaglets; or, as Mr. Malthus
would say, the pressure of the birds on the means of
subsistence.

Those who doubt the populating influence of foundling hospitals insist on their moral effects. Mercier, in
his Tableau de Paris, says [2] that since the establishment of foundling hospitals in Paris, infanticide has
been rare: yet Boisgelin, speaking of the more serious
crimes at Stockholm, mentions child-murder, though
a foundling hospital exists in that city. But suppose
that such receptacles lessened what is called infanticide—do they not occasion a suite of vices? Mr. Grahame says [3], " Foundling hospitals, although they may
multiply illegitimate births, do not multiply instances
of illicit intercourse." That is to say, illegitimate births
may not proceed from illicit intercourse. They prevent
marriage, encourage licentiousness, and continue it:—
the woman who erred and suffered the penalty of rearing the fruit of her transgression, would probably have
ceased to sin; but relieve her of her child, and she se-
duces or is again seduced. Thus it happens that two
or three lewd mothers and their consuming brood,

[1] Ὁς τρια μεν τικτει, δυω δ' εκλεπει εν δε αλεγιζει. Aristot. de
Animalibus, lib. 4. c. 6. t. 1. p. 864.
[2] p. 237.
[3] On Population, p. 227.

waste the means of a virtuous family. Suppose the children die; all that was expended on them is lost. If some be reared, what is the profit? Children so reared are pale, feeble and sickly. If we consider foundling hospitals as receptacles for spurious children, they deprive crimes of inflicting their own punishments: or if they be considered as a resource to the lower orders, they encourage improvidence, tend to lessen the love of parents and children, and to separate generation from paternity. Those children who escape the various deaths that beset them, and pass abroad, are without kindred, attachment, or character. A report of one of the foundling hospitals in France states [1], that the young persons so reared became vagabonds. Foundling hospitals may prevent a few violent deaths; but this is gained at the expense of many lives, and some licentiousness. The account stands thus: A few may be saved from individual violence, that many may suffer by a sentimental confederacy. Nothing is more startling than infanticide:—but in hope of escaping this crime, should we authorize a tenfold mortality? Compare the deaths in foundling hospitals with the ordinary loss of infants, superadding those wilfully destroyed, in any country at any time, and it will appear that one child has been saved at the loss of one hundred. And though in offices of humanity the expense can hardly be calculated, yet here we must consider this particular; for the expense is increased not for the preservation but the waste of mankind.

This requires further observations. Supposing that foundling hospitals induce illicit intercourse and preg-

[1] Annual Register, 1761, p. 133.

nancy and the premature death of children, without estimating the charges of the hospital establishment, they occasion a public loss. A child costs so much before he is born, as the mother by her pregnancy is prevented from earning:—a child is then so much capital: if he die, he is so much capital lost; and a child preserved is so much capital redeemed. Mrs. Newby, matron of the lying-in hospital, it is said [1], recovered five hundred still-born children. She then was a benefactor to the amount of the cost of their production: or more properly speaking, according to the language of debtor and creditor, their restoration is to be deducted from the expenditure of the establishment; for on this view expense and life are convertible terms. Let it not be supposed that I mean by this statement that the 500 saved were added to the whole population of the state; I should rather say, supposing the pregnancy of each mother of the 500 children reduced her labour 3*l*., and that a child cost 50*l*. before he can provide for himself, the saving of 500 still-born children was equal to the production of 30 men. I state this as merely explanatory of my views, without any regard or interest respecting accuracy—which is not attainable. In the West Indies it has been the subject of a very nice estimate; and though it comes from an unholy source, I subjoin it. Monsieur Dauberteuil says [2] that the loss during the last three months pregnancy and fifteen months nursing causes

---

[1] Highmore's Pietas Londinensis, p. 202. In the Annual Register, 1805, p. 389, the number of recovered still-born children is stated at one hundred.

[2] Steele and Dickson, p. 246.

a loss of 9*l.* sterling : at ten years the child is worth 44*l.* : at fifteen 60*l.* : having at this period earned 35*l.*

A child then represents as much stock as has been expended on him ; therefore his death is a loss to that amount. And it is to be observed, that if from excess of people he could not have been reared, the mere producing him was a loss also, so much labour prevented during parturition being so much lost to the community. If then the death of a child be a loss, how much more must be the death of a man ! The first erases the spring from the year, but this blots out the year from the round of time. What a benefactor then is the minister of peace ! for every man killed, beside the assassination, is a death cast on posterity : a debt which oppresses the living, whether the expenditure be met by annual taxes, or whether time and taxation interminably unite. But I must restrict myself here to peace, and the peaceful means of preserving human life.

The value of mankind seems to Mr. Malthus very inconsiderable : he says, in his loose dialect [1], " The effects of the dreadful plague in London in 1666 were not perceptible fifteen or twenty years afterward. It may even be doubted whether Turkey and Egypt were upon an average much less populous for the plagues which periodically lay it waste." The inference implied is false : for even if London recovered its number and its opulence in twenty years, its progress in both was retarded. The operation of diseases on Turks and Egyptians, who are afflicted by a tyranny which is so much more pernicious than bodily infirmities, is

[1] vol. 1. p. 563.

not easily estimated. Indeed in a great measure the plague may be referred to despotism; for the plague is of moral, not of physical origin. The plague was unknown anciently in Asia Minor and at Constantinople even under the Roman tyranny. Despotism induces predestination, heedlessness and apathy. When Guy wrote [1], no precautions were used against it: he says, " When the deaths exceed a certain number, public prayers are offered." Even when Thornton wrote [2], the Greek priests of the hospital constantly sold the clothes of those who perished by the plague, which the government knew and disregarded. At Smyrna, latterly [3], the population has become more cautious and the sale of the clothes of infected persons is a capital offence. This they have learned probably from foreigners resident among them; who, enjoying a portion of freedom in this land of slaves, have an interest in their lives, are proportionably circumspect, and thus they escape the death that surrounds them.

That the Turkish government should neglect the health of its people, and that the people should be indifferent respecting life, is not unaccountable. But careless as the English government always has been respecting the people, it is mysterious why rational measures have not been adopted to prevent the introduction of the plague into England. This country has more than once suffered by that calamity. In 1604 one fifth of the people of London died of the plague [4]. La-

[1] Letter 30.

[2] State of Turkey, vol. 2. p. 213. It is remarkable that in this country of the plague, canine madness is unknown, though dogs abound and feed on the worst garbage. Vol. 2. p. 161.

[3] Hobhouse, Travels, p. 642.   [4] Hume's History, vol. 6. p. 14.

zarettos are established in Leghorn, Marseilles, in Venice; and the rules and tariffs of the last seemed to Howard [1] to have regulated all similar establishments in Europe. England has no lazaretto. A proposal was made to build one in England, which was negatived, because, it was said, the profits of the Turkish trade were unequal to erect such an edifice. Nor is this all; as every person who has spoken of the quarantine laws, Howard [2], General Cockburn, &c., have treated them as in the highest degree impotent and absurd [3].

It is among the chief caprices of nations, that one of the greatest improvements in the health and life of European society was derived from the insensate Turks. Inoculation, which Niebuhr says [4] has been practised time immemorial among the Bedoins, was notoriously introduced into England by Lady Wortley Montagu, a century ago, from Constantinople. The destructiveness of the small-pox has been general. The Galla, the Mahas [5], and the Indians bordering on the fur-traders, have suffered considerably from its effects. In 1759 [6], of 4335 burials in Copenhagen, 1079 were the effects of the small-pox. Yet this was less than the mortality of the casual small-pox in London; for it

[1] On Lazarettos, p. 12. [2] Ibid. p. 28 et seq.

[3] Travels, vol. 2. p. 214. See also Medico-Chirurgical Transactions, vol. 6.

A fond theorist might use this indifference as a reason for the escape of the English from the plague; as Hobhouse says, all conjectures respecting this disease attribute the diffusion, *in a great measure, to the terror of the plague.* Travels, p. 642.

[4] Travels, c. 129. [5] Travels of Lewis and Clarke.

[6] Annual Register, 1761, p. 116.

appears that of those so afflicted, 25 in 100 perished, according to the registries of the inoculating hospitals[1]; while only 4 in 100 died, of those who were inoculated. Mr. Malthus could not be ignorant of similar results. He notices them. How? With joy? No. His miserable philosophy, blindfold and blundering, knows not cheerfulness. In answer to Dr. Haygarth, "I am far from doubting[2] that millions and millions of human beings have been destroyed by the small-pox. But were its devastations, as Dr. Haygarth supposes, many thousand degrees greater than the plague, I should still doubt whether the average population of the earth had been diminished by them. The small-pox is certainly one of the channels, and a very broad one, which *nature* has opened for the last thousand years to keep down the population to the level of the means of subsistence : but had this been closed, others would have become wider, or new ones would have been formed." What disastrous doctrine! and how absurd! He supposes that though men should be destroyed by diseases many thousand times more mortal than the plague, the average population on the earth would still be the same. He supposes that always an excess of population crowds the world; which must be destroyed by diseases : and that to provide these is *Nature's* business. Here Nature, the το παν of Mr. Malthus, branches into the *fatal sisters.* If

---

[1] Highmore's Pietas Londinensis, p. 284. Moore in his History of the Small Pox says, that for the last 30 years of the last century, the annual deaths by the small-pox were from 34 to 36,000 in Great Britain and Ireland.

[2] vol. 2. p. 29.

this be not fatalism, what is folly? Cure one disease, you render another more mortal, or you generate *new ones*. Then the Boards of Health, the education of physicians, all preventives against disease, even attention to health, are ineffectual to add one more to the society of the world. They merely oblige *Nature* to task her ingenuity, or to manifest her power, by inventing new maladies, which shall restore the balance between life and provisions. This certainly exhibits in an interesting and original view *the house of woe.* Plutarch said [1] reprovingly, Some have made panegyrics on vomiting and fever, and have been praised. Mr. Malthus has done more : he has introduced with much applause into political œconomy,

> "——————————————all maladies,
> Dropsies and asthmas, and joint-racking rheums,
> Convulsions, epilepsies, fierce catarrhs,
> Marasmus, and wide-wasting pestilence."

And these are among his *materia medica* for purging off the surfeit of population.

It is remembered to the disgrace of the faculty of medicine of Paris, that in 1768 thirty-two voted against twenty-three who wished to tolerate inoculation [2]. And the argument of B. Moseley, physician to the royal military hospital of Chelsea, did astonish many, who proved *à priori*, " that the cow-pox cannot be a preventive of the small-pox [3]." Yet this was sage and humane—exhibiting a great reach of thought—in comparison to the broad channel and minor drains of Mr. Malthus, which Nature and her eternal equiva-

---

[1] Plutarch. Moral. p. 28.   [2] Annual Register, 1768, p. 66.
[3] Preface to " Lues Bovilla."

lents prepare, in order to preserve a *dead* level between subsistence and population. Yet truly, Nature, according to the announcement of her high-priest, is but a sorry artist at destruction. Would not famishing the surplus people as directly and as expeditiously effect her high behests, as cutaneous complaints? And let me ask Mr. Malthus to signify to us under what head of checks the small-pox is to be ranked : for the children of all descriptions of people are affected by it—the rich and the poor. Thus the philosophy of Mr. Malthus, at every turn of his argument, is feeble and confounding. The death of children or adults, forsooth, is no loss; no reduction of life; no preventive of human increase : that whether we be ailing or vigorous, communicating being, or spreading infection, it is the same. Thus the ancients made Æsculapius and Circe brother and sister, and both children of Apollo. How absurd are the Egyptians, who hail the falling of the dew, as this stops the plague! How absurd are the people of Dembia [1], who rejoice at the fall of rain—for this stops the fever! How have all people mistaken their interest, who have respected the preservation of health and the diminution of disease! All wrong, says Mr. Malthus; vain wisdom all, and false philosophy. If you stop the broad channel of this disease, you but divert the current of mortality. If inoculation reduced the deaths from 25 to 4 per cent., so many more children perish by measles and kincough; the *new* disorders, the croup and scarlatina, have been added by nature to the old ones, to effect the necessary waste of human life. As to vac-

[1] Bruce's Travels, vol. 2. p. 452.

cination, this is no doubt worse than all the others; as it has unhappily rendered the small-pox innocuous. Dr. Jenner is much to blame; for who does not see with Mr. Malthus, that as vaccination advanced among the young, Nature was agitated; and from her monstrous womb issued battle and murder and sudden death against all full-grown persons! For breed you will, says Mr. Malthus, beyond the level of the means of subsistence; and die you must in proportion. And yet La Place, a man who knows as much as Mr. Malthus of ratios and geometric and arithmetic, in his *Essai sur les Probabilités* says, " The ratio of the population to the number of births would be increased, if we could diminish or destroy any disease that is dangerous or common :"—he adds, " that Monsieur Duvillard has found that the mean duration of human life is increased more than three years by vaccination."

Whatever preserves health, serves society; for sickness, besides its vexation, occasions a loss of property, a loss of time, and often it involves both the property and the time of others. There is nothing in which the moderns have so improved as in attention to health. The jail fever in Elizabeth's reign [1] was communicated to the court; and the chief baron, sheriff, and three hundred others perished by it.—It appears also, that from fifty to a hundred died annually in the Savoy [2]: yet from 1749 to 1752 inclusive, only four died, in consequence of proper ventilation, &c. In short, the jail fever has disappeared; a disease which Howard attributed to the " want of air and exercise." Other fevers have been greatly reduced. In London a society

[1] State Trials, Preface, p. 14.　　[2] Annual Register, 1764, p. 47.

to remove fever has subsisted from 1801 : they have an hospital to which the afflicted poor are moved. In 1802 the deaths by fevers were reduced from 3000 to 2,201 : and in 1807 the mortality was still further reduced to 1,033.—It is also remarkable, that in a Report to the House of Commons, the disease is not only declining, but that the mortality of the infected declines in the hospitals of Dublin, Waterford, Manchester. The Romans built temples to Fever [1] and Fear ; we build hospitals to Fever and Confidence. In this respect at least, the superstition of the Pagans has not infected us.

In various ways human life has been an important concern. Captain Cook first proved that health and a tedious navigation were not incompatible.—He circumnavigated the globe, and he restored the crew entire to their country. The Russian Kreusenstern, though absent three years, was equally fortunate. And it is most satisfactory that the complement of men employed in our navy is upheld by one third less expense of lives than formerly.

It seems also that the English are generally more attentive to health than they were in preceding times : —coffee and tea have been in many cases substituted for fermented liquors and ardent spirits. Yet I believe this improvement would have arisen, had China and the plantations never existed : for it originated (though I am aware of the increase of crime) in the more active and intelligent habits of the *whole* people. It has been supposed, though Shakespear's Caliban exists, that an ingenious and a drunken artist is nearly the

_____
[1] Febris fanum palatio, Cicero, t. 4. p. 249. 11.

same : just as a good soil absurdly was reputed injurious to industry. The human mind is strengthened by every advance in ability; and morals and intelligence imply each other. Drunkenness is the grossest of all vices: it is not even sensual, but insensate, and is an epitome both of phrensy and death. Savages are its saddest victims; while the wisest men are the most temperate. The greater temperance where the people have the means of excess, might almost determine their civilization. In this respect the English are far superior to the Russians. It is said that the mortality in St. Petersburg of persons from 20 to 60 years of age is as 817 to 1000 : and in London the mortality of persons of the same ages is as 720 to 1000 : which is referred to the greater use of ardent spirits in the Russian metropolis[1].

It is therefore my opinion, and it seems a truism, were it not confidently contradicted, that to extirpate a disease, to lessen its virulence, to enable the ailing, to fortify the sound, increases the happiness and the numbers of the people; as the time lost in a sick bed might have been employed in profitable labour, and thus, instead of burthening the labour of others, have added to the common stock; and thus to the means of increasing the people. A sickly family is seldom opulent—seldom numerous :—so of states. And considering men as so much productive industry, a plague or epidemic, which Mr. Malthus calls a necessary channel for carrying off the nuisance of a surplus population, is in fact a national loss, more hideous than the forty thousand bankrupts during the late war.

All inventions, except the very expensive, generally

[1] Tooke's Russia, p. 541.

speaking, which secure life, increase being: and this is acknowledged by the greater price required for those articles which are obtained at a greater hazard of life. Life is a private and public concern. He who secures a labourer's life cheapens the produce of industry, or prevents its enhancement with the general rise of prices. Let those who are insensible to their kind, regard them at least as an item in the general account. Sir H. Davy's safety lamp may be considered an actual discovery of richer mines; for it lessens the labour of extracting coal, by adding all those labourers free of expense, who would otherwise have been destroyed by the fire-damp, and by confirming the whole body of miners in their arduous employment. To substitute machinery for climbing boys, will probably add something to the amount of human life; not only as redeeming victims from premature death, but as promoting humanity. The attention to these wretches, and to the lunatic poor, (nor should the names of Mr. Wakefield and Mr. Bennet be forgotten) evinces increasing humanity; and in my estimation, this proves increasing population. Whatever generally promotes health, promotes life; and with increasing years an increase of people. Some old men are helpless and burthensome—I speak in the unfeeling phrase. However, I have no doubt but that nation whose people are longer lived (all things else being the same) will be more numerously inhabited.—Yet according to Blumenbach, not more than 78 persons in a thousand die of old age. I have spoken long, I hope not tediously, on health, and on the preservation of the lives of young and old: and with some shame I admit, according to a sordid arithmetic. But thus we must meet the new philosophy. I have considered each child as representing so much stock as was expended in his generation and nurture, which, should he die prematurely, would be lost. I have considered the death of an adult as the destruction of a machine in full work;—and in some respects the loss to population is the same, whether life be ended by intemperance or suicide, by tyranny or violence, on the scaffold or in the field. Each individual

" —————like ripe fruit should drop
Into his mother's lap, or be with ease
Gather'd, not harshly pluck'd, by death mature."

Such is my philosophy respecting an important particular connected with the increase of population; in which there is neither contradiction nor dilemma; and in which the best parts of knowledge concur with the charities and affections of mankind.

CHAPTER II.

Further means that have been adopted to increase the people by tributes of men and women—by total transfers of people. Catharine of Russia's ruinous projects—Mr. Malthus's projects—Sir John Sinclair's, &c.—Agriculture—pasture—manufactures—colonial policy as means of increasing population. Spence's—Southey's—Preston's, &c.—to feed the people with fish. Count Rumford's cookery.—Mr. Gray proposes eating-houses, &c.

MANY attempts have been made to increase the numbers of a state by the introduction of foreigners. The first great cause of this practice was war and conquest. Minos imposed an annual tribute of seven

young men and as many maidens on the Athenians.
These seem to have cohabited, and to have increased
so much that they became troublesome to the Cretans,
who sent them to Delphi. Thence they passed to
Italy, and finally settled in Thrace, under the name
of Bottiæans. The Turks practised the same impost;
exacting from the conquered provinces so many Christian children; with whom they recruited the janisaries.
Thus they intended to save their own people, and
waste the enemies of their faith. In the same spirit
the Protestant charter-shools were established in Ireland; their original object being expressly to increase
the Protestants by proselyting the children of the oppressed and persecuted Catholics.

After the *children of the tribute* (for so the Turks
called the young recruits from the Christian provinces) we may notice tributary women. It is said
that Darius ordered the neighbouring nations to send
a stipulated number of women to Babylon, who were
to be married to those Babylonians whose wives had
perished during the siege [1]. In Turkey, Persia, &c.,
the mode of recruiting the harams of potentates and
chiefs is not at present so summary. They obtain the
objects of their wishes after the European manner—
money is first exacted; and this, through the wants
and wishes of the people, commands men, women and
children.

The inhabitants of cities and districts have been
transferred to increase the population of provinces
and nations, *Roma interim crescit Albæ ruinis* [2].

---

[1] Herodotus, lib. 3. c. 139.   [2] Livius, lib. 1. c. 30.

Ancus Marcius [1] afterward transplanted a whole people to Rome, dividing them among the tribes of the city. The savage hordes of America also, on whom Mr. Malthus has founded his observations on the ravening *nature* of war, having overpowered the enemy, frequently adopt their prisoners into their society. A Mahomet [2], to secure advantages which he had gained, transferred the inhabitants of Podolia to the eastern side of the Danube: Sobieski defeated this policy. Shah Abbas built Ferabad [3]; and to people this intended metropolis, he swept towns and provinces of their inhabitants. This mode of populating effects directly a double destruction, beside its ruinous consequences.

Machiavel [4] says that, to obtain empire, (he ought to have said to sustain freedom, for that is the consideration,) a nation should be populous; that for this purpose two means are applicable—to increase the people by a forcible transfer from abroad; or to win the entry of foreigners by a liberal policy. There is a third which he has omitted, and, for the present, I shall not obtrude it on the reader. I have spoken of the compulsory mode; of the second, or *per amore* of Machiavel I now speak. Mr. Tooke [5] informs us, that Catharine of Russia employed millions of rubles " to increase the population from without." For this purpose, she published apostolically to all

[1] Dion Halicarnassus, lib. 3. c. 37.
[2] Palmer's Life of John Sobieski.
[3] Pietro della Valle, in Pinkerton, vol. 9. p. 51.
[4] Discorsi, lib. 2. c. 3.
[5] History of Russia, vol. 1. p. 621.

nations, in effect, " that her burthen was easy and her service light,"—that she would grant liberty of conscience—land—the means of reclaiming it, and that she would support those who should accede to her proposal, till they reached their destination. In consequence, in 1765 and 1766, multitudes were shipped from different countries, and disembarked in the land of promise, at Cronstad. The Empress, and her sage advisers, were surprised and alarmed that her call was honoured by many. As they landed, they were moved forward and lodged, in huts, at Oranienbaum. By a contagious disease 100,000 were reduced to 40,000, who were incapable of any exertions. This conclusion is not mentioned by Mr. Tooke, but by J. B. Flages [1], who was one of the government agents in this mighty requisition; but Mr. Tooke does inform us, that " no prince in modern times has ever made the subject of population so intimate a concern of government, as the late empress." Wonderful woman! and she established a *tutelary chancery*, whose special care was to regulate these foreign accessions. Yet a worse fate attended the 75,000 Christians, who were transferred from the Crimea to inhabit the country which had been abandoned by the Nogai Tartars. In a few years they were reduced to a tenth; a similar catastrophe attended other schemes of imperial population. This Pallas [2] ascribes to the want of those requisites which the Empress expected. Why did she expect them, unless she had faith in the tales of

[1] Etat de Russie.   [2] Voyage, &c. t. 5. p. 5.

Deucalion and Pyrrha? Yet such potentates, and their ministers, and their tutelary chanceries, pursuing schemes impossible, and exhausting as our Botany Bay establishment, rail at reformers; while, Adonislike, they fall in love with their own furrowed image in the rippling stream. The Empress might as well have expected, that an ukase should prolong her snow palace to a summer residence, as to populate Russia by such practical reveries.

Creation is not among the prerogatives of princes. What Catharine could not effect in her empire, Augustus failed to effect in his. Augustus exhausted provinces to people Nicopolis, that short-lived monument of vanity and victory, which the concentrated rays of Roman majesty could not quicken, even for one age, into vigorous life. Nicopolis, in the reign of Honorius, became the property of one woman; yet, I do not mean to suggest, that corresponding means will not people countries, will not establish cities. Timoleon called on Greece for people, and ten thousand supplied the deficiency: "a proof," says Hume, "that the maxims of ancient polity affected populousness more than riches;" and he speaks of the good effects of those maxims; and all this he justly refers "to ideas of equality." So when the Lombard league wished to construct a rational monument to their glory, they built Alexandria; to people which, they transplanted thither the inhabitants of the surrounding villages, and from the first year of the existence of this city it could send fifteen thousand men into the field. Thus the exertion of freemen was completely successful; while the actions of despots end with aggravated loss. Can it be otherwise? The Spanish kings expelled Jews and Moors, and transplanted the palatinates, at immense and ruinous expense, into their misgoverned country. While a branch of the same royal house, Don Carlos, king of Naples, was so anxious in his invitation of foreigners, that even Jews were accepted by the edict of 1740; but it was proclaimed by the same royal document, that he would not permit said *Jews*[1], *after the manner of our subjects, to cry about the streets old clothes to sell.*

Various other means have been proposed, for increasing or preserving our population. Mr. Malthus[2], to console mankind, as the angel does Adam, says, that Great Britain may contain in centuries, a treble and thrice happier population than it at present possesses. Wonderful! " It would have made *nature* immortal, and death should have played for lack of work." Taxed, indebted, and tormented, as we are, how is this possible? Mr. Malthus affords an innuendo on improved industry. What industry could effect such a prodigy? Mr. Malthus has proposed also, that agriculture should be promoted by the most perverse and extraordinary measures—Corn laws, and bounties on exportation. And as if this were not abundantly absurd, he would throw all the land into great farms, leaving the labourer to subsist on the wages of labour; for one of his axioms is, " It is quite obvious, that a peasantry which depends principally on its possessions in land[3], must be more ex-

---

[1] Beawes's Lex Mercatoria, p. 599.
[2] vol. 1. p. 80.   [3] vol. 2. p. 466.

posed to it (scarcity) than one which depends on the general wages of labour." I can only say here, (as the subject comes properly under another head,) that what is an obvious truth to Mr. Malthus, is to me a manifest error ; all my experience, and I have some on this point, goes directly to confirm an opposite conclusion—that the labourer is more secure, who has a small portion of land attached to his cottage ; and though I am far from admiring Arthur Young's cow system and the like, or insisting that a plot of ground with each cottage could relieve the country from the poor's rates ; yet the contrary practice has tended to the increase of paupers. A country labourer without any land, has no locality, no stake, no store, nothing like property to refresh his sight about him ; he is a manufacturer, without the pleasures of manufacturing society; and though his wages are not so fluctuating, they are inferior.

Mr. Malthus[1] proposes also the inclosure of land. He says, " It seems to be the clear and express duty of every government to remove all obstacles, and give every facility to the inclosure and cultivation of land." But observe, that this is introduced by stating, "I am inclined to think that we often draw very inconsiderate conclusions against the industry and government of states, from the appearance of uncultivated lands in them." Thus, he hushes governments, before he dares to offer the most obvious advice to the constituted authorities. But he should have told them that they prevent the cultivation of the soil, and the strength and numbers of the people,

[1] vol. 2. p. 217.

by preferring a few officers to the population of the empire. The fact is, that the parliament has no sympathy with the people; otherwise they would facilitate inclosures,—so far, I mean, as not subjecting every tract of common to a special bill, as at present; which prohibits improvement, inasmuch as it imposes a grievous tax on agricultural capital and industry. For instance, the bill for inclosing Holy Island in Northumberland, consisting of 1020 acres of common, cost 1267*l.* [1] Why is there not one general act for inclosure? Because some officers of parliament, the patronage of a few, would lose some fees by this reform.

Sir B. H. Hobhouse does not rise so high into the possibilities of population as Mr. Malthus : he supposes only, " that, if all the waste lands of Great Britain were cultivated, it would contain thirty millions." Yet many think we have cultivated too much, and that capital has been diverted from more profitable pursuits. Nor do I doubt but gentlemen and noblemen farm perniciously, that is, their returns are far beneath their expenses. I do not say, however, that their money, should they withdraw it from agriculture, would be more profitably employed. Sir John Sinclair favours agriculture of course, and no doubt he expects an extensive population in consequence. His summary proposal is, that the English should employ North Britons; and these agriculturists, he concludes, would alone multiply the produce of England *two-fold :* he also proposes that twelve millions be lent to the agricultural interest. Yet while he recommends agriculture and bounties, his countrymen in the Highlands

[1] Board of Agriculture, vol. 6.

follow Cato the Censor's advice, who sententiously preferred pasturing in the first and second degree of utility, placing aration in the fourth[1].

The agricultural and pastoral states have had their times of mutual dominion in England. When the agricultural was preferred, penal laws were passed against sheep-keeping, and the penalties were exacted :—in 1636 Sir Anthony Roper paid a fine of 4000*l.* for having more sheep than were allowed by the law: and long after that time it was the opinion of Fortrey and Davenant[2], that it was "more the national interest of England to employ its land to the breeding and feeding of cattle than to the produce of corn," because "tallow, hides, flesh, wool, are of much greater value abroad, than the like yield of the earth would be in corn."

Besides those who refer all to agriculture, and those who patriotically respect pasture, without sufficiently regarding the state of society and the intercourse of nations; others again are the patrons of manufactures. Sir James Steuart, though distinguishing agriculture, says, "Let it never be said that there are too many manufacturers employed in a country; it is the same as if it were said, there are too few idle persons, too few beggars, and too many husbandmen[3]."

Say refers the misery of Poland to its want of manufactures and commerce; he says, "*Elle reste pauvre et dépeuplée. C'est parce qu'elle borne son industrie à l'agriculture, tandis qu'elle devroit être en même temps*

[1] Cicero de Officiis, lib. 2. t. 4. p. 387.
[2] Works, vol. 2. p. 229.
[3] Political Œconomy, book 1. c. 6.

manufacturière et commerçante[1]." He might as well affirm that Switzerland should become maritime : or, what is equally absurd, state with Michel[2], that "Poland is the granary of Europe because it is the least populous;" for Holland, the most populous country, and least productive of corn in Europe, has been the granary of Europe. Poland was agricultural because it was poor, and it was poor because it was wretchedly governed. Lloyd designated it truly "a government in which the king was nothing, and the people slaves[3]." The Poles are now nearly in the same state as their Scythian progenitors in the time of Herodotus, of whom the historian says, "They sowed corn not to eat, but to sell it[4]." The land is laboured by boors, and what they should receive in necessaries, is seized by their lords and exchanged for foreign luxuries.

While some expect populousness from manufactures, or commerce, or agriculture, Mr. Dawson apprehends still greater effects from colonial policy. He first says, " that if the country was fully supplied with food, the population, which was six millions at the Revolution, in 1810 would be sixty millions instead of twelve millions[5]," which he explains afterwards :—" it has been shown in the fifth section of this chapter, that if there always had been plenty of food, (which would have been the case if importation had been free, and if colonies had been settled in America and Africa for the purpose of raising food,) the number of the people in Britain would, upon common chances, have exceed-

[1] t. 1. p. 18.   [2] On Legislature, p. 119.
[3] Bibliotheque de l'Homme Publique, t. 11. p. 83.
[4] Lib. 4. c. 17.   [5] p. 156. On the Poverty, &c.

ed sixty millions in the year 1812[1]." After all these, and in direct opposition to them, came Mr. Spence,—though no Spencean except in extravagance,—who insisted that commerce is nothing, or worse than nothing; that England is *totus teres atque rotundus*, and that any external addition but impairs the completeness of our demi-paradise.—This man's book, I believe, reached seven editions.

There are various subdivisions of such grand schemes, as to preserve the transit duties on linen, prohibit the export of wool, limit the foreign sale of cotton-twist, regulate the import of butter and cheese,—that is, tax them,—raise the admissible price of grain into Britain; and particularly, it is the chorus to all the reports to the Board of Agriculture, Let no foreign grain be warehoused in Great Britain. And as some have expressed a wish or hope that all our wastes might become arable, others, in this special time of distress—a time always of projects and fanaticism—propose that the waste lands should be purchased with public money, to be held as national domains, on which the state should establish disbanded soldiers and sailors, and all persons in want of employment. This scheme is patronized by Mr. Southey, who also recommends (the government having been parsimonious the last twenty-five years) as *a means of alleviating the present distress, a liberal expenditure.* Much is added about educating children in the Protestant religion as established by law. And a modern writer in a critical journal where we should be least likely to meet any approximation

[1] P. 191. This is the only extravagant assertion in his book; he is sincere and intelligent.

to the maudlin projects of Mr. Vansittart, proposes planting of churches throughout the land, as a remedy for poor's rates and mendicity.

Mr. Preston, while he advises the extension of husbandry, recommends that three millions sterling should be laid out on a great national road, to relieve the distress and support our population. But beside some graver objections, he should prove to the Rev. Mr. Warner of Bath the utility of roads; for the reverend gentleman condemns them; and even when he is most conciliatory he says, "Allowing thus much, however, I would still contend, we are yet without sufficient proof that the improvement of our public roads is promotive of the real happiness of the people." This sceptic in roads has, however, no doubts of the thirty-nine articles; and in the same year, 1810, he says, that "they [who doubt this compendium of the national religion, and national education] are unrepressed by evidence, unabated by candour, unsatisfied with fact." This reverend preacher had better add one more to the thirty-nine; the mystic Pythagoras has prepared it for him, "Decline highways." Nor is Mr. Warner single in his lament. Dr. Whitaker, vicar of Whalley and rector of Heysham, in his Topography, piteously repines at the good roads of Britain; his reason is "The returns of coroner's inquests within these districts for the last fifty years, would prove, I am persuaded, that the increased number of casualties is much greater than the increase of population." Here is a lover of population with the same sympathies as Mr. Malthus; for Mr. Whitaker, as I have quoted, expressly condemned populousness, and with melancholy lamented

Hunslet, which once enjoyed a *slender and obsequious population*.

Many plans have been adopted or proposed for increasing the people by the mode of feeding them. Fielding hoped that we should be able " to fill the mouths of the poor, if not with loaves, at least with fishes:" but hitherto the Fishmongers' Company, which abhors reform as much as the House of Commons, have defeated every effort towards relieving even the poor of the capital. Count Rumford proposed stews and soups, and in a letter to Majendie he says[1], " I verily believe that the inhabitants of Great Britain might be well nourished, their hunger perfectly satisfied, their health and strength preserved, and the pleasure they enjoy in eating increased, with two-thirds of the food they now consume, were the art of cookery better understood."

Mr. Gray[2], who favours population, differs from all these proposals.—That he favours populousness, read the following paragraph : " The additional population born in a country consisting of the surplus arising from the births exceeding the deaths, has a slower influence on a nation's *circuland*: but the operation of this influence is sure and powerful.—They are indeed just so many new customers, who add to the income of the great body of the old dealers much more than they take away, [then paupers are bankers] stimulate the *circulandary* powers, and operate towards rendering the whole national mass more extensive circulators." One would suppose that after this view the

[1] Society for bettering the Condition of the Poor, vol. 2. p. 338.
[2] On the Happiness of States.

author would give himself little trouble about feeding them, as provisions would of course rise like an exhalation. Yet Mr. Gray proposes to increase the population of Great Britain 500,000 by its inhabitants feeding on horses. This may seem original; though among the various projects about the year 1768[1], in consequence of the high price of provisions, the extirpation of horses was also proposed. To induce the eating of horses, Mr. Gray, *on the Happiness of States, Population, &c.*, says, "that it would tend greatly also to diminish the miseries endured by a generous animal." So much for pathos: but fearing that this would not be sufficiently operative, he praises the daintiness of horse-flesh: to determine which, without appeal, he states, "We have the authority of Tartar epicures for its excellence." These Tartar epicures, according to Rubruquis[2], eat all animals except mice and rats, and even those which die of sickness and old-age. Such are the means suggested by different writers for the improvement of population;—but why might not the greater part of them be simultaneously adopted? Suppose we enabled the farmers, by loans and bounties, and Scotch stewards, to cultivate superlatively,—that we settled all the vagrant and poor in fens made salubrious, and on moors made productive,—that we advanced our home trade and manufactures by obstructing the approaches of foreign commerce,—built churches, impaired by-roads, and stopped the leading ones,—required our colonies to act the Grecian daughter to Great Britain, and finally place Mr. Gray's

[1] Annual Register, 1768, p. 194.
[2] Pinkerton, Travels, &c. vol. 7. p. 30.

horses in Count Rumford's soup-kettles;—were all these adopted, then would England be the envy of nations and the admiration of the world, for her people would be as the sands of the sea.

CHAPTER III.

Modes of checking or destroying population—emasculation—absolute celibacy. Mr. Malthus—Tibet—celibacy of priests, &c.—protracted celibacy by law—custom. Mr. Malthus and Swiss political peasant. Mr. Malthus advises late marriages—praise of the Norwegians, that they are better off than the English, exposed—his sermon on marrying, &c. Polyandry. Abstinence of married people from cohabiting—total separation—protracting the time of suckling children—abortion—infanticide—exposing children—infants employed in manufactures—selling children—Spartan Cryptia. Persecutions—depopulation by Highland proprietors unparalleled—monopolies tend to depopulate—bad government—civil war—foreign war—conquests. Slavery injurious—destroyed the population at Rome—Servile wars. Mistake of Mons. Say respecting the cheapness of slaves' work. Mr. Malthus supposes in all countries, except West Indies, slaves will support their population—False—by different examples—as slavery destroys, liberty restores population.

At present, populousness is rather dreaded than hoped. This is not altogether a new sentiment; for Hippodamus, the Milesian legislator[1], Phædon of Corinth[2], Plato[3], and Aristotle[4], have expressed their apprehensions of an excess of people. In my opinion, the existing alarm has no foundation, and merely evinces an ordinary fluctuation of public opinion.

[1] De Repub. lib. 2. c. 7. Aristot.
[2] See Bodin de la République, p. 546.
[3] De Republica, lib. 5. p. 657. de Legib. lib. 5. p. 847.
[4] De Republica, lib. 7. c. 16.

What we wanted we persist in wistfully demanding,
while the completion of our wishes often surfeits the
appetite. It has also happened, that lofty expressions
respecting population were inordinately protracted;
while the present contemptuous language concerning
the many, as that men are a nuisance, does not so much
express an opinion as a defiance: yet it must be observed, that mercenary despotism has assisted this
vilifying language. Schiller said, The people, so powerful and conspicuous in ancient times, are now little
more than an abstract idea. Since he wrote they are
less, for monarchies have increased at the expense and
extinction of commonwealths. I proceed to state various obstructions to population. The first in effect is
emasculation: this the Gheyssiquas practise on themselves, which different travellers ascribe to an intention of preventing an extraordinary increase of their
families.

After this I may mention celibacy, which in some
countries is honoured. Buchanan mentions a tribe
who distinguish with temples and offerings those who
die unmarried[1]. In Tibet it is powerfully recommended; and the especial country of the Grand Lama
seems more perversely governed, civilly and religiously,
than even that of the Pope, particularly in preventing
population. Tibet is the country of checks. Here is a
world formed according to the *exemplar* in Mr. Malthus's mind; here is check and countercheck; and
Mr. Malthus adds, " Tibet is, perhaps, the only
country where these habits are universally encouraged
by the government, and where to repress rather than

[1] Pinkerton, Travels, vol. 8. p. 677–680.

to encourage population seems to be a public object[1]."
Yet this country is poor and beggarly.

Whatever caused the institutions of this ecclesiastical country, it is probable that celibacy enjoined by
the Catholic church had no regard to restricting the
numbers of the people. As polygamists, through jealousy, employ eunuchs in their harams, and as Asiatic
tyrants have used the same contemptible and envious
wretches as their ministers of state,—so the papacy separated, by celibacy, its agents from all civil and kindred affections; the priests were not permitted to
marry, that they might be *papists*; and monasteries, or
spiritual barracks, were built and encouraged, to dis-
sociate the spiritual soldiery from all lay intercourse.
As men were subtracted from society, women were removed also; just as in India, when a husband died, a
wife was burned. All these practices, though for a different purpose, checked population; and whether it will
surprise Mr. Malthus or not, it increased the poor, for
it increased the idle. The celibacy of any description
of persons could not retard population; for society
might be divided into breeders and workers, and population advance :—celibacy must be excessive, to
withdraw so many as to leave insufficient breeders to
support the stock. When Lorenzo de Medici, on an
envoy from Cairo asking him how so few madmen
were at Florence, pointed to a monastery, saying
" We shut them up in such houses," his jocularity was
beneath the evil; for such houses and establishments
are a bounty on the worst infatuation, which not only
withdraws so many from contributing to society, but

[1] vol. 1. p. 237.

withdraws so much and so many from the state, as
those monkeries and nunneries require to maintain them.
Thus, if if we should say that Spain had ten millions
of people, of which 200,000 were of the sacred order,
we should, in speaking of effectives, deduct with the
200,000 all those who contributed to their support; so
that the effective force of the country, instead of ten
would not be nine millions; whereas, if these 200,000
monks were citizens under a tolerable government, instead of being a reduction of power and numbers, they,
on the contrary, would effectually multiply both. This
sort of celibacy is pernicious to population, as it wastes
produce, and makes no return. Similar, or connected
with monkeries as affecting population, is the custom
in Catholic countries, particularly where the law of
primogeniture triumphs in its iniquity, of sending the
younger females to nunneries, that they may not impair the family fortune by requiring a dowry, nor *disgrace* their family by a plebeian marriage. This is a
sample of the connexion of church and state. These
sad sisterhoods and holy fraternities, the eulogy of Mr.
Burke, have been restored by the twice restored Louis
the Eighteenth :—the revolution swept away the nui-
sances, Louis labours to re-establish them. Yet Louis
the Fifteenth passed an ordonnance directing that no
religious community should receive a novice under the
age of twenty-four[1]; he should have doubled the age,
and thus approached the permissive years of an offi-
ciating Pythoness. I should observe that celibacy and
libertinism are frequently companions ; the husband
of none is often the paramour of many.

[1] Annual Register, 1766, p. 25.

Next to absolute celibacy is protracted celibacy. Edmonton says that in the Zetland islands, " no man was allowed to marry who had not fifty pounds Scots of free gear to set up house upon, or some lawful trade whereby to subsist, nor such as cannot read, and is in some way capable to demean himself as a christian master of a family." The peasants in Berne are obliged to possess warlike arms and accoutrements before they can obtain permission to marry. This Mr. Malthus[1] admires. Yet he does not expressly advise any legal enactment against marriages. He remembered, perhaps, that Paul had placed forbidding to marry among *the doctrines of devils;* therefore he adopts the pastoral advice of the same apostle, " He that marrieth doth well, but he that marrieth not doth better." This truly is the professor's text.

Mr. Malthus seems much surprised that his discoveries had not been anticipated :—the surprise is, that such reveries ever occurred to any one. Mr. Malthus, however, found a kindred spirit in the mistress of an inn at Jura ; but he encountered a rare political œconomist in the person of a peasant, who officiated as guide in the same place[2]. He said " early marriages might really be called *le vice du pays;*" and he thought a law should be enacted, by which men of forty should only be allowed to marry, and then only to *vieilles filles.* This genius married very young; and as with his superiors, his feelings pointed his philosophy. Mr. Malthus's conclusion is worth quoting verbatim. " The only point in which he failed as to his philosophical knowledge of the subject, was in confining his rea-

[1] vol. 1. p. 412.   [2] vol. 1. p. 417.

sonings too much to barren and mountainous countries, and not extending them into the plains." Thus
Mr. Malthus, who knows " each hill, and dale, and
bushy dell of this tall wood," for *le vice du pays* reads
le vice du monde. We shall therefore leave the Swiss,
who, according to the hostess and the guide, resemble the people of Abdera, who plagued with madness,
chanted the Andromeda of Euripides, and particularly the verse " Oh! love, tyrant of gods and men [1]."

Mr. Malthus recommends late marriages; and for
bad prose let me substitute the verses of an original
poet [2]:

> " If poor, delay for future want prepares,
> And eases humble life of half its cares;
> If rich, delay shall brace the thoughtful mind
> T"endure the ills that even the happiest find."

Mr. Malthus says also, that women would cheerfully
and readily acquiesce, if they could look forward with
just confidence to marriage at twenty-eight or thirty.
This, I find, is the matrimonial age by law in Formosa [3]. I doubt the benefit of this regulation, were it
practicable. It seems probable to me, when society
is numerous, that some should not marry, or marry
old, while others marry young; I do not mean boys

---

[1] Lucian quotes the verse in his ridicule of historiographers.
Opera, p. 347.

[2] Crabbe's Poems, p. 71. So wrote Ovid;

> Nubere si qua voles, quamvis properantibus ambo
> Differ; habent parvæ commoda magna moræ.

Fasti, lib. 3.

[3] Ferguson, on Civil Society, quotes a collection of Dutch voyages.

and girls, but in fresh maturity [1]. Mr. Malthus, in ardour for his preventive check and late marriages, forgets that late children are early orphans. Nor do I know one evil in society more lamentable, or more destructive, than children deserted by the death of their parents: few care for them, and they are equally heedless of themselves. I have shown the effects of celibacy in Tibet; I shall show the operation of late marriages in a country greatly vaunted by Mr. Malthus.

He says [2], " I believe that Norway is almost the only country in Europe where a traveller will hear any apprehension of a redundant population, and where the danger to the happiness of the lower classes of the people from this cause is in some degree seen and understood." To effect this, he says [3] " there are so many farms, having so many houses, according to the size of the farms, and that until one of these houses becomes vacant, no marriage can take place; the priests have also a negative, and may refuse to marry those who have not a probable means of supporting a family." Mr. Malthus says, " a redundant population is thus prevented from taking place, instead of being destroyed after it has taken place." And he contrasts the superior state of the Norwegians to the Swedes, referring the advantage of the former, when the Swedes were starving in 1799, to those preventive checks employed by the Norwegians. I do not deny this statement, except its generality in one case

[1] Sera juvenum Venus, eoque inexhausta pubertas : neque virgines festinantur : eadem juventa, similis proceritas, pares validique miscentur.   [2] vol. 1. p. 235.   [3] vol. 1. p. 310, 311.

and its specification in the other. Could not Mr. Malthus raise his view a little higher? Could he not perceive that the mighty evil was the mad government of that king, who is now the only unrestored of all the fallen legitimates ; of his despotism furiously abused ; of [1] mismanagement infinitely aggravated ; of a luxurious [2] aristocracy and more luxurious court; of a people of course imitating the heedlessness and prodigality of their superiors, who would drink though they should starve? This very people, who submitted without a murmur to the despotism of Gustavus the Third, repeatedly resisted the attempts of the same Gustavus to prevent private distillation. These circumstances just as rationally account for the misery of nations, as whether they eat out of a platter or a

[1] This stupid government has been these seventy years prohibiting ruffles, wines, &c. See Annual Register, 1770, p. 45. When I was in Sweden edicts were issued against coffee. Last year these edicts have been renewed ; though coffee, being a cheap and wholesome substitute for spirits, was a double good, saving of grain, &c.

[2] The whole state is deranged. Dr. Thomson in his late Travels observes, that in 1772 Stockholm contained 72,442 inhabitants ; in 1812 it contained 72,652. He remarks with much surprise that in 1730 there were 60 bakers, and in 1797 only 32 ; and that millers had declined from 44 to 20, though goldsmiths, jewellers, painters, &c. had increased. Here we find, with the increase of nobles, luxuries gaining ground on necessaries. There is a passage in Plutarch which may reveal the mystery to Dr. Thomson. " Would we could content ourselves with those things that are necessary for the life of man ! But excess and daintiness hath engendered usurers, as the same hath bred goldsmiths, silversmiths, confectioners, perfumers, dyers of gallant colours." I quote an old English version, to prove that I do not frame the quotation for the purpose.

dish, or marry at twenty-eight or thirty, or the like. The Norwegians were a considerate people ; and the English ministry, in their scheme of liberation, has transferred them from a bad to a worse government. Observe too, that in Norway there was no law which compelled the farmers to furnish post horses to travellers; which Mr. Malthus [1] admits, according to the Swedish œconomists, is, as I have stated, a waste of labour in horses and men equal to 300,000 tons of grain. In Norway [2] also the tithes were not required in kind; nor were the tithes seized by the parson, but divided between the king, the incumbent, and the church.

This, however, is but a portion of Mr. Malthus's extravagances on this point : having found the Norwegians pupils of his theory, he considered himself obliged to praise their *seeming* [3]. " And I particularly remarked that the sons of housemen, and farmers boys, were fatter, larger, and had better calves to their legs, than boys of the same age and in similar situations in England." Really? Then, possibly, our most wise ministry did fear for the honour of England ; and that as they transferred France to the Bourbons, lest the English should love reform, seeing its effects, they starved the full-fed Norwegians into submission to Sweden, lest the English should long for the plethoric board of the inhabitants of the scragg of Scandinavia. Why did not Mr. Malthus take a hint from Ramus, who insisted that Norway was the Ogygia of Homer, and that Ulysses [4] was the god

[1] vol. 1. p. 340. [2] Wollstonecraft's Letters on Norway, p. 111.
[3] vol. 1. p. 316.
[4] Kerguelin's Voyage. Pinkerton, &c. vol. 1. p. 769.

Outin? How differently do men, not devoted to an hypothesis, see the same things and persons! Lamotte describes the Norwegians as small and meagre; Leems [1] speaks of " parts of Norway in which you find paupers sometimes in herds together." Mr. Malthus, on the contrary, beheld an enviable people, eminently enjoying the preventive check, with limbs like a brawny prizer; whose poor [2] " were on the average better off than in England." Yet he admits that this favoured people " are obliged occasionally to mix the inner bark of the pine with their bread." Are the English brought occasionally to a worse state than this? Is there a worse state? Is it not Mr. Malthus's own account of the people about Nootka Sound, whom, when he wishes to excite the most poignant distress, he describes [3] *living very miserably on a paste made of the inner bark of the pine tree and cockles ?* There is no greater display of misery in his relations of the savages in Terra del Fuego; or on the islands of Adaman and New Holland, where he exhibits a wretch picking a maggot from a corrupted bone.—Yet Mr. Malthus has not described all the wretchedness of Norway. Von Buch [4], who also mentions the paste of bark, says, that food undergoes a double digestion; that the dung of horses is gathered and given with a mixture of meal, to cows, swine, sheep, &c. who eagerly devour it. This is a landscape with cattle fit to make a back-ground to Sir J. Reynolds's picture of Count Ugolino starving in prison.

[1] On Danish Lapland. Pinkerton, vol. 1. p. 382.

[2] vol. 2. p. 335.   [3] vol. 1. p. 74.   [4] Travels, p. 535.

Mr. Malthus, who favours Norway and its felicities, does not propose that the priest should have a power of denying marriage to the parties; he proposes only that "the [1] clergyman of each parish, after the publication of banns, should read a short address stating the strong obligations in every man to support his own children, the impropriety and even immorality of marrying without a prospect of being able to do this, the evil, &c." Truly this is not classical, for the priestess of [2] Ceres officiated at the marriage ceremony of the ancients: and does it not occur that this advice would be a little inopportune, if not inauspicious, and savour of Priuli's after-wish—" continual discord and a barren bed attend you both?" Might it not tend, if the preacher were very eloquent, to forbid the banns? nay, to change the passion of the parties from love to its antipathy? And we read that Hegesias [3], though no preacher, spoke so movingly of abstinence, that many died voluntarily of hunger. Another difficulty also occurs—Who is to officiate for this prudential purpose? No married curate, many married rectors, and all clergymen whatever who are disposed to marry or are married, and cannot or do not save sufficient to educate and provide for their families.

Mr. Malthus says [4], " it is clearly the duty of each individual not to marry till he has a prospect of supporting his children." Certainly. But this remark is limited to the laborious part of the community. In consequence he talks infinitely [5] " of the more general

[1] vol. 2. p. 321.   [2] Plutarch. Moral. p. 84.   [3] Ibid. p. 261.
[4] vol. 2. p. 242.   [5] vol. 2. p. 411.

prevalence of prudential habits with respect to marriage among the poor, from which alone any permanent and general improvement of their condition can arise." This accords with the proceedings of the Society for the Suppression of Vice. Are none improvident but those who should preparatory to marriage strike the double average between a day's wages[1] and the quartern loaf? What is wasted in health and property by the rich on mistresses, far exceeds the evils of improvident marriages among the laborious. But suppose not: Do not princes marry and beget children which they cannot provide for? Who is so considerate as William the Third, who when stadtholder and pressed by Temple[2] to marry, said " his fortunes were not in a condition for him to think of a wife?" Do not princes marry? Yet while a beggar's brat is a parish charge, a prince's child oppresses the nation. So of the sons of great commoners, and of lords, and earls, and marquises, and dukes, who save nothing for their younger children, and being idle by right of their cast, are supported by places, and sinecures, and pensions. These are the poor that oppress. Each one of these seizes the provision and wastes the produce of many toiling parsimonious men. These are the poor whose support pauperizes the multitude. They are the tiger's cubs in the dog's litter—they first exhaust and then devour their nurse. Yet Mr. Malthus has nothing to say to these improvident procreators; it is the poor who monopolize all his animadversions : he that has thousands and ten thousands and leaves his brood unprovided, passes unno-

[1] See vol. 2. p. 462.   [2] Works, vol. 1. p. 397.

ticed. Of him and his fellows he speaks more gently than Bottom, when he lisps with a *monstrous little voice*; but on the improvidence of a poor man's marriage, he acts the lion's part, and roars that *the duke will say, Let him roar again.*

After protracted marriages as a check to population, I may mention marriages of many women to one man, or polygamy; but having discussed it in a former division of the work, I shall not repeat the topic. Polyandry, or many men married to one woman, I shall defer to a future publication, when I shall detail marriage and its incidents.

Of occasional abstinence of married people I may begin with the nine holy days to Isis [1], during which it was unlawful for man and wife to cohabit. This enjoined reserve was probably a mere priest's trick to profit by an exception, and one of the old Catholic means of helping the exchequer of the temple. The conduct of the Parsees seems however to regard population; they consider one of the *five* sins to have commerce with a woman when she is suckling. This perhaps was intended to prevent repeated pregnancy, or that the mother might contribute her whole strength to the maintenance of her offspring. The ancient Druids it is said cohabited but once a year with their wives. And in Korea [2], sons on a father's death are prohibited from lying with their wives for

---

[1] Ille petit veniam quoties non abstinet uxor
    Concubitu sacris observandisque diebus.

    Juvenal, Sat. 6. ver. 535.

[2] Hamel in Pinkerton's Travels, vol. 7. p. 533.

three years, and any children produced during that interval are held illegitimate.

After these partial divorces, total separation follows. The Tapyri, according to Strabo [1], were accustomed to concede their wives in marriage to others, when they had brought them two or three sons; and Aristotle [2] says, the Cretans might divorce themselves if they had too many children.

Different modes have been practised to check generation. The ancient Romans [3] suckled their children till they were three years old. Parke [4] mentions that a negro woman suckles her child for the same period; so do the Morlacchi [5], or longer, for four or five years.

Need I notice abortion? This great abuse was not uncommon I fear in most countries. Among savages it is generally permitted; it was allowed in ancient Rome *visceribus suis vim inferre.* But Plato [6], having fixed the manners of population in his imaginary republic, enforces the practice: so cruel and absurd are the fantastical! Nor can Aristotle [7] be excused. If we believe writers concerning Formosa, women who

[1] lib. 11. t. 2. p. 127.   [2] De Repub. lib. 2. c. 10.

[3] Infantes non ante triennium mamma depellebantur.

Gravina, lib. 3. p. 355.

[4] Travels, p. 265.

[5] Travels by l'Abbé Fortis in Dalmatia. Protracted suckling is I believe common in most nations—it is used in Ireland. I have seen in England a child sucking its mother, who was so old as to wear pattens.

[6] De Republica, lib. 5. p. 657. de Legib. lib. 5. p. 847.

[7] De Republica, lib. 7. c. 16.

are pregnant before thirty [1], or according to some before thirty-six [2], habitually cause abortion.

Infanticide or exposure of infants has been tolerated in some countries, and some philosophers have spoken of it with shocking indifference. The Roman [3] father might destroy a monstrous child; but the force of legislation contravened this crime from the origin of the state. Romulus [4] ordered that all the male children and the first born females, Θυγατε-ρων τας πρωτογονους, should be preserved; and that no one should expose a child till he was three years old, and then not until he had shown it to five neighbours, and received their approbation. Yet Warburton supposes that Virgil, by placing the weeping [5] shadows of violated babes in the porch of the nether world, intended to discourage infanticidè. He might as well have said that Virgil anticipated the satire of Lucian, and employed it in his Epicurean character in contempt of Saturn the *voracious*. Virgil fancied these phantoms merely to complete his group. Exposure of infants was not uncommon in Greece, and a tragedy of the strongest interest depends on that circumstance. It is satisfactory to be able to state, that the Theban [6] law forbad any man on pain of death to expose his child: if however

[1] Ogylby's Japan, p. 51.   [2] Ferguson's Authorities.
[3] Pater insignem ad deformitatem puerum cito necato.
                                        Gravina, p. 184
[4] Dion Halicarnassus, lib. 2. c. 15. Hierocles said it was agreeable to nature, that all children should be reared, or the most of them η τα γε πλειστα.   Apud Stobæum, serm. 73. p. 448.
[5] Infantium animæ flentes in limine primo.
[6] lib. 2. c. 7.

the parent were in great necessity, he was to bring
the child to the magistrate, who was to sell it at a
small price, and take security from the purchaser
that he would rear the child honestly—the service of
the child was considered an equivalent for its education.

It is remarkable that the two general instances of
modern infanticide are by those of the higher orders,
and that the poor are exempted from the crime. Mr.
Malthus admits that the Earreeoie societies *consist
exclusively of the higher classes*—their children as
soon as produced are frequently suffocated [1]. **Mr.**
Malthus says, that this " is probably often adopted
as a fashion rather than a resort of necessity;" which
admission is unfavourable to his theory. The other
instance is from India. Mr. Moor [2] says, that some
tribes in Hindostan destroy their female children from
their inability to portion and marry them : that is, according to a certain aristocratical scale, just as the
French nobility immersed their daughters in con-
vents. This Hindoo infanticide has been abolished
not by law, not by the missionaries, not by the new
hierarchy of India, but by Colonel Walker [3]; he suggested to parents the wickedness and inhumanity of
the practice, and they reformed.

I have placed among the checks of population infanticide; yet Mr. Hume (and Mr. Malthus [4] subscribes to the doctrine) says that the permission to
commit infanticide generally contributes to increase

[1] vol. 1. p. 88, 89.   [2] Hindoo Infanticide, p. 25.
[3] Cormack's Account of the Abolition of Female Infanticide.
[4] vol. 1. p. 90.

the population of a country; because by removing the dread of a too numerous family, it promotes marriage; and children being by this means produced, tenderness for the offspring obliges the parents to labour for their support. This is refinement. A people who could tolerate infanticide by law, must be sadly obtuse in their feelings. How far it might operate among the middle orders, I do not say; but with the extremes of society, I fear that in settling the account it would appear that more were lost than gained by the license. The higher orders extinguish their infants in Otaheite, and the superior casts in India follow the same *fashion*, to use an expression of Mr. Malthus. And do we not hear and see how the higher orders treat their infants in civilized Europe, in England? how fashionable mothers, in their meats and drinks and hours, treat both the embryo and the infant? and that sooner than abstain from a life of senseless dissipation, they abandon their children to another's care? nay, a noble and a rich mother places her child in a pauper's bosom. And thus the female of fashion improves on that monster among birds, which substitutes its own egg in the nest of its attendant; for the lady often causes the death of the nurse's infant, and of her own, by the double transfer of children from their mothers :—and this comes of poverty and riches.

Next to infanticide and exposure of children is the custom of employing infants in manufactures [1]; for I

---

[1] Stat. 42 Geo. III. requires cotton-mills to be kept clean and airy, fixes the clothing of apprentices, that they should be taught

consider not only what is intended to check population, but what actually has that effect. This deserves legislative consideration much more than the misery of climbing-boys, who are comparatively few —and who commonly are hired by their parents; while the others are numerous, and frequently farmed by the directors of parish charities to master manufacturers [1]. To be sure, these often are great men, members of parliament; while perhaps no master-sweep has one vote in county or borough in the empire. Yet we may wonder how the infuriate enemies of negro slavery abroad tolerate this greater slavery at home. What is the reply? In effect, just what the friends of slavery asserted, that encouraging a mart for slaves was a sort of extra philanthropy. For infant task-masters insist that they are not overworked by unremitting labour for thirteen or fourteen hours in the twenty-four. Besides, Dr. Jarrold [2] says, evidence has been adduced that the heated rooms are not unfriendly to life. Then medical evidence can be had at the price of a prescription. I wonder they have not been recommended as a medicated atmosphere for consumptive habits. To be sure, the Doctor admits that the flying particles are injurious to young lungs. Has any of my readers seen an infant gang issuing from a spinning manufactory,

once every day for the four first years reading, writing, and arithmetic.

[1] The magistrates of the West Riding of Yorkshire would not sanction this practice.—Report of Society for bettering the Condition of the Poor, vol. 4.

[2] Dissertation on Man.

immeshed in one web of filth, ghastly and gulping convulsedly the air like fish flung from the water on the land! We are obliged to Dr. Aikin and Dr. Percival [1] for proving to those, who take their opinions from the faculty, the injuriousness of such labour and confinement; and we are still more obliged to Sir S. Romilly, for stating (June 7, 1811) among other atrocities, that at Manchester, two hundred children, who had been bound to a manufacturer, were on his bankruptcy marched to the work-house; that among other evils attending the present disposal of parish apprentices, the crime of murder was not unfrequently committed by masters; and that he knew instances that would fill the house with horror. Sir J. Hippesley Coxe confirmed this statement. To what will this reach? for I perceive that by the parliamentary debates in 1812, a bill was passed to enable the parish of Stroud to bind apprentices out of England [2].

Next to this, if not the same, was the custom of the Thracians [3], who sold their children for export. They thought perhaps, as those mentioned in the Gothic history of Jornandes, " *satius deliberant in-*

[1] Works, vol. 2. p. 356.

[2] The improvements proposed are almost as bad as the practice in the cantons of Zurich. It is said a benevolent regulation has been adopted, that children shall be nine years of age, and not worked more than 14 hours in the day. I have seen a paragraph signifying the great kindness of a master manufacturer in the north of England, because he reduced the time of working from 13 to 12 hours in the day. Dr. Baillie says, that seven years old is the earliest age at which children should be employed in factories.

[3] Herodotus, lib. 5. c. 6.

genuitatem perire quam vitam. Thus the English[1] in the time of Giraldus Cambrensis disposed of their children; and so late as the reign of Henry the Seventh the people of Bristol had a regular market for the same purpose, where the Irish were purchasers. Abominable as this practice appears, the present treatment of infant children under the sentimental name of charity is worse; it is only less terrific than the conduct of the Carthaginians[2], who sacrificed their sons to Saturn, thinking it holy; and of the Jews, who idolized

> —— Moloch, horrid king, besmear'd with blood
> Of human sacrifice, and parents' tears.

The modern idolatry is Mammon, " the least erected spirit that fell from heaven."

Various means have been adopted to destroy or weaken the population in different states in ancient and modern times; as the Cryptia in Sparta, the object of which, however disguised, was simply to destroy the Helotes. The sincere Thucydides relates a dreadful tale to this effect of Spartan policy: a number of Helotes had been offered their freedom; some joyfully presented themselves for manumission: the whole was an artifice to distinguish the more generous spirits: thus they made themselves known, and they were secretly and unaccountably all murdered. Such have been, in some respect, the persecutions in different states from religion or faction. England has been a victim, but Ireland has afforded under various titles a per-

---

[1] See Anglia Sacra, respecting the collection and sale of boys and girls, t. 1. p. 256. This traffic was practised along both coasts of the British Channel, and along those of the Baltic, &c.

[2] Plato, Minos. Opera, p. 565.

petual sacrifice. Scotland has also exhibited occasions of the same depopulating conduct. When the church of England wished to episcopize this Presbyterian country, the Cryptia was a common engine of the orthodox, and the massacre of Glenco ranks among the worst butcheries on record.

There is another act, not of church or state, but of the Highland proprietors, which I shall notice at some length. Britain, like most other conquered countries, was held by a few great proprietors, who had increased their territories by grants of confiscated estates, and by private war; manufactures were for domestic use, and commerce a paltry barter: rent was paid in kind, which was in part returned in barbarous hospitality in the great hall. Commerce advanced; and strange as it may appear, in these countries it operated to the reduction of agriculture, and the increase of pasturing. Hume says, that in the reign of Edward the Sixth " a great demand arose for wool, both abroad and at home ; pasturage was found more profitable than unskilful tillage—whole estates were laid waste by inclosures— the tenants, regarded as a useless burthen, were expelled their habitations[1]." Sir T. More, regarding this situation of England, says in his Utopia, " that a sheep was a'more voracious animal than a wolf."

This also was the progress of Scotland in some degree; but the bonds of the feudal state were more equal and more affectionate in Scotland. Each man, except the highest and the lowest, was at once lord and vassal; and it is remarkable, that the authority of the superior increased as the seignory descended; the

[1] vol. 4. p. 328.

vassal had the greater dominion, however light it might appear[1], over the sub-vassal, and loyalty to the king[2] was always secondary and subordinate to allegiance to the chieftain. This state of society, though compounded of many gradations, produced considerable equality and perpetual intercourse; chiefs were equals by right, and their vassals by courtesy[3]. The richer contributed, the poorest were fed, as among the Germans[4]; and the distinction between chiefs and followers specified their intimacy; they sat above and below the salt. In this situation, the interest of Scotland was also affected by the demand for wool; and we find that William the Lion attempted to encourage agriculture, by repressing the multitude of sheep[5]. Latterly sheep have again become the prime concern, nor has one voice been raised in favour of mankind.

To excuse the conduct of proprietors and agents in the Highlands, it is said Scotland was overpeopled by clanship; that a greater population should not be reserved in a country than can be profitably employed; that we are to look to the surplus produce only; that whatever is more productive should be preferred—pasture to agriculture, beasts to mankind:—therefore it

[1] Chalmers's Caledonia, vol. 1. p. 454.

[2] Laing's History, vol. 3. p. 47.

[3] Our anti-reformers, having mentioned the word vassal, conclude that few had any right or any power or countenance in elder time; yet du Haillan derives le mot vassal du vieux mot Allemand Geselle, compagnon d'armes.—Bibliothèque de l'Homme, &c. t. 3. p. 68.

[4] Nam epulæ et quamquam incomptæ, largitatem apparatus pro stipendio cedunt. Tacitus de Morib. Germ. c. 14.

[5] Chalmers's Caledonia, vol. 1. p. 791.

is fitting that the sons of those who redeemed the wilderness from nought should be expelled, and that sheep should be substituted for men.

Sir James Steuart imagined this case exactly[1]—I quote it for the benefit of his conclusion—He says, "A Machiavelian stands up (of which there are some in every country) and proposes, in place of multiplying the inhabitants by rendering agriculture more operose, to diminish their number, by throwing a quantity of corn-fields into grass;" adding, "If I propose a reform, it is only to augment the surplus upon which all the state, except the husbandmen, are fed; if the surplus after the reform is greater than at present, the plan is good; although 250 farmers should thereby be forced to starve for hunger,—*though no man is, I believe, capable to reason in so inhuman a style.*" This hypothetical impossibility is not only mooted now, but determined; and hundreds of rare thinkers, profound political œconomists, propose such damnable practices, and many have actually adopted them. They dispossessed families as they would grub up coppice-wood, and they treated villages and their people, as Indians harassed with wild beasts do, in their vengeance, a jungle with tigers. In parts of England, cottages have been prostrated, lest they should afford an asylum for paupers; but in Scotland the people dispossessed were not paupers, they afforded a rent, but they could not afford a raised rent. Concerning this conduct of proprietors in England, but in a much inferior degree, Davenant said[2], "thinking thereby to advance their rent, which proceeds from a narrow mind and short views." Is

[1] Political Œconomy, b. 1, c. 20.   [2] vol. 1, p. 89. Works.

it credible, that in the 18th century, in this missionary age, in this Christian æra, man shall be bartered for a fleece or a carcass of mutton, nay, held cheaper? The Highlander cannot pay an advanced rent; but the sheep which pay no taxes can; and thus, the man's title to his father's land,—whose fathers made it land,—is vitiated. There is nothing more hateful than this conduct; it was unknown to the Spartans[1], who received the ancient rent from the Helotes, nor desired more from them. Nothing is more detestable in the details of modern sordidness and modern tyranny; it surpasses the cruelty of the Russian lord to his boors, and of the slave-masters in the Indies, who dismiss the exhausted negro, for his labour cannot afford a surplus produce. Why, how much worse is it than the intention of the Moguls[2], who, when they had broken into the northern provinces of China, proposed in council to exterminate the inhabitants, and convert the land into pasture! This proposal many Highland proprietors have effected in their own country against their own countrymen; yet the Scotch are called well-educated, *national*, that is, excessively attached to each other; yet the rich have banished their poorer countrymen by families, by hundreds, by districts, and they have been exchanged for herds.—No matter whether wool is sought, or, according to Lord Selkirk[3], flesh-meat is now more relished by townsmen—the act was monstrous. Hindostan

---

[1] Οι δε ειλωτες αυτοις ειργαζοντο την γην, αποφοραν την ανωθεν εσταμενην—ουτοι μη πλεον επιζητωσιν. Plutarch. Laconica. Moralia, p. 142.

[2] Gibbon, c. 34.   [3] On Emigration, p. 63.

has no such sin to atone. "The ryots or farmers have no property in the ground, but it is not usual to turn any man away so long as he pays the customary rent. *Even in the reign of Tippoo*, such an act would have been looked upon as an astonishing grievance [1]."

Mark the consequences. The Scotch resorted to towns, there to contend for life with men who were inured to city-labour; for, when the proprietors dispossessed them for sheep, they obtained a law to prevent emigration to America. Some, however, were forced abroad poor and vagabond, some to St. John's Island, some to Canada, and to places which, compared with Botany Bay, are as hell to heaven. Yet happier were they in these ruthless regions than their friends who lingered at home, where the fields of Ceres had relapsed to the monster Polyphemus. They struggled, and struggle with misery. The survivors, driven from the country, and unable to exist in the towns, turned their desperate thoughts towards the sea; there they exhibited a picture scarcely less hideous than that presented by Dr. Vincent of the Ichthyophagi [2]: and it is to be remarked, that their misery was at the expense of the state; for a bill was brought into parliament in the 26th of Geo. III. (probably by the means of those who first ejected them, and then stopped their emigration) " for the building of free towns, villages, piers, and fishing. in the Highlands and islands of North Britain." Bounties also were passed, and facilities granted respecting salt-duties, &c. And what

[1] Buchanan in Pinkerton's Travels, &c. vol. 8. p. 699.
[2] View of the Highlands, published in 1784.

has been the result? Why, we are told [1] "the indulgence must be enlarged, more towns must be built," &c.

Such is the national *profit* of this merciless policy; by this a few may have obtained larger rents, but the public is at the expense, while Scotland has not supported its relative proportion; and I am persuaded the absolute strength of the people has declined. Could Scotland now array the numerical force that in 1639 [2] was prepared to march into England?

But we shall never want men, perhaps, for the future; yet in 1764 the magistrates of Edinburgh [3], with the Committee of Convention of Royal Boroughs, petitioned his majesty to revoke the license for recruiting in Scotland for the Scotch regiment in the Dutch service, on account of the scarcity of hands. They were wanting, and were found by Mr. Pitt, the greatest of that name. In every year for the last twenty-eight years they were wanted, for we subsidized foreigners; and in 1815, 16,000 Germans were introduced into Britain to preserve the peace of this country. This was done by act of parliament: and in 1816 and 1817, without act of parliament, it is said 30 or 40,000 alien mercenaries are mingled with our native troops. Thus it happens, that while England passes laws for the preservation of game, for saving flax seed, and for the growth of wool; and that to bury in woollens continues to be law, because this *promotes* manufactures and sheep-breeding, there is no saving law for man; a surplus man is a nuisance,

---

[1] Quarterly Review.   [2] Laing's History, vol. 3. p. 162.
[3] Annual Register, 1764, p. 70.

a surplus sheep capital stock. There is a passion or a madness in Britain about breeding beasts, and ox-weighing, and pig-fatting, and sheep-showing and sheep-shearing [1]. The genealogy of a ram or a bull is as elaborate as a pedigree prepared with a view to a claim of peerage. If such subjects be so very interesting to our gentry, it is certain that other questions are sadly neglected. When Rome became imperial, men amused themselves in raising grapes without stones, and the like. Palladius relates the fact. The Cappadocians [2], whether they carried their curiosity into the vineyard and herbary I don't know, had brute heralds; some of their horses were ennobled: and Strabo [3] mentions the extreme sottishness of the same people, who refused liberty, preferring royalty to a republic. Yet the Highland proprietors think they have made a happy exchange: for mere men of Scottish blood they have now sheep [4] from Spain crossed and recrossed, each sheep the sum of a labyrinth of perfections. These shall rival the sacred flock of Apollonius [5]; every Highland lord and his shep-

---

[1] We approach Egyptian brute worship : yet how differently do we show our love of sheep ! We fat and eat them, and bury our corpses in the fleece. The priests of Isis would not in their respect wear woollens nor eat mutton. Plutarch. Moral. p. 262.

[2] Hi mores in genere equorum præstantissimo reperientur. Nam qui infra nobilitatem sunt sati, nulla documenta sui præbuerunt. Polyhistor. lib. 1. c. 47.

[3] lib. 12. v. 2. p. 169.

[4] Cicero was not of this grazing school. Oves quid aliud afferunt, nisi ut earum villis confectis atque contextis homines vestiantur ? t. 4. p. 238. Opera.

[5] Herodotus, lib. 9. c. 93.

herd shall be recorded with Hercules and the Argo-
nauts. Would that Ferdinand the Beloved had made
them ninth knights of the order of the golden fleece [1]!
The Ettrick shepherd and the doggrels, and Dyer's
Fleece, and

" Nuceus [2] sweet Hinckleian swain,"

all rival Pan and Arcady. Thus the land was purged,
and men were the draff and the disease. Many cot-
tagers were forced into towns, who were again pushed towards the sea, like the ancient inhabitants of
this island, when they addressed " the Groans of the
Britons " to Rome. Excellent œconomists! rare politicians! as if man were not the first object, and humanity the first virtue, the sovereign boon. Yet to
complete the drama according to the modern theatre,
this tragedy concludes with a farce, and a Caledonian
asylum has been established to educate Highlanders
in the midst of London—an act worthy of a crazy
personage in one of the crazed modern melodrames,
who is represented

" Tending young lambs all in the setting sun."

After the instances of depopulation by which children are forced from their infancy to add to the surplus produce of master manufacturers at the expense
of their health and strength and life, and men are banished, come what come may with them, because a
thing affords a few shillings more by the poll, while
mutton or wool sells at an enhanced price,—we come
to those who, so far from adding to the surplus pro-

[1] He conferred that order on our beloved prince.
[2] To this verse in Dyer is appended a note—" Joseph Nutt, an
eminent apothecary at Hinckley."

dúce that they diminish it. And the instances I shall adduce, I insist, exhibit an improvement on the foregoing practice of lengthening a thread by shortening a life; it is also more simple, and squares admirably with the principles of the *superlucrative* science; for it does not merely bid the obtruder, as at Mr. Malthus's *mighty feast of nature*, begone, but it actually serves up the surplus men at table as surplus produce, and thus converts the feast of nature, while it supports the insatiate argument of Mr. Malthus *of eat a village*, into " the feast of reason and the flow of soul." Thus the Caspii [1] when old were killed; so were the followers of Woden; so were the Heruli [2] when they became old or diseased. Stephanus [3], on the authority of Menander, says there was a law at Ceos, that those who could not live well should die, and that those who had attained sixty years of age should end life by combat. Ælian [4] says, they were forced to die, in order that there might be sufficient subsistence for those who remained; and Strabo [5] agrees with Ælian in the edible part of his observations. Those subject to the Sardoan [6] law killed their parents, as did the Triballians [7] and the Derbices [8]— the last ate them. Polyhistor [9] adds to the summary.

[1] Strabo, lib. 11. t. 2. p. 136.

[2] Procopius de Bello Gothico, lib. 2. c. 14.

[3] De Urbibus, p. 332.

[4] Του διακειν τοις αλλοις την τροφην. Hist. Varia, lib. 3. c. 37.

[5] Ut reliquis cibaria sufficerent. lib. 10. t. 2. p. 81.

[6] Ælian. Hist. Varia, lib. 4. c. 1.

[7] Aristot. de Topicis, lib. 2. c. ult.

[8] Qui genere proximi sunt, ejus carnes absumunt. Strabo, lib. 11. p. 136.   [9] c. 55.

Nor do we want authorities in modern times: the Battas in the East Indies, Dr. Leyden says[1], kill and eat their parents when infirm. This seems to be the maximum of that consummate science, which disregarding sympathy or affection, wishes to convert life and death, the young and old and middle-aged, to profit, and which resolves the *happiness of countries to the proportion which the population and the food bear to each other*[2]. With such lights in political œconomy as I have here afforded, no one can want plenty while relations are ill or parents old.

Among the means of depopulation, or of preventing the wholesome increase of the people, is superstition. Human sacrifices are an obvious ruin; but beside the destruction of men by the Druids in their gigantic wicker works, and the many hecatombs[3] of human beings by Montezuma's priests, there are other modes of fanatic desolation, and they have been practised in the country of the Druids, and by the successors of Montezuma. It is not merely how many in South America have been prevented from existing by the sacred mismanagement of that vast continent, and they may be calculated by the comparatively increased advance of the population in the United Provinces of North America, but how many have actually perished in the dungeons of the Inquisition; nor do I refer to the numbers burned in Smithfield, but to those

[1] Asiatic Researches, v. 10. article 3.

[2] vol. 1. p. 577. Malthus.

[3] It is said that there were 30,000 killed the year preceding the coming of the Spaniards. Temple's Works, vol. 1. p. 206. This was said probably to discredit them, and was false.

who have been oppressed for their belief, trodden to poverty, forced abroad, baited at home. " How wretched am I !" said Anderson [1], a Catholic ; " if I go out of the kingdom, it is said I have with my religion renounced my natural allegiance ; and if I stay, by law I forfeit my life." It was in Ireland, however, that a Protestant government exhibited the full extent of sectarian malignity; and ministry continues it as far as weakness and malice and the episcopacy can succeed. The pure destruction of ghostliness is an endless tale ; every great sect claims its murderers and martyrs : the devotees of Juggernaut; the loving widows of Hindoo husbands, who rival the Thracian women [2]; the convulsionaries in France; the assassins in Denmark for righteousness sake, which has in some measure been revived by Peschel in Germany. There is no respite or end to the destructive horrors of superstition. At present, at Tripoli [3], it is said that one third of the people buried by the pious precipitation of their friends are alive.

All partial and iniquitous governments check population. A monopoly, a bounty, favouring towns or country, or manufactures or commerce, every operation which prevents or even diverts the inherent disposition to improve, increase, or accumulate, affects population, either in their number or their efficiency. I speak, however, of the more obvious iniquities of government, as the penal laws by which, in the time of Sir Thomas More, men were hanged by scores,

[1] State Trials, vol. 2. p. 1082.
[2] lib. 1. c. 16.
[3] Narrative of Ten Years Residence at Tripoli.

and thousands were annually executed. This swift destruction was diminished; and in 1649[1] an act was passed to transplant felons reprieved to the Summer Islands, and to other English plantations in America; but as these outlets were insufficient or incommodious, in 1651[2] sixty persons convicted of petty larcenies were shipped for Ireland. Thus England, such is the vicissitude of things, which was a receiving place for felons when a province of Rome[3], in its turn vomited forth the wretches of its domestic misrule on its dependencies.

Bad government operates by ten thousand modes of destruction, and it is at once tortuous and direct. When Polycrates[4], *tyrant* of Samos, one of Mr. Mitford's slandered good and great princes, wished to crush the high-minded Samians, he surreptitiously sought Cambyses that he would solicit his assistance. The Samians were armed, and sent to serve the great king, on condition that Polycrates should hear no more of them. In like manner Periander sent three hundred youths of the first families of Corcyra, to be emasculated at Sardis; and it was proposed by the Irish house of commons, less than a century ago, that the Irish priests should be castrated, for no matter the amount of the villany perpetrated in any age or nation, Ireland can afford a parallel enormity.

Thus tyranny disperses some, destroys others, excites general discontent, exasperates all the passions, causes seditions, insurrection, civil wars, which effect changes not less than the flaming sword of Milton, when

---

[1] Whitelock's Mem. p. 400.　　[2] Ibid. p. 465.
[3] Marcellinus, lib. 21. c. 1.　　[4] Herodotus, lib. 3. c. 44.

Eden's temperate clime felt the hot air of the Libyan desert. Such was the war between the people and Charles the First, which had so miserable a progress and so sad an issue; and who suffered himself, " by all the laws that he had left the people[1]." But the great destruction and confusion were in Ireland: there the inhabitants were swept away by craft and force and falsehood; the world seemed too narrow for their dispersion. " Many Irish transplanted by agreement[2]." " Articles were agreed to transplant the Munster tories to Flanders[3]." Such was the desolation in Ireland, that it became a void, a receptacle for all comers. Scotch[4] and others entered on all sides, as air into a vacuum. Sir W. Temple[5] could not account for the depopulation in England for the last fifty years, except " by the great numbers of English resorting into Ireland upon the desolations arrived there."

[1] This man obtained the crown of martyrdom by the union of church and state. But it was shocking to punish him, as it is shocking that there is no law to punish the greatest criminals. It is said he was willing to grant every thing, &c. But what security was there for his veracity ? Hume speaks of Charles's *frequent evasive messages during the session*, vol. 6. p. 255. Charles revived monopolies, *so solemnly abolished*, p. 374. Charles had impeached Lord Kimbolton and the five members of treason, p. 465. On which Hume says, " How could such an attempt be considered as treason after the act of oblivion which had passed ?" p. 468. The historian adds other instances. The loyal should inform us how often a king may lie, and yet be believed. A citizen loses all credit by a single lie, but kings have a large prerogative in this respect; and the magnanimous allies, by common consent, have increased it. [2] Whitelock's Memorials, p. 528.

[3] Ibid. p. 565. [4] Laing's History, vol. 4. p. 37.

[5] On Popular Discontents. Works, vol. 1. p. 267.

As civil wars proceed from bad government, foreign wars are frequently the sequel of both. The contest of England with her American colonies excited warfare in Europe and in the East. The civil war in France committed the whole world in arms during twenty-five years of infinite destruction. Yet the ruin in the field of battle, the ten and twenty thousands and thirty thousands killed, of which some have read with such joy,—and for which Christian states have alternately sung praises to God, as if they ,adored homicidal Mars,—is the smallest portion of the mortality occasioned by glorious war. Indeed, some think with the *now* ultra-royalist Chateaubriand,—when this shifting flatterer told Bonaparte, amidst his havoc of mankind, that he only expended the superfluous population by his armies,—that war is a blood-letting of the body politic, sick with plethora even to apoplexy. Certainly war is a mighty medicine for a great disease[1]. The massacre in battle is decisive, and readily counted; but the loss of the fugitives, the loss of prisoners, (of which the three hundred horsemen annually devoted to Swetovid[2], a pagan god of Russia,) is but typical of the victims which Christian sovereigns of the same country offer to the God of peace. Mark, that the massacre on the assault of towns,—though every inhabitant perished, as when the populous city of Urgentz[3] was captured by Zengis Kan,—that the massacre in the heat of battle and in the pursuit, is comparatively unimportant to the destruc-

---

[1] Bellis atque seditionibus plures deleti sunt quam omni reliqua calamitate. Cicero, t. 4. p. 476.   [2] Tooke's Russia, vol. 1. p. 118.
[3] Pinkerton's Travels, vol. 9. p. 327.

tive consequences of war. " La faim moissonna encore plus de Français que le fer pendant la guerre de la succession d'Espagne[1]." This is not peculiar:—a soldier's life embraces every possible calamity, and every circumstance of perdition[2]. Lacy[3] and Munich lost half their armies in their campaigns with the Tartars, without meeting an enemy in the field. We have had some experience of this swift depopulation in the isle of Walcheren and in the West Indies. Mr. Stephen[4] proved by authentic returns, that from 1796 to 1802 the English lost by sickness in the Windward Islands, exclusive of St. Domingo and Jamaica, 17,173 men out of 19,670. Suppose, however, they were not destroyed ; suppose them the triumphant survivors. Sir J. M'Gregor states, that from December 1811 to June 1814, (in two years and a half,) there were treated in the British hospitals of the Peninsula, 346,108 diseases and wounds. Consider these, ye shallow boasters! for these form the obverse of the medal of Victory. I have not spoken of the pestilences which war has a thousand times originated, from the siege of Troy to the battle of Leipsic. Wars cause waste of substance[5], destruction of capital, habits of idleness, violence, and a general derangement of society, in all its comfortable, consolatory, and ge-

---

[1] Say, t. 2. p. 351.   [2] Milites incuria, fame, morbo, vastitate consumpti. Cicero, t. 2. p. 507.   [3] Annual Register, 1769, p. 3.

[4] Steele and Dickson, &c. p. 11.

[5] Of two contracts by the English commissariat in Egypt in 1812: one for corn, which was spoiled and useless ; the other for horses, which were destroyed in Spain lest they should be possessed by the French.

nerous relations. Conquests, the object of war, enforce evil and continue it. By conquest, perpetual enmity is entailed in some cases. M. Peron[1] mentions four descriptions of people in Timor,—the aborigines in the interior armed with the bow and the club; the Malays nearer the shore; and the Portuguese and their conquerors,—who are all hostile to each other. Such is the situation of many people in Africa and along the Mediterranean. In Barbary there are three races. The Moors along the shore, who repelled the Arabs, who now inhabit the plains, and who had driven back the Berebbers, who now inhabit the mountains, and are shepherds or hunters. The Berebbers are the aborigines; they extend far into the interior, even above the Cataracts, and are probably, though occasionally recruited, descendants of the Bucoli, who harassed the agriculturists of Egypt from the remotest reach of history. This may seem extravagant;—yet what was the state of Ireland, or what is the state of Ireland after six centuries? The law of William the Conqueror in England is now law in Ireland : the curfew is revived; and not long since, the inhabitants of the plains and of the mountains, of the towns and the deserts, were as distinctive as the Moors and Berebbers, the Malays and Portuguese; and this in a great measure continues, in consequence of the sacred union of church and state, under the superlative characters of Protestants and Catholics.

These depopulating consequences of war and conquest are incalculably heightened by the innovation of standing armies. Soldiers are not merely so many

[1] Pinkerton's Travels, vol. 11. p. 804.

deducted from the common stock of industry: they must be fed and clothed by others; and a soldier consumes twice as much or more than a labourer : thus each soldier, in effect, deducts three or more from the profitable industry of the state.

No country exhibits the evil of war in this respect more strongly than England. Every island and promontory which she gains, though purposely to insure her strength, constantly adds to her army, to her expense, till she has raised a debt, the interest of which equals the present rental of her land. All these,—war, conquest, standing armies,—directly and incidentally waste the substance, destroy the people, and enslave them. And in my mind slavery contains all sorts of depopulation : though so perversely disposed are· the apprehensions of some men, that slavery has been considered a means of extreme populousness and extraordinary profits.

By slavery, it is said, those who would have been slain are saved; and no doubt murder has sometimes been respited by avarice: but to insinuate that all who are enslaved would have been slain, were men not marketable, is most false. Slave-making is a trade in the first instance by the captors. Whatever was the project of Julius Cæsar in disturbing the British[1], the Romans soon learned that they could obtain nothing from that island, if Cicero be an authority[2], except

---

[1] Raleigh's observations may afford a hint. " Enterprises done in countries remote are more praiseable : for the less they are known, the greater the glory to achieve them." Cabinet Council, p. 142.

[2] " Illud jam cognitum est neque argenti scriptum esse ullum

ignorant slaves. And it is certain when the Romans ceased to conquer they ceased to import slaves : as we learn that the number of slaves brought to Constantinople[1] depended on the success of the wars of the Tartars. Slave-making has been a trade, and the ransom of a prisoner and the price of a slave were equally ascertained in various nations. It appears from Leo Africanus[2], that his majesty of Borno invaded the neighbouring territories every year to obtain slaves, which he exchanged for the wants of his royal household. Nations seem not merely to traffic in slaves procured by war ; but also to attempt, by a concatenated depredation, to preserve a balance of this trade in their favour. The Shangalla[3] make inroads on the Agows, seize their children, and sell them to the Mahometans at Guba. Thus they endeavour to indemnify themselves for their losses in the same way by the Abyssinians[4]. This hunting begins with the dry season ; and every governor from Baharnagash to the Nile is obliged to pay a certain tribute of slaves. It is remarkable that many thousand Christian slaves are sent from Africa to Asia by Christians[5], and that these slaves lose at once their liberty and their religion. These observations come from Bruce, who is an unexceptionable testimony, as he favours the slave-trade,

---

in illa insula, neque ullam spem prædæ, nisi ex mancipiis,'ex quibus nullos puto te litteris aut musicis eruditos expectare. Cicero ad Atticum, t. 3. p. 246.

[1] Ricaut, b. 1. c. 18.   [2] lib. 7.
[3] Bruce's Travels, vol. 2. p. 40.   [4] Ibid. vol. 3. p. 156.
[5] vol. 2. p. 29. There is an account of a number sent by the king of Ethiopia to Aurengzebe, and some of them fit to be made eunuchs of. Pinkerton's Travels, vol. 8. p. 107.

and condemns the attempt to abolish it as *relaxation
and effeminacy*[1], and tending to the *decay of trade
and navigation.* Slave-making is not then, generally,
a redemption from death ; it is a mere trade. Thus
the people of Madagascar fit out expeditions against
the tranquil inhabitants of the Comoro Islands, for
the purpose of seizing and carrying them off, that they
may sell them. The slave-trade, so far from relieving
humanity, has added to the sufferings of many nations.
Mr. Meredith, in his " Account of the Gold Coast[2],"
speaking of the Fantees, says, " their punishments are
fines and slavery, which amount to nearly the same
thing ; for, if the guilty person cannot pay the fine, he
is by law adjudged to be a slave." And it is ascertained
that when the slave-trade flourished without check or
molestation, the most trifling offence was punished in
the slave country by loss of liberty. This trade in Africa,—the European slave-trade in Africa, —was carried
on along 3000 miles of coast[3], from the river Senegal
to Cape Negro :—it has been narrowed ; it has been
reduced ; and some tribes which seized men in their
incursions, are now satisfied with pillaging cattle[4]. But
the limitation of the slave-market has augmented the
hardships of those districts which continue within the
sphere of its operation. Salt[5] speaks of slaves marched nine hundred miles to be sold. And it has been remarked, that though the mouths of the Senegal and
Gambia are freed from witnessing this traffic, or rather

[1] Bruce's Travels, vol. 2. p. 30.   [2] p. 312.
[3] Clarkson on the Slave Trade, vol. 1. p. 22.
[4] Fifth Report of the African Institution.
[5] Travels in Abyssinia, p. 32.

this murder and robbery, the wretches are now driven more expeditiously to the Spanish and Portuguese slave-dealers at Benin. We are told that the slave-trade does not depopulate; that "the supply is always equal to the demand:" yet both banks of Rio Grande were unpeopled by the slave-trade. If the slave-trade should not depopulate, nothing is destructive of the race of man.—"The supply equal to the demand!!" Do animals hunted in the wilderness increase as they are destroyed? Why the hunters of these beasts, the fur traders in America, by vitiating the simple lives of the savages[1], and supplying them with spirits, have impaired their slender population; and thus populous villages have dwindled into a few wandering families.—I proceed to another view of this hideous subject.

Wallace imagined that slaves anciently were more available than inferior free-men in after-times toward the increase of the people; and Sir James Steuart[2] to the same purpose esteemed *slavery, or a violent method of making mankind labour, as the third principle of multiplication.* And again he says[3], " From these principles it appears, that slavery in former times had the same effect in peopling the world, that trade and industry have now. Men were then forced to labour, because they were slaves to others; men are now forced to labour, because they are slaves to their own wants." Some French writers seem to carry

---

[1] The Europeans have corrupted the Africans. Meredith says that those of the interior, in consequence, are much less vicious than those on the coast.

[2] vol. 1. p. 90.   [3] vol. 1. p. 40.

this error a gradation further. Mons. Chateaubriand considers that slavery enabled the Greeks and Romans to succeed in works of art; as did Mons. Thomas [1]: " Il falloit nécessairement à un pareil peuple la liberté, le loisir, l'aisance; il falloit des esclaves chargés de travailler pour eux et de suppléer à tous les soins de la vie." In this rhetorician's mind slavery is as necessary to the cultivation of the arts, as in a West Indian planter's apprehension Negroland is to the growth of sugar-canes.

I am as yet to learn the progress of the Spartans in the arts, who had more slaves than any other Grecian people. As to the liberty, leisure, and ease of the Romans,—when did these concur? A few observations on this people will, beside other instruction, evince the futility of the assertion.

At Rome every year there was a levy of citizens, and every citizen could only attain civil appointments by a ten years warfare [2]. The life of a Roman was war—his object plunder. The state grew and increased by both. Five hundred years Rome employed in conquering Italy: in two hundred [3] she mastered the world. During this whole period the Romans, those humanizers of mankind, who, according to many, prepared by supreme appointment the world for the reception of Christianity, carried on unabated war; for the temple of Janus was only shut [4] three

[1] Eloges, t. 2. p. 98.
[2] Polybius, lib. 6. p. 466.
[3] Florus, lib. 2. c. 1. Polybius says in 53 years. Preface.
[4] A. Victor, de Viris illustribus, p. 100. V. Paterculus, lib. 2. c. 38.

times for short periods. Indeed, the last of these seems to have been an order unexecuted; for Dion Cassius[1] says the temple of Janus was decreed to be shut, but the passage of the frozen Ister prevented it. Florus says it was shut by Augustus, and he laments the event—" pronum in omnia mala[2];" so intimately were war and fortune fixed in a Roman's mind.

The kings and patricians of Rome,—for the people were nothing, or worse than nothing,—surpassed our modern politicians in their progress to universal empire. Romulus[3] took Cameria; he transplanted half its inhabitants to Rome, and sent double their number of Romans to Cameria. The Ausoni[4] were exterminated; Capua and Carthage rased; of Corinth scarcely a vestige remained,—and this Cicero[5] justified in his speech on the Agrarian law. On the defeat of Perseus[6] 150,000 slaves were made in Epirus, and seventy cities sacked. These are specimens of their steps to empire, for the Roman government, proceeded by repeating similar deeds.

What was the consequence? Incessant rebellions and insurrections abroad; and at home in continual jeopardy from the Gauls, or Carthaginians, or Cimbri, &c. of being themselves extinguished, either by foreign nations or by the Italian states, as in the

[1] lib. 54. c. 36. He says in a preceding book, however, that Augustus shut it. lib. 53. c. 26.

[2] Last page of his History.

[3] Plutarch. in Romulo.

[4] Deletaque Ausonum gens. Livius, lib. 9. c. 25.

[5] t. 2. p. 304.

[6] Plutarch. in P. Æmilio.

Social war, or by their slaves [1]. The Servile war, ended by Pompey, Cicero [2] reserves for the consummation of Pompey's military glory.

The world mistakes the Roman state: few governments have been weaker. The Romans were distressed by pirates [3], and scarcely succeeded against them. Balba [4] with six hundred robbers plundered Italy unchecked for six years. This man, on being taken, answered the prefect Papinian, who asked him by what right he exercised robbery? " By that which made you prefect." And Variathus [5], a leader of a band of outlaws, made war on the Romans and frequently worsted them.

What did the Roman *people* gain by all these wars? Misery, loss of power, poverty, annihilation :—the wars immersed them in debt and prison. Before the banishment of Tarquin, and just when they feared his return, the patricians condescended [6] to conciliate the people; but afterwards they treated them servilely,

[1] Florus says, Quid autem bella servilia ? Unde nobis, nisi ex abundantia familiarum. lib. 3. c. 12.

[2] Pro Lege Manilia, t. 2. p. 240. Their wars with the gladiators was a servile war also : that in which Spartacus commanded against them was most dangerous—Quorum numerus in tantum adolevit, ut quia ultimo dimicavere acie X L millia hominum se Romano exercitui opposuerunt. V. Paterculus, lib. 2. c. 30.

[3] This was another achievement of Pompey. Xiphilin. p. 4.

[4] Dion Cassius, lib. 76. c. 10.

[5] A. Victor, de Viris illustribus, p. 90. V. Paterculus says, Ita varia fortuna gestum est, ut sæpius Romanorum gereretur adversus. lib. 2. c. 1.

[6] Æquo et modesto jure :—But afterward, servili imperio patres plebem exercere, de vita atque tergo regio more consulere, &c. Salust. Fragm. 1. Historia.

according to the royal practice. The patricians possessed all the territory, all the wealth of the state;
while the people were so abject, that as common
labourers they were neglected for slaves. Nay, a
law was passed by the interest of Licinius Stolo [1],
ordering that every proprietor should employ a certain number of free-men on his land. This of course
was nugatory. Hence the remnant of the Roman
people was supported by poor laws and occasional
gratuities. They had been declining to this situation
from a very early period. It is true, execration is
pronounced in the Twelve Tables [2] on the fraudulent
patron; and Virgil [3] places such among the climax of
sinners. But patronage was in truth a monopoly of
power, and clients [4] the items in the account. Patricians might boast the connexion, just as Cicero [5]
called the dominion of Rome its patronage of the
world; and as Augustus, who sacrificed three hundred
human victims to Divus Julius [6], exhibited plays to
Honour and Virtue [7].

We have seen the operation of slaves on the Roman *people:* their effects on the patricians were
equally ruinous. Having subjected the world and ex-

---

[1] Appian. de Bello Civili, p. 354.

[2] Patronus si clienti fraudem faxit, sacer esto.

[3] —————Fraus innexa clienti.

[4] —————Illa turba clientium
　　Sit major.　　　　　Horatius, ode 1. lib. 3.

[5] Nos magis patronatum orbis terrarum suscepimus quam im-
perium.

[6] Trecentos ex deditiis electos ex utriusque ordinis ad aram Divo
Julio extructam, idibus Martiis hostiorum more mactatos. Suetonius, lib. 2. c. 15.

[7] Της Τιμης και Αρετης. Dion Cassius, lib. 54. c. 18.

tinguished their native citizens, and made Italy a prison-house, they themselves sunk under the most deplorable despotism, morally and physically, that ever afflicted any nation that had ever advanced towards civilization. The whole order perished repeatedly. Yet we are told that anciently slavery multiplied mankind ;—though slave-making occasioned immediate death or swift destruction ; though slavery converted the free hands into armed task-masters to enforce labour and suppress insurrections. In the time of calamity the slave fled [1] to the enemy; or retaliated [2] privately, as did the Roman slaves on the sack of Rome by Alaric, the stripes and ignominy of their masters ; or publicly, as in the servile wars in Scythia [3]; at Tyre [4], where they massacred their masters; in Sicily [5], where their slaughter was so excessive, that it was said locusts arose from the blood of the unburied, and consumed the corn of the island [6]. In short, of such importance and variety were these starts of vengeance and efforts for redemption, that Cæcilius [7] the rhetorician composed a book on the servile wars, Περι των δουλικων πολεμων.

I know no difference betwixt ancient and modern slavery, nor any distinction except the greater or less slavery; and this has no regard to times past or present, or to this or that religion ; for the people of every religion, ancient and modern, have had slaves, and none more than the Christians, and the Christians of

[1] Thucydides, lib. 8. p. 581.
[2] Gibbon, c. 31. v. 3. p. 203.
[3] Justin. lib. 2. c. 5.
[4] Ibid. lib. 18. c. 5.
[5] Florus, lib. 3. c. 19.
[6] Plutarch. Moralia, p. 522.
[7] Athenæus, lib. 6. p. 272.

all denominations. It is true, some nations have regulated the state of slavery. The Greeks, when they
loved liberty, said Philostratus[1], would not sell a slave
beyond the boundaries of Greece. The Jews also,
though they admitted the servitude of their men, prohibited that of their women: " If a man sell his daughter to be a maid-servant, she shall not go out as the
men-servants do[2]:" which is followed by the Turks :—
no woman of Turkish birth can be a slave[3]. Portions of the world in all ages have expressed a kindness for the most unfortunate. Julius Pollux speaks
of places of refuge for slaves[4]. It appears also that
Dupolis[5] in Libya conferred liberty on whatever
slave entered it. But signal and distinguished among
the ancients were the Locrians and Phoceans[6], who
employed no slaves ; as were the Indians, who, if Ar-
rian[7], Strabo[8], Diodorus Siculus[9], report truly, were
equally liberal and enlightened.

It is true, the Romans were not the worst masters ; and the Athenians were distinguished for liberality to their abject inmates. An Athenian slave

[1] Apol. Tyan. Vita, lib. 8. c. 7.   Callicratidas did more. When
the allies proposed the sale of the Methymnæans, he said " that
where he commanded no Grecian should be reduced to slavery."
Xenophon. Historia Græca, lib. 1. p. 444.

[2] Exodus, chap. 21.

[3] Dallaway's Constantinople, p. 33.

[4] Και ιεροις οροις, εφ' οσον τοις οικεταις ασφαλεια, sacros termi-
nos, in quibus servis securitas præbetur. Onomasticon, lib. 1.
c. 1. 10.

[5] Stephanus de Urbibus, p. 243.

[6] Athenæus, lib. 6. p. 264.   [7] In Indice, c. 10.

[8] lib. 15. t. 2. p. 452.   [9] lib. 2.

might on ill usage by his master demand[1] a sale (πρασιν αιτειν). A slave might also be redeemed[2] by paying his master his price. The Athenian slave had some yearly wages, by which in time he might purchase his freedom. Yet still I have no doubt but slavery in this mitigated form was pernicious; freemen would have been more productive labourers, and therefore the whole population of Attica would have been multiplied had all been free. Consider the price which Nicias received for his slaves per day; he farmed them to his overseer. Those who were employed in the mines only procured him a current profit of one obolus a day[3]. If ever slavery could be profitable, it must have been at Athens, a most commercial state, where slaves were bought for two minæ[4]. Yet at Rome, in Cato the Censor's time[5], the price of a slave was seven times more. An obolus was inconsiderable in any circumstances for a man's day's labour: but how small must have been the returns from slaves' work, when Demosthenes, who inherited fifty-two from his father (and some of them artisans), was not distinguished for opulence!—Indeed, from his remarks on Midias, he was the reverse. Nor can his situation be attributed entirely to the fraud of his guardians. Does any one

[1] Plutarch. Moral. p. 100. The same is said to be the case in the Caraccas:—the slave may be bought by law if ill used for 300 dollars.

[2] Petit, L. Att. p. 179.   [3] Xenophon de Rat. Redita.

[4] Demosthenes adv. Spudiam, p. 1018.

[5] Fifteen hundred drachmæ seems the common price at that time. Plutarch. in Catonem C.

believe that a free labourer at Athens would not, if he had the means of employment, raise more than an obolus a day beyond the cost of his maintenance?

Yet does Mons. Say, a friend of liberty and a judicious œconomist, actually insist on the greater productiveness of the labour of slaves—an absurdity which I thought never could be revived by any generous and intelligent man. He says, " I have no doubt that the labour of the slave yields a greater surplus of production over consumption than the labour of free-men [1]." And he would prove this, because the slave is urged to the utmost, goaded by the avarice of his master to the extent of his faculties. In the second edition [2] of his Essay, though not quite so decisive, he still insists that the labour of slaves is the best for the planters; and he thinks it conclusive on this point: " l'opiniâtreté seule qu'ils mettent à defendre l'esclavage, prouve qu'il est une économie pour eux." If this reasoning be just, no prince would reduce his subjects to tyranny: for I hope it will not be contested that slaves are less available as a nation than free-men. If this reasoning were just, all despots would introduce representative governments. Yet now despots, sooner than acquit their promises to this effect, endanger their own pre-eminence. All sorts of government act with similar desperation. The Genoese so treated Corsica. It was truly said of them on that occasion,—that so they were sovereigns, they cared not if they governed rocks

[1] I quote this from Ganilh, p. 147, (Eng. version,) not having seen the first edition of Say's work, in 1803.

[2] t. 1. p. 286.

without people. In the same spirit the English made war in America, as now does Ferdinand the Beloved. Nor do I remember an aristocracy or a prince who could divest themselves of an expensive dependency, or reinstate any people in their rights, since the time of Nero [1], who having depopulated Greece left it free.

I know there are men who speak in the highest terms of the care taken of slaves in the West Indies, and of their happiness. Brian Edwards [2] tells a tale of a slave who said, " Since me come to white man's country, me lub life too much :"—that the state of a negro slave was a felicity dangerous to salvation. From such statements we should suppose that flogging was a slander of innovators and reformers ; or that if indeed castigation ever was used, it was performed in the philosophical spirit of Plato [3], who desired Xenocrates to beat his slave, for he was angry and dared not ; and moreover that the colonial legislatures and colonial judges were guardian angels. What is the fact? The health of the slave is disregarded, to the injury of the master's returns :—murders are committed. Who has not heard of Huggins and Hodges? The latter, a planter of Tortola, was of his majesty's council. It was sworn that the severity of his punishments killed sixty negroes. What signify laws in such circumstances? At Barbadoes a law was passed, that a slave should not receive more

---

[1] Πασαν μεν 'Ελλαδα ελεηλατησε καιπερ ελευθεραν αφεις.
                                        Dion Cassius, lib. 63. c. 11.

[2] History, p. 70.   [3] Diogenes Laertius, p. 209.

than 39 lashes at *one time* [1] : and the consequence was, on the 39 lashes being given, there was a halt for a short time, when the lashing recommenced. Suppose we had no damning facts of cruelty to slaves; what must have been committed in these outlying countries, where for many years our soldiers were repeatedly flogged, contrary to the acknowledged law of Great Britain? The judges of the West Indies were like their fellows, and power directed the judicatures. Dr. Pinkard states the opinion of a judge, published by himself and subscribed by his name in a colonial gazette, " That the authority of the master over his negroes is not to be encumbered with official formalities." That judge among us who would be executioner also, could not say more. Such being the conduct of the constituted authorities and the masters, the same tyranny descends of course to factors and assistants. It appears that the white servants of Barbadoes, and consequently of other colonies, " *understood* [2]" that the power of the masters over the negroes belonged to them; and they frequently killed them with impunity.

Mons. Say is mistaken when he supposes that men will follow their interest sordidly considered, when they possess absolute dominion; for this creates a hundred wayward passions. Mons. Say has however the opinion of William Pitt, as expressed to Mr. Clarkson, in favour of his belief. But how potently soever selfishness operates, it is perpetually

[1] Clarkson on the Slave Trade, vol. 2. p. 248.
[2] Steele and Dickson, p. 146.

disturbed by the blind will of tyranny. Inchiquin the Jesuit said truly, " Man will not labour, where he can substitute slaves : and wherever man does not labour, he will abuse his time and his faculties." The whites will not labour the land, but they will scourge the labourer, scourge him. Not long since an advertisement appeared in a Jamaica newspaper[1], in which 134 runaways, who went off together, were advertised : it stated that 48 of them were branded, one had his ears cropt, and another *both nose and ears cut off.* It is the slave-master's interest to treat slaves with humanity : yet Mr. Collins, who did so, and who realized 70,000*l.* by hiring slaves, is mentioned as an extraordinary character, who has had few imitators. The slave-master disregards man, himself, .his property ;—slavery is a common destruction. A law was passed, that for every ten negroes in Jamaica there should be one acre of ground cultivated for provisions ; yet it appears that the provision grounds were not a fourth of the quantity required by law[2].

[1] Steele and Dickson, p. 435.
[2] Sir W. Young, p. 14, states the produce of Jamaica in 1799 :

Coffee plantation...... 15,343 acres
Sugar ditto. 105,232
Provision grounds. 7771

The number of the slaves in this year I do n't recollect ; but in

1810 they were 313,683
1811 326,830
1812 319,912
1813 317,424
1814 315,385
1815 313,814

In Botany Bay in 1810 there were 10,454 persons ; they had then 21,000 acres in cultivation : and in 1800, when the popula-

By this neglect they submitted to the mercy of the Americans for their existence. Such is the misrule, the outrage, the self-destructiveness of absolute power.

The reasoning of Mons. Say is wrong generally, and in its specific application. It affords no colour for believing that slave servants are profitable, because they are not relinquished for free hands; for the pleasure of dominion to mischievous men is above all price. It appears to me that it was in consequence of slavery, and, of course, indifference to human toil, that so few improvements were made in mechanism formerly, compared to those in after-times [1]. Consider their mode of lifting masses of stone in different countries;—a mound was raised, one surface being an inclined plane, up which the stones were rolled. Thus, to erect an edifice they accumulated a mountain. Strabo [2] speaks of one hundred and fifty captives in Egypt employed in carrying water from the river. It is the essence of slavery to sink the man beneath the beast; for the master rates his own dignity by the other's depression. I wonder how Mons. Say could so transgress : for facts are as hostile to his assumption, as is the philosophy of man. In the West Indies,

tion was 6,000, they had nearly as much in cultivation for food as in Jamaica (as above stated) for its hundred thousands.

[1] I am ashamed to support this remark by a statement of Sutcliff in his Travels in North America. " It is pleasant to observe on this outlet (of the lake Skaneatetes) a number of mills sufficient to do the work of some thousands of Virginian slaves. It is greatly to be lamented that the absurd policy of the Southern states has placed these poor creatures as a barrier against every improvement in mechanics, &c." [2] lib. 17. vol. 2. p. 613.

approaching the slave to a freeman (that is, paying slaves for their labour[1]) serves their owners. And the same authors[2] mention, that a planter's slaves, *when paid*, did all his holing for less than a fourth part of the three pounds currency per acre which it had cost him *before they were paid*. As an approach to liberty cheapens labour, an approach to slavery enhances it; as it has been ascertained that the labour of colliers in Scotland suffering a moderate vassalage, was doubly more expensive than that of free hands in the same country. To talk of the cheapness of slave's labour at this time is a monstrous error. Those who labour by slaves, obtain produce always enhanced[3]. Mons. le Poivre long since spoke largely and wisely on the absurdity of cultivating cheaply sugar by slaves; and he exemplified his reasoning by the culture of sugar in Cochin China by free hands, concluding, " The earth which multiplies productions with profusion under the hands of freemen, shrinks into barrenness under the sweat of a slave." To urge in any way the advantage of slave labour, is to revive the absurdity of Columella[4], who could not see the evil, though he witnessed the decline of agriculture in Italy, and lamented it.

While discussing the subject of population as af-

---

[1] Steele and Dickson, p. 13.   [2] Ibid. p. 447.

[3] Mr. Greenleaf affords another exemplification of the expense of slave labour. He supposes the average number of inhabitants in New England before the population exceeds, to be about forty to a square mile; though, he adds, the *slave-holding* states cannot retain their population so long. Statistical View, &c.

[4] De Re Rustica, lib. 1. c. 7.

fected by slavery, an extraordinary assertion of Mr. Malthus occurs to me. He says[1], "It appears from a very general survey of different countries, that under every form of government, however unjust or tyrannical; in every climate of the world, however unfavourable to health; it has been found, that population, with the sole exception above alluded to, (the West Indies,) has been able to keep itself up to the level of the means of subsistence." Without inquiring into the accuracy or confusion of his *up-and-down level*, he has expressly contradicted this dogma[2]. For instance: of Otaheite, he says, "the population is at present repressed considerably below the average means of subsistence[3]." Does he not admit that the same is apparent in Africa, where the herds of cattle are vast, and the soil of wonderful fertility[4]? Does he not state, that the produce of Russia is above its consumption[5]? And of Southern Siberia, does he not say, that population does not increase in proportion to the *nature* of the soil[6]? So much for consistency. But what could so stupefy the mind or the eye of Mr. Malthus, as to insist that, no matter how mortal the disease or how oppressive the tyranny, men would support their numbers provided they were fed? This is the purport of his doctrine. Are there not countries and districts,

---

[1] vol. 2. p. 432.

[2] He says, "Population must always be kept down to the level of the means of subsistence." Preface, p. 7. This up-and-down was the wonder of the Euripus. Ὅσπερ Ευριπος ανω και κατω φερεται. Aristides, Orat. t. 2. p. 380. Does he mean, that men starved will die?   [3] vol. 1. p. 97.   [4] vol. 1. p. 170.

[5] vol. 1. p. 368.   [6] vol. 1. p. 199.

once populous now desert? If, then, we subscribe to Mr. Malthus's statement, the food ceased before the people declined. This is astonishing. Then, whether a battle or a pestilence sweeps off the multitude, subsistence had diminished somehow by anticipation.

But suppose we allow Mr. Malthus to mend his expression, or explain his meaning by a large allowance. Suppose we should insert *permanently*, or any word that might extend it beyond a sudden casualty. Have not many populous nations declined in numbers? and why must we disbelieve that their provisions, and, what is the same, the productive land, declined subsequently to the depopulation? Was not the population of Spain reduced by the banishment of Moors and Jews? Were they banished because the Spaniards were famished? No. Nor did the Catholic Spaniards replenish the seats of the banished Hebrews and Mahometans. What then became of all their conveniencies of living, of their houses, of their arts, of their cultivated grounds? Wherever there is good land, there is the means of subsistence; and wherever it is not cultivated, where cultivation is known, there population is repressed by other causes than want of subsistence. Moors and Jews and native Spaniards all declined by ecclesiastical tyranny. For the Inquisition, which was instituted by Ferdinand purposely to purge Granada of all remains of Mahometanism and Judaism[1], seized in 1726 three hundred and sixty families convicted of Mahometanism, and confiscated their fortunes[2]; which partial violence was in effect an

[1] Giannone, Storia de Napoli, lib. 22. p. 549.
[2] Swinburne's Travels, p. 168.

act of hostility against the whole population. Shall we say with Mr. Malthus, that the population of Spain, under such circumstances, has kept itself up to the level of the means of subsistence? *or*, that tyranny has ruined the people, their industry,—and that with this declension, subsistence, which includes all the means of living, declined also?

Egypt was comparatively populous, so was Sicily; yet they declined in people, not because there was want of provisions, for they supplied Italy with grain: they declined from tyranny; the provisions continued, but they were swept away by the robbers of mankind.

Mr. Malthus concludes that those who are fed must breed:—this is a beastly opinion. No matter, says he, how unjust or tyrannical is the form of government, and how pernicious the climate, population will keep itself up to the level of subsistence. Truly Mr. Malthus is no sentimentalist; he does not even divide the soul, like some of the ancients, into the sensitive [1] and the nutritive: the extent of a man's platter measures all his capabilities. How many beasts die, sooner than eat when confined! how many who live, disdain to produce their kind! Yet feed man, and he will breed; nay, breed in proportion to his feeding; no matter where, though he be doubly plagued both by climate and despotism.

Miserable philosopher! have you never heard of men, of women devoting themselves and their children to death, sooner than submit to their enemies?—of the Sidonians, when besieged by Artaxerxes [2]?—of the

Aristot. de Anima, lib. 3. c. 11.   [2] Diodorus Siculus, lib. 16.

people of Abydos, when besieged by Philip[1]?—of the Phoceans and Acarnanians?—of the Carthaginians[2]? These were promised security if they would emigrate. No, they resisted: the men and women fought to extremity, and then consumed themselves and city, sooner than suffer the triumph of their enemies. Ancient history abounds with examples of similar daring. Carthage, fired by its own people, burned for seventeen days.

But these were republican times, it may be said; the people nourished then extravagant notions of liberty and independence. Certainly the horrors of our monarchical æra, at man's daring to manage his own concerns, were then less distressing than at present. Yet without referring to the conduct of republicans, of whom courtiers and king-adoring parasites can have no idea, I will recall the reader's attention to some particulars within our own acquaintance, and more intelligible to the subjects of kings and princes. I say, slaves frequently will not breed, though fed; frequently they will not live. It is not merely the vagabond Alemanni[3], who roamed licentiously, that will not survive their freedom; nor the citizens of Grecian states, who felt that the only liberty left them was to die[4]:—it is common to many nations. In Asia[5], those who run *amuck* are slaves, who kill to be killed. In

---

[1] Polybius, lib. 16. c. 16.   [2] Florus, lib. 2. c. 15.

[3] Dion Cassius says that the women of the Alemanni were asked whether they would be killed or sold;—they answered, Killed. They were sold, and they killed themselves. lib. 77. c. 14.

[4] Τις δ'εστι δουλος; του θανει αφροντιστων. Plutarch. Moral. p.65.

[5] Pinkerton's Travels, &c. vol. 11. p. 186.

Africa, in capturing the Shangalla [1] many are slain, many precipitate themselves down steeps, or run mad, or hang themselves, or obstinately refuse food and starve themselves. Park [2] mentions also, that the slaves in their passage from the interior to the coast frequently eat clay to destroy themselves. Follow those poor savages to their sad voyage; they not unfrequently fling themselves overboard. And Clarkson [3] mentions on the credit of an eye-witness, that some in the act of drowning wave their hands in triumph of their escape. Accompany them on shore; see the wretched relics of the slaves of Africa labouring in gangs:—judge of their lives by their deaths. Dr. Pinkard and Captain Wilson [4] both attest that the funerals, which in Africa are accompanied with lamentations, are attended in the West Indies with joy and exultation.

This feeling is general. The original inhabitants of St. Domingo, when conquered by the Spaniards, frequently poisoned themselves in parties with the juice of the manioc; and they purposely neglected to cultivate their lands, in order to starve their oppressors. Do these afford a proof of Mr. Malthus's dogma—that men will breed if they are fed? I have shown that beasts will not breed, though indulged with superfluity of food. Why trees, and shrubs, and herbs will not vegetate if they be overtopped, some which grow will not fruit, others will not blossom;—yet man, Feed him, and he will flourish!

Mr. Malthus, in effect, refers man's race to a lower

[1] Bruce's Travels, vol. 3. p. 156. [2] Travels, p. 327.
[3] History of the Slave Trade, vol. 2. p. 223. [4] vol. 3. p. 67.

origin than those who derived him from the ape, or from a quadruped, or with Maillet from the piscatory tribes. Slavery and man are incompatible:—I speak of man as a rational moral being. Slavery stuns and stupefies the civilized creature:—Then how must it operate on those who have not enjoyed habits of intellectual culture? Slavery weakens the arms, and bows the body, the mind, the senses[1]; the appetites, except those which injure, are impaired by it; and it is alike destructive both of the oppressed and their oppressors.

It was so at Rome. Rome, to whom all nations were tributary, lost her people. Even in the time of the Gracchi the free citizens had greatly declined[2]: every effort was made to recruit them; there was a general naturalization, yet they could not support their numbers. Various laws were made to induce the marriage of the people, by rewards, honours, prerogatives, penalties; and these applied to males and females. Soldiers were solicited to marry, contrary to the ancient discipline[3]; and Julius Cæsar ordained that those who bred cattle should have one third of their shepherds freemen:—still the citizens decreased. Marriage became irksome. At first, duty prevailed over convenience, and Metellus reputed marriage a necessary grievance; at last it became intolerable. Did this class of society support its population up to the level of the means of subsistence, and were they celibataries from want? No, rather the contrary: con-

---

[1] It is the remark of all who have witnessed Europeans on their return from slavery. They are indifferent, doltish, &c.

[2] Plutarch. in Tib. Gracchum.   [3] Suetonius, lib. 1. c. 43.

quest and plunder, and a throng of domestic slaves depraved all orders; the women were bad wives, men of course avoided matrimony. Tacitus[1] laments the unchastity of the women; and he ascribes to this vice the ruin of there public. In Claudian's reign, so many free women abandoned themselves to the embraces of slaves[2], it was enacted, that she who, after warning from the master respecting her intercourse with his slave, continued the offence, should become the slave of the master of her paramour[3]. This was one means by which generation was impaired : I have spoken elsewhere of other causes of the ruin of the Roman people. Yet with all means of living, amidst Italy,—supplied with provisions from every shore of the Mediterranean,—even Britain contributed grain to the Romans,—the people were unproductive; they disregarded the continuance of their family[4] : there was no succession from father to son; races frequently ceased with the individuals; and thus, from age to age, the population declined[5].

Did this happen for want of subsistence?—there was a monstrous superfluity. Crates imputed the ruin of

[1] Impudicitia magnum reip. malorum initium fuit. Annal. 13. c. 45.

[2] Gliscebat supra modum amor ingenuarum mulierum erga servos alienos. Gravina, p. 325.

[3] Nec credi potest qua obsequiorum diversitate coluntur homines sine liberis Romæ. A. Marcellinus, lib. 14. c. 6.

[4] Telemachus particularly laments, ωδε γαρ ὑμετερην γενεην μονυωσε Κρονιων.

[5] ———— Cælibem vitam prebet
Sterilis juventus : hoc erit quicquid vides
Unius ævi turbæ. Seneca Hippol. ver. 465.

tyrannies to excessive food and opulence[1] ; and Florus[2] expressly attributed the decline of the Romans to the extent of their possessions and riches. The people were poor, and they obtained bread and plays ; but the patricians were not poor, but so rich that no order ever possessed such riches. Apicius considered himself lost, when the residue of his fortune amounted to about 80,000 pounds sterling ; and Crassus denied that a man was rich, who could not by his private income support an army[3]. Thus the Romans disappeared,—high and low, plebeians, patricians, and slaves, — though they had the world for their negro-land, and though even the strongest motives were proposed to ensure the procreation of slaves; for female slaves had their *jus trium liberorum*[4], and that boon of their fruitfulness was freedom: yet they all decayed, though the whole known world was the domain of Rome ; and *Roman*, from being an epitome of honour among mankind, became the last term of disgrace among barbarians[5]. It was slavery, and with this, want of moral virtue, that wore away the population of Rome; and these will ever, according to their intensity, produce the same consequences. In a tract by Franklin, published at Philadelphia so early as 1751, among the causes of depopulation he principally mentions "the introduction of slaves. The negroes brought into the English sugar-islands have greatly diminished the

[1] Δια τρυφην και πολυτελειαν. Moral. p. 77.　　[2] lib. 3. c. 12.
[3] Cicero, vol. 4. p. 439.
[4] Fœminis quoque fœcundioribus otium nonnunquam et libertatem dedimus, &c.　Columella de Re Rustica, lib. 1. c. 8.
[5] Pliny, at least, said so :—Gentium in toto orbe præstantissima una omni virtute haud dubie Romano. Hist. Nat. lib. 7. c. 40.

whites there : the poor are by this means deprived of employment, while a few families acquire vast estates, which they spend in foreign luxuries, and educating their children in the habits of those luxuries : the same income is needed for the support of one, that might have maintained one hundred. The whites who have slaves, not labouring are enfeebled, and therefore not so generally prolific : the slaves being worked too hard and ill-fed, their constitutions are broken, and the deaths among them are more than the births; so that a continual supply is needed from Africa. The northern colonies having few slaves, increase in whites," &c.

Here we have an abstract of the declension of imperial Rome in the perverted progress of a sugar-plantation. Italy had been laboured by freemen, and it was opulent in all productions; but under the culture of slaves it became sterile and effete. In St. Domingo the ground was cultivated by whites, and it is now cultivated by them. But what is still more important, St. Domingo[1], which required an annual importation of 29,000 negroes before the revolution, and though multitudes of its people perished during that crisis, 500,000 adults being reduced to 300,000; though violence, outrage, and war continued ; though the females and males have been very disproportioned; yet under the semblance of freedom the children in St. Domingo have greatly increased. Did food prepare the way for freedom, or liberty provide food?—ask, Does the yellow corn impart rays to the sun? or does the sun infuse its splendour into the ripened grain? On the same ground, the same people who perished under

[1] Malouet, Mem. t. 1. p. 52.

a Christian government of white people, at the rate of thirty thousand men annually,—under a new government of negroes, lately slaves, and during the fury of a revolution, increased prodigiously in people and their comforts.

Liberty is the want of man. Von Sach, speaking of the slaves in Surinam, says, though well-treated, they are declining in number, while the Bush Negroes, who escaped from this wasting colony into the woods, have increased so as to press on the possessions of their former masters. Did they find a feast of nature in the wilderness? No; but they carried with them an independent spirit; and this procured for them what their masters and fellow-countrymen, with their cultivated fields, and capital, and accommodations, could not attain.

CHAPTER IV.

Some writers superciliously indifferent respecting the possibility of increasing population.—Dr. Jarrold's mind-check.—Surgeon Birck.—Mr. Malthus.—Mr. Weyland.

WHILE some are anxious to increase the people heedlessly, without regarding their wants or their wishes,—as Mr. Anderson [1], who in his " Calm Investigation" considers it stronger than gospel, " *that the means of subsistence must rather be augmented than diminished by the augmentation of its population;*"—others, on the contrary, regard an increase of people

[1] Mr. Anderson has not studied Sir Anthony Absolute's character, " Can't be calm like me," when the old man suffers a paroxysm of passion.

as a tide without ebb, which must eventually extinguish human life by an excess of human beings. It might be hoped that such extravagancies would countervail each other; that the former would have ceased, as it has in the Highlands: " His (the Highlander's) glory and felicity consisted in the extent of his fold and the number of his family; he could never have too many children or too many cows, however great the difficulty might be of rearing the first to maturity, or providing fodder for the last." This superstition of the Highlands has changed, as I have shown, for its opposite.

Not so, however, in England. Both extremes have their advocates. Mr. Gray thinks there cannot be too many people; Mr. Malthus, that there cannot be too few. Indeed Dr. Gillum embraces in some measure both parties, in which he is not particular. He says, that if inoculation had been wisely practised so late as 1665, " the lives of one hundred thousand inhabitants might have been saved, exclusive of their offspring, and *nati natorum et qui nascuntur ab illis.*" Here Dr. Gillum propagates by the geometrical scale of Mr. Malthus, and feeds them by Mr. Anderson's sympathizing ratio.

> "———————— I the praise
> Yield thee, so well this day thou hast purvey'd."

While some consider, in the vulgar phrase, " the more mouths the better cheer;" or, on the contrary, with Mr. Malthus, that many include misery; some assume a rare indifference, and superciliously discredit the possibility of a superabundant population. Dr.

Jarrold proclaims his checks as well as his opponent Mr. Malthus; and the chief is the improvement of the mind. Not, observe, as teaching prudence, but as stinting the generative faculty. He says; " As man sinks down to the animal, he is prolific; as he ascends above, his fruitfulness decreases [1]." I thought man was an animal [2]; and that the savage, the lowest gradation of mankind, was the least fruitful. In the sequel it seems to have occurred to Dr. Jarrold, that savages are unproductive : but this no way impedes his doctrine; and according to the custom of such theorists, it confirms it: " In a word, mental apathy as strongly characterizes this class (peasants), as vigilance and anxiety do those of the savage and the philosopher [3]." Happy classification! the mind-check embraces others:—" Those who enjoy any rank in a civilized country; who stand at its head, either in intellect or power; stretch their capacity to the utmost, that they may acquit themselves with credit in the stations they fill. This exertion of the mind is, in the view I take of the subject, the efficient cause of the few generations an estate is enjoyed by such a family, or rather that such a family exists to possess it [4]." This is the height of genius; as it invents a fact, and then draws a fanciful consequence from its own imagination. No doubt the straining of royal

[1] Dissertations on Man, p. 250.

[2] Charles Abbot, in his Parochial Divinity, makes the same distinction. He speaks of Hydra and Cerberus, and " the animal, the feathered, and the vegetable classes." p. 122.

[3] Dissertations, &c. p. 269.

[4] This writer admits the fact of the quick extinction of such families. I have given another reason.

wit is agony—for lately, nine out of the ten legitimate ruling princes of Europe were drivellers or insane. The Doctor considers it a vulgar error, that prostitutes are barren on account of *their promiscuous intercourse ;* he says, *They owe their sterility to the influence of their mind*[1].

Dr. Jarrold, having so reasoned on the intellectual check, quotes Gibbon, who said that the Athenians fell from 30,000 to 21,000 in the best days of their republic. I repeat, that during the interval of the two census many thousand Athenians were disfranchised, and the latter census succeeded immediately a great plague. So much for history :—Now for existing facts and speculations. He says, " The present inhabitants of America will in a few centuries people that continent ; but the rate will not continue to be as it is now, it will diminish in proportion as the mental faculties are exerted[2]." The Americans, then, now think little. He also says, " It is my aim establish the fact,—that the most thoughtful people, taken as a body, are the least prolific[3]." How does this agree with the *thinking people* of Britain, and their increase from 1800 to 1810? Or is this a random stroke at the insensate state of the public mind for the last half century, from hostilities begun at Boston about a three-penny tea-duty, to............

Surgeon Birch[4] is equally at his ease in contemplating the excess of population, provided diseases have fair play. He says, " that when such pains are taken to magnify the victims to the small-pox, why is

[1] Dissertations, &c. p. 258.   p. 281.   [3] p. 273.
[4] Fatal Effects of Cow-pox.

it not remembered that, in the populous parts of the metropolis, this pestilential disease is considered a merciful provision on the part of Providence to lessen the burthen of a poor man's family?" This does approach the new doctrines of population and production, as far as medicine is comparable to political œconomy. This disregards man, and depopulates to procure a surplus produce for the survivors—while that would cherish a mortal disease in pure love of humanity. How far Mr. Malthus may be classed with Mr. Birch, I leave to the reader to decide from the following passage. Having mentioned, among the causes, foreign trade and colonial emigrations [1], he adds, " and the extreme unhealthiness of a great part of the country, which occasions a much greater average mortality than is common in other states. These I conceive were the unobserved causes which principally contributed to render Holland so famous for the management of her poor, and able to employ and support all who applied for it." Here, distinctly, disease and rapid mortality are reputed the principal causes by which Holland was enabled to support its poor with distinguished facility.—Towards the conclusion of this work I shall explain the true cause of Holland's superiority in providing for its poor.

Some again treat as notional the possibility of an excessive population in England; for, say they, one-

[1] vol. 2. p. 334. Emigration is no cause: for he elsewhere admits that the population of Holland was not upheld by propagation, as there was a great influx of foreigners. vol. 1. p. 376. And in other places he speaks of the bad effects of unhealthy countries to population—But he wanted a reason.

third of the people live in towns large enough to prevent the inhabitants from reproducing their numbers ;
that is, the excess of births in the country must find a
premature death in the towns.   This mortal consolation is mentioned by Mr. Weyland, jun. in his " Essay
on Population and Production," who seems on this
occasion to pride himself on a discovery.   The greater
mortality of towns was known for ages, and to none
more than the English.   But mark the different conclusions of three English writers.   Mr. Weyland considers the mortality of towns a remedy for any excess
of population ; Dr. Price, a ruin ; while Mr. Malthus,
somewhat melancholy, says, " In spite of our increasing towns and manufactures, the demand on the
country for people is by no means very pressing[1]."
Yet Ireland still more perplexes their science : it is a
country concerning which more nonsense has been
uttered than of all European nations together.   What
Africa was formerly[2], Ireland is now ; for Libya and
novelty, we must substitute Ireland and wonders.

CHAPTER V.

Dissertation on Population in Ireland.—Mr. Malthus's—Mr. Wey-
land's—Mr. Ricardo's—Mr. Grahame's opinions, &c. exposed.—
The poverty and populousness of Ireland truly explained.

THE people of Ireland are numerous and poor.—
On this association sages infer, either that they are poor
because they are numerous, or that they are nume-

[1] vol. 1. p. 466.

[2] Ὅτι ἀει φερει τι Λιϐυη καινον.   Aristot. Hist. Animal. lib. 8.
c. 28.

rous because they are poor. Other reasons are assigned for the populousness of Ireland. Sir John Davies states their infinite multiplication *from living on the milk of the cow.* Mr. Arthur Young [1] rails against the linen manufacture; Lawrence [2] against the great plenty of provisions, which he says is a main impediment to the trade and wealth of Ireland. Mr. Malthus concentrates his rage against potatoes. These are samples of the philosophy on Ireland. The sages have proposed remedies accordingly. Mr. Weyland [3]

[1] Tour in Ireland, vol. 2. p. 132.   [2] State of Ireland, p. 7.

[3] Mr. Curwen also, in his Letters on Ireland, published in 1818, says: "The greatest political alteration that could take place in this distressed country, would be a dislike to potatoes, and a general preference in the rising generation to bread and animal food." vol. 2. p 31. Does he imagine the Irish have Hindoo prejudices, and abhor animal food? Suppose them flesh-eaters—would this reduce the tithes paid by a Catholic people to a Protestant clergy And the composition for these tithes he admits is greater in Ireland than in England. vol. 1. p. 385. Will eating bread and beef exonerate their manufactures and commerce? Will it liberate the Catholics in respect to the Protestants? or both in respect to their rights? Will it send the Englishman, whose ancestor obtained mighty districts by confiscation, to reside on his iniquitous inheritance? Will it stop the emigration, in consequence of the Union, of lords and commoners, and restore the three millions of rents annually wrested from the laborious poor of Ireland, and sent to absentees? which three millions, considering that the taxation of Ireland can only be made to produce one-eleventh of the public revenue of Great Britain, are equal to thirty-three millions annually transferred from Great Britain. The Irish have only eaten potatoes for two centuries; but for many centuries they have suffered the tyranny of Great Britain: and they have been miserable, as have been all oppressed nations, eat what they may. Mr. Curwen says, truly, " Place man in that state in which, as a rational creature, he ought to be, and Ireland would be the delight of all beholders." p. 71.

calls the imputed excess of people in Ireland a *nuisance*; and talks of " the mere excrescence of the body politic eradicated to its great relief, if the operation could be effected without infringing the laws of humanity [1]." He probably feared to be more precise; as Swift, indignant at the oppressions of the Irish, had said ironically, " I am touched with a sensible pleasure when I hear of a mortality in a country, parish, or village." Mr. Weyland should know that the radical remedy had been applied to Ireland—the population of Ireland had been eradicated; and I have already quoted a passage from Temple to that purport. Mr. Weyland would correct the nuisance by " the method of absorption, slow and tedious as the process may be." While Mr. Malthus takes summary vengeance on the Irish, calling them *degraded* [2]; *in total want of decent pride; that they propagate their species like brutes* [3]. Whence this outrage? The Irish are prolific; but so were the Jews in Egypt [4]: And what proof is there that the Jews were more comfortable than the Irish? The Irish, it is true, negative one of Mr. Malthus's mighty dogmas—that population can never be very rapid, except where the price of labour is very high. Yet the price of Jewish labour was not higher perhaps in Egypt than labour in Ireland. Mr. Malthus proposes an *absorption* of potatoes, those peccant humours of a fertile soil: they are perniciously cheap [5]; for, speaking of Ireland, this

---

[1] On Population and Production, p. 220.

[2] vol. 2. p. 332.　　　　　[3] vol. 2. p. 336.

[4] Mr. Malthus, the reader may remember, has assumed this increase; and on his assumption I argue.　　　[5] vol. 1. p. 504.

accurate reasoner prefers food which is dear—that is, which is scarce—that is, plenty is misery in Ireland, though it is all things elsewhere. He would absorb potatoes, and substitute some dearer food (this is literally his project), which would extinguish all those people who are now enabled to live by the cheaper food. What is the use of machinery, or improved tillage, or encouragement to fishing; but to abridge labour, increase production,—in fine, cheapen the means of living? To favour a dearer food is to prefer operose agriculture, sterile land, and an inhospitable climate. Thus this soi-disant *friend to population when it follows its natural order*, decisively recommends extinguishing the people by enhancing their food. A capital concern of society is to produce the greatest benefit with the least toil. That potatoes are beneficial, all may witness : the Irish feel they are good. If then they satisfy those who use them, and those who use them are vigorous—what could they gain by eating wheat or rice, &c.? I cannot perceive that Mr. Malthus would object to potatoes, if they were double their present price. As he found a philosopher in Swisserland among the peasants, he might find another in Ireland :—" Master Hamilton," said a labourer, " you may talk of your new-fangled plans and all that; but there never was plenty in the county of Meath, since every plough had not six horses, and every horse had not a leader." If the Irish were fed by wheat, or even by potatoes produced by such a retinue, what a reformation would take place in the *rags and mud cabins* of Ireland ! Food would be most felicitously dear.

Mr. Ricardo [1] also prescribes: "The remedy for the evils under which Poland and Ireland suffer, which are similar to those experienced in the South Seas, is to stimulate exertion, to create new wants, and to implant new tastes: for those countries must accumulate a much larger amount of capital before the diminished rate of production will render the progress of capital necessarily less rapid than the progress of population. The facility with which the wants of the Irish are supplied, permits that people to pass a great part of their time in idleness: if the population were diminished, this evil would increase, because wages would rise; and therefore the labourer would be enabled, in exchange for a still less portion of his labour, to obtain all that his moderate wants require." As Mr. Malthus classes the Spaniards and Irish with the brutes, Mr. Ricardo places the Poles and Irish with the savages of the South Seas. But there is this difference; Mr. Malthus would feed the Irish on the dearer substance, and he would have their wages regulated by it [2]. How could this serve the capitalist? for raising the price of food would diminish the population, and increasing the wages of labour would lessen the profits of capital.

Mr. Ricardo is not so absurd: he does not propose a dearer food or higher wages,—but to excite new appetites, and so straighten their facility of living as to counteract this imputed habitual idleness of the Irish. The increase of wages is hostile to his whole system. He says [3]: " It has been my endeavour to

---

[1] Political Œconomy, p. 101.   [2] vol. 2. p. 383.
[3] Political Œconomy, p. 154.

show throughout this work, that the rate of profits can never be increased but by a fall of wages; and there can be no permanent fall of wages, but in consequence of a fall of the necessaries on which wages are expended." Mr. Ricardo is consequential in error, a happiness which Mr. Malthus rarely possesses.—I must however withdraw my doubtful praise of Mr. Ricardo's consistency, when he says; "Give to the Irish labourer a taste for the comforts and enjoyments which habit has made essential to the English labourer, and he would then be content to devote a further portion of his time to industry, that he might be enabled to obtain them." His own substantive account[1] of an English labourer is no object of admiration. What! are poor's-rates and workhouses among his comforts and enjoyments? Yet they are essential to him. But how are these tastes to be excited in Irish labourers? Is it supposed they are not like other human creatures? but that they make choice of privations? Perhaps Mr. Ricardo abstained from offering a special remedy, being deterred by the failure of Mr. Malthus's grand specific for poverty in Ireland.

If Mr. Ricardo,—whose general sentiments and character I should willingly praise, if I could stop to eulogize an individual when I resented a nation's wrongs,—has afforded no hints how these *tastes* are to be excited, Mr. Weyland has adopted Mr. Malthus's nostrum with marvellous mysticism[2]: " The very extent of the population (of Ireland) offers something like a physical impediment to the improvement of their society. But I am not entirely without hope

[1] p. 111.   [2] On Population, p. 102.

that the check which has lately been given to the exportation of corn from Ireland, by reducing its price and encouraging its consumption among the lowest ranks of the people, may tempt them to desert their potatoes for bread, which would advance them more rapidly towards better habits than may at first sight be imagined." How? unless the potatoe be the forbidden fruit, and wheat the bread of life!

Observe, that from these writers nothing escapes respecting the government, or the laws, or the judicature, or the state of property, or tithes, or tenancy, &c. No, the Irish are the sinners, and the scapegoat is the potatoe. Feed them on corn! Why the Poles do not eat potatoes, and they are poor and miserable. Are potatoes and wretchedness homogeneous in Ireland?—The Irish were miserable before a potatoe was planted in Europe.

Mr. Malthus riots in his abuse of the Irish, while no breath escapes him of the wide-wasting mischiefs which have immemorially beset this people. He talks of the Irish now as Strabo did. *The details of their population*, says Mr. Malthus [1], *are little known*: and oh! hideous! they eat potatoes! So the geographer [2]: " Nihil dicere manifestum habemus, hoc duntaxat excepto, quod longe magis quam Britanni sylvestres illius sunt incolæ anthropophagi manduconesque magni." And as abuse is never complete without a contrasting panegyric, he opposes the Scotch to the Irish [3]: " the quiet and peaceable habits of the instructed Scotch peasant compared with the turbulent disposition of the ignorant Irishman." Sup-

[1] vol. 1. p. 504. [2] lib. 4. t. 1. p. 365. [3] vol. 2. p. 344.

pose this to be true, which is false,—what causes the difference between the Scotch and Irish? The northern Irish are principally Scotch, and each country had the same name [1], as they possessed a common people. Besides, the Highlanders particularly eat potatoes like the Irish, and have increased in consequence. Lord Selkirk says, that in 1755 the population of the Highlands amounted to 255,845, and in 1801 they increased to 296,844. This he attributes to the universal use of potatoes, which were scarcely known at the time of the former calculation. Now the Scotch were something more than turbulent in 1717 and 1745, when they did not eat potatoes. Since that time potatoes have been a sedative to them ; though they have been so inflammatory in Ireland, saving and excepting in the year 1817, when Ireland was tranquil, and non-potatoe-eating England was insurrectionary and treasonable.

Mr. Malthus says nothing of provincial misrule ; nothing of one-tenth of the people absorbing exclusively all honours and profits ; nothing of middlle-men and subsetting ; nothing of absentees draining through a thousand conduits, thousands and millions, and affording no return ; nothing of a severe tithing system, which robs a Catholic population to enrich a Protestant ministry, who do not administer ; nothing of exciting disgust, exasperating animosity, inflaming sectarian hate—an aggravated and multifarious iniquity, which for length of time and excesses· has

[1] Temple says : Ireland and Scotland were called Scotia, and the north-west parts of Ireland and Scotland were called Ierne. Works, vol. 2. p. 533.

no parallel. Nay, Mr. Grahame, another writer on population, says [1] : "A system of misgovernment and oppression, *long since abandoned,* has bred among the people of Ireland a tendency to mistake the cause of their sufferings, and consequently the remedy of which they admitted : it has bred a habit of considering their government as the source of every evil, and of resorting to indolent clamour and furious rebellion against this imaginary cause of hardship, in place of that active exertion which is the natural consequence and the natural remedy of the only hardships-to which they are exposed." Here is another *natural* philosopher : "That a monster should be such a natural !"

I shall briefly relate the conduct of England to Ireland up to the present hour.—Henry the Second [2] came to assist M'Murough of Leinster ; and, as usual with such friends, he attempted to conquer Ireland for himself. To effect this, he was of course moved by the worthiest motives, and we find loyalty and true religion,—Adrian the Third cooperating with Henry the Second in this good office ; for the Irish were once independent both of England and Rome ; church and state being then under *domestic nomination*[3]. Popes and kings continued their joint achieve-

---

[1] p. 299.   [2] Macartney's Post. Works, vol. 2. p. 97.

[3] The Irish are very much altered. Some time since they were such papists !—That was the cry. Now, since the English restored the Pope, they are not papists enough !—in short, any thing for the benefit of an objection. The Irish Catholics were once notorious for their superstition ; " De tous les Catholiques Romains, il n'y en a point de si superstitieux, ni qui ayent une si grande veneration pour tout ce qui vient de Rome, que les Irlan-

ments. In Edward the Second's reign, says Hume [1],
" the horrible and absurd oppressions which the Irish
suffered under the English governments made them
at first fly to the Scots, whom they regarded as deli-
verers." The same historian, reflecting cumulatively
on all the British acts towards Ireland, calls them *to
the last degree absurd.* The army was supported by
free quarters. " Thrown [2] out of the protection of
justice, the natives could find no security but in force;
and flying the neighbourhood [3] of cities, which they
could not approach with safety, they sheltered themselves in their marshes and forests from the insolence
of their inhuman masters; being treated like wild
beasts, they became such," &c. There never was so
flagitious a government. Spenser [4] mentions a law,
which declared, that if an Irishman converse with an
Englishman he shall be condemned as a spy. The
Irish bards were murdered for those virtues which

dois; parce qu'il n'y en a point si ignorants." Wickefort, Ambas-
sadeurs, &c. p. 433. Their knowledge is improved mightily by
their treatment of Quarantotie's document.

[1] vol. 2. p. 342.   [2] vol. 5. p. 396.

[3] I have seen on different hills, or rather mountains, the marks
of ridges which have not been cultivated in the memory of any
living person. I imagine these remote and inhospitable tracts were
the refuge of some during these desolations. It is so in other
places: Bruce, speaking of the Mountains of the Moon, says they
are excellent soil; but as this unfortunate country has been for
ages the theatre of war, the inhabitants have only ploughed and
sown the tops of them. Travels, vol. 4 p. 262. So Van Egmont
laments the fine plain near Tiberias left barren; the inhabitants
cultivating the mountains to avoid the Arabs. Travels, vol. 2.
p. 38.

[4] State of Ireland, p. 48.

crowned the bravest names of Greece with imperish-
able glory ; and Spenser [1], a traitor to poetry and
patriotism, justified the crime. The harp, in which
the Irish excelled, was proscribed, in order that history,
and private reputation, and all the brave, generous,
mild, and endearing passions might eventually perish. What country ever so suffered ? Not Sicily, not
Greece, which has endured all sorts of barbarians
from Goths to Ottomans for twenty-three successive
centuries.

With Elizabeth's reign a new distinction arose.
The inhabitants in Ireland had been distinguished by
the English, and the *mere Irish*. Then they were
divided into Protestants and Catholics. As the Irishry
were persecuted before, so were the Catholics afterward. Coke, in his pleading against Essex, accuses
him, that when chief governor of Ireland he granted
" a public toleration of an idolatrous religion." As
by 4 Hen. V. c. 6. no Irishman was to be promoted in the church of Ireland, so no Catholic subsequently was to be advanced in the army : and Stafford [2] in his defence declared, " he never preferred
any captain, lieutenant, or ensign, to be of that army,
that was a papist." The policy of James, so vaunted
respecting Ireland, was principally to dispossess the
Irish and substitute British colonists. Thus the Irish
were persecuted, oppressed, subjected to free quarters. Stafford says [3], *Ireland had been at all times*

---

[1] p. 123.

[2] State Trials, vol. 1. p. 825. This exclusion was not peculiar.
4 Hen. IV. no Welshman was to be an officer in Wales. Law
Dict. vol. 2. p. 755.   [3] State Trials, vol. 1. p. 838.

accustomed to such summary proceedings. The Irish, desperate by their suffering, and seconded by the insurrection in Scotland and the civil war in England, endeavoured to resume their rights; as did Boadicea, Caractacus, and Alfred, to liberate Britain.

Hume (and I rather quote from this cautious author) says of the English, " By continuing their violent persecution, and still more violent menaces, against priests and papists, they confirmed the Irish Catholics in their rebellion.—By disposing before-hand of all the Irish forfeitures to subscribers or adventurers, they rendered all men of property desperate, and seemed to threaten a total extirpation of the natives." The hatred of the British to the Irish, which descended to the Catholics, inflamed the British against the English Catholics. Chief Justice North [1] said on Collyer's trial, " for I must tell you, the papists are best extirpated and suppressed by a steady prosecution of the laws against them." And another Chief Justice, Pemberton [2], said respecting the Popish plot, which no anti-Catholic however fanatic now credits, " There is *digitus Dei* in the discovery of it."

William the Third signed the treaty of Limerick the 3d of October 1689, and on the 22d of the same month this solemn act was broken : the English parliament excluding Catholics from both houses of the Irish parliament, by requiring each member, preparatory to admission, to take the oath of supremacy. In 1695 the Catholics were deprived of all means of educating their children—of being their guardians, &c [3].

[1] State Trials, vol. 3. p. 461.　　[2] Ibid. vol. 2. p. 747.

[3] Jura sanguinis nullo jure civili dirimi potest, says the Digest.

On the 4th of March 1704 it was enacted, That any son of a Catholic who should apostatize to the Protestant faith, should immediately succeed to the family estate. An entailed estate (Catholics being esteemed civilly dead) was to be enjoyed by the next Protestant in succession. Catholics could not purchase land, nor be tenants for life. Observe, these and the following statutes were enacted without provocation, the Irish being tranquil and submissive. In 1709, wives of Papists apostatizing were to receive increased jointures. No Papist was to keep a school. For discovering a Papist usher, the informer was to receive 10*l.*; for discovering a priest, 20*l.*; for discovering a bishop, 50*l.* Justices of the peace were enabled to force Papists to inform against Popish priests. By 1 Geo. II. c. 9., no Papist was allowed to vote for a member of parliament. These goads and torments were continued, were repeated, were aggravated. Submission was unavailing; suffering could not assuage; reason, policy, character could not control. In the mean time a shout of liberty across the Atlantic was heard, and the fears of Britain brought hope to Ireland. So much for the political situation of Ireland at the commencement of the American war.

Consider the duress and persecution of the Irish trade and manufactures, of its tillage and pasturing.

The legislation of Ireland is in direct opposition to all maxims of equity; yet in all periods the Irish lawyers praised the excellent constitution of church and state, and the beauty of the Irish jurisprudence. Thus in Scotland the small-pox is honoured with an attribute of Venus by the vulgar.

By 18 Charles II. c. 2. importations of cattle from Ireland were declared a nuisance; by the 30th of the same king, the introduction of mutton and lamb was prohibited [1]. The same brooding mischief blasted its agriculture. And observe, this was not against the Irishry or the Catholics, but against Ireland, which the rascal policy of England would render poor and wretched, a burthen and a disgrace to her. With regard to Ireland's agriculture, it was proposed that the Irish farmer should lay out five acres in every hundred in tillage; which the English interest discountenanced, not because it was absurd,—no, but lest Ireland should become agricultural.

It may be said, This is true ;—but then how careful has England been in protecting the staple of Ireland —the linen manufacture! England's attention to this manufacture was a mere imposition. The measures for the promotion of the growth of flax, &c. constantly attended the attempt directly to destroy the woollen manufacture. Stafford's politics, Sir William Temple's [2] recommendations, Davenant's advice, favoured the one to aid the ruin of the other. The English woolcombers and weavers persuaded their countrymen that the woollen manufactures were the wealth of Britain : and so insensate were their best writers on this point, that Davenant [3], who saw clearly, and who said that the prohibition of the import of Irish cattle was to serve the northern and western counties at the expense of England, could not see that the prohibition of Irish woollens was to serve

[1] Law Dict. vol. 2. p. 438. Decker on Trade, p. 52.
[2] Miscellanies, vol. 1. p. 113.   [3] Works, vol. 1. p. 46.

certain manufacturing districts at the general expense of the nation. On this point his heart was as hard, as his eye was dull; for of the laws respecting the woollens of Ireland he says, " Where the commonwealth is truly concerned, and where her safety is in question, they have very narrow minds who let their compassion be too much extended to private objects [1]."

In 1698 the English commons addressed William, stating " that the wealth and peace of England do in a great measure depend in preserving the woollen manufacture as much as possible entire to that realm:" and they request him to extinguish the woollen trade of Ireland. His majesty graciously answered that he would fulfil their wishes; and his conduct in consequence should be remembered by those who are interested for the veracity of princes. The woollen manufacture was destroyed in Ireland, where it had flourished for centuries; as it appears by a paper of Lord Charlemont's in the Irish Transactions, that in the fourteenth century Ireland had a considerable reputation at Florence for such manufactures. The manufacture was extinguished at once; for the king and parliament, and their officers, made an ultra-Luddite war on the woollen manufacture of the whole nation. In 1699, says Dr. Ledwich, " the town of Burros, and indeed the whole parish, were filled with combers and weavers; but after the passing of the act they converted their property into money, and became farmers [2]:" that is, with the wreck of their property they began to struggle in a new trade to support their existence. Shall we then be told of this and that man, and this

---

[1] Works, vol. 2. p. 246.   [2] Account of Aghaboe, p. 88.

and that law to promote the linen manufacture, as a set-off for this barbarity? What were these laws? One was passed in 1672, obliging farmers to sow so much flax-seed. This appears to have operated as a grievous penal law; for Temple says, " A general neglect in the execution and common guilt has rendered the penalties impracticable [1]." Long before Stafford's arrival in Ireland (the supposed creator of the linen manufacture in Ireland) it existed. It is clear, from the 13th of Elizabeth, that the Irish had habitually, at least a century preceding this act, exported wool, flax, linen and woollen yarns. Then, why are we to suppose that linen cloth was not made, when yarn was spun abundantly? It is perfectly certain that they who grow flax, and manufacture and export linen yarn, do not require the imputed magic of a slender bounty [2] to convert it into drapery. The Dublin Society, in their wisdom, attempted to form a silk manufacture in Ireland, by giving three per cent. to the wholesale purchasers of Irish silks who should retail them. What did this bounty effect?

The sordid cowardice of Britain having ended the woollen manufacture in Ireland, the free export [3] of wool from Ireland was also prohibited by the 1st of William and Mary, c. 32. s. 6. No wool was to be shipped from Ireland, except from particular ports, in order the more securely to monopolize the Irish wool

[1] vol. 1. p. 114.

[2] Anderson says it had never exceeded in any year 13,000*l.* History of Commerce, vol. 5. p. 384.

[3] Decker says, the export of woollens being prohibited, the wool was exported to France. On Trade, p. 55.

for the British manufacturers. This was further enforced by the 12th Geo. II. Ships also, by act of parliament, were directed to cruize round Britain and Ireland, to prevent the unlawful export of woollens. 5 Geo. II. c. 21, Ireland could neither export nor import except through England. Before 1780 Ireland could not export directly to the British West Indies, beef, pork, &c.; and when she obtained, by the 24th Geo. II. c. 13, a relaxation in her favour, and was permitted to import directly West India produce, there were excepted from the privilege, " sugars, tobacco, indigo, cotton, wool, molasses, ginger, pitch, tar, turpentine, masts, spars, bowsprits, speckee, woad, Jamaica wood," &c. that is, the numerous exceptions negatived the general permission. This might be considered an insult; yet such were British indulgencies to Ireland.

I shall not speak of the pernicious projects of Irish politicians according to their notions of serving Ireland, nor of the crimes of the Irish leaders in parliament, who, for the tenth of the tithe of the nation's substance, sold and resold their country to the English ministry, but come at once to the reign of George the Third. Here we are greeted by a new æra. Supposing that wisdom displaced folly, the virtue of one reign could have imperfect influence in redeeming a country from centuries of misrule. With this new æra the parliament of Ireland in 1768, which had been of indefinite duration, was made octennial [1]. The next year, 1769, a question occurred relative to the mode of originating money-bills. Sir

[1] Annual Register, 1768, p. 231.

G. Macartney, the secretary, told the Irish Commons, "that the money-bill taking its rise in the privy council, was a tax the commons of Ireland paid for a continuance of their constitution[1]." Mark the precious constitution, and its price! At this period, and long preceding, the pension-list far exceeded in amount the whole expense of the civil list. In 1771, in Lord Townshend's administration, this auxiliary fund, and all other modes of bribery, were inadequate; and the lord lieutenant, to ensure a majority, found it necessary to create "new places, new pensions, new boards[2]." The American war forced the English government to reflect; and in 1782 an arrangement was made between the two countries, which was called a *final adjustment*.

Ireland had been left defenceless during the American war. On this the Irish arose and formed a popular army for their defence. The weakness of England revealed the strength of the Irish; and the French revolution heightened the presumption of the oppressed. Nine-tenths of the people were and are rejected even from the possibility of enjoying the higher offices in their own country. At this time a vain unprincipled youth determined to depress his country by means which no honest man would use for its exaltation. Pitt wanted a substitute, and Castlereagh presented himself: "Make not thyself an underling to a foolish man." Castlereagh made himself that underling; and what the government spy Oliver was at Derby, &c. Castle-

---

[1] Annual Register, 1769, p. 156.
[2] Hardy's Life of Lord Charlemont, p. 292.

reagh[1] was in Ireland. Castlereagh began by advo-
cating parliamentary reform, and he annihilated the
parliament of his own country. His assistance in
subverting and transferring forcibly, Norway, Genoa, Saxony, Venice, Ragusa, to despots, is but a
self-attestation of his domestic treachery.

By what means and at what time was this measure
carried? During martial law, during rebellion pro-
voked and rebellion purposely continued[2], while the
guard-rooms were open theatres of torture[3]. Yet
these means, and the utmost prodigality to seduce the
sordid, failed. In the next year the measure was resumed; when more peerages were granted, more pen-

[1] Some have compared him to Poynings. It is a slander on that
monster to assimilate them. Bacon says, " Poynings the better
to make compensation of his service in the wars called a parliament." But Castlereagh's compensation in the fomented civil
wars was to annihilate the parliament

[2] This sort of grand policy is not peculiar Relative to the rebellion in Scotland, Temple says, " Lord Shaftesbury showed plainly
in council, and in other places, that he was unwilling the rising
should be wholly or too soon suppressed," &c. Temple vol. 1.
p. 339. To this may be added a statement of Franklin : He says
he was, when in England, informed that a great personage studied
much a book entitled *Arcana Imperii.* In this, he says " a particular king is applauded for his politically exciting a rebellion among
his subjects at a time when they had not strength to support it ; that
he might, in subduing them, take away their privileges which were
troublesome to them," &c. p. 252. The Irish were troublesome ;
they voted the regency of Ireland to the Prince of Wales before
William Pitt had granted leave and fixed the conditions.

[3] Lord Moira (speech 1812, Examiner, No. 218,) could once
say so. Judkin Fitzgerald, afterwards ennobled, boasted of his
torturing.

sions, places, promises, were given;—seven of the twelve Irish judges were the immediate judicial fruits of passing the Union

Now what has England gained by this? what has England lost? thou impotent in wickedness! What has Ireland lost?—A total disregard to her affairs. The Irish chancellor of the exchequer, and the last she is ever to possess, said "he hoped that the house would do him the justice of admitting he troubled them upon that subject (Ireland) as seldom as possible." Trouble to hear the affairs of many millions of people, whose duty is to attend to the petition of the meanest individual! Yet no doubt the chancellor of the exchequer understood his audience. The affairs of Ireland are very contemptible, when the whole state was committed to a stranger, to Mr. Peel, an English boy from an English college, who eulogized Orangemen, and posted to Calais to run his head against a pistol. He was the representative, the executive, and the *dernier ressort* of all that concerned Ireland[1]. No inquiry concerning the state of Ireland[2], though it wanted, beside other military, 25,000 regular troops; and though the curfew, the policy of William the Norman, was declared necessary for the existence of government.

[1] Last year it was proposed to stop distillation. Mr. Peel insisted, in the House of Commons, that there were plenty of provisions in Ireland: in consequence the distillers continued; the beggarly government received the excise; and the people suffered, first by the general enhancement of the grain, then by famine, and its consequence a wide-spreading malignant typhus fever.

[2] This is an old complaint. Lord Charlemont said, Neither the removal, nor even the investigation, has ever been seriously attempted. Hardy's Life of Lord Charlemont, p. 173.

Such have been the consequences of the union; a measure beyond the power of the House of Commons of Ireland to determine, unless a trust for a few years by self-appointment can become a property for ever, and a servant by self-will justify a mastery over his lord. What has been the consequence? An abuse of public money that is incredible; salaries of viceroys, ministers, judges, &c., greatly increased; boards added, large sums voted to them, and these in a great measure absorbed by their chief officers. The inland navigation board has been marked for prodigality even in this country, and the principal canal company has become insolvent. With the union, also, the national debt (so little was due before that event, may be said to have originated; and such is its amount, that the whole revenue, taxed and retaxed as the people are, is inadequate to the amount of many millions to pay the general expenditure. Yet did Lord Castlereagh, in February 1800, insist that "the union, by establishing a fair principle of contribution, tends to release Ireland from an expense of one million in time of war, and of 500,000 in time of peace." And, like every other promise, the taxes of Ireland have been disproportionably advanced in respect to England. Ireland has been so oppressed since the union, that, having no domestic store, she was forced to borrow millions abroad to liquidate part of the interest of the national debt forced on her, beside millions to supply her current expenses; while her revenue, her produce, and her commerce decline. To this sad distress and monstrous bankruptcy has Ireland been reduced since the union. Yet in the middle of the last century, when power ran in the narrowest channels, and the *under-takers* thrived[1]; the revenue exceeded the expenditure, and a surplus actually accumulated in the treasury. It is also remarkable, that while in 1816 seventeen millions of taxes were taken off the British, three hundred and forty thousand pounds only were taken off Ireland; and that in 1817, when 1,500,000*l.* were granted to relieve the British, only 250,000*l.* were granted to the Irish, who are at least half as numerous as the British, and poorer, and want the relief of poor laws. Consider the effects of the union in other respects:—the terms of that contract have been construed exactly in the same spirit in which they were imposed. The English parliament, to favour the British distillers, have repeatedly infringed the Act of Union. Lord Castlereagh and Mr. Fitzgerald, both ministers of the crown, declared this iniquity. To which Mr. Vansittart replied, "That no gentleman had a greater respect for the Act of Union than he had, and no person was more sincerely determined to support it; *but* on account of certain ambiguities in that act, they were obliged *at times* to have recourse to temporary measures for the purpose of carrying its provisions *fairly* into effect." Yet is it a rule in construing conventions, that in case of ambiguity, the articles shall always be interpreted in favour of the capitulating party. Not so for the Irish at the bar of the House of Commons of the imperial parliament.

[1] These undertakers, being paid, engaged to do the king's business. Such were the Beresfords, Fitzgibbons, Fosters, Castlereaghs: they correspond to what Machiavel calls *famiglie fatali,* who rise by the ruin of their country. p. 92.

But, says Mr. Vansittart, the prætor of the Latins in addressing the fraudulent Romans used *but* differently: —"Nam si etiam sub umbra fœderis æqui, *servitutem* pati possumus, &c."

If the law be broken, promises have been bravely disregarded. The Catholics were to be emancipated; yet, as if the government rejoiced in insulting that vast population, no man is so likely to rise to power as the most furious and lying of their enemies[1]. Instances of this prosperous hate occurred last year. I have in other publications spoken at large on this subject; I shall therefore only say, that, considering the general improvement in thinking, the conduct of the British church and state to the Catholics degrades the British government beneath the Russian, Austrian, and Prussian tyrannies, and sinks it to the low level of the priestridden governments of Portugal and Spain.

What has the union effected for the Protestants, Dissenters, and Catholics—the whole people of Ireland—respecting tithes? Mr. Pitt, when debating the union, said, that the mode of collecting tithes in Ireland was a great practical evil. Has this been reformed? has any show of reform been attempted? The English ministry can force the union, raise an immense debt without the possibility of paying the interest, throng the country with troops, revive the

---

[1] Mr. Peel, in his speech against the Catholics in 1817, became a representative of an university. In this speech he alluded to a great outrage in the county of Louth as if the violence had been committed by Catholics against Protestants; yet all were Catholics. If he did not know this, it is part of his usual ignorance; if he did know it, the deception was flagitious.

curfew;—but regulate tithing in Ireland! in this they are powerless,—powerless to do good, their energy being evil.

It has been proved on oath, that two guineas an acre for meadow were demanded and enacted for tithes in Armagh; that forty acres of potatoes in the South[1] were charged five pounds an acre; and that in five counties in one year 1421 decrees were issued against paupers for non-payment of tithes. For the national church of Ireland, that is, Protestant clergymen, exact in proportion to their neglect and their utter uselessness[2], for those they charge are generally Catholics[3]. No wretch so miserable that they will not pursue in order to seize part of his pittance. In this respect these ghostly men are only to be compared to the Ricaras, a savage tribe in North America, who descend to rob the field-mice of their stores.

No good has been done for Ireland; no interest is excited respecting it;—with the loss of its parliament all is lost, even hope; for the chances suggested by desperation come not of hope, but of hope deferred. Had the parliament of Ireland been reformed, and the people been reinstated in their rights and liberties. Ireland would have been a happy, a peaceable, and a powerful ally. But England in fear and envy made

---

[1] In Cashel. Sir John Newport stated this.

[2] The Bishop of Limerick told Mr. Wakefield, (State of Ireland,) "that there were parishes in his diocese which had never seen a Protestant clergyman."

[3] In some parishes there is not one Protestant. Sir J Blaquiere (Feb. 20, 1792) said in the House of Commons, that in the parish where he resided there were fifteen thousand Catholics, and he himself the only Protestant.

it a servant—a servant of servants; and she must enjoy the consequence: "Inter dominum et servum nulla amicitia—etiam in pace belli tamen jura serventur[1]." Twenty-five thousand troops in Ireland justify the remark. The evil of the connexion is increased to Ireland by the union in a thousand ways, and by none so much as by the numerous absentees—an evil recognised in Richard the Third's reign[2], and which induced him to publish an ordinance against absentees from Ireland. This evil occasioned Mr. Flood to propose a measure to the same purpose in the beginning of the present reign, to which Lord North seems to have acceded; and lately Mr. Peel and Mr. Fitzgerald had similar projects. The want of resident proprietors has rendered the West India islands of England inferior to the French[3]; and this want, which has acted against Ireland in the remotest periods, has increased by every violation of humanity and justice in this ill-fated land. Thus of 511,456 acres which escheated at once to the crown, 209,800 were bestowed on Londoners. The union has multiplied this mischief a thousand-fold. Though some lament that Ireland has not her share in the members of the imperial parliament[4], having less than a fifth in the

---

[1] Q. Curtius, lib 7. c. 8.   [2] Davies's State of Ireland, p. 223.

[3] Nine-tenths of the proprietors reside on them, according to Robinet. Dictionnaire de l'Homme d'Etat. Barbadoes is called Little England, because there is a greater proportion of resident proprietors there than in any other sugar-island. Steele and Dickson, p. 441. The twelve principal companies of London are seised of Irish estates in Ulster: James sold them for 60,000l. Hume, vol. 6. In Charles the First's reign, also, large tracts were forfeited.

[4] Mr. Newenham shows that Ireland should have had 150 or

Commons though she contains half the population of Britain; yet the more she should gain in equity of representation, the more she must lose in her proprietary population. Thus a larger representation would increase the mischief—so fundamentally pernicious is that measure. Yet all *loyal* Irishmen are bound to bless the union, and their glorious constitution in church and state! this union, which has not left them what the paltriest West Indian colony enjoys—a resident legislature; and which was preserved to the Isle of Man, for the Manx have their Tynwald still: yet Ireland has been thought unworthy of a minor session. Excellent Irish constitution! which requires strangers to direct the national affairs; and who, being collated to the ministry in Ireland, are then re-exported to attend to parliamentary affairs at London. A wonderful constitution! consisting of alien ministers and refugee legislators!

The loss by absentees to Ireland, in exhausting the sources of its prosperity, is enormous. When Arthur Young wrote his Tour in Ireland[1], he enumerated the absentees, and calculated the amount of their income, which they drew from Ireland, at 732,700*l.* a year. Different writers on the currency of Ireland in 1804, estimated it at 2,000,000[2]:—such was the evidence of Messrs. Paget and Bainbridge. Lord Lauderdale, in 1805, supposed that Ireland paid to her absentees

---

170 representatives. Scotland was better treated in forming her partnership. Laing's History, vol. 4. p. 330.

[1] vol. 2. p. 193.

[2] Mr. Wakefield calculated it generally between two and three millions in his elaborate work on Ireland.

2,890,000*l.*, exclusive of 1,500,000*l.* as interest on the money borrowed in England: for the last twelve years, in war and peace, the debt, the interest, and the draught by absentees, have fearfully increased the amount of her debt: I need not calculate it, for it can never be liquidated. Mark the loss to Ireland by her absentees only:—Estimate it at three millions, or less, annually for the last twenty-four years; this sum transferred to England, for which nothing is given, and nothing returned,—not even an imperial promissory note,—nearly equals all the subsidies granted by Britain during the war to the voracious allies. Yet these subsidies are supposed to have deranged the currency of opulent England, and some main branches of her industry. Yet England only lost what she had obtained gratuitously from Ireland: to her it was the loss of a gain; while to Ireland it was an entire loss, a perpetual loss; for it continues through all vicissitudes of domestic outrage, foreign war, and general tranquillity :—besides, three millions to Ireland equal thirty millions to Great Britain.

To this wholesale impoverishment by absentees, originating in the first outrageous connexion between the two islands, augmented by escheats and forfeitures, and by the last and greatest penalty —the forfeiture of the legislature; we must add the ruinous consequences of the monstrous disjunction of men from their property, extending in infinite detail. The absentee has an agent, who, as the price of a lease, receives a bribe equivalent to a fine. The tenants are frequently middlemen, who reset the land; as they have been squeezed, they, in their turn, crush their cotters. I know nothing like the Irish middleman: he does not resemble the American land-jobber, who is in some degree a retail dealer; nor the forestaller, who often relieves the seller by affording him a prompt market, and who gains little more than what his time and the use of his capital deserve; nor like the middlemen, who deal in slaves in the West Indies[1]. Tytler indeed compares Indian middlemen to them: they rent so much, and set this in portions at a rack-rent[2]. A writer in the Edinburgh Review[3] doubts if they are injurious; yet conduct similar to theirs in Ireland, was noticed by the Scotch proprietors, and remedied. Stair says, "Rentals do ordinarily contain a clause not to subset, assign, or analyse; which if it be contravened, not only the assignation or substraction is void, but the rental itself[4]." This subinfeudation of tenants comes by deputation from proprietors who are absentees; for no one could witness his land and those who reside on it abused together, and not prevent its recurrence. Let it not be supposed, however, that the oppression of the terre-tenant proceeds entirely from middlemen: this misery is of long-standing. In Spenser's time, a lease was considered a sort of bondage[5].

[1] These are reputed very pernicious, and resolutions have been passed to prevent the practice.

[2] At something more;—rack-rent is defined the full yearly value let by lease. Law Dict. vol. 2. p. 573. [3] No. for July, 1813.

[4] Stair's Institutions, &c. p. 317.

[5] "The poor husbandman either dare not bind himself to him for a longer term, or thinketh, by his continual liberty of change, to keep his landlord the rather in awe from wringing him." State of Ireland, p. 133. The same is now the case in the Zetland Islands. Edmonton says, There are few leases; the tenants seem to entertain as much repugnance to leases as the landlords, c. 7. Mr. Malthus, vol. 1. p. 489, has noticed, from the Statistical Ac-

To set at rack-rent is not unknown to proprietors. I have heard from a gentleman of the south of Ireland, that many of his cast esteem a *rise of rent equal to two manurings*. So that the English writers and talkers, who think that all the misery of Ireland proceeds from the idleness of the people,—and this from the coarseness of their living,—may learn that the life of an Irishman is not a continued holiday of indolence and relaxation.

Let then those who arraign the Irish people, recall their slanders, and Mr. Malthus chiefly; and let them direct their vengeance against the causes of the afflictions of Ireland. Does he not himself say, that the indigence, which is hopeless, destroys all vigorous exertions, and confines all efforts to the attainment of a bare existence? Whence then his abhorrence of the Irish?—that *they breed like beasts;* and his disgust at their mud-cabbins and rags, expressed like that popinjay, who railed because a dead body was brought between the wind and his nobility. The Irish are taxed *de haut et de bas*; they are taxed infinitely more than when Clarendon was viceroy, who dared say "the poor are miserably harassed that a few may gain." For, besides the sums which, having entered the exchequer, issue in a thousand polluted channels,—how miserably are they taxed by the agents of absentees, those farm-

count of Scotland, that in Bressay, Burra, and Quarff in Shetland, "the young are encouraged to marry young: the consequence is poverty and distress." Yet in the same paragraph, he says, "They fish for their masters, who either give them a fee totally inadequate, or take their fish at a low rate." He might as well say they were robbed, because they married: tyranny and oppression of this kind are quite sufficient to keep Scotch or Irish poor.

ers-general of the rental of Ireland! and by middle-men—creatures, half fly and half reptile, between the locust and the mole!—then the protestant clergyman and the tithe proctor, who would have been without similitude, in reality or fancy, had not Milton allegorized Sin and Death. Yet these things are perpetually acted; and the people are called turbulent, idle, ignorant, beastly breeders:—yet against the government and superior orders nothing transpires—

.... omnis
Turba tacet, nec causidicus nec præco loquitur [1].

Nay, the provincial government is praised and the imperial greatly eulogized, though it has imposed a military police yeomen and a standing army of 20,000, and is bankrupt to more than the amount of the whole national debt[2]: but England has adopted Ireland's insolvency. How could she do otherwise?—and she passed the intercourse act in admitting the import of Irish grain into England. Wonderful! Then must we honour the 14 Geo. II., by which Ireland was permitted, in time of dearth, to send victuals to Scotland. England accepted grain from Ireland when England want-

---

[1] Juvenal, sat. 6. ver. 437.

[2] Sir W. Petty said, "England hath constantly lost these 500 years, by their [her] meddling with Ireland." Polit. Anatomy, p. 28. This is certain, that by taxing Ireland far beyond her power, England has reduced Ireland's efficiency in various ways. Taxes paid into the exchequer in 1815, 5,750,000*l*; in 1816, 4,540,000*l*. Bushels of malt, which paid duty in 1815, 670,000; in 1816, 480,000. Duties on tea, 1815, 576,000*l*.; 1816, 443,000*l*. Total revenue this year, 4,338,000*l*.; current expense 4,865,000*l*. Thus 427,000*l*. added to 6,500,000*l*. interest on the debt, exhibit the amount of Ireland's insolvency and burthen to England by the Union.

ed provisions ;—Prodigious kindness ! If England resisted the import of Irish grain, how were the increasing absentees to receive their rents, and how was Ireland to contribute to the war of the monarchy ? The
English wanted money—Ireland had none ; but she
had grain, which was, in fact, the war [1] contribution of
Ireland : it was the conversion price, which the vassal
paid his lord when summoned to battle.

The productiveness of Ireland is immense. In
1808-9-10, the grain exported from Ireland amounted
to 2,170,000 quarters ; in 1814, Ireland exported
nearly three millions worth of grain, the greater part
of which passed to Great Britain. The average annual
export of butter from Ireland during 1812-13-14-15,
was 440,000 cwts., value 5*l.* 10*s.* per cwt. The export of beef and pork is equally extensive. In short,
Ireland exported eight millions of agricultural produce, the greater part of which was not given in barter, but sent to absentees, or paid as the war contribution, &c.; and this was absolutely lost to Ireland
without any return. Yet the Irish peasant is to be
abused because he is poor :—Who makes him so ?

> " The swain, with tears, his frustrate labour yields,
> And famish'd, dies amidst his ripen'd fields."

He is idle, forsooth. Labour is said to have been
imposed on man as a punishment; but the revilers of
the Irish must consider labour a luxury. Why should

---

[1] This kindness of Great Britain resembles the boast of Lord
Harcourt in his speech to the Irish parliament, October 1775.
" The act which allows the clothing and accoutrements necessary
for his majesty's forces, paid from the revenues of this kingdom, to
be exported from Ireland, is a particular mark of the royal favour."

the Irish be industrious, who will not receive the profit of their industry? Yet the Irish toil and struggle; and under every political and civil disadvantage they raise food for six millions of people at home, and a vast surplus produce for strangers. It is said that Ireland is overpeopled, and that this proceeds from the beastly propensities of the people to generate. There are many wretchedly poor in Ireland, but I deny that this misery is of the people's making; for the produce of the land and labour of Ireland is transferred from the Irish to others: nay, that which remains is still further perverted by the monstrous injustice of the ruling orders. The domestic state of Ireland, in this respect, resembles an account by Howard [1], "Certain keepers of Bridewell, who farmed what little food was allowed the prisoners, and who engaged to furnish each prisoner with two penny-worth of bread a day; I have known that shrink to one half." And yet the Irish, and not the government,—those who tax and tithe and carry away and waste and plunder,—are to be slandered by a host of men, who take the tone of vituperation from Mr. Malthus. " Are ye such fools, ye sons of Israel, that without examination, or knowledge of the truth, ye have condemned a daughter of Israel!" Yet these, without knowledge or examination, condemn a whole nation.

If any could be gratified by vengeance on such senseless declaimers, a review of their remedies for the excessive populousness of Ireland would amply gratify that passion. Feed them on the dearer food; on grain instead of potatoes—stimulate exertions—create new

[1] On Prisons, sect. I. p. 4.

wants [1]—implant new tastes. As if the Irish, by choice, were of the school of Diogenes. How little do such men know of human nature! The same objections have been habitually made to the Russians; yet Dr. Clarke, who has no predilection for that people, says of them, " With regard to the idleness of the lower classes here (Russia), of which we have heard great complaints, it appears that where they have an interest in exertion, they by no means want industry, and have just the same wish for luxuries as other people." Suppose the population of Ireland had as many wants as the Sybarites—how are they to relieve them in their present circumstances? Away with sick men's dreams! Give them a better government, a self-government: let the people enjoy the fruits of their labours; their disposition to enjoy all comforts is as certain as their senses. Create new wants! Try the experiment on Tantalus; and when you have succeeded in redeeming him from misery, you will have one proof, at least, for the potency of your charm.

Mr. Malthus and others seem to think, that by exciting new desires, and feeding the Irish on the dearer grain, the numbers of the Irish will be diminished, and their wages will rise (which Mr. Ricardo deprecates). But the people were not more comfortable when they were fewer than they are now [2]. The Irish

---

[1] This is not new; for bishop Berkeley, among his queries, " whether the bulk of our natives are not kept from thriving by a cynical content in dirt and beggary."

[2] Sir William Temple repeatedly complains of *scarcity of people* in Ireland, vol. 1. p. 6. Again he says, " The want of trade in Ireland proceeds from want of people." vol. 1. p. 110.

are now just as the Gauls [1] were when they suffered servitude; and their distresses continued their oppression.

I have now exhibited in a rapid view the state of the population of Ireland, and have endeavoured to show the true causes of the misery of the people, which does not arise from their numbers or their idleness, but from the circumstances, civil, political, and sectarian, to which they are subjected; and this inquiry, while it relieves a large portion of mankind from unmerited obloquy, preserves the simplicity of truth, promotes the science of government, and the comforts of society. The Irish are numerous and miserable; but they are not miserable because they are numerous; for six would be as wretched under the same misrule as six thousand, or six hundred thousand. It is utterly absurd to imagine, that because many have little, if they were reduced to few, those remaining must enjoy abundance; for this supposes that the poor must perish and the rich survive. Pursue this scheme, and I admit that having narrowed the population of the world to a few families, each individual would be kindred to a king; and by a further reduction, Adam and Eve might be restored to Paradise, of which there is a remote resemblance in England. I quote the passage for the benefit of those who favour a population of original exility. "It (the parish of Twiford near Harrow) contains only one house; the

---

[1] Plerique, quum aut ære alieno, aut magnitudine tributorum, aut injuria potentiorum premuntur, sese in servitutem dicant nobilibus. In hos eadem omnia sunt jura quæ dominis in servos. Cæsar de Bel. Gall. lib. 6. c. 13.

farmer who occupies it is perpetual churchwarden of a church which has no incumbent, and in which no duty is performed." The account concludes, " an overseer of the poor is unnecessary."

By this review I wish to inculcate that Ireland is not overpeopled, but undergoverned ; that the evils under which the country labours are referable to its military subjection and military possession ; to the perpetual politics of the British ministry in Ireland, creating dissension and mistrust among the natives, and thus humiliating all through their passions and their misery, which is continued by the existing army in Ireland ; by the degradation of the Catholics; by the immense tyranny of the law officers in prosecuting for libels ; and the peculiarly flagitious law under which they prosecute the object of their hate, by attainting all independent principles and liberal inquiry, in which crusade Provost Elrington [1] is as ardent as Attorney-General Saurin. Yet Lord Liver-

[1] Dr. James Wood has done as much for Cambridge ; but this was in consequence of the bills passed in 1817 against freedom. Dr. Elrington anticipated, prophetically, the authentic will of ministers. First he obstructed the meeting of the Historical Society, in which the students debated : having regulated and abridged, he finally abolished it. He also proposed that Locke on Government should be read in the *Course*, with his precious notes—the students were satisfied with the text. Then the *Board*, by and with the advice of the annotator, dismissed Locke on Government, and substituted Butler's Analogy, which, beside the baseness of the attempt, shows how incompetent a junta of priests are to educate citizens. Such is the fate of Locke !—banished when a student from the University of Oxford, and now banished as an author from the University of Dublin. The harmony of Universities ! !

pool and the like talk of educating the people, when the means of knowledge and the benefits of education to the higher classes of society are negatived or perverted by the officers of the crown and the heads of the universities. The evils of Ireland are referable also to strange ministers and a foreign legislature; to a taxation, which having swept away the capital of the country, has fallen into an abyss of unparalleled insolvency; to the flood of wealth to absentees, which never ebbs or stops, but flows on with an increasing tide:—to the pillage of the people by middlemen, and tithe proctors and clergymen. The Irish are called free; yet the serfs and boors of Hungary [1] (an appendant country like Ireland) do not pay altogether more than what the Catholics of Ireland pay to the Protestant clergy. Yet we are told, that morally to reform the Irish we must feed them on grain. We must give them new tastes—we must educate them [2]. They know their wrongs; to advance their

[1] Townson says, that the peasants of Hungary pay the ninths of their produce, which with duty days may amount to about our tithes. Travels in Hungary, p. 115–131.

[2] The Irish are as well educated as most people, better generally than the English. Formerly the ministerial cant was *the great benefit to be derived from charter schools*, which were literally depôts where Catholic children were charitably apostatized. Every Lord Lieutenant's speech, time immemorial, was seasoned with recommending them to parliament. In 1770 a tax on hawkers and pedlars was appropriated to their support; and they receive an annual grant of 40,000*l*. Now *these great sources of industry, virtue, and true religion* (Speech in 1767), are declared nought, while the expense of them continues. But Lord Liverpool, Mr. Peel, and the rest, talk of the diffusion of knowledge and true religion by education.—This must have an end.

knowledge would but inflame them against their enemies. It racks man's frame; it makes his nerves shrink; it fixes aching in his brain, and wears his anatomy, to hear incessantly millions of toiling fellow-men belied and abused—and for what and for whom? But it stuns and stupifies when these things are done, and not one raises his voice in the defence of the oppressed. I know the theme is ungrateful, and he that utters it adopts the load and odium he would relieve. " Let not the reverence of any man cause thy fall; and refrain not to speak when there is occasion to do good." Others fear to speak the truth—I should fear to be silent. Indeed, few think more of Ireland than of the dead. The public mind is lost in dismay or indignation, while busy *gentlemen* are selfish and sordid; or if a few be moved to better things, they are banded in some puny association—a horticultural society, which distributes prizes for best grapes and best gooseberries; or which under the style and title of Royal Academy, or Dublin Society, trifle so anxiously and so absurdly. The only public feeling that has been lately expressed, regards a tax on windows. Thus the voltaic battery twitches the eye or ear or lip of a thing no more. Your legislature was wrung from you, and all its accompanying consolations, and now you bluster about a window-tax.—" Ita sunt stulti ut amissa republica piscinas suas fore salvas sperare videantur."

CHAPTER VI.

No free nation distressed by excess of people.—Ill-governed nations distressed, whether having few or many people.—Population declining and misery increasing with the viciousness of the government;—and the reverse—population increasing and comfort with liberty.—Examples—Egypt—Crete—Rhodes—Cyprus—Sparta —Athens—Italy.

THOUGH I do not say that no free nation can become too populous, I presume that when the government is essentially vicious, the cause of the people's misery is more decisively referable in the first instance to the badness of the government than to the improvidence of the people. This is strictly just; for we know that nations formerly poor and thinly inhabited, have with a better government increased in numbers and comforts; and, on the contrary, that nations populous and opulent, have with the debasement of their laws and constitution, declined not more in people than in their enjoyments of life. Yet am I ignorant of any nation, which possessing confirmed liberty and equal laws, has become miserable merely by the excess of its people.

These positions are proved by the whole stream of history; first, by Egypt, which was so populous and has always been so productive. Herodotus [1] says of it, that " until the reign of Rhampsinitus, Egypt was remarkable for its *abundance* and *excellent law*;" but that under his successors all things were altered, and the people were grievously oppressed by toil and tyranny. Still the people were numerous; for the go-

[1] lib. 2. c. 124.

vernment, with all its evils, continued to be Egyptian. It became a Roman province :—the people declined ; enmity and jealousy were infused among the Egyptians, and they continued to be diminished by the greater provincial misrule, down to the present time. Those people who ate much flesh-meat in the time of Moses [1], who were so dainty in the time of Herodotus [2] that they despised barley and wheat as food, afterwards were satisfied [3] with bread and beer ; while now, those who reside in the territories of Adowa and Tchagassa, with their triple harvests [4], scarcely support a poor and dispersed people. The people have uniformly declined with their oppressions—with the increased viciousness of the government; and that country which was a refuge to the miserable of other nations, which alone of all Europe escaped famine in the time of Polybius [5], could not latterly support its own diminished population, as in 1784 and 1785 the towns of Syria and the neighbouring countries were filled with famishing [6] Egyptians. Such are the concomitants of a people falling from equal laws, if Theocritus be an authority for the ancient state of Egypt, to provincial subjection, till at present Egypt is literally the servant of servants, Mameluke [7] signifying a military slave.

Sicily exhibits the same eventful tale. When the

[1] Dion Cassius, lib. 71. c. 4.   [2] lib. 2. c. 36.
[3] Athenæus, lib. 10. p. 418.   [4] Bruce, vol. 3. c. 7.
[5] Excerpt. c. 2.
[6] Volney's Voyage en Syrie, t. 1. p. 173.
[7] Ibid. t. 1. p. 90.   These slaves, Mr. Legh says, took Ibrim : "The population was partly carried off by the Mamelukes, and partly removed to Dehr."

Athenians enjoyed the greatest power and opulence, a small portion of this island resisted an invading army of 60,000 men attended by a mighty fleet. Then the cities of Sicily were free, and a number of them cemented their common strength by a representative assembly [1]. After this, it fell under the dominion of Rome. At first the Romans ruled humanely. Cicero [2] says, Sicily was eminently favoured by enjoying the use of its own laws. Cato called Sicily the *cella penaria* of Rome; and Cicero, to the same purpose, "hac alimur ac sustinemur [3]." Rome, however, from the beginning enacted corn laws, and the Sicilians were not permitted to export grain to any power except by a license from Rome, which they granted to the Rhodians and other Greeks on their application [4]. As the Roman government sunk at home, it fell abroad: slavery was extended in Sicily, and the slaves were most abused. They were chained while they worked [5]; prisons for refractory slaves were frequent:—thence the Servile war began, and it continued till 60,000 men formed the insurrectionary force. Verres [6] assisted the depopulation of the island by his tyranny; and thus Sicily [7], even the

[1] Οι αλλοι Σικελιωται ξυνελθοντες ες γελαν απο πασων των πολεων πρεσζεις, &c. Thucydides, lib. 4. p. 289. Some suppose that representation is a modern invention; it was known to the ancients in every possible way. See "Nat. Government." I could add to the account in that work various authorities.

[2] t. 2. p. 121.   [3] Ibid. p. 89.   [4] Polybius, Excerpt. 73.

[5] Hic ad cultum agri frequentia ergastula catenatique cultores, materiam bello præbuere. Florus, lib. 3. c. 19.

[6] Siciliam provinciam C. Verres per triennium depopulatus esse, t. 2. p. 47.   [7] Ibid. p. 126.

Etnean part, which was most fertile, was rendered incult and unprofitable. After this, the island was subjected to Saracens and Normans and Spaniards ; under the last, the inhabitants of Messina [1] were excluded from all employments civil and military, even of being enrolled as common soldiers. Sicily latterly became an appendage to Naples. It may be remarked, in passing, that England, while it purchased the destruction of the parliament of Ireland by artifice, power, and subsidies, restored a parliament [2] to Sicily : and thus while it sunk Ireland to provincial vassalage, it effectually raised Sicily to a state-companion [3]. But the king of Naples on his restoration rather followed the example of England to Ireland, than England's missionary politics in Sicily. Sicily has now lost her parliament guaranteed by England, and she submits to the transmarine government of Ferdinand the Fourth, probably the worst sovereign that she ever experienced. The whole population of the island about the middle of the last century was not more, according to Amico, than 1,093,163 ; of

[1] Van Egmont's Travels, vol. 1. p. 60.

[2] The English wished to give the Sicilians the British constitution :—for the English suppose it must suit all people. Thus Mr. Campbell the missionary gave the Griquaas, the descendants of Griqua, a code founded on the English constitution. All the grand deeds of British legislation in Sicily are overborne. Thus, after having supported the Sicilian government by a subsidy of 300,000*l.* annually from 1805, and having expended a million and a half annually to support their army, we have restored legitimacy, and thus undid the constitution that we guarantied.

[3] As was said on another occasion, La signoria che noi concedemmo gia a i reali de Napoli fu compagnia, et non servitu. Machiavel Storia, p. 73.

which the religious orders were a thirteenth. The people are enormously oppressed, paying nearly all the ordinary and extraordinary contributions, the nobility and clergy contributing only an eighteenth. Large sums are raised every year for roads, which are never repaired [1]. Sicily has *corn-laws* and a corn-company [2]. The Sicilian landholder consigns his farm to his steward, as in Spain [3]; where the stewards of great estates cultivate them on their master's account.

Thence depopulation and poverty are spread in every direction: Mr. Vaughan speaks of tracts "to the extent of ten miles, containing neither farmers nor inhabitants." "Nothing," says Mr. Thompson, "is seen in Sicily but misery and oppression; on all sides a government sunk into the last stage of weakness." No matter in what direction, the country is desert and the people wretched: even Scolietta [4], which has a considerable trade, consists of a miserable collection of huts. Every thing declines:—sugar, which some time since was much cultivated in Sicily, is now confined to a small spot near Avola. Such is the consequence of bad government; with the finest climate, the most commercial situation, amidst a sea abounding in fish, possessing the most productive soil, which fed a numerous population, and supplied even in its provincial abasement, Rome [5], and the Archipelago, and Greece; Sicily, the abode of Ceres and Bacchus, has not now

[1] Cockburn's Voyage, vol. 2. p. 26.   [2] Ibid. p. 228.

[3] Travels, vol. 2. p. 25.

[4] General Cockburn cannot account for this, vol. 2. p. 81. Yet the reason is obvious.   [5] Cicero, t. 2, p. 148.

one-tenth [1] of its most fertile soil in tillage; and in 1812 it actually imported wheat to the amount of nearly a million of dollars. Such is the state of Sicily under Ferdinand, who, according to the *classical* [2] Mr. Eustace, possesses a happy royal medium understanding fittest for governing nations. Sicily, which boasted Syracuse, invented comedy and tragedy [3], educated Archimedes, which expelled the Carthaginians, repulsed confederated Greece,—is now without opulence or authority or people, except a few peasants who have survived to testify against king, barons, and clergy, for freedom and their fathers [4]. Here then are two nations which declined in people and their comforts in proportion to the degradation of their government; and these instances embrace a period, or rather a series of periods, co-extensive with the range of history. It is a common consequence: such has been the fate of Crete, called the *happy island* (μα-

[1] Vaughan, p. 316.

[2] This prosing author, though admired by our critics, says of this same monarch, that he observed in conversation, "All the world were Turks before the birth of our Saviour." This Ferdinand is the choice one of his father; his elder brother being set aside for idiocy. Mr. Eustace would be thought a great admirer of ancient literature. Hume says, that passionate admirers of the ancients are zealous partisans of civil liberty. Essays, vol. 1. t. 401.

[3] Plato. Minos. p. 569.

[4] Mr. Blaquiere speaks with horror of the higher orders, the *Corinthian capitals*. General Cockburn praises the *people* frequently. "The lower orders are by far the best, and naturally a fine people ruined by their government and their priests." vol. 2. p. 97. "In sixteen voyages with them, I have found them faithful, sober, scrupulously honest, and obliging." p. 74.

καρονησος), the parent of laws, navigation, and lite-rature[1],—of Rhodes, of Cyprus, which according to Olivier does not now contain 60,000 persons ; and mark that here the people have declined most in number, and here the people are most miserable[2] while in Thessaly, where the population has suffered the least, the people are the least wretched.

As the people disappear by bad government, so they re-assemble with the improvement of their laws and a reform of their constitution. Such effects are imputed to the laws of Lycurgus, and the establishment of the ephori; but as the government became deteriorated, and luxury and treachery and tyranny were manifest, the people declined[3]. Thence the loss at Leuctra was irre-parable[4]. For it was not the destruction of many citi-zens in that battle which could not be recruited ; they were estimated only at one thousand by Plutarch[5], and Aristotle says Laconia could support 1,500 horse and 30,000 foot[6]. The Spartans had supported great

[1] Strabo says, that Minos made the liberty of the subject the object of all his institutions. lib. 10. p. 480. Polyhistor. lib. 1. c. 17. It appears that Jupiter did for Crete (Aristot. t. 1. p. 1157.) what St. Patrick did for Ireland.

[2] Thornton's Turkish Empire, p. 19.

[3] There is a theatrical account of the abstinence of Pausanias after the battle of Platæa, Herod. lib. 9. c. 82. but he soon declined into the Asiatic taste. When he ceased simplicity, he betrayed his country to the great king. Thucydides, lib. i. p. 85.

[4] They governed unjustly:—thus, says Cicero, all their allies deserted them. t. 4. p. 377.

[5] In Agesil. Vitam.

[6] De Politicis, lib. 2. This is not the whole population. At Platæa there were five thousand Spartans, and each was accom-panied with seven armed helotes. Herod. lib. 9. c. 10.

wars, and they had frequently restored their ranks either by citizens, or by raising helotes to freedom[1]: but they had lost with the debasement of their institutions their indomitable spirit. Thucydides mentions the submission of the besieged Spartans at Sphacteria, though reduced from 420 to 292, as the most extraordinary event of that eventful war[2]: for it was imagined by all the Grecians, that they would never be taken alive. Thus public spirit and institutions declined together under the generalship of Pausanias, the royalty of Cleomenes, and the despotism of Nabis; those people, says Polybius, submitted to the tyrant Nabis, who formerly could not brook even the name of tyranny[3].

Athens and Greece exhibited the harmony between liberty and population, between a vicious government and a waning people; and the flood of life rose or fell according to the fluctuations of freedom or slavery. When, says Herodotus[4], the Athenians were subject to tyrants, (Mr. Mitford's much injured men,) they were not superior to their neighbours; but with freedom, when each man exercised his talents on his own account, they stood chief among mankind. How could it be otherwise? Their oath of allegiance was not to Pisistratus, for they execrated kings, but to their country, which they swore to leave better and greater than they found it[5]. And they were true to their promise, for their constitution was a democracy. "It is called a democracy," says Pericles, "because it regards not the profit of the few but of the

---

[1] Thucydides, lib 7. p. 501.   [2] lib. 4.   [3] lib. 4. c. 81.
[4] lib. 5. c. 78.   [5] Apud Stobæum, sermo 41. p. 243.

many[1]." The Athenian constitution held principles directly opposed to the British: for Xenophon says[2], The people deservedly have more power than the nobles and the rich, because the people support the navy and the state. At this time the people increased in number and enjoyments. They increased in *men,* —not as Mr. Malthus counts them, animals who live to eat,—but men who have left eternal monuments of their taste and genius. The democracy was displaced, and oligarchy substituted ; and assassination, chiefly managed by the young men of the *best families,* confirmed the short reign of the thirty tyrants[3]. How they must have reduced the population we may conjecture,. as the treaty with Antipater[4] (which deprived all those who had not two thousand drachmæ of the civil government) expatriated indignantly two-thirds of the Athenians. Affairs were reinstated, liberty restored, the people returned, and the genius of Pericles revived, in the eloquence of Demosthenes. But the Athenian republic had suffered too many and too great shocks quickly repeated to cope with Philip's power. Thus the Athenians, who commanded a force,

[1] Thucydides, lib. 2. p. 123.   [2] De Rep. Athen. p. 691.

[3] Mitford says, " The means by which the oligarchical party in Athens itself had in the meantime advanced far in their purpose, do no honour either to the Athenian government or the Athenian character. The principal was assassination, and it seems to have been chiefly managed by the young men of the best families," &c. c. 19. s. 5. It is no attaint to the Athenian character that the aristocrats were assassins ; for it is a common consequence that his *best* families should be the worst, at Athens as elsewhere.

[4] Plutarch, Antipater, Diodorus Siculus.

even after their defeat at Syracuse, of 40,000 combatants[1], could oppose Philip's domination with 2,000 men[2], 500 only of which were Athenians. Why Greece, which opposed the Persians with 150,000 men when Greece was free, could not raise in Plutarch's time 3,000 men[3]; a number which one city, Megara, sent to the battle of Platæa.

Modern reports also accord with ancient story. In the wreck of Italy—where all means failed to preserve the population; where slaves and freemen declined together; where the finest tracts, even Campania, the paradise of the world[4], became desert; where neither absence from tribute[5], nor the grant in propriety of waste lands, with many favours to those who should reclaim them[6], (a circumstance unhappily intelligible to the English of the present time[7],) could redeem

[1] Thucydides, lib. 7. p. 548.

[2] Truly this is the whole amount, with a few horse that Demosthenes proposed raising. First Philippic. Philip was a tolerable master: he would not garrison Athens, saying to his captains who advised him, Ὑπερ δοξης παντα ποιουντα και πασχοντα. Plutarch. Moral. p. 107.

[3] Moral. p. 186.

[4] Omnium non modo Italiæ sed toto orbe terrarum pulcherrima plaga est. Florus, lib. 1. c. 16. It was pestilential when Condamine travelled; it is so now, and must continue so under its present management.

[5] Three hundred and thirty thousand acres had been exempted from tribute. Gibbon, vol. 2. p. 65.

[6] As, to be ten years free from tribute and from all public avocations. Herodian, lib. 2. p. 92.

[7] The Duke of Bedford in 1816 stated, that he knew two farms in Norfolk, one of 5,000 and another of 3,000 acres, which had

from sterility;—the casual return of a free government, a self-government, though beset with mighty enemies, and obliged to incorporate the remains of a Gothic nobility, multiplied at once men and all things: all which sunk when the republics merged into principalities. Such was the state of Tuscany. Again: They arose from their misery with returning freedom. Capriata dwells on the exhausted state of Genoa, and on its restoration; on its liberty, and with liberty the increase of people, and their activity and opulence[1]. Van Egmont[2] also contrasts the debased state of Tuscany, and the sudden and ravishing change on passing from Tuscany into the republic of Lucca; which felicitous appearance he again saw contrasted with Pistoia, which had lost its liberty and its people.

been offered to any one who would cultivate them, rent free; and that the offer was not accepted.

[1] Storia di Genoa, p. 632.   [2] Travels, vol. 1. p. 29.

PART III.

CHAPTER I.

Various considerations respecting what should determine the mean-
ing of Populousness—or the contrary—as different states of so-
ciety—situation — climate—soil—unhealthiness—salubrity—ari-
dity— commodities — customary food—habits — intemperance—
abstemiousness—luxury—government.

Having reviewed the state of population in different countries and in dissimilar situations, I conclude
that neither the populousness of a nation nor the paucity of its inhabitants is alarming. It is bad government and unequal laws and disproportioned property
that are dreadful;—these render the few and the many
miserable : while a nation well governed, or rather not
misgoverned, increases in people, and enlarges their
store and their comforts. Thus the United Provinces
when they spurned the domination of Spain,—thus
the American provinces on their emancipation from
Britain,—increased in numbers, opulence, and authority. I also deny that any country in Europe is overpeopled, though Mr. Malthus states the reverse ; and
I am persuaded, on re-examination, few will believe
that the misery of Europe proceeds from superfœta-
tion, but from the rapacity and extravagance of the
ruling orders.

The *principle of population,* and all the devils which

a partial, unpopular, and hypochondriacal view saw emerging with the children of mankind, do not affright me. Men are surely as much the produce of the earth as the luxuriant crop and the folded sheep; and a populous country is as interesting as the plains of Poland or the pasturing districts of Spain. Perhaps we should consider the import of a populous state; some having calculated the square leagues and their inhabitants, pronounce such a state populous, and such the reverse. These conclusions are drawn from the narrowest premises; for the amount of the superficies of a country is probably the least interesting among a hundred particulars respecting the populousness of a country.

Speaking, then, of populousness or the contrary, we should consider the situation of the people, as savage, pastoral, agricultural, manufacturing, commercial; or how far these combine in forming their habits. Climate is most important. A country so inhospitable as to require a month's labour to procure fuel, —whether it be felling and carrying timber, or cutting and carting peat, or mining coal,—limits the people. A climate of this austerity also requires time to procure heavy or warm clothing, and to raise or sink dwellings;—even a temperate climate often requires much fuel. Dr. John Clarke imputes a large portion of the mortality of children in London to cold and moisture, —suppose the coal enhanced, the mortality would be greater of course.

Some climates have a tendency to disease. Ethiopia has been pestilential from early times: Thucydides says the pestilence of Athens descended from that country ; and Evagrius [1] speaks of another which proceeded from the same region, and wasted Europe for fifty-two years. Some are subjected to insects, which are rather the creatures of climate than of soil, of which locusts seem to be the most desolating : some are afflicted with vermin or poisonous reptiles, or large and voracious beasts. Some countries are subject to noxious winds or hurricanes or earthquakes, which, beside their actual destruction, may affect population through its morality, as this frequently promotes heedlessness or predestination.

As countries are doomed to sterility by a perpetual winter, others suffer by the contrary, and regions of ice are not less inhospitable than the burning desert. In countries so arid that there is no stream, and that wells (the only supply) must be sunk 300 feet few can live where so much labour is required to procure a drink of water. Countries where the rivers are few or small, or which are absorbed in their course, or spread into marshes, prevent many commodities, and of course affect population. Changing from the line to the pole :—In Lapland, where three or four hundred rein-deer are required for the subsistence of a family, one man may represent a hundred in a favoured region, and perhaps he is less comfortable than the last of a million. Some countries produce scarcely any thing; as that of the Ichthyophagi, who have not altered these 3000 years; still they eat, drink, and live on fish. Some of the Orkneys resemble the shores of the Ichthyophagi [2]; as in them even the

---

[1] Evagrius Scholasticus, lib. 4. c. 28.

[2] Other people are Ichthyophagi also, as the Laplanders along

sheep and rabbits live on sea-ware. Countries vary in their productiveness in various ways. The Babylonians praised in song the date-tree [1], as affording 360 necessary things. The Indians equally admire the cocoa-nut tree[2]. In the Spice Islands sago [3] affords the people food for three-fourths of the year :—All these vary in the facility of their cultivation and their nutritiousness. Other species of food vary still more in those respects; as rice, potatoes, millet, the plantain. It is computed that an acre of potatoes will produce three times more solid nourishment than an acre of wheat [4]. There is a dispute concerning the respective excellence of the potatoe and rice. Millet is very productive, returning in Switzerland 160 for 1 [5]; maize from 50 to 300 [6]. The plantain or banana seems to afford the greatest nourishment for man of all the vegetable classes. Humboldt says, the same ground, planted with the plantain, will produce 133 times more food than the same planted with wheat, and 44 times more than the same planted with potatoes [7]. Some say an acre of it will feed fifty persons for a year [8]. Yet the productiveness of the crop

the coast. Leems, c. 7.—Ehrenmalm. Pinkerton, vol. 1. p. 369. So are the people about Astracan, flesh and bread being so scarce. Ibid. t. 9. p. 387.

[1] Plutarch. Moral. p. 573.

[2] Mrs. Graham says it is the true riches of India. p. 5.

[3] Dampier, vol. 1. p. 4. Pinkerton, &c.

[4] This is A. Smith's calculation. A. Young says four times.

[5] Annual Register, 1765, p. 153.

[6] Monthly Review for January 1812, p. 40.

[7] Essai Politique sur la Nouvelle Espagne, c. 9.

[8] Steele and Dickson : He says also, some reduce the number to seventeen. p. 494.

is not the sole consideration. Millet is easily spoiled
in various stages. The banana, in the West Indies,
is apt to be overturned, particularly at the equinoxes.
Some sorts of food store with difficulty ; and others
cannot be preserved except for a short time, or for a
year ; while others may be preserved from year to
year, or through a succession of years, without any
material injury.

Population is regulated by the habitual food of the
people. If there be fish-eaters, there are many more
eaters of flesh among men. The Ethiopians lived on
flesh[1], and reproached the Persians who ate bread,
calling bread dung. So did the Parthians[2] and Celtæ[3],
and Usbecks and Turcomans and South Americans[4].
Of the last, Mawe says, " The constant diet of the
people, morning, noon, and night, is beef eaten almost
always without bread, and frequently without salt."

Some nations are comparatively indifferent what
they eat; as the Tartars, Mr. Gray's epicures already
mentioned, who feast on the vilest reptiles. The Bos-
jesman are rejoiced with bread made of pounded locusts. Dampier also speaks of a people living on
locusts[5], which, he says, they eat as we do shrimps ;
and Horneman[6] mentions, that in the Fezzan country
locusts, when dried, are esteemed a luxury.

There is also an abstemiousness in nations compared to others in the same state of society, which
operates materially on the numbers of the respective

---

[1] Herodotus, lib. 3. c. 22.   [2] Justin, lib. 41. c. 3.

[3] Athenæus, lib. 4. c. 13. p. 150.

[4] Pinkerton, &c. vol. 9. p. 331.   [5] Ibid. vol. 11. p. 49.

[6] Travels, p. 59. See Niebuhr also, c. 44.

countries. The Bœotians were reproached as great eaters, and of corresponding stupidity[1]; while the Athenians were most mercurial, and ate once, or at most twice a day. The ancient Iberians[2] taxed those who exceeded the measure of their girdle; nor are their descendants less abstemious. Mackinnon mentions, "that the population of Portugal is immense, compared to its cultivation;—they live on little; one third of the number of Britons would starve on such slender means of support."

The English have been long remarked for their Bœotian propensities. "To cram like an Englishman" was a simile in the time of Erasmus. And Shakespeare makes Macbeth say, "Then fly, false Thanes, and mingle with the English epicures." The English preserve the same character; it has been remarked, that what are called necessaries in England are esteemed in Sweden as inducing plethora and inflammation. Thence it happens, partly, that the English do not advance in proportion to their opportunities; while the Scotch, though less favourably situated in many respects, having more thrift and being sparer feeders, preserve nearly their relative population; and that Ireland, amidst all its horrors and afflictions, advances on the numbers of its masters; for though the Irish, like the Jews in Egypt, the more they afflicted them they multiplied and grew[3], exhibit

---

[1] Plutarch. Moral. p. 364. This eating had much more effect than the climate. The thick atmosphere and stupidity of Bœotia and its people are referable to their full feeding. The Milanese are remarkable among the Italians for eating, and are called *lupi Lombardi*.

[2] Apud Stobæum, sermo 5. p. 74.   [3] Exod. chap. 1.

nothing miraculous in their increase,—the climate is good, the land productive, and potatoes are congenial to soil, climate, and people, while affliction has been to the people a course of philosophy. Misgovernment, which diminished their comforts, imposed on them a rigid parsimony, which has eventually supported their numbers; or rather, these circumstances have enabled them to exceed the rate of increase among the British:—Nay more, these circumstances in a great degree have assisted the Catholic Irish[1] to advance on the Protestant Irish, though the Protestants possessed every advantage, for the Catholics obtained in effect merely the leavings of the English settlers and of their orthodox associates;—the property of the Irish or Catholics was confiscated, their industry and persons persecuted, and all public emoluments of every kind were conferred on strangers or enemies.

Temperance in drinking makes the greatest difference in the population of different kingdoms. I do not singly speak of besotted habits and dram-drinking, which are so notoriously injurious to savages, and to the young men in St. Petersburg, and to the mothers and infant children in London, and to the colonists in New South Wales, but to the unnecessary use of various liquors[2]. Fondness or abhorrence of

[1] Plunket said that in the whole province of Ulster the Catholics, men, women, and children, did not amount to 70,000. State Trials, vol. 3. p. 353. Not long since there was not a Catholic in Belfast;—there are now 4,000. The same is said of Derry.

[2] It appears that Governor Bligh's suppression of the barter of spirits occasioned the mutiny which deposed him.

ardent spirits distinguishes the same people. Thus Park speaks of " Kafirs and Soonakies, i. e. men who drink strong waters." The loss to population is considerable, independent of the demoralizing enfeebling effects of excessive drinking, by the waste of subsistence and labour that attends generally this habit. The religion of Mahomet then, so far as it prohibits the use of wine and spirits, tends to increase the number of the people, however destructive it is in other respects to population.

Besides these circumstances, luxurious propensities are most ruinous : " it consumes its means, and eventually itself." The destruction of human life by luxury is faintly evinced by the Roman who fed his fish with slaves : thousands of men are destroyed in the most senseless pursuits of fashion. How many individuals die, or are rendered infirm and diseased, by one winter's fashionable campaign in London!—The waste also of the means of life in such pursuits is incalculable. In luxury, one man may consume the labour of a hundred, or a thousand, or a hundred thousand : a large standing army is frequently a mere enhancement of the luxuriousness of prodigal royalty. Population not only depends on the constitution of the government, but every particular,—domestic, civil, and political, —restricts or expands population. Rent, taxes, duty, excise, every law or regulation respecting property and liberty, operates as a medicine or a malady on human life. Equity, freedom, security, quicken inert matter into human beings, and sustain human happiness.

---

[1] In the East if there be 100 dishes, the guest must taste of each.

How shallow and partial are those, who would determine the amount of population by the quantity of provisions [1],—when œconomy or prodigality in the use of food, extrinsic of all other considerations, alters immensely the relations of subsistence and population!

CHAPTER II.

The considerations in the preceding chapter considered by a review of the population in China—perhaps no sufficient reasons for disbelieving its immense imputed population.—The Chinese never advanced beyond the second or middle state.

I SHALL exemplify the foregoing remarks by reviewing the supposed population of China. The embassy to that country, under the auspices of Lord Macartney, were informed that the Chinese amounted to 333 millions. This approaches the population of the whole earth according to Sir W. Petty's calculation, which he fixed at about 350 millions. The population [2] was disbelieved merely on account of the enor-

---

[1] One half of the world, it is supposed, live on rice and water. There are people who consume, man for man, in comparison to these, ten times as much. If the former live, can the latter be said barely to exist? This contrast is still stronger when we are told, " Certainly an Englishman would be dying for want of food, before he accepted an invitation to dine with the king of Lattakoo." Yet this king's prerogative seemed to Campbell to consist mainly in sitting near the pot that contained the boiled beans.

[2] It has been the fashion to decry the Chinese, because they had been inordinately eulogized, and they will not fraternize with us. Some have attempted to prove them comparatively a new people. Mons. de Guines is the most violent impugner of Chinese antiquity.

mity, without any regard to the combination of circumstances which authorize this statement. I have not seen any reason for denying it. Ministers to be sure are disposed to multiply the people of their respective states; but after an excessive number what can be gained by exaggeration? The repetition of 3 might appear suspicious: and I perceive that Dr. Price [1] assumes the sum to be paid off 33,333,000*l*, and that Sir James Steuart's [2] random conjecture is 333,333. How far this circumstance may operate against the 333 millions, I leave to the ingenuity of the reader.

It is said that in the reign of Tching-tsong [3] a census was made in China of all those who cultivated the ground, and that they amounted to 21,976,965. In Canghi's reign the census was repeated [4], when the population amounted to 59,788,364, exclusive of the learned and magistrates, and soldiers, and of those who lived on rafts and on the rivers. A census in 1761 makes the people, it is said, amount to 198,214,553. Since that time, independent of the

Instead of subsisting, he says, 3000 years before Christ, he will not admit their empire " reuni d'une manière stable de depuis 529 ans." He might as truly determine the age of the French by the time when Guienne, Burgundy, &c. were resumed by the King of France. I am very indifferent whether China is young, or old, or middle-aged; but I may state that Mons. Delandine says, p. 140, that he found among the manuscripts at Lyons one in Chinese, which notices an astronomical observation made in China, which he specifies. He adds, that the conjunction alluded to, took place the 28th of February, 2549 years before the Christian æra.

[1] Annuities, &q. p. 117.   [2] vol. 1. p. 79.
[3] Duhalde's China, vol. 1. p. 428.   [4] Ibid. vol. 2. p. 20.

multiplication of the people, the dominion of China has been enlarged.

All travellers through China agree respecting the apparently immense population of China. Missionaries and ambassadors all concur with Lord Macartney, who says, " The number of villages is wonderful : the population is almost incredible [1]." It has been calculated [2] that 333 millions would be only 256 persons to a square mile : this, supposing the Chinese territory is not taken too low, is less than the population of the United Provinces, which contained 270 to a square mile ; and is only about a fifth more than the population of Bengal, that harassed province [3], which according to Mr. Colebrooke contains 25 millions of persons, or 203 to a square mile.

The reasons for believing the populousness of China are many. The climate is good [4]; the soil is generally fertile ; and tillage is universally encouraged by the laws of property and inheritance, and by the moderate impost on the land. It pays no tithe, little rent ; the taxation of the empire is inconsiderable, amounting to 12,140,625*l.*, each person being charged about eight-pence a-year [5]. By the law of succession

[1] Post. Works, vol. 2. p. 203.   [2] Barrow's Travels, p. 576.

[3] According to Tytler, the waste land in Bengal is immense. vol. 1. p. 99. He says again : the villages through Bengal are at great distance, and the lands only in their immediate vicinity are cultivated. p. 112. *Nearly one half of the country is a wild and useless jungle* ; nay worse, for it harbours buffaloes and wild hogs, which ravage on every side. This account renders the imputed excess of people in China to India probable.

[4] Duhalde, vol. 2. p. 25.

[5] Mr Tombe says the Chinese are taxed for their long nails— Who told him this ?

land is subdivided by every generation, and any unoccupied land is grantable and granted by the government to any one who will cultivate it.

Such a system is favourable to agriculture. Lord Macartney[1] believes " there is not an acre of cultivable land in China which is not cultivated." Mr. Barrow's[2] account does not harmonize with this position: he supposes that for want of agricultural instruments a very considerable portion, *perhaps of the richest land*, remains untilled. Had he said of ordinary or inferior land, he would be intelligible and just. Du Halde speaks of uncultivated heaths; and Mr. Ellis noticed large tracts untilled. Mons. de Guines[3], as Mr. Barrow says, dispraisingly—" en général ils labourent peu profondement : la charrue n'entre guerre au dela de quatre ou cinque pouces dans la terre, où l'on seme le riz." Should it go deeper? The fact is, that the plough is little used in China comparatively to the spade. The value or meaning of these authors is problematical. Mr. Barrow[4] denies that the Chinese have much merit as agriculturists; contrary to Lord Macartney[5], who asserts, " The Chinese are certainly the best husbandmen in the world." Yet Mr. Barrow bears testimony " to their skill and industry in raising the greatest possible quantity of vegetables from a given piece of ground :" thus distinguishing between agriculturists and horticulturists. The disagreement between these writers is indifferent to me ; for the Chinese mode of agriculture favours

[1] Post. Works, vol. 2. p. 379.   [2] China, p. 567.
[3] Voyage en Pekin, t. 3. p. 327.   [4] p. 568.
[5] Post. Works, vol. 2. p. 360.

the great population of China. It exhibits the remedy of Hobbes for a numerous people, " to live closer, and cultivate each spot exactly." The Chinese are excellent labourers. The Europeans who possessed Ceylon could not raise vegetables for the table; yet the Chinese succeeded. Mrs. Graham says, " I saw not only esculent vegetables of every kind, but thriving sugar-canes, under their management[1]."

Œconomy is a fundamental law in China; an officer must not use horses when the ordinance specifies asses[2]. This I have no doubt regards thrift. The Hebrews also were prohibited from multiplying horses.

The Chinese assiduously convert every refuse thing to some account: whatever is edible they eat; but rice is so perpetually their food[3], that it enters into every compound which signifies eating. They eat little flesh[4], are temperate perhaps beyond any other people, though some indulge in spiced wine and a ——, like Chou-ta-gin; and others delight in edible swallows nests, for which China affords the best market. The people are disposed to marriage, as are all unsophisticated people. Infanticide, or exposing

[1] India, p. 94. They did not succeed in Trinidad; for they became sickly by the voyage, and had been accustomed at home to use cattle in the cultivation of sugar-canes.

[2] Chinese Code, p. 258. Marco Polo says, In Persia asses are dearer than horses, because they eat little, carry much, and travel far. Pinkerton, vol. 7. p. 112.

[3] Barrow, p. 547.

[4] There is a discourse in Chinese, delivered in the person of an ox, dehorting from eating beef. This is held a monstrous fable by him, who says it has great effect, and prevents one in ten, or one in twenty, from eating beef. What is there monstrous in this fable that is not in other fables? Rev. R. Morrison's Horæ Sinicæ.

children, as a custom with which the Chinese have been charged, is unfounded [1]. That a city inhabited by three millions of people should contain many improvident and miserable, is necessary : but of the children supposed to be purposely destroyed, many are still-born. Sir G. T. Staunton says [2], infanticide is seldom committed, except in cases of very defective formation, or in the anguish of hopeless poverty.

> " Die, little wretch ! ere yet thy sorrows live,
> Take the last boon thy helpless sire can give."

In Tonquin it is expressly affirmed that exposing children is unknown.

Education in China seems comparatively excellent. I have already noticed its particulars in " National Education." I shall therefore merely say, that in China the object is not to teach the least in the longest time, and to destroy both the temper and the mind, by forcing scragged and futile and fanatical systems on infancy : Chinese teachers inculcate what is useful [3]. Literature is in the highest honour, and each man is his own patron. " These (literary) pursuits [4] are professedly the sole channel of introduction to

[1] I wonder Mons. Say could write of " la grande destruction d'enfans à la Chine," &c. t. 2. p. 145. It has been said that children have been eaten as a specific in certain diseases. Osbeck's China, vol. 2. p. 235. It might as well be said they eat men in France, because l'Homme appears at the head of a French Materia Medica.

[2] Preface to Chinese Code, p. 10.

[3] Ils (les Chinois) veulent que les jeunes gens aient un fond d'idées, de connoissances, de reflexions, et de vues, &c. Mémoires des Missionnaires, &c. t. 9.

[4] Sir G. T. Staunton's Chinese Code, p. 12.

political advancement in the state; to offices, rank, and honours of almost every description." Useful knowledge, that which leads to practical wisdom, forms the basis of their studies; the tenour of all their literature is moral. Du Halde says[1] that the Chinese novels are moral historical romances. Their fables have the same object. All these things emphatically educate the people. What they are at home we may learn by their conduct abroad. A writer in the Quarterly Review[2], from actual knowledge, says, that in Java the Chinese are industrious and peaceable; that they are chief proprietors in every town and village in the island; and that they are selected as chief magistrates, on account of their probity and sagacity. Such are some of the reasons for the populousness of China.

Those which deduct from the full measure of this conclusion are: first the monarchy; and next the Tartar conquest of the country, which has increased the evils of the monarchy, for the soldiery are Tartars[3]; and a Tartar is frequently associated with a Chinese, not so much to assist him, as to countervail the danger of a pure Chinese magistracy to a Tartar dynasty. The monarchy is extensive: yet the evil of extent has some peculiar advantages in China. If Mirabeau had any good grounds for stating that the excessive population in China induces moderation in the government, we may add that the vast circle of

[1] vol. 3. p. 113. [2] December 1811, p. 500, 508.
[3] " Every Tartar male child is accordingly enrolled." Barrow, p. 412.

China ensures an active administration [1], for any great remissness must dissolve such unwieldy province .

There are peculiarities respecting the monarchy of China, which render it infinitely less oppressive than the monarchies of Europe [2], or even than some of those states which presume to be free. The monarchy is at once hereditary and elective—the eldest son of the last emperor does not necessarily succeed. There are various checks to the wilfulness of the monarch, and to the component parts of the administration. His proclamations at least exhibit some decency. The broad lie is not the sum of the state papers of the overweening king, as in Christendom, and self-reproach often accompanies his public reproof. In another point the emperor of China may be contrasted with the kings of Europe :—With a revenue of twelve millions, Kien-long, the last emperor, upheld a mighty army [3]; provided for all the expenses of the

---

[1] From Pekin to Canton is 1200 miles. Government despatches have arrived the 12th day. Staunton, p. 252.

[2] It is thought to be more ceremonious :—it may be so ; but the court ceremonies in Europe are amazing to a common apprehension. The mere circumstances of *sieges à bras*, and *sieges à dos*, and their placing, would require a treatise. See Wickfort, p. 488. 525. The court of Louis the XIVth was rich in topics of this learning.

[3] It may be thought that a million in China is much more valuable in exchange than a million in England ; yet if we calculate the soldier's pay of the two countries, it is not so very unequal. A horseman receives three ounces three-tenths of silver, at 6s. 8d. each, and fifteen measures of rice. A foot soldier one ounce and six-tenths of silver, and ten measures of rice. Macartney, vol. 2. p. 480. Which is about 5d. a day, with rice, for a foot soldier. This was not much less than the pay of a foot soldier in England before the last war.

government; distributed large sums in charity; and beside restoring the taxes to particular provinces, he five times remitted all the taxes payable in specie[1], and three times all the taxes paid in kind throughout the empire.

The chief reason of this œconomy is; the Chinese monarchy has no Gothic incumbrances. There is no antiquated nobility; all titles, except those enjoyed by the descendants of Confucius preceding 1644, being resumed[2]. The few hereditary nobles are principally Tartar chieftains reduced to vassalage[3]; these are the only Corinthian capitals of this immense monarchy, with the exception of the princes of the imperial family[4], who enjoy prerogatives, one of which is, that they only shall educate castrated children for eunuchs.

The monarchy of China subsists without an ecclesiastical establishment; not one bishop, priest, or deacon belongs to the Chinese empire, though it has been found that a bishop and the like are required for British India; they have no religious establishment[5], no clergy, no religious assemblies, no stated season for public or private prayer, and the teachers of tolerated sects are actually under *surveillance* as troublesome and perfidious, and are obliged to wear a particular dress[6]. The Christian doctrines are particularly offensive to the emperor[7], who has been incensed by the surreptitious efforts of the missionaries; and he stigmatizes

[1] Staunton, p. 479.　　　　　　[2] Ibid. p. 49.
[3] Chinese Code, p. 391.　　　　[4] Chinese Code, p. 412.
[5] Barrow, Daniell, Staunton, p. 42.　[6] Staunton, p. 186.
[7] See Appendix to Sir G. T. Staunton's Chinese Code.

certain doctrines with the most contemptible epithets[1]: nor is it improbable, that the conduct of the followers of peace-loving Christianity in his neighbourhood, has induced him to believe that Christians are confessed hypocrites.

Some things are particularized in favour of this monarchy, which to me are the reverse. The great doctrine, respect to parents[2], is consummate: but this, like other maxims, is forced by a fictitious diversion to signify obedience from the subject to the prince, he being considered the father of his people. This is the tone of the canting Catharine, the *soi-disant* " tender mother" of the Poles. The prince who addresses his subjects with paternity, rejoices rather in their weakness than his own equity. The justice of a master to his slave, says Aristotle[3], is not identical with that of a parent to his child, $\alpha\lambda\lambda'$ $\delta\mu o\iota o\nu$: that is, in practice it is absolute. In consequence, flogging is very general in China; or, if we believe Sir G. T. Staunton[4], we should rather say *has been* general in China. This

[1] The emperors of China seem to have had little faith from olden time. It is said, that some drawing an omen from some storks, Tai-tsong remarked, " What signifies it to me ! it is a happy omen to have wise men about me." Duhalde, vol. 1. p. 392 ; which equals Homer's reply to the seer.

[2] It is of great antiquity in Greece. Apud Stobæum, sermo 77, p. 458–461.

[3] Ethic. ad Eudem. lib. 4. c. 4. t. 2. p. 235.

[4] He says, " Though every page of the following translation may seem, at first sight, to bear testimony to the universality of corporal punishments in China; yet so many exceptions and mitigations will be found, that the penal system will be found to abandon almost entirely that part of its apparent character." Preface, p. 27.

is intelligible, as few husbands *correct* their wives[1] in England, as they might have done by the common law; and masters have also disclaimed a similar abuse of their servants[2]. But it has amazed me exceedingly, that so many intelligent English should wince at the bambooing of all orders of Chinese—mandarins and peasants, &c. That this might have alarmed a Roman, when the *lex Porcia*[3] prohibited a Roman citizen from being beaten with rods; or a Frank, who was equally inviolate by the Salique law[4], is easily understood;—but the English have no right to be startled at this practice, as their own soldiers are flogged and re-flogged[5] contrary to acknowledged law: and if flogging be admitted, which I deprecate, there is no reason why chiefs should not suffer as well as subordinates: except we take a comment on equity from the votes of the Commons of England[6], and the judgements of the Lords.

[1] Blackstone's Commentaries, b. 1. c. 15.

[2] " If the master designeth correction to his servant, and accordingly useth it; and the servant, by some misfortune, dieth thereof; this is not murder, but *per infortunium*; because the law alloweth him to use moderate correction ; and therefore the deliberate purpose thereof is not *ex malitia præcognita*." Hale's Pleas of the Crown, vol. 1. p. 454.

[3] Cicero, t. 2. p. 311. 37.   [4] Pastoret, part 2. p. 87.

[5] General Ferguson stated that he knew, at Fort Charles, 300 men receive in two years 54,000 lashes. There is no country like England in this respect:—the janizaries, when flogged, seldom receive more than forty blows, and they are so given as not to disable the sufferer from marching. Thornton, vol. 1. p. 228. The Spanish soldiers in South America are not flogged. Pike's Travels.

[6] Thus a tinman offered a bribe to a prime minister,—and the attorney-general prosecuted the gnat. Lord Melville admitted that he had disposed of 10,000*l.* of the public money contrary to act of parliament,—and his peers acquitted him on an impeachment.

There is no distinction but the greater or less crime. If we regard persons, certainly the greater the person the greater the crime, and of course the more exemplary should be his punishment; which is the law of China[1]. This is not the place for comparing the laws of China, or judging minutely their merit : they err, as in other monarchies, particularly in the penalties pronounced against treason[2]; and they excell in their tenderness towards women, as daughters and wives[3]; far surpassing, or rather they are contrasted with the English laws[4] in this respect, as they are to that execrable judicial dogma[5], That he who cannot pay in his purse shall pay in his person.

Much has been written against their jealousy of admitting the entry of foreigners, and of permitting the departure of their own people. This is pernicious to population, did it merely prevent the acquisition of knowledge from abroad : but its operation in this instance is more direct ; for the bar to the intercourse with foreigners, as it has prevented the small islands along the coast from being inhabited by the Chinese[6], and their government not having shipping to give effect to this regulation, the islands are occupied by pirates. Here again the jealousy of the government impairs the entire prosperity of the people : from the same suspicion, they are passive in their foreign commerce,

[1] Chinese Code, p. 384.   [2] Ibid. p. 269.   [3] Ibid. p. 150. 459.
[4] " The indecent, wanton, and cruel custom of putting irons on the weaker sex in prisons, is not practised in any of the most uncivilized countries that I have visited." Howard on Lazarettos, p. 176.
[5] Chinese Code, p. 365.   [6] Staunton, p. 238.

which is limited to a single port. Yet considering the immensity of China,—its rivers, canals communicating with the great canal, which is only less wonderful than the great wall,—we might say, internal commerce in China is also foreign commerce. Lord Macartney [1] expressed the utmost admiration at the number of vessels in the Pæyho; and Mr. Barrow [2], who is of a less sanguine temperament, has no difficulty in saying, " I firmly believe that all the floating vessels in the world besides, taken collectively, would not equal either in number or tonnage those of China."

From all these circumstances, and others which I omit for brevity, I do not perceive any reason for doubting the population ascribed to China. Mr. Barrow says [3], it is not overstocked with people. And Mr. Ellis indirectly says more [4]. Yet a better government would increase the comforts of society in China, or abate its misery. In fact, it appears that, except in moral instruction, and perhaps gardening [5],

[1] Post. Works, vol. 2. p. 182.   [2] p. 399.

[3] p. 579. Duhalde says, the Chinese have recourse to every invention to procure subsistence. vol. 2. p. 125.

[4] " I have been much struck in all Chinese towns and villages, with the number of persons apparently of the middle classes. From this I am inclined to infer a wide diffusion of the substantial comforts of life, and the consequent financial capacity of the country. However absurd the pretensions of the emperor of China may be to universal supremacy, it is impossible to travel through his dominions without feeling that he has the finest country, within an imperial ring-fence, in the world." p. 323.

[5] The Chinese gardening is the reverse of the Mogul taste. At Surat, parterres are the taste; and so to plant them that they may exhibit a Turkey carpet is the effort. Forbes, p. 23.

" .... which not nice art
  In beds and curious knots, but nature boon
  Pour'd out profuse on hill and dale and plain,"

the Chinese have never advanced beyond the secondary stages: nor is this strange, when we consider their pertinacious adherence to custom. So little have the course of time and the progress of events altered their habits, that it is said, the expressions and style of modern writers differ little from the language of Confucius and that of his immediate followers.

The whole system may be pronounced secondary and inferior :—a monarchy directly sprung from the patriarchal state, with the obligation of a council, which probably rules when the emperor is inert or inefficient, and which is a mere name when he is strenuous and intelligent. The laws are minute in the extreme, prohibiting by lines and punishing by units. The details respecting mourning are extreme[1], and the penalties on transgression numerous. The sumptuary laws regard houses, apartments, carriages, dress, and furniture; while custom overpowers and impedes the business and pursuits of life with forms and ceremonies[2]. The laws respecting domestic industry evince the same spirit: To manufacture silks, satins, gauzes, or other stuffs, according to the prohibited pattern of the *lung*[3] or the *fung-whang*, is punishable by forfeiture of goods and a hundred blows. The exclusion of their people from foreign trade equals their internal regulations : yet the Chinese government seems to

[1] Chinese Code, p. 75, 112, 113, 487.
[2] Chinese Code, p. 185. Du Halde says there are three invitations to the same feast. vol. 2. p. 191.   [3] Ibid. p. 467.

have much juster notions on some points of trade than England's ambassador, who was amazed that the Hong merchants were not sensible of any disadvantage from the export of silver from Canton to India[1]; and still juster than our laws, which rejoice in error and contradiction :—by them, to export a few guineas is penal, but millions may be transferred at once without inquiry or offence.

The currency of the country is in the same inferior state : they have copper coin, but large payments are made by ingots[2]:—thus things are rather bartered than sold. They use the hoe and the spade, seldom employing the plough. Barrow's words are[3], "Two-thirds of the land in China are cultivated by the spade and hoe, without the aid of draft cattle." This is an advance beyond the people mentioned by Park: "The application of animal labour to the purposes of agriculture is no-where adopted, the plough therefore is wholly unknown (in the Negro territories); the chief implement used in husbandry is the hoe." The use of men instead of cattle in the more operose parts of agriculture is partly unfavourable to tillage, though it may generally increase the amount of the people; as does the practice of using men to carry what in other countries are borne by horses[4]. It may be remarked, that when New Spain was conquered, a numerous

[1] His words are : " I have been told, that some silver has of late been carried away by the country-ships from Canton to India; and that the Hong merchants, considering silver as a mere merchandise, did not appear sensible of any disadvantage from the trade." Post. Works, vol. 2. p. 517.

[2] Staunton, p. 124. In some of the provinces Spanish dollars have been introduced. [3] p. 585. [4] Duhalde, vol. 2. p. 158.

class of the people was employed in carrying burthens on the highways ; and it continues. In this respect China and South America coincide.

A thousand circumstances denote an early improvement and a sudden stop in China. This observation is corroborated by many instances. Their signs for sounds are not letters, but abbreviated symbols or pictures. They consist of 214 elementary characters, which in their combination constitute 80,000 words [1], a cumbrous and inefficient machinery. Though long acquainted with printing, they have not attained the discovery of metallic or moveable types [2]. Though literary, or rather a moralizing people, they have little taste for composition ; and none of their various works exhibits harmony or grace in its design or execution. Their novels, as I said, are mere romances; and the better theatrical pieces, novels represented; which, with some exceptions, are a mixture of comedy, tragedy, and song; and are just as much below the true drama, as the Italian Opera is beyond it [3]. Their tragedies in their moral tone, represent the philosophers and heroes of the nation [4], and correspond to those exhibited in Peru, according to the report of Garcillasso della Vega [5]. The scene is absolutely representative : If a wife kill her husband, he appears with a bloody gash above his eyes, and reels and falls on the stage. If a man be executed, the audience beholds the deed; the head rolls on the stage, and the body staggers after

---

[1] Lord Macartney, vol. 2. p. 492.   [2] Dubalde, vol. 1. p. 351, 416.
[3] See Duhalde, vol. 3. p. 195-196.
[4] Acosta, part. 9. lib. 6. c. 6.   [5] c. 17.

it[1]: and Mons. de Guines mentions[2], that the chief personage in a piece *devint grosse, et accoucha sur le théâtre d'un enfant.* Nor does it appear that at court theatrical exhibitions are of a higher cast: tumblers, mountebanks, and laureats seem to regale the majesty of China; which, however, are not so absurd or expensive as the masques and mummeries exhibited in the reigns of Elizabeth, James, and Charles: nor does it appear that the emperor participates, as Charles the Martyr did, in a court masque[3], and as Louis the Fourteenth did in a ballet. I have spoken of the tenour of the Chinese dramas: for "The Heir in his Old Age," translated by Mr. Davis, and eight hundred years old, resembles the Grecian drama, which seems to me at least one degree less advanced than the best English tragedies.

The Chinese are excellent imitators, which they enjoy with the Russians; as artists they have little merit; in painting, they exhibit the whole face. This agrees with Abyssinian art: "The Abyssinians in their pictures always strangely exaggerate the dominion of the eye, and invariably draw the figures with full face[4]." They are so fond of fact in their designs, that they cannot endure relief. Thus their taste conforms to queen Elizabeth's judgement[5], as exhibited in her own portraits, who would be painted without shadow.

Chinese architecture is mean, and only an improve-

[1] Mr. Barrow mentions the former, and Mr. Wathen this instance. [2] t. 2. p. 324.

[3] Finet Ambassadors, p. 48.   [4] Salt's Travels, p. 395.

[5] According to the Pythagoreans, souls don't wink nor cast shadows. Plutarch. Moral. p. 181.

ment on tents. They have no mirrors, nor windows of glass[1]; metal serves for the one, and oyster-shells for the other. They have neither wind- nor water-mills[2], employing querns or handmills, which is just an improvement on the negro practice of beating the grain in a mortar[3]. Their travelling carriages are not better than a higgler's cart[4]; and they are very deficient in practical mechanics[5], in medicine, in surgery—a fracture being commonly attended with death[6]. In ship-building they are equally deficient: for though they admire European ships, it would be criminal to improve their own rude vessels[7]; which all those among us who dread reform[8], and decry it as an innovation, must greatly admire. Their vessels therefore resemble the tub-formed merchant-ships of the ancients; and like them they keep close to the shore[9], except when the voyage obliges a bolder navigation: in short, they seem to be now, what the Seres were two or three thousand years ago. *Seres mites quidem sed et ipsi feris persimiles, cœtum reliquorum mortalium fugiunt cum commercia expectant*[10]. Thus I have partially sketched the mode of estimating the populousness of countries, by a view of the circumstances and condition of the Chinese; which may

[1] Macartney, vol. 2. p. 480.
[2] Duhalde, vol. 2. p. 125.
[3] Park's Travels, p. 10.
[4] Macartney, vol. 2. p. 420.
[5] Barrow, p. 90.
[6] Macartney, vol. 2. p. 364.
[7] Duhalde, vol. 2. p. 136.

[8] We have again failed in an embassy:—Who can read the difficulties on the bows, and not be enamoured of court ceremonies? The kou-tou is a ceremony of the Empire;—we knew this: then why do we furnish an embassy, and resist compliance?

[9] Barrow, p. 39.　　　　[10] Plin. Nat. Hist. lib. 6. c. 17.

also advance or explain other particulars in the philosophy of man. The account of the population of China may be exaggerated: yet, considering the climate, the soil and extent of China; the disposition to marry; the state of property; the cultivation of the land; that they are thrifty, industrious, managing, and abstemious; that they pay little rent, few taxes, no tithes; that no ecclesiastical establishment is charged on the people's labour, nor nobles, nor paupers, nor colonies;—considering all these things, and that there are few wars, and an immense internal trade, it does not appear to me improbable, though I by no means say it is authenticated,—that the immense territory of China contains 333 millions of people.

CHAPTER III.

On populous cities.

HAVING illustrated some prominent points respecting population, by a commentary on the most populous country that ever existed; I repeat that I do not dread the populousness of nations, nor am I alarmed by any local excess or partial throng of inhabitants. I fear bad government and external violence. Ten thousand times a country has become too populous for the subsistence, by the devastations of war and conquest. The same has inordinately increased the population of neighbouring states. Foreign misery has had this effect. The suffering of traders in 1810 and 1811 increased and incommoded the population of the Isle of Man. Rome latterly has exhibited every vicissitude of evil. It wanted people when the pope transferred his court to Avignon; the population having declined, it is said, in these seventy-two years of absence, to 30,000; and it increased intolerably by the ship-loads of Jesuits which were consigned to the holy father when this society was disgraced.

Delos lost its people by a fantasy of the Athenians, who carried off wholly the inhabitants from the island [1]. On the contrary, when the Romans destroyed Corinth, and dealt ruin largely through the Mediterranean states, Delos was a second time re-born, and became an entrepôt of Greece, Italy, and Asia [2]. The deficiency and excess of people in either case were imposed on the Delians; therefore they were not responsible for the inconvenience, but the governments which prepared or obliged these extraordinary situations. In like manner the government which fondles and pampers a manufacture, and with it forces a population, is answerable for the evils attending this exotic multiplication of mankind. Thus the misery which now afflicts society through every class and profession is not referable to the people, but to our warring wasting government, which squandered the property or perverted the capital of the state; and thus for the time greatly encouraged labour and pro-

---

[1] Thucydides, lib. 5. p. 343. They afterwards replaced them by order of the Oracle. p. 366.

[2] Eo enim negotiatores commigrarunt, præsertim cum templi immunitas accesserit, et ipsius portus invitat occasio. Etenim ex Italia et e Græcia in Asiam navigantibus, &c. Strabo, lib. 10. Cicero pro Lege Manilia, t. 2. p. 250.

duce, and of course called numbers into life and activity, who now, while the means which employed them are lost or mortgaged to satisfy the public creditor, want occupation altogether, or are insufficiently remunerated by their wages, which are further so diminished by taxation, that they relapse incessantly on the parish. I repeat, I am not afraid of population. If the people over-breed, as they suffer, they will remedy the evil. What is dreadful, is bad government, monstrous projects, tyranny, and conquest; because these press hardly on the innocent multitude, and lightly on the infatuated : " Quicquid delirant reges, plectuntur Achivi." This, and not over-breeding, is dreadful: for here the punishment is not retributory ; the crime is the rulers', while the satisfaction is reserved for the people.

Much contradiction has been expressed relative to great cities. By great cities I mean the capital and secondary cities in Europe. The supposed evils resulting from them, when they were very inferior to what they are at present, caused limitary laws to be enacted respecting them in different countries. By the 35th of Elizabeth, c. 6, the erection of new buildings within three miles of London or Westminster was prohibited. The fear of an increasing capital was common in the reigns of James[1] and Charles and during the Commonwealth. Whitelock says[2], " that in 1657 there was much debate on the bill for restraint of buildings in and about London :"—it passed. The same was proposed in Charles the Second's reign,

[1] Hume, vol. 6. p. 169. James proclaimed and warned and exhorted.   [2] Memorials, p. 661, 662.

which was abandoned, according to Clarendon [1], because it seemed to interfere with the liberty of the people. An ordinance was made in 1545 in France, prohibiting the increase of Paris, expressly through terror of populousness: "que les sujets multiplians," &c. [2] Harrington is therefore inaccurate in his reflections on this particular [3]; for the French government wished to limit not only Paris, but all the great cities [4]. Whether any law was enacted to the same effect in Holland, I do not know; but we hear from Temple, that many thought the enlargement of Amsterdam was injurious to the state [5]. This dread of populous cities has not been confined to modern legislators. Pheidon of Corinth prohibited the increase of houses in Corinth [6]. Aristotle relates the fact; who, though disagreeing with Pheidon, seems not unfriendly to some restrictions on population, as he says it is almost impossible to govern well a very populous

[1] History, book 4. p. 212.

[2] Bodin de la Republique, liv. 5. p. 546. This policy equalled the knowledge of that time :—Paris was then supposed to contain three millions. Duhalde's China, vol. 2. p. 10.

[3] He says, "But should a man tell them at Paris, or Grand Cairo, (in the latter whereof the plague is more frequent and furious than happens with us,) that they are not to build houses nor increase so much, lest they should have the plague; or that children should not be born so fast, lest they die,—they would think it strange news." Oceana, p. 302.

[4] L'ancien gouvernement de France bornait l'extension des grandes villes. Rien ne peut justifier ce système, si ce n'est la mauvaise humeur des fermiers generaux, qui n'aimaient pas voir s'établir hors des barriers des cabarets, où l'ou ne payait point de droit. E. Polit. tom. 2. p. 167.

[5] Works, vol. 1. p. 69.   [6] De Repub. lib. 2. c. 6.

state[1]. When we read of such expressions and terrors concerning states of twenty or thirty or a hundred thousand inhabitants, we must not smile at the *naïveté* of a lady at St. Helena, who remarked, that " the arrival of the India fleet in England must make London very gay."

Authors have followed and probably preceded legislators; they have spoken of great cities with unmeasured reprobation. Filangieri rails without reasoning, calling cities sumptuous sepulchres which a dying nation raises and enlarges to receive its very ashes[2]. Dr. Price rails and calculates and graduates, that London, which required six thousand recruits annually in the time of Graunt, did, when he himself wrote, consume ten thousand persons more than it produced; that the expectation of lives in great towns was twenty-one, of middling towns twenty-five, of the country thirty-seven.

Some on the contrary are consoled by the destruction of life in great towns; which, though they cannot advance it to the dignity of a final cause, is in their estimate a demand fully sufficient to destroy Mr. Malthus's geometrical supply. This observation has been claimed as an invention by Mr. Weyland, just as truly as Mr. Malthus's dogma is the creation of his genius. Sir James Steuart, who admits the unhealthiness of great cities, and "that the prolongation of life is more a private than a public concern[3]," insists that Paris has purged the country of idle mouths[4]. Thus Sir James Steuart patronized consumption as

[1] lib. 7. c. 4.   [2] Della Legislazione, tom. 1. p. 372.
[3] vol. 1. p. 53.   [4] vol. 1. p. 103.

much as Mr. Weyland, or as the British legislators, who, to serve the staple, command that all shall be buried in woollen. He says, "If the same number of inhabitants in the city of Paris consume four times as much of any necessary article as formerly, I hope it will be allowed that the production of such necessaries must be four times as abundant[1]." This does not follow; for the expenditure does not prove the existence of a proportionate supply, it only proves that there is a supply. Those who regard consumption as a good, or as a remedy, should honour plagues and conflagrations.

I do not wish to conceal the evils of populous cities. Those who consider long life, with the Chinese, one of the few instances of human felicity, must be distressed by the more rapid dissolution of mankind in great cities. They are particularly destructive to infant children. In Stockholm and Vienna, one half that are born die before they are two years old[2], while in the country the majority attain the age of thirty-five or forty years. As is the effort to live, such is the chance against existence. The pulsations of the heart of infants are about 140 in a minute; hence the purity of the air is more particularly necessary to infants. Cities are fatal to men of all ages. In Stockholm the mortality is as one to nineteen; while in Stoke-Damarel in Devonshire deaths are as one to fifty-four[3]. Yet it does also appear that towns are not mortal in proportion to their populousness. London

[1] vol. 1. p. 143.
[2] Percival's Works, vol. 2. p. 356. Bishop Hough says one-third.
[3] Percival's Works, vol. 2. p. 324.

is less fatal to children than Stockholm; and London may be still more improved, though it can never, I fear, be rendered equally kind to life as the country. Yet should London be dissipated, were it possible, and its people be planted on dry hills, because we are told the Macrobii lived on Athos[1]?

Besides the constantly greater consumption of life in cities, occasional mortalities are incomparably more numerous; they sometimes exhibit not merely deaths, but desolation. In 1771, in the course of nine months 56,672 person died in Moscow[2]; and it is remarkable, that neither in these nine months of mortality, nor in the six months succeeding, does a single birth appear in the statistical table.

What is pernicious to life frequently impairs generation, and that which escapes death is often imperfect. The natives of London are comparatively small. Here let me observe, that writers on population have disregarded the different characters of man, as animals and as intelligent beings. They talk of population as of abstract numbers, though ten times the number may not have half the strength of another nation[3]. Colquhoun says[4] (it is no calculation), that when he was inspector of the balloted militia, twenty-five or thirty were under size in London. It would appear that as London increased in people, it decreased in *men*. Fitzstephen says[5], that

[1] Polyhistor, lib. 1. c. 17.

[2] Tooke's History of Russia, vol. 1. p. 602.

[3] As when the youth have been cut off, or the men leaving women and children, &c.

[4] On Indigence, p. 159.

[5] Barrington's Ancient Statutes, p. 108.

in Henry the Second's reign London could muster
20,000 horse and 60,000 infantry; yet in Henry the
Eighth's reign the muster did not exceed 15,000 men[1].
How many warriors could now be arrayed out of its
1,050,000 inhabitants, including major Sturgeon and
the six regiments of trained bands in its battle, I
cannot guess. The decline is not peculiar to our metropolis. Costanza makes a similar remark respecting Naples; which Giannone[2] pursues, saying, that
this city, which abounded with illustrious cavaliers,
could now (when he wrote) raise with difficulty one
thousand men completely armed. Naples is one of
the most populous cities in Europe. It is to be observed, that the reduction of the animal man does
not entirely depend on the extent of cities. The individual generally declines with the increase of numbers. Holland and Venice increased in people and
decreased in active citizens. How inferior are the
most warlike nations in Europe, considering their population and combatants, to the vilest tribe of savages! When France had 650,000 troops, Peuchet
computed that there was not one in seventy of the
whole population under arms. This, though excessive, is trifling in comparison to the armed people
of some of the dependencies of that country. Mil-
bert says that the white population in the Isle of
France is 14,000, of whom 3000 are capable of
bearing arms. Yet this is exceeded by its neighbouring island. Orme[3] says, that the families settled
in Bourbon have multiplied to 4000, of whom 1000

[1] Hume's History, vol. 4. p. 271.   [2] lib. 24. p. 277.
[3] vol. 1. p. 93. History of Hindostan.

are capable of bearing arms. This is again outdone by the Indians sixty miles from James' Town [1]. Of a population of 5000, 1500 were warriors; and the Belootches, consisting of 20,000 families, sent 10,000 horse into the field [2].

Capital cities may be comparatively immoral. I speak doubtfully of this:—yet they afford facilities, provoke the appetites, and equally minister to vice and its concealment. In London is aggregated all that is absurd and fantastical, abject and insulting, fraudulent and false; plotters and counterplotters, impostors and prostitutes; whores and mystagogues. "And upon her forehead was written Mystery, Babylon the great, the mother of harlots and abominations of the earth [3]."

The depredations committed in London of every kind are immense. It was said, that three-fourths of all the smuggling in England are effected through the port of London. The vice of the capital is so excessive that it overflows on its purlieus; and it appears that in one year Middlesex [4], which contains about the same population as Yorkshire, arraigned 1217 offenders, and Yorkshire 245. Yet we must not suppose that London, as a populous city, is peculiarly vicious. Crimes are committed at Pekin and Canton [5], which are unknown in minor cities, or in the country: and it appears from Bradford [6], that in Pennsylvania three-fourths of the convictions for

[1] Jefferson's Notes on Virginia, p. 139.
[2] Ayeen Akbari, vol. 2. p. 142.   [3] Rev. chap. 17. ver. 5.
[4] Colquhoun's Police of the Metropolis, p. 613.
[5] Duhalde, vol. 2. p. 126.   [6] Opinions, &c. p. 268.

robbery, burglary, &c. were committed in Philadelphia the capital of the province. Thus the chief cities of the oldest and newest people, unhappily, concur in their criminal excesses. Hence, I may remark, the most injudicious opinions are formed of
nations. Individuals whose knowledge of the Spaniards was confined to Madrid, and of the Portuguese to Lisbon, condemned both, as base and profligate and incorrigible poltroons. They had only seen
the platform and steps and Corinthian capitals, the
frieze and cornice of royalty : but they had not seen
the people, the vassals[1], the audacious rabble, who
dare speak without faltering on the unblenched majesty of Spain, and of his *faithful* brother. The nobles, the king, as either Louis and their noblesse, fled
—while the basis of the columns and architrave remained.

" Iberia ! oft thy crestless peasantry
  Have seen thy plumed hidalgo quit thy side ;—
  Have seen, yet dauntless stood, 'gainst fortune fought, and died."

Victor Alfieri[2], Sir John Moore, Nelson, had
looked beyond the court and its minions ; had seen
the people,—and were true prophets of what they
could accomplish. The Portuguese at least equalled
the Spaniards. Mackinnon says of the former (and
it is delightful to bear good testimony for the oppressed), " At a distance from the capital I know
not any nation where there appears to be more pu-

---

[1] It is stated as a part of a penal sentence by the court of Lisbon,—that he *is divested of the honours and privileges of a vassal
and servant.* Ann. Register, 1759, p. 220.
  [2] Memoirs.

rity of morals than in Portugal." He also mentions, " The occupation of a servant is here by no means so degrading as in England and most parts of Europe." Can man for a moment think to whom and for what this people and the Spaniards are subjected, and not sicken when he reflects at the sad catastrophe to which England, at the expense of property and character, has boastingly reduced them ?

To the government, political depravity, and to this, extensive moral debasement, is directly referable. It is the custom of some princes to oblige their principal subjects to reside near their court. Such has been the policy of the Spanish crown ; such of Richlieu, who, under the show of annihilating warfare in the provinces, demolished all the chateaux ; and thus he actually drove their proprietors into the capital. This same capital became populous, that the crown may possess hostages for the allegiance of the aristocracy.

Such objections may be made to populous cities. Yet some of these evils are not necessary ; some may be palliated ; and others are in direct opposition to the assemblage of many men.

First : It is not necessary that populous cities should be more vicious than the country ; and I know villages that are comparatively more profligate than cities. No doubt thieves resort to the metropolis ;— so do they to forests and mountains, and to the frontiers of nations. In London, one of the great causes of subordinate profligacy is the destitution of all police ; or rather, as has appeared, by magistrates and their minions actually pandering to keepers of public-houses [1], whose company often consists of prostitutes and rogues. The nefarious partiality in the licensing magistrates, and in all those minor agents of order and equity, constables and thief-catchers, who prepare the crime and prompt wretches to crush them—have been exposed principally by the zeal and industry of Mr. Bennet. That populous cities abounding in property may be more honest than the country parts of other nations, I could believe. Fortunately the position is not conjectural :—the fact is proved by Mirabeau, who by the by, in a letter [2] to Frederic Guillaume of Prussia the Second, on his accession to the throne said, " Sans doute encore il faut limiter l'étendue des villes, où il se crée, par l'excessive population, un nombre de choses qui corrompt tout." Mirabeau alluded by this observation to Berlin : yet the same writer speaking of another capital declared [3], " Amsterdam contient plus de deux cents mille ames. Je mets en fait que c'est la grande ville de l'Europe, où il se commet le moins d'assassinats et de desordres ; j'y ai resté dix mois, pendant lesquels on n'a compté qu'un seul meurtre et très peude vols considérables." There are reasons why Amsterdam should be more vicious than Berlin :—it was more populous, there was a perpetual tide of strangers ; and the floating property of Amsterdam equalled the fee-simple of sterile Prussia. Yet the bare difference between a monarchy with its vices, and a state though

[1] Vintners and prostitutes are classed together by the Hindoos. Moor's Hindoo Infanticide, p. 167.

[2] Appended to l'Histoire Secrete, &c. t. 2. p. 326.

[3] Lettres de Cachet, &c. t. 1. p. 223.

declined, yet possessing the institutions of a republic, produced this contrast; for the police was much more rigid in Berlin than Amsterdam.

The mortality of towns may be greatly reduced ; and it has been so in London, by opening the leading passages, by the allineation of the streets, by preventives against the spread of diseases.

The third objection directly contravenes the expectable result from large associations of men ; for instead of weakness, they should be a security against tyranny. "The people," said Demosthenes [1], "being singly inferior to many individuals, who are supported by their friends and their opulence, associate to resist their insults and oppression." Hence originate those unions which vicious governments force the people to assume in their self-defence, and which such governments assail by laws and their infraction. Men confederate in hamlets, hundreds, towns, cities, and states, to resist foreign or domestic outrage. According to Strabo, when the Carians by sea and the Bœotians by land wasted Attica, Cecrops, to protect, collected the people into twelve cities ; and it is said Theseus [2] concentrated the inhabitants of Attica in Athens for their further security. It is certain that the Athenians, who were the most free, had the reputation of having first built towns [3].

Men are indisposed to live in strict associations, which cities imply, because men would be free : towns

[1] Adversus Midiam, p. 626.

[2] Pausanias, lib. 1. c. 22. Stephanus de Urbibus, p. 27.

[3] Πρωτοι γαρ Αθηναιοι τα αστη και τας πολεις εὑρειν ἱστορουνται. Stephanus de Urbibus, p. 28 ; and again, p. 131.

require regulations; to these men would not submit except to avoid greater evils. This opinion is supported by the human disposition and by facts. Elis was sacred and inviolable on account of the games; in consequence the people were so rural, that Polybius [1] says many of them did not visit the capital for two or three ages. Probably men would no more live by choice in cities than in fortified castles, or travel in caravans: yet in the ninth and tenth centuries this was the only secure mode of travelling in Europe; and until the accession of Henry the IVth in France, the mansions of all country gentlemen were fortified.

Danger is of different kinds. The kings of Europe were awed by their confederate conquerors, and to protect themselves they instituted many towns. Henry the Fowler, who began to reign in 920, built towns, ordering every tenth man, says Robertson [2], every ninth man, says Pütter [3], to remove from the country to them. Otho in the tenth century encouraged the citizens to form themselves into communities, in order to control the power of the court. Barbarossa and Philip the Gross pursued the same policy: so did Ximenes [4] on being appointed regent of Castille. Some of the British kings followed these examples; whether by imitation of the continental sovereigns, or that similar circumstances induced similar measures.

[1] lib. 4. The people of Epidaurus were the same, and called for that reason κονιποδες, "dusty feet." Plutarch. Moral. p. 176.

[2] Charles the Fifth, No. 17, p. 208.

[3] Germanic Constitution, b. 2. c. 2.

[4] This was altered after his death, and caused much confusion. Townsend's Travels, vol. 1. p. 200.

As men associated (I speak not of family connexions) from danger, and submitted their private will to general discipline, cities confederated for the same cause;—such originated the Grecian and Ionian confederacies, the associations along the Rhine, in Swisserland, the Hanseatic league, and the like.

Fear or danger operated in consolidating the less and greater aggregates of men. In Corsica the houses are collected in villages [paeses]. Boswell [1] says, In no place are the houses scattered as in England. Sir J. Steuart [2] makes the same remark respecting the difference of living in France and England, and he attributed it to the insecurity of the French. And Hume [3] supposes that the decay of towns complained of by parliament in the reign of Henry the Eighth, if true, proceeded from the greater security, which enabled the people to leave the provincial towns and reside in the country. Whether my conjectures be just or not in this particular, I have no hesitation in believing that cities tend to strengthen the people, though they have frequently effected their subjection. Yet their good effects have been evinced by the instances I have enumerated: and it is remarkable that Pisistratus was not less anxious that the Athenians should retire from Athens, than the friends of liberty had been to compact them together. Mr. Mitford [4], of course, the patron of tyrants, refers this conduct to his loving-kindness and patriotism. What was the object of James the First in repelling the great English proprietors from London, I cannot aver: he has been

[1] Corsica, p. 21. [2] Polit. Œconomy, vol. 1. p. 102.
[3] History, vol. 4. p. 277. [4] History of Greece, vol. 1. p. 271.

praised, among his animadversions on that topic, for saying, " England will shortly be London, and London England [1]."

Lest I should be mistaken, I say distinctly that I favour large cities :—they, with all their imperfections, tend to strengthen the feebleness of individuals, and relieve the many from oppression. A populous city commands respect by its multitude, and the most populous city is commonly the least abused ; which proceeds as much from the numbers of the people as from their being the seat of government. Constantinople is an instance : " The rajahs there have been denominated free and happy, when their condition has been compared with that of the tributary subjects, who are placed at a greater distance from the centre of this vast monarchy [2]." In some respect, then, it is not inaptly called " the refuge of the world [3]." It is not only the capital that is so distinguished : Volney speaks of the chief cities of the provinces as the only places that escape the tyranny of the seraglio [4].

Citizens are much more alive to their rights, have a quicker apprehension, and are more on the advance, than country gentlemen and their rustic companions, " whose talk is of oxen." " Pardon me, Phædrus [5]," said Socrates, " I am anxious to learn ;—trees can teach me nothing, but men in a city," &c. Voltaire

[1] Hobhouse says, One person asked him whether England was London, or London England. p. 594. The wisdom of a king is often folly in a subject.

[2] Thornton's Turkish Empire, vol. 2. p. 19.

[3] Hobhouse, p. 820.

[4] Voyage en Syrie, &c. t. 2. p. 268. Walpole says the same of the people of Asia Minor. [5] Plato, Phædrus. Opera, p. 1211.

urged Marmontel [1] to visit Paris, " seule école du
gout où peut se former le talent." In towns there is
every opportunity of improvement; the mind of each
is multiplied by the intelligence of all. What a fond
wandering creature is a rural genius in our times! We
have seen a politician, a poet, and a preacher, who
lived and loitered in the fields, and made vertigo their
divinity. In general, country-people continue their
prejudices longer than their fashions, in which they
are always unfashionable. They not only want taste
but knowledge; they cannot know, for they have not
seen, have not heard. Thus while France generally
had escaped from the bondage of *le grand monarque*
at Paris, and the monarch at Rome, the inhabitants of
the Bocage,—where there is no great town, few small
ones, and little intercourse,—worshipped their priests,
and adored the Bourbons as fervently as the English
Jacobites did James the Second.

Though I favour cities, I object to every prerogative, privilege, and favour towards them. The seat of
government unavoidably collects many: but when a
court and an accredited nobility are superadded, the
evil is increased without any countervailing advantage. These great proprietors distress each other in
efforts of prodigality. The rents of their tenants [2] are

[1] Memoires, t. 1. p. 162.

[2] Sir J. Steuart says, " The high price of most things in large
cities is surely a benefit, not a loss, to the country." vol. 1. p. 54.
Every one has heard of a fête by such a one, and the claim on the
tenants to pay up, to enable the master to provide the fête : What
good is this to the country ? A hundred tenants are pressed to sell
their grain prematurely, that the proprietor may produce fifty
dishes of insipid things out of season.

raised, to supply their senseless profusion; their lands are mortgaged; and thus those who rivalled the prince in waste, become paupers—eventually state paupers and royal parasites. This happens without one atom of good, without a memorial of their folly. Yet I remember one: a commander of the forces in Ireland, Sir John Irwin (I note the idiot's name for the honour of all great captains), exhibited at an entertainment to the Lord Lieutenant, the siege of Gibraltar in confectionary, which cost 1500*l.*

The flocking of seigneurs to the city is a pernicious increase to the capital; and Sully was sincere in wishing that the noblesse should live on their domains [1]. Yet the evil was as necessary in that monarchy, as absentees from Ireland under the double exhaustion of a foreign monarchy and an expatriated legislature.

Another cause of increasing illegitimately the capital of England, is the national debt. The funds oblige a large portion of the population to reside in the capital; and this for various reasons.

Another cause of the increase of London is the concentration of the East Indian trade, which alone is supposed to occupy 50,000 persons. Had this accumulation originated in the absolute liberty of commerce, which swelled the trade of Leghorn; or had it arisen from the lowness of the customs, which increased the commerce of the United Provinces,—there

---

[1] Il desiroit sur-tout que la noblesse habitât dans ses terres. Thomas, Eloges, t. 3. p. 340. Mezeray says of this minister, He retrenched in his office all little tricks and projects, and made it appear that to discharge his office there was only wanting diligence and a knowledge of vulgar arithmetic. Anno 1599.

could be no objection to it; the abundance would then have been a boon: but on the contrary it depended on a monopoly.

London is a great manufacturing town; and this has been effected in some cases by favouritism. Indeed towns have been specially favoured at the expense of the country. The 25th of Henry the Eighth enacted that cloth should be manufactured only in certain towns, which was intended to prevent country tradesmen from exerting their industry. The corporations which were opened in the former reign, were reclosed [1], and they continue so. These are the principal causes of the excessive increase of London. Yet it does not now bear a greater relative proportion to the state than it did in Davenant's time [2], if he were accurate, who computed its inhabitants at a tenth of the whole kingdom.

Cities have originated in superstition [3], and many have been enlarged by its operation; as Mecca, Jerusalem, &c. The Jews were obliged to come to Jerusalem [4] three times a-year, to thank God, and to maintain a friendly correspondence with one another. Such congregations were not unknown in Egypt. Herodotus [5] speaks of one at Bubastis, where seven hundred thousand people beside children assembled.

[1] Hume, vol. 4. p. 279.　　　[2] Works, vol. 1. p. 52.

[3] Niebuhr. Pinkerton's Travels, &c. vol. 10. p. 75.

[4] Josephus, lib. 4. c. 8. There is a sort of a New Jerusalem at Tromsoe. Many of the parishioners have fifty English miles to travel to hear divine service. Every proprietor in the parish has a wooden hut near the church, where he resides with his family during his devotion.　　　[5] lib. 2. c. 60.

Such is Benares, where the rajahs have resident ambassadors purposely to perform ablutions, &c.

If such be onerous and absurd, the custom of sacrificing the provinces to the capital is not less pernicious. Constantinople, which arose out of the ruins of the world, is supported by general depredation. When it wants provisions, says Volney [1], ten provinces are famished to afford it a supply. In Paris, it has been the practice to sell bread cheaper than the true price; the government, that is the nation, affording the means of this partiality.

Neither should any general tax be imposed, nor should any sums be diverted from the public funds to supply the capital with accommodations, as for constructing water-works and the like; nor with theatrical exhibitions, as at ancient Rome, and which is now common in all the capitals of the continent : the theatre at Copenhagen is said to cost the state 60 or 70,000 dollars. Nor should the public money be employed in building churches. The chancellor of the exchequer menaced the nation with applying the public money to build churches in the city. This is to make the Protestant church something more than a national establishment; and is in every view a gross perversion of public property. If the people of London want churches, why do they not provide them themselves? Are they not able? Are not the members of the Protestant church established by law far more opulent than Dissenters, who are barely tolerated?

[1] Voyage en Syrie, t. 2. p. 237. See Thornton also, vol. 2. p. 23.

Yet the Dissenters—the rejected—without property or honour or office, out of their proper funds have raised more temples of worship than those of the national establishment, whose sons possess all things. Yet this is not all :—Why should churches be built by the nation for the London clergy? James the First[1] declared, " The sickness and decay of all churches since the beginning of the world, have been pride, ambition, and avarice :" and he was right. And Dr. Hickes spoke also truly, " I would never have any clergyman govern himself by the practice of the clergy in London, where I may say as Justinian said of Rome—" Non quæ Romæ facta tam spectanda sunt quam quæ fieri debent." The purpose of Mr. Vansittart, which for that session was defeated by the misery of the finances, was iniquitous. This Christian chancellor of the exchequer should take a lesson from the Turkish law, which does not permit the sultan to appropriate to pious uses any part of the money consecrated to the necessities of the state[2]. Nothing should be built or supported in the capital at the nation's expense, which was not directly national.

[1] Basilikon Doron, p. 38.
[2] Thornton's State of Turkey, vol. 2. p. 44.

CHAPTER IV.

Population neither forced nor defrauded not alarming—population to be encouraged—how—natives and foreigners admitted absolute liberty of entry and egress.—Iniquitous conduct of the English government.—Error of Gibbon on the policy of some ancient states, Roman, Athenian, &c. respecting their increasing their population from abroad.—All not criminals to have the same right to labour, and trade, and sojourn—foreigners not to possess civil authority, except in extraordinary cases.

I DO not fear population which is not forced nor defrauded ; I fear bad government, conquest, and its consequences. Why should a nation's inhabitants,—I speak not of individuals,—overbreed their resources? The power of communicating life must always be controlled among rational beings, not by vice and misery, but by intelligence, by self-interest : selfishness alone would anticipate the summary destruction by vice and misery, unless we conclude that the human kind are among the lowest animals, worse than summer-flies, whose noisome offspring quicken amidst putrefaction, and perish amidst the ruin of their birth. I favour population as a proof (unless under peculiar circumstances) of good laws, or rather of laws and government not intolerable. As I favour population, I would promote the increase of men by an equitable distribution of property, by equal and authentic laws, an œconomical and a prompt distribution of justice; and by a constitution founded on common consent and universal utility, embracing each man's power, and all men's sagacity. As for the direct means of populating, which I have enumerated, by penalties, by bounties, immunities, and the like, I should as soon recommend Hermes Trismegistus, or advocate the *multiplying* of gold and silver.

Let the lowest species of labour be uncontrolled, and all the prime necessaries of life be untaxed; let each man labour when and where and at what rate he pleases, and let him look to his own exertions for his maintenance: until this be done, society is bound to provide for the wanting in their distress. The government has made the people what they are: and having distorted them to their fancy, they must continue to support them; as they trained them to dependence, they must uphold them. Every man should be perfect master of his time, his motions, and his labour; and the lowest labourers should be exonerated from every charge, directly or indirectly, on their food, clothes, and accommodations. If these be taxed, the tax must be returned in some way; or manufacturers and labourers must decline, and ultimately disappear.

The first concern in every state should be the labouring people; they should be free to adopt any profession in any place that suited their ability and wishes. This liberty should be granted to natives, and to all people. I am equally against soliciting foreigners, or repelling them: to repel the stranger, is only less hideous than banishing citizens iniquitously:—it may be worse, as it is a breach of hospitality. It was a dogma of pagan charity, "The stranger and the poor are from Jove."

To repel strangers is churlish, cowardly, and savage. The greatest barbarity is to kill strangers. Such it attributed to the Scythians [1], who, it is said, sacrificed

[1] Philostratus Tyan. Vita, lib. 6. c. 20.

them to Diana; and to Busiris, an Egyptian king, who wished to render his country inaccessible by such outrages. The next is the seizure of strangers, and enslaving them. Adelan had advanced beyond this stage; as Bruce[1], on offering him a present, said, "I will not refuse it, but it is quite unnecessary. I have faults like other men, but to hurt or ransom strangers was never one of them." Are we thence to infer, that presents from strangers are a compromise for forfeited freedom[2]? The next step, if it should not have preceded the former, is the utter rejection of foreigners. The Galla[3] admit no strangers to live among them: and the Abyssinians, while they admit them, resist their return[4] The Chinese suffer the entry of foreigners with great difficulty and various precautions, and it appears that they utterly exclude women. Bell[5], who was attached to the Russian embassy by land, says, that as it was about to pass the frontiers, the conductor, on seeing some women in the fields, said " they had women enough at Pekin already; and as there never had been an European woman in China, he could not admit them without a special order from the emperor." What was a surmise of the Chinese conductor is law in Japan. Tombe says, that on a ship approaching Japan, it is visited in order to ascertain that it does not con-

---

[1] Travels, vol. 5. p. 193.

[2] I fear that it is not a mere conjecture. Barrow mentions, that at Tonqueen, strangers, to free themselves from the exactions of insolent courtiers, become adopted by some potent citizen, to whom they make presents, &c. Pinkerton's Travels, vol. 9. p. 668.

[3] Bruce, vol. 2. p. 407.   [4] Bruce, vol. 2. p. 287.

[5] In Pinkerton's Travels, vol. 7. p. 365.

tain women or books[1], " for the approach of any woman, or the introduction of any book into this island,
is severely prohibited by law." This we call monstrous: and yet there was an English law, which prohibited, not the entry, but the exit of women, because
they were popishly inclined[2]. And in the Scotch law,
Mackenzie mentions, among crimes punished arbitrarily, " bringing home of erroneous books, and the
troublers of churchmen[3]." This miserable jealousy is
confined to particular places in particular countries.
The sanctuary at Mecca is reserved for the eyes of believers : and respecting Constantinople, " no foreigner
is allowed to reside in the city itself, not even the
minister of a friendly nation[4]."

No nation has exhibited more caprice and contradiction than the English, in respect to populating from
abroad. While foreign artificers were encouraged by
law[5], as by the 14th and 15th Henry VIII., strangers
using any handicraft, whether denizen or not, were
prohibited from taking an apprentice, or having more
than two journeymen, unless they were natural-born

[1] The books, I suppose, regard religion. The entry and translation of such books are censured by the emperor of China in Sir
G. T. Staunton's Chinese Code. When Langsdorff was at Japan,
all acts of religious worship by the embassy were prohibited.

[2] I quote this on the authority of the late Lord Stanhope's speech,
July 3, 1812, who knew more of law than the House of Lords
all together. If I mistake not, he alone protested against the last
war, when England was free to determine.

[3] Institutions, &c. p. 390.

[4] Hobhouse's Travels, p. 824. This, he says, is not of ancient
usage, but of modern policy.

[5] Reeves's Hist. English Law, vol. 4. p. 229.

subjects : that is, foreign artisans were requested to
enter, but they were disabled from teaching their sons
their profession. By the 25th of the same king, and
re-enacted by the 33d, c. 4, strangers born were excluded from working in pewter. Nonsense, absurdity, and contradiction ; whether these laws regarded
peopling, or promoting domestic industry. Again, by the
13th Geo. II. c. 3. foreign seamen serving two years
upon proclamation in time of war were naturalized ;
and by 2 Geo. II. c. 39. foreign protestants serving
two years in America were naturalized also. Yet with
these efforts to win the service of foreign soldiers and
sailors, England continues the most hideous of all
conscriptions—pressing,—which incites British sailors
to abandon their country for any other; for none can
be more hostile to man's interest and dignity, than the
British government is to the safe and sincere defenders
of the empire.

Later times have brought a no less serious charge
against the hospitality of England. Some years since,
about the time that the crown and judicature achieved
their joint exploits against Muir and Palmer, when
military torture was exercised in Ireland on many,—
for which some were nobly paid, and Judkin Fitzgerald knighted[1],—Napper Tandy fled from Ireland to
Hamburg; and contrary to the law of nations he was
demanded from that submissive city, and seized, forced
back to Ireland, and capitally condemned. In this
spirit the war was pursued at home ; and in the temper it began it has ended. By a system of outrage and

[1] Verres did not worse;—yet how did Cicero dwell on one Roman citizen being beaten !

lying, the English ministry helped to re-impose a Bourbon on the French throne[1], contrary to their proclaimed intention and the manifest wishes of the French people. To support this measure, certain individuals were to be abandoned to the vengeance of the intruding government. To this universal hostility against a few men; to this eagerness of crowned heads to seize and commit to the vengeful enemy,—compare the conduct of the town of Rotterdam, respecting Charles the Second's demand, through his minister, for the apprehension of Joyce, who had seized Charles the First at Holdenby, and carried him to the army. But Holland, though verging to a monarchy, was still a republic: it was then as were the free states of Greece, which equally increased in power and people by their easy access and general humanity. Temple[2] specifies, among the causes of Holland's extensive population, " the esteem in which it has passed, of being a refuge to men miserable at home, or persecuted by their own government."

How different is England now that she has leagued with despots[3]! Certain miserable men shall live only in the three great military prisons, Russia, Austria, and Prussia. To this she has re-enacted the alien

[1] Let no one suppose that I favour Bonaparte; I always abhorred him. He did much good; but he would just as soon have done evil, if such would have served his selfish views. The friends of our ministry are Bonaparte's associates:—both hold no sympathy with mankind.

[2] Works, vol. 2. p. 439.

[3] It is in common hatred of liberty. The patriots of South America were refused protection by the English officers at Curacoa and Trinidad,—which they found from Petion.

bill. The confederacy of the magnanimous allies has reduced the people of Europe to that lamentable state, under which it laboured during the Roman empire, when all men were linked together by one chain. The triumphant comparison by Gibbon between modern and ancient Europe has ceased; while the eulogium on the British,—that by Magna Charta they made the freedom of foreigners a portion of domestic liberty,— has become, by the alien bill, a stinging reproach. Yet let it be remembered, that the alien bill preceded but a little the bill for the suspension of the habeas corpus; and if in ancient times the barons made the rights of strangers and natives a common cause, their substitutes at present have attainted the rights of both together.

The alien bill is contrary to Magna Charta, to the 27th Edward the Third, which ensured to merchant strangers and others free entry, a safe sojourn, and an easy return. Why should the pride of Englishmen be so sadly humbled? Lord Liverpool the minister said, "it was not safe that Great Britain should be overrun with foreigners." Yet the amount of this overwhelming body was, according to the computation of Mr. H. Addington, (one of the warmest advocates of the bill,) not more than twenty thousand individuals; a number considerably less than the foreign mercenaries in England, who are employed by the crown contrary to the laws of the land and all laws of prudence; as foreign mercenaries ever have been, and must be, the satellites of despotism. This alien bill (the perniciousness of which no man can apprehend who knows not the jeopardy and terror with which it struck foreigners) was re-enacted in peace, when all the European powers were banded against one man and his baffled and expatriated adherents. Amidst songs of triumph on the 31st of May, 1816, it was passed, on the same day that in the committee of supply 40,000*l.* were voted by the titular representatives of the commons of the empire to the royalist emigrants from France. What a perversion of honour and interest! To prevent the possible entry of a few French unfriendly to the Bourbons, the British ministry obliged their creatures in parliament to subvert the national institutions and stifle the calls of humanity. At the very time that the British nation was menaced with insolvency, and while the ministry rejected the emigrants of one French party, it received and pensioned those of another;— it continued to pension the royalist emigrants, when their king of kings was restored. Excellent ministry! triumphant people! who fought for twenty-five years that a Bourbon might reign, and succeeded by chance, at the expense of honour, truth, and national solvency. There never was an act more disgraceful, more unfeeling, more dastardly and despotic, than this; and it substantiates an observation of Montesquieu, whom the overweening English love to quote, That the English, should they lose their liberty, will be among the most degraded slaves on the earth[1], most degraded! Rome, when basest[2], refused to return the

---

[1] S'ils venoient à la (liberté) perdre, ils seroient un des peuples des plus esclaves de la terre. liv. 2. c. 4. Esprit des Loix.

[2] Socrates Scholasticus, lib. 7. c. 18.

refugees from Persia, though claimed by the Persian king.

Having spoken so much on the generous and just conduct of nations respecting the admission of people from abroad, I wish to notice an error of Gibbon; and certainly not so much to disabuse the reader of his pages, as to redeem the injured from unmerited censure, and to advance a liberal policy among nations. The historian of the "Decline and Fall of the Roman Empire" says: "The narrow policy of preserving without foreign mixture the pure blood of the ancient citizens, had checked the fortune and hastened the ruin of Athens and Sparta. The aspiring genius of Rome sacrificed vanity to ambition; and deemed it more prudent, as well as honourable, to adopt virtue and merit for her own, wheresoever they were found—among slaves or strangers, enemies or barbarians." This is one of those ambitious passages in which extremes are violently associated, and truth ingloriously sacrificed to effect.

The exceeding hospitality of the Romans, and afterward their undistinguishing reception of strangers, are problematical;—the first in fact, the latter in policy. On the authority of Cicero [1], among the ancient Ro-

[1] t. 4. p. 345. Park comparing the Moors and the Arabs:—This wandering and restless way of life, while it inures them to hardships, strengthens at the same time the bonds of their little society, and creates in them an aversion towards strangers which is almost insurmountable. Travels, p. 159. What was Romulus, and his troop? Gika, the present king of the Caffres, was surprised when he was remonstrated with for the murder of the shipwrecked Englishmen. He said he could not understand any impropriety in the act; as, being strangers, they had no more right

mans *enemy* was equivalent to *stranger* : " Hostis apud majores nostros nunc peregrinum dicimus." The facility of incorporation is also questionable, when we reflect that the plebeians were prohibited from connecting themselves with patrician families. Did not the Lex Fusia Caninia and the Lex Ælia Sentia, &c. designedly obstruct the manumission of slaves? And was not the Social war caused by the indisposition of the Romans to admit the people of Italy to the fellowship of the Roman state? These at last won their right by force, and were distributed into eight new tribes [1]. So much for one portion of Gibbon's praise of Roman policy. They afterward, it is true, did admit promiscuously all descriptions of people [2]. But how did their conduct deserve his encomium respecting their adoption of *virtue* and *merit ?* Cicero [3] laments that the right of citizenship was granted not only to individuals but to provinces and nations. Dion of Halicarnassus says [4], it was conferred on robbers and prostitutes, and on every wretch. This exhibits in a lively manner the adoption of *virtue* and *merit* wherever they were found.

to enter his country than wolves. The Missionary account says, Gika was estimable in many respects.

[1] For security to the old, after whom they gave the votes, &c. Paterculus, lib. 2. p. 20.

[2] Data cunctis promiscue civitas Romana.   Aurelius Victor de Cæsaribus, p. 133.

[3] t. 2. p. 602.   50.

[4] Οἱ μεν απολησειας και τοιχωρυχιας και πορνειας και παντος αλλου πονηρου χρηματισαμενοι, &c. lib. 4. c. 24. Dion Cassius says, This right, which was once sold so high, might now be obtained for a trifle. lib. 60. c. 17.

As well might he praise the armies of Rome, when they were composed of foreign mercenaries [1], of Carthaginians [2], of Gauls, Syrians, &c. The fact is, that when Rome became *colluvies omnium gentium*, (a miscellany of the refuse of mankind,) it reverted to its original inanity—" imaginem urbis magis quam urbem fecerat : incolæ deerant [3]."

In Gibbon's contrast of the Greeks, he is equally erroneous. The Spartans adopted slaves by hundreds ; to incorporate foreigners they were averse, as were the Megareans, who boasted that they never admitted any one except Hercules and Alexander. But, generally speaking, the Greeks were free in communicating the *city* to men of desert [4] : and with respect to the Athenians, the historian's contrast is absolutely fantastic. Buzyges, who taught the use of the plough at Athens, execrated those who did not receive foreigners with hospitality [5]. Hospitality was praised by Theophrastus [6]; and Strabo enumerates this virtue, especially in his eulogy of the Athenians [7]. They enrolled the refugee Platæans [8], they incorporated the Gephyreans [9] whom the Bœotians had ex-

[1] Tacitus, Annal. lib. 3. c. 40.

[2] Herodian speaks of a Carthaginian who was consul. lib. 7. c. 377.   [3] Florus, lib. 1. c. 1.

[4] Cicero pro Archia Poeta, t. 2. p. 387.

[5] Or, who did not show the way to one wandering. Petit, L. Att. p. 557.

[6] Recte etiam in Theophrasto est laudata hospitalitas. Cic. t. 4. p. 383.

[7] Athenienses autem, sicuti reliquis in rebus, hospitium et externorum studiosi perstiterunt, &c. lib. 10. t. 2. p. 53.

[8] Auger's Lysias, p. 70.   [9] Herodotus, lib. 5. c. 57.

patriated : they admitted not only individuals but tribes. Thucydides says [1], that formerly the Athenians were free in conferring the right of citizenship : but he adds, it has been otherwise, latterly, on account of the multitude. Observe the progress of the Athenian and Roman states: Rome lost its people as it advanced, and no means could recruit them ; while the Athenians so increased that they were obliged to limit their accustomed generosity ;—for liberty declined at Rome as it advanced at Athens. Though the Athenians through necessity became select in their incorporation of foreigners, they always with alacrity cherished the votaries of popular liberty ; and were not less exemplary for being a common refuge for the miserable, than being the resort of philosophy, literature, and all the arts.

On the topic of entertaining foreigners with reference to population, it is obvious that in new planted countries every facility and encouragement should of course be granted to settlers : but as the population thickens, the want being remedied, the same facility should not be continued. I object to all prerogatives granted to strangers in any circumstances. It is said that Ferdinand, to encourage the silk manufactures, placed foreign artificers on the same footing as native Italians, and that they should *be sued only before their own consuls.* This, Giannone [2] says, induced many artificers to resort to Naples ; and in 1480 he pursued the same course with respect to workers in woollen ; and that one half of the inhabitants of Naples was supported by the profits of these manufac-

[1] lib. 1. c. 3.   [2] Storia de Napoli, lib. 27. p. 386.

tures. The propriety of this is doubtful, though it succeeded. Besides, it supposes a bad native government, for which I do not write : for, were the government equitable, would not this be sufficiently attractive to artisans? I would not even invite professors of the liberal arts, as Julius Cæsar [1] did, by granting them, as of course, the privileges of citizens. The masters in the liberal arts are surely among the most distinguished, yet an ingenious man may be a bad citizen.

Is it not obvious that all prerogatives granted to strangers prejudice the native citizen, and are a sort of fraudful solicitation of foreigners to abandon their country? The practice of England to gain sailors during a war, by the promise of naturalizing them, is of problematical advantage, and of course it causes re-action. Neither was the conduct of Lysander creditable; who proposed to increase the pay of the sailors in order to induce the mariners to withdraw from the Athenian fleets. Pericles treated a similar attempt as "a weak device of the enemy [2]." What! said that statesman and orator, do you fear they will abandon us for a few days' pay? Yet this was a temptation: but the promise of naturalization in England as a boon seems egregiously absurd. Why should a foreign sailor wish to become even a native British sailor, who is subjected to the harshest of all conscriptions? I have seen a petition of one (not a sailor) in this country to be disnaturalized.

I also particularly object to sudden and mighty incorporations; though it is said the 200,000 Egyp-

---

[1] Suetonius, lib. 1. c. 43.   [2] Thucydides, lib. 1. p. 96.

tians who settled in Ethiopia civilized it[1]; and though there are other accounts of wonders performed for nations by accessions of foreigners. It is to be remarked, that foreigners are less prolific, and more subject to complaints, than natives. It is so in Russia[2] and in the West Indies, it may here be remarked, that a country-born negro or negress is valued at double one imported[3].

It should be considered that a good citizen must possess peculiar knowledge, must be acquainted with the laws and institutions of the country:—How can a stranger obtain this intelligence? I speak not of a necessary defectiveness in the love of country in new-adopted citizens; for that affection which is not founded in knowledge is a blindfold passion. How are those who possess the right of granting admission to understand his pretensions? For these reasons, the most liberal nations have required a period of apprenticeship or probation preparatory to civil incorporation. Few, however, have been satisfied with mere residence. The Venetian laws required three years' abode[4]—" Firmum domicilium et habitationem cum familia"—to be assured by the state only; that is, to a right of residence. The French, when most disposed to profuse hospitality and excess in all things, required five years' residence in the republic:—" Et qui en outre ont épousé une Française ou acquit un

[1] Theagenes et Chariclea, p. 206.

[2] Tooke says that stillborn children of native women in Russia are seven in a thousand; of foreign women fifteen in a thousand. History, vol. 1. p. 540.

[3] Steele and Dickson, &c. p. 160.   [4] De Statutis Venet. p. 263.

immeuble, ou formé un établissement de commerce, ou obtenu dans quelque ville des lettres de bourgeoisie, sont reputés Français[1]." The Athenians in the strength of the commonwealth had various degrees of association; all were entertained who came, all were secured : but they had domiciliated strangers, to whom were assigned guardians or patrons to protect them, and to secure the state[2]. A person to be a citizen must have been a native by father and mother; and no one could be naturalized who had not transferred himself and family for ever to Athens[3]. He must have had considerable pretensions, either as an artist, ($\epsilon\pi\iota$ $\tau\epsilon\chi\nu\eta$[4],) or as having been a public benefactor[5]; he must also have been first admitted by the senate, and his admission confirmed by six thousand Athenians. Nations cannot be too circumspect in adopting foreigners as active citizens. There is a medium to be respected between those kings of Egypt who repulsed all, and Psammetichus who adopted all. All persons should be entertained who conduct themselves becomingly; all professions should be open to their industry; and all should have liberty of trade and commerce : but to interfere with political matters, this should not be granted except in rare and extraordinary cases. Length of residence may justify the admission to minor interests, but for the higher they must be incompetent[6].

[1] Decret du 30 Avril 1790. Code Français, partie 2. p. 280.
[2] Petit, L. Att. p. 170.   [3] Ibid. p. 129.   [4] Ibid. p. 425.
[5] Ibid. p. 130.
[6] Thus there are various distinctions in our laws; alien friends, —denizens—naturalized. So among other nations, the Athenians, the Jews, &c. some strangers were " hospites justitiæ," who were

The conclusion I draw on this point, relative to population, is the same respecting every other topic connected with this subject,—that good government will be sufficiently attractive.

CHAPTER V.

No cause of fearing over-populousness.—Should people exceed, why not migrate ?—Mr. Malthus.—Colonizing.—India,—the effects of that country on the commerce and opulence of Great Britain.—The British in India, and on their return.—The monstrous and confused government of British India.—Its ruinous effects in India.—The remedy suggested to convert the Hindoos to Christianity.—The government despotic; yet considered, particularly by Sir W. Jones, as necessary, and appointed by Providence.—The vices of the Asiatics referable to their governments.—The Asiatics equal to the Europeans proved, by examples from ancient and modern times.—The Hindoos no way peculiar—yet they must be treated as no other people ever were;—exemplified —No colonization; no community of interest, language, &c.—What should be done in respect to India.—I no advocate for colonizing.—Colonies seldom succeed.—Losses by West Indian colonies to Great Britain.—If colonies be planted, to be treated with the utmost liberality.—Ancient opinions on that subject.

But may not a nation become too attractive, and thus become uncomfortably multitudinous? May not the people, as according to Mr. Malthus, over-breed, over-populate their means of subsistence? I have read

" pari jure cum Israelitis." Grotius de J. B. et Pacis, lib. 1. c. 1. § 16. A stranger by becoming a Jew lost all kindred with his Gentile relatives. Selden, c. 16. Circumcision was the formality of being admitted. In later times, among Christians, baptism. Gipseys induct their converts by rubbing or dyeing the face with walnut oil. Annual Register 1797, p. 128.

(and I wish to give Mr. Malthus and his school all the advantage they can derive from my reading) in Hero·dotus, of a people who were, in respect to their starving condition, not unlike the generations of men who now hugely press against the limits of subsistence. The historian says they were greatly oppressed by famine; that they sported and starved every other day alternately. "Thus they lived for the space of eighteen years: but when the calamity remitted nothing of its violence, but rather increased, the king divided the whole nation into two parts, one of which was to continue at home and the other to emigrate[1]." Why may not our reprobate people, if they be excessively numerous, pass abroad? Mr. Malthus indeed says[2], " Europe affords no resource by emigration, as its states *have nearly all rather a redundant than a deficient population.*" Yet are all other quarters of the globe full? If Mr. Malthus thinks so, they are full to him as Banquo's chair was to Macbeth. The conduct of our wise men fixes the same belief on them, for they have adopted the last remedy—war; "which," Hobbes says, "provideth for every one by death or victory[3]." Theirs is the heroical check; it is of great antiquity and celestial descent. Wars, says Chrysippus[4], were instituted by Jupiter—the Saviour, the Generator, the father of *justice* and *peace*—in order to purge states of their population; and he quotes Euripides, who attributed the Trojan war to this necessary purgation. Could any theologian among the

---

[1] Herodotus, lib. 1. c. 94. [2] vol. 2. p. 69.
[3] Leviathan, part 2. c. 30. [4] Plutarch. Moral. p. 468.

modern Babel-builders comprise more contradictions in fewer words?

We have tried war; and whether it was entertained directly or indirectly against the people, it has been a remedy without a relief. Millions have been *killed off* (to use Mr. Windham's business-like expression), yet after twenty-five years' war we have not been comforted, nor have any of the belligerents gained *more food or room* by the general desolation.

I then ask, *if* we are over-populous, why do we not transplant our superfluous people? Plato furnishes a hint for transplanting a supernumerary population, and affording them at the same time the benefit of war. "Those," said he, "who through want of food are willing to enlist themselves under a leader, and to assail those who have abundance; let those deadly enemies of the state be expatriated under the honourable title of a colony[1]."

Of all countries, though many have vacillated in their colonial policy, the British have been most contradictory. They persecute or dishonour a large body of their subjects, yet obstruct their departure. In 1762[2] a proposal was made by certain Catholic lords to raise five regiments of Catholic Irish for the king of Portugal. This was resisted by the Irish parliament,—that is, by the English government,—while all means were employed to waste and exterminate the Catholics. Still the emigration of the Irish is obstructed. Some time since no American vessel could take more passengers from Ireland than one for every

[1] De Legib. lib. 5. p. 845.   [2] Annual Register 1762, p. 76.

five tons burthen;—now I believe one passenger is assigned to every three tons. This, to be sure, was intended for the convenience of the Irish emigrants: and thus the government, which never performed a just act unforced to the Irish at home, watched over their accommodation in their farewell passage across the Atlantic. Yet observe, when the British government proposed transplanting Wurtemburgers to South Carolina, the advertisement for shipping rated the individuals according to the tons; and two hundred persons were the complement for a ship of two hundred tons[1]. It is difficult to say whether this is more iniquitous or absurd. The Irish are treated as no people so circumstanced ever were treated : persecuted at first, then rejected, always belied and scorned and pillaged. They are solicited to remain at home by accounts, fabricated by the authority of government or under its auspices, of the uncomfortable state of the laborious in America, while they are precluded by the ratios of tonnage and passengers. This conduct seems as much to spite the Americans as to harass the Irish. Yet the government wishes to encourage settlers in Canada[2]; and here again the Irish are discredited. In short, the Irish are only fit to live in Ireland, under martial law and the curfew, and hear praises of their inimitable constitution.

This is one instance of the contradiction of the British government; and their foreign policy is a suite of similar outrages. England, which has been as fond of colonizing as its gentry of travelling, (for which I

[1] Annual Register 1760, p. 195.
[2] Strachan's Letters to Lord Selkirk.

sincerely honour them,) granted permission to Captain
Beaver to colonize Bulama; yet the colony was prevented from sailing, though every step to its final
equipment was undertaken with the knowledge of Mr.
Pitt, because a *constitution* for the colony was framed
and published for the management of the settlers.
Captain Beaver says[1], that the government had no objection to the sailing of the colonists without any constitution. Thus it appears that a constitution was as
alarming as Jacobinism; the friends of social order
dreaded a new constitution at Bulama, and actually
preferred anarchy to the chance of order.

As the French revolution had thus paralysed the
brave and stupified the wise, American independence
effected a counter policy in Britain to Asia. Formerly
England, when she ruled America, adopted every
mode to increase its population: so late as the 13th
of George the Second, foreigners were invited to the
American colonies by a law naturalizing them after a
residence of seven years[2]; and for the same purpose
lots of land were granted to sailors, soldiers, and
officers, in 1763. Sir W. Young[3] not inaptly characterized the British government in saying, " I know
of no instance of a Spaniard, Portuguese, or Dutch-
man, colonizing other than national settlements; but
the English seem colonizing mad—they would colonize for the French, for the Dutch, for all the world:"
and they continue this phrensy. Having possessed
Gibraltar, they must make another step in advance.

[1] African Memoranda, p. 18 and 19.
[2] Annual Register, 1763, p. 21.
[3] Colonial Common Place Book, p. 182.

Malta falls to them in the grand bustle. This is called our bulwark in the Mediterranean. This bulwark is again dependent on other countries for provisions, to secure which different writers have advised England to possess itself of Sicily. England is obliged, however, to be contented with patronizing the Ionian Isles, and increasing its strength, by extending its dominions; and its resources, by adding to its expenditure : but then they increase patronage [1], and employ an army of 10,000 men.

In another direction the English have been equally apt to colonize. How many British settlements there are at this side of the Cape of Good Hope, which is called our *grand outwork of India* ; and how many more on the other side, on the way to the *work* itself, it is unnecessary to enumerate : but in India the passion of colonizing is neutralized. In India no colony can be planted; and no Briton, generally speaking, is admissible. Then why rail at the jealousy of the Spaniards respecting the South American dependencies, which their timid policy happily cannot secure? or at the precautions of the Chinese? for the conduct of the British is more suspicious and dastardly than both. It is worse than that of the Sodomites [2], one of whose crimes was hatred of strangers ; for the British government in India is averse to their own countrymen, and repels them. Lee Lewes was sent back from India by Lord Cornwallis in 1788, because he had not obtained the special permission of the Court of Directors at London.

[1] Austria enjoys every trading advantage possessed by England.
[2] Josephus, lib. 1. c. 11.

We are told that the Anglo-Indian government is wonderful. Yes, truly! a few merchant-adventurers obtained the privilege of a factory, which China will not grant to our fraternizing government; and Bombay became held of the English crown by the East India Company, as *part of the manor of East Greenwich in the county of Kent*; just as beyond the Atlantic a portion of the world is reputed, if I mistake not, part of the see of London. Wonderful truly! and thus sixty millions of people in the opposite hemisphere are possessed by two thousand individuals in England, whose right of dominion consists in their possession of ten millions commercial capital, which sum does not equal one-third of their debts; that is, in right of a bankruptcy of more than twenty millions, two thousand insolvents, called proprietors of stock, command 380,000 square miles, and sixty millions of people.

This oligarchy elect twenty-four directors, six of whom vacate their places annually by rotation. Over these, or under them, (for they are like Trinculo in his viceroyalty,) is the Board of Control [1]. This arrangement may be called the maximum of British sagacity; as by it the happy balance of the constitution is

[1] This famous Board (Mr. Creevey says) while he was secretary, for fourteen months, did not meet, nor had there been a Board for twenty-two years before. Yet the Earl of Buckinghamshire, 12th July 1814, chairman of the Board, sent to the chairman of the East India Company, suggesting that pensions of 5,000*l*. a-year should be granted to the Marquis of Wellesley and Lord Melville; and that Lord Melville's debts, 20,000*l.*, should be paid :—and all this as contrary to law, and to the nature of a Board of Control, as a curb is to a spur.

trimmed with improved felicity. For, said **Mr. Pitt** and his party, if the patronage of India be granted according to Mr. Fox's bill, the minister would be greater than the crown. And anon, said Lord Castlereagh in his circumlocutories, if the crown possessed the patronage of India, this would be dangerous to our liberties. How interested for liberty! Hear this, his country, Ireland—and Norway, and Genoa, and Italy, and Ragusa, and Europe. This very man, who had been convicted of exchanging a place in India for a seat in parliament for his creature Lord Clancarty, talks thus, and is endured! When did not the ministry command the patronage of India? General Smith, before the existence of the Board of Control, stated, " it was notorious that for years past there had not been a single appointment in India which was not managed by ministers [1]." And Lord Melville, in 1806, affirmed in the House of Lords, that the exercising at pleasure the power of recalling the governors of India, *enabled his majesty's ministers to gain the entire patronage of India.* Yet we shall be told, India is not dangerous to our liberties; and that Pitt's bill, or Castlereagh's bill, operates as a patent engine to suspend India between the Gothic scales of our surprising constitution. What a world is this, when Lord Castlereagh, whose merit consists in a subterfuge for talents, can deprive matter of its weight and man of his passions! Then say, that falling bodies, which hitherto have declined to the *East*, as they partook of the rotary motion of the earth, fall plump down,—for a wise and veracious minister said so.

[1] Parliamentary Debates, 1781, p. 404.

Much praise has been justly given to the resolutions of the Commons in 1782, which were followed by corresponding resolutions by the Court of Directors; and to the acts of parliament of 1784 and 1793, which decided, " that to pursue schemes of conquest and extension of dominion in India, are measures repugnant to the wish, the honour and the policy of this nation [1]." Yet what has been the consequence? Though the law required that no hostile measures even of preparation or alliance should be effected, before the territories of the Company were attacked; yet every successive war has been waged in utter contempt of such laws and orders. Indeed, Sir John Malcolm stoutly affirms, that India has been saved by disobeying them. Thus Hastings, Cornwallis, Wellesley, and the rest, have constantly disregarded the home government and the imperial law: yet amidst this mighty disobedience, how exactly they followed the orders of their employers, when Lee Lewes, a poor player, was not permitted to fret his hour on the stage, but was rejected from India, as had he sinned against Louis and legitimacy! Thus has the government in India proceeded from war to conquest; from violence to spoliation; from interference to absolute dominion. But (say the friends of the Company) the acquisition of territory has been *forced*

---

[1] It was also stated by the court of France, long since: " Il seroit avantageux que les compagnies de deux nations aux Indes Orientales s'abstenissent à jamais de toutes vues militaires et de conquêtes, pour se restreindre et s'entr'aider dans les vues de commerce qui leur sont propres," &c. Mably, Droit Publ. t. 3. p. 274.

on them. This is just the *suite d'événemens* [1] of which the French East India Company spoke, and on which Bonaparte acted. It is difficult to understand the morality of that government, whose existence depends on universal domination. Sir John Malcolm speaks intelligibly in saying, It was gained by the sword, and by the sword we must maintain it.

As at home, the Directors and the Board of Control divide the civil authority over India. India is ruled by two incongruous military forces, the Company's and the King's; the partiality shown to one of them occasions enmity, jealousy, and dissension. Yet because the King appoints the commander of his troops, and the Directors nominate the commander of theirs, the eulogists of " things as they are," insist that this was wisely conceived, for it does not *halve* the responsibility, but *doubles* it. Perhaps, as we have heard of the ingenious mode of preventing the patronage in India from affecting even-handed Justice, who always holds the balance of our wonderful constitution, these adverse military establishments operate as the centrifugal and centripetal forces on the planetary system. At all events we are told the government is good;— that of this there can be no doubt, for it has been successful. What has been its success? It has in half a century overrun a great tract of Asia. If this be a subject for moral gratulation, fall down before Alexander—raise a temple to Tamerlane—call the " locusts [2] warping on the Eastern wind," harbingers

[1] Mably, Droit Publique, t. 3. p. 347.

[2] Buchanan speaks of a flight of locusts three miles long, a hundred yards wide, and fifty feet thick : they overspread every thing.

of the divine presence; and the simoon the divinity itself, for it is swiftest of all created things, and its breath is destruction.—What has been the success of Britain in India?

First consider the individuals who pass to India. They go—but their object is to return. Yet it appears by official documents, that the mortality of the British in India was as eighty-three to one. Mr. Grant computes the present mortality as four out of five. Mr. Forbes is more detailed: In 1755 he went to India with seventy-four gentlemen: of these, in 1777, three only had returned to England with fortunes; forty-eight had died in India, of whom eight had acquired or were acquiring fortunes when they died; but twenty-five had died bankrupts; the other fifteen were in indifferent circumstances. Thence it appears that the chance of these fortune-hunters to return to England is desperate, and that two fail for one who succeeds; yet the chant and chorus is the riches derived from the East, because now and then a wealthy individual returns from India, who plants and drains, and builds, and levels;

" Diruit, ædificat, mutat quadrata rotundis."

If such incidents prove a boon to the nation, then was the assessment of the crown revenue in France a national gain; for farmers-general made the same exhibitions through France in a supereminent degree, as nabobs do in Britain. Calculate the expense of the rearing and education and the outfit of all those who escape to India; kill nine in ten of them; let two parts be bankrupt;—why the survivors who return to England should have large fortunes, barely to indemnify the nation for the expenses and losses on all those who passed abroad and perished. Of those who escaped death and bankruptcy, and who return enriched, what joys do they feel or communicate? They have been unmade for Europe; they are puling valetudinarians, sickly and unsightly—a Lascar cast among the British people. So much for the Indian-British as individuals.— Let us now consider India in reference to Great Britain in its commercial relations.

The Directors asserted that their ships were excellent for the warlike defence of commerce : they were tried when William Pitt alarmed the English, and they were found insufficient. The Directors also insisted " that the trade of their company has been highly beneficial to the public, in affording a nursery for seamen in time of war." This,—if the Directors were capable of jesting,—might seem a satire on the law for burying in woollen, as serving the British staple :—this nursery for seamen is their grave.

The India trade the Directors have repeatedly declared to be a positive loss; and to such extent that it would be intolerable without the exclusive commerce with China being secured to the Company. Can such a system serve Great Britain? With respect to the China trade, the ordinary teas cost the Company from eight-pence a pound to two shillings at Canton [1]. Yet at what enormous prices are these teas sold in Great Britain and Ireland! The enhancement arises partly from the duty. This payment

[1] Barrow's China, p. 573.

into the exchequer the East India Company credits
their trade: as if teas could only be had through
their means; as if the duty was not paid by the
British consumer; as if the enhancement of the price
of teas was not in a considerable degree to support
the ruinous Indian trade of the Company,—which,
like all other companies, would lose, though private
traders should gain. It is farcical to talk of the de-
licacy of regulating the Chinese trade. American
republicans trade to Canton without a company: and
there are reasons equal to the jealousy of the Chinese, why private traders would be better received
than the servants of the East India Company. Yet
we are told of the advantages which the nation derives from this Company, when the whole trade of
Calcutta does not equal the present reduced trade of
Bristol. These exaggerated statements have induced
the continental writers to consider the East Indies
the source of British opulence. Suppose the Indian
trade employs 115,000 tons of shipping, navigated
by 10,000 men. The ships rot, the men are destroyed, and the *produce* is confessedly a *loss*, for
which loss the Company is indemnified by the exclusive commerce of China. Thus tea-drinkers are
taxed to support the Company: and they are informed that the bad teas are not brought to market, but,
sunk at the Nore. This is precisely the consolation
afforded by the Fishmongers' Company: they, generous souls! are anxious that the London epicures
should have nothing but the daintiest fish; yet it has
been ascertained "that whatever fish arrive beyond

the extended demand of the fishmongers, *however fresh and good*[1], is thrown into the Thames and destroyed before it reaches Billingsgate."

We come now to the English in India[2]. Those who go abroad from England are boys[3], who have made some progress in a nondescript seminary between a school and a college. From scholastic extravagance of all kinds, they proceed directly to exercise absolute power in civil, military, and judicial departments over sixty millions of men ; without any knowledge of man or government, and entirely ignorant of those whom they are deputed to manage. It was proposed to educate in India those intended to conduct the affairs of India : but this was negatived, principally lest the governors might thence acquire certain sympathies with the governed. Yet we are told by a Lord and traveller, of the blessedness of the East India Company's government. The eulogium is not unlike a Persian poet's address to Sir John Macpherson[4], "exalted as the sky, prosperous in thy undertakings, who like the sun receivest even atoms on thy beams. I have composed a poem in words of truth, beginning with a panegyric on the

[1] I do not mean to insinuate that the East India Company destroy their fresh teas : teas keep, and they supply the market to uphold the price.

[2] Mrs. Graham signifies that the white people in India are vulgar and ignorant. India, p. 134. The Quarterly Review says, The manners of the British are much changed for the worse. No. 23, p. 183.

[3] Aristotle holds that a young man may be a good mathematician, but not a good politician.

[4] Sir W. Jones's Life, p. 324.

Company." Some do not speak so poetically : Lord Cornwallis said the government of the East India Company " was sound and good for all practical purposes."—To the facts.

It is stated as an act of wonderful abstinence, that no European should possess lands in India. Nor could a Welshman formerly have purchased lands in the next English counties [1]. Yet who ever praised the generosity of this law? When the Athenians prohibited any Athenian from holding land beyond Attica [2], at the same time that they returned to the ancient proprietors all the land which they had conquered from them, they acted wisely, and were honoured for their disinterested conduct. But what relation has the British legislation to the Athenian? The non-appropriating interdict is part of the non-colonizing policy, and this proceeds from monstrous jealousy. The Indian British are not proprietors, but usufructuaries. Their conduct and their self-praise on this point resemble the egotism of the Jewish priesthood. The law was divided among the tribes; but *the tribe of Levi received no land, the Lord is their inheritance.* Yet mark the difference between the Levites and the British in India; the former received through godliness the largest share, but the British receive the half of the produce of the soil. Mr. Richards [3] made this statement in 1813

---

[1] 2 Henry IV. Law Dict. vol. 2. p. 755.

[2] Diod. Siculus, lib. 15.

[3] He said, (if the newspapers reported truly,) that the zemindars receive one half, that the government took 10–11ths of that half.

in the House of Commons. The self-denying ordinance, then, is merely an act begun in jealousy and
ending in rapine. If this be the amount of their
magnanimity,—what is the merit of the government in
points which are not prominently displayed or di-
stantly insinuated?

It is impossible that this government can be good;
it is of foreigners, of boys who go abroad with the certainty of not settling in the place of their government,
who leave their own country for the sole purpose of
money-making, and who are induced by their greediness, and their suffering from the climate, to quicken
their rapacity, that they may be enabled as soon as
possible to recoil on Europe. The state of the country
confirms the account: The government *broke promise* with the ryots[1], who are consigned to the mercy
of zemindars—creatures between Irish agents and middlemen. The Company squeezes the zemindars, who,
as in Ireland, double their snake-folds round the farmers; and as they had their flesh bruised, they break the
bone. Take one characteristic specimen of the effects
of this boasted government. Buchanan says, that
in Bengal the crop cannot be cut till the rent is paid;
and that in other places, though cut, it cannot be removed[2]: that is, the farmers are obliged to pay in advance; to insure which, the crop is of course distressed or impounded, to the danger of the whole crop or
its injury:—in consequence, the people are literally
ejected. Considering that men hardly live under better
treatment, it is inconceivable how life is continued

[1] Tytler's State of India, Introduction, p. 16.
[2] Pinkerton's Travels, &c. vol. 8. p. 574.

under such rapacity : every thing, however, declines ;
no new houses are building, and the old are in ruins.
Tytler has specified many towns and villages that are
in various gradations of dilapidation[1]. Buchanan[2], in
his journal, says, " The country is exceedingly bare,
and the population scanty; all the houses are collected in villages :—the smallest village of five or six
houses is fortified[3]." Dacoity or gang-robbery is admitted universally to have increased. Thus it happens, that in Bengal, which Bernier[4] thinks the most
productive country in the world,—and he specifies his
reasons, where "less than half a penny procures enough
of turmeric, spice, salt, and ghee, to season the whole
rice eaten in a day by a labourer and his wife and
five or six children ; the vegetables and acids that he
requires are found in every hedge[5];" even here, with
this facility of living, this people, *mild, laborious, and
patient,* says Niebuhr[6] : so patient, says Lord Va-

[1] Observations on India, vol. 1. p. 375 et seq.

[2] Pinkerton's Travels, &c. vol. 8. p. 587. The favourers of the
Company contrast their government with that of the Moguls. Suppose it better,— what merit could they derive from this comparison ?
It is certain that what is here said by Buchanan, is said by Bernier
of the Mogul's territories. Pinkerton, &c. vol. 8. p. 135. Forster
says the same of Persia, when most wretched ; that the smallest
hamlets are surrounded with walls, as a shelter against robbery.
Ibid. vol. 9. p. 308.

[3] Yet Lord Hastings said in his last speech at the College of Calcutta, "We have reared the bulwark of security round the humble
hovels of the helpless." Times Newspaper, January 17, 1818. Thus
his lordship re-edits St. Pierre's Chaumiere Indienne ;—all is less
secure, crimes increase as the population has become more poor.

[4] Pinkerton's Travels, &c. vol. 8. p. 226.

[5] Graham's India.   [6] Travels, c. 155.

lentia, that during the whole of the great famine [1]
they permitted the grain to pass through their villages
to Poonah, though their inhabitants were perishing
with hunger;....yet this people, in this productive country, are forced into gangs of robbers, and the population and cities disappear: this is the *blessed* government, *good for all practical purposes.* We talk of
Negroland, and Huggins and Hodge;—look to the
Molimgres or salt-boilers, a numerous population, who
suffer the most hideous slavery under the Bengal government; they are forced to work at this trade, and
a cordon of troops surround them to prevent their
escape: but the government derives a large income
from this monstrous tyranny. Can any government
be worse, and have subjects? What worse can befall
subjects than to live thus miserably, and thus prematurely perish?

What is the remedy? No one has taken a hint from
Mr. Malthus's project for relieving the miserable Irish
—to feed them on the dearest grain. No, the Indians
must be taught the divine precepts of Christianity;
they believe in Juggernaut, and some of them are as
superstitious as the Christian convulsionaries, and fall
down to be crushed by the idol's chariot[2]. The present Christian bishop of London only requires a *pro-
stration of the intellect.* Some Hindoo wives also burn
themselves with the remains of their husbands; yet
this is confessedly no part of the religion of Brahma.

[1] A famine probably attributable to the government. In the
Quarterly Review, No. 23, p. 194, &c. it is said, The Malabars are
often subjected to hunger by dearths, which the government rather
than the seasons occasion.

[2] This idol affords a revenue to the Company.

It is easily frustrated. Bernier says [1] he stopped a widow, who was determined to burn herself, by telling her she would thus leave her children without father or mother. Some parents of certain sects also exposed their female infants; yet, as I have said, Col. Walker's simple appeal to the humanity of the parents ended the practice. It appears, then, that the Hindoos are not unreasonable; yet they are to be reformed by being converted to Christianity. And for that purpose, the government at home, ever attentive to the wants of the people, lately sent Dr. Middleton to India under the title of bishop of Calcutta;—no doubt he will be as effective as his brethren in England [2]. To the bishop and his suffragans, missionaries have been recommended, who have been as resolutely opposed by the East India Company. When permission was asked from Governor Duncan for a missionary to go up the country, he answered, To be sure: but let him begin with the presidency, and first let him make Padre Burroughs (resident chaplain) a Christian:—this to be sure was before the episcopal appointment. The fact simply is, that the Company's servants are afraid that the missionaries would be too zealous, and endanger all things; and Dr. Buchanan, the star in the East, when he says " It is the duty of a Christian na-

[1] Pinkerton's Travels, &c. vol. 8. p. 177.

[2] As all this recalls the puritanical times, why do we not first christianize our own country? Sir Thomas Bernard supposes that two-thirds of the population of London know no more of Christianity than the Caffres. In the puritanical æra they began at home, "Every Friday ordered for debate how the gospel might be preached in some dark places of this kingdom." Whitelocke, p. 222. 275.

tion to propagate Christianity as long as a nation shall be found upon earth which is ignorant of it," does not give much security for their discretion[1]. This rage for converting the Heathen is new to us. In Willoughby's directions for his people, nothing transpires of that passion[2]. in the puritanical times also, I only remember an account of four men of Somersetshire, who had an immediate call from God to go and preach the gospel in Galilee[3]. Yet now we have 208 missionaries in active service, and more may be expected; as the Rev. Mr. Daltry, in his speech prior to dismissing four missionaries to India at the beginning of the year 1814, reminded them of the words of our Saviour, " The labourers are few, but the harvest is great." Whatever be the intention of the missionaries, whether this world or the next; whether they are to be classed with John Kelsey[4], who went in 1769 to Constantinople to convert the Grand Seignor, or not,—this is certain, that there are more vouchers for the virtues of the Hindoos[5] than for the morality of British Chri-

[1] Colonial Establishment, p. 431. Archdeacon Nares spoke of thousands of Brahmins being converted. Mr. Waring so curtailed this number that the Archdeacon recanted, and attributed his error to Dr. Buchanan's Memoir on the Expediency of a Church Establishment in India. It appears that in seven years they made 109 converts, called *rice* Christians. This has been called proof of their diligence and success; yet Joanna Southcote had 40,000 believers.

[2] See item 22. in the Ordinance for the Crew.

[3] Whitelocke, p. 454.   [4] Annual Register 1769, p. 297.

[5] Niebuhr says, " All who have opportunities of observing the lives of the Hindoos admire their patience, probity, and benevolence." Travels, c. 155. Col. Monroe speaks of their hospitality and charity among themselves, their tenderness and attachment to the women, among the particulars in which they exceed the Bri-

stians in or out of India; that there are infinite causes
of dissension; that the two orders of military have
little concord; that the ryots are discontented ; that
the peons, by being deprived of their pikes and dag-
gers, are equally dissatisfied, and more dangerous ; and
that the mutiny at Vellore was, according to Lord
Teignmouth, in some measure occasioned by the apprehension that Christianity would be forced upon the
natives: and what occasioned the insurrections at
Mundy-droog, Palam-cottah, Benares, and Banga-
pore?

Such is church and state in Hindostan ; and it is

tish. In Dekkan, containing 300,000 people, the numbers convicted for ten years did not amount to nine annually ;—in one year
in our capital they amounted to 1663. Sir H. Montgomery. Abu
Taleb was surprised that the houses in England were kept shut
through fear of thieves. Barrow says, " I give full credit to all that
Mr. Vaillant has said with regard to the fidelity and attachment he
experienced from this race of men, of whom the natural character
and disposition seem to approach nearer to those of the Hindoos than
any other nation." Tytler, who is least kind of those not missionaries to the Hindoos, admits that they possess " patience, mildness,
obedience, hospitality, sobriety, temperance." Observations on India, vol. 1. p. 258. " They are neither quarrelsome nor revenge-
ful." Ibid. p. 304. " They are in general humane." Ibid. p. 304.
"Affection to relatives I have repeatedly witnessed, and often has it
induced me to love and respect the native." p. 310 He also speaks
with the highest praise of the honesty of house-servants, p. 310,
and in the first volume, " Servants in India will always be what
their masters make them; and if a kind master, you will probably
keep the same servants as long as you are in the country." vol. 1.
p. 68. Let the Hindoos be what they may, I perfectly agree with
Dr. Watson, bishop of Landaff, " I do not, indeed, expect much
success in propagating Christianity by missionaries from any part
of Christendom, but I expect much from the extension of science
and commerce." Life, &c. p. 198.

dogmatically insisted, that it cannot be improved. Yet these political necessarians express surprise that the Hindoos believe in predestination—the sad resource of those who overcome desperation; but it is wonderful to me, that the Hindoos should be doomed to eternal misery. When I heard Sir J. Malcolm's declaration, that the sword gained India, and by the sword it must be preserved; association recalled the Gordian knot. When I read Mr. Grant's statement, that the government of India "moves in a trajectory of its own,"I heard unmeaning monstrous phraseology. But when I read that Sir W. Jones predestinated and damned the Hindoos to everlasting subjection, I own I was surprised. He (alluding to the popular tract for which the bishop of St. Asaph was tried) says, "As to the doctrines in that tract, though I shall certainly not preach them to the Indians, *who must and will be governed by absolute power*[1]; yet I shall go through life with a persuasion that they are just and rational; that substantial freedom is both the daughter and parent of virtue, and that virtue is the only source of public virtue and private felicity." What does this announce? That the Indians are necessarily subjected to vice and misery. Whence the necessity of this thraldom? An opinion is too general, that the Asiatics are preordained slaves. I must resist this conclusion at some extent, but with the utmost brevity.

Agesilaus said[2], The Asiatics are bad freemen, but good slaves. This royal paradox is met directly by Xenophon[3], who attributes the vices of the people of

[1] His Life, by Lord Teignmouth, p. 288.
[2] Plutarch. Moral. p. 114.   [3] Instit. Cyri, lib. 8. p. 239.

Asia to their governors, as subjects assume their character from their rulers:—thus the Asiatics had declined from their former rank. Hippocrates also[1], though he refers something to climate, considers that they are milder and less warlike in consequence of their laws; the greater part of Asia being oppressed by monarchy. He says, Men who are slaves do not fight for themselves; and if they labour, they do not enjoy the fruits of their industry. To prove that these are the ruling causes for the disposition of these Asiatics, he adds, that Greeks and foreigners in Asia, who are not despotically governed, but who enjoy their own laws, are industrious and brave.——Now for facts.

No people of ancient times are more repeatedly contemned for their baseness than the Lydians[3]; they were the lowest ministers to luxury:—yet they were brave in Homer's age. Herodotus[3] also speaks of them as a hardy valiant race. But adds the historian[4], when they were conquered they were deprived of their arms; then they became impotent and dastardly. And Æschylus calls them an effeminate rabble[5]. They declined in every art and sentiment: their music, which had been spirited, was harmonized for softness and pleasures[6].

With the Lydians the Phrygians[7] were frequently

---

[1] Περι αερων, &c.

[2] Quis unquam Græcus comœdiam scripsit, in qua servus primarum partium non Lydus esset? Cicero pro Flacco, t. 2. p. 364.

[3] lib. 1. c. 79. Justin says, Gens industriâ quondam potens.

[4] lib. 1. c. 156. [5] Αϐροδιαιτων Λυδων οχλος. Persæ, ver. 127.

[6] Επιτηδειον προς Θρηνον. Plutarch. Moral. p. 439.

[7] Ælian. Hist. Var. lib. 10. c. 14.

associated for their common baseness, as the Phrygians were contrasted with the Arcadians : " Slaves from Phrygia, from Arcadia auxiliaries[1]." Yet the Phrygians were probably a military people, as the Phrygian harmony was reserved for warlike representations. The Cappadocians also were reviled by the universal voice of antiquity, for what now would be their eulogy; they preferred the rule of a king to a democracy. Cicero assails them with outrageous contempt; "sine sensu, sine sapore, elinguem tardum vecordem Cappadocem[2]." Yet the Cappadocian cavalry had been distinguished for their discipline and bravery. Cicero condemns the whole of Asia Minor to disgrace and slavery: Jews and Syrians, he says, were *natis servituti*[3]. He might as well have said, they were by nature eunuchs, as we learn from him that many Syrians were emasculated[4]. And though the Jews were *despectissima pars servientium*, they were once a warlike and conquering people,—a quality I abhor in them, and which was their destruction : but whether praised or blamed, the Jews and every other nation of Asia have been conquerors equally as the Europeans. Europe, Asia, and Africa have alternately triumphed : nor is it so long, that we should forget the subjection of a large part of Europe to Asiatics, and the danger of their absolute dominion over the whole continent. I speak now, however, of its ancient circumstances. Asia conquered, and was conquered by, the Greeks: it was conquered by the Romans, and under their

---

[1] Ανδραποδ' εκ Φρυγιας, απο δ' Αρκαδιας επικυρυς. Athenæus, lib. 1. p. 27.
[2] Opera, t. 2. p. 398.   [3] t. 2. p. 508.   [4] t. 4. p. 464.

chief governors it was miserably abused. Volesus[1], pro-consul to the god Augustus, struck off three hundred heads, and glorified himself as having performed a royal achievement. Under such mal-administration the people, of course, declined not less in virtue than in number.

Passing further into Asia, we shall find that the vigour of the people was impaired or destroyed by the wickedness and tyranny of their rulers. Xenophon[2] speaks of the warlike Chaldæans. Such were the Babylonians: they were subjected; and after an ineffectual effort to escape the yoke of Xerxes[3] they were disarmed, and then they abandoned themselves to trivial pastimes. Advancing still further towards Hindostan,—the cause of this brief digression in defence of a continent of people,—the Medes and Persians were distinguished for their indomitable bravery[4]. Prior to the battle of Marathon, they were the terror of the Greeks[5]. Herodotus also says[6], The Barbarians were not inferior to the Greeks in strength and courage: and Thucydides[7], that they were only surpassed by the Athenians in discipline. The Persians declined in their institutions: they had honoured truth and ab-

[1] Volesus, nuper sub divo Augusto proconsul Asiæ, cum trecentos una die securi percussisset, incedens inter cadavera vultu superbo, quasi magnificum quiddam conspiciendumque fecisset, Græce proclamavit: O rem regiam! &c. Seneca de Ira, lib. 2. c. 5.

[2] De Instit. Cyri, lib. 3. p. 71.   [3] Plutarch. Moral.

[4] Medes and Persians are confounded by Herodotus, lib. 6. c. 112. So were Cappadocians and Syrians, lib. 1. c. 72. lib. 7. c. 63. So were Syrians and Assyrians, &c.

[5] Herodotus, lib. 6. c. 112.   [6] lib. 9. c. 42.

[7] lib. 6. p. 459.

horred falsehood[1]; they were patient of labour[2]; devoted to exercise[3]; eating but once a day[4], and frugally this single meal[5]. They conquered the Medes: then their virtues were attainted; they became effeminate in their habits[6], incapable of fatigue[7], luxurious, plethoric[8]. The officers of the army were encumbered with trappings, the camp incommoded with baggage, the soldiers lost their hardihood, and the people became so base and parasitical as to express more anxiety for the safety of Xerxes than for the fleet and army[9];—and they were treated accordingly: for the Persian kings consigned to their many wives, different cities, which became tributary to the toilets of the women of the polygamists[10]. The monarchy debased the people, ruined their morals and institutions; the people became stupidly loyal, deplorable royalists. The Assyrians and Medes, said Philostratus[11], adore

[1] Herodotus, lib. 6. c. 138.   [2] Xenophon, p. 197.

[3] I have thought that the *houses of strength*, mentioned by Franklin the traveller, where men contend with clubs, wrestle, dance violently to music, may be remnants of the ancient education or discipline of the Persians. Franklin in Pinkerton, vol. 9. p. 243.

[4] Xenophon says so expressly. De Instit. Cyri, lib. 8. p. 240; and indirectly to have been the royal custom; as Megacreon of Abdera advised his countrymen to rejoice that Xerxes did not eat two meals in the same day. Herodotus, lib. 7. c. 120.

[5] Xenophon, p. 122.   [6] Ibid. p. 241.   [7] Ibid. p. 197.
[8] Ibid. p. 655.   [9] Herodotus, lib. 9. c. 99.

[10] Solere aiunt barbaros reges Persarum ac Syrorum plures uxores habere, his autem uxoribus civitates attribuere, hoc modo : hæc civitas mulieri in redimiculum præbeat, hæc in collum, hæc in crines, ita populos habent universos non solum conscios libidinis suæ verum etiam ministros. tom. 2. p. 132, in Verrem.

[11] Philostratus, Apoll. Vita, lib. 1. c. 35.

tyrannies. The government of Persia is still hideous; *espionage* is unrivalled in that sad country. Franklin says[1], " Freedom of conversation is unknown in Persia; as that ' walls have ears' is proverbially in the mouth of every one."

We have now reached India, which anciently was not enslaved. Socrates said[2], the Indians enjoyed consummate liberty: and Pliny[3] speaks of Indian nations which were not subjected to kings, but were freemen. Let us, however, abandon ancient records, and see if we cannot defend the right or pretensions of the Hindoos to freedom by existing circumstances.

This will be considered Utopian, romantic, reforming. Orme states[4], that " the richness of the soil of part of Bengal, concurring with the unelastic atmosphere, has debased the essential qualities of the human race ; and that the people are without industry, and without energy, and of a stupidity which neither wishes

---

[1] Pinkerton, &c. vol. 9. p. 258.

[2] Ælian. Hist. Var. lib. 10. c. 14.   [3] lib. 6. c. 20.

[4] vol. 2. p. 3 et seq. History, &c. Much in the same tone of philosophy Mr. Tytler says, " The mild and regular climate of their country, and the fertility of their soil, easily supplying their wants and making them averse to labour, the regularity and simplicity of their diet may account for the apparent laziness of the Brahmins and lower classes, which is as remarkable as the industry and activity of the middle orders." Then the middle orders live under a wholly different climate from the other orders. The causes of the laziness of the Brahmins are truly the causes of all prerogative laziness; and Mr. Tytler himself refers the true cause of the apathy of the lower orders to the zemindary system, concluding, " successive subdivisions to an unlimited extent thus enhance the rent of the land, and it at length falls on the actual cultivator with a weight which for ever crushes all hopes of gain." vol. 1. p. 317.

nor seems to be capable of extending its operation into any variety of mechanic dexterity." This is the materialism which never alarms the righteous. The doctrine of submission can never be wrong in causes or consequences. Here the dullness of the people of Bengal is referred to a rich soil and an unelastic atmosphere. Had this historian ever heard of Newton's conjectures respecting a vibrating æther? Yet this apologist for the British in India says, in the succeeding page, concerning these very people aërially predisposed to indolence, " that a dread of extortion or violence from the officers of the district makes it prudent in him to appear and *to be poor.*"

Another charge against the Hindoos is, that they are deficient in truth. Lying is as much the effect of tyranny, as poverty and stripes. The Greeks were so, but not formerly, says Cicero[1]; and he refers their deceit and acquiescence to their daily oppression. The Romans were sincere; but they became most false when overrun by the Barbarians[2]. Are not Jews throughout the world the victims of persecution and intolerance? Who but a fanatic imagines they are what they are by magic? Observe that Swinburne's account of the Mahometans in Grenada[3], as being extremely humble and smooth-tongued, is a counterpart of a description of the Jews; while in Greece the Christian personates

[1] Sin vero fallaces sunt permulti et leves, et diuturna servitute ad nimiam assentationem eruditi. Epistola ad Atticum, tom. 3. p. 402.

[2] Hoc solo id est quidvis luxuriæ, quidvis mendacii, imo quidvid vitiorum est comprehendens, &c. Luitprand. Muratori Script. Ital. tom. 2. p. 1.

[3] Travels in Spain, p. 170.

the Jew. " But," says Hobhouse[1], " I saw nothing in his face (though he was a Christian) of the cringeing downcast timid look of the Greek peasant." I may add, that the Mussulman in Grenada is another being when placed in other circumstances. Thornton says[2], " Honesty is the characteristic of the Turkish merchant, and distinguishes him from the Jew, the Greek, and the Armenian ; against whose artifices no precaution can suffice." The falsehood of the Hindoos Dr. Heyne properly attributes to their political servitude. Were they better governed, they would improve in sincerity; were they less tormented by exactions, they would be more industrious:—but Mr. Orme says they find it *prudent to be poor*. Indeed! The Hindoos seem to excel in industry. Captain Pottinger says of them, " whose indefatigable industry is conspicuous wherever they are to be met with."

I see nothing among the Hindoos which should consign them irremediably to British despotism. A considerable portion of the Hindoos are weakly;—considering their repeated conquests and the grinding oppressions of their conquerors, it is marvellous that they exist. Riley's narrative shows how a strong robust man may be reduced ; and what race could support its character after centuries of penury[3]! Yet still many tribes and nations remain in Hindostan to claim their rank in manhood : " The palanquin-bearers

[1] Travels, p. 99.   [2] Turkey, vol. 2. p. 197.
[3] Mr. Malthus says, " In most countries, among the lower classes, there appears to be something like a standard of wretchedness." And this he actually attributes to any thing but the oppression from above.

are called rhois, and are remarkable for strength and swiftness[1]. Mrs. Graham[2] speaks of tribes of athletæ who use thirty-two kinds of weapons. Of the athletæ at Mysore Wilks says, "The whole world does not produce more perfect forms." Orme[3], who says he wrote his History principally to give a just idea of the superiority of European arms when opposed to those of Hindostan, speaks thus, "Each horseman was attended with his groom on foot[4]. This servant in India is by habit capable of keeping pace for several hours with the horse, although going at a great rate." He says of the Colleries[5], that "they are tall, well-made, and well-featured. Their arms are lances and pikes, and bows and arrows, rockets and matchlocks; but whether with or without other weapons, every man wears a sword and shield. In battle the different arms move in distinct bodies; the lances are eighteen feet long."

Sir John Malcolm, in his Evidence, &c., thus testifies for the Hindoos of Benares and those of the interior: "They are not more distinguished by their lofty statures and robust frame of body, than they are for some of the finest qualities of the mind; they are brave, generous, and humane, and as remarkable for truth as courage." He lays a stress on those inhabiting the interior: and I perceive in Pinkerton's Collection[6], that while those along the coast and in cities are comparatively degraded, because the intercourse with their conquerors is there frequent and direct, those inland being less tormented by misrule are

[1] Graham's India, p. 128. [2] Ibid. p. 17. [3] vol. 1. p. 219.
[4] vol. 2. p. 166. [5] Ibid. p. 568. [6] vol. 11. p. 264 et seq.

eminently superior. The distinction is marked in the Alforese, who are removed from the coast, and who are brave and vigorous, while those who approach the sea are feeble and dastardly. The people of Hindostan are not very wretches: they are, when in tolerable circumstances, strong and vigorous; they do not want bravery. I have quoted unexceptionable authorities for the fact. According to Colonel Wilks, in single combat native officers are more than equal to Europeans. Lieutenant Pottinger says, The Scindeans are remarkable for personal bravery; so are the Sikhs; so are the Peons, haughty and warlike. Wathen relates, that an Englishman having hastily struck a Peon for improperly loosing a greyhound, the Peon, who was a Rajahpoot, immediately said, I am your servant and have long eaten your rice: he then plunged the dagger into his bosom. Bernier says[1] the Rajahpoots can endure much hardship, and only want order and discipline to be excellent soldiers. I trust I have done justice to the abused Hindoos; who have been represented, with all the Asiatics, as base born, mean in person, feeble in mind, poltroons, creatures made by God to be abused by the lordly Europeans, *who must and will be governed*, says Sir W. Jones, *by absolute power*; who are irretrievably indolent, says Orme, in consequence of *an unelastic atmosphere and the richness of the soil.*

> " Need we the influence of the northern star
> To string our nerves and steel our hearts to war ?
> And where the force of nature laughs around
> Must sickening virtue fly the tainted ground ?
> Unmanly thought !"

---

[1] Pinkerton's Travels, &c. vol. 8. p. 136.

Miserable philosophers! hateful governors! Sir W. Jones is not satisfied with *must and will*, and the dire necessity of absolute misrule: he makes Heaven a partner in this fated despotism. He says[1], " In these Indian territories, which *Providence* has thrown into the arms of Britain for their protection and welfare, the religion, manners, and laws of the natives prevent even the idea of political freedom." Then Providence has made us absolute masters of India; which mastery, he informs us,—and I have quoted his words,—ensures vice and misery! This gross contradiction, this execrable declaration, militates also against his general sentiments respecting mankind; as "it was a favourite opinion of Sir W. Jones[2], that all men are born with an equal capacity for improvement." To such extent will a little power and profit besot and stupify man's reasoning, apprehension, and principles. I declare I see nothing peculiar in the Hindoos:—oppression is the key to all their apparent obliquities. By craft and authority, a tribe, probably of foreigners[3], obtained dominion over the minds of this people, and their descendants still assume unqualified superiority. Formerly they reputed themselves gods[4], now they are

[1] Life, by Lord Teignmouth, p. 481. Sir John Malcolm, though a soldier, is not so horrible in his statements of the absolute necessity. He only regards their security to England. Yet sixty millions of people are little in the account of either. Political History of India, p. 459.

[2] L fe, &c. p. 489.

[3] Broughton says, " The Brahmins are fair, have prominent features and comely persons; the rest are dark, with broad full faces, small features," &c.

[4] Philostratus, Apollonii Vita, lib. 3. c. 18.

lower. "The cast of the Brahmins is the highest; even above that of the kings. They say they were formerly the kings of the whole country, and presume to this day the privilege of commuting capital punishment, when merited, by the loss of their eyes[1]." This is not peculiar; it is theocratic, and agrees with the pretensions of Druids, Levites, Jesuits, ecclesiastics, &c. When they were gods they could do no wrong, now they enjoy the *benefit of clergy*. I see nothing in their religion that is not common to a hundred sects. They recount the battles of their gods; and they appeal for its truth to the spots on the sun and moon as marks of the contest. They had gods also of a higher form, generated of purest æther[2]. They have their ceremonies, their creeds, their misgivings, their consolations, their fancies, their particular providences. The Hindoos, says Scott[3], regard the failure of rain a sign of Divine displeasure. It is usual in times of drought for the emperor, attended by many religious persons, to go out to pray for rain. Scott adds, they generally choose a time when the clouds are heavy and promise an accomplishment of their petition. They have their paradise and their hells, in which they exhibit an elaborate imagination. They have their penances and processions. Maurice says[4], drawing an idol in a carriage obtains a remission of sins. With a theme of super-human virtue they are often

[1] Orme's Dissertation, p 4.

[2] Αιθηρ ον ηγεισθαι χρη γενεσιν Θεων ειναι. Philostratus, &c. lib. 3. c. 34.

[3] Ferishta's History of Dekkan, vol. 1. p. 102, note.

[4] Maurice's Hindostan, vol. 1. p. 104.

absurd and contradictory. The Morattoes[1] would not kill an insect that molested them, yet they delight in war; and as an atonement for the blood of their species they sacrifice a buffalo, as others have sacrificed human beings.

These things do not seem to me to be extraordinary; and certainly I cannot perceive how their *religion, manners, and laws, must prevent even the idea of political freedom*, as Sir W. Jones dogmatizes. They are not more attached to their religion than other people: if they are tenacious of their customs —who are not? A Jew will not eat pork, and a Russian in Peter's time would rather lose his head than his beard. The Hindoos have already relinquished injurious habits: burning of widows has declined; Hindoo infanticide has ceased; the Hindoos leave their country; Sepoy regiments passed by sea to Egypt in 1801;—and thus they overcame their prejudices with respect to eating and drinking[2]. Did not the Brahmins submit their laws to be digested by an European[3]? The immovability, then, of the Indian character is fictitious. On this particular the change in the conduct and opinions of the Sikhs is conclusive. Goru Govind wished to extinguish the arrangement of casts, and to effect the equality of all the Sikhs[4],

[1] Orme's History, b. 1. p. 41.

[2] Macgregor's Medical Sketches.

[3] Lord Teignmouth says, " It may be remarked as an occurrence of no ordinary nature, that the professors of the Brahminical faith should so far renounce their reserve and distrust, as to submit to the direction of a native of Europe the compiling a digest of their laws." Life of Sir W. Jones, p. 391.

[4] See Asiatic Researches, vol. 11. They have so frequently du-

in order that each might be obliged to depend on his individual character and exertions. In consequence, from being the victims of inveterate prejudices, and stupid through fear and abuse, this people soon became free and warlike. I see nothing, morally, which prevents the Hindoos from liberty. Even now the associated chiefs of the Sikhs resemble the baronial state of Europe when the king was general. In other parts of India,—in that through which Buchanan travelled,—a council of elders seems to supervise every village or district. It is remarkable, that in almost every village there are schools; and that from these sources some facilities of teaching the elements of learning in Great Britain have been derived. Add to this, their disposition to peace, their industry, temperance, their aptness to imitate [1], and their adroitness in manufactures—executing the most delicate work with the coarsest materials. As I must believe that they would rather use better than worse instruments in manufactures, and that by them they would improve their fabrics; so must I believe they would rather be well-governed than ill-governed: and I am persuaded that their profits, and the profits of their

---

ring the last war crossed the sea, that this capital prejudice is effectually extinct. Tytler also speaks of a relaxation respecting casts—that an intermixture of trades and professions has commenced, and that education is now no longer confined to the higher casts. Observations on India, vol. 1. p. 250.

[1] This is of ancient remark: Ostendens præterea Indos valde studiosos esse circa artes. Dicit quod cum spongiam apud Macedones vidissent, mox eam sunt imitati, &c. Strabo, lib. 15. vol. 2. p. 464.

governors, would be essentially advanced by every amelioration of their circumstances.

This must not be granted, because it might endanger the dominion of England in India. This is heartless, selfish, rascal policy. What have been India's transgressions to Great Britain? India has not preached the rights of man, nor made visionary war on the British constitution. What has England gained by India, that England should be interested in upholding her wickedness towards India? It never afforded slaves, the grand object of England's commercial policy, when her politicians triumphantly obtained the assiento contract [1]. It has afforded no tribute;—while the military force, the marine, the Cape of Good Hope, and the other stages by sea and land to the East, consume much more than all the sweepings and savings of the few fortunate adventurers who escape death and bankruptcy. Suppose that Madras was El Dorado, and Bombay, the golden city of Cathay; that the Ganges were Pactolus; that the wars in the East, instead of debt and waste, produced more prisoners than S. Gracchus' [2] conquest of Sardis;—that the wealth transmitted to Great Britain by Hastings and Wellesley and Moira, equalled the treasures which Pompey sent to Rome on the conquest of Asia; and those which P. Æmi-

[1] By this treaty of 1750, all disputes between England and Spain were settled. Beawes's Lex Mercatoria, p. 511. Mably, the philosopher, laments that his countrymen did not participate in the slave trade. Droit Publique, t. 2. p. 394.

[2] S. Gracchus tantum captivorum adduxit ut longa venditione res in proverbium venerat, Sardi Venales. A Victor, p. 79.

lius transmitted on the conquest of Macedonia, which it is said relieved the Romans from taxation for 125 years; and those which Cæsar [1] carried to Rome on the conquest of Ægypt, which were so great that they effectually reduced the interest of money, and raised the price of land;—What then? should England support a tyranny, a grinding despotism, a suspicious miserable misrule, for money's-worth? We should, forsooth, risk our dominion by a liberal policy; " Eh bien! périssent les colonies plutôt que les principes!" said Barnave, the eloquent and strenuous friend of liberty. But we gain nothing. Gain! we lose much. This Eastern empire has grievously perverted the independence of the people of Britain;—it is a source of immense patronage to the crown;—it affords a retreat to those who can conscientiously enjoy a bribe payable abroad: And this is its value.

What can be more miserable and suspicious than the British government in India? No one must enter this Eastern world, though largely inhabited by Moors, Arabs, Persians, Portuguese, Guebres, Tartars,—except he has obtained the dread authority of the rulers in Leadenhall-street; none enters it except a servant of the Company. Who then has cognisance of the state of India, but a companion? So that the little that transpires is by accident, and from one under the shrewd suspicion of being more favourable to the Company than to truth. This circumstance is, however, sufficiently descriptive of the wretchedness

[1] Suetonius, lib. 2. c. 57. Cæsar had a supplication to the God of fifty days length. Dion Cassius, lib. 43. c. 42. Te Deums are of great antiquity.

of the government. They seem to fear that the English should become Indian, or the Indian approach the British. No effort is made to facilitate the connexion of the two people. Bonaparte employed a company of players when he invaded Egypt, " as an amusement to the army, and as a means of changing the manners of the country." Nothing of this kind is permitted in the presidencies.

If Bonaparte can afford us no lesson but wickedness—learn of ancient Rome. Rome laboured to introduce the Latin language into all her dependencies: for this purpose she established, in each of the seventeen provinces of Gaul, schools professedly to introduce the Latin dialect, and the Romance language was eventually the consequence of this policy ; what was Romance in France was provincial [Provençale] at Rome. Rome pursued the same conduct in Britain. The use of the imperial language as a means of government is forcibly inculcated by Machiavel [1], and the affiliation it ensures between independent states is explained with equal justness by Talleyrand [2]. Instead of attracting by the mind, the ear, and the tongue, the people of Hindostan, Francis Wrangham recommends founding a Christian cast. Sir William Jones [3] recommends *translations into Sanscrit and Persian of such chapters of the Prophets, and particularly Isaiah, as are indisputably evangelical, and dispersed among the well-educated.* Dr. Buchanan recommends " that the parables of the Gospels alone be distributed among a barbarous peo-

[1] Il Principe, p. 4.   [2] Mémoire, &c. p. 11.
[3] Life, p. 453.

ple," &c. Some would have the whole Bible propounded, as means of governing India; some a few prayers. Long since Cosmo de Medici [1] said, States are not to be preserved by Pater-nosters.

Nothing effectual is done to conciliate the natives, or any part of them. Indian-built ships, by a quibble on the 26th of Geo. III. c. 69, are prevented from the benefit of registry, even when England wants ships, and so wants timber, that though she cannot feed her people, a portion of her domain is reserved for the growth of oak. England has made conquests, but she has not taken one effectual step to secure them. The Romans knew,—it was their maxim,—" Plus est provinciam retinere quam facere [2]." And Florus [3] gives the reason—" viribus parantur, jure retinentur." The Romans, when they conquered they colonized. A colony represents the state, is the patron of the province, and so far it tends to justice : it promotes in various ways the fellowship or union of the subject and the sovereign. In India, this is not to be tolerated in the remotest manner. The India Company is more suspicious than their Catholic and Faithful Majesties in South America ; than the successors of Mahomet in Europe [4], or in the East [5]. The admission into India

[1] Che gli stati non si tenevano con Pater Nostri in mano. Machiavel Storia, lib. 7. p. 248.

[2] Florus, lib. 2. c. 17.   [3] lib. 4. c. 12.

[4] " It is not permitted to Mussulmans to make a fixed residence in either principality. Those whom commercial or state affairs occasionally bring into the country, are lodged in the khans or hotels expressly built for their accommodation in Yassy or Bucharest." Thornton, &c. vol. 2. p. 355.

[5] Indeed the Mogul empire in the East was as becoming as the

of a Briton, not serving the Company, is more wonderful than man's descent to Avernus in Pagan story. Nothing approaching colonization is tolerable even in discourse [1], though by colonization Rome's authority in Italy was unassailable by the genius and fortune of Hannibal. Colonization began with the Roman power [2]; and by this, far n*o*re than by the arms of Rome, the dominion of Rome was confirmed. But observe, the Roman colonies carried abroad the image of the Roman government [3]. They were to Rome, what the American Provinces were to Britain [4]. It is most melancholy that sixty millions of people are doomed to endure slavery, as long as it can be imposed, to a mere trading company. It is vexatious that the London companies should in con-

English is base, in a religious view, in Great Britain and Ireland. " The religion of Bengal by law established is Mahometan ; yet for one Mahometan there are above an hundred Pagans ; and the public offices and posts of trust are filled promiscuously with men of both persuasions." Hamilton's Account of the East Indies. Pinkerton, &c. vol. 8. p. 414.

[1] There is an exception :—The Tannah establishment in Bengal, a tract of country a hundred miles long, was a few years ago a mere jungle for tigers and robbers. It was given to old soldiers and their families, who have converted it into fine fields and villages. Malcolm, Polit. Hist. of India, p. 526. He is favourable to colonizing India, p. 475.

[2] Diop Halicarnassus, lib. 2. c. 16. It continued in full force to the time of Julius Cæsar. He sent 80,000 citizens to the transmarine colonies. Suetonius, lib. 1. p. 43.

[3] Decuriones quidem dictos aiunt ex eo, quod initio coloniæ deducerentur decima pars eorum, qui ducerentur, consilii publici gratia conscribi solita est.

[4] The establishment of these provinces was highly honourable—their taxation was vicious and absurd.

sequence of misrule appropriate lands in the north of Ireland; but that a company in London, a tea monopoly, from having a warehouse-guard [1] to secure goods from common theft, should conquer the continent that unsuspiciously received them, and there rule despotically sixty millions of men;—nay, that this populous world cannot, *in the nature of things*, be relieved, is to combine all monstrous thoughts in the same image.

Yet true to the adage—That perdition and infatuation are twin-born of vice—the governors of India will not admit the customary mode of strengthening their empire. No ; they will not even use the means which present themselves, which obtrude on their attention for their security. It is calculated that the half-cast children, born of native women and European fathers, amount to 30,000 :—one would imagine that these should be particularly considered by the government. Quite the reverse — abandoned by their sordid fathers, they are rejected by the government. They cause regret, not as being memorials of British incontinence and British baseness : the regret is, " They are forming," says Lord Valentia [2], " the first step to colonization, by creating a link of union between the English and the natives." So speaks the single and sole favourite of the company and government of India. What is to be done with these infinitely abused beings? I have read some right merry dogmas in a presumptuous journal, of violating nature—and crossing breeds—and obliquity of

---

[1] Malcolm's Polit. Hist. p. 480.

[2] Travels, vol. 1. p. 241.

disposition in consequence (though the same authors fervently believe that Adam and Eve were the parents of mankind). D'Azara, on the contrary, says that an Indian and European exhibit better specimens of man, than Creoles produced from Spanish parents. I doubt both the reputed excellence and inferiority in either case; but it is certain, if Humboldt be an authority, that the children of Indian women by Spaniards under the Spanish tyranny, possessed, with few exceptions, all the privileges of children born of Spanish mothers by Spanish fathers. Yet the half-cast children in India are utterly excluded from the military and civil service of the Company.

This treatment of the half-cast children resembles the conduct of those crusaders who possessed Palestine, to their spurious offspring. These Christian warriors associated with the females of the country : their children were called poulains, and despised :—yet it has been remarked, that by a different conduct these would have recruited the power of their fathers and sustained their empire. This government, which compared to the Indian was founded on adamant, lasted only 150 years, which is shorter than the dominion of the Assassins [1]. Yet the Indian empire of Britain is comparatively of yesterday, and it has suffered many desperate shocks ; and such is its wretchedness, that the government systematically adds to its enemies this perpetually increasing half-cast population. Have they never heard of the Parthenoi in Sparta?—probably not. But they may have heard of the policy of the Egyptian king, who tampered with

[1] It subsisted 170 years.

nurse-tenders, to procure the abortion of the increasing Hebrew slaves in his dominions. As this failed, it may be useful to suggest a more efficacious remedy : —it relates to the Carthaginians, who like the British were addicted to foreign commerce, and from factories established dominations. Aristotle says [1], that the Carthaginians established themselves in a fertile island beyond the columns of Hercules. The settlers contracted marriages with the natives. On this the Carthaginian government ordered that no one should henceforward enter the island, on pain of death; and they extirpated the settlers and their children, lest they should by their marriages injure Carthaginian supremacy, by obtaining themselves the sovereignty of the island. This was more decisive and kinder policy than the conduct of the British in India to the children of their servants. They are considered enemies, and this treatment must create or increase their enmity. Be kind and princely, and despatch them. It suits the Prince's government, according to Machiavel's display of cabinet councils, and it accords with the philosophy of Hobbes, " that while men are afraid of one another, nobody can have better security than by prevention : so that every one should endeavour to oppress all others, either by violence or fraud, while there are any remaining to be afraid of [2]."

Such then is the state of our Indian empire, that while we read of successes round the circle of our frontiers, we cannot be assured that then one vestige of our Eastern government remains, or that one of

[1] Opera omnia, t. 1. p. 1157.
[2] Leviathan, c. 13. De Cive, c. 5.

our institutions survives our banishment, to excite a kind recollection or transient regret in the native of India; or one consolation to the British people, for all the evils they have done and suffered. We have planted no monument of art or industry in India; we have communicated no lights of science, nor established any government that may hereafter assist their wants or their wishes or their rights; our literature is unknown, our language is untaught. It was Plato's[1] dread that Sicily might pass to the Phœnician dynasty, and that thus the colonies of Greece in that island might lose the Grecian tongue[2]. With language—arts, science, deeds, philosophy, institutions are communicated, confirmed, consecrated; nor is there one existing language, so affluent and so vigorous as the English—none which contains so many subjects of the truest fancy, the loftiest imagination, the intensest interest, with all that is useful

---

[1] Epist. 8. p. 1296. Opera.

[2] A writer in the Edinburgh Review, No. 28, p. 329, says, " It is not easy to assign the precise notion which the early Greeks annexed to the term Barbarian, unless we consider it as synonymous with stranger or foreigner." Barbarian regarded the language — Βαρβαρος ουκ επι εθνους, αλλ' επι φωνης ελαμβανετο. Stephanus de Urbibus, p. 153. Dion of Halicarnassus says, The Tarentines, who were Greeks, treated the Roman ambassador with contempt, because he spoke Greek incorrectly; and on that account Βαρβαρον εκαλουν. Excerpt. 4. p. 710. So Aristophanes, Equites, ver. 17. Βαρβαριζει ως δουλος. Strabo says, Omnes itaque qui crasse loquuntur Barbari dicuntur: quales sunt nationes omnes præter Græcos. Lib. 14. t. 2. p. 373. So Ovid,
In paucis extant Græcæ vestigia linguæ;
Hæc quoque jam Getico barbara facta sono.
Trist. lib. 5.

to men and nations. Suppose that a liberal and enlightened policy tended eventually to liberate India from England, I can perceive no reason why such policy should not be adopted. Under such circumstances, so long as it remained subject, it would be more profitable, as a free servant is more serviceable than a slave. I speak not of the profit of one man or a few, whose advantage is often in direct opposition to that of the nation. I speak for the nation, for its justice, its honour, and glory :—true political glory rules rather by authority than by power, and makes the interest of all minister to universal obedience. The best present government would be, that which soonest enabled the inhabitants of India to enjoy liberty and property, independent of the control, assistance, or supervision of Great Britain ; and this would be a glorious retribution to the Indians for British conquest, rapacity, and outrage.

I am no advocate for colonizing. Colonies are attended with a train of evils : they divert attention from domestic affairs; increase patronage, and corrupt the ministers of power, as they are removed from responsibility and control. If colonies be intended for commerce, as those anciently by the Phœnicians [1], the merchant, from bartering with the natives, soon endeavours to command them and their productions.

In every way I object to colonies as they have been planted and appointed. The supposition of their service to the parent state is among the greatest of vulgar errors. Mr. G. Grant lately said that Jamaica exports 98,000 hogsheads of sugar, which

[1] Thucydides, lib. 6. p. 412.

pays 2,000,000*l.*, and that England in return exported 3,000,000*l.* of manufactures. Suppose so; the duty is no gift of the colonial trade: and the three millions of manufactures might be exported, or more, if the West Indian colonies were emancipated. Suppose not; the three millions of manufactures are not a gain of three millions; they afford a profit of eight or ten per cent., perhaps, that is 3 or 400,000*l.* This is the whole amount of the benefit—But what is this sum, compared to the expenditure for the military protection of the island? How many British soldiers perished in this island in the last war! 17,000 troops died by sickness in the Windward Islands, *exclusive* of the mortality in St. Domingo and Jamaica, from 1786 to 1802 : and what sum is to be charged for their protecting navy? Would the profits of a few hundred thousand pounds on merchandise indemnify the state for this various and enormous expenditure? Why John Glasfurd (one individual) drew six millions of bills on the treasury, from 1798 to 1805, during seven of the twenty-five years war, and his accounts are yet inaudited.

But many derive large incomes from the West Indies. Sir W. Young's [1] testimony is decisive on this subject. He says, " A speculative purchaser may receive, for some very few years, 12 per cent. ; but the epidemic diseases among the negroes, the effect of war, insurrections, &c. will at once and for ever reduce the computation of large interest for his purchase money." He also says, " that the hereditary landholder, who by himself or family has shared the losses

[1] Colonial Common Place Book, p. 26.

incident to the nature of his property in every course
of years, does not, I will venture to assert, receive
four per cent. on the capital laid out in original settlement, adding sums of money since expended in occasionally restoring his estates." Can property be invested less productively? All that Great Britain enjoys from her colonial commerce are the profits derived from the manufactures exported. Yet rate these
as highly as possible[1], we must, beside the ruinous
cost in protecting the colonies, deduct from the profits mentioned the enhancement of the sugar to the
consumers. I am persuaded that the surcharge on
the article to the British people exceeds the profits on
their exported industry; for the sugar of the West
Indies is brought into market through a labyrinth of
difficulties, and loaded—loaded perversely and mon-
strously—by the state-monopoly, by the shipping
interest, by the refiners[2], by a long succession of
oppressors down to the slave-owners and the masters
of the gangs. This last gradation or degradation of
human misery would, singly, inordinately enhance the

[1] Take one instance. On the 6th of Feb. 1804, the West India
merchants petitioned the king and parliament, stating, " That the
planters in the sugar colonies could neither subsist their negroes,
nor provide package for their produce, without supplies from America of provisions and lumber, and that a circuitous passage of
British ships, *via* America, would not only incur a surcharge of
freight and commission most heavy, but by accidents would prevent
their use when they arrived; and that the medium of ordinary exchange in the sugar-colonies, for lumber and provisions, was rum,
which America would take, and which the merchants of Great
Britain would not take." Yet for nine years, till 1793, government
resisted this application, in order to gratify the shipping interest.

[2] This part of the evil was lamented in Davenant's time.

article. Long since, Mons. de Poivre said, respecting the extraordinary cheapness of sugar in Cochin China by free hands, "Compare the price of the Cochin China production, with the same commodity which is cultivated and prepared by the wretched slaves of our European colonies."

Colonies, in whatever way they are presented to the unprejudiced, are expensive, and their expenditure constantly exceeds the ratio of their return. In 1814, the revenue of the Cape of Good Hope increased to 129,575*l*. 6*s*. 4*d*., but the disbursements of the same year amounted to 244,138*l*. 6*s*. 4*d*. They cause presumption, and thus they exasperate envy and hatred. Athens and Sparta alternately became victims of ambitious colonization. Athens, after its double triumph, colonized the land of the Hippobatæ with 4000 men[1]; they also transmitted the same number to the country of the Chalcidians[2]. Athens also, under Pericles[3], sent out many colonies, not for want of food and room, as Mr. Malthus would probably insist, but expressly to increase the interest of Athens. Yet these, while they gave present power, ensured eventual weakness; from being beloved, the Athenians were detested, and they declined till their existence was in peril. Distress taught them wisdom, and they resumed their moral dominion by renouncing all their colonies and conquests. The Spartans followed the same course, and they sunk like the Athenians; but wanting the excessive vitality of most popular institutions, they fell without the means of regeneration. Considering co-

[1] Herodotus, lib. 5. c. 78.　　[2] Ibid. lib. 5. c. 77.
[3] Plutarch, p. 361.

lonies, particularly in respect to the present subject, as a means of relieving an extreme populousness, should it occur, they are a desperate remedy if we judge from the results. Talleyrand[1] speaks of *des milliers de François* who perished in the expedition to the Mississippi, Cayenne, &c. 12,000 individuals, who were sent by the French government to Guiana, were also lost. How destructive was the Scotch expedition to Darien! Emigration to Newfoundland has failed; and now the inhabitants in that island are in the utmost misery[2], as are those on the continent along the Red River. America, notwithstanding its eventual success and portentous consequences, records an aggregate of failures. Colonization has failed in other quarters of the world. Wadstrom's project, in 1799, of establishing a republic on the coast of Africa, failed; so did Captain Beaver's attempt at Bulama. So at Sierra Leone; of seventeen hundred persons who arrived at that settlement in 1799, in 1800 twelve only survived. From ignorance of the time suited to such establishments, from unfitness of settlers for a new and unexpected life, from irrational hope and diverse causes, colonization, as a relief from a crowded population, is a vain effort, and at best a temporary expedient; the vacancy must soon be supplied, if the emigrants do not transport with themselves much more than their persons. My objection is directly the reverse of those who fear depopulation from emigration; for emigration, regarding merely the egress of people, leaves

[1] Mémoire.

[2] See debate on Mr. M. A. Taylor's motion last year on this subject.

the swift means of increase behind. Besides, I cannot
perceive any necessity, from the population of nations,
that they should recur to colonization. The sums of
money that have been wasted on such projects, would
have supported those at home who perished abroad ;
not that I recommend, for on the contrary I condemn,
all such tampering with people and their industry, as
has been latterly proposed for the English poor. Observe, that while much capital has been lost in the outfit of colonies, and in their protection, the same countries which furnished the colonists, have increased in
numbers vastly beyond their complement, when those
issues were thought indispensable to the ease of the
people. I detest the notion of taking from one class to
give to another, and all that cabinet curiosity in politics, where a minister, or a board, presumes to regulate what should be submitted to the dominion of circumstances ; but I say, if we are to be meddlers and
transplanters at a common cost, I would rather see
capital perverted on a colony at home, than at Labra-
dor, or at Caucasus, or Samoyda, or Upper Canada,
where men with double labour scarcely raise half produce, and who are more wasted by the pains of memory than by hunger and fatigue. If colonies be sent
abroad, let them go, not as servants, but equals[1]; let
them be dismissed sincerely, and with a surety of their
success. Plato says, let so many colonists (a hundred)
be accompanied by as many of the oldest of the Cnos-
sians ; let these act as fathers, until all things be set-

---

[1] Tullus said, It is not just that the parent-state should command
their colonies. Dion Halicarnassus, lib. 3.

tled, and then return to Cnossus[1]. This is paternal, and shows a perfect apprehension of equity and benevolence. Other particulars were equally understood by Plato; in the same page he says, there has been, and will be, much strife between parent-states and their colonies. It was a topic familiar even to the oracle, who answered Timesias, who consulted her on the propriety of planting a colony, " Your swarm of bees will soon become wasps[2]." This must ever be the case when colonies are treated with insult and oppression; for, as Thucydides says, men become colonists, not that they should be slaves, but equals[3]; nor is any thing good, or safe, or profitable, but equity and equality. The first sea-fight on record was between the Corinthians and their own colony of Corcyra[4], and the last between England and America.

CHAPTER VI.

Corn Laws.—Bounties.—Prohibition to import foreign corn, &c.

I HAVE considered population under various aspects, and my conclusions have often been the inverse of those of Malthus. While he esteems government, that is laws, institutions, and their administration, of inconsiderable influence compared to *misery deep-seated in*

[1] De Legib. lib. 6. p. 857.

[2] Σμηνα μελισσαων, ταχα τοι και σφηκε εσονται. Plutarch, Moral. p. 58.

[3] Ου γαρ επι τω δȣλοι αλλ' επι τω ομοιοι ειναι εκπεμπον.

[4] Thucydides, lib. 1. c. 13. To her next colony, to Epidamnus, she was wiser : it was established επι τη ιση και ομοια.

human nature : I, regarding civilized man, esteem bad laws and iniquitous government as the paramount and pregnant source of the calamities of nations. Indeed Mr. Malthus argues the subject of population, as if he had received a license for lecturing since the session of 1817, when political questions were prohibited. Any and all things are chargeable with infirmity by him in his categories, but government, which is openly defended, or treated with mysterious respect. Nature prompts, man and woman are nothing loth ; they breed unwittingly at the rate of 1, 2, 4, 8, and food grows as 1, 2, 3, 4. *Ergo*, men press against subsistence; and because miserable individuals appear in various countries, the accelerated increase of mankind beyond food is substantiated by facts. These propositions are to me more extravagant in themselves, and in their connexion, than the themes of Pindar's eulogy and his transitions.

All vices and follies of fathers and mothers,—idleness, company-keeping, gambling, epicurism, gluttony, drunkenness, silly projects, hazardous speculations, profusion, and prodigality of all kinds, which reduce families or keep them distressed, are all identified by Mr. Malthus with overbreeding. There is misery ; but how does misery prove that overbreeding is the cardinal and catholic sin ? Men breed heedlessly; but this vice or folly is but one of the many causes of man's misery. If the savage wants, there, says Mr. Malthus, you behold the effect of overbreeding, though there are few children and absolute improvidence :—if manufacturers be out of employment, this is overbreeding also. About twenty-five years ago, wearing shoe-buckles and torturing the head ceased to be indispensable; thence many workers in metal and hair-dressers were discharged, and they were distressed. Count them, says Mr. Malthus, and here behold the crime and punishment of overbreeding. During the war, few watches were imported from the continent: of course this manufacture increased in Great Britain, but the peace introduced foreign watches; in consequence several thousand watch- and clock-makers in London were reduced to poverty. Here, says Mr. Malthus, you perceive my theory is demonstrated by those five thousand mendicant artists and their wanting families. During the war, our most prodigal government wasted, by loans, so largely the capital of the country, that important branches of industry wanted the funds necessary for their success, which, with other causes, paralysed industry and enterprise. Many of course, who had been fully paid and fully occupied, could only obtain half work or half wages, and some were absolutely discharged : Triumphant proofs, cries Mr. Malthus, of an heedlessly overbreeding people. Men will breed, and must starve. Nature predetermined this consequence, and I first revealed the mighty truth.

Yet truly during this war, beside the loans by which capital was disssipated and extinguished, immense taxes were charged on every article which could bear an impost, and on many which sunk under the pressure. The nation was taxed so enormously, that the revenue, which had rapidly risen from the first year of the war, and whose gross produce in 1798 was 26,820,629l. 13s. 4d., amounted in 1815 to 81,334,292l. 9s. 0$\frac{1}{4}d$. Much of this charge fell directly on the labouring population, much indirectly. For mankind endeavour to shift the weight from themselves on others; and in the general effort to escape oppression, the weight falls on those on whom all falls, as surely as the entablature rests on the column, and this on its base. This enormously descending taxation, and the positive taxes on the people's necessaries without any adequate increase of wages, but, on the contrary, in some cases, with their positive reduction, also afflicted many with indigence, and plunged some into the abyss of poverty. On this Mr. Malthus cries, Triumphant principle of population! Oh, nature, and geometry, and all the satyrs, how the British breed! And thou arithmetic, and famine, and epidemics, and death, see how they starve!

Against the whole of this doctrine I demur—Whatever be the excess of people beyond employment, the excess is not attributable to the people, nor is their misery of their own making, unless we conclude that they wasted the capital of the state in foreign subsidies, in conquests east and west, &c.; unless we assume that they imposed taxes on their own soap, salt, leather, beer, tobacco, and bread; for every tax which affected agriculture tended to enhance the quartern loaf.

In 1815, the people were moderately employed, ill-paid, miserable. The legislature (the members of the House of Commons) turned their thoughts to the sufferings of the people; and this authentic organ of the public voice, to secure abundance for ever, passed that monument of sagacity and patriotism—the corn-law.

This subject implicates the foreign policy, the do-

mestic industry, and the subsistence of the people of
Great Britain and Ireland. From the earliest period Britain exported corn to Rome[1] : grain also
during the Saxon government was a constant article
of commerce. The Normans, conquerors and tyrants, aggravated all that was evil, while they introduced many new calamities into the state. The estates of many Britons were seized on the first spoliation, or by subsequent confiscations, and granted to
captains and followers of the conqueror. The intercourse of citizens was abridged; trades became crafts,
professions gilds[2]. Commerce suffered a similar
violation; and though a privilege to break the law
was among the ways and means of a rapacious government, the export of grain was prohibited. It
seems to have been with few exceptions the policy of
ancient British statesmen to secure plenty at home,
by withholding the export of victuals. Banks (the
attorney-general) against Hampden[3], in the great
cause respecting ship-money, said : " In all ages he
(the king) hath commanded no victuals shall be transported. Claus. 24 Edw. III. m. 7 dors. 5 Dec.
4 Hen. VIII. 11 Hen. VII. 23." This, however,
admits of some exceptions; for by one of the early
chronicles[4] it appears that considerable quantities of
corn were exported. yet this must be esteemed extraordinary, as the fines for licenses to export corn
registered in the exchequer prove the rule and the

---

[1] Ammianus Marcellinus, lib. 18. c. 2. Strabo, lib. 4.
[2] Madox, Firma Burgi, c. 1. § 9. There were gilds among
the Saxons, something like Friendly Societies.
[3] State Trials, vol. 1. p. 665. Irish Edit.
[4] Gul. Pictaven, p. 210.

infraction [1]. It seems that the export of grain in those early periods resembled the license trade to France during the last war.

In 1425 the exportation of grain without licenses was permitted by law, subject however to duties, and liable to be restrained by the king in council. The 4 Hen. VI. c. 5. was followed by the 15 Hen. VI. c. 2. This, says Barrington [2] (and he is wrong), " is the first permission to export corn in the statute book." He adds in a note: " the good policy of this statute, *with the addition of the bounty upon exportation*, hath made England the granary of the world." This florid eulogy on the omnipotence of a bounty is transcribed from William of Poictou, who thus panegyrized England centuries before the existence of a bounty.

In 1463 the members of the House of Commons complained that an excessive import so depreciated corn in England, that English farmers were exposed to ruin. These patriots, from whom the modern corn-law-givers are directly descended, enacted, that wheat should not be imported until its price exceeded 6s. 8d.; nor rye, nor barley, till the first exceeded 4s. and the latter 3s. a quarter.

This was followed by the 12th, 15th, and 22d of Charles the Second. The last (c. 13) exhibited a graduated scale of obstructed import. When wheat did not exceed 53s. 4d. the quarter in the home market, it paid 16s. duty; and when it did not exceed 4l., 8s. duty. This has been considered a rare

[1] Madox has extracted some of them.

[2] Ancient Statutes, p. 307

effort of science; and an attempt was made by a reporting committee of the House of Commons in 1814 to improve this scale, by a longer and minuter scale of graduation. To the non-importing law of the 22d of Charles the Second, was added the 1st of William and Mary, which encouraged exportation by a bounty, when the quarter of wheat did not exceed 48s. This, according to country gentlemen and rural reasoners, and sage ministers, was honoured as the maximum of human legislation. Mr. Malthus admires it, and Mr. Western solicits its readoption : the latter would thus add debt to the mountains of taxation, that the English grower might undersell foreigners in their own market; though, he says, the English farmer, even were he to pay no rent, could not successfully meet the foreign grower in the British markets. If the corn laws passed in Charles the Second's reign, and the bounties granted by the 1st of William and Mary, be so excellent that they should be regarded as exemplary laws and standard statutes; we must admit that the authors of them were both wise and lucky : for when they passed them, few had any exact knowledge of any one particular fact respecting political œconomy : even Davenant, the most intelligent person of his time on such subjects, imagined that England in a plentiful year produced five times the stock of grain requisite for the consumption of its people.

When the corn law was agitated in 1815, the people were directed to the effects of the laws in Charles the Second's reign and William's. Why should the bounty-giving law of William and Mary have solicited their attention, when a bounty on export made no part of the projected statute of 1815? Suppose, however, that the export of grain about the time of the Revolution followed the laws of Charles and William;—a consequence is not an effect. The yam was introduced into South America by a slave-ship from Africa;—the slave trade and the increased subsistence of the Americans are not cause and consequence. To speak more directly to the purpose: If circumstances in sequel indicate causation, we must infer that the prohibition, after the conquest of Britain by the Normans, to export corn, raised the price of that article from three shillings to eighteen pounds the quarter; and that the law of 1804, which permitted exportation, doubled the price of wheat; though the enhanced price immediately on passing the act prevented the exportation of a single quarter. A consequence taken as an effect would also discredit the corn law of 1815 still more than it deserves; for it was succeeded with a sudden and excessive enhancement, and with general misery.

Suppose, however, that the 12th, 15th, and 22d of Charles the Second, and the 1st of William and Mary, were followed by the export of grain;—on what grounds should we conclude that these laws produced or ministered to this event? Though the export of grain was prohibited in William the Conqueror's reign, and in the reigns of his successors, grain was occasionally exported, and the grower paid the crown for the liberty. William of Poictou says [1], " Then England might be called the storehouse of

[1] Henry's History, vol. 3. b. 3. c. 6.

Ceres, out of which the world was supplied with corn." This extravagance (to which I have already alluded) proves that some grain was exported, when export laboured under obstructions and penalties. The export of corn continued under similar impediments. Hume says[1], "A judicious author of that [Elizabeth's] age confirms the vulgar observation, that the kingdom was depopulating, from the increase of inclosures and decay of tillage; and he ascribes the reason, very justly, to the restraints put on the exportation of corn." If corn was exported under difficulties, and that tillage and export declined by increasing difficulties, why should not both agriculture and export of corn have resumed their activity by the removal of these difficulties? It is therefore hypothetical and gratuitous to refer to the 22d of Charles the Second, and the 1st of William and Mary, for the resumed exportation of grain.

There is also another most important point for consideration. Corn may be exported, either when tillage is enlarged, or when the home consumption is reduced. It may therefore be questioned by those who consider that a succession of facts evince cause and effects, if the wonder-working laws so often mentioned of Charles and William did not reduce the people rather than increase their agriculture. Temple speaks frequently of the indisposition to marry, and of the depopulation of England[2]. That England was depopulated by the mismanagement of Charles the First, by the civil war, by Cromwell's tyranny, there

[1] History, vol. 5. p. 484.
[2] Popular Discontents. Works, vol. 1. p. 267.

is reason to believe. Besides, it is ascertained that the houses in Britain had decreased; and this decrease from 1690 to 1766, according to the estimation of Dr. Price [1], amounted to a million and a half of inhabitants. When I restate this, I am aware of all that I have written respecting the insufficiency of houses under any rate to determine the amount of the people: but here the reduction of houses is not questioned; and this occurred in the same country, and in the same uninterrupted tract of time. This would of itself utterly discredit the wonder-working laws of non-importation, and of bounty. Let us recur to the facts. By the tables of import and export of corn, it appears that the export increased to 1750: then there was a stop. And from 1760 to 1770, the exported corn exceeded the imported only as 429,017 quarters do 265,730 quarters. This brings us beyond the term of declining houses and a reduced consumption, as stated by Dr. Price. In the next ten years England exported 284,715 quarters, while she imported 613,083 quarters. During this interval population certainly increased; and then England from an exporting became decidedly an importing nation:—that is, tillage having succeeded to grazing, which was more profitable in Davenant's time, manufactures succeeded to tillage. The people increased, and the ratio of manufacturers exceeded the ratio of agriculturists.

Independent of these facts, it seems utterly absurd that the 22d of Charles could have enabled England to export. This law prohibited import of grain till

---

[1] Expectation of Lives, &c. Supplement, p. 299.

it reached certain prices. This could only increase the home growth for the home consumption; it could not enable the nation to raise cheaper grain for the foreign market: if England exported grain, it raised it more cheaply than the foreign grower; and if the British grain rivalled the foreign grain in the foreign market, the prohibition to import foreign grain into the English market was nugatory. The benefit, therefore, of the 22d of Charles is fantastic. There remains the law of William and Mary, which granted a bounty of 5 shillings a quarter on export, when wheat was under 48 shillings the quarter. Remark, that this bounty was granted in 1690; but the value of money declined from 1690 to 1750: yet the export of grain regularly increased to 1750. In 1701 the export was 139,866 quarters; in 1749, the export was 932,593 quarters. If the export was ruled by the bounty, how happened it that the export increased as the bounty declined virtually with the depreciation of money? These bounties forced capital out of its allotted course, and they cost the nation at least as much as the sum employed in this perversion; and by so much they impaired the nation's ability to subsist itself. These laws of restriction and bounty were imagined by the same penurious intellects which regulated the commerce of grain at home. By the 15th of Charles II. c. 7. s. 4, it is enacted, that when the quarter of wheat doth not exceed 48 shillings, rye 32 shillings, barley or malt 28 shillings, buck wheat 28 shillings, oats 13 shillings, peas and beans 32 shillings,—any person (not forestalling nor selling the same again in three months) may buy such corn, &c. in open market, at or under such price, and lay it up and sell the same again without incurring any penalty. These are the legislators to whom our present law-giving political œconomists refer their paternity. The judicature of that day equalled the legislature. At the assizes [1] of Kent an indictment was preferred against an individual for engrossing apples, pears, and cherries. He was found guilty. Judgement was arrested; and the body of the argument was, that costermongers were not victuallers by their charters.

Mr. Malthus is a pertinacious advocate for bounties and corn laws: yet he says, " that a rich and commercial nation is thus by the *natural* course of things led more to pasture than tillage [2]." I need not remind the reader how frequently he has used natural as right, and unnatural as wrong;—but what office does the delicate Ariel perform for Prospero on this occasion? Mr. Malthus in his alarms says [3] ; " It seems in a great measure to have escaped attention, that a nation which from its extent of territory and population must necessarily support the greater part of its people on the produce of its own soil, but which yet in average years draws a small portion of its corn from abroad, is in a much more precarious situation, with regard to the constancy of its supplies, than such states as draw almost the whole of their provisions from other countries." Why should

---

[1] Styl. 190.

[2] vol. 2. p. 191. *Nature* is very busy in this part of his work. *Nature* appears at p. 123 ; *natural* 124 ; *naturally* and *natural*, 125.   [3] vol. 2. p. 122.

the absurdity,—that a perpetual and almost entire deficiency of provisions is preferable to an occasional
and comparatively moderate want of them, have ever
been imagined ? He then compares the situation of
Hamburg and Holland with England : " If they (the
demands of Holland) increase gradually, and are not
subject from year to year to any great and sudden
variations ; but it is otherwise with such a country as
England: supposing it in average years to want about
400,000 quarters of wheat, such a demand will of
course be very easily supplied ; but a year of deficient crops occurs, and the demand is suddenly two
millions of quarters. If the demand had been on an
average two millions, it might have been adequately
supplied from the extended agriculture of those countries which are in the habit of exporting corn : but
we cannot expect that it can easily be answered thus
suddenly."

This is rare reasoning. If the average want be
400,000 quarters, and the extraordinary want be two
millions; this is worse, much worse, he says, than if the
average want were two millions. Suppose the average
want be two millions, I ask why should not the extraordinary want be twice two or twice four millions ?
for he assumes the average want 400,000 quarters,
and the extraordinary want five times greater than
the average want. Mr. Malthus, who would render
England independent of supplies from foreign nations even at the expense of bounties, argues, that
the enormity of an average want is an assurance
against all want whatever, ordinary and extraordinary.

Mr. Malthus says [1], " It has been already observed, that we are exactly in the situation in which a country feels most fully the effect of those common years of deficient crops, which in the *natural* course of things are to be expected." What are the facts? By an official return to parliament, it appears that from 1775 to 1786 the average quantity of grain imported into Great Britain amounted to 564,000 quarters; that from 1787 to 1798 the grain amounted annually to 1,136,000 quarters; and that from 1799 to 1810 the average was 1,471,000 quarters. I perceive nothing alarming in this account. Suppose that about 1765 the exported and imported grain were balanced; there is every reason to believe that the population increased considerably from that period to 1801;—and we possess documents which specify that the increase from 1801 to 1811 amounted to 1,654,157 inhabitants. The population has advanced beyond the tillage of the country, yet agriculture has not been inert.

Besides, why should the import of 1,500,000 quarters, which is only equivalent to the national consumption of grain for six weeks, alarm the British? Iceland does not produce grain for a single meal of its 48,000 inhabitants. Malta and Goza and the Sette Commune near Vicenza are dependent on foreigners for their grain, none of them raising corn for three months subsistence in the year. Holland did not grow food for two months in the twelve, said Temple [2]; *nor grain for those only who have the care of its dykes.*

vol. 2. p. 146. [2] Observations on the United Provinces.

Then why should corn laws be necessary to England which were not necessary to Holland? Lord Liverpool thinks, with Mr. Malthus, that the two countries afford no similarity or coincidence; as he said in the debate on the corn laws in 1815, " Great countries are not to be ruled as small ones." This is the misery of men who argue without principles. The longitude or latitude of a country, its dimensions, being peninsular or insular, triangular or rounded,—any and every variation, affords cause to them to except its people from liberality and justice. Lord Liverpool's inference,—that England was not to be ruled as Holland, because England contained much more people,—Mons. Necker applied to France in respect to England. France, said Necker[1], is twice and a fifth more populous than England, Scotland, and Ireland; therefore she cannot be so liberal in her policy in the commerce of grain. False in every respect! for Sully admitted the free export of grain, and by this means chiefly he retrieved agriculture, which had suffered by the civil wars; and Turgot in 1775 reverted to the practice of Sully[2], and with the same success. So much for Mons. Necker's sagacity! Yet is Lord Liverpool still more defenceless. In 1669 the United Provinces contained 2,400,000 inhabitants. Suppose that in 1815 Great Britain contained twelve millions. If Great Britain imported 1,500,000 quarters in that year, and Holland in 1669 did not raise grain for two months subsistence of its people; it fed only 400,000 with home produce, leaving two millions of

[1] Dernières Vues, &c. p. 470.
[2] Bibliothèque de l'Homme Publique, tom. 12. p. 116.

its people dependent on supplies from abroad; while England required grain only for one million and a half of all its people.

Thus Mr. Malthus and Lord Liverpool argue; and I should not notice their misstatements and absurdities if they had been, as far as I know, already exposed. It appears that Mr. Malthus has no doubts of his own sagacity, even while he impugns the conclusions of Adam Smith. On the contrary, he continues an obstinate defender of the corn laws. When the last law, in 1815, was agitated, he published a pamphlet in aid of the ministers and the country gentlemen; in which he stated, " I own it appears to me, that the necessary effect of a change in the measure of value in the weight of a large national debt, is alone sufficient to make the question fundamentally different from that of a simple question about a free and a restricted trade." Had Holland no debt, no taxes? Had she no wars for liberty? and wars in which mighty deeds were executed with inconsiderable means? Twenty-five thousand troops[1], headed by a young man of twenty-two years of age, resisted 130,000 French troops, led by Vauban, Luxembourg, Turenne, and Condé. Yet the Dutch had no corn law;—nor had they a king's splendour to maintain; nor had they ministers with immense salaries and sinecures; nor had they a pensioned nobility:—prince, ministers, and people were laborious, thrifty, and honest. They had not only no corn laws, but the trade of the United Provinces moved on principles the reverse of those of Great Britain: " Lowness of customs and easiness

[1] Voltaire. Louis XIV. c. 9.

of paying them, which, with the freedom of their
ports, invite strangers and nations to bring commodities
hither, not only as to a market, but as to a magazine,
where they lodge till they are invited abroad to other
and better markets." Here is a difference indeed!
Holland might be called a free port, while England's
coast suffers a partial blockade. During the debate on
the corn bill in 1815, an argument for the non-importation of foreign corn, except under pains and difficulties, was drawn from the general illiberality of
the English commercial code; by which about two
hundred articles were similarly repressed by the laws
of Great Britain, in order to protect domestic produce
or manufactures. The argument was irresistible. Thus
the parliament legislated on the same grounds that
Macbeth moralized :—

> "——————— I am in blood
> Stept in so far, that, should I wade no more,
> Returning were as tedious as go o'er."

Precedents are legislators' leading-strings.

The excellence of precedents was illustrated by the
select committee in their Report on the corn trade in
1813, which Report was the parent of the corn law
of 1815. The committee, inverting the order of ancient oratory, began pathetically,—lamented the high
price of foreign grain, and the large sums it had cost
the country for the last twenty-one years. *Among the
evils of so great an importation* they stated *the established high prices of corn.* Yet the average price,
according to their statement, for the last twenty-one
years, was 77s. 3d. From these deplorable twenty-
one years they turn with some satisfaction to 1812 :

because, say they, this did in some manner restore the good old times prior to 1764. In 1812 England resumed the happy custom of exporting grain to foreign countries ; the exported grain being in that year 1,493,229 quarters, and the imported only 1,213,850. Here then, in 1812, we may behold precisely the state to which the legislators in 1815 wished permanently to reduce the people of Great Britain ; for their bill is but a modification of the report ; and both report and bill were passed by the same parliament, and supported by the same individuals. Look to the much-lauded 1812, and the circumstances of the people in that year. In this model year, 1812, the quartern loaf for eight months was at 1s. 6½d., and the quarter of wheat in March was enhanced to 122s. 8d. To this state a patriotic legislature, whose first concern was the labourer and the mechanic, would reduce the people!

We have enjoyed the corn law;—and what promise of its advocates has it fulfilled? It was to keep grain low-priced ; and the price was to be the same, or nearly so, at all times and in all years. Besides, it was said to be necessary to our existence as farmers ; lest we should, by leaving our ports open, be inundated with grain from France. Yet a few months after the passing of this law, a portion of the imported grain was re-shipped to France ; and in June 1817, Mr. Ponsonby, one of the most strenuous advocates for the corn law, called the attention of government to the export of corn from England to France. And so far was the wonder-working corn law from counter-vailing the intemperance of the air and the seasons, and the like, that scarcely had the legislative machinery begun to act, when this self-regulating instrument became irregular; the pendulum lengthened and increased its swing, its motion was accelerated, and from oscillating it became rotary.

Admirable legislators! who pass laws on the lawyers' dogma—the omnipotence of parliament. You vote that the Walcheren expedition was planned with skill and executed with ability;—that a golden guinea and a pound note with a shilling were of equal value; and you re-affirmed the same the subsequent session, though at these very periods the law-officers of the crown prosecuted Jews and turnpike-men for selling guineas for twenty-seven shillings in bank of England notes;—and you passed corn laws *to serve the people,* to increase the quantity of corn, and to fix and reduce its price! Acts of parliament of prohibition and bounty, to promote agriculture and to reduce prices! To these Mr. Malthus subscribes. Yet he says[1], " The prejudices on the subject of population bear a very striking resemblance to the old prejudices about specie." And this remark appears in a chapter entitled *"On the prevailing errors respecting population and plenty."* There are no greater prejudices than those in favour of bounties on the exportation of corn.

But then, as memory is stronger than reason, the consequence of the laws of William and Mary and Charles the Second! Suppose that these laws effected the consequences ascribed to them—whence the superlative benefit to the British of eating their own wheat without the mixture of foreign grain? Home-

[1] vol. 2. p. 208.

made, home-fed, home-bred, says the housewife: and, to exalt the illustration, the Persian kings could drink only of the water of the Euphrates. Why is it best, or good, that Britain should grow her own wheat exclusively? For the first fifty years of the last century England exported grain,—from 1783 to 1793 she imported largely;—was she less prosperous or powerful during that interval than in the exporting periods of her history? If we are to be ruled by precedents, let us revive the whole alimentary code. By the 31st of Edward I. the chancellor is ordered to regulate the buying and selling of stock-fish of St. Botolph and salmon of Berwick. And in Henry the Eighth's reign the chancellor's office was extended to the appraisement of poultry, beef, veal, cheese, and butter. Let no one say that all this is obsolete, for in 1815, when the parliament passed the corn law,—that grand assize of grain,—it also extended its saving sagacity to native cheese and domestic butter.

These are not the only monstrous views which this subject exhibits. We were told, that if we did not prohibit importation we should be overborne with foreign grain ; while we were advised to consider that other countries produced so little beyond their own consumption, that if we did not cultivate grain,— no matter at what cost and inconvenience,—we should subject ourselves to want, scarcities, and famine. Of all terrors and conceits, that of starving an opulent powerful nation is the most fantastic. England tried to intercept the supply of provisions to France ; and England, by Bonaparte's decrees and her own orders in council, was excluded from foreign assistance more effectually than any combination of enemies could possibly accomplish. A rich approachable country is always the least insecure of want of provisions; no matter whether it grows them or not. A rich country will be supplied before a less opulent or poorer one; though this produced the grain, the richer country will command it; for the holders of the produce will prefer those who pay the largest price, and those are the richest. It is therefore, not whether more or less is grown or exported or imported; the richest nation is the most secure from want. Where there are riches, there will be comparative plenty; and this must continue so long as men are moved by pleasure, and wealth is an agent in human affairs. Poland produced much of that grain which fed the Hollanders; and Poland and other agricultural countries have wanted food when Holland was amply provided. So in other particulars, Sir W. Temple says[1], there is more silver seen in Holland than brass in Spain and France.

The corn law was absurd and vicious, and it was lyingly and insultingly proposed and carried. The parliament passed it to serve the people! Legislators said so; though it was avowedly enacted to enhance the price of home-grown corn. Then it serves the people to pay a higher price for their bread; and therefore Peter, in the Tale of a Tub, was a matter-of-fact reasoner. If the parliament passed it to serve the people, it stands in the code as the city in the wilderness—wonderful in itself, and still more marvellous by the contrast which surrounds it—for where shall we find another statute sympathizing with the

[1] vol. 1. p. 66.

people! The fact is, the corn law was a short-sighted attempt to indemnify the country gentlemen who supported the war, by giving them and their farmers a monopoly of the prime necessary against all the people. Who believes that monopolies serve any but the monopolists? The corn law proposed that monopoly for the proprietors of land. The reign of Queen Elizabeth was disgraced by grants of various monopolies: " When a list of them," says Hume, " was read in the house, a member cried, Is not bread a monopoly? Bread! said every one with astonishment. Yes, I assure you, replied he, if affairs go on at this rate, we shall have bread reduced to a monopoly before next parliament [1]." This the parliament of 1815 endeavoured to effect.

CHAPTER VII.

Principal causes of poverty in England—the expense of the monarchy—namely, many courts, the nobility, the ecclesiastical establishment, the House of Commons, the national debt, subsidies, wars, military establishments, pensioners, sinecurists,—which are contrary to custom and precedents, to common sense and common honesty. The circumstances of England and America contrasted. —Reform.

The people are poor, and growing poorer. The cause of this seems to me no mystery. Some say, The more you give them the more they want. The misapplication of funds may increase the mendicant order, I admit; but the poor in England increase not by what is given, but by what is subtracted from the

[1] History, vol. 5. p. 439.

people. The wealth of states was derived from labour, and by labour it must be sustained. It seems equally clear that a certain profit is necessary to support capital, and certain wages to support labour. Thence it follows, that after a certain charge on capital it will escape abroad or perish at home; that this will affect the wages of labour, as it curtails the means of employment; and should wages, beside their depreciation in consequence, be lessened by direct or indirect charges, poverty must ensue. That this has happened, I shall evince by a recital of the repeated and enormous impositions on the people of England [1].

The British constitution is excellent. This has been ardently asserted at all times, and by the best authorities; by the commons house of parliament and its chiefs; by the lords, by the king, by the bishops, by the judges, by Lord Ellenborough, by Lord Mansfield, by Jefferies, by Finch, who insisted " None other can share with him (the king) his absolute power [2];" by Coventry, who defended ship-money ; " so gracious," said this lord-keeper, " is the frame and constitution of the king's government [3]." In short, the British constitution is always best, whatever changes it may undergo; and its excellence is commonly most applauded, when the greatest crimes are perpetrated against liberty under its supposed sanction : nor have I any doubt but that the beauty of the law and constitution was praised, as we have heard it praised, in Richard the

---

[1] This chapter refers to the poverty of the English. In another work I shall take a general view of the poor;— this present chapter is a restricted disquisition.

[2] State Trials, vol. 1. p. 769.   [3] Ibid. vol. 1. p. 566.

Second's reign, when Sir Thomas Haxey[1] was condemned to die the death of a traitor, for having moved in the house of commons that œconomy should be promoted at court; and that to attain this purpose the court should not be so much frequented by *bishops and ladies*. The constitution may then be called sacred,—consecrated by prescription; it is the best that ever existed. Then why should it not be the dearest; and why should not it, as it grows better than the best, annually increase its incredible expense according to its superlative perfection?

First stands the king, the πϑ στω, the *point d'appuie* of the system. The crown, so far back as 1810, received of droits 7,344,000*l.*; it received also, as far back as 1812, of $4\frac{1}{2}$ per cent. Leeward Island duties, 1,600,000*l.* The Prince Regent received also the revenues of the duchies of Cornwall and Lancaster[2], which revenues would of themselves support four or five hundred working families. The debts of the crown and of the prince have also been frequently paid by the people. Yet these enormous sums are but the extraordinaries of the royal revenue. The civil list amounts to nearly two millions a year. Above half a million[3] of the civil list is expended on the personal accommodation and private account of the Prince Regent.

---

[1] Cotton's Abridgement, p. 362. Reeves, &c. vol. 3. p. 218.

[2] How much does he receive from crown lands in Hanover?

[3] That is the sum allowed: yet it appears by an account presented to the house of commons, that for one quarter of a year ending 5th July 1814, the sum expended was 199,195*l.*; nor did this include the whole expense of that quarter.

This has alarmed many: but they should be told, indeed they cannot be told too often, the maxim is self-evident, That the king can do no wrong,—which is essentially true; for, according to the constitution, he can do nothing [1], say nothing. The constitution considers his acts in council, and speeches in parliament, the acts and speeches of ministers. The king of England, no matter who, is by nature angelic, and his government a mysterious energy. If then a minister, to whom the constitution attributes actions and language, receive ten or twenty thousand pounds a year, on the supposition that he exercises his functions [2], the king, or his *locum tenens*, whose characteristic is goodness, and whose power is divine, is not overpaid by many millions.

Besides, those who censure such prodigality err in supposing that, because these sums are charged to the prince or to the crown, they are expended for individual or private purposes. Who has hot heard of the splendour of the throne? A Spanish ambassador, being irritated by his master, who rebuked him for quitting congress for a ceremony, replied, "A ceremony! your majesty is but a ceremony." All talk—loyalists and reformers speak so much of the splendour of the throne, and so little of the virtue and wisdom and

[1] We now and then hear of a king and a prince writing a letter *with his own hand:*—this we should say emphatically of one who had marvellously recovered the use of his members, of which he had long been deprived.

[2] Horace Walpole says, that on the Duke of Newcastle leaving the ministry a closet of dispatches from America was found unopened.

knowledge of kings, that an over-curious person might be disposed to inquire into the paramount importance of burnishing the royal arms, and the chair of state, and the sceptre. Whom does this splendour serve? Not the king; for it is doubtful if a summer-fly rejoices in its hues even when it plays Adonis, and overlooks the flood. Can it serve the people? can it captivate them? Few have an opportunity of a transitory glance at the splendour of the throne. The splendour of the throne can serve few but carvers and gilders, and the like.

But I may be told that the splendour of the throne regards the palace, the equipage, the officers of the household, the gentlemen pensioners, and servants " plastered with gold." This brings the royal majesty within the circle of final causes; for Chrysippus said, A peacock was made for the beauty of his tail[1]. Of the court which costs so much, and where the crown exhibits all its glories, Sir W. Temple says[2], "A court, properly a fair, the end of it trade or gain, for none would come to be jostled in a crowd that is easy at home, nor go to service, that thinks he has enough to live with himself." The contemporary of Temple,

---

[1] Ο ταως ενεκα της ωρας γεγονε δια το καλλος αυτης. Plutarch. Moral. p. 465.

[2] Works, vol. 1. p. 312. Madame de Stael has given, in her "Germany," a most humiliating account of the nobles and court of Austria: yet to these, twenty-five millions of men, got together by every violence, are sacrificed,—and this is legitimacy. The disposition of the government is to sink men of superior merit. p. 63. " Noblemen of rank take their promenade on horses or in carriages of the greatest magnificence and good taste :—all their amusement consists in bowing in an alley of the Prater to those whom they

John Milton, when the expense of the monarchy was
not equal to one item in the modern account-royal,
lamented the cost of a monarchy. Johnson, who
called Milton a surly republican, resists the charge,
stating that Milton is ignorant and absurd; " that
the support and expense of a court are for the most
part only a particular kind of traffic, by which money
is circulated without any national impoverishment."
This is a new view of commerce. A court is therefore a national mart, in which the king's mistress is a
great trader. How ignorant then were " they of Tar-
sus and Mallos, (who) made insurrection because they
were given to the king's concubine," of political œconomy. According to this mercantile doctrine, though
" they that wear soft clothing are in king's houses,"
yet are they factors; and henceforward the court calendar must be considered as an appendix to the list
of merchants and traders. The whole of this topic
—the splendour of the crown, its traffic, &c.—is exemplified by a circumstance related by Park [1]. This
traveller was introduced to an original king of Africa.
His majesty, under various pretences, courteously deprived him of a variety of articles. At last he begged
Park's coat, which of course he obtained; but he assured Park that he would wear it on all public occasions for his sake.

have just left in a drawing-room." p. 75. " All the good company
transports itself, *en masse*, from one drawing-room to another three
or four times every week. A certain time is lost in the duties of
the toilet, which are necessary in these great assemblies; more is lost
in the streets and on the staircases, waiting till the carriages draw
up in order; still more in sitting three hours at table." p. 82.

[1] Travels, p. 55.

Beside the crown and court-royal, there are other courts: the king's court at Windsor is upheld at an expense of 220,000*l.* a year. Then the queen's court—*hic domus est triplex.* Besides these are many minor principalities; and all of them have had their treasures increased, in proportion to the debts and incumbrances of the monarchy: nay, in the midst of the national distress in 1816, 260,000*l.* were added to the civil list; and the ministers Castlereagh and Vansittart, in the same year, requested that 6000*l.* might be added to the Duke of Cumberland's pension, that the duke and duchess might live with *proper dignity and splendour;*—such were the words of their application.

To the expense of the crown succeeds that of the nobility. Judge Blackstone informs us, " A body of nobility is also more particulary necessary in our mixed and compounded constitution, in order to support the rights of both the crown and people, by forming a barrier to withstand the encroachments of both." Then the constitution consists of king and commons, and the nobility form an armed neutrality. Excellent commentator! Yet suppose it, How are the people's rights to be protected by having their chief men withdrawn by the king from among themselves, and placed among his own favourites[1]? To support the people against the crown, by the prerogative listing the chiefs of the people in the king's service, may be considered among the peculiar felicities of our constitution.

[1] Hominum nobilium non fere quisquam nostræ industriæ favit, nullis nostris officiis benevolentiam illorum allicere possumus ; quasi natura et genere disjuncti sunt, ita dissident a nobis animo ac voluntate. Cicero in Verrem, t. 2. p. 217.

Blackstone[1] announces another dogma, which is more to the present purpose. Having praised the right of the king to ennoble, he adds, "in order to reward such as are eminent for their services to the public, in a manner the most desirable to individuals, and yet without a burthen to the community." The remark is shallow and false: a body of nobility is an expense, merely as so many are separated and elevated above the people. Part of Sweden's misery is referable to its increasing nobles, and the lazzaroni are the effects of a numerous Neapolitan nobility[2]. Where there are many eminences there will be corresponding valleys; and as the hill ascends, the land becomes sterile and the climate austere; while the surrounding country, north, east, and west, is swept with the chill of its circling shadow. But it is not merely by removing men from citizens to a lordly state, that now in England and Ireland they become burthensome—a title and a pension are common associates[3].

Blackstone and the eulogists of king-ennobling may talk of the indescribable propriety of granting a title to men *eminent for their services,* "Et nobilitatur Rhegium patinis." But how can a British title ennoble, except technically; when not long after the Revolution, a draft was made from the commons to the house of lords, to effect a ministerial majority? when for a similar purpose, in 1777, another batch was drafted

[1] Commentaries, b. 1. c. 2. p. 157.
[2] Scipione Mazzelli considered that he eulogized his country, by saying that Naples had more nobility than all Italy. Storia, &c. p. 607.
[3] This adjunct was refused by Lord Hopetoun.

into the House of Lords:—and how often did William Pitt follow the same regimental precedent! in 1797 ten peers were made. He nearly created the order of marquises; he made ten marquises in England, where there was one; and nine in Ireland, where there were none—all men of course eminent for their *services*. He also rivalled King James in conferring knighthood on all men eminent for their services ; Sir Judkin Fitzgerald and the like. What is transubstantiation to this?

Without questioning whether one man can ennoble another, it may be doubted, when individuals are sent to the upper house as freeholders are sent to the pollbooth, whether true honour is not tarnished by the peerage. I believe this would have been determined in the affirmative by Queen Elizabeth. She was asked to create General Vere a baron; she answered, " that in her estimation he was above it already; and to make him one, would be to hazard that repute upon a carpet, that his valour had already earned in the field[1]." How many have been carpet-wrecked!—Saville, Pulteney, Pitt. Honour Pitt with the title of Lord Chatham, add 3000*l*. to support the splendour of his nobility ! Glorious prerogative of royalty ! Then sacred be Nero's latest egotism, "A consummate artist dies[2]." Nero gilded a statue of Phidias, and George the Third ennobled William Pitt.

Now the nobility are a direct charge: first, the man of merit is minted, and then the royal arms must be emblazoned, that his lordship may live in becoming

---

[1] Cayley's Life of Sir Walter Raleigh, p. 72.
[2] Qualis artifex pereo.

splendour; for in every thing the nobleman partakes of the monarch, just as radiant caloric is a constituent part of the solar ray. The king enjoys hundreds of thousands; so does the old peer a potent sinecure, or the new one a large pension. The last-made peer, Mr. Abbot, having enjoyed lucrative offices all his life, and having profited by them, was called to the upper house: and *to support the peerage*—such is the court cant—beside a sinecure of 1,500*l.* in Ireland for his *eminent services* in that country, a pension of 4000*l.* was added by the House of Commons[1]. Thus the public money is squandered, and the people impoverished. When England comparatively had no debt, Sir James Steuart, who saw the character of a nobility differently from Justice Blackstone, said, "If you cannot afford to have a nobility, let it die away[2]." But now, when we are with pretences and expedients, lotteries, exchequer bills *provided for* by redrawing others, and loans from the Bank, and paper issues, respiting the day of national insolvency; we increase our nobility, and their pensions also.

Whether the ecclesiastical establishment should not precede in these strictures the nobility, may be doubted. Perhaps I should at once demand forgiveness; for as Finch gave precedence to kings before the commons in respect of time, Laud, who asserted "No bishop no king," also presumed "there were Christian bishops before there were Christian kings."

---

[1] It is said that the house, furniture, &c. of Mr. Abbot cost the nation 200,000*l.*; but then he was such a Speaker! So was Mr. Addington.

[2] Political Œconomy, vol. 1. p. 65.

That *episcopus* appears in the New Testament is certain, and *episcopus* is translated *bishop;* but to infer a similarity of office between existing bishops and bishops in the apostolical age, on account of identity of name, might startle a mere grammarian. If names decidedly fix the characters of those to whom they are ascribed, parasite and bishop are one and the same ; as formerly parasite was a revered and sacred title[1], and his office particularly regarded the holy food[2]. Again, if a title determine the kindred, our bishops might be reputed successors of the priesthood of Diana; for there was in Pagan times, Diana the episcopal[3]. Mosheim speaks thus of bishops, past and present; " Let no one confound the bishops of this primitive and golden period of the church, with those of whom we read in the following; for though they were both designated by the same name, yet they differed extremely in many respects. A bishop during the first and second century had the care of one Christian assembly, in which he acted not so much with the authority of a master, as with the zeal and diligence of a faithful servant."

Bishops in after-times reversed this character; and, in defiance of the rebuke of him, whom they call their master, to his disciples, " Whosoever will be chief among you, let him be your servant," bishops assume

---

[1] Το τ8 παρασιτ8 ονομα παλαι ην σεμνον και ιερον. Athenæus, lib. 4.

[2] Την τ8 ιερου σιτ8 εκλογην αιρουμενος. Crates de Attic. Dialect. lib. 2.

[3] Plutarch. Moral. p. 182.

superiority over all laymen[1], and over each other:
nay Burke, uttering in oracular terms his Delphic
raptures,

"Os rabidum, fera corda domans, fingitque premendo,"

insists, "We [our provident constitution] will have her
[religion] to exalt her mitred front in courts and parliaments"—"We can see without pain or grudging,
an archbishop precede a duke[2]." False throughout!
We grudge it—the people grudge it, and they show
their dissatisfaction by separating from the establishment, the only way their wretched representation admits them to express their sentiments. A lord may
rejoice at seeing a bishop at levee; for he is probably
his brother, or cousin, or tutor. The people grudge—
for what do the bishops for their stipend? Old Lati-
mer reviled *unpreaching prelates,* and he directed them,
"Learn of the devil to be diligent in doing of your
office."

What do the aspirants at episcopacy? They labour
not. Spencer says that in Hebrew and in Greek, "Six
days shalt thou labour" is a command[3]. And Paolo
Sarpi says, "Men were commanded to eat bread by
the sweat of their brow. Now the clergy might as well
pretend to have been created free from original sin
as from this curse; though they are the executioners
of it, by selling again to the laity that bread which

---

[1] The presumption of the clergy that they are the church, is not
apostolical, it is among the corruptions of after ages.

[2] Reflections on the French Revolution, p. 152.

[3] De Legib. Hebr. p. 46.

they received from their ancestors under the title of alms[1]." But our constitution will not allow them to work. St. Paul did work with his hands, that he might not be a burthen to his congregation : but Mr. Burke would have surmounted his head with a mitre, and given him precedence in the courts of Tiberius and Nero.

What do the superior clergy? I speak not of the bishops professionally as spiritual pastors. Do they not preclude the most credulous from believing they can perform any service for the salaries they wring from the people? Some years since, a bill was brought into parliament to enforce residence. On this, the penalties incurred for non-residence were so numerous, that in a following session an indemnity bill was introduced, exonerating these unjust stewards from paying their forfeitures. Thus the parliament stultified its own laws, and an innovated benefit of clergy was passed, in order to evince the perfect union between church and state. In Henry the Eighth's time there were 200 dispensations for pluralities, now there are 2000 ; and last session, Mr. Gordon, in the debate on Mr. Sutton's 'Clergy Residence Bill,' said he knew a clergyman who was dignitary in no less than six cathedrals. Lord Redesdale also, when the same bill was debated in the House of Lords, said, that the mischiefs arising from the non-residence of the *lower* clergy were experienced in all parts of the kingdom ; —he said curates had been non-residents. Nearly one half of the clergy of the established church are non-residents.

[1] Rights of Sovereigns, p. 180.

Yet resident or non-resident, the clergy of the establishment are paid by the people; by the very labour of the people; by tithes, which Paley truly denominated most pernicious. It is a rent uncertain and inequitable; for the tithe may be the whole profit of the crop: it is a rent in advance; a tax on labour and capital; a penalty on agriculture; a prohibition to improve inferior lands, for lands will pay one rent, which cannot pay both proprietor and priest; and lands will return a profit to the cultivator, which cannot afford either rent or tithe. All these lands by tithing are condemned to barrenness. Few can imagine the ruin of this vexatious and barbarous imposition on population and tillage. Observe the effect of an inconsiderable impost. Mathison says, in his Notices on Jamaica, that in 1810 the tillage of 87,000 acres was suspended, in order to escape the payment of three-pence an acre. What then must be the effect of tithes in the present state of this country?

Yet, what import these considerations? Have the clergy reduced their tithes? Have the non-residents and pluralists taken counsel of St. Paul, who said, that those who do not work neither shall they eat; and stinted their appetite? No; they show their orthodoxy as Bel did his godship:—the priests of Bel having daily consumed twelve measures of fine flour and forty sheep and six vessels of wine, Babylon's king exclaimed, " Great art thou, O Bel! and with thee is no deceit." No species of property has advanced so rapidly as the stipends of the clergy[1]: in

1 See the Communications to the Board of Agriculture, vol. 5.

14 years (from 1790 to 1804) tithe had increased forty-eight per cent.

This was a subject for parliamentary investigation and legislative amendment; and not a corn law prohibiting the people from foreign grain. Yet during the debates on the corn bill in 1815, nothing was suggested respecting tithes. Compare this silence with the loquacity of a former period. The House of Commons in the 6th of Henry IV. proposed, in place of granting new supplies, that the temporalities of the church should be seized for the exigencies of the state : and they assigned as their reason, that the riches of the clergy disqualified them from their duties. They repeated the same in the 11th of the same king, when they required that fifteen thousand parish priests, with moderate stipends, should be substituted for the church establishment then existing. Hume expresses justly his surprise at such extraordinary efforts against the church ; when by the by he says, " The Commons showed a laudable zeal for liberty in their transactions with the crown." Four hundred years after (in 1815), the Commons showed no disposition for liberty or justice.

The proposal of the British Commons has been executed, and at no greater distance from England than the breadth of the Tweed. The Scotch reformed their church : and, fortunately for their own dignity and the good of posterity, they were not, like our valetudinarians on principle, unmeaning moderate reformers. The king and the parliament unanimously favoured an ecclesiastical establishment —the people resisted. They resisted James the First, who from a presbyterian apostatized to episopacy. This very James, who said[1], "If you aim at Scottish presbytery, it agrees as well with monarchy as God and the devil." They resisted Charles the Martyr, who said, No bishop no king : and Charles the Profligate, who insisted that presbyterianism was not a religion for a gentleman ; whose vigorous government declared that non-abjuring the presbyterian religion was a capital offence[2]; and which hunted and shot the conventiclers in pure love of king, and bishops, and Christianity. The Scotch immoderately and wisely resisted and reformed the clerical orders, in opposition to church and state, and kings, nobles, bishops, parliament and military; and the Scotch now live without bishops[3], without tithes, and effectually without poor laws.

What is the consequence ? The clergy are all sufficiently paid ;—none are mendicants and houseless, none are wallowing in wealth and literally enthroned in palaces : the business of the Scottish church is competently executed ; and the people profit by the advice and example of their pastors. This reform operates morally and physically. The Scotch, with a harsher climate and less grateful soil, pay greater rents than the English, are better farmers, and make their land more productive. The reason is obvious :

[1] Hume, vol. 6. p. 14.

[2] "In 1684 the privy council ordained that whosoever owned, or refused to disown, the declaration (adherence to the Presbyterian form of worship), should be put to death in the presence of two witnesses, though unarmed when taken." Bowyer's History of the University of Edinburgh, vol. 1. p. 307.

[3] There are some inconsiderable remains of that system.

they are not tormented with tithe proctors and tithing parsons—publicans and sinners. They know
what they are to pay ; their rent is fixed in consequence of a civil contract for an equivalent ; tithe,
which is as barbarous as lefsilver—(a fine paid
by the customary tenant to the lord for leave to
plough and sow) they suffer not. No other cause
can sufficiently explain how Scotland, which a century
ago was so poor, so wretched, so ignorant, so immoral—now equals England in all circumstances which
deserve competition,—but the better footing of its
church establishment. Superior climate and soil
and situation England still possesses ; and she had
enjoyed without rivalry superior wealth, improved
machinery, and more civilized habits, many years before Scotland had emerged from the depths of feudal
barbarism : yet now all is inverted, and England follows North Britain. The Scotch have no poor-rates ;
they have no tithe ; the people are better educated ;
they have parochial schools ; they have a diligent
moralizing clergy, springing from the people, and not
falling among them from aloft like meteoric stones,
they know not whence. As the clergy are derived
from the people, they in gratitude and duty serve the
people.

We are told, a tree is known by its fruit. But this
is not here directly the consideration, but the pauperizing effects of the ecclesiastical establishment.
Compare its charges—its onerous charges on population and subsistence, and the freewill offerings to
the Scottish clergy ; who when Adam Smith wrote
were supported for 60 or 70,000*l.* ;—while the clergy

of the ecclesiastical establishment of England and Ireland cost the people in tithe and territory eight or ten millions sterling. Nor are they satisfied with these sums; every year 100,000*l.* (perhaps all the Scottish clergy do not cost more) is granted by parliament to the clergy of this very establishment: nay, churches are built out of the exchequer of the state. The fact is, the church establishment has no sympathy with the people. Mr. Simeon says [1]; "There are about 11,000 places of worship in the established church, and about as many out of it." There are more: yet by this account it appears that there is no want of zeal in the people, as the Dissenters from the church, though taxed to support the establishment, build churches and support their ministers out of their own unassisted funds, which is an improvement on the Presbyterian church of Scotland; and unless we suppose that Protestants would have less regard for their clergy, if they were not forced on the people, there is no reason for concluding that a Protestant ministry should not be treated with equal affection and more generosity; as in this country Protestants are the opulent order. Yet we must not think of reforming this church establishment when the separatists are so numerous, and though they increase prodigiously. It has been estimated, that though during the first years of his majesty's reign Dissenting places of worship had increased beyond all former periods, they have during the last 14 years exceeded the first 14 years of this reign as

[1] Sermon on the Excellency of the Liturgy, preached before the University of Cambridge.

five to one. Thus while churches empty, the conventicle fills. In the parish of St. Pancras, there is one church which can contain about 200 persons : the population amounts to 40,000 ; yet the parishioners think this church sufficient. If the people's money is forced one way, while they go another, second-sight is not necessary to perceive that there must be a radical reform in the church establishment.

Having placed ecclesiastics after the nobility, (for which I request their excuse,) I proceed to the House of Commons—the double belt of Jupiter.

To exhibit this gratuitous representation of the people, of which less than two hundred individuals nominate a majority, would be a wretched office. I speak only of their expense to the nation, and by this expense their pauperizing effects. It may be truly said, that the great majority of seats in parliament are bought and sold, and many bought and sold with perjury and bribery and the subornation of many vices. What they want in honour is required in emolument; and thus a seat is considered a presentation for self, or, what is more common, for children and dependants, to various offices and emoluments. The frame of the House of Commons is new, is an innovation not only in the prolongation of parliament, but in respect to the views and conduct of its members. No one formerly presumed to consider the representation of the people in parliament a vested interest; and yet the porers into legendary lore affect to be ruled by precedents. A *printed* petition,—monstrous! Then Mr. Wynn, the speaker in expectation, says, that this question was agitated in 1656, and that a petition from Nottingham was rejected in 1813 : these entries[1], he says, established the rule. So in these legitimate times the House of Commons can take a precedent from Cromwell's creatures! and on this ground 468 petitions of the people were rejected. No reason was suggested; the parliament stuck to the precedent of 1656. It was a desperate hint to pregnant imaginations, and might lead to unreasonable precedents. Yet while the Commons rejected 468 petitions on this quiddit, started originally by a revolutionary government, the ministry prosecuted Mr. Wooler for ridiculing the right of petitioning, and which they made more than ridiculous. I remember, that some years since a determination not to petition was considered evidence of proneness in the people to sedition. What if it were proved that for centuries the House of Commons received only written petitions? and that before this, petitions were *viva voce?* for printing succeeded writing, and writing discourse. Suppose it were the practice during the Norman, Danish, and Saxon dynasties—what then? "Antiquissimum id habendum est quod optimum[2]."—But I speak of the expense of the house.

Bribery and seat-selling are later than the grand period of rejecting printed petitions. We read, in-

---

[1] Why are amendments printed? Is this practice older than 1656?

[2] Cicero, tom. 4. p. 338. Coke says of parliament; " Si antiquitatem spectes vetustissima, si dignitatem honoratissima, si jurisdictionem capacissima." 4 Instit. 36. And of the law of parliament he says, " Ab omnibus quærenda, a multis ignorata, a paucis cognita." 1 Instit. 11.

deed, of a mayor who in 1571 received four pounds for a seat in parliament; which Hume[1] supposes were given, as the seat afforded a privilege from arrest:—a seat in parliament being them burthensome. We read also of *undertakers*[2] who were employed to obtain a majority in James the First's time. But according to Sir W. Temple[3], and there is no better authority, bribery and seat-selling came with the Restoration. Temple says, the court party grew numerous in parliament " by a practice introduced by Lord Clifford, of downright buying off one man after another as they could make the bargain." It was a good precedent, and thrived wonderfully ;

> " In the porch Briareus stands,
> Shows a bribe in all his hands."

H. Walpole writes, that his father, Sir R. Walpole, used to say, it was fortunate few could be principal ministers, as thus few could thoroughly know the shocking wickedness of mankind. At last the world begins to know a little of the grand management of the House of Commons, the guardian in advance of our inimitable constitution. And most certainly the prize offered by George the Third in 1769 to the students of the Royal Academy, for the best painting on TIME DISCOVERING TRUTH, should be awarded to the present ministers. The plot, the reports of the secret committees, the seditious meetings bill, the suspension of the habeas corpus act—that outlawry of all the people—the relegation of the electors of Westminster from Palace-yard, Lord Sidmouth's circular,

---

[1] Hume, vol. 5, p. 183.   [2] Ibid. vol. 6. p. 71.   [3] vol. 1. p. 458.

the fomented insurrection, the trials, the convictions, the acquittals, the moral ostensible agents—Reynolds[1] and Castles, and Oliver and Bradley, and their parliamentary compurgators,—exhibit the *truth* of parliaments and ministers, to use a poet's expression, " all naked and raw life."

Of all modern departures from ancient practice by the House of Commons, none is more flagrant and enormous than their huge prodigality of the public money, emphatically the people's money. On this point their predecessors had been always chary. In all times tyranny could not force, fear could not extort, even an assurance of thrifty application and on occasions of great pith and moment was ineffectual to induce the House of Commons to lavish the public money. Hume[2], speaking of Elizabeth's reign, " Nor could the authority of that princess, which was otherwise almost absolute, ever extort from them the requisite supplies." Yet during the present reign the minister—no matter who, when, or for what,—ever wanted supplies, whatever was the amount of his demand. The reason is obvious. In the former periods of our history, the money voted was paid equally by the voters and their families and the people; and little was returned either to the voters or their families. Now, when the House of Commons votes millions, a share of this supply they or their families or dependants receive in advance by premiums on loans, by enhancing the price of money, by contracts, by

[1] On Oliver Bond's trial I heard him admit in detail, that he five times perjured himself.
[2] vol. 6. p. 202.

offices, by pensions, &c. The perniciousness of loans was exhibited by the failure of the income tax. Here the legislators counted that they should pay more than they and theirs could gain by the impost. Had the ministry reconnoitred the money market, as they did afterward, by means of the bank directors, œconomy would have been echoed as feebly as reform ; for the commons house of parliament voted the estimates and sanctioned a loan, equal to the income tax.

The waste of the people's money by the House of Commons is almost incredible. William Pitt attributed former wars to the corruption of the House of Commons[1]; and he insisted, that without reform the nation would be hurried into new debts and new wars, and that no honest minister could serve the nation. He gave the argument and the example—the prophet marvellously accomplished his own prediction.

It is wonderful how any nation could support such universal waste. The British subsidized almost every nation in Europe with many millions ; and she alternately fought and subsidized the same nation; she became security also for some, and of course liquidated their debts. She bound herself for Austria to her own money-lenders ; and she pays them, and must continue to pay them. She remitted ten millions ster-

---

[1] He called in 1782 the defect of the representation the *national disease ;* adding, " Without a parliamentary reform the nation will be plunged into *new wars ;* without a parliamentary reform you cannot be secure against bad ministers, nor can good ministers be of use to you. No honest man, according to the system, can be minister."

ling to the French[1], due for the maintenance of their prisoners, as part of the bonus for their submission to Louis. She pensioned the emigrant French priests, and continues to pay them. She paid Ferdinand's travelling expenses from Valencia to Madrid; Louis the Eighteenth's from London to Paris; the Pope's from Bologna to Rome. She, to please the Prince, raised a monument to the last of the Stuarts. Yet all these were but the outward flourishes of the waste and prodigality of our sad government.

For what has been the waste of our own warlike achievements? Mons. Calonne argued[2], that since the French revolution, four campaigns, with all the profusions, dilapidations, expenses, &c. did not cost France one-fourth of the expenditure of England in one year of war. And it is ascertained by accounts printed by order of the House of Commons, that for 1797, the year after Calonne made this observation, to January 1817, the gross revenue of Great Britain amounted to twelve hundred and ninety-two millions one hundred and eighty thousand five hundred and ninety-two pounds five shillings and three half-pence. This has vanished, and a debt has accumulated during

---

[1] This immense sum was remitted under the subterfuge of a comparatively inconsiderable sum being paid to private creditors of the French crown. Yet the most scandalous delays and subterfuges have been practised by the legitimate government of Louis; and in no instance has a substantial payment been made of the debts authenticated by the commissioners in 1814. And the same conduct is now pursued respecting the support of the army of occupation, who will soon retreat.

[2] Tableau de l'Europe jusqu'au Commencement de 1796. p. 68.

the same period of eight hundred millions. If to these sums we add four years' expense from the beginning of the war in 1793 to 1797, and all the local charges connected with the war, providing substitutes for the militia, &c.—this war, in favour originally of the Gallican church, and the noblesse of France, and the Bourbons, against reformation and the people's rights, from its beginning to the second restoration of Louis, cost Great Britain and Ireland thirty hundred millions sterling. Who supplied this? The people, constitutionally speaking, the commonalty of this realm. Yet the means by which these mighty sums were wrung from the people aggravated the enormity. Have the overweening friends of the constitution supported precedent on these occasions, either in the waste of the people's substance, or in the means of extracting it from them? At the Revolution of England, two shillings on every fire-hearth was taken off[1], "because," says the preamble of the repealing act, "it was not only a great oppression to the poorer sort, but a badge of slavery on the whole people; exposing every man's house to be entered into and searched at pleasure by persons unknown to him." What was this tax to *extents in aid*, which have ceased in some degree as flames on ship-board cease by the sinking of the vessel? What was the hearth-tax to that inquisitorial tax on income, when a man's cabinet was laid open, and he sworn to his secret drawers? What was the hearth-tax to the more inquisitorial

---

[1] Ireland still suffers this tax of course.

tax than that on income, the 55th of Geo. III. c. 184. respecting duties on legacies [1], &c.? What was the hearth-tax to the taxes on soap, leather, tobacco, salt? At Droitwich salt costs thirty-one pounds the ton, thirty pounds of which are duty; this is twenty times a greater tax than the hearth-tax. The senate of Rome—no very sentimental body—remitted the tax on salt, saying it was enough for the poor to support their children [2].

In consequence of such sums so extorted, the distribution of justice is a vain name; and the people become poorer and more vicious—" The vice of the poor is their poverty :"—and because the people would resume their rights, would elect those who are called the representatives of the people, would have *actual* representatives, (let their opponents enjoy *virtual* pensions and *virtual* sinecures,) &c. they are treated as outcasts and rebels. The ministry are fond of recurring to precedents. Chateaubriand's authority will not be questioned by the friends of the king and legitimacy: he says, " No sooner did the spirit of liberty make its appearance [prior to the French revolution] than *lettres de cachet* were multiplied : these letters caused, no doubt, more noise than mischief; but they were, it must be confessed, subversive of every legitimate principle [3]." This precedent the British ministry has followed; and many last year were imprisoned

[1] I have known the heir charged more for the tax or duty than he derived from the inheritance.

[2] See Machiavel's Discorsi, p. 61.

[3] Essay on the Revolution, p. 61.

without charge or trial. The church also followed a precedent at home [1]; and all good Protestants prayed against the madness of the people. Let the ministry remember, that it is proved by repeated publications, that kindness is the most effectual means of curing the insane, and that bad usage frequently drives the diseased to fury. Yet the remedies applied to the popular disposition for reform and œconomy are severe laws drawn strictly; new and severe interpretations; laws against meetings, against associations, against personal liberty; imprisonment without trial; trials in which a copy of the information would not be granted; for, said Lord Ellenborough in the case of Hone, *we have no funds out of which to pay the expense of making the copy.* Yet funds were at hand to array some twelve or twenty lawyers to prosecute the dupes of Oliver, the government spy. It was however signified to Mr. Hone that he might have copies on paying nine pounds. All no doubt conformable to the maxim of administering justice in mercy [2], and to

Hume, speaking of the clergy in the reign of Charles the Martyr, says, " So disgusted were all friends of civil liberty at the doctrines promoted by the clergy, that these invectives were received without control." vol. 6. p. 384.

We heard last session of the king's jails, and the mercy taught on that occasion. I imagine, considering some trials, &c. as Muir's and Lord Halifax's, that the axiom should be—Justice and mercy. Thus a friend to liberty obtains justice, as Muir, and is transported for fourteen years, for telling a friend he will find a certain book in his great-coat pocket. But a minister who would murder liberty obtains mercy. Halifax, who acted against freedom, obtained a privy seal from the king, that he should be indemnified for any damages granted by a jury for his wickedness. Annual Register, 1769, p. 151. This is mercy, and the brightest jewel in the crown!

Magna Charta, by which kings swore they would not sell, deny, or delay justice.

" L'injustice à la fin produit l'indépendence."

The people groan under aggravated oppression, and they are insulted, spurned, slandered ;—told of the splendour of the monarchy, and of the dignity of the peerage—of legitimacy, of precedents. Precedents cannot be too old or too new, if anti-popular ; and one from the Protectorate is irrefragable, because it impairs security and freedom. Septennial parliaments ; how old are they ? for the same wicked reason, they are most constitutional. Barracks, which Swift thought required explanation, are necessary to preserve military discipline, and to secure the soldier from the dangers of civil society : yet, if we believe Lord Eldon, when the Earl of Essex was dragooned in Pall Mall, every soldier is a citizen according to the constitution. Worthy interpreter of virtual laws made by virtual representatives! " Words are the daughters of earth, and things are the sons of heaven."

Nicholas Bacon [1] saw this subject in a different view from such dreamers. He said, " Henry the Seventh's guard he only pretended was a ceremony of state, brought from the French court ; and yet it is strange it went so well down with a free people. For that prince that will keep guards about his person in the midst of his own people, may as well double them into the pitch of an army whensoever he pleases to be fearful, and so turn the royal power of law into force of arms [2]." The military establishment was imitated

[1] On Government, part 2. p. 114.   [2] State Trials, vol. 3. p. 850.

from France, and is not older than Henry the Seventh. His soldiers were called pensioners, then yeomen of the guard, afterwards life-guardsmen; now they are denominated household troops. These now amount to 12,000 men, exactly the number of Louis the Eighteenth's Swiss guards; and the whole military establishment is from 130,000 to 140,000. Where is the precedent for this standing army, or any standing army? Lord Liverpool assures us, " the military establishment in 1792 will not now suit the state, as the population of Great Britain has increased since that period above two millions." Then the increase of the military is for home service. But are the British people more dangerous to king, lords, bishops, and their nominees in the House of Commons, and pluralists and sinecurists, than Bonaparte and all his means of destruction, when he menaced boastingly the British shores? Yet in 1817 the British government have a larger military establishment for their defence and their favourites, than Great Britain when that insolent despot threatened this nation with jeopardy; and in this same year the military establishment costs more by 400,000*l.* than the whole national expense in 1792. How is this to be defended? Not in respect to our finances, unless we recur to Dr. Johnson's correction of Milton; and as the money received by the crown, according to the critic, was on a mercantile account, we infer that the many millions paid to the military are also *a kind of traffic, by which money is circulated without any national impoverishment.* Had he said so, he would have been supported by royal authority; for Frederic II.

of Prussia wrote, in a letter to D'Alembert, " Mes nombreuses armées font circuler les espèces, et repandent dans les provinces avec une distribution égale les subsides que les peuples fournissent au gouvernement." If there be no royal road to mathematics, it appears that there is a royal and military road to political œconomy.

Let us inquire into this circumstance. In 1794 the subsidy to Prussia was calculated at 30*l.* a man for the troops he engaged to furnish, and the subsidy to Sweden was calculated at 40*l.* a man. Such were the prices of man in the cheap markets for belligerent consumption. In another part of the world, in Barbadoes, it is said, " An acre of plantable and productive land is sufficient to supply three persons with food ; and that a tenement for a foot soldier must be two acres, and for a horseman four [1]." Here, then, a foot soldier requires land sufficient for six persons, and a horseman requires land sufficient for twelve. In England, considering the bounty, the loss by desertions, the training and clothing the citizen before he becomes a citizen-soldier, according to Lord Eldon, costs a considerable sum, which, with his pay and allowances and accoutrements and lodging, raises his charge on the people to double and treble that of the wages of a day-labourer. If so, supposing a labourer to support himself, 100,000 troops require two or three times their number of labouring people to feed and clothe them ; and thus all these soldiers and supporters, to the amount of three or four hundred thousand, are deducted from the productive popula-

[1] Steele and Dickson, &c. p. 174.

tion of the state. This is restricting the remark to the common soldier; for if we consider the aristocracy of the army, field-marshals, generals, colonels[1], an army of 100,000 men pauperizes half a million of labourers, consuming more than they produce. The standing army, this huge appendage of the monarchy, cost in 1817, exclusive of the navy, a sum approaching to seven millions sterling. Considering this item of expense, is it wonderful that the people are poor, oppressed, that they wince, and are irritated? irritated, when they find the military increased beyond any former example—increased in peace beyond its excess in war when the nation was encompassed with peril and disasters—and when a thousand trials are making to find how much may be done by military means, by foreign mercenaries[2], with impunity;— when the military monarchs of Europe afford court models for orders of honour, and the birth-day is kept according to the continental calendar!

We come now to a motley and monstrous assemblage of pensioners, sinecurists, pluralists, who may

[1] In 1816 there were 4 field-marshals, 103 generals, 205 lieutenant-generals, 294 major-generals, 270 colonels, 880 lieutenant-colonels, &c.

[2] Earl Grey asked by what law Colonel Quintin, a German, was employed in the British service? *No answer from ministers.* What wretches are ministers who will serve such purposes! In a fortnight after this question a bill was brought into parliament, in which a clause was inserted, stating that foreigners might be appointed to commissions in British regiments. Mr. Horner noted the anomaly proposed; on which the Speaker said it was so important that he should move that the chairman should report progress. —How many foreigners are now soldiers in the British army?

be called generally state paupers. According to the interpreters of our excellent constitution, the crown must enjoy a prodigious revenue, that the prince may live in splendour. Then the archbishop must enjoy a mighty revenue, and the bishops, that the ecclesiastical halo may accompany with becoming brightness the royal luminary. The splendour of the throne declines with scrupulous minutiæ; and as the day, verging through hours and minutes to the west, ends at midnight, the archbishop, who has twenty or thirty thousand pounds a-year, and who d s nothing, sets in a curate having 50*l.*, or even less, who does every thing; for, said the bishop of Worcester, on Lord Harrowby's Curate's Stipend Bill, " on the subject of inequality in the church, it was necessary on a principle of human nature that there should be distinctions[1]." A begging curate and a prince bishop are a bishop's exemplifications of the inequality of human nature. Lord Ellenborough, in the same debate, declared in his usual manner;

" Turbidus hîc cœno vastaque voragine gurges
     Æstuat—— "

" that inequality of rank was as necessary in the church as the state[2]." Admirable constitutionalist!

[1] In 1813.

[2] That the clergy should pauperize the laity is not strange, considering that they have no bowels for their own profession. Year after year bills were brought into parliament by Sir W Scott and Mr. Perceval, in 1805 and 1808, to relieve the curates; and they failed by the opposition of the ecclesiastics. Thus they forced their body to apply to parliament for 100,000*l* a year. Begging is also customary in the rich diocese of Durham. There the revenue of the clergy amounts to about 200,000*l.* a year; yet every year

But why, when the bishop is crowned with a mitre, are not curates, as subdeacons were formerly, inducted by the delivery of an empty platter?

By parity of reasoning the commander-in-chief also must enjoy a princely revenue; and the descending scale must also be preserved in pay and in prize-money. When the British took the Havannah under Lord Albemarle, the commander's share of the prize-money was 20,000*l.*, while the privates received 13*s.* 5*d.*; and Lord Palmerstone said, last session [1], that prize money during the late war was distributed on the same principle as in former wars. Thus the commander is esteemed equal to twenty or thirty thousand private soldiers;—and thus the church is directed by the state, and both regulate the army [2]:—admirable harmony!

> " Where order in variety we see,
> And where, though all things differ, all agree."

And for aught I know, this happy adjustment and special concordance is as old as Linus, who sung

> " Omnia sunt unum, sunt omnis singulæ partes."

Of course ministers must live in splendour, and all their families possess offices, emoluments, pensions,

there is a general begging for the poor clergy and their families. If it be not continued, the reform is attributable to the public exposure of this baseness by William Burdon, a scholar, a thinker, and a sincere and strenuous friend of liberty and truth.

[1] 26th June 1817.

[2] So of the navy. In 1813, when there was not an enemy at sea, there were 180 admirals, 798 captains, 595 commanders, besides superannuated officers. These I do not object to, nor to those pensions enjoyed by the naval officers; but to the relative situation

sinecures, &c. Observe, the placeman s salary, though excessive, is not enough ; sinecure employments must be added. Mr. Malthus descanted on an over-breeding people, and thence deduced their poverty. Yet Lord Bathurst, in 1815, received of public money as much as the amount of the whole poor rates of the city of Norwich. George Canning, too, was not satisfied with 18,000*l.* a year [1], and the dignity of ambassador during his attendance on a sick child at Lisbon, nor with pensions to his mother and sisters. Nay, he proved to an admiring parliament that this office was put upon him ; that it was a losing trade. He indeed is worth his hire. He disdains to reprove innovations [2] which embraces every improvement from the savage state onward, as beneath his high displeasure ; he will not tolerate the word reform ; — for while some recommend oxygen, or pure vital air, to cure consumptions, this *docteur en droit* prescribes the damps of jails as the only medi-

of the chiefs of the naval establishment, and of the sailors. Lord Albemarle obtained 20 000*l* and a sailor 13*s*. 5*d*. Yet of the droits of the crown, amounting to millions, a sailor obtains not one penny. There is another point :—To educate 71 boys at the Naval Asylum costs 400,000*l*. The sailors, during the expenditure of these sums by the crown and the aristocracy, starve, die in the streets, or are hanged. Yet these are things that should not be reformed, or moderately reformed. We must speak of them with temper :— political quietism is the worst state-heresy.

[1] He had an office in the alien department, worth annually four days of his pay at Lisbon.

[2] Hume says: " And though many constitutions, and none more than the British, have been improved even by violent innovations, the praise bestowed on those patriots, &c." History, vol. 5. p. 452.

eated atmosphere. Mr. Canning is an orator and an ambassador—so was Demosthenes. But Demosthenes damned Philip and tyrants. Mr. Canning descants against Spence and the Spenceans. When Demosthenes was sent by the republic of Athens to negotiate with the ablest monarch of the age, his salary was about one shilling a day. When Mr. Canning was sent about nothing to nobody, he had fifty pounds a day. Yet who dare doubt the patriotic virtues of Mr. Canning? His virtues shine through him ;—nay, virtue is in him like the motion of light in diaphanous bodies ;—yet does this miserable man call the people fickle, rebellious, insensate[1]. When has the public voice been declared? The people distinctly condemned the slave-trade, the corn bill ; and they have spoken decisively in favour of reformation and œconomy. Time has justified and will justify their determinations. A sneaking enemy, a truckling associate, this sordid man calls all reformers profligates and criminals. Thus, as he exposes his own unprincipled greediness, he riots in popular abuse; and thus he resembles the orator Demades, who sold his country to Philip and Antipater, of whom it was said, He was as a beast after sacrifice, of which nothing remained but the tongue and paunch.

Sinecures pointedly aggravate the rapacity of the holders. The lord treasurer is his own auditor, attorneys-general chief judges, a chief judge his own jailor. Then there is a chief justice of the forest, as

---

[1] Machiavel says, " La moltitudine e piu savia e piu costante ch' un principe;" and this he proves in one of his longest Discorsi. p. 102.

there was and is possibly an admiral of Connaught. The apostate Wentworth enjoyed the office. But we are told by some, whose high names disgrace the opposition[1], and help the undistinguishing contempt of all parties, that sinecures are necessary to the crown[2], to attract men of talents, and to reward them for their public services. What have been the services of Lord Arden, or Mr. Knox the prothonotary, whose brother possesses also from sixteen to twenty thousand pounds in the church? What have been the mighty deeds and achievements of George Rose[3], who recommends saving banks to the people while he opens the vomitories of the treasury, and who himself, besides lucrative offices, enjoys a sinecure of 8000*l*. a year, which is confirmed to his son in succession? If the public money were forced out of its direct channels to relieve the necessitous and the distinguished, there might be some colour of argument for the abuse. But what has this sinecurist performed, which might not have been adequately and congenially paid by secret service money? Thus it is in other parts of the world.

[1] The bill introduced by the ministry, which was opposed by sinecurists and patriots, proposed to reduce in *twelve years* places amounting to 57,000*l.*, to pensions amounting to 42,000*l.*

[2] Those men consider the power of the crown and the authority of the people as directly opposed. Sir N. Wraxall was attacked by all parties. I wonder his sighing over the extinction of some places did not excuse him a little; he said, " it deprived the crown of that species of majesty produced by the operation of time and the hoar of ages ;—and that this was calculated to protect and perpetuate the sanctity of the monarchical office." vol. 2. p. 182.

[3] He wrote an answer to Charles Fox's History, and every observation was false without exception. The whole was a tissue of falsehood. He wrote a pamphlet to prove that the influence of

At Surat, says Niebuhr, there is no hospital for human beings; but there is an extensive one for inferior animals. I saw a great tortoise in it; it was blind, helpless, and very old.

No point is more *constitutional* in Great Britain, than that because a man had an opulent office, he should enjoy, on quitting it, a large pension or sinecure. Why one who had been chancellor, or ambassador, or prime minister, or lord of the admiralty, and was enormously paid in office, should have, on his retirement from office, pensions or sinecures, is inconceivable[1]; except it be a maxim, that every one connected with the government enjoys a right of commonage over the whole property of the people. For it is not only Lord Sandwich, who on his retiring from the admiralty became ranger of the park, and his son Lord Hinchinbroke master of the buck-hounds;—but from these mighty ones spring another retinue of sinecurists and

the crown had not increased; when no family, that pretends to gentility, is without a placeman or an expectant. In this pamphlet he bears testimony to Mr. Pitt's extravagance, who had in 1789 greatly embarrassed himself, and who refused a subscription from ship owners, &c. to relieve him. This he eulogizes. I was informed by the person who was deputed to the editor and the printer of a Sunday newspaper, who were imprisoned for two years, and fined a thousand pounds; that if they chose their fine should be paid, and they should never be made acquainted with the means of the payment. Yet these men, who had not thousands a year, and who were suffering in a public cause—the cause of truth—refused to accept my friend's offer, and actually paid the fine out of their own narrow funds.

. [1] If there be honour in the officer or the office, he should be paid less than the marketable loss in obtaining the office. At Venice ambassadors received no salary. Wickfort, p. 113.

pensioners, as it is said the locusts arose from the blood of the giants. Mr. Edward Cooke, Lord Castlereagh's under secretary, retires with 4000*l.* compensation for his eminent services; and this man has another minor retinue, who under gracious names are quartered on the community [1].

Such are the pregnant causes of the people's poverty, which Mr. Malthus and his school could not see, do not see, and will not understand. Nature and overbreeding!! No, it is what made Catiline poor—*alieni appetens, sui profusus ;* it is what impoverished the Roman state, *rapti largiuntur.* Is not this the state of Britain? Is not the treasury pennyless? Is not the prince poor, aye, the poorest? " What," says Temple, " is the fantastic calculation of riches and poverty that is current in the world, by which a man that wants a million is a prince, he that wants a groat is a beggar [2]!" Are not the nobles poor? they are pensioners and immersed in debt. Are not the members of the House of Commons poor? poor in every sense : having appropriated the rights of the people, they have squandered their fortunes ; while mendicant ministers require their sa-

Pension on retirement..	£1500
Compensation of a reversion	500
Ex-revenue officer.....................	400
Keeper of the Irish Records	1000
His wife keeper of Dublin-castle, which she keeps as he does the records.	600
	£4000

Compare Secretary Walsingham, in Hume's History, vol. 5. p. 521, to this under-secretary. In short, England now pays inversely as she is served.　　　　* United Provinces, p. 50.

laries to be continued when they do nothing, even when they are discharged. Very different are they, nay, in direct opposition to the thrifty yet generous individuals of the time of Queen Elizabeth. Then large private fortunes were expended for public purposes. "Such," says Hume, "was the spirit of Elizabeth's reign [1]." If distress pervade the higher orders, even those " who stand in the gap and trade of more preferments," when many escape to the continent or America, and families are expatriated by taxation, must not the people be poor, who support themselves and all others? a tremendous train—the crown ; many courts; principalities; an increasing pensioned nobility; a House of Commons, bought and sold frequently in a single session; an ecclesiastical establishment, which costs yearly eight or ten millions, with tithing which ruins more than it extorts ; a military establishment, whose annual charge to the people exceeds six millions sterling; a crowd of pensioners, sinecurists, placemen, pluralists, who are again involved in an atmosphere of consuming insects, each of which, like the blistering cantharis that exudes a clinging grub, generates a self-ravening disease; for now placemen and pensioners, having exhausted the people, prey on each other, through habitual craving and insatiable voracity. These are the causes of the increase of the poor, and of the accelerated advance of general delinquency.

The friends of the commonalty have solicited reform, have appealed to records against the duration of parliament; against the nomination of the Commons by lords and individuals, and against the monstrous waste and prodigality of the national substance through the

[1] vol. 5. p. 379.

means of parliament. They have been repelled, contemned, slightingly told that ancient times suit not modern circumstances. They then unwillingly, being precluded from learning of their ancestry in Britain, are forced to regard the conduct of their children beyond the Atlantic.

Those who originally left England for America were few and poor[1], and not remarkable for their morality. It is computed[2], that about 80,000 persons left these countries prior to the middle of the last century. In 1749, the whole white population in the United States was estimated at 1,046,000[3]. In 1782, by a return to congress, the population amounted to 2,389,300. In 1790, the inhabitants amounted to 3,929,326. In 1800, to 5,309,758; in 1810, to 7,239,903. It is probable, that now the population reaches eight and a half or nine millions ;—such is the advance of the United States, to which, so lately as 1766, England transported her criminals.

This advance, though partly attributable to situation, soil, &c. is mainly to be referred to the constitution and the government of these provinces; for South America, which is equally favoured, halts comparatively in its progress. The constitution of America is determinate[4] and *written*[5], and acknowledges

---

[1] Davenant's Works, vol. 2. p. 3. [2] Ann. Register, 1760, p. 195.

[3] I take these numbers from Pitkin's Statistical View, p. 174. 250.

[4] Hume says, " The sacred veil which had hitherto covered the English constitution, and which threw an obscurity upon it so advantageous to royal prerogative," &c. vol. 6. p. 117. Yet it appears that the *ambiguous nature*, as he elsewhere calls it, promoted the destruction of Charles. p. 207.

[5] The vagrant character of the English constitution I have exposed in Defects, &c. of the English Laws.

no hereditary sovereign; the president is elected every four years, and he receives 25,000 dollars (not 6,000*l*.), about the sixth part of Lord Arden's sinecure.

America has no hereditary legislators, no house of lords; the senators are elected every six years.

The house of representatives is elected every two years, almost by universal suffrage, and districts increase their numbers by one representative for every 30,000 additional voters. There are no boroughs, close or open. The ordinary congress or parliament cannot alter a fundamental law[1], nor advance their own trust to three and seven years; there is no undefined privilege[2] belonging to the American parliament. There is no ecclesiastical establishment; no state religious establishment; no tithes; no intolerance for faith sake; all sects are equally eligible to all offices.

There is no court of equity; no ex-officio informations; no special juries. Paine's Politics and *Reason*, and the like, are published with equal indifference and security in America[3]. There are no sinecure places; no pensions to ministers and minions; no secret service money, which in 1810 in England amounted to 270,000*l*. and in 1815 to 175,000*l*.

The salaries of the public officers are small; the

[1] The president, December 2, 1817, signified that congress cannot, by the constitution, enact a law for roads and canals through the United Provinces, and that congress must request an enlargement of their powers for this purpose. Yet the Irish parliament committed suicide.

[2] " These privileges are at present as undetermined as were formerly the prerogatives of the crown." Hume, vol. 6. p. 459. More so.

[3] Vanderkemp laments that infidelity is general in North America, and that Paine's works are found in the lowest cottages.

second in dignity in the state receives only 5000 dollars (about 1100*l*.) a year. Yet the common seamen in the service of the American government receive four times greater wages than British sailors; in America there is no pressing. There are few soldiers in the American states; but there are 800,000 militia. America had contracted debts in attaining her liberty and securing her power, and in 1809 her government extinguished 33,580,000 dollars of debt, the whole that could be liquidated according to the original contract with the public creditor. At present, having purchased Louisiana and Florida, having increased by peaceful means her provinces from thirteen to twenty, having concluded a war of difficulty and expense,—Mr. Monroe, the president of America, December 2, 1817, called on congress to repeal all the internal taxes [1], America being restored to the situation it enjoyed under Mr. Jefferson, when a tax-gatherer was unknown in the United States. Such are the products of popular representation. It increases the people, and it increases still more their opulence, their agriculture, their manufactures: in 1790, America did not possess a single cotton-mill; after a few years it counted a score; they now exceed a hundred.

Let the British learn of their children to redeem themselves from the abyss into which ministry has forced them; let them resume their rights. The constitution of Great Britain is essentially popular—all who are

---

[1] Yet England, taxed till the heart-strings of her people crack, after paying the interest on the debt and sinking fund, amounting to 44 millions, has seven millions for the current expenses of the empire—the revenue being 51 millions: I omit fractions.

not king and nobles are the people, are designated the commonalty. How utterly absurd then is the doctrine, that king and lords and people are coequal ! unless we speak *virtually.* James the First called himself the great servant of the public : the king is the chief officer of the state,—how then can one man paid by the people be esteemed tantamount to the people? How can the nobles, who spring from the king, countervail the commons? To say so is miserable flattery, beginning with crown lawyers and ending with the laureat's choir :

" For 'tis their duty, all the learned think,
T'espouse the cause by whom they eat and drink."

Yet this has infatuated kings, maddened nobles, and ruined the people. They (the minions of the crown) told the king, " Creation's heir, the world, the world is thine," that the more he spent the circulation of wealth was quickened : though truly the expenditure of kings (I speak not of what is necessary for them, but of their regimental state and their prerogative prodigality,) is a greater loss than the burning decrees of Bonaparte to British merchandise. Œconomists talk of the cost of production; but there is a cost of consumption—a *superlucrative* loss; for where much is to be consumed, much is often consumed in that consumption. Besides, a fête at court, some gewgaw of furniture or equipage, and the like, occasions a general imitation, and waste and want succeed. Hence every man connected with the crown, directly or indirectly, is paid excessively, and is excessively distressed—even to Trip, who raises money by way of annuity.

Œconomy is slighted as a shop-keeping article. Hence immense salaries, sinecures, pensions; hence political prodigality, bribery, and corruption[1]. Money must be had; lands are mortgaged, the peer is bought, and his price purchases many. Money must be had: the government confederates with the Bank; and the late rational Mr. Horner characterized truly their intimacy, " as exhibiting the most profligate profusion on one part, and the greatest rapacity on the other." Hence arises a national debt, which has utterly changed the property, the character of property in this country; for the proprietors of lands and houses are in fact tenants to public creditors, who are usufructuaries, and who, in some degree, are an unproductive order. Thus to the landed gentry have been added moneyed gentlemen, who are a load and an impoverishment. " Let states," said Bacon, "that aim at greatness, take heed how their nobility and gentlemen multiply too fast; for that makes the common subject grow to be a peasant and base swain driven out of heart, and in effect but a gentleman's labourer; so that there will be great population and little strength."

The government has increased its nobility and its gentlemen; and instead of relieving the people, it labours to support perversely the creatures of its vices

[1] Ambassadors were called court-spies:—they are something more now. Coxe says, that except Eugene, all the Austrian ambassadors received largesses from Riperda's agents, " Even the emperor himself did not blush to encourage this venal traffic by his own example." Eugene said, Much may be done in London by the same means. What are these snuff-boxes of 1000*l.* value, but bribes ?

and its mismanagement. The government endeavours to support the landed interest by corn laws. Shallow ministers! Locke long since said [1], " The public expenses of government will fall on the land ; —the labourer cannot, the merchant will not;—therefore the landholder must." This is particularly true in England, where wages are ruled directly by statute, and indirectly by the poor-rates. The corn law also, as I have said, is of the same description; which, if it succeeded by enhancing the quartern loaf and upholding the price of land, must be nugatory or worse, for the poor-rates must increase in proportion. Sir James Steuart said [2], " If therefore, according to modern œconomy, the lowest species of labour must be kept cheap in order to make manufactures flourish, the state must be at the expense of the children." This has been the case, and exhibits truly the wondrous sentimentality of the poor laws. On this reasoning, supposing that the corn laws effected their intended purpose, the state must have been at the expense not only of the children but of their parents also.

The expedients of the government to support its being by its extravagance, might be exemplified by a starving animal gnawing its own members. Mark their dilemma :—the supporters of government prepare to fall off, if they are not paid for the discredit attached to their service ; and the people are incapable, were they willing, of still affording the means of bribing their enemies to their own destruction. This

<hr>

[1] Observations, &c. p. 95.   [2] vol. 1. p. 153.

the ministry at one time call Jacobinism, at another rebellion; sometimes also a transition from war to peace. It is the transition of the prodigal who prepares to settle his accounts. Transition! It is of bad to worse—when the leprous disease having overspread the body falls inward on the sources of life. It is a transition from worse to worst; and the government would correct it accordingly:—they outlaw the nation, suborn the base, abuse the unsuspecting, drive the objects of their hate from town to country, sink them in prisons—in prisons where they (contrary to law) consign them, unheard and unseen, to their own solitary executioners; prosecute day after day, on the same lying charge, the same victim : their impotence and malice correspond, like the torpedo, whose shocks when dying quicken in number as they decrease in force.

The people will not bear this maltreatment much longer; they cannot:—they must resume their rights. The situation of the governors and the governed approaches the state antecedent to order—when levity contended with weight, and darkness with light[1]; it is of the few against many, of one against all. Under such abuse of power and property Lord Liverpool might well be affrighted by the increasing population of Great Britain. He is not particular in this respect: the multitude was troublesome to Egyptian sovereigns[2], who, to secure their despotism, effeminated[3] the men, and introduced sectarian dissension

[1] Mollia cum duris, sine pondere habentia pondus.

[2] Plutarch says, υπο πληθους. Moral. p. 278.

[3] Scholia in Œdip. Coloneus of Sophocles.

among the people [1]. This has been the resource of the enemies of toleration and liberty in the British councils. But it will not again avail. Many, which are the wicked one's weakness, are the people's strength. Besides, the many think, they understand, they have long felt; the people have determined;—the crisis approaches ; and if justice be not promptly rendered to the people, the *choice of Hercules* must be achieved by the *force of Hercules*.

CHAPTER VIII.

Conclusion—Summary view.

I do not say that none propagate improvidently ; but that the improvidence of the people, in this respect, is only one cause in many of the miseries of the people's making. And in saying this I exonerate government and the laws—the chief causes of public misery—from many human afflictions. Every vice and imprudence occasion a portion of misery ; and if the propagation of mankind now ceased, misery would continue ; unless we conclude that the sterility and the perfectibility of the human race are identical expressions. Mr. Malthus geometrizes, multiplies the bred into breeders ; wonders and cries with Archimedes, " I have discovered it !" as if all hurried together, like the atoms of Democritus. On the contrary, the moral check, which escaped Mr. Malthus

[1] The very bill that was the cause of the preceding ministry abandoning their situation—and against which the present ministry raised the *No Popery* yell,—the same ministry introduced themselves last session, and it passed without notice.

entirely in the first edition of his work, and crossed him only in vision in the second, perpetually operates in every class of society; and perhaps few have reached a certain age without having suffered frequently its admonitions and control. What are all the laws of marriage, but this moral providence authenticated by the supreme authority of nations?

I do not see *deep-seated causes of evil in nature* (to use Mr. Malthus's expression). There are accidents which no prudence can prevent, and malignant and pinching seasons intervene. I say seriously and sincerely, I cannot call these evil;—they may be necessary, they may be good, they may be indifferent. But when Mr. Malthus refers a propensity to breed to the same abyss of mysterious evil, I deny the imputation. Without any pretensions to reason beyond experience, I call this propensity a manifest good, without which man and woman separately would exhibit incomplete creatures.

The power to generate is strenuous, but not self-destructive; and the ability to increase rapidly the species is essentially beneficial. Thus society is enabled to retrieve its occasional losses and criminal mortality. The Romans lived in perpetual warfare; every year four legions were raised of 4000 foot and 200 horse[1], each of which occasionally was increased to 5000 foot and 300 horse[2]. At the battle of Cannæ, of 80,000 foot and 6000 horse[3] (the whole

[1] Polybius, lib. 1. c. 16.

[2] Ibid. lib 3. c. 107. Ten legions were enrolled against the Volsci, of 4000 each. Dion Hal. lib. 6. c. 42.

[3] d. c. 113.

army), 70,000 were slain[1]. Yet after this destruction and the immense waste of men in this war, the consuls again brought into the field a powerful army. The followers of Odin were still more incessant in their wars; and so prodigal were they of life, that a death not violent was ignominious[2]. What destruction of people in France during the last 25 years —forced emigrations, murders on the scaffold, civil wars! Hoche computed that the war of La Vendée cost the republic 600,000 Frenchmen; —wars by sea and land throughout the world. In 1794 France counted 750,000 in the field, and nearly 400,000 in the reserve or sick. In 1798 it was decreed that every Frenchman was a soldier, and the conscription affected all men from 20 to 25 years of age. Mons. Pradt estimates the loss of the French in six campaigns in the Peninsula at 600,000. Jomini states the levy in 1812 and 1813 at 1,307,000, and specifies their situation and duties. Of the 524,000 who assailed Russia, of which a considerable body was French, few returned. Yet the next year the French, after many sanguinary battles, brought 170,000 Frenchmen into the field at Leipsic. And the next year they fought the allies, and suffered severely. Yet after these monstrous losses in men France contained, according to Mons. Mentelle, after the treaty

[1] Polybius, lib. 6. c. 56. Paterculus says, that a few years after Rome was taken by the Gauls it became very populous. lib. 1. c. 14.

[2] Mallet, vol. 1. p. 102. Temple was shown by Oxenstiern, a bay in Sweden where those *past all military action threw themselves.* Works, vol. 1. p. 216.

of Paris, 28,246,360 inhabitants, which corresponds with the calculation of Mons. Calonne [1] of the population of France in 1797.

> " Les débris s'animaient, la mort était féconde,
> Et la déstruction renouvellait le monde."

Such is the disposition of the people to repair the ruin of their rulers—of life to have an heir—of matter to be organized. This passion, this energy, is evinced in various countries and situations. Park says [2], " Notwithstanding the exterminating system, it is surprising to behold how soon an African town is rebuilt and repeopled." The spirit of reviviscence is singularly exhibited in Smyrna. Previous to 1675 it had been six several times partially destroyed;—in 1688 it was assailed with three of the greatest calamities—a fire, an earthquake, and an inundation of the sea;—repeated convulsions, annual pestilences, are its visitants:—yet even amidst the Turkish empire it continues and increases; and when Mr. Hobhouse wrote, the population, amounted to 150,000 inhabitants [3]. The tenacity of life, the disposition to continue existence, is evinced by the Berebbers, sons of the descendants of those who probably possessed Carthage before the Tyrian colonists;—by the Copts, no inefficient population the representatives of the ancient Egyptians;—by the Pariars of Hindostan; the Poolears of Malabar, who are also esteemed the aborigines of the country, though they are loathed and abhorred;—by the Parsees, a considerable body

---

[1] Tableau de l'Europe, p. 10.   [2] Travels, p. 291.
[3] Travels, p. 616.

living at Guzarat, who fled a thousand years ago (in 767) from Kirman, to avoid the persecution of the Mahometans. Regard the Gipsies; whether they are descended from the vagrants mentioned by Juvenal, or from Indian refugees who escaped the cruelties of Timour, or whether they are descended from Egyptians, according to Mons. Gebelin,—they live in spite of all privations of life.

Thus do I show no disposition to lessen the argument of those who travail in their discourse about the propensity of men to propagate their race. Grant that man is as prone to breed as matter to descend, and that gravitation and generation are twins of one necessity. Yet, unhappily, there is a power which can neutralize desire and extinguish the sources of generation. It is true, men survive ages and centuries of persecution; and though they inhabit the pole and the line, and promontories and rocks the most inhospitable, yet they shall not outlive despotism. True, Ormus [1], a barren rock of volcanic formation, the basis salt, without a spring or rivulet, having little rain, producing no food, the heat intolerable, was populous and opulent; while in an opposite extremity Samoida [2], which to the misery of a disastrous climate and sterile land endures taxation, is inhabited. So is Finmark, though the inhabitants are tithed for the fish [3] they catch with diffi-

[1] Vincent's Nearchus, p. 322 et seq.—Pinkerton's Voyages, vol. 9. p. 405.

[2] Every one who pulls a bow is to pay a skin worth 25 copecs. Pinkerton, vol. 1. p. 530.

[3] This was divided by Christian the Fifth, (of glorious memory,

culty. So under the 69th degree of latitude, on the banks of the Mosenelo, which the wandering Laplanders seldom visit, a colony of Norwegians established themselves; and they have never required foreign assistance. Hamerfest also, which may be called midway between earth and Erebus, where the smaller vegetables will not germinate nor trees grow, which labours under a continual fog; yet counts forty inhabitants. True: and let those who insist upon the original sin of breeding by a compound ratio, or a geometrical series; let all revilers of the poor, among whose greatest miseries are such slanders, take advantage of these facts: nay, if it serve them, let them know that the population of Lapmarken in Swedish Finland, from 1751 to 1801, has increased from 26,000 to 52,000.

Such is the power of generation and of life in mankind;—man will live and increase where the land is rock, the water ice, under perpetual night; where "the air burns frore, and cold performs the effect of fire." Yet despotism is worse than all these together; and man perishes under misgovernment, though surrounded with a wilderness of enjoyments. What other cause reduced many populous countries to deserts, and continues them so? Have they become effete? has mortality struck the elements of their composition? There can be no competent cause assigned for the immense tracts of land once populous, and equally fruitful now as then, but misrule; for we find with liberty,

says Leems,) between the king, the church, and the clergyman. Pinkerton, vol. 1. p. 446.

which approaches to self-government[1], the same countries resume their populousness and opulence, though otherwise they are the least productive and inviting; while throughout the world, the utmost bounties of soil, climate, and situation are attended with misery and distress. Mons. le Poivre says, " In the midst of all this luxuriance of nature, the Malay is miserable : the culture of the land, abandoned to slaves, is fallen into contempt[2]." Bernier[3] speaks also of the Mogul's territories, " that even of those that would be fertile, there is much that is not used for want of workmen, some of which have perished by the too evil treatment of the governors, who often take from their necessary livelihood, and their very children whom they make slaves." So in Tehama[4]; the land gives three crops, and the people are miserable. So in Egypt; Bruce has spoken of the abundance of the land and the misery of the people ; and Legh, one of the last travellers in that country, says, " that the productiveness of the soil and the destitution of the inhabitants are contrasted." So in Elis, which also had its triple harvests[5]. So at Titza[6], the inhabitants are " employed

[1] Hydra, the Aristera of the ancients, is a rock about a league from the main land of Cape Skyllo, almost bare, having only one town, which, however, contains inhabitants sufficient to man eighty ships of 300 tons burthen ; they have purchased of the Porte the independent election of their own magistrates, &c. Hobhouse's Travels, p. 600.

[2] Ann. Register, 1769, p. 243.   [3] Pinkerton.

[4] Niebuhr, c. 131.

[5] ————τριπολοις σπορον εν νειοισιν

Εσθ' οτε βαλλοντες, &c.   Theocrit. Idyl. 25. ver. 25.

[6] Hobhouse's Travels, p. 85.

in the cultivation of a rich soil, and in the tending numerous flocks ; their wine, their corn, their meat, the
fleeces and skins and even the milk of their sheep and
goats, all were to be sold to raise so exorbitant a tax,
that they were starving in the midst of abundance." It
was from observing that men were desolate amidst
the prodigality of all things, that some writers have
declared that the productiveness of the land was unfriendly to industry. It is true, the wretchedness of a
country may serve the population. Thus Landt says,
" The Feroe Islands contain a happy and comparatively ingenious people, which they derive from their
unpromising soil and situation, which have preserved
them from the oppression of Denmark." A rich country is miserable, because it is worth oppressing; and a
poor one happy, because it is abandoned to its own
management, in despair of extorting any profit amidst
its wants. Burnet says, in his Travels, " The bailage
of Lugano is the worst country, the least productive,
the most exposed to cold, and the least capable of trade
of any in all Italy, and yet it is the best-peopled. If
ever this country is brought under a yoke like that
which the rest of Italy bears, it will soon be abandoned ; for nothing draws so many people to live in so
bad a soil, when they are in sight of the best soil in
Europe, but the easiness of the government." Here
is the secret. For it is most absurd to fancy that
richness of soil, genial influence of climate, convenience
of the situation, should occasion idleness and sloth; it
might be as well said that men would be remiss in proportion to the returns of their labour ; that is, they
would be unaffected inversely according to their mo-

tives to action. The dread of excessive population is a vain terror; the true terrors, which should be repeated perpetually in adamantine terms, are unpopular rulers, perverse laws, wasteful institutions, the bad growing worse, and no hope, except through ruin, of reformation. If the soil and climate be inhospitable, freedom will make life easy ;—if the soil be generous and the climate kind, no matter how few the people, they will be wretched under misrule. Italy, in Burnet's time, was thinly peopled, and of the few many were beggars; yet during its æra of republics it was populous and rich, and cultivated to admiration. It is now more miserable than Ireland. Spain also,—at once continental and insular, with every facility for commerce, with all opportunities for the most varied productions,—was and is thinly peopled, and abounds and abounded in mendicants of every description; while Holland, a province of that empire, by breaking its bondage became the most populous of modern nations, and considering its territory pre-eminently opulent, and this opulence was transmitted down to the lowest orders of the people. This Mr. Malthus is obliged to admit: but ignorantly or wilfully mistaking, he refers principally to the greater average mortality as the cause " which contributed to render Holland so famous for the management of her poor, and able to employ and support all who applied for relief[1]:" which is contrary to his own sentiments, as he speaks on other occasions[2] of the benefit of healthy situations. The fact is, Holland was a republic; it was therefore not oppressed with courts; and patron-

[1] vol. 2. p. 334.   [2] vol. 2. p. 129.

age, which costs so much among the necessary and elegant appendages of royalty, was unknown. There were no tithes; the dignity of the peerage was also unknown as an expense. The states-general cost nothing in direct bribes, or places, or pensions, or sinecures. De Witt, though a minister among the richest citizens in the world, had a small salary for incessant application to the public business. The ambassadors of Holland were men of business[1], and they received no snuff-boxes and the like ambiguous presents: all were popularly governed, and all were busily employed. In 1669 the United Provinces contained 2,400,000 inhabitants, and those who were not actively and productively employed amounted only to 200,000, which included " gentry without calling, statesmen, officers, usurers, soldiers, beggars." " The Dutch," says Temple[2], " increased in wealth by the utmost thrift, the utmost industry and temperance of living, almost sordid." These habits enabled them to support the greatest expenditure without suffering; and as no man wasted, all were supplied.

In Holland the people were most numerous and most opulent ;—such circumstances commonly coincide. Thus Thucydides[3] speaks of the city of Amphilochia as most *wealthy and populous*; and he adds, that becoming distressed, they incorporated the Ambraciots with themselves : thence it appears, that they considered an increase of people an increase of riches. The same historian[4] speaks of Athens, that after the plague it recovered *its people and riches*. Attica, says Poly-

<hr>

[1] Wickfort, p. 541, is angry at their reserve.
[2] vol. 2. p. 66. Works.   [3] lib. 2. p. 144.   [4] lib. 6. p. 430.

bius, was most populous, and richer than all Peloponnesus[1]. Xenophon[2] speaks of countries universally inhabited, and abounding in sheep, corn, &c. So Machiavel[3] describes Florence, that the city never was more happy, full of riches and credit, the citizens fit to bear arms 30,000, and those of the surrounding country 70,000. Few people imply generally a poor state[4].

Yet some have actually, in this age of spasmodic philosophy and desperate politics, reasoned, that to reduce the people would improve their power and comforts. This is just as original as the argument, that the national debt was a mine of wealth. How superior is Mr. Malthus to Aristotle, who said that a state to be powerful must abound with inhabitants[5]! and to Hume[6], that "the happiness of any society and its populousness are necessary attendants."

---

[1] Polybius, lib. 2. c. 62.   [2] p. 112.   [3] Storia, p. 52.

[4] Procopius says, that Britain was so populous, that the British, with their wives and families, often emigrated to the Franks. De Bello Gothico, lib. 4. c. 20. It was poor, but it could not have been populous. In the ancient writers *mansa carnicata familia* (a hide of land) was considered land sufficient for one family; this quantity of land, it was supposed, one plough could cultivate in a year. It is computed at 100 or 120 acres. And I find Spenser rates Ulster according to ancient records at 9000 plough lands, each of which containing 120 acres, value forty shillings. State of Ireland. England is, perhaps, four times as populous as it was in the time of Procopius; and if so, forty times more rich. To cultivate land or manufactures supposes capital; and to cultivate either or any branch of industry to the highest advantage, implies accumulated capital. So much again for ratios geometric and arithmetic, and of people pressing against subsistence.

[5] δει δε μαλλον μη εις το πληθος, εις δε δυναμιν αποβλεπειν· ου γαρ ταυτον μεγαλη τε πολις και πολυανθρωπος. De Repub. lib. 7. c. 4.   [6] Essays, vol. 1. p. 405.

I profess myself decidedly in favour of populousness. Without an increasing population, what would have induced savages to emancipate themselves from their immediate wants? How would they have extended their domain? The Numidians[1] were prevented from cultivating their fertile land until they had won it from the beasts; and to this day there is a tribe of Arabs[2], who are freed from tribute because they hunt lions, or, in the language of the country, live on the flesh of lions. Had not mankind increased, they would have held a doubtful empire over the earth, and never have advanced beyond the hunting-state.

By their continued multiplication mankind have passed from hunters to shepherds; and thence, from shifting as the sward was cropped, and wandering over a waste world, they stopped, and of the rude earth made tilth. Then agriculture became an art, cultivation a science, and many men were born. These, improving in power as they increased in numbers, reduced rivers within their banks, purified swamps or made them arable. By increasing population and successive exertion the atmosphere was tempered, and even the Euxine ceased to freeze. By many men seas have been repressed, the Baltic subsides; while with the decline of population all is reversed. The inhabitants of Persia, who formerly made fertile the parched land by subterranean aqueducts, cannot now cultivate the richest valleys; while in Egypt the means of health formerly have now become a source of disease. In Sparta, Argos, Corinth, along the banks of the Alpheus, and particularly at Patros, the stagnant water causes

[1] Strabo, lib. 2.   [2] Bruce's Travels, Introduct. p. 26.

epidemics. How wretched is Campania! Ask the cause; the answer is, The want of people. The medicine for this want is better government; man revives of course with freedom. Eustace, speaking of the country along the Tyrrhene sea, says, " It is still disastrous in the heats of summer, though every method has been employed to drain the marshes and purify the atmosphere. Of all those methods, the increase of population occasioned by the commerce of Leghorn has been the most effectual." Leghorn was a free port.

It is by increasing and increased population that nations have been enabled to effect a police among themselves. " In Arabia," says Niebuhr[1], " as in all other thinly inhabited countries, robbery is practised." Until people have accumulated, how can the division of hundreds and the like be made available for intercourse or security? The *petite guerre*, the confusion of the middle ages, arose as much from the unsupported state of population as from immorality and barbarism. Men are merchandise, without referring to the slave trade. They are money, without being stamped at the mint. Many men are themselves a great machine. How could the division of labour have originated or been serviceable, if men were not multiplied and condensed? In a thinly peopled country, each man is his own artist; and in a state a little more advanced, the same mechanic jobs at many trades, and he succeeds accordingly. Smith says[2], " It is the great multiplication of the production of all the different arts, in consequence of the division of

[1] c. 108.   [2] Wealth of Nations, b. 1. c. 1.

labour, which occasions, in a *well-governed society*, that universal opulence which extends itself to the lowest ranks of the people." And this opulence did extend to many of the lowest English, though not well governed, before the last dreadful-and treacherous war, which has confounded all orders, and reduced all to want, and many to poverty and ruin.

When I praise populousness, I mean distinctively freemen. Of slaves I speak not;—a slave makes one miserable and two vicious. Whatever approaches slavery deranges mind, body, feeling, and language[1].

Populousness is good, if the government be good ; and, as Hume says, "every country will abound with people and their comforts as . it is well governed." Under a well-organized constitution, authentic laws, and their prudent administration, the people will improve their intelligence ; and this will regulate their number, by ascertaining their wants and conveniencies. That constitution is best which effects the greatest good to all without injuring any. If one obtains more than his usefulness merits, if one obtains less than his usefulness deserves, society is disturbed, and in proportion to the amount of the iniquity. Every one should possess absolutely his time and the profits of his labour : and as the pains to obtain things teach prudence in their use, he who earns will best employ the produce of his industry. In like manner, those who contribute to the public should not merely determine the necessity and quantity of the supply, but super-

---

[1] Ker Porter, speaking of forty persons employed on a wind-instrumen, says, " I inquired who the instrument belonged to; by that word both pipes and men are included."

intend its expenditure:—therefore, that representation is most secure which is most popular; and that administration is most efficient which introduces domestic œconomy into the management of public affairs. Tillage without tithes, trade without excise, intercourse without toll, commerce without duties, professions without enforced apprenticeships, wages without statutory limitation, industry without control, or formulary, or tax;—these establish liberty and security, and consummate human enjoyment. In consequence, whatever lessens expense is good: for expense is supported by labour, labour is onerous, and the burthen is the people's. Utility should be regarded in all political concerns, and utility can only be learned of the people, through the people;—the people are the eye, the light, the object, and the mirror.

Far be it from my philosophy to adorn one with the attributes of all, and to starve the board of many, that he who supports a *royal servitude* may sicken with plethora and kill sense with enjoyment. Still further be it from me to prefer the few to the many : for this multiplies a single mischief; transforms the dog to Cerberus, and the snake to Hydra. The people, the many, the commonalty—these are the only legitimate objects of philosophical legislation. What are patricians as contradistinguished to the people? Parentage. What nobles? The will of one man,—of one weak man, made weaker by flattery and dominion. It is that monstrous perversion—counting the many as ciphers, and one or the few as millions—which has occasioned disaster, distraction, revolutions in states and societies, and which has confounded, outraged, overwhelmed mankind in all countries and ages. The wickedness and infatuation of ambitious individuals to move a great weight by an inferior force, and to continue the extravagance, may be called the *great war*. It contravenes the principles of matter, of mind, of the earth, and universe. As this world is to itself, so should citizens be to each other, and all to the state. The world has no prerogative atoms, no negative masses, none which are acted on and do not actuate. The attraction of the earth is not at either pole, nor at its centre, nor at its surface; it is the result of the gravitation of all its parts.

ERRATA.

Page.	Line.	
28	9, *after* them *insert* ".	
31	8, *for* Polowhe *read* Polo.	
50	19, *after* of *insert* the.	
58	14 and 15, *dele* " and at line 17 *place* " *after* united.	
69	26, *for* despotism *read* despotisms.	
101	4, *for* 100,000 *read* 10,000.	
107	16, *for* women *read* woman.	
137	17, *for* chime *read* chine.	
252	5, *for* there public *read* the republic.	